2012

GAAS

PRACTICE MANUAL

Current SASs, SSAEs, and SSARSs in Practice

GEORGE GEORGIADES

.CCH

a Wolters Kluwer business

This publication is designed to provide accurate and authoritative information in regard to the subject matter covered. It is sold with the understanding that the publisher is not engaged in rendering legal, accounting, or other professional services. If legal advice or other professional assistance is required, the services of a competent professional person should be sought

—From a *Declaration of Principles* jointly adopted by a Committee of the American Bar Association and a Committee of Publishers and Associations

ISBN: 978-0-8080-2653-2

© 2011 CCH. All Rights Reserved.
4025 W. Peterson Ave.
Chicago, IL 60646-6085
1 800 248 3248
http://CCHGroup.com

No claim is made to original government works; however, within this Product or Publication, the following are subject to CCH's copyright: (1) the gathering, compilation, and arrangement of such government materials; (2) the magnetic translation and digital conversion of data, if applicable; (3) the historical, statutory and other notes and references; and (4) the commentary and other materials.

Portions of this work were published in a previous edition.

Printed in the United States of America

SUSTAINABLE FORESTRY INITIATIVE   Certified Fiber Sourcing

www.sfiprogram.org

GAAS Practice Manual

by George Georgiades

Highlights

CCH's *GAAS Practice Manual* provides practitioners with a comprehensive, quick reference to the current effective pronouncements of AICPA Statements on Auditing Standards (SASs), Statements on Standards for Attestation Engagements (SSAEs), Statements on Standards for Accounting and Review Services (SSARSs), and the interpretations of those standards. In addition to providing answers for over 600 frequently asked questions on how to implement the standards, the *Manual* contains more than 350 illustrations, including checklists and practice aids. Special practice aids are also included on the accompanying CD-ROM.

2012 Edition

The 2012 Edition of *GAAS Practice Manual* has been updated for new pronouncements through the issuance of Statement on Auditing Standards (SAS) No. 121 titled, "Revised Applicability of Statement on Auditing Standards No. 100, *Interim Financial Information*"; Statement on Standards for Attestation Engagements (SSAE) No. 17 titled, "Reporting on Compiled Prospective Financial Statements When the Practitioner's Independence Is Impaired"; and Statement on Standards for Accounting and Review Services (SSARS) No. 20 titled, "Revised Applicability of Statements on Standards for Accounting and Review Services."

Coverage in the 2012 Edition of *GAAS Practice Manual* includes the following:

- AU Section 110, "Responsibilities and Functions of the Independent Auditor," which discusses the issuance of (1) a final clarified Statement on Auditing Standards (SAS), "Overall Objectives of the Independent Auditor and the Conduct of an Audit in Accordance with Generally Accepted Auditing Standards," and the issuance of "Preface to Codification of Statements on Auditing Standards, *Principles Underlying an Audit Conducted in Accordance with Generally Accepted Auditing Standards*," and (2) a proposed SAS, "Omnibus Statement on Auditing Standards—2011."

- AU Section 120, "Defining Professional Requirements in Statements on Auditing Standards," which discusses the issuance of (1) a final clarified SAS, "Overall Objectives of the Independent Auditor and the Conduct of an Audit in Accordance with Generally Accepted Auditing Standards," and the issuance of "Preface to Codification of Statements on Auditing Standards, *Principles Underlying an Audit Conducted in Accordance with Generally*

Accepted Auditing Standards," and (2) a proposed SAS, "Omnibus Statement on Auditing Standards—2011."

- AU Section 150, "Generally Accepted Auditing Standards," which discusses the issuance of (1) a final clarified SAS, "Overall Objectives of the Independent Auditor and the Conduct of an Audit in Accordance with Generally Accepted Auditing Standards," and the issuance of "Preface to Codification of Statements on Auditing Standards, *Principles Underlying an Audit Conducted in Accordance with Generally Accepted Auditing Standards,"* and (2) a proposed SAS, "Omnibus Statement on Auditing Standards—2011."

- AU Section 161, "The Relationship of Generally Accepted Auditing Standards to Quality Control Standards," which discusses the issuance of (1) a final clarified SAS, "Quality Control for an Engagement Conducted in Accordance with Generally Accepted Auditing Standards," and (2) Statement on Quality Control Standards (SQCS) No. 8, "A Firm's System of Quality Control *(Redrafted).*"

- AU Section 201, "Nature of the General Standards," which discusses the issuance of (1) a final clarified SAS, "Overall Objectives of the Independent Auditor and the Conduct of an Audit in Accordance with Generally Accepted Auditing Standards," and the issuance of "Preface to Codification of Statements on Auditing Standards, *Principles Underlying an Audit Conducted in Accordance with Generally Accepted Auditing Standards,"* and (2) a proposed SAS, "Omnibus Statement on Auditing Standards—2011."

- AU Section 210, "Training and Proficiency of the Independent Auditor," which discusses the issuance of (1) a final clarified SAS, "Overall Objectives of the Independent Auditor and the Conduct of an Audit in Accordance with Generally Accepted Auditing Standards," and the issuance of "Preface to Codification of Statements on Auditing Standards, *Principles Underlying an Audit Conducted in Accordance with Generally Accepted Auditing Standards,"* and (2) a proposed SAS, "Omnibus Statement on Auditing Standards— 2011."

- AU Section 220, "Independence," which discusses the issuance of (1) a final clarified SAS, "Overall Objectives of the Independent Auditor and the Conduct of an Audit in Accordance with Generally Accepted Auditing Standards," and the issuance of "Preface to Codification of Statements on Auditing Standards, *Principles Underlying an Audit Conducted in Accordance with Generally Accepted Auditing Standards,"* and (2) a proposed SAS, "Omnibus Statement on Auditing Standards—2011."

- AU Section 230, "Due Professional Care in the Performance of Work," which discusses the issuance of (1) a final clarified SAS, "Overall Objectives of the Independent Auditor and the Conduct of an Audit in Accordance with Generally Accepted Auditing Standards," and the issuance of "Preface to Codification of Statements on Auditing Standards, *Principles Underlying an Audit Conducted in Accordance with Generally Accepted Auditing Standards,"* and (2) a proposed SAS, "Omnibus Statement on Auditing Standards—2011."

- AU Section 311, "Planning and Supervision," which discusses the issuance of (1) a final clarified SAS, "Planning an Audit," and (2) a final clarified SAS, "Terms of Engagement."

- AU Section 312, "Audit Risk and Materiality in Conducting an Audit," which discusses the issuance of a final clarified SAS, "Materiality in Planning and Performing an Audit."

- AU Section 314, "Understanding the Entity and Its Environment and Assessing the Risks of Material Misstatement," which discusses the issuance of a final clarified SAS, "Understanding the Entity and Its Environment and Assessing the Risks of Material Misstatement."

- AU Section 315, "Communications between Predecessor and Successor Auditors," which discusses the issuance of (1) a final clarified SAS, "Opening Balances—Initial Audit Engagements, Including Reaudit Engagements," and (2) a final clarified SAS, "Terms of Engagement."

- AU Section 316, "Consideration of Fraud in a Financial Statement Audit," which discusses the issuance of a final clarified SAS, "Consideration of Fraud in a Financial Statement Audit (*Redrafted*)."

- AU Section 317, "Illegal Acts by Clients," which discusses the issuance of a final clarified SAS, "Consideration of Laws and Regulations in an Audit of Financial Statements."

- AU Section 318, "Performing Audit Procedures in Response to Assessed Risks and Evaluating the Audit Evidence Obtained," which discusses the issuance of a final clarified SAS, "Understanding the Entity and Its Environment and Assessing the Risks of Material Misstatement."

- AU Section 324, "Service Organizations," which discusses the issuance of a final clarified SAS, "Audit Considerations Relating to an Entity Using a Service Organization."

- AU Section 325, "Communicating Internal Control Related Matters Identified in an Audit," which discusses the issuance of a final clarified SAS, "Communicating Internal Control Related Matters Identified in an Audit (*Redrafted*)."

- AU Section 326, "Audit Evidence," which discusses the issuance of a final clarified SAS, "Audit Evidence (*Redrafted*)."

- AU Section 328, "Auditing Fair Value Measurements and Disclosures," which discusses the issuance of a final clarified SAS, "Auditing Accounting Estimates, Including Fair Value Accounting Estimates and Related Disclosures."

- AU Section 329, "Analytical Procedures," which discusses the issuance of a final clarified SAS, "Analytical Procedures (*Redrafted*)."

- AU Section 330, "The Confirmation Process," which discusses the issuance of a final clarified SAS, "External Confirmations."

- AU Section 331, "Inventories," which discusses the issuance of a final clarified SAS, "Audit Evidence—Specific Considerations for Selected Items."

- AU Section 332, "Auditing Derivative Instruments, Hedging Activities, and Investments in Securities," which discusses the issuance of a final clarified SAS, "Audit Evidence—Specific Considerations for Selected Items."

- AU Section 333, "Management Representations," which discusses the issuance of a final clarified SAS, "Written Representations."

- AU Section 334, "Related Parties," which discusses the issuance of a final clarified SAS, "Related Parties (*Redrafted*)."

- AU Section 336, "Using the Work of a Specialist," which discusses the issuance of a final clarified SAS, "Using the Work of an Auditor's Specialist."

- AU Section 337, "Inquiry of a Client's Lawyer Concerning Litigation, Claims, and Assessments," which discusses the issuance of a final clarified SAS, "Audit Evidence—Specific Considerations for Selected Items."

- AU Section 339, "Audit Documentation," which discusses the issuance of a final clarified SAS, "Audit Documentation (*Redrafted*)."

- AU Section 342, "Auditing Accounting Estimates," which discusses the issuance of a final clarified SAS, "Auditing Accounting Estimates, Including Fair Value Accounting Estimates and Related Disclosures."

- AU Section 350, "Audit Sampling," which discusses the issuance of a final clarified SAS, "Audit Sampling (*Redrafted*)."

- AU Section 380, "The Auditor's Communication with Those Charged with Governance," which discusses the issuance of (1) a final clarified SAS, "The Auditor's Communication with Those Charged with Governance (*Redrafted*)," and (2) a proposed SAS, "Omnibus Statement on Auditing Standards—2011."

- AU Section 390, "Consideration of Omitted Procedures after the Report Date," which discusses the issuance of a final clarified SAS, "Consideration of Omitted Procedures After the Report Release Date."

- AU Section 410, "Adherence to Generally Accepted Accounting Principles," which discusses the issuance of a final clarified SAS, "Forming an Opinion and Reporting on Financial Statements."

- AU Section 411, "The Meaning of *Present Fairly in Conformity with Generally Accepted Accounting Principles*," which indicates that the Auditing Standards Board has withdrawn AU Section 411 and its related auditing interpretation.

- AU Section 420, "Consistency of Application of Generally Accepted Accounting Principles," which discusses the issuance of a final clarified SAS, "Consistency of Financial Statements."

- AU Section 431, "Adequacy of Disclosure in Financial Statements," which discusses the issuance of a final clarified SAS, "Modifications to the Opinion in the Independent Auditor's Report."

- AU Section 508, "Reports on Audited Financial Statements," which discusses the issuance of: (1) a final clarified SAS, "Forming an Opinion and Reporting on Financial Statements," (2) a final clarified SAS, "Modifications to the Opinion in the Independent Auditor's Report," (3) a final clarified SAS, "Emphasis-of-Matter Paragraphs and Other-Matter Paragraphs in the Independent Auditor's Report," and (4) a proposed SAS, "Omnibus Statement on Auditing Standards—2011."

- AU Section 530, "Dating of the Independent Auditor's Report," which discusses the issuance of a final clarified SAS, "Forming an Opinion and Reporting on Financial Statements."

- AU Section 532, "Restricting the Use of an Auditor's Report," which discusses the issuance of a proposed SAS, "Alert as to the Intended Use of the Auditor's Written Communication."

- AU Section 534, "Reporting on Financial Statements Prepared for Use in Other Countries," which discusses the issuance of a proposed SAS, "Financial Statements Prepared in Accordance with a Financial Reporting Framework Generally Accepted in Another Country."

- AU Section 543, "Part of Audit Performed by Other Independent Auditors," which discusses the issuance of a final clarified SAS, "Special Considerations—Audits of Group Financial Statements (Including the Work of Component Auditors)."

- AU Section 544, "Lack of Conformity with Generally Accepted Accounting Principles," which discusses the issuance of a final clarified SAS, "Special Considerations—Audits of Financial Statements Prepared in Accordance with Special Purpose Frameworks."

- AU Section 550, "Other Information in Documents Containing Audited Financial Statements," which discusses the issuance of a proposed SAS, "Omnibus Statement on Auditing Standards—2011."

- AU Section 552, "Reporting on Condensed Financial Statements and Selected Financial Data," which discusses the issuance of a final clarified SAS, "Engagements to Report on Summary Financial Statements."

- AU Section 560, "Subsequent Events," which discusses the issuance of a final clarified SAS, "Subsequent Events and Subsequently Discovered Facts."

- AU Section 561, "Subsequent Discovery of Facts Existing at the Date of the Auditor's Report," which discusses the issuance of a final clarified SAS, "Subsequent Events and Subsequently Discovered Facts."

- AU Section 623, "Special Reports," which discusses the issuance of: (1) a final clarified SAS, "Special Considerations—Audits of Financial Statements Prepared in Accordance with Special Purpose Frameworks," (2) a final clarified SAS, "Special Considerations—Audits of Single Financial Statements and Specific Elements, Accounts, or Items of a Financial Statement," and (3) a proposed SAS, "Reporting on Compliance with Aspects of Contractual Agreements or Regulatory Requirements in Connection with Audited Financial Statements (*Redrafted*)."

- AU Section 625, "Reports on the Application of Accounting Principles," which discusses the issuance of a final clarified SAS, "Reports on Application of Requirements of an Applicable Financial Reporting Framework."

- AU Section 634, "Letters for Underwriters and Certain Other Requesting Parties," which discusses the issuance of a proposed SAS, "Letters for Underwriters and Certain Other Requesting Parties (*Redrafted*)."

- AU Section 711, "Filings Under Federal Securities Statutes," which discusses the issuance of a final clarified SAS, "Filings with the U.S. Securities and Exchange Commission Under the Securities Act of 1933."

- AU Section 722, "Interim Financial Information," which discusses the issuance of: (1) SAS-121, "Revised Applicability of Statement on Auditing Standards No. 100, *Interim Financial Information*," and (2) a proposed SAS, "Interim Financial Information."

- AU Section 801, "Compliance Audits," which discusses the issuance of a proposed SAS, "Omnibus Statement on Auditing Standards—2011."

- AU Section 901, "Public Warehouses—Controls and Auditing Procedures for Goods Held," which discusses the issuance of a final clarified SAS, "Audit Evidence—Specific Considerations for Selected Items."

- AT Section 101, "Attest Engagements," which discusses the issuance of Interpretation No. 8, "Including a Description of Tests of Controls or Other Procedures, and the Results Thereof, in an Examination Report."

- AT Section 301, "Financial Forecasts and Projections," which discusses the issuance of Statement on Standards for Attestation Engagements (SSAE) No. 17, "Reporting on Compiled Prospective Financial Statements When the Practitioner's Independence Is Impaired."

- A new AT Section 801, "Reporting on Controls at a Service Organization," which provides detailed coverage of SSAE No. 16, "Reporting on Controls at a Service Organization."

- A new AR Section 60, "Framework for Performing and Reporting on Compilation and Review Engagements," which provides detailed coverage of Statement on Standards for Accounting and Review Services (SSARS) No. 19, "Compilation and Review Engagements."

- A new AR Section 80, "Compilation of Financial Statements," which provides detailed coverage of SSARS-19.

- A new AR Section 90, "Review of Financial Statements," which provides detailed coverage of SSARS-19 and SSARS-20, "Revised Applicability of Statements on Standards for Accounting and Review Services."

- AR Section 110, "Compilation of Specified Elements, Accounts, or Items of a Financial Statement," which has been updated for SSARS-19.

- AR Section 120, "Compilation of Pro Forma Financial Information," which has been updated for SSARS-19.

- AR Section 200, "Reporting on Comparative Financial Statements," which has been updated for SSARS-19.

- AR Section 300, "Compilation Reports on Financial Statements Included in Certain Prescribed Forms," which has been updated for SSARS-19.

IMPORTANT NOTICE ABOUT THE AUDITING STANDARDS BOARD CLARITY PROJECT

Overview

In 2004, in light of the creation of the Public Company Accounting Oversight Board (PCAOB), as well as the move toward globalization of auditing standards, the AICPA's Auditing Standards Board (ASB) contemplated the best way to achieve its mission. The ASB concluded that a plan should be undertaken to make U.S. GAAS easier to read, understand, and apply. Accordingly, the ASB devised a plan to clarify U.S. GAAS and converge them with the International Standards on Auditing (ISAs) issued by the International Auditing and Assurance Standards Board (IAASB), while at the same time avoiding or mitigating unnecessary conflict with PCAOB standards.

A basic foundation of the Clarity Project is the establishment of an objective for each auditing standard, which is intended to better reflect a principles-based approach to standard-setting. In order to accomplish its goal to improve clarity and reduce the length and complexity of the redrafted auditing standards as well as newly issued standards, the ASB has adopted clarity drafting conventions, which include the following:

- Establishing objectives for each of the standards;

- Including a definitions section, if relevant, in each standard;

- Separating requirements from application and other explanatory material;

- Numbering application and other explanatory material paragraphs using an "A" prefix and presenting them in a separate section following the requirements section;

- Using formatting techniques, such as bulleted lists, to enhance readability;

- Including, where appropriate, special considerations relevant to audits of smaller, less complex entities within the text of the standard; and

- Including, where appropriate, special considerations relevant to audits of governmental entities within the text of the standard.

In some cases, extant individual AU Sections are being clarified "one for one" into individual clarified standards. In other cases, some AU Sections are grouped together and clarified into one or more clarified standards. As a result, topics currently associated with certain AU Section numbers might be re-titled and assigned different AU Section numbers.

The ASB is working toward completing the Clarity Project in 2011. Once all of the ASB's clarified standards have been finalized, the ASB will issue all of the clarified standards in one Statement on Auditing Standard (SAS) that will be codified in "AU Section" format.

To address practice issues, certain SASs have been issued in advance. These standards have been assigned numbers and include SAS No. 117, which deals with compliance audits, and SAS Nos. 118, 119, and 120, which deal with supplementary information.

Effective Date and Adoption

Because SAS Nos. 117–120 have been issued, their effective dates have already been established as discussed below. The effective date for all other clarified SASs is for audits of financial statements for periods ending on or after December 15, 2012. The ASB believes having a single effective date will ease the transition to, and implementation of, the redrafted standards.

Access to Clarified Final Standards and Exposure Drafts

To assist in training, including development of training materials and implementation, the ASB has begun releasing the finalized redrafted standards as they are approved. The ASB does recognize that conforming changes may need to be made to approved, redrafted standards as a result of the clarification of other standards. However, the ASB expects these changes will be minor (e.g., wording, placement of material), rather than substantial.

As each clarified auditing standard is finalized, it is made available on the "Final Clarified Statements on Auditing Standards" page on the AICPA's web site. However, it should be noted that finalized clarified auditing standards are not effective yet.

In addition, as each *exposure draft* of a clarified auditing standard is issued, it is made available on the "Improving the Clarity of ASB Standards" page on the AICPA's web site.

Coverage in 2012 GAAS Practice Manual

Extant individual AU Sections that are affected by the Clarity Project contain "Practice Points" that address the issuance of (1) exposure drafts of clarified auditing standards, or (2) final clarified auditing standards, as applicable. In addition, the ASB has issued SAS Nos. 117–120, with early application explicitly permitted. Because early application of the SASs is explicitly permitted, the Manual also includes detailed coverage of these standards. The four standards and their effective dates are as follows:

- SAS-117 (AU Section 801), *Compliance Audits*, which is effective for compliance audits for fiscal periods ending on or after June 15, 2010; early application is permitted.

- SAS-118 (AU Section 550), *Other Information in Documents Containing Audited Financial Statements*, which is effective for audits of financial statements for periods beginning on or after December 15, 2010; early application is permitted.

- SAS-119 (AU Section 551), *Supplementary Information in Relation to the Financial Statements as a Whole*, which is effective for audits of financial statements for periods beginning on or after December 15, 2010; early application is permitted.

- SAS-120 (AU Section 558), *Required Supplementary Information*, which is effective for audits of financial statements for periods beginning on or after December 15, 2010; early application is permitted.

CCH Learning Center

CCH's goal is to provide you with the clearest, most concise, and up-to-date accounting and auditing information to help further your professional development, as well as a convenient method to help you satisfy your continuing professional education requirements. The CCH Learning Center* offers a complete line of self-study courses covering complex and constantly evolving accounting and auditing issues. We are continually adding new courses to the library to help you stay current on all the latest developments. The CCH Learning Center courses are available 24 hours a day, seven days a week. You'll get immediate exam results and certification. To view our complete accounting and auditing course catalog, go to: **http:/cch.learningcenter.com.**

Accounting Research Manager™

Accounting Research Manager is the most comprehensive, up-to-date, and objective online database of financial reporting literature. It includes all authoritative and proposed accounting, auditing, and SEC literature, plus independent, expert-written interpretive guidance. And, in addition to our standard accounting and SEC libraries, you can enjoy the full spectrum of financial reporting with our Audit library.

---

* CCH is registered with the National Association of State Boards of Accountancy (NASBA) as a sponsor of continuing professional education on the National Registry of CPE Sponsors. State boards of accountancy have final authority on the acceptance of individual courses for CPE credit. Complaints regarding registered sponsors may be addressed to the National Registry of CPE Sponsors, 150 Fourth Avenue North, Nashville, TN 37219-2417. Telephone: 615-880-4200.

*CCH is registered with the National Association of State Boards of Accountancy as a Quality Assurance Service (QAS) sponsor of continuing professional education. Participating state boards of accountancy have final authority on the acceptance of individual courses for CPE credit. Complaints regarding QAS program sponsors may be addressed to NASBA, 150 Fourth Avenue North, Suite 700, Nashville, TN 37219-2417. Telephone: 615-880-4200.

The Audit library covers auditing standards, attestation engagement standards, accounting and review services standards, audit risk alerts, and other vital auditing-related guidance. You'll also have online access to our best-selling *GAAS Practice Manual, Knowledge-Based Audit Procedures, Compilations & Reviews, CPA's Guide to Effective Engagement Letters, CPA's Guide to Management Letter Comments,* and be kept up-to-date on the latest authoritative literature via the *GAAS Update Service.*

With **Accounting Research Manager,** you maximize the efficiency of your research time while enhancing your results. Learn more about our content, our experts, and how you can request a FREE trial by visiting us at **http:/ www.accountingresearchmanager.com.**

09/11

Contents

Our Peer Review Policy

Thank you for ordering the 2012 *GAAS Practice Manual*. Each year we bring you the best accounting and auditing reference guides. To confirm the technical accuracy and quality control of our materials, CCH, a Wolters Kluwer business, voluntarily submitted to a peer review of our publishing system and our publications (see the Peer Review Statement on the following page).

In addition to peer review, our publications undergo strict technical and content reviews by qualified practitioners. This ensures that our books meet real-world standards and applicability.

Our publications are reviewed every step of the way—from conception to production—to ensure that we bring you the finest guides on the market.

Updated annually, peer reviewed, technically accurate, convenient, and practical—the 2012 *GAAS Practice Manual* shows our commitment to creating books and practice aids you can trust.

Peer Review Statement

 **Caldwell, Becker, Dervin, Petrick & Co., L.L.P.**
CERTIFIED PUBLIC ACCOUNTANTS

Quality Control Materials Review Report

November 12, 2009

Executive Board
CCH, a Wolters Kluwer business
and the National Peer Review Committee

We have reviewed the system of quality control for the development and maintenance of GAAS Practice Manual (2010 Edition) (hereafter referred to as *materials*) of CCH, a Wolters Kluwer business (the organization) and the resultant materials in effect at October 31, 2009. Our quality control materials peer review was conducted in accordance with the Standards for Performing and Reporting on Peer Reviews established by the Peer Review Board of the American Institute of Certified Public Accountants. The organization is responsible for designing a system of quality control and complying with it to provide users of the materials with reasonable assurance that the materials are reliable aids to assist them in conforming with those professional standards that the materials purport to encompass. Our responsibility is to express an opinion on the design of the system and the organization's compliance with that system based on our review. The nature, objectives, scope, limitations of, and the procedures performed in a Quality Control Materials Review are described in the standards at www.aicpa.org/prsummary.

In our opinion, the system of quality control for the development and maintenance of the quality control materials of CCH, a Wolters Kluwer business was suitably designed and was being complied with during the year ended October 31, 2009, to provide users of the materials with reasonable assurance that the materials are reliable aids to assist them in conforming with those professional standards the materials purport to encompass. Also, in our opinion, the quality control materials referred to above are reliable aids at October 31, 2009. Organizations can receive a rating of *pass, pass with deficiency(ies)*, or *fail*. CCH, a Wolters Kluwer business has received a peer review rating of *pass*.

CALDWELL, BECKER, DERVIN, PETRICK & CO, LLP.
CALDWELL, BECKER, DERVIN, PETRICK & CO., L.L.P.

20750 Ventura Boulevard, Suite 140 • Woodland Hills, CA 91364
(818) 704-1040 • FAX (818) 704-5536

Preface

The primary objective of the *GAAS Practice Manual* is to provide a complete, quick, and valuable reference source for the practitioner of the currently effective pronouncements of AICPA Statements on Auditing Standards (SASs), Statements on Standards for Attestation Engagements (SSAEs), Statements on Standards for Accounting and Review Services (SSARSs), and the interpretations of these standards. The Sections in this book follow the sequence of sections of the AICPA's *Codification of Statements on Auditing Standards, Codification of Statements on Standards for Attestation Engagements,* and *Codification of Statements on Standards for Accounting and Review Services,* which are found in the AICPA's *Professional Standards.* Therefore, the practitioner can easily cross the bridge from the AICPA's original language to implementing the standards confidently, efficiently, and proficiently as discussed in this book. The most important benefits that the *GAAS Practice Manual* offers the practitioner are that it:

- Provides answers to over 600 frequently asked questions on how to implement the standards. These are practical answers to the most commonly encountered questions raised in applying the official pronouncements. The questions are based on real-life practice issues. The answers are presented in clear conversational style in order to assist in fully understanding the technical requirements.

- Provides over 350 illustrations, including checklists and other practice aids, to clarify application and compliance with the standards. These illustrations are designed to show the practitioner a cost-effective approach for conducting high-quality engagements and for enhancing the quality of the CPA's practice.

To facilitate the use of this *Manual,* each Section is divided into the following three easy-to-read and easy-to-understand major parts:

1. **What Every Practitioner Should Know.** This section provides a clear and concise discussion of the specific standard and its basic requirements and the practitioner's essential responsibilities.

2. **Practice Issues and Frequently Asked Questions.** This section focuses on techniques for applying the standard by using a "Question and Answer" format designed to provide practical discussion, advice, and specific implementation guidance.

3. **Illustrations and Practice Aids.** This section includes numerous checklists, questionnaires, sample working papers, sample correspondence letters, and sample accountant's reports. The functionality and abundance of the illustrations and practice aids in this section are designed to assist the practitioner in performing accounting, auditing, and attest engagements effectively and efficiently.

Throughout, this *Manual* features various efficiency and effectiveness practice tips to help the practitioner better plan and execute accounting, auditing, and attest engagements and to quickly integrate the standards into practice.

The *GAAS Practice Manual* is current through the following pronouncements:

→ SAS-121 (Revised Applicability of Statement on Auditing Standards No. 100, "Interim Financial Information")

→ SSAE-17 (Reporting on Compiled Prospective Financial Statements When the Practitioner's Independence Is Impaired)

→ SSARS-20 (Revised Applicability of Statements on Standards for Accounting and Review Services)

The *GAAS Practice Manual* is updated annually with more "Questions and Answers" and Illustrations and Practice Aids. Therefore, the author and publisher welcome comments, suggestions, and recommendations to improve this *Manual*. These will be considered for incorporation in future revisions of the *Manual*. Please send your comments to:

Sandra Lim

Developmental Editor

CCH, a Wolters Kluwer business

76 Ninth Avenue

7th Floor

New York, NY 10011

sandra.lim@wolterskluwer.com

Acknowledgments

Thanks are due to the staff of CCH, and especially to Sandra Lim, developmental editor, for her constructive input and efforts in producing the *Manual*, and to Curt Berkowitz for his care and skill in bringing this edition to press. The author and publisher also thank Vincent J. Love, CPA, for his thoughtful, thorough review and comments on this book.

In addition, I thank my wife, Caroline, for her continuous patience and support, and my sons, Alex and Dmitri, for their inspiration and constant source of energy and joy.

George Georgiades

Laguna Niguel, California

About the Author

George Georgiades, CPA, has more than 30 years of experience in public accounting, including seven years with an international public accounting firm. He currently has his own firm and consults exclusively with CPA firms on technical accounting, auditing, and financial reporting and disclosure issues. In writing this *Manual*, Mr. Georgiades has capitalized on the extensive experience he has gained from association with clients and with international, national, regional, and local accounting firms. He has been involved personally in more than 600 audit engagements and related financial statements of both small, closely held companies as well as large, publicly held enterprises. He has personally conducted more than 75 peer reviews, consulting reviews, and inspections. In this *Manual*, he has provided the benefit of his extensive hands-on experience in performing independent technical reviews of accounting, auditing, and attestation engagements.

Mr. Georgiades is also the author of *GAAP Financial Statement Disclosures Manual* and the *GAAS Update Service.* He is a member of the American Institute of Certified Public Accountants and the California Society of Certified Public Accountants, and served on the California Society of CPAs Peer Review Committee.

AU Section 100
STATEMENTS ON AUDITING STANDARDS—INTRODUCTION

AU SECTION 110
RESPONSIBILITIES AND FUNCTIONS OF THE INDEPENDENT AUDITOR

PRACTICE POINT: As part of its Clarity Project, the American Institute of Certified Public Accountants' (AICPA's) Auditing Standards Board (ASB) has finalized a clarified standard that includes: (1) Preface to Codification of Statements on Auditing Standards, *Principles Underlying an Audit Conducted in Accordance with Generally Accepted Auditing Standards* ("Preface"), and (2) Statement on Auditing Standards (SAS), "Overall Objectives of the Independent Auditor and the Conduct of an Audit in Accordance with Generally Accepted Auditing Standards."

The Preface contains the principles underlying an audit conducted in accordance with U.S. generally accepted auditing standards (GAAS). These principles are not requirements and do not carry any authority. The ASB has developed the principles to provide a framework that is helpful in understanding and explaining an audit. The principles are organized to provide a structure for the Codification of Statements on Auditing Standards. This structure addresses the purpose of an audit, personal responsibilities of the auditor, auditor actions in performing the audit, and reporting.

The SAS addresses the independent auditor's overall responsibilities when conducting an audit of financial statements in accordance with GAAS. Specifically, it sets out the overall objectives of the independent auditor and explains the nature and scope of an audit designed to enable the independent auditor to meet those objectives. It also explains the scope, authority, and structure of GAAS and includes requirements establishing the general responsibilities of the independent auditor applicable in all audits, including the obligation to comply with GAAS.

The ASB is expected to issue many of the clarified standards in *one* SAS that will be codified in "AU Section" format. The ASB has decided that the effective date of the clarified SASs that have not yet been issued is for audits of financial statements for periods ending on or after December 15, 2012. Auditors should be alert to and monitor further developments in this area.

PRACTICE POINT: In March 2011, the American Institute of Certified Public Accountants' (AICPA's) Auditing Standards Board (ASB) issued an exposure draft (ED) of a proposed Statement on Auditing Standards (SAS) titled, "Omnibus Statement on Auditing Standards—2011." This proposed SAS, which is part of the AICPA's Clarity Project, would amend the following SASs that have been issued in the clarity format and are currently effective:

- SAS-117 (AU Section 801) (Compliance Audits). The amendment to SAS-117 conforms the auditor's report on compliance to the requirements of the clarified SAS, "Forming an Opinion and Reporting on Financial Statements." In addition, the amendment revises the appendix in SAS-117, "AU Sections That Are Not Applicable to Compliance Audits," to reflect conforming changes to affected references to AU Sections as a result of the ASB's Clarity Project.

- SAS-118 (AU Section 550) (Other Information in Documents Containing Audited Financial Statements). The amendment to SAS-118 clarifies the requirements with respect to identified material inconsistencies by categorizing the requirements based on when the inconsistencies are identified (prior to the date of the auditor's report on the audited financial statements; after the date of the auditor's report but prior to the report release date; and after the report release date). It also adds application material addressing electronic sites to include guidance from an interpretation of AU Section 550 (Other Information in Documents Containing Audited Financial Statements), which the ASB determined was appropriate to include in SAS-118.

In addition, in order to address other changes necessitated by the ASB's overall Clarity Project, the proposed SAS would amend the following clarified SASs that have been finalized and released, but not yet issued as authoritative:

- Clarified SAS, "Overall Objectives of the Independent Auditor and the Conduct of an Audit in Accordance with Generally Accepted Auditing Standards."

- Clarified SAS, "Modifications to the Opinion in the Independent Auditor's Report."

- Clarified SAS, "Reports on Application of Requirements of an Applicable Financial Reporting Framework."

- Clarified SAS, "The Auditor's Communication with Those Charged with Governance (Redrafted)."

- Clarified SAS, "Audit Documentation (Redrafted)."

The proposed SAS would be effective for audits of financial statements for periods ending on or after December 15, 2012, except for the amendment to the clarified SAS, "Reports on Application of Requirements of an Applicable Financial Reporting Framework," which would be effective for engagements ending on or after December 15, 2012.

WHAT EVERY PRACTITIONER SHOULD KNOW

Basic Objective

The objective of an audit of financial statements pursuant to GAAS is to express an opinion on the fairness of presentation, in all material respects, of financial position, results of operations, and cash flows in conformity with generally accepted accounting principles or another comprehensive basis of accounting. The auditor is required to identity those circumstances in which accounting principles have not been consistently applied in the current period financial statements, when compared to those of the preceding period.

Responsibilities of the Auditor

The auditor's responsibilities include:

a. Expressing an opinion on the financial statements.

b. Obtaining reasonable assurance about whether the financial statements are free of material misstatement resulting from error, fraud, or certain illegal acts.

c. Exercising due skill and care in the conduct of the audit.

d. Complying with standards established by the profession (e.g., the AICPA's *Code of Professional Conduct*) and by the state boards of accountancy in those states where they practice.

Responsibilities of Management

Management's responsibilities include:

a. Adopting sound accounting policies and methods.

b. Establishing and maintaining an adequate system of internal controls.

c. Accepting responsibility for the integrity, reliability, and objectivity of the financial statements.

PRACTICE ISSUES AND FREQUENTLY ASKED QUESTIONS

Issue 1: Is the auditor responsible for detecting misstatements that are not material to the financial statements?

No. The auditor has no responsibility to plan and perform the audit to obtain reasonable assurance that misstatements that are not material to the financial statements are detected. This is true regardless of whether such immaterial misstatements are caused by errors or fraud.

PRACTICE POINT: See AU Section 312 (Audit Risk and Materiality in Conducting an Audit) for additional guidance on the auditor's consideration of materiality when conducting an audit in accordance with generally accepted auditing standards.

Issue 2: How does the auditor respond to a perception that an audit guarantees the financial statements to be free from misstatements?

Communicating with and "educating" the audit client and third-party users are crucial in clarifying and distinguishing between the auditor's responsibilities and those of management. The financial statements are management's responsibility; the auditor's responsibility is to express an opinion on those financial statements. Throughout auditing literature, the concept of *reasonable assurance* (rather than absolute assurance) recognizes that the cost of internal control should not exceed the benefits expected to be derived. Therefore, the auditor is *not* expected to disregard all costs and all time constraints in order to achieve total precision and absolute accuracy. In addition, the concept of *inherent limitations* of the auditing process is based on time and cost considerations; accordingly, audits incorporate many tests of samples of transactions as opposed to 100% testing. Therefore, since absolute proof and truth are unknown in the audit process and the auditor's judgment is not infallible, the auditor cannot "guarantee" that an entity's financial statements are free from misstatements.

Issue 3: The auditor often drafts financial statements or notes for the client. Does this change the auditor's responsibility for those financial statements?

The responsibility for the financial statements always rests with management. The statements are management's representations, not the auditor's. An auditor may draft the financial statements or notes for the client, or may assist the client in doing so, especially when management lacks sufficient experience and expertise. However, in these circumstances it is important that the auditor discuss the financial statements and notes with management in order to enable management to make an informed decision about accepting responsibility for their content. Finally, although the auditor may make recommendations about such matters as the form and content of financial statements, or the adoption of accounting policies or internal controls, the decision to implement these recommendations always rests with management, not with the auditor. In other words, management does not discharge its obligation and responsibility by engaging the auditor.

Issue 4: Can the auditor rely on the advice of other professionals in exercising his or her judgment about matters pertinent to the audit?

Yes. Auditing often involves exercising informed judgment about matters outside the scope of the accounting profession's normal expertise, such as legal issues or valuations of assets and liabilities. An independent auditor does not purport to act in the capacity of another profession or occupation. In some cases, it is necessary for an auditor to consult other experts, such as attorneys, appraisers, or actuaries, in order to obtain audit evidence. The auditor may appropriately rely on the advice and opinion of such experts in matters that come within the scope of their professions' expertise.

PRACTICE POINT: During the course of an audit, the auditor may encounter matters that require special skill or knowledge and, therefore, require using the work of a specialist to obtain competent sufficient evidence. In such cases, the auditor should refer to AU Section 336 (Using the Work of a Specialist), which provides guidance to auditors who use the work of a specialist in performing an audit in accordance with GAAS.

Issue 5: Is it appropriate to include on each page of the basic audited financial statements a reference to the auditor's report such as "The accompanying notes and auditor's report are an integral part of these financial statements"?

No. The financial statements are the responsibility of the client and management and should be clearly distinguished from the auditor's responsibility. Therefore, the auditor's report cannot be an *integral part of the financial statements*. Accordingly, it is inappropriate to include such reference to the auditor's report as part of the reference to the notes to the financial statements. However, a note such as the following is appropriate: "The accompanying notes are an integral part of these financial statements."

ILLUSTRATIONS AND PRACTICE AIDS

ILLUSTRATION 1—MANAGEMENT'S RESPONSIBILITY FOR FINANCIAL REPORTING

Note: *The following is an example of a management report acknowledging management's responsibility for financial reporting. The report is typically signed by senior management (e.g., the chief executive officer), including the chief financial officer.*

Management's Responsibility for Financial Reporting

Management is responsible for the preparation, integrity, and objectivity of the Company's financial statements and notes thereto. These financial statements have been prepared in conformity with accounting principles generally accepted in the United States of America and, accordingly, include certain amounts that represent management's best estimates and judgments. Actual amounts could differ from those estimates.

Management maintains internal control systems to assist it in fulfilling its responsibility for financial reporting. These systems include business, accounting, and reporting policies and procedures, selection of personnel, segregation of duties, and an internal audit function. Although no system can ensure elimination of all errors and fraud, the Company's systems, which are reviewed and modified in response to changing conditions, have been designed to provide reasonable assurance that assets are safeguarded, policies and procedures are followed, and transactions are properly executed and reported. The concept of reasonable assurance is based on the recognition that there are limitations in all systems and that the costs of such systems should not exceed their benefits.

The Audit Committee of the Board of Directors, which is composed of directors who are neither officers nor employees of, nor consultants to, the Company, meets regularly with the Company's senior financial personnel, internal auditors, and independent certified public accountants to review audit plans and results, as well as the actions taken by management in discharging its responsibilities for accounting, financial reporting, and internal control systems. The Audit Committee reports its findings and recommends the selection of independent certified public accountants to the Board of Directors. The Company's management, internal auditors, and independent certified public accountants have direct and confidential access to the Audit Committee at all times.

The independent certified public accountants are engaged to conduct the audits of and report on the financial statements in accordance with auditing standards generally accepted in the United States of America. These standards require a review of the systems of internal controls and tests of transactions to the extent considered necessary by the independent certified public accountants for purposes of supporting their opinion as set forth in their report.

AU SECTION 120
DEFINING PROFESSIONAL REQUIREMENTS IN STATEMENTS ON AUDITING STANDARDS

PRACTICE POINT: As part of its Clarity Project, the American Institute of Certified Public Accountants' (AICPA's) Auditing Standards Board (ASB) has finalized a clarified standard that includes: (1) Preface to Codification of Statements on Auditing Standards, *Principles Underlying an Audit Conducted in Accordance with Generally Accepted Auditing Standards* ("Preface"), and (2) Statement on Auditing Standards (SAS), *Overall Objectives of the Independent Auditor and the Conduct of an Audit in Accordance with Generally Accepted Auditing Standards.*

The Preface contains the principles underlying an audit conducted in accordance with U.S. generally accepted auditing standards (GAAS). These principles are not requirements and do not carry any authority. The ASB has developed the principles to provide a framework that is helpful in understanding and explaining an audit. The principles are organized to provide a structure for the Codification of Statements on Auditing Standards. This structure addresses the purpose of an audit, personal responsibilities of the auditor, auditor actions in performing the audit, and reporting.

The SAS addresses the independent auditor's overall responsibilities when conducting an audit of financial statements in accordance with GAAS. Specifically, it sets out the overall objectives of the independent auditor and explains the nature and scope of an audit designed to enable the independent auditor to meet those objectives. It also explains the scope, authority, and structure of GAAS and includes requirements establishing the general responsibilities of the independent auditor applicable in all audits, including the obligation to comply with GAAS.

Upon the issuance of all clarified SASs, one SAS will be issued containing all clarified SASs in codified format. The ASB has decided that the effective date of the clarified SASs that have not yet been issued is for audits of financial statements for periods ending on or after December 15, 2012.

Auditors should be alert to and monitor further developments in this area.

PRACTICE POINT: In March 2011, the American Institute of Certified Public Accountants' (AICPA's) Auditing Standards Board (ASB) issued an exposure draft (ED) of a proposed Statement on Auditing Standards (SAS) titled, "Omnibus Statement on Auditing Standards—2011." This proposed SAS, which is part of the AICPA's Clarity Project, would amend the following SASs that have been issued in the clarity format and are currently effective:

- SAS-117 (AU Section 801) (Compliance Audits). The amendment to SAS-117 conforms the auditor's report on compliance to the requirements of the clarified SAS, "Forming an Opinion and Reporting on Financial Statements." In addition, the amendment revises the appendix in SAS-117, "AU Sections That Are Not Applicable to Compliance Audits," to reflect conforming changes to affected references to AU Sections as a result of the ASB's Clarity Project.

- SAS-118 (AU Section 550) (Other Information in Documents Containing Audited Financial Statements). The amendment to SAS-118 clarifies the requirements with respect to identified material inconsistencies by categorizing the requirements based on when the inconsistencies are identified (prior to the date of the auditor's report on the audited financial statements; after the date of the auditor's report but prior to the report release date; and after the report release date). It also adds application material addressing electronic sites to include guidance from an interpretation of AU Section 550 (Other Information in Documents Containing Audited Financial Statements), which the ASB determined was appropriate to include in SAS-118.

In addition, in order to address other changes necessitated by the ASB's overall Clarity Project, the proposed SAS would amend the following clarified SASs that have been finalized and released, but not yet issued as authoritative:

- Clarified SAS, "Overall Objectives of the Independent Auditor and the Conduct of an Audit in Accordance with Generally Accepted Auditing Standards."
- Clarified SAS, "Modifications to the Opinion in the Independent Auditor's Report."
- Clarified SAS, "Reports on Application of Requirements of an Applicable Financial Reporting Framework."
- Clarified SAS, "The Auditor's Communication with Those Charged with Governance (Redrafted)."
- Clarified SAS, "Audit Documentation (Redrafted)."

The proposed SAS would be effective for audits of financial statements for periods ending on or after December 15, 2012, except for the amendment to the clarified SAS, "Reports on Application of Requirements of an Applicable Financial Reporting Framework," which would be effective for engagements ending on or after December 15, 2012.

WHAT EVERY PRACTITIONER SHOULD KNOW

Basic Objectives and Requirements

This Section defines the terminology the AICPA uses to describe the degree of responsibility that the auditing standards impose on auditors. It specifically defines two types of responsibility that the standards impose on auditors: (1) unconditional responsibility to comply with a requirement in all cases, for which responsibility is communicated by the terms "must" or "is required" and (2) presumptive responsibility to comply with a requirement in all cases, for which responsibility is communicated by the term "should" and which places the burden of proof on the auditor if he or she departs from the presumptive requirement.

Categories of Professional Requirements

This Section uses, describes, and imposes the following two categories of professional requirements on the auditor:

- *Unconditional requirements*—The auditor is required to comply with a requirement in all cases in which the circumstances exist to which the requirement applies. An unconditional requirement is indicated by the words "must" or "is required."

- *Presumptively mandatory requirements*—The auditor is also required to comply with a presumptively mandatory requirement in all cases in which the circumstances exist to which the presumptively mandatory requirement applies. In rare circumstances, the auditor may depart from a presumptively mandatory requirement provided he or she documents the justification for departure and how alternative procedures performed in the circumstances were sufficient to achieve the objectives of the presumptively mandatory requirement. A presumptively mandatory requirement is indicated by the word "should."

The following is a summary of the imperatives/terms used in this Section and the degrees of responsibility they impose on auditors:

Imperatives/Terms	What They Mean
"must" and "is required"	These words impose an unconditional responsibility or requirement on the auditor to comply with requirements of this type specified in professional standards.
"should"	This indicates a presumptively mandatory requirement. Compliance with requirements of this type specified in professional standards is required, unless the auditor can demonstrate that the alternative procedures or actions that he or she applied were appropriate and sufficient to accomplish the objectives of the particular standard.
"should consider"	This indicates that the consideration of the procedure or action provided in professional standards is presumptively required; however, carrying out the action or procedure is not required.
"may," "might," and "could"	These words do not impose a professional requirement for the auditor to perform the suggested procedures or actions. Rather, these words impose on the auditor a responsibility to consider certain actions, procedures, or matters specified in professional standards. Whether and how the auditor implements these matters in the conduct of an audit is subject to the auditor's professional judgment.

Required Documentation When a Presumptively Mandatory Requirement Is Not Complied With

The imperative "should" indicates a presumptively mandatory activity. There are only rare circumstances in which the auditor would be able to meet the objectives of the standards by alternative means. Therefore, if the auditor departs from a presumptively mandatory requirement, the auditor must document in the working papers the following: (1) the reasons why the presumptively mandatory requirement was not complied with and (2) how the alternative procedures performed adequately achieved the objectives of the presumptively mandatory requirement. Since the auditor must already document the work performed as part of an audit, adding a concise explanation as to why the auditor chose to perform the alternative procedures should not increase the volume of documentation to an unreasonable level.

PRACTICE ISSUES AND FREQUENTLY ASKED QUESTIONS

Issue 1: Do the words "may," "might," and "could" impose a professional requirement for the auditor to perform the suggested procedures or actions described in professional standards?

No. Professional standards generally include explanatory material that provides further clarification or guidance on the professional requirements, or identifies and describes other procedures or actions relating to the auditor's activities. Such explanatory material generally explains why the auditor might consider certain particular procedures and provides additional information for the auditor to consider in exercising professional judgment in performing the audit engagement. The words *may, might*, and *could* are typically used to describe these actions and procedures. Therefore, explanatory material that uses such terms is not intended to impose a professional requirement for the auditor to perform the suggested procedures or actions. Rather, these procedures or actions require the auditor's attention and understanding; accordingly, how and whether the auditor carries out the suggested procedures or actions depends on the exercise of professional judgment in the specific engagement.

ILLUSTRATIONS AND PRACTICE AIDS

There are no illustrations and practice aids for this Section.

AU SECTION 150
GENERALLY ACCEPTED AUDITING STANDARDS

PRACTICE POINT: As part of its Clarity Project, the American Institute of Certified Public Accountants' (AICPA's) Auditing Standards Board (ASB) has finalized a clarified standard that includes: (1) Preface to Codification of Statements on Auditing Standards, *Principles Underlying an Audit Conducted in Accordance with Generally Accepted Auditing Standards* ("Preface"), and (2) Statement on Auditing Standards (SAS), *Overall Objectives of the Independent Auditor and the Conduct of an Audit in Accordance with Generally Accepted Auditing Standards.*

The Preface contains the principles underlying an audit conducted in accordance with U.S. generally accepted auditing standards (GAAS). These principles are not requirements and do not carry any authority. The ASB has developed the principles to provide a framework that is helpful in understanding and explaining an audit. The principles are organized to provide a structure for the Codification of Statements on Auditing Standards. This structure addresses the purpose of an audit, personal responsibilities of the auditor, auditor actions in performing the audit, and reporting.

The SAS addresses the independent auditor's overall responsibilities when conducting an audit of financial statements in accordance with GAAS. Specifically, it sets out the overall objectives of the independent auditor and explains the nature and scope of an audit designed to enable the independent auditor to meet those objectives. It also explains the scope, authority, and structure of GAAS and includes requirements establishing the general responsibilities of the independent auditor applicable in all audits, including the obligation to comply with GAAS.

Upon the issuance of all clarified SASs, one SAS will be issued containing all clarified SASs in codified format. The ASB has decided that the effective date of the clarified SASs that have not yet been issued is for audits of financial statements for periods ending on or after December 15, 2012.

Auditors should be alert to and monitor further developments in this area.

PRACTICE POINT: In March 2011, the American Institute of Certified Public Accountants' (AICPA's) Auditing Standards Board (ASB) issued an exposure draft (ED) of a proposed Statement on Auditing Standards (SAS) titled, "Omnibus Statement on Auditing Standards—2011." This proposed SAS, which is part of the AICPA's Clarity Project, would amend the following SASs that have been issued in the clarity format and are currently effective:

- SAS-117 (AU Section 801) (Compliance Audits). The amendment to SAS-117 conforms the auditor's report on compliance to the requirements of the clarified SAS, "Forming an Opinion and Reporting on Financial Statements." In addition, the amendment revises the appendix in SAS-117, "AU Sections That Are Not Applicable to Compliance Audits," to reflect conforming changes to affected references to AU Sections as a result of the ASB's Clarity Project.

- SAS-118 (AU Section 550) (Other Information in Documents Containing Audited Financial Statements). The amendment to SAS-118 clarifies the requirements with respect to identified material inconsistencies by categorizing the requirements based on when the inconsistencies are identified (prior to the date of the auditor's report on the audited financial statements; after the date of the auditor's report but prior to the report release date; and after the report release date). It also adds application material addressing electronic sites to include guidance from an interpretation of AU Section 550 (Other Information in Documents Containing Audited Financial Statements), which the ASB determined was appropriate to include in SAS-118.

In addition, in order to address other changes necessitated by the ASB's overall Clarity Project, the proposed SAS would amend the following clarified SASs that have been finalized and released, but not yet issued as authoritative:

- Clarified SAS, "Overall Objectives of the Independent Auditor and the Conduct of an Audit in Accordance with Generally Accepted Auditing Standards."
- Clarified SAS, "Modifications to the Opinion in the Independent Auditor's Report."
- Clarified SAS, "Reports on Application of Requirements of an Applicable Financial Reporting Framework."
- Clarified SAS, "The Auditor's Communication with Those Charged with Governance (Redrafted)."
- Clarified SAS, "Audit Documentation (Redrafted)."

The proposed SAS would be effective for audits of financial statements for periods ending on or after December 15, 2012, except for the amendment to the clarified SAS, "Reports on Application of Requirements of an Applicable Financial Reporting Framework," which would be effective for engagements ending on or after December 15, 2012.

WHAT EVERY PRACTITIONER SHOULD KNOW

Basic Objectives and Requirements

This Section establishes three levels in the generally accepted auditing standards (GAAS) hierarchy: (1) auditing standards, (2) interpretive publications, and (3) other auditing publications.

There are ten generally accepted auditing standards approved by the AICPA that are divided into three groups:

1. *General Standards*—There are three standards in this group that relate to the professional qualifications, independence, and personal integrity of the auditor.

2. *Standards of Field Work*—There are three standards in this group that set forth quality criteria for the actual conduct of the audit, including the proper design and execution of auditing procedures.

3. *Standards of Reporting*—There are four standards in this group that guide the auditor to the ultimate objective of an audit: to issue the audit report and provide an opinion on the financial statements.

The SASs are codified within the framework of the ten standards. Therefore, the auditor should have sufficient knowledge of the SASs to identify those that are applicable to his or her audit, and should be prepared to justify departures from them.

In addition, the auditor should be aware of and consider *interpretive publications* applicable to his or her audit. *Interpretive publications*, for example, Auditing Interpretations of the SASs, are recommendations on the application of the SASs in specific circumstances. Therefore, if the auditor does not apply the guidance included in an applicable interpretive publication, the auditor should be prepared to explain how he or she complied with the SAS provisions addressed by such auditing guidance in the applicable interpretive publication.

Other auditing publications (e.g., auditing articles in the *Journal of Accountancy*, textbooks) have no authoritative status, but may be indicative of the practice in specific areas not addressed in the authoritative literature. If an auditor applies the auditing guidance included in an "other auditing publication," the auditor should be satisfied that such guidance is both appropriate and relevant to the audit engagement.

PRACTICE ISSUES AND FREQUENTLY ASKED QUESTIONS

Issue 1: What is the difference between "auditing standards" and "auditing procedures" as they appear in professional literature?

"Auditing procedures" are acts that an auditor performs in an audit engagement in order to meet the standards. Procedures are specific in nature and have the primary purpose of gathering evidence to support particular financial statement assertions. "Auditing standards" are broader, more authoritative, and are criteria for the quality of audit performance. They deal with the objectives to be accomplished by those procedures, the quality of their performance, and the auditor's judgment in performing and reporting on an audit. Auditing procedures vary depending on the size, nature, complexity, and other unique characteristics of each engagement, whereas auditing standards do not change from engagement to engagement and provide guidance and requirements for all audits.

Issue 2: How does the concept of materiality affect an auditor's judgment in developing "auditing procedures"?

Items that are relatively more important to the financial statements, or that are more susceptible to misstatement, should generally be given greater attention than those of lesser importance, or that are less susceptible to misstatement. For example, inventory is usually a significant item in the financial statements of most manufacturers. The audit procedures applied to inventory would therefore be more extensive and would typically take more time than those applied to an item of lesser importance, such as prepaid expenses. Strong evidence of the existence of inventory, for example, would be provided by an observation of physical counts by the auditor. Detailed testing of inventory pricing might be performed by vouching inventory costs to vendors' invoices to support management's assertion about the inventory value. On the other hand, simple analytical procedures, such as comparison to prior years' balances, might suffice for small prepaid expense balances that are clearly immaterial to the financial statements.

PRACTICE POINT: See AU Section 312 (Audit Risk and Materiality in Conducting an Audit) for additional guidance on the auditor's consideration of materiality when conducting an audit in accordance with generally accepted auditing standards.

Issue 3: The third general standard states that the auditor must exercise due professional care in the performance of an audit and the preparation of the audit report. What is generally meant by "due professional care"?

The exercise of due professional care requires that the auditor develop a healthy skepticism when conducting the audit. This is generally exhibited by a disposition to question and test all material assertions made by management, whether they are oral, written, or incorporated into the accounting records. At the same time, such an attitude of skepticism should be balanced by an open mind about the integrity of management; in other words, the auditor should not blindly assume that management is dishonest, nor should the auditor assume that management is perfectly and unquestionably honest. For further discussion, see AU Section 230 (Due Professional Care in the Performance of Work).

PRACTICE POINT: Illustration 1 in the section below provides a comparison between generally accepted auditing standards and attestation standards.

Issue 4: What are "interpretive publications" under generally accepted auditing standards?

Interpretive publications are recommendations on the application of the SASs in specific circumstances and in engagements involving specialized industries. Interpretive publications consist of:

1. Auditing Interpretations of the SASs;
2. Appendices to the SASs;
3. Auditing guidance included in AICPA Audit and Accounting Guides; and
4. AICPA auditing Statements of Position.

While interpretive publications are not auditing standards, the auditor is expected to apply the auditing guidance included in an applicable interpretive publication. If the auditor does not apply such applicable auditing guidance in an audit, he or she should be prepared to explain how the SAS provisions addressed by such auditing guidance were complied with.

Issue 5: Is the auditor required or expected to follow the auditing guidance included in an other auditing publication, for example an article in the **Journal of Accountancy** *or other such professional journals?*

No. *Other auditing publications* have no authoritative status, although they may help the auditor understand and apply the auditing standards. *Other auditing publications* under this Section include:

- AICPA auditing publications other than SASs and interpretive publications
- Auditing articles in the *Journal of Accountancy* and other professional journals
- Auditing articles in the AICPA *CPA Letter*
- Continuing professional education programs
- Other instruction materials
- Textbooks
- Guide books
- Audit programs and checklists
- Other auditing publications from state CPA societies, other organizations, and individuals

If an auditor applies the auditing guidance included in an "other auditing publication" such as the ones listed above, the auditor should be satisfied that such guidance is both appropriate and relevant to the specific circumstances of the audit engagement.

ILLUSTRATIONS AND PRACTICE AIDS

ILLUSTRATION 1—COMPARISON BETWEEN GENERALLY ACCEPTED AUDITING STANDARDS AND ATTESTATION STANDARDS

Generally Accepted Auditing Standards	Attestation Standards
General Standards	
1. The auditor must have adequate technical training and proficiency to perform the audit.	1. The practitioner must have adequate technical training and proficiency to perform the attestation engagement.
	2. The practitioner must have adequate knowledge of the subject matter.
	3. The practitioner must have reason to believe that the subject matter is capable of evaluation against criteria that are suitable and available to users.
2. The auditor must maintain independence in mental attitude in all matters relating to the audit.	4. The practitioner must maintain independence in mental attitude in all matters relating to the engagement.
3. The auditor must exercise due professional care in the performance of the audit and in the preparation of the report.	5. The practitioner must exercise due professional care in the planning and performance of the engagement and in the preparation of the report.

Generally Accepted Auditing Standards	Attestation Standards

Standards of Field Work

1. The auditor must adequately plan the work and properly supervise any assistants.

2. The auditor must obtain a sufficient understanding of the entity and its environment, including its internal control, to assess the risk of material misstatement of the financial statements whether due to error or fraud, and to design the nature, timing, and extent of further audit procedures.

3. The auditor must obtain sufficient appropriate audit evidence by performing audit procedures to afford a reasonable basis for an opinion regarding the financial statements under audit.

1. The practitioner must adequately plan the work and properly supervise any assistants.

2. The practitioner must obtain sufficient evidence to provide a reasonable basis for the conclusion that is expressed in the report.

Standards of Reporting

1. The auditor must state in the auditor's report whether the financial statements are presented in accordance with generally accepted accounting principles.

2. The auditor must identify in the auditor's report those circumstances in which such principles have not been consistently observed in the current period in relation to the preceding period.

1. The practitioner must identify the subject matter or the assertion being reported on and state the character of the engagement in the report.

2. The practitioner must state his or her conclusion about the subject matter or the assertion in relation to the criteria against which the subject matter was evaluated in the report.

Generally Accepted Auditing Standards	Attestation Standards
3. When the auditor determines that informative disclosures are not reasonably adequate, he or she must state so in the auditor's report.	3. The practitioner must state all of his or her significant reservations about the engagement, the subject matter, and, if applicable, the assertion related thereto in the report.
4. The auditor must either express an opinion regarding the financial statements, taken as a whole, or state that an opinion cannot be expressed, in the auditor's report. When the auditor cannot express an overall opinion, the auditor should state the reasons therefor in the auditor's report. In all cases where an auditor's name is associated with financial statements, the auditor should clearly indicate the character of the auditor's work, if any, and the degree of responsibility the auditor is taking in the auditor's report.	4. The practitioner must state in the report that the report is intended solely for the information and use of the specified parties under the following circumstances: • When the criteria used to evaluate the subject matter are determined by the practitioner to be appropriate only for a limited number of parties who either participated in their establishment or can be presumed to have an adequate understanding of the criteria. • When the criteria used to evaluate the subject matter are available only to specified parties. • When reporting on subject matter, and a written assertion has not been provided by the responsible party. • When the report is on an attestation engagement to apply agreed-upon procedures to the subject matter.

AU SECTION 161
THE RELATIONSHIP OF GENERALLY ACCEPTED AUDITING STANDARDS TO QUALITY CONTROL STANDARDS

PRACTICE POINT: As part of its Clarity Project, the American Institute of Certified Public Accountants' (AICPA's) Auditing Standards Board (ASB) has finalized a clarified Statement on Auditing Standards (SAS) titled, "Quality Control for an Engagement Conducted in Accordance with Generally Accepted Auditing Standards," which supersedes SAS-25 (AU Section 161) (The Relationship of Generally Accepted Auditing Standards to Quality Control Standards).

Extant AU Section 161 contains no requirements addressing specific responsibilities of the auditor regarding quality control procedures for an audit of financial statements. However, the clarified SAS contains requirements and application material that address such auditor responsibilities. Among other matters, the clarified SAS:

- Specifies quality control procedures at the engagement level that assist the auditor in achieving the objectives of the quality control standards.

- Addresses the engagement quality control review process for those audit engagements, if any, for which the firm has determined that an engagement quality control review is required. The reference to "engagement quality control review" in the clarified SAS is synonymous with what is commonly referred to as "concurring review" or "second partner review." The clarified SAS does not require such a review. However, for audit engagements, if any, for which the firm has determined that an engagement quality control review is required, the clarified SAS prescribes certain specified procedures to be performed by the engagement quality control reviewer.

- Provides that certain matters be included in the audit docu mentation.

The ASB is expected to issue many of the clarified standards in *one* SAS that will be codified in "AU Section" format. The ASB has decided that the effective date of the clarified SASs that have not yet been issued is for audits of financial statements for periods ending on or after December 15, 2012. Auditors should be alert to and monitor further developments in this area.

PRACTICE POINT: Also, the American Institute of Certified Public Accountants' (AICPA's) Auditing Standards Board (ASB) has issued Statement on Quality Control Standards (SQCS) No. 8 titled, "A Firm's System of Quality Control (Redrafted)," which supersedes SQCS-7 (QC Section 10) of the same name. To facilitate convergence with the International Standards on Quality Control (ISQCs), the SQCS-8 has been drafted using ISQC No. 1 (ISQC-1), "Quality Control for Firms That Perform Audits and Reviews of Financial Statements, and Other Assurance and Related Services Engagements," as a base.

SQCS-8, which reflects a more principles-based approach to standard setting, does not change or expand extant SQCS-7 in any significant respect. SQCS-8 contains a requirement that procedures established for dealing with differences of professional opinion should enable a member of the engagement team to document that member's disagreement with the conclusions reached after appropriate consultation. This requirement is presently included in Statement on Auditing Standards (SAS) No. 108 (AU Section 311) (Planning and Supervision); however, the ASB believes that this requirement is more appropriately placed at the firm level for all engagements.

SQCS-8 is applicable to a CPA firm's system of quality control for its accounting and auditing practice as of January 1, 2012.

WHAT EVERY PRACTITIONER SHOULD KNOW

Basic Requirement

A firm of independent auditors must have a quality control system to provide reasonable assurance that generally accepted auditing standards and the quality control standards are being observed in each engagement. The specific controls to be established are discussed in the AICPA's Quality Control Standards.

Elements of Quality Control

The elements of quality control are identified in Statement on Quality Control Standards (SQCS) No. 7, "A Firm's System of Quality Control." In establishing quality control policies and procedures, a firm should address the following six elements of quality control:

1. *Leadership responsibilities for quality within the firm* ("tone at the top")—A firm's system of quality control should include policies for:

   a. Assigning management responsibilities to ensure that commercial considerations do not override the quality of work performed;

   b. Addressing performance evaluation, compensation, and advancement of its personnel; and

   c. Devoting adequate resources for the development, communication, and support of the firm's quality control policies and procedures.

2. *Relevant ethical requirements*—This element of quality control requires a firm to establish policies and procedures to provide it with reasonable assurance that the firm and its personnel comply with relevant ethical requirements, including those relating to integrity, objectivity, independence, and due care.

3. *Acceptance and continuance of client relationships and specific engagements*— In order to minimize the likelihood of association with a client whose management lacks integrity, a firm should establish controls for deciding whether to accept or continue a client relationship and whether to perform a specific engagement for that client.

4. *Human resources*—A firm's system of quality control should include policies and procedures to address (a) recruitment and hiring; (b) determining capabilities and competencies; (c) assigning personnel to engagements; (d) professional development; and (e) performance evaluation, compensation, and advancement.

5. *Engagement performance*—A firm's policies and procedures should be designed to provide reasonable assurance that engagements are consistently performed in accordance with professional standards and regulatory and legal requirements, and that the firm's reports are appropriate in the circumstances. Such policies and procedures should address engagement performance, documentation, and supervision and review responsibilities.

6. *Monitoring*—A firm's system of quality control should include monitoring procedures that are sufficiently comprehensive for the firm to assess compliance with all applicable professional standards and regulatory requirements, and the firm's quality control policies and procedures.

PRACTICE ISSUES AND FREQUENTLY ASKED QUESTIONS

Issue 1: Do a firm's quality control policies and procedures have to be documented?

Yes. In determining the extent of such documentation, the firm should consider the size, structure, and nature of its practice. For example, documentation of a firm's quality control policies and procedures generally would be less extensive in a small firm than in a large or multi-office firm.

Issue 2: How do quality control standards affect a firm's audit practice?

Quality control standards relate to the conduct of a firm's audit practice as a whole, whereas auditing standards relate to the conduct of individual audit engagements. Quality control standards deal with a firm's system to provide it with reasonable assurance that its audit engagements meet the requirements of generally accepted auditing standards (GAAS).

Issue 3: With respect to accepting a new client, is a CPA firm required to have the necessary expertise to conduct an audit engagement as a condition to accepting the engagement?

No. A CPA firm is not precluded from accepting an audit engagement which the firm is not fully qualified to execute at the time the engagement is accepted. Therefore, the CPA may accept an engagement in an industry in which the CPA does not have experience, as long as he or she obtains the necessary expertise before the engagement is completed.

Issue 4: Do deficiencies in a firm's quality control system indicate that an audit engagement was not performed in accordance with GAAS?

No. This Section specifically states that deficiencies in a firm's quality control system, or noncompliance therewith, do not in and of themselves necessarily indicate that an audit engagement was not performed in accordance with GAAS.

ILLUSTRATIONS AND PRACTICE AIDS

ILLUSTRATION 1—CLIENT ACCEPTANCE AND RETENTION EVALUATION FORM

Client Name: _____

Date of Financial Statements: _____

Instructions

This form should be used to document the screening of prospective new clients or for evaluating the retention of existing clients. This form is only a guide; the auditor should exercise professional judgment to determine how the form should be modified by revising questions listed or adding questions where appropriate. This form should be updated at least annually, and the engagement executive should review it to determine whether to retain or terminate the client.

Section I—Background and Basic Information

1. Entity legal name: _____

2. Key contact name and title: _____

3. Entity address and telephone number: _____

     _____

     _____

     _____

4. Type of entity (e.g., partnership, Subchapter S, public): _____

5. Fiscal year end: _____

6. Principal stockholders, officers, and directors: _____

Name	Position
_____	_____
_____	_____
_____	_____
_____	_____

7. Describe how contact initially was established:

     _____

     _____

     _____

8. Entity's attorneys:

     Name: _____

     Name: _____

9. Entity's banking relationships:

     Name: _____

     Name: _____

10. Describe the nature of the entity's business and products or services provided, including any economic dependence or concentrations.

     _____

     _____

     _____

11. Explain management's reasons for changing CPA firms and how frequently the entity has changed CPA firms.

     _____

_____

_____

12. Describe what services and reports are requested and their required completion dates.

_____

_____

_____

13. Describe why the entity desires audited financial statements and what parties may potentially rely on them (e.g., regulatory requirements, banks).

_____

_____

_____

Section II—Entity Financial Condition and Nature of Transactions

Note: Any "Yes" answers to the following questions indicate a higher level of risk than normal, and the auditor should expand on those answers.

	Yes	No	N/A
1. Is cash flow or working capital inadequate to meet operating requirements, debt payments, dividends, etc.?	___	___	___
2. Are there significant demands for new debt or equity capital?	___	___	___
3. Have loan agreement covenants been waived or violated?	___	___	___
4. Is there any doubt about the ability of the entity to continue in existence?	___	___	___
5. Have sales, gross margins, or income trends deteriorated significantly in recent years?	___	___	___
6. Is the entity's industry unfavorable, unusually litigious, or considered risky (e.g., construction companies)?	___	___	___
7. Does the entity engage in significant related-party transactions?	___	___	___
8. Does the entity usually engage in significant unusual transactions during the year or near year end?	___	___	___
9. Does the entity lack the financing necessary to carry out its business plans?	___	___	___
10. Is there evidence of complex accounting issues or transactions that are difficult to audit?	___	___	___
11. Is financing by third parties contingent on the entity's meeting certain minimum financial ratios?	___	___	___
12. Does the company engage in the use of derivatives?	___	___	___

Section III—Management Integrity and Business Risk Exposure

Note: Any "Yes" answers to the following questions indicate a higher level of risk than normal, and the auditor should expand on those answers.

	Yes	No	N/A

1. Has the entity, or any of its principals, ever been charged with violating any federal, state, or local laws?

2. Is there any pending litigation or regulatory investigation against the entity or any of its principals?

3. Are there significant disagreements or lawsuits among the owners?

4. Are any mergers, acquisitions, or dispositions planned or likely?

5. Has there been a high turnover of key management?

6. Is the entity dependent on one major customer for most of its revenue or on one major supplier for most of its products?

7. Does management have a reputation for taking unusual or unnecessary risks?

8. Is management reluctant to provide necessary documents regarding major transactions or generally uncooperative or unreasonable?

9. Is management unwilling to correct material misstatements in the financial statements?

10. Is there any indication that management representations are not reliable?

11. Does management place undue pressure on meeting financial goals or reducing income taxes?

12. Does top management lack the experience necessary to operate the business?

13. Is top management lacking a financial and accounting officer who is knowledgeable about the business and the decisions made?

14. Does management lack the commitment to adopt and apply appropriate accounting principles?

15. Are the company's internal controls inadequate for the size and organizational structure of the business?

16. Is the company's corporate governance structure inappropriate or inadequate?

17. Does management lack the commitment to implement and maintain an effective internal control system?

18. Does management lack the commitment to implement and maintain antifraud programs and controls?

19. Are key management employees compensated based on the results of the entity's operations?

20. Is management aware of any instances of fraud or illegal acts?

Section IV—Communication with Predecessor Accountants

Note: Any "Yes" answers to the following questions indicate a higher level of risk than normal, and the auditor should expand on those answers.

	Yes	No	N/A
1. Are you aware of any situations that might bear on the integrity of management?			
2. Have you had any significant disagreements with management over the application of accounting principles, practices, or financial statement disclosures?			
3. Has management ever attempted to restrict or direct the scope of the audit?			
4. Are you aware of any incidents of management intervention in, or circumvention of, the company's internal control?			
5. Is management unwilling to accept primary responsibility for the content of the financial statements?			
6. Does management discourage its key employees from cooperating fully with the independent auditor?			
7. Have you had any communications with management regarding fraud, illegal acts, or internal control related matters?			
8. Are you aware of any pending or threatened litigation or regulatory investigations against the company?			
9. Are you aware of any material contingencies affecting the company?			
10. Are you aware of any matters that might raise substantial doubt about the entity's ability to continue as a going concern?			
11. Are you aware of any significant deficiencies or material weaknesses in internal control?			
12. Are you willing to reissue your report or otherwise provide a consent with respect to the previously issued financial statements (if applicable)?			

13. Inquire of the predecessor auditor about his or her understanding of reasons for change in auditors and summarize:

_____

_____

14. Name of predecessor auditor: _____

15. Name and position of person inquired of: _____

_____

16. Date of inquiry: _____

Section V—Independence and Ability to Provide Services Requested

	Yes	No	N/A
1. Does the entity appear to have appropriate completeness procedures to ensure that accounting transactions are entered into the accounting system?			

2. Does the accounting system appear to provide records sufficient to permit application of cost-effective audit procedures?   _____ _____ _____

3. Does the firm have the required technical skills and expertise in the entity's industry?   _____ _____ _____

4. Does the firm or any of its staff have any existing relationship with the entity that would impair its independence?   _____ _____ _____

5. Are there any services that the firm has already provided, is in the process of providing, or will be providing (e.g., appraisal, valuation, and actuarial services) that impair independence?   _____ _____ _____

6. Are there any relationships between firm personnel and officers and directors of the client that impair independence?   _____ _____ _____

7. Are there any business relationships between the firm and the client that impair independence?   _____ _____ _____

8. Is the client potentially significant to the firm in terms of fees, status, or other factors that would impair independence?   _____ _____ _____

9. Are there any indications that the firm might have a problem billing or collecting its fees?   _____ _____ _____

Section VI—Additional Comments

Note: Use this section to elaborate on any of the answers above or to provide additional comments about matters that increase the overall engagement risk.

_____

_____

_____

Section VII—Conclusion

Acceptance decision:

☐ YES   ☐ NO

Prepared by: _____ Date: _____

Partner's signature: _____ Date: _____

Concurring Partner's signature: _____ Date: _____

Updated in subsequent years as follows:

Year	Updated by	Date
_____	_____	_____
_____	_____	_____
_____	_____	_____
_____	_____	_____

AU Section 200
THE GENERAL STANDARDS

AU SECTION 201
NATURE OF THE GENERAL STANDARDS

PRACTICE POINT: As part of its Clarity Project, the American Institute of Certified Public Accountants' (AICPA's) Auditing Standards Board (ASB) has finalized a clarified standard that includes: (1) Preface to Codification of Statements on Auditing Standards, *Principles Underlying an Audit Conducted in Accordance with Generally Accepted Auditing Standards* ("Preface"), and (2) Statement on Auditing Standards (SAS), "Overall Objectives of the Independent Auditor and the Conduct of an Audit in Accordance with Generally Accepted Auditing Standards."

The Preface contains the principles underlying an audit conducted in accordance with U.S. generally accepted auditing standards (GAAS). These principles are not requirements and do not carry any authority. The ASB has developed the principles to provide a framework that is helpful in understanding and explaining an audit. The principles are organized to provide a structure for the Codification of Statements on Auditing Standards. This structure addresses the purpose of an audit, personal responsibilities of the auditor, auditor actions in performing the audit, and reporting.

The SAS addresses the independent auditor's overall responsibilities when conducting an audit of financial statements in accordance with GAAS. Specifically, it sets out the overall objectives of the independent auditor and explains the nature and scope of an audit designed to enable the independent auditor to meet those objectives. It also explains the scope, authority, and structure of GAAS and includes requirements establishing the general responsibilities of the independent auditor applicable in all audits, including the obligation to comply with GAAS.

The ASB is expected to issue many of the clarified standards in *one* SAS that will be codified in "AU Section" format. The ASB has decided that the effective date of the clarified SASs that have not yet been issued is for audits of financial statements for periods ending on or after December 15, 2012. Auditors should be alert to and monitor further developments in this area.

PRACTICE POINT: In March 2011, the American Institute of Certified Public Accountants' (AICPA's) Auditing Standards Board (ASB) issued an exposure draft (ED) of a proposed Statement on Auditing Standards (SAS) titled, "Omnibus Statement on Auditing Standards—2011." This proposed SAS, which is part of the AICPA's Clarity Project, would amend the following SASs that have been issued in the clarity format and are currently effective:

- SAS-117 (AU Section 801) (Compliance Audits). The amendment to SAS-117 conforms the auditor's report on compliance to the requirements of the clarified SAS, "Forming an Opinion and Reporting on Financial Statements." In addition, the amendment revises the appendix in SAS-117, "AU Sections That Are Not Applicable to Compliance Audits," to reflect conforming changes to affected references to AU Sections as a result of the ASB's Clarity Project.

- SAS-118 (AU Section 550) (Other Information in Documents Containing Audited Financial Statements). The amendment to SAS-118 clarifies the requirements with respect to identified material inconsistencies by categorizing the requirements based on when the inconsistencies are identified (prior to the date of the auditor's report on the audited financial statements; after the date of the auditor's report but prior to the report release date; and after the report release date). It also adds application material addressing electronic sites to include guidance from an interpretation of AU Section 550 (Other Information in Documents Containing Audited Financial Statements), which the ASB determined was appropriate to include in SAS-118.

In addition, in order to address other changes necessitated by the ASB's overall Clarity Project, the proposed SAS would amend the following clarified SASs that have been finalized and released, but not yet issued as authoritative:

- Clarified SAS, "Overall Objectives of the Independent Auditor and the Conduct of an Audit in Accordance with Generally Accepted Auditing Standards."
- Clarified SAS, "Modifications to the Opinion in the Independent Auditor's Report."
- Clarified SAS, "Reports on Application of Requirements of an Applicable Financial Reporting Framework."
- Clarified SAS, "The Auditor's Communication with Those Charged with Governance (Redrafted)."
- Clarified SAS, "Audit Documentation (Redrafted)."

The proposed SAS would be effective for audits of financial statements for periods ending on or after December 15, 2012, except for the amendment to the clarified SAS, "Reports on Application of Requirements of an Applicable Financial Reporting Framework," which would be effective for engagements ending on or after December 15, 2012.

WHAT EVERY PRACTITIONER SHOULD KNOW

Basic Objective

The general standards deal with an auditor's qualifications and the quality of his or her work. There are three general standards that deal with the auditor's:

1. *Training and proficiency*—Covered in AU Section 210 (Training and Proficiency of the Independent Auditor).
2. *Independence*—Covered in AU Section 220 (Independence).
3. *Due professional care*—Covered in AU Section 230 (Due Professional Care in the Performance of Work).

PRACTICE ISSUES AND FREQUENTLY ASKED QUESTIONS

Issue 1: What is the difference between the general standards and the standards of fieldwork and standards of reporting?

The general standards deal with an auditor's qualifications and the quality of his or her work, whereas the standards of fieldwork set forth quality criteria for the actual conduct of the audit, and the standards of reporting deal with auditors' reports and related opinions on the financial statements.

ILLUSTRATIONS AND PRACTICE AIDS

There are no illustrations and practice aids for this Section.

AU SECTION 210
TRAINING AND PROFICIENCY OF THE INDEPENDENT AUDITOR

PRACTICE POINT: As part of its Clarity Project, the American Institute of Certified Public Accountants' (AICPA's) Auditing Standards Board (ASB) has finalized a clarified standard that includes: (1) Preface to Codification of Statements on Auditing Standards, *Principles Underlying an Audit Conducted in Accordance with Generally Accepted Auditing Standards* ("Preface"), and (2) Statement on Auditing Standards (SAS), "Overall Objectives of the Independent Auditor and the Conduct of an Audit in Accordance with Generally Accepted Auditing Standards."

The Preface contains the principles underlying an audit conducted in accordance with U.S. generally accepted auditing standards (GAAS). These principles are not requirements and do not carry any authority. The ASB has developed the principles to provide a framework that is helpful in understanding and explaining an audit. The principles are organized to provide a structure for the Codification of Statements on Auditing Standards. This structure addresses the purpose of an audit, personal responsibilities of the auditor, auditor actions in performing the audit, and reporting.

The SAS addresses the independent auditor's overall responsibilities when conducting an audit of financial statements in accordance with GAAS. Specifically, it sets out the overall objectives of the independent auditor and explains the nature and scope of an audit designed to enable the independent auditor to meet those objectives. It also explains the scope, authority, and structure of GAAS and includes requirements establishing the general responsibilities of the independent auditor applicable in all audits, including the obligation to comply with GAAS.

The ASB is expected to issue many of the clarified standards in *one* SAS that will be codified in "AU Section" format. The ASB has decided that the effective date of the clarified SASs that have not yet been issued is for audits of financial statements for periods ending on or after December 15, 2012. Auditors should be alert to and monitor further developments in this area.

PRACTICE POINT: In March 2011, the American Institute of Certified Public Accountants' (AICPA's) Auditing Standards Board (ASB) issued an exposure draft (ED) of a proposed Statement on Auditing Standards (SAS) titled, "Omnibus Statement on Auditing Standards—2011." This proposed SAS, which is part of the AICPA's Clarity Project, would amend the following SASs that have been issued in the clarity format and are currently effective:

- SAS-117 (AU Section 801) (Compliance Audits). The amendment to SAS-117 conforms the auditor's report on compliance to the requirements of the clarified SAS, "Forming an Opinion and Reporting on Financial Statements." In addition, the amendment revises the appendix in SAS-117, "AU Sections That Are Not Applicable to Compliance Audits," to reflect conforming changes to affected references to AU Sections as a result of the ASB's Clarity Project.

- SAS-118 (AU Section 550) (Other Information in Documents Containing Audited Financial Statements). The amendment to SAS-118 clarifies the requirements with respect to identified material inconsistencies by categorizing the requirements based on when the inconsistencies are identified (prior to the date of the auditor's report on the audited financial statements; after the date of the auditor's report but prior to the report release date; and after the report release date). It also adds application material addressing electronic sites to include guidance from an interpretation of AU Section 550 (Other Information in Documents Containing Audited Financial Statements), which the ASB determined was appropriate to include in SAS-118.

In addition, in order to address other changes necessitated by the ASB's overall Clarity Project, the proposed SAS would amend the following clarified SASs that have been finalized and released, but not yet issued as authoritative:

- Clarified SAS, "Overall Objectives of the Independent Auditor and the Conduct of an Audit in Accordance with Generally Accepted Auditing Standards."

- Clarified SAS, "Modifications to the Opinion in the Independent Auditor's Report."

- Clarified SAS, "Reports on Application of Requirements of an Applicable Financial Reporting Framework."

- Clarified SAS, "The Auditor's Communication with Those Charged with Governance (Redrafted)."

- Clarified SAS, "Audit Documentation (Redrafted)."

The proposed SAS would be effective for audits of financial statements for periods ending on or after December 15, 2012, except for the amendment to the clarified SAS, "Reports on Application of Requirements of an Applicable Financial Reporting Framework," which would be effective for engagements ending on or after December 15, 2012.

WHAT EVERY PRACTITIONER SHOULD KNOW

Basic Objective

This Section deals with the first general standard, which states that the auditor must have adequate technical training and proficiency to perform the audit.

Training and Proficiency

The auditor meets his or her responsibility through formal education, experience in the profession, and experience specifically in the field of auditing. The auditor also must continue to learn and stay abreast of new accounting and auditing authoritative pronouncements as they are issued. This necessitates that auditors obtain continuing professional education periodically in order that their training and proficiency can be maintained at an adequate level.

PRACTICE ISSUES AND FREQUENTLY ASKED QUESTIONS

Issue 1: How does a junior staff member just entering an auditing career fulfill his or her responsibility to meet the training and proficiency requirements?

The profession recognizes the importance of both formal education and professional experience. No matter how talented a junior assistant is, training and experience in the field of auditing are essential if that person is to be an auditor. Formal education alone will seldom entirely enable an individual to develop the seasoned judgment born of many years of experience within a particular industry, or to deal with emerging business issues, or complex and unusual transactions. Therefore, a junior assistant should obtain his or her professional experience with the proper review and supervision of his or her work by a more experienced auditor (i.e., through on-the-job experience). The auditor with final responsibility for the engagement should determine the extent of supervision and review of the subordinate's work necessary on any particular engagement.

Issue 2: What role does self-study and self-development play in an auditor's training?

In addition to studying and applying new accounting and auditing pronouncements, an auditor must understand and be aware of general business, economic, and regulatory developments. Day-to-day reading of publications that relate to the business environment in general and to the specific industries in which the auditor practices are important because formal courses of study may not always be developed in time to enable the auditor to keep pace with these changes. Similarly, conversation and consultation with colleagues or other business professionals, whether within the context of formal meetings of professional societies or in an informal setting, help to increase the auditor's proficiency.

Issue 3: Is the auditor expected to gain technical knowledge and training in other disciplines that might be needed to successfully complete an audit engagement?

No. Adequate training and proficiency for an auditor do not go beyond the boundaries of accounting and auditing knowledge. When the auditor encounters situations requiring specialized knowledge, it may be necessary to consult a specialist. Examples include using an appraiser when evaluating the replacement cost of specialized inventory and an actuary for determining the appropriateness of the recorded value of insurance loss reserves. The auditor should have a sufficient understanding of the client's business to recognize the need for a professional with specialized knowledge and training. AU Section 336 (Using the Work of a Specialist) provides guidance to auditors for selecting specialists and reviewing their work to successfully complete an audit engagement.

Issue 4: What are some of the policies and procedures that a CPA firm might adopt to obtain reasonable assurance that its staff has adequate technical training and proficiency as auditors?

There are several policies and procedures that a CPA firm can adopt to obtain reasonable assurance that its staff has adequate technical training and proficiency as auditors, including the following:

- Develop criteria to identify the attributes, achievements, and experience desired in entry-level and experienced personnel.
- Establish criteria to evaluate personal characteristics, such as integrity, competence, and motivation.
- Designate an appropriate person in the firm to be responsible for assigning personnel to engagements based on factors such as:
  — Engagement size and complexity.
  — Specialized experience or expertise required.
  — Personnel availability and involvement of supervisory personnel.
  — Timing of the work to be performed.
  — Opportunities for on-the-job training.
  — Situations where independence or objectivity concerns exist.
- Require personnel to participate in general and industry-specific continuing professional education and professional development activities that enable them to satisfy responsibilities assigned and fulfill applicable continuing professional education requirements.
- Require personnel selected for advancement to have specified qualifications necessary to fulfill the responsibilities they will be called on to assume.
- Provide adequate supervision during the course of an engagement.
- Consult with appropriate individuals within the firm and outside the firm when certain specified issues or specialized situations arise.
- Maintain an adequate and up-to-date reference library or resource that is accessible to all professional personnel that includes materials related to clients served.

ILLUSTRATIONS AND PRACTICE AIDS

There are no illustrations and practice aids for this Section.

AU SECTION 220
INDEPENDENCE

PRACTICE POINT: As part of its Clarity Project, the American Institute of Certified Public Accountants' (AICPA's) Auditing Standards Board (ASB) has finalized a clarified standard that includes: (1) Preface to Codification of Statements on Auditing Standards, *Principles Underlying an Audit Conducted in Accordance with Generally Accepted Auditing Standards* ("Preface"), and (2) Statement on Auditing Standards (SAS), "Overall Objectives of the Independent Auditor and the Conduct of an Audit in Accordance with Generally Accepted Auditing Standards."

The Preface contains the principles underlying an audit conducted in accordance with U.S. generally accepted auditing standards (GAAS). These principles are not requirements and do not carry any authority. The ASB has developed the principles to provide a framework that is helpful in understanding and explaining an audit. The principles are organized to provide a structure for the Codification of Statements on Auditing Standards. This structure addresses the purpose of an audit, personal responsibilities of the auditor, auditor actions in performing the audit, and reporting.

The SAS addresses the independent auditor's overall responsibilities when conducting an audit of financial statements in accordance with GAAS. Specifically, it sets out the overall objectives of the independent auditor and explains the nature and scope of an audit designed to enable the independent auditor to meet those objectives. It also explains the scope, authority, and structure of GAAS and includes requirements establishing the general responsibilities of the independent auditor applicable in all audits, including the obligation to comply with GAAS.

The ASB is expected to issue many of the clarified standards in *one* SAS that will be codified in "AU Section" format. The ASB has decided that the effective date of the clarified SASs that have not yet been issued is for audits of financial statements for periods ending on or after December 15, 2012. Auditors should be alert to and monitor further developments in this area.

PRACTICE POINT: In March 2011, the American Institute of Certified Public Accountants' (AICPA's) Auditing Standards Board (ASB) issued an exposure draft (ED) of a proposed Statement on Auditing Standards (SAS) titled, "Omnibus Statement on Auditing Standards—2011." This proposed SAS, which is part of the AICPA's Clarity Project, would amend the following SASs that have been issued in the clarity format and are currently effective:

- SAS-117 (AU Section 801) (Compliance Audits). The amendment to SAS-117 conforms the auditor's report on compliance to the requirements of the clarified SAS, "Forming an Opinion and Reporting on Financial Statements." In addition, the amendment revises the appendix in SAS-117, "AU Sections That Are Not Applicable to Compliance Audits," to reflect conforming changes to affected references to AU Sections as a result of the ASB's Clarity Project.

- SAS-118 (AU Section 550) (Other Information in Documents Containing Audited Financial Statements). The amendment to SAS-118 clarifies the requirements with respect to identified material inconsistencies by categorizing the requirements based on when the inconsistencies are identified (prior to the date of the auditor's report on the audited financial statements; after the date of the auditor's report but prior to the report release date; and after the report release date). It also adds application material addressing electronic sites to include guidance from an interpretation of AU Section 550 (Other Information in Documents Containing Audited Financial Statements), which the ASB determined was appropriate to include in SAS-118.

In addition, in order to address other changes necessitated by the ASB's overall Clarity Project, the proposed SAS would amend the following clarified SASs that have been finalized and released, but not yet issued as authoritative:

- Clarified SAS, "Overall Objectives of the Independent Auditor and the Conduct of an Audit in Accordance with Generally Accepted Auditing Standards."

- Clarified SAS, "Modifications to the Opinion in the Independent Auditor's Report."

- Clarified SAS, "Reports on Application of Requirements of an Applicable Financial Reporting Framework."

- Clarified SAS, "The Auditor's Communication with Those Charged with Governance (Redrafted)."

- Clarified SAS, "Audit Documentation (Redrafted)."

The proposed SAS would be effective for audits of financial statements for periods ending on or after December 15, 2012, except for the amendment to the clarified SAS, "Reports on Application of Requirements of an Applicable Financial Reporting Framework," which would be effective for engagements ending on or after December 15, 2012.

WHAT EVERY PRACTITIONER SHOULD KNOW

Basic Objective

This Section deals with the second general standard, which requires the auditor to maintain independence in mental attitude in all matters relating to the audit engagement.

Preserving Independence

Independence is the true cornerstone of the auditing profession. Auditors must be independent—not only *in fact,* but in *appearance* as well. Independence in fact exists when the auditor is able to develop and maintain an unbiased attitude throughout the audit; that is, the auditor should not subordinate his or her judgment to others and should be disassociated from influences, actions, or conditions that might impair his or her judgment. On the other hand, independence in appearance primarily depends on a third party's perception of whether or not the auditor is independent; for example, accepting gifts from clients can create the appearance that an auditor is not independent.

PRACTICE ISSUES AND FREQUENTLY ASKED QUESTIONS

Issue 1: How does an auditor respond to critics who say that auditors cannot be truly independent when their fees are paid by the clients they audit?

There is probably no clear or satisfactory answer to this question, but the following points are worth addressing:

- One possible alternative to the engagement of the CPA and payment of audit fees by management would be the use of government or quasi-government auditors. It is questionable whether the audit function would be performed better or more effectively or efficiently by a public sector body.

- Critics can be comforted in knowing that the business risks and penalties associated with litigation, monetary loss, and adverse business exposure that auditors face are far more severe than the loss of audit fees.

- CPA firms are required to have quality control policies and procedures that monitor compliance with the independence standards and rules. Firms monitor compliance with the independence rules by requiring their professional employees to disclose any conditions that might impair independence. Firms are also required to have a peer review every three years to evaluate the firm's system for addressing independence.

Issue 2: What are some of the methods that a CPA firm might use to obtain reasonable assurance that its professional employees maintain independence in fact and in appearance?

There are several methods that a CPA firm can use to obtain reasonable assurance that its professional employees are independent, including the following:

- Explain the firm's interpretations of professional and regulatory requirements on independence to the staff and provide guidance for identifying and resolving potential issues or situations.

- Designate a senior member of the firm to answer questions and resolve matters and, if necessary, consult with sources outside the firm on independence issues.

- Obtain written representations from personnel upon hire and on an annual basis stating whether they are aware of any situations or conditions that might impair the firm's independence.

PRACTICE POINT: Illustration 1 in the section below provides an example of a form that a CPA firm might use in obtaining written representations from its staff regarding independence issues.

- Periodically review unpaid fees from clients to determine whether any outstanding balances impair the firm's independence.

- Periodically review the nature and scope of other professional services provided to audit clients and evaluate their effect on independence. See Illustration 2.
- In connection with the firm's quality control policies and procedures, specify procedures for staff to follow when they believe a member of the engagement team (or the firm) lacks independence.

Issue 3: What are some examples of auditors' personal impairments that are likely to affect a third party's perception of whether the auditor is independent?

Personal impairments that are likely to cause a third party to question whether the auditor is independent include:

- Professional, personal, financial, or official relationships that might cause an auditor to limit the extent of his or her inquiry, to limit disclosure, or to slant audit findings in any way.
- Preconceived ideas about individuals, groups, or organizations that could bias the audit.
- Biases (e.g., political or social convictions) that result from employment in or loyalty to a particular group or organization.
- Subsequent performance of an audit by the same individual who, for example, had previously approved invoices, payrolls, claims, and other proposed payments of the entity being audited.
- Concurrent or subsequent performance of an audit by the same person who maintained the accounting records.
- Financial interest, direct or indirect, in the entity being audited.

ILLUSTRATIONS AND PRACTICE AIDS

ILLUSTRATION 1—INDEPENDENCE REPRESENTATION FORM

PRACTICE POINT: This form can be used by a CPA firm to obtain written representations from staff regarding independence issues.

Employee name:_____

The Firm's quality control policies and procedures relating to independence require obtaining written representations from personnel, upon hire and on an annual basis, regarding independence with respect to the firm's clients. Completion of this form is required in order to determine that the firm and its personnel are in compliance with the independence rules, regulations, interpretations and rulings of the AICPA, the *(name of state)* CPA Society, the *(name of state)* Board of Accountancy, and state statutes. Therefore, please answer the following questions, sign, date, and return the form by *(date)* to *(name of person)*. If you have any questions about completing this form, or if you are aware of a matter that may impair the firm's independence, please contact *(name of partner)* to discuss and resolve the issue.

		Yes	*No*
1.	Do you have a direct or indirect material financial interest in a client or its subsidiaries and affiliates?	_____	_____
2.	Do you have a financial interest in any major competitors, investees, or affiliates of a client?	_____	_____
3.	Do you have any outside business relationship with a client or an officer, director, or principal stockholder having the objective of financial gain or who is in a position to influence the operations of the client?	_____	_____
4.	Do you owe any client any debt, such as notes or advances?	_____	_____
5.	Do you have any note or account receivable from a client?	_____	_____
6.	Do you have the authority to sign checks or to make management decisions for a client?	_____	_____
7.	Are you connected with a client as a promoter, underwriter or voting trustee, director, officer or in any capacity equivalent to a member of management or an employee?	_____	_____
8.	Do you serve as a director, trustee, officer, or employee of a not-for-profit organization that is a present client?	_____	_____
9.	Has your spouse or minor child been employed by a client?	_____	_____
10.	Has anyone in your legal family, or any blood relative, been employed in any type of managerial position by a client?	_____	_____
11.	Are any billings delinquent for any clients that are your responsibility?	_____	_____

I have read and understand the firm's independence policies and procedures and the independence requirements of the (1) American Institute of Certified Public Accountants, (2) *(State)* Board of Accountancy, (3) *(State)* Society of Certified Public Accountants, and (4) Government Auditing Standards. *(Specify any other regulatory agencies where applicable.)*

Also, I have read the attached listing of the firm's accounting, auditing, and attestation clients. To the best of my knowledge and belief, I am independent with respect to all of the clients on the list as required by the applicable requirements listed above except as follows (**Note:** For every "Yes" answer to the independence checklist, give details as to names, addresses, amounts, and other pertinent facts. If there are no exceptions, write "None"):

_____

_____

_____

_____   _____

Employee signature   Date

_____   _____

Form reviewed and approved by   Date

ILLUSTRATION 2—EFFECT ON INDEPENDENCE OF PERFORMANCE OF CERTAIN OTHER NONATTEST SERVICES FOR AN ATTEST CLIENT

PRACTICE POINT: Interpretation 101-3 of the AICPA Code of Professional Conduct, titled "Performance of Nonattest Services" indicates that, before a member performs other nonattest services for an attest client, he or she must evaluate the effect of such services on his or her independence. The examples below are based on Interpretation 101-3 and identify the effect that performance of other services for an attest client can have on a member's independence.

Type of Other Service	Independence Would Not Be Impaired	Independence Would Be Impaired
Bookkeeping	• Record transactions for which management has determined or approved the appropriate account classification, or post coded transactions to a client's general ledger. • Prepare financial statements based on information in the trial balance. • Post client-approved entries to a client's trial balance. • Propose standard, adjusting, or correcting journal entries or other changes affecting the financial statements to the client, provided the client reviews the entries and the member is satisfied that management understands the nature of the proposed entries and the impact the entries have on the financial statements.	• Determine or change journal entries, account codings or classification for transactions, or other accounting records without obtaining client approval. • Authorize or approve transactions. • Prepare source documents or originate data. • Make changes to source documents without client approval.

Type of Other Service	Independence Would Not Be Impaired	Independence Would Be Impaired
Payroll and Other Disbursement	• Use payroll time records provided and approved by the client, generate unsigned checks, or process client's payroll. • Transmit client-approved payroll or other disbursement information to a financial institution provided the client has authorized the member to make the transmission and has made arrangements for the financial institution to limit the corresponding individual payments as to amount and payee. In addition, once transmitted, the client must authorize the financial institution to process the information. • Make electronic payroll tax payments in accordance with U.S. Treasury Department guidelines, provided the client has made arrangements for its financial institution to limit such payments to a named payee.	• Accept responsibility to authorize payment of client funds, electronically or otherwise, except as specifically provided for with respect to electronic payroll tax payments. • Accept responsibility to sign or cosign client checks, even if only in emergency situations. • Maintain a client's bank account or otherwise have custody of a client's funds or make credit or banking decisions for the client. • Sign payroll tax returns on behalf of client management. • Approve vendor invoices for payment.
Benefit Plan Administration	• Communicate summary plan data to plan trustee. • Advise client management regarding the application or impact of provisions of the plan document. • Process transactions (e.g., investment/benefit elections or increase/decrease contributions to the plan; data entry; participant confirmations; and processing of distributions and loans) initiated by plan participants through the member's electronic medium, such as an interactive voice response system or Internet connection or other media. • Prepare account valuations for plan participants using data collected through the member's electronic or other media. • Prepare and transmit participant statements to plan participants based on data collected through the member's electronic or other media.	• Make policy decisions on behalf of client management. • When dealing with plan participants, interpret the plan document on behalf of management without first obtaining management's concurrence. • Make disbursements on behalf of the plan. • Have custody of assets of a plan. • Serve a plan as a fiduciary as defined by ERISA.

Type of Other Service	Independence Would Not *Be Impaired*	Independence Would *Be Impaired*
Investment— Advisory or Management	• Recommend the allocation of funds that a client should invest in various asset classes, depending upon the client's desired rate of return, risk tolerance, etc. • Perform record keeping and reporting of client's portfolio balances, including providing a comparative analysis of the client's investments to third-party benchmarks. • Review the manner in which a client's portfolio is being managed by investment account managers, including determining whether the managers are (1) following the guidelines of the client's investment policy statement, (2) meeting the client's investment objectives, and (3) conforming to the client's stated investment styles. • Transmit a client's investment selection to a broker-dealer or equivalent, provided the client has authorized the broker-dealer or equivalent to execute the transaction.	• Make investment decisions on behalf of client management or otherwise have discretionary authority over a client's investments. • Execute a transaction to buy or sell a client's investment. • Have custody of client assets, such as taking temporary possession of securities purchased by a client.
Corporate Finance— Consulting or Advisory	• Assist in developing corporate strategies. • Assist in identifying or introducing the client to possible sources of capital that meet the client's specifications or criteria. • Assist in analyzing the effects of proposed transactions including providing advice to a client during negotiations with potential buyers, sellers or capital sources. • Assist in drafting an offering document or memorandum. • Participate in transaction negotiations in an advisory capacity. • Be named as a financial advisor in a client's private placement memoranda or offering documents.	• Commit the client to the terms of a transaction or consummate a transaction on behalf of the client • Act as promoter, underwriter, broker-dealer, or guarantor of client securities, or distributor of private placement memoranda or offering documents. • Maintain custody of client securities.

Type of Other Service	Independence Would Not Be Impaired	Independence Would Be Impaired
Appraisal, Valuation or Actuarial	• Actuarial valuation that does not require a significant degree of subjectivity (e.g., valuation of a client's pension or postemployment benefit liabilities). • Appraisal, valuation, and actuarial services performed for nonfinancial statement purposes (e.g., tax planning or tax compliance, estate and gift taxation, and divorce proceedings).	• Appraisal, valuation, or actuarial service for which the results of the service, individually or in the aggregate, would be material to the financial statements and the appraisal, valuation, or actuarial service involves a significant degree of subjectivity (e.g., valuations in connection with employee stock ownership plans and business combinations).
Executive or Employee Search	• Recommend a position description or candidate specifications. • Solicit and perform screening of candidates and recommend qualified candidates to a client based on client-approved criteria (e.g., required skills and experience). • Participate in employee hiring or compensation discussions in an advisory capacity.	• Commit the client to employee compensation or benefit arrangements. • Hire or terminate client employees.
Business Risk Consulting	• Provide assistance in assessing the client's business risks and control processes. • Recommend a plan for making improvements to a client's control processes and assist in implementing these improvements.	• Make or approve business risk decisions. • Present business risk considerations to the board or others on behalf of management.
Information Systems— Design, Installation, or Integration	• Install or integrate a client's financial information system that was not designed or developed by the member (e.g., an off-the-shelf accounting package). • Assist in setting up the client's chart of accounts and financial statement format with respect to the client's financial information system. • Design, develop, install, or integrate a client's information system that is unrelated to the client's financial statements or accounting records. • Provide training and instruction to client employees on an information and control system.	• Design or develop a client's financial information system. • Make other than insignificant modifications to source code underlying a client's existing financial information system. • Supervise client personnel in the daily operation of a client's information system. • Operate a client's local area network (LAN) system.

Type of Other Service	Independence Would Not *Be Impaired*	Independence Would *Be Impaired*
Internal Audit Assistance Services	• Separate evaluations focused on the continued effectiveness of a client's internal control, including separate evaluations of the client's ongoing monitoring activities. • Performing services considered to be extensions of the audit scope applied in the audit of the client's financial statements (e.g., confirming of accounts receivable and analyzing fluctuations in account balances), even if the extent of such testing exceeds that required by GAAS.	• Perform ongoing monitoring activities or control activities (e.g., reviewing customer credit information as part of the customer's sales authorization process) that affect the execution of transactions or ensure that transactions are properly executed, accounted for, or both. • Perform routine activities in connection with the client's operating or production processes that are equivalent to those of an ongoing compliance or quality control function. • Determine which recommendations for improving the internal control system should be implemented. • Report to the board of directors or audit committee on behalf of management or the individual responsible for the internal audit function. • Approve or be responsible for the overall internal audit work plan, including the determination of the internal audit risk and scope, project priorities, and frequency of performance of audit procedures. • Be connected with the client as an employee or in any capacity equivalent to a member of client management (e.g., be referred to by title or description as supervising, or in charge of, the client's internal audit function).

AU SECTION 230
DUE PROFESSIONAL CARE IN THE PERFORMANCE OF WORK

PRACTICE POINT: As part of its Clarity Project, the American Institute of Certified Public Accountants' (AICPA's) Auditing Standards Board (ASB) has finalized a clarified standard that includes: (1) Preface to Codification of Statements on Auditing Standards, *Principles Underlying an Audit Conducted in Accordance with Generally Accepted Auditing Standards* ("Preface"), and (2) Statement on Auditing Standards (SAS), "Overall Objectives of the Independent Auditor and the Conduct of an Audit in Accordance with Generally Accepted Auditing Standards."

The Preface contains the principles underlying an audit conducted in accordance with U.S. generally accepted auditing standards (GAAS). These principles are not requirements and do not carry any authority. The ASB has developed the principles to provide a framework that is helpful in understanding and explaining an audit. The principles are organized to provide a structure for the Codification of Statements on Auditing Standards. This structure addresses the purpose of an audit, personal responsibilities of the auditor, auditor actions in performing the audit, and reporting.

The SAS addresses the independent auditor's overall responsibilities when conducting an audit of financial statements in accordance with GAAS. Specifically, it sets out the overall objectives of the independent auditor and explains the nature and scope of an audit designed to enable the independent auditor to meet those objectives. It also explains the scope, authority, and structure of GAAS and includes requirements establishing the general responsibilities of the independent auditor applicable in all audits, including the obligation to comply with GAAS.

The ASB is expected to issue many of the clarified standards in *one* SAS that will be codified in "AU Section" format. The ASB has decided that the effective date of the clarified SASs that have not yet been issued is for audits of financial statements for periods ending on or after December 15, 2012. Auditors should be alert to and monitor further developments in this area.

PRACTICE POINT: In March 2011, the American Institute of Certified Public Accountants' (AICPA's) Auditing Standards Board (ASB) issued an exposure draft (ED) of a proposed Statement on Auditing Standards (SAS) titled, "Omnibus Statement on Auditing Standards—2011." This proposed SAS, which is part of the AICPA's Clarity Project, would amend the following SASs that have been issued in the clarity format and are currently effective:

- SAS-117 (AU Section 801) (Compliance Audits). The amendment to SAS-117 conforms the auditor's report on compliance to the requirements of the clarified SAS, "Forming an Opinion and Reporting on Financial Statements." In addition, the amendment revises the appendix in SAS-117, "AU Sections That Are Not Applicable to Compliance Audits," to reflect conforming changes to affected references to AU Sections as a result of the ASB's Clarity Project.

- SAS-118 (AU Section 550) (Other Information in Documents Containing Audited Financial Statements). The amendment to SAS-118 clarifies the requirements with respect to identified material inconsistencies by categorizing the requirements based on when the inconsistencies are identified (prior to the date of the auditor's report on the audited financial statements; after the date of the auditor's report but prior to the report release date; and after the report release date). It also adds application material addressing electronic sites to include guidance from an interpretation of AU Section 550 (Other Information in Documents Containing Audited Financial Statements), which the ASB determined was appropriate to include in SAS-118.

In addition, in order to address other changes necessitated by the ASB's overall Clarity Project, the proposed SAS would amend the following clarified SASs that have been finalized and released, but not yet issued as authoritative:

- Clarified SAS, "Overall Objectives of the Independent Auditor and the Conduct of an Audit in Accordance with Generally Accepted Auditing Standards."

- Clarified SAS, "Modifications to the Opinion in the Independent Auditor's Report."

- Clarified SAS, "Reports on Application of Requirements of an Applicable Financial Reporting Framework."

- Clarified SAS, "The Auditor's Communication with Those Charged with Governance (Redrafted)."

- Clarified SAS, "Audit Documentation (Redrafted)."

The proposed SAS would be effective for audits of financial statements for periods ending on or after December 15, 2012, except for the amendment to the clarified SAS, "Reports on Application of Requirements of an Applicable Financial Reporting Framework," which would be effective for engagements ending on or after December 15, 2012.

WHAT EVERY PRACTITIONER SHOULD KNOW

Basic Objective

This Section deals with the third general standard, which requires the auditor to exercise due professional care in performing the audit and in preparing the audit report.

Exercising Due Professional Care

Due *professional care* requires the auditor to:

1. Fulfill his or her duties diligently and carefully, including considering the completeness of the working papers, the sufficiency of the audit evidence, and the appropriateness of the audit report.

2. Conduct proper supervision and review, at every appropriate level, of the work done and the judgments made by those working on the engagement.

3. Exercise *professional skepticism.* In other words, the auditor should neither assume that management is dishonest nor assume unquestioned honesty. In difficult audit areas that are subject to an increased level of professional judgment, the auditor should recognize the increased importance of factors that bear on management integrity.

4. Obtain *reasonable assurance* that the financial statements are free of material misstatement, whether caused by errors or fraud. Reasonable assurance is a high (but not absolute) level of assurance that audit risk is limited to a low level. Because audits incorporate many tests of samples of transactions, there is a risk that material errors or fraud, if they exist, will not be detected. Therefore, the auditor is not an insurer and his or her report does not constitute a guarantee.

PRACTICE ISSUES AND FREQUENTLY ASKED QUESTIONS

Issue 1: What are some practical considerations that the auditor should keep in mind when exercising "professional skepticism" with respect to available audit evidence?

A lack of critical assessment of audit evidence and lack of management integrity have been found to exist in the great majority of significant accountants' liability cases. Following are some of the questions that the auditor should ask when exercising professional skepticism:

- Are there differences in control accounts and subsidiary records, or similar discrepancies within the double-entry accounting system?
- Are there confirmations that disclose discrepancies in reported accounts and customers' representations?
- Are there abnormally low response rates to confirmations, relative to the rates expected?
- Are there unusual transactions at or near the year-end?
- Are there significant disagreements or lawsuits among the owners?
- What is the reputation of top management and/or majority owners in the business community?
- Is there any significant pending litigation against the entity?
- Is there high turnover in key financial positions?
- Does top management lack the experience necessary to operate the business?

Issue 2: What factors should the auditor evaluate in determining whether an entity is auditable?

Although an entity and expected users of the financial statements may want an audit, certain factors (e.g., inadequate accounting system, unavailability of accounting records, concerns about management integrity) might preclude the auditor from auditing the entity and expressing an opinion on the financial statements. The auditor should inquire of management about the availability of documents to substantiate the transactions recorded in the accounting records.

The auditor should determine if the accounting records include *at least* the following information:

- A description of the type of transactions in sufficient detail to permit appropriate classification in the financial statements. The accounting records generally need to indicate only broad classes of transactions (such as sales, cost of sales, payroll). The transactions should be described in a manner that permits the recording of monetary value in the financial statements.

- The period in which the transactions occurred to permit the recording of transactions in the appropriate accounting period.

The form and degree of detail of accounting records maintained by the client primarily will depend on the nature of the client's business, its size, and its organizational structure. A formalized and complex accounting system or sophisticated internal controls are not necessarily required for a business to be auditable. Many small businesses do not have elaborate or computerized accounting systems and adequate segregation of duties, but do have the basic elements of accounting records described above and, therefore, are auditable.

The client's accounting system must provide sufficient evidence to support the transactions that have occurred. The accounting system should also ensure that all transactions that should be recorded have, in fact, been recorded. If the auditor has concerns about the accounting system, he or she may conclude that it is unlikely that sufficient competent evidence will be available to support an opinion on the financial statements.

Issue 3: Who has the ultimate responsibility on an engagement to ascertain that due professional care has been exercised?

Due professional care imposes a responsibility on each professional, across all levels within a CPA firm, to observe professional standards on an engagement. However, in all audit engagements, the auditor with final responsibility for the engagement (i.e., the person signing the audit report) bears the burden of deciding on the nature, extent, competency, and sufficiency of audit evidence. For example, a casual review of the working papers often reveals comments made by auditors to not pursue certain items and to dispose of them as immaterial. The concept of due professional care, in this case, should be tempered by the more seasoned review and judgment of the auditor with final responsibility for the engagement regarding (1) the item's materiality, (2) whether it is an isolated incident or indicates pervasive disregard to the entity's internal controls, and (3) whether users of the financial statements are likely to perceive the item as material.

Issue 4: Does subsequent discovery of material misstatements that exist in financial statements mean that the auditor did not perform the audit according to professional standards?

No. An auditor's opinion is based on reasonable, not absolute, assurance. Obtaining reasonable assurance involves applying good faith judgment in evaluating audit evidence, but does not ensure that the auditor will detect all misstatements. Similarly, mistakes and errors in professional judgment do not, by themselves, necessarily imply a lack of due professional care. Furthermore, because of the characteristics of fraud (e.g., collusion among management), a properly executed audit may not detect a material misstatement.

Issue 5: What responsibility does an auditor have to detect falsified documentation?

A properly planned audit does not ordinarily include procedures specifically designed to detect falsified documentation. Auditors normally are not trained in techniques of document authentication and are not expected to be experts in this field. Also, falsified documentation can be concealed through collusion within the entity or by outside parties. Therefore, an audit of financial statements in accordance with generally accepted auditing standards is not directed toward detecting such falsified documentation. However, information, such as an irregular signature on a canceled check, may come to an auditor's attention and arouse suspicion that documents may be falsified; in such situations, as a matter of due professional care, the auditor should obtain reasonable assurance of the document's authenticity.

Issue 6: What are some of the more significant allegations that auditors have faced in litigation regarding the lack of exercise of due professional care and professional skepticism?

Some of the more persistent and significant allegations auditors have faced in litigation regarding the lack of exercise of due professional care in the performance of audit work include:

- Willingness by the auditor to accept management's representations without corroboration.
- Allowing the client to unduly influence the scope of auditing procedures.
- The failure to identify risky situations, or ignoring identified audit risks by not applying professional skepticism and revising auditing procedures appropriately.
- Inadequate allocation of audit time and effort to high-risk, complex, and unusual transactions.
- Inadequate supervision and review of less experienced staff.
- Lack of timely and sufficient involvement and review by the auditor with final responsibility for the engagement.
- Inadequate documentation in the working papers of the work performed and the conclusions reached, including why certain factors were considered more relevant and persuasive than others in reaching the conclusions.
- Failure to obtain timely representations and confirmations from management, client legal counsel, and other third parties.

ILLUSTRATIONS AND PRACTICE AIDS

There are no illustrations and practice aids for this Section.

AU Section 300
THE STANDARDS OF FIELD WORK

AU SECTION 311
PLANNING AND SUPERVISION

PRACTICE POINT: As part of its Clarity Project, the American Institute of Certified Public Accountants' (AICPA's) Auditing Standards Board (ASB) has finalized a clarified Statement on Auditing Standards (SAS) titled, "Planning an Audit," which supersedes paragraphs .01–.04 and .11–.33 of AU Section 311 (Planning and Supervision), as amended. The clarified SAS does not change or expand existing requirements in extant AU Section 311 in any significant respect. Requirements included in paragraphs .05–.10 of AU Section 311, addressing the auditor's responsibilities about the early appointment of the independent auditor and establishing the terms of the engagement, have been included in the clarified SAS, "Terms of Engagement" (see "Practice Point" below). Requirements included in paragraphs .28–.32 of AU Section 311, addressing supervision in an audit, have been included in the clarified SAS, "Quality Control for an Engagement Conducted in Accordance with Generally Accepted Auditing Standards" (see AU Section 161). The placement of these requirements does not create a difference between extant SASs as a whole and the clarified SASs as a whole.

The ASB is expected to issue many of the clarified standards in *one* SAS that will be codified in "AU Section" format. The ASB has decided that the effective date of the clarified SASs that have not yet been issued is for audits of financial statements for periods ending on or after December 15, 2012. Auditors should be alert to and monitor further developments in this area.

PRACTICE POINT: As part of its Clarity Project, the American Institute of Certified Public Accountants' (AICPA's) Auditing Standards Board (ASB) has finalized a clarified Statement on Auditing Standards (SAS) titled, "Terms of Engagement," which supersedes (*a*) paragraphs .05–.10. of AU Section 311 (Planning and Supervision), as amended, and (*b*) paragraphs .03, .05–.10, and .14 of AU Section 315 (Communications between Predecessor and Successor Auditors), as amended. Among other matters, the clarified SAS:

- Requires the auditor to determine whether the financial reporting framework to be applied in the preparation of the financial statements is acceptable. The auditor's responsibility for determining the acceptability of the applicable financial reporting framework, which is necessary in order to express an opinion on the financial statements, has been implicit in GAAS. Therefore, this change in requirements is not expected to affect current practice.

- Requires the auditor to obtain the agreement of management that it acknowledges and understands its responsibility for selecting the appropriate financial reporting framework, establishing and maintaining internal control, and providing access and information to the auditor. Paragraph .08 of extant AU Section 311 requires the auditor to establish an understanding with management and requires that the understanding include management's responsibilities. Paragraph .09 of extant AU Section 311 includes management's responsibility for the selection and application of financial reporting, establishing and maintaining internal control, and making all financial records and related information available to the auditor as matters that may be included in the understanding established with the client. Therefore, a level of detail that is suggested in extant AU Section 311 is required in the clarified SAS. The ASB believes that it is appropriate to require that management's responsibilities be explicit in the engagement letter because there is no point in starting an audit if management will not acknowledge its responsibilities.

• Requires that if management or those charged with governance of an entity that is not required by law or regulation to have an audit impose a limitation on the scope of the auditor's work in the terms of a proposed audit engagement such that the auditor believes the limitation will result in the auditor disclaiming an opinion on the financial statements as a whole, the auditor should not accept such a limited engagement as an audit engagement unless the audit is required by law or regulation. Also, unless required by law or regulation to do so, the auditor should not accept the engagement if the auditor has determined that the applicable financial reporting framework is not acceptable or if the agreement of management referred to above has not been obtained. Existing GAAS does not contain these requirements. Therefore, these changes in requirements will affect current practice.

• Requires the auditor to assess for recurring audits whether circumstances require the terms of the audit engagement to be revised. If the auditor concludes that the terms of the engagement need not be revised, the auditor should remind the entity of the terms of the engagement. This may be accomplished by means of a new engagement letter or a reminder, either written or oral, that the responsibilities in the previous terms of engagement still apply. Extant AU Section 311 requires the auditor to establish an understanding with the client for each engagement, which in practice may not result in a reminder each year for recurring audits. The clarified SAS also requires that the reminder, which may be written or oral, should be documented. These requirements may affect current practice, depending on how existing GAAS has been interpreted.

• Addresses situations in which the auditor is requested to change the audit engagement to an engagement that conveys a lower level of assurance. These situations are addressed in Statements on Standards for Accounting and Review Services (SSARS). Therefore, including these requirements in GAAS will not affect current practice.

• Addresses situations in which law or regulation prescribes the layout or wording of the auditor's report in a form or in terms that are significantly different from the requirements of GAAS. Existing GAAS requires that in such circumstances, the auditor reword the prescribed form or attach a separate report. The clarified SAS includes the explicit requirement that if the auditor determines that rewording the prescribed form or attaching a separate report would not be permitted or would not mitigate the risk of users misunderstanding the auditor's report, the auditor should not accept the engagement. Therefore, this change in requirement may affect current practice.

The ASB is expected to issue many of the clarified standards in *one* SAS that will be codified in "AU Section" format. The ASB has decided that the effective date of the clarified SASs that have not yet been issued is for audits of financial statements for periods ending on or after December 15, 2012. Auditors should be alert to and monitor further developments in this area.

Auditors should be alert to and monitor further developments in this area.

WHAT EVERY PRACTITIONER SHOULD KNOW

Basic Objectives and Requirements

This Section provides guidance on planning and supervising the audit, including: (1) establishing an understanding with the client regarding the services to be performed; (2) performing procedures regarding the continuance of the client relationship, including the specific audit engagement, and compliance with ethical requirements (e.g., independence); (3) establishing an overall audit strategy, including determining the extent of involvement of specialists and supervision of assistants; and (4) considering additional matters in initial audit engagements. In addition, this Section:

1. Requires the auditor to develop an audit plan in which the auditor documents the audit procedures to be used that are expected to reduce audit risk to an acceptably low level.

2. Provides guidance on the use of an information technology (IT) professional to understand the effect of IT on the audit.

3. Indicates that the work performed by each assistant and the related audit documentation should be reviewed to determine whether it was adequately performed and documented, and to evaluate the results obtained and the conclusions reached in the auditor's report.

4. Provides guidance on the responsibility of assistants for the resolution of accounting and auditing issues.

Establishing an Understanding with the Client

The auditor is required to obtain an understanding of the entity, its environment, and its internal control in connection with planning the audit. However, before the auditor accepts an audit engagement he or she should: (1) determine whether circumstances are likely to allow an adequate audit and to express an unqualified opinion on the entity's financial statements, and if not, (2) discuss with the client that it might be necessary to issue a qualified or disclaimer of opinion on the entity's financial statements.

This Section requires the auditor to establish, for each engagement, an understanding with the client regarding the services to be performed and to document such understanding through a written communication (e.g., engagement letter) with the client. Such an understanding should include the following:

- *Objectives of the engagement*—Essentially, the primary objective of the audit is to express an opinion on the financial statements.

- *Management's responsibilities*—Management is responsible for the following:

— The entity's financial statements.

— Selecting and applying the entity's accounting policies.

— Establishing and maintaining effective internal control over financial reporting.

— Designing and implementing programs and controls to prevent and detect fraud.

— Identifying and ensuring that the entity complies with the laws and regulations applicable to its activities.

— Making all financial records and related information available to the auditor.

— Providing the auditor, at the conclusion of the audit, with a letter that confirms certain representations made during the audit.

— Adjusting the financial statements to correct material misstatements.

— Affirming to the auditor in the representation letter that the effects of any uncorrected misstatements, resulting from errors or fraud, aggregated by the auditor during the current engagement and pertaining to the latest period presented are immaterial, both individually and in the aggregate, to the financial statements taken as a whole.

- *Auditor's responsibilities*—The auditor is responsible for the following:

— Conducting the audit in accordance with generally accepted auditing standards (GAAS).

— Obtaining reasonable, rather than absolute, assurance about whether the financial statements are free of material misstatement, whether caused by error or fraud; and, therefore, a material misstatement may remain undetected.

— Determining whether to decline to express an opinion or to issue a report on the financial statements, if the auditor is unable to complete the audit or is unable to form an opinion.

— Obtaining an understanding of the entity and its environment, including its internal control, sufficient to assess the risks of material misstatement of the financial statements and to design the nature, timing, and extent of further audit procedures to be performed.

— Ensuring that those charged with governance are aware of any significant deficiencies that come to the auditor's attention.

- *Limitations of the engagement*—An audit conducted in accordance with GAAS is not designed to:

— Detect error or fraud that is immaterial to the financial statements.

— Provide assurance on internal control or to identify significant deficiencies.

PRACTICE POINT: Illustration 1 below provides a sample engagement letter.

PRACTICE POINT: The auditor should decline to accept or perform the engagement if he or she believes that an understanding with the client has not been established regarding the services and terms for the engagement.

PRACTICE POINT: Statement on Quality Control Standards No. 7, "A Firm's System of Quality Control," indicates that a firm should establish policies and procedures requiring that the identity and role of the engagement partner be communicated to management and those charged with governance. One way to comply with this requirement is to make the communication in the engagement letter.

Other matters that may be included when establishing an understanding with the client In addition to the required matters discussed above, this Section indicates that an understanding with the client also may include other matters, such as the following:

- The overall audit strategy.
- Arrangements regarding involvement of specialists or internal auditors.
- Arrangements involving a predecessor auditor.
- Arrangements regarding fees and billings.
- Any limitation of or other arrangements regarding the liability of the auditor or the client, for example, indemnification to the auditor for liability arising from knowing misrepresentations to the auditor by management (certain regulators may restrict or prohibit such liability limitation arrangements).
- Conditions under which access to audit documentation may be granted to others.
- Additional services to be provided relating to regulatory requirements.
- Arrangements regarding other services to be provided in connection with the engagement, for example, preparation of tax returns.

Individuals with whom the auditor is required to establish an understanding This Section does not indicate a specific person with whom the auditor is required to establish an understanding regarding the services to be performed. Deciding with whom to establish this understanding depends on several factors, including whether the person representing the client has the authority to act on the company's behalf. Therefore, this Section envisions that the understanding will be established with persons charged with such responsibility, for example: management, the board of directors, the audit committee, or similar other bodies charged with governance and responsible for approving the financial statements. Generally, it is preferable to have one or two members of senior management sign the engagement letter to confirm that such an understanding has been established. It is equally important that the person signing the engagement letter understands the terms and limitations of the engagement.

Preliminary Engagement Activities

At the beginning of the current audit engagement, the auditor is required to:

- Perform procedures relating to the continuance of the client relationship and the specific audit engagement.
- Evaluate the auditor's compliance with ethical requirements, including independence.

The auditor should perform these procedures prior to performing other significant activities for the current audit engagement. In addition, as conditions and circumstances change during the course of the audit, the auditor should continue to consider the client continuance and ethical requirements.

Relationship between the Overall Audit Strategy and the Audit Plan

The auditor is required to develop an overall audit strategy and an audit plan for each engagement. The overall audit strategy is a *broad* approach regarding how the audit will be conducted and takes into consideration factors such as the following: the scope of the engagement; deadlines for performing the audit and issuing the report; and recent financial reporting developments. On the other hand, the audit plan is a more *detailed* map that describes the nature, timing, and extent of audit procedures to be performed that are expected to reduce audit risk to an acceptably low level.

The new standard recognizes that establishing the overall audit strategy and developing the audit plan are not necessarily separate or sequential activities; rather, they are strongly interconnected and changes in one may result in changes to the other. Therefore, although auditors may establish the overall audit strategy before developing the detailed audit plan, they need to keep in mind the close relationship that exists between these two planning activities.

Overall audit strategy In connection with establishing the overall audit strategy for the audit, the auditor is required to address the following matters:

- *Characteristics of the engagement*—The auditor should determine the scope of the engagement, for example: (1) the basis of reporting; (2) the industry-specific reporting requirements; and (3) the locations of the entity.
- *Reporting objectives of the engagement*—The auditor should establish and plan the timing of the audit and the nature of the communications required, for example: (1) deadlines for interim and final reporting and (2) pertinent dates for expected communications with management and those charged with governance.
- *Significant factors affecting the audit team's efforts*—The auditor should consider the main factors that will determine the focus of the audit team's efforts, for example: (1) appropriate materiality levels; (2) audit areas with higher risks of material misstatement; (3) material locations and account balances; and (4) recent significant entity-specific, industry, financial reporting, or other relevant developments.
- *Results of preliminary engagement activities*—The auditor should consider the results of preliminary engagement activities, for example: (1) any

issues with management integrity and (2) the auditor's ethical and independence requirements.

The auditor is also required to update and document any significant revisions to the overall audit strategy to respond to changes in circumstances.

Audit plan In connection with establishing the audit plan for the audit, this Section requires the auditor to include the following matters in the audit plan:

- A description of the nature, timing, and extent of planned risk assessment procedures sufficient to assess the risks of material misstatement. Risk assessment procedures include inquiries, observation, inspection, and analytical procedures.

- A description of the nature, timing, and extent of planned further audit procedures at the relevant assertion level for each material class of transactions, account balance, and disclosure. Further audit procedures, which may include tests of controls, should be responsive to the assessed risk of material misstatement at the relevant assertion level. The auditor should also provide a clear linkage between the understanding of the entity, the risk assessments, and the design of further audit procedures.

- A description of other audit procedures to be performed to comply with GAAS (e.g., communicating with the client's lawyers regarding litigation, claims, and assessments).

The auditor should document changes made to the original audit plan.

Involvement of Professionals Having Specialized Skills

When the auditor encounters situations requiring specialized knowledge, it may be necessary to consult a specialist. Examples include using a diamond expert when evaluating the replacement cost of diamonds and an actuary for determining the appropriateness of the recorded value of insurance loss reserves. The auditor should have a sufficient understanding of the client's business to recognize the need for a specialist. Proper planning is necessary to make sure that a specialist is available when needed and that he or she is both competent and preferably independent of the client.

PRACTICE POINT: See AU Section 336 (Using the Work of a Specialist), for further guidance on the requirements for selecting specialists and reviewing their work.

This Section requires the auditor to consider whether specialized skills are needed in performing the audit. If the auditor plans on using a professional with specialized skills, the auditor should determine whether the professional will effectively function as a member of the audit team. If such a professional is part of the audit team, the auditor should supervise him or her consistent with the auditor's responsibilities for supervising assistants. In addition, in such circumstances, the auditor should:

- Have sufficient knowledge and understanding of the scope and objectives of the other professional's work.

- Evaluate whether the specified audit procedures will meet the auditor's objectives.

- Evaluate the results of the audit procedures performed as they relate to the nature, timing, and extent of further planned audit procedures.

Involvement of professionals possessing information technology skills An entity's use of information technology (IT) may affect any of the five components of internal control relevant to the achievement of the entity's financial reporting, operations, or compliance objectives, and its operating units or business functions. The auditor should consider whether specialized skills are needed to determine the effect of IT on the audit, to understand the IT controls, or to design and perform tests of IT controls or substantive tests. In determining whether a professional with IT skills is needed on the audit team, this Section indicates that the auditor should consider factors, such as:

- The complexity of the entity's systems and IT controls and the manner in which they are used in conducting the entity's business.

- Whether changes are made to existing systems and the significance of such changes.

- Whether new systems have been implemented.

- The nature and extent of data shared among systems.

- The nature and extent of the entity's participation in electronic commerce.

- Whether the entity uses emerging technologies.

- The significance of audit evidence that is available only in electronic form.

Communication with Those Charged with Governance

The auditor is required to provide to those charged with governance an overview of the planned scope and timing of the audit, for example:

- The auditor's approach to internal control relevant to the audit.

- The concept of materiality in planning and executing the audit.

- The extent to which the auditor will use the work of internal auditors, where applicable.

- The views of those charged with governance about the entity's business risks that may result in material misstatements and significant communications with regulators.

- The actions of those charged with governance in response to previous communications with the auditor.

See AU Section 380 (The Auditor's Communication with Those Charged with Governance) for further guidance on communicating the planned scope and timing of the audit.

Additional Procedures for Initial Audit Engagements

New engagements usually call for the auditor to perform special procedures, primarily because the auditor generally lacks any previous experience with the client, management, and those charged with governance. Accordingly, this Section requires the auditor to perform the following procedures in initial audit engagements:

1. *Before starting an initial audit, perform procedures regarding the acceptance of the client relationship and the specific audit engagement*—In order to minimize the likelihood of association with a client whose management lacks integrity, a firm should establish controls for deciding whether to accept or continue a client relationship and whether to perform a specific engagement for that client.

2. *Before starting an initial audit, communicate with the previous auditor, where applicable*—In evaluating a potential client that has been audited previously by another auditor, the predecessor auditor is a primary source of information about the client. AU Section 315 (Communications between Predecessor and Successor Auditors) requires the successor auditor to communicate with the predecessor auditor. If the successor auditor cannot obtain required information from the predecessor auditor because of client restrictions, the successor auditor should carefully consider the implications of such restrictions in evaluating whether to accept the engagement.

3. *In developing the overall audit strategy and audit plan, consider additional matters including the following*:

   a. Arrangements to be made with the predecessor auditor (e.g., to review the predecessor auditor's audit documentation).

   b. Any major issues discussed with management or those charged with governance involving the initial selection as auditors and how these issues affect the overall audit strategy and audit plan.

   c. The planned procedures to obtain audit evidence regarding opening balances.

   d. The assignment of personnel possessing the appropriate characteristics and qualifications to enable them to perform competently and to successfully execute the engagement.

   e. Other procedures required by the firm's quality control system for initial audit engagements, for example, the involvement of another senior individual to review the overall audit strategy before starting the audit or to review the audit report before it is issued.

PRACTICE POINT: Illustration 2 below includes additional examples of audit procedures that might be applicable for initial audit engagements.

Supervision

Assigning the appropriate staff to the engagement and directing the efforts of assistants are important to meet generally accepted auditing standards and to promote audit efficiency.

Supervision also involves reviewing the audit effort and related audit judgments made by assistants to determine whether these judgments are appropriate in the circumstances. This Section indicates that elements of supervision include:

- Instructing assistants.
- Staying abreast of significant issues encountered during the audit.
- Reviewing the work performed by assistants to determine that it is adequate and that the results are consistent with the conclusions to be presented in the auditor's report.
- Dealing with differences of opinion among firm personnel.

Required discussions and communications with assistants The timing and nature of supervision provided to assistants will vary greatly depending on the assistants' experience and training, and the characteristics of the engagement. Although reviews of working papers and financial statements are indispensable supervisory procedures, it is doubtful that effective supervision can be achieved without the involvement, in all phases of the audit, of the auditor with final responsibility for the audit. Such involvement by the auditor with final responsibility for the audit (1) keeps the audit team focused on the big picture and significant issues affecting the audit, (2) helps avoid potential inefficient or ineffective auditing procedures, and (3) compensates for overauditing or underauditing tendencies on the part of the assistants.

This Section requires that certain particular communications with assistants take place in connection with every audit engagement. Specifically:

1. The auditor with final responsibility for the audit should communicate with members of the audit team regarding:
   a. The susceptibility of the entity's financial statements to material misstatement due to error or fraud, with special emphasis on fraud.
   b. The need to maintain a questioning mind and to exercise professional skepticism in gathering and evaluating audit evidence throughout the audit.
   c. The need to bring to the attention of the auditor with final responsibility for the audit the accounting and auditing issues that were raised during the audit that the assistant believes are significant to the financial statements or auditor's report.

2. Assistants assigned to the audit engagement should be informed of:
   a. Their responsibilities and the objectives of audit procedures to be performed.
   b. Matters that may affect the nature, timing, and extent of audit procedures to be performed, for example, the nature of the entity's business and possible accounting and auditing issues.
   c. The need to bring to the attention of appropriate individuals in the firm difficulties encountered in performing the audit, for example: missing documents; limiting access to information sought by the audit team; client refusal to respond to auditor inquiries; or other similar imposed restrictions.

Reviewing the work performed by assistants This Section states: "The work performed by each assistant, including the audit documentation, should be reviewed to determine whether it was adequately performed and documented and to evaluate the results, relative to the conclusions to be presented in the auditor's report." However, this Section provides only general guidance and, therefore, a firm's practice for reviewing engagements will vary depending on the size of the firm and the complexity of the engagement. The review of work performed by assistants is ordinarily conducted by the person with final responsibility for the audit. However, such person may choose to delegate parts of the review responsibility to other assistants.

The primary objectives of the review of the work performed on each audit engagement, including the audit documentation, are to determine whether:

- The audit has been appropriately planned.
- The scope of the audit is sufficient to support the auditor's opinion on the entity's financial statements.
- The audit has been conducted in accordance with firm and professional standards.
- Technical differences of opinion are addressed in accordance with professional standards.
- The accounting and auditing issues have been evaluated properly and the financial statements meet accepted standards of presentation and disclosure.
- The firm's audit report is appropriate.

PRACTICE POINT: The practice aid in Illustration 3 below can be used by a CPA firm to document its review of the audit documentation.

Differences of opinion During the conduct of an audit engagement, differences of opinion may occur regarding the significance or implications of accounting and auditing issues. These differences may surface during the course of the audit, including the supervision phase of the engagement. This Section indicates that each assistant has a professional responsibility to voice concerns about, and bring to the attention of appropriate individuals in the firm, any disagreements or concerns the assistant might have with respect to accounting and auditing issues he or she believes are significant to the financial statements or auditor's report.

Both the auditor with final responsibility for the audit and assistants should be aware of the procedures to be followed when such differences of opinion exist. This Section specifically states that procedures should allow assistants to document their positions if they disagree with the way a particular accounting or auditing issue was resolved. When such differences of opinion remain and an assistant decides to disassociate himself or herself from the resolution of the matter, the basis for the final resolution should be documented.

Once this is completed, an assistant who disagrees with the way a particular accounting or auditing issue was resolved has essentially met the requirements of professional standards for the subject matter and, therefore, has no further responsibility regarding any related decisions made by supervisory personnel.

PRACTICE POINT: The practice aid in Illustration 4 below can be used by a CPA firm to address differences of professional opinion among firm personnel.

PRACTICE ISSUES AND FREQUENTLY ASKED QUESTIONS

Planning Issues

Issue 1: Is the use of engagement letters required by generally accepted auditing standards?

Yes. This Section requires the auditor to establish, for each engagement, an understanding with the client regarding the services to be performed and to document such understanding in the form of an engagement letter. The engagement letter is intended to:

- Document the contractual duties agreed to by the auditor and the client.
- Explain the auditor's and the client's responsibilities.
- Explain the nature of the services to be rendered by the auditor, including limitations of the engagement.
- Avoid misunderstandings with the client and among the staff.
- Help protect the auditor from legal liability.

PRACTICE POINT: Illustration 1 below provides a sample engagement letter.

Issue 2: What are some of the matters that should or should not be discussed in engagement letters?

There are no strict or standard procedures that the auditor should follow in engagement letters. However, as a result of the persistent and significant allegations auditors have faced in litigation, the following reminders of engagement letter dos and don'ts are offered.

DOs	DON'Ts

- State the purpose of the engagement and the auditor's responsibilities.
- Define the scope of the engagement (i.e., specifically actions that will and will not be taken).
- Describe management's responsibilities (e.g., management is responsible for the entity's financial statements and for establishing and maintaining effective internal control).
- Specify known negative conditions or adverse situations.
- Note client instructions, responsibilities, and delivery dates.
- Note reliance on facts provided by the client.
- Outline the terms of fee collections and the consequences of late payment.
- Request the client's signature and instruct the client to return the signed letter.
- Explain the inherent limitations of the internal control.
- Explain the limitations regarding financial statement distribution.
- Explain the conditions for engagement termination procedures.

- Do not use absolutes, superlatives, and words that expand rather than limit the auditor's responsibilities.
- Do not use legal jargon or ambiguous terms, abbreviations, or words only a CPA would understand.
- Avoid including forms of marketing or promotional information. The engagement letter is a contract and should be composed accordingly.
- Do not make adverse comments about other auditors.

Issue 3: What action should the auditor take if a potential client refuses to sign an engagement letter?

An auditor should not accept or perform an engagement when he or she believes that an understanding with the client has not been established. Management's reluctance to sign an engagement letter is a clear indication that the required understanding with the client has not been established. The auditor should consider the reasons for the client's reluctance and determine if they can be overcome through discussions.

Issue 4: When establishing an understanding with the client regarding the services to be performed, with whom specifically is the auditor required to establish this understanding?

Professional standards do not indicate a specific person or level of person with whom the auditor is required to establish an understanding regarding the services to be performed. Deciding with whom to establish this understanding depends on several factors, including whether the person representing the client has the authority to act on the company's behalf. Therefore, the standards envision that the understanding will be established with persons discharged with such responsibility, for example, senior management, the board of directors, and the audit committee. Generally, it is preferable to have one or two members of senior management sign the engagement letter to confirm that such an understanding has been established. It is equally important that the person signing the engagement letter understands the terms and limitations of the engagement.

Issue 5: Can an auditor accept an appointment to an audit engagement after an entity's year end?

Yes. However, early appointment is preferable in order to allow adequate time for proper audit planning. When the appointment comes near or after the year end, the auditor should consider the effect on the timing and nature of the audit work. One of the most common issues the auditor faces in these situations is the observation of year-end inventory counts. In some cases, where the controls over inventory are effective and adequate, a physical count can be observed after the year end. In other instances, appointment to an audit engagement after year end might preclude the auditor from obtaining sufficient evidence to express an unqualified opinion. In this case, the matter should be discussed with the client before accepting the engagement, including the possibility of issuing a qualified or disclaimer of opinion.

Issue 6: What are some of the procedures that the auditor can use to obtain an understanding and knowledge of the client's business and industry?

Obtaining an understanding and knowledge of the client's business and industry can be accomplished in various ways, including the following:

1. *Review current developments*—The auditor's objective is to identify new environmental factors or changes in prior-year factors that could increase or decrease the auditor's risk. Early discussions with key operating and financial executives will help the auditor identify current developments that are of concern to management and that may affect the current audit. The auditor also should make use of pertinent articles from trade journals or general business publications when planning the audit. Meetings with client personnel should include discussion of:

   a. Interim financial results, major new products or services, new contracts or contingencies, and planned acquisitions or discontinued operations.

   b. Changes in accounting systems and methods.

   c. New accounting or auditing pronouncements that may affect the audit.

   d. Important accounting systems, the status of documentation, and the need for updating existing documentation.

   e. Implementation of internal controls to address comments the auditor made in previous audits, or related cost/benefit analysis.

2. *Review results of previous audits*—Prior-year workpapers usually contain a wealth of information regarding the client and its business, organizational structure, and other operating characteristics.

3. *Review the permanent files*—By reviewing the permanent files, the auditor often is able to gather valuable information about the client, including the history of the entity, debt and leasing information, and the account-

ing principles used. Studying this information and discussing it with client personnel aids in understanding the business.

4. *Tour the plant and offices*—A tour of the client's facilities is helpful in obtaining a better understanding of the client's business and operations because it provides an opportunity to meet key personnel and observe operations firsthand.

5. *Perform analytical procedures*—Analytical procedures are commonly used to obtain information about the client's business and industry. The use of analytical procedures is discussed in detail in AU Section 329 (Analytical Procedures).

Issue 7: Are there any additional audit procedures that the auditor should perform in connection with new audit engagements?

Yes. New audit engagements usually require the auditor to perform special procedures. In addition to obtaining an understanding of the client's business and industry as described above, the auditor should perform additional procedures, such as the following for new engagements:

- Communicate with the predecessor auditor (see AU Section 315, [Communications between Predecessor and Successor Auditors]).

- Establish the reasonableness of beginning balances for significant balance sheet accounts. For example, the auditor should determine the basis of the property accounts (both book and tax) and should examine evidence of title to at least the principal real estate.

- Prepare or obtain a summary of shareholders' equity or proprietary accounts, from inception if practicable, with particular attention to prior reorganizations, revaluations of assets, issuance of stock for other than cash, and other unusual equity transactions.

- Determine the origin of other continuing accounts, such as intangibles and deferrals.

PRACTICE POINT: Illustration 2 below includes additional examples of audit procedures that might be applicable for initial audit engagements.

Issue 8: What benefits do time budgets provide, particularly in light of the fact that oftentimes they are not met?

Time budgets have many benefits, including:

- Providing guidelines for the auditor to schedule staff.

- Providing the staff an overall idea about the allocation of audit effort and the relative importance of various audit areas.

- Serving as a basis for establishing audit fees.

- Providing a basis for monitoring the progress of the audit.

The auditor should recognize, however, that time budgets are only guidelines and that the auditor may find it necessary to deviate from the time budget because of changes in engagement conditions. Although it is important to meet time budgets, this is not the objective of the audit.

Issue 9: What specific audit planning tips might be useful to the auditor in order to conduct an effective and efficient audit, and increase the likelihood of meeting time budgets?

Each audit engagement is unique and is likely to require specific planning considerations. However, the following general audit planning tips should be useful. An auditor should:

- Determine areas where work can be shifted to the client and transfer as much nonprofessional work to the client as possible. For example, client assistance often is available to prepare account analyses, locate documents, and reconcile accounts.

- Encourage the client to take additional responsibility for the financial statements. For example, have the client determine the amounts of certain accounts, such as depreciation and income taxes, and draft the financial statements.

- Avoid getting into the habit of performing the same audit procedures in every audit without considering the different circumstances that exist with each client.

- Avoid asking the client to prepare schedules or analyses that the auditor would not prepare himself or herself. Remember that if the schedule or analysis does not contribute enough audit evidence to the audit, it should not be included in the workpapers.

- Ask the client to prepare and update schedules that involve monthly analyses of accounts. For example, a schedule of property and equipment additions for the year can be prepared monthly by the client as the accounting records are prepared.

- Generally provide the client with examples and samples of workpapers. This may be accomplished by providing copies of prior-year audit workpapers. (**Note:** It might be necessary to delete the audit comments made on the workpapers.)

- Prepare a control list of schedules to be provided by the client. A control list assists the auditor in fixing client responsibility and should include: (1) the name of analysis or schedule to be prepared, (2) the deadline for the preparation of each schedule, (3) the client personnel assigned to prepare the schedule, (4) the space for client personnel to sign-off upon completion of the work, and (5) the space for the auditor to fill in the date on which the schedule is received from the client.

- Before preparing, or asking the client to prepare, an audit workpaper, ask whether the workpaper will contribute to the expression of opinion on the financial statements. If the answer is "no," the auditor should consider omitting the workpaper.

Supervision Issues

Issue 10: What is an assistant's responsibility when a significant disagreement about the financial statements or auditor's report is not resolved to his or her satisfaction?

Every professional on an audit engagement has a responsibility to voice concerns to the appropriate individuals in the firm about auditing and accounting issues that he or she believes are important to the engagement. This responsibility results from the particular work assigned to individual professionals in each engagement. If an assistant is not satisfied that those concerns have been resolved, the assistant has the right to disagree and document that disagreement in the working papers. Once this is done, the assistant has met the requirements of professional standards for the matter and has no further responsibility regarding any decisions made by supervisory personnel.

Issue 11: Some entry level professionals might be reluctant to document a disagreement with their supervisors. What considerations should govern a decision to reduce a disagreement to writing?

First, entry level staff should carefully consider and evaluate all facts and circumstances surrounding such situations and obtain a strong understanding of the applicable professional standards for the particular issue. Statements on Quality Control Standards (SQCS) require CPA firms to establish adequate consultation policies and procedures; often these policies and procedures result in designating experts either within or outside the firm, who should be consulted on difficult or unusual matters. Staff members should consider referring to these designated persons in order to clarify the issue and evaluate the alternatives available, if any.

Furthermore, SQCS require CPA firms to establish mechanisms for resolving differences of professional opinion within an engagement team. Therefore, the audit staff should understand the firm's policies and procedures for resolving such differences and make sure to follow them in considering a course of action.

Finally, although the decision to document a disagreement should not be affected by personal or political influences, due consideration should be given to whether such documentation in the working papers might increase a firm's exposure if the particular engagement is subjected to litigation at a later date.

PRACTICE POINT: The practice aid in Illustration 4 below can be used by a CPA firm to address differences of professional opinion among firm personnel.

Issue 12: Can the objective of adequately supervising assistants be achieved strictly through the engagement partner's review of the audit workpapers and financial statements at the completion of the audit?

No. The timing and nature of supervision provided to assistants will vary greatly depending on the assistants' experience and training, and the characteristics of the engagement. Although reviews of working papers and financial statements are indispensable supervisory procedures, it is doubtful that effective supervision can be achieved without the engagement partner's involvement in all phases of the audit. One of the significant allegations auditors have faced in litigation is the lack of, or inadequate, engagement partner involvement in critical aspects of the audit.

Experienced auditors generally would agree that involvement by the engagement partner in the planning phase of an audit is critical, prudent, and beneficial. Establishing an understanding with the client, approving audit programs, informing assistants about their assignments, and discussing specific matters, such as accounting problems or difficult issues relating to the engagement, can save time later in the engagement. Such involvement by the engagement partner (1) keeps the audit team focused on the big picture, (2) helps avoid potential inefficient or ineffective auditing procedures, and (3) compensates for overauditing or underauditing tendencies on the part of the staff.

Issue 13: Do all of the planning and supervision standards apply to a sole practitioner whose audit practice consists of a few small, privately held businesses in one industry?

As with all auditing standards, the planning and supervision standards are written broadly and cannot, and do not, take into account all possible circumstances. However, it is important to consider the intent and objectives of this or any other standard as it relates to the auditor's specific situation. For example, provisions of the standard that deal with directing the work of assistants would not be relevant to a sole practitioner with no professional staff.

One of the dangers inherent in highly stable and homogenous practices is that due consideration will not be given to changes in the client's business and industry situation, or in accounting and auditing standards. Therefore, planning procedures should target and emphasize these matters.

Although many sole practitioners see supervision procedures in the final review stage of their audits as problematic, this can be mitigated in a number of ways. One is to set an engagement aside for a day or more before issuing the financial statements and return to it with a fresh perspective for a final review. The use of practice aids, such as reporting disclosure checklists and supervisory review checklists, is not required by GAAS, but most sole practitioners feel that a well-designed set of practice aids is a valuable self-supervision tool when used as part of their final review process. Finally, some sole practitioners form "mutual assistance arrangements" with colleagues under which they provide one another with second-party reviews on engagements involving unusually complex or contentious issues.

Documentation Issues

Issue 14: Is a written "audit program" required for every audit engagement?

Yes. Prior to the issuance of SAS-108 (Planning and Supervision), the audit plan, as discussed in this Section, was referred to as the "audit program." Under this Section, the audit plan (which includes audit programs) should include a description of the following:

- A description of the nature, timing, and extent of planned risk assessment procedures sufficient to assess the risks of material misstatement.

- A description of the nature, timing, and extent of planned further audit procedures at the relevant assertion level for each material class of transactions, account balance, and disclosure.

- A description of other audit procedures to be performed to comply with GAAS (e.g., communicating with the client's lawyers regarding litigation, claims, and assessments).

Audit programs represent a series of tests, procedures, activities, and steps designed to collect specific types of audit evidence that allows the auditor to form an opinion on the financial statements. In other words, an audit program outlines the evidence-gathering steps the auditor plans to use. Audit programs provide:

- Evidence of proper audit planning.

- A record of the work performed during the audit.

- Guidance to assistants regarding specific procedures to be performed.

- A mechanism by which to determine the audit steps that have been performed and steps that need to be performed, thereby providing better control over the engagement.

Issue 15: Once the initial audit plan is prepared and approved, can it be modified later during the course of the engagement?

Yes. The auditor should recognize that the initial audit plan is designed early in the audit and may need to be modified because of changes in conditions and circumstances in the engagement. Modifications of the initial audit plan are *not* unusual because it is often difficult to anticipate all conditions unique to a specific engagement. For example, when designing the initial audit plan, the auditor may anticipate that control risk will be low for accounts receivable and, therefore, may design an audit step to confirm only a few accounts receivable balances. However, the auditor may later determine that control risk is higher than anticipated and, therefore, may decide to increase the number of accounts receivable confirmations.

Issue 16: Should a list of points generated for further consideration, commonly called a "to-do" list, be retained in the working papers?

There is no requirement to either retain or discard a "to-do" list. However, the current trend in the profession points overwhelmingly toward discarding the "to-do" list once all the points have been resolved. The rationale for this thinking is that other documentation techniques ordinarily employed, such as initialing of workpapers, sign-offs on program steps, completion of checklists, and memoranda or notations in the workpapers themselves are sufficient for this purpose. Many practitioners believe that leaving "to-do" lists in the files can provide a road map to an adversary, could be used against the auditor in challenging his or her work, and unnecessarily exposes the auditor to liability.

ILLUSTRATIONS AND PRACTICE AIDS

ILLUSTRATION 1—SAMPLE ENGAGEMENT LETTER

(Prepared on auditor's letterhead)

December 18, 20X2
Seliga Enterprises
2960 Champion Way
Tustin, California 92782

To the Board of Directors:

We are pleased to confirm our understanding of the services we are to provide for Seliga Enterprises for the year ended December 31, 20X2. We will audit the balance sheet of Seliga Enterprises as of December 31, 20X2, and the related statements of operations, stockholders' equity, and cash flows for the year then ended. Also, the document we submit to you will include the following additional information that (will or will not) be subjected to the auditing procedures applied in our audit of the financial statements:

(List additional information)

Our audit will be made in accordance with U.S. generally accepted auditing standards and will include tests of the accounting records of Seliga Enterprises and other procedures we consider necessary to enable us to express an unqualified opinion that the financial statements are fairly presented, in all material respects, in conformity with U.S. generally accepted accounting principles. If our opinion is other than unqualified, we will fully discuss the reasons with you in advance. If, for any reason, we are unable to complete the audit, we will not issue a report as a result of this engagement.

Our procedures will include tests of documentary evidence that support the transactions recorded in the accounts, tests of the physical existence of inventories, and direct confirmation of cash, investments, and certain other assets and liabilities by correspondence with customers, creditors, and financial institutions. Also, we will request written representations from your attorneys as part of the engagement, and they may bill you for responding to that inquiry. At the conclusion of our audit, we will also request certain written representations from you about the financial statements and related matters.

An audit includes examining, on a test basis, evidence supporting the amounts and disclosures in the financial statements; therefore, our audit will involve judgment about the number of transactions to be examined and the areas to be tested. Our audit is designed to provide reasonable, not absolute, assurance about whether the financial statements are free of material misstatement, whether due to error, fraudulent financial reporting, misappropriation of assets, or violations of laws or governmental regulations. Because of this concept of reasonable assurance and because we will not examine all transactions, there is a risk that material misstatements may exist and not be detected by us. Also, an audit is not designed to detect error or fraud that is immaterial to the financial statements. The Company's management is responsible for establishing and maintaining a sound system of internal control, which is the best means of preventing or detecting errors, fraudulent financial reporting, misappropriation of assets, or violations of laws or governmental regulations. Our responsibility as auditors is limited to the period covered by our audit and does not extend to matters that might arise during any later periods for which we are not engaged as auditors.

An audit includes obtaining an understanding of the entity and its environment, including its internal control, sufficient to assess the risks of material misstatement of the financial statements and to design the nature, timing, and extent of further audit procedures. An audit is not designed to provide assurance on internal control or to identify significant deficiencies. However, we will ensure that those charged with governance are aware of any significant deficiencies that come to our attention.

We understand that you will provide us with the basic information required for our audit and that you are responsible for the accuracy and completeness of that information. We may advise you about appropriate accounting principles and their application and may assist in the preparation of your financial statements, but the responsibility for the financial statements remains with you. This management responsibility includes: (a) establishing and maintaining adequate records and related internal control policies and procedures, (b) selecting and applying accounting principles, (c) safeguarding assets, and (d) identifying and ensuring that the entity complies with laws and regulations applicable to its activities.

Management is responsible for making all financial records and related information available to us. Management is also responsible for adjusting the financial statements to correct material misstatements and for affirming to us in the management representation letter that the effects of any uncorrected misstatements, resulting from errors or fraud, aggregated by us during the current engagement and pertaining to the latest period presented are immaterial, both individually and in the aggregate, to the financial statements taken as a whole. In addition, management is responsible for: (a) the design and implementation of programs and controls to prevent and detect fraud, (b) for informing us about any fraud or suspected fraud affecting the entity involving management, employees who have significant roles in internal control, or others where the fraud could have a material effect on the financial statements, and (c) for informing us about any allegations of fraud or suspected fraud affecting the entity received in communications from employees, former employees, analysts, regulators, short sellers, or others.

We understand that your employees will prepare all confirmations we request and will locate any documents or invoices selected by us for testing.

If you intend to publish or otherwise reproduce the financial statements and make reference to our firm, you agree to provide us with printers' proofs or masters for our review and approval before printing. You also agree to provide us with a copy of the final reproduced material for our approval before it is distributed.

During the course of the engagement, we may communicate with you or with the company personnel via fax or e-mail, and you should be aware that communication in those mediums contains a risk of misdirected or intercepted communications.

The timing of our audit will be scheduled for performance and completion as follows: (insert dates)

	Begin	*Complete*
Document internal control and preliminary tests		
Observe physical inventories		
Mail confirmations		
Perform year-end audit procedures		
Issue audit report		

Our fees are based on the amount of time required at various levels of responsibility, plus actual out-of-pocket expenses. Invoices will be rendered every two weeks and are payable upon presentation. We estimate that our fee for the audit will be between $35,000 and $45,000. We will notify you immediately of any circumstances we encounter that could significantly affect this initial fee estimate. Whenever possible, we will attempt to use your Company's personnel to assist in the preparation of schedules and analyses of accounts. This effort could substantially reduce our time requirements and facilitate the timely conclusion of the audit.

We will also prepare the Company's federal and state (insert names of states) income tax returns for the fiscal year ended December 31, 20X2. The fee for tax return preparation is not expected to exceed $5,000.

Further, we will be available during the year to consult with you on the tax effects of any proposed transactions or contemplated changes in business policies.

During the course of the audit we may observe opportunities for economy in, or improved controls over, your operations. We will bring such matters to the attention of the appropriate level of management, either orally or in writing.

If the foregoing is in accordance with your understanding, please indicate your agreement by signing the duplicate copy of this letter and returning it to us. If you have any questions, please let us know.

We appreciate the opportunity to be your certified public accountants and look forward to working with you and your staff.

Very truly yours,

_____

[*Signature*]

_____

[*Firm name*]
****

RESPONSE:

This letter correctly sets forth the understanding of Seliga Enterprises.

Approved by: _____

Title: _____

Date: _____

PRACTICE POINT: The auditor should customize the engagement letter for the unique circumstances of the client and engagement. The auditor must also ensure that the engagement letter contains, at a minimum, the objectives of the engagement, management's responsibilities, the auditor's responsibilities, and limitations of the engagement, including the following:

- The objective of the audit is the expression of an opinion on the financial statements.

- Management is responsible for the entity's financial statements and the selection and application of the accounting policies.

- Management is responsible for establishing and maintaining effective internal control over financial reporting.

- Management is responsible for designing and implementing programs and controls to prevent and detect fraud.

- Management is responsible for identifying and ensuring that the entity complies with the laws and regulations applicable to its activities.

- Management is responsible for making all financial records and related information available to the auditor.

- At the conclusion of the engagement, management will provide the auditor with a letter that confirms certain representations made during the audit.

- The auditor is responsible for conducting the audit in accordance with generally accepted auditing standards. Those standards require that the auditor obtain reasonable rather than absolute assurance about whether the financial statements are free of material misstatement, whether caused by error or fraud. Accordingly, a material misstatement may remain undetected. Also, an audit is not designed to detect error or fraud that is immaterial to the financial statements. If, for any reason, the auditor is unable to complete the audit or is unable to form or has not formed an opinion, he or she may decline to express an opinion or decline to issue a report as a result of the engagement.

- An audit includes obtaining an understanding of the entity and its environment, including its internal control, sufficient to assess the risks of material misstatement of the financial statements and to design the nature, timing, and extent of further audit procedures. An audit is not designed to provide assurance on internal control or to identify significant deficiencies. However, the auditor is responsible for ensuring that those charged with governance are aware of any significant deficiencies that come to his or her attention.

- Management is responsible for adjusting the financial statements to correct material misstatements and for affirming to the auditor in the management representation letter that the effects of any uncorrected misstatements aggregated by the auditor during the current engagement and pertaining to the latest period presented are immaterial, both individually and in the aggregate, to the financial statements taken as a whole.

PRACTICE POINT: Statement on Quality Control Standards No. 7, "A Firm's System of Quality Control," indicates that a firm should establish policies and procedures requiring that the identity and role of the engagement partner be communicated to management and those charged with governance. One way to comply with this requirement is to include a statement such as the following in the engagement letter: "John Doe, CPA, is the engagement partner responsible for supervising the engagement and for signing, or authorizing an individual to sign, the auditor's report and has the appropriate authority to do so."

PRACTICE POINT: The auditor may wish, and in some cases may be required by law, regulation, or audit contract, to confirm in writing with the client that the auditor may be required to provide a regulator access to the audit documentation. In such circumstances, the auditor may use sample language such as the following in the engagement letter:

The audit documentation for this engagement is the property of (name of auditor) and constitutes confidential information. However, we may be requested to make certain audit documentation available to (name of regulator) pursuant to authority given to it by law or regulation. If requested, access to such audit documentation will be provided under the supervision of (name of auditor) personnel. Furthermore, upon request, we may provide copies of selected audit documentation to (name of regulator). The (name of regulator) may intend, or decide, to distribute the copies of information contained therein to others, including other governmental agencies.

PRACTICE POINT: If the auditor performs nonattest services (e.g., tax return preparation) for an audit client, the auditor should document his or her understanding with the client regarding the nonattest services to be performed. Such documentation can be either in the working papers or in the engagement letter. In order to satisfy the documentation requirement, the auditor may add the following additional language to the engagement letter, following the description of the nonattest services engagement:

The Company's management is responsible for (a) making all management decisions and performing all management functions; (b) assigning a competent individual to oversee the services; (c) evaluating the adequacy of the services performed; (d) evaluating and accepting responsibility for the results of the services performed; and (e) establishing and maintaining internal controls, including monitoring ongoing activities.

ILLUSTRATION 2—ADDITIONAL AUDIT PROCEDURES FOR INITIAL AUDIT ENGAGEMENTS

1. Communicate with the predecessor auditor (see AU Section 315).

2. Review the predecessor auditor's report on the financial statements; management letter or communication of significant deficiencies (including material weaknesses) in internal control; attorney response letters to audit inquiries; the management representation letter; and permanent file documents that are pertinent to the audit, such as articles of incorporation and significant agreements and legal documents.

3. Review the predecessor auditor's working papers for all significant audit areas, including documentation of planning, internal control, audit results, conclusion memos, and other matters of continuing accounting and auditing significance (e.g., stockholder's equity accounts) and copy the applicable working papers and files.

4. Assess the reasonableness of opening balances of significant balance sheet accounts (e.g., cash, accounts receivable, and property and equipment). In making this assessment, review the predecessor auditor's working papers and consider whether the predecessor auditor:

   a. Confirmed cash balances and tested the client's cash reconciliations and cash cutoff.

   b. Confirmed and tested investments and determined the reasonableness of recorded values.

   c. Confirmed accounts receivables (and the coverage was adequate); tested the adequacy of the allowance for doubtful accounts; and performed sales cut-off procedures.

   d. Observed inventory and made appropriate test counts; performed inventory price tests; identified any excess, slow-moving, or obsolete inventory; performed shipping and receiving cut-off procedures; and considered inventory valuations for lower of cost or market.

   e. Tested property, plant, and equipment giving appropriate consideration to significant additions and retirements, depreciation methods, useful lives, and impairment issues.

   f. Tested prepaid expenses, deferred charges, intangible assets, and other assets and considered the reasonableness of the remaining asset balances.

   g. Performed a search for unrecorded liabilities and tested the validity and adequacy of accrued liabilities.

   h. Analyzed the income tax-related accounts and addressed significant temporary differences and related deferred tax asset valuation allowances.

   i. Confirmed debt terms and balances and tested the reasonableness of interest expense.

      j. Examined authorization and supporting documentation for significant equity transactions, including stock issuance, retirement, and dividends.

5. Identify the accounting principles and methods used by the entity in the prior period and determine if there have been any changes in such accounting principles and methods.

6. Review the predecessor auditor's year-end adjusting journal entries and any unrecorded audit differences (passed adjusting journal entries) and evaluate their potential impact on the current period's audit.

7. Determine the effect of any misstatement of the opening balances on the current period's financial statements.

8. Read the Company's minutes of meetings of shareholders and directors for a reasonable period of time (e.g., the previous three years, and prior years if it is considered necessary).

9. Review the Company's income tax returns and revenue agents' reports for a reasonable period of time (e.g., the previous three years, and prior years if it is considered necessary).

ILLUSTRATION 3—AUDIT REVIEW AND APPROVAL CHECKLIST

Client Name: _____

Date of Financial Statements: _____

	Yes	No	N/A

Detailed Review

Based on my review, I am satisfied that:

1. We adequately performed and documented risk assessment procedures to:
   a. Obtain an understanding of the entity and its environment.
   b. Obtain an understanding of internal controls and evaluate their design.
2. Identified risks of material misstatement, including fraud and other significant risks, which are clearly linked to the procedures performed to address those risks.
3. The conclusions of engagement personnel are consistent.
4. Audit procedures addressed relevant assertions for all significant accounts, classes of transactions, and disclosures.
5. Audit documentation is complete and clearly demonstrates the work performed, sources of information, and conclusions reached, and we have:
   a. Completed the audit programs and cross-referenced the steps to supporting documentation.
   b. Properly indexed, cross-referenced, signed, and dated audit documentation.

	Yes	No	N/A

c. Obtained management representation letters, legal counsel confirmations letters, and other important representations and confirmations.

6. All significant issues, findings, and other matters have been adequately resolved, including uncorrected misstatements and omitted disclosures.

7. We modified the nature, timing, and extent of audit procedures in response to evidence obtained during the audit, as needed.

8. The nature, timing, and extent of audit procedures were sufficient in view of the audit evidence obtained to conclude that:

    a. Risk assessments remain appropriate.

    b. The final audit strategy and audit plan were appropriate.

    c. Audit risk has been reduced to an appropriately low level.

9. The audit was conducted in accordance with generally accepted auditing standards and firm policies and procedures.

10. The financial statements are presented in accordance with generally accepted accounting principles (or another comprehensive basis of accounting):

    a. They are complete and agree with the audited trial balance.

    b. Disclosures are appropriately presented, complete, and understandable.

11. We have communicated material misstatements to management in a timely manner.

12. We have communicated matters to management and the audit committee (or others charged with governance) in accordance with professional standards.

13. Assistants were properly supervised and informed of their responsibilities and the nature of any matters that had an impact on the audit procedures they performed.

14. The opinion expressed in the auditor's report is appropriate.

Detailed reviewer's signature:_____ Date:_____

Principal Review

Based on my review, I am satisfied that:

1. Risk assessment procedures were performed sufficiently to identify risks of material misstatement and to develop an appropriate audit plan to address risks of material misstatements.

2. A detailed review has been performed of all audit procedures and audit areas.

	Yes	No	N/A
3. I have conducted an adequate review of audit documentation relevant to significant accounting, auditing, and reporting issues, and additional audit documentation as deemed necessary.	____	____	____
4. The audit was conducted in accordance with generally accepted auditing standards.	____	____	____
5. Audit procedures addressed relevant assertions for all significant accounts, classes of transactions, and disclosures.	____	____	____
6. We obtained a timely and appropriate representation letter from management.	____	____	____
7. We obtained timely and appropriate confirmation letters from the entity's legal counsel.	____	____	____
8. Appropriate consideration was given to all unrecorded audit adjustments and audit differences.	____	____	____
9. We held appropriate and timely discussions among the audit engagement personnel about the susceptibility of the entity's financial statements to risks of material misstatement, including those due to fraud.	____	____	____
10. I reminded engagement personnel of the need to exercise professional skepticism, to critically assess audit evidence, and to consult with other team members or experts in the firm, where appropriate.	____	____	____
11. We communicated matters to management and the audit committee (or others charged with governance) in accordance with professional standards.	____	____	____
12. The financial statements are presented in accordance with generally accepted accounting principles (or another comprehensive basis of accounting) and disclosures are appropriately presented, complete, and understandable.	____	____	____
13. The opinion expressed in the auditor's report is appropriate.	____	____	____

Principal reviewer's signature:_____ Date: _____

	Yes	No	N/A

Independent/Concurring Review

Based on my review, I am satisfied that:

	Yes	No	N/A
1. The financial statements are presented in accordance with generally accepted accounting principles (or another comprehensive basis of accounting) and disclosures are appropriately presented, complete, and understandable.	____	____	____
2. The firm's report on the financial statements is in accordance with generally accepted auditing standards and the opinion expressed in the auditor's report is appropriate.	____	____	____
3. I have performed an objective review of significant accounting, auditing, and reporting issues, including:			

	Yes	No	N/A
a. Discussions with the audit partner in charge of the engagement.	_____	_____	_____
b. Review of audit documentation relevant to significant accounting, auditing, and reporting considerations to the extent required by firm policies.	_____	_____	_____
c. Review of reports or other communications to management and those charged with governance required in conjunction with the audit (e.g., communication of significant deficiencies and material weaknesses).	_____	_____	_____

Independent/concurring reviewer's signature: _____ Date: _____

ILLUSTRATION 4—DIFFERENCES OF PROFESSIONAL OPINION FORM

Client Name: _____

Date of Financial Statements: _____

Instructions

This form should be used when differences of opinion concerning accounting and auditing issues exist among firm personnel involved in the audit. The form is designed to enable an audit staff member to document his or her disagreement with the conclusions reached if, after appropriate consultation, he or she believes it necessary to disassociate himself or herself from the resolution of the matter.

Names and titles of audit staff with differences of professional opinion:

Name	Title
_____	_____
_____	_____
_____	_____
_____	_____

Briefly describe the accounting or auditing issue causing differences of opinion among firm personnel.

_____

_____

Cite professional literature discussed, names of any consultants with whom the issue was discussed, and conclusion of consultant.

_____

_____

_____

Summarize final resolution and basis for conclusion.

_____

_____

_____

Final resolution approved by:

Partner	Date
_____	_____
_____	_____
_____	_____
_____	_____
_____	_____

The following personnel disassociate themselves from the final resolution of the matter discussed above:

Name	Date
_____	_____
_____	_____
_____	_____
_____	_____

ILLUSTRATION 5—UNCONDITIONAL AND PRESUMPTIVELY MANDATORY REQUIREMENTS OF AU SECTION 311

Unconditional Requirements

The following unconditional requirements, which are identified by the words "must" or "is required," obligate the auditor to:

- Adequately plan the audit work.
- Properly supervise any assistants.
- Plan the audit so that it is responsive to the assessment of the risk of material misstatement based on the auditor's understanding of the client and its environment, including its internal control.
- Develop an audit plan that documents the audit procedures to be used that are expected to reduce audit risk to an acceptably low level.

Presumptively Mandatory Requirements

Presumptively mandatory requirements are identified by the word "should" and place the burden of proof on the auditor if he or she departs from the presumptive requirement. Presumptively mandatory requirements are required to be performed in all applicable circumstances unless the auditor can justify in the audit documentation a reason for not doing so and demonstrate how other audit procedures that the auditor performed have met the audit objectives. AU Section 311 states that the auditor *should*:

1. Before accepting an audit engagement at or near the close of the entity's fiscal year:

    a. Ascertain whether circumstances are likely to permit an adequate audit and the expression of an unqualified opinion; and

    b. If an unqualified opinion is not likely, discuss with the client the possibility of a qualified opinion or disclaimer of opinion.

2. Evaluate certain communications with the predecessor auditor before accepting an audit engagement.

3. Establish, for each engagement, an understanding with the client regarding the services to be performed and document such understanding in a written engagement letter with the client, including the following items:

    a. *The objectives of the engagement*—Essentially, the primary objective of the audit is to express an opinion on the financial statements.

    b. *Management's responsibilities*—Management is responsible for the following:

       (1) The entity's financial statements;

       (2) The selection and application of the entity's accounting policies;

       (3) Establishing and maintaining effective internal control over financial reporting;

       (4) Designing and implementing programs and controls to prevent and detect fraud;

       (5) Identifying and ensuring that the entity complies with the laws and regulations applicable to its activities;

       (6) Making all financial records and related information available to the auditor;

       (7) Providing the auditor, at the conclusion of the audit, with a letter that confirms certain representations made during the audit;

       (8) Adjusting the financial statements to correct material misstatements; and

       (9) Affirming to the auditor in the representation letter that the effects of any uncorrected misstatements, resulting from errors or fraud, aggregated by the auditor during the current engagement and pertaining to the latest period presented are immaterial, both individually and in the aggregate, to the financial statements taken as a whole.

    c. *The auditor's responsibilities*—The auditor is responsible for the following:

       (1) Conducting the audit in accordance with GAAS;

       (2) Obtaining reasonable, rather than absolute, assurance about whether the financial statements are free of material misstatement, whether caused by error or by fraud; and, therefore, a material misstatement may remain undetected;

> (3) Determining whether to decline to express an opinion or to issue a report on the financial statements, if the auditor is unable to complete the audit or is unable to form an opinion;
>
> (4) Obtaining an understanding of the entity and its environment, including its internal control, sufficient to assess the risks of material misstatement of the financial statements and to design the nature, timing, and extent of further audit procedures to be performed; and
>
> (5) Ensuring that those charged with governance are aware of any significant deficiencies that come to the auditor's attention.
>
> d. *Limitations of the engagement*—An audit conducted in accordance with GAAS is not designed to:
>
> > (1) Detect error or fraud that is immaterial to the financial statements; and
> >
> > (2) Provide assurance on internal control or to identify significant deficiencies.

4. At the beginning of the current audit engagement, and before performing other significant audit activities, perform procedures relating to the continuance of the client relationship and the specific audit engagement.

5. At the beginning of the current audit engagement, and before performing other significant audit activities, evaluate the auditor's compliance with ethical and independence requirements.

6. Establish the overall audit strategy by performing the following procedures:

   a. Determining the characteristics and scope of the engagement (e.g., the basis of reporting; industry-specific reporting requirements; and locations of the entity).

   b. Establishing and planning the timing of the audit and the nature of the communications required (e.g., deadlines for interim and final reporting; and pertinent dates for expected communications with management and those charged with governance).

   c. Considering the main factors that will determine the focus of the audit team's efforts (e.g., materiality levels; high risk audit areas; material locations and account balances; and recent significant entity-specific, industry, financial reporting, or other relevant developments).

   d. Considering the results of preliminary engagement activities (e.g., any issues with management's integrity; and the auditor's ethical and independence requirements) and experience gained on other engagements with the client.

7. Update and document significant revisions to the overall audit strategy to respond to changes in circumstances occurring during the audit, if any.

8. Include in the audit plan descriptions of:

   a. The nature, timing, and extent of planned risk assessment procedures.

   b. The nature, timing, and extent of planned further audit procedures at the relevant assertion level for each material account balance, transaction class, and disclosure.

   c. Other audit procedures to be performed (e.g., direct communication with the organization's legal counsel).

9. Document changes to the original audit plan.

10. Consider whether specialized skills are needed to perform the audit and, if so:

   a. Seek assistance from a professional with those skills.

   b. Determine whether that professional will function effectively as a part of the audit team.

   c. Have sufficient knowledge to communicate the objectives and evaluate the results of the specialist's work.

   d. Consider a number of specific factors relative to the need to engage an information technology specialist.

11. Be cautious not to compromise the effectiveness of the audit when discussing the audit strategy or audit plan with those charged with governance, such as by disclosing details about the nature, timing, or extent of planned audit procedures.

12. Before starting an initial audit, perform certain client and engagement acceptance procedures and, where applicable, communicate with the predecessor auditor.

13. Consider a number of additional specific matters (e.g., assignment of appropriate firm personnel) in developing the overall audit strategy and audit plan for initial audits.

14. Communicate to audit team members the susceptibility of the entity's financial statements to material misstatement due to fraud or error, with special emphasis on fraud.

15. Emphasize to audit team members the need to maintain independence in mental attitude, and for exercising professional skepticism and a questioning mind in gathering and evaluating audit evidence.

16. Inform assistants about:

   a. Their responsibilities.

   b. The objectives of the audit procedures they are to perform.

   c. Matters that may affect the nature, timing, and extent of the audit procedures they are to perform.

17. Direct assistants to:

   a. Bring significant accounting or auditing issues to the attention of the auditor with final responsibility for the audit (e.g., engagement partner).

    b. Bring difficulties encountered in performing the audit (e.g., missing documents, restricted access to information) to the attention of appropriate individuals in the firm.

18. Review the work performed by each assistant to determine that it was adequately performed and documented and to evaluate its results.

19. Be aware of the firm's procedures for addressing differences of professional opinion among the audit team relating to accounting and auditing issues, including documenting those disagreements and their resolution.

AU SECTION 312
AUDIT RISK AND MATERIALITY IN CONDUCTING AN AUDIT

PRACTICE POINT: As part of its Clarity Project, the American Institute of Certified Public Accountants' (AICPA's) Auditing Standards Board (ASB) has finalized a clarified Statement on Auditing Standards (SAS) titled, "Materiality in Planning and Performing an Audit." This clarified standard along with the clarified standard, "Evaluation of Misstatements Identified during the Audit," supersedes AU Section 312 (Audit Risk and Materiality in Conducting an Audit).

The clarified SAS, "Materiality in Planning and Performing an Audit," does not change or expand existing requirements in extant AU Section 312 in any significant respect. Extant AU Section 312 addresses audit risk, materiality, and the evaluation of misstatements identified during the audit. To make the standard clearer and consistent with ISA 320, "Materiality in Planning and Performing an Audit," and ISA 450, "Evaluation of Misstatements Identified during the Audit," AU Section 312 has been separated into two standards. The clarified SAS, "Materiality in Planning and Performing an Audit," addresses the use of materiality in planning and performing the audit. The clarified SAS, "Evaluation of Misstatements Identified during the Audit," addresses the evaluation of misstatements identified during the audit.

Also, the definition of audit risk and its components are now defined in the clarified SAS, "Overall Objectives of the Independent Auditor and the Conduct of an Audit in Accordance with Generally Accepted Auditing Standards." Paragraphs .62–.67 of extant AU Section 312 address the auditor's responsibilities to evaluate the overall effect of audit findings on the auditor's report. These requirements have been included in the clarified SAS, "Forming an Opinion and Reporting on Financial Statements." The placement of these requirements does not create a difference between extant SASs as a whole and the clarified SASs as a whole.

The ASB is expected to issue many of the clarified standards in *one* SAS that will be codified in "AU Section" format. The ASB has decided that the effective date of the clarified SASs that have not yet been issued is for audits of financial statements for periods ending on or after December 15, 2012. Auditors should be alert to and monitor further developments in this area.

WHAT EVERY PRACTITIONER SHOULD KNOW

Basic Objectives and Requirements

This Section provides guidance on the auditor's consideration of audit risk and materiality when performing an audit of an entity's financial statements. Specifically, this Section:

1. Requires the auditor to have an appropriate basis for all risk assessments and eliminates the concept of assessing risk "at the maximum" without support.

2. Discusses the auditor's determination of materiality for the financial statements as a whole when planning the audit and provides examples

of benchmarks that might be appropriate, for example: total revenues, gross profit, and profit before tax.

3. Requires the auditor to reconsider the appropriateness of the initial assessment of the level of materiality, including the levels of tolerable misstatement, as the audit progresses.

4. Requires the auditor to accumulate all known and likely misstatements during the audit and to communicate them to management on a timely basis.

5. Discusses the auditor's evaluation of audit findings and requires the auditor to include the effect on the current period's financial statements of those prior-period misstatements and consider the qualitative aspects of the misstatements.

6. Requires the auditor to evaluate whether the financial statements as a whole are free of material misstatement and to satisfy himself or herself that the entity has adjusted the financial statements to reduce the risk of material misstatement to an appropriate low level.

7. Requires the auditor to communicate with those charged with governance (e.g., audit committee or board of directors) about materiality and misstatements.

8. Requires the auditor to document (a) the levels of materiality and tolerable misstatement used in the audit and any changes thereto; (b) a summary of uncorrected misstatements and conclusion as to whether the uncorrected misstatements cause the financial statements to be materially misstated; and (c) all known and likely misstatements identified by the auditor that have been corrected by management, other than those considered to be trivial.

Definition of Audit Risk

This Section defines *audit risk* as "the risk that the auditor may unknowingly fail to appropriately modify his or her opinion on financial statements that are materially misstated" and, therefore, the risk that financial statements will include material misstatements. The auditor addresses materiality and audit risk at an overall financial statement level to develop an audit strategy that will provide sufficient evidence to enable him or her to reasonably evaluate whether the financial statements are materially misstated. At the individual account balance, class of transactions, relevant assertion, or disclosure level, audit risk (AR) is made up of inherent risk (IR), control risk (CR), and detection risk (DR). This combination is multiplicative and is usually stated as follows:

$$AR = IR \times CR \times DR$$

Inherent risk *Inherent risk* is the susceptibility of a relevant financial statement assertion to a material misstatement, either individually or when aggregated with other misstatements, assuming there are no related controls.

Control risk *Control risk* is the risk that a material misstatement that could occur in a relevant financial statement assertion, either individually or when aggregated with other misstatements, will not be prevented or detected on a timely basis by the entity's internal control.

Detection risk *Detection risk* is the risk that the auditor will not detect a material misstatement that exists in a relevant financial statement assertion, either individually or when aggregated with other misstatements. Detection risk can be disaggregated into additional components of tests of details risk and substantive analytical procedures risk.

This Section refers to the combination of inherent risk and control risk as the risk of material misstatement.

Considerations of Audit Risk at the Financial Statement Level

The auditor is required to consider audit risk and to determine a materiality level for the financial statements taken as a whole in order to accomplish the following:

- Determine the extent and nature of risk assessment procedures.
- Identify and assess the risks of material misstatement.
- Determine the nature, timing, and extent of further audit procedures.
- Evaluate whether the financial statements taken as a whole are presented fairly, in all material respects, in conformity with generally accepted accounting principles (GAAP).

The auditor's consideration of audit risk at the financial statement level includes general planning decisions such as staffing, extent of review, and degree of professional skepticism. The auditor is not required to make an involved analysis or to quantify the audit risk; however, he or she is required to perform the audit to reduce audit risk to a low level that is appropriate for expressing an opinion on the entity's financial statements. Therefore, consideration of audit risk is necessarily judgmental and not mathematical and, accordingly, the auditor may assess audit risk in quantitative or nonquantitative terms.

In addressing audit risk at the overall financial statement level, the auditor should:

- Consider risks of material misstatement that relate pervasively to the financial statements taken as a whole and potentially affect many relevant assertions. Generally, such risks relate to the entity's control environment and may be particularly relevant to the auditor's consideration of the risks of material misstatement arising from fraud.
- Consider matters such as the following in developing responses to the risks of material misstatement at the overall financial statement level: (a) the knowledge, skill, and ability of personnel assigned to the engagement; (b) whether the involvement of a specialist is needed; and (c) the appropriate level of supervision of assistants.
- For an entity with operations in multiple locations or components, consider the extent of procedures to be performed at selected locations or components. Factors that could influence such selection include the following:

— The amount and nature of assets and transactions executed at the individual location or component.

— The degree of centralization of records or information processing.

— The effectiveness of the control environment.

— The frequency, timing, and scope of monitoring activities.

— Judgments about materiality of the location or component.

— Risks associated with the location (e.g., political or economic instability).

Considerations of Audit Risk at the Individual Account Balance, Class of Transactions, or Disclosure Level

The auditor is required to consider audit risk at the individual account balance, class of transactions, or disclosure level. The auditor's objective in such consideration is primarily to (1) determine the nature, timing, and extent of further audit procedures and (2) seek to reduce audit risk at the individual balance, class, or disclosure level in such a way to enable the auditor to express an opinion on the financial statements taken as a whole at an appropriately low level of audit risk. In determining the nature, timing, and extent of audit procedures to be applied to a specific account balance, class of transactions, or disclosure, the auditor should design audit procedures to obtain reasonable assurance of detecting misstatements that could be material (when aggregated with misstatements in other balances, classes, or disclosures) to the financial statements taken as a whole.

The consideration of audit risk at the account balance, class of transactions, relevant assertion, or disclosure level is a function of (1) the combination of inherent risk and control risk that the relevant assertions related to balances, transaction classes, or disclosures contain misstatements that could be material to the financial statements when aggregated with misstatements in other relevant assertions related to balances, classes, or disclosures and (2) the risk that the auditor will not detect such misstatements (i.e., *detection risk*).

The auditor combines the assessment of inherent risk and control risk to assess the risk of material misstatement. The auditor may use quantitative terms (e.g., percentages) or qualitative terms (e.g., low, medium, or high risk) to express the assessments of inherent risk and control risk. It should be noted that this Section and others describe the risk of material misstatement as the auditor's combined assessment of inherent risk and control risk; however, the auditor may make separate assessments of inherent risk and control risk. In addition, the auditor may implement these audit risk concepts in different ways, which necessarily involves professional judgment and depends on the auditor's approach or methodology.

Regardless of the auditor's approach or methodology, this Section requires the auditor to assess the risk of material misstatement at the relevant assertion level as a basis for further audit procedures. In addition, the auditor should have an appropriate basis for that assessment, which may be obtained through:

- The risk assessment procedures performed to obtain an understanding of the entity and its environment, including its internal control; and

- The performance of tests of controls to obtain audit evidence about the operating effectiveness of controls, where appropriate.

Materiality Concepts and Tolerable Misstatement

Determining materiality for the financial statements as a whole Materiality for the financial statements as a whole is the maximum amount that the auditor believes the financial statements could be misstated and still fairly present the entity's overall financial statements. The auditor's estimate of materiality requires professional judgment, based on the understanding of the client's business and the specific circumstances of the engagement. Since materiality is relative, rather than absolute, it is common to have benchmarks for establishing whether misstatements are material. Common benchmarks include income before income taxes, gross profit, total revenues, and total assets. In practice, auditors calculate materiality by applying an appropriate percentage to a relevant benchmark.

When establishing the overall audit strategy for the audit, the auditor should determine a materiality level for the financial statements taken as a whole. When determining an appropriate materiality level, the auditor is required to consider: (1) prior periods' financial results and financial positions, (2) the period-to-date financial results and financial position, and (3) budgets or forecasts for the current period.

Considerations of lower materiality levels that may influence decisions of financial statement users The auditor should consider whether misstatements of particular items of lesser amounts than the materiality level determined for the financial statements taken as a whole could, in the auditor's judgment, reasonably be expected to influence decisions of financial statement users in the specific circumstances of the entity. In making such determination, this Section provides that the auditor should consider factors such as the following:

- Whether accounting standards, laws, or regulations affect users' expectations regarding the measurement or disclosure of certain items.

- The key disclosures in relation to the industry and the environment in which the entity operates.

- Whether attention is focused on the financial performance of a particular subsidiary or division that is separately disclosed in the consolidating financial statements.

Tolerable misstatement Tolerable misstatement is the maximum monetary misstatement the auditor is willing to accept in a population (e.g., at the account balance or class of transactions level) without causing the financial statements to be materially misstated.

Tolerable misstatement is generally lower than materiality for the financial statements as a whole. When the auditor audits an account balance, class of transactions, or disclosure based on a specified level of materiality, it is possible that some misstatement below that level is present even if the auditor observes no errors. As a result, if the auditor uses materiality for specific audit tests, the auditor leaves no margin for the aggregate effect of undetected misstatements. Consequently, it is only logical that the amount of tolerable misstatement that the auditor establishes for each audit area should be less than materiality.

The auditor should set tolerable misstatement for each class of transactions, account balance, and disclosure to such a low level of risk that the total of undetected misstatements, detected misstatements, and judgmental differences (e.g., differences between management and the auditor regarding the allowance for doubtful accounts) from all audit areas will exceed materiality.

Considerations of materiality as the audit progresses The auditor's judgment about materiality for planning purposes may differ from the judgment about materiality used in evaluating the audit findings. As the audit progresses, the auditor may find it necessary to reconsider the levels of materiality initially established to set the overall scope of the audit. This Section provides the following additional guidance:

- If the auditor concludes that a lower materiality level than that initially established is appropriate, the auditor should reconsider the related levels of tolerable misstatement and appropriateness of the nature, timing, and extent of further audit procedures.

- If identified misstatements indicate that other misstatements may exist that in the aggregate could be material, the auditor should consider whether the overall audit strategy and audit plan need to be revised.

- If the aggregate of known and likely misstatements that the auditor has identified approaches the materiality level, the auditor should consider whether there is a greater than acceptable low level of risk that undetected misstatements, when taken with the aggregate identified misstatements, could exceed the materiality level. If so, the auditor should reconsider the nature and extent of further audit procedures.

Communication of Misstatements to Management

The auditor is required to accumulate all known and likely misstatements during the audit (other than those deemed to be trivial) and to communicate them to management on a timely basis. When communicating the details of misstatements to management, the auditor should:

- Distinguish between known misstatements and likely misstatements.

- Request management to record the adjustments needed to correct all known misstatements, including the effect of prior-period misstatements (other than those deemed to be trivial).

- Where the amount of likely misstatements from a sample in a class of transactions, account balance, or disclosure is material, either individually or in the aggregate with other misstatements, request management to examine the class of transactions, account balance, or disclosure in order to identify and correct misstatements therein.

- Where a likely misstatement involves differences in estimates (e.g., difference in a fair value estimate), request management to review the assumptions and methods used in developing management's estimate.

After management has addressed the auditor's communication of the details of likely misstatements, the auditor should reevaluate the amount of likely misstatements and perform additional audit procedures, if necessary. For example, if management has reviewed the assumptions and methods used in developing an estimate for which the auditor has identified a likely misstatement, the auditor should reevaluate the amount of likely misstatements and perform additional audit procedures, if necessary.

If management decides not to correct some or all of the known and likely misstatements that the auditor believes should be corrected, this Section directs the auditor to (1) obtain an understanding of management's reasons for not making the corrections, (2) consider the qualitative aspects of the entity's accounting practices, and (3) consider the implications for the auditor's report.

Evaluating Audit Findings, Adjustments, and Differences

Evaluating the findings of the audit procedures and documenting conclusions are important aspects of the audit process. A major step in this process is summarizing the misstatements and judgmental differences uncovered in the audit. During evaluation, the following factors may affect the auditor's judgment about whether misstatements uncovered are material to the overall financial statements: (1) types of misstatements, (2) qualitative characteristics of the misstatements, and (3) analysis of unrecorded audit differences (commonly referred to as "passed adjusting journal entries"). Each of these factors is discussed in greater detail below.

Types of Misstatements

Misstatements can result from errors or fraud and may consist of items such as the following: (1) difference between the amount, classification, or presentation of an item, account, or element reported in the financial statements and the amount, classification, or presentation that is required to be reported under GAAP; (2) incorrect, unreasonable, or inappropriate accounting estimates; and (3) inaccurate data from which financial statements are prepared.

Corrected misstatements During the course of the audit, the auditor may uncover misstatements that are material. In such cases, the auditor proposes adjusting journal entries for these material misstatements in order for the financial statements to be presented fairly in conformity with GAAP. The auditor typically proposes these adjustments, and management determines whether to accept them. Therefore, the auditor should have management approve any adjusting journal entries before they are recorded. Typically, the auditor reviews the adjustments with the client and provides the client with the list of adjustments so that they are recorded in the accounting records. These adjusting journal entries should not be included in the analysis of unrecorded audit differences discussed below.

Uncorrected misstatements In addition to the misstatements that have been corrected, the auditor should evaluate the combined effect of misstatements that the client has not corrected and decide whether the financial statements could be materially misstated. Therefore, the auditor should consider the effect, both individually and in the aggregate, of misstatements on important financial statement amounts, totals, or subtotals (e.g., current assets, current liabilities, and gross profit). This Section contains a specific requirement for evaluating uncorrected misstatements:

> In evaluating whether the financial statements are presented fairly, in all material respects, in conformity with generally accepted accounting principles, the auditor must consider the effects, both individually and in the aggregate, of misstatements (known and likely) that are not corrected by the entity. In making this evaluation, in relation to particular classes of transactions, account balances, and disclosures, the auditor should consider the size and nature of the misstatements and the particular circumstances of their occurrence, and determine the effect of such misstatements on the financial statements taken as a whole.

In aggregating misstatements at the conclusion of the audit, the auditor should include both known misstatements and likely misstatements. *Known misstatements* are amounts of misstatements specifically identified and *likely misstatements* represent the auditor's best estimate of total misstatements in the account balances or classes of transactions that he or she has examined. Likely misstatements include both (1) uncorrected known misstatements that the auditor identifies in the account balances or classes of transactions and (2) the auditor's estimate of additional misstatements as a result of applying audit sampling and substantive analytical procedures.

Before the auditor considers the aggregate effect of identified uncorrected misstatements, this Section directs the auditor to consider each misstatement separately to evaluate:

- The effect of the misstatement on the relevant individual classes of transactions, account balances, or disclosures.
- Whether misstatements of particular items of lesser amounts than the materiality level determined for the financial statements as a whole could reasonably be expected to influence economic decisions of financial statement users.
- Whether it is appropriate to offset misstatements.
- The effect of misstatements uncorrected in prior periods on the current period's financial statements.

In aggregating known and likely misstatements that the entity has not corrected, the auditor may designate an amount below which misstatements need not be accumulated ("trivial" amounts). This amount should be set so that any such misstatements, either individually or when aggregated with other such misstatements, would not be material to the financial statements, after the possibility of further undetected misstatements is considered.

Misstatements in accounting estimates Management often makes estimates about the effect of future events on the valuation of certain amounts in its financial statements (e.g., allowances for uncollectible accounts receivable and obsolete inventory, accruals for warranty costs, losses from plant closing, and income taxes). AU Section 342 (Auditing Accounting Estimates) requires the auditor to evaluate the reasonableness of accounting estimates made by management in the context of the financial statements taken as a whole. In evaluating the reasonableness of accounting estimates, the auditor should concentrate on fundamental factors and assumptions that are (1) significant to an estimate, (2) sensitive to variations, (3) different from past patterns, and (4) highly subjective. Furthermore, the auditor should obtain an understanding of the way management developed the estimate and perform one or a combination of the following procedures:

1. Review and test management's accounting estimation process.

2. Develop an independent estimate.

3. Review subsequent events or transactions.

Considering the Qualitative Characteristics of Misstatements

The auditor should not rely exclusively on quantitative benchmarks, or rules of thumb, to determine whether an item is material to the financial statements. A numerical threshold may provide the basis for a preliminary assumption that an amount is unlikely to be material; however, it is not a substitute for a full analysis. Statement of Financial Accounting Concepts No. 2, *Qualitative Characteristics of Accounting Information*, defines *materiality* as "the magnitude of an omission or misstatement of accounting information that, in the light of surrounding circumstances, makes it probable that the judgment of a reasonable person relying on the information would have been changed or influenced by the omission or misstatement."

The auditor should carefully evaluate qualitative factors on all audits. In many instances, qualitative factors are more important than the quantitative guidelines applied to the balance sheet and income statement. The intended uses of the financial statements and the nature of the information on the statements, including footnotes, must be carefully evaluated, since certain types of misstatements are likely to be more important to users than others, even if the dollar amounts are the same.

Analysis of Unrecorded Audit Differences (Passed Adjusting Journal Entries)

Differences encountered during the audit for which the client does not make adjustment, including misstatements both in recorded amounts and in accounting estimates, should be aggregated to evaluate the materiality of their combined effect on the financial statements as a whole. The auditor generally accumulates all such differences on a worksheet that typically distinguishes between (1) the effect on the income statement and the balance sheet and (2) the significant classifications within these statements. The auditor then considers whether the individual or combined effect of these audit differences is material to the financial statements.

To maximize efficiency, it is generally appropriate to set a nominal amount below which the auditor will not carry differences noted during the audit to the worksheet. In this situation, the auditor should document in the analysis the nominal amount used.

Uncorrected prior-year misstatements In prior periods, misstatements may not have been corrected by the entity because they did not cause the financial statements for those periods to be materially misstated. However, when evaluating whether the current period's financial statements are free of material misstatement, the auditor should consider what cumulative effect misstatements not corrected in the prior year will have on the current-year financial statements. Uncorrected misstatements from the prior year encompass misstatements that are specifically identified (i.e., known) and projected (i.e., likely misstatements, including differences in accounting estimates), as previously discussed. An immaterial uncorrected misstatement from the prior year might cause, for example, current-year net income to be materially misstated when it is considered along with current-year uncorrected misstatements.

Evaluating Whether the Financial Statements as a Whole Are Free of Material Misstatement

This Section requires the auditor to evaluate whether the financial statements, as a whole, are free of material misstatement. This evaluation involves both quantitative and qualitative considerations and requires the use of professional judgment.

As the aggregate effect of uncorrected misstatements gets closer to the amount that the auditor considers material, the auditor should give more consideration to possible further undetected misstatements. If the auditor believes that the risk of further undetected misstatements is unacceptably high, he or she should perform additional audit procedures to support the audit opinion on the entity's financial statements or satisfy himself or herself that the entity has adjusted the financial statements to reduce audit risk to an appropriately low level.

If the auditor believes that the financial statements, taken as a whole, are materially misstated, the auditor should request management to make the necessary corrections. If management refuses to make the corrections, the auditor must determine the implications for the auditor's report and follow the guidance in AU Section 508 (Reports on Audited Financial Statements).

Documentation Requirements

This Section requires the auditor to document the following items pertaining to materiality, uncorrected misstatements, and conclusion as to whether the uncorrected misstatements cause the financial statements to be materially misstated:

1. Materiality levels for the financial statements as a whole when establishing the overall audit strategy and tolerable misstatement, including any changes thereto, and the basis on which those levels were determined.

2. A summary of uncorrected misstatements (other than those that are trivial) related to known and likely misstatements.

3. The auditor's conclusion as to whether uncorrected misstatements (individually or in aggregate) cause the financial statements to be materially misstated and the basis for that conclusion.

4. All known and likely misstatements that the auditor identified during the audit (other than those that are trivial) and that have been corrected by management.

5. Uncorrected misstatements in a manner that reflects consideration of:

a. The separate effects of known and likely misstatements, including the effects of uncorrected misstatements identified in prior periods on the current period's financial statements.

b. The aggregate effect of misstatements on the financial statements.

c. The qualitative factors deemed relevant for evaluating whether misstatements are material.

PRACTICE ISSUES AND FREQUENTLY ASKED QUESTIONS

Issue 1: Is the auditor's business risk the same as audit risk?

No. The auditor's business risk is the risk of potential litigation costs from an alleged audit failure and the risk of other costs (whether an audit failure is alleged or not), such as fee realization and effects on the auditor's reputation resulting from association with the client. On the other hand, the auditor's audit risk is the risk that the auditor may unknowingly fail to appropriately modify his or her opinion on financial statements that are materially misstated.

Issue 2: Is the auditor required to quantify his or her assessment of risk in a financial statement audit?

No. Auditing standards require only that the concepts of inherent risk, control risk, and detection risk (all of which make up audit risk) be considered for each significant account balance or transaction class. Risk assessments may be expressed in general terms, such as high, moderate, or low. Auditing literature often describes audit risk as being the product of the probabilities of misstatement from the three categories of risks. However, the standards do not specify, for example, at what level or threshold of misstatement a risk crosses over from low to moderate or from moderate to high.

Issue 3: What are the steps involved to effectively and efficiently apply the concept of materiality in a financial statement audit?

The following steps summarize how the auditor should apply the concept of materiality in a financial statement audit:

1. Establish preliminary judgment about materiality during the initial planning phase of the audit engagement.

2. Relate planning materiality to the scope of tests of transactions and balances.

3. Summarize total misstatements. This step includes (a) known misstatements (i.e., the amount of errors specifically identified when performing audit procedures) and (b) likely misstatements (i.e., an estimate or a projection of actual errors because only a sample, rather than the entire population, is audited).

4. Compare total misstatements with materiality at the end of the audit and evaluate whether audit procedures have been sufficient to detect material misstatements.

5. If significantly lower materiality levels become appropriate in evaluating the audit findings, reevaluate the sufficiency of the auditing procedures that were performed.

Steps 1 and 2 are performed in the planning stage, before audit procedures are applied. Steps 3, 4, and 5 are performed in the evaluation stage, after the audit procedures are applied.

Issue 4: Have any authoritative quantitative guidelines for materiality judgments been established in the accounting or auditing standards?

No. Authoritative guidance does not currently exist, and the FASB and AICPA are unwilling to provide specific guidelines for quantifying a dollar amount regarding materiality. The concern is that the auditor would apply such guidelines without considering all the complexities that should affect his or her final decision. Both auditing and accounting standards recognize that materiality judgments involve both quantitative and qualitative considerations.

Although an auditor's judgment about materiality necessarily involves calculations and is expressed in quantitative terms, the auditor's judgment is generally influenced by his or her perception of the needs of a reasonable user of the financial statements. In practice, a wide variety of methods exist for calculating materiality. Some practitioners use a fixed percentage of a financial statement measure such as total assets, stockholder's equity, revenues, or net income, while others use a graduated percentage scale based on financial statement measures. (See Issue 5 below for additional guidance in this area.) Still, others use an amount that they believe the client or other user of the financial statements perceives as significant, without specific regard to financial statement measures. Any of these methods, as long as they are documented in the workpapers, meet the requirements of professional standards.

Issue 5: What are some of the general guidelines commonly used by accounting firms as a practical approach to establishing materiality?

Although there are no authoritative standards for percentage guidelines on materiality, the following general guidelines and concepts are commonly used by accounting firms, large and small, and are reasonable as a practical approach to establishing materiality:

- *General guidelines*—Because materiality is relative, rather than absolute, it is necessary to have benchmarks for establishing whether misstatements are material. Typically, operating results are the most important measurement benchmarks that external financial statement users utilize to make decisions. Also, a misstatement generally becomes material to income long before it becomes material to the balance sheet. Since the auditor's opinion usually relates to the financial statements taken as a whole, rather than to an individual financial statement, the most useful guide is the smaller materiality amount. It also is important to determine whether the misstatements could materially affect the reasonableness of other possible benchmarks, such as current assets, current liabilities, and stockholders' equity. Common benchmarks used by accounting firms include income before income taxes, total revenues, and total assets. In practice, auditors calculate materiality by applying an appropriate percentage to a relevant benchmark (e.g., 5% of pretax income).

- *Materiality judgments based on operating results or financial position*—Generally, 5% of pretax income would be regarded as a reasonable and conservative percentage for most businesses. Whether to use the preceding year's actual income, annualized current-year income, or an average of previous years' income is a judgmental decision based on the entity's trend of earnings and current economic conditions. In many situations, it would be appropriate to challenge the reasonableness of the different methods by computing materiality each way as a cross-check on the various methods. If the entity operates at or near the breakeven point or fluctuates between net income and net loss from year to year, pretax income may not be the most appropriate basis for computing planning materiality. Instead, total revenue or gross profit may be more appropriate. In certain situations, planning materiality based on operating results will not make sense to the auditor. For example, if an entity's operating results have been so poor that liquidity or solvency has become a major concern, it probably would be more appropriate to compute planning materiality based on financial position. In deciding what percent of stockholders' equity to use, the auditor should consider the relationship of stockholders' equity to the entity's total operations and financial position. For example, an entity that is experiencing losses, declining sales, and liquidity problems probably would be at the low end of the range.

The table in Illustration 2 below summarizes certain guidelines used by CPA firms to calculate materiality based on operating results or financial position.

Issue 6: What constitutes a "misstatement" for purposes of determining whether the financial statements are materially misstated under this Section?

A misstatement may consist of any of the following:

- A difference between the *amount* of an item, account, or element reported in the financial statements and the *amount* that is required to be reported under GAAP.

- A difference between the *classification* of an item, account, or element reported in the financial statements and the *classification* that is required to be reported under GAAP.

- A difference between the *presentation* of an item, account, or element reported in the financial statements and the *presentation* that is required to be reported under GAAP.

- An item that is omitted from the financial statements.

- A disclosure that is not presented in accordance with GAAP.

- Omitted information that is required to be disclosed under GAAP.

- Incorrect, unreasonable or inappropriate accounting estimates.

- Unreasonable or inappropriate accounting policies.
- Inaccurate data from which financial statements are prepared.

Issue 7: What is a common example of "likely misstatements" when evaluating audit findings?

The most common example of determining likely misstatements is in audit sampling, statistical or nonstatistical. For example, if the auditor sampled 20% of the accounts receivable balance and found total misstatements of $2,000 (the known misstatements), the auditor could project this misstatement to the account balance as $10,000 (the likely misstatements)—$2,000 divided by 20%. The likely misstatements of $10,000 include the known misstatements of $2,000 because the known misstatements are projected to the total accounts receivable balance. However, if the client corrects the known misstatements of $2,000, then the likely misstatements would be only $8,000 ($10,000 − $2,000).

Issue 8: Does the judgment about materiality used to plan the audit have to be used in evaluating the impact on the financial statements at the conclusion of the audit?

No. Judgment about materiality that is used to plan the audit is the auditor's *preliminary* judgment and is used to develop the overall scope of audit procedures. Oftentimes referred to as *planning materiality,* it is used to identify critical audit areas and is different than materiality in the evaluation stage. Planning materiality is used to determine the scope or effectiveness of audit procedures, whereas materiality in the evaluation stage is used to determine whether the financial statements are materially misstated. When planning the audit, the auditor establishes planning materiality to design effective and efficient audit procedures. However, at the completion of the audit, the auditor will have gathered additional evidence that may cause him or her to take a more or less conservative position, depending on the circumstances of the engagement, and change his or her judgment about materiality.

Therefore, the amount that the auditor considers material at the end of the audit may differ from planning materiality because ordinarily it is not feasible to anticipate all of the circumstances that may ultimately influence the auditor's judgment about materiality.

Issue 9: What considerations should the auditor give to "differences in accounting estimates" when evaluating whether financial statements are materially misstated?

Management often makes estimates about the effect of future events on the valuation of certain amounts in its financial statements (e.g., allowances for uncollectible accounts receivable and obsolete inventory, accruals for warranty costs, losses from plant closing, and income taxes). The auditor is required to evaluate the reasonableness of accounting estimates made by management in the context of the financial statements taken as a whole.

The auditor's analysis and evaluation of these estimates often lead to a range of acceptable amounts. If the auditor concludes management's recorded estimate falls within the range of acceptable amounts, the auditor ordinarily would conclude that the recorded amount is reasonable and there is no likely misstatement in the account balance or class of transactions. In other situations, management's recorded estimate will not fall within the auditor's acceptance range. This may result primarily because of different expectations about future events between the auditor and management or because of management's inappropriate consideration of relevant facts and circumstances. In these situations, the auditor should treat the difference between management's estimated recorded amount and the closest estimate of the auditor's acceptance range as a likely misstatement.

For example, the auditor may believe that the allowance for obsolete inventory should be between $20,000 and $35,000. If management's recorded estimate is $25,000, the auditor would conclude that the recorded amount is reasonable because it falls within the acceptable range. Therefore, the auditor would conclude that there are no likely misstatements in the inventory balance. On the other hand, if management's recorded estimate is $15,000, the auditor would conclude that an audit difference of $5,000 ($20,000 − $15,000) exists. Therefore, the auditor would treat such difference as a likely misstatement in the inventory balance and aggregate it with other likely and known misstatements for an overall evaluation on the financial statements.

If management's recorded estimates are clustered at either end of the auditor's range of acceptable amounts, thereby indicating a possible management bias, the auditor should reconsider whether other recorded estimates reflect a similar bias and should perform additional audit procedures that address those estimates. Also, the auditor should be alert to whether management's recorded estimates were clustered at one end of the auditor's range of acceptable amounts in the preceding year and clustered at the other end of the range in the current year; this indicates that management might be using swings in accounting estimates to offset higher or lower than expected earnings. In these circumstances, the auditor should consider whether these matters should be communicated to those charged with governance.

Issue 10: Why should the auditor consider the cumulative effect of uncorrected prior-year misstatements on the current period's financial statements?

The auditor should consider what cumulative effect misstatements not corrected in the prior year will have on the current-year financial statements. This is important because an immaterial uncorrected misstatement from the prior year might cause current-year net income to be materially misstated when it is considered along with current-year uncorrected misstatements. Consider the following scenario.

Assume that an auditor is evaluating audit differences at the conclusion of the December 31, 2002, audit of ABC Company and the only uncorrected misstatements noted in the current and prior-period audits are unrecorded liabilities. Assume that accrued expenses are understated by $15,000 at December 31, 2002, and overstated by $10,000 at December 31, 2001, and the auditor considers a $20,000 misstatement of ABC Company's pretax income to be material.

In evaluating audit differences, the auditor combines the understatement of accrued expenses of $15,000 at December 31, 2002, with the overstatement of accrued expenses of $10,000 at December 31, 2001. This produces a $25,000 overstatement of 2002 pretax income. This is because the $10,000 of expenses were erroneously charged in 2001, which causes year 2002 expenses to be understated and, therefore, results in an overstatement of year 2002 pretax income. Note that the auditor would have reached the wrong conclusion if he or she considered only the $15,000 misstatement at December 31, 2002, when evaluating the audit differences.

Uncorrected misstatements in the prior year's closing balance sheet carry over to the current-period income statement and the auditor should consider the reversing effect of these carryover differences on the current-period financial statements.

In addition, the auditor should provide to management and those charged with governance a summary of uncorrected financial statement misstatements.

Issue 11: What approaches are commonly used in practice to evaluate the effect on the current year's financial statements of uncorrected prior-year misstatements?

The evaluation of materiality of uncorrected misstatements requires the evaluation of the effect on the financial statements of misstatements that originated in the current year as well as misstatements that originated in prior years (i.e., prior-year misstatements). Three primary approaches are commonly used in practice to evaluate the effect on the current year's financial statements of uncorrected prior-year misstatements: (1) the rollover approach, (2) the iron curtain approach, and (3) the dual approach, which is a combination of the first two approaches.

Rollover approach The rollover, or income statement, approach quantifies the effect of a prior-year misstatement on the current year's financial statements based on the effect of correcting the misstatement in the current year's income statement, including the reversing or rollover effect of prior-year misstatements. Under the rollover approach, the reversal or correction of a prior-year misstatement in the current year is considered an error in the current year and offsets the income statement effect of errors originating in the current year. The main weakness of the rollover approach is that prior-year misstatements that were deemed immaterial and that remain uncorrected at the end of the year are allowed to develop to a potentially material amount on the end-of-year balance sheet. Therefore, erroneous items are allowed to accumulate on the balance sheet to the point where eliminating the improper asset or liability in a later year would itself result in a material misstatement in the income statement in the year adjusted.

Iron curtain approach The iron curtain, or balance sheet, approach quantifies the effect of a misstatement based on the effect of correcting the misstatement existing in the balance sheet at the end of the current year, regardless of the year the misstatement originated. In essence, the iron curtain approach assumes that once a prior-period misstatement is properly determined to be immaterial to the prior-year financial statements, an iron curtain falls on that year, and correcting the prior-year misstatement in a future year is the proper accounting. Therefore, under the iron curtain approach, the correction of a prior-year misstatement in the current year, which could materially misstate the current year's income statement, is not considered an error in the current year's financial statements, which is the primary weakness in the iron curtain approach.

Dual approach Generally, companies and their auditors choose one approach or the other. However, because of the aforementioned weaknesses in the rollover or iron curtain approaches when used separately, best practice is to quantify and evaluate a prior-period misstatement under both the rollover and iron curtain approaches known as the dual approach. Under the dual approach, an entity's financial statements would need to be adjusted if a misstatement would be material under either the rollover or iron curtain approach, after considering all relevant quantitative and qualitative factors. The dual approach is a more comprehensive approach and results in more accurate financial reporting.

PRACTICE POINT: Currently, AICPA professional standards neither discuss nor require the use of these alternative approaches, but rather provide neutral guidance on the consideration of uncorrected prior-period misstatements. However, the SEC currently mandates that registrants and their auditors quantify and evaluate uncorrected prior-period misstatements under both the rollover and iron curtain approaches known as the dual approach. Under the dual approach, a registrant's financial statements would need to be adjusted if a misstatement would be material under either the rollover or iron curtain approach, after considering all relevant quantitative and qualitative factors. The SEC believes that the dual approach is a better approach, primarily because of the aforementioned inherent weaknesses of either the rollover or iron curtain approach when applied separately.

Issue 12: What types of qualitative considerations of misstatements should the auditor look for when evaluating audit findings?

Certain misstatements may have significance even though the dollar amount may not be as large as the auditor typically would assume to be material. Therefore, the nature of the misstatement (i.e., its qualitative characteristic) will help the auditor determine (1) the potential for additional misstatements of a similar type and (2) the need for changes in audit procedures. Therefore, the auditor should carefully evaluate qualitative factors on all audits. In many instances, qualitative factors are more important than the quantitative guidelines applied to the balance sheet and income statement. The intended uses of the financial statements and the nature of the information on the statements, including footnotes, must be carefully evaluated, since certain types of misstatements are likely to be more important to users than others, even if the dollar amounts are the same. Some examples include the following:

- *Errors versus fraud*—Amounts involving fraud generally are considered more critical than unintentional errors of equal dollar amounts. This is because fraud reflects on the integrity of management and the reliability of management representations.

- *Considerations of contractual obligations*—Misstatements that are otherwise minor may be material if adverse consequences are likely to arise from contractual obligations. An example is when net working capital included in the financial statements is only a few hundred dollars more than the required minimum in a loan agreement. The qualitative characteristic of the misstatement makes it material because the loan would be in default.

- *Effect on trend of earnings*—Misstatements that are otherwise immaterial may be material if they affect the entity's trend of earnings. For example, an error that would cause an entity's income to be reported as a loss would be of great significance.

- *Offsetting of "hard" and "soft" differences*—An agreement with management to waive "hard" debit audit differences (e.g., inventory pricing errors) because it has identified that offsetting "soft" credit differences (e.g., the reduction of bad debt or warranty reserve) can result in problems. Experience has shown that "soft" differences may not materialize, particularly when they are discovered by management at the last minute after it is informed of "hard" differences.

- *Expectations and perceptions of financial statement users*—Boards of directors, audit committees, and outsiders (e.g., attorneys, regulators) who become aware of unrecorded audit differences sometimes question why those differences were not recorded, especially if they are (a) marginally below materiality thresholds, (b) errors, or (c) clear deviations from GAAP.

In addition, AU Section 312 indicates that the auditor may find it important to consider the following qualitative factors for evaluating misstatements:

- The potential effect of the misstatement on trends, particularly profitability trends.

- A misstatement that changes a loss into income (or vice versa).

- The potential effect of the misstatement on the entity's compliance with loan covenants, other contractual agreements, and regulatory provisions.

- The existence of statutory or regulatory reporting requirements that affect materiality thresholds.

- A misstatement that masks a change in earnings or other trends.

- A misstatement that has the effect of increasing management's compensation.

- The sensitivity of the circumstances surrounding the misstatement (e.g., the implications of misstatements involving fraud and possible illegal acts, violations of contractual provisions, and conflicts of interest).

- The significance of the financial statement element affected by the misstatement.

- The effects of misclassifications (e.g., misclassification between operating and nonoperating income or recurring and nonrecurring income items).

- The significance of the misstatement relative to reasonable user-needs, for example:

— The significance of earnings to investors, earnings per share to public company investors, and equity amounts to creditors.

— The magnifying effects of a misstatement on the calculation of purchase price in a transfer of interests (e.g., in buy/sell agreements).

— The effect of misstatements of earnings when contrasted with expectations.

- The definitive character of the misstatement (e.g., the precision of an error that is objectively determinable versus a misstatement that inherently involves a degree of subjectivity through estimation, allocation, or uncertainty).

- The motivation of management with respect to the misstatement.

- The existence of offsetting effects of individually significant, but different, misstatements.

- The likelihood that a misstatement that is currently immaterial may have a material effect in future periods because of a cumulative effect.

- The cost of making the correction (i.e., it may not be cost-beneficial for the client to develop a system to calculate a basis to record the effect of an immaterial misstatement).

- The risk that possible additional undetected misstatements could affect the auditor's evaluation.

Issue 13: Is there a practical and effective approach that the auditor can use to consider whether financial statements are materially misstated at the conclusion of the audit?

Differences encountered during the audit for which the client does not make adjustments, including misstatements both in recorded amounts and in accounting estimates, should be summarized to evaluate the materiality of their combined effect on the financial statements. It is common practice for auditors to accumulate all such differences on a workpaper that typically distinguishes between (1) the effect on the income statement and the balance sheet and (2) the significant classifications within these statements. The auditor then considers whether the individual or combined effect of these audit differences is material to the financial statements.

Illustration 3 includes such a worksheet that the auditor can use to summarize, analyze, and evaluate the materiality of uncorrected misstatements. To maximize efficiency, it is generally appropriate to set a nominal amount below which the auditor will not carry differences noted during the audit to the worksheet.

Issue 14: AU Section 312 requires the auditor to accumulate all known and likely misstatements identified during the audit, other than those that the auditor believes are trivial, and communicate them to the appropriate level of management. What is considered "trivial" for purposes of this requirement?

This Section indicates that matters that are trivial are amounts designated by the auditor below which misstatements need not be accumulated. This amount is set so that any such misstatements, either individually or when aggregated with other such misstatements, would not be material to the financial statements, after considering the possibility of further undetected misstatements.

Issue 15: If inherent risk is assessed as low, can an auditor ignore the assessment of control risk in connection with his or her assessment of the combined risks of material misstatement?

No. Paragraph 23 of AU Section 312 states, in part:

> The auditor should assess the risk of material misstatement at the relevant assertion level as a basis for further audit procedures. Although that assessment is a judgment rather than a precise measurement of risk, the auditor should have an appropriate basis for that assessment.

The *risk of material misstatement* is defined as the product of inherent risk and control risk. Generally accepted auditing standards do not require separate assessments of inherent risk and control risk to be performed. However, they do require an assessment of risk of material misstatement that includes control risk. Therefore, because an auditor is required to assess the combined risk of material misstatement, an auditor cannot ignore control risk regardless of his or her assessment of inherent risk.

In situations in which the auditor's methodology makes separate assessments of inherent risk and control risk, the auditor's assessment of inherent risk should exclude the effect of any related controls. Therefore, if an auditor assesses inherent risk as low, the auditor should be careful whether his or her judgment was influenced by the effect of certain controls.

ILLUSTRATIONS AND PRACTICE AIDS

ILLUSTRATION 1—INHERENT RISK ASSESSMENT FORM

Client Name: _____

Date of Financial Statements: _____

Instructions

The auditor may use this form to document the assessment of inherent risk for all significant account balances, classes of transactions, and disclosures. The form includes the typical audit account balances and related assertions. Any account balances that are not applicable or significant to the engagement should be removed. The auditor also should add any account balance, class of transaction, or disclosure not included in this form that is significant to the engagement.

Inherent risk is the susceptibility of a relevant financial statement assertion to a misstatement that could be material, either individually or when aggregated with other misstatements, assuming that there are no related controls.

The column headings in the table below correspond to the following questions:

- *Entity and Environment*—Are there high risk factors in the entity and its environment (e.g., a weak control environment or a high risk industry)?

- *External Factors*—Are there high risk external factors (e.g., technological developments that might make a particular product obsolete)?

- *Complexity of Calculations*—Does the recorded amount involve difficult-to-audit transactions or complex accounting issues?
- *Susceptibility to Theft or Fraud*—Is the recorded amount susceptible to theft or fraud, including both misappropriation of assets and fraudulent financial reporting?
- *Judgment and Estimates*—Does the recorded amount consist of amounts derived from accounting estimates that are subject to significant measurement uncertainty or judgment?
- *Competence of Client Personnel*—Do the personnel responsible for processing the transactions lack the proper experience and supervision?
- *Prior Period Misstatements*—Are prior-year misstatements in the recorded amount significant?

For each of the inherent risk factors, indicate your assessment of inherent risk as Maximum (MAX), Slightly Below Maximum (SBM), Moderate (MOD), or Low. The overall assessment of inherent risk for an assertion in column 9 is the result of the auditor's consideration of each inherent risk factor in columns 2 through 8. The consideration of inherent risk factors is a qualitative rather than a quantitative judgment. Low inherent risk factors do not necessarily compensate for high inherent risk factors, so the determination of inherent risk is not an average of the risk factors for each assertion. Rather, consideration of each inherent risk factor will help the auditor to identify those factors that may indicate that an assertion has an overall higher inherent risk. For example, an assertion assessed as MAX for *Susceptibility to Theft or Fraud* and MAX for the *Degree of Judgment Required and Extent of Estimates Involved* may have a MAX inherent risk even though each of the other risk factors is LOW.

(1) Area/Assertion	(2) Entity and Environment	(3) External Factors	(4) Complexity of Calculations	(5) Susceptibility to Theft or Fraud	(6) Degree of Judgment Required and Extent of Estimates Involved	(7) Competence of Client Personnel	(8) Prior Period Misstatements	(9) Overall Assessment (Max, SBM, Mod, Low)
Cash								
Existence and Occurrence								
Rights and Obligations								
Completeness								
Accuracy								
Cut-off								
Classification								
Valuation and Allocation								
Presentation and Disclosure: Occurrence and Rights and Obligations								
Presentation and Disclosure: Completeness								
Presentation and Disclosure-Understandability and Classification								

(1) Area/Assertion	(2) Entity and Environment	(3) External Factors	(4) Complexity of Calculations	(5) Susceptibility to Theft or Fraud	(6) Degree of Judgment Required and Extent of Estimates Involved	(7) Competence of Client Personnel	(8) Prior Period Misstatements	(9) Overall Assessment (Max, SBM, Mod, Low)
Presentation and Disclosure: Accuracy and Valuation								
Accounts Receivable and Sales								
Existence and Occurrence								
Rights and Obligations								
Completeness								
Accuracy								
Cut-off								
Classification								
Valuation and Allocation								
Presentation and Disclosure: Occurrence and Rights and Obligations								
Presentation and Disclosure: Completeness								

(1) Area/Assertion	(2) Entity and Environment	(3) External Factors	(4) Complexity of Calculations	(5) Susceptibility to Theft or Fraud	(6) Degree of Judgment Required and Extent of Estimates Involved	(7) Competence of Client Personnel	(8) Prior Period Misstatements	(9) Overall Assessment (Max, SBM, Mod, Low)
Presentation and Disclosure: Understandability and Classification								
Presentation and Disclosure: Accuracy and Valuation								
(Insert additional audit areas, for example, inventory, and the related assertions.)								

We considered the following additional factors in assessing inherent risk:

Prepared by: _____   Date: _____

Approved by: _____   Date: _____

ILLUSTRATION 2—GUIDELINES TO CALCULATE MATERIALITY BASED ON OPERATING RESULTS OR ON FINANCIAL POSITION

Benchmark	Planning Materiality Is:
Total Revenue	1/2%–1% of Total Revenue
Total Assets	1/2%–1% of Total Assets
Pretax Income	5%–10% of Pretax Income
Gross Profit	1%–2% of Gross Profit
Stockholders' Equity	1%–5% of Stockholders' Equity

ILLUSTRATION 3—WORKSHEET FOR ANALYSIS OF UNCORRECTED MISSTATEMENTS

XYZ, Inc.
Analysis of Uncorrected Misstatements
Financial Statement Date: 12/31/20X2

Date:
Prepared By:
Reviewed By:

Over/(Under) Statement of

Workpaper Reference	Description	Total Current Year Amount	Assets		Liabilities		Equity	Pretax Income	Income Taxes	Net Income
			Current	Non Current	Current	Non Current				
AF-4	Overstatement of Allowance for Doubtful Accounts	(16,000)	(16,000)	0	0	0	(10,600)	(16,000)	(5,400)	(10,600)
AG-5	Understatement of Inventory Obsolescence Reserve	15,000	15,000	0	0	0	9,900	15,000	5,100	9,900
LA-9	Understatement of Accounts Payable-Unentered Liabilities	12,000	0	(3,000)	(12,000)	0	5,900	9,000	3,100	5,900
	Uncorrected Misstatements—Current Year	11,000	(1,000)	(3,000)	(12,000)	0	5,200	8,000	2,800	5,200
	Effect of Prior-Year Uncorrected Misstatements on Current-Year Income							13,000	4,400	8,600
	Net Effect on Current Year		(1,000)	(3,000)	(12,000)	0	5,200	21,000	7,200	13,800

ILLUSTRATION 4—UNCONDITIONAL AND PRESUMPTIVELY MANDATORY REQUIREMENTS OF AU SECTION 312

Unconditional Requirements

The following unconditional requirements, which are identified by the words "must" or "is required," obligate the auditor to:

- Consider audit risk and determine a materiality level for the financial statements taken as a whole in order to accomplish the following:
    - Determine the extent and nature of risk assessment procedures;
    - Identify and assess the risks of material misstatement;
    - Determine the nature, timing, and extent of further audit procedures; and
    - Evaluate whether the financial statements taken as a whole are presented fairly, in all material respects, in conformity with GAAP.
- Perform the audit to obtain reasonable assurance of detecting misstatements that could be large enough either individually or in the aggregate, in the auditor's judgment, to be quantitatively material to the financial statements.
- Accumulate all known and likely misstatements identified in the audit, other than trivial amounts, and communicate them to the appropriate level of management. *Trivial* amounts are amounts designated by the auditor below which misstatements need not be accumulated.
- Consider the effects, both individually and in the aggregate, of known and likely misstatements that are not corrected, in evaluating whether the financial statements are fairly presented.
- Evaluate whether the financial statements, as a whole, are free of material misstatement.
- Determine the implications for the auditor's report if management refuses to make necessary corrections.
- Determine the implications for the auditor's report if he or she concludes that, or is unable to conclude whether, the financial statements are materially misstated.

Presumptively Mandatory Requirements

Presumptively mandatory requirements are identified by the word "should" and place the burden of proof on the auditor if he or she departs from the presumptive requirement. Presumptively mandatory requirements are required to be performed in all applicable circumstances unless the auditor can justify in the audit documentation a reason for not doing so and demonstrate how other audit procedures that the auditor performed have met the audit objectives. AU Section 312 states that the auditor *should*:

- Consider the implications for the integrity of management or employees, and the possible effects on other aspects of the audit, when he or she encounters evidence of potential fraud, even if immaterial.
- Consider audit risk in relation to the relevant assertions related to individual account balances, classes of transactions, and disclosures and at the overall financial statement level.
- Perform risk assessment procedures to assess the risks of material misstatement at both the financial statement and relevant assertion levels.

- Perform the audit to reduce audit risk to an appropriately low level for expressing an opinion on the financial statements.

- Consider the risks of material misstatement that relate pervasively to the financial statements as a whole and that potentially affect many relevant assertions, when considering audit risk at the overall financial statement level. Generally, such risks relate to the entity's control environment and may be particularly relevant to the auditor's consideration of the risks of material misstatement arising from fraud.

- Consider the knowledge, skills, and abilities of staff assigned significant engagement responsibilities, the need for specialists, and the appropriate level of supervision of assistants when developing responses to the risks of material misstatement at the overall financial statement level.

- Consider the extent to which it is necessary to perform audit procedures at selected locations or components of an entity with multiple locations or components, based on several factors including:

  — The amount and nature of assets and transactions executed at the individual location or component;

  — The degree of centralization of records or information processing;

  — The effectiveness of the control environment;

  — The frequency, timing, and scope of monitoring activities;

  — The judgments about materiality of the location or component; and

  — The risks associated with the location (e.g., political or economic instability).

- Design audit procedures to obtain reasonable assurance of detecting material misstatements to the financial statements as a whole, when determining the nature, timing, and extent of audit procedures to be applied to a specific account balance, class of transactions, or disclosure.

- Consider audit risk (including the risk of understatement as well as overstatement) at the account balance, class of transactions, or disclosure level. The consideration of such audit risk is a function of (1) the combination of inherent risk and control risk that the relevant assertions related to balances, transaction classes, or disclosures contain misstatements that could be material to the financial statements when aggregated with misstatements in other relevant assertions related to balances, classes, or disclosures and (2) the risk that the auditor will not detect such misstatements (i.e., *detection risk*).

- Seek to reduce audit risk at the individual account balance, transaction class, or disclosure level to enable the auditor to express an opinion on the financial statements as a whole at an appropriately low level of audit risk.

- Assess the risk of material misstatement at the relevant assertion level as a basis for further audit procedures and have an appropriate basis for that assessment.

- Perform substantive procedures for all relevant assertions related to material account balances, transaction classes, and disclosures.

- Determine a materiality level for the financial statements as a whole when establishing an overall strategy for the audit.

- Consider the following factors when determining materiality: (a) prior periods' financial results and financial positions, (b) the period-to-date financial results and financial position, and (c) budgets or forecasts for the current period.
- Consider materiality when planning the audit and evaluating misstatements regardless of the client's inherent business characteristics.
- Consider whether misstatements of particular items that are less than materiality level for the statements as a whole could reasonably be expected to influence users' decisions, in light of several specific factors, such as:
  - Whether accounting standards, laws, or regulations affect users' expectations regarding the measurement or disclosure of certain items;
  - The key disclosures in relation to the industry and the environment in which the entity operates; and
  - Whether attention is focused on the financial performance of a particular subsidiary or division that is separately disclosed in the consolidating financial statements.
- Allow for the possibility that certain misstatements lower than the materiality levels could, in the aggregate, result in a material misstatement of the financial statements.
- Determine one or more levels of tolerable misstatement that are normally lower than the materiality level.
- Be alert for misstatements that could be qualitatively material, even though it is not usually practical to design audit procedures to detect them.
- Reconsider the levels of tolerable misstatement and the appropriateness of the nature, timing, and extent of further audit procedures when the auditor concludes that a materiality level lower than that initially determined is appropriate.
- Consider whether, in the face of identified misstatements, the overall audit strategy and audit plan need to be revised.
- Not assume that a misstatement is an isolated occurrence.
- Consider whether the risk of undetected misstatements is greater than an acceptably low level, if the aggregate known and likely misstatements approach the materiality level.
- Reconsider the nature and extent of further audit procedures if there is a greater than acceptably low level of risk that undetected misstatements could exceed the materiality level.
- Communicate all known and likely misstatements to the appropriate level of management on a *timely* basis. (**Note:** *Communication* is an unconditional requirement. *Timeliness* of the communication is presumptively mandatory.)
- Distinguish between known and likely misstatements in communicating the details of misstatements.
- Request management to correct all known misstatements (other than those that are deemed trivial), including the effects of prior period misstatements.
- Request management to examine the account balance, transaction class, or disclosure to identify and correct misstatements therein when a likely material misstatement is identified in a sample.

- Request management to review the assumptions and methods used in developing accounting estimates, when likely misstatements are identified involving differences in estimates.

- Reevaluate the amount of likely misstatement after management has (*a*) examined a class of transactions, account balance, or disclosure and corrected misstatements therein and (*b*) challenged the assumptions and methods used in developing an estimate for which the auditor has identified a likely misstatement.

- Obtain an understanding of management's reasoning for not correcting some or all of the known or likely misstatements identified by the audit, and take that into account when considering qualitative aspects of the client's accounting practices and implications for the audit report.

- Consider the size and nature of uncorrected misstatements and the specific circumstances of their occurrence and determine their effects on the financial statements as a whole.

- Consider and aggregate *both* likely and known misstatements in a way that facilitates assessment of their effects on individual amounts, subtotals, or totals within the financial statements in relation to the financial statements as a whole.

- Consider each misstatement separately, before considering the aggregate effect of identified uncorrected misstatements, in order to evaluate:
  — The effect of each misstatement in relation to the relevant individual classes of transactions, account balances, or disclosures.
  — Whether it is appropriate to offset misstatements.
  — The effect of misstatements related to prior periods.

- Include the effects of prior period misstatements on the current period's financial statements, in aggregating misstatements.

- Consider the aggregate effects of uncorrected misstatements in determining whether the financial statements are free of material misstatement.

- Expand audit procedures and request management to investigate, when substantive analytical procedures indicate that a misstatement might exist, but the approximate amount is not known.

- Project the amount of known misstatements identified in the sample to the items in the balance or class from which the sample was selected.

- Treat the difference between estimated amounts in the financial statements and the closest reasonable estimate that is supported by audit evidence as a likely misstatement.

- Consider whether the difference between estimates that are best supported by audit evidence and individually reasonable estimates included in the financial statements indicate a possible management bias.

- Consider whether management's apparent use of accounting estimates to "smooth over" earnings or otherwise manipulate financial statements should be communicated to those charged with governance.

- Consider the implications of misstatements that are, or may be, the result of fraud in relation to other aspects of the audit, even if the effect of the misstatement is not material.

- Consider, when evaluating whether the financial statements as a whole are free of material misstatement, the evaluation of known and likely misstatements and certain qualitative factors.
- Consider, when concluding whether the misstatements are material individually or in the aggregate, the nature and amount of the misstatements in relation to the nature and amount of items in the financial statements.
- Request management to make the necessary corrections when the auditor believes that the financial statements as a whole are materially misstated.
- Consider the effects of undetected misstatements in concluding whether the financial statements are fairly stated.
- Perform additional audit procedures or satisfy himself or herself that management has adjusted the financial statements to reduce audit risk to an appropriately low level, if the auditor believes that audit risk is unacceptably high.
- Document the following:
    - Materiality levels for the financial statements as a whole when establishing the overall audit strategy and tolerable misstatement, including any changes thereto, and the basis on which those levels were determined;
    - A summary of uncorrected misstatements (other than those that are trivial) related to known and likely misstatements;
    - The auditor's conclusion as to whether uncorrected misstatements (individually or in aggregate) cause the financial statements to be materially misstated, and the basis for that conclusion;
    - All known and likely misstatements that the auditor identified during the audit (other than those that are trivial) and that have been corrected by management; and
    - Uncorrected misstatements in a manner that reflects consideration of (1) the separate effects of known and likely misstatements, including the effects of uncorrected misstatements identified in prior periods on the current period's financial statements; (2) the aggregate effect of misstatements on the financial statements; and (3) the qualitative factors deemed relevant for evaluating whether misstatements are material.

AU SECTION 314
UNDERSTANDING THE ENTITY AND ITS ENVIRONMENT AND ASSESSING THE RISKS OF MATERIAL MISSTATEMENT

PRACTICE POINT: As part of its Clarity Project, the American Institute of Certified Public Accountants' (AICPA's) Auditing Standards Board (ASB) has finalized a clarified Statement on Auditing Standards (SAS) titled, "Understanding the Entity and Its Environment and Assessing the Risks of Material Misstatement," which supersedes AU Section 314 of the same name. The clarified SAS does not change or expand existing requirements in extant AU Section 314 in any significant respect. The requirement included in paragraph .19 of extant AU Section 314 for the auditor to perform the audit with professional skepticism has been included in the clarified SAS, "Overall Objectives of the Independent Auditor and the Conduct of an Audit in Accordance with Generally Accepted Auditing Standards." The requirement included in paragraph .45 of extant AU Section 311 for the auditor to consider whether the entity has disclosed a particular matter appropriately has been included in the clarified SAS, "Forming an Opinion and Reporting on Financial Statements." The placement of these requirements does not create a difference between extant SASs as a whole and the clarified SASs as a whole.

The ASB is expected to issue many of the clarified standards in *one* SAS that will be codified in "AU Section" format. The ASB has decided that the effective date of the clarified SASs that have not yet been issued is for audits of financial statements for periods ending on or after December 15, 2012. Auditors should be alert to and monitor further developments in this area.

WHAT EVERY PRACTITIONER SHOULD KNOW

Basic Objectives and Requirements

This Section provides guidance on implementing the second standard of field work, which states:

> The auditor must obtain a sufficient understanding of the entity and its environment, including its internal control, to assess the risk of material misstatement of the financial statements whether due to error or fraud, and to design the nature, timing, and extent of further audit procedures.

Specifically, this Section requires the auditor to:

1. Perform risk assessment procedures to obtain an understanding of the entity and its environment, including its internal control. These procedures include:

    a. Inquiries of management.

    b. Inquiries of others within the entity (e.g., production, marketing, and sales personnel; employees with different levels of authority).

    c. Analytical procedures.

    d. Observation (e.g., observation of entity activities and operations).

e. Inspection (e.g., review documents, controls manuals, written business plans, and strategies).

2. Discuss the susceptibility of the entity's financial statements to material misstatements with members of the audit team.

3. Determine whether changes have occurred to information obtained in prior periods, such as internal control and risk assessments, that would affect its relevance to the current audit if the auditor plans to rely on that information.

4. Obtain an understanding of the audited entity's:

   a. Industry, regulatory, and other external factors.

   b. Nature of operations, including the entity's ownership, investments, and how it is structured and financed.

   c. Objectives, strategies, and related business risks that may result in a material misstatement of the financial statements.

   d. Measurement and review of its financial performance (e.g., key performance indicators, budgets, variance analysis, and departmental reports).

   e. Internal control, including (1) the control environment, (2) the risk assessment process, (3) information and communication systems, (4) control activities, and (5) monitoring controls.

5. Identify and assess the risks of material misstatement at the financial statement level and at the relevant assertion levels for classes of transactions, account balances, and disclosures.

6. Determine which of the identified risks require special audit attention, evaluate the entity's controls over those risks, and determine whether they have been implemented.

7. Identify the risks for which it is impossible or impracticable to reduce the risks of material misstatement at the relevant assertion level to an appropriately low level solely by substantive procedures, evaluate the design and implementation of controls over those risks, and determine whether they have been implemented.

8. Include specific audit documentation, such as discussions among the audit team, understandings of the entity and the risk assessment process, identified risks and evaluated related controls, and results of the auditor's risk assessments.

Risk Assessment Procedures and Sources of Information about the Client

This Section states that the procedures the auditor performs to obtain an understanding of the entity and its environment are referred to as *risk assessment procedures*, which encompass (1) inquiries of management and others within the entity, (2) analytical procedures, and (3) observation and inspection. Auditors are not required to perform each of these procedures for each of the five aspects of the understanding of the entity and its environment. However, all of these risk assessment procedures should be performed during the process of obtaining the required understanding of the entity and its environment. Therefore, the auditor cannot default to assessing control risk at the maximum without support; rather, the risk assessment procedures the auditor performs provide the audit evidence needed to support the risk assessment.

Inquiries of management and others within the entity Much of the information necessary for the audit can be obtained by inquiries of management and persons responsible for financial reporting. However, it is important to inquire not only of financial management personnel, but of others. Deciding to whom inquiries should be directed and the exact nature and extent of those inquiries is a matter of professional judgment in which the auditor should consider what information might be obtained that would assist in identifying risks of material misstatement.

PRACTICE POINT: Issue 1 below provides additional guidance about inquiries of others within the entity.

Analytical procedures Analytical procedures are particularly useful in considering the risk of material misstatement because they highlight unexpected or unusual relationships, transactions, balances, and events within the financial statements. The requirements for analytical procedures in general appear in AU Section 329 (Analytical Procedures). When using analytical procedures in connection with risk assessment, the auditor should:

- Develop expectations about relationships that might plausibly exist;
- Compare the results of the analytical procedures to those expectations; and
- Consider unusual or unexpected relationships in identifying risks of material misstatement.

It is important to note that analytical procedures performed at a high level of aggregation, such as those usually applied in the planning and final review stages of an audit, might give only broad indications of whether material misstatements exist. Analytical procedures at a more microscopic level, such as a gross profit test by location, product line, or shorter periods such as on a monthly basis, may have a greater chance of detecting a misstatement. Therefore, the auditor should consider the results of analytical procedures in connection with other information obtained in identifying the risks of material misstatement.

Observation and inspection Observation and inspection provides information about the entity and its environment and may also corroborate information gained through inquiries. Such procedures typically include:

- Observing the entity's activities and operations.
- Inspecting documents.
- Reading reports prepared by management, internal auditors, or persons charged with governance.
- Visiting the entity's facilities.
- Tracing transactions through the information system.

Other sources of information about the client An audit of an entity's financial statements is an integrated and coordinated process that includes relevant information from different sources that assist the auditor in identifying the risks of material misstatements. The auditor should consider the following sources of information that provide a relevant understanding about the client and assist in identifying the risk of material misstatement:

- The results of the assessment of the risk of material misstatement due to fraud, as addressed in AU Section 316 (Consideration of Fraud in a Financial Statement Audit).

- Information obtained from procedures performed in connection with the client acceptance or continuance process.

- Information and experience gained on other engagements performed for the entity.

In addition, when using information from prior periods such as internal control evaluations, the auditor should make inquiries and perform other audit procedures (e.g., walk-throughs of systems) to ascertain whether that information has changed.

Discussion among the Audit Team

This Section requires that the engagement team discuss the susceptibility of the financial statements to material misstatements. This discussion normally occurs during the planning process, covers critical issues, and should be recorded in the audit documentation. The discussion should include the auditor with final responsibility for the engagement, and the key members of the audit team.

PRACTICE POINT: Issue 2 below provides additional guidance about the objectives of the discussion among the audit team.

PRACTICE POINT: Issue 3 below provides additional guidance about the critical issues that should be covered in the discussion among the audit team.

Normally, it is efficient for this discussion to occur concurrently with the discussion about fraud risk required under AU Section 316. If the audit involves multiple locations, multiple discussions may take place. Even when the audit is performed by one person, consideration of the matters above should be documented.

Understanding the Entity and Its Environment

The auditor is required to obtain an understanding of the following five aspects of the entity and its environment on every audit: (1) industry, regulatory, and other external factors; (2) nature of the entity; (3) objectives, strategies, and related business risks; (4) measurement and review of financial performance; and (5) internal control.

PRACTICE POINT: Appendix A to AU Section 314 contains detailed discussion and examples of understanding the entity and its environment.

Industry, regulatory, and other external factors The auditor should gain an understanding of the pertinent industry, regulatory and other external factors, including:

- Competitive environment.
- Customer and supplier relationships.
- General economic conditions.
- Political and legal environment.
- Environmental matters.
- Regulatory environment.
- Technological developments.

An entity's industry may be subject to particular risks of material misstatement due to the nature of its business, government regulation, or other external factors. In this case, the auditor should consider whether the audit team has sufficient expertise to address these matters and whether it is necessary to use the work of specialists.

Nature of the entity The auditor should gain an understanding of the entity's nature in order to understand the classes of transactions, balances, and disclosures expected to appear in the financial statements. An entity's nature is comprised of many characteristics, which include the nature of its:

- Operations;
- Ownership, including the structure of the ownership and whether it has complex characteristics that may increase the risk of material misstatement;
- Investments, including subsidiaries, joint ventures, investments accounted for by the equity method, other current or future planned investments, and special purpose entities;
- Governance;
- Financing;
- Management;
- Key personnel; and
- Related-party transactions.

Objectives, strategies, and related business risks Businesses operate in the context of industry, regulatory, and other internal and external factors, which create business risks. Within this context, an entity defines overall plans for its business, which are commonly referred to as objectives. Strategies are management's operational approaches toward achieving those objectives.

The concept of business risk is broader than, but includes, the risk of material misstatement to the financial statements. When significant business risks exist, an entity's ability to carry out its strategies and accomplish its objectives may be critically impaired. Although auditors do not have to identify or assess every business risk, a solid understanding of business risk greatly increases the likelihood of identifying risks of material misstatement. Business risk can arise from:

- Setting inappropriate objectives or strategies;
- Conditions or events that adversely affect an entity's ability to reach its objectives or to execute its strategies;
- Change or the failure to recognize a need to change, such as from the development of new products that fail or inadequate markets or design flaws in the product that result in liability or damage to a business reputation; and
- Complexity, such as in long-term construction projects that carry risks in estimating the percentage of completion, pricing, costing, design, and project management.

The guidance in this Section illustrates the relationship of business risk to the risk of material misstatement with the example of a competitor that has brand recognition and economies of scale entering a new marketplace. This causes a *business risk* to existing manufacturers' ability to command retail shelf space and to compete on price. The *risks of material misstatement* to the existing manufacturers' statements, in this case, include inventory obsolescence or excess production of inventory that would have to be sold at a discount.

Most business risks have financial consequences, but not all risks give rise to the risk of material misstatement. The auditor's consideration of whether a business risk leads to the risk of material misstatement is made within the context of the entity's circumstances.

Measurement and review of financial performance Performance measures and their review signal to the auditor the aspects of the entity's performance that are the most important to management and others. They create pressures that may give management incentives either to improve performance or to misstate the financial statements. For these reasons, auditors should understand how an entity measures and reviews its financial performance.

Management's review of performance measures is intended to assess whether the entity's performance meets the objectives set by management or by outside parties such as lenders or financial analysts. This process is different from monitoring internal controls, which is solely concerned with the effective operations of those controls.

In setting performance measures, management may use both internally generated and external information. Internal measures may signal to management, by unusual or unexpected results or trends, a need to take corrective action. They may also indicate to the auditor the possibility of material misstatement. Examples of internally generated performance measures include:

- Financial key performance indicators.
- Nonfinancial key performance indicators.

- Budgets and forecasts.
- Variance analyses.
- Subsidiary, divisional, or departmental information.
- Comparisons of performance with competitors.

An unusually rapid growth or high profitability combined with performance-based management bonuses may, for example, indicate a risk of management bias in financial statement preparation.

External performance measures may provide useful perspectives for the auditor's understanding of the entity and its environment. These may include information such as analysts' or credit rating agencies' reports.

When using internally generated information for the audit, such as performing analytical procedures, the auditor should be careful to consider whether that information provides a reliable basis and is sufficiently precise and relevant to detect material misstatements.

Internal control This Section discusses internal control within the context of the well-known *Internal Control—Integrated Framework*, published by the Committee of the Sponsoring Organizations of the Treadway Commission (COSO). It stresses that the auditor's primary consideration is whether and how a particular control prevents or detects and corrects material misstatements at the relevant assertion level. Therefore, auditors may use frameworks or terminology other than the COSO model, as long as all of the internal control components described in this Section are addressed.

The following discussion provides further guidance on the required understanding of internal control.

Understanding of Internal Control

The auditor should develop an understanding of how the entity selects and applies its accounting policies and should consider their appropriateness. This understanding should include (1) methods of accounting for significant and unusual transactions; (2) the effects of significant accounting policies in emerging or controversial areas for which consensus or authoritative guidance is lacking; (3) identification of new financial reporting standards and regulations pertinent to the entity, including how the entity will implement them; and (4) changes in the entity's accounting policies, including consideration of the reasons for and the appropriateness of the changes.

The auditor should also consider the financial statement disclosures and whether they are appropriate in form, arrangement, and content. This includes the terminology used, level of detail presented, classification of items presented, and bases of the amounts.

Internal control components This Section states that the auditor should gain an understanding of the five elements of internal control described below. This understanding should be sufficient to assess the risk of material misstatement in the financial statements caused by fraud or error and to design the nature, timing, and extent of further audit procedures. The auditor should also perform risk assessment procedures to evaluate the design and implementation of controls relevant to the audit. The knowledge gained in this process should be used to (1) identify types of possible misstatements, (2) consider factors affecting the risk of material misstatement, and (3) design tests of controls and substantive procedures.

The five components of internal control are:

1. *Control environment*—The control environment is the foundation for all the other components because it sets the tone of the entity and influences the control consciousness of its personnel.

2. *Entity's risk assessment process*—The entity's risk assessment process is its identification and analysis of risks that pertain to the achievement of its objectives. This assessment forms the basis for management of the identified risks.

3. *Information and communication systems*—These systems support the identification, capture, and exchange of information in such form and within such time periods as will enable personnel to carry out their duties.

4. *Control activities*—Control activities are policies and procedures designed to assure that management's directives are executed.

5. *Monitoring of controls*—Monitoring is the process that evaluates the quality of internal control performance over time.

PRACTICE POINT: Issues 4 through 8 below provide further guidance on each of the five components of internal control.

PRACTICE POINT: AU Section 314 (paragraphs 67 through 101) and Appendix B to AU Section 314 include a detailed discussion of each of the five components of internal control.

Relevant controls Internal control applies to the entire entity, including all of its business functions and operating units. Controls that are relevant to the audit, however, pertain to preparing the financial statements. An understanding of internal control pertaining to each unit and function, or an assessment of all controls, may not be necessary when assessing the risk of material misstatement and designing and performing audit procedures.

The auditor should focus on significant risks and evaluate the design and implementation of the controls relevant to those risks. In addition, the auditor should consider the following particular control components and factors:

- The entity's size.
- Materiality.
- The nature of the entity's business.
- The entity's organization and ownership characteristics.
- The complexity and diversity of operations.

- The legal and regulatory requirements.
- The nature and complexity of the systems that make up the internal control system.
- The use of service organizations.

An entity usually has operational controls that do not directly relate to the audit, such as a production scheduling system. Ordinarily, these controls need not be considered in the audit. However, controls over operations and compliance objectives may be pertinent to the audit if they relate to information that may be evaluated or used in the audit procedures. The controls over nonfinancial data, such as production statistics, are relevant to the audit if that data is to be used in performing analytical procedures. Similarly, controls designed to detect noncompliance with income tax laws and regulations would likely have a direct and material bearing on the financial statements and, therefore, would be relevant to the audit.

Depth of understanding of internal control The auditor's understanding of internal control consists of two elements: (1) evaluating the design of the control and (2) determining if it has been implemented. In evaluating a control's design, the auditor considers whether it is capable of preventing or detecting and correcting material misstatements. Auditors should consider control design before considering the related control's implementation. This is an efficient audit approach because an ineffectively designed control will not work even if it is implemented and, therefore, need not be tested for implementation. However, an improperly designed control may represent a significant deficiency or material weakness in internal control. The auditor should consider communicating such deficiencies in internal control to management and those charged with governance.

The auditor is reminded to perform risk assessment procedures to gain an understanding of internal control. Such procedures may include:

- Inquiries of entity personnel.
- Observation of the application of specific controls.
- Inspection of reports and documents.
- Tracing transactions through the financial reporting system.

Inquiry alone, however, is not sufficient to evaluate the design of a control or to determine if it has been implemented. Neither is obtaining an understanding of controls sufficient, in itself, as a test of their operating effectiveness, unless they are automated controls operating within an environment of effective information technology (IT) general controls.

Automated internal control elements The extent to which an entity uses IT-based systems affects the five components of internal control relevant to its financial reporting, operational, or compliance objectives and its operating units and business functions. IT may be used as stand-alone systems that support specific activities, functions, or business units, such as an accounts receivable system or a system that controls the operation of production equipment. These systems may not be integrated with other IT systems. Conversely, an entity may have complex and highly integrated IT systems that share data and support the entire range of its financial reporting, operational, and compliance objectives.

Systems that employ IT may use automated procedures to initiate, authorize, record, process, and report transactions. Electronic records typically replace paper documents in these systems. Controls in such systems are both automated and manual. For example, there may be controls embedded in a computer program that report transactions over a specified size, but the follow-up on those transactions may be a manual process.

While IT provides potential benefits of effectiveness and efficiency for an entity's internal control, IT systems also pose specific risks to an entity's internal control. The following are some of the key benefits and risks associated with IT systems:

Benefits of IT Systems	Risks of IT Systems
• Consistent processing of large volumes of data or transactions using predefined rules and complex calculations. • Enhanced delivery of timely, accurate, and accessible information. • Ease of additional analyses of information. • Enhanced ability to monitor entity performance. • Reduced risk that controls will be circumvented. • Strengthened segregation of duties through implementation of security controls in applications, databases, and operating systems.	• Reliance on systems or programs that inaccurately process data. • Reliance on systems or programs that process inaccurate data. • Unauthorized access to data, resulting in (a) destruction of data, (b) recording of unauthorized or fictitious transactions, and (c) inaccurate recording of transactions. • Unauthorized changes to master files, programs, or systems. • Failure to make required changes to programs or systems. • Improper manual intervention. • Potential loss of data. • Potential inability to access data as needed.

Manual internal control elements The extent to which an entity uses manual systems affects the five components of internal control relevant to its financial reporting, operational, or compliance objectives and its operating units and business functions. Manual systems employ manual procedures and generate paper records. Controls in these systems are also manual and may consist of processes such as approvals, reviews, and reconciliations. Manual controls may be best suited to areas that require high degrees of judgment in situations, circumstances, or events that involve:

- Large transactions;
- Unusual or nonrecurring transactions;
- Misstatements that are difficult to define, predict, or anticipate;
- Activation of controls that are outside the scope or capability of existing automated controls; and
- Monitoring the effectiveness of automated controls.

Manual controls, on the other hand, are more susceptible to error than automated controls and can be more easily evaded or circumvented. Because of the human element involved, manual controls cannot be assumed to be operating consistently. They may be less suitable than automated controls in the following situations:

- High volume or recurring transactions.

- Transactions in which anticipated errors are likely to be detected or prevented by automated controls.

- Control activities where specific ways to carry out an activity can be adequately designed and automated.

Limitations of internal control There are inherent limitations in all systems of internal control. Lapses in internal control may be due to misunderstandings, poor judgment, carelessness, or fatigue. In addition, a properly designed and implemented system can be circumvented through collusion or by inappropriate management override of controls.

Management must recognize its responsibility to maintain and monitor an entity's internal control and to recognize the need for changes in the system in response to changing conditions. In addition, the design of the internal control must include a consideration of the costs and benefits of developing such a system. Therefore, the entity cannot possibly design or maintain a perfect internal control system. Internal control, no matter how well designed and operated, can provide only reasonable but not absolute assurance of achieving an entity's control objectives.

Assessing the Risks of Material Misstatement

The auditor should identify and assess risks of material misstatement on two levels: (1) the financial statement level and (2) the relevant assertion level for classes of transactions, account balances, and disclosures. As a part of this process, this Section requires the auditor to:

- Identify risks throughout the process of gaining an understanding of the entity, its environment, and its internal control.

- Relate those specific identified risks to potential misstatements at the relevant assertion level.

- Consider whether the *magnitude* of those identified risks could result in material misstatement of the financial statements.

- Consider whether it is *likely* that the identified risks could result in material misstatement of the financial statements.

- Use the audit evidence obtained in performing risk assessment procedures (e.g., inquiries, observation, inspection, and analytical procedures) to support the risk assessment.

- Use the risk assessment in determining the nature, timing, and extent of additional audit procedures.

- Perform appropriate tests of controls when the risk assessment is based on the auditor's expectation that controls are operating effectively at the relevant assertion level.

- Determine whether identified risks are isolated to particular relevant assertions associated with certain classes of transactions, account balances, or disclosures or are more pervasive and likely to affect the financial statements as a whole.

- Identify controls that are likely to prevent or detect and correct material misstatements in certain relevant assertions.

- Communicate significant deficiencies in internal control to those charged with governance.

- Consider whether the audit report should be modified (i.e., a qualified opinion or disclaimer of opinion) or whether the auditor should withdraw from the engagement, when serious engagement conditions exist, such as concerns about the (a) auditability of the financial statements, (b) integrity of management, and (c) condition and reliability of the entity's records.

PRACTICE POINT: Appendix C to AU Section 314 contains examples of conditions and events that may be indicative of risks of material misstatement. See Issue 21 below.

Special audit consideration for significant risks As part of the auditor's risk assessment, the auditor is required to identify significant risks, which are defined as those risks that require special audit consideration. Determining risks that are significant and thus require special audit consideration is subject to a high degree of professional judgment. In making this determination, the auditor should consider the following factors:

- Inherent risk (i.e., the susceptibility of a relevant financial statement assertion to a material misstatement assuming there are no related controls).

- Likelihood of multiple misstatements.

- Nature of the related business risks.

- Risk of fraud.

- Whether the risk is related to significant recent developments in the economy or in accounting.

- Complexity of the transactions.

- Related-party transactions.

- Degree of subjectivity involved.

- Whether the risk involves significant nonroutine or unusual transactions.

Nonroutine transactions and judgmental matters involving accounting estimates are normally regarded as areas in which significant risks are likely to be identified. The nature of nonroutine transactions makes it difficult for management to design and implement control over them. In addition, nonroutine transactions often exhibit one or more of the following characteristics which cause them to have higher risk:

- Complex accounting principles or calculations.

- Greater management intervention to control the accounting treatment.

- Greater manual intervention in data collection and processing.
- Related-party transactions.

Judgmental matters may arise in accounting principles that are subject to differing interpretations or may involve significant estimates or uncertainties, such as assumptions about future events.

The auditor should evaluate the design and implementation of the entity's internal controls related to significant risks. Where controls are absent or ineffective and such limitations represent significant deficiencies or material weaknesses, the auditor should communicate the matters to those charged with governance and consider their effects on the risk assessment.

Significant risks are likely to arise in most audits. When the auditor has determined that an assessed risk of material misstatement at the relevant assertion level is a significant risk, the audit procedures should include, but not be limited to, the following procedures prescribed in AU Section 318 (Performing Audit Procedures in Response to Assessed Risks and Evaluating the Audit Evidence Obtained):

- Perform substantive procedures that are specifically designed to address and be responsive to the identified significant risk.
- If the auditor plans to rely on the operating effectiveness of controls intended to mitigate the significant risk, perform tests of controls in the current period to obtain audit evidence about the operating effectiveness of such controls. (**Note:** The auditor cannot and should not rely on audit evidence about the operating effectiveness of controls over such risks obtained in a prior audit.)

Situations in which substantive procedures alone are not effective In some cases, auditors may find it impossible to design substantive procedures that are effective in providing sufficient appropriate audit evidence to support relevant financial statement assertions. This often occurs when routine daily business transactions permit highly automated processing and entities use IT to initiate, process, and record transactions with little or no manual intervention. Telecommunications companies or Internet service providers, for example, provide service to customers through electronic media and use IT to log the services provided, initiate and process billings, and automatically record the transactions in the accounting records.

In these cases, audit evidence may exist only in electronic form, and its appropriateness and sufficiency are highly dependent on the effectiveness of the related controls. The auditor should identify those risks for which it is not possible or practicable to reduce detection risk at the relevant assertion level to an acceptably low level by means of substantive procedures alone; in such circumstances, the auditor should then evaluate the design and implementation of controls, including relevant control activities over those identified risks.

When transaction initiation and processing is highly automated (such as for revenues, purchases, cash receipts, or disbursements), risks ordinarily relate to those specific classes of transactions. Those risks include incomplete or inaccurate processing, and improper initiation or alteration of information.

Therefore, testing of controls becomes important in these situations because stronger controls provide an environment in which risks of misstatement are reduced. Consequently, a combination of audit evidence obtained through both tests of controls and substantive tests can reduce detection risk at the relevant assertion level to an acceptably low level.

Revision of risk assessment Risk assessment is a dynamic process that occurs throughout the audit. As a result of applying audit procedures, the auditor may discover, for example, that internal controls are not operating as expected or that misstatements have occurred in amounts or frequencies that are greater than is consistent with the initial risk assessment. When this occurs, the auditor should (1) revise the risk assessment and (2) modify the planned audit procedures appropriately to respond to the revised risk assessment.

Specific Audit Documentation Requirements

AU Section 339 (Audit Documentation) provides authoritative guidance on the form and content of audit documentation. There is considerable professional judgment involved in deciding the exact manner in which these elements are to be documented. For example, properly used narrative memoranda, question-naires, checklists, and flowcharts can be effective documentation techniques. As a general rule, audit documentation becomes more extensive as the complexity of the entity, its environment, its internal control, and the extent of the audit procedures applied increases. Specific audit methodologies and technologies used also affect the form and extent of the audit documentation.

In addition, this Section requires the auditor to specifically document the following four elements related to an understanding of the entity and its environment, and the assessment of the risk of material misstatement:

1. The audit team's discussion about the susceptibility of the financial statements to material misstatement, whether caused by fraud or error. This documentation should include:

   a. How the discussion occurred.

   b. When it occurred.

   c. Names of the participants.

   d. Subjects discussed.

   e. Significant decisions regarding planned audit responses at the financial statement and relevant assertion levels.

2. Significant elements of the auditor's understanding of the entity and its environment obtained to assess the risk of material misstatement of the financial statements, the sources from which the understanding was obtained, and the risk assessment procedures performed to obtain such understanding. This documentation should encompass the auditor's understanding of each of the following aspects of the entity, its environment, and its internal control:

   a. Industry, regulatory, and other external factors.

   b. Nature of the entity.

    c. Objectives, strategies, and related business risks that may result in a material misstatement of the financial statements.

    d. Measurement and review of the entity's financial performance.

    e. Entity's internal control, including the selection and application of accounting policies.

    f. Five components of the entity's internal control: (1) control environment, (2) risk assessment, (3) information and communication systems, (4) control activities, and (5) monitoring.

3. The assessment of the risks of material misstatement at both the financial statement and the relevant assertion levels, including the basis for such assessment.

4. The risks identified and related controls evaluated, including:

    a. Risks that require special audit consideration.

    b. Risks for which it is not possible or practicable to reduce detection risk at the relevant assertion level to an acceptably low level by substantive procedures alone.

PRACTICE ISSUES AND FREQUENTLY ASKED QUESTIONS

Risk Assessment Procedures and Sources of Information about the Client

Issue 1: Besides making inquiries of management, to whom within the entity might the auditor direct his or her inquiries when performing risk assessment procedures?

Deciding to whom, besides management, inquiries should be directed and the exact nature and extent of those inquiries is a matter of the auditor's professional judgment. However, other persons within the entity to whom inquiries might be directed generally include:

- *Persons charged with governance (such as the audit committee or board of directors)*—To gain an understanding of the environment in which the financial statements are prepared.

- *Internal auditors*—To obtain information about their activities concerning the design and effectiveness of internal control and about management's responses to internal audit findings.

- *Operating personnel who are not directly involved in financial reporting (such as marketing, sales, or production personnel)*—To obtain information about changes in the entity's strategies and trends or in its contractual relationships.

- *Employees involved in initiating, authorizing, recording, or processing unusual or complex transactions*—To assist the auditor in evaluating the appropriateness of the accounting policies used.

- *In-house legal counsel*—To acquire information about matters such as contracts, compliance with laws and regulations, fraud, litigation, warranties, and post-sale obligations.

Discussion among the Audit Team

Issue 2: What is the objective of the engagement team's discussion of the susceptibility of the financial statements to material misstatements?

The discussion among the audit team of the susceptibility of the financial statements to material misstatements is intended to accomplish the following:

- Provide the audit team with a better understanding of the potential for material misstatement due to fraud or error.
- Assist audit team members in understanding how the results of the audit procedures they perform may impact other audit areas.
- Offer more experienced team members an opportunity to share their knowledge about the entity.
- Enable team members to exchange information about the entity's business risk and the susceptibility of the financial statements to material misstatement.

Issue 3: What are some of the critical issues that should be covered in the engagement team's discussion of the susceptibility of the financial statements to material misstatements?

The discussion among the audit team of the susceptibility of the financial statements to material misstatements should cover critical issues, such as:

- Areas of significant audit risk.
- Areas susceptible to management override of controls.
- Unusual accounting procedures used.
- Significant control systems.
- Materiality at the financial statement and account levels.
- The effect of materiality on the scope of testing.
- The entity's application of generally accepted accounting principles.
- Risk of material misstatement due to fraud.
- Fraud risk factors.
- Audit responses to assessed fraud risks.
- The need to perform the audit with an attitude of professional skepticism, to be alert for and follow up on indications of material misstatements, and to exercise professional judgment.

Understanding the Entity and Its Environment

Issue 4: How might the auditor apply the guidance in AU Section 314 to obtain an understanding of the control environment component of internal control?

The auditor should obtain sufficient knowledge of the control environment to understand management's and the board of directors' attitude, awareness, and actions concerning the control environment. Because an entity may establish controls but not act upon them, the auditor should concentrate on the substance of controls rather than their form. For example, management may establish a formal code of conduct but act in a manner that condones violations of that code.

Control environment factors include the following:

- Communication and enforcement of integrity and ethical values.
- Commitment to competence.
- Participation of those charged with governance.
- Management's philosophy and operating style.
- Organizational structure.
- Assignment of authority and responsibility.
- Human resource policies and practices.

PRACTICE POINT: Illustration 1 includes a questionnaire that the auditor can use to obtain an understanding of the control environment.

Issue 5: How might the auditor apply the guidance in AU Section 314 to obtain an understanding of the risk assessment component of internal control?

The auditor should obtain sufficient knowledge of the entity's risk assessment process to understand how management considers risks relevant to financial reporting objectives and decides about actions to address those risks. Such knowledge might include understanding how management identifies risks, estimates their significance, assesses the likelihood of their occurrence, and relates them to financial reporting.

Risks can occur due to the following factors:

- Changes in operating environment.
- New personnel.
- New or revamped information systems.
- Rapid growth.
- New technology.
- New business models, products, or activities.
- Corporate restructurings.
- Expanded foreign operations.
- New accounting pronouncements.

PRACTICE POINT: Illustration 2 includes a questionnaire that the auditor can use to obtain an understanding of the risk assessment.

Issue 6: How might the auditor apply the guidance in AU Section 314 to obtain an understanding of the control activities component of internal control?

Generally, control activities that may be relevant to an audit include those relating to authorization, segregation of duties, safeguarding of assets, and asset accountability. The auditor should obtain an understanding of the policies and procedures that help ensure that management directives are carried out, including how information technology affects control activities that are relevant to the audit. In addition, the auditor should obtain an understanding of the process of reconciling detail to the general ledger for significant accounts.

Examples of specific control activities include the following:

- Authorization.
- Segregation of duties.
- Safeguarding.
- Asset accountability.

PRACTICE POINT: Illustration 3 includes a questionnaire that the auditor can use to obtain an understanding of the control activities.

Issue 7: How might the auditor apply the guidance in AU Section 314 to obtain an understanding of the information and communication components of internal control?

The auditor should obtain sufficient knowledge of the accounting information system to understand:

1. The major classes of transactions of the entity's operations (e.g., major sources of revenue and major types of expenditures).

2. The procedures (both automated and manual) by which transactions are initiated, authorized, recorded, processed, and reported from their occurrence to their inclusion in the financial statements.

3. The accounting records (both electronic and manual), supporting information, and specific accounts in the financial statements involved in initiating, authorizing, recording, processing, and reporting transactions (e.g., journals, ledgers, invoices, and checks).

4. How the information system captures other events and conditions that are significant to the financial statements.

5. The financial reporting process followed by the entity to prepare the financial statements, including accounting estimates and disclosures.

In obtaining an understanding of the financial reporting process, the auditor should understand the automated and manual procedures an entity uses to prepare financial statements and related disclosures and how misstatements may occur. Such procedures include those used to (1) enter transaction totals into the general ledger; (2) initiate, authorize, record, and process journal entries in the general ledger; (3) initiate and record recurring and nonrecurring adjustments to the financial statements that are not reflected in formal journal entries (e.g., consolidating adjustments, report combinations, and reclassifications); (4) combine and consolidate general ledger data; and (5) prepare financial statements and related disclosures. In addition, the auditor should obtain sufficient knowledge of the means the entity uses to communicate financial reporting roles and responsibilities and significant matters relating to financial reporting.

PRACTICE POINT: Illustration 4 includes a questionnaire that the auditor can use to obtain an understanding of the information and communication components of internal control.

Issue 8: How might the auditor apply the guidance in AU Section 314 to obtain an understanding of the monitoring component of internal control?

Monitoring is a process that assesses the quality of internal control performance over time. It involves assessing the design and operation of controls on a timely basis and taking necessary corrective actions. The following are examples of ongoing monitoring activities:

- *Communications from external parties*—Communications from external parties corroborate internally generated information or indicate problems. For example, customers implicitly corroborate billing data by paying their invoices, or customer complaints about billings could indicate system deficiencies in the processing of sales transactions. Similarly, bankers, regulators, or other outside parties may communicate with the company on matters of accounting significance.

- *Performance of critical control functions by employees*—Employees may be required to "sign off" as evidence of the performance of critical control functions. The sign-off allows management to monitor the performance of these functions.

- *Recommendations by external auditors*—External auditors regularly provide recommendations on the way internal control can be strengthened. Auditors may identify potential weaknesses and make recommendations to management for corrective action.

The auditor should obtain sufficient knowledge of the major types of activities the entity uses to monitor internal control over financial reporting, including how those activities are used to initiate corrective actions.

PRACTICE POINT: Illustration 5 includes a questionnaire that the auditor can use to obtain an understanding of monitoring.

Issue 9: Is the auditor required to consider and understand all controls that exist within an entity?

No. Generally, controls that are relevant to an audit pertain to the entity's objective of preparing its financial statements that are fairly presented in conformity with GAAP or other comprehensive basis of accounting. Entities typically have additional controls that are not necessarily relevant to an audit and, therefore, need not be considered. Examples include controls relating to the effectiveness, economy, and efficiency of certain management decision-making processes, such as whether to make expenditures for certain research and development or advertising activities.

In addition, although internal control is relevant to the entire entity or to any of its operating units or business functions, an understanding of internal control relevant to each of the entity's operating units and business functions may not be necessary.

Generally speaking, a financial audit would concentrate primarily on the controls over financial reporting because these are the controls that are the most likely to be meaningful to the audit. However, it may be helpful to assess controls in other areas that are relevant to the audit work, such as the development of production statistics to be used in analytical procedures. Controls over compliance with laws and regulations such as employment practices and occupational health and safety although important to the company, ordinarily do not have a direct impact on the financial statements and therefore need not be assessed.

Issue 10: What are the primary reasons for the auditor's required understanding of any internal control system?

The auditor's understanding of any internal control system must, at a minimum, accomplish the following:

- Determine whether the entity is auditable. The auditor must obtain information about the integrity of management and the nature and extent of the entity's accounting records to be satisfied that sufficient competent evidence is available to support the financial statements.

- Identify the types of potential misstatements whether caused by error or fraud that could occur in the financial statements.

- Consider factors that affect the risk that material misstatements will occur.

- Design tests of controls, when applicable.

- Design substantive tests. The information obtained should allow the auditor to design effective tests of financial statement balances, including tests of details of transactions and balances, and analytical procedures.

Issue 11: What factors should the auditor consider when evaluating the effectiveness of the board of directors or audit committee?

An entity's control consciousness is influenced significantly by the entity's board of directors and audit committee. Factors that the auditor should consider that can affect the effectiveness of the board of directors or audit committee include:

- Its independence from management.

- Experience and stature of its members.

- Extent of its involvement and scrutiny of activities.

- Appropriateness of its actions.

- Degree to which difficult questions are raised and pursued with management.

- Its interaction with internal and external auditors.

Issue 12: What are some signals that typically should increase the auditor's concern about the effectiveness of an entity's control environment?

The following are some signals that generally should increase the auditor's concern about the effectiveness of an entity's control environment:

- High turnover in management positions, particularly financial management.

- Managerial talent and qualifications not commensurate with the growth of the business.

- Increased dependence on computer processing for decision-making purposes, but without adequate knowledge of computer operations.

- Diversified activities, each with its own accounting system.

- Decentralized operations and record keeping, with a centralized management.

- Inadequate internal audit function.

Issue 13: Should the auditor's understanding of an entity's financial reporting information system include the accounting system maintained by the service organization?

Yes. Many entities use service organizations (e.g., banks, brokerage firms, or electronic data processing service centers) to perform some or all of their data processing. Entities that process certain transactions in-house have complete control and responsibility for that function. On the other hand, entities that use service organizations generally lose a certain degree of control over the portion of their financial reporting information system maintained by the service organization; they generally have limited ability and authority to define or enforce control activities to be adopted or followed by the service organization.

Therefore, the auditor's understanding of an entity's financial reporting information system should include the accounting system maintained by the service organization. See AU Section 324 (Service Organizations) for further discussion and guidance on the use of service organizations and their effect on the audit.

Issue 14: What are some of the procedures that the auditor can use to obtain an understanding of internal control?

The auditor often obtains an understanding of internal control through previous experience with the entity and through the performance of risk assessment procedures, such as:

- *Inquiries of management, supervisory, and staff personnel within the entity*— For example, the auditor may inquire about the types of accounting documents used to process sales transactions and about the entity's control activities that have been implemented for authorizing a credit sale.

- *Observation of client activities and the application of specific controls*—The auditor can observe client personnel in the process of preparing accounting records and documents and carrying out their assigned accounting and control functions.

- *Inspection of documents, reports, or electronic files*—By inspecting actual completed documents, reports, or electronic files, the auditor can better understand their application to the entity's internal control.

- *Reviewing an entity's policy and systems manuals*—This includes both (1) policy manuals and documents, such as a corporate code of conduct and (2) systems manuals and documents, such as an accounting manual and an organization chart.

Observation of activities and inspection of accounting documents and records can provide knowledge about the design of controls and whether they have been implemented. They can be conveniently and effectively combined in the form of a transaction walk-through. With that procedure, the auditor selects the appropriate documents for the initiation of a transaction type and traces them through the entire accounting process. Furthermore, at each stage of the processing steps, the auditor makes inquiries, observes personnel activities, and inspects completed documentation for the transactions selected.

Issue 15: Is a specific form of documentation required in the working papers for the auditor's understanding of an entity's internal control?

No. Although the auditor is required to document his or her understanding of an entity's internal control, the form and extent of the documentation is flexible and is influenced by various factors such as the following: (1) the risks of material misstatement at both the financial statement and the relevant assertion levels; (2) the nature and complexity of the entity's internal control; and (3) the nature of the entity's documentation of internal control. The documentation could take the form of memoranda, flowcharts, questionnaires, decision tables, or a combination of these. For most small business audits, memoranda of the understanding may be sufficient. The documentation should be more extensive for larger and more complex entities.

Illustrations 1 through 5 contain practice aids that the auditor can use in documenting an understanding of the five components of the entity's internal control.

Issue 16: What factors might auditor consider in determining whether a professional with IT skills is needed on the audit team?

In determining whether a professional with IT skills is needed on the audit team, the auditor might consider factors, such as:

- The complexity of the entity's systems and IT controls and the manner in which they are used in conducting the entity's business.

- The significance of changes made to existing systems or the implementation of new systems.

- The extent to which data is shared among systems.

- The extent of the entity's participation in electronic commerce.

- The entity's use of emerging technologies.

- The significance of audit evidence that is available only in electronic form.

Issue 17: What compensating controls should the auditor consider when there is a lack of segregation of duties in a small business?

Smaller entities may find that certain types of control activities are not relevant because of highly effective controls applied by management. Management of a small business is often dominated by an individual who has an ownership interest in the business. Therefore, a major compensating control available in a small entity is the knowledge and concern of the top operating person, who is frequently an owner-manager. The close involvement of the owner-manager usually compensates for inadequate separation of duties. Therefore, even companies with only a few employees may be able to assign their responsibilities to achieve appropriate controls. For example, internal control of a small business can be significantly strengthened if the owner-manager performs duties, such as:

- Reviewing supporting documents for disbursements before signing the checks.

- Reviewing bank reconciliations prepared by the accounting clerk and following up on major unusual reconciling differences.

- Reviewing customer accounts receivable statements before they are mailed.

- Approving credit to customers.

- Approving write-offs of accounts receivable balances considered uncollectible.

- Approving draw-downs on lines of credit.

Issue 18: What are some opportunities to implement cost-saving measures in understanding and documenting an entity's internal control and in assessing the risks of material misstatement?

There are opportunities to implement cost-saving measures in understanding and documenting an entity's internal control and in gathering evidence to assess the risks of material misstatement. The following are some cost-saving measures that auditors can use to improve audit efficiency and effectiveness:

- When documenting the accounting system, use client documentation and obtain client assistance in preparing or updating documentation.

- If the use of flowcharts is considered effective, supplement flowcharts with narrative descriptions to help explain transaction flows. Also, eliminate unnecessary detail from the flowcharts. For example, there is no need to document the flow of copies of a document not related to the achievement of specific control objectives (e.g., documents used for production statistics).

- Eliminate documentation of insignificant accounting systems.

- The partner in charge of the engagement should take the time during the planning phase of the engagement to share with the engagement staff everything he or she knows about the client that could be relevant to the audit.

- During the planning phase of the engagement, segregate the various transaction classes and account balances into the following three categories:
  - Those that are so insignificant that misstatement could not have a material effect on the financial statements. These typically include various small prepaid items, accruals, and small income and expense accounts. Generally, no audit effort needs to be expended on this group.
  - Those that could have a material effect on the financial statements, but are made of a few large dollar items and are, therefore, going to have 100% tests of details. These generally include notes payable and property and equipment.
  - Those that are material in total, but because they are made up of a large number of small amounts or transactions, they cannot reasonably be tested 100%. These generally include inventory, accounts receivable, cash receipts, and cash disbursements.
- Analytical procedures are a very effective and efficient type of substantive test. For example, relating depreciation expense to asset balance, after giving effect to additions and disposals, and average depreciation rate or relating payroll expense to the average number of employees and the average pay per period are effective and efficient substantive tests.

Issue 19: Is there such a thing as a "perfect" internal control system?

No. There are inherent limitations in all systems of internal control. Lapses in internal control may be due to misunderstandings, poor judgment, carelessness, or fatigue. In addition, controls can be overridden through collusion and through management intervention. In addition, the design of the internal control must include a consideration of the costs and benefits in developing such a system. Therefore, an entity cannot possibly design or maintain a perfect internal control; internal control, no matter how well designed and operated, can provide only reasonable assurance of achieving an entity's control objectives.

Issue 20: Is the auditor required to obtain an understanding of internal control where the auditor does not expect the entity to have effective internal control and if he or she intends to design a substantive audit approach and not rely on controls?

Yes. Paragraph 40 of AU Section 314 states, in part:

> The auditor should obtain an understanding of the five components of internal control sufficient to assess the risk of material misstatement of the financial statements, whether due to error or fraud, and to design the nature, timing, and extent of further audit procedures. The auditor should obtain a sufficient understanding by performing risk assessment procedures to evaluate the design of controls relevant to an audit of financial statements and to determine whether they have been implemented.

When the auditor believes, based on the understanding of controls, that controls are not capable of preventing or detecting and correcting material misstatements, the auditor would (1) assess control risk as maximum and (2) plan and perform substantive procedures to appropriately respond to the identified risks. If, in such circumstances, the auditor identifies missing or ineffective controls, the auditor must evaluate the identified control deficiencies and determine whether they are, individually or in combination, significant deficiencies or material weaknesses. In addition, the auditor needs to be satisfied that performing substantive procedures alone would enable the auditor to design and perform an appropriate audit strategy and provide sufficient appropriate audit evidence to support his or her audit opinion.

Assessing the Risks of Material Misstatement

Issue 21: What are some examples of conditions and events that may indicate the existence of risks of material misstatement?

Appendix C to AU Section 314 contains examples of conditions and events that may be indicative of risks of material misstatement. The following examples cover a broad range of conditions and events, which are adapted from Appendix C to AU Section 314:

Entity, industry, and regulatory conditions and events

- Operations in regions that are economically unstable (e.g., countries with significant currency devaluation or highly inflationary economies).
- Operations exposed to volatile markets (e.g., futures trading).
- High degree of complex regulation.
- Going concern and liquidity issues (e.g., loss of significant customers).
- Marginally achieving explicitly stated strategic objectives.
- Constraints on the availability of capital and credit.
- Changes in the industry in which the entity operates.
- Changes in the supply chain.
- Developing or offering new products or services, or moving into new lines of business.
- Expanding into new locations.
- Changes in the entity (e.g., large acquisitions, reorganizations, or other unusual events).
- Entities or divisions likely to be sold.
- Complex alliances and joint ventures.
- Use of off-balance-sheet finance, special-purpose entities, and other complex financing arrangements.
- Significant transactions with related parties.
- Inquiries into the entity's operations or financial results by regulatory or government bodies.
- Pending litigation and contingent liabilities (e.g., sales warranties, financial guarantees, and environmental remediation).

Internal control conditions and events

- Lack of personnel with appropriate accounting and financial reporting skills.

- Changes in key personnel, including departure of key executives.
- Weaknesses in internal control, especially those not addressed by management.
- Inconsistencies between the entity's information technology (IT) strategy and its business strategies.
- Changes in the IT environment.
- Installation of significant new IT systems related to financial reporting.

Financial reporting conditions and events

- Past misstatements, history of errors, or a significant amount of adjustments at period-end.
- Significant amount of nonroutine or nonsystematic transactions, including intercompany transactions and large revenue transactions at period-end.
- Transactions that are recorded based on management's intent (e.g., debt refinancing, assets to be sold, and classification of marketable securities).
- Application of new accounting pronouncements.
- Complex processes related to accounting measurements.
- Events or transactions that result in significant measurement uncertainty, including accounting estimates.

ILLUSTRATIONS AND PRACTICE AIDS

ILLUSTRATION 1—QUESTIONNAIRE FOR UNDERSTANDING THE CONTROL ENVIRONMENT COMPONENT OF INTERNAL CONTROL

	Yes	No	N/A
1. Does management adequately convey the message that integrity cannot be compromised?	——	——	——
2. Does a positive control environment exist, whereby there is an attitude of control consciousness throughout the organization, and a positive "tone at the top"?	——	——	——
3. Is the competence of the entity's people commensurate with their responsibilities?	——	——	——
4. Is management's operating style, the way it assigns authority and responsibility, and organizes and develops its people appropriate?	——	——	——
5. Does management understand the requirements of laws and regulations pertinent to its business?	——	——	——
6. Does management adequately consider the potential effects of taking unusual business risks?	——	——	——
7. Are financial statements submitted to and reviewed by management, the board of directors, or the audit committee at regular intervals?	——	——	——
8. Does management demonstrate concern about and willingness to correct important weaknesses in the system of internal control?	——	——	——

	Yes	No	N/A
9. Does the entity maintain up-to-date accounting policies and a procedures manual? If yes, obtain copies.	___	___	___
10. Is a chart of accounts maintained and does it describe the nature of each account? If yes, obtain a copy.	___	___	___
11. Does management periodically review insurance coverage?	___	___	___
12. Does management have a history of establishing reliable accounting estimates?	___	___	___
13. Is there a low turnover of accounting, IT, and key management positions?	___	___	___
14. Are key operating positions adequately staffed, therefore avoiding constant crisis?	___	___	___
15. Is there adequate coordination between accounting and information technology departments, resulting in timely reports and closings?	___	___	___
16. Is there an organization chart that reflects the areas of responsibility and the line of reporting? If yes, obtain a copy.	___	___	___
17. Are there formal job descriptions that clearly set out duties and responsibilities?	___	___	___
18. Are backgrounds and references of applicants for financial, IT, and key management positions investigated?	___	___	___
19. Are personnel policies and employee benefit plans documented and communicated to employees?	___	___	___
20. Is a formal conflict of interest policy or code of conduct in effect? If yes, obtain a copy.	___	___	___
21. Are employees who handle cash, securities, and other valuable assets bonded?	___	___	___
22. Do related employees, if any, have job assignments that minimize opportunities for collusion?	___	___	___
23. Are employees adequately trained to meet their assigned responsibilities?	___	___	___
24. Is rotation of duties enforced by mandatory vacations?	___	___	___
25. Is job performance periodically evaluated and reviewed with employees?	___	___	___
26. Has management established adequate policies and procedures for the development, modification, and use of computer programs and data files?	___	___	___
27. Does the entity have a board of directors or an audit committee? If yes:	___	___	___
a. Does the board or committee take an active role in over-seeing the entity's policies and practices?	___	___	___
b. Does the board or committee approve the appointment of the entity's independent auditors?	___	___	___
c. Does the board or committee have sufficient knowledge, experience, and time to serve effectively?	___	___	___

	Yes	No	N/A

d. Does the board or committee constructively challenge management's planned decisions and take appropriate action if necessary (for example, conducting special investigations)? _____ _____ _____

e. Does the board or committee meet in a timely manner with the chief accounting officer and internal and external auditors to discuss the reasonableness of the financial reporting process, the system of internal control, and other significant matters? _____ _____ _____

f. Does the board or committee review the scope of activities of the external and internal auditors at least annually? _____ _____ _____

g. Does the board or committee regularly receive and review key information, such as financial statements, major marketing initiatives, significant contracts, and negotiations? _____ _____ _____

h. Does a process exist for informing the board or committee in a timely manner of sensitive information, investigation, and improper acts (e.g., significant litigation, investigations by regulatory agencies, embezzlement, misuses of corporate assets)? _____ _____ _____

i. Is there appropriate oversight in determining the compensation and benefits of executive officers? _____ _____ _____

j. Is the board or committee sufficiently involved in establishing and evaluating the effectiveness of the "tone at the top" (e.g., approving the entity's code of conduct or policy and procedure manual)? _____ _____ _____

Additional Comments—Control Environment

_____

_____

_____

_____

ILLUSTRATION 2—QUESTIONNAIRE FOR UNDERSTANDING THE RISK ASSESSMENT COMPONENT OF INTERNAL CONTROL

	Yes	No	N/A

1. Has management established clear entity-wide objectives and are they consistent with its business plans and budgets? _____ _____ _____

2. Has management established objectives for key activities and are they consistent with and linked to the entity-wide objectives and strategies? _____ _____ _____

3. Has management identified the resources and critical factors that are important to achieving its objectives (e.g., financing, personnel, facilities, or technology)? _____ _____ _____

	Yes	No	N/A

4. Does management consider risks arising from external sources (e.g., supply sources, creditors' demands, competitors' actions, regulation, natural events)?

5. Does management consider risks arising from internal sources (e.g., retention of key personnel or changes in their responsibilities, compensation and benefit programs to keep the entity competitive, the adequacy of back-up systems in the event of failure of systems that could significantly affect operations)?

6. Does management identify and monitor significant shifts in the entity's industry (e.g., changes in customer demographics, preferences, or spending patterns)?

7. Does management consult with its legal counsel regarding the implications of any new legislation?

8. Are new employees in key positions adequately supervised to ensure that they understand and perform in accordance with the entity's policies and procedures?

9. Are procedures in place to assess the effects of new or redesigned information systems and to monitor new technologies?

10. Are procedures in place to handle rapidly increasing volumes of information?

11. When considering development of new product lines, does management give appropriate consideration to major factors such as customer demand, production capabilities, and profitability implications?

12. In connection with corporate restructurings, are staff reassignments and reductions appropriately analyzed for their potential effect on operations or on the morale of the remaining employees?

13. Does management keep abreast of the political, regulatory, business, and social culture of areas in which foreign operations exist and are personnel made aware of accepted customs and rules?

14. Is management aware of the existence of new accounting or reporting pronouncements and how they may affect the entity's financial reporting practices?

Additional Comments—Risk Assessment

_____

_____

_____

_____

ILLUSTRATION 3—QUESTIONNAIRE FOR UNDERSTANDING THE CONTROL ACTIVITIES COMPONENT OF INTERNAL CONTROL

	Yes	No	N/A
1. Does management have clear objectives in terms of budget, profit, and other financial and operating goals? If yes, are such objectives:			
a. Clearly written?	___	___	___
b. Actively communicated throughout the entity?	___	___	___
c. Actively monitored?	___	___	___
2. Do the planning and reporting systems in place:			
a. Adequately identify variances from planned performance?	___	___	___
b. Adequately communicate variances to the appropriate level of management?	___	___	___
3. Does the appropriate level of management:			
a. Adequately investigate variances?	___	___	___
b. Take appropriate and timely corrective action?	___	___	___
4. Has management established procedures to prevent unauthorized access to, or destruction of, documents, records, and assets?	___	___	___
5. Has management established policies for controlling access to programs and data files?	___	___	___
6. Does management adequately monitor such policies?	___	___	___
7. Are amounts recorded by the accounting system periodically compared with physical assets?	___	___	___
8. Are control and subsidiary accounts reconciled regularly and discrepancies reported to appropriate personnel?	___	___	___
9. Are signatures required to evidence the performance of critical control functions, such as reconciling accounts?	___	___	___
10. Are general journal entries, other than standard entries, required to be approved by a responsible official not involved with their origination?	___	___	___
11. Are accounting estimates and judgments made only by knowledgeable and responsible personnel?	___	___	___
12. Does the accounting system provide in a timely manner the necessary information for the preparation of financial statements and related disclosures in accordance with generally accepted accounting principles or another comprehensive basis of accounting?	___	___	___
13. Are financial statements and related disclosures prepared and reviewed by competent personnel who are knowledgeable of the factors affecting the company's financial reporting requirements?	___	___	___

Additional Comments—Control Activities

_____

_____

_____

ILLUSTRATION 4—QUESTIONNAIRE FOR UNDERSTANDING THE INFORMATION AND COMMUNICATION COMPONENT OF INTERNAL CONTROL

	Yes	No	N/A

Information

1. Does the organization have mechanisms in place to obtain relevant external information (e.g., on market conditions, competitors' programs, legislative or regulatory developments, and economic changes) and internally generated information critical to the achievement of the organization's objectives? ____ ____ ____

2. Is the information provided to the right people in sufficient detail and on time to enable them to carry out their responsibilities efficiently and effectively? ____ ____ ____

3. Is the development or revision of information systems over financial reporting based on a strategic plan and interrelated with the entity's overall information systems and is it responsive to achieving the entity-wide and activity-level objectives? ____ ____ ____

4. Does management commit the appropriate human and financial resources to develop the necessary financial reporting information systems? ____ ____ ____

Communication

5. Does management communicate employees' duties and control responsibilities in an effective manner? ____ ____ ____

6. Are communication channels established for people to report suspected improprieties? ____ ____ ____

7. Does communication flow across the organization adequately (e.g., from shipping to accounting) to enable people to discharge their responsibilities effectively? ____ ____ ____

8. Does management take timely and appropriate follow-up action on communications received from customers, vendors, regulators, or other external parties? ____ ____ ____

9. Do other parties outside the organization review and follow (e.g., an active review of bank loan agreements)? ____ ____ ____

Additional Comments—Information and Communication

_____

_____

_____

_____

ILLUSTRATION 5—QUESTIONNAIRE FOR UNDERSTANDING THE MONITORING COMPONENT OF INTERNAL CONTROL

	Yes	No	N/A
1. Is operating information used to manage operations integrated or reconciled with data generated by the financial reporting system?	___	___	___
2. Are customer complaints about billings investigated and any internal control deficiencies corrected?	___	___	___
3. Are communications from vendors and monthly statements of accounts payable used as control monitoring techniques?	___	___	___
4. Are internal control recommendations made by external auditors (and internal auditors, if applicable) implemented?	___	___	___
5. Does management receive feedback from training seminars, planning sessions, and other meetings on whether controls operate effectively?	___	___	___
6. Does the organization take a fresh look at the internal control system from time to time and evaluate its effectiveness? If yes:			
a. Does the evaluation process include checklists, questionnaires, or other tools?	___	___	___
b. Are the evaluations documented?	___	___	___
7. Does the entity have an adequate internal audit function? If yes, do the internal auditors:			
a. Possess adequate training and experience?	___	___	___
b. Adhere to applicable professional standards?	___	___	___
c. Have an adequate documentation of the organization's internal control?	___	___	___
d. Perform tests of controls and substantive tests?	___	___	___
e. Have adequate documentation of their work?	___	___	___
f. Submit reports on their findings to the board of directors or audit committee in a timely manner?	___	___	___
g. Follow up on corrective actions taken by management?	___	___	___
h. Have direct access to the board of directors or audit committee?	___	___	___
i. Have direct access to records and the scope of their activities is not limited?	___	___	___

Additional Comments—Monitoring

_____

_____

_____

_____

_____

_____

ILLUSTRATION 6—UNCONDITIONAL AND PRESUMPTIVELY MANDATORY REQUIREMENTS OF AU SECTION 314

Unconditional Requirements

AU Section 314 identifies one unconditional requirement, in which it restates the second standard of field work:

> The auditor must obtain a sufficient understanding of the entity and its environment, including its internal control, to assess the risk of material misstatement of the financial statements whether due to error or fraud, and to design the nature, timing, and extent of further audit procedures.

AU Section 314 positions obtaining an understanding of the entity and its environment, including its internal control, as an essential part of the auditor's risk assessment process. The procedures the auditor performs to obtain an understanding of the entity and its environment are referred to as *risk assessment procedures*, which encompass (1) inquiries of management and others within the entity, (2) analytical procedures, and (3) observation and inspection.

Presumptively Mandatory Requirements

Presumptively mandatory requirements are identified by the word "should" and place the burden of proof on the auditor if he or she departs from the presumptive requirement. Presumptively mandatory requirements are required to be performed in all applicable circumstances unless the auditor can justify in the audit documentation a reason for not doing so and demonstrate how other audit procedures that the auditor performed have met the audit objectives. AU Section 314 states that the auditor *should*:

- Assess risk at the financial statement and relevant assertion levels based on an appropriate understanding of the client and its environment, including its internal control.

- Apply the provisions of AU Section 314 in conjunction with other AU sections, particularly with respect to the auditor's responsibility to consider fraud in an audit of financial statements, as discussed in AU Section 316 (Consideration of Fraud in a Financial Statement Audit).

- Perform the risk assessment procedures previously discussed in order to obtain an understanding of the entity and its environment, including its internal control, and use professional judgment to determine the extent of such understanding.

- Consider information that might be helpful in identifying risks of material misstatement when determining what inquiries to make or the extent of those inquiries.

- Apply analytical procedures in planning the audit, including (1) developing expectations about plausible relationships that are reasonably expected to exist and (2) considering the results of the analytical procedures performed, along with other information gathered, in identifying the risks of material misstatement.

- Determine whether changes have occurred to information obtained in prior periods (e.g., internal control and risk assessments) that may affect the relevance of such information in the current audit, when the auditor is planning to rely on that information.

- Consider the following sources of information that provide relevant understanding about the client and assist in identifying the risk of material misstatement: (1) the results of the assessment of the risk of material misstatement due to fraud, as addressed in AU Section 316; (2) other relevant information, such as that obtained from procedures performed in connection with the client acceptance or continuance process; and (3) information and experience gained on other engagements performed for the entity.

- Discuss the susceptibility of the client's financial statements to material misstatements with members of the audit team and use professional judgment in deciding the extent of the discussion, which members of the audit team to include in the discussion, and how and when the discussion should occur. In addition, the discussion should (1) involve the auditor with final responsibility for the engagement (e.g., audit partner) and key members of the audit team; (2) cover certain specific critical issues; (3) address the application of GAAP to the client's facts and circumstances, and in light of the client's accounting policies; and (4) emphasize the need to exercise professional skepticism, to be alert for indications that a material misstatement may have occurred, and to be rigorous in following up on such indications. The auditor with final responsibility should consider which matters are to be communicated to members of the engagement not involved in the discussion. When the entire engagement is performed by a single auditor, the auditor should nonetheless consider and document the susceptibility of the entity's financial statements to material misstatements and consider other factors that may be necessary in the engagement (e.g., personnel possessing specialized skills).

- Plan and perform the audit with professional skepticism.

- Obtain an understanding of the entity's industry, regulatory, and other external factors.

- Obtain an understanding of the entity's operations, including its ownership, governance, the types of investments in which it engages, and how it is structured and financed.

- Obtain an understanding of the entity's objectives, strategies, and related business risks that may result in a material misstatement of the financial statements.

- Obtain an understanding of the entity's measurement and review of its financial performance (e.g., key performance indicators, budgets, variance analysis, and departmental reports).

- Obtain a sufficient understanding of the entity's internal control, by performing risk assessment procedures to evaluate the design of controls relevant to the audit and to determine whether they have been implemented. This understanding should encompass the five components of internal control. The knowledge gained in this process should be used to

(1) identify types of possible misstatements, (2) consider factors affecting the risks of material misstatement, and (3) design tests of controls and substantive procedures.

- Obtain an understanding of the entity's selection and application of accounting principles, including their appropriateness for the business and their consistency with GAAP (or with another comprehensive basis of accounting) and industry practice.

- Identify new financial reporting standards and regulations and consider how and when the client will adopt them.

- Consider the reasons for changes in the selection or application of accounting policies, and whether they are appropriate and consistent with GAAP.

- Consider whether disclosures in the financial statements are adequate in light of circumstances and facts at the time.

- Form a professional judgment as to which controls should be tested, considering the circumstances, the applicable control component, and certain other specific factors.

- Evaluate the design and implementation of controls over financial reporting, including control activities for areas of significant risk.

- Consider the design of a control in determining whether to consider its implementation.

- Consider whether to communicate improperly designed controls to management and to those charged with governance.

- Perform the following procedures in obtaining an understanding of, and evaluating the design of, the entity's control environment:

  — Consider the design and implementation of entity programs and controls to address fraud risk.

  — Consider the following elements and how they have been incorporated into the client's processes: (1) communication and enforcement of integrity and ethical values; (2) commitment to competence; (3) participation of those charged with governance; (4) management's philosophy and operating style; (5) organizational structure; (6) assignment of authority and responsibility; and (7) human resource policies and practices.

  — Obtain sufficient knowledge of the control environment to understand the actions, attitudes, and awareness of those charged with governance concerning internal control.

  — Concentrate on the implementation of controls because controls may be established but not acted upon.

  — Consider the independence of the directors and their ability to evaluate the actions of management.

  — Consider whether there is a group of those charged with governance that understands the client's business transactions and evaluates the financial statements.

— Consider whether the control environment elements have been implemented.

— Consider the collective effect on the control environment of strengths and weaknesses in various control environment elements.

— Consider the effect of other components of internal control in conjunction with the control environment when assessing the risks of material misstatement.

- Perform the following procedures in obtaining an understanding of, and evaluating the design and implementation of, the entity's risk assessment process:

— Obtain an understanding of how management considers and addresses risks relevant to financial reporting objectives.

— Consider how management identifies business risks relevant to financial reporting, estimates the significance of the risks, assesses the likelihood of their occurrence, and decides how to manage them.

— Focus on aspects of the internal control framework that affect risks of material misstatement in financial reporting.

— Inquire about business risks that management has identified and consider whether they may result in material misstatement to the financial statements.

— Consider why the client's risk assessment process failed, in cases where management did not identify risks, and whether the process is appropriate.

— Discuss with management how business risks are identified and addressed in smaller entities that do not have formal risk assessment processes.

- Perform the following procedures in obtaining an understanding of the entity's information system:

— Obtain an understanding of how the incorrect processing of transactions is resolved.

— Obtain an understanding of the client's automated and manual procedures for preparing financial statements and disclosures, and how misstatements may occur.

— Be aware, in planning the audit, that automatic transfer of information via information technology systems may leave little or no visible evidence.

— Obtain an understanding of the client's information system related to financial reporting that is appropriate to the client's circumstances.

- Obtain an understanding of how the client communicates financial reporting roles and responsibilities and significant matters related to financial reporting.

- Perform the following procedures in obtaining an understanding of those control activities relevant to the audit:

— Consider the knowledge about the presence or absence of control activities obtained from an understanding of the other components of internal control in determining whether it is necessary to obtain an additional understanding of control activities.

— Obtain an understanding of the process of reconciling detail to the general ledger for significant accounts.

— Obtain an understanding of how information technology affects control activities that are relevant to planning the audit.

— Assess general information technology controls in relation to their effect on applications and data that become part of the financial statements.

— Consider whether the client has adequately responded to risks arising from information technology by establishing effective controls.

• Perform the following procedures in obtaining an understanding of the major types of activities that the entity uses to monitor internal control over financial reporting:

— Follow the guidance in AU Section 322 (The Auditor's Consideration of the Internal Audit Function in an Audit of Financial Statements) when obtaining an understanding of the internal audit function.

— Obtain an understanding of the sources and reliability of the information that management uses for its monitoring activities.

• Perform the following procedures in connection with identifying and assessing the risks of material misstatement at the financial statement level and at the relevant assertion level related to classes of transactions, account balances, and disclosures:

— Identify risks throughout the process of gaining an understanding of the entity, its environment, and its internal control.

— Relate those specific identified risks to potential misstatements at the relevant assertion level.

— Consider whether the *magnitude* of those identified risks could result in material misstatement of the financial statements.

— Consider whether it is *likely* that the identified risks could result in material misstatement of the financial statements.

— Use the audit evidence obtained in performing risk assessment procedures (e.g., inquiries, observation, inspection, and analytical procedures) to support the risk assessment.

— Use the risk assessment in determining the nature, timing, and extent of additional audit procedures.

— Perform appropriate tests of controls when the risk assessment is based on the auditor's expectation that controls are operating effectively at the relevant assertion level.

— Determine whether identified risks are isolated to particular relevant assertions associated with certain classes of transactions, account balances, or disclosures, or are more pervasive and likely to affect the financial statements as a whole.

— Identify controls that are likely to prevent or detect and correct material misstatements in certain relevant assertions.

- Communicate significant deficiencies in internal control to those charged with governance.

- Consider whether the audit report should be modified (i.e., qualified opinion or a disclaimer of opinion) or whether the auditor should withdraw from the engagement, when serious engagement conditions exist, such as concerns about the (a) auditability of the financial statements; (b) integrity of management; and (c) condition and reliability of the entity's records.

- Determine which of the identified risks require special audit consideration ("significant risks").

- Consider inherent risk in determining significant risks.

- Consider certain matters in addressing the nature of a significant risk, including (1) whether it is a fraud risk; (2) whether it is related to recent significant economic, accounting, or other developments; (3) the complexity of the transactions; (4) whether related-party transactions are involved; (5) the degree of subjectivity involved; and (6) whether the risk involves significant nonroutine or unusual transactions.

- Evaluate the design and determine the implementation of controls related to significant risks and develop a sufficient understanding of them to develop an effective audit approach.

- Communicate to those charged with governance and consider the implications for the auditor's risk assessment, when management has not implemented controls over significant risks and, as a result, the auditor believes a significant deficiency or material weakness in internal control over financial reporting exists.

- Evaluate the design and determine the implementation of controls over risks for which it is not possible or practicable to reduce detection risk to an acceptably low level at the relevant assertion level through substantive procedures alone.

- Revise the risk assessment and modify the planned audit procedures when evidence obtained during the audit contradicts the original risk assessment.

- Document the following:

— Discussion among the audit team about the susceptibility of the financial statements to material misstatement.

— Key elements of the auditor's understanding about the entity and its environment, the sources from which the understanding was obtained, and the risk assessment procedures performed to obtain such understanding.

— Assessment of the risk of material misstatement at the financial state-ment and relevant assertion levels, including the basis for such assessment.

— The risks identified and related controls evaluated.

AU SECTION 315
COMMUNICATIONS BETWEEN PREDECESSOR AND SUCCESSOR AUDITORS

PRACTICE POINT: As part of its Clarity Project, the American Institute of Certified Public Accountants' (AICPA's) Auditing Standards Board (ASB) has finalized a clarified Statement on Auditing Standards (SAS) titled, "Opening Balances—Initial Audit Engagements, Including Reaudit Engagements," which supersedes paragraphs .01–.02, .04, .11–.13, and .15–.23 of AU Section 315 (Communications between Predecessor and Successor Auditors). The clarified SAS incorporates guidance from ISA 510, "Initial Audit Engagements—Opening Balances," which requires the auditor to obtain sufficient appropriate audit evidence about whether:

- Opening balances contain misstatements that materially affect the current period's financial statements;

- Accounting policies reflected in the opening balances have been consistently applied in the current period's financial statements; and

- Changes in the accounting policies have been properly accounted for and adequately presented and disclosed in accordance with the applicable financial reporting framework.

The clarified SAS strengthens existing standards by making clear that reviewing a predecessor auditor's audit documentation cannot be the only procedure performed to obtain sufficient appropriate audit evidence regarding opening balances. The clarified SAS clarifies that initial audit engagements include reaudit engagements, and it eliminates from AU Section 315 requirements and guidance directed to reaudits that are repetitive with other SASs.

The ASB is expected to issue many of the clarified standards in *one* SAS that will be codified in "AU Section" format. The ASB has decided that the effective date of the clarified SASs that have not yet been issued is for audits of financial statements for periods ending on or after December 15, 2012. Auditors should be alert to and monitor further developments in this area.

PRACTICE POINT: As part of its Clarity Project, the American Institute of Certified Public Accountants' (AICPA's) Auditing Standards Board (ASB) has finalized a clarified Statement on Auditing Standards (SAS) titled, "Terms of Engagement," which supersedes (*a*) paragraphs .05–.10. of AU Section 311 (Planning and Supervision), as amended, and (*b*) paragraphs .03, .05–.10, and .14 of AU Section 315 (Communications between Predecessor and Successor Auditors), as amended. Among other matters, the clarified SAS:

- Requires the auditor to determine whether the financial reporting framework to be applied in the preparation of the financial statements is acceptable. The auditor's responsibility for determining the acceptability of the applicable financial reporting framework, which is necessary in order to express an opinion on the financial statements, has been implicit in GAAS. Therefore, this change in requirements is not expected to affect current practice.

- Requires the auditor to obtain the agreement of management that it acknowledges and understands its responsibility for selecting the appropriate financial reporting framework, establishing and maintaining internal control, and providing access and information to the auditor. Paragraph .08 of extant AU Section 311 requires the auditor to establish an understanding with management and requires that the understanding include management's responsibilities. Paragraph .09 of extant AU Section 311 includes management's responsibility for the selection and application of financial reporting, establishing and maintaining internal control, and making all financial records and related information available to the auditor as matters that may be included in the understanding established with the client. Therefore, a level of detail that is suggested in extant AU Section 311 is required in the clarified SAS. The ASB believes that it is appropriate to require that management's responsibilities be explicit in the engagement letter because there is no point in starting an audit if management will not acknowledge its responsibilities.

- Requires that if management or those charged with governance of an entity that is not required by law or regulation to have an audit impose a limitation on the scope of the auditor's work in the terms of a proposed audit engagement such that the auditor believes the limitation will result in the auditor disclaiming an opinion on the financial statements as a whole, the auditor should not accept such a limited engagement as an audit engagement unless the audit is required by law or regulation. Also, unless required by law or regulation to do so, the auditor should not accept the engagement if the auditor has determined that the applicable financial reporting framework is not acceptable or if the agreement of management referred to above has not been obtained. Existing GAAS does not contain these requirements. Therefore, these changes in requirements will affect current practice.

- Requires the auditor to assess for recurring audits whether circumstances require the terms of the audit engagement to be revised. If the auditor concludes that the terms of the engagement need not be revised, the auditor should remind the entity of the terms of the engagement. This may be accomplished by means of a new engagement letter or a reminder, either written or oral, that the responsibilities in the previous terms of engagement still apply. Extant AU Section 311 requires the auditor to establish an understanding with the client for each engagement, which in practice, may not result in a reminder each year for recurring audits. The clarified SAS also requires that the reminder, which may be written or oral, be documented. These requirements may affect current practice, depending on how existing GAAS has been interpreted.

- Addresses situations in which the auditor is requested to change the audit engagement to an engagement that conveys a lower level of assurance. These situations are addressed in Statements on Standards for Accounting and Review Services (SSARS). Therefore, including these requirements in GAAS will not affect current practice.

- Addresses situations in which law or regulation prescribes the layout or wording of the auditor's report in a form or in terms that are significantly different from the requirements of GAAS. Existing GAAS requires that in such circumstances, the auditor reword the prescribed form or attach a separate report. The clarified SAS includes the explicit requirement that if the auditor determines that rewording the prescribed form or attaching a separate report would not be permitted or would not mitigate the risk of users misunderstanding the auditor's report, the auditor should not accept the engagement. Therefore, this change in requirement may affect current practice.

The ASB is expected to issue many of the clarified standards in *one* SAS that will be codified in "AU Section" format. The ASB has decided that the effective date of the clarified SASs that have not yet been issued is for audits of financial statements for periods ending on or after December 15, 2012. Auditors should be alert to and monitor further developments in this area.

WHAT EVERY PRACTITIONER SHOULD KNOW

Basic Objectives

This Section applies in the following situations:

1. Whenever an independent auditor is considering accepting an engagement to audit or reaudit financial statements in accordance with generally accepted auditing standards and after such auditor has been appointed to perform such an engagement.

2. Whenever a successor auditor is replaced before completing an audit engagement and issuing a report.

This Section also provides guidance on communications between predecessor and successor auditors when:

1. A change of auditors is in process or has taken place.

2. Possible misstatements are discovered in financial statements reported on by a predecessor auditor.

Communication Requirements before Accepting an Engagement

The successor auditor should ask the prospective client to grant permission to discuss the impending engagement with the predecessor auditor, and to authorize the predecessor auditor to respond fully to the successor auditor's inquiries. The main objective of such communication is to find out any information that is relevant to deciding whether to accept the engagement. Therefore, the successor auditor should make specific and reasonable inquiries of the predecessor, including:

1. Information that might bear on the integrity of management.

2. Disagreements with management over the application of accounting principles, auditing procedures, or other similarly significant matters.

3. Communications to those charged with governance, audit committees, or others with equivalent authority and responsibility (e.g., board of directors, or the owner in a small business) regarding fraud, illegal acts by clients, and internal-control-related matters.

4. The predecessor auditor's understanding as to the reasons for the change of auditors.

In addition to the required inquiries mentioned, the successor auditor may want to address with the predecessor auditor other pertinent matters, such as:

- Adequacy of internal control.
- Pending or threatened litigation or regulatory investigations.
- Material contingencies.
- Going concern issues.
- Whether the predecessor auditor will be willing to reissue his or her report or otherwise provide a consent with respect to previously issued financial statements, if applicable.

PRACTICE POINT: Illustration 1 provides a form that the successor auditor can use when making inquiries of the predecessor auditor.

Other Communications

The successor auditor should request the client to authorize the predecessor auditor to allow a review of the predecessor's working papers. The predecessor auditor may wish to request a consent and acknowledgment letter from the client to document this authorization in an effort to reduce potential misunderstandings about the scope of the communications being authorized.

PRACTICE POINT: Illustration 3 below is an example of such a client consent and acknowledgment letter, which is included in SAS-84 (AU Section 315).

PRACTICE POINT: Before permitting access to the working papers, the predecessor auditor may wish to obtain a written communication from the successor auditor as to the use of the working papers. Illustration 4 below is an example of such a successor auditor acknowledgment letter, which is included in SAS-84 (AU Section 315).

The successor auditor's review of the predecessor auditor's working papers may affect the nature, timing, and extent of the successor auditor's procedures regarding the opening balances and consistency of accounting principles. However, the audit evidence used in analyzing such effect and any conclusions reached are solely the responsibility of the successor auditor. Therefore, in reporting on the audit, the successor auditor should not make reference to the report or work of the predecessor auditor as the basis, in part, for the successor auditor's own opinion.

PRACTICE POINT: Illustration 2 is an audit work program that the successor auditor can use when reviewing the predecessor auditor's working papers and planning the new audit engagement.

Communication Requirements in Connection with Audits of Financial Statements That Have Been Previously Audited by a Predecessor Auditor

If an auditor is asked to audit financial statements that have been previously audited (i.e., a reaudit), the auditor considering acceptance of the reaudit engagement is also a successor auditor, and the auditor who previously reported is also a predecessor auditor. In addition to the communication requirements discussed above, the successor should in these circumstances, state that the purpose of his or her inquiries is specifically to obtain information about whether to accept the "reaudit" engagement. If the successor auditor accepts the reaudit engagement, the information obtained merely from reviewing the predecessor's working papers, report, and inquiries of the predecessor do not represent sufficient appropriate audit evidence and, therefore, do not provide the successor a reasonable basis for expressing an opinion on the reaudited financial statements.

Under no circumstances should the successor auditor assume responsibility for the work of the predecessor auditor or issue a report that reflects divided responsibility for the audit. The successor auditor should obtain sufficient appropriate audit evidence to support his or her own opinion on the financial statements.

If the successor auditor is unable to obtain sufficient appropriate audit evidence in a reaudit engagement that will enable him or her to express an opinion on the financial statements, a scope limitation exists. Therefore, the successor auditor should either express a qualified opinion or disclaim an opinion on the financial statements in these situations.

The successor auditor should request access to working papers of the predecessor auditor for (1) the period under reaudit and (2) the period prior to the reaudit period. However, the extent, if any, to which the predecessor auditor permits access to the working papers is a matter of judgment.

In a reaudit, the successor auditor generally will be unable to observe inventory or make physical counts at the reaudit date as prescribed by professional standards. Therefore, if inventory is material, the successor auditor performing the reaudit should observe or perform some physical inventory counts at a date subsequent to the reaudit date and apply appropriate tests of intervening transactions to reconcile the subsequent count to the client's count.

Discovery of Possible Misstatements in Financial Statements Reported on by a Predecessor Auditor

During the audit or reaudit, the successor auditor may become aware of certain information that leads him or her to believe that financial statements reported on by the predecessor auditor may require revision. In such cases, the successor auditor should request that the client inform the predecessor auditor and arrange for the three parties to discuss the situation.

If the successor is not satisfied with the results of the matter or if the client refuses to inform the predecessor, the successor auditor should:

1. Evaluate possible implications on the current engagement.
2. Evaluate whether to resign from the engagement.

3. Consider consulting with legal counsel to determine an appropriate course of action.

The successor auditor should communicate to the predecessor any information that the predecessor may need to consider in accordance with AU Section 561 (Subsequent Discovery of Facts Existing at the Date of the Auditor's Report).

PRACTICE ISSUES AND FREQUENTLY ASKED QUESTIONS

Issue 1: What additional assurances might the successor auditor give the predecessor auditor to obtain broader access to the predecessor's working papers?

Experience has shown that the predecessor auditor may be willing to grant the successor auditor broader access to his or her working papers if the successor auditor provides additional assurance concerning the use of the predecessor's working papers. Accordingly, the successor auditor might consider agreeing to the following limitations on the review of the predecessor auditor's working papers in order to obtain broader access:

- The successor auditor will not comment, orally or in writing, to anyone as a result of the review as to whether the predecessor auditor's engagement was performed in accordance with generally accepted auditing standards.

- The successor auditor will not provide expert testimony or litigation support services or otherwise accept an engagement to comment on issues relating to the quality of the predecessor auditor's audit.

- The successor auditor will not use the audit procedures or results thereof documented in the predecessor auditor's working papers as audit evidence in rendering an opinion on the client's financial statements, except as contemplated in this Section.

The successor auditor can incorporate the aforementioned points in the acknowledgment letter to the predecessor auditor, as shown in Illustration 4 below.

Issue 2: Is a successor auditor required to comply with the communication requirements of this Section when the most recent financial statements have been compiled or reviewed?

No. When the most recent financial statements have been compiled or reviewed in accordance with Statements on Standards for Accounting and Review Services, the accountant who reported on those financial statements is *not* considered a "predecessor auditor" for purposes of this Section. However, the successor auditor may still find the matters discussed in this Section useful in determining whether to accept the prospective engagement in these circumstances.

Issue 3: What steps can the successor auditor take if the predecessor auditor will not provide a comprehensive response to the successor's inquiries?

The successor auditor should seriously consider the desirability of accepting a prospective client, without considerable other investigation, if the predecessor auditor will not provide a comprehensive response to the successor's inquiries. In practice, many CPA firms investigate the prospective client to determine its acceptability. Sources of information include local attorneys, banks, other CPAs, and other businesses. In some cases, the auditor may hire a professional investigator to obtain information about the reputation, background, and integrity of key members of management.

Issue 4: Are there any circumstances under which the predecessor auditor might decide not to respond fully to the inquiries made by the successor auditor?

Yes. Because of unusual circumstances, such as impending, threatened, or potential litigation; disciplinary proceedings; or such other unusual circumstances, the predecessor auditor might decide not to respond fully to the inquiries made by the successor auditor. In such circumstances, the predecessor should clearly state that his or her response is limited. The predecessor auditor should also consider consulting with legal counsel before responding to the successor auditor's inquiries under such circumstances.

Issue 5: May a successor auditor make a proposal for an audit engagement before communicating with the predecessor auditor?

Yes. However, the auditor should not *accept* an audit engagement until the communications described in this Section have been evaluated. One way to accomplish this is to make the audit firm's final acceptance of the engagement conditioned upon satisfactory responses from the predecessor auditor.

Issue 6: Are the communications between successor and predecessor auditors required to be in writing?

No. The communications between successor and predecessor auditors may be either written or oral.

Issue 7: Are there any specific types of predecessor auditor's working papers that the successor auditor is required to review in connection with a new audit engagement?

No. However, the successor auditor is required to obtain sufficient appropriate audit evidence to afford a reasonable basis for expressing an opinion on the financial statements, including evaluating the consistency of the application of accounting principles. Although the audit evidence used is a matter of professional judgment, it generally includes the following:

- The most recent audited financial statements and the predecessor auditor's report thereon.
- Management letter or communication of significant deficiencies and material weaknesses in internal control.
- Attorney response letters to audit inquiries.
- The management representation letter.
- Significant audit areas, including documentation of planning, internal control, audit results, conclusion memos, and other matters of continuing accounting and auditing significance (e.g., stockholder's equity accounts).

PRACTICE POINT: In addition to the above, the successor auditor can use the audit work program in Illustration 2 below to gather sufficient appropriate audit evidence for such new audit engagements.

Issue 8: Is a successor auditor prohibited from accepting a prospective audit engagement if the predecessor does not respond, or provides only a limited response, to the successor auditor's inquiries?

No. This Section does *not* prohibit a CPA firm from accepting an audit engagement when the predecessor auditor does not respond, or limits his or her response, to the successor auditor's inquiries. Such situations, however, should lead to a heightened awareness on the part of the successor that matters relating to the potential client's integrity or to disagreements over accounting issues may exist. Accordingly, additional client acceptance inquiries are prudent in these circumstances. The auditor can use the "Client Acceptance and Retention Evaluation Form" in AU Section 161 (Illustration 1) to make such inquiries.

Issue 9: How should the communications between the successor and predecessor auditors be documented?

Professional standards do not require any formal letters between any of the parties, or any specific documentation as a result of the communications. However, good business practice suggests that notations in the working papers indicating the names of the persons communicated with, the dates of communication, and the substance of the conversations, as a minimum level of documentation. In addition, while the letters in Illustrations 3 and 4 below, regarding client consent and acknowledgment, and successor auditor acknowledgment, respectively, are not required by professional standards, it is good practice to obtain such acknowledgment letters and include them in the workpapers.

ILLUSTRATIONS AND PRACTICE AIDS

ILLUSTRATION 1—COMMUNICATION WITH PREDECESSOR AUDITOR FORM

Note: Any "Yes" answers to the following questions indicate a higher level of risk than normal, and the auditor should expand on those answers.

Client Name: _____

Date of Financial Statements: _____

	Yes	No	N/A
1. Are you aware of any situations that might bear on the integrity of management?	___	___	___
2. Have you had any significant disagreements with management over the application of accounting principles, practices, or financial statement disclosures?	___	___	___
3. Has management ever attempted to restrict or direct the scope of the audit?	___	___	___
4. Are you aware of any incidents of management intervention in, or circumvention of, the company's internal control?	___	___	___

	Yes	No	N/A
5. Is management unwilling to accept primary responsibility for the content of the financial statements?	_____	_____	_____
6. Does management discourage its key employees from cooperating fully with the independent auditor?	_____	_____	_____
7. Have you had any communications with management regarding fraud, illegal acts, or internal control related matters?	_____	_____	_____
8. Are you aware of any pending or threatened litigation or regulatory investigations against the company?	_____	_____	_____
9. Are you aware of any material contingencies affecting the company?	_____	_____	_____
10. Are you aware of any matters that might raise substantial doubt about the entity's ability to continue as a going concern?	_____	_____	_____
11. Are you aware of any significant deficiencies or material weaknesses in internal control?	_____	_____	_____
12. Are you willing to reissue your report or otherwise provide a consent with respect to the previously issued financial statements (if applicable)?	_____	_____	_____

13. Inquire of the predecessor auditor about his or her understanding of reasons for change in auditors and summarize:

_____

_____

_____

14. Name of predecessor auditor:

_____

15. Name and position of person inquired of:

_____

16. Date of inquiry:

_____

ILLUSTRATION 2—AUDIT PROGRAM FOR REVIEWING THE PREDECESSOR AUDITOR'S WORKING PAPERS AND PLANNING THE NEW AUDIT ENGAGEMENT

Client Name: _____

Date of Financial Statements: _____

1. Consider the predecessor auditor's reputation, independence, and general competence, by communicating with the AICPA, applicable state society, other auditors, or bankers.

2. Review the most recent audited financial statements and the predecessor auditor's report thereon; management letter or communication of significant deficiencies (including material weaknesses) in internal control; attorney response letters to audit inquiries; the management representation letter; and permanent file documents that are pertinent to the audit

such as articles of incorporation and significant agreements and legal documents.

3. Review the predecessor auditor's working papers for all significant audit areas, including documentation of planning, internal control, audit results, conclusion memos, and other matters of continuing accounting and auditing significance (e.g., stockholder's equity accounts) and copy the applicable working papers and files.

4. Assess the reasonableness of opening balances of significant balance sheet accounts (e.g., cash, accounts receivable, property and equipment). In making this assessment, review the predecessor auditor's working papers and consider whether the predecessor auditor:

   a. Confirmed cash balances and tested the client's cash reconciliations and cash cutoff.

   b. Confirmed and tested investments and determined the reasonableness of recorded values.

   c. Confirmed accounts receivables (and the coverage was adequate); tested the adequacy of the allowance for doubtful accounts; and performed sales cut-off procedures.

   d. Observed inventory and made appropriate test counts; performed inventory price tests; identified any excess, slow- moving, or obsolete inventory; performed shipping and receiving cut-off procedures; and considered inventory valuations for lower of cost or market.

   e. Tested property, plant, and equipment giving appropriate consideration to significant additions and retirements, depreciation methods, useful lives, and impairment issues.

   f. Tested prepaid expenses, deferred charges, intangible assets, and other assets and considered the reasonableness of the remaining asset balances.

   g. Performed a search for unrecorded liabilities and tested the validity and adequacy of accrued liabilities.

   h. Analyzed the income tax related accounts and addressed significant temporary differences and related deferred tax asset valuation allowances.

   i. Confirmed debt terms and balances and tested the reasonableness of interest expense.

   j. Examined authorization and supporting documentation for significant equity transactions, including stock issuance, retirement, and dividends.

5. Identify the accounting principles and methods used by the entity in the prior period and determine if there have been any changes in such accounting principles and methods.

6. Review the predecessor auditor's year-end adjusting journal entries and any unrecorded audit differences (passed adjusting journal entries) and evaluate their potential impact on the current period's audit.

7. Determine the effect of any misstatement of the opening balances on the current period's financial statements.

8. Read the Company's minutes of meetings of shareholders and directors for a reasonable period of time (e.g., the previous three years, and prior years, if it is considered necessary).

9. Review the Company's income tax returns and revenue agents' reports for a reasonable period of time (e.g., the previous three years, and prior years, if it is considered necessary).

ILLUSTRATION 3—CLIENT CONSENT AND ACKNOWLEDGMENT LETTER

[*Date*]

ABC Enterprises
[*Address*]

You have given your consent to allow [*name of successor CPA firm*], as successor independent auditors for ABC Enterprises, access to our working papers for our audit of the December 31, 20X1, financial statements of ABC Enterprises. You also have given your consent to us to respond fully to [*name of successor CP A firm*]'s inquiries. You understand and agree that the review of our working papers is undertaken solely for the purpose of obtaining an understanding about ABC Enterprises and certain information about our audit to assist [*name of successor CPA firm*] in planning the audit of the December 31, 20X2, financial statements of ABC Enterprises.

Please confirm your agreement with the foregoing by signing and dating a copy of this letter and returning it to us.

Attached is the form of the letter we will furnish [*name of successor CPA firm*] regarding the use of the working papers.

Very truly yours,

[*Predecessor auditor*]

By: _____

Accepted:

ABC Enterprises

By: _____ Date: _____

ILLUSTRATION 4—SUCCESSOR AUDITOR ACKNOWLEDGMENT LETTER

[*Date*]

[*Successor auditor*]
[*Address*]

We have previously audited, in accordance with auditing standards generally accepted in the United States of America [or for audits performed in accordance with PCAOB standards, " . . . in accordance with the standards of the Public Company Accounting Oversight Board (United States)"], the December 31, 20X1, financial statements of ABC Enterprises (ABC). We rendered a report on those financial statements and have not performed any audit procedures subsequent to the audit report date. In connection with your audit of ABC's 20X2 financial statements, you have requested access to our working papers prepared in connection with that audit. ABC has authorized our firm to allow you to review those working papers.

Our audit, and the working papers prepared in connection therewith, of ABC's financial statements were not planned or conducted in contemplation of your review. Therefore, items of possible interest to you may not have been specifically addressed. Our use of professional judgment and the assessment of audit risk and materiality for the purpose of our audit mean that matters may have existed that would have been assessed differently by you. We make no representation as to the sufficiency or appropriateness of the information in our working papers for your purposes.

We understand that the purpose of your review is to obtain information about ABC and our 20X1 audit results to assist you in planning your 20X2 audit of ABC. For that purpose only, we will provide you access to our working papers that relate to that objective.

Because your review of our working papers is undertaken solely for the purpose described above and may not entail a review of all our working papers, you agree that (1) the information obtained from the review will not be used by you for any other purpose; (2) you will not comment, orally or in writing, to anyone as a result of that review as to whether our audit was performed in accordance with generally accepted auditing standards; (3) you will not provide expert testimony or litigation support services or otherwise accept an engagement to comment on issues relating to the quality of our audit; and (4) you will not use the audit procedures or results thereof documented in our working papers as audit evidence in rendering your opinion on the 20X2 financial statements of ABC, except as contemplated in Statement on Auditing Standards No. 84.

Upon request, we will provide copies of those working papers that provide factual information about ABC. You agree to subject any such copies or information otherwise derived from our working papers to your normal policy for retention of working papers and protection of confidential client information. Furthermore, in the event of a third-party request for access to your working papers prepared in connection with your audits of ABC, you agree to obtain our permission before voluntarily allowing any such access to our working papers or information otherwise derived from our working papers, and to obtain on our behalf any releases that you obtain from such third party. You agree to advise us promptly and provide us a copy of any subpoena, summons, or other court order for access to your working papers that include copies of our working papers or information otherwise derived therefrom.

Please confirm your agreement with the foregoing by signing and dating a copy of this letter and returning it to us.

Very truly yours,

[*Predecessor auditor*]

By: _____

Accepted: _____

[*Successor auditor*]

By: _____   Date:_____

AU SECTION 316
CONSIDERATION OF FRAUD IN A FINANCIAL STATEMENT AUDIT

> **PRACTICE POINT:** As part of its Clarity Project, the American Institute of Certified Public Accountants' (AICPA's) Auditing Standards Board (ASB) has finalized a clarified Statement on Auditing Standards (SAS) titled, "Consideration of Fraud in a Financial Statement Audit (Redrafted)," which supersedes AU Section 316 (Consideration of Fraud in a Financial Statement Audit), as amended. The clarified SAS does not change or expand extant AU Section 316 in any significant respect. The definition of *fraud* has been revised to converge with ISA 240, "The Auditor's Responsibilities Relating to Fraud in an Audit of Financial Statements," while avoiding unnecessary differences with Public Company Accounting Oversight Board standards. The ASB believes that the definition of fraud, when read in conjunction with the objective of the clarified SAS, does not create differences between the application of extant AU Section 316 and the application of the clarified SAS.
>
> The ASB is expected to issue many of the clarified standards in *one* SAS that will be codified in "AU Section" format. The ASB has decided that the effective date of the clarified SASs that have not yet been issued is for audits of financial statements for periods ending on or after December 15, 2012. Auditors should be alert to and monitor further developments in this area.

WHAT EVERY PRACTITIONER SHOULD KNOW

Basic Requirement

In a financial statement audit, the auditor has a responsibility to obtain *reasonable* (not absolute) assurance regarding whether the financial statements are free of material misstatement, whether caused by error or fraud. Because of the concept of "reasonable assurance," even a properly planned and executed audit may not detect material misstatements resulting from fraud.

Types of Misstatements

There are two types of misstatements that are relevant to a financial statement audit:

1. *Misstatements resulting from fraudulent financial reporting*—This type of fraud is usually committed by management to deceive financial statement users and may be concealed by falsifying or forging documents, or through collusion among management, employees or third parties.

2. *Misstatements resulting from misappropriation of assets*—This type of fraud involves the theft of an entity's assets, most often by employees, and can be accomplished in ways such as embezzling cash, stealing or misusing assets, and causing an entity to pay for goods or services not received.

This Section identifies three conditions that are generally present when fraud occurs:

1. Management or employees are under *pressure* or have an *incentive* to commit fraud *("incentives/pressures")*.

2. *Opportunities* exist (e.g., ineffective controls, management's ability to override controls) for the fraud to be committed *("opportunities")*.

3. The persons involved possess an *attitude*, character, or set of ethical values that allow them to *rationalize* committing a fraudulent act *("attitudes/rationalizations")*.

Importance of Professional Skepticism

This Section requires the auditor to apply professional skepticism in gathering and evaluating audit evidence. It emphasizes the importance of exercising professional skepticism by affirming that the auditor should:

- Have a mindset that fraud could exist in any audit.
- Set aside his or her existing beliefs about management's honesty and integrity in considering how fraud could occur.
- Question whether the evidence gathered may be indicative that fraud has occurred.
- Challenge any evidence that is less less-than-persuasive, regardless of his or her belief about management's honesty.

Having a skeptical attitude can lead to additional or more effective audit procedures. For example, the auditor may decide to (1) design additional or different audit procedures to obtain more reliable evidence, and (2) obtain additional corroboration of management's explanations, for example by obtaining third-party confirmations or using a specialist.

Brainstorming among the Audit Team Members about the Risks of Fraud

This Section requires, as part of planning the audit, that a discussion among the audit engagement personnel takes place about the risks of material misstatement due to fraud. Such discussion should include:

1. Sharing ideas, or "brainstorming," about the following matters:
   a. How and where the financial statements might be materially misstated due to fraud.
   b. How management could perpetrate and conceal fraudulent financial reporting (e.g., capitalizing certain operating expenses in fixed assets).
   c. How the perpetrators could misappropriate company assets.
   d. Known external and internal factors affecting the entity that might (1) create incentives/pressures to commit fraud, (2) provide the opportunity for fraud to take place, and (3) reveal attitudes or rationalizations about why fraud is acceptable behavior.
   e. The risk of management override of controls.
   f. How best to respond to these fraud risks through the design of audit procedures.

2. Reminding all engagement personnel of the need to emphasize professional skepticism, to critically assess audit evidence, and to consult with other team members or experts in the firm where appropriate.

The discussion of the matters above should always include the person with final responsibility for the audit and, ordinarily, other key members of the audit team (e.g., managers, seniors). Also, depending on the nature and complexity of the engagement, if specialists are assigned to the engagement, consideration should be given to involving such specialists in the forum. Furthermore, such discussions should continue throughout the audit, including when evaluating audit evidence at or near the completion of field work.

Procedures Required When Obtaining Information Needed to Identify the Risks of Fraud

There are no boilerplate-type procedures that the auditor can use when obtaining information needed to identify the risks of fraud. The size, complexity, and ownership characteristics of the entity also have a significant influence on the identification of relevant risk factors during this process. Therefore, the auditor should use professional judgment when developing the procedures to be performed. However, this Section requires that the specified procedures discussed herein be performed on *every* audit engagement when gathering information necessary to identify the risks of fraud.

Inquire of management, and others within the entity, about the risks of fraud
This Section requires the auditor to make certain inquiries of management, those charged with governance (or the audit committee or at least its chair), appropriate internal audit personnel (where applicable), and others within the entity (e.g., operations management). Such inquiries should include:

1. Inquiries of the entity's management about:

    a. Whether it is aware of actual or suspected fraud.

    b. Whether it is aware of any allegations of fraud (e.g., communications from employees or others).

    c. Its understanding about the risks of fraud within the entity, including any specific risks identified or areas where fraud is likely to occur.

    d. The programs and controls that it has established to mitigate fraud risks and how it monitors such programs and controls.

    e. The nature and extent of monitoring of operating locations or business segments (for an entity with multiple locations), and whether there are particular units for which a risk of fraud may be more likely to exist.

    f. Whether and how management communicates to employees its views on business practices and ethical behavior.

    g. Whether management has reported to those charged with governance (or the audit committee or its equivalent) on how the entity's internal control monitors the risks of material fraud.

2. Inquiries of those charged with governance (or the audit committee or at least its chair) about:

   a. Their views about the risks of fraud and whether they have knowledge of any actual fraud or suspected fraud.

   b. How they exercise their oversight of the entity's assessment of risks of fraud and the programs and controls the entity has adopted to mitigate those risks.

3. Inquiries of appropriate internal audit personnel, where applicable, about:

   a. Their views of the risks of fraud.

   b. Any procedures they performed to identify or detect fraud during the period under audit.

   c. Management's response to the findings.

   d. Whether they have knowledge of any actual fraud or suspected fraud.

4. Inquiries of others within the entity about any actual fraud or suspected fraud. The nature and extent of such inquiries, and to whom they should be directed, are up to the auditor's judgment. For example, the auditor may decide to direct inquiries to:

   a. Employees with different levels of authority in the company.

   b. Operational personnel not directly involved in the financial reporting process.

   c. Employees involved in initiating, recording, or processing complex or unusual transactions.

   d. In-house legal counsel.

Consider the results of the analytical procedures performed in planning the audit When performing analytical procedures during the planning stages of the audit, the auditor develops certain expectations about important financial and operating relationships based on his or her understanding of the client's business and industry. Results of analytical procedures that differ from the auditor's expectations should increase his or her overall skepticism, and the auditor should consider those results in identifying the risks of fraud.

This Section requires the auditor to perform "analytical procedures relating to revenue with the objective of identifying unusual or unexpected relationships involving revenue accounts that may indicate a material misstatement due to fraudulent financial reporting." Examples of such procedures include:

- Comparison of sales volume, based on recorded revenue amounts, with production capacity; recorded sales volume in excess of capacity should raise a red flag about potential fictitious sales.

- Comparison of monthly sales and sales returns during the period under audit with periods subsequent to the reporting period; this may disclose the existence of significant returns which might indicate that revenues were improperly recognized during the reporting period.

- Comparison of revenue reported by month and by product line or business segment during the current reporting period with comparable prior periods.

- Analysis of relationships between financial statement items (i.e., ratio analysis) for the current reporting period with comparable prior periods; for example, a significant decrease in the ratio of cost of sales to sales might indicate that revenues are overstated.

Consider whether one or more fraud risk factors exist The auditor may identify the following three conditions that are generally present when fraud exists: (1) incentives/pressures to commit fraud, (2) opportunities to carry out the fraud, (3) and attitudes/rationalizations to justify the fraudulent action. This Section refers to such conditions as "fraud risk factors" and includes examples of risk factors related to fraudulent financial reporting and misappropriation of assets that are classified based on these three conditions. Illustrations 1 and 2 below provide examples of risk factors relating to fraudulent financial reporting and to misappropriation of assets, respectively.

Consider certain other information This Section states that the auditor should consider other information that may be relevant in identifying risks of fraud, including:

- The discussion among engagement personnel (as discussed above).

- Information from the results of procedures relating to the acceptance and continuance of clients and engagements.

- Information from the results of reviews of interim financial statements.

- Inherent risk identified as part of the consideration of audit risk at the individual account balance or class of transaction level.

Identifying Risks that May Result in a Material Misstatement Due to Fraud

---

PRACTICE POINT: AU Section 314 (Understanding the Entity and Its Environment and Assessing the Risks of Material Misstatement) requires the auditor to identify and assess the risk of material misstatement at the financial statement level and at the relevant assertion level for classes of transactions, account balances, and disclosures. For further guidance, see AU Section 314.

This Section requires the auditor to "evaluate whether identified risks of material misstatement due to fraud can be related to specific financial-statement account balances or classes of transactions and related assertions, or whether they relate more pervasively to the financial statements as a whole." Based on this assessment, the auditor will be in a better position to determine the nature, timing, and extent of audit procedures to be performed. When identifying the risk of material misstatement due to fraud, the auditor should consider the attributes of such risk, including the following:

- The *type* of risk—that is, does it involve fraudulent financial reporting or misappropriation of assets?

- The *significance* of the risk—that is, could the magnitude of the risk lead to a possible material misstatement in the financial statements?

- The *likelihood* of the risk—i.e., is it likely that the risk will result in a material misstatement in the financial statements?

- The *pervasiveness* of the risk—that is, is the risk related to specific financial-statement account balances or classes of transactions and related assertions, or is it related to the financial statements as a whole?

This Section indicates that, regardless of any conclusions reached about the existence of specific fraud risks, the auditor should (1) ordinarily presume that improper revenue recognition is a fraud risk, and (2) address the risk that management override of controls could occur in every audit.

Assessing the Identified Risks after Taking into Account an Evaluation of the Entity's Programs and Controls

This Section requires the auditor to assess the identified risks that may result in a material misstatement due to fraud, taking into account an evaluation of the entity's programs and controls. Specifically, the auditor should assess these risks as follows:

- Evaluate, in connection with the understanding of internal control, whether the entity has appropriately designed and placed in operation programs and controls that address identified risks of material misstatement due to fraud. Such programs and controls may be broad in nature (e.g., a code of conduct that promotes honesty and integrity), or may include specific controls (e.g., inventory items of high value are locked); and

- Consider whether such programs and controls mitigate the identified risks or whether specific control deficiencies may increase the risks.

The Auditor's Response to the Results of the Fraud Risk Assessment

PRACTICE POINT: AU Section 318 (Performing Audit Procedures in Response to Assessed Risks and Evaluating the Audit Evidence Obtained) requires the auditor to (a) determine overall responses to address the assessed risks of material misstatement at the financial statement level (e.g., assigning more experienced staff or using specialists) and (b) design and perform additional audit procedures that are responsive to the assessed risks of material misstatement at the relevant assertion level. For further guidance, see AU Section 318.

The way the auditor responds to the results of the fraud risk assessment depends on the nature and significance of the fraud risks identified and on the entity's programs and controls that address such risks. This Section indicates that auditors respond to the results of the fraud risk assessment in three ways: (1) an overall response as to how the audit is conducted; (2) specific responses involving modification of the nature, timing, and extent of procedures to be performed; and (3) responses to further address the risk of management override of controls.

Overall response as to how the audit is conducted This Section indicates that an overall response affects how the audit is conducted and involves more general considerations apart from the specific procedures otherwise planned. The auditor should incorporate the following overall responses in every audit:

- *Assignment of personnel and supervision*—The auditor should determine that the level and qualifications of staff needed to perform and supervise the engagement are commensurate with the engagement risk. For example, the auditor may assign to the engagement more experienced persons or personnel with specialized skills or knowledge, such as information technology specialists.

- *Accounting principles*—The auditor should consider management's selection and application of significant accounting principles and whether collectively they indicate a bias that could be material to the financial statements. The auditor should particularly scrutinize those accounting principles involving subjective measurements and complex transactions.

- *Unpredictability of auditing procedures*—The auditor should test areas, locations, and accounts that otherwise might not be tested. The audit procedures and tests should include an element of unpredictability from the client's viewpoint, for example: (1) testing certain account balances and assertions not otherwise tested due to their materiality or risk; (2) changing the timing of testing from that otherwise expected (e.g., from year-end date to interim date); (3) using differing sampling methods; and (4) performing procedures at locations on an unannounced basis.

In addition to the above, the auditor may determine that other overall responses are appropriate, for example, corroborating client explanations or representations with others outside the entity.

Specific responses involving modification of the nature, timing, and extent of procedures to be performed Judgments about the risk of material misstatement due to fraud may prompt the auditor to modify the nature, timing, and extent of audit procedures in the following ways:

- *Nature* of auditing procedures—More reliable evidence or additional corroborative information may be obtained, such as more audit evidence from independent sources outside the company. The auditor may also choose to use computer-assisted audit techniques to gather more extensive evidence about data contained in significant accounts or electronic files. Also, inquiries of additional members of management or others may be made to identify issues and corroborate evidence.

- *Timing* of auditing procedures—The auditor may conclude that substantive procedures need to be performed at or near the end of the reporting period. On the other hand, because an intentional misstatement may have been initiated in an interim period, the auditor might elect to apply substantive tests to transactions occurring earlier or throughout the period.

- *Extent* of auditing procedures—The auditor may decide to increase sample sizes or perform analytical procedures at a more detailed level. In addition, computer-assisted audit techniques may be used for more extensive testing of electronic transactions and account files.

The specific auditing procedures performed will vary depending on the types of risks identified and the account balances, classes of transactions, and assertions that may be affected. Specific responses may involve both substantive tests and tests of controls. However, because of the risk that management may override controls, it is unlikely that tests of controls alone can reduce audit risk to an appropriately low level.

Responses to further address the risk of management override of controls This Section indicates that, because management override of controls can occur in unpredictable ways, the auditor should perform the following procedures to address that risk:

1. *Examine journal entries and other adjustments for evidence of possible material misstatement due to fraud.* The auditor is required to design procedures to test the appropriateness of journal entries recorded in the general ledger and other adjustments (e.g., entries posted directly to financial statement drafts) made in the preparation of the financial statements. Specifically, the auditor should:

    a. Obtain an understanding of the entity's financial reporting process. Such an understanding typically would include the sources of significant debits and credits to an account; who can initiate entries to the general ledger or transaction processing systems; what approvals are required for such entries; and how journal entries are recorded (e.g., online with no paper trail, or in paper form and entered in batch mode).

    b. Obtain an understanding of the design of the controls over journal entries and other adjustments and determine whether they are suitably designed and have been placed in operation. For example, an entity may have designated certain individuals to propose adjustments, and which may only be recorded by a supervisor.

    c. Test selected journal entries and other adjustments. In determining the nature, timing, and extent of such testing, the auditor should consider:

        — The auditor's assessment of the risk of material misstatement due to fraud. For example, the auditor's assessment may reveal specific classes of journal entries that have a higher risk of misstatement.

        — The effectiveness of controls that have been implemented over journal entries and other adjustments.

        — The entity's financial reporting process and the nature of the evidence that can be examined. The auditor should select from the general ledger journal entries to be tested and examine related support, regardless of whether they exist in electronic or paper form.

— The characteristics of fraudulent entries or adjustments. For example, entries made (a) to unrelated, unusual, or seldom-used accounts; (b) by individuals who typically do not make journal entries; (c) with little or no explanation or description; (d) before or during the preparation of the financial statements that do not have account numbers; or (e) that contain round numbers or a consistent ending number.

— The nature and complexity of the accounts. For example, suspicious accounts may include those that contain (a) unusual or complex transactions, (b) significant estimates and period-end adjustments, (c) unreconciled differences, and (d) intercompany transactions.

— Journal entries or other adjustments processed outside the normal course of business. Additional emphasis should be placed on nonstandard entries; for example, those made to record a business combination or an asset impairment, consolidating adjustments, report combinations, and reclassifications.

d. Determine the timing of the testing. This Section indicates that the auditor's testing of journal entries and other adjustments ordinarily should focus on those made at the end of a reporting period because fraudulent entries are often made at that time. However, the auditor should consider whether to test also journal entries throughout the audit period.

e. Inquire of individuals involved in the financial reporting process about inappropriate or unusual activity relating to the processing of journal entries and other adjustments.

2. *Review accounting estimates for biases that could result in material misstatement due to fraud.* The auditor should consider whether differences between estimates supported by audit evidence and those included in the financial statements indicate a possible management bias. If such a bias exists, the auditor is required to reconsider the estimates. In addition, the auditor should:

a. Perform a retrospective review of significant accounting estimates reflected in the prior year's financial statements to determine whether there is possible management bias. The estimates selected for testing should include those that involve highly sensitive assumptions or judgments made by management. This retrospective review is intended to provide the auditor with additional information about whether a possible management bias exists in making the current-year estimates.

b. Evaluate whether circumstances producing a management bias represent a risk of a material misstatement due to fraud (e.g., a risk that management instructed employees to record certain adjustments in order to inflate earnings).

3. *Evaluate the business rationale for significant unusual transactions.* The auditor should obtain an understanding of the business rationale for significant unusual transactions and whether that suggests the transactions may have been entered into to engage in fraudulent financial reporting or conceal misappropriation of assets. In obtaining such an understanding, the auditor should consider:

a. Whether the structure of such transactions is unnecessarily complex (e.g., involving multiple entities within a consolidated group or unrelated third parties).

b. Whether management has informed those charged with governance about the nature of and accounting for such transactions.

c. Whether management is emphasizing the need for a particular accounting treatment over the underlying economics of the transaction.

d. Whether those charged with governance have reviewed and approved transactions that involve unconsolidated related parties, including special purpose entities.

e. Whether the transactions involve previously unidentified related parties or parties that are unable to support the transaction without assistance from the entity being audited.

The Auditor's Evaluation of Audit Evidence

The auditor's assessment of the risks of material misstatement due to fraud is an ongoing and a cumulative process. This Section indicates that for purposes of evaluating audit evidence, the auditor should:

1. Assess the risks of material misstatement due to fraud throughout the audit. In connection with such assessment, the auditor should carefully consider conditions that either change or support the auditor's judgment. For example, such conditions include:

a. Discrepancies in the accounting records (e.g., unauthorized transactions; last-minute adjustments that significantly affect the financial statements).

b. Conflicting or missing audit evidence (e.g., unusual or irreconcilable discrepancies between the company's records and confirmation replies; inconsistent or implausible responses by the company's personnel to auditor inquiries).

c. Problematic or unusual relationships between management and the auditor (e.g., unusual delays in providing information requested for the audit; unreasonable time constraints to resolve complex issues or to complete the audit).

2. Evaluate whether analytical procedures that the auditor performed as substantive tests or in the overall review stage of the audit indicate a risk of material misstatement due to fraud that was previously unrecognized. In connection with this evaluation, this Section indicates that the auditor, at a minimum, should:

    a. Perform analytical procedures relating to revenue through the end of the period being audited.

    b. Focus attention on unusual relationships involving year-end revenue and income (e.g., unusual transactions or unusually large amounts of income being reported in the last couple of weeks of the reporting period; income that is inconsistent with trends in cash flows from operations).

    c. Consider unusual or unexpected analytical relationships that may have been identified (e.g., company's profitability or bad debt write-offs that are inconsistent with industry trends; unexpected or unexplained relationship between sales volume compiled from the accounting records and production data maintained by operations personnel).

    d. Consider whether management responses to audit inquiries throughout the audit have been vague, implausible, or inconsistent.

3. Evaluate whether the risks of material misstatement due to fraud at or near the completion of fieldwork affect the assessment the auditor made when first planning the audit. This evaluation process is primarily qualitative in nature and requires the use of the auditor's professional judgment. However, this Section indicates that, as part of this evaluation, the auditor with final responsibility for the audit should:

    a. Ascertain that there has been appropriate communication with the other audit team members throughout the audit regarding information or conditions indicative of risks of material fraud.

    b. Consider having another discussion among audit team members about the risks of material fraud.

The auditor's response to misstatements that may be the result of fraud When audit test results identify a misstatement in the financial statements, the auditor should evaluate whether such misstatement may be indicative of fraud. The auditor's response depends on whether the effect of the misstatement is material or not material to the financial statements. This Section provides the following guidance.

- *Effect of misstatement is not material to the financial statements.* If the auditor has determined that a misstatement is or may be the result of fraud, but the effect of the misstatement is not material to the financial statements, this Section nevertheless requires the auditor to evaluate the implications. In making this evaluation, the auditor should particularly consider the organizational level of the employee involved. For example, fraud involving petty cash theft entrusted to a non-management employee generally would be of little significance. Conversely, the problem may be more pervasive if the matter involves a higher level management position, although the amount itself is not considered material to the financial statements. Under such circumstances, this Section indicates that the auditor should reevaluate the assessment of the risk of material misstatement due to fraud and its impact on: (1) the nature, timing, and extent of the tests of balances or transactions, and (2) the assessment of the effectiveness of controls if control risk was assessed below the maximum level.

- *Effect of misstatement is unknown or is material to the financial statements.* If the auditor has determined that a misstatement is or may be the result of fraud, and the effect of the misstatement is material to the financial statements, or the effect could not be determined, the auditor should:

  — Attempt to obtain sufficient appropriate audit evidence to determine if material fraud in fact exists and, if so, its impact on the financial statements and the auditor's report.

  — Consider the implications for other aspects of the audit, as discussed in the preceding section, by reevaluating the nature, timing, and extent of the tests performed, and the assessment of control risk.

  — Discuss the matter and an appropriate course of action with management (at least one level above those involved) and with senior management and those charged with governance.

  — Recommend that the client consult with legal counsel.

If the auditor determines that a significant risk of fraud exists, the auditor should consider withdrawing from the engagement and communicating the reasons for withdrawal to those charged with governance. Such situations might include unresolved questions about the integrity of management and lack of cooperation by management in investigating the fraud. In these circumstances, the auditor should consider consulting with legal counsel.

If, subsequent to the date of the report on the financial statements, the auditor becomes aware of facts that existed at that date which might have affected the auditor's report, the auditor should follow the guidance in AU Section 561 (Subsequent Discovery of Facts Existing at the Date of the Auditor's Report). Also, if financial statements reported on by a predecessor auditor are affected, the successor auditor should attempt communication with the predecessor as required by AU Section 315 (Communications between Predecessor and Successor Auditors).

The Auditor's Communications about Fraud to Management, Those Charged with Governance, and Others

This Section requires the auditor to communicate matters involving fraud to an appropriate level of management. This is generally appropriate even if the matter might be considered inconsequential, such as a minor defalcation by an employee at a relatively low level. Fraud involving senior management, and fraud that causes a material misstatement of the financial statements, should be reported directly to those charged with governance.

The auditor should reach an understanding with those charged with governance regarding the expected nature and extent of communications with them about misappropriations by lower-level employees.

As a result of the assessment of the risk of material misstatement due to fraud, the auditor may identify certain fraud risks that have continuing control implications. The auditor should evaluate whether these fraud risks represent significant deficiencies relating to the entity's internal control that should be communicated to management and those charged with governance. AU Section 325 (Communicating Internal Control Related Matters Identified in an Audit) provides guidance to auditors about communication of certain matters regarding the entity's internal control that come to the auditor's attention during the audit. In addition, the auditor should consider whether the absence of, or deficiencies in, an entity's programs and controls to adequately address specific fraud risks represent significant deficiencies that should be included in such communication.

Communications to third parties outside the entity This Section indicates that, generally, the auditor is not responsible to notify third parties—other than the client's senior management and those charged with governance—of fraud-related matters. However, the auditor may have a duty to disclose these matters to parties outside the entity in the following circumstances:

- To comply with certain legal and regulatory requirements, such as the SEC disclosure requirements regarding a change in auditors.

- To comply with the communication requirements of AU Section 315 when a successor auditor makes inquiries of a predecessor auditor. Under AU Section 315, communications between predecessor and successor auditors require the specific permission of the client.

- To respond to a subpoena.

- To comply with governmental audit requirements applicable to entities that receive governmental financial assistance from a funding or other specified agency.

Because of the potential conflicts of the confidential relationship between the auditor and the client, the auditor may find it advisable to contact legal counsel before fraud-related matters are disclosed to parties outside the entity. This is particularly important because unjustified third-party notification could result in a lawsuit against the auditor for damages, slander, or similar reasons.

Documentation of the Auditor's Consideration of Fraud

This Section requires the auditor to document the following:

1. The discussion among audit team members in planning the audit regarding the susceptibility of the entity's financial statements to material misstatement due to fraud, including:

   a. How the discussion occurred;

   b. When the discussion occurred;

   c. The audit team members who participated; and

   d. The subject matter discussed.

2. The procedures performed to obtain information necessary to identify and assess the risks of material misstatement due to fraud.

3. Specific risks of material misstatement due to fraud that the auditor identified, and a description of his or her response to those risks.

4. If improper revenue recognition was not identified as a risk of a material misstatement due to fraud, the reasons regarding how the auditor overcame that presumption.

5. The results of the procedures the auditor performed to address the risk of management override of controls.

6. Other conditions and analytical relationships that led the auditor to believe that additional auditing procedures, or other responses, were required and any further responses the auditor concluded were appropriate to address such risks or other conditions.

7. The nature of the communications about fraud made to management, those charged with governance, and others.

PRACTICE ISSUES AND FREQUENTLY ASKED QUESTIONS

Differences between Fraud, Errors, and Forensic Investigations

Issue 1: What is the primary factor that differentiates fraud from error?

The primary factor that differentiates fraud from error is whether the underlying action that results in the financial statement misstatement is intentional or unintentional. AU Section 316 acknowledges that intent is often difficult, if not impossible, to determine, particularly in matters involving accounting estimates and the application of accounting principles. Although the auditor has no responsibility to determine intent, the auditor's responsibility to plan and perform the audit to obtain reasonable assurance about whether the financial statements are free of material misstatement is relevant in either case.

Issue 2: How does the consideration of fraud as part of a financial statement audit differ from a forensic investigation or fraud audit?

An audit pursuant to GAAS has the objective of expressing an opinion on the fairness of the financial statement presentation. The auditor's responsibility for fraud detection in a financial statement audit is still addressed in terms of materiality and reasonable assurance. The auditor is required to design audit tests to provide *reasonable assurance* that fraud would be detected in the audit if it were *material* to the company's financial statements as a whole.

On the other hand, a fraud audit or a forensic investigation is not intended to express opinion on a set of financial statements taken as a whole. Generally, in such situations a fraud is either alleged or discovered and the question is how far and widespread does it go? The purpose is, in other words, to find out the who, what, when, where, and how of the fraud, generally without regard to their materiality to the financial statements taken as a whole.

Brainstorming/Discussion among Engagement Personnel

Issue 3: Does this Section provide any requirements regarding who should attend the brainstorming session to discuss the potential for a material misstatement in the financial statements due to fraud?

No. Although brainstorming/discussion among engagement personnel is a required procedure, the fraud standard does not provide any requirements on who should attend such session. However, the fraud standard states that the brainstorming/discussion among engagement personnel ordinarily should involve key members of the audit team, including those responsible for planning, performing, and supervising key aspects of the audit, including the auditor with final responsibility for the audit. If a key member of the audit team is unable to attend the brainstorming session, pertinent issues discussed should be communicated to that person.

Issue 4: Does this Section require the brainstorming/discussion among engagement personnel to be conducted face-to-face?

No. This fraud standard does not require the brainstorming/discussion among engagement personnel to be conducted face-to-face. However, while such sessions can be conducted over the phone or via e-mail, they are generally more effective when they are conducted face-to-face.

Issue 5: How can the brainstorming/discussion among engagement personnel be made more productive, effective, and valuable?

The brainstorming/discussion among engagement personnel can be more productive, effective, and valuable if all participants have a similar level of understanding about the client's business, its industry, its management, and its current financial performance. Therefore, before the brainstorming session, auditors might find it beneficial to perform procedures such as the following:

- Review the most current financial information, interim financial statements of the current year, and prior year's financial statements.

- Review communications issued to the client about significant deficiencies, material weaknesses, or other management letter comment items.

- Review selected working papers from the prior year's audit, for example: summary of recorded and unrecorded audit differences, documentation about internal control, and legal letters.

- Review current information released by the client, for example: press releases and marketing literature.

- Review current information about the client's industry and common frauds in that industry.

Issue 6: Does this standard require the brainstorming/discussion among engagement personnel to include specific questions that should be addressed and answered?

No. The main objective of brainstorming is to identify "how and where the entity's financial statements might be susceptible to material misstatement due to fraud and to reinforce the importance of adopting an appropriate mindset of professional skepticism." In order to achieve this objective, it is beneficial to pose specific questions to generate practical ideas and discussion about areas that are susceptible to fraud. The following are examples of such questions:

- If you were in charge of accounts receivable or accounts payable, how could you embezzle funds and get away with it?

- What are some ways that the entity might underreport expenses?

- If you were in the shipping or receiving inventory area, how could you steal inventory and not get caught?
- If you wanted to get bank financing or increase the existing credit facility, how could you manipulate the financial statements to obtain a favorable response?

Issue 7: How does a sole practitioner with no staff comply with the requirement to conduct a brainstorming session under this fraud standard?

This fraud standard does not specifically address how a sole practitioner with no staff complies with the requirement to conduct a brainstorming session. However, AICPA Practice Aid, "Fraud Detection in a GAAS Audit: SAS No. 99 Implementation Guide," indicates that this lack of guidance does not mean that a sole practitioner is exempt from the spirit of what the standard requires. The Practice Aid also indicates that "introspection and reflection upon the guidance contained in this Practice Aid and the standard itself would be one way in which the sole practitioner could comply with the spirit of the requirement." The sole practitioner should document his or her thoughts in this regard.

Issue 8: Does this standard require documentation of the brainstorming session?

Yes. This standard requires the auditor to document the following items, at a minimum, regarding the brainstorming session:

1. How it occurred.
2. When it occurred.
3. The members who participated.
4. The subject matter discussed.

Assessment of the Risk of Material Misstatement Due to Fraud

Issue 9: What are "fraud risk factors" for purposes of this standard?

Fraud risk factors are events or conditions that indicate:

- Incentives or pressures to perpetrate fraud.
- Opportunities to carry out the fraud.
- Attitudes or rationalizations to justify a fraudulent action.

The guidance in this standard indicates that, although fraud risk factors do not necessarily indicate the existence of fraud, they are often present in circumstances where fraud exists.

Issue 10: Is there a specific model that the auditor can use to assess the risk of material misstatement due to fraud?

No. There is no specific model that the auditor can use to assess the risk of material misstatement due to fraud. The size, complexity, and ownership characteristics of the entity have a significant influence on the identification of relevant risk factors. Therefore, the auditor should use professional judgment when evaluating the significance of risk factors, individually or in the aggregate. Illustration 3 below includes a "Fraud Risk Assessment Form" that may be used in connection with such evaluation.

Issue 11: Is the auditor required to assess the risk of material misstatement due to fraud if he or she intends to assess control risk at the maximum?

Yes. The auditor should assess the risk of material misstatement due to fraud regardless of whether the auditor plans to assess inherent risk or control risk at the maximum. In addition, the auditor should inquire of management regarding its view regarding the risk of material misstatement due to fraud. The auditor's inquiry may include subsidiary locations, business segments, types of transactions, account balances, or financial statement categories where fraud risk factors may exist and how management may be addressing these risks.

Issue 12: Is the auditor always required to consider all the fraud risk factors listed in AU Section 316 when assessing the risk of material misstatement due to fraud?

No. The auditor should use professional judgment in considering the fraud risk factors that are applicable to each particular audit engagement. This standard, like most pronouncements, cannot and does not anticipate every circumstance that might apply across a wide variety of organizations. Therefore, if the auditor becomes aware of additional risk factors not identified in AU Section 316, those risk factors should be equally considered. Similarly, not all of the risk factors listed in AU Section 316 will necessarily apply in all circumstances.

Issue 13: What additional or specific audit procedures should the auditor apply to determine if fraud risk factors are present?

Many of the steps that are normally applied in the course of planning an audit and performing field work can serve as fraud risk evaluation procedures. Some of these procedures include:

- Reviewing minutes of board of directors.
- Reviewing legal invoices and corresponding with attorneys.
- Reviewing correspondence with regulatory agencies.
- Confirmations with third parties, for example, customers, vendors, banks.
- Researching public records, newspapers, or other published sources.
- Performing tests of controls.
- Performing analytical procedures.
- Inquiries of management and employees.

If the auditor identifies fraud risk factors present in specific audit areas (e.g., inventory, accounts receivable) the auditor should consider applying additional audit procedures as described in the section below "Common Fraud Schemes and Related Audit Procedures."

Issue 14: Is the auditor required to assess the risk of fraud at a specific level, such as "high," "moderate," or "low" under this standard?

No. The auditor is not required to quantify the fraud risk assessment, such as "high," "moderate," or "low." Rather, the auditor is required to assess the identified risks to determine where the entity is most vulnerable to material misstatements due to fraud, how the client is likely to conceal such material misstatements, and the types of fraud that are most likely to occur.

Inquiries and Communication Issues

Issue 15: Is the auditor required to communicate immaterial instances of fraud not involving senior management?

Yes. The auditor is required to bring to the attention of an appropriate level of management all matters involving fraud, even if the matter might be considered inconsequential (e.g., minor defalcation by an employee at a low level in the entity's organizational structure). In addition, in such situations, the auditor should:

- Evaluate the fraud implications to other aspects of the audit.

- Communicate the matter to those charged with governance if it meets the agreed-upon criteria established by the auditor and those charged with governance regarding the expected type and extent of auditor communications concerning fraud by lower-level personnel.

- Consider whether any fraud risk factors identified represent significant deficiencies that should be communicated as required by AU Section 325 (Communicating Internal Control Related Matters Identified in an Audit).

Issue 16: What type of communication should the auditor initiate when the fraud perpetrator is the owner-manager of a small business?

If the fraud perpetrator is the owner-manager of a small business, the auditor should communicate directly with the perpetrator and has little choice but to withdraw from the engagement. However, when considering withdrawal from an engagement, the auditor should consult with his or her legal counsel regarding the contemplated course of action and the nature of the communications with the client.

Issue 17: How should the auditor respond to a situation where he or she has concluded that it is unlikely that auditing procedures can be economically applied to sufficiently address the risk of fraud in an audit?

This would be a most extreme case and the auditor has little choice but to withdraw from the engagement. However, the auditor should always communicate the reasons for withdrawal to those charged with governance. The responsiveness of management and the board of directors in investigating and taking action in such sensitive scenarios will weigh heavily on the auditor's decision to withdraw. Also, it is good business practice for the auditor to consult with legal counsel when considering a withdrawal from an engagement due to fraud.

Issue 18: In connection with the requirement for the auditor to make inquiries of management about the risks of fraud, who specifically is "management"?

This fraud standard does not define "management" for purposes of the auditor's inquiries. However, as a practical matter, management includes the same individuals who sign the management representation letter. AU Section 333 (Management Representations) states that the letter should be signed by:

> . . . those members of management with overall responsibility for financial and operating matters whom the auditor believes are responsible for and knowledgeable about, directly or through others in the organization, the matters covered by the representations. Such members of management nor-

mally include the chief executive officer and chief financial officer or others with equivalent positions in the entity.

In addition, the auditor should consider making inquiries of the (1) controller and (2) the owner, in the case of an owner-managed business.

Effect of Fraud on Auditor's Reports

Issue 19: What is the effect on the auditor's report if the client refuses to revise financial statements due to misstatements resulting from fraud ?

The auditor should always insist that the financial statements be revised for misstatements resulting from fraud. If the client refuses to revise the financial statements, the auditor should express a qualified or adverse opinion. An adverse opinion would be appropriate if the auditor believes the financial statements are misleading and cannot, and should not, be relied on.

Issue 20: What is the effect on the auditor's report if the auditor is precluded from obtaining needed evidence considered necessary to evaluate the risk of fraud in the financial statements?

If the auditor is precluded from obtaining needed evidence considered necessary to evaluate the risk of fraud in the financial statements, the auditor should disclaim an opinion on the financial statements or withdraw from the engagement. If the auditor disclaims an opinion, a separate paragraph should be added to the auditor's report to explain the restriction. If the auditor decides to withdraw from the engagement, he or she should consider consulting with legal counsel.

Common Fraud Schemes and Related Audit Procedures

Issue 21: What are some common fraud schemes relating to cash and example audit procedures that may help detect material misstatements resulting from such frauds?

Common Fraud Schemes Relating to Cash

- Items are sold for cash but the sale is not recorded and cash is misappropriated.
- Checks received are deposited but not recorded; checks are written to employees for the same amount and also are not recorded.
- Customer remittances are misappropriated and collectible accounts are written off or otherwise credited.
- Lapping (cash receipts misappropriated and shortages concealed by delaying postings of cash receipts—for example, payment from customer A is diverted by the employee; payment from customer B is applied to customer A's account; customer C's payment is applied to customer B's account; and so on).
- Duplicate payments of invoices are made.
- Vendor invoices are altered and photocopied to conceal alteration; payment benefits third parties.
- Check signature or endorsement is forged.

- Checks are issued for benefit of employees or third parties, and payees are changed in the cash disbursements journal.
- Cash disbursements journal is overstated; the overstated amount is recorded and the difference is misappropriated.
- Kiting (exploiting the time required for a check to clear the bank, commonly referred to as the "float" period, to conceal shortage of cash).

Example Audit Procedures That May Be Performed in Response to Cash Fraud Schemes

- Perform a proof of cash, rather than a mere review of the client's bank reconciliation.
- Perform surprise cash counts.
- Compare payees with approved vendor lists.
- Compare sales price to the price list.
- Search for and investigate disbursements payable to "cash" or unusual sounding vendors.
- Search for and investigate non-payroll check disbursements made to employees and related parties.
- Expand tests of cancelled checks and scrutinize unusual payees, authorized signatures, endorsements, and amounts.
- Examine supporting documentation for held checks.
- Investigate void checks and analyze void transactions.
- Test interbank transfers.
- Obtain cutoff bank statements in addition to obtaining bank confirmations.
- Compare bank deposits to cash receipts, noting any time lags in deposit dates.
- Examine cancelled checks noting unusual patterns, for example, time lags between the disbursement date per books versus the date the check cleared the bank.
- Match sales returns to original sales.
- Confirm returned sales with customers.
- Perform tests of controls over cash receipts and cash disbursements.

Issue 22: What are some common fraud schemes relating to investments and example audit procedures that may help detect material misstatements resulting from such frauds?

Common Fraud Schemes Relating to Investments

- Investments made are not authorized.
- Investments are purchased but not recorded.
- Investments are recorded but not owned by the entity.
- Investments are sold but not recorded; investments are recorded as sold but not sold.
- Investments are valued incorrectly.

- Unwarranted investment losses are incurred or potential investment gains are not realized.

- Unauthorized pledging of investments occurs for the benefit of employees or third parties.

- Investment income or gains are misappropriated or diverted.

- Improper classification of marketable securities such as trading, available-for-sale, or held-to-maturity.

- Unreasonable or unsupportable fair value estimates.

Example Audit Procedures That May Be Performed in Response to Investment Fraud Schemes

- Consider using the work of a specialist in determining the fair value of the securities or derivatives, and scrutinize the specialist's qualifications, integrity, and results.

- Verify the fair value of securities using multiple brokers or third parties.

- Perform predictive tests of investment income and scrutinize amounts that look out of line with expectations.

- Evaluate the underlying assumptions used in valuing the securities or derivatives and scrutinize valuations that look out of line with expectations.

- Evaluate the legitimacy and financial viability of the custodian when confirming investments, including verifying the proper address of the custodian.

- Insist on inspecting original supporting documents rather than copies, e.g., original security certificates, brokers' statements.

- Expand tests of details and trace all transactions to the appropriate accounts.

- Trace sales proceeds and investment income to bank or brokerage statements.

- Trace cost of investment purchases to cancelled checks and bank statements.

- Review all journal entries related to investments and examine supporting documents.

- Scrutinize and investigate investments acquired in exchange for non-cash assets or company stock.

- Perform tests of controls over investments.

Issue 23: What are some common fraud schemes relating to accounts receivable and example audit procedures that may help detect material misstatements resulting from such frauds?

Common Fraud Schemes Relating to Accounts Receivable

- Goods are shipped or services are rendered but not billed; accounts receivable are not recorded.

- Billings are recorded, but goods are not shipped or services are not rendered at all or are not rendered until the following period.
- Customers are billed at incorrect amounts.
- Revenues are recorded in the wrong period to achieve desired earning trends, commissions, bonuses, or profit-sharing goals.
- Revenues are understated to reduce taxes, royalties, or rentals based on sales volume.
- Revenues are recognized while the customer's obligation to pay is contingent on future events.
- Orders from customers with poor credit are accepted and normal or favorable credit terms are granted.
- Orders are accepted at terms other than those established by management.
- Unwarranted credits or discounts are granted under a kickback arrangement.
- Accounts receivable are aged incorrectly, and potentially uncollectible amounts are not recognized.
- Accounts receivable are improperly written off to conceal misappropriation of cash receipts.
- Credits issued for returns or allowances are not earned or are not in accordance with company policy.
- Revenues are recognized while there is substantial continuing involvement by the company.
- Lapping (cash receipts misappropriated and shortages concealed by delaying postings of cash receipts—for example, payment from customer A is diverted by the employee; payment from customer B is applied to customer A's account; customer C's payment is applied to customer B's account; and so on).

Example Audit Procedures That May Be Performed in Response to Accounts Receivable Fraud Schemes

- Perform analytical procedures and predictive tests of key ratios.
- Review monthly sales levels and compare to monthly inventory levels.
- Review sales returns and inspect credit memos.
- Confirm account activity (not just the balance) and the terms of unusual arrangements directly with customers.
- Confirm returned sales with customers.
- Confirm amounts written off that appear unusual, such as writeoffs of balances due from continuing customers.
- Identify and test large, complex, or unusual transactions, particularly those occurring around the end of the year.
- Investigate material cash payments to customers and inquire about the nature of such payments.

- Examine supporting documents for entries made to the allowance for doubtful accounts.
- Examine supporting documents for significant reconciling items appearing in the accounts receivable reconciliation.
- Match sales returns to original sales. Compare sales price to list price.
- Ascertain that shipped merchandise actually arrived at the customer's location and that the merchandise was not shipped to a warehouse or location controlled by the client.
- Ascertain that shipping documents and invoices are pre-numbered sequentially and accounted for.
- Examine original documents for sales invoices and shipping documents and be alert for possible alterations.
- Telephone customers directly and confirm items such as: unusual payment terms, sales returns, credit memos, side agreements, merchandise receipt date, or other concerns.
- Review customer complaints and look for unusual trends.
- Consider circumstances where salespeople are trying to meet or exceed sales goals in order to achieve quotas or increase their commissions or bonuses.
- Agree daily cash receipts detail to the bank statements and investigate unusual lags.
- Perform a proof of cash.

NOTE: Also, see Issue 32 below for common types of revenue recognition fraud and related example audit procedures that may be performed.

Issue 24: What are some common fraud schemes relating to inventory and example audit procedures that may help detect material misstatements resulting from such frauds?

Common Fraud Schemes Relating to Inventory

- Including nonexistent inventory items in physical count (e.g., empty boxes).
- Transfers from raw materials or work in process are improperly recorded or recorded in the wrong period.
- Unauthorized adjustment of inventory records is made to conceal misappropriation of assets.
- Inventory records are manipulated to improve performance picture.
- Increasing or otherwise altering the inventory counts for those items the auditor did not test count.
- Programming the computer to produce fraudulent physical quantity tabulations or priced inventory listings.

- Manipulating the inventory counts/compilations for locations not visited by the auditor.
- Double-counting inventory in transit between locations.
- Physically moving inventory and counting it at two locations.
- Including in inventory merchandise recorded as sold but not yet shipped to a customer.
- Arranging for false confirmations of inventory held by others.
- Including inventory receipts for which corresponding payables have not been recorded.
- Overstating the stage of completion of work-in-process.
- Manipulating the "rollforward" of an inventory taken before the financial statement date.
- Scrap sales not reported.
- Physical loss of, or deterioration in, inventory occurs but is not accounted for.

Example Audit Procedures That May Be Performed in Response to Inventory Fraud Schemes

- Observe all inventory locations simultaneously.
- Account for all inventory tags used during the physical count and obtain copies of all inventory count sheets or tags before leaving the physical inventory sites.
- Open containers and match contents to description, noting salability.
- Perform extensive test counts during the physical inventory observation.
- Confirm inventories at locations outside the entity.
- Scrutinize any material book to physical inventory adjustments and examine supporting documents.
- Examine consignment agreements and determine proper accounting method.
- Examine production records for indications of stage of completion.
- Perform analytical procedures and predictive tests of key ratios.
- Expand testing of receiving and shipping cutoff.
- Examine supporting documents for significant reconciling items appearing in the inventory account reconciliations.
- Examine individual entries in the general ledger inventory account to search for expenses or other items that are improperly charged to inventory.
- Examine journal entries made to the inventory accounts subsequent to year-end.
- Compare carrying amounts to recent sales amounts.
- Confirm vendors' invoices and unusual terms.
- Test direct labor rates and the calculation of overhead rates.

- Analyze scrap sales.
- Analyze inventory shortages by location or product type.
- Look for evidence of bulk sales at steep discounts which could indicate a declining value for the products.
- Perform tests of controls over inventory.

Issue 25: What are some common fraud schemes relating to property and equipment and example audit procedures that may help detect material misstatements resulting from such frauds?

Common Fraud Schemes Relating to Property and Equipment

- Purchases of property are not recorded.
- Employees are able to conceal unauthorized purchases for their own benefit.
- Property remains in the accounting records after disposal.
- Sales of property are not recorded, and proceeds are misappropriated.
- Wrong lives or residual values are assigned to property, resulting in miscalculation of depreciation.
- Property accounts include inventory manufacturing costs or research and development costs.
- Improper capitalization of costs that should have been expensed.
- Failure to recognize impairment losses on long-lived assets.
- Property is used for personal benefit rather than company business.
- Recognizing assets that the company does not have title to.
- Unreasonable or unsupportable fair value estimates.
- Improper expensing of capital items to obtain a tax benefit.

Example Audit Procedures That May Be Performed in Response to Property and Equipment Fraud Schemes

- Physically inspect significant assets and major additions, and agree serial numbers with invoices or other supporting documents.
- Carefully scrutinize appraisals and engineering reports that seem out of line with reasonable expectations, and challenge the underlying assumptions.
- When vouching fixed asset additions, accept only original invoices, purchase orders, receiving reports, or similar supporting documentation.
- Confirm the terms of significant property additions with the counterparty to the transaction.
- Review journal entries made to property accounts.
- For self-constructed assets, examine supporting documents for labor, materials, capitalized interest, and other direct and indirect costs included in the capitalized asset.
- Examine miscellaneous cash receipts records and other income accounts for evidence of proceeds from fixed asset disposals.

- Examine supporting documents for significant reconciling items appearing in the reconciliation between the detail records and the general ledger.
- Review capital expenditures plan and compare to minutes of board meetings for approval.
- Use the work of a specialist for material asset valuations and indications of impairment.
- Perform extensive review of depreciation calculations, depreciation methods, estimated useful lives, and residual values.
- Ascertain that the entity has title to reported assets by reviewing relevant legal documents or public records.

Issue 26: What are some common fraud schemes relating to other assets and example audit procedures that may help detect material misstatements resulting from such frauds?

Common Fraud Schemes Relating to Other Assets

- Misclassifications conceal unauthorized expenditures for the benefit of employees.
- Amortization period exceeds the period of benefit.
- Assets remain on the books after disposal or expiration of the benefit period.
- Costs that should be charged to expense are deferred.
- Intangible assets are carried in excess of value.
- Sales of other assets are not recorded; proceeds are misappropriated.
- Failure to recognize impairment losses on long-lived assets.
- Other assets are used for personal benefit rather than company business.
- Recognizing assets that the company does not have title to.
- Using fair value estimates that are unreasonable or unsupportable.

Example Audit Procedures That May Be Performed in Response to Other Assets Fraud Schemes

- Scrutinize documentation supporting amounts capitalized.
- Vouch and trace transactions to original documents (not copies), including examination of cancelled checks and bank statements.
- Confirm significant deposits and assets held by others.
- Obtain a list of the detail of all suspense accounts and scrutinize activity for unusual or large items.
- Review journal entries made to the general ledger accounts.
- Test current-period amortization and evaluate the reasonableness of carrying amounts, amortization periods, and methods.
- Use the work of a specialist for material asset valuations and indications of impairment.
- Confirm the terms of significant intangibles additions with the counterparty to the transaction.

Issue 27: What are some common fraud schemes relating to accounts payable and example audit procedures that may help detect material misstatements resulting from such frauds?

Common Fraud Schemes Relating to Accounts Payable

- Unauthorized purchases are incurred.
- Purchases are recorded but goods or services are not received.
- Liability is incurred but not recorded.
- Purchase amount is recorded incorrectly.
- Purchase is charged to wrong account or is recorded in wrong period.
- Purchases at other than favorable terms are made to facilitate side deals for the personal benefit of employees.
- Purchases are misclassified to conceal lack of authorization.
- Improper deferrals of income are recorded in order to shift income to future periods.
- Purchase discounts are taken but not recorded and amounts of discounts are misappropriated.
- Employees conceal unauthorized purchases for their own benefit.
- Contingent liability is understated or not recorded.
- Kickbacks paid by vendors to the company's purchasing agent.

Example Audit Procedures That May Be Performed in Response to Accounts Payable Fraud Schemes

- Send blank confirmations to vendors requesting them to furnish information about all outstanding invoices and other pertinent items such as payment terms, payment histories, etc. Include new vendors and accounts with small or zero balances.
- Confirm collectibility of debit memos with vendors.
- Match vendor names and addresses per invoices with master vendor list.
- Search for unusual or large year-end transactions and adjustments, for example, transactions not containing normal processing initials, not going through normal processes, or not having normal supporting documentation.
- Review vendor files for unusual items, such as manual and not customized forms; different delivery addresses; and vendors that have multiple addresses.
- Examine disbursements made for items that do not require delivery of goods.
- Examine voided checks.
- Examine supporting documents for payments for amounts just under the threshold required for approval.

- Examine original canceled checks and scrutinize for items such as discrepancies between cancelled checks, invoices, and the disbursements journal; multiple endorsements; the identity of the endorsees.
- Examine supporting documents for significant reconciling items appearing in the reconciliation between the aging and the general ledger.
- Expand testing of receiving cutoff.
- Perform analytical procedures and predictive tests of key ratios.
- Search public records (e.g., UCC filings).
- Perform tests of controls over accounts payable.

Issue 28: What are some common fraud schemes relating to payroll and example audit procedures that may help detect material misstatements resulting from such frauds?

Common Fraud Schemes Relating to Payroll

- Unauthorized work or work not performed is accrued.
- Accrual of employee benefits (e.g., vacation pay, sick leave) is recorded but not earned.
- Fictitious employees ("ghost employees") are on the payroll.
- Employees' earnings are overaccrued or underaccrued because of the use of improper rates or computation errors.
- Payroll costs, expenses, or related liabilities are misclassified.
- Payroll is recorded in period paid rather than in period earned.
- Time cards or reports are padded.
- Terminated employees remaining on payroll.

Example Audit Procedures That May Be Performed in Response to Payroll Fraud Schemes

- Observe payroll distributions.
- Follow up on payroll checks that have not been cashed.
- Scrutinize payroll records for employees with little or no deductions.
- Review personnel files for compensation rates.
- Test payroll calculations and deductions.
- Confirm amounts paid to employees who are at remote locations working without direct supervision.
- Examine payroll disbursements subsequent to year-end and compare with accrued payroll at the balance sheet date.
- Scrutinize the payroll registers and the payroll check registers for unusual items such as: names of former employees; duplicate names, duplicate addresses; unusual pay rates; unusual number of hours worked; and same social security numbers for two different people.
- Compare list of current employees in the personnel department to the payroll journal.

- Scrutinize payroll records for unusual pay rates or number of hours worked.
- Examine cancelled payroll checks for suspected fictitious employees.
- Perform tests of controls over payroll transactions.

Issue 29: What are some common fraud schemes relating to income taxes and example audit procedures that may help detect material misstatements resulting from such frauds?

Common Fraud Schemes Relating to Income Taxes

- Required estimated tax payments are not made.
- Provision for income taxes or related tax liability is not reflected in the accounting records or is reflected at incorrect amounts.
- Incorrect tax returns are filed; subsequent audits by taxing authorities result in material unrecorded liabilities.
- Tax expense is intentionally misstated to enhance results of operations or financial position.
- A valuation allowance is not established.

Example Audit Procedures That May Be Performed in Response to Income Taxes Fraud Schemes

- Confirm tax payments and tax refunds directly with taxing authorities.
- Examine supporting documents for significant entries in the income tax related accounts.
- Examine supporting documents to determine the adequacy of the valuation allowance.
- Determine the latest years that tax returns have been examined by taxing authorities and any periods contested, and examine reports prepared by revenue agents.

Issue 30: What are some common fraud schemes relating to debt obligations and example audit procedures that may help detect material misstatements resulting from such frauds?

Common Fraud Schemes Relating to Debt Obligations

- Unauthorized borrowing.
- Pledged assets or collateral are not identified and disclosed; unauthorized pledging of assets exists.
- Violations of debt covenants or lease agreements are not reported to lenders or lessors.
- Capital leases are recorded as operating leases or vice versa.
- Interest expense is recorded in the wrong period or at the wrong amount, is not recorded, or is misclassified.
- Debt proceeds are used for other than business purposes.
- Loan proceeds are recorded as sales.
- Debt is recorded as equity.

- Entire loan payments are charged to either principal or interest.

Example Audit Procedures That May Be Performed in Response to Debt Obligations Fraud Schemes

- Perform search of public records (e.g., UCC filings).
- Vouch and trace loan proceeds and debt payments.
- Contact lenders and creditors.
- Insist on inspecting original supporting documents rather than copies.
- Agree detail of debt terms to authorization in minutes of board meetings.
- Confirm compliance with loan covenants directly with lenders.

Issue 31: What are some common fraud schemes relating to equity and example audit procedures that may help detect material misstatements resulting from such frauds?

Common Fraud Schemes Relating to Equity

- Sale of shares is not authorized and violates loan covenants or other legal requirements.
- Sale of shares is recorded incorrectly or not recorded at all.
- Stock options exercised are not authorized or not in accordance with the terms of options granted.
- Dividends paid violate restrictive documents or other legal requirements.
- Dividends are paid to wrong parties or at incorrect amounts.
- Proceeds from sale of shares are misappropriated.
- Stock is pledged without authorization.
- Receivables from sale of stock are not recognized.

Example Audit Procedures That May Be Performed in Response to Equity Fraud Schemes

- Account for and vouch all proceeds from stock issues.
- Confirm terms of equity arrangements and shares held directly with shareholders.
- Confirm funds received from and dividends paid to shareholders.
- Confirm with shareholders whether there are any side agreements.
- Scrutinize transactions and determine whether the terms and substance of the arrangements indicate that the proceeds should be recorded as debt, rather than equity.
- Request confirmation of stock issued from the registrar and transfer agent.

Issue 32: What are some common fraud schemes relating to revenue recognition and example audit procedures that may help detect material misstatements resulting from such frauds?

Common Fraud Schemes Relating to Revenue Recognition

- Recording sales to nonexistent customers.

- Recording phony sales to legitimate customers.
- Shipping goods to a warehouse that is undisclosed to the auditor, and creating a shipping document to indicate that the goods were shipped to a customer.
- Entering into "bill-and-hold" sales transactions—a customer agrees to purchase the goods but the seller retains physical possession until the customer requests shipment to designated locations.
- Recognizing revenue when right of return exists beyond the normal sales return privileges.
- Recording sales upon shipment of a product to customers who have been given a free tryout period after which the customer can return the product with no obligation.
- Recognizing sales when customers have unilateral cancellation or termination provisions.
- Recognizing sales in which evidence indicates the customer's obligation to pay for the product is contingent on resale to another party or on receipt of financing from another party.
- Purchase orders are recorded as completed sales.
- Holding the books open until after the shipment has occurred to record revenue in the desired (improper) period.
- Side agreements are used to alter the terms and conditions of sales in order to entice customers to accept delivery of the goods (e.g., relieving the customer of some of the risks and rewards of ownership).
- "Channel stuffing"—A practice used to boost sales by inducing distributors to buy substantially more inventory than they can resell and is usually accompanied by side agreements, such as provisions for the return of unsold merchandise.
- Recording sales of the same inventory back and forth among affiliated entities or related parties.
- Sales of merchandise that are shipped in advance of the scheduled shipment date without evidence of the customer's agreement or consent.
- Pre-invoicing of goods that are in the process of being assembled or invoicing prior to, or in the absence of, actual shipments.
- Altered dates on contracts or shipping documents.

Example Audit Procedures That May Be Performed in Response to Revenue Recognition Fraud Schemes

- Perform analytical procedures and predictive tests of key ratios.
- Confirm with customers relevant contract terms and the absence of side agreements, such as (1) acceptance criteria; (2) delivery and payment terms; (3) the absence of future or continuing vendor obligations; (4) the right to return the product; (5) guaranteed resale amounts; and (6) cancellation or refund provisions.

- Inquire of the entity's personnel (e.g., sales and marketing personnel or in-house legal counsel) about sales or shipments near year-end and whether they are aware of any unusual terms or conditions in connection with these transactions.

- Be physically present at the client's location at year-end to observe the shipment of goods or the processing of returned goods and perform extended sales and inventory cutoff procedures.

- When revenue transactions are electronically initiated, processed, and recorded, test controls to determine whether they provide assurance that recorded revenue transactions occurred and are properly recorded.

- Review monthly sales levels and compare to monthly inventory levels.

- Review sales returns and inspect credit memos.

- Confirm directly with customers: account activity (not just the balance); sales returns; credit memos; merchandise receipt date; and amounts written off that appear unusual, such as write-offs of balances due from continuing customers.

- Identify and test large, complex, or unusual transactions, particularly those occurring around the end of the year.

- Investigate material cash payments to customers and inquire about the nature of such payments.

- Examine supporting documents for the following:
  - Entries made to the sales, accounts receivables, and allowance for doubtful accounts.
  - Significant reconciling items between the accounts receivable subsidiary ledger and the general ledger.
  - Significant reconciling items between the sales journal and the general ledger.
  - Reversals of sales or large returns in the period subsequent to the balance sheet date.

- Match sales returns to original sales.

- Compare sales price to the price list.

- Ascertain that shipped merchandise actually arrived at the customer's location and that the merchandise was not shipped to a warehouse or location controlled by the client.

- Examine original documents for sales invoices and shipping documents and be alert for possible alterations.

- Ascertain that shipping documents and invoices are pre-numbered sequentially and accounted for.

- Review customer complaints and look for unusual trends.

- Consider circumstances where salespeople are trying to meet or exceed sales goals in order to achieve quotas or increase their commissions or bonuses.

- Compare details of units shipped with revenues and production records and consider whether revenues are reasonable compared to levels of production and average sales price.

- Compare the number of weeks of inventory in distribution channels with prior periods for unusual increases that may indicate channel stuffing.

- Analyze and review deferred revenue accounts for propriety and reasonableness of deferral.

- Agree daily cash receipts detail to the bank statements and investigate unusual lags.

NOTE: See Issue 23 above for common types of accounts receivable fraud and related example audit procedures that may be performed.

ILLUSTRATIONS AND PRACTICE AIDS

ILLUSTRATION 1—FRAUD RISK FACTORS RELATING TO MISSTATEMENTS ARISING FROM FRAUDULENT FINANCIAL REPORTING

The following are examples of fraud risk factors relating to misstatements arising from fraudulent financial reporting that are included in AU Section 316.

Incentives/Pressures

- Financial stability or profitability is threatened by economic, industry, or entity operating conditions, such as (or as indicated by):

  — High degree of competition or market saturation, accompanied by declining margins.

  — High vulnerability to rapid changes, such as changes in technology, product obsolescence, or interest rates.

  — Significant declines in customer demand and increasing business failures in either the industry or overall economy.

  — Operating losses making the threat of bankruptcy, foreclosure, or hostile takeover imminent.

  — Recurring negative cash flows from operations or an inability to generate cash flows from operations while reporting earnings and earnings growth.

  — Rapid growth or unusual profitability, especially compared to that of other companies in the same industry.

  — New accounting, statutory, or regulatory requirements.

- Excessive pressure exists for management to meet the requirements or expectations of third parties due to the following:

  — Profitability or trend level expectations of investment analysts, institutional investors, significant creditors, or other external parties (particularly expectations that are unduly aggressive or unrealistic), including expectations created by management in, for example, overly optimistic press releases or annual report messages.

— Need to obtain additional debt or equity financing to stay competitive, including financing of major research and development or capital expenditures.

— Marginal ability to meet exchange listing requirements or debt repayment or other debt covenant requirements.

— Perceived or real adverse effects of reporting poor financial results on significant pending transactions, such as business combinations or contract awards.

- Information available indicates that management or the board of directors' personal financial situation is threatened by the entity's financial performance arising from the following:

— Significant financial interests in the entity.

— Significant portions of their compensation (for example, bonuses, stock options, and earn-out arrangements) being contingent upon achieving aggressive targets for stock price, operating results, financial position, or cash flow.

— Personal guarantees of debts of the entity.

- There is excessive pressure on management or operating personnel to meet financial targets set up by the board of directors or management, including sales or profitability incentive goals.

Opportunities

- The nature of the industry or the entity's operations provides opportunities to engage in fraudulent financial reporting that can arise from the following:

— Significant related-party transactions not in the ordinary course of business or with related entities not audited or audited by another firm.

— A strong financial presence or ability to dominate a certain industry sector that allows the entity to dictate terms or conditions to suppliers or customers that may result in inappropriate or non-arm's-length transactions.

— Assets, liabilities, revenues, or expenses based on significant estimates that involve subjective judgments or uncertainties that are difficult to corroborate.

— Significant, unusual, or highly complex transactions, especially those close to period end that pose difficult "substance over form" questions.

— Significant operations located or conducted across international borders in jurisdictions where differing business environments and cultures exist.

— Significant bank accounts or subsidiary or branch operations in tax-haven jurisdictions for which there appears to be no clear business justification.

- There is ineffective monitoring of management as a result of the following:
  - — Domination of management by a single person or small group (in a nonowner-managed business) without compensating controls.
  - — Ineffective oversight over the financial reporting process and internal control by those charged with governance.
- There is a complex or unstable organizational structure, as evidenced by the following:
  - — Difficulty in determining the organization or individuals that have controlling interest in the entity.
  - — Overly complex organizational structure involving unusual legal entities or managerial lines of authority.
  - — High turnover of senior management, counsel, or board members.
- Internal control components are deficient as a result of the following:
  - — Inadequate monitoring of controls, including automated controls and controls over interim financial reporting (where external reporting is required).
  - — High turnover rates or employment of ineffective accounting, internal audit, or information technology staff.
  - — Ineffective accounting and information systems, including situations involving significant deficiencies.

Attitudes/Rationalizations

- Ineffective communication, implementation, support, or enforcement of the entity's values or ethical standards by management or the communication of inappropriate values or ethical standards.
- Nonfinancial management's excessive participation in or preoccupation with the selection of accounting principles or the determination of significant estimates.
- Known history of violations of securities laws or other laws and regulations, or claims against the entity, its senior management, or board members alleging fraud or violations of laws and regulations.
- Excessive interest by management in maintaining or increasing the entity's stock price or earnings trend.
- A practice by management of committing to analysts, creditors, and other third parties to achieve aggressive or unrealistic forecasts.
- Management failing to correct known significant deficiencies on a timely basis.
- An interest by management in employing inappropriate means to minimize reported earnings for tax-motivated reasons.
- Recurring attempts by management to justify marginal or inappropriate accounting on the basis of materiality.

- The relationship between management and the current or predecessor auditor is strained, as exhibited by the following:
  - Frequent disputes with the current or predecessor auditor on accounting, auditing, or reporting matters.
  - Unreasonable demands on the auditor, such as unreasonable time constraints regarding the completion of the audit or the issuance of the auditor's report.
  - Formal or informal restrictions on the auditor that inappropriately limit access to people or information or the ability to communicate effectively with those charged with governance.
  - Domineering management behavior in dealing with the auditor, especially involving attempts to influence the scope of the auditor's work or the selection or continuance of personnel assigned to or consulted on the audit engagement.

ILLUSTRATION 2—FRAUD RISK FACTORS RELATING TO MISSTATEMENTS ARISING FROM MISAPPROPRIATION OF ASSETS

The following are examples of fraud risk factors relating to misstatements arising from misappropriation of assets that are included in AU Section 316.

Incentives/Pressures

- Personal financial obligations may create pressure on management or employees with access to cash or other assets susceptible to theft to misappropriate those assets.
- Adverse relationships between the entity and employees with access to cash or other assets susceptible to theft may motivate those employees to misappropriate those assets. For example, adverse relationships may be created by the following:
  - Known or anticipated future employee layoffs.
  - Recent or anticipated changes to employee compensation or benefit plans.
  - Promotions, compensation, or other rewards inconsistent with expectations.

Opportunities

- Certain characteristics or circumstances may increase the susceptibility of assets to misappropriation. For example, opportunities to misappropriate assets increase when there are the following:
  - Large amounts of cash on hand or processed.
  - Inventory items that are small in size, of high value, or in high demand.
  - Easily convertible assets, such as bearer bonds, diamonds, or computer chips.
  - Fixed assets that are small in size, marketable, or lacking observable identification of ownership.

- Inadequate internal control over assets may increase the susceptibility of misappropriation of those assets. For example, misappropriation of assets may occur because there is the following:

  — Inadequate segregation of duties or independent checks.

  — Inadequate management oversight of employees responsible for assets, for example, inadequate supervision or monitoring of remote locations.

  — Inadequate job applicant screening of employees with access to assets.

  — Inadequate recordkeeping with respect to assets.

  — Inadequate system of authorization and approval of transactions (for example, in purchasing).

  — Inadequate physical safeguards over cash, investments, inventory, or fixed assets.

  — Lack of complete and timely reconciliations of assets.

  — Lack of timely and appropriate documentation of transactions, for example, credits for merchandise returns.

  — Lack of mandatory vacations for employees performing key control functions.

  — Inadequate management understanding of information technology, which enables information technology employees to perpetrate a misappropriation.

  — Inadequate access controls over automated records, including controls over and review of computer systems event logs.

Attitudes/Rationalizations

- Disregard for the need for monitoring or reducing risks related to misappropriations of assets.

- Disregard for internal control over misappropriation of assets by overriding existing controls or by failing to correct known internal control deficiencies.

- Behavior indicating displeasure or dissatisfaction with the company or its treatment of the employee.

- Changes in behavior or lifestyle that may indicate assets have been misappropriated.

ILLUSTRATION 3—FRAUD RISK ASSESSMENT FORM

PRACTICE POINT: AU Section 316 does not specify how the fraud risk assessment should be documented. Therefore, documentation may take the form of a checklist, a memo, or combination of both, or some other form.

I. **Brainstorming among Audit Team Members about the Risks of Fraud**

1. Indicate the date(s) the discussion occurred.

_____

_____

_____

2. Indicate the team members who participated (Note: The discussion should always include the person with final responsibility for the audit and, ordinarily, other key members of the audit team, for example, managers and seniors).

Name	Title
_____	_____
_____	_____
_____	_____
_____	_____

3. Indicate how the discussion occurred (e.g., face-to-face meeting, conference call).

_____

_____

_____

4. Describe the subject matter discussed, including:

   a. How and where the financial statements might be materially misstated due to fraud.

   b. How management could perpetrate and conceal fraudulent financial reporting (e.g., capitalizing certain operating expenses in fixed assets).

   c. How the perpetrators could misappropriate company assets.

   d. Known external and internal factors affecting the entity that might (1) create incentives/pressures to commit fraud, (2) provide the opportunity for fraud to take place, and (3) reveal attitudes or rationalizations about why fraud is acceptable behavior.

   e. The risk of management override of controls.

   f. How best to respond to these fraud risks through the design of audit procedures.

   g. The need for engagement personnel to emphasize professional skepticism, to critically assess audit evidence, and to consult with other team members or experts in the firm where appropriate.

_____

_____

_____

II. Inquiries about the Risks of Fraud

1. Inquire of the company's management about whether it is aware of (1) actual or suspected fraud, or (2) any allegations of fraud (e.g., communications from employees or others). Describe.

   _____

   _____

   _____

2. Inquire of the company's management about its understanding of the risks of fraud within the company, including any specific risks identified or areas where fraud is likely to occur. Describe.

   _____

   _____

   _____

3. Inquire of the company's management about the programs and controls that it has established to mitigate fraud risks and how it monitors such programs and controls. Describe.

   _____

   _____

   _____

4. Inquire of the company's management about the nature and extent of monitoring of operating locations or business segments, where applicable, and whether there are particular units for which a risk of fraud may be more likely to exist. Describe.

   _____

   _____

   _____

5. Inquire of the company's management about whether and how it communicates to employees its views on business practices and ethical behavior. Describe.

   _____

   _____

   _____

6. Inquire of the company's management about whether it has reported to those charged with governance (or the audit committee or its equivalent) on how the entity's internal control monitors the risks of material fraud. Describe.

   _____

   _____

   _____

7. Inquire of those charged with governance (or the audit committee or at least its chair) about (1) their views about the risks of fraud, (2) whether they have knowledge of any actual fraud or suspected

fraud, and (3) how they exercise their oversight of the entity's assessment of risks of fraud and the programs and controls the entity has adopted to mitigate those risks. Describe.

_____

_____

_____

8. Where applicable, inquire of the internal audit personnel about: (1) their views of the risks of fraud, (2) any procedures they performed to identify or detect fraud during the period under audit, (3) management's response to the findings, and (4) whether they have knowledge of any actual fraud or suspected fraud. Describe.

_____

_____

_____

9. Inquire of others within the company (e.g., operating personnel not directly involved in the financial reporting process and employees with different levels of authority) about any actual fraud or suspected fraud. Describe.

_____

_____

_____

10. Inquire of individuals involved in the financial reporting process about inappropriate or unusual activity relating to the processing of journal entries and other adjustments. Describe.

_____

_____

_____

III. **Consideration of Fraud Risk Factors Relating to Fraudulent Financial Reporting**

	Yes	No	N/A
Incentives/Pressures			
1. Is the company experiencing a high degree of competition or market saturation, accompanied by declining margins?	___	___	___
2. Is the company highly vulnerable to rapid changes, such as changes in technology, product obsolescence, or interest rates?	___	___	___
3. Is the company's industry, or overall economy, experiencing significant declines in customer demand and increasing business failures?	___	___	___
4. Is the company having operating losses that make the threat of bankruptcy, foreclosure, or hostile takeover imminent?	___	___	___

	Yes	No	N/A

5. Is the company experiencing recurring negative cash flows, or is unable to generate cash flows, from operations while reporting earnings and earnings growth? _____ _____ _____

6. Has the company been experiencing unusually rapid growth or profitability, especially compared to that of other companies in the same industry? _____ _____ _____

7. Are there new accounting, statutory, or regulatory requirements that could impair the financial stability or profitability of the company? _____ _____ _____

8. Is management facing excessive pressure to meet the requirements or expectations of third parties due to factors such as the following:

   a. Profitability or trend level expectations of investment analysts, institutional investors, significant creditors, or other external parties (particularly expectations that are unduly aggressive or unrealistic), including expectations created by management in overly optimistic press releases or annual report messages? _____ _____ _____

   b. Need to obtain additional debt or equity financing to stay competitive, including financing of major research and development or capital expenditures? _____ _____ _____

   c. Marginal ability to meet exchange listing requirements or debt repayment or other debt covenant requirements? _____ _____ _____

   d. Perceived or real adverse effects of reporting poor financial results on significant pending transactions, such as business combinations or contract awards? _____ _____ _____

9. Are there any indications that management or the board of directors' personal financial situation is threatened by the company's financial performance arising from factors such as the following:

   a. Significant financial interests in the company? _____ _____ _____

   b. Significant portions of their compensation (e.g., bonuses, stock options, and earn-out arrangements) being contingent upon achieving aggressive targets for stock price, operating results, financial position, or cash flow? _____ _____ _____

   c. Personal guarantees of debts of the entity? _____ _____ _____

10. Is there excessive pressure on management or operating personnel to meet financial targets set up by the board of directors or management, including sales or profitability incentive goals? _____ _____ _____

11. Other fraud risk factors that were considered:

	Yes	No	N/A

12. Document whether events or conditions exist that indicate *incentives/pressures* to perpetrate fraud and intentionally misstate the entity's financial statements.

	Yes	No	N/A

Opportunities

1. Are there significant related-party transactions not in the ordinary course of business or with related entities not audited or audited by another firm?

2. Does the company have a strong financial presence or the ability to dominate a certain industry sector that allows it to dictate terms or conditions to suppliers or customers that may result in inappropriate or non-arm's-length transactions?

3. Are the company's assets, liabilities, revenues, or expenses based on significant estimates that involve subjective judgments or uncertainties that are difficult to corroborate?

4. Are there significant, unusual, or highly complex transactions, especially those close to year-end, that pose difficult "substance over form" questions?

5. Does the company have significant operations located or conducted across international borders in jurisdictions where differing business environments and cultures exist?

6. Does the company have significant bank accounts or subsidiary or branch operations in tax-haven jurisdictions for which there appears to be no clear business justification?

7. Is there ineffective monitoring of management as a result of the following:

   a. Domination of management by a single person or small group (in a nonowner-managed business) without compensating controls?

   b. Ineffective oversight over the financial reporting process and internal control by those charged with governance?

8. Does the company have a complex or unstable organizational structure, as evidenced by the following:

	Yes	No	N/A

a. Difficulty in determining the organization or individuals that have controlling interest in the entity? _____ _____ _____

b. Overly complex organizational structure involving unusual legal entities or managerial lines of authority? _____ _____ _____

c. High turnover of senior management, counsel, or board members? _____ _____ _____

9. Are the company's internal control components deficient as a result of:

a. Inadequate monitoring of controls, including automated controls and controls over interim financial reporting (where external reporting is required)? _____ _____ _____

b. High turnover rates or employment of ineffective accounting, internal audit, or information technology staff? _____ _____ _____

c. Ineffective accounting and information systems, including situations involving significant deficiencies? _____ _____

10. Other fraud risk factors that were considered:

_____

_____

_____

11. Document whether events or conditions exist that indicate *opportunities* to carry out the fraud and intentionally misstate the entity's financial statements.

_____

_____

_____

	Yes	No	N/A

Attitudes/Rationalizations

1. Does management fail to effectively communicate, implement, support, or enforce the company's values or ethical standards, or does it communicate inappropriate values or ethical standards? _____ _____ _____

2. Does nonfinancial management excessively participate in, or display an excessive preoccupation with, the selection of accounting principles or the determination of significant estimates? _____ _____ _____

3. Is there a known history of violations of securities laws or other laws and regulations, or claims against the company, its senior management, or board members alleging fraud or violations of laws and regulations? _____ _____ _____

	Yes	No	N/A

4. Is there excessive interest by management in maintaining or increasing the company's stock price or earnings trend?   _____ _____ _____

5. Does management have a tendency to commit to analysts, creditors, and other third parties to achieve aggressive or unrealistic forecasts?   _____ _____ _____

6. Has management failed to correct known significant deficiencies on a timely basis?   _____ _____ _____

7. Does management pursue inappropriate means to minimize reported earnings for tax-motivated reasons?   _____ _____ _____

8. Are there recurring attempts by management to justify marginal or inappropriate accounting on the basis of materiality?   _____ _____ _____

9. Does management have frequent disputes with its auditors on accounting, auditing, or reporting matters?   _____ _____ _____

10. Does management place unreasonable demands on the auditor, such as unreasonable time constraints regarding the completion of the audit or the issuance of the auditor's report?   _____ _____ _____

11. Does management impose formal or informal restrictions on the auditor that inappropriately limit access to people or information or the ability to communicate effectively with those charged with governance?   _____ _____ _____

12. Does management exhibit domineering behavior in dealing with the auditor, especially involving attempts to influence the scope of the auditor's work or the selection or continuance of personnel assigned to or consulted on the audit engagement?   _____ _____ _____

13. Other fraud risk factors that were considered:

_____

_____

_____

14. Document whether events or conditions exist that indicate *attitudes/ rationalizations* to justify the fraud and intentionally misstate the entity's financial statements.

_____

_____

_____

IV. Consideration of Fraud Risk Factors Relating to Misappropriation of Assets

	Yes	No	N/A

Incentives/Pressures

1. Are there any indications that management or employees with access to cash or other assets susceptible to theft have personal financial obligations that may create pressure to misappropriate assets? ___ ___ ___

2. Are there any conditions that may create adverse relationships between the company and employees with access to cash or other assets susceptible to theft, such as the following:

   a. Known or anticipated future employee layoffs? ___ ___ ___

   b. Recent or anticipated changes to employee compensation or benefit plans? ___ ___ ___

   c. Promotions, compensation, or other rewards inconsistent with expectations? ___ ___ ___

3. Other fraud risk factors that were considered:

   _____

   _____

   _____

4. Document whether events or conditions exist that indicate *incentives/pressures* to perpetrate fraud and misappropriate assets.

   _____

   _____

   _____

	Yes	No	N/A

Opportunities

1. Does the company have large amounts of cash on hand or process significant cash transactions? ___ ___ ___

2. Does the company's inventory consist of small-size, high-value, or high-demand items that are susceptible to theft? ___ ___ ___

3. Does the company have easily convertible assets, such as bearer bonds, diamonds, or computer chips? ___ ___ ___

4. Does the company have fixed assets that are susceptible to misappropriation, such as ones that are small in size, marketable, or lacking observable ownership identification? ___ ___ ___

5. Is there a lack of appropriate segregation of duties or independent checks? ___ ___ ___

6. Is there a lack of appropriate management oversight of employees responsible for assets (e.g., inadequate supervision or monitoring of remote locations)? ___ ___ ___

	Yes	No	N/A
7. Is there a lack of job applicant screening procedures relating to employees with access to assets?	___	___	___
8. Does the company have inadequate recordkeeping with respect to assets?	___	___	___
9. Is there a lack of appropriate system of authorization and approval of transactions (e.g., in purchasing)?	___	___	___
10. Does the company have poor physical safeguards over cash, investments, inventory, or fixed assets?	___	___	___
11. Is there a lack of complete and timely reconciliations of assets?	___	___	___
12. Is there a lack of timely and appropriate documentation of transactions (e.g., credits for merchandise returns)?	___	___	___
13. Is there a lack of mandatory vacations for employees performing key control functions?	___	___	___
14. Does management have an inadequate understanding of information technology, which enables information technology employees to perpetrate a misappropriation?	___	___	___
15. Are access controls over automated records inadequate (including controls over, and review of, computer systems event logs)?	___	___	___

16. Other fraud risk factors that were considered:

_____

_____

_____

17. Document whether events or conditions exist that indicate *opportunities* to carry out the fraud and misappropriate assets.

_____

_____

_____

	Yes	No	N/A

Attitudes/Rationalizations

1. Do employees who have access to assets susceptible to misappropriation show:			
a. Disregard for the need for monitoring or reducing risks related to misappropriations of assets?	___	___	___
b. Disregard for internal control over misappropriation of assets by overriding existing controls?	___	___	___
c. Disregard for internal control over misappropriation of assets by failing to correct known internal control deficiencies?	___	___	___

2. Do employees who have access to assets susceptible to misappropriation exhibit behavior indicating displeasure or dissatisfaction with the company or its treatment of its employees? _____ _____ _____

3. Have you observed any unusual or unexplained changes in behavior or lifestyle of employees who have access to assets susceptible to misappropriation? _____ _____ _____

4. Other fraud risk factors that were considered:

_____

_____

_____

5. Document whether events or conditions exist that indicate attitudes/ rationalizations to carry out the fraud and misappropriate assets:

_____

_____

_____

V. Other Considerations Relating to Fraud

1. Describe any additional fraud risk factors or conditions identified as being present, and whether there are specific controls that mitigate the risk.

_____

_____

_____

2. Describe the current risks affecting the company's financial stability or profitability, and how these risks create pressure on the company to report improved financial results.

_____

_____

_____

3. Describe the company's revenue recognition policies and whether the company engages in (1) bill-and-hold-transactions, (2) barter transactions, (3) transactions involving side agreements, and (4) transactions with related parties.

_____

_____

_____

4. If improper revenue recognition was not identified as a risk of material misstatement due to fraud, describe the reasons regarding how that presumption was overcome.

_____

_____

_____

5. Describe the company's process for recording journal entries and other adjustments to the financial statements and specific controls over them, including: (1) who can initiate entries, (2) what approvals are required for such entries, (3) the sources of significant debits and credits to an account, and (4) how such entries are recorded, for example, online with no paper trail.

6. Describe the company's significant accounting estimates that are vulnerable to manipulation (e.g., provision for doubtful accounts and inventory obsolescence; asset impairment issues; accrued warranty reserves; restructuring charges).

7. Describe whether the company has entered into significant unusual transactions that are outside the normal course of business and, if so, describe the business rationale for such transactions.

8. Describe the company's values and ethical standards and how they are communicated, supported, and enforced.

9. Describe under what circumstances management might waive or bypass established policies and procedures and whether any policies and procedures were waived or bypassed during the period under audit.

VI. Response to Fraud Risks

The way the auditor responds to the results of the fraud risk assessment depends on the nature and significance of the fraud risks identified and on the entity's programs and controls that address such risks. Auditors respond to the results of the fraud risk assessment in three ways: (1) an overall response as to how the audit is conducted; (2) specific responses involving modification of the nature, timing, and extent of procedures to be performed; and (3) responses to further address the risk of management override of controls.

1. *Overall response*—Describe your overall responses to identified fraud risks, including: (1) assignment of personnel and supervision, (2) scrutiny of management's selection and application of significant accounting principles, and (3) including an element of unpredictability in audit procedures and tests.

_____

_____

_____

2. *Specific response*—Describe your specific responses to identified fraud risks, including modification of the nature, timing, and extent of audit procedures.

_____

_____

_____

3. *Response to address management override of controls*—Because management override of controls can occur in unpredictable ways, the risk of management override of controls is always an identified fraud risk and the auditor is required to perform certain specified procedures to respond to such risk. These procedures relate to (1) examining journal entries and other adjustments, (2) reviewing accounting estimates for biases, and (3) evaluating the business rationale for significant unusual transactions.

_____

_____

_____

Prepared by: _____ Date: _____

Approved by: _____ Date: _____

AU SECTION 317
ILLEGAL ACTS BY CLIENTS

PRACTICE POINT: As part of its Clarity Project, the American Institute of Certified Public Accountants' (AICPA's) Auditing Standards Board (ASB) has finalized a clarified Statement on Auditing Standards (SAS) titled, "Consideration of Laws and Regulations in an Audit of Financial Statements," which supersedes AU Section 317 (Illegal Acts by Clients). The clarified SAS requires the performance of procedures to identify instances of noncompliance with those laws and regulations that may have a material effect on the financial statements. Also, it specifically requires the auditor to inspect correspondence, if any, with the relevant licensing or regulatory authorities. This procedure is not required by extant AU Section 317. Therefore, this change in requirements will affect current practice.

In addition, extant AU Section 317 states that an audit performed in accordance with GAAS provides no assurance that noncompliance with laws and regulations will be detected or that any contingent liabilities that may result will be disclosed. However, the clarified SAS states that because of the inherent limitations of an audit, some material misstatements in the financial statements may not be detected, even though the audit is properly planned and performed in accordance with GAAS. The concept of "no assurance" is different from the concept described as "inherent limitations of an audit." However, the differing descriptions of these concepts will not affect current practice.

Furthermore, the requirement in extant AU Section 317 to obtain a written representation from management concerning the absence of noncompliance with laws or regulations has been placed in the clarified SAS, "Written Representations."

The ASB is expected to issue many of the clarified standards in *one* SAS that will be codified in "AU Section" format. The ASB has decided that the effective date of the clarified SASs that have not yet been issued is for audits of financial statements for periods ending on or after December 15, 2012. Auditors should be alert to and monitor further developments in this area.

WHAT EVERY PRACTITIONER SHOULD KNOW

Basic Requirements

The auditor is required to plan and perform the audit to provide reasonable assurance that misstatements resulting from illegal acts having a *material and direct* effect on the financial statements will be detected. Also, the auditor should be aware of the possibility that other illegal acts having *material but indirect* effects on the financial statements may have occurred; if the auditor suspects that such other illegal acts might have occurred, he or she should apply audit procedures specifically designed to detect illegal acts.

Audit Procedures When There Is No Evidence of Illegal Acts

Typically, the audit engagement does not include audit procedures specifically directed toward identifying illegal acts when no specific information has come to the auditor's attention suggesting that any illegal acts occurred. Nonetheless, the auditor should inquire of management about the following:

1. The entity's compliance with laws and regulations.

2. The entity's policies designed to prevent illegal acts.

3. The entity's directives, and periodic representations obtained by the entity from appropriate levels of management, concerning compliance with laws and regulations.

In addition, the auditor should request a written representation from management stating no violations or possible violations of laws or regulations have occurred that may require accrual or disclosure in the financial statements.

Audit Procedures When There Is Evidence of Illegal Acts

If the auditor is aware of information concerning an illegal act, the auditor should (1) understand the nature of the act, (2) understand the circumstances surrounding the act, and (3) obtain sufficient information to evaluate the effects of the act on the financial statements. If possible, the auditor should deal with management at least one level above those involved in the act.

When management cannot provide sufficient information to demonstrate that an illegal act did not take place, the auditor should:

1. Consult with the entity's legal counsel or other specialists (the entity should make the arrangements for the auditor to meet with its legal counsel).

2. Perform additional procedures, if deemed necessary, to obtain a further understanding of the illegal act, such as:

   a. Inspect supporting documentation (e.g., canceled checks, invoices) and compare it with accounting records.

   b. Confirm significant information with other parties to the transaction or intermediaries.

   c. Determine if the transaction has been properly authorized.

   d. Consider whether similar transactions have occurred and, if they have, attempt to identify them.

Audit Implications of Illegal Acts

When the auditor determines that an illegal act has occurred, or may have occurred, the auditor should evaluate the effects of the illegal act and determine if it is material. The auditor should evaluate the materiality of an illegal act on both a quantitative and a qualitative basis. To evaluate materiality, the auditor should consider:

1. Possible effects on amounts presented in the financial statements, including any loss contingencies. All costs relating to the loss, such as penalties and fines, should be considered. The need for accrual and/or disclosure in the financial statements should be evaluated in the context of guide-

lines established by FASB Accounting Standards Codification (ASC) 450, Contingencies.

2. Potential effects on the operations of the entity (e.g., possible loss of a significant business relationship or of assets).

3. The implications of the illegal act on other aspects of the audit. Of primary concern is the auditor's ability to rely on management's representations and the validity and accuracy of records and documents obtained during the audit.

Communication Requirements

The auditor should make sure that those charged with governance are adequately informed about illegal acts that come to his or her attention. However, if members of senior management are involved in the illegal act, the auditor should communicate directly with those charged with governance. The communication can be written or oral and, in both cases, should be adequately documented in the workpapers. Such communication should include (1) a description of the illegal act, (2) the circumstances surrounding the illegal act, and (3) the effect on the financial statements.

Notification of Illegal Acts to Parties Outside the Client

Generally, the auditor has no duty to notify third parties outside the client of an illegal act. However, the auditor may have a duty to notify parties outside the entity in the following circumstances:

1. To comply with certain legal and regulatory requirements, such as the SEC disclosure requirements regarding a change in auditors on Form 8-K.

2. To comply with the communication requirements of AU Section 315 (Communications between Predecessor and Successor Auditors), when a successor auditor makes inquiries of a predecessor auditor.

3. To respond to a subpoena.

4. To comply with governmental audit requirements applicable to entities that receive governmental financial assistance from a funding or other specified agency.

PRACTICE POINT: Because of the potential conflicts of the confidential relationship between the auditor and the client, the auditor may find it advisable to consult with legal counsel before matters relating to illegal acts are disclosed to parties outside the entity. This is particularly important because unjustified third-party notification could result in a lawsuit against the auditor for damages, slander, or similar reasons.

Effect on the Auditor's Report

If the effects of an illegal act are material and have not been properly accounted for or disclosed in the financial statements, the auditor should express either a qualified or an adverse opinion (depending on materiality) because of the lack of conformity with GAAP. If the entity does not allow the auditor to collect sufficient appropriate audit evidence to determine whether an illegal act has taken place or whether an illegal act has a material effect on the financial statements, the auditor generally should disclaim an opinion. If the entity refuses to accept the modified auditor's report, the auditor should withdraw from the engagement and notify those charged with governance of the reasons for the withdrawal.

PRACTICE ISSUES AND FREQUENTLY ASKED QUESTIONS

Issue 1: What is meant by "illegal acts having a material and direct effect on the financial statements"?

An illegal act would have a *direct and material effect* on the financial statements if the law or regulation, if violated, would affect the determination of financial statement amounts in a material sense. For example, if the client being audited is required by the terms of its contract to adhere to certain government regulations, such as Department of Defense regulations, and the revenue earned from the contract is material, then the auditor should test for compliance with those particular regulations. Failure by the client to adhere to those regulations would likely affect the continuing stream of revenue and potentially could result in sanctions and penalties.

All laws and regulations that have a direct effect on the financial statements have one common characteristic: requirements that affect the valuation or classification of a line-item financial statement amount. Therefore, the auditor's concern for compliance with these laws and regulations is not necessarily derived from their legality but from their effect on financial statement amounts.

Issue 2: What is meant by "illegal acts having material indirect effect on the financial statements"?

Many laws and regulations may have a *material but indirect effect* on the financial statements. Illegal acts of this type are generally related to the operations of the organization rather than to the financial and accounting aspects of the entity. These acts might include insider trading, antitrust violations, and safety and health violations. The effects of illegal acts of this type are often indirect in that they might lead to contingent liabilities and require disclosure in the financial statements. Illegal acts of this type are not detectable by traditional audit procedures, although documents normally inspected during an audit, inquiries of management, and responses from the client's lawyers may provide an indication that such an illegal act has been committed.

Issue 3: What are examples of illegal acts that, from an auditor's perspective, have considerably different audit implications?

Two examples of illegal acts are a violation of federal tax laws and a violation of the federal environmental protection laws. From an auditor's perspective, there is considerable difference in these two laws. In the case of federal tax law violations, the laws directly affect income tax expense and accrued income taxes in the financial statements; also, the auditor is likely to be more knowledgeable about tax laws because they are within most auditors' expertise. On the other hand, environmental protection violations affect the financial statements only if there is a fine or sanction; also, auditors are unlikely to be knowledgeable about environmental protection laws or their interpretation.

Issue 4: Is the auditor expected to be actively searching for the existence of illegal acts in a financial statement audit?

No. Many audit procedures normally performed on audits to search for errors and fraud may also uncover illegal acts. Examples include (1) reading minutes of meetings of the board of directors; (2) making inquiries of the client's legal counsel regarding litigation, claims, and assessments; and (3) performing substantive tests of details of transactions or balances. However, the auditor generally is not required to, and usually does not, design specific audit procedures to detect illegal acts, unless there is reason to believe they may exist.

Issue 5: Does the auditor's consideration of possible illegal acts extend to personal misconduct by the client's personnel?

No. Illegal acts by clients do not include personal misconduct by the entity's personnel unrelated to their business activities. Say, for example, during the course of an audit, the auditor reads in the newspaper that a member of the client's personnel has been arrested for drunk driving. The auditor might conclude that the employee's alleged conduct is a personal affair that is not business related, and, therefore, would not apply any auditing procedures with respect to this matter. However, if the person involved is a key member of management, the auditor might consider the ramifications of this incident on his or her assessment of the reliability of that person's representations made as a part of the audit. Also, possible financial pressures caused by this person's situation might need to be taken into account in connection with the auditor's consideration of fraud risk factors.

Issue 6: What is the main difference between illegal acts and fraud?

Fraud is always an intentional act, but not all illegal acts are intentional. Auditing literature describes fraud, generally, as an intentional act involving financial reporting or misappropriation of assets. Illegal acts, on the other hand, are violations of laws or governmental regulations. As such, consideration of illegal acts covers a much broader range of issues, such as occupational safety and health, employment practices, environmental protection, and antitrust laws. Illegal acts may not always be intentional and may not always have an effect on the financial statements.

Issue 7: Why should an auditor be concerned with illegal acts that are not material to or that do not have a direct effect on the financial statements?

Because of the wide variety of matters that can be considered illegal acts, the auditor must use professional judgment in considering their effects in the context of the financial statements taken as a whole. Consider, for example, the case of an illegal bribe payment of $10,000 in a $100 million-size company. Although the small amount involved might be considered immaterial, such an act takes on greater qualitative significance if it jeopardizes the loss of a significant contract, a business license, or the right to operate in a foreign country. In this case, the auditor should evaluate the adequacy of disclosure in the financial statements of the potential effects of the illegal act on the entity's operations.

Similarly, the direct effects of illegal transactions maybe properly recorded in the financial statements, but indirect effects that could be material may not be disclosed. Consider, for example, the purchase or sale of securities based on illegal insider information. Although the direct effects of the transaction may be recorded appropriately, its indirect effect (i.e., the possible contingent liability for violating securities laws) may not be appropriately disclosed.

ILLUSTRATIONS AND PRACTICE AIDS

ILLUSTRATION 1—EXAMPLES OF RED FLAGS THAT MAY RAISE QUESTIONS ABOUT THE EXISTENCE OF ILLEGAL ACTS

- Unauthorized transactions, improperly recorded transactions, or transactions not recorded in a complete or timely manner in order to maintain accountability for assets.
- Investigation by a governmental agency, an enforcement proceeding, or payment of unusual fines or penalties.
- Violations of laws or regulations cited in reports of examinations by regulatory agencies made available to the auditor.
- Large payments for unspecified services to consultants, affiliates, or employees.
- Sales commissions or agents' fees that appear excessive in relation (1) to those normally paid by the client or (2) to the services actually received.
- Unusually large payments in cash, purchases of bank cashiers' checks in large amounts payable to bearer, transfers to numbered bank accounts, or similar transactions.
- Unexplained payments made to government officials or employees.
- Failure to file tax returns or pay government duties or similar fees common to the entity's industry or the nature of its business.

AU SECTION 318
PERFORMING AUDIT PROCEDURES IN RESPONSE TO ASSESSED RISKS AND EVALUATING THE AUDIT EVIDENCE OBTAINED

> **PRACTICE POINT:** As part of its Clarity Project, the American Institute of Certified Public Accountants' (AICPA's) Auditing Standards Board (ASB) has finalized a clarified Statement on Auditing Standards (SAS) titled, "Understanding the Entity and Its Environment and Assessing the Risks of Material Misstatement," which supersedes AU Section 318 (Understanding the Entity and Its Environment and Assessing the Risks of Material Misstatement). The clarified SAS does not change or expand existing requirements in extant AU Section 318 in any significant respect.
>
> The ASB is expected to issue many of the clarified standards in *one* SAS that will be codified in "AU Section" format. The ASB has decided that the effective date of the clarified SASs that have not yet been issued is for audits of financial statements for periods ending on or after December 15, 2012. Auditors should be alert to and monitor further developments in this area.

WHAT EVERY PRACTITIONER SHOULD KNOW

Basic Objectives and Requirements

This Section provides guidance about implementing the third standard of field work, which states:

> The auditor must obtain sufficient appropriate audit evidence by performing audit procedures to afford a reasonable basis for an opinion regarding the financial statements under audit.

Specifically, this Section requires the auditor to:

1. Determine overall responses to address the assessed risks of material misstatement at the financial statement level (e.g., assigning more experienced staff or using specialists).

2. Design and perform additional audit procedures that are responsive to the assessed risks of material misstatement at the relevant assertion level. Such audit procedures include substantive procedures and, where relevant and necessary, tests of the operating effectiveness of controls.

3. Design and perform substantive procedures for all relevant assertions related to each material class of transactions, account balance, and disclosure, regardless of the assessed risk of material misstatement.

4. Agree the financial statements and accompanying notes to the entity's underlying records and examine material journal entries and other adjustments made during the course of preparing the financial statements.

5. Perform tests of controls to obtain evidence about their operating effectiveness when (a) the auditor's risk assessment includes an expectation of the operating effectiveness of controls or (b) when substantive proce-

dures alone do not provide sufficient appropriate audit evidence at the relevant assertion level.

6. When the auditor is performing audit procedures at an interim date:

  a. Determine what additional evidence should be obtained for the remaining period when tests of controls are performed during an interim period; and

  b. Perform further substantive procedures or a combination of substantive procedures and tests of controls for the remaining period to provide a reasonable basis for extending audit conclusions based on substantive procedures performed at an interim date to the period-end.

7. When an auditor plans to carry forward and rely on evidence about specific controls from previous audits in the current audit:

  a. Inquire, observe, and inspect documentation to determine if they have changed;

  b. Test their operating effectiveness in the current audit, if they have changed; and

  c. Test the operating effectiveness of such controls at least once every third year in an annual audit, if they have *not* changed.

8. Include the following documentation as part of every audit:

  a. The auditor's overall responses to the risk assessment at the financial statement level.

  b. The nature, timing, and extent of audit procedures performed.

  c. The linkage of audit procedures to the assessed risks at the relevant assertion level.

  d. The results of audit procedures.

  e. The conclusions reached regarding the use in the current audit of evidence about the operating effectiveness of controls that was obtained in a prior audit.

Overall Responses

This Section provides guidance on determining overall responses to address risks of material misstatement at the financial statement level. Those responses may include:

- Emphasizing to engagement personnel the need to maintain an attitude of professional skepticism in performing the audit.
- Assigning more experienced staff to the engagement.
- Assigning specialists or those with special skills to the engagement.
- Providing additional supervision to the audit team.
- Introducing elements of unpredictability in the selection of audit procedures.
- Changing the nature, timing, or extent of audit procedures.

The auditor's consideration of the control environment has a significant impact on the assessment of the risks of material misstatement at the financial statement level and, therefore, on the general approach to the audit. When weaknesses are noted in the control environment, the auditor should consider appropriate responses. These might include:

- Performing a substantive procedure such as confirmation at year-end rather than at an interim date.
- Making more extensive use of substantive procedures.
- Changing the nature of audit procedures to obtain more persuasive evidence.
- Increasing the number of locations to be included in the audit scope.

Responses to Risks of Material Misstatement at the Relevant Assertion Level

This Section advances the concept of a linkage between the audit tests performed and the risks assessed. While not a new concept, it gives additional emphasis to the idea that the auditor should design and perform further audit procedures whose nature, timing and extent are responsive to the assessed risks of material misstatement at the relevant assertion level. In doing so, the auditor should consider:

- The significance of the risk.
- The likelihood of material misstatement.
- The characteristics of the class of transactions, account balances, or disclosures involved.
- The nature of the entity's controls and whether they are automated or manual.
- Whether audit evidence will be obtained regarding the effectiveness of controls.

Stated in other terms, audit procedures should be proportional to the assessed risk, with areas of higher risk receiving more attention from the audit team. Usually, this entails developing an audit approach that contains elements of substantive procedures, tests of controls, and analytical procedures in varying degrees to achieve an appropriate level of assurance for each relevant assertion.

This Section further develops the concept of linking audit tests and the risks assessed by discussing the relationship between the level of assessed risk and the nature, timing, and extent of audit procedures. It notes that information developed in an effective internal control environment is generally more reliable than information that is not. Effective internal control thus reduces, but does not eliminate, the risk of material misstatement. In an effective internal control environment, tests of controls can therefore reduce, but not eliminate, the need for substantive procedures. Conversely, it is not necessary to perform tests of the operating effectiveness of controls in an audit area where substantive procedures alone are, in the auditor's judgment, sufficient to reduce detection risk to an acceptably low level, or in an area where effective controls appear to be lacking.

Likewise, analytical procedures may be sufficient in areas where balances or transaction classes are immaterial and assessed at low risk of material misstatement. However, in some areas, it is appropriate to bolster the evidence obtained through analytical procedures with substantive tests. This Section cites the example of an estimation process, such as allowance for doubtful accounts, in which subsequent collection tests would be used to strengthen evidence developed through analytical procedures.

Often, a combined approach using both tests of controls and substantive procedures is effective. However, the auditor is not precluded from adopting a substantive audit approach provided that the auditor has documented an appropriate basis for this approach. In addition, this Section briefly discusses small entities, in which control activities cannot be identified and, therefore, a primarily substantive approach must be taken. In such cases, auditors are cautioned to consider whether it is possible to obtain appropriate audit evidence.

Nature of further audit procedures The nature of audit procedures is a qualitative determination, in which the auditor uses professional judgment in selecting the type of procedures, such as inspection, observation, inquiry, recalculation, reperformance, or analytical procedures, that are likely to be the most effective and efficient in obtaining audit evidence. In selecting audit procedures, the auditor considers the risk of misstatement in the particular class of transactions, account balance, or disclosure. This includes considering the reasons for the risk assessment. For example, if the particular characteristics of a class of transactions have low inherent risk without regard to controls, it may be appropriate to use substantive analytical procedures alone. Conversely, if the assessed control risk is low and the auditor intends to design substantive procedures based on the effectiveness of those controls, it will be necessary to perform tests of those controls.

It is also necessary to gather evidence to support the accuracy and completeness of information produced by the entity's information system when that data is used in performing audit procedures. For example, this is the case when budget or nonfinancial data is used in performing substantive analytical procedures.

Timing of further audit procedures In determining when to perform auditing procedures, the auditor should consider:

- The control environment.
- When relevant information will become available.
- The nature of the risk.
- The date or period to which the evidence relates.

Tests of controls or substantive procedures may be performed at an interim date, or at period-end. Performing tests at an interim date may enable the auditor to identify significant matters early in the audit and thus either resolve them with management's assistance or develop an effective audit approach to deal with them. However, when substantive procedures or tests of the operating effectiveness of controls are performed at an interim date, the auditor should consider what additional evidence is necessary for the remaining period.

On the other hand, the auditor is more likely to perform substantive tests at or near the period-end or at unannounced or unpredictable times when there is a high assessed risk of misstatement. In addition, certain procedures can be performed only at or after the period-end, such as examining adjustments made during financial statement preparation and agreeing the financial statements to the underlying accounting records. For example, when there is an assessed risk of improper cutoffs or other improper transactions or adjustments near the period-end, the auditor should inspect transactions near that time and perform other procedures to specifically address that risk.

Extent of further audit procedures Determining the extent of audit procedures is a quantitative process, in which the auditor decides matters such as sample sizes or the number of observations of a control activity. This process involves the auditor's professional judgment, which takes into account:

- Tolerable misstatement.
- Assessed risk of material misstatement.
- Degree of assurance to be obtained.

In general, more extensive audit procedures, such as larger sample sizes, yield a higher degree of assurance. However, it is important not to confuse quantity with the relevance of the procedure to a particular assertion. A substantive procedure, such as inspecting all of the vendors' invoices to support recorded accounts payable, provides strong support for the existence of those payables but does nothing to assure the completeness of accounts payable. Similarly, in sampling applications, an inappropriate selection methodology or sample size, or the failure to follow up on exceptions will affect the validity of the auditor's conclusions. Therefore, it is the nature of the audit procedure and not its extent that is the most important consideration.

This Section encourages the use of different audit procedures in combination with each other, such as tests of the operating effectiveness of controls together with substantive or analytical procedures. However, auditors should be careful to consider whether the extent of testing is sufficient when using different procedures in combination.

Tests of Controls

The auditor should perform tests of controls (1) when the risk assessment includes an expectation of the operating effectiveness of those controls or (2) when substantive procedures do not by themselves provide sufficient appropriate evidence at the relevant assertion level.

The consideration of tests of controls consists of the following three steps, which normally are performed in order as a matter of audit efficiency:

1. Determine that the relevant control exists and that the entity has implemented it by performing risk assessment procedures (e.g., inquiries, observation, and inspection).

2. Determine that the relevant control is suitably designed to prevent or detect a material misstatement in a relevant assertion. This determina-

tion is important because if the control is not suitably designed, it will not be necessary or efficient to test for its operating effectiveness.

3. Determine that the relevant control is operating effectively. This includes gathering evidence about how the control was applied at relevant times during the period, the consistency of its application, and by what means or by whom the control was applied.

In some cases, the auditor's risk assessment procedures to assess the design and implementation of controls may also serve as tests of those controls. For example, IT controls generally are consistent in their application; therefore, the determination that they have been implemented may also serve as a test of their operating effectiveness.

Auditors often find that it is efficient to test internal controls concurrently with substantive tests of details on the same transaction. In so doing, consideration should be given to the effect that the result of substantive testing has on the control testing and vice versa. A material misstatement revealed by the auditor's substantive procedures that went undetected by the entity would usually be considered a significant deficiency in internal control. On the other hand, control weaknesses noted in the test of controls may indicate that the auditor should consider whether the planned extent of the substantive procedure, such as the sample size, is adequate.

Nature of tests of controls Procedures to test the operating effectiveness of controls usually include:

- Inquiries of entity personnel.
- Inspection of documents, reports, or electronic files that indicate the performance of the control.
- Observation of the control's application.
- Reperformance of the control's application.

Neither inquiry nor observation are sufficient procedures by themselves and should be used in combination with other procedures to obtain sufficient evidence about the operation of a control. When selecting audit procedures, the auditor should consider the degree of assurance about operating effectiveness that is needed. As the planned level of assurance increases, so should the reliability or extent of the audit evidence. In such circumstances, the auditor should use different audit procedures in concert to supplement each other. For example, evidence provided by a combination of inquiry and inspection or reperformance ordinarily provides a higher degree of assurance than evidence obtained by inquiry and observation alone.

The auditor should also consider indirect controls on which direct controls depend for their effectiveness. For example, the usefulness of a review of an exception report of credit sales in excess of customer limits, the direct control, depends on both the IT controls used to generate the data and the effectiveness of the user's review. In many cases, evidence about the operation of these indirect controls will have been obtained in the performance of the risk assessment procedures, particularly risk assessment procedures addressing IT controls and entity-level controls. In other cases, the auditor may need to design tests of these indirect controls.

Timing of tests of controls Controls should be tested throughout the period or as of a point in time that the auditor plans to rely on them. Observations at a point in time, such as physical inventory observation, may be sufficient when the controls pertain only to that time. However, when the auditor plans to rely on controls throughout a period, point-in-time observations or tests performed in interim periods should be supplemented with other procedures that are capable of providing evidence that the control operated effectively throughout that period. In such circumstances, consideration should be given to:

- The significance of the assessed risks of material misstatement at the relevant assertion level.
- The specific controls tested on an interim basis.
- The degree to which audit evidence about their effectiveness was obtained.
- The length of the remaining period.
- The extent to which reliance on the controls to reduce the extent of substantive procedures is contemplated.
- The control environment.
- The nature and extent of any significant changes in internal control subsequent to the interim period.

This Section provides that, if the auditor plans to rely on controls that have not changed since they were last tested, such controls should be tested at least once every third year of an annual audit. This marks a significant departure from the previously existing practice, in which internal control documentation was routinely rolled over from one audit to the next at the auditor's discretion. When planning to rely on evidence obtained about the operating effectiveness of controls in previous audits, the auditor should:

- Determine that the controls are not being relied on to mitigate a risk identified as a significant risk, as these controls must be tested each year.
- Perform and document audit procedures to identify significant changes in internal control, including changes in the information system, processes, and personnel that occurred subsequent to the period last tested (if controls have changed since they were last tested, the auditor should test the operating effectiveness of such controls in the current audit).

This Section offers significant guidance for determining when, and whether, it is appropriate to use audit evidence obtained in a prior audit. It states that the auditor should consider:

- The effectiveness of other internal control elements, including the entity's (1) control environment, (2) monitoring of controls, and (3) risk assessment process.
- The risks arising from the characteristics of the control, including whether controls are automated or manual.

- The effectiveness of IT general controls.
- The control's effectiveness and its application by the entity, including the nature and extent of deviations in its application noted in prior audits.
- Whether changing circumstances have not caused a change in a particular control.
- The risk of material misstatement.
- The extent of reliance on the control.

As the risk of material misstatement or the planned reliance on controls increases, the interval of time that elapses between tests is likely to shorten. The presence of the following indicators ordinarily results in not relying on evidence obtained in prior audits or shortening the period for retesting a control:

- Weak control environment.
- Weak monitoring controls.
- Weak general IT controls.
- Significant personnel changes that affect control application.
- Changes in circumstances that indicate a need for changes in the control.

In any case, the auditor should perform some testing of the operating effectiveness of controls every year. This approach provides evidence about the continuing effectiveness of the particular controls tested and of the control environment, and contributes to the decision about whether reliance on evidence obtained in prior audits is appropriate. In addition, it avoids the possibility that the auditor would test all relevant controls in one period and perform no tests in the subsequent two periods. Accordingly, the auditor should plan to test a portion of the controls each period, so that each control is tested at least once in every three annual audits.

An important exception to the "three-year rule" exists when the auditor has determined that there is a significant assessed risk of material misstatement at the relevant assertion level. In this case, when the auditor plans to rely on a control to mitigate that risk, the operating effectiveness of that control should be tested in the current period.

Extent of tests of controls The auditor should design tests of controls to provide sufficient appropriate evidence that they are operating effectively throughout the period of reliance. In determining the extent of tests of controls, the following factors may be considered:

- The frequency with which the control is performed.
- The length of time during the audit period the auditor is relying on the control.
- The relevance and reliability of the evidence supporting the control's effectiveness in preventing, detecting, or correcting material misstatements at the relevant assertion level.
- The extent of evidence obtained about other controls pertinent to the relevant assertion.
- The extent of planned reliance on the control in the assessment of risk.

- The expected deviation from the control.

When a control operates frequently, such as a control over daily transactions, consideration should be given to employing an audit sampling technique to obtain reasonable assurance about its operating effectiveness. When a control operates only on a periodic or infrequent basis, the auditor should consider applying the guidance for testing smaller populations, such as testing the control application for two months of the year and reviewing evidence of its application or scanning for unusual items in other months.

The greater the level of reliance on control effectiveness in the risk assessment process, the greater the extent of testing. However, when a high incidence of deviation is expected, the auditor should consider whether tests of controls will be sufficient to reduce control risk at the relevant assertion level. In such cases, the auditor may decide that tests of controls would be inappropriate or inefficient.

IT processing is inherently consistent, thus the auditor may able to limit the extent of tests to one or a few instances of operation. However, having once determined that the control is operating as intended, the auditor should perform tests to assure that it continues to function effectively.

Substantive Procedures

Substantive procedures should be planned and performed to be responsive to the related assessed risk of material misstatement. When the assessed risk of material misstatement at the relevant assertion level is determined to be significant, substantive procedures specifically responsive to that risk should be performed. Regardless of the assessment of the risk of material misstatement, substantive procedures should be designed and performed for all relevant assertions related to each material class of transactions, account balance, and disclosure on every audit. These procedures should include the following steps related to the financial reporting process:

1. Agreeing the financial statements and accompanying notes to the underlying accounting records.
2. Examining material adjustments and journal entries made in the preparation of the financial statements.

Nature of substantive procedures Substantive procedures should be designed to respond to the planned level of detection risk. Such procedures consist of both (1) tests of details and (2) substantive analytical procedures. The decision as to which procedures are to be applied, or in what combination, is influenced by whether the auditor has gathered evidence about the operating effectiveness of controls.

Tests of details are usually most appropriate to gather audit evidence pertaining to certain relevant assertions about account balances, such as valuation and existence. On the other hand, substantive analytical procedures generally lend themselves to situations involving large transaction volumes that are relatively predictable over time. Substantive procedures may be sufficient in situations of low assessed risk where the auditor has determined that the relevant controls are operating effectively or they may be used in combination with limited tests of details.

When designing substantive analytical procedures, consideration should be given to:

- The suitability of substantive analytical procedures for the given assertion.
- The reliability of the data from which ratios or expectations are derived, including the controls over the preparation of that data.
- The risk of management override of controls.
- The degree of precision of the expectation relative to the levels of materiality and desired assurance.
- The acceptable variance between expectations and recorded amounts.

In deciding to use substantive analytical procedures and in evaluating their results the auditor should be cognizant of their limitations. In particular, they may not be well suited for detecting certain types of fraud involving management override of controls, in which financial statement amounts have been manipulated to create a false appearance of normality or consistency and thus cause the auditor to accept them erroneously.

Analytical procedures can provide weak or strong evidence depending on how they are designed and performed. Analytical procedures can be strengthened by:

- Using knowledge of the entity in developing an accurate expectation, including using relationships between financial data or nonfinancial data and the balance being tested to predict and quantify the current-year expected balance.
- Increasing precision by disaggregating data (i.e., evaluating monthly sales instead of annual sales).
- Corroborating inquiries made to explain variances with additional information, such as inquiries of others, links to work done in other areas, and other supporting documentation.
- Testing the accuracy and completeness of source information.

Inquiry is not a sufficient detail test by itself and should be used in combination with other procedures. Inquiry should involve:

- Considering the knowledge, objectivity, experience, responsibility, and qualifications of the individual questioned.
- Asking clear, concise, and relevant questions.
- Using open or closed ended questions appropriately
- Listening actively and effectively.
- Considering the reactions and responses and asking follow-up questions.
- Evaluating the response.

Timing of substantive procedures When considering whether to perform substantive procedures at the period-end or at an interim date, the auditor should consider:

- The control environment and relevant controls.
- The availability of necessary information at a date after the interim date.
- The objective of the substantive procedure.
- The assessed risk of material misstatement, including fraud risk.
- The nature of the account balance or class of transactions and the relevant assertions.
- The entity's procedures for analyzing and adjusting balances and transaction classes at interim dates.
- The entity's procedures for establishing proper cutoffs.
- The capability of the information system to permit investigation of (1) significant, unusual transactions or entries; (2) causes of significant or expected fluctuations that did not occur; and (3) changes in the composition of account balances or classes of transaction during the remaining period.
- The ability to reduce detection risk at the period-end with (1) further substantive procedures or (2) a combination of control tests and substantive procedures.

If substantive procedures are performed at an interim date, the auditor's detection risk at period-end increases. In order to mitigate this risk, the auditor should, at a minimum, perform further substantive procedures. While it is not always necessary to perform tests of the operating effectiveness of controls for the interim period to provide a reasonable basis for projecting the audit conclusions from the interim date to the period-end, the auditor should consider whether the interim substantive procedures alone provide a sufficient basis. When the auditor determines that the interim substantive procedures do not adequately support conclusions about the remaining period, additional period-end substantive procedures or a combination of control tests and substantive procedures over the remaining period should be performed.

Audit procedures performed between the interim date and the period-end may include:

- Comparison and reconciliation of interim and period-end balances.
- Identification and investigation of amounts that appear unusual.
- Substantive analytical procedures applied to balances and transaction classes that are reasonably predictable.
- Tests of details.

When material misstatements are detected at an interim date, consideration should be given to modifying the nature, timing, or extent of the substantive procedures covering the remaining period or to repeating the audit procedures at the period-end.

Audit evidence obtained from substantive procedures applied in previous audits is not sufficient to reduce detection risk to an acceptably low level in the current period. When considering whether to use such evidence in the current audit, the evidence and related subject matter must not have fundamentally changed. The auditor should perform tests in the current period to establish its continuing relevance.

This Section lists the following other timing considerations for substantive tests:

- Coordinating audit procedures for related-party transactions and balances in light of the risks of material misstatements.
- Coordinating tests of interrelated accounts and cutoffs.
- Maintaining temporary audit control over negotiable assets.
- Simultaneously testing such assets and cash on hand, bank loans, and other related items.

Extent of substantive procedures Determination of the extent of substantive tests of details to be performed is usually thought of in quantitative terms, primarily related to sample sizes. In making this determination, a higher level of assessed risk of misstatement usually indicates the need for more extensive substantive procedures. However, consideration of the operating effectiveness of internal controls and the relevance of the planned procedure to the specific risk should also enter into this determination.

Consideration should be given to the qualitative aspects of specific populations to be detail-tested and whether it may be more effective to use other methods of selection, such as selecting large or unusual items from a population or stratifying the population into homogeneous subsets for sampling.

When using substantive analytical procedures, the auditor should determine how large of a variance from expectation is acceptable. This involves considering tolerable misstatement and the desired level of assurance, and the possibility that a combination of misstatements could aggregate to a material level.

Adequacy of Presentation and Disclosure

This Section places additional emphasis on the auditor's responsibility to evaluate the financial statements for their fairness of presentation and disclosure. This evaluation should take place within the context of the assessed risk of material misstatement at the relevant assertion level. Procedures targeted toward this objective should include consideration of whether:

- Financial statements and related notes are in accordance with generally accepted accounting principles in their overall presentation and are appropriate in (1) form, (2) arrangement, and (3) content.
- Financial statements and related notes contain proper (1) classifications, (2) descriptions, (3) terminology, (4) levels of detail, (5) bases of amounts set forth, and (6) adequate disclosure of material matters.
- Individual financial statements reflect appropriate classification and description of financial information.

- Management has, or should have, disclosed a particular matter in light of the facts and circumstances of which the auditor is aware.

Evaluating the Sufficiency and Appropriateness of Audit Evidence

This Section states that "An audit of financial statements is a cumulative and iterative process." This recognizes that evidence builds up throughout the audit, as audit procedures are performed, and that assumptions about the risk of material misstatement may change in light of this evidence. It is important that the auditor view the audit process as an integrated whole rather than as a series of sequentially applied procedures. This involves careful consideration, both during and at the end of the audit, of whether preliminary assumptions about risk continue to be valid and whether the audit procedures respond adequately to the assessed risks. Factors that may cause the auditor to reevaluate the initial risk assessment include:

- Differences between information upon which risk assessments were based and information that subsequently comes to the auditor's attention.
- Extent of misstatements detected by substantive procedures.
- Effect of those misstatements on the auditor's assessment of the effectiveness of controls.
- Whether misstatements due to fraud or error are isolated instances and how their detection affects the assessed risk of material misstatement.
- Extent of deviations in the application of control procedures detected by tests of controls.
- Whether the tests of controls provide sufficient basis for reliance upon the controls.

Finally, the auditor should conclude as to whether sufficient appropriate evidence has been obtained to reduce the risk of material misstatement to an appropriately low level. This determination is a matter of the auditor's professional judgment. In reaching this conclusion, the auditor should consider:

- All relevant audit evidence, whether it appears to support or contradict the relevant financial statement assertions.
- The significance of the potential misstatement in the relevant assertion.
- The likelihood of the potential misstatement having a material effect on the financial statements, either individually or when aggregated with other misstatements.
- The effectiveness of management's controls and responses to risks.
- The experience from previous audits with respect to similar potential misstatements.
- The results of audit procedures performed.
- Whether audit procedures identified specific instances of fraud or error.
- The sources and reliability of information.
- The persuasiveness of audit evidence.
- The understanding of the entity, its environment, and its internal control.

When the auditor concludes that sufficient appropriate evidence has not been obtained with respect to material financial statement assertions, attempts should be made to obtain additional evidence. If sufficient appropriate audit evidence cannot be obtained, the auditor should express a qualified opinion or disclaim an opinion.

Inconsistencies in audit evidence, findings, and estimates The auditor should perform additional procedures to resolve inconsistencies in the audit evidence, findings that indicate the possibility of other misstatements, and estimates that fall outside the range of acceptability. The amount of additional evidence needed is a matter of judgment but should be sufficient to allow the auditor to form a conclusion as to the accuracy of the assertion being tested.

Matters of significance to the financial statements or auditor's report, or difficulties encountered in the audit, should be brought to the attention of the auditor with final responsibility for the audit. In addition, assistants should be instructed to bring these matters to the attention of the auditor with final responsibility for the audit. Misstatements discovered in one aspect of an audit may affect other areas; for example, the auditor should:

- Address the effects of misstatements discovered in the performance of interim procedures on period-end substantive tests.

- Consider misstatements detected in performing substantive tests on the assessment of the operating effectiveness of controls. For example, a misstatement detected in a substantive test may indicate that the related controls are not operating effectively, even though tests of those controls did not reveal any deficiencies.

Deviations from prescribed controls and misstatements in substantive tests If deviations from prescribed controls are discovered in the sample testing of internal controls, the auditor may have to increase the extent (i.e., sample size) of internal controls testing until it is no longer cost beneficial or the control is deemed unreliable.

If misstatements are discovered in sampling for substantive tests, those known misstatements should be projected to the sampling population in order to estimate the likely misstatement in the entire population.

If the auditor is unable to test certain items as planned in a substantive sample, the auditor should perform alternative procedures on those sample items. In addition, the auditor should consider the reasons that such items could not be tested as planned. For example, if certain invoices needed as part of a sample to test inventory prices are unavailable because the purchase date of the inventory part is too old, there may be an issue with inventory valuation due to obsolescence.

In sampling for substantive tests, the auditor should consider substantive evidence obtained in previous stages of the audit, including results of journal entries tested.

Specific Audit Documentation Requirements

AU Section 339 (Audit Documentation) provides authoritative guidance on the form and content of audit documentation. There is considerable professional judgment involved in deciding the exact manner in which these elements are to be documented. For example, properly used narrative memoranda, questionnaires, checklists, and flowcharts can be effective documentation techniques. As a general rule, audit documentation becomes more extensive as the complexity of the entity, its environment, and its internal control and the extent of the audit procedures applied increase. Specific audit methodologies and technologies used also affect the form and extent of the audit documentation.

In addition, this Section requires the auditor to specifically document the following elements of the audit procedures performed in response to assessed risks and the evaluation of the audit evidence obtained through those procedures:

- The overall responses to the risk assessment at the financial statement level.
- The nature, timing, and extent of audit procedures performed.
- The linkage of audit procedures to the assessed risks at the relevant assertion level.
- The results of audit procedures.
- The conclusions reached concerning the use in the current audit of evidence about the operating effectiveness of controls that was obtained in a previous audit.

PRACTICE ISSUES AND FREQUENTLY ASKED QUESTIONS

Issue 1: What does the phrase "expectation of the operating effectiveness of controls" mean in the context of the auditor's requirement to perform tests of controls when the auditor's risk assessment includes an expectation of the operating effectiveness of controls?

AU Section 318 requires the auditor to perform tests of controls when (1) the auditor's risk assessment includes an expectation of the operating effectiveness of controls or (2) substantive procedures alone do not provide sufficient appropriate audit evidence at the relevant assertion level. The phrase *expectation of the operating effectiveness of controls* means that (1) the auditor's understanding of the five components of internal control provides a basis to initially assess control risk at less than maximum and (2) the auditor's strategy contemplates a combined approach of designing and performing tests of controls and substantive procedures. It should be noted that the auditor's initial assessment of control risk is preliminary and is subject to the satisfactory results of the tests of the operating effectiveness of those controls.

Issue 2: May the auditor follow an all substantive audit approach even if the auditor's understanding of internal control causes him or her to believe that controls are designed effectively?

Yes. Paragraph 8 of AU Section 318 states, in part:

In some cases, the auditor may determine that performing only substantive procedures is appropriate for specific relevant assertions and risks. In those circumstances, the auditor may exclude the effect of controls from the relevant risk assessment. This may be because the auditor's risk assessment procedures have not identified any effective controls relevant to the assertion or because testing the operating effectiveness of controls would be inefficient.

The auditor's decision about whether to test the operating effectiveness of controls may be considered within a cost-benefit framework. If the auditor believes that the benefit of testing the operating effectiveness of controls is less than the cost of testing controls, the auditor may wish to adopt an audit strategy that excludes testing controls, and perform substantive procedures that respond to the assessed risks for specific assertions. However, the extent of substantive testing cannot be reduced based on the premise of effective controls, unless the auditor has tested the effective operation of such controls.

Issue 3: Why should the auditor bother performing substantive tests at an interim date?

The auditor might find it useful to perform substantive tests at an interim date for several reasons, such as:

- *To smooth out the CPA firm's peak work schedule periods*—If significant portions of the firm's audit practice is concentrated within a short time period, time pressure can often be alleviated by scheduling test work during off-peak times.

- *To meet tight client deadlines for audited financial statements*—For example, if a December year-end client needs the financial statements issued by no later than January 31, the auditor might perform substantive tests at an interim date to meet the client deadline.

- *To deal with potential unusual difficulties or complex transactions*—For example, when significant adjustments or difficulties in applying auditing procedures are anticipated, it is often more efficient to perform test procedures early; by doing so, the auditor lengthens the time frame available to assess and resolve complex, unusual, or contentious issues that may arise as a result of the audit.

- *To relieve any undue pressure on the client's accounting staff*—Clients generally are not receptive to having their accounting staff perform audit assistance tasks during a compressed time frame, which might interfere with their regular work schedule and lead to overtime.

Issue 4: How long is the remaining period between the interim test date and the balance sheet date?

This Section does not impose any specific requirements or offer any specific guidance with respect to the length of the remaining period. However, it indicates that applying substantive tests as of an interim date potentially increases the risk that misstatements that may exist at the balance sheet date will not be detected by the auditor; therefore, the potential for such increased audit risk tends to become greater as the remaining period is lengthened. In practice, most auditors tend to limit the length of the remaining period to two or three months.

Still, auditors who wish to control audit risk to a more acceptable level tend to limit the length of the remaining period to one month.

Generally, the length of the remaining period depends on the nature of the test. For example, certain transactions, such as property additions or new debt, occurring on the first day of the client's fiscal year could be audited on that day because that test work substantiates the occurrence of the transaction. On the other hand, procedures such as physical inventory observation that seek to support the existence of an asset at the balance sheet date are usually most effective when performed at or near the balance sheet date.

Issue 5: What are some of the risks and challenges that the auditor faces when deciding on the timing of audit procedures as of an interim date?

A timing decision is made for virtually every type of audit procedure. The nature of the audit area may affect the timing of the auditor's procedures. In areas where the year-end balance may not be predictable two or three months prior to year-end (e.g., inventories for a retailer), the auditor should plan to perform the audit procedures as near to year-end as possible. The most difficult aspect of the timing decision is the determination of how early in the year audit procedures can be effectively and efficiently performed. Timing will depend primarily on the likelihood of material misstatement, particularly as it is affected by control risk, and on the nature of the audit procedures. In addition, timing will depend on client deadlines and staff scheduling considerations.

Effective internal control leads the auditor to expect that controls tested at an interim date before year-end will continue to function during the entire year. Therefore, the effectiveness of internal control is also a factor in determining how early in the year the auditor can perform tests of controls.

When there is a strong internal control environment and control objectives are being achieved, the auditor may decide to perform most of the direct tests of balances as of two or three months before year-end. However, the auditor will have to perform tests of intervening transactions to provide persuasive evidence as the auditor deems necessary. This approach would not be appropriate where, for example, there is a history of substantial inventory adjustments, unless there is a reasonable basis for providing for the adjustment from the inventory date to year-end.

The auditor should keep in mind that a weak or ineffective internal control environment, or a condition in which the internal control objectives are not being achieved in an audit area, should lead the auditor to challenge whether audit procedures should be performed as of an interim date. If the auditor is not able to rely on controls for the remaining period, he or she should consider whether the effectiveness of the procedures for the period is impaired. For example, the effectiveness of roll-forward tests and comparisons of balances may be impaired when the auditor has not established a basis for relying on the proper recording of interim transactions. Therefore, the auditor should consider whether it is more efficient to perform the additional tests necessary to establish a basis for relying on the propriety of interim transactions or to perform direct tests at year-end.

Issue 6: What are some of the typical substantive tests applied as of an interim date?

In practice, substantive tests as of an interim date typically occur for the following types of tests:

- Tests of transactions on balance sheet accounts (e.g., details of the additions to and reductions of accounts such as property, investments, debt, and equity)
- Tests of details of transactions on income and expense accounts (e.g., vouching expense charges over a predetermined dollar amount)
- Tests of accounts that are not to be audited by testing the details of items comprising the balance (e.g., warranty reserves or deferred charges)
- Analytical procedures (e.g., computing monthly gross profit percentages)

Performance of these tests as of an interim date often can be both efficient and effective. The auditor can perform these substantive tests even if the planned assessed level of control risk is high. For example, if performing tests of transactions for debt, the auditor must vouch new debts for the early part of the year as well.

Issue 7: What are some examples of additional procedures that the auditor might perform on the remaining period between the interim test date and the balance sheet date for accounts receivable balances?

The extent of the additional audit procedures to be performed depends on, among other things, the materiality of the account balance and the transactions occurring during the remaining period. For accounts receivable confirmed on a date other than the balance sheet date, the auditor might prepare, or obtain from the client, an analysis of transactions (e.g., cash receipts or sales) between the confirmation date and the balance sheet date, and perform the following:

- Trace the balance as of the confirmation date to the aged trial balance.
- Trace cash received during the remaining period to the cash receipts journal or bank statements.
- Trace sales/revenue amounts during the remaining period to the sales/ revenue journal.
- Determine the reasonableness and propriety of any other reconciling items.
- Trace the ending balance per the analysis to the trial balance as of the balance sheet date.

PRACTICE POINT: Illustration 2 below is a sample workpaper analysis that the auditor can use when performing an accounts receivable roll-forward from an interim date to the balance sheet date.

Issue 8: What are some examples of additional procedures that the auditor might perform on the remaining period between the interim test date and the balance sheet date for inventory account balances?

The extent of the additional audit procedures to be performed depends on, among other things, the materiality of the account balance and the transactions occurring during the remaining period. If the inventory physical count was taken as of an interim date, the auditor might prepare, or obtain from the client, an analysis and reconciliation of the inventory per the physical count to the inventory per the balance sheet and perform the following:

- Review and analyze the general ledger inventory control accounts from the date of the physical count to the balance sheet date.

- Trace inventory additions to appropriate sources, such as the purchases journal and cost accounting records.

- Trace inventory reductions to cost of sales.

- Compare the current activity between the physical count date and balance sheet date to activity of the comparable period in the preceding year, and investigate unusual fluctuations.

- Determine the propriety and reasonableness of any other reconciling items.

PRACTICE POINT: Illustration 3 below is a sample workpaper analysis that the auditor can use when performing inventory reconciliation from the interim physical observation date to the balance sheet date.

ILLUSTRATIONS AND PRACTICE AIDS

ILLUSTRATION 1—EXAMPLES OF SUBSTANTIVE PROCEDURES FOR INVENTORIES

Note: This example is adapted from the appendix, "Illustrative Financial Statement Assertions and Examples of Substantive Procedures Illustrations for Inventories of a Manufacturing Company" of SAS 110 (Performing Audit Procedures in Response to Assessed Risks and Evaluating the Audit Evidence Obtained). This example illustrates the use of financial statement assertions in designing substantive procedures and does not illustrate tests of controls. The examples of substantive procedures are not intended to be all-inclusive, nor is it expected that all of the procedures would be applied in an audit. Rather, the particular substantive procedures to be used in each circumstance depend on the auditor's risk assessments and tests of controls.

Illustrative Assertions about Account Balances	*Examples of Substantive Procedures*
Existence	
Inventories included in the balance sheet physically exist.	• Physically examining inventory items.
	• Obtaining confirmation of inventories at locations outside the entity.
	• Inspecting documents relating to inventory transactions between a physical inventory date and the balance sheet date.

Illustrative Assertions about Account Balances	*Examples of Substantive Procedures*
Inventories represent items held for sale or use in the normal course of business.	• Inspecting perpetual inventory records, production records, and purchasing records for indications of current activity.
	• Reconciling items in the inventory listing to a current computer-maintained sales catalog and subsequent sales and delivery reports using computer-assisted audit techniques (CAATs).
	• Questioning production and sales personnel.
	• Using the work of specialists to corroborate the nature of specialized products.
Rights and Obligations	
The entity has legal title or similar rights of ownership to the inventories.	• Examining paid vendors' invoices, consignment agreements, and contracts.
	• Obtaining confirmation of inventories at locations outside the entity.
Inventories exclude items billed to customers or owned by others.	• Examining paid vendors' invoices, consignment agreements, and contracts.
	• Inspecting shipping and receiving transactions near year-end for recording in the proper period.
Completeness	
Inventory quantities include all products, materials, and supplies on hand.	• Observing physical inventory counts.
	• Analytically comparing the relationship of inventory balances to recent purchasing, production, and sales activities.
	• Inspecting shipping and receiving transactions near year-end for recording in the proper period.
Inventory quantities include all products, materials, and supplies owned by the company that are in transit or stored at outside locations.	• Obtaining confirmation of inventories at locations outside the entity.
	• Analytically comparing the relationship of inventory balances to recent purchasing, production, and sales activities.
Inventory listings are accurately compiled and the totals are properly included in the inventory accounts.	• Inspecting shipping and receiving transactions near year-end for recording in the proper period.
	• Examining the inventory listing for inclusion of test counts recorded during the physical inventory observation.
	• Reconciling all inventory tags and count sheets used in recording the physical inventory counts using CAATs
	• Recalculating an inventory listing for clerical accuracy using CAATs.

Illustrative Assertions about Account Balances	*Examples of Substantive Procedures*
	• Reconciling physical counts to perpetual records and general ledger balances and investigating significant fluctuations using CAATs.
Valuation and Allocation	
Inventories are properly stated at cost (except when market is lower).	• Examining paid vendors' invoices and comparing product prices to standard cost build-ups. • Analytically comparing direct labor rates to production records. • Recalculating the computation of standard overhead rates. • Examining analyses of purchasing and manufacturing standard cost variances.
Slow-moving, excess, defective, and obsolete items included in inventories are properly identified.	• Examining an analysis of inventory turnover. • Analyzing industry experience and trends. • Analytically comparing the relationship of inventory balances to anticipated sales volume. • Performing a walk-through of the plant for indications of products not being used. • Inquiring of production and sales personnel concerning possible excess, or defective or obsolete inventory items. • Addressing logistic and distribution business processes (e.g., cycle time, volume of returns, or problems with suppliers).
Inventories are reduced, when appropriate, to replacement cost or net realizable value.	• Inspecting sales catalogs or industry publications for current market value quotations. • Recalculating inventory valuation reserves. • Analyzing current production costs. • Examining sales after year-end and open purchase order commitments.

Illustrative Assertions about Presentation and Disclosure	*Examples of Substantive Procedures*
Rights and Obligations	
The pledge or assignment of any inventories is appropriately disclosed.	• Obtaining confirmation of inventories pledged under loan agreements.
Completeness	
The financial statements include all disclosures related to inventories specified by generally accepted accounting principles.	• Using a disclosure checklist to determine whether the disclosures included in generally accepted accounting principles were made.
Understandability	

Illustrative Assertions about Presentation and Disclosure	Examples of Substantive Procedures
Inventories are properly classified in the balance sheet as current assets.	• Examining drafts of the financial statements for appropriate balance-sheet classification.
Disclosures related to inventories are understandable.	• Reading disclosures for clarity.
Accuracy and Valuation	
The major categories of inventories and their bases of valuation are accurately disclosed in the financial statements.	• Examining drafts of the financial statements for appropriate disclosures.
	• Reconciling the categories of inventories disclosed in the draft financial statements to the categories recorded during the physical inventory observation.

ILLUSTRATION 2—ACCOUNTS RECEIVABLE ROLL-FORWARD FROM CONFIRMATION DATE TO BALANCE SHEET DATE

XYZ, Inc.

Accounts Receivable—Rollforward from Confirmation Date to
Balance Sheet Date
Financial Statement Date: 12/31/20X2

Date:
Prepared By:
Reviewed By:

Balance per Books @ 10/31/20X2			$4,700,000
Intervening Period Activity:			
Add:	Sales	6,758,000	
	NSF Checks	17,000	6,775,000
Deduct:	Cash Receipts	(5,883,000)	
	Credit Memos	(125,000)	
	Sales Discounts	(100,000)	
	Write offs	(315,000)	(6,423,000)
Balance per Books @ 12/31/20X2			$5,052,000

ILLUSTRATION 3—INVENTORY RECONCILIATION FROM INTERIM PHYS-ICAL OBSERVATION DATE TO BALANCE SHEET DATE

XYZ, Inc.
Inventory—Reconciliation from Physical to
Balance Sheet Date
Financial Statement Date: 12/31/20X2

Date:
Prepared By:
Reviewed By:

	Raw Materials	Work in Process	Finished Goods	Other

Unadjusted Balance per Books @ Date of Physical 10/31/20X2	$4,542,000	$1,073,000	$5,756,000	$121,000
Adjustments of Book to Physical	(293,000)	195,000	(382,000)	0
Balance per Physical @10/31/20X2	4,249,000	1,268,000	5,374,000	121,000
Intervening Period Activity:				
Purchases	1,920,000			12,000
Requisitions	(1,472,000)	1,472,000		
Direct Labor		455,000		
Overhead		279,000		
		2,206,000		
Cost of Goods Manufactured		(1,654,000)	1,654,000	
			7,028,000	
Cost of Goods Sold			(2,738,000)	
Balance per Books 12/31/20X2	$4,697,000	$1,820,000	$4,290,000	$133,000

ILLUSTRATION 4—UNCONDITIONAL AND PRESUMPTIVELY MANDATORY REQUIREMENTS OF AU SECTION 318

Unconditional Requirements

Essentially, there are two unconditional requirements in AU Section 318. In one of the requirements, AU Section 318 recites the third standard of field work, which states that:

> The auditor must obtain sufficient appropriate audit evidence by performing audit procedures to afford a reasonable basis for an opinion regarding the financial statements under audit.

The second unconditional requirement indicates that, in order for evidence from a prior audit to be used as substantive evidence in the current audit, the audit evidence and the related subject matter must not fundamentally change.

Presumptively Mandatory Requirements

Presumptively mandatory requirements are identified by the word "should" and place the burden of proof on the auditor if he or she departs from the presumptive requirement. Presumptively mandatory requirements are required to be performed in all applicable circumstances unless the auditor can justify in the audit documentation a reason for not doing so and demonstrate how other audit procedures that the auditor performed have met the audit objectives. AU Section 318 states that the auditor *should*:

- Determine overall responses to address the assessed risks of material misstatement at the financial statement level, and consider an appropriate response if there are weaknesses in the control environment (e.g., perform audit procedures as of the period-end rather than at an interim date).

- Design and perform further audit procedures that are responsive to the assessed risks of material misstatement at the relevant assertion level.

- Consider certain specific matters in designing further audit procedures (e.g., the significance of the assessed risk, the likelihood that a material misstatement will occur).

- Design and perform substantive procedures for all relevant assertions related to each material class of transactions, account balance, and disclosure.

- Consider whether, in the case of very small entities in which further audit procedures are primarily substantive, it is possible to obtain sufficient appropriate audit evidence in the absence of controls.

- Consider the reasons for the assessment of the risk of material misstatement at the relevant assertion level for each class of transactions, account balance, and disclosure.

- Test controls to obtain evidence about their operating effectiveness if the auditor intends to design substantive tests with the expectation that the controls are effective.

- Obtain audit evidence about the accuracy and completeness of information produced by the client's information system (nonfinancial information, budget data) when that information is to be used in performing audit procedures, including substantive analytical procedures.

- Consider, when performing tests of controls or substantive procedures before the period-end, what additional evidence is necessary for the remaining period.

- Take into account certain specific matters in determining when to perform audit procedures (e.g., the control environment; when the information is available; the nature of the risk; and the period or date to which the evidence relates).

- Inspect transactions near the period-end and perform other responsive procedures, if there is a risk of improper sales contracts or transactions that may not have been finalized at period-end.

- Consider whether the extent of testing is appropriate when performing different audit procedures in combination.

- In connection with *tests of controls*:

    — Test controls when the risk assessment includes an expectation of their operating effectiveness or when substantive procedures alone do not provide sufficient appropriate evidence at the relevant assertion level.

    — Test controls when it is not possible or practicable to reduce detection risk at the relevant assertion level to an acceptably low level through substantive procedures alone.

— Determine that the relevant controls exist and that the client is using them when obtaining evidence about control implementation by performing risk assessment procedures.

— Obtain evidence that controls operate effectively when performing tests of controls, including how controls were applied, the consistency with which they were applied, and by whom or by what means they were applied.

— Consider each control separately if substantially different controls were used at different times during the audit period.

— Consider whether some risk assessment procedures that are not specifically designed as tests of controls may nevertheless provide sufficient evidence about the operating effectiveness of the related controls.

— Select audit procedures to obtain assurance about the operating effectiveness of controls, seeking more reliable or extensive evidence as the planned level of assurance increases.

— Perform tests of controls to obtain a higher level of assurance about their operating effectiveness in circumstances in which the audit approach consists primarily of tests of controls.

— Perform other audit procedures in combination with inquiry to test the operating effectiveness of controls.

— Supplement observations of the operation of internal controls with inquiries of client personnel.

— Consider, when designing tests of controls, the need to obtain audit evidence supporting the effective operation of controls directly related to the relevant assertions, as well as other indirect controls on which these controls depend.

— Consider the design and evaluation of tests intended to be performed concurrently as a test of controls and a test of details on the same transaction, including how the results of the tests of controls may affect the extent of substantive procedures to be performed, such as by increasing the sample size when controls are found to be ineffective.

— Consider the implications of misstatements detected in performing substantive procedures when assessing the operating effectiveness of the related controls.

— Regard a material misstatement that was not identified by the client as at least a significant deficiency, and possibly as a material weakness in internal control, that should be communicated to management and those charged with governance.

— Test controls for the particular time or throughout the period for which reliance on those controls is planned.

— Determine what additional evidence should be obtained for the remaining period when testing the operating effectiveness of controls during an interim period, taking into consideration the (1) significance of the assessed risk of material misstatement at the relevant assertion level, (2) specific controls tested during the interim period, (3) degree to which evidence about their operating effectiveness was obtained, (4) length of the remaining period, (5) extent to which reduction of further substantive procedures based on reliance of controls is planned, (6) control environment, and (7) nature and extent of significant changes in internal control in the remaining period.

— Obtain evidence (by a combination of observation, inquiry, and inspection) about whether changes in controls have occurred since the prior audit, if planning to use in the current audit evidence about the operating effectiveness of such controls that was obtained in prior audits.

— Perform audit procedures to establish the continuing relevance of evidence obtained in prior periods when planning to use that evidence in the current audit.

— Test the operating effectiveness of controls that have changed since they were last tested, if planning to rely on them in the current audit.

— Test the operating effectiveness of controls at least once every third year in an annual audit, if the auditor plans to rely on controls that have not changed since they were last tested.

— Consider a number of specific factors in deciding whether it is appropriate to use evidence about the operating effectiveness of controls obtained in prior audits, and the length of time that may elapse before retesting a control.

— Test the operating effectiveness of *some* controls each year (so that each control is tested at least every third audit) when there are a number of controls for which the auditor determines that it is appropriate to use audit evidence obtained in prior audits.

— Test in the current period the operating effectiveness of controls over areas of significant risks when the auditor plans to rely on such controls that are intended to mitigate those significant risks.

— Design sufficient tests of controls to obtain sufficient appropriate audit evidence that the controls are operating effectively throughout the period of reliance.

— Consider using an audit sampling technique in control testing to obtain reasonable assurance about the operation of the control when the control is applied on a transaction basis (e.g., matching approved purchase orders to vendor invoices) and operates frequently.

— Consider guidance appropriate for testing smaller populations (e.g., testing the control application for two months and reviewing other months for unusual items) when a control is applied on a periodic basis (e.g., monthly reconciliation of accounts receivable subsidiary ledger to the general ledger).

— Increase the extent of tests of controls when more reliance is placed on the operating effectiveness of controls in the assessment of risk, or as the rate of expected deviation from a control increases.

— Consider whether the rate of expected deviation in a control over a particular assertion is expected to be so high as to render tests of controls ineffective and inappropriate.

— Test automated controls to determine that they continue to function effectively.

• In connection with *substantive procedures*:

— Plan and perform substantive procedures to be responsive to the related assessment of the risk of material misstatement.

— Design and perform substantive procedures for all relevant assertions related to each material class of transactions, account balance, and disclosure, regardless of the assessed risk of material misstatement.

— Perform substantive procedures related to the financial statement reporting process, including (1) agreeing the financial statements and notes to the underlying accounting records and (2) examining material journal entries and other adjustments made during the financial statement preparation.

— Perform substantive procedures that are specifically responsive to significant assessed risks of material misstatement at the relevant assertion level.

— Consider the specific guidance in AU Section 318 on the nature, timing, and extent of substantive procedures when the audit approach to significant risks consists only of substantive procedures.

— Plan substantive procedures to be responsive to the planned level of detection risk, and design tests of details that are responsive to the assessed risk.

— Select from items contained in a financial statement amount and obtain the relevant audit evidence when testing the existence or occurrence assertions.

— Select from audit evidence indicating that an item should be included in the relevant financial statement amount, and ascertain whether it is included, when testing the completeness assertion.

— Consider the following when designing substantive analytical procedures: (1) the suitability of the procedures to the assertions; (2) the reliability of the data from which the expectations are developed; (3) the precision of the expectation; and (4) the amount of an acceptable difference between recorded amounts and expected values.

— Consider testing the controls over the client's preparation of information that is used by the auditor in analytical procedures.

— Evaluate the risk of management override of controls, and whether adjustments might have been made to the financial statements outside of the normal period-end financial reporting process when designing substantive analytical procedures.

— Perform further substantive procedures or substantive procedures combined with tests of controls to cover the remaining period when substantive procedures are performed at an interim date.

— Consider certain specific factors when performing substantive procedures at an interim date, for example: (1) the control environment; (2) the objective of the substantive procedure; and (3) the nature of the account balance or transaction class and the relevant assertions.

— Consider whether substantive procedures alone are sufficient to cover the period from an interim date to the period-end and, if not deemed sufficient, perform tests of the operating effectiveness of relevant controls or perform substantive procedures as of the period-end.

— Consider whether substantive procedures might best be performed at or near the period-end when addressing an identified risk of material misstatement due to fraud.

— Consider the following matters when performing substantive analytical procedures to cover the intervening period between an interim test date and the reporting period-end: (1) whether the period-end balances are reasonably predictable with respect to amount, relative significance, and composition; (2) whether the client's procedures for analyzing and adjusting account balances and classes of transactions at interim dates are appropriate; (3) whether the client's procedures for establishing cutoffs are appropriate; and (4) whether the financial reporting information system will provide sufficient information about balances at period-end and transactions in the remaining period.

— Consider modifying the risk assessment and the planned nature, timing, or extent of substantive procedures covering the remaining period when misstatements are detected at an interim date.

— Perform audit procedures in the current period to establish the continuing relevance of audit evidence obtained in a prior period that is to be used in the current audit.

— Make decisions about coordinating related audit procedures in the light of the risks of material misstatement and of the particular audit procedures that could be applied.

— Consider, in designing tests of details, whether it is more effective to use selective means of testing (e.g., selecting large or unusual items from a population) as opposed to performing sampling.

— Increase the desired level of assurance as the planned level of detection risk increases when designing substantive analytical procedures.

• Evaluate whether the overall presentation of the financial statements and disclosures is in accordance with generally accepted accounting principles (GAAP), taking into consideration (1) whether the individual financial statements reflect appropriate classification and description of financial information; (2) whether management should have disclosed a particular matter in light of the surrounding facts and circumstances; and (3) the assessed risk of material misstatement at the relevant assertion level.

- Evaluate the sufficiency and appropriateness of audit evidence obtained and whether the assessments of the risks of material misstatement at the relevant assertion level remain appropriate.

- Reevaluate the planned audit procedures when the auditor discovers information that is significantly different from the information on which the initial risk assessments were based.

- Make specific inquiries to understand deviations from prescribed controls and their potential consequences.

- Consider whether misstatements detected by substantive procedures change the auditor's judgment about the effectiveness of the related controls, and determine whether (1) tests of controls performed provide an appropriate basis for reliance; (2) whether additional tests of controls are necessary; or (3) whether the potential risks of misstatement need to be addressed using substantive procedures.

- Consider how the detection of an instance of fraud or error affects the assessed risks of material misstatement without assuming that it is an isolated occurrence.

- Evaluate, before the conclusion of the audit, whether audit risk has been reduced to an appropriately low level, taking into account reconsideration of (1) the nature, timing, and extent of substantive procedures; (2) the evidence of the operating effectiveness of relevant controls; and (3) the client's risk assessment process.

- Conclude whether there is sufficient appropriate evidence to reduce the risk of material misstatement in the financial statements to an appropriately low level, by considering all relevant evidence, regardless of whether it appears to support or contradict the relevant financial statement assertions.

- Attempt to obtain further audit evidence if sufficient appropriate evidence has not been obtained for a material financial statement assertion; and if further audit evidence cannot be obtained, a qualified opinion or a disclaimer of opinion should be issued.

- Document certain specific elements of the audit procedures performed in response to assessed risks and the evaluation of the audit evidence obtained through those procedures.

AU SECTION 322
THE AUDITOR'S CONSIDERATION OF THE INTERNAL AUDIT FUNCTION IN AN AUDIT OF FINANCIAL STATEMENTS

WHAT EVERY PRACTITIONER SHOULD KNOW

Basic Requirements

When obtaining an understanding of internal control, the independent auditor should obtain an understanding of the internal audit function sufficient to identify those internal audit activities that are relevant to planning the audit. The independent auditor ordinarily should make inquiries of appropriate management, those charged with governance, and internal audit personnel about the internal auditors':

1. Organizational status within the entity.
2. Application of professional internal audit standards.
3. Audit plan, including the nature, timing, and extent of audit work.
4. Access to records and whether there are limitations on the scope of their activities.

Assessing the Competence and Objectivity of the Internal Auditors

If the independent auditor decides that it would be efficient to consider how the internal auditors' work might affect the nature, timing, and extent of audit procedures, he or she should assess the competence and objectivity of the internal audit function in light of the intended effect of the internal auditors' work on the audit.

Effect of the Internal Auditors' Work on the Audit

When the work of the internal auditors is expected to affect the audit, the independent auditor should (a) consider the extent of the effect on the audit, (b) coordinate audit work with internal auditors, and (c) evaluate and test the effectiveness of the internal auditors' work.

Evaluating the Effectiveness of the Internal Auditors' Work

The independent auditor should perform procedures to evaluate the quality and effectiveness of the internal auditors' work that significantly affect the nature, timing, and extent of the independent auditor's procedures. In connection with this, the independent auditor should consider whether the internal auditors':

- Scope of work is appropriate to meet the objectives.
- Audit programs are adequate.
- Working papers adequately document the work performed, including evidence of supervision and review.
- Conclusions are appropriate in the circumstances.

- Reports are consistent with the results of the work performed.

Testing the Effectiveness of the Internal Auditors' Work

The independent auditor should test some of the internal auditors' work related to the significant financial statement assertions. These tests may be accomplished by either (a) examining some of the controls, transactions, or balances that the internal auditors examined or (b) examining similar controls, transactions, or balances not actually examined by the internal auditors. Then, the independent auditor should compare the results of his or her tests with the results of the internal auditors' work.

Using Internal Auditors to Provide Direct Assistance during the Audit

When internal auditors provide direct assistance to the independent auditor during the audit, the independent auditor should:

- Assess the internal auditors' competence and objectivity.
- Supervise, review, evaluate, and test the work performed by internal auditors to the extent appropriate in the circumstances.
- Inform the internal auditors of their responsibilities, the objectives of the procedures they are to perform, and matters that may affect the nature, timing, and extent of audit procedures, such as possible accounting and auditing issues.
- Inform the internal auditors that all significant accounting and auditing issues identified during the audit should be brought to the auditor's attention.

PRACTICE ISSUES AND FREQUENTLY ASKED QUESTIONS

Issue 1: What factors should the auditor consider when assessing the competence of the internal auditors?

When assessing the competence of internal auditors, the auditor should obtain information about such factors as the following:

- Educational level and professional experience of internal auditors.
- Professional certification and continuing education.
- Audit policies, programs, and procedures.
- Practices regarding assignment of internal auditors.
- Supervision and review of internal auditors' activities.
- Quality of working paper documentation, reports, and recommendations.
- Evaluation of internal auditors' performance.

Issue 2: What factors should the auditor consider when assessing the objectivity of the internal auditors?

When assessing the objectivity of internal auditors, the auditor should obtain information about such factors as the following:

- The organizational status of the internal auditor responsible for the internal audit function, including:
  — Whether the internal auditor reports to an officer of sufficient status to ensure broad audit coverage and adequate consideration of, and action on, the findings and recommendations of the internal auditors.
  — Whether the internal auditor has direct access and reports regularly to those charged with governance.
  — Whether those charged with governance oversee employment decisions related to the internal auditor.
- Policies to maintain internal auditors' objectivity about the areas audited, including:
  — Policies prohibiting internal auditors from auditing areas where relatives are employed in important or audit-sensitive positions.
  — Policies prohibiting internal auditors from auditing areas where they were recently assigned or are scheduled to be assigned on completion of responsibilities in the internal audit function.

Issue 3: What are some key areas in which the work performed by the internal auditors may provide useful information to the independent auditor?

Procedures performed by the internal auditors may provide useful information to the independent auditor when:

- *Obtaining an understanding of the entity's internal control*—For example, internal auditors may develop a flowchart of a new computerized sales and receivables system. The independent auditor may review the flowchart to obtain information about the design of the related controls. In addition, the auditor may consider the results of procedures performed by the internal auditors on related controls to obtain information about whether the controls have been placed in operation.

- *Assessing the risk of material misstatement at the financial statement level*—The independent auditor's assessment of risk at the financial statement level often affects the overall audit strategy. The entity's internal audit function may influence this overall assessment of risk as well as the auditor's resulting decisions concerning the nature, timing, and extent of auditing procedures to be performed. For example, if the internal auditors' plan includes relevant audit work at various locations, the auditor may coordinate work with the internal auditors and reduce the number of the entity's locations at which the independent auditor would otherwise need to perform auditing procedures.

- *Assessing the risk of material misstatement at the account-balance or class-of-transaction level*—When planning and performing tests of controls, the independent auditor may consider the results of procedures planned or performed by the internal auditors. For example, the internal auditors' scope may include tests of controls for the completeness of accounts payable. The results of internal auditors' tests may provide appropriate information about the effectiveness of controls and change the nature, timing, and extent of testing the independent auditor would otherwise need to perform.

- *Performing substantive procedures*—For example, internal auditors, as part of their work, may confirm certain accounts receivable and observe certain physical inventories. Therefore, the independent auditor may be able to change the timing of the confirmation procedures, the number of accounts receivable to be confirmed, or the number of locations of physical inventories to be observed.

Issue 4: Can the independent auditor always use the work of internal auditors alone to reduce audit risk to an acceptable level and eliminate testing directly by the independent auditor?

No. For assertions related to material financial statement amounts where the risk of material misstatement or the degree of subjectivity involved in the evaluation of the audit evidence is high, the auditor should perform directly sufficient procedures in those areas. Assertions about the valuation of assets and liabilities involving significant accounting estimates, and about the existence and disclosure of related-party transactions, contingencies, uncertainties, and subsequent events, are examples of such areas.

Conversely, for certain assertions related to less material financial statement amounts where the risk of material misstatement or the degree of subjectivity involved in the evaluation of the audit evidence is low, the independent auditor may decide that testing of the assertions directly by himself or herself is not necessary. Assertions about the existence of cash, prepaid assets, and fixed-asset additions are examples of such areas.

ILLUSTRATIONS AND PRACTICE AIDS

ILLUSTRATION 1—CHECKLIST FOR THE INDEPENDENT AUDITOR'S CONSIDERATION OF THE INTERNAL AUDIT FUNCTION

	Yes	No	Comments

Overall Understanding of the Internal Audit Function

1. Does the internal audit function have a charter, a mission statement, or similar directive from management or those charged with governance?

2. Is an internal audit schedule covering the scope of internal control activities established regularly?

3. Does the internal audit schedule reflect an overall audit strategy that is tailored to the critical areas of accounting, auditing, and concerns of management and those charged with governance?

4. Does the internal auditors' current year report include the scope of the internal audits conducted, findings, recommendations, and appropriate follow-up?

	Yes	No	Comments

5. Does management or those charged with governance follow up on recommendations and reports of internal auditors?   ____ ____ _____

Objectivity of the Internal Auditors

1. Is the internal audit function independent of top management and those charged with governance?   ____ ____ _____

2. Do internal auditors have unrestricted access to the entity's operations and records when performing an internal audit?   ____ ____ _____

3. Do internal auditors report regularly to those charged with governance?   ____ ____ _____

4. Are there policies prohibiting internal auditors from auditing areas where relatives are employed in important or audit-sensitive positions?   ____ ____ _____

5. Are there policies prohibiting internal auditors from auditing areas where they were recently assigned or are scheduled to be assigned on completion of the responsibilities in the internal audit function?   ____ ____ _____

6. Are temporary assignments of internal audit staff to other functions (e.g., accounting, operations) strictly prohibited?   ____ ____ _____

Competence of the Internal Auditors

1. Is the internal audit department adequately staffed and supervised?   ____ ____ _____

2. Is the educational level and professional experience of internal auditors commensurate with their responsibilities?   ____ ____ _____

3. Do internal auditors hold professional certification and engage in continuing education?   ____ ____ _____

4. Are internal auditors knowledgeable about the entity's operations, processes, and procedures?   ____ ____ _____

5. Are up-to-date audit manuals, policies, and procedures available?   ____ ____ _____

6. Do job assignments reflect formal job descriptions?   ____ ____ _____

7. Are internal audits periodically reviewed by superiors and by someone not participating in the particular examination?   ____ ____ _____

8. Is the work of internal audit staff members audited?   ____ ____ _____

9. Are the internal auditor's working papers, reports, findings, and recommendations adequate?   ____ ____ _____

10. Are the periodic evaluations of internal auditors' performance required?   ____ ____ _____

Evaluating the Work of Internal Auditors

	Yes	No	Comments

1. Is the scope of the internal audits adequate to meet the stated objectives?

2. Is the work performed by internal auditors independent of accounting functions?

3. Are written audit programs prepared and modified to respond to current circumstances?

4. Are all tests documented in detail in the working papers, including the specific procedures performed and the results obtained?

5. Are internal audit reports and conclusions appropriate in the circumstances and consistent with the results of the work performed?

6. Do the internal auditors' reports summarize all significant matters, with no influence by management?

7. Are the findings and recommendations reviewed with management?

8. Have the internal audit reports been followed up on and corrective actions taken regarding reported deficiencies?

9. Are operational and administrative controls reviewed on a cyclical basis?

AU SECTION 324
SERVICE ORGANIZATIONS

PRACTICE POINT: As part of its Clarity Project, the American Institute of Certified Public Accountants' (AICPA's) Auditing Standards Board (ASB) has finalized a clarified Statement on Auditing Standards (SAS) titled, "Audit Considerations Relating to an Entity Using a Service Organization," which supersedes AU Section 324 (Service Organizations). The clarified SAS contains guidance only for user auditors. Guidance for service auditors is contained in Statement on Standards for Attestation Engagements (SSAE) No. 16 (AT Section 801), "Reporting on Controls at a Service Organization." The clarified SAS changes AU Section 324 in the following ways:

- A user organization is now known as a *user entity*.

- A user auditor is permitted to make reference to the work of a service auditor in the user auditor's report to explain a modification of the user auditor's opinion. In such circumstances, the user auditor's report is required to indicate that such reference does not diminish the user auditor's responsibility for that opinion. However, as in extant AU Section 324, the user auditor is prohibited from making reference to the work of a service auditor in a user auditor's report containing an unmodified opinion.

- A user auditor is required to inquire of management of the user entity about whether the service organization has reported to the user entity any fraud, noncompliance with laws and regulations, or uncorrected misstatements. If so, the user auditor is required to evaluate how such matters affect the nature, timing, and extent of the user auditor's further audit procedures.

- In determining the sufficiency and appropriateness of the audit evidence provided by a service auditor's report, the user auditor should be satisfied regarding the adequacy of the standards under which the service auditor's report was issued.

The ASB is expected to issue many of the clarified standards in *one* SAS that will be codified in "AU Section" format. The ASB has decided that the effective date of the clarified SASs that have not yet been issued is for audits of financial statements for periods ending on or after December 15, 2012. Auditors should be alert to and monitor further developments in this area.

PRACTICE POINT: Statement on Standards for Attestation Engagements (SSAE) No. 16 (AT Section 801), "Reporting on Controls at a Service Organization," supersedes the guidance for service auditors in this AU Section 324 when the service auditor is reporting on periods ending on or after June 15, 2011. Earlier implementation of SSAE-16 is permitted. For further guidance and coverage of SSAE-16, see AT Section 801 (Reporting on Controls at a Service Organization) of this Manual.

WHAT EVERY PRACTITIONER SHOULD KNOW

Basic Objectives

This Section provides guidance for:

1. Independent auditors auditing the financial statements of an entity that uses a service organization to process certain transactions ("user auditor").

2. Independent auditors issuing reports on the processing of transactions by a service organization ("service auditor").

Requirements for User Auditors

Many entities use service organizations (e.g., banks, brokerage firms, electronic data processing service centers) to perform some or all of their data processing. Services provided by outside organizations range from performing specific tasks (e.g., maintaining custody of marketable securities) to replacing entire departments (e.g., performing all computer processing). Many entities use such service organizations because, generally, they do not have the internal expertise or skills to perform the services or it is cost effective to outsource the service.

As with any audit, the user auditor should obtain an understanding of the user organization's internal control sufficient to plan the audit. This understanding may encompass controls placed in operation by the entity and by service organizations whose services are part of the entity's information system. A service organization's services are part of an entity's information system if they affect any of the following:

1. Significant transactions in the client's financial statements.

2. The accounting processing involved from the initiation of the transactions to their inclusion in the financial statements.

3. The accounting records, supporting information, and specific accounts in the financial statements involved in initiating, recording, processing, and reporting of the client's transactions.

4. How the client's information system captures significant events and transactions.

5. The financial reporting process used to prepare the client's financial statements, including significant accounting estimates and disclosures.

The user auditor's consideration of the significance of the service organization's controls to those of the user organization The significance of the service organization's controls to those of the user organization depends primarily on the following:

1. *The nature and materiality of the transactions it processes for the user organization* If the transactions processed or accounts affected by the service organization are material to the user organization's financial statements, the user auditor may need to obtain an understanding of the controls at the service organization. In certain situations, the transactions processed and accounts affected may not appear to be material to the

user organization's financial statements, but the nature of the transactions processed may require that the user auditor obtain an understanding of those controls because improper processing may result in a material misstatement.

2. *The degree of interaction between the internal controls at the user organization and the controls at the service organization* The degree of interaction relates to the extent to which a user organization is able to and decides to implement effective internal controls over the processing performed by the service organization and on the nature of the services provided by the service organization. The following examples illustrate how the degree of interaction affects user organization controls:

   a. *High degree of interaction*—When the *user organization initiates transactions* and the service organization executes and does the accounting processing of those transactions, there is a high degree of interaction between the activities at the user organization and those at the service organization. If the user organization implements highly effective internal controls over the processing of transactions at the service organization, the user auditor may not need to gain an understanding of the controls at the service organization in order to plan the audit. For example, if the user organization has such controls, the user auditor could obtain an understanding of the controls by performing a walk-through at the user organization.

   b. *Low degree of interaction*—When the *service organization initiates, executes, and does the accounting processing* of the user organization's transactions, there is a lower degree of interaction between the activities at the user organization and those at the service organization; in these circumstances, it may not be practicable for the user organization to implement effective controls for those transactions. If the user organization has a low degree of interaction and has not placed into operation effective internal controls over the activities of the service organization, the user auditor would most likely need to gain an understanding of the relevant controls at the service organization in order to plan the audit.

The user auditor's consideration of available information to plan the audit
Information about the nature of the services provided by a service organization that are part of the user organization's information system and the service organization's controls over those services may be available from a wide variety of sources, such as the following:

- User manuals
- System overviews
- Technical manuals
- The contract between the user organization and the service organization
- Reports by service auditors, internal auditors, or regulatory authorities on the service organization's controls

If the services and the service organization's controls over those services are highly standardized, information obtained through the user auditor's prior experience with the service organization may be helpful in planning the audit.

After considering the available information, the user auditor has to determine whether a sufficient understanding of the internal control can be obtained to plan the audit. Such an understanding can be obtained generally in one of the following ways:

1. The user organization may have sufficient controls over the information processed by the service organization. This is typically the case in most small business audits in which the entity uses a payroll processing service. Ordinarily, the entity authorizes and verifies the payroll checks and related information produced by a payroll processing service.

2. If the user auditor concludes that the user organization does not have sufficient controls over the information processed by the service organization to plan the audit, the user auditor should obtain and review a copy of the service auditor's report on the service organization's description of its controls.

3. If the user auditor concludes that neither of the preceding two alternatives are possible to plan the audit, the user auditor must obtain his or her own understanding of the service organization's controls that are relevant to the user organization's internal control. This can be accomplished by performing procedures, such as the following:

   a. Contacting the service organization to obtain specific information.

   b. Visiting the service organization to make inquiries and observations, review documentation, and perform the necessary procedures.

   c. Requesting that a service auditor be engaged to perform procedures that will provide the necessary information.

If, after performing the steps identified above, the user auditor is unable to obtain sufficient competent evidence to accomplish the desired audit objectives, the user auditor should qualify his or her opinion or disclaim an opinion on the financial statements because of a scope limitation.

The user auditor's assessment of control risk at the user organization After the user auditor obtains an understanding of the relevant controls at both the user organization and the service organization and considers the factors that affect the risk of material misstatement, he or she should assess control risk for the financial statement assertions. To accomplish this, the user auditor should evaluate the type of evidence obtained about the operating effectiveness of relevant controls and conclude whether the type of evidence obtained allows him or her to reduce the assessed level of control risk below the maximum.

Control risk can only be assessed below the maximum if audit evidence is obtained using one or a combination of the following procedures:

- *By testing the user organization's controls over the activities of the service organization*—For example, if a user organization uses an EDP service center to process payroll transactions, the user organization may establish controls over input and output data to prevent or detect material misstatements. The user organization might recalculate the service organization's payroll computations on a test basis. In this situation, the user auditor may perform tests of the user organization's controls over data processing that would provide a basis for assessing control risk below the maximum for the assertions related to payroll transactions.

- *By obtaining a service auditor's report on controls placed in operation* and *tests of operating effectiveness, or a report on the application of agreed-upon procedures that describes relevant tests of controls*—If the user auditor decides to use a service auditor's report, the user auditor should consider the extent of the evidence provided by the report concerning the effectiveness of controls intended to prevent or detect material misstatements regarding the particular assertions. The user auditor remains responsible for evaluating the evidence presented by the service auditor and for determining the effect of this evidence on the assessment of control risk at the user organization. (**Note:** A service auditor's report on controls placed in operation at a service organization that does not include tests of operating effectiveness does not provide the user auditor with a basis for reducing the assessment of control risk below the maximum.)

- *By the user auditor performing appropriate tests of controls at the service organization*—No single specific test of controls is always necessary, applicable, or equally effective in every circumstance and every engagement. Therefore, the auditor should use professional judgment to determine what constitutes sufficient appropriate audit evidence under the specific circumstances of the engagement.

Illustration 1 summarizes the types of evidence that a user auditor may obtain about relevant controls at a service organization and whether such evidence provides a basis for the user auditor to assess control risk below the maximum at the user organization.

Requirements for Service Auditors

PRACTICE POINT: Statement on Standards for Attestation Engagements (SSAE) No. 16 (AT Section 801), "Reporting on Controls at a Service Organization," supersedes the guidance for service auditors in this AU Section 324 when the service auditor is reporting on periods ending on or after June 15, 2011. Earlier implementation of SSAE-16 is permitted. For further guidance and coverage of SSAE-16, see AT Section 801 of this Manual.

The service auditor is responsible for the representations in his or her report and for exercising due care in the application of procedures that support those representations. The service auditor should obtain written representations from the service organization's management that include the items listed in Illustration 2.

The service auditor may become aware of illegal acts, fraud, or uncorrected errors attributable to the service organization that may affect one or more user organizations. In such circumstances, the service auditor should determine from the appropriate level of management of the service organization whether this information has been communicated appropriately to affected user organizations, unless those matters are clearly inconsequential. If management has not communicated the information to affected user organizations and is unwilling to do so, the service auditor should inform those charged with governance of the service organization. If those charged with governance do not respond appropriately to the service auditor's communication, the service auditor should consult with an attorney and consider whether to resign from the engagement.

The service auditor may be requested to apply substantive procedures to user transactions or assets at the service organization. In such circumstances, the service auditor may make specific reference in his or her report to having carried out the designated procedures or may provide a separate report in accordance with AT Section 201 (Agreed-Upon Procedures Engagements). Either form of reporting should include a sufficient description of the nature, timing, extent, and results of the procedures to enable user auditors to decide whether to use the results as evidence to support their opinions.

Two types of reports may be issued by a service auditor:

1. *Report on controls placed in operation at the service organization*—This type of report includes (a) a description of the controls at the service organization that may be relevant to a user organization's internal control, (b) a description of whether such service organization's controls were suitably designed to achieve specific control objectives, and (c) whether such controls had been placed in operation as of a specific date.

2. *Report on controls placed in operation at the service organization and tests of operating effectiveness*—In addition to reporting on the system design as described in 1 above, the service auditor renders an opinion, based on tests of compliance with controls over a period of time, on whether the degree of compliance with the controls tested is sufficient to provide reasonable, but not absolute, assurance that the related specific control objectives have been achieved.

Each of these reports is discussed below. Illustration 3 provides a detailed comparison of what is included in each type of the service auditor's reports.

Report on controls placed in operation at a service organization To be able to report on controls placed in operation at the service organization, the service auditor should perform the following procedures when considering the service organization's description of controls placed in operation:

1. Obtain information on the controls through discussions with appropriate service organization personnel and through reference to various forms of documentation, such as system flowcharts and narratives.

2. Determine whether the description of controls provides sufficient information for user auditors to obtain an understanding of those controls that may be relevant to a user organization's internal control.

3. Determine whether the description of controls include the specific control objectives of the service organization that are relevant to user organizations.

4. Obtain evidence of whether controls have been placed in operation, which is ordinarily obtained through:

   a. Previous experience with the service organization.

   b. Inquiry of appropriate management, supervisory, and staff personnel.

   c. Inspection of service organization documents and records.

   d. Observation of service organization activities and operations.

5. Inquire about changes in the service organization's controls that may have occurred before the beginning of fieldwork. If the service auditor believes that the changes would be considered significant by user organizations and their auditors, those changes should be included in the description of the service organization's controls. If the service auditor concludes that the changes would be considered significant by user organizations and their auditors and the changes are not included in the description of the service organization's controls, the service auditor should describe the changes in his or her report.

6. Consider whether the description of controls is inaccurate or insufficiently complete for user auditors, in which case the service auditor's report should so state and should contain sufficient detail to provide user auditors with an appropriate understanding.

7. Consider whether the system was designed with the assumption that certain controls would be implemented by the user organization. If the service auditor is aware of the need for such complementary user organization controls, these should be delineated in the description of controls and the service auditor's report should be appropriately modified.

8. Consider conditions that come to his or her attention that, in the service auditor's judgment, represent significant deficiencies in the design or operation of the service organization's controls that preclude the service auditor from obtaining reasonable assurance that specified control objectives would be achieved.

9. Consider whether any other information, irrespective of specified control objectives, has come to his or her attention that causes him or her to conclude (a) that design deficiencies exist that could adversely affect the ability to record, process, summarize, or report financial data to user organizations without error and (b) that user organizations would not generally be expected to have controls in place to mitigate such design deficiencies.

The following sample service auditor's reports are provided in the Illustrations and Practice Aids section below:

- Illustration 4 is a sample service auditor's report on controls placed in operation at a service organization that is applicable when there are no exceptions.

- Illustration 5 is a sample service auditor's report on controls placed in operation at a service organization that is applicable when the description of controls is inaccurate or incomplete.

- Illustration 6 is a sample service auditor's report on controls placed in operation at a service organization that is applicable when significant deficiencies exist in the design or operation of the service organization's controls.

Report on controls placed in operation at a service organization *and* **tests of operating effectiveness** To be able to report on controls placed in operation and tests of operating effectiveness at the service organization, the service auditor should perform the procedures described above under "Report on controls placed in operation at a service organization." In addition, the service auditor should:

1. Perform tests of controls to determine whether specific controls are operating with sufficient effectiveness to achieve specified control objectives.

2. Determine which controls are, in his or her judgment, necessary to achieve the control objectives specified by management.

3. Determine the nature, timing, and extent of the tests of controls needed to evaluate operating effectiveness. Testing should be applied to controls in effect throughout the period covered by the report.

The following sample service auditor's reports are provided in the Illustrations and Practice Aids section below:

- Illustration 7 is a sample service auditor's report on controls placed in operation at a service organization and tests of operating effectiveness that is applicable when there are no exceptions.

- Illustration 8 is a sample service auditor's report on controls placed in operation at a service organization and tests of operating effectiveness that is applicable when the description of controls is inaccurate or incomplete.

- Illustration 9 is a sample service auditor's report on controls placed in operation at a service organization and tests of operating effectiveness that is applicable when significant deficiencies exist in the design or operation of the service organization's controls.

Service auditors' responsibilities for subsequent events Changes in a service organization's controls may occur subsequent to the period covered by the service auditor's report but before the date of his or her report (referred to as *subsequent events*). Although a service auditor has no responsibility to detect such subsequent events, he or she should consider information about the following types of subsequent events that come to his or her attention:

- *Events that provide additional information about conditions that existed during the period covered by the service auditor's report.* The service auditor should use this information in determining whether controls at the service organization that could affect user organizations' information systems were (a) placed in operation, (b) suitably designed, and (3) if applicable, operating effectively during the period covered by the engagement.

- *Events that provide information about conditions that arose subsequent to the period covered by the service auditor's report that are so significant that their disclosure is necessary to prevent users from being misled.* Generally, this type of subsequent event will not affect the service auditor's report, as long as the information is appropriately disclosed. Therefore, the service auditor should determine whether management has disclosed such information in the section of the service auditor's report titled "Other Information Provided by the Service Organization." If this information is not disclosed by the service organization, the service auditor should consider disclosing it in the section of his or her report titled "Other Information Provided by the Service Auditor" and/or in the service auditor's report.

Also, a service auditor should inquire of management about its knowledge of any subsequent events that would have a significant effect on user organizations. In addition, the service auditor should obtain a representation from management regarding subsequent events.

Considerations When Service Organizations Use the Services of Other Service Organizations (Subservice Organizations)

PRACTICE POINT: Statement on Standards for Attestation Engagements (SSAE) No. 16 (AT Section 801), "Reporting on Controls at a Service Organization," supersedes the guidance for service auditors in this AU Section 324 when the service auditor is reporting on periods ending on or after June 15, 2011. Earlier implementation of SSAE-16 is permitted. For further guidance and coverage of SSAE-16, see AT Section 801 of this Manual.

There may be situations when a service organization (e.g., bank trust department) uses the services of another service organization (e.g., an independent computer processing service organization) to perform its data processing. In these situations, the other service organization (i.e., the computer processing service organization) is considered a subservice organization. This section addresses certain specific issues when service organizations use the services of other service organizations.

Effect on a user auditor's and a service auditor's procedures when a service organization uses a subservice organization When a service organization uses a subservice organization, the user auditor should determine whether the processing performed by the subservice organization affects assertions in the user organization's financial statements and whether those assertions are significant to the user organization's financial statements. To plan the audit and assess control risk, a user auditor may need to consider the controls at both the service organization and the subservice organization. Therefore, the guidance discussed above should be interpreted to include the subservice organization. The following are the most important factors to consider in determining the significance of the subservice organization's controls to the user organization's internal control:

- The degree of interaction between the user organization, the service organization, and the subservice organization.

- The nature and materiality of the transactions processed by the service organization and the subservice organization.

Methods used by a user auditor to obtain information about controls at a subservice organization If a user auditor concludes that information about the subservice organization is needed in order to plan the audit or to assess control risk, the user auditor may perform the following procedures to obtain such information:

- Contact the service organization through the user organization.

- Contact the subservice organization either through the user organization or the service organization.

- Request that a service auditor be engaged to perform procedures that will supply the necessary information.

- Visit the service organization or subservice organization and perform such procedures.

Information about a subservice organization that should be included in the service organization's description of controls A service organization's description of controls should include a description of the functions and the nature of the processing performed by the subservice organization in sufficient detail for user auditors to understand the significance of the subservice organization's functions to the processing of the user organization's transactions. This is intended to alert user organizations and their auditors that another entity (i.e., the subservice organization) is involved in the processing of the user organization's transactions and to summarize the functions the subservice organization performs.

Generally, the identity of the subservice organization is not required to be disclosed, unless the service organization determines that such disclosure would be relevant to user organizations. In these situations, the name of the subservice organization may be included in the service organization's description of controls.

When a subservice organization performs services for a service organization, there are two equally acceptable methods of presenting the description of controls:

1. *The Carve-Out Method*—Under the carve-out method, the subservice organization's relevant control objectives and controls are excluded from the description and from the scope of the service auditor's engagement. The service organization states in the description that:

    a. The subservice organization's controls and related control objectives are omitted from the description.

    b. The control objectives in the report include only the objectives the service organization's controls are intended to achieve.

2. *The Inclusive Method*—Under the inclusive method, the subservice organization's relevant controls are included in the description and in the scope of the service auditor's engagement. The description should:

a. Clearly differentiate between controls of the service organization and those of the subservice organization.

b. Include all of the control objectives a user auditor would expect both the service organization and the subservice organization to achieve.

Under either method, the service organization should include in its description of controls a description of the functions and nature of the processing performed by the subservice organization. If the service organization does not disclose the existence of the subservice organization and the functions it performs, if considered significant to the processing of user organization transactions, the service auditor should consider modifying his or her report. In such situations, the service auditor may need to issue a qualified or adverse opinion as to the fairness of the presentation of the description of controls.

Effect of the presentation of information about the subservice organization on the service auditor's report If the service organization has adopted the carve-out method, the service auditor should:

1. Modify the scope paragraph of his or her report to briefly summarize the functions and nature of the processing performed by the subservice organization. Generally, this summary is briefer than the information provided by the service organization in its description of the functions and nature of the processing performed by the subservice organization.

2. Include a statement in the scope paragraph of his or her report indicating that the description of controls includes only those of the service organization and, therefore, the service auditor's examination does not extend to controls at the subservice organization.

Illustration 10 provides a sample scope paragraph of a service auditor's report using the carve-out method.

If the service organization has adopted the inclusive method, the service auditor should perform procedures such as the following:

1. Perform tests of the service organization's controls over the activities of the subservice organization.

2. Perform procedures at the subservice organization. Under this option, the service auditor should recognize that the subservice organization generally is not the client for the engagement and, therefore, the service organization should arrange for such procedures.

Illustration 11 provides a sample service auditor's report using the inclusive method.

PRACTICE ISSUES AND FREQUENTLY ASKED QUESTIONS

Issues Relating to User Auditors

Issue 1: What factors should a user auditor consider when using a service auditor's report that is intended to satisfy the needs of several different user auditors?

Because a service auditor's report may be intended to satisfy the needs of several different user auditors, a user auditor should determine whether the specific tests of controls and results in the service auditor's report are relevant to assertions that are significant in the user organization's financial statements. For those tests of controls and results that are relevant, a user auditor should consider whether the nature, timing and extent of such tests of controls and results provide sufficient evidence about the effectiveness of the controls to support the user auditor's desired assessment of the level of control risk. In evaluating these factors, the user auditor should also keep in mind that the shorter the time period covered by the tests of controls and the longer the time elapsed since the performance of the tests, the less support for control risk reduction the tests may provide.

Issue 2: What course of action should the user auditor take if he or she believes that the service auditor's report is not sufficient to meet his or her audit objectives?

If the user auditor believes that the service auditor's report may not be sufficient to meet his or her audit objectives, the user auditor should consider the following:

1. Discussing with the service auditor the scope and results of the service auditor's work in order to obtain a better understanding of the service auditor's procedures and conclusions.

2. Contacting the service organization, through the user organization, to request that the service auditor perform agreed-upon procedures at the service organization.

3. Performing the audit procedures deemed necessary at the service organization to accomplish the audit objectives

Issue 3: May the user auditor make reference to the report of the service auditor as a basis for his or her opinion on the user organization's financial statements?

No. There cannot be a division of responsibility for the audit of the user organization's financial statements because the service auditor did not audit any portion of that organization's financial statements. Therefore, the user auditor should not make reference to the report of the service auditor.

Issue 4: What should the user auditor do if the service organization's description of controls placed in operation is as of a date that precedes the beginning of the period under audit for the user organization?

A service organization's description of controls placed in operation is as of a specified date. Accordingly, the service auditor issues a report on whether the description presents fairly, in all material respects, the relevant aspects of the service organization's controls at a specified date. A report on controls placed in operation that is as of a date outside the reporting period of a user organization may be useful in providing a user auditor with a preliminary understanding of the controls placed in operation at the service organization, if the report is supplemented by additional current information from other sources. If the service organization's description is as of a date that precedes the beginning of the period under audit, the user auditor should consider updating the information in the description to determine whether there have been any changes in the service organization's controls relevant to the processing of the user organization's transactions. Procedures to update the information in a service auditor's report may include:

1. Discussions with user organization personnel who would be in a position to know about changes at the service organization.

2. A review of current documentation and correspondence issued by the service organization.

3. Discussions with service organization personnel or with the service auditor.

If the user auditor determines that there have been significant changes in the service organization's controls, the user auditor should attempt to gain an understanding of the changes and consider the effect of those changes on his or her audit.

Issue 5: Does the auditor of a small business that uses the services of an outside payroll service to process its payroll checks, payroll tax returns, and W-2s generally have to obtain a service auditor's report in connection with the audit?

Probably not. Small businesses that hire payroll processing services typically control both the input and the output of the process. In any case, it is usually easy for an auditor to verify the accuracy of the payroll independently of either the client's or the service organization's system of controls. In this case, it would not be necessary to obtain a service auditor's report. However, a prudent auditor would address this concept in his or her working papers to show awareness and consideration of the issue involving the use of service auditors' reports.

Issue 6: Does the auditor of a user organization that has significant cash receipts collected through a bank lock-box arrangement, with different locations and accounts in several cities, need to obtain a service auditor's report for the bank's lock-box operation?

Probably yes. Many organizations engage the services of a bank to process their cash receipts and provide the organizations with posting detail to customers' accounts. Generally, such organizations' operations involve large numbers of cash receipts from a wide variety of customers. If the population consists of a large number of small amounts, confirmations are not likely to be an economical and effective means of assuring the completeness of cash receipts.

In such cases, a service auditor's report is probably important. Because the auditor will not be in a position to observe or test the controls over the cash receipts function at the bank, a service auditor's report on the bank's controls placed in operation and tests of operating effectiveness, or a service auditor's report on the application of agreed-upon procedures that describe controls over the bank's cash receipts processing, would enable the user auditor to assess control risk below the maximum. Typically, analytical procedures alone would not provide sufficient evidence in such a case.

Issue 7: What should a user auditor do in deciding whether a service auditor's report is satisfactory and competent to meet the objectives of his or her audit engagement?

The user auditor will usually make inquiries about the service auditor's professional reputation. The American Institute of Certified Public Accountants, and state societies can generally respond to certain inquiries about a firm's membership standing, enrollment in peer review programs, and the status of certain kinds of disciplinary proceedings. State Boards of Accountancy can usually verify licensing status and respond to certain questions about disciplinary actions. Other CPAs, bankers, attorneys, and persons in the business community can also provide relevant information. The user auditor can also visit the service auditor to discuss the procedures applied and the conclusions reached, and to review audit programs and workpapers.

Issues Relating to Service Auditors

PRACTICE POINT: Statement on Standards for Attestation Engagements (SSAE) No. 16 (AT Section 801), "Reporting on Controls at a Service Organization," supersedes the guidance for service auditors in this AU Section 324 when the service auditor is reporting on periods ending on or after June 15, 2011. Earlier implementation of SSAE-16 is permitted. For further guidance and coverage of SSAE-16, see AT Section 801 of this Manual.

Issue 8: In connection with a service auditor's engagement to report on the processing of transactions by a service organization, is it necessary for the service auditor to be independent from each user organization?

No. It is not necessary for the service auditor to be independent from each user organization. However, the service auditor should be independent from the service organization.

Issue 9: May the service auditor prepare the description of controls and control objectives in connection with his or her engagement to report on controls placed in operation at the service organization?

Yes. The service auditor may prepare the description of controls and control objectives for reports on controls placed in operation at the service organization; however, the representations in the description remain the responsibility of the service organization. Also, the description of controls and control objectives required for these reports may certainly be prepared by the service organization.

Issue 10: When service auditors issue reports on controls placed in operation and tests of operating effectiveness, what information and how much detail should they include in the reports about the tests performed and the results obtained?

A service auditor's report expressing an opinion on a description of controls placed in operation at a service organization and tests of operating effectiveness should contain a description of tests of operating effectiveness. Such a description should include:

- The controls that were tested.
- The objectives that the controls were intended to achieve.
- The tests applied to the controls.
- The results of the tests applied.
- An indication of the nature, timing, and extent of the tests in sufficient detail to enable user auditors to determine the effect of such tests on user auditors' assessments of control risk.
- Relevant information about exceptions discovered by the service auditor, including causative factors and corrective actions taken.

When considering what information and how much detail should be included in the description of the "tests applied" and the "results of the tests," the service auditor should:

1. Provide sufficient information to enable user auditors to assess control risk for financial statement assertions affected by the service organization.

2. Indicate whether the items tested represent a sample or all of the items in the population, but need not indicate the size of the population.

3. Include exceptions and other information in describing the results of the tests that could be relevant to user auditors. Such exceptions and other information should be included for each control objective, regardless of whether the service auditor concludes that the control objective has been achieved. The description of exceptions noted, if any, should include:

    a. The size of the sample, when sampling has been used.

    b. The number of exceptions noted. If no exceptions or other information that could be relevant to user auditors are identified by the tests, the service auditor should so indicate, for example, "No relevant exceptions noted."

    c. The nature of the exceptions.

Issue 11: Is a service auditor required to identify in his or her report a service organization's design deficiencies that do not affect processing during the period covered by his or her examination, but that may present potential problems in future periods?

No. This Section does not apply to design deficiencies that potentially could affect processing *in future periods.* Therefore, a service auditor is not required to identify in his or her report design deficiencies that do not affect processing during the period covered by his or her examination, but that may present potential problems in future periods.

However, according to an auditing interpretation of this Section, the service auditor may, in his or her professional judgment, choose to:

1. Communicate such deficiencies to the service organization's management, and

2. Advise management to disclose this information and its plans for correcting the design deficiencies in a section of the service auditor's document titled "Other Information Provided by the Service Organization." If the service organization includes information about the design deficiencies in this section of the document, the service auditor should:

    a. Read the information and consider the guidance in AU Section 550 (Other Information in Documents Containing Audited Financial Statements), and

    b. Include a paragraph in his or her report disclaiming an opinion on the information provided by the service organization. The following is an example of such a paragraph:

        The information in section [X] describing ABC Service Organization's plans to modify its disaster recovery plan is presented by the Service Organization to provide additional information and is not a part of the Service Organization's description of controls that may be relevant to a user organization's internal control. Such information has not been subjected to the procedures applied in the examination of the description of the controls applicable to the processing of transactions for user organizations and, accordingly, we express no opinion on it.

In addition, a service auditor may consider communicating information about the design deficiencies in the section of his or her document titled "Other Information Provided by the Service Auditor."

Issue 12: May a service auditor expand his or her report to describe the risk of projecting to the future conclusions about the effectiveness of a service organization's controls?

Yes. This Section requires a service auditor to include in his or her report a statement of the inherent limitations of the potential effectiveness of controls at the service organization and of the risk of projecting to future periods any evaluation of the description. The sample auditor's reports in the Illustrations below include examples of how such a statement might read. The following sentence appears in the illustrative auditor's reports:

Furthermore, the projection of any conclusions, based on our findings, to future periods is subject to the risk that changes may alter the validity of such conclusions.

A service auditor may expand the above description to describe the risk of projecting to the future conclusions about the effectiveness of controls. This may be accomplished by modifying the aforementioned sentence to read as follows:

Furthermore, the projection of any conclusions, based on our findings, to future periods is subject to the risk that changes made to the system or controls, or the failure to make needed changes to the system or controls, may alter the validity of such conclusions.

ILLUSTRATIONS AND PRACTICE AIDS

ILLUSTRATION 1—TYPES OF EVIDENCE THAT MAY OR MAY NOT PROVIDE A USER AUDITOR WITH A BASIS TO ASSESS CONTROL RISK BELOW THE MAXIMUM AT THE USER ORGANIZATION

PRACTICE POINT: Statement on Standards for Attestation Engagements (SSAE) No. 16 (AT Section 801), "Reporting on Controls at a Service Organization," supersedes the guidance for service auditors in this AU Section 324 when the service auditor is reporting on periods ending on or after June 15, 2011. Earlier implementation of SSAE-16 is permitted. For further guidance and coverage of SSAE-16, see AT Section 801 of this Manual.

Type of Evidence Obtained about Relevant Controls at the Service Organization	Does Type of Evidence Obtained Allow the User Auditor to Reduce the Assessed Level of Control Risk below the Maximum?
1. A service auditor's report on a service organization's controls placed in operation.	No
2. A service auditor's report on a service organization's controls placed in operation *and* tests of operating effectiveness.	Yes
3. A service auditor's report on the application of agreed-upon procedures that describes relevant tests of controls at the service organization.	Yes
4. User auditor testing of the user organization's controls over the activities of the service organization.	Yes
5. User auditor testing of controls at the service organization that are relevant to significant assertions embodied in the user organization's financial statements.	Yes

ILLUSTRATION 2—ITEMS TO BE INCLUDED IN A SERVICE ORGANIZA-TION MANAGEMENT REPRESENTATION LETTER TO THE SERVICE AUDITOR (APPLICABLE TO BOTH TYPES OF REPORTS)

PRACTICE POINT: Statement on Standards for Attestation Engagements (SSAE) No. 16 (AT Section 801), "Reporting on Controls at a Service Organization," supersedes the guidance for service auditors in this AU Section 324 when the service auditor is reporting on periods ending on or after June 15, 2011. Earlier implementation of SSAE-16 is permitted. For further guidance and coverage of SSAE-16, see AT Section 801 of this Manual.

---

1. Acknowledgment of management's responsibility for establishing and maintaining appropriate controls relating to the processing of transactions for user organizations.

2. Acknowledgment of the appropriateness of the specified control objectives.

3. A statement that the description of controls presents fairly, in all material respects, the aspects of the service organization's controls that may be relevant to a user organization's internal control.

4. A statement that the controls, as described, had been placed in operation as of a specific date.

5. A statement that management believes its controls were suitably designed to achieve the specified control objectives.

6. A statement that management has disclosed to the service auditor the following items:

   a. Any significant changes in controls that have occurred since the service organization's last examination.

   b. Any illegal acts, fraud, or uncorrected errors attributable to the service organization's management or employees that may affect one or more user organizations.

   c. All design deficiencies in controls of which it is aware, including those for which management believes the cost of corrective action may exceed the benefits.

   d. Any subsequent events that would have a significant effect on user organizations.

7. If the scope of the service auditor's work includes tests of operating effectiveness, a statement that management has disclosed to the service auditor all instances, of which it is aware, when controls have not operated with sufficient effectiveness to achieve the specified control objectives.

ILLUSTRATION 3—CONTENTS OF SERVICE AUDITORS' REPORTS ON SERVICE ORGANIZATIONS' DESCRIPTION OF CONTROLS

PRACTICE POINT: Statement on Standards for Attestation Engagements (SSAE) No. 16 (AT Section 801), "Reporting on Controls at a Service Organization," supersedes the guidance for service auditors in this AU Section 324 when the service auditor is reporting on periods ending on or after June 15, 2011. Earlier implementation of SSAE-16 is permitted. For further guidance and coverage of SSAE-16, see AT Section 801 of this Manual.

		Report on Controls Placed in Operation	Report on Controls Placed in Operation and Tests of Operating Effectiveness
1.	Reference to the description of applications covered at the service organization. The report should have as an attachment a description of the service organization's controls that may be relevant to a user organization's internal control.	Yes	Yes
2.	Description of the scope and nature of the service auditor's procedures.	Yes	Yes
3.	Identification of the party specifying the control objectives.	Yes	Yes
4.	Indication about the purpose of the service auditor's engagement which is to obtain reasonable, but not absolute, assurance about the service organization's controls and their operation as of a specific date.	Yes	Yes
5.	A disclaimer of opinion on the operating effectiveness of the controls.	Yes	No
6.	The service auditor's opinion on the fair presentation of the description of the controls and their suitability in achieving specific control objectives.	Yes	Yes
7.	Reference to a description of controls for which tests of operating effectiveness were performed, the specified control objectives intended to be achieved by those controls, the tests applied, and the results of those tests.	No	Yes
8.	The period covered by the service auditor's report on tests of operating effectiveness.	No	Yes
9.	The service auditor's opinion on whether the controls tested were operating to provide reasonable, but not absolute, assurance that specified control objectives were achieved.	No	Yes

	Report on Controls Placed in Operation	Report on Controls Placed in Operation and Tests of Operating Effectiveness
10. A statement that the scope of the service auditor's engagement did not include tests to determine whether control objectives not listed in the description of controls were achieved and a disclaimer of opinion on such.	No	Yes
11. A statement that the relative effectiveness and significance of specific controls at the service organization and their effect on assessments of control risk at user organizations are dependent on their interaction with the controls and other factors present at individual user organizations.	No	Yes
12. A statement that the service auditor has performed no procedures to evaluate the effectiveness of controls at individual user organizations.	No	Yes
13. A statement of the inherent limitations of the potential effectiveness of controls at the service organization and of the risk of projecting to the future any evaluation of the description or any conclusions about the effectiveness of controls in achieving control objectives.	Yes	Yes
14. The parties for whom the service auditor's report is intended.	Yes	Yes

ILLUSTRATION 4—SAMPLE SERVICE AUDITOR'S REPORT ON CONTROLS PLACED IN OPERATION AT A SERVICE ORGANIZATION—NO EXCEPTIONS

PRACTICE POINT: Statement on Standards for Attestation Engagements (SSAE) No. 16 (AT Section 801), "Reporting on Controls at a Service Organization," supersedes the guidance for service auditors in this AU Section 324 when the service auditor is reporting on periods ending on or after June 15, 2011. Earlier implementation of SSAE-16 is permitted. For further guidance and coverage of SSAE-16, see AT Section 801 of this Manual.

To XYZ Service Organization:

We have examined the accompanying description of controls related to the [*identify application*]application of XYZ Service Organization. Our examination included procedures to obtain reasonable assurance about whether (1) the accompanying description presents fairly, in all material respects, the aspects of XYZ Service Organization's controls that may be relevant to a user organization's internal control as it relates to an audit of financial statements; (2) the controls included in the description were suitably designed to achieve the control objectives specified in the description, if those controls were complied with satisfactorily[1]; and (3) such controls had been placed in operation as of [*identify specific date.*] The control objectives were specified by [*identify party that specified the control objectives.*] Our examination was performed in accordance with standards established by the American Institute of Certified Public Accountants and included those procedures we considered necessary in the circumstances to obtain a reasonable basis for rendering our opinion.

We did not perform procedures to determine the operating effectiveness of controls for any period. Accordingly, we express no opinion on the operating effectiveness of any aspects of XYZ Service Organization's controls, individually or in the aggregate.

In our opinion, the accompanying description of the aforementioned application presents fairly, in all material respects, the relevant aspects of XYZ Service Organization's controls that had been placed in operation as of [*identify specific date*]. Also, in our opinion, the controls, as described, are suitably designed to provide reasonable assurance that the specified control objectives would be achieved if the described controls were complied with satisfactorily[1].

The description of controls at XYZ Service Organization is as of [*identify specific date*] and any projection of such information to the future is subject to the risk that, because of change, the description may no longer portray the controls in existence. The potential effectiveness of specific controls at the XYZ Service Organization is subject to inherent limitations and, accordingly, errors or fraud may occur and not be detected. Furthermore, the projection of any conclusions, based on our findings, to future periods is subject to the risk that changes may alter the validity of such conclusions.

This report is intended solely for use by the management of XYZ Service Organization, its customers, and the independent auditors of its customers.

PRACTICE POINT: [1]If the application of controls by user organizations is necessary to achieve the stated control objectives, the service auditor's report should be modified to include the phrase "and user organizations applied the controls contemplated in the design of XYZ Service Organization's controls" following the words "complied with satisfactorily" in the scope and opinion paragraphs.

ILLUSTRATION 5—SAMPLE SERVICE AUDITOR'S REPORT ON CONTROLS PLACED IN OPERATION AT A SERVICE ORGANIZATION—DESCRIPTION OF CONTROLS IS INACCURATE OR INCOMPLETE

PRACTICE POINT: Statement on Standards for Attestation Engagements (SSAE) No. 16 (AT Section 801), "Reporting on Controls at a Service Organization," supersedes the guidance for service auditors in this AU Section 324 when the service auditor is reporting on periods ending on or after June 15, 2011. Earlier implementation of SSAE-16 is permitted. For further guidance and coverage of SSAE-16, see AT Section 801 of this Manual.

To XYZ Service Organization:

We have examined the accompanying description of controls related to the [*identify application*]application of XYZ Service Organization. Our examination included procedures to obtain reasonable assurance about whether (1) the accompanying description presents fairly, in all material respects, the aspects of XYZ Service Organization's controls that may be relevant to a user organization's internal control as it relates to an audit of financial statements; (2) the controls included in the description were suitably designed to achieve the control objectives specified in the description, if those controls were complied with satisfactorily[1]; and (3) such controls had been placed in operation as of [*identify specific date*]. The control objectives were specified by [*identify party that specified the control objectives*]. Our examination was performed in accordance with standards established by the American Institute of Certified Public Accountants and included those procedures we considered necessary in the circumstances to obtain a reasonable basis for rendering our opinion.

We did not perform procedures to determine the operating effectiveness of controls for any period. Accordingly, we express no opinion on the operating effectiveness of any aspects of XYZ Service Organization's controls, individually or in the aggregate.

The accompanying description states that XYZ Service Organization uses operator identification numbers and passwords to prevent unauthorized access to the system. Based on inquiries of staff personnel and inspections of activities, we determined that such procedures are employed in Applications A and B but are not required to access the system in Applications C and D.

In our opinion, except for the matter referred to in the preceding paragraph, the accompanying description of the aforementioned application presents fairly, in all material respects, the relevant aspects of XYZ Service Organization's controls that had been placed in operation as of [*identify specific date*]. Also, in our opinion, the controls, as described, are suitably designed to provide reasonable assurance that the specified control objectives would be achieved if the described controls were complied with satisfactorily[1].

The description of controls at XYZ Service Organization is as of [*identify specific date*] and any projection of such information to the future is subject to the risk that, because of change, the description may no longer portray the controls in existence. The potential effectiveness of specific controls at the XYZ Service Organization is subject to inherent limitations and, accordingly, errors or fraud may occur and not be detected. Furthermore, the projection of any conclusions, based on our findings, to future periods is subject to the risk that changes may alter the validity of such conclusions.

This report is intended solely for use by the management of XYZ Service Organization, its customers, and the independent auditors of its customers.

PRACTICE POINT: [1]If the application of controls by user organizations is necessary to achieve the stated control objectives, the service auditor's report should be modified to include the phrase "and user organizations applied the controls contemplated in the design of XYZ Service Organization's controls" following the words "complied with satisfactorily" in the scope and opinion paragraphs.

ILLUSTRATION 6—SAMPLE SERVICE AUDITOR'S REPORT ON CONTROLS PLACED IN OPERATION AT A SERVICE ORGANIZATION—SIGNIFICANT DEFICIENCIES EXIST IN THE DESIGN OR OPERATION OF THE SERVICE ORGANIZATION'S CONTROLS

PRACTICE POINT: Statement on Standards for Attestation Engagements (SSAE) No. 16 (AT Section 801), "Reporting on Controls at a Service Organization," supersedes the guidance for service auditors in this AU Section 324 when the service auditor is reporting on periods ending on or after June 15, 2011. Earlier implementation of SSAE-16 is permitted. For further guidance and coverage of SSAE-16, see AT Section 801 of this Manual.

To XYZ Service Organization:

We have examined the accompanying description of controls related to the [*identify application*]application of XYZ Service Organization. Our examination included procedures to obtain reasonable assurance about whether (1) the accompanying description presents fairly, in all material respects, the aspects of XYZ Service Organization's controls that may be relevant to a user organization's internal control as it relates to an audit of financial statements; (2) the controls included in the description were suitably designed to achieve the control objectives specified in the description, if those controls were complied with satisfactorily[1]; and (3) such controls had been placed in operation as of [*identify specific date*]. The control objectives were specified by [*identify party that specified the control objectives*]. Our examination was performed in accordance with standards established by the American Institute of Certified Public Accountants and included those procedures we considered necessary in the circumstances to obtain a reasonable basis for rendering our opinion.

We did not perform procedures to determine the operating effectiveness of controls for any period. Accordingly, we express no opinion on the operating effectiveness of any aspects of XYZ Service Organization's controls, individually or in the aggregate.

As discussed in the accompanying description, from time to time XYZ Service Organization makes changes in application programs to correct deficiencies or to enhance capabilities. The procedures followed in determining whether to make changes, in designing the changes, and in implementing them do not include review and approval by authorized individuals who are independent from those involved in making the changes. There are also no specified requirements to test such changes or provide test results to an authorized reviewer prior to implementing the changes.

In our opinion, the accompanying description of the aforementioned application presents fairly, in all material respects, the relevant aspects of XYZ Service Organization's controls that had been placed in operation as of [*identify specific date*] Also in our opinion, except for the deficiency referred to in the preceding paragraph, the controls, as described, are suitably designed to provide reasonable assurance that the specified control objectives would be achieved if the described controls were complied with satisfactorily[1].

The description of controls at XYZ Service Organization is as of [*identify specific date*] and any projection of such information to the future is subject to the risk that, because of change, the description may no longer portray the controls in existence. The potential effectiveness of specific controls at XYZ Service Organization is subject to inherent limitations and, accordingly, errors or fraud may occur and not be detected. Furthermore, the projection of any conclusions, based on our findings, to future periods is subject to the risk that changes may alter the validity of such conclusions.

This report is intended solely for use by the management of XYZ Service Organization, its customers, and the independent auditors of its customers.

PRACTICE POINT: [1]If the application of controls by user organizations is necessary to achieve the stated control objectives, the service auditor's report should be modified to include the phrase "and user organizations applied the controls contemplated in the design of XYZ Service Organization's controls" following the words "complied with satisfactorily" in the scope and opinion paragraphs.

ILLUSTRATION 7—SAMPLE SERVICE AUDITOR'S REPORT ON CONTROLS PLACED IN OPERATION ATA SERVICE ORGANIZATION AND TESTS OF OPERATING EFFECTIVENESS—NO EXCEPTIONS

PRACTICE POINT: Statement on Standards for Attestation Engagements (SSAE) No. 16 (AT Section 801), "Reporting on Controls at a Service Organization," supersedes the guidance for service auditors in this AU Section 324 when the service auditor is reporting on periods ending on or after June 15, 2011. Earlier implementation of SSAE-16 is permitted. For further guidance and coverage of SSAE-16, see AT Section 801 of this Manual.

To XYZ Service Organization:

We have examined the accompanying description of controls related to the [*identify application*]application of XYZ Service Organization. Our examination included procedures to obtain reasonable assurance about whether (1) the accompanying description presents fairly, in all material respects, the aspects of XYZ Service Organization's controls that may be relevant to a user organization's internal control as it relates to an audit of financial statements; (2) the controls included in the description were suitably designed to achieve the control objectives specified in the description, if those controls were complied with satisfactorily[1]; and (3) such controls had been placed in operation as of [*identify specific date*]. The control objectives were specified by [*identify party that specified the control objectives*]. Our examination was performed in accordance with standards established by the American Institute of Certified Public Accountants and included those procedures we considered necessary in the circumstances to obtain a reasonable basis for rendering our opinion.

In our opinion, the accompanying description of the aforementioned application presents fairly, in all material respects, the relevant aspects of XYZ Service Organization's controls that had been placed in operation as of [*identify specific date*]. Also, in our opinion, the controls, as described, are suitably designed to provide reasonable assurance that the specified control objectives would be achieved if the described controls were complied with satisfactorily[1].

In addition to the procedures we considered necessary to render our opinion as expressed in the previous paragraph, we applied tests to specific controls, listed in Schedule X, to obtain evidence about their effectiveness in meeting the control objectives, described in Schedule X, during the period from [*identify specific date*]to [*identify specific date*]. The specific controls and the nature, timing, extent, and results of the tests are listed in Schedule X. This information has been provided to user organizations of XYZ Service Organization and to their auditors to be taken into consideration, along with information about the internal control at user organizations, when making assessments of control risk for user organizations. In our opinion the controls that were tested, as described in Schedule X, were operating with sufficient effectiveness to provide reasonable, but not absolute, assurance that the control objectives specified in Schedule X were achieved during the period from [*identify specific date*] to [*identify specific date*]. [*However, the scope of our engagement did not include tests to determine whether control objectives not listed in Schedule X were achieved; accordingly, we express no opinion on the achievement of control objectives not included in Schedule X.]*[2]

The relative effectiveness and significance of specific controls at XYZ Service Organization and their effect on assessments of control risk at user organizations are dependent on their interaction with the controls and other factors present at individual user organizations. We have performed no procedures to evaluate the effectiveness of controls at individual user organizations.

The description of controls at XYZ Service Organization is as of [*identify specific date*], and information about tests of the operating effectiveness of specific controls covers the period from [*identify specific date*] to [*identify specific date*]. Any projection of such information to the future is subject to the risk that, because of change, the description may no longer portray the controls in existence. The potential effectiveness of specific controls at XYZ Service Organization is subject to inherent limitations and, accordingly, errors or fraud may occur and not be detected. Furthermore, the projection of any conclusions, based on our findings, to future periods is subject to the risk that changes may alter the validity of such conclusions.

This report is intended solely for use by the management of XYZ Service Organization, its customers, and the independent auditors of its customers.

PRACTICE POINT: [1]If the application of controls by user organizations is necessary to achieve the stated control objectives, the service auditor's report should be modified to include the phrase "and user organizations applied the controls contemplated in the design of XYZ Service Organization's controls" following the words "complied with satisfactorily" in the scope and opinion paragraphs.

[2]This sentence should be added when all of the control objectives listed in the description of controls placed in operation are not covered by the tests of operating effectiveness. This sentence would be omitted when all of the control objectives listed in the description of controls placed in operation are included in the tests of operating effectiveness.

ILLUSTRATION 8—SAMPLE SERVICE AUDITOR'S REPORT ON CONTROLS PLACED IN OPERATION AT A SERVICE ORGANIZATION AND TESTS OF OPERATING EFFECTIVENESS—DESCRIPTION OF CONTROLS IS INACCURATE OR INCOMPLETE

PRACTICE POINT: Statement on Standards for Attestation Engagements (SSAE) No. 16 (AT Section 801), "Reporting on Controls at a Service Organization," supersedes the guidance for service auditors in this AU Section 324 when the service auditor is reporting on periods ending on or after June 15, 2011. Earlier implementation of SSAE-16 is permitted. For further guidance and coverage of SSAE-16, see AT Section 801 of this Manual.

To XYZ Service Organization:

We have examined the accompanying description of controls related to the [*identify application*]application of XYZ Service Organization. Our examination included procedures to obtain reasonable assurance about whether (1) the accompanying description presents fairly, in all material respects, the aspects of XYZ Service Organization's controls that may be relevant to a user organization's internal control as it relates to an audit of financial statements; (2) the controls included in the description were suitably designed to achieve the control objectives specified in the description, if those controls were complied with satisfactorily[1]; and (3) such controls had been placed in operation as of [*identify specific date*]. The control objectives were specified by [*identify party that specified the control objectives*]. Our examination was performed in accordance with standards established by the American Institute of Certified Public Accountants and included those procedures we considered necessary in the circumstances to obtain a reasonable basis for rendering our opinion.

The accompanying description states that XYZ Service Organization uses operator identification numbers and passwords to prevent unauthorized access to the system. Based on inquiries of staff personnel and inspections of activities, we determined that such procedures are employed in Applications A and B but are not required to access the system in Applications C and D.

In our opinion, except for the matter referred to in the preceding paragraph, the accompanying description of the aforementioned application presents fairly, in all material respects, the relevant aspects of XYZ Service Organization's controls that had been placed in operation as of [*identify specific date*]. Also, in our opinion, the controls, as described, are suitably designed to provide reasonable assurance that the specified control objectives would be achieved if the described controls were complied with satisfactorily[1].

In addition to the procedures we considered necessary to render our opinion as expressed in the previous paragraph, we applied tests to specific controls, listed in Schedule X, to obtain evidence about their effectiveness in meeting the control objectives, described in Schedule X, during the period from [*identify specific date*]to [*identify specific date*]. The specific controls and the nature, timing, extent, and results of the tests are listed in Schedule X. This information has been provided to user organizations of XYZ Service Organization and to their auditors to be taken into consideration, along with information about the internal control at user organizations, when making assessments of control risk for user organizations. In our opinion the controls that were tested, as described in Schedule X, were operating with sufficient effectiveness to provide reasonable, but not absolute, assurance that the control objectives specified in Schedule X were achieved during the period from [*identify specific date*] to [*identify specific date*]. [*However, the scope of our engagement did not include tests to determine whether control objectives not listed in Schedule X were achieved; accordingly, we express no opinion on the achievement of control objectives not included in Schedule X.*][2]

The relative effectiveness and significance of specific controls at XYZ Service Organization and their effect on assessments of control risk at user organizations are dependent on their interaction with the controls and other factors present at individual user organizations. We have performed no procedures to evaluate the effectiveness of controls at individual user organizations.

The description of controls at XYZ Service Organization is as of [*identify specific date*], and information about tests of the operating effectiveness of specific controls covers the period from [*identify specific date*] to [*identify specific date*]. Any projection of such information to the future is subject to the risk that, because of change, the description may no longer portray the controls in existence. The potential effectiveness of specific controls at XYZ Service Organization is subject to inherent limitations and, accordingly, errors or fraud may occur and not be detected. Furthermore, the projection of any conclusions, based on our findings, to future periods is subject to the risk that changes may alter the validity of such conclusions.

This report is intended solely for use by the management of XYZ Service Organization, its customers, and the independent auditors of its customers.

PRACTICE POINT: [1]If the application of controls by user organizations is necessary to achieve the stated control objectives, the service auditor's report should be modified to include the phrase "and user organizations applied the controls contemplated in the design of XYZ Service Organization's controls" following the words "complied with satisfactorily" in the scope and opinion paragraphs.

[2]This sentence should be added when all of the control objectives listed in the description of controls placed in operation are not covered by the tests of operating effectiveness. This sentence would be omitted when all of the control objectives listed in the description of controls placed in operation are included in the tests of operating effectiveness.

ILLUSTRATION 9—SAMPLE SERVICE AUDITOR'S REPORT ON CONTROLS PLACED IN OPERATION AT A SERVICE ORGANIZATION AND TESTS OF OPERATING EFFECTIVENESS—SIGNIFICANT DEFICIENCIES EXIST IN THE DESIGN OR OPERATION OF THE SERVICE ORGANIZATION'S CONTROLS

PRACTICE POINT: Statement on Standards for Attestation Engagements (SSAE) No. 16 (AT Section 801), "Reporting on Controls at a Service Organiza-tion," supersedes the guidance for service auditors in this AU Section 324 when the service auditor is reporting on periods ending on or after June 15, 2011. Earlier implementation of SSAE-16 is permitted. For further guidance and cover-age of SSAE-16, see AT Section 801 of this Manual.

To XYZ Service Organization:

We have examined the accompanying description of controls related to the [*identify application*]application of XYZ Service Organization. Our examination included procedures to obtain reasonable assurance about whether (1) the ac-companying description presents fairly, in all material respects, the aspects of XYZ Service Organization's controls that may be relevant to a user organization's internal control as it relates to an audit of financial statements; (2) the controls included in the description were suitably designed to achieve the control objectives specified in the description, if those controls were complied with satisfactorily[1]; and (3) such controls had been placed in operation as of [*identify specific date*]. The control objectives were specified by [*identify party that specified the control objectives*]. Our examination was performed in accordance with standards established by the American Institute of Certified Public Accountants and included those procedures we considered necessary in the circumstances to obtain a reasonable basis for rendering our opinion.

As discussed in the accompanying description, from time to time XYZ Service Organization makes changes in application programs to correct deficiencies or to enhance capabilities. The procedures followed in determining whether to make changes, in designing the changes, and in implementing them do not include review and approval by authorized individuals who are independent from those involved in making the changes. There are also no specified requirements to test such changes or provide test results to an authorized reviewer prior to implementing the changes.

In our opinion, the accompanying description of the aforementioned application presents fairly, in all material respects, the relevant aspects of XYZ Service Organization's controls that had been placed in operation as of [*identify specific date*]. Also in our opinion, except for the deficiency referred to in the preceding paragraph, the controls, as described, are suitably designed to provide reasonable assurance that the specified control objectives would be achieved if the described controls were complied with satisfactorily[1].

In addition to the procedures we considered necessary to render our opinion as expressed in the previous paragraph, we applied tests to specific controls, listed in Schedule X, to obtain evidence about their effectiveness in meeting the control objectives, described in Schedule X, during the period from [*identify specific date*]to [*identify specific date*]. The specific controls and the nature, timing, extent, and results of the tests are listed in Schedule X. This information has been provided to user organizations of XYZ Service Organization and to their auditors to be taken into consideration, along with information about the internal control at user organizations, when making assessments of control risk for user organizations. In our opinion the controls that were tested, as described in Schedule X, were operating with sufficient effectiveness to provide reasonable, but not absolute, assurance that the control objectives specified in Schedule X were achieved during the period from [*identify specific date*] to [*identify specific date*]. [*However, the scope of our engagement did not include tests to determine whether control objectives not listed in Schedule X were achieved; accordingly, we express no opinion on the achievement of control objectives not included in Schedule X.*][2]

The relative effectiveness and significance of specific controls at XYZ Service Organization and their effect on assessments of control risk at user organizations are dependent on their interaction with the controls and other factors present at individual user organizations. We have performed no procedures to evaluate the effectiveness of controls at individual user organizations.

The description of controls at XYZ Service Organization is as of [*identify specific date*], and information about tests of the operating effectiveness of specific controls covers the period from [*identify specific date*] to [*identify specific date*]. Any projection of such information to the future is subject to the risk that, because of change, the description may no longer portray the controls in existence. The potential effectiveness of specific controls at XYZ Service Organization is subject to inherent limitations and, accordingly, errors or fraud may occur and not be detected. Furthermore, the projection of any conclusions, based on our findings, to future periods is subject to the risk that changes may alter the validity of such conclusions.

This report is intended solely for use by the management of XYZ Service Organization, its customers, and the independent auditors of its customers.

PRACTICE POINT: [1]If the application of controls by user organizations is necessary to achieve the stated control objectives, the service auditor's report should be modified to include the phrase "and user organizations applied the controls contemplated in the design of XYZ Service Organization's controls" following the words "complied with satisfactorily" in the scope and opinion paragraphs.

[2]This sentence should be added when all of the control objectives listed in the description of controls placed in operation are not covered by the tests of operating effectiveness. This sentence would be omitted when all of the control objectives listed in the description of controls placed in operation are included in the tests of operating effectiveness.

ILLUSTRATION 10—SAMPLE SCOPE PARAGRAPH OF A SERVICE AUDITOR'S REPORT USING THE CARVE-OUT METHOD

PRACTICE POINT: Statement on Standards for Attestation Engagements (SSAE) No. 16 (AT Section 801), "Reporting on Controls at a Service Organization," supersedes the guidance for service auditors in this AU Section 324 when the service auditor is reporting on periods ending on or after June 15, 2011. Earlier implementation of SSAE-16 is permitted. For further guidance and coverage of SSAE-16, see AT Section 801 of this Manual.

To the Board of Directors of Example Trust Company:

We have examined the accompanying description of the controls of Example Trust Company applicable to the processing of transactions for users of the Institutional Trust Division. Our examination included procedures to obtain reasonable assurance about whether (1) the accompanying description presents fairly, in all material respects, the aspects of Example Trust Company's controls that may be relevant to a user organization's internal control as it relates to an audit of financial statements; (2) the controls included in the description were suitably designed to achieve the control objectives specified in the description, if those controls were complied with satisfactorily, and user organizations applied the controls contemplated in the design of Example Trust Company's controls; and (3) such controls had been placed in operation as of June 30, 20X2. Example Trust Company uses a computer processing service organization for all of its computerized application processing. The accompanying description includes only those control objectives and related controls of Example Trust Company and does not include control objectives and related controls of the computer processing service organization. Our examination did not extend to controls of the computer processing service organization. The control objectives were specified by the management of Example Trust Company. Our examination was performed in accordance with standards established by the American Institute of Certified Public Accountants and included those procedures we considered necessary in the circumstances to obtain a reasonable basis for rendering our opinion.

[*The remainder of the report is the same as the standard service auditor's reports presented in Illustrations 4 to 9 above.*]

ILLUSTRATION 11—SAMPLE SERVICE AUDITOR'S REPORT USING THE INCLUSIVE METHOD

PRACTICE POINT: Statement on Standards for Attestation Engagements (SSAE) No. 16 (AT Section 801), "Reporting on Controls at a Service Organization," supersedes the guidance for service auditors in this AU Section 324 when the service auditor is reporting on periods ending on or after June 15, 2011. Earlier implementation of SSAE-16 is permitted. For further guidance and coverage of SSAE-16, see AT Section 801 of this Manual.

To the Board of Directors of Example Trust Company:

We have examined the accompanying description of the controls of Example Trust Company and Computer Processing Service Organization, an independent service organization that provides computer processing services to Example Trust Company, applicable to the processing of transactions for users of the Institutional Trust Division. Our examination included procedures to obtain reasonable assurance about whether (1) the accompanying description presents fairly, in all material respects, the aspects of Example Trust Company's and Computer Processing Service Organization's controls that may be relevant to a user organization's internal control as it relates to an audit of financial statements; (2) the controls included in the description were suitably designed to achieve the control objectives specified in the description, if those controls were complied with satisfactorily, and user organizations applied the controls contemplated in the design of Example Trust Company's controls; and (3) the controls had been placed in operation as of June 30, 20X2. The control objectives were specified by the management of Example Trust Company. Our examination was performed in accordance with standards established by the American Institute of Certified Public Accountants and included those procedures we considered necessary in the circumstances to obtain a reasonable basis for rendering our opinion.

In our opinion, the accompanying description of the aforementioned controls presents fairly, in all material respects, the relevant aspects of Example Trust Company's and Computer Processing Service Organization's controls that had been placed in operation as of June 30, 20X2. Also, in our opinion, the controls, as described, are suitably designed to provide reasonable assurance that the specified control objectives would be achieved if the described controls were complied with satisfactorily and user organizations applied the controls contemplated in the design of Example Trust Company's controls.

In addition to the procedures we considered necessary to render our opinion as expressed in the previous paragraph, we applied tests to specific controls, listed in Schedule X to obtain evidence about their effectiveness in meeting the control objectives, described in Schedule X, during the period from January 1, 20X2, to June 30, 20X2. The specific controls and the nature, timing, extent, and results of the tests are listed in Schedule X. This information has been provided to user organizations of Example Trust Company and to their auditors to be taken into consideration, along with information about internal control at user organizations, when making assessments of control risk for user organizations. In our opinion the controls that were tested, as described in Schedule Y, were operating with sufficient effectiveness to provide reasonable, but not absolute, assurance that the control objectives specified in Schedule X were achieved during the period from January 1, 20X2, to June 30, 20X2.

The relative effectiveness and significance of specific controls at Example Trust Company and Computer Processing Service Organization, and their effect on assessments of control risk at user organizations are dependent on their interaction with the controls and other factors present at individual user organizations. We have performed no procedures to evaluate the effectiveness of controls at individual user organizations.

The description of controls at Example Trust Company and Computer Processing Service Organization is as of June 30, 20X2, and information about tests of the operating effectiveness of specific controls covers the period from January 1, 20X2, to June 30, 20X2. Any projection of such information to the future is subject to the risk that, because of change, the description may no longer portray the controls in existence. The potential effectiveness of specific controls at the Service Organization and Computer Processing Service Organization is subject to inherent limitations and, accordingly, errors or fraud may occur and not be detected. Furthermore, the projection of any conclusions, based on our findings, to future periods is subject to the risk that changes may alter the validity of such conclusions.

This report is intended solely for use by the management of Example Trust Company, its users, and the independent auditors of its users.

AU SECTION 325
COMMUNICATING INTERNAL CONTROL RELATED MATTERS IDENTIFIED IN AN AUDIT

PRACTICE POINT: As part of its Clarity Project, the American Institute of Certified Public Accountants' (AICPA's) Auditing Standards Board (ASB) has finalized a clarified Statement on Auditing Standards (SAS) titled, "Communicating Internal Control Related Matters Identified in an Audit (Redrafted)," which supersedes AU Section 325 Communicating Internal Control Related Matters Identified in an Audit). The clarified SAS makes explicit the following requirements that are implied in extant AU Section 325:

- The requirement to determine whether, on the basis of the audit work performed, the auditor has identified one or more deficiencies in internal control; and

- The requirement to include specific matters in a written communication stating that no material weaknesses were identified during the audit that are similar to those in the written communication of significant deficiencies and material weaknesses. Extant AU Section 325 implies that these matters be included by presenting them in the second example of exhibit A of AU Section 325, which is an illustrative written communication indicating that no material weaknesses were identified.

The clarified SAS adds the following requirements that were not included in AU Section 325:

- The requirement to communicate, in writing or orally, only to management other deficiencies in internal control identified during the audit that have not been communicated to management by other parties and that, in the auditor's professional judgment, are of sufficient importance to merit management's attention. The ASB does not view this new requirement as a difference between extant AU Section 325 and the clarified SAS because auditor judgment is the sole determinant regarding whether a deficiency, other than a material weakness or a significant deficiency, is of sufficient importance to communicate to management. Similarly, extant AU Section 325 does not preclude the auditor from communicating other internal control matters to management if the auditor believes it is important to do so.

- The requirement to include in the written communication an explanation of the potential effects of the significant deficiencies and material weaknesses identified. The ASB believes management and those charged with governance need this information to enable them to take appropriate remedial action. Further, the ASB does not believe this requires additional effort by the auditor because the potential effects would have been considered as part of the evaluation of the severity of the deficiency. The clarified SAS includes guidance addressing that the potential effects need not be quantified.

The ASB is expected to issue many of the clarified standards in *one* SAS that will be codified in "AU Section" format. The ASB has decided that the effective date of the clarified SASs that have not yet been issued is for audits of financial statements for periods ending on or after December 15, 2012. Auditors should be alert to and monitor further developments in this area.

WHAT EVERY PRACTITIONER SHOULD KNOW

Basic Objectives and Requirements

This Section establishes standards and provides guidance to auditors on communicating matters related to an entity's internal control over financial reporting (herein referred to as "internal control" or ICFR) observed during a financial statement audit. Specifically, this Section:

1. Requires the auditor to communicate in writing no later than 60 days following the report release date to management and those charged with governance significant deficiencies and material weaknesses in internal control.

2. Provides guidance on evaluating (a) deviations in the operation of controls and whether they constitute control deficiencies and (b) severity of control deficiencies.

3. Identifies indicators of material weaknesses in internal control and includes examples of circumstances that may be control deficiencies, significant deficiencies, or material weaknesses.

4. If the auditor determines that a deficiency (or combination of deficiencies) is not a material weakness, requires the auditor to consider "whether prudent officials, having knowledge of the same facts and circumstances, would likely reach the same conclusion."

The Auditor's Evaluation of Deficiencies in Internal Control Identified as Part of a Financial Statement Audit

This Section provides the following definitions related to deficiencies in internal control over financial reporting:

- *Deficiency*—A deficiency in internal control exists when the design or operation of a control does not allow management or employees, in the normal course of performing their assigned functions, to prevent, or detect and correct, misstatements on a timely basis. There are two types of deficiencies:

  — *Deficiency in design*—A deficiency in design exists when (a) a control necessary to meet the control objective is missing, or (b) an existing control is not properly designed so that, even if the control operates as designed, the control objective would not be met.

  — *Deficiency in operation*—A deficiency in operation exists when (a) a properly designed control does not operate as designed, or (b) the person performing the control does not possess the necessary authority or competence to perform the control effectively.

- *Significant deficiency*—A deficiency, or a combination of deficiencies, in internal control that is less severe than a material weakness, yet important enough to merit attention by those charged with governance.

- *Material weakness*—A deficiency, or a combination of deficiencies, in internal control, such that there is a reasonable possibility that a material misstatement of the entity's financial statements will not be prevented, or detected and corrected, on a timely basis.

This Section requires the auditor to evaluate the severity of each deficiency in ICFR identified as part of the audit to determine whether the deficiency, individually or in combination, is a significant deficiency or a material weakness. The severity of a deficiency in internal control does not depend on whether a misstatement actually occurred. Rather, it depends on both of the following:

1. *The magnitude of the potential misstatement.* Factors that affect the magnitude of a misstatement include (a) the financial statement amounts exposed to the deficiency; (b) the number of transactions exposed to the deficiency; (c) the volume of activity in the account or class of transactions exposed to the deficiency in the current period; and (d) the volume of activity in the account or class of transactions exposed to the deficiency that is expected in future periods.

2. *Whether there is a reasonable possibility that the entity's controls will fail to prevent, or detect and correct, a misstatement of an account balance or disclosure.* Factors that affect whether there is a reasonable possibility that a deficiency will result in a misstatement of an account balance or disclosure include (a) the nature of the financial statement accounts, classes of transactions, disclosures, and assertions; (b) whether the related assets or liabilities are susceptible to loss or fraud; (c) the subjectivity, complexity, or extent of judgment required to determine the amount involved; (d) the interaction or relationship of the control with other controls; (e) the interaction of the control deficiency with other control deficiencies; and (f) the possible future consequences of the deficiency.

The auditor should determine whether deficiencies that affect the same significant account or disclosure, relevant assertion, or component of internal control collectively result in a significant deficiency or a material weakness.

Effects of compensating controls Compensating controls are controls that can limit the severity of a control deficiency. Although compensating controls can mitigate the effects of a control deficiency, they do not eliminate the control deficiency. This Section does not require the auditor to consider the effects of compensating controls for the purpose of communicating significant deficiencies or material weaknesses. However, the auditor may consider the effects of compensating controls related to a deficiency in operation of a control only if the auditor has tested the compensating controls for operating effectiveness as part of the financial statement audit.

The prudent official test In connection with the auditor's evaluation of whether a deficiency, or a combination of deficiencies, in internal control is not a material weakness, this Section indicates that the auditor should consider whether prudent officials having knowledge of the same facts and circumstances would likely reach the same conclusion as the auditor. Although the term *prudent official* is not defined, the concept is that an auditor should stand back and take another objective look at the deficiency much as would a regulator or someone from an oversight agency.

Form and Content of Communication of Significant Deficiencies and Material Weaknesses

This Section requires the auditor to communicate, in writing, to management and to those charged with governance significant deficiencies or material weaknesses identified in connection with each audit. This requirement is also applicable to significant deficiencies or material weaknesses that the auditor previously communicated to these parties in connection with previous audits, but that have not yet been remediated; however, the auditor may refer to previously issued written communication and the date of that communication that describes the significant deficiencies or material weaknesses that have not yet been remediated.

The auditor's written communication to address significant deficiencies and material weaknesses regarding an entity's ICFR should include the following items:

- A statement that the purpose of the auditor's consideration of internal control was to express an opinion on the financial statements and not to express an opinion on the effectiveness of the entity's internal control.
- A statement that the auditor does not express an opinion on the effectiveness of the entity's internal control.
- A statement that the auditor's consideration of internal control was not designed to identify all deficiencies in internal control that might be significant deficiencies or material weaknesses.
- A definition of *material weakness* and, where relevant, *significant deficiency.*
- A description of the significant deficiencies identified and, if applicable, an identification of those significant deficiencies that are considered material weaknesses.
- A statement that the communication is intended solely for the information and use of management, those charged with governance, and others within the organization and, when applicable, specific regulatory agencies that have requested copies of the report.

An audit is not designed to detect all matters that might be significant deficiencies and does not provide a basis for expressing such assurance. The auditor is prohibited from issuing a written communication stating that no significant deficiencies were identified because of the potential for a reader misinterpreting the limited assurance associated with such a statement.

If no material weaknesses are noted, the auditor may, but is not required to, include a statement in the written communication that no material weaknesses were identified during the audit. In addition, if one or more significant deficiencies have been identified, but none is deemed to be a material weakness, the auditor may so state in the written communication to management and those charged with governance.

Timing of Communication of Significant Deficiencies and Material Weaknesses

This Section provides that the auditor's written communication should preferably be made by the release date of the auditor's report on the audited financial statements, but no later than 60 days following the report release date (i.e., the date the auditor grants the entity permission to use the auditor's report in connection with the audited financial statements).

In addition, in certain situations, the auditor may determine that it is important to initiate early communication of significant deficiencies and material weaknesses during the course of the audit, rather than when the auditor's report is released. In such circumstances, the form of the interim communication is affected by the nature and relative significance of the deficiencies identified and the need for immediate corrective action. Although these matters need not be communicated in writing during the audit, all significant deficiencies and material weaknesses identified should ultimately be included in the written communication even if they were remediated during the audit.

Communication of Other Matters Related to Internal Control

The auditor often observes less significant internal control-related matters, as well as opportunities for the client to improve or strengthen operational and administrative controls. Although the auditor is not required to communicate such matters to the client, he or she may decide to do so to better serve the client. As a matter of good practice, most auditors will issue a letter of recommendations to management. Usually, such a letter is separate from, and not combined with, the letter communicating significant deficiencies or material weaknesses, even though combining these matters is not specifically precluded. Communication of other such matters related to internal control may be made either orally or in writing. However, if other matters related to an entity's internal control are communicated orally, this Section indicates that the auditor should document the communication.

Management's Written Response to the Auditor's Communication

Sometimes an entity may decide or be required by a third party to respond to the auditor's communication regarding identified significant deficiencies or material weaknesses. In addition, management's response may include, for example, a corrective action plan or comments regarding the impracticality of taking any corrective actions. If management's written response is included in a document that contains the auditor's written communication to management and those charged with governance, this Section indicates that the auditor may add an additional paragraph to his or her written communication disclaiming an opinion on such information. For example:

> ABC Company's written response to the significant deficiencies [*and material weaknesses*] identified in our audit was not subjected to the auditing proce-

dures applied in the audit of the financial statements and, accordingly, we express no opinion on it.

PRACTICE ISSUES AND FREQUENTLY ASKED QUESTIONS

Issue 1: Is the auditor required to apply specific procedures to detect significant control deficiencies in financial statement audits?

No. The auditor is not obligated to search for significant control deficiencies in connection with an audit of an entity's financial statements. In addition, a financial statement audit is not structured to identify all significant control deficiencies in internal control over financial reporting. Control deficiencies may be discovered during various phases of the audit engagement, including the evaluation of internal control, the consideration of fraud, and the tests of financial statement balances. However, once discovered, control deficiencies that the auditor believes are significant deficiencies or material weaknesses should be communicated to management and those charged with governance.

Issue 2: If the auditor identifies a control deficiency but has not identified an actual misstatement related to that deficiency, can the auditor automatically conclude that the deficiency is not a significant deficiency or a material weakness?

No. The severity of a deficiency in internal control does not depend on whether a misstatement actually occurred. If the auditor identifies a control deficiency but has not identified an actual misstatement related to that deficiency, the auditor cannot automatically conclude that the deficiency is not a significant deficiency or a material weakness. If the auditor has identified a misstatement, the auditor should consider the potential for further misstatements in the financial statements being audited.

Issue 3: Is the auditor required to consider the possible mitigating effects of compensating controls on an identified control deficiency?

No. This Section does not require the auditor to consider the effects of compensating controls for the purpose of communicating significant deficiencies or material weaknesses. However, the auditor may consider the effects of compensating controls related to a deficiency in operation of a control only if the auditor has tested the compensating controls for operating effectiveness as part of the financial statement audit.

Issue 4: When determining whether a deficiency, or combination of deficiencies, is not a material weakness, how does the auditor address the requirement to consider whether prudent officials would likely reach the same conclusion as the auditor's?

If the auditor determines that a deficiency, or a combination of deficiencies, is not a material weakness, the auditor is required to consider whether prudent officials, having knowledge of the same facts and circumstances, would likely reach the same conclusion. However, this Section does not define the term "prudent official" and does not provide any specific examples of how the auditor might achieve such conclusion. Practically, the auditor would have to take into account various factors, such as the following:

- The severity of the deficiency.
- Ineffective oversight of the entity's ICFR.
- Whether other controls accomplish the same control objective.
- Compensating controls.

The concept of the prudent official test is that an auditor should "stand back" and objectively assess the severity of the deficiency through the skeptical eyes of a prudent official, such as a regulator or an official from an oversight agency. If the auditor does not have a robust basis for his or her conclusion and would not be comfortable defending such conclusion, the auditor should reconsider his or her evaluation of the significance of the deficiency.

Issue 5: What are some indicators of material weaknesses in internal control?

Indicators of material weaknesses in internal control include:

- Identification of fraud on the part of senior management, regardless of materiality.
- Restatement of previously issued financial statements for material misstatement(s).
- Identification by the auditor of a material misstatement in circumstances that indicate that the misstatement would not have been detected by the entity's internal control.
- Ineffective oversight of the entity's financial reporting and internal control by those charged with governance.

Issue 6: If no significant deficiencies were noted during the audit, can the auditor issue a written report stating that no significant deficiencies were noted?

No. An audit is not designed to detect all matters that might be significant deficiencies and does not provide a basis for expressing such assurance. The auditor is prohibited from issuing a written report stating that no significant deficiencies were noted because of the potential for a reader misinterpreting the limited assurance associated with such a statement.

Issue 7: Is the auditor required to separately identify material weaknesses in the communication of significant deficiencies?

Yes. The auditor is required to evaluate the control deficiencies noted during the audit and separately identify and communicate those that are considered to be significant deficiencies and those that are considered to be material weaknesses.

Issue 8: If no material weaknesses are identified, is the auditor required to include a statement in a written report to that fact?

No. If no material weaknesses are noted, the auditor may, but is not required to, include a statement in a written report that no material weaknesses were identified during the audit.

Issue 9: Is the auditor required to include in the written communications of significant deficiencies statements regarding the inherent limitations of internal control or the extent of the auditor's consideration of the entity's internal control during the audit?

No. The auditor may wish, but is not required, to include additional statements regarding the inherent limitations of internal control, including management override of controls, or the specific nature and extent of the consideration of an entity's internal control during the audit, or other matters regarding the basis for the comments made.

Issue 10: Is the auditor required to communicate again in the current period under audit significant deficiencies and material weaknesses communicated in previous audits that have not yet been remediated?

Yes. If the auditor communicated significant deficiencies and material weaknesses in previous audits and those deficiencies have not yet been remediated, the auditor is required to communicate them again in the current period under audit. The auditor may make such communication by referring to the previously issued written communication and the date of that communication. In some circumstances, management and those charged with governance may have made a conscious decision to accept the degree of risk associated with identified significant deficiencies and material weaknesses because of cost or other considerations. While management is responsible for that decision, the auditor is nevertheless responsible for continuing to communicate significant deficiencies and material weaknesses, regardless of management's decision.

Issue 11: What is the relationship, if any, between significant deficiencies and "management letter comments"?

In addition to significant deficiencies, the auditor often observes less significant internal control-related matters, as well as opportunities for the client to improve or strengthen operational and administrative controls. Although the auditor is not required to communicate such matters to the client, he or she may decide to do so to better serve the client. As a matter of good practice, most auditors will issue a letter of recommendations to management. Usually, such a letter is separate from, and not combined with, the letter communicating significant deficiencies or material weaknesses, even though combining these matters is not precluded. Such a letter may be presented in any format the auditor wishes. If the auditor decides to communicate orally such other matters related to internal control, the auditor should document the communication in the working papers.

Issue 12: Is the auditor required to recommend a specific course of action for the significant deficiencies noted?

No. Although the auditor is not required to recommend a specific course of action for the significant deficiencies noted, he or she may do so as a matter of client service.

Issue 13: What are some examples of deficiencies in the design of controls that may be control deficiencies, significant deficiencies, or material weaknesses?

Examples (adapted from the Appendix to AU Section 325) of circumstances involving deficiencies in the design of controls that may be control deficiencies, significant deficiencies, or material weaknesses are:

- Inadequate design of controls over the preparation of the financial statements being audited.

- Inadequate design of controls over a significant account or process.
- Inadequate documentation of the five components of internal control: (1) control environment, (2) risk assessment, (3) control activities, (4) information and communication, and (5) monitoring.
- Insufficient control consciousness within the entity (e.g., the tone at the top and the control environment).
- Absent or inadequate segregation of duties within a significant account or process.
- Absent or inadequate controls over the safeguarding of assets (this applies to controls that the auditor determines would be necessary for effective internal control over financial reporting).
- Inadequate design of information technology (IT) general and application controls that prevent the information system from providing complete and accurate information consistent with financial reporting objectives and current needs.
- Employees or management who lack the qualifications and training to fulfill their assigned functions. For example, in an entity that prepares financial statements in accordance with GAAP, the person responsible for the accounting and reporting function lacks the skills and knowledge to apply GAAP in recording the entity's financial transactions or preparing its financial statements.
- Inadequate design of monitoring controls used to assess the design and operating effectiveness of the entity's internal control over time.
- Absence of an internal process to report deficiencies in internal control to management on a timely basis.

Issue 14: What are some examples of failures in the operation of internal control that may be control deficiencies, significant deficiencies, or material weaknesses?

Examples (adapted from the Appendix to AU Section 325) of circumstances involving failures in the operation of internal control that may be control deficiencies, significant deficiencies, or material weaknesses are:

- Failure in the operation of effectively designed controls over a significant account or process (e.g., failure of a control such as dual authorization for significant disbursements within the purchasing process).
- Failure of the information and communication component of internal control to provide complete and accurate output because of deficiencies in timeliness, completeness, or accuracy (e.g., failure to obtain timely and accurate consolidating information from remote locations that is needed to prepare the financial statements).
- Failure of controls designed to safeguard assets from loss, damage, or misappropriation.

PRACTICE POINT: This circumstance may need careful consideration before it is evaluated as a significant deficiency or material weakness. For example, a company uses security devices to safeguard its inventory (preventive controls) and also performs periodic timely physical inventory counts (detective control) in relation to its financial reporting. Although the physical inventory count does not safeguard the inventory from theft or loss, it prevents a material misstatement of the financial statements if performed effectively and timely. Therefore, given that the definitions of material weakness and significant deficiency relate to the likelihood of misstatement of the financial statements, the failure of a preventive control such as inventory tags will not result in a significant deficiency or material weakness if the detective control (physical inventory) prevents a misstatement of the financial statements. Material weaknesses relating to controls over the safeguarding of assets would only exist if the company does not have effective controls (considering both safeguarding and other controls) to prevent or detect a material misstatement of the financial statements.

- Failure to perform reconciliations of significant accounts (e.g., accounts receivable subsidiary ledgers are not reconciled to the general ledger account in a timely or accurate manner).

- Undue bias or lack of objectivity by those responsible for accounting decisions (e.g., consistent understatement of expenses or overstatement of allowances at the direction of management).

- Misrepresentation by client personnel to the auditor (an indicator of fraud).

- Management override of controls.

- Failure of an application control caused by a deficiency in the design or operation of an IT general control.

- An observed deviation rate that exceeds the number of deviations expected by the auditor in a test of the operating effectiveness of a control.

ILLUSTRATIONS AND PRACTICE AIDS

ILLUSTRATION 1—AUDITOR'S COMMUNICATION TO CLIENT WITH SIGNIFICANT DEFICIENCIES OR MATERIAL WEAKNESSES

(*Date*)

(*Name and Address of Client*)

In planning and performing our audit of the financial statements of (*insert name of client*) as of and for the year ended (*insert date*), in accordance with auditing standards generally accepted in the United States of America, we considered (*insert name of client*)'s internal control over financial reporting ("internal control") as a basis for designing our auditing procedures for the purpose of expressing our opinion on the financial statements, but not for the purpose of expressing an opinion on the effectiveness of the Company's internal control. Accordingly, we do not express an opinion on the effectiveness of the Company's internal control.

Our consideration of internal control was for the limited purpose described in the preceding paragraph and was not designed to identify all deficiencies in internal control that might be significant deficiencies or material weaknesses and therefore, there can be no assurance that all deficiencies, significant deficiencies, or material weaknesses have been identified. However, as discussed below, we identified certain deficiencies in internal control that we consider to be material weaknesses [*and other deficiencies that we consider to be significant deficiencies*].

A deficiency in internal control exists when the design or operation of a control does not allow management or employees, in the normal course of performing their assigned functions, to prevent, or detect and correct misstatements on a timely basis. A material weakness is a deficiency, or a combination of deficiencies, in internal control, such that there is a reasonable possibility that a material misstatement of the entity's financial statements will not be prevented, or detected and corrected, on a timely basis. [*We consider the following deficiencies in the Company's internal control to be material weaknesses:*]

[*Describe the material weaknesses that were identified.*]

A significant deficiency is a deficiency, or a combination of deficiencies, in internal control that is less severe than a material weakness, yet important enough to merit attention by those charged with governance. We consider the following deficiencies in the Company's internal control to be significant deficiencies:

[*Describe the significant deficiencies that were identified.*]

This communication is intended solely for the information and use of management, [*identify the body or individuals charged with governance, for example, audit committee, board of directors*], others within the organization, and [*identify any specified governmental authorities*] and is not intended to be and should not be used by anyone other than these specified parties.

(*Signature of Auditor*)

PRACTICE POINT 1: Control deficiencies identified during the audit that, upon evaluation, are considered significant deficiencies or material weaknesses should be communicated in writing to management and those charged with governance as a part of each audit, including significant deficiencies and material weaknesses that were communicated to management and those charged with governance in previous audits that have not yet been remediated. (Significant deficiencies and material weaknesses that previously were communicated and have not yet been remediated may be communicated in writing by referring to the previously issued written communication and the date of that communication.)

PRACTICE POINT 2: The auditor may include additional statements in the communication regarding the general inherent limitations of internal control, including the possibility of management override of controls, or the specific nature and extent of the auditor's consideration of internal control during the audit.

PRACTICE POINT 3: The auditor should not issue a written communication stating that no significant deficiencies were identified during the audit because of the potential for misinterpretation of the limited degree of assurance provided by such a communication.

PRACTICE POINT 4: Management may wish or may be required by a regulator to prepare a written response to the auditor's communication regarding significant deficiencies or material weaknesses identified in the audit. Such management communications may include a description of corrective actions taken by the entity, the entity's plans to implement new controls, or a statement indicating that management believes the cost of correcting a significant deficiency or material weakness would exceed the benefits to be derived from doing so. If such a written response is included in a document containing the auditor's written communication to management and those charged with governance concerning identified significant deficiencies or material weaknesses, the auditor should add a paragraph to the written communication disclaiming an opinion on such information. Following is an example of such a paragraph:

> (*Insert name of client*)'s written response to the significant deficiencies [*and material weaknesses*] identified in our audit has not been subjected to the auditing procedures applied in the audit of the financial statements and, accordingly, we express no opinion on it.

ILLUSTRATION 2—AUDITOR'S COMMUNICATION TO CLIENT WITH NO MATERIAL WEAKNESSES

(*Date*)

(*Name and Address of Client*)

In planning and performing our audit of the financial statements of (*insert name of client*) as of and for the year ended (*insert date*), in accordance with auditing standards generally accepted in the United States of America, we considered (*insert name of client*)'s internal control over financial reporting ("internal control") as a basis for designing our auditing procedures for the purpose of expressing our opinion on the financial statements, but not for the purpose of expressing an opinion on the effectiveness of the Company's internal control. Accordingly, we do not express an opinion on the effectiveness of the Company's internal control.

A deficiency in internal control exists when the design or operation of a control does not allow management or employees, in the normal course of performing their assigned functions, to prevent, or detect and correct misstatements on a timely basis. A material weakness is a deficiency, or a combination of deficiencies, in internal control, such that there is a reasonable possibility that a material misstatement of the entity's financial statements will not be prevented, or detected and corrected, on a timely basis.

Our consideration of internal control was for the limited purpose described in the first paragraph and was not designed to identify all deficiencies in internal control that might be deficiencies, significant deficiencies, or material weaknesses. We did not identify any deficiencies in internal control that we consider to be material weaknesses, as defined above.

This communication is intended solely for the information and use of management, [*identify the body or individuals charged with governance, for example, audit committee, board of directors*], others within the organization, and [*identify any specified governmental authorities*] and is not intended to be and should not be used by anyone other than these specified parties.

[*If one or more significant deficiencies have been identified, the auditor may add the following sentence to the third paragraph of the communication:*

> *However, we identified certain deficiencies in internal control that we consider to be significant deficiencies, and communicated them in writing to management and those charged with governance on [date]. A significant deficiency is a deficiency, or a combination of deficiencies, in internal control that is less severe than a material weakness, yet important enough to merit attention by those charged with governance.*]

(*Signature of Auditor*)

PRACTICE POINT 1: Control deficiencies identified during the audit that, upon evaluation, are considered significant deficiencies or material weaknesses should be communicated in writing to management and those charged with governance as part of each audit, including significant deficiencies and material weaknesses that were communicated to management and those charged with governance in previous audits that have not yet been remediated. (Significant deficiencies and material weaknesses that previously were communicated and have not yet been remediated may be communicated in writing by referring to the previously issued written communication and the date of that communication.)

PRACTICE POINT 2: The auditor may include additional statements in the communication regarding the general inherent limitations of internal control, including the possibility of management override of controls, or the specific nature and extent of the auditor's consideration of internal control during the audit.

PRACTICE POINT 3: The auditor should not issue a written communication stating that no significant deficiencies were identified during the audit because of the potential for misinterpretation of the limited degree of assurance provided by such a communication.

PRACTICE POINT 4: Management may wish or may be required by a regulator to prepare a written response to the auditor's communication regarding significant deficiencies or material weaknesses identified in the audit. Such management communications may include a description of corrective actions taken by the entity, the entity's plans to implement new controls, or a statement indicating that management believes the cost of correcting a significant deficiency or material weakness would exceed the benefits to be derived from doing so. If such a written response is included in a document containing the auditor's written communication to management and those charged with governance concerning identified significant deficiencies or material weaknesses, the auditor should add a paragraph to the written communication disclaiming an opinion on such information. Following is an example of such a paragraph.

> (*Insert name of client*)'s written response to the significant deficiencies [*and material weaknesses*] identified in our audit has not been subjected to the auditing procedures applied in the audit of the financial statements and, accordingly, we express no opinion on it.

AU SECTION 326
AUDIT EVIDENCE

PRACTICE POINT: As part of its Clarity Project, the American Institute of Certified Public Accountants' (AICPA's) Auditing Standards Board (ASB) has finalized a clarified Statement on Auditing Standards (SAS) titled, "Audit Evidence (Redrafted)," which supersedes AU Section 326 (Audit Evidence). The clarified SAS does not change or expand extant AU Section 326 in any significant respect. The requirements in paragraphs .14–.19 of AU Section 326, addressing the auditor's use of assertions in obtaining audit evidence, have been placed in the clarified SAS, "Understanding the Entity and Its Environment and Assessing the Risks of Material Misstatement (Redrafted)."

The ASB is expected to issue many of the clarified standards in *one* SAS that will be codified in "AU Section" format. The ASB has decided that the effective date of the clarified SASs that have not yet been issued is for audits of financial statements for periods ending on or after December 15, 2012. Auditors should be alert to and monitor further developments in this area.

WHAT EVERY PRACTITIONER SHOULD KNOW

Basic Objectives and Requirements

This Section provides guidance on how the auditor obtains sufficient appropriate audit evidence by performing audit procedures to afford a reasonable basis for an opinion on the financial statements. Specifically, this Section:

1. Defines *audit evidence* as "all the information used by the auditor in arriving at the conclusions on which the audit opinion is based and includes the information contained in the accounting records underlying the financial statements and other information."

2. Categorizes assertions into the following three major categories:

   a. Assertions about classes of transactions and events, which include: (1) occurrence, (2) completeness, (3) accuracy, (4) cutoff, and (5) classification.

   b. Assertions about account balances, which include: (1) existence, (2) rights and obligations, (3) completeness, and (4) valuation and allocation.

   c. Assertions about presentation and disclosure, which include: (1) occurrence and rights and obligations, (2) completeness, (3) classification and understandability, and (4) accuracy and valuation.

3. Describes how the auditor uses the aforementioned assertions to assess the risks of material misstatement and to design and perform audit procedures.

4. Discusses qualitative aspects of evidence that the auditor considers in determining whether audit evidence obtained is sufficient and appropriate (e.g., audit evidence is more reliable when it exists in documentary form rather than as an oral representation).

5. Provides guidance on the reliability of various kinds of audit evidence. For example, audit evidence obtained from independent parties outside the entity, such as confirmations, is more reliable than evidence obtained internally from the entity.

6. Indicates that the auditor should perform risk assessment procedures on all audits.

7. Indicates that evidence obtained solely by performing risk assessment procedures is not sufficient to support the auditor's opinion on the financial statements. The auditor will need to supplement such procedures by others, in the form of tests of controls and substantive procedures, to be able to support his or her opinion.

8. Provides guidance on the uses and limitations of "inquiry" as an audit procedure. For example, the auditor is prohibited from using inquiry alone to obtain audit evidence about the operating effectiveness of controls.

Concept and Characteristics of Audit Evidence

The overall objective of an audit of financial statements is to render an opinion on whether the client's financial statements are presented fairly, in all material respects, in conformity with generally accepted accounting principles (GAAP). In order for the auditor to render an opinion on the entity's financial statements, the auditor must first gather and evaluate sufficient appropriate audit evidence as a basis for his or her opinion. The third standard of field work states:

> The auditor must obtain sufficient appropriate audit evidence by performing audit procedures to afford a reasonable basis for an opinion regarding the financial statements under audit.

Audit evidence can be defined as any information that has an impact in determining whether financial statements are fairly presented in accordance with GAAP, including the information contained in the accounting records underlying the financial statements. Although a variety of information may have some impact on the auditor's decision process, it is well recognized that both the quality and quantity of evidence must be evaluated. The third standard of field work refers to these two characteristics as *sufficient* (quantity) and *appropriate* (quality).

Audit evidence can be classified as (1) underlying accounting data and (2) corroborating evidence. *Underlying accounting data* consists of general and specialized journals, ledgers, manuals, and supporting worksheets and other analyses. Generally, underlying accounting data is tested by retracing transactions through the accounting system, recomputing allocations, and performing other mathematical calculations. Although underlying accounting data is an important part of audit evidence, such data alone is not sufficient to determine whether financial statements are fairly presented in accordance with GAAP. The auditor must collect corroborating evidence before an opinion on the financial statements can be expressed. *Corroborating evidence* consists of documentary evidence, such as vendors' invoices, confirmations, and observations.

Appropriate audit evidence This Section indicates that audit evidence is appropriate when it is both *reliable* and *relevant*; however, these terms are not defined. Generalizing about what constitutes reliable evidence is difficult because the particular audit circumstances must be considered. Nevertheless, recognizing the possibility that exceptions exist, this Section indicates that reliable evidence usually has the following characteristics:

- Audit evidence is more reliable if it is obtained from an independent, knowledgeable source outside the entity.

- The more effective the internal controls, the more reliable the audit evidence.

- Audit evidence obtained directly by the auditor, for example, through physical examination, observation, computation, and inspection is more reliable than evidence obtained indirectly or by inference. For example, the auditor's calculation of the gross profit percentage and comparison with prior years provides more reliable evidence than if the auditor relied on the client's calculations.

- Audit evidence is more reliable when it exists in documentary form (e.g., a written record of a meeting is more reliable than subsequent oral representation of matters discussed in the meeting).

- Original documents provide more reliable audit evidence than photocopies or facsimiles of such documents.

Audit evidence should be capable of proving or disproving an assertion made by the client in its financial records. Therefore, evidence must pertain or be relevant to the audit objective or the assertion the auditor is testing before it can be persuasive. Relevance can be considered only in terms of specific audit objectives or assertions, and evidence may be relevant to one specific audit objective or assertion but not to another. For example, assume that the auditor is concerned with whether all shipments made to customers are being billed by the client (completeness assertion). If the auditor selects a sample of duplicate sales invoices (i.e., using the sales invoices as the population) and traces them to the related shipping documents, the evidence would not be relevant for the completeness assertion. A relevant procedure would be to select a sample of shipping documents (i.e., using the shipping documents as the population) and compare them with the related duplicate sales invoices to determine if the customers had been billed. In this example, when the auditor traces from the duplicate sales invoices to the related shipping documents, the evidence would be relevant to the existence or occurrence assertion and not to the completeness assertion.

Sufficient audit evidence It is relatively difficult to define, and this Section does not define, *sufficient* audit evidence because the term refers simply to the amount of evidence collected. Nevertheless, the auditor must exercise considerable judgment when determining whether sufficiency is achieved. This Section offers the following guidance for determining whether sufficient audit evidence has been collected:

- The concept of sufficient audit evidence recognizes that the auditor can never reduce audit risk to zero and, therefore, the accumulation of evidence should be persuasive rather than conclusive. The auditor is seldom convinced beyond all doubt with respect to all aspects of the financial statements being audited. However, to obtain reasonable assurance, the auditor must be satisfied that the audit evidence collected is persuasive.

- The auditor is not free to collect unlimited amounts of evidence, since he or she must work within economic limits. However, cost cannot be the sole basis for the quantity or quality of audit procedures, and the difficulty and expense of a test is not a valid reason for omitting it.

- The auditor should not form an opinion on the entity's financial statements until he or she has obtained sufficient appropriate audit evidence to remove any substantial doubt about a material assertion. Otherwise, the auditor should express a qualified opinion or a disclaimer of opinion on the financial statements.

Identifying Management's Assertions and the Auditor's Use of Assertions in Obtaining Audit Evidence

Assertions are implied or expressed representations by management about the recognition, measurement, presentation, and disclosure of information in the financial statements and related disclosures. For example, if the entity's financial statements show cash of $50,000, this means that management asserts that cash of $50,000 exists, is owned by the entity, and includes funds at all locations, funds with custodians, and deposits in transit as of the balance sheet date. Furthermore, unless otherwise disclosed in the financial statements or notes thereto, management also asserts that the cash was unrestricted and available for the entity's general operating purposes. Similar assertions exist for each asset, liability, equity, revenue, and expense item in the financial statements.

One of the first steps in the audit process is to identify management's assertions regarding each material component of the entity's financial statements. The auditor must test these assertions or propositions by gathering evidence to support or rebut them. The assertions identified in this Section may be classified in three broad categories:

1. Assertions about classes of transactions and events for the period under audit.

2. Assertions about account balances at the period-end.

3. Assertions about presentation and disclosure.

Assertions about classes of transactions and events for the period under audit
This Section indicates that assertions about classes of transactions and events for the period under audit address whether recorded transactions and events:

- Have in fact occurred and relate to the entity (*occurrence*);

- Include all transactions and events that should have been recorded (*completeness*);

- Have been properly recorded based on appropriate amounts and other data (*accuracy*);

- Have been recorded in the correct accounting period (*cutoff*); and

- Have been recorded in the proper accounts (*classification*).

Assertions about account balances at the period-end This Section indicates that assertions about account balances at the period-end address whether:

- Assets, liabilities, and equity interests exist (*existence*);
- The entity holds or controls the rights to assets, and liabilities are the obligations of the entity (*rights and obligations*);
- All assets, liabilities, and equity interests that should have been recorded have been recorded (*completeness*); and
- Assets, liabilities, and equity interests are included in the financial statements at appropriate amounts and any resulting valuation or allocation adjustments are appropriately recorded (*valuation and allocation*).

Assertions about presentation and disclosure This Section indicates that assertions about presentation and disclosure address whether:

- Disclosed events and transactions have occurred and relate to the entity (*occurrence and rights and obligations*);
- All disclosures that should have been included in the financial statements have been included (*completeness*);
- Financial information is appropriately presented and described and disclosures are clearly expressed (*classification and understandability*); and
- Financial and other information are disclosed fairly and at appropriate amounts (*accuracy and valuation*).

The auditor's use of assertions in obtaining audit evidence This Section requires the auditor to determine the *relevance* of each of the financial statement assertions described above for each significant class of transactions, account balance, and presentation and disclosure. The auditor should use the identified relevant assertions to assess the risks of material misstatements in the financial statements and to design further audit procedures that are responsive to the assessed risks. The auditor should evaluate the following aspects in determining whether a particular assertion is relevant:

1. The nature of the assertion.
2. The volume of transactions or data related to the assertion.
3. The nature and complexity of the systems the entity uses to process and control information supporting the assertion.

Developing Audit Tests and Procedures for Obtaining Evidence

To determine what type of evidence to obtain, the auditor develops specific audit objectives related to each relevant assertion. When determining audit objectives, the auditor should evaluate each of the relevant assertions as they relate to the specific account balance, class of transactions, or presentation and disclosure. For example, if the auditor is attempting to gather evidence on the assertions of existence of inventory, the auditor's objective would be to gather evidence that the inventory included in the balance sheet physically existed as of the balance sheet date. Having identified specific audit objectives, the auditor should then develop methods to achieve them.

The methods used by the auditor to achieve the audit objectives are referred to by auditors using terminology such as *audit procedures, audit techniques,* and *audit tests.* These terms represent the evidence-gathering methods the auditor uses and involve the following considerations:

- The audit procedures that should be used (i.e., the *nature* of audit tests);

- The proper time for performing the procedures (i.e., the *timing* of audit tests); and

- The particular items that should be subject to such procedures (i.e., the *extent* of audit tests).

This Section indicates that the auditor should perform the following types of procedures:

- *Risk assessment procedures*—These are audit procedures performed to obtain an understanding of the entity and its environment, including its internal control, to assess the risks of material misstatement at the financial statement and relevant assertion levels. Risk assessment procedures must be performed in all audits. Examples of risk assessment procedures include inspection of documents or tangible assets, and analytical procedures.

- *Tests of controls* (when relevant or necessary)—These are audit procedures performed to test the operating effectiveness of controls in preventing or detecting material misstatements at the relevant assertion level. The auditor should perform tests of controls in the following two circumstances:

- When the auditor's risk assessment includes an expectation of the operating effectiveness of controls, the auditor should test those controls to support the risk assessment.

- When the substantive procedures alone do not provide sufficient appropriate audit evidence, the auditor should perform tests of controls to obtain audit evidence about their operating effectiveness.

Substantive procedures—These are audit procedures performed to detect material misstatements at the relevant assertion level and include tests of details of classes of transactions, account balances, and disclosures, and substantive analytical procedures. Regardless of the assessed risk of material misstatement, substantive procedures must be performed in all audits for all relevant assertions related to each material class of transactions, account balance, and disclosure.

Types of audit procedures This Section indicates that the auditor should use one or more types of the audit procedures described below when performing risk assessment procedures, tests of controls, or substantive procedures:

- *Inspection of records and documents*—Inspection involves the auditor's examination, other than vouching or tracing, of documents and records to substantiate the information that is or should be included in the financial statements. This procedure is usually applied to documents such as lease agreements, debt agreements, contracts, and minutes of meetings of the board of directors. Inspection addresses all of the financial statement assertions because of the variety of documents the auditor may inspect.

- *Inspection of tangible assets*—Inspection of tangible assets is the physical examination or count by the auditor of a tangible asset. This type of evidence-gathering procedure is most often associated with cash, securities, inventory, and property and equipment. The primary audit assertion tested by physical examination is existence; however, physical examination can also provide evidence about the valuation or allocation and rights and obligations assertions.

- *Observation*—Observation focuses on client activities to understand who performs them, or how or when they are performed. Observation differs from physical examination: the former usually is used to gather evidence that leaves no audit trail (e.g., the auditor may observe that cash is deposited daily by a specific clerk); the latter involves counting or inspecting a specific tangible asset (e.g., cash or inventory) to determine its existence. While observation satisfies all financial statement assertions, it is rarely sufficient by itself. Rather, it is often necessary for the auditor to follow up with other kinds of corroborative evidence.

- *Inquiry*—Responses to an inquiry made by the auditor may be oral or in writing. The auditor often makes inquiries of various individuals to determine who performs a particular activity, or how or when the activity is done. For example, the auditor may inquire of client personnel about who deposits cash and how often it is done. Testing of internal control activities that leave no audit trail of documentary evidence is usually accomplished by inquiry. Inquiry can also be used as a substantive test. For example, inquiries of management regarding subsequent events would be a substantive test because they provide evidence concerning the adequacy of disclosures in the financial statements. Although considerable evidence is obtained from the client through inquiry, it usually cannot be regarded as conclusive; therefore, it is normally necessary for the auditor to obtain further corroborating evidence through other procedures. Inquiries are useful in testing all of the financial statement assertions. In some cases, the auditor should obtain replies to inquiries in the form of written representations from management.

- *Confirmation*—Confirmation procedures include primarily written and sometimes oral responses from specific third parties regarding particular items affecting the financial statements. The primary assertions tested by confirmation are existence and rights and obligations, although confirmation can also provide evidence about the other financial statement assertions. Typically, confirmations are used to verify cash and accounts receivable balances. To be considered reliable evidence, confirmations must be controlled by the auditor from the time their preparation is completed until they are returned to the auditor.

- *Recalculation*—Recalculation involves testing the mechanical accuracy and rechecking of computations and transfers of information made by the client. This includes such procedures as extending sales or vendor invoices, adding journals and ledgers, and checking the calculation of depreciation expense. Recalculation can be performed through the use of information technology and computer-assisted audit techniques (CAATs).

- *Reperformance*—Reperformance is the auditor's independent execution of procedures or controls that were originally performed as part of the entity's internal control, either manually or through the use of CAATs.

- *Analytical procedures*—Analytical procedures use comparisons and relationships to determine whether account balances appear reasonable. An example is comparing the gross margin percentage in the current year with the percentage from the preceding year. Analytical procedures satisfy all assertions and are so important that they are required on *all* audits. For certain audit objectives or small account balances, analytical tests alone may be sufficient evidence. However, in most cases, additional evidence beyond analytical procedures is necessary to satisfy the requirement for sufficient competent evidence.

PRACTICE POINT: AU Section 329 (Analytical Procedures) states that analytical procedures are performed at any of three stages during an audit, as follows:

- They are *required* to be performed during the planning phase to help the auditor determine the nature, extent, and timing of work to be performed.

- They are often used as substantive tests during the testing phase of the engagement to obtain audit evidence about particular assertions.

- They are *required* to be used during the completion phase of the audit as a final review for material misstatements or financial problems, and to help the auditor take a final objective look at the audited financial statements.

PRACTICE ISSUES AND FREQUENTLY ASKED QUESTIONS

Issue 1: What do assertions about "existence" or "occurrence" deal with?

Existence or occurrence assertions deal with whether assets, liabilities, and equities included in the balance sheet actually existed as of the balance sheet date and whether transactions and events that have been recorded have actually occurred during the period covered by the financial statements and pertain to the entity. For example, management may assert that inventory included in the entity's balance sheet exists and is available for sale as of the balance sheet date. Similarly, management may assert that sales and purchases presented in the income statement represent transactions that have actually taken place.

Issue 2: What do assertions about "completeness" deal with?

The completeness assertion deals with (1) whether all transactions and events that should have been recorded have been recorded and (2) whether all assets, liabilities, and equity interests that should have been recorded have been recorded. For example, management may assert that all sales of goods are recorded and included in the financial statements. Therefore, failure to record a sale that did occur would violate the completeness assertion. Recording a sale that did not take place also would be a violation of the occurrence assertion.

Issue 3: What do assertions about "rights and obligations" deal with?

Rights and obligations assertions deal with whether recorded assets are actually rights of the entity and whether liabilities are actually obligations of the entity. For example, although certain assets, such as inventory held on consignment, may be in the client's possession, they may not be owned by the client and should not be included in the balance sheet.

Issue 4: What do assertions about "valuation and allocation" deal with?

Valuation and allocation assertions deal with whether assets, liabilities, equities, revenues, and expenses have been included in the financial statements in the appropriate amounts and any resulting valuation or allocation adjustments are appropriately recorded. Proper valuation of financial statement items is specified by GAAP (e.g., FIFO, LIFO, or average-cost method for the valuation of inventory). Allocation is a part of proper valuation for many financial statement items. For example, management may assert that property is recorded at historical cost and that such cost is systematically allocated to appropriate accounting periods through depreciation.

Issue 5: What do assertions about "accuracy" deal with?

Assertions about accuracy deal with whether amounts and relevant data relating to recorded transactions and events have been recorded appropriately. For example, management may assert that the company's inventory listings are accurately compiled and the totals are properly included in the inventory accounts. Similarly, management may assert that the major categories of inventories (e.g., materials, work-in-process, and finished goods) are accurately disclosed in the financial statements.

Issue 6: What do assertions about "cutoff" deal with?

Assertions about cutoff deal with whether transactions and events have been recorded in the correct accounting period. For example, management may assert that shipping and receiving transactions pertaining to inventories near year-end have been recorded in the proper period.

Issue 7: What do assertions about "classification" deal with?

Assertions about classification deal with whether transactions and events have been recorded in the proper accounts. For example, management may assert that materials, work-in-process, and finished goods inventories have been recorded in their appropriate respective categories and that the total inventories are properly classified in the balance sheet as current assets.

Issue 8: What do assertions about "presentation and disclosure" deal with?

Presentation and disclosure assertions are concerned with whether components of the financial statements and related information are properly classified, described, and disclosed. Proper classification includes presentation of assets and liabilities as current and noncurrent. Proper description includes the use of specific account titles, such as "trade accounts payable." Proper disclosure is concerned with whether information presented in the financial statements and notes thereto adequately informs financial statement users about matters to which it relates.

Issue 9: Do management's written representations and the auditor's assessment of control risk constitute sufficient audit evidence about the completeness assertion?

No. Management's written representations about the completeness assertion and the auditor's assessment of control risk do not, by themselves, constitute sufficient appropriate audit evidence about the completeness assertion. The auditor should obtain other evidence by performing substantive tests, including analytical procedures and tests of details of accounts. In addition, the auditor should consider that for some transactions (e.g., revenues that are received primarily in cash, such as those of a charitable organization) it may be necessary to perform tests of controls.

Issue 10: Why is the completeness assertion considered to be the most difficult of all the financial statement assertions in obtaining evidence?

The completeness assertion is the most difficult financial statement assertion to verify because gathering evidence to support the completeness assertion involves searching a seemingly infinite universe for transactions and accounts that may have been improperly omitted from the statements, while the other assertions are confined to the finite universe of those that are shown on the financial statements. Therefore, to obtain evidence about the completeness assertion, the auditor has to narrow the infinite universe in which potentially unrecorded items may reside to an economically manageable range for audit purposes. A good starting place is to consider where omissions are most likely to occur within the financial statements. Procedures can then be applied to those financial statement elements to detect unrecorded transactions and accounts.

One efficient technique is the application of analytical procedures to the financial statements in the planning phases of the audit. Pronounced decreases in like balances from one period to the next, absent explanation, may signal a lack of completeness. Likewise, a lack of consistency between relationships within the statements may indicate that data is not complete.

Because the search for evidence about completeness is necessarily concerned with items that are, for the present, outside of the financial statements, it is useful to draw upon sources and data outside of the financial statements, the accounting department, or the company itself to obtain assurances. For example, comparing records of units of production, which are maintained outside the accounting department, to cost of sales and inventory records, can provide additional evidence about the completeness of cost of sales. Statements of third parties who may have knowledge about the company, such as confirmations or correspondence with banks, attorneys, insurers, customers, or suppliers, may also provide strong evidence. Furthermore, reading of minutes, contracts, and legal documents may reveal items such as commitments or contingencies that should be reported or disclosed in the statements. Substantive tests applied to transactions at locations or during time periods that are considered to be at high risk for misstatement are also appropriate. Finally, the auditor's personal observations and general knowledge about the client and the industry provide important evidence about completeness.

Issue 11: Does an auditor's review of a client's past due accounts receivable aging with the credit manager provide sufficient evidence regarding the collectibility of accounts receivable?

Probably not. The credit manager's comments are representations of management. Furthermore, they are subjective evaluations. While they are important as a starting point, objective evidence or evidence obtained directly by the auditor from sources outside the company would generally be needed to corroborate the credit manager's assertions. The auditor's direct observation of subsequent collections would provide convincing evidence of their collectibility, and observation of their noncollection after a significant period following the balance sheet date would tend to support noncollectibility. Similarly, statements about intentions or capability to pay obtained directly from the customers as a part of the confirmation process, or data from independent credit information services would provide far more persuasive evidence.

Issue 12: What are the implications to the auditor for not being able to obtain sufficient appropriate audit evidence relating to income tax accruals?

The client is responsible for the income tax accruals and for the adequacy of related disclosures in the financial statements. An auditing interpretation, titled *The Effect of an Inability to Obtain Audit Evidence Relating to Income Tax Accruals*, addresses various practice issues concerning audit evidence with respect to income tax accruals in connection with an audit. The following discussion is based on the guidance in the auditing interpretation:

- When a client either (1) does not provide the auditor with adequate information to support the income tax accruals and related disclosures or (2) restricts the auditor's access to such information, the auditor faces a scope limitation that precludes the issuance of an unqualified opinion on the financial statements.

- Audit documentation of relevant information about the income tax accruals generally would be considered insufficient if it does not include pertinent items, such as:

  — Significant elements of the client's analysis of tax contingencies or reserves, including roll-forward of material changes to such reserves.

  — The client's position and support for income tax-related disclosures, such as its effective tax rate reconciliation and support for its intraperiod allocation of income tax expense or benefit to continuing operations and to items other than continuing operations.

  — The client's basis for assessing deferred tax assets and related valuation allowances.

- The auditor may not be able to adequately substantiate the tax accruals and related disclosures merely by accepting the conclusions of a third-party tax adviser who has been engaged by the client for such a purpose.

Issue 13: Do accounting records alone provide sufficient appropriate audit evidence on which to base an audit opinion on the financial statements?

No. Accounting records alone do not provide sufficient appropriate audit evidence on which to base an audit opinion on the financial statements. Therefore, the auditor should obtain other audit evidence from other sources, such as the following:

- Minutes of meetings of the board of directors or relevant committees

- Confirmations from third parties

- Industry analysts' reports

- Comparable data about competitors (benchmarking)

- Controls manuals

- Information obtained through inquiry, observation, and inspection

Issue 14: Are there any specific circumstances under which the auditor is required to test controls?

Yes. This Section states that tests of controls are necessary in the following two circumstances:

1. When the auditor's risk assessment includes an expectation of the operating effectiveness of controls. In this circumstance, the auditor should test those controls to support the risk assessment.

2. When the substantive procedures alone do not provide sufficient appropriate audit evidence. In this circumstance, the auditor should perform tests of controls to obtain audit evidence about their operating effectiveness.

ILLUSTRATIONS AND PRACTICE AIDS

ILLUSTRATION 1—INTEGRATION OF FINANCIAL STATEMENT ASSERTIONS AND SUBSTANTIVE PROCEDURES FOR INVENTORIES

Note: This example is adapted from the appendix, "Illustrative Financial Statement Assertions and Examples of Substantive Procedures Illustrations for Inventories of a Manufacturing Company" of SAS No. 110 (AU Section 318) titled, "Performing Audit Procedures in Response to Assessed Risks and Evaluating the Audit Evidence Obtained." This example illustrates the use of financial statement assertions in designing substantive procedures and does not illustrate tests of controls. The examples of substantive procedures are not intended to be all-inclusive, nor is it expected that all of the procedures would be applied in an audit. The particular substantive procedures to be used in each circumstance depend on the auditor's risk assessments and tests of controls.

Illustrative Assertions about Account Balances	*Examples of Substantive Procedures*
Existence	
Inventories included in the balance sheet physically exist.	• Physically examining inventory items. • Obtaining confirmation of inventories at locations outside the entity. • Inspecting documents relating to inventory transactions between a physical inventory date and the balance sheet date.
Inventories represent items held for sale or use in the normal course of business.	• Inspecting perpetual inventory records, production records, and purchasing records for indications of current activity. • Reconciling items in the inventory listing to a current computer-maintained sales catalog and subsequent sales and delivery reports using computer-assisted audit techniques (CAATs). • Questioning production and sales personnel. • Using the work of specialists to corroborate the nature of specialized products.
Rights and Obligations	
The entity has legal title or similar rights of ownership to the inventories.	• Examining paid vendors' invoices, consignment agreements, and contracts. • Obtaining confirmation of inventories at locations outside the entity.
Inventories exclude items billed to customers or owned by others.	• Examining paid vendors' invoices, consignment agreements, and contracts. • Inspecting shipping and receiving transactions near year-end for recording in the proper period.
Completeness	
Inventory quantities include all products, materials, and supplies on hand.	• Observing physical inventory counts. • Analytically comparing the relationship of inventory balances to recent purchasing, production, and sales activities. • Inspecting shipping and receiving transactions near year-end for recording in the proper period.
Inventory quantities include all products, materials, and supplies owned by the company that are in transit or stored at outside locations.	• Obtaining confirmation of inventories at locations outside the entity. • Analytically comparing the relationship of inventory balances to recent purchasing, production, and sales activities.

Illustrative Assertions about Account Balances	*Examples of Substantive Procedures*
Inventory listings are accurately compiled and the totals are properly included in the inventory accounts.	• Inspecting shipping and receiving transactions near year-end for recording in the proper period. • Examining the inventory listing for inclusion of test counts recorded during the physical inventory observation. • Reconciling all inventory tags and count sheets used in recording the physical inventory counts using CAATs. • Recalculating inventory listing for clerical accuracy using CAATs. • Reconciling physical counts to perpetual records and general ledger balances and investigating significant fluctuations using CAATs.

Valuation and Allocation

Inventories are properly stated at cost (except when market is lower).	• Examining paid vendors' invoices and comparing product prices to standard cost build-ups. • Analytically comparing direct labor rates to production records. • Recalculating the computation of standard overhead rates. • Examining analyses of purchasing and manufacturing standard cost variances.
Slow-moving, excess, defective, and obsolete items included in inventories are properly identified.	• Examining an analysis of inventory turnover. • Analyzing industry experience and trends. • Analytically comparing the relationship of inventory balances to anticipated sales volume. • Performing a walk-through of the plant for indications of products not being used. • Inquiring of production and sales personnel concerning possible excess, or defective or obsolete inventory items. • Addressing logistic and distribution business process (e.g., cycle time, volume of returns, or problems with suppliers).
Inventories are reduced, when appropriate, to replacement cost or net realizable value.	• Inspecting sales catalogs or industry publications for current market value quotations. • Recalculating inventory valuation reserves. • Analyzing current production costs. • Examining sales after year-end and open purchase order commitments.

Illustrative Assertions about Presentation and Disclosure	*Examples of Substantive Procedures*

Rights and Obligations

The pledge or assignment of any inventories is appropriately disclosed.	• Obtaining confirmation of inventories pledged under loan agreements.

Completeness

The financial statements include all disclosures related to inventories specified by generally accepted accounting principles.	• Using a disclosure checklist to determine whether the disclosures included in generally accepted accounting principles were made.

Understandability

Inventories are properly classified in the balance sheet as current assets.	• Examining drafts of the financial statements for appropriate balance sheet classification.
Disclosures related to inventories are understandable.	• Reading disclosures for clarity.

Accuracy and Valuation

The major categories of inventories and their bases of valuation are accurately disclosed in the financial statements.	• Examining drafts of the financial statements for appropriate disclosures. • Reconciling the categories of inventories disclosed in the draft financial statements to the categories recorded during the physical inventory observation.

ILLUSTRATION 2—UNCONDITIONAL AND PRESUMPTIVELY MANDATORY REQUIREMENTS OF AU SECTION 326

Unconditional Requirements

The following unconditional requirements, which are identified by the words "must" or "is required," obligate the auditor to:

- Obtain sufficient appropriate audit evidence by performing audit procedures to afford a reasonable basis for the audit opinion. Audit evidence can be classified as (a) underlying accounting data and (b) corroborating evidence. *Underlying accounting data* consists of general and specialized journals, ledgers, manuals, and supporting worksheets and other analyses. *Corroborating evidence* consists of documentary evidence, such as vendors' invoices, confirmations, and observations.

- Not be satisfied with evidence that is less than persuasive. The concept of sufficient audit evidence recognizes that the auditor can never reduce audit risk to zero and, therefore, the accumulation of evidence should be persuasive rather than conclusive.

- Perform risk assessment procedures to provide a satisfactory basis for the assessment of risks at the financial statement and relevant assertion levels. *Risk assessment procedures* are audit procedures performed to obtain an understanding of the entity and its environment, including its internal control, to assess the risks of material misstatement at the financial statement and relevant assertion levels.

- Supplement risk assessment procedures with substantive procedures, and, when relevant or necessary, with tests of controls.

Presumptively Mandatory Requirements

Presumptively mandatory requirements are identified by the word "should" and place the burden of proof on the auditor if he or she departs from the presumptive requirement. Presumptively mandatory requirements are required to be performed in all applicable circumstances unless the auditor can justify in the audit documentation a reason for not doing so and demonstrate how other audit procedures that the auditor performed have met the audit objectives. AU Section 326 states that the auditor *should*:

1. Obtain audit evidence by testing the accounting records.

2. Obtain other audit evidence, because accounting records alone do not provide sufficient appropriate audit evidence on which to base an audit opinion.

3. Consider the sufficiency and appropriateness of audit evidence to be obtained when assessing risks and designing further audit procedures. *Sufficiency* refers to the quantity of audit evidence, and *appropriateness* refers to the quality of audit evidence.

4. Consider the reliability of the information to be used as audit evidence. Audit evidence is more reliable if it is obtained from an independent knowledgeable source outside the entity. In addition, the more effective the internal controls, the more reliable the audit evidence. Furthermore, audit evidence obtained directly by the auditor, for example, through physical examination, observation, computation, and inspection is more reliable than evidence obtained indirectly or by inference.

5. Obtain audit evidence about the accuracy and completeness of client-prepared information when using that information to perform further audit procedures.

6. Determine what additional audit procedures are necessary to resolve inconsistencies in audit evidence obtained from different sources.

7. Use professional judgment and exercise professional skepticism in evaluating the quantity and quality of audit evidence to support the audit opinion.

8. Use relevant assertions for classes of transactions, account balances, and presentation and disclosure in sufficient detail to form a basis for assessing the risks of material misstatement and for designing and performing further audit procedures.

9. Use relevant assertions in assessing risks by considering the types of misstatements that might arise and designing further audit procedures to respond to those risks.

10. Determine the relevance of each of the financial statement assertions for each significant class of transactions, account balance, and presentation and disclosure.

11. Determine the source of likely potential misstatements in each significant class of transactions, account balance, and presentation and disclosure, in order to identify relevant assertions.

12. Evaluate the nature of the assertion, the volume of transactions or data related to the assertion, and the nature and complexity of the entity's systems for purposes of determining whether a particular assertion is relevant to a significant account balance or disclosure.

13. Obtain audit evidence on which to base the audit opinion by performing the following procedures:

    a. Risk assessment procedures.

    b. Tests of controls (when relevant or necessary). These are audit procedures performed to test the operating effectiveness of controls in preventing or detecting material misstatements at the relevant assertion level.

    c. Substantive procedures. These are audit procedures performed to detect material misstatements at the relevant assertion level and include tests of details of classes of transactions, account balances and disclosures, and substantive analytical procedures.

14. Perform tests of controls in the following two circumstances: (a) when the auditor's risk assessment includes an expectation of the operating effectiveness of controls and (b) when the substantive procedures alone do not provide sufficient appropriate audit evidence.

15. Plan and perform substantive procedures to be responsive to the related planned level of detection risk.

16. Design and perform substantive procedures for all relevant assertions related to each significant class of transactions, account balance, and disclosure, regardless of the assessed risk of material misstatement.

17. Use one or more types of audit procedures described below when performing risk assessment procedures, tests of controls, or substantive procedures:

    a. *Inspection of records and documents*—Inspection involves the auditor's examination, other than vouching or tracing, of documents and records to substantiate the information that is, or should be, included in the financial statements.

    b. *Inspection of tangible assets*—This type of evidence-gathering procedure is most often associated with cash, securities, inventory, and property and equipment.

    c. *Observation*—Observation focuses on client activities to understand who performs them, or how or when they are performed. While observation satisfies all financial statement assertions, it is rarely sufficient by itself; it is often necessary for the auditor to follow up with other kinds of corroborative evidence.

    d. *Inquiry*—Although considerable evidence is obtained from the client through inquiry, it usually cannot be regarded as conclusive; therefore, it is normally necessary for the auditor to obtain further corroborating evidence through other procedures.

    e. *Confirmation*—To be considered reliable evidence, confirmations must be controlled by the auditor from the time their preparation is completed until they are returned to the auditor.

    f. *Recalculation*—Recalculation involves testing the mechanical accuracy and rechecking of computations and transfers of information made by the client. Recalculation can be performed through the use of information technology and CAATs.

g. *Reperformance*—Reperformance is the auditor's independent execution of procedures or controls that were originally performed as part of the entity's internal control, either manually or through the use of CAATs.

h. *Analytical procedures*—Analytical procedures satisfy all assertions and are so important that they are required on *all* audits. For certain audit objectives or small account balances, analytical tests alone may be sufficient evidence. In most cases, however, additional evidence beyond analytical procedures is necessary to satisfy the requirement for sufficient competent evidence.

18. Perform procedures to establish the continuing relevance of evidence obtained in previous audits, where that evidence is to be used in the current audit.

19. Obtain, in some cases, replies to inquiries in the form of written management representations; for example, when obtaining oral responses to inquiries, the nature of the response may be so significant that it warrants obtaining written representation from the respondent.

20. Perform additional audit procedures to resolve significant inconsistencies in the information or evidence obtained.

21. Perform audit procedures in addition to the use of inquiry to obtain sufficient appropriate evidence. This is because inquiry alone ordinarily does not provide sufficient appropriate audit evidence to detect a material misstatement at the relevant assertion level.

AU SECTION 328
AUDITING FAIR VALUE MEASUREMENTS AND DISCLOSURES

PRACTICE POINT: As part of its Clarity Project, the American Institute of Certified Public Accountants' (AICPA's) Auditing Standards Board (ASB) has finalized a clarified Statement on Auditing Standards (SAS) titled, "Auditing Accounting Estimates, Including Fair Value Accounting Estimates and Related Disclosures," which supersedes AU Section 328 (Auditing Fair Value Measurements and Disclosures) and AU Section 342 (Auditing Accounting Estimates). The clarified SAS combines the requirements and guidance from AU Section 328 and AU Section 342, and it does not change or expand those AU Sections in any significant respect.

The ASB is expected to issue many of the clarified standards in *one* SAS that will be codified in "AU Section" format. The ASB has decided that the effective date of the clarified SASs that have not yet been issued is for audits of financial statements for periods ending on or after December 15, 2012. Auditors should be alert to and monitor further developments in this area.

WHAT EVERY PRACTITIONER SHOULD KNOW

Responsibility for Fair Value Measurements and Disclosures in the Financial Statements

It is management's (not the auditor's) responsibility to make the fair value measurements and disclosures in the financial statements. In connection with its responsibility, management needs to:

- Establish an accounting and financial reporting process for determining the fair value measurements and disclosures.
- Select appropriate valuation methods.
- Identify and support significant assumptions used.
- Prepare the valuation.
- Ensure that the presentation and disclosure of the fair value measurements are in conformity with GAAP.

The auditor should gather audit evidence to provide reasonable assurance that fair value measurements and disclosures are in accordance with GAAP. The auditor obtains such evidence based on information available to him or her at the time of the audit; therefore, the auditor is not responsible for predicting future conditions, transactions, or events that may affect management's actions or assumptions.

Obtaining an Understanding of the Entity's Process for Determining Fair Value Measurements and Disclosures and of the Relevant Controls, and Assessing Risk

For some entities, the measurement of fair value and the process established by management to determine fair value may be simple and reliable; for example, to determine fair value for its marketable securities, management may simply refer to published price quotations. For other entities, fair value measurements are inherently more complex and involve uncertainty about the occurrence of future events or their outcome; therefore, for such entities, management may need to develop assumptions which involve the use of judgment.

The guidance in this Section states that the auditor "should obtain an understanding of the entity's process for determining fair value measurements and disclosures and of the relevant controls sufficient to develop an effective audit approach." When obtaining this understanding, the auditor is required to consider various factors, such as the following:

- The entity's controls over the process used to determine fair value measurements.
- The qualifications of the persons determining the fair value measurements.
- The extent to which information technology is involved in the process.
- The types of accounts or transactions requiring fair value measurements or disclosures (e.g., whether they are the result of routine and recurring transactions, or nonroutine or unusual transactions).
- Whether the entity relies on a service organization to provide fair value measurements or data that supports the measurement. In such circumstances, the auditor should consider the requirements of AU Section 324 (Service Organizations).
- Whether the entity uses the work of a specialist in determining fair value measurements and disclosures. In such circumstances, the auditor should consider the requirements of AU Section 336 (Using the Work of a Specialist).
- The significant assumptions management has used to determine fair value.
- The documentation management prepared supporting the assumptions used.
- The methods used to develop and apply management assumptions and to monitor changes thereto.
- Relevant controls over valuation models and information systems, including approval processes and controls over the consistency, timeliness, and reliability of the data used in valuation models.

The auditor uses his or her understanding of the entity's process and the related controls when assessing the risk of material misstatement and for determining the nature, timing, and extent of audit procedures.

Evaluating Conformity of Fair Value Measurements and Disclosures with GAAP

This Section requires the auditor to evaluate whether an entity's fair value measurements and disclosures are in accordance with GAAP. Specifically:

1. The auditor should evaluate management's intent and ability to carry out specific courses of action, where relevant to the fair value measure-

ments and disclosures. The extent of evidence to be obtained about management's intent and ability is a matter of professional judgment. Ordinarily, the auditor's procedures include inquiries of management. In addition, the auditor corroborates management's responses, for example, by considering management's:

   a. Past history of carrying out its stated intentions.

   b. Stated reasons for choosing a particular course of action.

   c. Ability to carry out a particular course of action given the entity's economic circumstances, including the implications of its contractual commitments.

   d. Written plans and other documentation (e.g., budgets, minutes).

2. Where there are no observable market prices and the entity estimates fair value using a valuation method, the auditor should determine whether the entity's method of measurement is appropriate in the circumstances. In making this evaluation, the auditor should use professional judgment and consider the following:

   a. Management's rationale for selecting a particular method, and discuss with management its reasons for selecting the valuation method;

   b. Whether management has properly evaluated and applied the criteria, if any, provided by GAAP to support the selected method;

   c. Whether the valuation method is appropriate in the circumstances;

   d. Whether the valuation method is appropriate in relation to the business, industry, and environment in which the entity operates; and

   e. If management has determined that different valuation methods result in a range of significantly different measurements, how the entity has resolved these differences in establishing its fair value measurements.

3. The auditor should evaluate whether the entity has applied its fair value measurements consistently and whether the consistency is appropriate considering (a) possible changes in the environment or circumstances affecting the entity, or (b) changes in accounting principles. If management has changed the method for determining fair value, the auditor should be satisfied that the new method is more appropriate or that it is supported by a change in the GAAP requirements or a change in circumstances.

Using the Work of a Specialist

This Section indicates that the auditor should consider whether to engage a specialist and whether to use that specialist's work in performing substantive tests. If the auditor plans to use a specialist in auditing fair value measurements, the auditor should obtain an understanding of the assumptions and methods used by the specialist, and should consider:

- The requirements of AU Section 336 (Using the Work of a Specialist).
- Whether the specialist's understanding of the definition of fair value and the method that he or she will use to determine fair value are consistent with those of management and with GAAP.

Testing the Entity's Fair Value Measurements and Disclosures

The auditor should test the entity's fair value measurements and disclosures. The nature, timing, and extent of the auditor's procedures depend on (1) the complexity of the fair value measurements, (2) the auditor's understanding of the reliability of management's process for determining fair value measurements, and (3) the auditor's assessment of the level of risk of material misstatement associated with the entity's process for determining fair values. This Section provides the following examples of items to consider when developing audit procedures:

- The evidence furnished by an entity to support its fair value measurements (e.g., an independent valuation by an appraiser) may be as of a date that is different from the date that the entity is required to measure and report that information in its financial statements. Under such circumstances, the auditor should ascertain that management has appropriately considered the effect of intervening events, transactions, and changes in circumstances (i.e., those occurring between the date of fair value evidence and the reporting date).

- Where collateral is an important factor in measuring the fair value of an investment or evaluating its carrying amount, the auditor should (1) gather audit evidence about the existence, value, rights, and access to or transferability of such collateral; (2) determine whether appropriate liens have been filed; and (3) ascertain that appropriate disclosures about the collateral have been made in the financial statements.

- Some situations may require the auditor to apply additional audit procedures (e.g., inspection of an asset) to obtain adequate evidence about the appropriateness of a fair value measurement. For example, the auditor may need to inspect an investment property to gather information about the current physical condition of the asset relative to its fair value.

The auditor's testing of the entity's fair value measurements may involve (a) testing management's significant assumptions, the valuation model, and the underlying data; (b) developing independent fair value estimates; or (c) reviewing subsequent events and transactions. Each of these methods is discussed in the following paragraphs.

Testing management's significant assumptions, the valuation model, and the underlying data When testing the entity's fair value measurements and disclosures, the auditor should assess whether:

1. *Management's assumptions are reasonable and consistent with market information*—The auditor should (1) evaluate the source and reliability of evidence supporting management's assumptions, (2) consider the assumptions in light of historical and market information and whether

they are consistent with the entity's plans and past experience, (3) consider whether management has identified the significant assumptions and factors influencing the measurement of fair value, and (4) determine whether management's reliance on historical financial information, if any, in developing assumptions is justified.

2. *Management used an appropriate model, if applicable, when determining the fair value measurement*—If the entity used a valuation model, the auditor should review the model and evaluate whether the assumptions used are reasonable and the model is appropriate.

3. *Management used relevant information that was reasonably available at the time*—The auditor should (1) test the data used to develop the fair value measurements and disclosures and (2) evaluate whether the fair value measurements have been properly determined from such data and management's assumptions. Such tests may include: verifying the source of the data, mathematical recomputation, and reviewing information for internal consistency.

Developing independent fair value estimates This Section indicates that the auditor may make an independent estimate of the entity's fair value to corroborate management's measurement. Specifically, the auditor may:

1. Develop his or her own model.

2. Develop an independent estimate using management's assumptions. In such cases, the auditor should evaluate management's assumptions as discussed above.

3. Develop an independent estimate using his or her own assumptions. In such cases, the auditor should nevertheless understand management's assumptions. The auditor uses that understanding to (1) determine the appropriateness of the assumptions that he or she developed, (2) ascertain that his or her independent estimates take into account all significant variables, and (3) evaluate any significant differences from management's estimate.

Reviewing subsequent events and transactions Certain transactions and events may occur after the end of the period being reported on but before completion of the audit (e.g., a sale of investment property after the period end) which may provide audit evidence about management's fair value measurements as of the end of the period. The auditor should consider the effect of subsequent events on an entity's fair value measurements and disclosures and refer to the guidance in AU Section 560 (Subsequent Events). When using a subsequent event or transaction to substantiate a fair value measurement, the auditor should consider only those events or transactions that reflect circumstances existing at the balance sheet date.

Auditing Disclosures about Fair Values

The auditor should determine whether the disclosures about fair values in an entity's financial statements are in conformity with GAAP. In connection with his or her evaluation, the auditor should:

1. Ascertain that the valuation principles are appropriate under GAAP and have been consistently applied.

2. Determine that the method of estimation and significant assumptions used are adequately disclosed.

3. Assess whether the disclosures adequately inform users about any measurement uncertainty.

When an entity omits the required fair value disclosures because it is not practicable to determine fair value, the auditor should evaluate the adequacy of disclosures required in the circumstances and whether the financial statements are materially misstated.

Obtaining Management Representations

In connection with obtaining written representations from management, as required by AU Section 333 (Management Representations), the auditor ordinarily should obtain representations regarding the reasonableness of significant assumptions and whether they appropriately reflect management's intent and ability to carry out specific courses of action.

In addition, depending on the nature, materiality, and complexity of fair values, the guidance in this Section indicates that the auditor may want to obtain representations about whether:

1. The measurement methods and related assumptions used in determining fair value are appropriate and have been consistently applied.

2. The disclosures related to fair values are complete and adequate.

3. Subsequent events require adjustment to the fair value measurements and disclosures included in the financial statements.

Communicating with Those Charged with Governance

The auditor should ascertain that those charged with governance are informed about (a) the process that management uses in formulating sensitive accounting and fair value estimates and (b) the basis for the auditor's conclusions regarding the reasonableness of those estimates. For example, the auditor should consider communicating the nature of significant assumptions used in fair value measurements, the degree of subjectivity involved in developing the assumptions, and the relative materiality of the items being measured at fair value to the financial statements as a whole.

When determining the nature and form of communication with those charged with governance, the auditor should consider the guidance in AU Section 380 (The Auditor's Communication with Those Charged with Governance).

Auditing Interests in Trusts Held by a Third-Party Trustee and Reported at Fair Value and Auditing Investments in Securities Where a Readily Determinable Fair Value Does Not Exist

There may be circumstances where the auditor has determined that the nature and extent of auditing procedures should include verifying the existence and testing the measurement of investments held by a third party (e.g., trustee or hedge fund). For example, entities may have interests in trusts held by a third-party trustee that are required to be reported at fair value or an investment in a hedge fund that is reported at fair value. Also, in some circumstances, the fair value of such holdings may be estimated because a readily determinable fair value does not exist (e.g., investments in limited partnership interests or other private equity securities). As part of the auditor's procedures, the auditor generally would satisfy the existence assertion through direct confirmation with the third party, examination of legal documents, or other means. In the case of independent third-party confirmation, the third party may only provide the fair value, in aggregate, of investments held and may not necessarily provide management or the auditor with detailed information about specific investments held or about the basis and method for measuring the entity's investments.

A key factor to consider is whether simply receiving a confirmation from a third party (e.g., trustee, hedge fund) regarding a company's investments, either in the aggregate or on an investment-by-investment basis, would constitute adequate audit evidence with respect to the existence and valuation assertions. Auditing interpretations of AU Section 328 and AU Section 332 provide the following guidance regarding audit evidence obtained with respect to the valuation and existence assertions:

- *Valuation assertion*—In circumstances where the auditor determines that the nature and extent of auditing procedures should include testing the measurement of investments held by a trust or investments in securities, simply receiving a confirmation from a third party *either in the aggregate or on an investment-by-investment basis* does not constitute adequate audit evidence with respect to the valuation assertion.

- *Existence assertion*—In circumstances where the auditor determines that the nature and extent of auditing procedures should include verifying the existence of investments held by a trust or investments in securities, simply receiving a confirmation from a third party for investments *in the aggregate* does not constitute adequate audit evidence with respect to the existence assertion. To illustrate, confirmations in the aggregate such as "$500,000 of total investments" or "$200,000 of total investments in private equity securities; $175,000 of total investments in interests in limited partnerships; and $125,000 of total investments in debt securities" do not constitute adequate audit evidence with respect to the existence assertion. However, receiving confirmation from the third party on an *investment-by-investment basis* typically would constitute sufficient audit evidence with respect to the existence assertion; such a confirmation on an investment-by-investment basis might read as follows: "800 shares of common stock of private company ABC, with a fair value of $130,000; 600 shares of preferred stock of private company DEF, with a fair value of $90,000; 30 units of limited partnership interest XYZ, with a fair value of $220,000; and real estate Property A2Z, with a fair value of $500,000."

In addition, the auditing interpretations indicate that if the auditor is unable to audit the existence or measurement of interests in trusts or investments in securities at the financial statement date, a scope limitation exists. In such circumstances, the auditor is required to consider whether it is necessary to qualify his or her opinion or to disclaim an opinion on the entity's financial statements, as discussed in AU Section 508 (Reports on Audited Financial Statements).

PRACTICE ISSUES AND FREQUENTLY ASKED QUESTIONS

Issue 1: Is the auditor responsible for making the fair value measurements and disclosures that are included in an entity's financial statements?

No. It is management's (not the auditor's) responsibility to make the fair value measurements and disclosures that are included in an entity's financial statements. However, the auditor is responsible for gathering audit evidence to provide reasonable assurance that fair value measurements and disclosures are in accordance with GAAP.

Issue 2: What factors should the auditor consider when evaluating the reasonableness of management's assumptions underlying the fair value measurements?

Assessing the reasonableness of management's assumptions is a matter of professional judgment. However, the guidance in this Section indicates that, to be reasonable, management's assumptions should be realistic and consistent with the following items:

- The general economic environment
- The economic environment of the entity's specific industry
- The entity's economic circumstances
- Existing market information
- Management's plans and expectations of the outcome of specific objectives and strategies
- Assumptions made in prior periods, if appropriate
- The entity's prior experience, to the extent currently applicable
- Other matters relating to the financial statements (e.g., management's assumptions for accounting estimates)
- The risk associated with cash flows, if applicable

Issue 3: How precise should fair value estimates be?

Fair value estimates are inherently imprecise. This is primarily because the estimates may be based on assumptions about future conditions, transactions, or events whose outcome is uncertain and is subject to change over time. Most users of fair value information are aware of this fact and they understand that fair value information has limitations. Therefore, the cost to provide such information must be reasonable in relation to the benefits derived. Also, materiality should be considered in relation to users' expectations.

Issue 4: What are common valuation methods that valuation specialists generally use when estimating fair values?

Many valuation methods are used in practice. However, all such methods can generally be classified as variations of one of the following three approaches:

1. *Cost approach*—The general principle under this approach is the valuation of an asset by determining its replacement cost—that is the amount that would have to be paid currently to replace the same or a similar asset.

2. *Market approach*—This approach bases the fair value measurement on what an asset could be sold at a particular time in an orderly sale (i.e., other than in a forced sale).

3. *Income approach*—The principal notion behind the income approach is that fair value measurement is based on expectations of future income and cash flows.

Because fair value estimates are inherently imprecise, valuation specialists generally consider more than one of these approaches when determining fair value.

Issue 5: Are there any specific items for which historical amounts can be used to approximate fair value, therefore without necessarily requiring significant amounts of audit time?

Yes. There are several assets and liabilities for which fair value often approximates historical amounts, including typically the following:

- Short-term trade accounts receivable or trade accounts payable
- Short-term loans receivable or loans payable
- Variable rate long-term loans
- Materials inventory that turn more than twice a year
- Prepaid and accrued items

Issue 6: What are some circumstances where the specialist's relationship to the client might impair the specialist's objectivity?

If the client has the ability to directly or indirectly control or significantly influence the specialist, then the specialist's objectivity might be impaired. The client's ability to influence the specialist might arise from employment, ownership, contractual right, family relationship, or otherwise. Circumstances that might impair the specialist's objectivity include the following:

- The specialist is an affiliate of the client, whereby the client is able to directly or indirectly control or significantly influence the specialist.
- The specialist is a shareholder or director of the client.
- The specialist is a member of the client's management.
- The specialist is related by blood to management or principal owners, for example, spouse, brother, sister, parent, or child.

Issue 7: In order to place reliance on the work of a specialist, must he or she be hired directly by the auditor, or may the specialist be retained by the client?

An auditor may potentially rely on the work of a specialist in either case. However, there is a presumption that specialists retained by the audit firm will be more objective, because they are removed from the client's influence. When the client hires the specialist, the auditor should assess the degree of influence that the client will likely be able to wield. In light of this assessment, the auditor should also consider the susceptibility of the matter to judgment, and the risk of misstatement and relative importance of the matter to the financial statements.

Issue 8: Should the auditor refer to the work or findings of a valuation specialist in his or her report on an entity's financial statements?

No. Generally, the auditor should not refer to the work or findings of a valuation specialist in his or her report on an entity's financial statements. This is because such reference might be misunderstood by financial statements users to be a qualification of the auditor's opinion or a division of responsibility.

ILLUSTRATIONS AND PRACTICE AIDS

ILLUSTRATION 1—AUDIT PROGRAM FOR AUDITING FAIR VALUE MEASUREMENTS AND DISCLOSURES

	Performed By	Workpaper Reference
1. Obtain an understanding of the entity's transactions and environment relating to fair value measurements and disclosures, as follows:		
a. Identify the types of accounts or transactions requiring fair value measurements or disclosures (e.g., whether the accounts arise from the recording of routine and recurring transactions or whether they arise from nonroutine or unusual transactions).	_____	_____
b. Identify any special risks associated with these accounts or transactions.	_____	_____
c. Consider those accounts or transactions whose fair value measurements have an inherently higher degree of uncertainty due to factors such as the following:		
(1) The length of the forecast period.	_____	_____
(2) The number of significant and complex assumptions associated with the fair value measurement process.	_____	_____
(3) A higher degree of subjectivity associated with the assumptions and factors used in the process.	_____	_____
(4) A higher degree of uncertainty associated with the future occurrence or outcome of events underlying the assumptions used.	_____	_____
(5) Lack of objective data when highly subjective factors are used.	_____	_____
d. Consider the requirements of AU Section 324 (Service Organizations) when the entity uses a service organization.	_____	_____
2. Obtain an understanding of the entity's process for determining fair value measurements and disclosures and of the relevant controls, by considering factors such as the following:		

		Performed By	Workpaper Reference
a.	The qualifications of the persons determining the fair value measurements.	_____	_____
b.	The extent to which information technology is involved in the process.	_____	_____
c.	Whether the entity uses the work of a specialist in determining fair value measurements and disclosures.	_____	_____
d.	The significant assumptions management has used to determine fair value.	_____	_____
e.	The documentation management prepares supporting the assumptions used.	_____	_____
f.	The methods used to develop and apply management assumptions and to monitor changes thereto.	_____	_____
g.	Relevant controls over valuation models and information systems, including approval processes.	_____	_____
h.	Relevant controls over the consistency, timeliness, and reliability of the data used in valuation models.	_____	_____

3. If a specialist is engaged to estimate fair values, perform the following procedures:

		Performed By	Workpaper Reference
a.	Evaluate the expertise, objectivity, and experience of the specialist.	_____	_____
b.	Consider the specialist's relationship to the entity for which the valuation is performed.	_____	_____
c.	Obtain an understanding of the objective and scope of the specialist's work.	_____	_____
d.	Obtain an understanding of the methods or assumptions used, or to be used, and any nonclient data that will be used.	_____	_____
e.	Determine whether the specialist's understanding of the definition of fair value and the method that he or she will use to determine fair value are consistent with those of management and with GAAP.	_____	_____
f.	Identify the data to be furnished by the client to the specialist and determine whether it should be subjected to audit testing.	_____	_____
g.	Compare the current methods and significant assumptions with the methods and assumptions used in valuations of assets acquired in previous valuations (or business combinations).	_____	_____
h.	Evaluate any restrictions on the specialist's access to necessary key entity personnel, records, or files.	_____	_____
i.	Verify the valuation specialist's understanding that the valuation findings will be used during the audit to evaluate the related assertions in the financial statements.	_____	_____

	Performed By	Workpaper Reference

j. Consider the anticipated timing of the availability of the valuation conclusions and specialist's report and identify possible timing issues that might affect reporting and auditing of the fair value estimates. _____ _____

k. Identify whether the specialist's valuation report will include the specific items that will be needed to perform the evaluation and support the audit procedures. _____ _____

l. Consider the requirements of AU Section 336 (Using the Work of a Specialist). _____ _____

4. Based on the circumstances and available information, test the fair value measurements by using one or more of the following approaches:

a. *Test management's significant assumptions, the valuation model, and the underlying data.* When using this approach, perform the following steps:

(1) Evaluate the source and reliability of evidence supporting management's assumptions. _____ _____

(2) Consider the assumptions in light of historical and market information and whether they are consistent with the entity's plans and past experience. _____ _____

(3) Consider whether management has identified the significant assumptions (e.g., those that are sensitive to variation or bias) and factors influencing the measurement of fair value. _____ _____

(4) If management has not identified particularly sensitive assumptions, consider techniques to identify those assumptions. _____ _____

(5) Ensure that there are no contrary data indicating that marketplace participants would use different assumptions (e.g., discount rates that do not appear to reflect current market assumptions). _____ _____

(6) Identify any sources of documented support for management's assumptions. _____ _____

(7) Determine whether management's reliance on historical financial information, if any, in developing assumptions is justified. _____ _____

(8) Review related written plans and other documentation such as budgets and minutes. _____ _____

(9) If the entity used a valuation model, review the model and evaluate whether the assumptions used are reasonable and the model is appropriate. _____ _____

(10) Test the data used to develop the fair value measurements and disclosures (e.g., by verifying the source of the data, mathematical recomputation, and reviewing information for internal consistency). _____ _____

	Performed By	Workpaper Reference

(11) Evaluate whether the fair value measurements have been properly determined from such data and management's assumptions.   _____   _____

b.   *Develop independent fair value estimates to corroborate management's measurement.* Under this approach the auditor can use his or her own developed model, or develop an independent estimate to corroborate management's measurement. In such circumstances, the auditor nevertheless should understand management's assumptions and use that understanding to:

(1) Determine the appropriateness of the assumptions that he or she developed.   _____   _____

(2) Ascertain that his or her independent estimates take into account all significant variables.   _____   _____

(3) Evaluate any significant differences from management's estimate.   _____   _____

c.   *Review subsequent events and transactions.* Under this approach, consider those subsequent events or transactions that reflect circumstances existing at the balance sheet date and their effect on the entity's fair value measurements and disclosures.   _____   _____

5.   Evaluate whether the entity's fair value measurements and disclosures are in accordance with GAAP, as follows:

a.   Evaluate management's intent and ability to carry out specific courses of action, where relevant to the fair value measurements and disclosures, by making inquiries of management and considering management's: _____   _____

(1) Past history of carrying out its stated intentions.   _____   _____

(2) Stated reasons for choosing a particular course of action.   _____   _____

(3) Ability to carry out a particular course of action given the entity's economic circumstances, including the implications of its contractual commitments.   _____   _____

(4) Written plans and other documentation (e.g., budgets, minutes).   _____   _____

b.   Where there are no observable market prices and the entity estimates fair value using a valuation method, determine whether the entity's method of measurement is appropriate in the circumstances by considering the following:

(1) Management's rationale for selecting a particular method, and discuss with management its reasons for selecting the valuation method.   _____   _____

(2) Whether management has properly evaluated and applied the criteria, if any, provided by GAAP to support the selected method.   _____   _____

	Performed By	*Workpaper Reference*

(3) Whether the valuation method is appropriate in the circumstances. _____ _____

(4) Whether the valuation method is appropriate in relation to the business, industry, and environment in which the entity operates. _____ _____

(5) If management has determined that different valuation methods result in a range of significantly different measurements, how the entity has resolved these differences in establishing its fair value measurements. _____ _____

c. Evaluate whether the entity has applied its fair value measurements consistently and whether the consistency is appropriate considering (1) possible changes in the environment or circumstances affecting the entity, or (2) changes in accounting principles. _____ _____

d. If management has changed the method for determining fair value, determine that the new method is more appropriate or that it is supported by a change in the GAAP requirements or a change in circumstances. _____ _____

e. Determine that the method of estimation and significant assumptions used are adequately disclosed. _____ _____

f. Assess whether the disclosures adequately inform users about any measurement uncertainty. _____ _____

g. If the required fair value disclosures have been omitted because it is not practicable to determine fair value, evaluate the adequacy of disclosures required in the circumstances and whether the financial statements are materially misstated. _____ _____

6. If an impending transaction to be realized is the basis for a fair value estimate, consider the following before relying on this anticipated event for the valuation:

a. Whether the transaction will meet the GAAP requirements for determining a fair value for the items in the transaction. _____ _____

b. The likelihood that a change in management's plans might result in a delay, modification, or cancellation of the transaction. _____ _____

c. The availability of an alternative source for the fair value estimate in case the anticipated transaction is not completed. _____ _____

d. Whether any factors (e.g., contractual contingencies, or the proximity of the transaction to the valuation date) might invalidate the use of the transaction as a fair value estimate at the date of the financial statements. _____ _____

	Performed By	Workpaper Reference

7. Consider whether transactions occurring subsequent to year end provide information that corroborates or questions the fair value estimates used in the financial statements. _____ _____

8. Consider applying additional audit procedures (e.g., inspecting an asset) to obtain adequate evidence about the appropriateness of a fair value measurement. _____ _____

9. If the fair value measurement was made as of a date that is different from the date that the entity is required to measure and report that information in its financial statements, ascertain that management has appropriately considered the effect of intervening events, transactions, and changes in circumstances (i.e., those occurring between the date of fair value evidence and the reporting date). _____ _____

10. If collateral is an important factor in measuring the fair value of an investment or evaluating its carrying amount, perform the following:

    a. Gather audit evidence about the existence, value, rights, and access to or transferability of such collateral. _____ _____

    b. Determine whether appropriate liens have been filed. _____ _____

    c. Ascertain that appropriate disclosures about the collateral have been made in the financial statements. _____ _____

11. In connection with obtaining written representations from management, obtain representations about the following:

    a. The reasonableness of significant assumptions and whether they appropriately reflect management's intent and ability to carry out specific courses of action. _____ _____

    b. Whether the measurement methods and related assumptions used in determining fair value are appropriate and have been consistently applied. _____ _____

    c. Whether the disclosures related to fair values are complete and adequate. _____ _____

    d. Whether subsequent events require adjustment to the fair value measurements and disclosures included in the financial statements. _____ _____

12. Ascertain that those charged with governance are informed about:

    a. The process that management uses in formulating sensitive accounting and fair value estimates. In connection with this, consider communicating the following:

        (1) The nature of significant assumptions used in fair value measurements. _____ _____

        (2) The degree of subjectivity involved in developing the assumptions. _____ _____

	Performed By	Workpaper Reference
(3) The relative materiality of the items being measured at fair value to the financial statements as a whole.	_____	_____
b. The basis for the auditor's conclusions regarding the reasonableness of those estimates.	_____	_____

AU SECTION 329
ANALYTICAL PROCEDURES

PRACTICE POINT: As part of its Clarity Project, the American Institute of Certified Public Accountants' (AICPA's) Auditing Standards Board (ASB) has finalized a clarified Statement on Auditing Standards (SAS) titled, "Analytical Procedures (Redrafted)," which supersedes AU Section 329 (Analytical Procedures). The clarified SAS does not change or expand the requirements of extant AU Section 329 in any significant respect. The use of analytical procedures as a risk assessment procedure performed in the planning stage of the audit, addressed in extant AU Section 329, has been placed in paragraph 6 and related application guidance of the clarified SAS, "Understanding the Entity and Its Environment and Assessing the Risks of Material Misstatement (Redrafted)."

The ASB is expected to issue many of the clarified standards in *one* SAS that will be codified in "AU Section" format. The ASB has decided that the effective date of the clarified SASs that have not yet been issued is for audits of financial statements for periods ending on or after December 15, 2012. Auditors should be alert to and monitor further developments in this area.

WHAT EVERY PRACTITIONER SHOULD KNOW

Basic Requirement

The auditor is required to use analytical procedures in the planning and overall review stages of all audits. Analytical procedures involve comparisons of recorded amounts, or ratios developed from recorded amounts, to expectations developed by the auditor. They range from simple comparisons to the use of complex models involving many relationships and elements of data.

Analytical Procedures Used in Planning the Audit

The auditor is required to use analytical procedures in the planning phase of the audit to accomplish the following:

1. Draw attention to audit areas with significant potential for misstatements.

2. Gain an understanding of the client's operations and the transactions and events that have occurred since the last audit date.

3. Assist in assessing risk at the financial statement level.

Analytical Procedures Used in the Overall Review

The auditor is required to use analytical procedures during the completion phase of the audit. Analytical procedures used in the overall final review phase of the audit assist the auditor in:

1. Assessing the validity of the conclusions reached.

2. Evaluating the overall financial statement presentation.

During this overall review, the auditor should read the financial statements and related notes and consider the following:

1. The adequacy of evidence collected in response to unusual or unexpected balances identified as part of the preliminary analysis.

2. The existence of unusual or unexpected findings not otherwise identified and addressed during the audit of the financial statements.

When the overall final review identifies unusual or unexpected balances not addressed during other phases of the engagement, the auditor should determine whether additional procedures should be performed before expressing an opinion on the financial statements.

Analytical Procedures Used as Substantive Tests

Although not required, the auditor may use analytical procedures during audit fieldwork as part of the substantive tests to achieve desired audit objectives or to achieve those objectives in an efficient manner. In determining whether and to what extent analytical procedures should be used for substantive testing, the auditor should consider the following four factors:

1. The nature of the assertion being tested—For example, the determination of whether an allowance for returned merchandise is properly stated may be more effectively tested by analytical procedures (e.g., review of sales volume, history of returned goods) than by tests of details (e.g., vouching actual sales returned).

2. Plausibility and predictability of the relationship between data.

3. Reliability and availability of the data used to develop the expectation.

4. Precision of the expectation—As the intended reliance on analytical procedures increases, so does the need for assurance that significant differences from the auditor's expectations do not represent errors or fraud.

Documentation of substantive analytical procedures When the auditor uses an analytical procedure as the principal substantive test of a significant financial statement assertion, the auditor should document the following items:

1. The expectation, if not readily determinable from the documentation of the work performed, and the factors the auditor considered in developing the expectation;

2. Results of the comparison of the expectation to the recorded amounts or ratios developed from recorded amounts; and

3. Any additional auditing procedures that the auditor performed in response to significant unexpected differences arising from the analytical procedure, and the results of such additional procedures.

PRACTICE ISSUES AND FREQUENTLY ASKED QUESTIONS

Issue 1: What are the main steps involved in performing analytical procedures?

There are three general steps in performing analytical procedures:

1. Develop an expectation for the account balance or item.

2. Compare the expected amount to the recorded balance.

3. Determine the desired nature and extent of further audit testing based on the difference between the recorded and estimated balance.

Issue 2: What are some of the most important reasons for utilizing analytical procedures?

The most important reasons for utilizing analytical procedures are to:

- *Obtain knowledge about the client's industry and business*—For example, a decline in gross profit percentages over time may indicate increasing competition in the company's market area.

- *Help in assessing the ability of the entity to continue as a going concern*—For example, if an entity has a higher than normal ratio of long-term debt to net worth, coupled with a declining current ratio, a relatively higher risk of financial failure may be indicated.

- *Signal the possible presence of errors and fraud in the financial statements*—For example, if the auditor notes that the ratio of the allowance for uncollectible accounts receivable to gross accounts receivable had decreased in the current period and, at the same time, accounts receivable turnover had decreased, this would indicate a possible understatement of the allowance.

- *Reduce detailed audit tests*—For example, if analytical procedures results of a certain account balance (e.g., prepaid insurance) are favorable, the auditor may be able to support a decision to reduce audit tests, eliminate the test entirely, or reduce sample sizes.

Issue 3: Are analytical procedures effective in providing evidence for all types of financial statement assertions?

No. Analytical procedures are normally ineffective in providing evidence about matters that are not recorded in the accounting system or that are not easily quantifiable. Evidence about rights and obligations, for example, must typically be developed through such procedures as reading contracts, minutes and legal correspondence. However, information derived from analytical procedures may alert the auditor to inquire about such matters. For example, an increase in expense under an operating lease may alert the auditor to the existence of a new lease agreement involving new obligations that must be disclosed. Similarly, it is unlikely that analytical procedures would highlight evidence about certain other disclosure matters, such as off-balance sheet risk for financial instruments.

Issue 4: What are some common types of analytical procedures that auditors use in practice?

There are various types of analytical procedures that auditors use to help plan the audit and to evaluate the reasonableness of the financial information. The following are three broad types of analytical procedures commonly used by auditors:

1. *Trend analysis*—The comparison of an account balance or item to the prior year balance or to a trend of balances from two or more prior periods. A common example is comparing the monthly totals for sales for the current and preceding year.

2. *Ratio analysis*—The comparison of a ratio calculated for the current period to a related or similar ratio for a prior period, an industry standard, or a budget. Financial and operating ratios are commonly classified into four major categories: liquidity, profitability, leverage, and activity ratios.

3. *Model-based procedures*—The use of client operating data and the relevant external data (industry information and general economic information) to develop an expectation for the account balance or item. These procedures typically use operating and external data in addition to financial data to perform reasonableness tests. For example, the number of employees can be used to determine the average wages or vacation pay per employee.

Issue 5: What are some of the strengths and weaknesses of each of the following three types of analytical procedures: trend analysis, ratio analysis and model-based procedures?

Trend analysis is a relatively simple procedure, because it is not necessary to obtain data from outside the client company to perform it. Like all analytical procedures, trend analysis is based on the premise that plausible relationships among data can reasonably be expected to exist, and to continue in the absence of known conditions to the contrary. Trend analysis can be highly effective in spotting fluctuations caused by misclassifications and mispostings, or by either the failure to post transactions or by duplicate postings. It also can alert the auditor to fluctuations that are not the result of accounting misstatements, such as changes in business conditions, which may have material bearing on the financial statements. Its primary weakness is that it can compare only like data to like, for example, discreet line items in financial statements, or units of production data, over one or more periods. For this reason, trend analysis, by itself, is not capable of bringing outside data to bear on an item. It is ineffective in detecting situations in which financial statement amounts should have changed but did not, or in detecting items that are consistently misstated over two or more periods.

Ratio analysis can also be applied without using data from outside the client company. One of the strengths that it offers over trend analysis is that relationships between accounts can be compared for inconsistencies. A pure trend analysis over a period of years, for example, would detect steady rises in both sales and cost of sales, but might fail to detect a gradual erosion of the gross profit percentage.

Research suggests that *model-based procedures* outperform both trend and ratio analysis. This is because they incorporate data from diverse sources, as by comparison of operating statistics to accounting information, or by comparison of client data to industry data. It is far less likely that data from outside the accounting system would incorrectly corroborate data from inside the system than it is that internally generated data would.

Issue 6: May the auditor use budgets and forecasts in applying analytical procedures?

Yes. The auditor may compare current financial data to budgets and forecasts in performing analytical procedures. However, when budgets or forecasts are used in performing analytical procedures, the auditor has two primary concerns:

1. The auditor must be satisfied that the budgets or forecasts are realistic, represent management's best estimate, and have been adequately prepared. Therefore, the auditor should discuss the budget procedures with the client to satisfy this concern.

2. There is a possibility that current financial information was changed by client personnel to conform to the budget or forecast. If that has occurred, the auditor would not uncover any differences in comparing actual results with budgets or forecasts, even if there are errors in the financial statements. The auditor's assessment of control risk and detailed audit tests of actual data are usually designed to minimize this likelihood.

When budgets or forecasts are used in performing analytical procedures, the auditor should (a) investigate and discuss with the client large variances and (b) analyze major revisions made to them during the year.

Issue 7: What are some of the pitfalls of using industry data when performing analytical procedures?

Although comparisons of client data with industry statistics can provide useful information, the auditor should be satisfied that the data is comparable. Meaningful comparisons can be difficult, primarily because of the following:

- The industry data are broad averages and the client's line of business is not the same as the industry standards.

- The organization of industry statistics by Standard Industry Classification (SIC) code may result in comparisons of diversified entities with an entity that operates in one industry.

- Different entities follow different accounting methods (e.g., FIFO vs. LIFO for inventory valuation, and straight-line vs. double-declining balance for depreciation).

This does not necessarily mean that industry comparisons should not be made. On the contrary, their principal value may be the questions they raise; however, the auditor should exercise judgment in selecting industry data for analytical procedures and in analyzing and evaluating the comparison results.

Issue 8: May the auditor use nonfinancial data from outside the accounting system or financial statements when applying analytical procedures?

Yes. When applying analytical procedures, the auditor may use data from outside the accounting system or financial statements. Examples of nonfinancial information that might be appropriate include: units purchased, units sold, units produced, number of customers, number of employees, and direct labor hours. For example, the number of employees can be used to determine the average wages or vacation pay per employee.

The primary concern in using nonfinancial data is the accuracy of such data. Therefore, the auditor should exercise judgment in using such nonfinancial data for analytical procedures and in analyzing and evaluating the results obtained.

Issue 9: What are some of the most common liquidity ratios used in practice?

Liquidity ratios are used to help measure an entity's ability to satisfy its short-term obligations as they become due and to provide an indication of the entity's solvency. The following are the two most common liquidity ratios used in practice.

$$\text{Current ratio} = \frac{\text{Current assets}}{\text{Current assets liabilities}}$$

The *current ratio* indicates whether the claims of short-term creditors can be met by current assets. In general, a business with less inventory and more collectible accounts receivable can operate more safely with a lower current ratio than a business having a high percentage of current assets in inventory.

$$\text{Quick or acid-test ratio} = \frac{\text{Current assets - inventory}}{\text{Current liabilities}}$$

The *quick* or *acid-test ratio* is a stringent test of liquidity and measures an entity's ability to satisfy claims of short-term creditors without relying on the sale of its inventory. Inventory is not included because it usually takes a relatively longer time to convert into cash. Therefore, this ratio represents a more conservative evaluation of liquidity than the current ratio. In general, the ratio should at least be equal to 1. A quick ratio of less than 1 implies that the entity is dependent on inventory to meet its current obligations.

Issue 10: What are some of the most common profitability ratios used in practice?

Profitability ratios measure how effectively the entity is being managed. The following are the most common profitability ratios used in practice.

$$\text{Gross profit ratio} = \frac{\text{Net sales - cost of goods sold}}{\text{Net sales}}$$

The *gross profit ratio* measures whether the business is earning a good return on the sale of its merchandise, and the entity's ability to pass cost increases through to its customers.

$$\text{Operating margin ratio} = \frac{\text{Income before income taxes and interest}}{\text{Net sales}}$$

The *operating margin ratio* measures the entity's operating profitability by measuring the extent to which operating expenses are covered by net sales.

$$\text{Net income ratio (or profit margin ratio)} = \frac{\text{Net income}}{\text{Net sales}}$$

The *net income ratio* indicates the entity's ability to generate earnings at a particular sales level, and, therefore, its return on sales.

$$\text{Return on total assets ratio} = \frac{\text{Net income + interest expense}}{\text{Average total assets}}$$

The *return on total assets ratio* measures how effectively the entity's resources have been used in operations and the entity's return on its assets.

$$\text{Return on equity ratio} = \frac{\text{Net income}}{\text{Average stockholders' equity}}$$

The *return on equity ratio* indicates the return on investment to stockholders.

Issue 11: What are some of the most common leverage ratios used in practice?

Leverage ratios measure the long-term financial strength of the entity. They indicate the extent to which the entity is financed by debt and provide a measure of the risk taken by the creditors. The following are the most common leverage ratios used in practice.

$$\text{Debt to assets ratio} = \frac{\text{Total debt}}{\text{Total sales}}$$

The *debt to assets ratio* indicates the percentage of total funds provided by all creditors.

$$\text{Debt to equity ratio} = \frac{\text{Long - term debt}}{\text{Stockholder's equity}}$$

The *debt to equity ratio* indicates the extent to which the entity's operations are financed through long-term debt versus owners' equity.

$$\text{Times interest earned ratio} = \frac{\text{Income before income taxes and interest}}{\text{Interest expense}}$$

The *times interest earned ratio* measures the extent to which earnings can decline and still provide the entity with the ability to meet its annual interest costs.

Issue 12: What are some of the most common activity ratios used in practice?

Activity ratios measure how effectively an entity uses its available resources. The following are the most common activity ratios used in practice.

$$\text{Inventory turnover} = \frac{\text{Cost of goods sold}}{\text{Average inventory}}$$

The *inventory turnover* rate estimates how many times a year inventory is sold. A low turnover rate may indicate overstocking or obsolescence.

$$\text{Average age of inventory} = \frac{360 \text{ days}}{\text{Inventory turnover}}$$

The *average age of inventory ratio* indicates the number of days of inventory on hand at year end.

$$\text{Accounts receivable turnover} = \frac{\text{Net sales}}{\text{Average accounts receivable}}$$

The *accounts receivable turnover ratio* estimates how many times a year accounts receivable are collected. The lower the turnover rate, the longer receivables are being held, and the less likely they are to be collected. Therefore, a low turnover rate may indicate that an allowance for doubtful accounts is needed.

$$\text{Days sales in accounts receivable} = \frac{360 \text{ days}}{\text{Receivable turnover}}$$

The *days sales in accounts receivable ratio* indicates the entity's average collection period or the number of days sales are not collected.

$$\text{Asset turnover} = \frac{\text{Net sales}}{\text{Total assets}}$$

The *asset turnover ratio* measures the client's ability to generate a sufficient volume of business to support its asset investment base.

Issue 13: What are some guidelines that the auditor can use in determining whether a fluctuation in an analytical procedure is material?

It is essential for the auditor to decide whether a fluctuation in an analytical procedure is material. When planning analytical procedures, the auditor typically sets the materiality thresholds for accepted deviations from expected amounts and results. Professional literature does not provide much guidance in this area. However, it is observed that, in practice, auditors use one or both of the following approaches:

1. *Deviation exceeds a preestablished dollar amount threshold*—For example, the auditor may decide that a $10,000 error is unacceptable in the audit of payroll taxes expense. If a difference exceeding that amount is uncovered, the auditor would perform additional detail testing; otherwise, payroll taxes expense would not be considered fairly stated.

2. *Deviation exceeds a preestablished percentage threshold*—Under this approach, the auditor compares, for example, the current year's general and administrative expense accounts with the prior year's and computes the percentage change. If the percentage change exceeds what the auditor believes is appropriate (e.g., 10%), the deviation would be considered material and would require further investigation. This approach, how-

ever, could result in more work than necessary if there are many small dollar account balances. This would cause the auditor, for example, to pursue an increase from $1,000 to $1,100 for a $10 million entity. More importantly, the auditor would fail to investigate an account for which there was no change when there should have been. Therefore, in using this approach, the auditor should exercise judgment and modify his or her definition of what would be considered a significant deviation. Such a definition might read as follows "account balances over $25,000 *and* showing increases or decreases of 10% or greater from the prior year."

Issue 14: What course of action should the auditor take when a significant deviation from an expected amount is encountered during the performance of analytical procedures?

When a significant deviation from an expected amount is encountered, the auditor should attempt to identify and corroborate explanations for the deviation. This process might include:

- Utilization of information obtained in other parts of the audit

- Explanation provided by the client

- Utilization of extended audit procedures

The corroborative process is employed to reasonably ensure that the significant deviation is caused by factors other than errors. The auditor should evaluate the reasonableness of the deviations on the basis of his or her knowledge of the client's business and the information already collected during the audit.

Issue 15: What are some audit efficiency tips that auditors can use when performing analytical procedures?

- Omit or limit comparisons of current-year financial data to budgets and forecasts if prior experience with the client has revealed that budgets and forecasts are unreasonable, unrealistic, or do not represent management's best estimate.

- Before performing analytical procedures involving comparisons with industry data, evaluate if the client's line of business is the same as the industry standards and whether there is significant variation in the data reported and in the structure of the companies.

- When planning analytical procedures, determine the extent and availability of client-prepared financial and operating data and become familiar with such information. Most entities develop a vast amount of information to help management analyze operations and make business decisions. Before spending the time to accumulate and analyze such information, the auditor should obtain any internally prepared management reports and analyses that would serve the same purpose.

- Sometimes auditors perform excessive analytical procedures and ratio analyses regardless of their relevance to the audit. Before performing an analytical procedure, the auditor should ask, "What useful evidence will this relationship provide?"

ILLUSTRATIONS AND PRACTICE AIDS

ILLUSTRATION 1—ANALYTICAL PROCEDURES RATIO ANALYSIS FORM

Liquidity Ratios

	20 __	20 __	20 __	20 __
1. Current ratio =				
Current assets				
———————————	____	____	____	____
Current liabilities				

Comments:

_____

_____

_____

	20 __	20 __	20 __	20 __
2. Quick or acid test ratio =				
Current assets - inventory				
———————————	____	____	____	____
Current liabilities				

Comments:

_____

_____

_____

Profitability Ratios

	20 —	20 __	20 __	20 __
1. Gross profit ratio =				
Net sales - cost of goods				
———————————	____	____	____	____
Net sales				

Comments:

_____

_____

_____

	20 __	20 __	20 __	20 __
2. Operating margin ratio =				
Income before income taxes and interest				
———————————	____	____	____	____
Net sales				

Comments:

_____

_____

_____

	20 __	20 __	20 __	20 __
3. Net income ratio (or profit margin ratio) =				

$$\frac{\text{Net income}}{\text{Net sales}}$$

	20 __	20 __	20 __	20 __
	___	___	___	___

Comments:

_____

_____

_____

		20 __	20 __	20 __	20 __

4.   Return on total assets ratio =

$$\frac{\text{Net income + interest expense}}{\text{Average total assets}}$$

	___	___	___	___

Comments:

_____

_____

_____

	20 __	20 __	20 __	20 __

5.   Return on equity ratio =

$$\frac{\text{Net income}}{\text{Average stockholders' equity}}$$

	___	___	___	___

Comments:

_____

_____

_____

Leverage Ratios

	20 __	20 __	20 __	20 __

1.   Debt to assets ratio =

$$\frac{\text{Total debt}}{\text{Total assets}}$$

	___	___	___	___

Comments:

_____

_____

_____

	20 __	20 __	20 __	20 __

2.   Debt to equity ratio =

$$\frac{\text{Long-term debt}}{\text{Stockholder's equity}}$$

	___	___	___	___

Comments:

_____

_____

_____

	20 __	20 __	20 __	20 __

3. Times interest earned ratio =
    Income before taxes and
    interest

    _____ ____ ____ ____ ____

    Interest expense
Comments:

_____

_____

_____

Activity Ratios

	20 —	20 __	20 __	20 __

1. Inventory turnover =
    Cost of goods sold

    _____ ____ ____ ____ ____

    Average inventory
Comments:

_____

_____

_____

	20 __	20 __	20 __	20 __

2. Average age of inventory =
    360 days

    _____ ____ ____ ____ ____

    Inventory turnover
Comments:

_____

_____

_____

	20 __	20 __	20 __	20 __

3. Accounts receivable turnover =
    Net sales

    _____ ____ ____ ____ ____

    Average accounts
       receivable
Comments:

_____

_____

_____

	20 __	20 __	20 __	20 __

4. Days sales in accounts receivable =

        360 days
    ─────────────────────────────   ─────   ─────   ─────   ─────

        Accounts receivable
            turnover

    Comments:

    _____

    _____

    _____

                                      20 __   20 __   20 __   20 __

5. Asset turnover =

            Net sales
        ─────────────────────   ─────   ─────   ─────   ─────

            Total assets

    Comments:

    _____

    _____

    _____

AU SECTION 330
THE CONFIRMATION PROCESS

PRACTICE POINT: As part of its Clarity Project, the American Institute of Certified Public Accountants' (AICPA's) Auditing Standards Board (ASB) has finalized a clarified Statement on Auditing Standards (SAS) titled, "External Confirmations," which supersedes AU Section 330 (The Confirmation Process). Although the clarified SAS does not change or expand AU Section 330 in any significant respect, the following are noteworthy variations:

- The presumptively mandatory requirement in AU Section 330 to confirm accounts receivable has been placed in the clarified SAS, "Audit Evidence (Redrafted)."

- The clarified SAS addresses the responsibilities of the auditor when management refuses to allow the auditor to send a confirmation request. These responsibilities include communicating with those charged with governance if the auditor concludes that management's refusal is unreasonable or if the auditor is unable to obtain relevant and reliable audit evidence from alternative audit procedures. These procedures are not currently required by AU Section 330.

- The clarified SAS includes application material and guidance regarding the use of oral responses to confirmation requests as audit evidence. Specifically, it clarifies that the receipt of an oral response to a confirmation request does not meet the definition of an external confirmation and provides guidance on how the response may be considered part of alternative procedures performed in order to obtain sufficient appropriate audit evidence.

The ASB is expected to issue many of the clarified standards in *one* SAS that will be codified in "AU Section" format. The ASB has decided that the effective date of the clarified SASs that have not yet been issued is for audits of financial statements for periods ending on or after December 15, 2012. Auditors should be alert to and monitor further developments in this area.

WHAT EVERY PRACTITIONER SHOULD KNOW

Basic Requirements

The auditor should:

1. Consider the use of confirmations when the combined assessed level of inherent risk and control risk is high.

2. Consider confirming the terms of unusual or complex transactions when the combined assessed level of inherent risk and control risk is high.

3. Assess whether the evidence provided by confirmations reduces audit risk for the related financial statement assertions to an acceptably low level; in making this assessment, the auditor should consider the materiality of the account balance and his or her assessment of inherent risk and control risk.

4. Perform additional procedures when he or she concludes that evidence provided by confirmations alone is not sufficient to reduce audit risk to an acceptably low level.

5. Exercise an appropriate level of professional skepticism throughout the confirmation process.

Designing the Confirmation Request

When designing the confirmation request, the auditor should consider the assertions being addressed and the factors that are likely to affect the reliability of the confirmations. In addition, the auditor should consider the following factors:

1. *Form of the confirmation request*—There are two common types of confirmation requests used: the positive confirmation and the negative confirmation. A *positive* confirmation request is addressed to the recipient requesting that it send directly to the auditor confirmation of whether the information stated on the confirmation request is correct or incorrect. A *negative* confirmation request is addressed to the recipient and requests a response only if the recipient disagrees with the stated information on the confirmation request.

2. *Auditor's prior experience with the client*—The auditor should consider information from prior experience with the client and with similar clients. This information includes response rates, knowledge of misstatements identified during prior years' audits, and any knowledge of inaccurate information on returned confirmations. Prior experience may suggest, for example, that a confirmation form was improperly designed or previous response rates were so low that audit procedures other than confirmation should be considered.

3. *Nature of information being confirmed*—The auditor should consider the types of information respondents will be readily able to confirm when determining what to include in the confirmation request. For example, when designing an accounts receivable confirmation, the auditor should consider whether respondents are more capable of verifying an individual account balance or transactions that make up a single account receivable balance.

4. *Characteristics of respondents*—Confirmation requests should be addressed to respondents who will generate meaningful and competent audit evidence. Factors to be considered in this regard include the following:

   a. *Competence of the recipient*—Recipients may be apathetic about the confirmation process, and management may have assigned responsibility to an individual who will sign and return the confirmation without adequate concern for its accuracy.

   b. *Knowledge of the respondent*—Confirmations may be signed by persons who have no knowledge of the account and no authority to respond.

c. *Objectivity of the respondent*—For example, the reliability of confirmations from related parties may be questionable.

Control over the Confirmation Requests

For confirmation procedures to be effective, the auditor should maintain control of the confirmations from the time they are prepared and mailed until they are returned by the respondent. The confirmation process should be executed so that the client does not have an opportunity to intercept requests when they are mailed or when they are returned from respondents. When positive confirmations are used and there is no response, the auditor should consider sending second and, possibly, third requests.

Confirmations Received Via Fax or Electronically and Oral Confirmations

When a fax or e-mail is received from a respondent as part of the confirmation process, some degree of uncertainty arises concerning the source of the information. To reduce that risk, the auditor should consider:

1. Verifying the source and content of the fax or e-mail by telephoning the respondent.

2. Requesting that the respondent mail the original confirmation directly to the auditor.

When information is confirmed orally, the content of, and circumstances surrounding, the confirmation should be documented in the workpapers. If the information confirmed orally is significant, the auditor should request the respondent to confirm the information in writing.

Alternative Procedures

If the auditor has not received replies to positive confirmation requests, he or she should apply alternative procedures to the non-responses to obtain the evidence necessary to reduce audit risk to an acceptably low level. However, it may be acceptable to omit the use of alternative procedures when the auditor has not received replies to positive confirmation requests if both of the following conditions are met:

1. The auditor has not identified unusual qualitative factors or systematic characteristics related to the nonresponses (e.g., all nonresponses pertain to year-end transactions).

2. When testing for overstatement of amounts, the nonresponses in the aggregate, when projected as 100% misstatements to the population and added to the sum of all other unadjusted differences, would not affect the auditor's decision about whether the financial statements are materially misstated.

The nature and extent of the alternative procedures selected will depend on (a) the assessed risk of material misstatement, (b) the nature of the account balance or other information the auditor attempted to confirm, and (c) the availability of audit evidence.

For negative confirmations, the auditor is not required to perform alternative procedures for nonresponses because the recipient was not requested to respond if the balance or information was correct.

Evaluating the Results of Confirmation Procedures

When all differences have been resolved, including those discovered when performing alternative procedures, the auditor should determine whether sufficient evidence has been obtained about all applicable assertions. In making this determination, the auditor should consider:

1. The reliability of evidence obtained through the confirmation process and alternative procedures.

2. The nature and implications of exceptions discovered.

3. The evidence obtained by the auditor through the use of procedures other than confirmation and alternative procedures.

4. Whether additional evidence is needed.

If the auditor concludes that audit evidence obtained through the confirmation process, alternative audit procedures, and other audit procedures is not sufficient to substantiate relevant assertions in the financial statements, additional evidence must be obtained. The additional evidence may be acquired by applying whatever procedures the auditor deems appropriate, including additional confirmations, tests of details, and analytical procedures.

Use of Electronic Confirmations

The use of an electronic confirmation process by the auditor, and consequently, the transmission or receipt of electronic confirmations, is not precluded by AU Section 330. An auditing interpretation of AU Section 330 (Use of Electronic Confirmations) indicates that the auditor's consideration of the reliability of the information contained in electronic confirmations includes consideration of the risks that:

- The confirmation response might not be from an authentic source.

- A respondent might not be knowledgeable about the information to be confirmed.

- The integrity of the transmission might have been compromised.

PRACTICE POINT: To address these risks, the auditor may decide to rely on a system or process that is in place to facilitate electronic confirmation between the auditor and the respondent. An assurance trust services report (e.g., Systrust) or another auditor's report may be available, which may assist the auditor in assessing the design and operating effectiveness of the controls with respect to that system or process. Otherwise, the auditor may find it necessary to perform additional procedures to address those risks.

The auditing interpretation indicates that confirmations obtained electronically can be considered reliable audit evidence if the auditor is satisfied that (1) the electronic confirmation process is secure and properly controlled, (2) the information obtained is a direct communication in response to a request, and (3) the information is obtained from a third party who is the intended respondent. The auditing interpretation also indicates that the auditor might use various means to verify the validity of the sender and whether the respondent is authorized to confirm the information requested by the auditor. It indicates that some of the means that may improve the security of the electronic confirmation process include the use of:

- *Encryption*—The use of encryption reduces the risk of unintended intervention in an electronic communication. It is the process of encoding electronic data so that it cannot be read without the other party using a matching encryption key.

- *Electronic digital signatures*—Digital signatures use different means to ensure that only the claimed signer of the document could have affixed the symbol. The signature and its characteristics are uniquely linked to the signer.

- *Web site authenticity*—Web site authenticity involves means to monitor data or a Web site to ensure that its content has not been altered without authorization. Webtrust or VeriSign certifications, which may be earned and affixed to a Web site, indicate that an active program is protecting the underlying content of the information.

In addition, to mitigate the risks associated with electronic confirmations, the auditor may perform procedures to verify the authenticity of information, such as the e-mail address of the purported sender, and may find it necessary to directly contact the purported sender (e.g., by telephone) to verify the validity and accuracy of the information transmitted.

Confirmation of Accounts Receivable

The confirmation of accounts receivable is a generally accepted auditing procedure. Therefore, it is presumed that the auditor will request the confirmation of accounts receivable during an audit, unless one of the following is true:

1. The accounts receivable balance is immaterial to the financial statements.

2. It is expected that the use of confirmations would be ineffective (e.g., prior experience might suggest that the response rate is too low or responses are expected to be unreliable). In such circumstances, the auditor should consider whether to modify the nature or extent of alternative procedures by applying a combination of procedures or applying the procedures to a larger number of items than would have been confirmed, in order to reduce audit risk to an acceptably low level.

3. The auditor's combined assessed level of inherent risk and control risk is low, and the assessed level, in conjunction with the evidence expected to be provided by analytical procedures or other substantive tests of details, is sufficient to reduce audit risk to an acceptably low level for the applicable financial statement assertions.

If the auditor has not requested confirmations of accounts receivable, the auditor should document how he or she overcame this presumption. The workpapers should include a full explanation and make a compelling case beyond mere convenience.

PRACTICE ISSUES AND FREQUENTLY ASKED QUESTIONS

Issue 1: What is the primary advantage and disadvantage of using blank confirmation requests?

The primary advantage of the use of blank confirmation requests is that they may provide a greater degree of assurance about the information confirmed; this is because there is a risk that recipients of positive confirmation requests may sign and return the confirmations without verifying that the information contained on the positive confirmation is correct. The primary disadvantage of using blank confirmation requests is that they might result in lower response rates because additional effort may be required of the recipients; as a result, the auditor may have to perform more alternative procedures.

Issue 2: Is the auditor required to limit to dollar amounts the information to be confirmed with respondents?

No. Information to be confirmed with respondents should not be limited to dollar amounts. For example, in complex transactions it may be appropriate to confirm terms of contracts or other documentation that supports such transactions. In addition, it may be appropriate to confirm information that is based on oral modifications and, therefore, not part of the formal documentation.

Issue 3: Is the evidence generated from the use of negative confirmation requests the same as the evidence generated from the use of positive confirmation requests?

No. A negative confirmation form requires the respondent to return the confirmation only if there is disagreement with the amount owed. When negative confirmations are not returned, the evidence generated is different from that generated when positive confirmations are used. That is, the lack of returned negative confirmations provides only implicit evidence that the information is correct. In other words, unreturned negative confirmations do not provide explicit evidence that the intended third parties received the confirmation requests and verified that the information contained on them is correct.

If the auditor decides to use negative confirmations, he or she should (1) consider performing other substantive procedures to supplement the use of negative confirmations and (2) investigate relevant information provided in responses to negative confirmations and determine their effects on the audit.

Issue 4: Under what conditions is the auditor likely to use negative confirmation requests?

The auditor is likely to use negative confirmation requests when the following conditions exist:

- The combined assessed level of inherent and control risk is low.

- The audit population contains a large number of relatively small individual balances.

- There is no reason to believe that respondents will not give adequate attention to confirmation requests.

Issue 5: What are some of the considerations that the auditor should take into account when deciding on a confirmation date?

The confirmation date relates to the timing of the confirmation procedures. Whether confirmations are requested as of year end or as of some other date will depend on the overall design of the audit approach, with the aim of making the examination more efficient or meeting client deadlines. A confirmation date other than year end can be justified when the internal control system is sufficiently reliable to produce reasonably accurate information between the confirmation date and year end. Otherwise, confirmations must be performed at or very near to the balance sheet date. Other factors the auditor should consider when deciding on a confirmation date include (1) the materiality of the account balance and (2) the auditor's exposure to lawsuits because of the possibility of client bankruptcy and similar risks.

If the auditor makes the decision to confirm account balances prior to year end, the auditor may find it necessary to test the transactions occurring between the confirmation date and the balance sheet date. For example, in the area of accounts receivable, the auditor would examine such internal documents as duplicate sales invoices, shipping documents, and evidence of cash receipts in addition to performing analytical procedures of the intervening period.

Issue 6: Is the auditor required to continue sending confirmation requests to recipients when the response rate in prior years has been low?

No. Auditing standards in general do not obligate an auditor to perform procedures that are likely to result in insufficient or unreliable evidence. A historically poor response rate is considered a valid reason not to request confirmations. However, the auditor should document this fact as the reason for not sending out confirmations. In addition, the auditor should obtain evidence from other sources, such as tests of subsequent collections in the examination of accounts receivable.

Issue 7: There is substantial divergence in practice on the question of whether the auditor, in requesting cash confirmations from a client's bank, should fill in the balances from the bank statement or leave them blank. What should the auditor consider in making this decision?

Proponents of providing balances on the form argue that there is a good faith presumption that a confirmation signed by a client's bank is accurate, and that filling in the balances is merely a clerical accommodation that speeds up the process and benefits all the parties. They cite the fact that the bank and its employees are in a position to be knowledgeable about a depositor's balance, and that it is in the general interest of the banking system to provide reliable information to auditors.

Proponents of leaving the confirmation request blank believe that filling in the balances may tempt the respondent to erroneously or negligently authenticate an incorrect balance. They cite as evidence against the presumption of correctness stated above the fact that confirmations sent out "in blank" are sometimes returned with erroneous information, such as balances at the date the confirmation is signed by the bank, rather than the date requested.

The auditor, in deciding on this issue, should consider his or her knowledge about the confirming bank, including previous experience. The degree of planned reliance on the confirmation as audit evidence, the level of assessed risk, and the feasibility and reliability of other audit procedures to obtain assurance about cash balances should all enter into this consideration.

Issue 8: What are some audit efficiency tips for the auditor when performing confirmation procedures?

- Challenge the number of confirmations to be mailed. Sometimes a few confirmations will cover a high dollar percentage of the accounts.

- When confirming accounts receivable, consider confirming invoices (individually significant items) instead of account balances if a significant amount of time is spent on alternative procedures.

- Limit the evidence gathered from alternative procedures on nonresponses. For example, in the case of accounts receivable, examine a subsequent cash receipt or a shipping record, rather than both.

- Ask the client to gather the documents for alternative procedures (e.g., cash receipts, sales invoices, shipping documents) and to reconcile confirmation exceptions. Limit your involvement to reviewing and testing the client's reconciliation.

- If account balances were confirmed as of an interim date, ask the client to prepare a rollforward analysis from the confirmation date to the balance sheet date and reconcile the balance to the general ledger control account.

Issue 9: What can the auditor do to improve the response rates to confirmation requests?

Practice Alert 2003-01 (Audit Confirmations) indicates that the following techniques may be used to improve the confirmation response rates:

- Request information that the recipient is likely and able to confirm.

- Include relevant information required for a response by the recipient (e.g., include a list of outstanding invoices, debits, credits, and other adjustments that comprise the account balance).

- Ask the respondent to indicate his or her understanding of the information requested (this is generally appropriate when the auditor is seeking confirmation of terms of a transaction, rather than amounts).

- Use clear wording.

- Send the confirmation to a specified individual (as opposed to "To whom it may concern").

- Identify the exact and full name of the organization being audited.

- Ask the client to hand-sign the confirmation request.

- Specify a deadline for the recipient to respond.

- Send second, and consider third, requests.

- Call the respondent to obtain oral confirmation and request the recipient to return the written confirmation.

Issue 10: What should the auditor do when confirmation requests are returned undelivered?

For positive and negative confirmation requests that were returned undelivered, the auditor should:

- Ascertain that the parties (e.g., customers, vendors) indeed exist.
- Normally report that information to the client's personnel not directly involved in the area subject to confirmation.
- Be mindful of the possible reasons for undeliverable requests, including the possibility of fraud.

Issue 11: What are common examples of alternative procedures?

Common examples of alternative procedures include examining the following documents:

- Cash receipt records, remittance advices, wire transfers, or other evidence of subsequent collection.
- Cash disbursement records, cancelled checks, wire transfers, or other evidence of disbursement.
- Shipping records.
- Receiving reports.
- Evidence of receipt of goods by the customer.
- Invoices.
- Customer or vendor correspondence.

Issue 12: How should the auditor evaluate responses to positive confirmation requests that include exceptions?

The auditor should investigate all differences between the client's records and the information provided by respondents. If such differences cannot be resolved or the auditor determines that they represent misstatements, the auditor should:

- Determine the cause of the misstatement;
- Extrapolate the misstatement (together with other misstatements included in the same sampling application, if applicable) over the population to determine whether additional audit evidence is required to reduce the risk of material misstatement to an appropriately low level;
- Consider the possibility that fraud may have occurred and whether an investigation may be necessary;
- Determine whether additional audit procedures are necessary to achieve the desired confirmation audit objectives;
- Report all unreconciled misstatements to a client personnel not directly involved in the area subject to confirmation; and
- Consider whether responses indicate matters that should be reported to those charged with governance (e.g., audit committee, board of directors).

Issue 13: What should the auditor do if a client requests that certain balances or other information not be confirmed by the auditor?

During selection of the accounts or other information for confirmation, it is important that the auditor has complete discretion and independence in choosing the items to be confirmed. However, clients sometimes request that certain accounts or information not be confirmed. In these cases, the auditor should determine (1) the client's reasons for the request and whether they are valid, (2) whether the amounts involved are material, and (3) whether it is possible to verify the balances in the accounts or the desired information by other means (e.g., testing subsequent collections in the case of accounts receivable).

If the auditor concludes that management's request to not send an external confirmation is reasonable and valid, then the auditor should:

1. Apply alternative procedures to obtain the necessary information that would have been the subject of the independent confirmation; and

2. Consider including in the client representation letter the accounts or information that were not confirmed and the reasons for management's request to not confirm such items.

If the client dictates which accounts to select or refuses to grant permission to confirm certain accounts and the auditor cannot confirm the validity of the accounts by other means, the auditor should evaluate the effect of this scope limitation on the overall audit and whether an unqualified opinion can still be issued on the financial statements. If the auditor concludes that management's restrictions significantly limit the scope of the audit, he or she should disclaim an opinion, or withdraw from the engagement.

Issue 14: Can the auditor use client personnel to assist him or her in auditing nonreplies or exceptions in the confirmation responses?

Yes. The auditor generally would use client personnel to maximize efficiency in auditing nonreplies or reconciling exceptions in the confirmation responses. The auditor can use client personnel to:

- List and accumulate data.

- Reconcile book and reported amounts for the auditor's follow-up and examination.

- Accumulate documents for the auditor's inspection and testing.

However, for confirmation procedures to be effective, the auditor should maintain control of the confirmations from the time they are prepared and mailed until they are returned by the respondent.

Issue 15: When does it become necessary for the auditor to confirm the terms of unusual or complex agreements or transactions?

While this is subject to the auditor's professional judgment, the auditor generally should confirm the terms of unusual or complex agreements or transactions, especially ones relating to the company's revenue recognition methods. Practice Alert 2003-01 (Audit Confirmations) emphasizes this point primarily based on AU Section 316 (Consideration of Fraud in a Financial Statement Audit), which indicates that the auditor should ordinarily presume that there is a risk of material misstatement due to fraud relating to revenue recognition. The Practice Alert indicates that it becomes increasingly necessary to confirm terms of transactions and the absence of side agreements if the auditor encounters any of the following items:

- Significant sales or high sales volume at or near the end of the reporting period.
- Contracts or contract clauses that are not standard.
- Use of letters of authorization as opposed to signed contracts or agreements.
- Dates on contracts or shipping documents that have been altered.
- Concurrent agreements or "linked" contracts and transactions.
- Lack of evidence, or insufficient evidence, of customer acceptance.
- Existence of bill-and-hold transactions.
- Existence of extended payment terms or non-standard installment receivables.
- Lack of involvement by accounting/finance department in sales transactions or in the monitoring of arrangements with distributors.
- Unusual sales volume to distributors or retailers.
- Sales (other than software sales) with commitments for future upgrades.
- Sales where significant uncertainties and/or obligations to the seller exist.
- Sales to value-added resellers and distributors lacking financial strength.
- Increasing receivables from customers that may indicate that payments are not due until resale to end users.
- Aggressive accounting policies or practices.

Issue 16: Under what circumstances might it be appropriate, or even necessary, for the auditor to confirm accounts payable?

Practice Alert 2003-01 (Audit Confirmations) indicates that confirmation of accounts payable may be appropriate or even necessary when the following situations exist:

- "Round-trip" or "linked" transactions have been identified as a risk. (*Round-trip* or *linked* transactions occur when a company enters into a sales transaction with a customer but sends all or some of the sales proceeds back to the customer in another purchase transaction.)
- Client controls over payables and cash disbursements are weak, thereby increasing the risk of unprocessed and unrecorded vendor invoices.
- Industry practices that may create a higher risk of unrecorded liabilities and/or inappropriate accounting (e.g., internet entities, software companies, real estate, energy, telecommunications).
- Complex business transactions that create an environment where unrecorded liabilities might exist (e.g., business combinations, royalty arrangements).

Issue 17: How can confirmation procedures be effectively designed to assist an auditor in detecting unrecorded accounts payable?

When seeking evidence about completeness, it is usually preferable to use blank confirmation requests, i.e., to request recipients to furnish balances, rather than asking them to verify a client-supplied balance. Also, the confirmation of accounts payable is likely to be more effective if the sample of vendors is selected from the universe of all vendors with whom the client deals, rather than from the accounts payable detail listing.

Practice Alert 2003-01 (Audit Confirmations) indicates that, in order to obtain the intended degree of assurance from confirmation of suppliers, the auditor should consider the following procedures:

- Review accounts payable/purchase subsidiary ledger, vendors' invoice files, and disbursement records or purchase volume records by supplier.
- Request the client's purchasing personnel to identify and list major suppliers.
- Identify other suppliers from which confirmation of the accounts payable balance is desired (e.g., suppliers with known or suspected disputed balances).

Issue 18: What are some of the considerations that the auditor should take into account when deciding on the number of accounts receivable to confirm?

The primary considerations affecting the decision on the number of accounts receivable confirmations to send are:

- The materiality of total accounts receivable (i.e., if the accounts receivable balance is highly material relative to the other asset balances, a larger number of accounts would be necessary than when the balance is immaterial).
- The number of accounts receivable.
- The distribution in the size of the accounts (i.e., if all the accounts are approximately the same size, fewer need to be confirmed than when their size is distributed over a wide range of values).
- The results of obtaining an understanding of the client's internal control and tests of transactions.
- The results of the confirmation tests in previous years.
- The type of confirmation being used (more confirmations usually are required for negative than for positive confirmations).
- The results of related analytical procedures.

Issue 19: When confirming accounts receivable, should the auditor place an additional emphasis particularly on any specific accounts?

Yes. In most audits, the auditor's emphasis should be on confirming accounts receivable with the following characteristics:

- Accounts with larger balances
- Accounts with older balances

- Accounts in dispute

- Accounts with credit balances

- Accounts with related parties

Issue 20: May the auditor perform, at the client request, confirmation procedures that go beyond the minimum scope requirements of the audit?

Yes. Occasionally, the client may ask the auditor to perform procedures that go beyond the minimum scope requirements of the audit. For example, the client may ask the auditor to confirm certain customer accounts receivable that are below the cutoff amount determined by the auditor or to confirm all customer accounts receivable. Although it is permissible for the auditor to accommodate the client's wishes, the auditor should indicate clearly in the workpapers which tests are being performed to be responsive to the client's expectations.

Also, errors noted while performing additional tests of accounts receivable balances at the client's request may receive different consideration. For example, the auditor may have decided to confirm all accounts receivable balances over $5,000 and 90 days past due as part of the audit procedures. Also, the client has requested that the auditor confirm all other balances over 90 days past due. In this case, alternative procedures may not be required on nonreplies for accounts less than $5,000. In addition, although the client should be notified of errors noted in accounts less than $5,000 for follow-up, the auditor need only summarize them, instead of obtaining an explanation for them, and consider them along with the results of errors noted in the confirmations that are within the scope of the auditor's procedures.

Issue 21: Does an auditor's online inquiry about a client's information meet the definition of "confirmation" under AU Section 330?

No. Auditors are sometimes able to directly access online information held by a third party concerning a client's account balance or other information. For example, a client's personnel may give the auditor the client's personal identification number to make an online inquiry about a client's bank balance information. While the auditor may be able to obtain the desired information, Practice Alert 2003-01 (Audit Confirmations) states that this procedure does not meet the definition of "confirmation" and, therefore, does not qualify as a confirmation response. AU Section 330.04 defines confirmation as a "direct communication from a third party in response to" a specific request. Therefore, AU Section 330 requires an active response from the third party. According to the Practice Alert, an auditor's online inquiry of the third party's database does not meet the auditor's confirmation responsibilities under AU Section 330; instead, it constitutes an alternative procedure.

ILLUSTRATIONS AND PRACTICE AIDS

ILLUSTRATION 1—ACCOUNTS RECEIVABLE CONFIRMATION AUDIT PROGRAM

	Performed By	Workpaper Reference

1. Prepare or obtain from the client an aged trial balance of trade accounts receivable and perform the following: ___ ___
   a. Test the arithmetical accuracy of the aged trial balance and the aging categories therein. ___ ___
   b. Reconcile the total balance to the general ledger control account balance. ___ ___
   c. Note and investigate any unusual entries. ___ ___
   d. Summarize the total of credit balances and make appropriate reclassification entry, if material. ___ ___
   e. On a selective basis, trace individual account balances in the aged trial balance to individual subsidiary ledgers and vice versa. ___ ___

2. Select customer accounts from the aged trial balance for confirmation procedures and perform the following:
   a. Arrange for confirmation requests to be mailed directly by the auditor and maintain control over the confirmation process at all times. ___ ___
   b. Trace balances included in individual confirmation requests to subsidiary accounts. ___ ___
   c. Mail confirmations using envelopes with the auditor's return address. ___ ___
   d. Prepare confirmation statistics. ___ ___
   e. If the client requests exemption from confirmation for any accounts selected by the auditor, obtain and document satisfactory explanation, and determine necessity for alternative procedures. ___ ___
   f. Obtain new addresses for confirmations returned by the post office as undeliverable, and remail. ___ ___
   g. Send second requests for positive confirmations on which there is no reply and consider registered or certified mail for second requests. ___ ___

3. Process the confirmation requests and replies and summarize the results of confirmation procedures as follows:
   a. For positive confirmation requests to which no reply was received, perform alternative procedures for those customers by examining cash receipts subsequent to the confirmation date and, if no cash has been received, by examining sales invoices and corresponding shipping documents. ___ ___
   b. For responses to positive confirmation requests that include exceptions, investigate all differences between the client's records and the information provided by respondents. If such differences cannot be resolved or they represent misstatements, perform the following:
      (1) Determine the cause of the misstatement. ___ ___

	Performed By	Workpaper Reference

(2) Extrapolate the misstatement (together with other misstatements included in the same sampling application, if applicable) over the population to determine whether additional audit evidence is required to reduce the risk of material misstatement to an appropriately low level. _____ _____

(3) Consider the possibility that fraud may have occurred. _____ _____

(4) Determine whether additional audit procedures are necessary to achieve the desired confirmation audit objectives. _____ _____

(5) Consider reporting all unreconciled misstatements to a client's personnel not directly involved in the area subject to the confirmation. _____ _____

(6) Consider whether responses indicate matters that should be reported to those charged with governance. _____ _____

c. For accounts exempted from confirmation at the client's request, perform the following:

(1) Determine the client's reasons for the request and whether they are valid. _____ _____

(2) Determine whether the amounts involved are material. _____ _____

(3) Determine whether it is possible to verify the balances in the accounts or the desired information by other means (e.g., testing subsequent collections). _____ _____

(4) If management's request to not send an external confirmation is reasonable and valid, apply alternative procedures to obtain the necessary information that would have been the subject of the independent confirmation,and consider including in the client representation letter the accounts or information that were not confirmed and the reasons for management's request not to confirm such items. _____ _____

(5) If the validity of the accounts cannot be established by other means, evaluate the effect of this scope limitation on the overall audit and whether an unqualified opinion can still be issued on the financial statements. _____ _____

4. For the positive and negative confirmation requests that were returned undelivered, perform the following:

a. Ascertain that the parties' customers indeed exist. _____ _____

	Performed By	Workpaper Reference

b. Report that information to a client's personnel not directly involved in the area subject to confirmation. _____ _____

c. Consider the possible reasons for undeliverable requests, including the possibility of fraud. _____ _____

d. Indicate the total accounts and balances confirmed without exceptions, confirmations reconciled, and nonreplies or exempted accounts with alternative procedures performed. _____ _____

5. For accounts receivable confirmed on a date other than the balance sheet date, prepare or obtain from the client an analysis of transactions (e.g., cash receipts, sales) between the confirmation date and the balance sheet date, and perform the following:

a. Trace the balance as of the confirmation date to the aged trial balance used in Step 2 above. _____ _____

b. Trace cash received per the analysis to the cash receipts journal and/or bank statements. _____ _____

c. Trace sales/revenue amounts per the analysis to the sales/revenue journal. _____ _____

d. Determine the reasonableness and propriety of any other reconciling items. _____ _____

e. Trace the ending balance per the analysis to the trial balance as of the balance sheet date. _____ _____

f. Scan the accounts receivable and sales activity during the period from the interim date to the balance sheet date and investigate any unusual activity. _____ _____

6. Perform the following procedures for confirmations received via fax or e-mail:

a. Verify the source and content of the fax or e-mail by telephoning the respondent. _____ _____

b. Request that the respondent mail the original confirmation directly to the auditor. _____ _____

ILLUSTRATION 2—CONFIRMATION REQUEST FOR CUTOFF BANK STATEMENT

(Prepared on client's letterhead)

(Date)

(Name and address of financial institution)

Dear _____:

In connection with an audit of the financial statements of *(insert name of client)* as of *(insert balance sheet date)* and for the *(insert period [e.g., year, quarter])* then ended, please mail the following information directly to our auditors *(insert name and address of auditors)*:

 1. For the account numbers listed below, a statement of our account and the related canceled checks, deposit slips, and documents sup-

porting other charges or credits to the account for the period from *(insert balance sheet date)* to *(insert cutoff date)*, inclusive.

Account Name	Account Number
_____	_____
_____	_____
_____	_____

Thank you for your anticipated timely cooperation with this request.

Respectfully,

(Name of client)

_____

(Client's authorized signature and title)

ILLUSTRATION 3—CONFIRMATION REQUEST FOR ACCOUNTS RECEIVABLE: POSITIVE REQUEST OF DOLLAR AMOUNTS

(Prepared on client's letterhead)

(Date)

(Customer's name and address)

Dear _____:

In connection with an audit of the financial statements of *(insert name of client)* as of *(insert date)* and for the *(insert period [e.g., year, quarter])* then ended, please confirm directly to our auditors *(insert name and address of auditors)* the amount of your indebtedness to us as of *(insert date)*, which according to our records amounted to $_____.

Please check the appropriate response below after determining whether this is in agreement with your records. If there are differences, please provide any information in sufficient detail to assist our auditors in reconciling the difference.

After checking the appropriate response below, please sign and date your reply and mail it directly to our auditors in the enclosed return envelope. **DO NOT SEND ANY PAYMENTS TO OUR AUDITORS.**

Thank you for your anticipated timely cooperation with this request.

Respectfully,

(Name of client)

_____

(Client's authorized signature and title)

****

RESPONSE:

To: *(Insert auditor's name)*

( ) The balance due *(insert client's name)* shown above as of *(insert date)* is correct.

( ) Our records show a balance of $_____ as of *(insert date)* and the difference may be due to the following:

_____

_____

_____

Signature: _____

Title: _____

Date: _____

ILLUSTRATION 4—CONFIRMATION REQUEST FOR ACCOUNTS RECEIVABLE: POSITIVE REQUEST OF OPEN INVOICES

(Prepared on client's letterhead)

(Date)

(Customer's name and address)

Dear _____:

In connection with an audit of the financial statements of *(insert name of client)* as of *(insert date)* and for the *(insert period [e.g., year, quarter])* then ended, please confirm directly to our auditors *(insert name and address of auditors)* the amounts on the invoices listed below *(or in the attached statement)* as shown by our records that you were indebted to us as of *(insert date)*. Please take notice that the invoices that our auditors have selected for confirmation purposes may represent only a portion of the total balance due from you.

Invoice Number	Invoice Date	Invoice Amount
_____	_____	_____
_____	_____	_____
_____	_____	_____
_____	_____	_____
_____	_____	_____

Please check the appropriate response below after determining whether this is in agreement with your records. If there are differences, please provide any information in sufficient detail to assist our auditors in reconciling the difference.

After checking the appropriate response below, please sign and date your reply and mail it directly to our auditors in the enclosed return envelope. **DO NOT SEND ANY PAYMENTS TO OUR AUDITORS.**

Thank you for your anticipated timely cooperation with this request.

Respectfully,

(Name of client)

_____

(Client's authorized signature and title)

****

RESPONSE:

To: *(Insert auditor's name)*

( ) The invoice balances due *(insert client's name)* shown above as of *(insert date)* are correct.

( ) The invoice balances due *(insert client's name)* shown above as of *(insert date)* are not correct. Our records show the following differences:

_____

_____

_____

Signature: _____

Title: _____

Date: _____

ILLUSTRATION 5—CONFIRMATION REQUEST FOR ACCOUNTS RECEIVABLE: NEGATIVE REQUEST

(Prepared on client's letterhead)

(Date)

(Customer's name and address)

Dear _____:

Our auditors *(insert name and address of auditors)* are conducting an audit of our financial statements as of *(insert date)* and for the *(insert period [e.g., year, quarter])* then ended. Our records show the amount of your indebtedness to us as of *(insert date)* to be $_____. If this amount is **not** correct, please report details of any differences directly to our auditors in the space provided below and use the enclosed return envelope.

IF YOU DO NOT WRITE TO OUR AUDITORS, THEY WILL CONSIDER THE BALANCE SHOWN ABOVE TO BE CORRECT. NO REPLY IS NECESSARY IF THE AMOUNT SHOWN ABOVE AGREES WITH YOUR RECORDS.

DO NOT SEND ANY PAYMENTS TO OUR AUDITORS.

Thank you for your anticipated timely cooperation with this request.

Respectfully,

(Name of client)

_____

(Client's authorized signature and title)

****

RESPONSE:

To: *(Insert auditor's name)*

The balance due *(insert client's name)* shown above as of *(insert date)* is **not** correct. Our records show a balance of $_____ and the difference may be due to the following:

_____

_____

_____

Signature: _____

Title: _____

Date: _____

ILLUSTRATION 6—CONFIRMATION REQUEST FOR NOTES RECEIVABLE

(Prepared on client's letterhead)

(Date)

(Borrower's name and address)

Dear _____:

Our auditors *(insert name and address of auditors)* are conducting an audit of our financial statements as of *(insert date)* and for the *(insert period [e.g., year, quarter])* then ended. Our records show the following information regarding your indebtedness to us as of *(insert date):*

Initial date of note *(insert date)*   _____

Original amount of indebtedness *(insert amount)* $_____

Unpaid principal balance *(insert amount)* $_____

Annual interest rate *(insert rate)*   _____%

Date interest was paid to *(insert date)*   _____

Due date of note *(insert date)*   _____

Description of collateral *(insert description; if none insert "None"):*

_____

_____

_____

Please check the appropriate response below after determining whether the information shown above is in agreement with your records. If there are differences, please provide any information in sufficient detail to assist our auditors in reconciling the difference.

After checking the appropriate response below, please sign and date your reply and mail it directly to our auditors in the enclosed return envelope. **DO NOT SEND ANY PAYMENTS TO OUR AUDITORS.**

Thank you for your anticipated timely cooperation with this request.

Respectfully,

(Name of client)

_____

(Client's authorized signature and title)

****

RESPONSE:

To: *(Insert auditor's name)*

( ) The information shown above regarding our note payable to *(insert client's name)* agrees with our records and is correct as of *(insert date).*

( ) The information shown above regarding our note payable to *(insert client's name)* does **not** agree with our records and is **not** correct as of *(insert date).* The following are exceptions and differences we have identified:

_____

_____

_____

Signature: _____

Title: _____

Date: _____

ILLUSTRATION 7—CONFIRMATION REQUEST FOR ACCOUNTS PAYABLE

(Prepared on client's letterhead) (Date)

(Vendor's name and address)

Dear _____:

Our auditors *(insert name and address of auditors)* are conducting an audit of our financial statements as of *(insert date)* and for the *(insert period [e.g., year, quarter])* then ended. Please confirm directly to them the amount of our liability to you as of *(insert date)*. If there is a balance due, please attach a statement of the items comprising such balance. If no balance is due, please indicate this by checking the appropriate box below.

After checking the appropriate response below, please sign and date your reply and mail it directly to our auditors in the enclosed return envelope.

Thank you for your anticipated timely cooperation with this request.

Respectfully,

(Name of client)

_____

(Client's authorized signature and title)

****

RESPONSE:

To: *(Insert auditor's name)*

( ) Our records indicate that a balance of $_____ was due from *(insert name of client)* as of *(insert date),* as shown in the attached statement.

( ) Our records indicate that no balance is due from *(insert name of client)* as of *(insert date).*

_____

_____

_____

Signature: _____

Title: _____

Date: _____

ILLUSTRATION 8—CONFIRMATION REQUEST FOR NOTES PAYABLE

(Prepared on client's letterhead) (Date)

(Creditor's name and address)

Dear _____:

Our auditors *(insert name and address of auditors)* are conducting an audit of our financial statements as of *(insert date)* and for the *(insert period [e.g., year, quarter])* then ended. Our records show the following information regarding our note payable to you as of *(insert date):*

Initial date of note *(insert date)*	_____
Original amount of note *(insert amount)*	$_____
Unpaid principal balance *(insert amount)*	$_____
Payment intervals *(insert monthly, quarterly, etc.)*	_____
Periodic payment required *(insert amount)*	$_____
Annual interest rate *(insert rate)*	_____%
Date interest was paid to *(insert date)*	_____
Due date of note *(insert date)*	_____

Description of collateral *(insert description; if none insert "None"):*

_____

_____

_____

Description of terms (e.g., demand provisions, prepayment penalties) *(insert description; if none, insert "None")*:

_____

_____

_____

Please check the appropriate response below after determining whether the information shown above is in agreement with your records. If there are differences, including any direct or contingent liabilities to you not otherwise indicated above, please provide information in sufficient detail to assist our auditors in reconciling the difference.

After checking the appropriate response below, please sign and date your reply and mail it directly to our auditors in the enclosed return envelope.

Thank you for your anticipated timely cooperation with this request.

Respectfully,

(Name of client)

_____

(Client's authorized signature and title)

****

RESPONSE:

To: *(Insert auditor's name)*

( ) The information shown above regarding the obligation from *(insert name of client)* agrees with our records and is correct as of *(insert date)*.

( ) The information shown above regarding the obligation from *(insert name of client)* does **not** agree with our records as of *(insert date)*. The following are exceptions and differences we have identified:

_____

_____

_____

Signature: _____

Title: _____

Date: _____

ILLUSTRATION 9—CONFIRMATION REQUEST FOR LEASE AGREEMENT

(Prepared on client's letterhead) (Date)

(Lessor's name and address)

Dear _____:

Our auditors *(insert name and address of auditors)* are conducting an audit of our financial statements and would like to confirm the following terms and provisions of the lease agreement dated *(insert date)* between *(insert name of client)* and *(insert name of lessor)* regarding *(insert a brief description, and address if applicable, of property under lease)*:

Part I

1. Lease term: from _____ to _____

2. Monthly rental amounts applicable under lease term *(insert amounts and respective dates per lease agreement [e.g., "From 1/1/X1 to 12/31/X2, $1,250/month," "From 1/1/X3 to 12/31/X3, $1,375/month"])*:

   _____

   _____

3. Amount of security deposit: *(insert amount; if none, insert "None")*: $_____

4. Purchase option *(if none, insert "None")*:   _____

   a. Purchase price *(insert amount or description [e.g., fair value of the property at the date the option becomes exercisable])* $_____

   b. The date the purchase option becomes exercisable *(insert date)*   _____

   c. Other *(insert pertinent provisions, if any, regarding purchase option)*

   _____

   _____

   _____

5. Renewal option *(if none, insert "None")*:   _____

   a. Renewal period *(insert dates)*

   _____

   b. Renewal amounts applicable under renewal period *(insert amounts and respective dates)*

   _____

   c. Other *(insert pertinent provisions, if any, regarding renewal option)*

   _____

   _____

   _____

6. Amount of outstanding delinquent payments as of *(insert balance sheet date)* *(insert amount; if none, insert "None")*:

   _____

7. Restrictions imposed by the lease agreement *(insert a brief description of such restrictions [e.g., payment of dividends, incurring additional debt, further leasing]; if none, insert "None")*:

   _____

   _____

   _____

Part II

In addition to confirming the above, please provide directly to our auditors the following related information:

1. A description of the basis on which contingent rental payment amounts, if any, are determined *(if none, please state "None")*:

   _____

   _____

   _____

2. A description of any violations or defaults:

_____

_____

_____

3. A description of any pertinent additional information that relates to the lease agreement (e.g., contingent liabilities) *(if none, please state* "None"):

_____

_____

_____

Please check the appropriate response below regarding whether the information shown in Part I above is in agreement with your records. If there are differences, please provide any information in sufficient detail to assist our auditors in reconciling the difference.

Please sign and date your reply and mail it directly to our auditors in the enclosed return envelope.

Thank you for your anticipated timely cooperation with this request.

Respectfully,

(Name of client)

_____

(Client's authorized signature and title)

****

RESPONSE:

To: *(Insert auditor's name)*

( ) The information shown in Part I above regarding the lease agreement agrees with our records and is correct as of *(insert balance sheet date)*.

( ) The information shown in Part I above regarding the lease agreement does **not** agree with our records and is **not** correct as of *(insert balance sheet date)*. The following are exceptions and differences we have identified:

_____

_____

_____

Signature: _____

Title: _____

Date: _____

ILLUSTRATION 10—CONFIRMATION CONTROL SUMMARY

Client Name:	Date:
	Prepared By:
Financial Statement Date:	Reviewed By:

Confirmation Control Number	Customer Name	Date Confirmation Sent		Date Received
		1st Request	2nd Request	
1				
2				
3				
4				
5				
6				
7				
8				
9				
10				

ILLUSTRATION 11—ACCOUNTS RECEIVABLE CONFIRMATION RESULTS SUMMARY

XYZ, Inc.
Accounts Receivable
   Confirmation Results Summary
Financial Statement Date: 12/31/20X2

Date: 2/10/20X3
Prepared By: *AKS*
Reviewed By: *TWG*

	Number of Accounts	Dollar Amount	Percent of Dollar Amount	Unreconciled Difference over (under) Statement
CIRCULARIZATION:				
Positives	40	$ 5,200,000	48.1%	*N/A*
Negatives	55	1,400,000	12.9%	*N/A*
Selected for Testing	95	6,600,000	61.0%	*N/A*
Accounts Not Sent	444	4,225,000	39.0%	*N/A*
Total Accounts Receivable	539	$10,825,000	100.0%	*N/A*
CONFIRMATION RESULTS:				
Positive Replies:				
No Exceptions	18	$ 2,300,000	34.8%	*N/A*
Exceptions Reconciled	9	1,500,000	22.7%	*N/A*
Unreconciled Exceptions	1	125,000	1.9%	(8,000)
Alternative Procedures on Positive Nonreplies:				
No Exceptions	11	1,175,000	17.8%	*N/A*

	Number of Accounts	Dollar Amount	Percent of Dollar Amount	Unreconciled Difference over (under) Statement
Unreconciled Exceptions (Including Balances Not Pursued)	1	100,000	1.6%	3,000
Summary/Positives	40	5,200,000	78.8%	(5,000)
Negative Replies:				
No Exceptions (Including Nonreplies)	45	1,167,500	17.7%	N/A
Exceptions Reconciled	9	225,000	3.4%	N/A
Unreconciled Exceptions (Including Balances Not Pursued)	1	7,500	0.1%	250
Summary/Negatives	55	1,400,000	21.2%	250
Total Selected for Testing	95	$ 6,600,000	100.0%	$ (4,750)

ILLUSTRATION 12—ACCOUNTS RECEIVABLE ROLL-FORWARD FROM CONFIRMATION DATE TO BALANCE SHEET DATE

XYZ, Inc.	Date: 2/10/X3
Accounts Receivable—Roll-Forward from	Prepared By: *AKS*
Confirmation Date to Balance sheet date	Reviewed By: *TWG*
Financial Statement Date: 12/31/X2	

Balance per Books @ 11/30/X2			$ 481,317
Add:	Sales	*S* 61,438	
	NSF Checks	*N* 3,717	
			65,155
Deduct:	Cash Receipts	*CR* 57,981	
	Credit Memos	*CM* 7,518	
	Sales Discounts	*N* 5,433	
	Writeoffs	*N* 4,115	
			(75,047)
Balance per Books @ 12/31/X2			$ 471,425

S — Traced to sales journal.

CR — Traced to cash receipts journal.

CM — *Examined credit memos issued.*

N — *No further procedures are deemed necessary. Amounts involved are relatively small and nature of items is reasonable.*

AU SECTION 331
INVENTORIES

PRACTICE POINT: As part of its Clarity Project, the American Institute of Certified Public Accountants' (AICPA's) Auditing Standards Board (ASB) has finalized a clarified Statement on Auditing Standards (SAS) titled, "Audit Evidence—Specific Considerations for Selected Items," which supersedes:

- AU Section 331 (Inventories);
- AU Section 332 (Auditing Derivative Instruments, Hedging Activities, and Investments in Securities);
- AU Section 337 (Inquiry of a Client's Lawyer Concerning Litigation, Claims, and Assessments);
- AU Section 337A (Appendix—Illustrative Audit Inquiry Letter to Legal Counsel); and
- AU Section 337C (Exhibit II—American Bar Association Statement of Policy Regarding Lawyers' Responses to Auditors' Requests for Information).

The clarified SAS also rescinds AU Section 337B (Exhibit I—Excerpts from Financial Accounting Standards Board Accounting Standards Codification 450, Contingencies) and AU Section 901 (Public Warehouses—Controls and Auditing Procedures for Goods Held).

The following are noteworthy changes from extant GAAS:

- The clarified SAS combines the requirements and guidance from extant AU Sections 331, 332, and 337.
- Many of the requirements of extant AU Section 332 are essentially the same as requirements in other clarified standards, primarily the risk assessment standards and the clarified SAS, "Auditing Accounting Estimates, Including Fair Value Accounting Estimates and Related Disclosures." Therefore, the ASB concluded that the application of those requirements in the other clarified standards to the subject matter addressed by extant AU Section 332 is most appropriately addressed as interpretative guidance in the AICPA Audit Guide, "Auditing Derivative Instruments, Hedging Activities, and Investments in Securities." Consideration of these requirements and related application guidance will be a specific focus in updating the audit guide.
- Requirements and guidance addressing auditing investments accounted for using the equity method have been excluded from this clarified SAS because the auditing of equity investees is addressed more broadly by the clarified SAS, "Special Considerations—Audits of Group Financial Statements (Including the Work of Component Auditors)."
- Extant AU Section 337 states, in part, that "the auditor should request the client's management to send a letter of inquiry to those lawyers with whom management consulted concerning litigation, claims, and assessments." In contrast, the clarified SAS takes a more principles-based approach and requires the auditor to seek direct communication with the entity's external legal counsel (through a letter of inquiry) if the auditor assesses a risk of material misstatement regarding litigation or claims, or

when audit procedures performed indicate that material litigation or claims may exist.

The ASB is expected to issue many of the clarified standards in *one* SAS that will be codified in "AU Section" format. The ASB has decided that the effective date of the clarified SASs that have not yet been issued is for audits of financial statements for periods ending on or after December 15, 2012. Auditors should be alert to and monitor further developments in this area.

WHAT EVERY PRACTITIONER SHOULD KNOW

Basic Requirements

The observation of inventories is a mandatory generally accepted auditing procedure. When inventory quantities are determined solely by means of a physical count, the auditor should ordinarily observe and test the count of the full physical inventory taken at year end or at an interim date. Tests of the accounting records alone will not be sufficient for the auditor to become satisfied about inventory quantities; therefore, it will always be necessary for the auditor to make, or observe, some physical counts of the inventory and apply appropriate tests of intervening transactions.

Perpetual Inventory Records

Companies that maintain perpetual inventory records may verify them in cycles continually throughout the year, never taking a complete shutdown physical inventory. In this case, the auditor should review the results of the company's cycle counts to make a preliminary assessment of the reliability of the system. If the system appears reliable, the auditor should test it. The auditor's tests will typically include a selection of items from the perpetual records for tracing to the physical inventory, and a selection from the physical inventory items for tracing to the perpetual records. These tests can be performed on either an interim or a year-end basis. If the system does not appear reliable, the company may have to take a full physical inventory at year end.

Inventory and Client Use of Statistical Sampling

If the client uses statistical sampling methods to determine inventory quantities, an annual physical count of each inventory item may not be necessary. However, in such circumstances the auditor should be:

1. Satisfied that the client's procedures or methods are sufficiently reliable to produce results substantially the same as those which would be obtained by a count of all items each year.

2. Satisfied that the sampling plan is reasonable and statistically valid, that it has been properly applied, and that the results are reasonable.

3. Present to observe some physical counts and become satisfied about the effectiveness of the counting procedures used.

Audit Considerations for Beginning of Period Inventories

Special problems arise regarding beginning inventory when an auditor is engaged to perform an audit of an entity for the first time. The auditor is typically engaged after the beginning inventory date (i.e., last year's ending inventory) and thus cannot substantiate beginning inventory by observation. Under these circumstances, and provided that the auditor is satisfied with ending inventory, the auditor may test beginning inventory by other procedures, such as the following:

1. Tests of prior transactions.

2. Reviews of the records of the prior counts.

3. Application of gross profit tests.

In addition, if the client has been audited by other auditors for the prior year, the auditor may become satisfied as to the beginning inventory by reviewing the predecessor auditor's report and/or workpapers.

If the client's internal control is not sufficiently reliable (e.g., if the client has weaknesses in its internal control system over inventories), the auditor may not be able to perform satisfactory alternative procedures and may have to disclaim an opinion on the current year's statements of income and cash flows. See Illustration 6 for a sample auditor's report.

Inventories Held in Public Warehouses

Inventories may be held in public warehouses or by other outside custodians. Generally, direct confirmation with the third party of such inventory provides sufficient evidence to validate the existence and ownership of the inventory. However, if the inventory held in public warehouses or by other outside custodians is significant in relation to current assets and total assets, the auditor should supplement confirmation of the inventory by performing additional procedures such as the following:

1. Test the client's control activities used in investigating and evaluating the performance of the warehouseman.

2. Observe the warehouseman's or client's count of goods whenever practical and reasonable.

3. If warehouse receipts have been pledged as collateral, confirm details with the lenders.

4. Obtain an independent auditor's report on the warehouseman's system of internal control relevant to custody of goods and, if applicable, pledge of receipts, or apply alternative procedures at the warehouse to gain reasonable assurance that information received from the warehouseman is reliable.

PRACTICE POINT: Sample letters requesting confirmation of inventories held at outside locations are included in Illustrations 1 and 2.

PRACTICE ISSUES AND FREQUENTLY ASKED QUESTIONS

Issue 1: What special considerations should the auditor take into account if the client desires to take the physical inventory prior to the balance sheet date?

If the client desires to take the physical inventory prior to the balance sheet date, the auditor should carefully consider whether effective substantive tests can be performed to cover the remaining period (i.e., the period between the date of the physical inventory and the balance sheet date). The auditor's assessed level of control risk for the existence assertion is an important factor in this consideration. The lower the assessed level of control risk, the more likely it will be that substantive tests for the remaining period will be effective. Regardless of when the inventory is taken, the auditor should address the following issues relating to inventory observation:

- Reviewing inventory-taking instructions.
- Performing inventory test counts.
- Determining proper inventory cutoff.
- Determining the extent of slow-moving, obsolete, or damaged inventory.

Issue 2: What factors should the auditor be concerned with in connection with his or her review of the client's inventory-taking instructions to facilitate an accurate count of the inventory?

The auditor's objective in reviewing the client's inventory-taking instructions is to determine if those procedures will produce a complete and accurate inventory count. The auditor should note items such as how the inventory counts are to be made (e.g., one person will count and another person will record the count), whether inventory tags are to be used and how these tags will be controlled, and how cutoff procedures will be handled. The auditor should then suggest any changes in the inventory-taking procedures before the count.

To facilitate an accurate count of the inventory, the auditor should ensure that:

- The inventory is neatly arranged to allow for easy access and counting.
- Movement of goods stops or is controlled during the count to avoid double counting.
- The counting teams use a systematic approach and do not skip around their assigned areas.
- Inventory tags are used sequentially and systematically, and all inventory tags are accounted for as used, unused, damaged, or voided.
- Inventory tags will not be removed before the auditor observing the count gives clearance by area.
- Client personnel will be available to assist the auditor in identifying parts or units of work-in-process.

Issue 3: What should the auditor do if he or she discovers errors when making test counts?

If the auditor discovers any errors when making test counts, he or she should request that they be corrected. Also, the auditor should make more test counts from the same area and from other areas counted by the same people. If the auditor finds a pattern of count discrepancies, he or she should request that the entire area be recounted.

Issue 4: What factors should the auditor consider when determining the number of inventory test counts to make?

The number of test counts the auditor makes is a matter of professional judgment. When determining the number of test counts, the auditor should consider such factors as:

- The significance of the inventory items, considered individually or as a group.
- The familiarity of the inventory taking team with the inventory.
- The use of second, independent count teams.
- The effectiveness of the client's procedures and methods for counting the inventory.
- The adequacy of the client's inventory taking instructions to employees.
- The receipts and shipments of inventory during the counts.
- The involvement of internal auditors, if any.

Issue 5: When making test counts, what consideration should the auditor give to work-in-process inventory?

Although counts of raw materials and finished goods may be relatively easy to test, the auditor may experience problems assessing the stage of completion for work-in-process inventory. The last operation completed on the work-in-process inventory must be identified on the tags to assist in valuation after the count. If possible, the auditor should obtain a routing sheet or other document to confirm that the last operation performed is appropriately identified on the tag. If the stage of completion is not evident, information such as parts listing, standard cost sheets, job cost sheets, discussion with production personnel, and the use of professional judgment may be helpful in evaluating the recorded stage of completion.

Issue 6: How can the auditor maintain control over the inventory counts to ensure that all items are included in the final inventory listing and to help avoid inclusion of fictitious items?

The auditor should maintain control over the count documentation to ensure that all items are included in the final inventory listing and to help avoid inclusion of fictitious items. This can be accomplished as follows:

- *When inventory tags are used*—During the observation, the auditor should ensure that all tags have been used, unused, or voided and should obtain details of such tag numbers. Later, after receiving the final inventory listing, the auditor can determine if unused tags appear on the inventory listing.

- *When count sheets are used*—During the observation, the auditor should obtain photocopies of the count sheets used by the client. If this is not practical, the auditor should consider placing an identifying mark on each count sheet and either listing selected items or photocopying some of the count sheets for subsequent follow-up.

Issue 7: What procedures should the auditor apply if he or she was appointed to the engagement after the physical count and was unable to observe the client's inventory count on the balance sheet date?

An auditor may not be able to observe the inventory count on the balance sheet date. For example, the auditor may have been appointed to the engagement after the physical count was completed. In this event, the auditor must use alternate audit procedures to support the existence of the inventory at the balance sheet date. Alternate audit procedures for the auditor primarily consist of the following:

- Making or observing inventory counts at a date subsequent to the balance sheet date, and reviewing intervening transactions at or near the balance sheet date to reconcile the subsequent count to the client's count.
- Testing and reviewing the documentation created by the client's physical count.

When the auditor does not observe the physical count of inventory and is not satisfied with the use of alternate audit procedures (e.g., the company did not make a count of its physical inventory), the audit report must be modified. See Illustration 7 for a sample auditor's report.

Issue 8: Is the report of an outside inventory-taking firm that takes independent inventory counts a satisfactory substitute for the auditor's own observation of the physical count of inventory?

No. The auditor's responsibility with regard to the count and other tasks performed by an inventory-taking company is similar to the tasks that normally would be performed directly by the client. Therefore, the report from an outside company that takes independent inventory counts is not, by itself, a satisfactory substitute for the auditor's own observation of the physical count of inventory. In such circumstances, the auditor should:

- Review the outside firm's inventory-counting program.
- Observe the outside firm's inventory-counting procedures and controls.
- Make or observe a test of physical counts.
- Recompute calculations of the submitted inventory on a test basis.
- Apply appropriate tests to the intervening transactions, if applicable.

The auditor ordinarily may reduce, but not eliminate, the extent of his or her work on the physical count of inventory if the procedures of the outside firm are deemed satisfactory.

Issue 9: May the auditor use the work of a specialist to determine whether certain special inventory actually is as represented by the client?

Yes. If the auditor is unfamiliar with the identification or measurement of quantity or quality of certain inventory (e.g., precious metals, diamonds, coal piles), the auditor may find it necessary to obtain the services of specialists to determine whether the inventory actually is as represented by the client. In these circumstances, the auditor should refer to AU Section 336 (Using the Work of a Specialist) for the appropriate procedures to be followed.

Issue 10: What procedures should the auditor perform with respect to information gathered at the physical observation in order to ensure the client's accuracy of the recording of the physical counts?

The auditor uses the information gathered during the inventory observation to check the client's accuracy of the recording of the physical counts. Therefore, the auditor agrees the test counts taken during the observation to the client's final inventory listing and reconciles any differences. In tracing the test counts to the final inventory listing, the auditor must take particular care to make sure that the unit of measure used in the inventory listing is the same as that recorded in the inventory test count.

Generally, the auditor applies the following procedures to test quantities on the final inventory listings:

- Trace test counts recorded during the inventory observation to the final inventory listings and determine if they are properly recorded on the listing with respect to description and quantities.

- Determine, by using the information gathered at the physical observation, if all inventory tags or count sheets used to record the physical count are accounted for in the final inventory listings.

- Determine, by using the information gathered at the physical observation, if no inventory tags or count sheets have been added subsequent to the inventory physical count.

- Compare the final inventory listings with perpetual inventory records, on a test basis, if the client uses perpetual records in the preparation of the final inventory listings.

Issue 11: What are some common analytical procedures that the auditor can use to test the reasonableness of inventory?

Analytical procedures applied to the inventory account are primarily used in testing inventory pricing, and in efforts to detect misclassification errors arising from improper inclusion of costs in, or exclusion of costs from, overhead. A secondary use of analytical review procedures is to provide a focus to determine if more work is needed in relation to obsolete inventory, inventory shrinkage, and cutoff.

Common analytical review procedures for inventory, which are often computed by product line or location, include:

- *Gross profit ratio*—For most companies, gross profit percentages remain fairly constant from one year to the next. Because the gross profit relationship is often predictable, the auditor frequently uses this ratio to gather evidence that inventories are fairly stated.

- *Inventory turnover ratio*—The inventory turnover ratio is the ratio of cost of goods sold to average inventory. A high ratio usually is favorable since it is an indication of efficient inventory policies; however, a high ratio might reflect unrecorded inventory. A low ratio might indicate an audit problem, such as obsolete or otherwise unsalable inventory, or an overstated inventory valuation.

- *Shrinkage ratio*—The shrinkage ratio is the ratio of inventory write-down to total inventory, which is used to highlight unusual write-down, and should be analyzed in conjunction with the inventory turnover ratio.

- *Analysis of the relationship between materials, labor, and overhead to total product cost*—These ratios can be used to analyze the composition of product costs over time and relative to the industry average. This analysis is effective in detecting the improper classification of cost items, especially in the overhead component. For example, costs such as selling and marketing expenses may be improperly included in overhead.

Issue 12: What are some common reported methods of fraudulently misstating inventories?

AICPA Practice Alert No. 94-2 (Auditing Inventories—Physical Observations) indicates that reported methods of fraudulently misstating inventory have involved the following:

- Including in inventory items that do not exist (e.g., empty boxes).

- Increasing or otherwise altering the inventory counts for those items the auditor did not test count.

- Programming the computer to produce fraudulent physical quantity tabulations or priced inventory listings.

- Manipulating the inventory counts/compilations for locations not visited by the auditor.

- Double-counting inventory in transit between locations.

- Physically moving inventory and counting it at two locations.

- Including in inventory merchandise recorded as sold but not yet shipped to a customer.

- Arranging for false confirmations of inventory held by others.

- Including inventory receipts for which corresponding payables have not been recorded.

- Overstating the stage of completion of work-in-process.

- Reconciling physical inventory amounts to falsified amounts in the general ledger.

- Manipulating the "rollforward" of an inventory taken before the financial statement date.

Issue 13: What are some audit efficiency tips for auditing inventories?

- Challenge the number of recorded test counts to be made during the inventory observation. Remember that the goal is to review and evaluate the reliability of the client's inventory procedures and not to take the inventory count for the client.

- Identify controls that will result in limiting the number of inventory locations observed, when the client has multiple locations.

- Challenge the extent of tests of the clerical accuracy of inventory extensions. Testing of inventory extensions often can be reduced.

- Maximize effective use of analytical procedures. For example, if the client's inventory includes work-in-process and manufactured finished goods, and their respective balances are not material to the total inventory balance or total assets, the testing of cost accumulation can be reduced and, potentially, eliminated. Analytical procedures usually are more effective in this instance.

- Challenge the need for any sampling applications. Determine if a few individually significant items will provide high dollar coverage.

- Select the items to be tested and have client personnel prepare analyses for inventory tests such as price tests, obsolescence, and cutoffs.

- Obtain client assistance in gathering documentation such as invoices, shipping records, receiving reports, etc.

- Coordinate receivables and payables cutoff tests with inventory procedures.

ILLUSTRATIONS AND PRACTICE AIDS

ILLUSTRATION 1—REQUEST FOR CONFIRMATION OF INVENTORIES HELD BY WAREHOUSES OR OTHER THIRD PARTIES WHEN LISTING OF INVENTORIES IS PROVIDED BY THE CLIENT AND ENCLOSED WITH THE CONFIRMATION REQUEST

(Prepared on client's letterhead)

(Date)

(Name and address of warehouse or other third party)

Dear_____:

Our auditors *(insert name and address of auditors)* are conducting an audit of our financial statements as of *(insert date)* and for the *(insert period [e.g., year, quarter])* then ended. We have furnished our auditors with a copy of the attached listing, which reflects the inventory held by you for our account as of *(insert date)*. Accordingly, please review the listing carefully and confirm directly to our auditors the information requested below as of *(insert date)*.

After completing the information in the space provided below, please sign and date your reply and mail it directly to our auditors in the enclosed return envelope.

Thank you for your anticipated timely cooperation with this request.

Respectfully,

(Name of client)

_____

(Client's authorized signature and title)

****

RESPONSE:

To: *(Insert auditor's name)*

1. The enclosed inventory listing is in agreement with our records as of *(insert date)* with the following exceptions, if any. (If no exceptions are noted, please state "None.")

    _____

    _____

    _____

2. The correctness of the quantities we are confirming to you was determined as follows (please check the appropriate items):
    — Physical count
    — Weight
    — Measure
    — Book record only
    — Other (specify) _____

3. The following is a list of negotiable and nonnegotiable warehouse receipts issued. (If none were issued, please state "None.") Also, please state whether such receipts have, to your knowledge, been assigned or pledged.

    _____

    _____

    _____

    _____

4. The following are known liens against the merchandise. (If none are known to your knowledge, please state "None.")

    _____

    _____

    _____

5. The amount of unpaid charges, if any, as of *(insert date)* is $_____.

Signature: _____

Title: _____

Date: _____

ILLUSTRATION 2—REQUEST FOR CONFIRMATION OF INVENTORIES HELD BY WAREHOUSES OR OTHER THIRD PARTIES WHEN LISTING OF INVENTORIES IS NOT PROVIDED BY THE CLIENT AND NOT ENCLOSED WITH THE CONFIRMATION REQUEST

(Prepared on client's letterhead)

(Date)

(Name and address of warehouse or other third party)

Dear _____:

Our auditors *(insert name and address of auditors)* are conducting an audit of our financial statements as of *(insert date)* and for the *(insert period [e.g., year, quarter])* then ended. Please furnish directly to our auditors the information requested below about merchandise held in your custody for our account as of *(insert date):*

1. Quantities on hand, including:
   a. Lot number _____
   b. Date received _____
   c. Type of merchandise _____
   d. Unit of measure or package including number of units and kind of units (e.g., box, can, dozen) _____

   In addition to the above-requested quantities, please complete the information requested below with respect to the merchandise. After completing the information requested, please sign and date your reply and mail it directly to our auditors in the enclosed return envelope.

   Thank you for your anticipated timely cooperation with this request.

Respectfully,

(Name of client)

_____

(Client's authorized signature and title)

****

RESPONSE:

To: *(Insert auditor's name)*

1. The correctness of the quantities we are confirming to you was determined as follows (please check the appropriate items):
   — Physical count
   — Weight
   — Measure
   — Book record only
   — Other (specify) _____

2. The following is a list of negotiable and nonnegotiable warehouse receipts issued. (If none were issued, please state "None.") Also, please state whether such receipts have, to your knowledge, been assigned or pledged.

   _____

   _____

   _____

3. The following are known liens against the merchandise. (If none are known to your knowledge, please state "None.")

   _____

   _____

   _____

4. The amount of unpaid charges, if any, as of *(insert date)* is _____.

Signature:_____

Title:_____

Date:_____

ILLUSTRATION 3—INVENTORY OBSERVATION CHECKLIST

Client Name:_____

Date of Financial Statements: _____

1. Summarize below the locations of the inventory, the date the client will be counting the inventory, the name of the client personnel in charge, and the percentage of inventory at each location in relation to the total inventory.

Location	Date of Count	Client Personnel In Charge	% of Total Inventory
_____	_____	_____	_____
_____	_____	_____	_____
_____	_____	_____	_____
_____	_____	_____	_____

	Yes	No	N/A
2. Do adequate detailed written inventory instructions and procedures exist? If yes, attach a copy.	____	____	____
3. Do inventory procedures give appropriate consideration to the location and arrangement of inventories? Describe.	____	____	____
4. Do inventory procedures give appropriate consideration to identification and description of inventories? Describe.	____	____	____
5. Is the method of determining inventory quantities specified (e.g., weight, count)? Describe.	____	____	____
6. Is the method used for recording items counted (e.g., count sheets, prenumbered tags) adequate? Describe.	____	____	____
7. Are inventory tags used? If yes:	____	____	____
a. Are they prenumbered?	____	____	____
b. Is accounting for inventory tags adequate and does it include control with respect to tags used, unused, and voided? Describe.	____	____	____

	Yes	No	N/A

_____

_____

_____

8. Are adequate procedures in place to identify inventory counted, to ensure that all items have been counted, and to prevent double counting? Describe.   _____ _____ _____

_____

_____

9. Are obsolete, slow-moving, or damaged inventories properly identified and segregated? Describe.   _____ _____ _____

_____

_____

10. Is the inventory reasonably identifiable for proper classification in the accounting records (e.g., description, stage of completion)? Describe.   _____ _____ _____

_____

_____

11. Are inventory counts subject to: _____ _____ _____
    a. Complete recounts by persons independent of the ones involved in the initial counts?   _____ _____ _____
    b. Recounts only of merchandise having substantial value?   _____ _____ _____
    c. Spot checks by supervisory personnel?   _____ _____ _____

_____

_____

12. Are counts performed by employees whose functions are independent of the physical custody of inventories and recordkeeping functions? Describe.   _____ _____ _____

_____

_____

13. Do proper accounting controls and procedures exist for the exclusion from inventory of merchandise on hand, which is not property of the client (e.g., customers' merchandise, consignments in)? Describe.   _____ _____ _____

_____

_____

	Yes	No	N/A

14. Do proper accounting controls and procedures exist for the inclusion in inventory of merchandise not on hand, but the property of the client (e.g., merchandise in warehouses, out on repair, consignments out)? Describe.

_____

_____

_____

15. Will identical inventory items in various areas be accumulated to allow a tie in total counts to a summary listing subsequent to the observation? Describe.

_____

_____

_____

16. Is the movement of inventory adequately controlled (e.g., shipping and receiving activities suspended) during the physical count to ensure a proper cutoff? Describe.

_____

_____

_____

17. Are significant differences between physical counts and detailed inventory records investigated before the accounting and inventory records are adjusted to match the physical counts? Describe.

_____

_____

_____

18. Will the client be using the services of a specialist? If yes, describe the arrangements that have been made.

_____

_____

_____

19. Will inventory at remote locations be counted? Describe.

_____

_____

_____

20. Will special counting procedures or volume conversions be necessary (e.g., items weighed on scale)? Describe.

_____

_____

_____

	Yes	No	N/A

21. How will work-in-process inventory be identified? Describe. ____ ____ ____

_____

_____

_____

22. How will the stage of completion of work-in-process inventory be identified? Describe. ____ ____ ____

_____

_____

_____

23. Describe any other matters that should be noted for the inventory count. ____ ____ ____

_____

_____

_____

Prepared by: _____ Date: _____

Approved by: _____ Date: _____

ILLUSTRATION 4—INVENTORY TEST COUNT SHEET

Client Name: Date:

                                               Prepared By:

Financial Statement Date: Reviewed By:

Tag Number or Reference	Inventory Description	Count		Difference Over/(Under) Client	Explanation
		Per Client	Per Auditor		

ILLUSTRATION 5—INVENTORY AUDIT PROGRAM

	Performed By	Workpaper Reference

Inventory Observation Procedures

1. Meet with client's personnel in charge of the inventory observation and perform the following planning procedures:

	Performed By	Workpaper Reference

a. Determine the physical inventory observation date, the locations of the inventory including outside locations and warehouses, client supervisory staff in charge of the inventory, the materiality of inventory levels at the respective locations, and whether any outside specialists will be used in counting the inventory. _____ _____

b. Obtain an understanding of the procedures that will be used by the client to count the inventory. Review any inventory instructions, location maps, samples of tags to be used, and other relevant information that will be used to document the inventory procedures. _____ _____

c. Tour the client's inventory locations and determine which inventory items will be material to the overall financial statements when priced and extended. _____ _____

d. Determine the nature and extent of any inventory held for the client by warehouses or other third parties and the need to confirm or observe such inventory. _____ _____

e. Determine the adequacy of audit staffing and hold a preplanning meeting to review the client's instructions and procedures. _____ _____

2. On the physical inventory date, perform the following procedures:

a. Tour the premises; evaluate the inventory arrangements; and recommend appropriate changes as needed. _____ _____

b. Determine whether property not owned by the client is clearly segregated and identified. _____ _____

c. Determine the appropriate cutoff control numbers for receiving and shipping documents and obtain copies. _____ _____

d. Ascertain that receiving and shipping departments are informed about appropriate cutoff procedures. _____ _____

e. Observe and note the client's practices and procedures regarding segregation and identification of slow-moving, damaged, or obsolete inventory. _____ _____

f. Examine samples of inventory items for source of identification, description, measure, and status of completion. _____ _____

g. Observe count teams and determine whether the client's instructions and procedures are being properly followed. _____ _____

h. Ascertain that prenumbered inventory tickets and/or count sheets are properly controlled and accounted for. _____ _____

	Performed By	Workpaper Reference

i. Make test counts, particularly of high-dollar items, and record test count information such as item number, description, stage of completion, quantity, and other pertinent information that would assist in tracing the inventory item to the final inventory listing. _____ _____

j. Observe any omissions from count and ask for recounts in case of errors. _____ _____

k. Note any inventory movement during the observation and obtain adequate explanations. _____ _____

l. Determine whether any inventory appears to be obsolete, slow-moving, damaged, or very old and whether the client has properly identified those items. Consider preparing a summary of these items. _____ _____

m. Determine if all inventory count sheets or tags have been accounted for. Obtain a summary of tags used, unused, voided, or damaged and summarize the sequences of tags or count sheets into these categories. _____ _____

n. Tour the shipping and receiving areas and obtain information about inventory items therein. Determine whether they should be counted in or excluded from the inventory. _____ _____

o. Determine the nature and extent of any inventory held by the entity on behalf of third parties and ensure that it is excluded from the inventory count. _____ _____

p. Prepare a memorandum of observation of the physical inventory. Include comments on the overall controls, arrangements, procedures used, and compliance therewith. _____ _____

Reconciliation and Valuation of Inventory

3. Obtain an understanding of the procedures used by the client to summarize, reconcile, and value the inventory and test these procedures as follows:

a. On a test basis, trace tag sequences of used, unused, voided, and damaged tags to the final inventory listing summary and ascertain consistent treatment. Investigate any tags that have been added or deleted. _____ _____

b. Trace test counts noted during the observation of the physical inventory to the final inventory listing summary and investigate any differences. _____ _____

c. Test the arithmetical accuracy of the final inventory listing summary with respect to both quantities and dollar value. _____ _____

	Performed By	Workpaper Reference

    d.   Reconcile the final inventory listing summary to the general ledger and review book to physical adjustments. Investigate large adjustments for possible inventory shrinkage, motives to overstate inventory, or weaknesses in the client's system. _____ _____

    e.   Trace confirmation of inventory items held by third parties to the final inventory listing summary. _____ _____

4.   Determine the inventory method used (FIFO, LIFO, average cost, etc.) and determine whether such method is consistently applied. _____ _____

5.   For raw materials and purchased finished goods on the FIFO method, test the cost as follows:

    a.   Vouch the cost to the most recent vendor's invoice and other external evidence; if the quantities on hand exceed the invoice total, vouch the excesses back to previous purchases until the quantity on hand has been built up. _____ _____

    b.   Determine that freight, duty, discounts, and allowances are consistently accounted for. _____ _____

    c.   Note the dates of purchase of the items tested and note items that appear to be slow-moving. _____ _____

    d.   Relate the cost of items tested to the costs of similar products and investigate significant variations. _____ _____

    e.   Relate the costs of other significant untested items to prices used in the prior year and investigate significant variations. _____ _____

    f.   Determine the dollar difference for each item tested, summarize total differences, and consider the impact of misstatements found on the overall population. _____ _____

6.   For work-in-process and finished goods manufactured by the company, perform the following:

    a.   Trace unit costs from the final inventory listing to the cost accounting records. _____ _____

    b.   Trace the raw material quantities used in producing the work-in-process items or the finished goods items to supporting documents (e.g., bills of material, requisition forms, production reports). _____ _____

    c.   Trace the cost of raw materials used to the vendor invoices, freight invoices, and other external documents, where appropriate. _____ _____

    d.   Trace the labor hours used in producing the work-in-process items or finished goods items to supporting documents (e.g., time cards, time studies). _____ _____

    e.   Agree actual labor rates used to payroll records. _____ _____

	Performed By	Workpaper Reference

f. For overhead, test the client's overhead rate as follows:

   (1) Review the costs included in the overhead pool for propriety. _____ _____

   (2) Determine that overhead costs are being charged to inventory in accordance with appropriate policy (e.g., as a percentage of direct labor). _____ _____

   (3) Identify disposition of variances between actual overhead costs incurred and overhead costs applied to production and inventory. Determine that variances are reasonable and that no excessive costs for idle plant are being charged to inventory. _____ _____

   (4) Compare the overhead rate to the prior year for reasonableness. _____ _____

7. For LIFO inventory cost calculations, perform the following:

  a. Obtain an understanding of the pricing elections made when the entity initially adopted LIFO, including the following:

   (1) The method used to determine the LIFO cost of the current year's increase in inventory (e.g., earliest, latest, or average acquisition cost). _____ _____

   (2) The method of valuing LIFO inventories (i.e., specific goods method or dollar-value method). _____ _____

   (3) The pools (i.e., the method of accumulating or grouping similar inventory items) used, including a description of each pool. _____ _____

   (4) If the dollar-value LIFO method is used, the technique of computing the LIFO value of the dollar value pools (i.e., double-extension, index, or link-chain). _____ _____

  b. Record in carryforward schedules the various layers of LIFO inventory cost. _____ _____

  c. If the specific goods LIFO (also known as "unit LIFO" or "specific item LIFO") is used, review the client's schedules for year-end quantities. Reconcile unit costs per the company's schedules to the carryforward schedules by layers for quantities not in excess of the preceding year's quantities. _____ _____

	Performed By	Workpaper Reference

    d.   If dollar-value LIFO is used, price all or a portion of the closing inventory at current-year cost and at base-year cost, and compute an index of aggregate current-year cost to base-year cost. Test prices and clerical accuracy of the final inventory listing at current year cost. Also, test the calculation of the index used for conversion from current-year cost to base-year cost.   _____   _____

    e.   Agree base-year costs with carry forward LIFO working papers and agree quantities with the final inventory listing.   _____   _____

    f.   State the closing inventory in terms of base-year cost for each LIFO pool. If base-year costs have not been extended 100%, they may be extended by applying the index to inventory totals at current-year cost.   _____   _____

8.   Perform the following procedures to test for slow-moving and obsolete items:

    a.   Obtain an understanding from the client with respect to the criteria and calculation used to determine what constitutes slow-moving and obsolete items.   _____   _____

    b.   Note dates per vendors' invoices during the inventory price test and be alert for slow-moving items.   _____   _____

    c.   Compare listing of slow-moving and obsolete inventory items noted during the inventory observation and trace to the client's final listing of slow-moving and obsolete inventory.   _____   _____

    d.   Compare items noted during the current period's review of slow-moving and obsolete items to the prior year's listing.   _____   _____

    e.   Check that significant items written down in prior years have not been written up in the current year; determine if further write-downs might be required.   _____   _____

9.   Perform the following procedures to determine lower of cost or market applications:

    a.   For purchased inventory items, compare, on a test basis, the unit price used in the final inventory listing summary to current price lists, recent sales invoices, or recent vendor invoices.   _____   _____

    b.   For work-in-process and finished goods manufactured by the company, compare, on a test basis, inventory carrying amounts and recent selling prices or sales invoices; ascertain stage of completion and estimated cost to complete for work-in-process items; and ascertain that such carrying amounts are not in excess of net realizable value.   _____   _____

	Performed By	Workpaper Reference

c.   Compare inventory turnover ratio and gross profit percentage of the current period to prior periods. _____ _____

d.   Compare quantities on hand for selected items with quantities noted on the sales invoices to determine that the quantities on hand are not excessive. _____ _____

10. Perform the following shipping and receiving cutoff procedures with respect to cutoff information obtained at the physical inventory observation date:

a.   On a test basis, determine whether the last few shipments of inventory before the physical inventory observation date have been excluded from inventory and included in sales for the period under audit. _____ _____

b.   On a test basis, determine whether the first few shipments of inventory after the physical inventory observation date have been included in inventory and excluded from sales for the period under audit. _____ _____

c.   On a test basis, determine whether the last few inventory items received before the physical inventory observation date have been included in inventory and accounts payable for the period under audit. _____ _____

d.   On a test basis, determine whether the first few inventory items received after the physical inventory observation date have been excluded from inventory and accounts payable for the period under audit. _____ _____

11. If the inventory physical count was taken as of an interim date, obtain an analysis and reconciliation of the inventory per the physical count to the inventory per the balance sheet and perform the following:

a.   Review and analyze the general ledger inventory control accounts from the date of the physical count to the balance-sheet date. _____ _____

b.   Trace inventory additions to appropriate sources, such as the purchases journal and cost accounting records. _____ _____

c.   Trace inventory reductions to cost of sales. _____ _____

d.   Compare the current activity between the physical count date and balance sheet date to activity of the comparable period in the preceding year, and investigate unusual fluctuations. _____ _____

e.   Determine the propriety and reasonableness of any other reconciling items. _____ _____

12. Perform the following analytical procedures to inventories and investigate any significant fluctuations or deviations from the expected balances:

		Performed By	Workpaper Reference

a. Compare the current year's account balances with the prior year's account balances for inventories and the reserves for slow-moving or obsolete items. ___ ___

b. Compare the current year's components of inventory (i.e., raw materials, work-in-process, finished goods) as a percentage of total inventory with the prior year's percentages. ___ ___

c. Compare the current year's composition of total product cost (i.e., materials, labor, and overhead) with the prior year's. ___ ___

d. Compute the following ratios for the current year and compare with the prior year's ratios:

   (1) Inventory turnover in total and by major product or division. ___ ___

   (2) Average age of inventory in total and by major product or division. ___ ___

   (3) Gross profit percentage in total and by major product or division. ___ ___

   (4) Shrinkage ratio (i.e., inventory write-offs to average inventory). ___ ___

13. If inventory held in public warehouses or by other outside custodians is significant in relation to current assets and total assets, perform one or more of the following procedures:

a. Confirm the inventory held in public warehouses or by other custodians. See sample confirmation letter requests included in Illustrations 1 and 2, which may be used to confirm such inventory. ___ ___

b. Test the client's control activities used in investigating and evaluating the performance of the warehouseman. ___ ___

c. Observe the warehouseman's or client's count of goods whenever practical and reasonable. ___ ___

d. If warehouse receipts have been pledged as collateral, confirm details with the lenders. ___ ___

e. Obtain an independent auditor's report on the warehouseman's system of internal control relevant to custody of goods and, if applicable, pledge of receipts, or apply alternative procedures at the warehouse to gain reasonable assurance that information received from the warehouseman is reliable. ___ ___

14. If the auditor is concerned about the risk of fraud, audit procedures such as the following should be considered in addition to the ones listed above:

a. Examine individual entries in the general ledger inventory account to search for expenses or other items that are improperly charged to inventory. ___ ___

	Performed By	Workpaper Reference

b.   Scrutinize any material book to physical inventory adjustments and examine supporting documents.   _____   _____

c.   Review year-end accruals and adjustments to the inventory account and ascertain that the entries are normal and required.   _____   _____

d.   Perform detailed price testing of labor and overhead rates.   _____   _____

e.   Look for evidence of bulk sales at steep discounts which could indicate a declining value for the products.   _____   _____

f.   Perform a detailed analysis of scrap sales.   _____   _____

g.   Examine journal entries made to the inventory account subsequent to year-end.   _____   _____

h.   Expand the inventory cutoff procedures.   _____   _____

i.   Confirm accounts payable.   _____   _____

j.   In connection with the inventory observation:

   (1)   Observe all inventory locations simultaneously.   _____   _____

   (2)   Obtain copies of all inventory count sheets or tags before leaving the physical inventory sites.   _____   _____

   (3)   Physically examine the inventory by opening boxes to assure that the purported inventory is actually present, and match content to the labels.   _____   _____

15.   Determine if any inventory is pledged or subject to liens.   _____   _____

16.   Determine if the inventory amount includes any significant intercompany profit that should be eliminated.   _____   _____

17.   Determine if the inventory is properly classified in the balance sheet and if adequate disclosure is made with respect to the valuation method, major components of inventory, and pledged inventory.   _____   _____

ILLUSTRATION 6—AUDITOR'S REPORT: DISCLAIMER OF OPINION— AUDITOR DID NOT OBSERVE BEGINNING INVENTORY

Independent Auditor's Report

Board of Directors and Stockholders
ABC Company

We have audited the accompanying balance sheet of ABC Company as of December 31, 20X2, and we were engaged to audit the related statements of income, retained earnings, and cash flows for the year then ended. These financial statements are the responsibility of the Company's management. Our responsibility is to express an opinion on these financial statements based on our audit.

Except as discussed in the following paragraph, we conducted our audit in accordance with auditing standards generally accepted in the United States of America. Those standards require that we plan and perform the audit to obtain reasonable assurance about whether the financial statements are free of material misstatement. An audit includes examining, on a test basis, evidence supporting the amounts and disclosures in the financial statements. An audit also includes assessing the accounting principles used and significant estimates made by management, as well as evaluating the overall financial statement presentation. We believe that our audit provides a reasonable basis for our opinion.

Because we were not engaged by the Company as auditors until after December 31, 20X1, we were not present to observe the physical inventory taken at that date, and we have not satisfied ourselves by means of other procedures concerning inventory quantities. The amount of the inventory at December 31, 20X1, enters materially into the determination of the results of operations and cash flows for the year ended December 31, 20X2. Therefore, we do not express an opinion on the accompanying statements of income, retained earnings, and cash flows for the year ended December 31, 20X2.

In our opinion, the balance sheet referred to above presents fairly, in all material respects, the financial position of ABC Company as of December 31, 20X2, in conformity with accounting principles generally accepted in the United States of America.

Seliga & Co., CPAs

March 14, 20X3

ILLUSTRATION 7—AUDITOR'S REPORT: DISCLAIMER OF OPINION— COMPANY DID NOT MAKE A COUNT OF ITS PHYSICAL INVENTORY

Independent Auditor's Report

Board of Directors and Stockholders
ABC Company

We were engaged to audit the accompanying balance sheets of ABC Company as of December 31, 20X2, and 20X1, and the related statements of income, retained earnings, and cash flows for the years then ended. These financial statements are the responsibility of the Company's management.

The Company did not make a count of its physical inventory in 20X2 or 20X1, stated in the accompanying financial statements at $_____ as of December 31, 20X2, and at $_____ as of December 31, 20X1. The Company's records do not permit the application of other auditing procedures to inventories.

Since the Company did not take physical inventories and we were not able to apply other auditing procedures to satisfy ourselves as to inventory quantities, the scope of our work was not sufficient to enable us to express, and we do not express, an opinion on these financial statements.

Seliga & Co., CPAs

March 14, 20X3

AU SECTION 332
AUDITING DERIVATIVE INSTRUMENTS, HEDGING ACTIVITIES, AND INVESTMENTS IN SECURITIES

PRACTICE POINT: As part of its Clarity Project, the American Institute of Certified Public Accountants' (AICPA's) Auditing Standards Board (ASB) has finalized a clarified Statement on Auditing Standards (SAS) titled, "Audit Evidence—Specific Considerations for Selected Items," which supersedes:

- AU Section 331 (Inventories);
- AU Section 332 (Auditing Derivative Instruments, Hedging Activities, and Investments in Securities);
- AU Section 337 (Inquiry of a Client's Lawyer Concerning Litigation, Claims, and Assessments);
- AU Section 337A (Appendix—Illustrative Audit Inquiry Letter to Legal Counsel); and
- AU Section 337C (Exhibit II—American Bar Association Statement of Policy Regarding Lawyers' Responses to Auditors' Requests for Information).

The clarified SAS also rescinds AU Section 337B (Exhibit I—Excerpts from Financial Accounting Standards Board Accounting Standards Codification 450, Contingencies) and AU Section 901 (Public Warehouses—Controls and Auditing Procedures for Goods Held).

The following are noteworthy changes from extant GAAS:

- The clarified SAS combines the requirements and guidance from extant AU Sections 331, 332, and 337.

- Many of the requirements of extant AU Section 332 are essentially the same as requirements in other clarified standards, primarily the risk assessment standards and the clarified SAS, "Auditing Accounting Estimates, Including Fair Value Accounting Estimates and Related Disclosures." Therefore, the ASB concluded that the application of those requirements in the other clarified standards to the subject matter addressed by extant AU Section 332 is most appropriately addressed as interpretive guidance in the AICPA Audit Guide, "Auditing Derivative Instruments, Hedging Activities, and Investments in Securities." Consideration of these requirements and related application guidance will be a specific focus in updating the audit guide.

- Requirements and guidance addressing auditing investments accounted for using the equity method have been excluded from this clarified SAS because the auditing of equity investees is addressed more broadly by the clarified SAS, "Special Considerations—Audits of Group Financial Statements (Including the Work of Component Auditors)."

- Extant AU Section 337 states, in part, that "the auditor should request the client's management to send a letter of inquiry to those lawyers with whom management consulted concerning litigation, claims, and assessments." In contrast, the clarified SAS takes a more principles-based approach and requires the auditor to seek direct communication with the entity's external legal counsel (through a letter of inquiry) if the auditor

assesses a risk of material misstatement regarding litigation or claims, or when audit procedures performed indicate that material litigation or claims may exist.

The ASB is expected to issue many of the clarified standards in *one* SAS that will be codified in "AU Section" format. The ASB has decided that the effective date of the clarified SASs that have not yet been issued is for audits of financial statements for periods ending on or after December 15, 2012. Auditors should be alert to and monitor further developments in this area.

WHAT EVERY PRACTITIONER SHOULD KNOW

Basic Requirements for Risk Assessment and Designing Substantive Procedures

The auditor should:

- Design procedures to obtain reasonable assurance of detecting misstatements of assertions about derivatives and securities that, when aggregated with misstatements of other assertions, could cause the financial statements taken as a whole to be materially misstated. When designing such procedures, the auditor should consider the inherent risk and control risk for these assertions.

- Obtain an understanding of internal control over derivatives and securities transactions and assess control risk for the related assertions. The auditor's understanding of internal control over derivatives and securities may encompass controls placed in operation by the entity and by service organizations whose services are part of the entity's information system. If the auditor plans to assess control risk below the maximum for one or more assertions about derivatives and securities, the auditor should:

  — Identify specific controls relevant to the assertions that are likely to prevent or detect material misstatements and that have been placed in operation by either the entity or the service organization, and

  — Gather audit evidence about the operating effectiveness of such controls.

- Consider the following in designing auditing procedures for assertions about derivatives and securities:

  — The size of the entity

  — The entity's organizational structure

  — The nature of the entity's operations

  — The types, frequency, and complexity of the entity's derivatives and securities transactions

  — The entity's controls over derivatives and securities transactions

- Consider whether special skills or knowledge are necessary to plan and perform auditing procedures for derivatives and securities.

- Use the assessed levels of inherent risk and control risk to determine the nature, timing, and extent of the substantive procedures to be performed to detect material misstatements of the assertions for derivatives and securities.

- Consider whether the results of other audit procedures conflict with management's assertions about derivatives and securities, and the impact of any such identified matters on management's assertions and on the sufficiency of audit evidence.

- Consider that derivatives may not involve an initial exchange of tangible consideration and, therefore, it may be difficult to limit audit risk for assertions about the completeness of derivatives to an acceptable level with an assessed level of control risk at the maximum. The auditor should not focus exclusively on evidence relating to cash receipts and disbursements, because derivatives may involve only a commitment to perform under a contract and not an initial exchange of tangible consideration. Therefore, when testing for completeness, the auditor should consider making inquiries, inspecting agreements, and reading other information (e.g., minutes of meetings of the board of directors or finance or other committees).

- Evaluate whether the presentation and disclosure of derivatives and securities are in conformity with GAAP.

Tests of Valuation Assertions

The auditor should design tests of valuation assertions according to the valuation method used for the measurement or disclosure under GAAP.

Valuation based on cost The auditor should evaluate management's conclusion about the need to recognize an impairment loss for a decline in the security's fair value below its cost that is other than temporary. To obtain evidence about the cost of securities, the auditor should apply procedures such as the following: (a) inspection of documentation of the purchase price, (b) confirmation with the issuer or holder, and (c) testing discount or premium amortization, either by recomputation or analytical procedures.

Valuation based on an investee's financial results For valuations based on an investee's financial results, including but not limited to the equity method of accounting, the auditor should obtain sufficient evidence in support of the investee's financial results. The auditor should read available financial statements of the investee and the accompanying audit report, if any. Financial statements of the investee that have been audited by an auditor whose report is satisfactory to the investor's auditor may constitute sufficient audit evidence.

If the investee's financial statements are not audited, or if the investee auditor's report is not satisfactory to the investor's auditor, the investor's auditor should apply, or should request that the investor arrange with the investee to have another auditor apply, appropriate auditing procedures to the investee's financial statements. In making this decision, the investor's auditor should take into consideration the materiality of the investment in relation to the financial statements of the investor.

In addition, the auditor should give adequate consideration to the following factors and perform the respective audit procedures:

- If the carrying amount of the security reflects factors that are not recognized in the investee's financial statements or fair values of assets that are materially different from the investee's carrying amounts, the auditor should obtain sufficient evidence in support of these amounts.

- Any time lag in reporting between the date of the financial statements of the investor and that of the investee should be consistent from period to period. If a time lag between the date of the entity's financial statements and those of the investee has a material effect on the entity's financial statements, the auditor should determine whether the entity's management has properly considered the lack of comparability. If a change in time lag occurs that has a material effect on the investor's financial statements, an explanatory paragraph should be added to the auditor's report because of the change in reporting period.

- The auditor should evaluate management's conclusion about the need to recognize an impairment loss for a decline in the security's fair value below its carrying amount that is other than temporary.

- With respect to subsequent events and transactions of the investee occurring after the date of the investee's financial statements but before the date of the investor auditor's report, the auditor should read available interim financial statements of the investee and make appropriate inquiries of the investor to identify subsequent events and transactions that are material to the investor's financial statements. Such events or transactions should be disclosed in the notes to the investor's financial statements and, where applicable, labeled as "unaudited information." For the purpose of recording the investor's share of the investee's results of operations, the auditor should give recognition to events or transactions of the type contemplated in AU Section 560 (Subsequent Events).

- The auditor should obtain evidence relating to material transactions between the entity and the investee to evaluate (a) the propriety of the elimination of unrealized profits and losses on transactions between the entity and the investee that is required when the equity method of accounting is used to account for an investment under GAAP and (b) the adequacy of disclosures about material related party transactions.

Valuation based on fair value The auditor should obtain evidence supporting management's assertions about the fair value of derivatives and securities measured or disclosed at fair value. The auditor should also determine whether GAAP specify the method to be used to determine the fair value of the entity's derivatives and securities and evaluate whether the determination of fair value is consistent with the specified valuation method.

If the determination of fair value requires the use of estimates, the auditor should consider the guidance in AU Section 342 (Auditing Accounting Estimates).

Consideration of sources of fair value and valuation models Quoted market prices obtained from sources such as the national exchanges and the National Association of Securities Dealers Automated Quotations System (NASDAQ), or from pricing services based on sources such as those, are generally considered to provide sufficient evidence of the fair value of the derivatives and securities.

If quoted market prices are not available for the derivative or security, the auditor may obtain estimates of fair value from broker-dealers or other third-party sources based on proprietary valuation models or from the entity based on internally or externally developed valuation models (e.g., market approach, income approach, or cost approach). However in such circumstances, the auditor should:

    a. Obtain an understanding of the method used by the broker-dealer or other third-party source in developing the estimate (e.g., whether a pricing model or a cash flow projection was used).

    b. Determine whether it is necessary to obtain estimates from more than one pricing source, which may be appropriate if either of the following occurs:

        (1) The pricing source has a relationship with an entity that might impair its objectivity (e.g., an affiliate or a counterparty involved in selling or structuring the product).

        (2) The valuation is based on assumptions that are highly subjective or particularly sensitive to changes in the underlying circumstances.

A derivative or security may be valued by the entity using a valuation model such as the following: present value of expected future cash flows, option-pricing models, matrix pricing, option-adjusted spread models, and fundamental analysis. In such circumstances, the auditor should obtain evidence supporting management's assertions about fair value determined using a model by performing procedures such as the following:

- Assessing the reasonableness and appropriateness of the model. The auditor should determine whether the valuation model is appropriate for the derivative or security to which it is applied and whether the assumptions used are reasonable and appropriately supported. The auditor may consider it necessary to involve a specialist in assessing the model.

- Calculating the value, for example, using a model developed by the auditor or by a specialist engaged by the auditor, to develop an independent expectation to corroborate the reasonableness of the value calculated by the entity.

- Comparing the fair value with subsequent or recent transactions.

Consideration of collateral in evaluating fair value If collateral (e.g., negotiable securities, real estate, and property) is an important factor in evaluating the fair value and collectibility of the security, the auditor should obtain evidence regarding the existence, fair value, and transferability of such collateral as well as the investor's rights to the collateral.

Impairment losses The auditor should evaluate management's conclusion about the need to recognize in earnings an impairment loss for a decline in fair value that is other than temporary. Specifically, the auditor should evaluate:

1. Management's consideration of factors that may indicate a decline in fair value that is other than temporary, and

2. Management's conclusions about the need to recognize an impairment loss.

The auditor's evaluation should include obtaining evidence about any factors that may corroborate or conflict with management's conclusions. When the entity has recognized an impairment loss, the auditor should gather evidence supporting the amount of the impairment adjustment recorded and determine whether the entity has appropriately followed GAAP.

In addition, the auditor should gather audit evidence to support the amount of unrealized appreciation or depreciation in the fair value of a derivative that is recognized in earnings or other comprehensive income or that is disclosed because of the ineffectiveness of a hedge.

Special Considerations about Hedging Activities

For transactions that are accounted for as hedges, the auditor should gather audit evidence in order to:

*   Determine whether management complied with the hedge accounting requirements under GAAP, including designation and documentation requirements.

*   Support management's expectation at the inception of the hedge that the hedging relationship will be highly effective and its ongoing effectiveness will be periodically assessed.

*   Support the recorded change in the hedged item's fair value that is attributable to the hedged risk.

*   Determine whether management has properly applied GAAP to the hedged item.

*   Evaluate management's determination of whether a forecasted transaction that is hedged is probable of occurring. **(Note:** GAAP require that the likelihood that the transaction will take place not be based solely on management's intent; rather, the transaction's probability should be supported by observable facts and the attendant circumstances.)

Assertions about Securities Based on Management's Intent and Ability

GAAP require that management's intent and ability be considered in valuing certain securities; for example, whether equity securities are classified as trading or available-for-sale depends on management's intent and objectives in investing in the securities. Under such circumstances, in evaluating management's intent and ability, the auditor should:

1. Obtain an understanding of the process used by management to classify securities as trading, available-for-sale, or held-to-maturity.

2. For an investment accounted for using the equity method, inquire of management as to whether the entity has the ability to exercise significant influence over the operating and financial policies of the investee and evaluate the attendant circumstances that serve as a basis for management's conclusions.

3. If the entity accounts for the investment contrary to the presumption established by GAAP for the use of the equity method, obtain sufficient evidence about whether that presumption has been overcome and whether appropriate disclosure is made regarding the reasons for not accounting for the investment in keeping with that presumption.

4. Consider whether management's activities corroborate or conflict with its stated intent.

5. Determine whether GAAP require management to document its intentions and specify the content and timeliness of that documentation. The auditor should inspect the documentation and obtain audit evidence about its timeliness.

6. Determine whether management's activities, contractual agreements, or the entity's financial condition provide evidence of its ability. For example, management's cash flow projections may suggest that it does not have the ability to hold debt securities to their maturity.

Management Representations

The auditor generally should obtain written representations from management confirming aspects of management's intent and ability that affect assertions about derivatives and securities, such as its intent and ability to hold a debt security until its maturity. The auditor also should consider obtaining written representations from management confirming other aspects of derivatives and securities transactions that affect assertions about them. See Illustration 5 for examples of management representations that may be appropriate in certain situations relating to derivatives and securities.

AU Section 333 (Management Representations) provides guidance to auditors in obtaining written representations from management.

Auditing Interests in Trusts Held by a Third-Party Trustee and Reported at Fair Value and Auditing Investments in Securities Where a Readily Determinable Fair Value Does Not Exist

There may be circumstances where the auditor has determined that the nature and extent of auditing procedures should include verifying the existence and testing the measurement of investments held by a third party (e.g., trustee or hedge fund). For example, entities may have interests in trusts held by a third-party trustee that are required to be reported at fair value or an investment in a hedge fund that is reported at fair value. Also, in some circumstances, the fair value of such holdings may be estimated because a readily determinable fair value does not exist (e.g., investments in limited partnership interests or other private equity securities). As part of the auditor's procedures, the auditor generally would satisfy the existence assertion through direct confirmation with the third party, examination of legal documents, or other means. In the case of independent third-party confirmation, the third party may only provide the fair value, in aggregate, of investments held and may not necessarily provide management or the auditor with detailed information about specific investments held or about the basis and method for measuring the entity's investments.

A key factor to consider is whether simply receiving a confirmation from a third party (e.g., trustee, hedge fund) regarding a company's investments, either in the aggregate or on an investment-by-investment basis, would constitute adequate audit evidence with respect to the existence and valuation assertions. Auditing interpretations of AU Section 328 and AU Section 332 provide the following guidance regarding audit evidence obtained with respect to the valuation and existence assertions:

- *Valuation assertion.* In circumstances where the auditor determines that the nature and extent of auditing procedures should include testing the measurement of investments held by a trust or investments in securities, simply receiving a confirmation from a third party *either in the aggregate or on an investment-by-investment basis* does not constitute adequate audit evidence with respect to the valuation assertion.

- *Existence assertion.* In circumstances where the auditor determines that the nature and extent of auditing procedures should include verifying the existence of investments held by a trust or investments in securities, simply receiving a confirmation from a third party for investments *in the aggregate* does not constitute adequate audit evidence with respect to the existence assertion. To illustrate, confirmations in the aggregate such as "$500,000 of total investments" or "$200,000 of total investments in private equity securities; $175,000 of total investments in interests in limited partnerships; and $125,000 of total investments in debt securities" do not constitute adequate audit evidence with respect to the existence assertion. However, receiving confirmation from the third party on an *investment-by-investment basis* typically would constitute sufficient audit evidence with respect to the existence assertion; such a confirmation on an investment-by-investment basis might read as follows: "800 shares of common stock of private company ABC, with a fair value of $130,000; 600 shares of preferred stock of private company DEF, with a fair value of $90,000; 30 units of limited partnership interest XYZ, with a fair value of $220,000; and real estate Property A2Z, with a fair value of $500,000."

In addition, the auditing interpretations indicate that if the auditor is unable to audit the existence or measurement of interests in trusts or investments in securities at the financial statement date, a scope limitation exists. In such circumstances, the auditor is required to consider whether it is necessary to qualify his or her opinion or to disclaim an opinion on the entity's financial statements, as discussed in AU Section 508 (Reports on Audited Financial Statements).

PRACTICE ISSUES AND FREQUENTLY ASKED QUESTIONS

Issue 1: What are some examples of factors that might affect the auditor's assessment of inherent risk for assertions about a derivative or a security?

The following are examples of factors that might affect the auditor's assessment of inherent risk for assertions about a derivative or security:

- **Management's objectives** For example, the entity may enter into derivatives as hedges, in response to management's objective of minimizing the risk of loss from changes in market conditions. The use of hedges is subject to the risk that market conditions will change so that the hedge is no longer effective. That increases the inherent risk for certain assertions about the derivatives because, in such circumstances, continued application of hedge accounting would not be in conformity with GAAP.

- **The complexity of the features of the derivative or security** For example, interest payments on a structured note may be based on two or more factors, such as one or more interest rates and the market price of certain equity securities.

- **Whether the transaction that gave rise to the derivative or security involved the exchange of cash** Derivatives that do not involve an initial exchange of cash are subject to an increased risk that they will not be identified for valuation and disclosure considerations. For example, a foreign exchange forward contract that is not recorded at its inception because the entity does not pay cash to enter into the contract is subject to an increased risk that it will not be identified for subsequent adjustment to fair value.

- **The entity's inexperience with the derivative or security** For example, under a new arrangement, an entity may pay a small deposit to enter into a futures contract for foreign currency to pay for purchases from an overseas supplier. The entity's lack of experience with such derivatives may lead it to incorrectly account for the deposit (e.g., treating it as inventory cost), thereby increasing the risk that the contract will not be identified for subsequent adjustment to fair value.

- **Whether a derivative is freestanding or an embedded feature of an agreement** Because embedded derivatives are less likely to be identified by management, the inherent risk for certain assertions increases. For example, an option to convert the principal outstanding under a loan agreement into equity securities is less likely to be identified for valuation and disclosure considerations if it is a clause in a loan agreement than if it is a separate freestanding agreement.

- **Whether external factors affect the assertion** A variety of risks related to external factors may affect assertions about derivatives and securities, such as:

- Credit risk (i.e., the risk of loss as a result of the issuer of a debt security or the counterparty to a derivative failing to meet its obligation).

- Market risk (i.e., the risk of loss from adverse changes in market factors that affect the fair value of a derivative or security, such as interest rates and foreign exchange rates).

- Basis risk (i.e., the risk of loss from ineffective hedging activities).

- Legal risk (i.e., the risk of loss from a legal or regulatory action that invalidates or otherwise precludes performance by one or both parties to the derivative or security).

The evolving nature of derivatives and the applicable GAAP As new forms of derivatives are developed, interpretive accounting guidance for them may not be issued until after the derivatives are broadly used in the marketplace.

Significant reliance on outside parties Entities that rely on external expertise may be unable to appropriately challenge the specialist's methodology or assumptions, such as when a valuation specialist values a derivative.

GAAP may require developing assumptions about future conditions As the number and subjectivity of those assumptions increase, the inherent risk of material misstatement increases for certain assertions.

Issue 2: May a valuation model be used to determine the fair value of a security when GAAP require that the fair value of a security be determined using quoted market prices?

No. A valuation model (e.g., present value of expected future cash flows, option-pricing models) should not be used to determine fair value when GAAP require that the fair value of a security be determined using quoted market prices.

Issue 3: What are some examples of factors that may indicate that a decline in fair is other than temporary?

The following are examples of factors that may indicate that a decline in fair value is other than temporary:

- Fair value is significantly below cost and:
  - The decline is attributable to adverse conditions specifically related to the security or to specific conditions in an industry or in a geographic area.
  - The decline has existed for an extended period of time.
  - Management does not possess both the intent and the ability to hold the security for a period of time sufficient to allow for any anticipated recovery in fair value.
- The security has been downgraded by a rating agency.
- The financial condition of the issuer has deteriorated.
- Dividends have been reduced or eliminated, or scheduled interest payments have not been made.
- The entity recorded losses from the security subsequent to the end of the reporting period.

Issue 4: What factors should the auditor consider when evaluating whether the presentation and disclosures of derivatives and securities are in conformity with GAAP?

When evaluating whether the presentation and disclosures of derivatives and securities are in conformity with GAAP, the auditor should consider whether:

- The accounting principles selected and applied have general acceptance.

- The accounting principles are appropriate in the circumstances.

- The financial statements, including the related notes, are informative of matters that may affect their use, understanding, and interpretation.

- The information presented in the financial statements is classified and summarized in a reasonable manner (i.e., neither too detailed nor too condensed).

- The financial statements reflect the underlying transactions and events in a manner that presents the financial position, results of operations, and cash flows stated within a range of acceptable limits that are reasonable and practicable.

In addition, the auditor should follow the guidance in AU Section 431 (Adequacy of Disclosure in Financial Statements) in evaluating the adequacy of disclosure that is not specifically required by GAAP.

Issue 5: When inspecting and counting a client's securities, what should the auditor watch for?

When inspecting and counting a client's securities, the auditor should watch for items such as the following:

- Name of issuer

- Name of registered owner

- Type of security, serial number, and face value or number of shares of stock

- Interest and dividend rates and payment dates

- Maturity dates

- Indication of collateral held

- Alterations and possible forgeries

Issue 6: How can an auditor appropriately substantiate a client's valuation of securities carried at fair value that are listed on a national exchange, but do not trade regularly?

In such circumstances, the auditor should consider independently obtaining estimates of fair value from broker-dealers or other third parties. In addition, it may be prudent to obtain fair-value estimates from more than one source, particularly if a pricing source has a relationship with the client that might cause it to lack objectivity. If the third-party source uses modeling techniques for valuation, the auditor might consider the guidance in AU Section 336 (Using the Work of a Specialist) regarding the use of specialists in an audit engagement. If the client uses a pricing service, the auditor might consider the guidance in AU Section 324 (Service Organizations) concerning service organizations.

Issue 7: How can an auditor go about gathering information about the nature of a service organization's services that are part of an entity's information system for derivatives and securities transactions?

An auditor may be able to gather information about the nature of a service organization's services that are part of an entity's information system for derivatives and securities transactions, or its controls over those services, from a variety of sources such as the following:

- User manuals
- System overviews
- Technical manuals
- The contract between the entity and the service organization
- Reports by auditors, internal auditors, or regulatory authorities on the information system and other controls placed in operation by the service organization
- Inquiry or observation of personnel at the entity or at the service organization
- The auditor's prior experience with the service organization, if the services and the service organization's controls over those services are highly standardized

Issue 8: What sources of information can an auditor use to assess inherent risk related to an entity's derivatives and securities activities?

There are a variety of sources that auditors can use when assessing inherent risk in connection with an entity's derivatives and securities activities, including the following:

- Actual contracts (e.g., interest rate swap agreements)
- Interim financial information that may include transactions relating to derivatives and securities activities
- Inquiries of management
- Minutes of meetings of the board of directors, finance or investment committee, or other committees
- Activity reports of transaction accounts (e.g., securities transaction account)
- Prior experience with the entity or with similar derivatives and securities
- Reports prepared by internal auditors, if any

Issue 9: What are some examples of a service organization's services for derivatives and securities that would be part of a client's information system?

The following are examples of services for derivatives and securities performed by a service organization for an entity that would be part of the entity's information system:

- A pricing service organization that provides fair values of derivatives and securities, through paper documents or electronically, that the entity uses for financial statement reporting.

- A service organization acting as investment adviser or manager that initiates the purchase or sale of equity securities.

- Collecting investment income (e.g., interest, dividends) and distributing that income to the entity.

- Receiving notification of security purchase and sale transactions.

- Receiving notification of corporate actions.

- Maintaining records of securities transactions for the entity.

- Receiving payments from purchasers and disbursing proceeds to sellers for security purchase and sale transactions.

Issue 10: This Section indicates that the auditor may obtain estimates of fair value from various sources, including internally or externally developed valuation models such as the Black-Scholes option-pricing model. What is the Black-Scholes option-pricing model?

The Black-Scholes option-pricing model is a mathematical model for estimating the fair value of options that uses the following five variables:

1. Time to expiration of the option.

2. Exercise or strike price of the option.

3. Risk-free interest rate.

4. Price of the underlying stock.

5. Volatility of the price of the underlying stock.

Although the Black-Scholes option-pricing model is not the only model for estimating the price of options, it is the best known and most widely used.

Issue 11: What attributes should the auditor consider confirming when designing confirmations for derivatives and securities?

When designing confirmations for derivatives and securities, the auditor should consider confirming the following attributes:

- The name of the issuer

- The complete description of the derivative or security

- The investment certificate numbers on the documents

- The name of the owner of the security or the parties to the derivative

- The number of shares of stock or face amount of debt securities

- The terms of the derivative or security

- Any restrictions on disposal

- Any evidence of pledging

ILLUSTRATIONS AND PRACTICE AIDS

ILLUSTRATION 1—REQUEST FOR CONFIRMATION OF SECURITIES HELD BY BROKERS OR OTHER THIRD PARTIES WHEN LISTING OF SECURITIES IS INCLUDED IN THE CONFIRMATION REQUEST

(Prepared on client's letterhead)

(Date)

(Name and address of broker or other third party)

Dear _____:

Our auditors *(insert name and address of auditors)* are conducting an audit of our financial statements as of *(insert date)* and for the *(insert period [e.g., year, quarter])* then ended. Our records show the following information regarding securities belonging to *(insert name of client)* that were held by you for our account as of *(insert date):*

Description	Par or Principal Amount	Number of Shares	Total Cost	Market Value
	$		$	$
	$		$	$
	$		$	$
	$		$	$
	$		$	$

Please check the appropriate response below after determining whether this is in agreement with your records. If there are differences, please provide information in sufficient detail to assist our auditors in reconciling the difference.

After checking the appropriate response below, please sign and date your reply and mail it directly to our auditors in the enclosed return envelope.

Thank you for your anticipated timely cooperation with this request.

Respectfully,

(Name of client)

_____

(Client's authorized signature and title)

****

RESPONSE:

To: *(Insert auditor's name)*

( ) The securities information listed above held for the account of *(insert name of client)* as of *(insert date)* is correct.

( ) The securities information listed above held for the account of *(insert name of client)* as of *(insert date)* is not correct. Our records show the following differences:

_____

_____

_____

Signature: _____

Title: _____

Date: _____

ILLUSTRATION 2—REQUEST FOR CONFIRMATION OF SECURITIES HELD BY BROKERS OR OTHER THIRD PARTIES WHEN LISTING OF SECURITIES IS NOT INCLUDED IN THE CONFIRMATION REQUEST

(Prepared on client's letterhead)

(Date)

(Name and address of broker or other third party)

Dear _____:

Our auditors *(insert name and address of auditors)* are conducting an audit of our financial statements as of *(insert date)* and for the *(insert period [e.g., year, quarter])* then ended. Accordingly, please send directly to them a statement of our account(s) with you as of *(insert date)*, indicating the following information:

    1. Description of securities held by you for our account, including (a) par or principal amount, (b) number of shares, (c) cost, and (d) market value:

        _____

        _____

        _____

    2. Description of securities out for transfer to our name, including (a) par or principal amount, (b) number of shares, (c) cost, and (d) market value:

        _____

        _____

        _____

    3. Amounts payable to or due from us, if any:

        _____

        _____

        _____

    4. A statement of trade activity during the period from *(insert date)* to *(insert date)*:

        _____

        _____

        _____

    Please mail your reply directly to our auditors in the enclosed return envelope. Thank you for your anticipated timely cooperation with this request.

Respectfully,

(Name of client)

_____

(Client's authorized signature and title)

ILLUSTRATION 3—COUNT SHEET OF SECURITIES

Client Name: Date:

                                                      Prepared By:

Financial Statement Date: Reviewed By:

Name of Issuer	Class of Security	Number of Shares	Serial Number	Interest Rate	Maturity Date

ILLUSTRATION 4—INVESTMENTS IN SECURITIES WORKPAPER

Client Name: Date:

                                                      Prepared By:

Financial Statement Date: Reviewed By:

Description of Securities	Beginning Balance		Additions			Disposals					Ending Balance		Market Value
	Number of Shares	Cost	Number of Shares	Date	Cost	Number of Shares	Date	Cost	Proceeds	Realized Gain (Loss)	Number of Shares	Cost	Market Value
Available for Sale													
Security 1													
Security 2													
Total													
Trading:													
Security 1													
Security 2													
Total													
Held to Maturity:													
Security 1													
Security 2													
Total													

ILLUSTRATION 5—EXAMPLES OF MANAGEMENT REPRESENTATIONS THAT MAY BE APPROPRIATE IN CERTAIN SITUATIONS RELATING TO DERIVATIVES AND SECURITIES

Situation/Condition	Illustrative Management Representation
• Management intends to, and has the ability to, hold to maturity debt securities classified as held-to-maturity.	• Debt securities that have been classified as held-to-maturity have been so classified due to management's intent to hold such securities to maturity and the entity's ability to do so. All other debt securities have been classified as available-for-sale or trading.
• Management considers the decline in value of debt or equity securities to be temporary.	• We consider the decline in value of debt or equity securities classified as either available-for-sale or held-to-maturity to be temporary.
• Management has determined the fair value of significant financial instruments that do not have readily determinable market values.	• The methods and significant assumptions used to determine fair values of financial instruments are as follows: [*describe methods and significant assumptions used to determine fair values of financial instruments*]. The methods and significant assumptions used result in a measure of fair value appropriate for financial statement measurement and disclosure purposes.
• There are financial instruments with off-balance-sheet risk and financial instruments with concentrations of credit risk.	• The following information about financial instruments with off-balance-sheet risk and financial instruments with concentrations of credit risk has been properly disclosed in the financial statements: (a) the extent, nature, and terms of financial instruments with off-balance-sheet risk; (b) the amount of credit risk of financial instruments with off-balance-sheet risk and information about the collateral supporting such financial instruments; and (c) significant concentrations of credit risk arising from all financial instruments and information about the collateral supporting such financial instruments.

Situation/Condition	Illustrative Management Representation
• There are unusual considerations involved in determining the application of equity accounting.	• The equity method is used to account for the Company's investment in the common stock of [*investee*] because the Company has the ability to exercise significant influence over the investee's operating and financial policies.
	• The cost method is used to account for the Company's investment in the common stock of [*investee*] because the Company does not have the ability to exercise significant influence over the investee's operating and financial policies

ILLUSTRATION 6—ILLUSTRATIVE AUDIT PROCEDURES FOR DERIVATIVE INSTRUMENTS, HEDGING ACTIVITIES, AND INVESTMENTS IN SECURITIES

	Performed By	Workpaper Reference
Audit Procedures for Investments in Securities (e.g., Bonds, Stocks, and Mutual Funds)		
1. Prepare or obtain from the client a detailed analysis of such investments, showing the following (see sample "Investments in Securities Workpaper" in Illustration 4):		
a. The classification of the securities (i.e., trading, held-to-maturity, or available-for-sale).	_____	_____
b. A detailed description of the security and its terms (e.g., interest rate, maturity date, dividend rate, etc.).	_____	_____
c. The nominal quantity (shares, face value) and the balance at cost, market, or other basis, as applicable, and the balance of unamortized premium or discount as of the end of the prior period.	_____	_____
d. Detail of additions, sales, or disposals for the current period.	_____	_____
e. The nominal quantity (shares, face value) and the balance at cost, market, or other basis, as applicable, and the balance of unamortized premium or discount as of the end of the current period.	_____	_____
f. Valuation allowances as of the beginning and end of the period, and changes in valuation allowances.	_____	_____
g. Detail of investment income.	_____	_____
2. Test the arithmetical accuracy of the analysis.	_____	_____

	Performed By	Workpaper Reference

3. Trace opening balances to the prior-period workpapers and year-end balances to the general ledger.

4. In the presence of the custodian, inspect the securities on hand and determine if they are owned by the client, note serial or certificate numbers, and obtain a signed receipt from the custodian.

5. For investments held by independent third parties, obtain positive confirmation of such securities.

6. If a service organization provides services that are part of a client's information system, determine if it is necessary to inspect supporting documentation, such as securities purchases and sales advices, located at the service organization's facilities.

7. Summarize the terms of preferred stock and debt securities.

8. Determine whether security transactions were properly authorized by examining minutes of board of directors meetings or other committee minutes.

9. Examine bank, broker, or custodian reports of transactions and vouch the cost of significant purchases and the proceeds from significant sales.

10. Trace payments to canceled checks and cash receipts to cash receipts journal.

11. Recompute amortization of premium and/or discount.

12. Compute realized and unrealized gains and/or losses for current and noncurrent portfolios, and ascertain that the method used in determining the cost of securities sold (e.g., first-in, first-out; specific identification; or average cost) was consistently applied.

13. Determine whether unrealized gains or losses have been properly presented and disclosed in the financial statements.

14. Test the reasonableness of investment income (dividends, interest income), if the amount is material.

15. Test the propriety of the classification of securities as trading, held-to-maturity or available-for-sale.

16. Determine whether any security has been pledged or assigned.

17. Determine that any transfers between categories of investments have been properly made and recorded in accordance with GAAP.

18. Consider management's intent and ability in valuing securities, as follows:

    a. Obtain an understanding of the process used by management to classify securities as trading, available-for-sale, or held-to-maturity, and determine that the securities are classified in accordance with GAAP.

	Performed By	Workpaper Reference

b. For investments classified as held-to-maturity, obtain a representation from management in the representation letter about the entity's ability and intent to hold such investments until maturity. _____ _____

c. Consider whether management's activities corroborate or conflict with its stated intent. For example, the auditor should evaluate management's assertion and intent to hold debt securities to maturity by examining evidence such as documentation of management's strategies and sales and other historical activities with respect to those securities and similar securities. _____ _____

d. Determine whether management's activities, contractual agreements, or the entity's financial condition provide evidence of its ability, for example as follows:

   (1) The entity's financial position, working capital needs, operating results, debt agreements, guarantees, alternate sources of liquidity, and other relevant contractual obligations, as well as laws and regulations, may provide evidence about the entity's ability to hold debt securities to their maturity. _____ _____

   (2) Management's cash flow projections may suggest that it does not have the ability to hold debt securities to their maturity. _____ _____

19. See steps 1 through 3 below under "Audit Procedures for Tests of Valuations" and step 1 under "Other Audit Procedures" for audit procedures regarding the valuation of securities, impairment losses, and adequacy of presentation and disclosure in the financial statements. _____ _____

Audit Procedures for Investments in Closely Held Corporations, Partnerships, Joint Ventures, and Investments Carried on the Equity Method

1. Prepare or obtain from the client a detailed analysis of such investments, showing the following:

   a. The name of each investee. _____ _____

   b. Percentage of ownership. _____ _____

   c. The accounting policies of the client/investor. _____ _____

   d. The difference, if any, between the amount at which the investment is carried and the amount of underlying equity in net assets. _____ _____

2. Read executed partnership or similar underlying agreements and other forms of supporting documentation. _____ _____

3. Determine the proper method of accounting for the investment (cost, equity, consolidation). _____ _____

	Performed By	Workpaper Reference

4. Obtain and review copies of the investee's most recent financial statements and the accompanying audit report, if any, and/or tax returns. If necessary, determine if an adjustment to record the current-year equity investment should be made.

5. Review information in the investor's files that relates to the investee (e.g., investee minutes; budgets and cash flows information about the investee).

6. Make inquiries of the investor's management about, and obtain sufficient evidence in support of, the investee's financial results.

7. Apply, or request that the investor arrange with the investee to have another auditor apply, appropriate auditing procedures to the investee's financial statements, if the investee's financial statements are not audited or if the investee auditor's report is not satisfactory.

8. If the carrying amount of the security reflects factors that are not recognized in the investee's financial statements or fair values of assets that are materially different from the investee's carrying amounts, obtain sufficient evidence in support of these amounts.

9. If a time lag between the date of the entity's financial statements and those of the investee has a material effect on the entity's financial statements, determine whether the entity's management has properly considered the lack of comparability.

10. Add an explanatory paragraph to the auditor's report, if a change in time lag occurs that has a material effect on the investor's financial statements.

11. Evaluate sufficiency of audit evidence because of significant differences in fiscal year-ends, significant differences in accounting principles, changes in ownership, changes in conditions affecting the use of the equity method, or the materiality of the investment to the investor's financial position or results of operations.

12. Obtain evidence about material transactions between the entity and the investee and evaluate (a) the propriety of the elimination of unrealized profits and losses on such transactions when the equity method of accounting is used to account for an investment under GAAP and (b) the adequacy of disclosures about material related-party transactions.

13. For subsequent events and transactions of the investee occurring after the date of the investee's financial statements but before the date of the investor auditor's report, read available interim financial statements of the investee and make appropriate inquiries of the investor to identify subsequent events and transactions that are material to the investor's financial statements.

	Performed By	Workpaper Reference

14. Determine whether the investment is properly classified in the financial statements and disclosure, if necessary, is made with respect to summarized information of assets, liabilities, and results of operations of the investee.

15. For an investment accounted for using the equity method, inquire of management as to whether the entity has the ability to exercise significant influence over the operating and financial policies of the investee and evaluate the attendant circumstances that serve as a basis for management's conclusions.

16. If the entity accounts for the investment contrary to the presumption established by GAAP for the use of the equity method, obtain sufficient evidence about whether that presumption has been overcome and whether appropriate disclosure is made regarding the reasons for not accounting for the investment in keeping with that presumption.

17. Evaluate management's conclusion about the need to recognize an impairment loss for a decline in the fair value of the investment below its carrying amount that is other than temporary.

Audit Procedures for Derivative Instruments and Hedging Activities

1. Confirm with counterparties the outstanding transactions as of the balance sheet date, including significant terms and the absence of any side agreements.

2. Confirm with counterparties settled and unsettled transactions.

3. Request counterparties who are frequently used, but with whom the accounting records indicate there are presently no derivatives, to state whether they are counterparties to derivatives with the client.

4. Physically inspect the derivative contract, underlying agreements, and any other forms of supporting documentation.

5. Inspect financial instruments and other agreements to identify embedded derivatives.

6. Inspect documentation, in paper or electronic form, for activity subsequent to the end of the reporting period.

7. If a service organization provides services that are part of a client's information system, determine if it is necessary to inspect supporting documentation, such as derivative contracts, located at the service organization's facilities.

8. Read other information, such as minutes of meetings of the board of directors or finance, investment, or other committees to identify the nature and extent of derivative instruments and hedging activities.

	Performed By	Workpaper Reference

9. Trace payments for purchases of derivatives to canceled checks or wire transfers. _____ _____

10. Gather sufficient appropriate audit evidence to support the amount of unrealized appreciation or depreciation in the fair value of a derivative that is recognized in earnings or other comprehensive income or that is disclosed because of the ineffectiveness of a hedge. _____ _____

11. For hedging activities:

  a. Determine whether management complied with the hedge accounting requirements under GAAP, including designation and documentation requirements. _____ _____

  b. Support management's expectation at the inception of the hedge that the hedging relationship will be highly effective and its ongoing effectiveness will be periodically assessed. _____ _____

  c. Support the recorded change in the hedged item's fair value that is attributable to the hedged risk. _____ _____

  d. Determine whether management has properly applied GAAP to the hedged item. _____ _____

  e. Evaluate management's determination of whether a forecasted transaction that is hedged has a probability of occurring. (Note: GAAP require that the likelihood that the transaction will take place not be based solely on management's intent; rather, the transaction's probability should be supported by observable facts and the attendant circumstances.) _____ _____

12. Obtain written representations from management confirming aspects of management's intent and ability that affect assertions about derivatives, such as to enter into a forecasted transaction for which hedge accounting is applied. _____ _____

13. See steps 1 through 3 below under "Audit Procedures for Tests of Valuations" and step 1 under "Other Audit Procedures" for audit procedures regarding the valuation of derivatives, impairment losses, and adequacy of presentation and disclosure in the financial statements. _____ _____

Audit Procedures for Tests of Valuations

1. For investments in securities and derivative instruments that are valued based on fair value, test such valuations as follows:

  a. Determine whether GAAP specify the method to be used to determine the fair value of the client's securities and derivatives and evaluate whether the determination of fair value is consistent with the specified valuation method. _____ _____

	Performed By	*Workpaper Reference*

b. Obtain quoted market prices from sources such as the following: financial publications, the exchanges, the National Association of Securities Dealers Automated Quotations System (NASDAQ), or pricing services based on sources such as those. _____ _____

c. If quoted market prices for securities or derivatives are obtained from broker-dealers who are market makers in them or through the "Pink Sheets" prices provided by Pink OTC Markets Inc., determine whether special knowledge is required to understand the circumstances in which the quote was developed. (For example, quotations published by Pink OTC Markets Inc. may not be based on recent trades and may only be an indication of interest and not an actual price for which a counterparty will purchase or sell the security or the derivative.) _____ _____

d. If quoted market prices are not available for the security or derivative, obtain estimates of fair value from broker-dealers or other third-party sources based on proprietary valuation models or from the entity based on internally or externally developed valuation models (e.g., market, income, or cost approach). Under these circumstances, also perform the following:

(1) Obtain an understanding of the method used by the broker-dealer or other third-party source in developing the estimate (e.g., whether a pricing model or a cash flow projection was used). _____ _____

(2) Determine whether it is necessary to obtain estimates from more than one pricing source, which may be appropriate if the pricing source has a relationship with the client that might impair its objectivity, or the valuation is based on assumptions that are highly subjective or particularly sensitive to changes in the underlying circumstances. _____ _____

e. For fair-value estimates obtained from broker-dealers and other third-party sources, consider the applicability of the guidance in AU Section 336 (Using the Work of a Specialist) or AU Section 324 (Service Organizations). (For example, the guidance in AU Section 336 may be applicable if the third-party source derives the fair value of the security or derivative by using modeling or similar techniques. On the other hand, if the entity uses a pricing service to obtain prices of securities or derivatives, the guidance in AU Section 324 may be appropriate.) _____ _____

	Performed By	Workpaper Reference

f. If a security or derivative is valued by the entity using a valuation model (e.g., present value of expected future cash flows, option-pricing models), obtain evidence supporting management's assertions about fair value by performing the following procedures, as deemed necessary:

    (1) Assess the reasonableness and appropriateness of the model. Determine whether the valuation model is appropriate for the derivative or security to which it is applied and whether the assumptions used are reasonable and appropriately supported. Consider involving a specialist in assessing the model. _____ _____

    (2) Calculate the value, for example, using a model developed by the auditor or by a specialist engaged by the auditor, to develop an independent expectation to corroborate the reasonableness of the value calculated by the entity. _____ _____

    (3) Compare the fair value with subsequent or recent transactions. _____ _____

g. In situations requiring considerable judgment, consider the guidance in:

    (1) AU Section 342 on obtaining and evaluating sufficient appropriate audit evidence to support significant accounting estimates. _____ _____

    (2) AU Section 336 on the use of the work of a specialist in performing substantive procedures. _____ _____

h. If collateral (e.g., negotiable securities, real estate, property, etc.) is an important factor in evaluating the fair value and collectibility of the security, obtain evidence regarding the existence, fair value, and transferability of such collateral as well as the investor's rights to the collateral. _____ _____

i. Determine if there have been material declines in market values subsequent to the balance sheet date. _____ _____

2. For investments in securities that are valued based on cost, test such valuations as follows:

a. Inspect documentation of the purchase price. _____ _____

b. Confirm the purchase price with the issuer or holder. _____ _____

c. Test discount or premium amortization, either by recomputation or analytical procedures. _____ _____

d. Evaluate management's conclusion about the need to recognize an impairment loss for a decline in the security's fair value below its cost that is other than temporary (see step 3 below). _____ _____

	Performed By	Workpaper Reference

3. Regardless of the valuation method used, evaluate the need to recognize in earnings an impairment loss for a decline in fair value that is other than temporary, as follows:

   a. Evaluate whether management has considered relevant information and factors such as the ones below in

   reaching its conclusions about the need to recognize an impairment loss:

   (1) Fair value is significantly below cost and:

   (i) The decline is attributable to adverse conditions specifically related to the security or to specific conditions in an industry or in a geographic area.   _____   _____

   (ii) The decline has existed for an extended period of time.   _____   _____

   (iii) Management does not possess both the intent and the ability to hold the security for a period of time sufficient to allow for any anticipated recovery in fair value.   _____   _____

   (2) The security has been downgraded by a rating agency.   _____   _____

   (3) The financial condition of the issuer has deteriorated.   _____   _____

   (4) Dividends have been reduced or eliminated, or scheduled interest payments have not been made.   _____   _____

   (5) The entity recorded losses from the security subsequent to the end of the reporting period.   _____   _____

   b. When the entity has recognized an impairment loss, gather evidence supporting the amount of the impairment adjustment recorded and determine whether the entity has appropriately followed GAAP.   _____   _____

Other Audit Procedures

1. Evaluate whether the presentation and disclosure of derivatives and securities are in conformity with GAAP as follows:

   a. Determine whether the accounting principles selected and applied have general acceptance.   _____   _____

   b. Determine whether the accounting principles are appropriate in the circumstances.   _____   _____

   c. Determine whether the financial statements, including the related notes, are informative of matters that may affect their use, understanding, and interpretation.   _____   _____

	Performed By	Workpaper Reference

d.   Determine whether the information presented in the financial statements is classified and summarized in a reasonable manner (i.e., neither too detailed nor too condensed).   _____   _____

e.   Determine whether the financial statements reflect the underlying transactions and events in a manner that presents the financial position, results of operations, and cash flows stated within a range of acceptable limits that are reasonable and practicable.   _____   _____

f.   Consider the form, arrangement, and content of the financial statements and their notes, including, for example, the terminology used, the amount of detail given, the classification of items in the statements, and the bases of amounts reported.   _____   _____

g.   Compare the presentation and disclosure with the requirements of GAAP.   _____   _____

h.   Follow the guidance in AU Section 431 (Adequacy of Disclosure in Financial Statements) in evaluating the adequacy of disclosure that is not specifically required by GAAP.   _____   _____

2.   If the auditor is concerned about the risk of fraud, audit procedures such as the following should be considered in addition to the ones listed above:

a.   Consider using the work of a specialist in determining the fair value of the securities or derivatives, and scrutinize the specialist's qualifications, integrity, and results.   _____   _____

b.   Verify the fair value of securities using multiple brokers or third parties.   _____   _____

c.   Perform predictive tests of investment income and scrutinize amounts that look out of line with expectations.   _____   _____

d.   Evaluate the underlying assumptions used in valuing the securities or derivatives and scrutinize valuations that look out of line with expectations.   _____   _____

e.   Evaluate the legitimacy and financial viability of the custodian when confirming investments, including verifying the proper address of the custodian.   _____   _____

f.   Insist on inspecting original supporting documents rather than copies (e.g., original security certificates, brokers' statements).   _____   _____

g.   Expand tests of details and trace all transactions to the appropriate accounts.   _____   _____

h.   Trace sales proceeds and investment income to bank statements.   _____   _____

i.   Trace cost of investment purchases to cancelled checks and bank statements.   _____   _____

	Performed By	Workpaper Reference

j. Review all journal entries related to investments and examine supporting documents.

k. Scrutinize and investigate investments acquired in exchange for non-cash assets or company stock.

3. For transfers of financial assets, determine that the transaction has been accounted for in accordance with GAAP, as follows:

    a. If a transfer of financial assets has been accounted for as a sale by the client, determine that all of the following conditions have been met:

        (1) The transferred assets have been isolated from the client—put

        presumptively beyond the reach of the client and its creditors, even in bankruptcy or other receivership.

        (2) Each transferee has the right to pledge or exchange the assets (or beneficial interests) it received, and no condition both constrains the transferee from taking advantage of its right to pledge or exchange and provides more than a trivial benefit to the client.

        (3) The client does not maintain effective control over the transferred assets.

    b. Upon completion of a transfer of assets by a client that satisfies the conditions to be accounted for as a sale as described in step a. above, determine that the client:

        (1) Has derecognized all assets sold.

        (2) Has recognized all assets obtained and liabilities incurred in consideration as proceeds of the sale, including: cash; put or call options held or written (for example, guarantee or recourse obligations); forward commitments (for example, commitments to deliver additional receivables during the revolving periods of some securitizations); swaps (for example, provisions that convert interest rates from fixed to variable); and servicing liabilities, if applicable.

        (3) Has initially measured at fair value assets obtained and liabilities incurred in a sale or, if it is not practicable to estimate the fair value of an asset or a liability, has applied alternative measures.

        (4) Has recognized in earnings any gain or loss on the sale.

    c. Upon completion of any transfer of financial assets in which the client is the transferor, determine that the client:

	Performed By	Workpaper Reference

(1) Has continued to carry in its statement of financial position any retained interest in the transferred assets, including, if applicable: servicing assets, beneficial interests in assets transferred to a qualifying special-purpose entity in a securitization, and retained undivided interests. _____ _____

(2) Has allocated the previous carrying amount between the assets sold, if any, and the retained interests, if any, based on their relative fair values at the date of transfer. _____ _____

d. If the client is the transferee, determine that the client has recognized all assets obtained and any liabilities incurred and initially measured them at fair value (in aggregate, presumptively the price paid). _____ _____

e. If a transfer of financial assets in exchange for cash or other consideration (other than beneficial interests in the transferred assets) does not meet the criteria for a sale in step a. above, determine that the transfer has been accounted for as a secured borrowing with pledge of collateral. _____ _____

AU SECTION 333
MANAGEMENT REPRESENTATIONS

PRACTICE POINT: As part of its Clarity Project, the American Institute of Certified Public Accountants' (AICPA's) Auditing Standards Board (ASB) has finalized a clarified Statement on Auditing Standards (SAS) titled, "Written Representations," which supersedes AU Section 333 (Management Representations). The clarified SAS does not change or expand existing requirements in extant AU Section 333 in any significant respect.

The ASB is expected to issue many of the clarified standards in *one* SAS that will be codified in "AU Section" format. The ASB has decided that the effective date of the clarified SASs that have not yet been issued is for audits of financial statements for periods ending on or after December 15, 2012. Auditors should be alert to and monitor further developments in this area.

WHAT EVERY PRACTITIONER SHOULD KNOW

Basic Requirements

The auditor should obtain a written letter of representations from management for all financial statements and periods covered by the auditor's report. Therefore, when reporting on comparative financial statements, the written letter of representations obtained at the completion of the most recent audit should address all periods being reported on. The management representations letter is not a substitute for other auditing procedures but nevertheless represents an essential component of audit evidence.

Contents of the Management Representations Letter

The specific written representations that the auditor obtains will depend on the circumstances of the engagement and the nature and basis of presentation of the financial statements. However, such representations ordinarily should cover the following matters:

1. Management's acknowledgment of its responsibility for the fair presentation in the financial statements of financial position, results of operations, and cash flows in conformity with GAAP.
2. Management's belief that the financial statements are fairly presented in conformity with GAAP.
3. Availability of all financial records and related data.
4. Completeness and availability of all minutes of the meetings of stockholders, directors, and committees of directors.
5. Communications from regulatory agencies concerning noncompliance with or deficiencies in financial reporting practices.
6. Absence of unrecorded transactions.
7. Management's belief that the effects of any uncorrected financial statement misstatements aggregated by the auditor during the current en-

gagement and pertaining to the latest period presented are immaterial, both individually and in the aggregate, to the financial statements taken as a whole. A summary of such items should be included in or attached to the representations letter.

8. Management's acknowledgment of its responsibility for the design and implementation of programs and controls to prevent and detect fraud.

9. Management's knowledge of any fraud or suspected fraud affecting the entity involving (1) management, (2) employees who have significant roles in the internal control, or (3) others where the fraud could be material.

10. Management's knowledge of any allegations of fraud or suspected fraud affecting the entity received in communications from employees, former employees, analysts, regulators, short sellers, or others.

11. Plans or intentions that may affect the carrying value or classification of assets and liabilities.

12. Information concerning related-party transactions and amounts receivable from or payable to related parties.

13. Guarantees, whether written or oral, under which the Company is contingently liable.

14. Significant estimates and material concentrations known to management that are required to be disclosed in accordance with the FASB Accounting Standards Codification (ASC) 275, *Risks and Uncertainties*.

15. Violations or possible violations of laws or regulations whose effects should be considered for disclosure in the financial statements or as a basis for recording a loss contingency.

16. Unasserted claims or assessments that the entity's lawyer has advised are probable of assertion and must be disclosed in accordance with ASC 450, *Contingencies*.

17. Other liabilities and gain or loss contingencies that are required to be accrued or disclosed by ASC 450.

18. Satisfactory title to assets, liens or encumbrances on assets, and assets pledged as collateral.

19. Compliance with aspects of contractual agreements that may affect the financial statements.

20. Information concerning subsequent events.

Management's representations may be limited to matters that are considered, either individually or collectively, material to the financial statements, provided management and the auditor have reached an understanding on the limits of materiality for this purpose. This materiality level may be stated explicitly in the representations letter, either qualitatively or quantitatively. However, materiality considerations do not apply to items that are not directly related to amounts included in the financial statements (for example, items 1, 3, 4, 5, and 8 above).

A "Management Representations Letter," which follows the authoritative guidance in this Section, is presented in Illustration 1. Illustration 2 provides examples of additional management representations that may be appropriate.

Signing and Dating Requirements

Management representations should be made as of the date of the auditor's report because the auditor is concerned with events occurring through the date of his or her report that may require adjustment to or disclosure in the financial statements. If the report is dual dated, the auditor should consider whether obtaining additional representations for subsequent events is needed. The representations letter should be signed by members of management who have overall responsibility for financial and operating matters and who are responsible for and knowledgeable about the items enumerated in the letter.

Updating Management's Representations Letter

The auditor should obtain an updated representations letter from management under certain circumstances, including the following:

- When a predecessor auditor is requested by a former client to reissue (or consent to the reuse of) his or her report on the financial statements of a prior period.

- When the auditor is performing subsequent events procedures in connection with filings under the Securities Act of 1933. Additional guidance is provided in AU Section 711 (Filings under Federal Securities Statutes) in these situations.

The updated management representations letter should state (a) whether any of the previous representations should be modified and (b) whether any subsequent events have occurred that would require adjustment to or disclosure in the financial statements.

An "Updating Management Representations Letter," which follows the authoritative guidance in this Section, is presented in Illustration 3.

Management's Refusal to Furnish Written Representations

Management's refusal to furnish the auditor with a written letter of representations constitutes a limitation on the scope of the auditor's examination sufficient to preclude an unqualified opinion. Therefore, the auditor should generally either disclaim an opinion or withdraw from the engagement. However, based on the nature of the representations not obtained or the circumstances of the refusal, the auditor may conclude that a qualified opinion is appropriate. The auditor also should consider and evaluate the effects of management's refusal to furnish a representations letter on his or her ability to rely on other management representations.

PRACTICE ISSUES AND FREQUENTLY ASKED QUESTIONS

Issue 1: What are the primary purposes for obtaining a management representations letter?

The primary purposes for obtaining a management representations letter are to (1) ensure that management accepts its responsibility for the assertions in the entity's financial statements and (2) document the responses from management to the auditor's inquiries about various aspects of the audit. The management representations letter provides written documentation of management representations in the event of a disagreement or a lawsuit between the auditor and the client.

Issue 2: Who generally should sign the management representations letter?

Generally, the chief executive officer and chief financial officer, or others in equivalent positions in the entity, should sign the representations letter. Other officers and employees whose functions include significant responsibility for the financial reporting process also may be asked to sign the letter.

Issue 3: What are the audit implications if current management was not present during all periods covered by the auditor's report and, therefore, is unwilling to provide certain representations relating to those periods?

If current management was not present during all periods covered by the auditor's report, the auditor should, nevertheless, obtain written representations from current management on all periods covered in the auditor's report. The specific written representations will depend on the circumstances of the engagement and the nature and basis of presentation of the financial statements. Management's representations may be limited to matters that are considered, either individually or collectively, material to the financial statements.

Legitimate reasons may exist for the new management's inability to make representations about the financial statements. The auditor must consider those reasons, and the adequacy of the representations that management is able, or willing to make. If the auditor is unable to obtain representations that are in his or her professional judgment necessary, a limitation on the scope of the audit exists that is sufficient to preclude an unqualified opinion. Furthermore, the auditor should consider the effect of management's refusal on his or her ability to rely on other management representations.

Issue 4: There appears to be an ongoing debate about whether the representations letter should include any discussion of materiality levels as permitted by this Section. What are the current practice trends on this issue?

Presently, some auditors choose not to have management quantify an understanding about materiality levels in the representations letter. Professional standards do not prohibit this. Those who choose not to do so point out that such a representation could, in the event of a misunderstanding, easily work to the auditor's detriment. They also argue that making a quantitative statement about the auditor's perception of materiality to management could facilitate its concealment of material misstatements.

On the other hand, proponents of including a discussion of materiality levels in the representations letter state that there may be good reasons for including this in the letter, such as previous misunderstandings with management, or simply a stated preference on management's part. They further point out that astute management will recognize that the auditor is always free to examine items that fall outside any stated or perceived range of materiality.

Issue 5: Can the owner-manager of a small company indicate in the management representations letter that his knowledge of GAAP is limited and that he places some reliance on the independent auditor for advice in this area?

Yes. The standards do not prohibit the owner from including language to the effect that his knowledge of GAAP is limited, and that he has engaged the auditor to advise him in fulfilling his responsibility, as long as the owner-manager expressly takes on that responsibility. Therefore, the owner must acknowledge in the management representations letter his responsibility for the financial statements, including their conformity with GAAP.

Issue 6: Why is a predecessor auditor who is requested by a former client to reissue his or her report on the financial statements of a prior period required to obtain an updating representations letter from management?

Because the predecessor auditor no longer serves as the company's auditor and because his or her opinion is to appear along with the successor auditor's report in a comparative presentation, the predecessor is not in a position to be aware of subsequent events that might affect the financial statements. Accordingly, the predecessor should request an update to the former client's representations through the current date, and a statement that no information has come to management's attention that would cause their previous representations to be modified, and that no events have occurred that would require adjustments to or disclosures in the previously issued financial statements. The updated letter should make reference to the original letter, but need not repeat each of its representations.

Issue 7: What implications does a qualified opinion on an audit due to a material departure from GAAP have on the management representations letter?

The representations of management and the auditor's report must be consistent with one another. There have been instances in practice in which an auditor has issued a qualified opinion for a GAAP departure, but where management has represented in the representations letter that the financial statements are fairly presented. This oversight most often results from failure to appropriately modify the standard language in a representations letter copied from a word processing template. This is a serious departure from professional standards, because it undermines the credibility of management's representations as a whole.

Issue 8: If the auditor audits the financial statements of a subsidiary but not those of the parent company, is he or she required to obtain representations from management of the parent company?

No. However, if the auditor performs an audit of the financial statements of a subsidiary but does not audit those of the parent company, he or she may want to obtain representations from management of the parent company concerning matters that may effect the subsidiary. Examples include significant related-party transactions or the parent company's intent to provide continuing financial support to the subsidiary.

Issue 9: What are the implications of a situation whereby the auditor is precluded from performing certain audit procedures with respect to a matter that management has given written representations about?

The auditor obtains written representations from management to complement other auditing procedures. Therefore, representations from management are not a substitute for the application of auditing procedures considered necessary by the auditor. If management precludes the auditor from performing procedures he or she considers necessary with respect to a certain matter that is material to the financial statements, even though management has given representations about the matter, a limitation on the scope of the audit exists. In these circumstances, the auditor should express a qualified opinion or disclaim an opinion on the financial statements.

Issue 10: As part of the management representations letter, the auditor is required to provide the client a summary of any uncorrected financial statement misstatements. Does this Section require the auditor to follow a specific format when providing this information to the client?

No. While the summary of any uncorrected financial statement misstatements should be included in or attached to the management representations letter, the format in which this information is provided to the client is flexible. The summary can simply be the auditor's passed audit adjustment worksheet that lists the adjustments the auditor determined to be immaterial, individually and in the aggregate, to the financial statements as a whole. Exactly how the auditor summarizes this information is a matter of professional judgment. Some auditors may wish to merely print the passed audit adjustment worksheet and make it an attachment to the representations letter; others may want to summarize the information in a narrative format. Illustration 3, "Worksheet for Analysis of Unrecorded Audit Differences," in AU Section 312 (Audit Risk and Materiality in Conducting an Audit) presents an example of a form that the auditor might use to provide the client such a summary.

In addition, in complying with this requirement in the management representations letter, the auditor should consider the following additional guidance:

1. If management believes that certain of the identified items are not misstatements, management's belief may be acknowledged by adding to the representations letter, for example: "We do not agree that items [X] and [Y] constitute misstatements because [*description of reasons*]."

2. The auditor may designate an amount below which misstatements need not be accumulated in the passed audit adjustment worksheet. Similarly, the summary of uncorrected misstatements included in, or attached to, the representations letter need not include such misstatements.

3. The summary of uncorrected misstatements should include sufficient information to provide management with an understanding of the nature, amount, and effect of the uncorrected misstatements.

4. Similar uncorrected misstatements may be aggregated.

5. If the client has recorded all the audit adjustments, including those determined to be immaterial, the representations letter may be modified

to indicate that there is no summary of unrecorded misstatements since all adjustments proposed by the auditor, material and immaterial, have been recorded.

ILLUSTRATIONS AND PRACTICE AIDS

ILLUSTRATION 1—MANAGEMENT REPRESENTATIONS LETTER

(Prepared on client's letterhead)

(Date)

To *(Independent auditor)*

We are providing this letter in connection with your audit(s) of the *(identify the financial statements, e.g., balance sheet, statement of operations, and statement of cash flows)* of *(name of entity)* as of *(dates)* and for the *(periods)* then ended, for the purpose of expressing an opinion as to whether the *(consolidated)* financial statements present fairly, in all material respects, the financial position, results of operations, and cash flows of *(name of entity)* in conformity with accounting principles generally accepted in the United States of America. We confirm that we are responsible for the fair presentation in the *(consolidated)* financial statements of financial position, results of operations, and cash flows in conformity with generally accepted accounting principles.

Certain representations in this letter are described as being limited to matters that are material. Items are considered material, regardless of size, if they involve an omission or misstatement of accounting information that, in the light of surrounding circumstances, makes it probable that the judgment of a reasonable person relying on the information would be changed or influenced by the omission or misstatement.

We confirm, to the best of our knowledge and belief, as of *(date of auditor's report)*, the following representations made to you during your audit(s).

1. The financial statements referred to above are fairly presented in conformity with accounting principles generally accepted in the United States of America.

2. We have made available to you all:

   a. Financial records and related data.

   b. Minutes of the meetings of stockholders, directors, and committees of directors, or summaries of actions of recent meetings for which minutes have not yet been prepared.

3. There have been no communications from regulatory agencies concerning noncompliance with or deficiencies in financial reporting practices.

4. There are no material transactions that have not been properly recorded in the accounting records underlying the financial statements.

5. We believe that the effects of the uncorrected misstatements in the financial statements summarized in the attached schedule and aggregated by you during the current engagement are immaterial, both individually and in the aggregate, to the financial statements taken as a

whole.[1] (If no uncorrected misstatements were identified, this item should be eliminated.)

6. We acknowledge our responsibility for the design and implementation of programs and controls to prevent and detect fraud.

7. We have no knowledge of any fraud or suspected fraud affecting the entity involving (1) management, (2) employees who have significant roles in internal control, or (3) others where the fraud could have a material effect on the financial statements.

8. We have no knowledge of any allegations of fraud or suspected fraud affecting the entity received in communications from employees, former employees, analysts, regulators, short sellers, or others.

9. The Company has no plans or intentions that may materially affect the carrying value or classification of assets and liabilities.

10. The following have been properly recorded or disclosed in the financial statements:

    a. Related-party transactions, including sales, purchases, loans, transfers, leasing arrangements, and guarantees, and amounts receivable from or payable to related parties.

    b. Guarantees, whether written or oral, under which the Company is contingently liable.

    c. Significant estimates and material concentrations known to management that are required to be disclosed in accordance with FASB Accounting Standards Codification (ASC) 275, *Risks and Uncertainties*. Significant estimates are estimates at the balance sheet date that could change materially within the next year. Concentrations refer to volumes of business, revenues, available sources of supply, or markets or geographic areas for which events could occur that would significantly disrupt normal finances within the next year.

11. There are no:

    a. Violations or possible violations of laws or regulations whose effects should be considered for disclosure in the financial statements or as a basis for recording a loss contingency.

    b. Unasserted claims or assessments that our lawyer has advised are probable of assertion and must be disclosed in accordance with ASC 450, *Contingencies*.[2]

    c. Other liabilities or gain or loss contingencies that are required to be accrued or disclosed by ASC 450.

12. The Company has satisfactory title to all owned assets, and there are no liens or encumbrances on such assets nor has any asset been pledged as collateral.

13. We have complied with all aspects of contractual agreements that would have a material effect on the financial statements in the event of noncompliance.

14. We represent to you the following for the Company's fair value measurements and disclosures:

    a. The underlying assumptions are reasonable and they appropriately reflect management's intent and ability to carry out its stated courses of action.

    b. The measurement methods and related assumptions used in determining fair value are appropriate in the circumstances and have been consistently applied.

    c. The disclosures related to fair values are complete, adequate, and in conformity with GAAP.

    d. There are no subsequent events that require adjustment to the fair value measurements and disclosures included in the financial statements.

(Add additional representations that are unique to the entity's business or industry. See Illustration 2 below for illustrative examples of additional representations.)

To the best of our knowledge and belief, no events have occurred subsequent to the balance sheet date and through the date of this letter that would require adjustment to or disclosure in the aforementioned financial statements.

_____

(Name of Chief Executive Officer and Title)

_____

(Name of Chief Financial Officer and Title)

PRACTICE POINT: [1]If management believes that certain of the identified items are not misstatements, management's belief may be acknowledged by adding to the representations letter, for example: "We do not agree that items [X] and [Y] constitute misstatements because [*description of reasons*]."

[2]If the entity has not consulted a lawyer regarding litigation, claims, and assessments, the auditor normally would rely on the review of internally available information and obtain a written representation from management regarding the lack of litigation, claims, and assessments (see AU Section 337 for additional guidance), such as the following:

> "We are not aware of any pending or threatened litigation, claims, or assessments or unasserted claims or assessments that are required to be accrued or disclosed in the financial statements in accordance with ASC 450, *Contingencies,* and we have not consulted a lawyer concerning litigation, claims, or assessments."

ILLUSTRATION 2—ADDITIONAL ILLUSTRATIVE MANAGEMENT REPRESENTATIONS

General

Interim Financial Information

Unaudited interim information accompanies the financial statements.

The unaudited interim financial information accompanying [*presented in Note X to*] the financial statements for the [*identify all related periods*] has been prepared and presented in conformity with generally accepted accounting principles applicable to interim financial information [*and with Item 302(a) of Regulation S-K*]. The accounting principles used to prepare the unaudited interim financial information are consistent with those used to prepare the audited financial statements.

Accounting Changes

The effect of a new accounting principle is not known.

We have not completed the process of evaluating the effect of adopting ASC [*XXX*], [*Title*], as discussed in Note [*X*]. The Company is therefore unable to disclose the effect that adopting ASC [*XXX*], [*Title*], will have on its financial position and the results of operations when such ASC Topic is adopted.

There is justification for a change in accounting principles.

We believe that [*describe the newly adopted accounting principle*] is preferable to [*describe the former accounting principle*] because [*describe management's justification for the change in accounting principles*].

Going Concern

Financial circumstances are strained, with disclosure of management's intentions and the entity's ability to continue as a going concern.

Note [*X*] to the financial statements discloses all of the matters of which we are aware that are relevant to the entity's ability to continue as a going concern, including significant conditions and events, and management's plans.

Variable Interest Entities

The company has a variable interest in another entity.

Variable interest entities (VIEs) and potential VIEs and transactions with VIEs and potential VIEs have been properly recorded and disclosed in the financial statements in accordance with U.S. GAAP.

We have considered both implicit and explicit variable interests in (a) determining whether potential VIEs should be considered VIEs, (b) calculating expected losses and residual returns, and (c) determining which party, if any, is the primary beneficiary.

We have provided you with lists of all identified variable interests in (i) VIEs, (ii) potential VIEs that we considered but judged not to be VIEs, and (iii) entities that were afforded the scope exceptions of FASB Accounting Standards Codification (ASC) 810, *Consolidation*.

We have advised you of all transactions with identified VIEs, potential VIEs, or entities afforded the scope exceptions of ASC 810.

We have made available all relevant information about financial interests and contractual arrangements with related parties, de facto agents and other entities, including but not limited to, their governing documents, equity and debt instruments, contracts, leases, guarantee arrangements, and other financial contracts and arrangements.

The information we provided about financial interests and contractual arrangements with related parties, de facto agents, and other entities includes information about all transactions, unwritten understandings, agreement modifications, and written and oral side agreements.

Our computations of expected losses and expected residual returns of entities that are VIEs and potential VIEs are based on the best information available and include all reasonably possible outcomes.

Regarding entities in which the Company has variable interests (implicit and explicit), we have provided all information about events and changes in circumstances that could potentially cause reconsideration about whether the entities are VIEs or whether the Company is the primary beneficiary or has a significant variable interest in the entity.

We have made and continue to make exhaustive efforts to obtain information about entities in which the Company has an implicit or explicit interest but that were excluded from complete analysis under ASC 810 due to lack of essential information to determine one or more of the following: whether the entity is a VIE, whether the Company is the primary beneficiary, or the accounting required to consolidate the entity.

Use of a Specialist

The entity has used the work of a specialist.

We agree with the findings of specialists in evaluating the [*describe assertion*] and have adequately considered the qualifications of the specialist in determining the amounts and disclosures used in the financial statements and underlying accounting records. We did not give or cause any instructions to be given to specialists with respect to the values or amounts derived in an attempt to bias their work, and we are not otherwise aware of any matters that have had impact on the independence or objectivity of the specialists.

Assets

Cash

Disclosure is required of compensating balances or other arrangements involving restrictions on cash balances, line of credit, or similar arrangements.

Arrangements with financial institutions involving compensating balances or other arrangements involving restrictions on cash balances, line of credit, or similar arrangements have been properly disclosed.

Financial Instruments/Derivatives

Management intends to, and has the ability to, hold to maturity debt securities classified as held-to-maturity.

Debt securities that have been classified as held-to-maturity have been so classified due to management's intent to hold such securities to maturity and the entity's ability to do so. All other debt securities have been classified as available-for-sale or trading.

Management considers the decline in value of debt or equity securities to be temporary.

We consider the decline in value of debt or equity securities classified as either available-for-sale or held-to-maturity to be temporary.

Management has determined the fair value of significant financial instruments that do not have readily determinable market values.

The methods and significant assumptions used to determine fair values of financial instruments are as follows: [*describe methods and significant assumptions used to determine fair values of financial instruments*]. The methods and significant assumptions used result in a measure of fair value appropriate for financial statement measurement and disclosure purposes.

There are financial instruments with off-balance-sheet risk and financial instruments with concentrations of credit risk.

The following information about financial instruments with off-balance-sheet risk and financial instruments with concentrations of credit risk has been properly disclosed in the financial statements: (a) the extent, nature, and terms of financial instruments with off-balance-sheet risk; (b) the amount of credit risk of financial instruments with off-balance-sheet risk and information about the collateral supporting such financial instruments; and (c) significant concentrations of credit risk arising from all financial instruments and information about the collateral supporting such financial instruments.

Receivables

Receivables have been recorded in the financial statements.

Receivables recorded in the financial statements represent valid claims against debtors for sales or other charges arising on or before the balance sheet date and have been appropriately reduced to their estimated net realizable value.

Inventories

Excess or obsolete inventories exist.

Provision has been made to reduce excess or obsolete inventories to their estimated net realizable value.

Investments

There are unusual considerations involved in determining the application of equity accounting.

- The equity method is used to account for the Company's investment in the common stock of [*investee*] because the Company has the ability to exercise significant influence over the investee's operating and financial policies.

- The cost method is used to account for the Company's investment in the common stock of [*investee*] because the Company does not have the ability to exercise significant influence over the investee's operating and financial policies.

Long-Lived Assets to Be Held and Used

The possibility exists that the value of specific significant long-lived assets or certain identifiable intangibles may be impaired.

We have reviewed long-lived assets and certain identifiable intangibles to be held and used for impairment whenever events or changes in circumstances have indicated that the carrying amount of the assets might not be recoverable, and have appropriately recorded the adjustment.

The entity's estimates of future cash flows are reasonable.

The entity's estimates of future cash flows are based on reasonable and supportable assumptions regarding the cash flows expected to result from the use of the assets and their eventual disposition.

Goodwill

Management's acknowledgment of its review of goodwill for impairment.

Management, using its best estimates based on reasonable and supportable assumptions and projections, reviews for impairment of goodwill whenever events or changes in circumstances indicate that the carrying amount of goodwill might not be recoverable. Management acknowledges that the entity has tested goodwill for impairment in accordance with the requirements of ASC 350, *Intangibles—Goodwill and Other*, and impairment losses have been recorded when required.

No impairment is recorded because the implied fair value of the reporting unit's goodwill exceeded its carrying amount.

Although the carrying amount of XYZ reporting unit [*identify the reporting unit*] exceeded its fair value, the entity has not recorded an impairment loss because the implied fair value of the reporting unit's goodwill exceeded its carrying amount.

Fair value measurements of reporting units and goodwill are reasonable.

The determination of fair value of reporting units and the implied fair value of goodwill were based on reasonable and supportable assumptions.

Deferred Charges

Material expenditures have been deferred.

We believe that all material expenditures that have been deferred to future periods will be recoverable.

Deferred Tax Assets

A deferred tax asset exists at the balance sheet date.

- The valuation allowance has been determined pursuant to the provisions of ASC 740, *Income Taxes*), including the entity's estimation of future taxable income, if necessary, and is adequate to reduce the total deferred tax asset to an amount that will more likely than not be realized. [*Complete with appropriate wording detailing how the entity determined the valuation allowance against the deferred tax asset.*]

- A valuation allowance against deferred tax assets at the balance sheet date is not considered necessary because it is more likely than not the deferred tax asset will be fully realized.

Liabilities

Debt

Short-term debt could be refinanced on a long-term basis and management intends to do so.

The entity has excluded short-term obligations totalling $[*amount*] from current liabilities, because the entity intends to refinance the obligations on a long-term basis. [*Complete with appropriate wording detailing how amounts will be refinanced, as follows:*]

- The entity has issued a long-term obligation (debt security) after the date of the balance sheet but prior to the issuance of the financial statements for the purpose of refinancing the short-term obligations on a long-term basis.
- The entity has the ability to consummate the refinancing, by using the financing agreement referred to in Note [X] to the financial statements.

Tax-exempt bonds have been issued.

Tax-exempt bonds issued have retained their tax-exempt status.

Taxes

Management intends to reinvest undistributed earnings of a foreign subsidiary.

We intend to reinvest the undistributed earnings of [*name of foreign subsidiary*].

Contingencies

Estimates and disclosures have been made of environmental remediation liabilities and related loss contingencies.

Provision has been made for any material loss that is probable from environmental remediation liabilities associated with [*name of site*]. We believe that such estimate is reasonable based on available information and that the liabilities and related loss contingencies and the expected outcome of uncertainties have been adequately described in the entity's financial statements.

Agreements may exist to repurchase assets previously sold.

Agreements to repurchase assets previously sold have been properly disclosed.

Pension and Postretirement Benefits

An actuary has been used to measure pension liabilities and costs.

We believe that the actuarial assumptions and methods used to measure pension liabilities and costs for financial accounting purposes are appropriate in the circumstances.

There is involvement with a multiemployer plan.

We are unable to determine the possibility of a withdrawal liability in a multiemployer benefit plan.

Postretirement benefits have been eliminated.

- We do not intend to compensate for the elimination of postretirement benefits by granting an increase in pension benefits.
- We plan to compensate for the elimination of postretirement benefits by granting an increase in pension benefits in the amount of $XX.

Employee layoffs that would otherwise lead to a curtailment of a benefit plan are intended to be temporary.

Current employee layoffs are intended to be temporary.

Management intends to either continue to make or not make frequent amendments to its pension or other postretirement benefit plans, which may affect the amortization period of prior service cost, or has expressed a substantive commitment to increase benefits obligations.

- We plan to continue to make frequent amendments to the entity's pension or other postretirement benefit plans, which may affect the amortization period of prior service cost.
- We do not plan to make frequent amendments to the entity's pension or other postretirement benefit plans.

Equity

There are capital stock repurchase options or agreements or capital stock reserved for options, warrants, conversions, or other requirements.

Capital stock repurchase options or agreements or capital stock reserved for options, warrants, conversions, or other requirements have been properly disclosed.

Income Statement

There may be a loss from sales commitments.

Provisions have been made for losses to be sustained in the fulfillment of, or from inability to fulfill, any sales commitments.

There may be losses from purchase commitments.

Provisions have been made for losses to be sustained as a result of purchase commitments for inventory quantities in excess of normal requirements or at prices in excess of prevailing market prices.

Nature of the product or industry indicates the possibility of undisclosed sales returns.

We have fully disclosed to you all sales terms, including all rights of return or price adjustments and all warranty provisions.

ILLUSTRATION 3—UPDATING MANAGEMENT REPRESENTATIONS LETTER

(Prepared on client's letterhead)

(Date)

To (Independent auditor)

In connection with your audit(s) of the [*identify the financial statements, e.g., balance sheet, statement of operations, and statement of cash flows*] of [*name of entity*] as of [*dates*] and for the [*periods*] then ended, for the purpose of expressing an opinion as to whether the [*consolidated*] financial statements present fairly, in all material respects, the financial position, results of operations, and cash flows of [*name of entity*] in conformity with accounting principles generally accepted in the United States of America, you were previously provided with a representation letter under date of [*date of previous representation letter*]. No information has come to our attention that would cause us to believe that any of those previous representations should be modified.

To the best of our knowledge and belief, no events have occurred subsequent to [*date of latest balance sheet reported on by the auditor*] and through the date of this letter that would require adjustment to or disclosure in the aforementioned financial statements.

[*Name of Chief Executive Officer and Title*]

[*Name of Chief Financial Officer and Title*]

PRACTICE POINT: If matters exist that should be disclosed to the auditor, they should be indicated in a list following the representation. For example, if an event subsequent to the date of the balance sheet has been disclosed in the financial statements, the final paragraph could be modified as follows:

"To the best of our knowledge and belief, except as discussed in Note [X] to the financial statements, no events have occurred . . . ."

AU SECTION 334
RELATED PARTIES

PRACTICE POINT: As part of its Clarity Project, the American Institute of Certified Public Accountants' (AICPA's) Auditing Standards Board (ASB) has finalized a clarified Statement on Auditing Standards (SAS) titled, "Related Parties (Redrafted)," which supersedes AU Section 334 (Related Parties). Extant AU Section 334 is premised on the applicability of the related-party requirements in FASB ASC 850, *Related Party Disclosures*, to the financial statements being audited. That is, extant AU Section 334 is focused on auditing the amounts and disclosures pursuant to accounting principles generally accepted in the United States (U.S. GAAP), and it is centered on the provisions of FASB ASC 850. In contrast, the clarified SAS is framework neutral, encompassing financial reporting frameworks in addition to U.S. GAAP, such as International Financial Reporting Standards as promulgated by the International Accounting Standards Board, as well as special purpose frameworks described in the clarified SAS, "Special Considerations—Audits of Financial Statements Prepared in Accordance with Special Purpose Frameworks." The objectives, requirements, and definitions in this clarified SAS are applicable irrespective of whether the applicable financial reporting framework establishes requirements for related-party disclosures.

The ASB is expected to issue many of the clarified standards in *one* SAS that will be codified in "AU Section" format. The ASB has decided that the effective date of the clarified SASs that have not yet been issued is for audits of financial statements for periods ending on or after December 15, 2012. Auditors should be alert to and monitor further developments in this area.

WHAT EVERY PRACTITIONER SHOULD KNOW

Basic Requirements

Although an audit cannot be expected to provide assurance that all related-party transactions will be discovered, nevertheless, the auditor should:

1. Obtain an understanding of management responsibilities and the relationship of each component to the total entity.
2. Consider controls over management activities and the business purpose served by the various components of the entity.
3. Be aware of the possible existence of material related-party transactions that could affect the financial statements.
4. Be aware of common ownership or management control relationships that are required to be disclosed by ASC 850, even though there are no transactions. Illustration 1 provides examples of related parties based on the definition in ASC 850.
5. Recognize that the substance of a particular transaction could be significantly different from its form and that financial statements should recognize the substance, rather than the legal form, of particular transactions. Illustration 2 provides examples of transactions that because of their nature may indicate the existence of related parties. Illustration 3

provides examples of conditions that may create motivation for related-party transactions.

6. Place emphasis on testing material transactions with parties known to be related to the entity being audited.

Auditing Procedures for Related Parties

The auditor should apply appropriate audit procedures to determine the existence of related parties and to identify material transactions with related parties. After identifying related-party transactions, the auditor should apply the procedures he or she considers necessary to obtain satisfaction concerning the purpose, nature, and extent of these transactions and their effect on the financial statements. Illustration 4 is a detailed audit program that the auditor can use for identifying and substantiating related-party transactions, based on the requirements of this Section.

Also, the auditor should consider obtaining a related-party confirmation letter from all directors, principal officers, and major stockholders if the following conditions exist:

1. The entity does not have adequate controls and processes in place to identify related-party transactions; and

2. The auditor has not otherwise been satisfied as to the extent of related-party transactions.

See Illustration 5 for a sample related-party confirmation letter in such circumstances.

In addition, if other auditors are involved in auditing a component of the entity (e.g., subsidiary or division), the auditor should consider communicating with the other auditors to facilitate a timely exchange of information regarding related-party issues. See Illustration 6 for a sample letter to other auditors in such circumstances.

Arm's-Length Transactions

Generally, it is not possible for the auditor to determine whether a particular transaction would have taken place if the parties had not been related, or what the terms and manner of settlement would have been assuming the transaction had taken place. Therefore, it is difficult for the auditor to substantiate management's representations that a transaction was consummated on terms equivalent to those that prevail in arm's-length transactions. If such a representation is included in the financial statements and the auditor believes that the representation is unsubstantiated by management and the transaction is material, he or she should express a qualified or an adverse opinion (depending on materiality) due to a departure from GAAP. A preface to a disclosure such as "Management believes that . . ." or "It is the Company's belief that . . ." does not change management's responsibility to substantiate the representation.

Disclosure in Financial Statements

The auditor should evaluate all the information available to him or her concerning the related-party transactions or control relationships identified, and be satisfied that they are adequately disclosed in the financial statements in accordance with GAAP. Illustration 7 summarizes the financial statement disclosure requirements for related-party transactions under GAAP. Illustration 9 provides sample financial statement disclosures.

PRACTICE ISSUES AND FREQUENTLY ASKED QUESTIONS

Issue 1: What are the audit implications in a situation where the auditor concludes there is a high risk of misstatement due to related-party transactions?

The higher the auditor's assessment of risk regarding related-party transactions, the more extensive or effective the audit tests should be. For example, the auditor's tests regarding valuation of a receivable from an entity under common control might be more extensive than for a trade receivable of the same size because the company's parent may be motivated to obscure the substance of the transaction. In order to understand the particular transaction, or obtain evidence regarding it, the auditor may have to perform one or more of the following procedures where the risk of assessment is high:

- Refer to audited or unaudited financial statements of the related party.
- Apply procedures at the related party.
- Audit the financial statements of the related party.
- Obtain representations from senior management and its board of directors about whether they or other related parties engaged in any transactions with the entity during the period under audit.

Issue 2: Is the auditor required to call attention to the existence of related-party transactions in the auditor's report?

No. The auditor is not required to call attention to the existence of related-party transactions in the auditor's report. However, the auditor is not precluded from calling the reader's attention to related-party transactions in the audit report by means of a separate explanatory paragraph. Illustration 8 provides an example of an auditor's report that contains an emphasis of a matter paragraph describing the existence of related-party transactions.

Issue 3: Does the existence of related-party transactions generally result in a high-risk audit engagement?

Not necessarily. Related-party transactions per se do not necessarily or inherently have negative implications for an audit engagement. The auditor's primary concern is that (1) all related-party transactions are properly recorded and reflect economic substance, rather than form and (2) all material related-party transactions are adequately disclosed in the financial statements.

Issue 4: Do privately held businesses generally present any concerns about related-party transactions?

Yes. Privately held businesses are very likely to have such related-party transactions as (1) notes or advances to or from owners, (2) operating leases between the company and a stockholder, (3) purchases or sales of goods or services involving an owner or other related entity, or (4) nonmonetary transactions. Because the controls over financial reporting in owner-managed businesses are particularly susceptible to owner override, related-party transactions may be more easily concealed.

Once these transactions are identified, it is especially important in this context that the auditor develop an understanding of the true substance of related-party transactions, rather than accepting *prima facie* their apparent form. This may be especially critical in the small company, where documentation may be less formal.

Issue 5: Can the auditor consult with the entity's legal counsel regarding related-party transactions?

Yes. As a matter of fact, the auditor may find consultation with the entity's legal counsel useful in identifying related parties and understanding related-party transactions. The auditor often needs to rely on the expertise of legal counsel in related-party matters.

Issue 6: Why is it often difficult to evaluate "substance over form" issues associated with related-party transactions?

Many related-party transactions have substance over form problems primarily because substance depends so much on the intentions of the parties and it is most difficult, if not impossible, to evaluate those intentions when the transactions between the parties are not at arm's length.

Related-party transactions can be described by their legal form, such as a loan, a lease, a purchase or sale of products or services, and so on. They also can be described by their economic substance, which may be different from their legal form. For example, what is legally a lease may in economic reality be a purchase.

The auditor should be aware that the substance of a particular transaction could be significantly different from its form and that financial statements should recognize the substance, rather than the legal form, of particular transactions.

Issue 7: Should the principal auditor and the other auditor exchange information on related parties?

Yes. The principal auditor and the other auditor should, at an early stage in the audit, obtain from each other the names of known related parties, their knowledge of existing related-party relationships, and the extent of management involvement in material transactions.

Issue 8: What are some of the factors that the auditor should consider when assessing the risk of material misstatement associated with related-party matters?

When assessing the risk of material misstatement associated with related-party matters, the auditor should consider whether the following factors exist:

- Highly complex business practices that enhance the ability of management to mask the economic substance of business transactions

- The existence of unique, highly complex, and material transactions close to year end that present difficult "substance over form" questions

- Overly complex corporate structures

- Entities that have material intercompany transactions with one another with audit responsibilities divided among two or more auditing firms, or in which one of the entities is not audited

- Significant bank accounts or subsidiary or branch operations in tax-haven jurisdictions for which there appears to be no clear business justification

- Difficulty in determining the party that controls an off-balance-sheet entity

Issue 9: Are transactions between related parties required to be disclosed in the financial statements even though they may not be given accounting recognition in the financial records?

Yes. Transactions between related parties are considered to be related-party transactions even though they may not be given accounting recognition in the financial records. Examples include an entity receiving or providing accounting, management, or other services at no charge; major stockholder absorbing corporate expenses; guarantee of debt without charge; and cash advances with no interest charges. These and other similar transactions should be adequately disclosed in the financial statements.

ILLUSTRATIONS AND PRACTICE AIDS

ILLUSTRATION 1—EXAMPLES OF RELATED PARTIES BASED ON THE DEFINITION IN ASC 850, RELATED PARTY DISCLOSURES

According to FASB Accounting Standards Codification (ASC) 850, *Related Party Disclosures*, a related party may be any of the following:

- *Affiliate*—An affiliate is a party that directly or indirectly controls, is controlled by, or is under common control with another party. *Control* means the direct or indirect power to determine or influence management and policies of an entity through ownership, by contract, or otherwise.

- *Principal owner*—A principal owner is the owner of record or known beneficial owner of more than 10% of the voting interests of an entity.

- *Management*—Persons having responsibility for achieving objectives of the entity and requisite authority to make decisions that pursue those objectives. This definition normally includes members of the board of directors, chief executive officer, chief operating officer, president, treasurer, any vice president in charge of a principal business function (e.g., sales, administration, finance), and any other individual who performs similar policymaking functions.

- *Immediate family of management or principal owners*—Generally, this includes spouses, brothers, sisters, parents, children, and spouses of these persons.

- *A parent company and its subsidiaries*—Generally accepted accounting principles define a *parent company* as an entity that "directly or indirectly has a controlling financial interest" in a subsidiary company.

Controlling financial interest is defined as "ownership of a majority voting interest" and, therefore, generally as "ownership by one enterprise, directly or indirectly, of over fifty percent of the outstanding voting shares of another enterprise."

- *Trusts for the benefit of employees*—Trusts for the benefit of employees include pension and profit-sharing trusts that are managed by, or under the trusteeship of, the entity's management.

- *Other parties*—Other parties include any other party that has the ability to significantly influence the management or operating policies of the entity, to the extent that it may be prevented from fully pursuing its own separate interests. The ability to exercise significant influence may be indicated in several ways, such as representation on the board of directors, participation in policymaking processes, material intercompany transactions, interchange of managerial personnel, or technological dependency.

ILLUSTRATION 2—EXAMPLES OF TRANSACTIONS THAT MAY BE INDICATIVE OF THE EXISTENCE OF RELATED PARTIES

- Contracts that carry no interest rate or an unrealistic interest rate
- Real estate transactions that are made at a price that is significantly different from appraised values
- Nonmonetary transactions that involve the exchange of similar assets
- Loan agreements that contain no repayment schedule
- Loans to parties that do not possess the ability to repay
- Sales without substance, including funding the other party to the transaction so that the sales price is fully remitted
- Services or goods purchased from a party at little or no cost to the entity
- Payment for services never rendered or at inflated prices
- Unnecessarily complex corporate structure
- Highly complex business practices that enhance the ability of management to mask their economic substance
- The existence of unusual, complex, and material transactions close to year-end that raise difficult "substance over form" questions
- Agreements under which one party pays expenses on behalf of another party
- Circular arrangements between parties (i.e., sales arrangements in which the seller of goods or services has concurrent obligations to the buyer to purchase goods or services or provide other benefits)
- Engaging in business deals, such as leases, at more or less than market value
- Sale of land with arranged financing
- Sale of securities at a significant discount from fair value
- Services or goods are purchased from a party at little or no cost
- Utilization of a party to mitigate market risks (e.g., creation of a "shell company" to help mitigate market risks on various equity transactions)

ILLUSTRATION 3—CONDITIONS THAT MAY CREATE MOTIVATION FOR RELATED-PARTY TRANSACTIONS

- Inadequate working capital or lines of credit

- Overly optimistic forecasts
- Dependence on few products, customers, suppliers, or transactions
- Many failures in the industry
- Excess capacity
- Significant legal problems
- Significant technological obsolescence exposure
- Management's desire for strong earnings to support the market price of the company

ILLUSTRATION 4—AUDIT PROGRAM FOR IDENTIFYING AND SUB-STANTIATING RELATED-PARTY TRANSACTIONS

	Performed By	Workpaper Reference
1. Perform the following procedures for determining the existence of related parties and for identifying related-party transactions:		
a. Inquire about and evaluate the entity's procedures for identifying, authorizing, accounting for, and disclosing related-party transactions.	_____	_____
b. Request from appropriate management personnel the names of all related parties and inquire whether there were any transactions with these parties during the period.	_____	_____
c. Review filings with the SEC and other regulatory agencies for: (i) the names of related parties, (ii) other businesses in which officers and directors occupy directorship or management positions, and (iii) information about material transactions with related parties.	_____	_____
d. Determine the names of all pensions and other trusts established for the benefit of employees and the names of their officers and trustees.	_____	_____
e. Review stockholder listings of closely held companies to identify principal stockholders.	_____	_____
f. Review prior years' working papers for the names of known related parties.	_____	_____
g. Inquire of predecessor, principal, or other auditors of related entities concerning their knowledge of existing relationships and the extent of management involvement in material transactions.	_____	_____
h. Review material investment and sales transactions to determine whether they may have created related parties.	_____	_____
i. Provide audit personnel or auditors of segments of the entity with the names of known related parties.	_____	_____
j. Review the minutes of meetings of the board of directors and executive or operating committees for information about material transactions authorized or discussed at their meetings.	_____	_____

	Performed By	Workpaper Reference
k. Review conflict-of-interests statements obtained by the company from its management.	_____	_____
l. Review the extent and nature of business transactions with major customers, suppliers, borrowers, and lenders for indications of previously undisclosed relationships.	_____	_____
m. Consider whether transactions are occurring, but are not being given accounting recognition (e.g., receiving or providing accounting, management, or other services at no charge; or a major stockholder absorbing corporate expenses).	_____	_____
n. Review accounting records for large, unusual, or nonrecurring transactions or balances, paying particular attention to transactions recognized at or near the end of the reporting period.	_____	_____
o. Review confirmations of compensating balance arrangements for indications of balances maintained for or by related parties.	_____	_____
p. Review invoices from law firms that have performed regular or special services for the company.	_____	_____
q. Review confirmations of loans receivable and payable for indications of guarantees. When guarantees are indicated, determine their nature and the relationships, if any, of the guarantors to the reporting entity.	_____	_____
r. Inquire as to the nature and terms of any off-balance-sheet arrangements or transactions involving special purpose entities (SPE) or such other structured financial arrangements.	_____	_____
s. Consider whether detailed tests of transactions and balances performed in other audit areas indicated the possibility that related parties or related-party transactions may exist.	_____	_____

2. In determining the scope of procedures to apply with respect to possible related-party transactions, perform the following:

	Performed By	Workpaper Reference
a. Obtain an understanding of management responsibilities and the relationships of each component of the total entity.	_____	_____
b. Consider controls over management activities.	_____	_____
c. Consider the business purpose served by the various components of the entity.	_____	_____
d. Consider the entity's business or organizational structure and whether they appear to be designed to conceal related-party transactions.	_____	_____

3. When related-party transactions are identified, perform the following:

	Performed By	Workpaper Reference
a. Obtain an understanding of the business purpose of the transaction.	_____	_____

		Performed By	Workpaper Reference
b.	Examine supporting documents (e.g., invoices, contracts) that substantiate the transaction.	_____	_____
c.	Determine whether the transaction has been approved by those charged with governance (e.g., by the board of directors).	_____	_____
d.	Test the reasonableness of numbers compiled for possible disclosures in the financial statements.	_____	_____
e.	If considered necessary, arrange for the audits of intercompany account balances and for the examination of specified transactions.	_____	_____
f.	Inspect, or confirm, and obtain sufficient competent evidence regarding the transferability and value of any collateral.	_____	_____
g.	If principal auditors are involved, inquire of the principal auditors regarding their knowledge of any plans of the parent, which may affect the subsidiary's assets or liabilities.	_____	_____
h.	For significant loans receivable and payable: (i) review for unusual interest rates, terms, and conditions, (ii) obtain confirmations and review for indications of guarantees, and (iii) if guarantees are indicated, determine their nature and the relationship of the guarantor with the company.	_____	_____

4. If the procedures performed above do not result in satisfactory audit evidence, consider performing the following extended audit procedures:

		Performed By	Workpaper Reference
a.	Confirm transaction amounts and terms and conditions with the related party.	_____	_____
b.	Inspect supporting documents and additional evidence in the possession of the other party.	_____	_____
c.	Confirm or discuss pertinent information with intermediaries (e.g., banks, guarantors, agents or lawyers).	_____	_____
d.	Verify the existence of the other party by referring to other sources (e.g., credit agencies, financial publications).	_____	_____
e.	Obtain information about the financial capability of the other party with respect to material uncollected balances, guarantees, and other obligations.	_____	_____
f.	Refer to audited or unaudited financial statements of the related party.	_____	_____
g.	Apply certain specific procedures at the related party.	_____	_____
h.	Audit the financial statements of the related party.	_____	_____

	Performed By	Workpaper Reference

5. Consider obtaining a related-party confirmation letter from all directors, principal officers, and major stockholders if the following conditions exist:

    a. The entity does not have adequate controls and processes in place to identify related-party transactions; and _____ _____

    b. The auditor has not otherwise been satisfied as to the extent of related-party transactions. _____ _____

6. Consider the effect, if any, of the related-party transactions on the tax provision and inform the tax engagement team of all such transactions for purposes of their review of the tax provision and the preparation of tax returns. _____ _____

7. Evaluate whether off-balance-sheet arrangements and transactions entered into with a special purpose entity (SPE) represent related-party transactions, and perform the following procedures:

    a. Determine whether the issuer of loans or investments held or the primary obligor of debt guarantees issued indicate that an SPE may be involved. _____ _____

    b. Review the nature and terms of any SPE or structured financial arrangements. _____ _____

    c. Review significant documents and agreements related to significant transactions involving SPEs. _____ _____

    d. Inquire about any modifications to existing SPEs that may have been made in the current period that could affect the accounting determined at the date of the transaction. _____ _____

    e. Tailor the management representation letter to include specific representations on critical issues and assumptions related to SPE transactions and to confirm that all relevant information and documents have been provided. _____ _____

    f. Consider conducting further procedures with respect to the books and records of the SPE. _____ _____

    g. Consider consulting with other technical experts regarding these types of structures and related transactions to ensure the appropriateness of accounting and disclosures. _____ _____

8. Consider the effect of related parties and related-party transactions on the fraud risk assessment and the possible need to perform additional procedures, such as the following:

    a. Reviewing material cash disbursements, advances, and investments to consider whether the company provided funds to a related entity. _____ _____

	Performed By	Workpaper Reference

    b.   Discussing with tax and consulting personnel, who have provided services to the client, their knowledge of the client's relationships and knowledge of related parties.

    c.   Discussing with intermediaries (e.g., lawyers, predecessor auditors, and others providing professional services to the client) their knowledge of the identity of principal parties to material transactions.

9.   Obtain written representations from management (in the representation letter) about the completeness of information provided regarding related parties and related-party transactions and the adequacy of related-party disclosures in the financial statements.

10. Ascertain that the financial statements adequately disclose related-party transactions.

11. Consider the following reporting issues:

    a.   If the financial statements disclose transactions with related parties that imply they were consummated on terms equivalent to those that prevail in arm's-length transactions and such representations are unsubstantiated by management, express a qualified or an adverse opinion (depending on materiality) because of a GAAP departure.

    b.   If sufficient appropriate audit assurance cannot be obtained regarding related parties and transactions with such parties, consider whether a report modification is necessary.

    c.   If there are significant transactions with related parties, consider whether to emphasize this matter by adding an explanatory paragraph to the auditor's report (e.g., if the entity is heavily dependent on parent financing, or if the entity had a significant sale to a related party).

ILLUSTRATION 5—RELATED-PARTY CONFIRMATION LETTER

(Prepared on client's letterhead)

(Date)

(Name and address of principal officer, major stockholder, or director)

Dear _____:

Our auditors *(insert name and address of auditors)* are conducting an audit of our financial statements for the year ended *(insert date)*. Please provide answers to the questions included in the attached questionnaire, sign your name, and return the questionnaire in the enclosed return envelope directly to our auditors. The questionnaire is designed to provide the auditors with information about the interests of officers, directors and other related parties in transactions with the Company.

Please answer all questions in the questionnaire. Certain terms used in the questions are defined at the end of the questionnaire. Please read the definitions carefully before answering the questions. If the answer to any question is "yes," please provide an explanation.

Thank you for your anticipated timely cooperation with this request.

Respectfully,

(*Name of client*)

_____

(*Client's authorized signature and title*)

****

(*Name of client*)

Related-Party Questionnaire

Please answer all questions in the questionnaire. Certain terms used in the questions are defined at the end of the questionnaire. Please read the definitions carefully before answering the questions. If the answer to any question is "yes," please provide an explanation.

		Yes	*No*
1.	Have you or any related party of yours had any interest, direct or indirect, in any sales, purchases, transfers, leasing arrangements or guarantees or other transactions since (*beginning of period of audit*) to which the Company (*or specify any pension, retirement, savings or similar plan provided by the client*) was, or is to be, a party?	_____	_____
2.	Do you or any related party of yours have any interest, direct or indirect, in any pending or incomplete sales, purchases, transfers, leasing arrangements, guarantees or other transactions to which the company (*or specify any pension, retirement, savings or similar plan provided by the client*) is, or is to be, a party?	_____	_____
3.	Have you or any related party of yours been indebted to the company (*or specify any pension, retirement, savings or similar plan provided by the client*) at any time since (*beginning of period of audit*)? [**Note:** Please exclude amounts due for purchases on usual trade terms and for ordinary travel and expense advances.]	_____	_____

The answers to the foregoing questions are correct to the best of my knowledge and belief.

Date: _____   Signature: _____

Definitions

- *Company*—Parent company, any subsidiary or investee for which investments are accounted for by the equity method.

- *Related Party*—Any: (1) party (other than the Company) of which you are an officer, director or partner or are, directly or indirectly, the beneficial owner of 10% or more of the voting interests, (2) trust or other estate in which you have a substantial beneficial ownership or for which you serve as trustee or in a similar fiduciary capacity, (3) any member of your immediate family, and (4) other party with which you may deal if you, or the other party, control or can significantly influence the other to an extent that either of you might be prevented from fully pursuing your own separate interests.

- *Control*—Possession, direct or indirect, of the power to direct or cause the direction of the management and policies of a party, whether through ownership, by contract or otherwise.

- *Party*—An individual, a corporation, a partnership, an association, a joint-stock company, a business trust or an unincorporated organization.

- *Beneficial owner*—A party who enjoys or has the right to secure benefits substantially equivalent to those of the ownership of securities, even though the securities are not registered in the party's name. Examples of beneficial ownership include securities held for the party's benefit in the name of others, such as nominees, custodians, brokers, trustees, executors and other fiduciaries; a partnership of which the person is a partner; and a corporation for which the party owns substantially all of the stock. Shares that are considered beneficially owned include: (1) shares held, individually or in a fiduciary capacity, by the party's spouse, the party's or his or her spouse's minor children or a relative of the party or his or her spouse who shares the same home with the party; or (2) shares as to which the party can vest or revest title in himself at once or at some future time.

ILLUSTRATION 6—LETTER TO OTHER AUDITORS REGARDING RELATED PARTIES

(Date)

(Name and address of other auditor)

Dear _____:

This letter is to help facilitate a timely exchange of information regarding known related parties and related-party transactions, in connection with our audit of the consolidated financial statements of ABC Company and its subsidiaries as of and for the year ended December 31, 20X2, in which you are participating as auditors of DEF Subsidiary. Enclosed is a list of related parties, as defined in FASB Accounting Standards Codification (ASC) 850, *Related Party Disclosures*, of which we are aware and a description of transactions with such parties. (*Note: If additional related parties or transactions are identified later in the engagement, a list of transactions with those parties should be forwarded to the other auditors.*)

Our primary audit objectives associated with related-party transactions are to accomplish the following:

- Determine the existence of related parties.
- Identify transactions with related parties.
- Examine identified related-party transactions.

- Determine the adequacy of disclosure.

As a participant in this audit engagement, you should refer to the enclosed list and should be alert for any transactions with related parties (those on the list or others that may come to your attention) during the conduct of your audit.

Based on your knowledge, please advise us of other related parties not included on the list and of transactions with related parties that differ from those described herein.

Very truly yours,

(*Auditor's name and signature*)

PRACTICE POINT: Before completion of the audit, it may be desirable to confirm matters with the other auditors, such as the following:

- A description of the transactions, including transactions to which no amounts or nominal amounts were ascribed, for each of the periods under audit.

- Dollar volume of transactions with related parties for each of the periods under audit and the effects of any change in the method of establishing the terms from that used in the preceding period.

- Amounts due to or from related parties as of the date of each of the balance sheets presented, along with the terms and manner of settlement.

ILLUSTRATION 7—FINANCIAL STATEMENT DISCLOSURE REQUIRE-
MENTS FOR RELATED-PARTY TRANSACTIONS (APPLICABLE TO NON-
PUBLIC COMPANIES)

1. The following disclosures should be made for material related-party transactions (other than compensation arrangements, expense allowances, and other similar items in the ordinary course of business):

   a. The nature of the relationship of the parties involved

   b. A description of the transactions, including transactions to which no amounts or nominal amounts were ascribed, for each of the periods for which income statements are presented, and such other information deemed necessary to an understanding of the effects of the transactions on the financial statements

   c. The dollar amounts of transactions for each of the periods for which income statements are presented and the effects of any change in the method of establishing the terms from those used in the preceding period

   d. Amounts due from or to related parties as of the date of each balance sheet presented and, if not otherwise apparent, the terms and manner of settlement

2. Disclosures concerning related-party transactions should be worded in a manner that does not imply that the transactions were consummated on terms equivalent to those that prevail in arm's-length transactions, unless such representations can be substantiated.

3. Disclosure should be made of the nature of the control relationship, even though there are no related-party transactions, when the client and one or more other enterprises are under common ownership or

management control and the existence of that control could result in operating results or financial position of the client significantly different from those that would have resulted if the client were autonomous.

4. Disclosures should be made of the nature and extent of leasing transactions with related parties.

ILLUSTRATION 8—AUDITOR'S REPORT INCLUDES EMPHASIS OF A MATTER PARAGRAPH TO DESCRIBE RELATED-PARTY TRANSACTIONS

Independent Auditor's Report

Board of Directors and Stockholders
ABC Company

We have audited the accompanying balance sheets of ABC Company as of December 31, 20X2, and 20X1, and the related statements of income, retained earnings, and cash flows for the years then ended. These financial statements are the responsibility of the Company's management. Our responsibility is to express an opinion on these financial statements based on our audits.

We conducted our audits in accordance with auditing standards generally accepted in the United States of America. Those standards require that we plan and perform the audit to obtain reasonable assurance about whether the financial statements are free of material misstatement. An audit includes examining, on a test basis, evidence supporting the amounts and disclosures in the financial statements. An audit also includes assessing the accounting principles used and significant estimates made by management, as well as evaluating the overall financial statement presentation. We believe that our audits provide a reasonable basis for our opinion.

In our opinion, the financial statements referred to above present fairly, in all material respects, the financial position of ABC Company as of December 31, 20X2, and 20X1, and the results of its operations and its cash flows for the years then ended in conformity with accounting principles generally accepted in the United States of America.

As discussed in Note [X] to the financial statements, the Company has had numerous significant transactions with businesses controlled by, and with people who are related to, the officers and directors of the Company.

[*Signature*]

[*Date*]

ILLUSTRATION 9—EXAMPLES OF FINANCIAL STATEMENT DISCLOSURES OF RELATED-PARTY TRANSACTIONS

Example 1: A director of the Company is a partner in the law firm that acts as counsel to the Company

A director of the Company is a partner in the law firm that acts as counsel to the Company. The Company paid legal fees and expenses to the law firm in the amount of approximately $375,000 in 20X2 and $210,000 in 20X1.

Example 2: A director of the Company is an owner in an insurance agency that has written policies for the Company

A director of the Company has an ownership interest in an insurance agency that has written general liability policies for the Company with premiums totaling $136,000 and $122,000 in 20X2 and 20X1, respectively.

Example 3: Related party supplies inventory materials to the Company

The Company has an agreement with Just, Inc., an entity in which a major stockholder of the Company owns a significant interest, which provides for purchases by the Company of electrical equipment, sub-assemblies, and spare parts. Purchases from Just, Inc. for 20X2 and 20X1 totaled $2,900,000 and $3,750,000, respectively. Accounts payable to Just, Inc. amounted to $1,010,000 and $1,236,000 at December 31, 20X2, and 20X1, respectively. In addition, in 20X2 the Company made advance payments to Just, Inc. for future inventory purchases in return for lower prices on certain components. Advance payments of $420,000 were included in prepaid expenses at December 31, 20X2.

Example 4: Company sells a substantial portion of its products to a related entity

The Company sells a substantial portion of its medical instruments products to Horizons, Ltd., an entity in which the Company's vice president of operations is a majority stockholder. During 20X2 and 20X1, the Company sold approximately $10,400,000 and $8,732,000 of products to Horizons, Ltd. Trade receivables from Horizons, Inc. were $1,923,000 and $1,544,000 at December 31, 20X2, and 20X1, respectively.

Example 5: Related parties reimburse the Company for allocated overhead and administrative expenses

The Company's managed limited partnerships reimburse the Company for certain allocated overhead and administrative expenses. These expenses generally consist of salaries and related benefits paid to corporate personnel, rent, data processing services, and other corporate facilities costs. The Company provides engineering, marketing, administrative, accounting, information management, legal, and other services to the partnerships. Allocations of personnel costs have been based primarily on actual time spent by Company employees with respect to each partnership managed. Remaining overhead costs are allocated based on the pro rata relationship of the partnership's revenues to the total revenues of all businesses owned or managed by the Company. The Company believes that such allocation methods are reasonable. Amounts charged to managed partnerships and other affiliated companies have directly offset the Company's general and administrative expenses by approximately $5,100,000 and $5,400,000 for the years ended December 31, 20X2, and 20X1, respectively.

Example 6: Company's corporate services agreement with a related entity provides for payment of a fee based on company's net sales

The Company has a corporate services agreement with Odeyssa, Inc., an entity that is controlled by the Company's Chairman of the Board and president. Under the terms of the agreement, the Company pays a fee to Odeyssa, Inc. for various corporate support staff, administrative services, and research and development services. Such fee equals 2.2% of the Company's net sales, subject to certain adjustments, and totaled $1,975,000 and $1,836,000 in 20X2 and 20X1, respectively.

Example 7: Companies under common control may experience change in operations

The Company's 80% shareholder also controls other entities whose operations are similar to those of the Company. Although there were no transactions between the Company and these entities in 20X2 or 20X1, the 80% shareholder is, nevertheless, in a position to influence the sales volume of the Company for the benefit of the other entities that are under his control.

Example 8: Guarantee of indebtedness of related entity

As of December 31, 20X2, the Company is contingently liable as guarantor with respect to $5,400,000 of indebtedness of Ecaped, Inc., an entity that is owned by the Company's stockholders. No material loss is anticipated by reason of such guarantee.

AU SECTION 336
USING THE WORK OF A SPECIALIST

PRACTICE POINT: As part of its Clarity Project, the American Institute of Certified Public Accountants' (AICPA's) Auditing Standards Board (ASB) has finalized a clarified Statement on Auditing Standards (SAS) titled, "Using the Work of an Auditor's Specialist," which supersedes AU Section 336 (Using the Work of a Specialist). Extant AU Section 336 addresses the use of the auditor's specialist and the use of management's specialist. The requirements and guidance addressing the use of management's specialist have been included in the clarified SAS, "Audit Evidence (Redrafted)," under the view that audit evidence produced by management's experts (internal or external) needs to be evaluated by the auditor for relevance and reliability like any other audit evidence. The placement of these requirements does not create a difference between extant SASs as a whole and the clarified SASs as a whole. Extant AU Section 336 specifically scopes out from the standard use of specialists employed by the firm who participate in the audit. In contrast, the clarified SAS encompasses in-firm specialists. The ASB believes that this change in the scope of the standard will affect current practice because it will create incremental documentation requirements.

The ASB is expected to issue many of the clarified standards in *one* SAS that will be codified in "AU Section" format. The ASB has decided that the effective date of the clarified SASs that have not yet been issued is for audits of financial statements for periods ending on or after December 15, 2012. Auditors should be alert to and monitor further developments in this area.

WHAT EVERY PRACTITIONER SHOULD KNOW

Basic Objectives

This Section provides guidance to the auditor who uses the work of a specialist in performing an audit. A *specialist* is a person or firm "possessing special skill or knowledge in a particular field other than accounting or auditing" and includes actuaries, appraisers, engineers, environmental consultants, and geologists. This Section also applies to auditors who use the work of a specialist as audit evidence in performing substantive tests to evaluate material financial statement assertions in the following situations:

- When management of the client engages or employs the specialist.

- When management engages a specialist employed by the auditor's firm to provide advisory services.

- When the auditor engages the specialist.

The auditor should have a sufficient understanding of the client's business to recognize the need for a specialist. Proper planning is necessary to make sure that a specialist is available when needed and that he or she is both competent and preferably independent of the client.

Qualifications of a Specialist

Before using and relying on the work of a specialist, the auditor should be satisfied with the specialist's qualifications in the particular field. Therefore, the auditor is required to consider the following in connection with his or her evaluation of the specialist's qualifications:

1. The professional certification, license, or other recognition of the competence of the specialist.

2. The reputation and standing of the specialist in the views of peers and others familiar with his or her work.

3. The specialist's experience in the type of work for which the auditor is considering using the specialist.

Work of a Specialist

After the auditor is satisfied with the qualifications of the specialist, he or she should obtain an understanding of the specialist's role and the nature of the work to be performed. The auditor's understanding should cover:

- The scope and objectives of the specialist's work.
- The specialist's relationship to the client.
- The methods and assumptions used.
- A comparison of the assumptions and methods used in the current engagement to those used in the preceding engagement.
- The appropriateness of using the specialist's work for the intended purpose or to support assertions made in the financial statements.
- A description of the form and content of the specialist's findings that would allow the auditor to use the findings in connection with the audit.

Relationship of the Specialist to the Client

The auditor should evaluate whether the specialist's relationship to the client might impair the specialist's objectivity. If the auditor believes the relationship might impair the specialist's objectivity, the auditor should perform additional procedures to determine whether the specialist's assumptions, methods, or findings are not unreasonable, or engage another specialist for that purpose.

Using the Specialist's Findings

The auditor should perform the following procedures when using the specialist's findings:

1. Obtain an understanding of the methods and assumptions used.

2. Make appropriate tests of data provided to the specialist.

3. Evaluate whether the findings support the related financial statement assertions.

4. If the specialist's findings are deemed unreasonable, apply additional procedures including obtaining the opinion of another specialist.

Effect on the Auditor's Report

If there is a material difference between the specialist's findings and the assertions in the financial statements, the auditor should apply additional procedures. If the matter cannot be resolved by applying additional procedures, the auditor should obtain the opinion of another specialist, unless it appears that the matter cannot be resolved. If the matter has not been resolved, the auditor ordinarily should qualify the opinion or disclaim an opinion due to a scope limitation.

If, after applying additional procedures, the auditor concludes that the assertions in the financial statements are not in conformity with GAAP, the auditor should express a qualified or an adverse opinion.

The auditor should not refer to the work or findings of the specialist or identify the specialist in the auditor's report, unless the specialist's findings cause the auditor to add explanatory language to his or her standard report or to depart from an unqualified opinion.

PRACTICE ISSUES AND FREQUENTLY ASKED QUESTIONS

Issue 1: What are some examples of common use of specialists?

Examples of common use of specialists include using:

- An actuary to determine the appropriateness of the recorded value of insurance loss reserves.
- An appraiser to determine the value of real estate.
- An inventory specialist to distinguish among various electronic components of a high-technology entity.
- An environmental consultant to determine environmental cleanup obligations.
- An attorney for legal interpretation of contracts or agreements.
- A precious metals expert to determine the valuation of certain special purpose inventory.
- An actuary to determine employee benefit obligations.
- A petroleum engineer to determine oil and gas reserves.

Issue 2: Is the auditor prohibited from using a specialist who has a relationship with the client?

No. The auditor is not prohibited from using a specialist who has a relationship with the client if circumstances warrant the use of such a specialist. However, the work of a specialist who does not have a relationship with the client clearly will provide the auditor with greater assurance of reliability. Nonetheless, the auditor is required to evaluate circumstances in which the specialist's objectivity might be impaired by the specialist's relationship with the client.

Issue 3: What are some circumstances in which the specialist's relationship to the client might impair the specialist's objectivity?

If the client has the ability to directly or indirectly control or significantly influence the specialist, then the specialist's objectivity might be impaired. The client's ability to influence the specialist might arise from employment, ownership, contractual right, family relationship, or otherwise. Circumstances that might impair the specialist's objectivity include the following:

- The specialist is an affiliate of the client, whereby the client is able to, directly or indirectly control or significantly influence, the specialist.
- The specialist is a shareholder or director of the client.
- The specialist is a member of the client's management.
- The specialist is related by blood to management or principal owners, for example, spouse, brother, sister, parent, or child.

Issue 4: Can the auditor use the work of an attorney as a specialist in situations relating to matters other than litigation, claims, or assessments?

Yes. The auditor may use the work of attorneys as specialists in situations relating to matters other than litigation, claims, or assessments. For example, the auditor can use the attorney's work in interpreting the provisions of contracts or technical requirements of regulations, and in determining legal title to property.

Note: AU Section 337 (Inquiry of a Client's Lawyer Concerning Litigation, Claims, and Assessments) applies to an attorney's response to audit inquiries concerning litigation, claims, and assessments.

Issue 5: In order to place reliance on the work of a specialist, must he or she be hired directly by the auditor, or may the specialist be retained by the client?

An auditor may potentially rely on the work of a specialist in either case. However, there is a presumption that specialists retained by the auditor will be more objective, because they are removed from the client's influence. When the client hires the specialist, the auditor should assess the degree of influence that the client will likely be able to wield. In light of this assessment, the auditor should also consider the susceptibility of the matter to judgment, and the risk of misstatement and relative importance of the matter to the financial statements.

Issue 6: What implications does the use of a specialist that is employed by the auditor's CPA firm have on the audit engagement?

If the client engages a specialist employed by the auditor's CPA firm to determine an amount or disclosure that is material to the financial statements, the auditor has to apply the same audit procedures that are required to be applied to the work of a specialist who is not employed by the CPA firm. Therefore, the auditor would have to obtain an understanding of the methods and assumptions used by the specialist, make appropriate tests of data provided to the specialist, and evaluate whether the specialist's findings support the related assertions in the financial statements.

On the other hand, if the auditor uses a specialist employed by the auditor's CPA firm to apply additional audit procedures when the client uses a related specialist, the specialist employed by the auditor's CPA firm functions as a member of the audit team. Under these circumstances, the provisions of this

Section do not apply and the auditor would have to provide proper supervision over the specialist in the same manner as any other member of the audit team.

Issue 7: Is it necessary or permissible for the auditor to refer to the specialist's work in the auditor's report?

If the auditor's report is unqualified, the auditor should not refer to the work or findings of the specialist, or identify the specialist, in the audit report. Such a reference might confuse the readers of the report and cause them to believe that it is qualified, or might lead them to believe that it offers a higher level of assurance because of the mention of the specialist. The auditor, in deciding to rely on the specialist's work, is always responsible for evaluating his or her competence, methods, and findings. A specialist is never in a position to have an auditor's knowledge about the client's financial statements.

Therefore, the auditor cannot divide the responsibility for the audit with the specialist in the same way that he or she could with another auditor who had audited a portion of the financial statements.

On the other hand, the auditor may, as a result of the specialist's report or findings, decide to add explanatory language to the standard audit report or depart from an unqualified opinion. In these circumstances, reference to and identification of the specialist may be made in the auditor's report if the auditor believes such reference will facilitate an understanding of the reason for the explanatory paragraph or the departure from the unqualified opinion.

Issue 8: How can the auditor or client effectively use the work of an environmental specialist for estimating environmental remediation liabilities?

The process of estimating environmental remediation liabilities usually is complex and involves many subjective factors and judgments. Therefore, management or the auditor often will use a specialist to perform this work. Such specialists include remediation technologies specialists, responsibility allocation specialists, environmental engineers, and environmental attorneys. Specialists might be involved at various stages of the estimation process to perform functions such as the following:

1. Identify situations for which remediation is required, such as releases from hazardous waste management units.

2. Develop or recommend a remedial action plan for the entity.

3. Collect, analyze, and evaluate data to be used in developing the estimates of remediation costs, such as performing a baseline risk assessment. Baseline risk assessment is the qualitative and quantitative evaluation performed in an effort to define the risk posed to human health, the environment, or both resulting from specific pollutants.

4. Provide management with relevant information to help the entity in its estimation process and financial statements disclosures of the related environmental remediation liabilities.

Issue 9: What type of procedures can the auditor perform to test the reliability of the source data used by the specialist when such data is significant to the accuracy of the specialist's findings and the financial statements?

The auditor can perform various procedures to test the reliability of the source data used by the specialist, including:

1. Corroborating accounting and non-accounting data that the client provided to the specialist.

2. Inquiring of the specialist about whether he or she is satisfied about the accuracy of the source data provided by the client.

3. Considering the reliability and relevance of the data provided by the client to the specialist.

For example, in connection with a pension plan's actuarial calculation, the auditor may perform the following procedures:

- Compare the demographic information to the client's personnel files;

- Compare the payroll information to the payroll registers;

- Review the rate of return on the plan portfolio for reasonableness; and

- Test the forecasted earnings stream and the cap rate used in the valuation.

Issue 10: If the auditor concludes that he or she will be using the findings of a specialist, can the auditor obtain a specific representation in the client representation letter about the client's responsibility for the findings of the specialist?

Yes. If the client has engaged a specialist, the auditor should always consider incorporating in the client representation letter a specific representation regarding the client's responsibility for the findings and qualifications of the specialist. The following is an example of such a representation, which is adapted from AU Section 333 (Management Representations):

> We assume responsibility for, and agree with, the findings of specialists in evaluating the [*describe assertion*] and have adequately considered the qualifications of the specialists in determining the amounts and disclosures used in the financial statements and underlying accounting records. We did not give or cause any instructions to be given to specialists with respect to the values or amounts derived in an attempt to bias their work, and we are not otherwise aware of any matters that have had impact on the independence or objectivity of the specialists.

ILLUSTRATIONS AND PRACTICE AIDS

ILLUSTRATION 1—CHECKLIST FOR USING THE WORK OF A SPECIALIST

1. Evaluate the specialist's qualifications and consider the following:

   a. The professional certification, license, or other recognition of the competence of the specialist.

   b. The reputation and standing of the specialist in the views of peers and others familiar with his or her work.

   c. The specialist's experience in the type of work for which the auditor is considering using the specialist.

2. Obtain an understanding of the specialist's role and the nature of the work to be performed, including the following:

   a. The scope and objectives of the work to be performed by the specialist.

    b. The specialist's relationship to the client.

    c. The methods and assumptions to be used by the specialist.

    d. A comparison of the assumptions and methods used in the current engagement and those used in the preceding engagement.

    e. The appropriateness of using the specialist's work for the intended purpose.

    f. A description of the form and content of the specialist's findings that would allow the auditor to use the findings.

3. Perform additional procedures if there is a material difference between the specialist's findings and the representations in the financial statements, or if the specialist's findings seem unreasonable.

AU SECTION 337
INQUIRY OF A CLIENT'S LAWYER CONCERNING LITIGATION, CLAIMS, AND ASSESSMENTS

PRACTICE POINT: As part of its Clarity Project, the American Institute of Certified Public Accountants' (AICPA's) Auditing Standards Board (ASB) has finalized a clarified Statement on Auditing Standards (SAS) titled, "Audit Evidence—Specific Considerations for Selected Items," which supersedes:

- AU Section 331 (Inventories);

- AU Section 332 (Auditing Derivative Instruments, Hedging Activities, and Investments in Securities);

- AU Section 337 (Inquiry of a Client's Lawyer Concerning Litigation, Claims, and Assessments);

- AU Section 337A (Appendix—Illustrative Audit Inquiry Letter to Legal Counsel); and

- AU Section 337C (Exhibit II—American Bar Association Statement of Policy Regarding Lawyers' Responses to Auditors' Requests for Information).

The clarified SAS also rescinds AU Section 337B (Exhibit I—Excerpts from Financial Accounting Standards Board Accounting Standards Codification 450, Contingencies) and AU Section 901 (Public Warehouses—Controls and Auditing Procedures for Goods Held).

The following are noteworthy changes from extant GAAS:

- The clarified SAS combines the requirements and guidance from extant AU Sections 331, 332, and 337.

- Many of the requirements of extant AU Section 332 are essentially the same as requirements in other clarified standards, primarily the risk assessment standards and the clarified SAS, "Auditing Accounting Estimates, Including Fair Value Accounting Estimates and Related Disclosures." Therefore, the ASB concluded that the application of those requirements in the other clarified standards to the subject matter addressed by extant AU Section 332 is most appropriately addressed as interpretative guidance in the AICPA Audit Guide, "Auditing Derivative Instruments, Hedging Activities, and Investments in Securities." Consideration of these requirements and related application guidance will be a specific focus in updating the audit guide.

- Requirements and guidance addressing auditing investments accounted for using the equity method have been excluded from this clarified SAS because the auditing of equity investees is addressed more broadly by the clarified SAS, "Special Considerations—Audits of Group Financial Statements (Including the Work of Component Auditors)."

- Extant AU Section 337 states, in part, that "the auditor should request the client's management to send a letter of inquiry to those lawyers with whom management consulted concerning litigation, claims, and assessments." In contrast, the clarified SAS takes a more principles-based approach and requires the auditor to seek direct communication with the entity's external legal counsel (through a letter of inquiry) if the auditor

assesses a risk of material misstatement regarding litigation or claims, or when audit procedures performed indicate that material litigation or claims may exist.

The ASB is expected to issue many of the clarified standards in *one* SAS that will be codified in "AU Section" format. The ASB has decided that the effective date of the clarified SASs that have not yet been issued is for audits of financial statements for periods ending on or after December 15, 2012. Auditors should be alert to and monitor further developments in this area.

WHAT EVERY PRACTITIONER SHOULD KNOW

Basic Requirements

The auditor should obtain audit evidence relevant to the following items with respect to litigation, claims, and assessments:

- Uncertainty as to possible loss to an entity arising from litigation, claims, and assessments
- The period in which the underlying cause for legal action occurred
- The degree of probability of an unfavorable outcome
- The amount or range of possible loss

As part of gathering such audit evidence, the auditor should perform certain mandated audit procedures, including inquiring of the client's lawyer about litigation loss contingencies.

In addition, this Section requires the auditor to document:

1. Either in the audit inquiry letter or in a separate letter to the client's lawyer, that the client has assured the auditor that it has disclosed all unasserted claims that the lawyer has advised the client are probable of assertion and must be disclosed in accordance with FASB Accounting Standards Codification (ASC) 450, Contingencies; and

2. The conclusion the auditor reached as a result of responses obtained in a conference with legal counsel relating to matters covered by the audit inquiry letter.

Required Audit Procedures

In addition to making inquiries of the client's lawyer, the auditor is required to perform the following audit procedures with respect to litigation, claims, and assessments:

- Inquire of, and discuss with, the client the policies and procedures established to identify, evaluate, and account for litigation, claims, and assessments.
- Obtain written assurances from management that it has disclosed all matters required to be disclosed by ASC 450 and all unasserted claims that the client's lawyer has advised are probable of assertion and must be disclosed under ASC 450.

- Review the legal correspondence file and examine legal invoices for indications of contingent liabilities.

- Review the minutes of board of directors, stockholders, and committee meetings for indications of lawsuits or other contingencies.

- Examine contracts, loan agreements, leases, and correspondence from government agencies to provide insight regarding the entity's current status and future prospects of potential loss contingencies.

- Obtain information concerning guarantees from bank confirmations.

- Inspect other documents for possible guarantees by the client.

Inquiry of a Client's Lawyer and Contents of Inquiry Letter

The auditor should ask the client's management to send inquiry letters to those lawyers with whom management consulted concerning litigation, claims, and assessments. The inquiry letter to the lawyer should be prepared on the client's letterhead and signed by a company official, and should include the following:

1. A list prepared by management of all material pending or threatened litigation, claims, or assessments with which the lawyer has had significant involvement. An alternative is for the letter to request the lawyer to prepare such a list. Such a list ordinarily should include (a) the nature of the matter, (b) the progress of the matter to date, (c) the way management is responding or intends to respond, and (d) an evaluation of the likelihood of an unfavorable outcome and an estimate, if one can be made, of the amount or range of potential loss.

2. A list prepared by management of material unasserted claims and assessments that are probable of assertion, in connection with which the attorney has had significant involvement. Such a list ordinarily should include (a) the nature of the matter; (b) the way management intends to respond, if the case is asserted; and (c) an evaluation of the likelihood of an unfavorable outcome and an estimate, if one can be made, of the amount or range of potential loss. If management believes that there are no unasserted claims or assessments to be specified to the lawyer for comment, the letter should include a statement indicating that the lawyer has not advised management of unasserted claims or assessments that are probable of assertion and that must be disclosed in accordance with ASC 450.

3. A request to identify any unlisted pending or threatened litigation, claims, and assessments, or a statement that the client's list is complete, when the client has prepared such a list.

4. A statement by the client noting that it is management's understanding that the lawyer has a professional responsibility to inform management whenever there is, in the lawyer's judgment, a legal matter requiring disclosure in the client's financial statements. The letter also should request that the lawyer confirm directly to the auditor that the client's understanding is correct.

5. A request that the lawyer identify the nature of, and reasons for, any limitations in the response.

6. A request that the lawyer specifies the effective date of his or her response and the date by which the lawyer's response should be sent to the auditor.

PRACTICE POINT: The audit inquiry letter may be either in long form, in which the client asks the lawyer to comment on the completeness of information provided by the client, or in short form, in which the lawyer is requested to prepare the information. A sample audit inquiry letter to a lawyer in long form is provided in Illustration 1. A sample audit inquiry letter to a lawyer in short form is provided in Illustration 2.

When the auditor is aware that a client has changed lawyers or that a lawyer engaged by the client has resigned, the auditor should consider the need to inquire concerning the reasons the lawyer is no longer associated with the client.

Evaluation of a Lawyer's Response and Effect on the Auditor's Report

A lawyer may appropriately limit his or her response to the following matters, which are *not* considered limitations on the scope of the audit and, therefore, would not require modifications of the auditor's report:

- Matters to which the lawyer has given substantive attention in the form of legal consultation or representation.

- Matters that are considered individually or collectively material to the financial statements, provided the lawyer and auditor have reached an understanding of the limits of materiality for this purpose.

On the other hand, the following limitations of a lawyer's response generally would preclude the auditor from rendering an unqualified opinion:

- *A lawyer's refusal to furnish, either in writing or orally, the information requested in an inquiry letter*—In such circumstances, the lawyer's refusal would be a limitation on the scope of the audit sufficient to preclude an unqualified opinion. Illustration 3 provides an example of an auditor report that is qualified due to lack of response by the client's attorney.

- *A lawyer's inability to respond concerning the likelihood of an unfavorable outcome of litigation, claims, or assessments or the amount or range of potential loss, because of inherent uncertainties*—In such circumstances, the auditor ordinarily would conclude that the financial statements are affected by an uncertainty concerning the outcome of a future event that is not susceptible to reasonable estimation; therefore, the auditor should follow the guidance in AU Section 508 (Reports on Audited Financial Statements), which generally results in the auditor qualifying or disclaiming an opinion on the financial statements.

The auditor should recognize that a lawyer may respond with statements that are clearly not acceptable for the auditor's purposes, such as "From what we presently know, it appears that the company has a good chance of prevailing" or,

"We are unable to express an opinion, but management believes . . . ." These types of statements do not corroborate the probability of outcome or the amount or range of loss. Illustration 4 provides some examples, based on the auditing literature, of lawyers' evaluations of litigation that are *not* clear about the likelihood of an unfavorable outcome. Illustration 5 provides some examples, based on the auditing literature, of lawyers' evaluations of litigation that may be considered sufficiently clear that the likelihood of an unfavorable outcome is "remote," although the lawyers do not use that term.

Accounting Considerations

The standards of financial accounting and reporting for loss contingencies, including those arising from litigation, claims, and assessments, are found in ASC 450. ASC 450 defines a *contingency* as an existing condition, situation, or set of circumstances involving uncertainty about possible gain or loss to an enterprise that will ultimately be resolved when one or more future events either occurs or fails to occur.

ASC 450 requires that a loss contingency be accrued in the entity's financial statements if both of the following conditions are met:

1. It is probable that an asset has been impaired or a liability has been incurred; and

2. The loss can be reasonably estimated.

Disclosure is required for loss contingencies not meeting both those conditions if there is a reasonable possibility that a loss may have been incurred.

If it is possible to reasonably estimate a range of loss, accrual of the most likely estimate of the loss within that range should be made. However, when no amount within that range is a better estimate than any other amount, the minimum amount in the range should be accrued. The auditor should recognize that management's ability to estimate a range of loss when the loss is probable indicates that a reasonable estimate can be made; therefore, accrual is required.

Accrual is not required if the amount of a probable loss cannot be reasonably estimated or if the loss is only reasonably possible, but disclosure in notes to the financial statements is. When the potential loss is remote, neither accrual nor disclosure is necessary. When disclosure is made in notes to the financial statements regarding loss contingencies, the notes should describe the nature and amount of the contingency to the extent they are known and the opinion of legal counsel and/or management regarding the expected outcome.

Illustration 6 provides examples of financial statement disclosures regarding litigation, claims, and assessments.

PRACTICE ISSUES AND FREQUENTLY ASKED QUESTIONS

Audit Inquiry Letters

Issue 1: What factors should the auditor consider for purposes of establishing materiality levels in the inquiry letter to the client's lawyer?

Generally, the audit inquiry letter will include a materiality amount that constitutes a material contingency for purposes of the lawyer's response. The amount defined as material in the letter should not be so low as to result in an unreasonable burden on the lawyer. The auditor should give consideration to using a materiality amount that is equal to planning materiality that the auditor has established for purposes of the audit. Generally, it is appropriate to ask the lawyer to report all contingencies that exceed planning materiality. However, under certain circumstances, the auditor may decide to use tolerable misstatement or even a lower amount because of specific engagement considerations (e.g., a client with a history of frequent litigation or an inadequate record of identifying and evaluating claims). However, whatever amount is defined as material, the audit inquiry letter should request that the lawyer report all claims that exceed the materiality amount in the aggregate so that the auditor will be made aware of smaller claims that could aggregate the material amount.

Issue 2: Should the audit inquiry letter to the client's lawyer request the lawyer to specify the effective date of the lawyer's response and the date by which the lawyer's response should be sent to the auditor?

Yes. The audit inquiry letter should include a request that the lawyer specify the effective date of his or her response (i.e., the latest date covered by his or her review) and the date by which the lawyer's response should be sent to the auditor. Ordinarily, a two-week period should be allowed between the specified effective date of the lawyer's response and the latest date by which it should be sent to the auditor. This is because it may require several days for law firms to complete the necessary internal review procedures in preparing their response. Therefore, it is common for law firms to specify an effective date of response that may be earlier than the date of the response. If the lawyer's response does not specify an effective date, the auditor can assume that the date of the response is the effective date.

Issue 3: If management represents to the auditor that the entity did not use the services of a lawyer in the period under audit for matters concerning litigation, claims, or assessments, is the auditor, nevertheless, required to send an inquiry letter to the client's lawyer?

No. The auditor is required to send an inquiry letter only to those lawyers with whom management consulted concerning litigation, claims, and assessments. Therefore, if management represents that it had used the services of a lawyer in the period under audit only for matters other than those concerning litigation, claims, or assessments (e.g., to pursue collection of past due accounts receivable from the entity's customers), an audit inquiry letter need *not* be sent. However, the auditor should obtain evidence about management's assertions by reviewing invoices received from the lawyer and related correspondence files. If the auditor discovers information contrary to management's assertions, the auditor should request that management send an inquiry letter to the lawyer. (See also Issue 15 below.)

Evaluation of a Lawyer's Response

Issue 4: Is an oral response from a client's attorney concerning matters covered by the audit inquiry letter acceptable audit evidence?

Yes. In special circumstances, oral representations made by the client's lawyer concerning matters covered by the audit inquiry letter constitute acceptable audit evidence. A conference between the auditor, the client, and the lawyer may provide a more detailed discussion and explanation than a written reply under special circumstances such as the following:

- The matter requires evaluation of the effect of legal advice concerning unsettled points of law.
- The effect of uncorroborated information on the matter in question is not clear.
- Complex judgments are required to render an evaluation of the matter in question.

In such special circumstances the auditor should adequately and thoroughly document conclusions reached about the need for accounting for or disclosure of litigation, claims, and assessments.

Issue 5: What should the auditor do if he or she is uncertain as to the meaning of the lawyer's response to the inquiry letter?

The auditor should compare the lawyer's response with the audit inquiry letter to determine if the lawyer has responded to all matters requested. When the auditor is uncertain as to the meaning of the lawyer's evaluation of litigation, claims, or assessments, he or she should request clarification, either in a follow-up letter or in a conference with the lawyer and the client. The clarification should be adequately documented in the workpapers.

In addition, there may be instances where the auditor's understanding of the facts based on information received differs from the information furnished in the lawyer's response. The auditor should resolve the difference by requesting a conference with the lawyer and management. The auditor also may find it necessary to obtain a revised written response from the lawyer.

The auditor should indicate disposition of significant matters identified in responses from lawyers. For example, an item of litigation may be indicated as having been disclosed in the notes to the financial statements, as not material enough to consider for disclosure, or as the cause of a qualified opinion.

Issue 6: Why is it usually difficult for the auditor to obtain information from the client's lawyer regarding unasserted claims?

Unasserted claims arise when certain events have occurred that may give rise to legal liability but no litigation has actually been initiated or threatened, and no settlement has been proposed. A lawyer may confirm an asserted claim not disclosed by the client in his or her response to the auditor's inquiry letter. However, in the case of an unasserted claim, no such disclosure option exists; therefore, a lawyer may not unilaterally provide information about unasserted claims unless the client specifically identifies such a claim and asks the lawyer to comment on it.

A lawyer's comments regarding pending or threatened litigation and asserted claims and assessments are not likely to constitute a waiver of the attorney-client privilege. However, a response regarding an unasserted claim could be a waiver. Unasserted claims are treated differently because a lawyer's knowledge and evaluation of unasserted claims probably result from confidential client communication. Assume, for example, that a company manufactures a product that injures consumers over time. This is an indication of an unasserted claim, until the injuries are discovered and legal action is initiated. A lawyer can advise a client about product liability only after the client has communicated relevant facts and information to the lawyer. In contrast, legal conclusions related to pending or threatened litigation come from a variety of sources, including depositions and the attorney's own research. Therefore, an audit response evaluating such legal action is not a waiver of privileged communication.

Limitations of a Lawyer's Response and Scope Restrictions

Issue 7: What course of action should the auditor take if the client's lawyer refuses to respond to the audit inquiry letter?

If the client's lawyer refuses to respond to the audit inquiry letter, the auditor should attempt to hold a conference with the lawyer and the client in order to (1) review the reasons for refusing to respond and (2) obtain oral confirmation. If the auditor receives an oral response, the auditor should write a letter of understanding regarding the meeting and send it to the attorney, with a copy furnished to the client.

If the auditor is unsuccessful and the client's lawyer (1) refuses to furnish the information requested, (2) refuses to evaluate litigation, or (3) responds in a manner that can be interpreted only as a refusal, the auditor is faced with a scope limitation, and a qualified opinion or disclaimer of opinion should be issued.

Issue 8: Is it common for a lawyer to restrict his or her response to those matters that he or she has devoted substantive attention to in the form of legal consultation or representation?

Yes. Both the auditing literature and the American Bar Association's "Statement of Policy Regarding Lawyers' Responses to Auditors' Requests for Information" recognize that it is appropriate for lawyers to restrict their responses to those matters that they have devoted substantive attention to in the form of legal consultation or representation. This essentially means that a lawyer does not, and is not required to, undertake to evaluate all legal exposures or reconsider earlier conclusions. Therefore, such lawyer responses are *not* considered limitations on the scope of the audit and, consequently, do not require modifications of the auditor's report.

Issue 9: Does a lawyer's response that includes explanatory comments emphasizing the preservation of the attorney-client privilege with respect to unasserted possible claims or assessments constitute a limitation on the scope of the audit?

No. Some lawyers include in their responses to audit inquiry letters explanatory comments that emphasize the preservation of the attorney-client privilege with respect to unasserted possible claims or assessments, such as:

It would be inappropriate for this firm to respond to a general inquiry relating to the existence of unasserted possible claims or assessments involving the company.

The inclusion of this or similar language in a lawyer's response does not result in a limitation on the scope of the audit.

Issue 10: Do comments about the attorney-client privilege in the audit inquiry letter or in the lawyer's response result in a limitation of the scope of an audit?

No. Some clients state in their letter of audit inquiry that the letter is not intended to infringe on the attorney-client privilege or the attorney work-product privilege. Likewise, the response to the letter by the lawyer may state that the lawyer has been advised by the client that the request for information is not intended to waive the privileged relationship with the client. Such comments in the audit inquiry letter or the lawyer's response to it simply make explicit what has always been implicit: that neither the client nor the lawyer intended a waiver. Therefore, such language does not result in a limitation of the scope of an audit.

Issue 11: Does an auditor's inability to review documents or correspondence that is subject to lawyer-client privilege constitute a scope limitation?

No. In recognition of the public interest in protecting the confidentiality of lawyer-client communications, the auditing literature is not intended to require an auditor to examine documents that the client identifies as subject to the lawyer-client privilege. The auditor may wish to confirm with the lawyer that such information is subject to that privilege and that the information was considered by the lawyer in responding to the audit inquiry letter.

Issue 12: May the auditor refer to or quote the lawyer's response in the client's financial statements without first consulting with the lawyer?

No. For example, a lawyer's response may contain information that could prejudice efforts to negotiate a favorable settlement of a pending litigation described in the response. Therefore, the lawyer should have an opportunity to review the footnote in full, if the auditor decides to quote verbatim or include the substance of the lawyer's reply in footnotes to the client's financial statements.

The auditor should also recognize that lawyers generally include specific language in their response, placing the burden on the auditor to obtain the lawyer's consent before making reference to or quoting the lawyer's response in the footnotes to the financial statements. Furthermore, the audit inquiry letter to the client's lawyer typically includes the following statement: "Your response will not be quoted or referred to in our financial statements without prior consultation with you." Therefore, when the auditor concludes that matters reported by the client's lawyer require disclosure in the entity's audited financial statements, the auditor should discuss the wording with the lawyer and the client before issuance of the financial statements.

Inside Counsel

Issue 13: Is audit evidence obtained from a client's inside general counsel or legal department a substitute for information outside counsel refuses to furnish?

No. An entity may employ an inside general counsel to handle its legal matters. The inside legal counsel is as fully bound by the American Bar Association Code of Professional Responsibility as is outside legal counsel. Accordingly, the auditor may obtain audit evidence from the client's inside counsel. However, a response from outside counsel usually is superior audit evidence to that received from inside counsel. Therefore, corroboration from inside general counsel is not a substitute for information that outside counsel refuses to furnish. If outside counsel has devoted substantive attention to a client's legal matters and refuses to respond to the audit inquiry letter, inside general counsel's opinion cannot be substituted.

Issue 14: Under what circumstances would the auditor's use of a client's inside counsel in the evaluation of litigation, claims, and assessments be considered adequate audit evidence?

The auditor should send audit inquiry letters to those lawyers, either inside counsel or outside lawyers, who have the primary responsibility for, and knowledge about, particular litigation, claims, and assessments. When inside counsel is involved, the following guidance applies:

- If inside counsel is handling litigation, claims, and assessments exclusively, their evaluation and response ordinarily would be considered adequate.
- If both inside counsel and outside counsel are handling the matters, but inside counsel has assumed the primary responsibility for the matters, inside counsel's evaluation may well be considered adequate.
- If the matters involve substantial overall participation by outside lawyers and are significant to the financial statements, the auditor should consider obtaining the outside lawyers' response that they have not formulated a substantive conclusion that differs materially from inside counsel's evaluation, even though inside counsel may have primary responsibility.
- If both inside counsel and outside lawyers have devoted substantive attention to a legal matter, but their evaluations of the possible outcome differ, the auditor should discuss the differences with the parties involved. If the lawyers fail to reach an agreement, the auditor should consider modifying the audit report.

Client Has Not Consulted a Lawyer

Issue 15: What is the auditor's responsibility in situations where the client has not consulted a lawyer?

The auditor's responsibility is limited expressly to inquiries of lawyers with whom management has consulted. Therefore, if the client has not consulted a lawyer during the period under audit, the auditor should rely on (1) the review of internal information available and (2) written representations of management regarding litigation, claims, and assessments. In such circumstances, the auditor should modify the management representation letter item regarding litigation, claims, and assessments to include the following wording (see also Issue 3 above):

"We are not aware of any pending or threatened litigation, claims, or assessments or unasserted claims or assessments that are required to be accrued or disclosed in the financial statements in accordance with FASB Accounting Standards Codification (ASC) 450, *Contingencies*, and we have not consulted a lawyer concerning litigation, claims, or assessments."

Updated Lawyer's Response

Issue 16: What factors should the auditor consider in determining whether to obtain an updated response from the client's lawyer if a significant amount of time has elapsed between the effective date of the lawyer's response and the completion date of the audit?

If a significant amount of time has elapsed between the effective date of the lawyer's response and the completion date of the audit, the auditor should consider obtaining an updated response. If the effective date of the lawyer's response is more than one month before the completion date of the audit, the auditor generally should obtain updated responses from lawyers to whom audit inquiry letters were sent. The auditor should use professional judgment in determining whether oral or written updates should be obtained. If the auditor obtains an oral update from the lawyer, and no significant changes have occurred, the auditor should document the discussion in the workpapers. If the auditor obtains an oral update from the lawyer and is informed that significant changes have occurred, the auditor should obtain an updated written response from the lawyer.

ILLUSTRATIONS AND PRACTICE AIDS

ILLUSTRATION 1—ILLUSTRATIVE AUDIT INQUIRY LETTER TO CLIENT LEGAL COUNSEL IF MANAGEMENT HAS PROVIDED DETAILS OF LEGAL ACTIONS

PRACTICE POINT: This letter generally should be used if the client prepares an audit inquiry letter that includes a list describing and evaluating all material pending or threatened litigation, asserted claims, and assessments. Therefore, the letter is sent to the client's legal counsel to obtain corroboration of information furnished by management to the auditor. If the client does not furnish the auditor with this information, but requests that legal counsel prepare such a list, the letter in Illustration 2 should be used.

(Prepared on client's letterhead)

(Date)

(Name and address of lawyer)

Dear_____:

In connection with an audit of our financial statements as of *(insert balance sheet date)* and for the *(insert period)* then ended, we have prepared and furnished to our independent auditors *(insert name and address of auditors)* a description and evaluation of certain contingencies, including those set forth below, involving matters with respect to which you have been engaged and to which you have devoted substantive attention on behalf of the Company (and any of its subsidiaries, if applicable) in the form of legal consultation or representation. These contingencies are regarded by us as material for this purpose if they involve claims amounting to more than *(insert materiality dollar amount)*, individually or in the aggregate.

Pending or Threatened Litigation, Asserted Claims, and Assessments

[The client should prepare a list describing all material pending or threatened litigation, asserted claims, and assessments. Ordinarily, such information would include (1) the nature of the matter, including (a) the proceedings, (b) the amount of monetary damages sought, or, if no amounts are indicated, a statement to that effect, (c) the extent to which potential damages are covered by insurance, and (d) the objectives sought by the plaintiff other than monetary or other damages, if any; (2) the progress of the matter to date; (3) how management is responding or intends to respond (e.g., to contest the case vigorously or to seek an out-of-court settlement); and (4) an evaluation of the likelihood of an unfavorable outcome and an estimate, if one can be made, of the amount or range of potential loss.]

Please furnish to our auditors such explanation, if any, that you consider necessary to supplement the foregoing information, including an explanation of those matters for which your views differ from those stated, and an identification of the omission of any pending or threatened litigation, claims, and assessments, or a statement that the list of such matters is complete. If you cannot express an opinion on the outcome of certain litigation, please so state, together with your reasons for that position.

Unasserted Claims and Assessments (considered by us to be probable of assertion, and, if asserted, to have at least a reasonable possibility of an unfavorable outcome)

[The client should prepare a list describing all such material contingencies. Ordinarily, management's information would include (1) the nature of the matter, (2) how management intends to respond if the claim is asserted, and (3) an evaluation of the likelihood of an unfavorable outcome and an estimate, if one can be made, of the amount or range of potential loss.]

Please furnish to our auditors an explanation, if any, that you consider necessary to supplement the foregoing information, including an explanation of those matters for which your views differ from those stated.

We understand that whenever, in the course of performing legal services for us with respect to a matter recognized to involve an unasserted possible claim or assessment that may call for financial statement disclosure, if you have formed a professional conclusion that we should disclose or consider disclosure concerning such possible claim or assessment, as a matter of professional responsibility to us, you will so advise us and will consult with us concerning the question of such disclosure and the applicable requirements of FASB Accounting Standards Codification (ASC) 450, *Contingencies* (excerpts of which can be found in the ABA's *Auditor's Letter Handbook*). Please specifically confirm to our auditors that our understanding is correct.

We have represented to and assured our auditors that the unasserted claims and assessments mentioned in this letter include all unasserted claims and assessments that you have advised us are probable of assertion and must be disclosed in accordance with ASC 450.

PRACTICE POINT: This section of the letter assumes that the client specifies certain unasserted claims and assessments. If management believes that there are no unasserted claims or assessments to be specified to the lawyer for comment that are probable of assertion and that, if asserted, would have a reasonable possibility of an unfavorable outcome, the unasserted claims and assessments section above should be replaced in its entirety by the following:

> **Unasserted Claims and Assessments**
>
> We have represented to our auditors that there are no unasserted possible claims or assessments that you have advised us are probable of assertion and must be disclosed in accordance with ASC 450 (excerpts of which can be found in the ABA's *Auditor's Letter Handbook*).
>
> We understand that whenever, in the course of performing legal services for us with respect to a matter recognized to involve an unasserted possible claim or assessment that may call for financial statement disclosure, if you have formed a professional conclusion that we should disclose or consider disclosure concerning such possible claim or assessment, as a matter of professional responsibility to us, you will so advise us and will consult with us concerning the question of such disclosure and the applicable requirements of ASC 450. Please specifically confirm to our auditors that our understanding is correct.

Other Matters

[The auditor may request the client to inquire about additional matters (e.g., specified information on certain contractually assumed obligations of the Company, such as guarantees of indebtedness of others).]

PRACTICE POINT: The auditor may wish to confirm with legal counsel the amount owed by the client for legal services. Accordingly, language similar to the following would be appropriate:

> Please indicate the amount owed to you for services and expenses, billed and unbilled, as of *(insert balance sheet date).*

Response

Your response should include matters that existed as of *(insert balance sheet date)* and additional information about those matters or new matters that arose during the period from that date to the effective date of your response.

Please specifically identify the nature of and reasons for any limitation on your response.

We expect to have our audit completed about *(insert expected completion date)*. Therefore, we appreciate receiving your reply by that date with a specified effective date no earlier than *(insert date)*.

Your response will not be quoted or referred to in the Company's financial statements without prior consultation with you.

Please send your response directly to our auditors, with a copy to me.

Thank you for your anticipated timely cooperation with this request.

Respectfully,

(Name of client)

(Client's authorized signature and title)

PRACTICE POINT: In some cases, to emphasize the preservation of the attorney-client privilege or the attorney work-product privilege, clients have included language similar to the following in the audit inquiry letter to legal counsel:

> We do not intend that either our request to you to provide information to our auditor or your response to our auditor should be construed in any way to constitute a waiver of the attorney-client privilege or the attorney work-product privilege.

The explanatory language about the attorney-client privilege or the attorney work-product privilege does not result in a limitation on the scope of the audit. Such language simply makes explicit what has always been implicit: that the client's request does not constitute an expression of intent to waive such privileges.

PRACTICE POINT: Ordinarily, a two-week period should be allowed between the specified effective date of the lawyer's response and the expected completion date of the audit.

ILLUSTRATION 2—ILLUSTRATIVE AUDIT INQUIRY LETTER TO CLIENT LEGAL COUNSEL IF MANAGEMENT HAS NOT PROVIDED DETAILS OF LEGAL ACTIONS

PRACTICE POINT: This letter generally should be used if the client has not included a list describing and evaluating all material pending or threatened litigation, asserted claims, and assessments. If the client has prepared and furnished the auditor with such information, the letter in Illustration 1 should be used.

(Prepared on client's letterhead)

(Date)

(Name and address of lawyer)

Dear _____:

In connection with an audit of our financial statements as of *(insert balance sheet date)* and for the *(insert period)* then ended, please furnish to our independent auditors *(insert name and address of auditors)* the following information concerning certain contingencies involving matters as to which you have devoted substantive attention on behalf of the Company (and any of its subsidiaries, if applicable) in the form of legal consultation or representation. These contingencies are regarded by us as material for this purpose if they involve claims amounting to more than *(insert materiality dollar amount),* individually or in the aggregate.

Pending or Threatened Litigation, Asserted Claims, and Assessments

Please furnish to our auditors a description and evaluation of all pending or threatened litigation, asserted claims, and assessments. Your response should include the following:

1. The nature of each matter, including (a) the proceedings; (b) the amount of monetary damages sought, or if no amounts are indicated, a statement to that effect; (c) the extent to which potential damages are covered by insurance; and (d) the objectives sought by the plaintiff other than monetary or other damages.

2. The progress of each matter to date.

3. The way we are responding or intend to respond (e.g., to contest the case vigorously or to seek an out-of court settlement).

4. An evaluation of the likelihood of an unfavorable outcome and an estimate, if one can be made, of the amount or range of potential loss. If you cannot express an opinion on the outcome of certain litigation, please so state, together with your reasons for that position.

Unasserted Claims and Assessments (considered by us to be probable of assertion, and, if asserted, to have at least a reasonable possibility of an unfavorable outcome)

[*The client should prepare a list describing all such material contingencies. Ordinarily, management's information would include (1) the nature of the matter, (2) how management intends to respond if the claim is asserted, and (3) an evaluation of the likelihood of an unfavorable outcome and an estimate, if one can be made, of the amount or range of potential loss.*]

Please furnish to our auditors an explanation, if any, that you consider necessary to supplement the foregoing information, including an explanation of those matters as to which your views may differ from those stated.

We understand that whenever, in the course of performing legal services for us with respect to a matter recognized to involve an unasserted possible claim or assessment that may call for financial statement disclosure, if you have formed a professional conclusion that we should disclose or consider disclosure concerning such possible claim or assessment, as a matter of professional responsibility to us, you will so advise us and will consult with us concerning the question of such disclosure and the applicable requirements of FASB Accounting Standards Codification (ASC) 450 *Contingencies* (excerpts of which can be found in the

ABA's *Auditor's Letter Handbook*). Please specifically confirm to our auditors that our understanding is correct.

We have represented to and assured our auditors that the unasserted claims and assessments mentioned in this letter include all unasserted claims and assessments that you have advised us are probable of assertion and must be disclosed in accordance with ASC 450.

PRACTICE POINT: This section of the letter assumes that the client specifies certain unasserted claims and assessments. If management believes that there are no unasserted claims or assessments to be specified to the lawyer for comment that are probable of assertion and that, if asserted, would have a reasonable possibility of an unfavorable outcome, the unasserted claims and assessments section above should be replaced in its entirety by the following:

Unasserted Claims and Assessments

We have represented to our auditors that there are no unasserted possible claims or assessments that you have advised us are probable of assertion and must be disclosed in accordance with ASC 450 (excerpts of which can be found in the ABA's *Auditor's Letter Handbook*).

We understand that whenever, in the course of performing legal services for us with respect to a matter recognized to involve an unasserted possible claim or assessment that may call for financial statement disclosure, if you have formed a professional conclusion that we should disclose or consider disclosure concerning such possible claim or assessment, as a matter of professional responsibility to us, you will so advise us and will consult with us concerning the question of such disclosure and the applicable requirements of ASC 450. Please specifically confirm to our auditors that our understanding is correct.

Other Matters

[*The auditor may request the client to inquire about additional matters (e.g., specified information on certain contractually assumed obligations of the Company, such as guarantees of indebtedness of others).*]

PRACTICE POINT: The auditor may wish to confirm with legal counsel the amount owed by the client for legal services. Accordingly, language similar to the following would be appropriate:

Please indicate the amount owed to you for services and expenses, billed and unbilled, as of *(insert balance sheet date)*.

Response

Your response should include matters that existed as of *(insert balance sheet date)* and additional information about those matters or new matters that arose during the period from that date to the effective date of your response.

Please specifically identify the nature of and reasons for any limitation on your response.

We expect to have our audit completed about *(insert expected completion date)*. Therefore, we appreciate receiving your reply by that date with a specified effective date no earlier than *(insert date)*.

Your response will not be quoted or referred to in the Company's financial statements without prior consultation with you.

Please send your response directly to our auditors, with a copy to me.

Thank you for your anticipated timely cooperation with this request.

Respectfully,

(Name of client)

(Client's authorized signature and title)

PRACTICE POINT: In some cases, to emphasize the preservation of the attorney-client privilege or the attorney work-product privilege, clients have included language similar to the following in the audit inquiry letter to legal counsel:

> We do not intend that either our request to you to provide information to our auditor or your response to our auditor should be construed in any way to constitute a waiver of the attorney-client privilege or the attorney work-product privilege.

The explanatory language about the attorney-client privilege or the attorney work-product privilege does not result in a limitation on the scope of the audit. Such language simply makes explicit what has always been implicit: that the client's request does not constitute an expression of intent to waive such privileges.

PRACTICE POINT: Ordinarily, a two-week period should be allowed between the specified effective date of the lawyer's response and the expected completion date of the audit.

ILLUSTRATION 3—AUDITOR'S QUALIFIED OPINION DUE TO CLIENT'S LAWYER NOT RESPONDING TO AUDIT INQUIRY LETTER

Independent Auditor's Report

Board of Directors and Stockholders
ABC Company

We have audited the accompanying balance sheets of ABC Company as of December 31, 20X2, and 20X1, and the related statements of income, retained earnings, and cash flows for the years then ended. These financial statements are the responsibility of the Company's management. Our responsibility is to express an opinion on these financial statements based on our audits.

Except as discussed in the following paragraph, we conducted our audits in accordance with auditing standards generally accepted in the United States of America. Those standards require that we plan and perform the audits to obtain reasonable assurance about whether the financial statements are free of material misstatement. An audit includes examining, on a test basis, evidence supporting the amounts and disclosures in the financial statements. An audit also includes assessing the accounting principles used and significant estimates made by management, as well as evaluating the overall financial statement presentation. We believe that our audits provide a reasonable basis for our opinion.

We were unable to obtain a response from the Company's legal counsel to our request regarding a discussion and evaluation of the pending litigation matter described in Note [X].

In our opinion, except for the effects of any adjustments and additional disclosures that might have resulted if the scope of our audit had not been limited by our inability to obtain satisfactory evidence relating to the pending litigation, the financial statements referred to above present fairly, in all material respects, the financial position of ABC Company as of December 31, 20X2, and 20X1, and the results of its operations and its cash flows for the years then ended in conformity with accounting principles generally accepted in the United States of America.

[Signature]

[Date]

ILLUSTRATION 4—EXAMPLES OF LAWYERS' RESPONSES THAT ARE NOT CLEAR ABOUT THE LIKELIHOOD OF AN UNFAVORABLE OUTCOME

- "This action involves unique characteristics wherein authoritative legal precedents do not seem to exist. We believe that the plaintiff will have serious problems establishing the company's liability under the act; nevertheless, if the plaintiff is successful, the award may be substantial."

- "It is our opinion that the company will be able to assert meritorious defenses to this action." (The term "meritorious defenses" indicates that the company's defenses will not be summarily dismissed by the court; it does not necessarily indicate counsel's opinion that the company will prevail.)

- "We believe the action can be settled for less than the damages claimed."

- "We are unable to express an opinion on the merits of the litigation at this time. The company believes there is absolutely no merit to the litigation." (If client's counsel, with the benefit of all relevant information, is unable to conclude that the likelihood of an unfavorable outcome is "remote," it is unlikely that management would be able to form a judgment to that effect.)

- "In our opinion, the company has a substantial chance of prevailing in this action." (A "substantial chance," a "reasonable opportunity," and similar terms indicate more uncertainty than an opinion that the company will prevail.)

ILLUSTRATION 5—EXAMPLES OF LAWYERS' RESPONSES THAT ARE CLEAR THAT THE LIKELIHOOD OF AN UNFAVORABLE OUTCOME IS REMOTE

- "We are of the opinion that this action will not result in any liability to the company."

- "It is our opinion that the possible liability to the company in this proceeding is nominal in amount."

- "We believe the company will be able to defend this action successfully."

- "We believe that the plaintiff's case against the company is without merit."

- "Based on the facts known to us, after a full investigation, it is our opinion that no liability will be established against the company in these suits."

ILLUSTRATION 6—EXAMPLES OF FINANCIAL STATEMENT DISCLOSURES REGARDING LITIGATION, CLAIMS, AND ASSESSMENTS

Example 1: No accrual is made for litigation because the likelihood of a material adverse outcome is remote

The Company is a defendant in a case entitled Jones vs. the Company, which is in the United States District Court in the Northern District of California. The case arose from claims by Mrs. Jones, a former employee, that the Company had discriminated against her during her employment at the Company. The suit seeks damages totaling $1,500,000. The Company believes that the claims are without merit and intends to vigorously defend its position. The ultimate outcome of this litigation cannot presently be determined. However, in management's opinion, the likelihood of a material adverse outcome is remote. Accordingly, adjustments, if any, that might result from the resolution of this matter have not been reflected in the financial statements.

Example 2: No accrual is made of potential liability because management does not believe it is probable

A former employee of the Company has filed a workers' compensation claim related to injuries incurred in connection with the September 20X2 fire at the Company's Temecula facility. In the claim, the employee is requesting payment of an additional 15% award of compensation, approximately $450,000, claiming the Company violated a state safety statute in connection with the occurrence of his injury. As of December 31, 20X2, the Company has not recorded a provision for this matter as management intends to vigorously defend these allegations and believes the payment of the penalty is not probable. The Company believes, however, that any liability it may incur would not have a material adverse effect on its financial condition or its results of operations.

Example 3: Accrual is made but exposure exists in excess of amount accrued

The Company is a defendant in a lawsuit, filed by a former supplier of electronic components alleging breach of contract, which seeks damages totaling $750,000. The Company proposed a settlement in the amount of $500,000, based on the advice of the Company's legal counsel. Consequently, $500,000 was charged to operations in the accompanying 20X2 financial statements. However, if the settlement offer is not accepted by the plaintiff and the case goes to trial, the amount of the ultimate loss to the Company, if any, may equal the entire amount of damages of $750,000 sought by the plaintiff.

Example 4: Unasserted claim relating to product defects

In September 20X2, the Company announced that it will conduct an inspection program to eliminate a potential problem with an electrical component supplied to various manufacturers of microwave ovens. The ultimate cost of the repair will not be known until the inspection program is complete, which could have a material impact on the Company's financial condition and results of operations.

Example 5: Contingent liability resulting from government investigation

The Company is currently the subject of certain U.S. government investigations. If the Company is charged with wrongdoing as a result of any of these investigations, the Company could be suspended from bidding on or receiving awards of new government contracts pending the completion of legal proceedings. If convicted or found liable, the Company could be fined and debarred from new government contracting for a period generally not to exceed three years.

Example 6: Litigation settlement is subject to a confidentiality agreement

In January 20X2, Stuart Construction Co. ("Stuart") filed suit against the Company alleging that the Company had failed to provide coated, welded pipe, fittings, and joints in accordance with contract specifications for a construction project in the Pacific Grove area. In November 20X2, the parties involved agreed to settle the suit. The financial terms of the settlement are subject to a confidentiality agreement; however, the settlement will not have a material impact on the Company's financial condition or results of operations.

AU SECTION 339
AUDIT DOCUMENTATION

PRACTICE POINT: As part of its Clarity Project, the American Institute of Certified Public Accountants' (AICPA's) Auditing Standards Board (ASB) has finalized a clarified Statement on Auditing Standards (SAS) titled, "Audit Documentation (Redrafted)," which supersedes AU Section 339 (Audit Documentation). The clarified SAS does not change or expand extant AU Section 339 in any significant respect. Requirements addressing the retention, confidentiality, integrity, accessibility, and retrievability of audit documentation in extant AU Section 339 have been placed in Statement on Quality Control Standards (SQCS) No. 7, "A Firm's System of Quality Control."

The ASB is expected to issue many of the clarified standards in *one* SAS that will be codified in "AU Section" format. The ASB has decided that the effective date of the clarified SASs that have not yet been issued is for audits of financial statements for periods ending on or after December 15, 2012. Auditors should be alert to and monitor further developments in this area.

PRACTICE POINT: In March 2011, the American Institute of Certified Public Accountants' (AICPA's) Auditing Standards Board (ASB) issued an exposure draft (ED) of a proposed Statement on Auditing Standards (SAS) titled, "Omnibus Statement on Auditing Standards—2011." This proposed SAS, which is part of the AICPA's Clarity Project, would amend the following SASs that have been issued in the clarity format and are currently effective:

- SAS-117 (AU Section 801) (Compliance Audits). The amendment to SAS-117 conforms the auditor's report on compliance to the requirements of the clarified SAS, "Forming an Opinion and Reporting on Financial Statements." In addition, the amendment revises the appendix in SAS-117, "AU Sections That Are Not Applicable to Compliance Audits," to reflect conforming changes to affected references to AU Sections as a result of the ASB's Clarity Project.

- SAS-118 (AU Section 550) (Other Information in Documents Containing Audited Financial Statements). The amendment to SAS-118 clarifies the requirements with respect to identified material inconsistencies by categorizing the requirements based on when the inconsistencies are identified (prior to the date of the auditor's report on the audited financial statements; after the date of the auditor's report but prior to the report release date; and after the report release date). It also adds application material addressing electronic sites to include guidance from an interpretation of AU Section 550 (Other Information in Documents Containing Audited Financial Statements), which the ASB determined was appropriate to include in SAS-118.

In addition, in order to address other changes necessitated by the ASB's overall Clarity Project, the proposed SAS would amend the following clarified SASs that have been finalized and released, but not yet issued as authoritative:

- Clarified SAS, "Overall Objectives of the Independent Auditor and the Conduct of an Audit in Accordance with Generally Accepted Auditing Standards."

- Clarified SAS, "Modifications to the Opinion in the Independent Auditor's Report."

- Clarified SAS, "Reports on Application of Requirements of an Applicable Financial Reporting Framework.."

- Clarified SAS, "The Auditor's Communication with Those Charged with Governance (Redrafted)."

- Clarified SAS, "Audit Documentation (Redrafted)."

The proposed SAS would be effective for audits of financial statements for periods ending on or after December 15, 2012, except for the amendment to the clarified SAS, "Reports on Application of Requirements of an Applicable Financial Reporting Framework," which would be effective for engagements ending on or after December 15, 2012.

WHAT EVERY PRACTITIONER SHOULD KNOW

Basic Requirements

This Section requires auditors to prepare and retain audit documentation in connection with each engagement conducted pursuant to generally accepted auditing standards (GAAS) established by the AICPA. Audit documentation, which is also commonly referred to as "work papers" or "working papers," includes the procedures the auditor performed, the evidence obtained, the source of the information, and the conclusions reached. The type, form, quantity, and content of audit documentation are matters of the auditor's judgment; however, they should be tailored to meet the circumstances of the individual engagement.

Audit documentation, which may be in the form of paper, electronic files, or other media, includes: audit programs, confirmations, management representation letters, correspondence (including e-mail), memoranda, analyses, abstracts or copies of client documents, and client-prepared or auditor-prepared schedules. When the original paper documentation is transferred or copied to another media, the auditor should make sure that none of the original documentation is compromised in the process, and the copy is identical to the original documentation.

Relevance and Sufficiency of Audit Documentation

Audit documentation should:

- Include the nature, timing, extent, and results of procedures performed by the auditor; the evidence obtained; the source of the evidence obtained; and the conclusions reached;

- Incorporate abstracts or copies of the entity's records, such as significant contracts and agreements, if necessary to understand the work performed and conclusions reached;

- Include significant audit findings or issues encountered during an engagement, including: (a) description of the findings or issues, (b) the actions taken to address them, (c) any additional evidence obtained as a result of the actions taken, and (d) the basis for the final conclusions reached; and

- Contain sufficient information to enable an *experienced auditor* with no previous connection to the engagement to understand and determine the following: (a) the nature, timing, and extent of the procedures performed; (b) the results and evidence obtained; (c) the conclusions reached on important and significant issues; and (d) that the client's accounting records agree or reconcile with the financial statements or other audited information. For purposes of this requirement, this Section defines an "experienced auditor" as an internal or external auditor who "possesses the competencies and skills that would have enabled him or her to perform the audit." This individual is expected to have an understanding of: audit processes; the SASs and relevant legal and regulatory requisites; the entity's business environment; and auditing and financial reporting issues pertinent to the industry in which the entity operates.

Oral explanations alone do not constitute adequate support for the work the auditor performed or the conclusions reached. Oral explanations should generally be limited to those situations where it is necessary to clarify or supplement information already included in the workpaper documentation and should not contradict the documented evidence.

Factors to Consider in Determining the Nature and Extent of Audit Documentation

This Section indicates that, in determining the nature and extent of the audit documentation to be included in the audit file for the specific engagement, the auditor should consider the following factors:

- The nature of the audit procedures used;
- The risk of material misstatement relating to the assertion, the account balance, or class of transactions, and related disclosures;
- The degree of professional judgment involved in performing the work and evaluating the results;
- The significance of the audit evidence obtained;
- The nature and extent of exceptions discovered; and
- The need to document a conclusion not readily determinable from the documentation of the work performed or evidence obtained.

Specific Documentation Requirements

While the type and extent of audit documentation is, to some degree, dependent on the characteristics of a particular engagement, this Section requires the auditor to include documentation of the following specific matters:

1. *Significant audit findings or issues*—The auditor should document significant audit findings or issues encountered during an engagement, includ-

ing: (a) a description of the findings or issues, (b) the actions taken to address them, (c) any additional evidence obtained as a result of the actions taken, and (d) the basis for the final conclusions reached. Significant audit findings or issues fall into one of the following categories:

a. Matters that both (i) are significant, and (ii) involve the selection, application, and consistency of accounting principles regarding the financial statements and related disclosures. Such matters may relate to: accounting for complex or unusual transactions; accounting estimates; management assumptions; and uncertainties.

b. Findings that indicate that (i) the financial information or disclosures could be materially misstated or (ii) the auditor's assessment of the risks of material misstatement, and the auditor's responses thereto, need to be modified.

c. Circumstances causing significant difficulty in the application of required or necessary audit procedures.

d. Findings that could lead to a modification of the standard auditor's report.

e. Audit adjustments. This Section defines an *audit adjustment* as "a correction of a misstatement of the financial information that is identified by the auditor, whether or not recorded by management, that could, either individually or when aggregated with other misstatements, have a material effect on the company's financial information."

2. *Discussions of significant matters with management and others*—The auditor is required to document discussions of significant matters with management and others (e.g., those charged with governance, those who have oversight responsibility of the financial reporting process, internal auditors); such documentation should include: (a) the significant matter discussed; (b) the individuals involved in the discussions; (c) the dates of the discussions; and (d) the responses obtained.

3. *Any information that the auditor identified that conflicts with, or is different from, the auditor's final conclusions about a significant matter, and how the auditor addressed the inconsistency*—However, it is not necessary to retain documentation that reflects incomplete or preliminary thinking; superseded drafts of working papers or financial statements; duplicates of documents; and previous copies of documents that have been corrected for typographical or other errors.

4. *The individuals who performed the audit work and the date the work was performed.*

5. *The individuals who reviewed the audit documentation and the date of their review.*

6. *Identification of specific items tested*—Where the audit procedures performed involve the inspection of documents or confirmation, including substantive tests of details and tests of operating effectiveness of controls, documentation should include identifying characteristics of the

specific items the auditor tested. This requirement may be satisfied by indicating the source from which the items were selected and the specific selection criteria. For example, the documentation would include:

a. The specific invoice numbers or check numbers of the items included in the sample, when an audit sample is selected from a population of documents.

b. A description of the scope and an identification of the population (e.g., all sales invoices over $50,000 from the October sales journal), when all items over a specified dollar amount are selected from a certain population.

c. An identification of the source of the documents and an indication of the starting point and the sampling interval (e.g., a systematic sample of shipping documents was selected from the shipping log for the period from June 1, 20X5 to October 31, 20X5, starting with shipping document number 249 and selecting every 75th shipping document from that point), when a systematic sample is selected from a population of documents.

7. *Abstracts or copies of the entity's records.*

8. *Any departures from a "presumptively mandatory requirement" that the auditor undertook that in his or her judgment were necessary to more effectively accomplish the objectives of the audit*—A "presumptively mandatory requirement" is indicated by the imperative "should." Compliance with requirements of this type specified in professional standards is required, unless the auditor can demonstrate that the alternative procedures or actions that he or she applied were appropriate and sufficient to accomplish the objectives of the particular standard. If the auditor departs from a presumptively mandatory requirement, the auditor must document in the working papers the following: (a) the reasons why the presumptively mandatory requirement was not complied with and (b) how the alternative procedures performed adequately achieved the objectives of the presumptively mandatory requirement.

Changes to Audit Documentation Subsequent to the Auditor's Report Date

The date of the auditor's report should not be earlier than the date on which the auditor has obtained sufficient appropriate audit evidence to support his or her opinion on the entity's financial statements. This Section explicitly states that sufficient appropriate audit evidence includes evidence that:

- The audit documentation has been reviewed;
- The entity's financial statements, including disclosures, have been prepared; and
- Management has asserted that it has taken responsibility for the entity's financial statements and related disclosures (e.g., obtained a representation letter to this effect).

Generally, the auditor's report date is very close to the report release date (i.e., the date the auditor grants the entity permission to use the auditor's report).

This Section specifies that the auditor should complete the assembly of the final audit file no later than 60 days following the report release date. The date that the audit file is completed is referred to as the "documentation completion date." The audit documentation should also include notation of the report release date.

Documentation of new information After the date of the auditor's report, the auditor may receive new information or discover that audit procedures may not have been performed, evidence may not have been obtained, or appropriate conclusions may not have been reached. This Section provides the following guidance for such circumstances:

- Based on the auditor's evaluation, the auditor may not be able to determine or demonstrate that the procedures performed were adequate, that the evidence obtained was sufficient, and that the conclusions reached were appropriate. In such circumstances, the auditor should comply with the provisions of AU Section 390, (Consideration of Omitted Procedures after the Report Date), including the documentation requirements of AU Section 390.

- Subsequent to the date of the auditor's report, the auditor may become aware of facts that existed at the date of the audit report, but were not known to him or her at that date, and that would have affected the audit report had he or she been aware of such facts. In such circumstances, the auditor should follow the guidance in AU Section 561, (Subsequent Discovery of Facts Existing at the Date of the Auditor's Report).

In each of these circumstances, the auditor should appropriately document the new information that the auditor became aware of subsequent to the audit report date. Also, if the auditor determines it is necessary to perform new audit procedures or reaches new conclusions, the auditor should appropriately document these changes. This Section indicates that such documentation should include the following:

- The date the changes were made;
- The individual who made the changes;
- The individual who reviewed the changes and the date of the review, if applicable;
- The specific reasons for the changes; and
- The effect of the changes on the auditor's conclusions.

Also, if the auditor deems it necessary to make any additions or amendments to the audit documentation after the documentation completion date, the auditor should document such changes and include the items listed above. However, the auditor is precluded from deleting or discarding audit documentation after the documentation completion date.

Ownership and Confidentiality of Audit Documentation

This section requires the auditor to adopt reasonable procedures and controls to accomplish the following:

1. Retain and access audit documentation for a period of time sufficient to meet the needs of the firm's practice and to satisfy legal or regulatory requirements for records retention, but not shorter than five years from the report release date;

2. Maintain the confidentiality of client information that is confidential and is contained in the audit documentation;

3. Determine when and by whom the audit documentation was created, changed, or reviewed;

4. Protect the integrity of the documentation at all stages of the audit;

5. Prevent unauthorized changes to the audit documentation; and

6. Allow authorized individuals access to the audit documentation to properly discharge their responsibilities.

Providing Access to or Copies of Audit Documentation to Regulators

Auditors are sometimes required by law, regulation, or audit contract to provide regulators access to the audit documentation. The term *regulator* includes federal, state, and local government officials with legal oversight authority over the entity. Regulators may request access to the auditor's audit documentation for various reasons, such as to fulfill a quality review requirement or to assist in establishing the scope of a regulatory examination. If the auditor is required by law, regulation, or audit contract to provide regulators access to the audit documentation, the auditor should:

1. Consider advising the client and the client's legal counsel that the regulator has requested access to, and possibly copies of, the audit documentation and that the auditor intends to comply with such a request. Illustration 2, which is from an AICPA Auditing Interpretation of AU Section 339, provides sample language that the auditor may use (either in an engagement letter or in a separate communication to the client) to confirm with the client the requirements to provide access to the audit documentation.

2. Make appropriate arrangements with the regulator for the review of the auditor's audit documentation.

3. Maintain control over the original audit documentation. This is necessary to ensure the confidentiality of the audit documentation and of client information.

4. Consider submitting a letter to the regulator that clarifies that an audit in accordance with generally accepted auditing standards is not intended to, and does not, satisfy a regulator's oversight responsibilities. Illustration 3, which is from an AICPA Auditing Interpretation of AU Section 339, provides an example of such a letter to regulators to avoid any misunderstanding.

Guidance when auditors are requested by a regulator to provide access to the audit documentation before the audit has been completed and the report released A regulator may request access to the audit documentation before the audit has been completed and the report released. When the audit has not been completed, the audit documentation is necessarily incomplete. Therefore, because the audit documentation may change prior to completion of the audit, the auditor ordinarily should not provide access to or copies of the audit documentation until the audit has been completed.

However, if access is provided prior to completion of the audit, the auditor should consider issuing the letter in Illustration 3, appropriately modified, and including additional language such as the following:

> We have been engaged to audit in accordance with auditing standards generally accepted in the United States of America the December 31, 20X1, financial statements of XYZ Company, but have not as yet completed our audit. Accordingly, at this time we do not express any opinion on the Company's financial statements. Furthermore, the contents of the audit documentation may change as a result of additional audit procedures and review of the audit documentation by supervisory personnel of our firm. Accordingly, our audit documentation is incomplete.

Guidance when regulators engage an independent party, such as another independent public accountant, to perform the audit documentation review on behalf of the regulator Some regulators may engage an independent party, such as another independent public accountant, to perform the audit documentation review on behalf of the regulatory agency. In such circumstances, the auditor should be satisfied that the party engaged by the regulator is subject to the same confidentiality restrictions as the regulatory agency itself. This can be accomplished by obtaining an acknowledgment, preferably in writing, from the regulator stating that the third party is acting on behalf of the regulator and an agreement from the third party that he or she is subject to the same restrictions on disclosure and use of audit documentation and the information contained therein as the regulator.

Guidance when a regulator requests the auditor to provide access to (and possibly copies of) audit documentation and the auditor is not otherwise required by law, regulation, or audit contract to provide such access Sometimes a regulator may request access to, and possibly copies of, audit documentation of an auditor who is not required by law, regulation, or audit contract to comply with such request. In such situations, the auditor should:

- Obtain an understanding of the reasons for the regulator's request for access to the audit documentation.
- Consider consulting with legal counsel regarding the request.
- Obtain the client's consent, preferably in writing, to provide the regulator access to the audit documentation if the auditor decides to comply with the request.

Illustration 4, which is from an AICPA Auditing Interpretation of AU Section 339, provides sample language that the auditor may use in the written communication to the client under such circumstances.

PRACTICE ISSUES AND FREQUENTLY ASKED QUESTIONS

Issue 1: Does this Section apply to audit documentation in electronic form as well?

Yes. This Section applies to all forms of audit documentation, including documentation in paper form, electronic form, or other media.

Issue 2: Can audit documentation be a substitute for the client's accounting records?

No. Although audit documentation often may be useful to the client, it is not a part of, nor is it a substitute for, the client's accounting records.

Issue 3: Who owns the audit documentation, the auditor or the client?

The auditor, not the client, owns the audit documentation. Some states have already recognized this right of ownership in their statutes. Audit documentation is the auditor's evidence of the procedures performed, evidence obtained, and conclusions reached. Therefore, they belong to the auditor and are necessary for the auditor to support any legal questions regarding the work performed. Audit documentation should be retained for a period that meets the legal requirements and the needs of the auditor.

Issue 4: What is the auditor's responsibility for confidential client information contained in audit documentation?

At a minimum, the auditor has an ethical responsibility and obligation to maintain the confidentiality of client information. In addition, in some cases, a legal obligation exists as well.

Rule 301 (ET Section 301) of the AICPA's Code of Professional Conduct, which requires the auditor to maintain the confidentiality of working papers, states:

> A member in public practice shall not disclose any confidential client information without the specific consent of the client.

During the course of an audit, auditors obtain a considerable amount of information of a confidential nature, including officers' salaries, product pricing, and advertising plans. Therefore, the auditor should not reveal information gathered in the course of an audit without the client's express consent. Rule 301, however, does *not* preclude the auditor from responding to a subpoena, a peer review, or an ethics inquiry. Communications between the client and the auditor are not considered privileged, unless declared privileged by statute.

Issue 5: Does preparation of audit working papers by the client impair the auditor's independence?

No. However, the auditor should apply appropriate audit procedures to test the information provided in the client-prepared working papers.

Issue 6: What are some common audit documentation deficiencies that the auditor should watch out for?

The auditor should be aware of the following common audit documentation deficiencies recurring in peer reviews:

- Failure to use a written audit program
- Failure to assess the risk of fraud
- Failure to document the auditor's consideration of internal control

- Failure to document analytical procedures
- Failure to obtain a management representation letter
- Failure to obtain a legal representation letter if an attorney was consulted
- Failure to make the required communications with those charged with governance

Issue 7: Should audit documentation contain all review notes, "to do" points, and "draft" versions of the financial statements generated in connection with an audit?

No. Review notes that are generated as a result of the different levels of review in a firm (e.g., detailed review, partner review) may require time to follow up in order to get the issues resolved before the audit is completed. Review or "to do" notes should be cleared and documented in the appropriate audit working papers. After the reviewer is satisfied that these notes have been appropriately addressed and resolved, they should be discarded and not be included in the working papers. Otherwise, they may provide a road map to an adversary and could be used against the auditor in challenging his or her work.

Similarly, superseded drafts of financial statements, schedules, memos, and reports, in both hard copy and electronic format, should be discarded. Such documents, like audit working papers, are subject to subpoena. Only final versions of such documents should be retained in the working papers.

Issue 8: Is the auditor specifically required to include a time budget for individual audit areas in the working papers?

No. However, although not required by professional standards, the working papers nevertheless generally include a time budget for individual audit areas. This is primarily because time budgets provide many benefits, including:

- Providing guidelines for the auditor to schedule staff
- Providing the staff an overall idea about the allocation of audit effort and the relative importance of various audit areas
- Serving as a basis for establishing audit fees
- Providing a basis for monitoring the progress of the audit

Issue 9: What type of audit documentation is generally included in so-called "permanent files"?

Permanent files generally include audit documentation of matters of a historical nature or of continuing interest (i.e., information that pertains to each year's audit and is essentially unchanged from year to year). Audit documentation in the permanent files typically include the following:

- Copies (or extracts) of significant documents of continuing importance, such as the articles of incorporation, bylaws, debt instruments, lease agreements, pension plan documents, and contracts.
- Information related to the understanding of the internal control and assessment of control risk, including organizational charts, flowcharts, questionnaires, and checklists. (Some CPA firms, however, prefer to include this information in the current period audit documentation files.)

Issue 10: What are some general considerations and mechanics for preparing working papers?

Although the mechanics of the format of working papers may differ among auditors, there are nevertheless certain similar characteristics. The following are some basic mechanics and considerations for the preparation of working papers:

- All working papers should include the following:
  — Name of client
  — Date of the financial statements being audited
  — Title description of the workpaper
  — Initials of the persons who prepared and reviewed the workpaper, along with the date of performance
  — Notation, such as "PBC," to indicate if the schedule was prepared by the client
  — Cross-reference to related working papers
  — Proper indexing
- Whenever practical, the auditor should use standard tick marks, and all tick marks should be adequately explained. Tick marks should be simple so that they communicate information clearly to the reviewer.
- The working papers should include documentation concerning all material facts, including (1) the scope of the audit work performed, (2) the sources of the information, and (3) the conclusions reached. The best way of preparing and evaluating a set of working papers is to consider whether, at some future date, another auditor with no previous connection with the engagement could review them and testify as to the audit work performed and related findings.
- Completed working papers must be legible and must clearly indicate the audit work performed. This is usually accomplished in one of the following ways:
  — By a written description in the form of a memorandum
  — By initialing the audit procedures in the audit program
  — By notations directly on the workpaper schedules

Issue 11: What are some practical considerations for the use of workpaper indexing and cross-referencing?

Many auditors use an indexing system for working papers. Standard index referencing aids in organizing, reviewing, and filing audit working papers. Indexing, in turn, permits cross-referencing of procedures in the audit program and the trial balances to the related audit working papers.

The auditor should avoid excessive use of cross-referencing. Accordingly, cross-referencing between working papers within the same audit area may not be necessary. For example, it would not be necessary to cross-reference the amount of outstanding checks on a bank reconciliation workpaper to the outstanding check list that follows the workpaper. On the other hand, it may be helpful to cross-reference amounts on an analysis of deferred income taxes to schedules in other audit areas from which they were derived, such as the depreciation analysis included in the fixed assets working papers.

Also, when there are several pages of an analysis, numbering of each page is not necessary if it will not facilitate organizing, reviewing, or filing the working papers.

Issue 12: Is the auditor required to let the working papers out of his or her custody in response to a regulator's request, pursuant to law or regulation, to access the working papers?

No. While the auditor is required in such circumstances to provide the regulator access to the working papers, authoritative literature specifically recognizes that the auditor should maintain custody of the working papers. This is necessary to insure their continued integrity. Therefore, the working papers may be made available to a regulator at the offices of the client, the auditor, or a mutually agreed-upon location, as long as the auditor maintains control. In addition, the auditor should take appropriate steps to maintain custody of the original working papers.

ILLUSTRATIONS AND PRACTICE AIDS

ILLUSTRATION 1—AUDIT DOCUMENTATION CHECKLIST

	Yes	No	N/A	Workpaper Reference
1. Did you establish an understanding with the client regarding the services to be performed, including any nonattest services, and document that understanding through a written communication (e.g., engagement letter) with the client? (SAS-108; AU Section 311; and Ethics Interpretation 101-3)	____	____	____	_____
2. Did you prepare, update, and document any significant revisions to the overall audit strategy to respond to changes in circumstances for this engagement? (SAS-108; AU Section 311)	____	____	____	_____
3. Did you prepare a written audit plan, which includes the audit procedures to be used that, when performed, are expected to reduce audit risk to an acceptably low level, for this engagement? (SAS-108; AU Section 311)	____	____	____	_____
4. Does audit documentation include instances of consultation (e.g., AICPA Technical Hotline, specialists, authoritative literature), the basis for the final resolution, and any differences of professional opinion? (SAS 108; AU Section 311)	____	____	____	_____

	Yes	No	N/A	Workpaper Reference

5. Did you document the levels of materiality and tolerable misstatement, including any changes thereto, used in the audit and the basis on which those levels were determined? (SAS-107; AU Section 312)

6. For misstatements discovered in the audit engagement, did you document the following (SAS-107; AU Section 312):

   a. A summary of uncorrected misstatements, other than those that are trivial, related to known and likely misstatements?

   b. Your conclusion as to whether uncorrected misstatements, individually or in aggregate, do or do not cause the financial statements to be materially misstated, and the basis for that conclusion?

   c. All known and likely misstatements identified by the auditor during the audit, other than those that are trivial, that have been corrected by management?

   d. Uncorrected misstatements in a manner that allows you to (1) separately consider the effects of known and likely misstatements, including uncorrected misstatements identified in prior periods; (2) consider the aggregate effect of misstatements on the financial statements; and (3) consider the qualitative factors that are relevant to your consideration whether misstatements are material?

7. In connection with your consideration of fraud in the entity's financial statement audit, does audit documentation include the following (SAS-99; AU Section 316):

   a. The procedures performed to obtain information necessary to identify and assess the risks of material misstatement due to fraud?

   b. Specific risks of material misstatement due to fraud that you identified, and a description of your response to those risks?

	Yes	No	N/A	*Workpaper Reference*

c.   If improper revenue recognition was not identified as a risk of a material misstatement due to fraud, the reasons regarding how you overcame that presumption?

d.   The results of the procedures performed to address the risk of management override of controls?

e.   Other conditions and analytical relationships that led you to believe that additional auditing procedures, or other responses, were required and any further responses you concluded were appropriate to address such risks or other conditions?

f.   The nature of the communications about fraud made to management, those charged with governance, and others?

8.   Did you document your discussion among the audit team regarding the susceptibility of the entity's financial statements to material misstatement due to error or fraud, including how and when the discussion occurred, the subject matter discussed, the audit team members who participated, and significant decisions reached concerning planned audit responses at the financial statement and relevant assertion levels? (SAS 99; AU Section 316 and SAS-109; AU Section 314)

9.   Did you document oral communications to the audit committee or others with equivalent authority and responsibility about illegal acts that have come to your attention, including: (a) a description of the illegal act; (b) the circumstances surrounding the illegal act; and (c) the effect on the financial statements? (SAS-54; AU Section 317)

	Yes	No	N/A	Workpaper Reference

10. In connection with your considerations of the entity's internal control, did you document key elements of the understanding obtained regarding each of the aspects of the entity and its environment, including each of the components of internal control, to assess the risks of material misstatement of the financial statements; the sources of information from which the understanding was obtained; and the risk assessment procedures performed to obtain such understanding? (SAS 109; AU Section 314)   _____ _____ _____ _____

11. In connection with your assessment of the risk of material misstatement, did you document (SAS 109; AU Section 314):

   a. The assessment of the risks of material misstatement both at the financial statement level and at the relevant assertion level and the basis for the assessment?   _____ _____ _____ _____

   b. The risks identified and related controls evaluated for significant risks that require special audit considerations and risks for which substantive procedures alone do not provide sufficient appropriate audit evidence?   _____ _____ _____ _____

12. Does the audit documentation include the written communication made to management and those charged with governance about significant deficiencies and material weaknesses in internal control? (SAS-115; AU Section 325)   _____ _____ _____ _____

13. If internal control-related matters, other than significant deficiencies and material weaknesses, (e.g., opportunities for the client to improve or strengthen operational and administrative controls) were communicated orally to the client, does the audit documentation include the nature of such communication? (SAS-115; AU Section 325)   _____ _____ _____ _____

14. Does audit documentation include the following items regarding income tax accruals (AU Section 9326.06–.23):

   a. Significant elements of the client's analysis of tax contingencies or reserves, including roll-forward of material changes to such reserves?   _____ _____ _____ _____

	Yes	No	N/A	Workpaper Reference

b. The client's position and support for income-tax-related disclosures, such as its effective tax rate reconciliation, and support for its intraperiod allocation of income tax expense or benefit to continuing operations and to items other than continuing operations? _____ _____ _____ _____

c. The client's basis for assessing deferred tax assets and related valuation allowances and support for applying the "indefinite reversal criteria," including management's plans for reinvestment of undistributed foreign earnings? _____ _____ _____ _____

d. If the client's support for the tax accrual or matters affecting it, including tax contingencies, is based on an opinion issued by an outside adviser, either (1) the actual advice or opinions rendered by an outside adviser or (2) other sufficient documentation or abstracts supporting both the transactions or facts addressed as well as the analysis and conclusions reached by the client and the adviser? _____ _____ _____ _____

15. In connection with your procedures to respond to assessed risks, did you document the following (SAS-110; AU Section 318):

a. The overall responses to address the assessed risks of material misstatement at the financial statement level? _____ _____ _____ _____

b. The nature, timing, and extent of the further audit procedures? _____ _____ _____ _____

c. The linkage of those procedures to the assessed risks at the relevant assertion level? _____ _____ _____ _____

d. The results of the audit procedures? _____ _____ _____ _____

e. The conclusions reached with regard to use in the current audit of audit evidence about the operating effectiveness of controls that was obtained in a prior audit? _____ _____ _____ _____

16. In connection with performing analytical procedures, did you document the following when an analytical procedure is used as the principal substantive test of a significant financial statement assertion (SAS-56; AU Section 329):

	Yes	No	N/A	Workpaper Reference
a. The expectation, if not readily determinable from the documentation of the work performed, and the factors you considered in developing the expectation?	_____	_____	_____	_____
b. Results of the comparison of the expectation to the recorded amounts or ratios developed from recorded amounts?	_____	_____	_____	_____
c. Any additional auditing procedures that were performed in response to significant unexpected differences arising from the analytical procedure, and the results of such additional procedures?	_____	_____	_____	_____

17. In connection with performing confirmation procedures, did you document the following (SAS-67; AU Section 330):

a. Oral confirmations?	_____	_____	_____	_____
b. If confirmations in the examination of accounts receivable were not requested, how you overcame this presumption?	_____	_____	_____	_____

18. Does audit documentation include appropriate written representations from management? (SAS-85; AU Section 333)

_____	_____	_____	_____

19. In connection with your inquiry of the client's lawyer concerning litigation, claims, and assessments (SAS-12; AU Section 337):

a. Did you document (either in the audit inquiry letter or in a separate letter to the client's lawyer) that the client has provided assurances that it has disclosed all unasserted claims that the lawyer has advised the client are probable of assertion and must be disclosed in accordance with ASC 450, *Contingencies*?	_____	_____	_____	_____
b. Did you document the conclusions reached as a result of responses obtained in a conference with legal counsel relating to matters covered by the audit inquiry letter?	_____	_____	_____	_____

20. Does the audit documentation include (SAS-103; AU Section 339):

	Yes	No	N/A	Workpaper Reference

a. The reconciliation of the accounting records to the audited financial statements or other audited information? ____ ____ ____ _____

b. Abstracts or copies of significant contracts or agreements that you examined to evaluate the accounting for significant transactions? ____ ____ ____ _____

c. For tests of operating effectiveness of controls and substantive tests of details that involve inspection of documents or confirmation, an identification of the items tested (e.g., the source from which the items were selected and the specific selection criteria)? ____ ____ ____ _____

d. Audit findings or issues that were deemed to be significant, the actions taken to address them, and the basis for the final conclusions reached, including:

  (1) Significant matters that involved the selection, application, and consistency of accounting principles regarding the financial statements, including related disclosures (e.g., accounting for complex or unusual transactions; estimates and uncertainties, management assumptions; or other financial reporting matters)? ____ ____ ____ _____

  (2) Results of audit procedures, which indicated (i) that the financial information or disclosures could be materially misstated or (ii) a need to revise your previous assessment of the risks of material misstatement and your responses to those risks? ____ ____ ____ _____

  (3) Circumstances that caused significant difficulty in applying necessary auditing procedures? ____ ____ ____ _____

  (4) Other findings that could result in modification of the auditor's report? ____ ____ ____ _____

  (5) Audit adjustments? ____ ____ ____ _____

		Yes	No	N/A	Workpaper Reference

e. Discussions of significant findings or issues with management and others (including those charged with governance), responses obtained, when the discussions took place, and with whom the discussions took place?

f. Information that contradicts or is inconsistent with the auditor's final conclusions about a significant matter, and how those contradictions or inconsistencies were addressed?

g. Who performed the audit work and the date such work was completed?

h. Who reviewed specific audit documentation and the date of such review?

i. Justification for any departure from a presumptively mandatory requirement under generally accepted auditing standards and how the alternative procedures performed were sufficient to achieve the objectives of the presumptively mandatory requirement?

j. The report release date?

21. In connection with your consideration of the entity's ability to continue as a going concern for a reasonable period of time, did you document the following (SAS-59; AU Section 341):

a. The conditions or events that led you to believe that there is substantial doubt about the entity's ability to continue as a going concern for a reasonable period of time?

b. The elements of management's plans that you considered to be significant to overcoming the adverse effects of the conditions or events?

c. The auditing procedures that you performed and the evidence obtained in connection with your evaluation of management's plans?

	Yes	No	N/A	*Workpaper Reference*

d. Your conclusion about whether substantial doubt about the entity's ability to continue as a going concern for a reasonable period of time remains or is alleviated? In connection with this item:

   (1) If substantial doubt remains, does documentation also include the possible effects of the conditions or events on the financial statements and the adequacy of the related disclosures? ____ ____ ____ _____

   (2) If substantial doubt is alleviated, does documentation also include the conclusion regarding the need to disclose the principal conditions and events that initially caused you to believe there was substantial doubt? ____ ____ ____ _____

e. Your conclusion regarding whether an explanatory paragraph should be included in the audit report to reflect that there is substantial doubt? ____ ____ ____ _____

f. If the related going-concern disclosures are inadequate, does documentation also include the conclusion as to whether to express a qualified or an adverse opinion for the GAAP departure? ____ ____ ____ _____

22. Did you document all matters that are required to be communicated with those charged with governance, when such matters have been communicated orally? Also, did you retain a copy of the communication, when matters that are required to be communicated with those charged with governance have been communicated in writing? (SAS-114; AU Section 380). ____ ____ ____ _____

23. Before reissuing or consenting to the reissue of a report previously issued on the financial statements of a prior period, did you obtain representation letters from management of the former client and from the successor auditor? (SAS-58; AU Section 508) ____ ____ ____ _____

	Yes	No	N/A	Workpaper Reference
24. If the engagement included reporting on financial statements prepared for use in another country, did you obtain written representations from management regarding the purpose and uses of such financial statements prepared in conformity with the accounting principles of the other country? (SAS-51; AU Section 534)	____	____	____	_____
25. For audits of governmental entities and recipients of governmental financial assistance in accordance with GAAS, did you document the oral communications to management and those charged with governance if you became aware that the entity is subject to an audit requirement that may not be encompassed in the terms of the engagement? (SAS-74; AU Section 801)	____	____	____	_____
26. Have all required audit programs and checklists been completed and signed off?	____	____	____	_____
27. Have all open or outstanding matters been resolved and have the resolutions been documented in the workpapers?	____	____	____	_____
28. Has evidence of workpaper preparation and review been documented in the workpapers?	____	____	____	_____
29. Have all reviewers' comments been properly addressed in the workpapers and removed?	____	____	____	_____
30. Have all superseded workpapers or support been removed from the audit file?	____	____	____	_____
31. Has a final copy of the financial statements and report been included in the audit file and have the financial statements and related notes been referenced to testing performed?	____	____	____	_____
32. Have appropriate back-ups of the audit file been made in accordance with Firm policy?	____	____	____	_____
33. Has assembly of the final audit file been completed within 60 days of the report release date?	____	____	____	_____

ILLUSTRATION 2—AUDITOR'S COMMUNICATION TO CLIENT WHEN THE AUDITOR MAY BE REQUIRED BY LAW, REGULATION, OR AUDIT CONTRACT TO PROVIDE ACCESS TO THE AUDIT DOCUMENTATION

(Date)

(Name and address of client)

The audit documentation for this engagement is the property of (*name of auditor*) and constitutes confidential information. However, we may be requested to make certain audit documentation available to (*name of regulator*) pursuant to authority given to it by law or regulation. If requested, access to such audit documentation will be provided under the supervision of (*name of auditor*) personnel. Furthermore, on request, we may provide copies of selected audit documentation to (*name of regulator*). The (*name of regulator*) may intend, or decide, to distribute the copies or information contained therein to others, including other governmental agencies.

(*Firm Signature*)

Agreed and acknowledged by:

_____

(*Name and title*)

_____

(*Date*)

ILLUSTRATION 3—AUDITOR'S LETTER TO REGULATOR PRIOR TO ALLOWING A REGULATOR ACCESS TO THE AUDIT DOCUMENTATION

(*Date*)

(*Name and address of regulatory agency*)

Your representatives have requested access to our audit documentation in connection with our audit of the December 31, 20X2, financial statements of (*name of client*). It is our understanding that the purpose of your request is (*state purpose: for example,* "to facilitate your regulatory examination").[1]

Our audit of (*name of client*) December 31, 20X2, financial statements was conducted in accordance with auditing standards generally accepted in the United States of America[2], the objective[3] of which is to form an opinion as to whether the financial statements, which are the responsibility and representations of management, present fairly, in all material respects, the financial position, results of operations and cash flows in conformity with accounting principles generally accepted in the United States of America.[4] Under auditing standards generally accepted in the United States of America, we have the responsibility, within the inherent limitations of the auditing process, to design our audit to provide reasonable assurance that errors and fraud that have a material effect on the financial statements will be detected, and to exercise due care in the conduct of our audit. The concept of selective testing of the data being audited, which involves judgment both as to the number of

---

[1] If the auditor is not required by law, regulation, or audit contract to provide a regulator access to the audit documentation but otherwise intends to provide such access, the letter should include a statement that: "Management of (*name of client*) has authorized us to provide you access to our audit documentation for (*state purpose*)."

[2] The auditor should appropriately modify this letter when the audit has been performed in accordance with auditing standards generally accepted in the United States of America and also in accordance with additional auditing requirements specified by a regulatory agency (for example, the requirements specified in *Government Auditing Standards* issued by the Comptroller General of the United States).

[3] In an audit performed in accordance with the *Single Audit Act of 1984*, and certain other federal

audit requirements, an additional objective of the audit is to assess compliance with laws and regulations applicable to federal financial assistance. Accordingly, in these situations, the above letter should be modified to include the additional objective.

[4] If the financial statements have been prepared in conformity with regulatory accounting practices, the phrase "financial position, results of operations and cash flows in conformity with accounting principles generally accepted in the United States of America" should be replaced with appropriate wording such as, in the case of an insurance company, the "admitted assets, liabilities . . . of the XYZ Insurance Company in conformity with accounting practices prescribed or permitted by the state of . . . insurance department."

transactions to be audited and as to the areas to be tested, has been generally accepted as a valid and sufficient basis for an auditor to express an opinion on financial statements. Thus, our audit, based on the concept of selective testing, is subject to the inherent risk that material errors or fraud, if they exist, would not be detected. In addition, an audit does not address the possibility that material errors or fraud may occur in the future. Also, our use of professional judgment and the assessment of materiality for the purpose of our audit means that matters may have existed that would have been assessed differently by you.

The audit documentation was prepared for the purpose of providing the principal support for our report on (*name of client*) December 31, 20X2, financial statements and to aid in the conduct and supervision of our audit. The audit documentation is the principal record of procedures performed, evidence obtained and conclusions reached in the engagement. The audit procedures that we performed were limited to those we considered necessary under auditing standards generally accepted in the United States of America[5] to enable us to formulate and express an opinion on the financial statements[6] taken as a whole. Accordingly, we make no representation as to the sufficiency or appropriateness, for your purposes, of either the information contained in our audit documentation or our audit procedures. In addition, any notations, comments, and individual conclusions appearing on any of the audit documentation do not stand alone, and should not be read as an opinion on any individual amounts, accounts, balances or transactions.

Our audit of (*name of client*) December 31, 20X2, financial statements was performed for the purpose stated above and has not been planned or conducted in contemplation of your (*state purpose: for example,* "regulatory examination") or for the purpose of assessing (*name of client*) compliance with laws and regulations.[7] Therefore, items of possible interest to you may not have been specifically addressed. Accordingly, our audit and the audit documentation prepared in connection therewith, should not supplant other inquiries and procedures that should be undertaken by the (*name of regulatory agency*) for the purpose of monitoring and regulating the financial affairs of the (*name of client*). In addition, we have not audited any financial statements of (*name of client*) since (*date of audited balance sheet referred to in the first paragraph above*) nor have we performed any audit procedures since (*date*), the date of our auditor's report, and significant events or circumstances may have occurred since that date.

The audit documentation constitutes and reflects work performed or evidence obtained by (*name of auditor*) in its capacity as independent auditor for (*name of client*). The documents contain trade secrets and confidential commercial and financial information of our firm and (*name of client*) that is privileged and confidential, and we expressly reserve all rights with respect to disclosures to third parties. Accordingly, we request confidential treatment under the Freedom of Information Act or similar laws and regulations[8] when requests are made for the audit documentation or information contained therein or any documents created by the (*name of regulatory agency*) containing information derived there from. We further request that written notice be given to our firm before distribution of the information in the audit documen-

---

[5] Refer to footnote 2.

[6] Refer to footnote 3.

[7] Refer to footnote 3.

[8] This illustrative paragraph may not in and of itself be sufficient to gain confidential treatment under the rules and regulations of certain regulatory agencies. The auditor should consider tailoring this paragraph to the circumstances after consulting the regulations of each applicable regulatory agency and, if necessary, consult with legal counsel regarding the specific procedures and requirements to gain confidential treatment.

tation (or copies thereof) to others, including other governmental agencies, except when such distribution is required by law or regulation.

Note: *If it is expected that copies will be requested, add the following:*

Any copies of our audit documentation we agree to provide you will be identified as "Confidential Treatment Requested by (*name of auditor, address, telephone number*)."

(*Firm signature*)

ILLUSTRATION 4—AUDITOR'S COMMUNICATION TO CLIENT WHEN THE AUDITOR IS NOT REQUIRED BY LAW, REGULATION, OR AUDIT CONTRACT TO PROVIDE ACCESS TO THE AUDIT DOCUMENTATION

(*Date*)

(*Name and address of client*)

The audit documentation for this engagement is the property of (*name of auditor*) and constitutes confidential information. However, we have been requested to make certain audit documentation available to (*name of regulator*) for (*describe the regulator's basis for its request*). Access to such audit documentation will be provided under the supervision of (*name of auditor*) personnel. Furthermore, on request, we may provide copies of selected audit documentation to (*name of regulator*).

You have authorized (*name of auditor*) to allow (*name of regulator*) access to the audit documentation in the manner discussed above. Please confirm your agreement to the above by signing below and returning to (*name of auditor, address*).

(*Firm signature*)

Agreed and acknowledged by:

_____

(*Name and title*)

_____

(*Date*)

AU SECTION 341
THE AUDITOR'S CONSIDERATION OF AN ENTITY'S ABILITY TO CONTINUE AS A GOING CONCERN

WHAT EVERY PRACTITIONER SHOULD KNOW

Basic Requirements

The auditor has a responsibility to evaluate whether there is substantial doubt about the entity's ability to continue as a going concern for a reasonable period of time. *Reasonable period of time* is defined as a period not to exceed one year beyond the date of the financial statements being audited. The auditor should perform the following procedures to evaluate going concern:

1. Consider conditions and events that indicate there could be substantial doubt about the entity's ability to continue as a going concern for a reasonable period of time.

2. Identify and evaluate management's plans for dealing with the conditions or events that prompted the substantial doubt conclusions and assess the likelihood that such plans can be effectively implemented.

3. Draw a conclusion concerning the existence of substantial doubt and consider the effect of this conclusion on disclosures in the financial statements and modifications of the auditor's report.

Illustration 1 includes an audit procedures checklist that the auditor can use in evaluating an entity's ability to continue as a going concern.

The Auditor's Consideration of Conditions and Events

Conditions and events that may raise a substantial doubt about an entity's ability to continue as a going concern include the following:

- Negative financial trends (e.g., recurring operating losses, working capital deficiencies, negative cash flows from operations, or adverse key financial ratios)

- Other indications of possible financial difficulties (e.g., default on loan or similar agreements, arrearages in dividends, denial of usual trade credit from vendors, need to seek new sources of financing or sell substantial assets, or restructuring of debt)

- Internal matters (e.g., labor difficulties such as work stoppages, substantial dependence on the success of a particular project, or uneconomic long-term commitments)

- External matters (e.g., loss of key customer or vendor, occurrence of uninsured or underinsured catastrophe such as earthquake or flood, legal proceedings or legislation, or loss of key franchise or license)

The Auditor's Consideration of Management's Plans

If conditions or events raise questions about the entity's ability to continue as a going concern for a reasonable period of time, the auditor should:

- Gather evidence about potentially mitigating or aggravating factors. For example, consider whether assets can be sold without disrupting operations or whether debt restructuring is feasible.

- Evaluate management's plans for dealing with conditions or events that raise questions and assess the likelihood that management's plans can be effectively implemented. If prospective financial information is available and considered relevant, the auditor should review and evaluate such information, including the fundamental assumptions used to prepare the prospective information.

Illustration 2 provides examples of management's plans and the corresponding factors that are relevant to the auditor's evaluation of management's plans.

Draw a Conclusion about Going-Concern Matters

If the auditor concludes that substantial doubt does not exist, he or she should consider whether the conditions or events that originally raised the question about going concern should be disclosed in the financial statements. The disclosure might include the possible impact of the conditions or events and mitigating factors, including management's plans.

If, on the other hand, the auditor concludes that substantial doubt exists, the effects of conditions or events should be considered as they relate to (1) adequate disclosures in the financial statements and (2) modifications to the auditor's report.

Adequate disclosures in the financial statements The auditor must ensure that disclosures in the financial statements properly reflect the recoverability and classification of assets and the amounts and classification of liabilities. In addition, the auditor should consider whether disclosures related to the possible discontinuance of operations are adequate in the financial statements. Pertinent disclosures might include the following:

- Conditions or events that gave rise to the substantial doubt concerning continued existence

- Possible effects of the conditions or events

- Management's assessments concerning the significance of the conditions or events

- Other factors that may aggravate or mitigate the conditions or events

- Management's plans that will attempt to deal with the adverse conditions or events

- Possible discontinuance of operations

If the auditor concludes that the required disclosures are omitted or inadequate, the auditor should qualify his or her opinion or express an adverse opinion on the financial statements.

Illustration 3 summarizes the disclosure requirements that are applicable to going-concern matters. Illustration 4 contains examples of financial statement disclosures regarding going-concern uncertainties.

Modifications to the auditor's report If the auditor concludes that substantial doubt exists about the continued existence of the client, the audit report should be modified. When the auditor believes that the financial statements still can be relied on, the report modification is limited to an explanatory paragraph (following the opinion paragraph) referring to the uncertainty in the report, but the opinion expressed is unqualified. The explanatory paragraph must include the phrase "substantial doubt about its [the entity's] ability to continue as a going concern," or similar wording. If similar wording is used, the terms "substantial doubt" and "going concern" must be used in the phrase.

The audit report should unequivocally convey the auditor's conclusion about the going-concern status of the entity. A conclusion that contains conditional terminology such as "If the company is unable to obtain financing, there may be substantial doubt about the entity's ability to continue as a going concern" is not definitive enough. The auditor is precluded from using such conditional language.

When the auditor concludes that the uncertainty related to the substantial doubt question is so significant that an opinion cannot be expressed on the financial statements, the auditor should express a disclaimer of opinion.

Illustration 5 provides an example of a modified auditor's report.

Documentation of Going-Concern Matters

In connection with the auditor's consideration of an entity's ability to continue as a going concern for a reasonable period of time, the auditor should document all of the following items:

1. The conditions or events that led the auditor to believe that there is substantial doubt about the entity's ability to continue as a going concern for a reasonable period of time.

2. The elements of management's plans that the auditor considered to be significant to overcoming the adverse effects of the conditions or events.

3. The auditing procedures the auditor performed and the evidence obtained in connection with his or her evaluation of management's plans.

4. The auditor's conclusion about whether substantial doubt about the entity's ability to continue as a going concern for a reasonable period of time remains or is alleviated. In connection with this item:

   a. If substantial doubt remains, documentation should also include the possible effects of the conditions or events on the financial statements and the adequacy of the related disclosures.

   b. If substantial doubt is alleviated, documentation should also include the conclusion regarding the need to disclose the principal conditions and events that initially caused the auditor to believe there was substantial doubt.

5. The auditor's conclusion regarding whether an explanatory paragraph should be included in the audit report to reflect that there is substantial doubt. If the related going-concern disclosures are inadequate, the auditor also should document the conclusion as to whether to express a qualified or an adverse opinion for the GAAP departure.

Communication with Those Charged with Governance

If the auditor concludes that substantial doubt exists about the entity's ability to continue as a going concern for a reasonable period of time, the auditor should communicate the following to those charged with governance:

- The nature of the events or conditions that have been identified.
- The possible effect on the financial statements and the adequacy of related disclosures in the financial statements.
- The effects on the auditor's report.

Reissued Reports and Going-Concern Matters

A client may ask an auditor to reissue the audit report on the entity's financial statements and remove a going concern explanatory paragraph after a situation giving rise to substantial doubt about the entity's ability to continue as a going concern has been resolved. In these circumstances, the auditor may, but is under no obligation to, reissue the audit report on the entity's financial statements.

However, if the auditor elects to reissue his or her report and is considering whether to eliminate the going-concern paragraph in a reissued report, the auditor should perform the following procedures:

1. Audit the event or transaction that caused the entity to request the auditor to reissue the audit report and eliminate the going- concern paragraph there from.

2. Perform the procedures that are generally applied in connection with subsequent events, as specified in AU Section 560 (Subsequent Events).

3. Reassess the going-concern status of the entity at the date of reissuance by (a) performing any procedures the auditor deems necessary and (b) reconsidering the conditions and events regarding the going-concern assumption as of the date of reissuance.

PRACTICE ISSUES AND FREQUENTLY ASKED QUESTIONS

Issue 1: Do professional standards presently offer definite thresholds at which an auditor must include a going-concern paragraph in the audit report?

No. The standards do not provide quantitative levels at which a going-concern matter must be reported. This is a qualitative judgment that must be made by the auditor in light of both quantitative data and other relevant facts and circumstances. However, the AICPA, in attempting to improve the effectiveness of the standards, has formed a group to research and evaluate the need to address financial reporting and auditing issues on the topic of financial capability.

Issue 2: Do the audit requirements to consider an entity's ability to continue as a going concern apply to an audit of financial statements based on the assumption of liquidation?

No. The audit requirements to consider an entity's ability to continue as a going concern do not apply to an audit of financial statements based on the assumption of liquidation, such as the following situations:

- When an entity is in the process of liquidation
- When the owners of a business have decided to commence dissolution or liquidation
- When legal proceedings, including bankruptcy, have reached a point at which dissolution or liquidation is probable

See AU Section 508 (Reports on Audited Financial Statements) for guidance in situations when the financial statements are prepared on a liquidation basis of accounting.

Issue 3: Is the auditor required to design specific audit procedures solely to assess the ability of an entity to continue as a going concern?

No. The auditing standards do not require the auditor to use any specific audit procedures especially and solely directed to assess the ability of an entity to continue as a going concern. The regular and usual audit procedures designed and performed to achieve other audit objectives should be sufficient for that purpose. Some of the usual audit procedures that may identify such conditions and events include:

- Applying analytical procedures.
- Reviewing subsequent events.
- Reviewing compliance with debt and loan agreements.
- Reading the minutes of meetings of stockholders, board of directors, and other important committees.
- Inquiring of the entity's lawyers about litigation, claims, and assessments.
- Confirming with related and third parties details of arrangements or agreements to provide or maintain financial support.
- Obtaining written representations from management.

Issue 4: If substantial doubt about an entity's going concern existed in a prior period but that doubt has been removed in the current period, should the auditor repeat the explanatory paragraph in the audit report on the comparative financial statements presented?

No. If substantial doubt about the entity' ability to continue as a going concern existed at the date of prior period financial statements that are presented on a comparative basis, and that doubt has been removed in the current period, the explanatory paragraph included in the auditor's report on the financial statements of the prior period should *not* be repeated.

Issue 5: Does doubt about an entity's continued existence as a going concern in the current year imply that such doubt existed in the prior year?

No. Doubt about an entity's continued existence as a going concern in the present does not imply that such doubt existed in the past. Most auditors consider the fact that the company was still in business a year later as convincing evidence that a going-concern problem did not exist in the prior year. Therefore, substantial doubt in the current year should not affect the auditor's report on the prior year, even when statements are presented on a comparative basis.

Issue 6: What considerations should the auditor take into account when evaluating going-concern matters of an entity that may be relying on significant financial support from third parties?

Many entities may be relying on significant financial support from third parties to support their deficit operations and mitigate any going-concern issues. Such third parties may include major stockholders, family members of the stockholders, or other affiliated entities. The auditor's decision not to modify the auditor's report for a going-concern uncertainty in such situations depends on receiving adequate evidence regarding the third party's future financial participation and support. Therefore, in these situations the auditor should consider obtaining written representations from such third parties confirming their intentions to continue providing the necessary financial support to the entity being audited.

Issue 7: What factors should the auditor consider when reviewing prospective financial information that is significant to management's plans regarding a going-concern matter?

When prospective financial information is especially significant to management's plans, the auditor should request management to provide that information and should consider the adequacy of support for significant assumptions underlying that information. The auditor should consider:

- Whether the assumptions are consistent with each other and reasonable.
- Whether the logical arguments or theory are reasonable.
- Whether the assumptions used deviate from the entity's historical trends.
- Whether the assumptions used are consistent with historical trends of the industry.
- Whether the data used in developing the assumptions are sufficiently reliable.
- Whether the computations made are mathematically correct and free from obvious errors.

It is not intended that such prospective financial information constitute prospective financial statements meeting the minimum presentation guidelines set forth in AT Section 301 (Financial Forecasts and Projections). In addition, the inclusion of prospective financial information in management's plans does not require the auditor to consider any procedures beyond those normally required by generally accepted auditing standards.

Issue 8: Should the auditor be concerned with events occurring subsequent to the balance sheet date for purposes of evaluating the entity's ability to continue as a going concern?

Yes. Going-concern issues may not always manifest themselves in the raw numbers of the financial statements. For instance, subsequent to the balance sheet date, the Company could lose a major customer, or a significant source of supply or financing, or key executives. Its production capacity could be impaired by an act of nature, or by governmental action. For this reason, thorough consideration of subsequent events is vital in reaching a conclusion about going-concern matters.

However, the auditor has no duty to perform any auditing procedures subsequent to the date of his or her audit report.

Issue 9: How does the auditor respond to the perception by some financial statement users that the absence of a going-concern paragraph in an auditor's opinion is a guarantee that the entity will continue to be solvent for the coming year?

First, an auditor's report is never a guarantee. The auditor provides only *reasonable assurance*. Therefore, it is always possible that a properly planned and executed audit will fail to detect an existing cause for doubt about going concern.

Second, doubt about going concern is, to a certain extent, a subjective consideration and involves considerable judgment. The auditing standards do *not* provide a quantitative threshold whereby if an entity fails to meet a certain financial measure, substantial going concern doubt is automatically raised. Therefore, there can be good faith differences of professional opinion based upon evaluation of facts as to whether substantial doubt exists in a situation.

Finally, it is important to remember that an auditor is responsible only for events arising through the date of the auditor's report. Events can, and often do, happen after the report is issued that cause companies to go bankrupt before their next year end. Many of these events, such as withdrawal of line of credit by a bank or natural disasters, cannot be reasonably predicted or avoided.

Issue 10: When an entity's ability to continue as a going concern is questionable in connection with an audit of financial statements on the cash basis or income tax basis of accounting (i.e., an other comprehensive basis of accounting), should the audit report include an explanatory paragraph that refers to this uncertainty?

Yes. Generally accepted auditing standards are applicable to *all* audit engagements, whether the financial statements are prepared in accordance with GAAP or with an other comprehensive basis of accounting (OCBOA).

ILLUSTRATIONS AND PRACTICE AIDS

ILLUSTRATION 1—AUDIT PROCEDURES CHECKLIST TO EVALUATE AND DOCUMENT GOING CONCERN

	Performed By	Workpaper Reference

1. Determine whether audit procedures performed during the audit have identified conditions that could raise substantial doubt about the entity's ability to continue as a going concern for a reasonable period of time. Consider the existence or occurrence of factors such as the following when making this determination:

   a. Negative financial trends:

(1) Recurring operating losses	_____	_____
(2) Working capital deficiencies	_____	_____
(3) Negative cash flows from operations	_____	_____
(4) Adverse key financial ratios	_____	_____

   b. Other negative trends:

(1) Default on loans or similar agreements	_____	_____
(2) Arrearages in dividends	_____	_____
(3) Denial of usual trade credit from vendors	_____	_____
(4) Need to seek new sources of financing	_____	_____
(5) Need to sell substantial assets	_____	_____
(6) Need to restructure debt	_____	_____
(7) Noncompliance with statutory or contractual capital requirements	_____	_____

   c. Internal matters:

(1) Labor difficulties, such as work stoppages	_____	_____
(2) Substantial dependence on the success of a particular project	_____	_____
(3) Uneconomic long-term commitments	_____	_____
(4) Need to significantly revise operations	_____	_____

   d. External matters:

(1) Loss of a key customer or supplier	_____	_____
(2) Occurrence of uninsured or underinsured catastrophe, such as earthquake or flood	_____	_____
(3) Legal proceedings or legislation	_____	_____
(4) Loss of a key franchise, patent, or license	_____	_____

2. If conditions or events raise substantial doubt about the entity's ability to continue as a going concern for a reasonable period of time, obtain information and gather evidence about management's plans, and perform the following:

   a. If management plans to dispose of assets, consider the potential effect of the following factors on such plans:

(1) Restrictions on disposal of assets, such as covenants limiting such transactions in loan, or similar agreements or encumbrances against assets	_____	_____

	Performed By	Workpaper Reference

    (2) Apparent marketability of assets that management plans to sell _____ _____

    (3) Possible direct or indirect effects of disposal of assets _____ _____

  b. If management plans to borrow money or restructure debt, consider the potential effect of the following factors on such plans:

    (1) Availability of debt financing, including existing or committed credit agreements, such as lines of credit or arrangements for factoring receivables _____ _____

    (2) Existing or committed arrangements to restructure or subordinate debt or to guarantee loans to the entity _____ _____

    (3) Possible effects on management's borrowing plans of existing restrictions on additional borrowing or the sufficiency of available collateral _____ _____

  c. If management plans to reduce or delay expenditures, consider the potential effect of the following factors on such plans:

    (1) Apparent feasibility of plans to reduce overhead or administrative expenditures, to postpone maintenance or research and development projects, or to lease rather than purchase assets _____ _____

    (2) Possible direct or indirect effects of reduced or delayed expenditures _____ _____

  d. If management plans to increase ownership equity, consider the potential effect of the following factors on such plans:

    (1) Apparent feasibility of plans to increase ownership equity, including existing or committed arrangements to raise additional capital _____ _____

    (2) Existing or committed arrangements to reduce current dividend requirements or to accelerate cash distributions from affiliates or other investors _____ _____

3. Evaluate management's plans for dealing with conditions or events that raise substantial doubt about the entity's ability to continue as a going concern, and assess the likelihood that management's plans can be effectively implemented. If prospective financial information is available and considered relevant, review and evaluate such information, including the fundamental assumptions used to prepare the prospective information. _____ _____

4. Evaluate the adequacy of related financial statement disclosures. _____ _____

	Performed By	Workpaper Reference
5. Consider the effects on the audit report.	_____	_____
6. Document the following matters in the audit files:		
a. The conditions or events that led you to believe that there is substantial doubt about the entity's ability to continue as a going concern for a reasonable period of time.	_____	_____
b. The elements of management's plans that you considered to be significant to overcoming the adverse effects of the conditions or events.	_____	_____
c. The auditing procedures that you performed and the evidence obtained in connection with your evaluation of management's plans.	_____	_____
d. Your conclusion about whether substantial doubt about the entity's ability to continue as a going concern for a reasonable period of time remains or is alleviated. In connection with this item:		
(1) If substantial doubt remains, documentation should also include the possible effects of the conditions or events on the financial statements and the adequacy of the related disclosures.	_____	_____
(2) If substantial doubt is alleviated, documentation should also include the conclusion regarding the need to disclose the principal conditions and events that initially caused you to believe there was substantial doubt.	_____	_____
e. Your conclusion regarding whether an explanatory paragraph should be included in the audit report to reflect that there is substantial doubt.	_____	_____
f. If the related going-concern disclosures are inadequate, documentation should also include the conclusion as to whether to express a qualified or an adverse opinion for the GAAP departure.	_____	_____
7. If substantial doubt exists about the entity's ability to continue as a going concern for a reasonable period of time, communicate the following to those charged with governance:		
a. The nature of the events or conditions that have been identified.	_____	_____
b. The possible effect on the financial statements and the adequacy of related disclosures in the financial statements.	_____	_____
c. The effects on the auditor's report.	_____	_____

ILLUSTRATION 2—EXAMPLES OF MANAGEMENT'S PLANS AND THE CORRESPONDING FACTORS THAT ARE RELEVANT TO THE AUDITOR'S EVALUATION OF MANAGEMENT'S PLANS

Management's Planned Action	Factors that Are Relevant to the Auditor's Evaluation of Management's Planned Action
Sale of assets	Existing restrictions on the sale of assets, e.g., loan covenants limiting such transactions
	Lack of marketability of assets
	Possible effects of disposal of assets, e.g., disruption of operations
Borrow money or restructure debt	Likelihood of raising funds based on existing or committed debt arrangements
	Existing or committed arrangements for restructuring debt or obtaining guarantees for loans
	Existing restrictions on ability borrow or use assets as collateral
Reduce or delay expenditures	Feasibility of reducing or postponing expenditures
	Possible effects of reducing or delaying expenditures on operations
Increase ownership equity	Feasibility of increasing ownership equity and raising additional capital
	Existing or committed arrangements to reduce current dividend requirements or to accelerate cash distributions from affiliates or other investors

ILLUSTRATION 3—DISCLOSURE REQUIREMENTS APPLICABLE TO GOING CONCERN

If, after considering management's plans, a conclusion is reached that there is substantial doubt about the entity's ability to continue as a going concern for a period of time not to exceed one year beyond the balance sheet date, the financial statements should include the following disclosures:

1. Pertinent conditions and events giving rise to the assessment of substantial doubt about the entity's ability to continue as a going concern for a period of time not to exceed one year beyond the balance sheet date.

2. The possible effects of such conditions and events.

3. Management's evaluation of the significance of those conditions and events and any mitigating factors.

4. Possible discontinuance of operations.

5. Management's plans (including relevant prospective financial information).

6. Information about the recoverability or classification of recorded asset amounts or the amounts or classification of liabilities.

When substantial doubt about the entity's ability to continue as a going concern for a period of time not to exceed one year from the balance sheet date is alleviated, the financial statements should include the following disclosures:

1. The principal conditions and events that initially caused the auditor to believe there was substantial doubt.

2. The possible effects of such conditions and events, and any mitigating factors, including management's plans.

ILLUSTRATION 4—EXAMPLES OF FINANCIAL STATEMENT DISCLOSURES REGARDING GOING-CONCERN UNCERTAINTIES

Example 1: Going-concern issues arising from recurring losses and cash flow problems

As shown in the accompanying financial statements, the Company has incurred recurring losses from operations and as of December 31, 20X2, the Company's current liabilities exceeded its current assets by $800,000 and its total liabilities exceeded its total assets by $1,900,000. These factors raise substantial doubt about the Company's ability to continue as a going concern. Management has instituted a cost reduction program which included a reduction in labor and fringe costs. In addition, the Company has redesigned certain product lines, increased sales prices on certain items, obtained more favorable material costs, and has instituted more efficient management techniques. Management believes these factors will contribute towards achieving profitability. The financial statements do not include any adjustments that might be necessary if the Company is unable to continue as a going concern.

Example 2: Company's successful operations are dependent on those of its parent

The Company has historically relied on its parent to meet its cash flow requirements. The parent has cash available in the amount of approximately $83,000 as of December 31, 20X2, and a working capital deficit of $80 million. The Senior Secured Notes in the amount of $65 million have been reclassified because the Company's parent does not currently have sufficient funds to make the next interest payment (in the approximate amount of $6 million) due in May 20X3. Failure by the parent to make such payment could allow the holders of the Notes to declare all amounts outstanding immediately due and payable. The Company and its parent will need additional funds to meet the development and exploratory obligations until sufficient cash flows are generated from anticipated production to sustain operations and to fund future development and exploration obligations.

The parent plans to generate the additional cash needed through the sale or financing of its domestic assets held for sale and the completion of additional equity, debt or joint venture transactions. There is no assurance, however, that the parent will be able to sell or finance its assets held for sale or to complete other transactions in the future at commercially reasonable terms, if at all, or that the Company will be able to meet its future contractual obligations.

ILLUSTRATION 5—AUDITOR'S UNQUALIFIED OPINION INCLUDING AN EXPLANATORY PARAGRAPH REGARDING A GOING-CONCERN UNCERTAINTY

Independent Auditor's Report

Board of Directors and Stockholders
ABC Company

We have audited the accompanying balance sheet of ABC Company as of December 31, 20X2, and the related statements of income, retained earnings, and cash flows for the year then ended. These financial statements are the responsibility of the Company's management. Our responsibility is to express an opinion on these financial statements based on our audit.

We conducted our audit in accordance with auditing standards generally accepted in the United States of America. Those standards require that we plan and perform the audit to obtain reasonable assurance about whether the financial statements are free of material misstatement. An audit includes examining, on a test basis, evidence supporting the amounts and disclosures in the financial statements. An audit also includes assessing the accounting principles used and significant estimates made by management, as well as evaluating the overall financial statement presentation. We believe that our audit provides a reasonable basis for our opinion.

In our opinion, the financial statements referred to above present fairly, in all material respects, the financial position of ABC Company as of December 31, 20X2, and the results of its operations and its cash flows for the year then ended in conformity with accounting principles generally accepted in the United States of America.

The accompanying financial statements have been prepared assuming that the Company will continue as a going concern. As discussed in Note [X] to the financial statements, the Company has suffered recurring losses from operations and has a net capital deficiency that raises substantial doubt about its ability to continue as a going concern. Management's plans in regard to these matters are also described in Note [X]. The financial statements do not include any adjustments that might result from the outcome of this uncertainty.

[*Signature*]

[*Date*]

AU SECTION 342
AUDITING ACCOUNTING ESTIMATES

PRACTICE POINT: As part of its Clarity Project, the American Institute of Certified Public Accountants' (AICPA's) Auditing Standards Board (ASB) has finalized a clarified Statement on Auditing Standards (SAS) titled, "Auditing Accounting Estimates, Including Fair Value Accounting Estimates and Related Disclosures," which supersedes AU Section 328 (Auditing Fair Value Measurements and Disclosures) and AU Section 342 (Auditing Accounting Estimates). The clarified SAS combines the requirements and guidance from AU Section 328 and AU Section 342, and it does not change or expand those AU Sections in any significant respect.

The ASB is expected to issue many of the clarified standards in *one* SAS that will be codified in "AU Section" format. The ASB has decided that the effective date of the clarified SASs that have not yet been issued is for audits of financial statements for periods ending on or after December 15, 2012. Auditors should be alert to and monitor further developments in this area.

WHAT EVERY PRACTITIONER SHOULD KNOW

Basic Requirements

The auditor must collect sufficient audit evidence to determine whether accounting estimates established by management are reasonable in the context of the financial statements taken as a whole. An *accounting estimate* is "an approximation of a financial statement element, item, or account." Accounting estimates are made to measure past transactions or events (e.g., loss contingency arising from pending lawsuits) or to measure assets (e.g., net realizable value of accounts receivable) or liabilities (e.g., accrual related to warranty contracts). Illustration 1, which is adapted from the appendix to AU Section 342, includes examples of accounting estimates that are included in financial statements.

The auditor should evaluate accounting estimates to obtain reasonable assurance that:

1. Management has developed all accounting estimates that could be material to the financial statements.

2. The accounting estimates are reasonable.

3. The accounting estimates are presented in conformity with GAAP and are properly disclosed in the financial statements.

Because of the uncertainty related to accounting estimates and the higher possibility of misstatement, the auditor must have a greater degree of skepticism when planning and performing procedures related to the audit of accounting estimates.

Internal Control Related to Accounting Estimates

Many factors, such as the availability of reliable data and the required complexity of the evaluation process, have an effect on the risk of material misstatement in the financial statements because of unreasonable accounting estimates. In addition, when assessing the risk factor for misstatement, the auditor should consider the entity's internal control relating to the development of accounting estimates. Relevant aspects of an entity's internal control related to accounting estimates include the following:

1. Management's communication of the need for proper accounting estimates.

2. Accumulation of relevant, sufficient, and reliable data.

3. Preparation of accounting estimates by competent personnel.

4. Adequate review and approval of accounting estimates by appropriate personnel, including the review of relevant factors and assumptions and the need for specialists.

5. Comparison of prior accounting estimates with actual results.

6. Determination that accounting estimates are consistent with management's plans.

Identifying Circumstances that Give Rise to Accounting Estimates

To determine whether the entity has identified all circumstances that require accounting estimates, the auditor should consider the entity's operating characteristics and the industry in general, including any new pronouncements that affect the industry. On the basis of a review of these factors, the auditor should consider performing the following procedures:

1. Read the financial statements and identify those assertions implied in the financial statements that may require an accounting estimate.

2. Evaluate information obtained in performing other procedures during the audit, such as:

   a. Information about changes made or contemplated by the entity or the industry that would affect the operations of the business.

   b. Changes in the methods of accumulating information.

   c. Information about identified litigation, claims, and assessments.

   d. Information from reading available minutes of the board of directors, stockholders, and other significant committees.

   e. Information contained in regulatory or examination reports, supervisory correspondence, and similar materials from applicable regulatory agencies.

3. Inquire of management about the existence of circumstances that may indicate the need to make an accounting estimate.

Evaluating Reasonableness of Accounting Estimates

In evaluating the reasonableness of accounting estimates, the auditor should obtain an understanding of how management developed the estimate. Based on that understanding, the auditor should use one or a combination of the following approaches:

1. *Review and test the accounting estimation process used by management*—Procedures that the auditor should consider when he or she decides to review and test the accounting estimation process used by management include the following:

   a. Identify management controls and supporting data.

   b. Identify sources of data and factors used by management.

   c. Consider whether data and factors are relevant, reliable, and sufficient to support the estimate.

   d. Determine whether other factors or assumptions are appropriate.

   e. Determine if assumptions are internally consistent with other assumptions and supporting data.

   f. Determine that historical data used are comparable and consistent with data of the period under audit and such data are reliable.

   g. Determine whether changes in the current period require that other factors be considered in developing assumptions.

   h. Review documentation supporting assumptions used to make accounting estimates.

   i. Inquire about other plans that may have been adopted by management that could have an effect on assumptions related to accounting estimates.

   j. Determine whether a specialist is needed to evaluate assumptions.

   k. Recompute calculations made to convert assumptions and key factors into the accounting estimate.

2. *Develop an independent expectation of the estimate to corroborate the reasonableness of management's estimate*—The auditor may test the reasonableness of accounting estimates by making an independent calculation. In making the calculation, the auditor should use other factors or alternative assumptions that he or she considers relevant.

3. *Review subsequent events or transactions occurring prior to completion of fieldwork*—The auditor may decide to test the reasonableness of accounting estimates by reviewing subsequent events or transactions that occur after the date of the balance sheet through the date of the auditor's report. Such information may make it unnecessary to evaluate factors and assumptions related to the accounting estimate. In other circumstances, the uncertainty related to the evaluation of factors and assumptions may be significantly reduced.

Performance and Reporting Guidance Related to Fair Value Disclosures

Some entities may disclose the fair value information required by FASB Accounting Standards Codification (ASC) 825, *Financial Instruments*. In addition, some entities may disclose *voluntarily* the fair value of financial instruments not encompassed by ASC 825, as amended. In such situations, the auditor should obtain, for both required and voluntary disclosures, reasonable assurance that:

1. The valuation principles are acceptable, consistently applied, and supported by underlying documentation.

2. The method of estimation and significant assumptions used are properly disclosed.

Only required fair value information is presented When an entity discloses in its basic financial statements only information required by ASC 825, the auditor may issue a standard unqualified opinion, assuming no other report modifications are necessary. The auditor may add an emphasis-of-matter paragraph describing the nature and possible range of such fair value information. If the entity has not disclosed the required fair value information, the auditor should consider whether a qualified or an adverse opinion is required due to the departure from GAAP.

Both required and voluntary fair value information are presented When voluntary fair value information is presented in addition to required information, the auditor may audit the voluntary information only if *both* of the following conditions exist:

1. The measurement and disclosure criteria used to prepare the fair value financial information are reasonable; and

2. Competent persons using the measurement and disclosure criteria would ordinarily obtain materially similar measurements or disclosures.

Voluntary fair values may be presented as a complete balance sheet presentation or a presentation of less than a complete balance sheet. When the audited disclosures constitute a complete balance sheet presentation, the auditor should add a paragraph to the report, similar to the one presented in the audit report in Illustration 2.

When the audited disclosures do not constitute a complete balance sheet presentation and are located on the face of the financial statements or in the footnotes, the auditor may issue a standard unqualified opinion and need not mention the disclosures in the report. When the audited disclosures do not constitute a complete balance sheet presentation and are included in a supplemental schedule or exhibit, the auditor should add an additional paragraph to the report, similar to the one presented in the audit report in Illustration 3.

In some situations, the auditor may not be engaged to audit the voluntary information or may be unable to audit it. When the unaudited voluntary disclosures are included in an auditor-submitted document and located on the face of the financial statements, the footnotes, or in a supplemental schedule to the basic financial statements, the voluntary disclosures should be labeled "unaudited" and the auditor should disclaim an opinion on the unaudited information, as shown in the audit report in Illustration 4.

When the unaudited voluntary disclosures are included in a client-prepared document and are located on the face of the financial statements, the footnotes, or in a supplemental schedule, the voluntary disclosures should be labeled "unaudited." When such unaudited information is not presented on the face of the financial statements, in the footnotes, or in a supplemental schedule, the auditor should consider the guidance in AU Section 550 (Other Information in Documents Containing Audited Financial Statements).

PRACTICE ISSUES AND FREQUENTLY ASKED QUESTIONS

Issue 1: Is the client's management or the auditor responsible for establishing accounting estimates?

It is the responsibility of management to establish reasonable accounting estimates. Such estimates are established by reviewing past experiences and evaluating these experiences in the context of current and expected future conditions. Therefore, accounting estimates are based on both objective factors (past transactions and events) and subjective factors (projecting the likely outcome of future transactions and events). Although management is responsible for establishing accounting estimates, the auditor must collect sufficient audit evidence to determine whether accounting estimates are reasonable.

Issue 2: What are the implications of unreasonable accounting estimates that the auditor becomes aware of?

The purpose of the audit of accounting estimates is to determine whether estimates are reasonable. Therefore, the auditor might conclude, based on available evidence, that an estimate is not reasonable or is not necessarily the best estimate. Generally, the difference between the reasonable estimate and best estimate should not necessarily be treated as a misstatement; however, if most estimates appear to reflect a particular bias, such as the tendency to understate expenses, the auditor should consider whether all misstatements combined result in a material misstatement.

If, after due consideration, the auditor nevertheless believes the estimated amount is unreasonable, he or she should treat the difference between that estimate and the closest reasonable estimate as a likely misstatement and aggregate it with other likely misstatements.

Issue 3: What should the auditor do when his or her analysis and evaluation of the client's accounting estimates lead to a range of acceptable amounts and the client's recorded amount does not fall within the auditor's range?

The auditor's analysis and evaluation of the client's accounting estimates often lead to a range of acceptable amounts. If the auditor concludes management's recorded estimate falls within the range of acceptable amounts, the auditor ordinarily would conclude that the recorded amount is reasonable and there is no likely misstatement in the account balance or class of transactions.

In other situations, management's recorded estimate will not fall within the auditor's acceptable range. This may result primarily because of different expectations about future events between the auditor and management, or because of management's inappropriate consideration of relevant facts and circumstances. In these situations, the auditor should treat the difference between management's estimated recorded amount and the closest estimate of the auditor's acceptable range as a likely misstatement.

For example, the auditor may believe that the allowance for obsolete inventory should be between $20,000 and $35,000. If management's recorded estimate is $25,000, the auditor would conclude that the recorded amount is reasonable because it falls within the acceptable range. Therefore, the auditor would conclude that there are no likely misstatements in the inventory balance. On the other hand, if management's recorded estimate is $15,000, the auditor would conclude that an audit difference of $5,000 ($20,000 − $15,000) exists. Therefore, the auditor would treat such difference as a likely misstatement in the inventory balance and aggregate it with other likely and known misstatements for an overall evaluation on the financial statements.

Issue 4: What are some common practices for documenting the auditing procedures applied to accounting estimates?

The standards do not prescribe specific methods for documenting the auditing procedures applied to accounting estimates. However, the following three approaches have been observed in common practice:

1. *Make notations about the evaluations of estimates directly on the working papers of the specific accounts or elements*—An example of this approach would be a notation on a depreciation schedule that depreciable lives and methods are reasonable for the client's industry. This method is economical and is generally sufficient for small entities with estimates that are few in number and simple in nature.

2. *Use a narrative memorandum*—Some auditors use a narrative memorandum to document their evaluations of the various accounting estimates contained in the financial statements. This method has the advantage of placing all of the evaluations in one place, so that omissions of necessary estimates or tendencies toward aggregate misstatements are more easily spotted. Many auditors, however, feel that this method requires undue time and might be inefficient.

3. *Use an "estimates lead sheet" which lists the significant accounting estimates within the financial statements and references the specific working paper on which they are evaluated*—Some firms incorporate this information directly into their audit programs, while others have a program step that refers to a separate accounting estimates lead sheet or checklist. As engagements become larger and estimates more numerous and complex, common practice appears to favor this approach as both effective and reasonably economical.

Issue 5: How might the auditor respond to a client's controller who indicates that the entity does not need to establish internal controls over accounting estimates?

Like any other element of financial statements, accounting estimates should be developed and reviewed or approved by competent personnel. Therefore, systems should be in place to ensure that the entity can identify circumstances requiring estimates, and that sufficient reliable data is available for their development. Estimates should be compared with actual results periodically by management to ensure that they are reasonable. All of these items are key components of a sound system of internal control. Because of the inherent uncertainty surrounding all accounting estimates, the risk of misstatement is higher than it might be with other financial statement elements of the same size. For this reason, internal control is as important in developing accounting estimates as it is in other accounting areas.

Issue 6: If the client has identified to the auditor the accounting estimates that are believed to be significant to the financial statements and the auditor is satisfied with the reasonableness and presentation of such estimates, does the auditor need to perform any additional procedures?

Yes. One of the most important steps is identifying circumstances that give rise to accounting estimates. Asking the client to identify accounting estimates is only one means toward this end, because by itself it is not effective in detecting circumstances in which the client has failed to make accounting estimates that are required. Therefore, in such situations, the auditor should read the financial statements in order to identify assertions that may require estimates. For example, the presentation of accounts receivable on the balance sheet almost always indicates the need for an estimate of an allowance for doubtful accounts. In addition, the auditor should consider other evidence, both financial and non-financial, gathered during the audit, that might indicate the need for accounting estimates.

Issue 7: What are the implications in audits of small businesses where management does not record during the year certain accounting estimates, such as uncollectible receivables and depreciation, and request the auditor to record them through audit adjustments at year-end?

Like all the other elements of the financial statements, the estimates, even though calculated by the auditor, are management's responsibility. In such situations, the auditor has a responsibility to review those estimates with management, so that management can make an informed decision as to their reasonableness and can take responsibility for them. The auditor also has the responsibility to consider other circumstances that require accounting estimates that might not have been identified by management.

Issue 8: When a client uses Internal Revenue Service (IRS) guidelines in establishing the estimated useful lives of fixed assets, can the auditor accept these estimates as reasonable without further consideration?

Not necessarily. Although in many cases the IRS guidelines result in a reasonable estimate of an asset's expected life, the auditor needs to evaluate the reasonableness of such estimates based on relevant factors, such as historical patterns of the client and industry characteristics. For example, office and transportation equipment that may reasonably be expected to last seven years in one company might last half as long, or twice as long, in other companies.

ILLUSTRATIONS AND PRACTICE AIDS

ILLUSTRATION 1—EXAMPLES OF ACCOUNTING ESTIMATES

Receivables:

Uncollectible receivables
Allowance for loan losses
Uncollectible pledges

Revenues:

Airline passenger revenue
Subscription income
Freight and cargo revenue
Dues income
Losses on sales contracts

Inventories:

Obsolete inventory
Net realizable value of inventories where future selling prices and future costs are involved
Losses on purchase commitments

Contracts:

Revenue to be earned
Costs to be incurred
Percent of completion

Financial instruments:

Valuation of securities
Trading versus investment security classification
Probability of high correlation of a hedge
Sales of securities with puts and calls

Leases:

Initial direct costs
Executory costs
Residual values

Litigation:

Probability of loss
Amount of loss

Productive facilities, natural resources, and intangibles:

Useful lives and residual values
Depreciation and amortization methods
Recoverability of costs
Recoverable reserves

Rates:

Annual effective tax rate in interim reporting
Imputed interest rates on receivables and payables
Gross profit rates under program method of accounting

Accruals:

Property and casualty insurance company loss reserves
Compensation in stock option plans and deferred plans
Warranty claims
Taxes on real and personal property
Renegotiation refunds
Actuarial assumptions in pension costs

Other:

Losses and net realizable value on disposal of segment or restructuring of a business
Fair values in nonmonetary exchanges
Interim period costs in interim reporting
Current values in personal financial statements

ILLUSTRATION 2—AUDITOR'S REPORT WHEN THE AUDITED FAIR VALUE DISCLOSURES CONSTITUTE A COMPLETE BALANCE SHEET PRESENTATION

Independent Auditor's Report

Board of Directors and Stockholders
ABC Company

We have audited the accompanying balance sheet of ABC Company as of December 31, 20X2, and the related statements of income, retained earnings, and cash flows for the year then ended. These financial statements are the responsibility of the Company's management. Our responsibility is to express an opinion on these financial statements based on our audit.

We conducted our audit in accordance with auditing standards generally accepted in the United States of America. Those standards require that we plan and perform the audit to obtain reasonable assurance about whether the financial statements are free of material misstatement. An audit includes examining, on a test basis, evidence supporting the amounts and disclosures in the financial statements. An audit also includes assessing the accounting principles used and significant estimates made by management, as well as evaluating the overall financial statement presentation. We believe that our audit provides a reasonable basis for our opinion.

In our opinion, the financial statements referred to above present fairly, in all material respects, the financial position of ABC Company as of December 31, 20X2, and the results of its operations and its cash flows for the year then ended in conformity with accounting principles generally accepted in the United States of America.

We have also audited in accordance with auditing standards generally accepted in the United States of America the supplemental fair value balance sheet of ABC Company as of December 31, 20X2. As described in Note [X], the supplemental fair value balance sheet has been prepared by management to present relevant financial information that is not provided by the historical-cost balance sheets and is not intended to be a presentation in conformity with accounting principles generally accepted in the United States of America. In addition, the supplemental fair value balance sheet does not purport to present the net realizable, liquidation, or market value of ABC Company as a whole. Furthermore, amounts ultimately realized by ABC Company from the disposal of assets may vary significantly from the fair values presented. In our opinion, the supplemental fair value balance sheet referred to above presents fairly, in all material respects, the information set forth therein as described in Note [X].

[*Signature*]

[*Date*]

ILLUSTRATION 3—AUDITOR'S REPORT WHEN THE AUDITED FAIR VALUE DISCLOSURES DO NOT CONSTITUTE A COMPLETE BALANCE SHEET PRESENTATION AND ARE INCLUDED IN A SUPPLEMENTAL SCHEDULE OR EXHIBIT

Independent Auditor's Report

Board of Directors and Stockholders
ABC Company

We have audited the accompanying balance sheet of ABC Company as of December 31, 20X2, and the related statements of income, retained earnings, and cash flows for the year then ended. These financial statements are the responsibility of the Company's management. Our responsibility is to express an opinion on these financial statements based on our audit.

We conducted our audit in accordance with auditing standards generally accepted in the United States of America. Those standards require that we plan and perform the audit to obtain reasonable assurance about whether the financial statements are free of material misstatement. An audit includes examining, on a test basis, evidence supporting the amounts and disclosures in the financial statements. An audit also includes assessing the accounting principles used and significant estimates made by management, as well as evaluating the overall financial statement presentation. We believe that our audit provides a reasonable basis for our opinion.

In our opinion, the financial statements referred to above present fairly, in all material respects, the financial position of ABC Company as of December 31, 20X2, and the results of its operations and its cash flows for the year then ended in conformity with accounting principles generally accepted in the United States of America.

Our audit was conducted for the purpose of forming an opinion on the basic financial statements taken as a whole. The accompanying fair value information in schedule [X] is presented for purposes of additional analysis and is not a required part of the basic financial statements. Such information has been sub-jected to the auditing procedures applied in the audit of the basic financial statements and, in our opinion, is fairly stated in all material respects in relation to the basic financial statements taken as a whole.

[*Signature*]

[*Date*]

ILLUSTRATION 4—AUDITOR'S DISCLAIMER OF OPINION ON UNAUDITED VOLUNTARY FAIR VALUE DISCLOSURES INCLUDED IN AN AUDITOR-SUBMITTED DOCUMENT

Independent Auditor's Report

Board of Directors and Stockholders
ABC Company

We have audited the accompanying balance sheet of ABC Company as of December 31, 20X2, and the related statements of income, retained earnings, and cash flows for the year then ended. These financial statements are the responsi-bility of the Company's management. Our responsibility is to express an opinion on these financial statements based on our audit.

We conducted our audit in accordance with auditing standards generally accepted in the United States of America. Those standards require that we plan and perform the audit to obtain reasonable assurance about whether the financial statements are free of material misstatement. An audit includes examining, on a test basis, evidence supporting the amounts and disclosures in the financial statements. An audit also includes assessing the accounting principles used and significant estimates made by management, as well as evaluating the overall financial statement presentation. We believe that our audit provides a reasonable basis for our opinion.

In our opinion, the financial statements referred to above present fairly, in all material respects, the financial position of ABC Company as of December 31, 20X2, and the results of its operations and its cash flows for the year then ended in conformity with accounting principles generally accepted in the United States of America.

Our audit was conducted for the purpose of forming an opinion on the basic financial statements taken as a whole. The accompanying fair value information in schedule [X] is presented for purposes of additional analysis and is not a required part of the basic financial statements. Such information has not been subjected to the auditing procedures applied in the audit of the basic financial statements, and, accordingly, we express no opinion on it.

[*Signature*]

[*Date*]

AU SECTION 350
AUDIT SAMPLING

PRACTICE POINT: As part of its Clarity Project, the American Institute of Certified Public Accountants' (AICPA's) Auditing Standards Board (ASB) has finalized a clarified Statement on Auditing Standards (SAS) titled, "Audit Sampling (Redrafted)," which supersedes AU Section 350 (Audit Sampling). The clarified SAS does not change or expand AU Section 350 in any significant respect.

The ASB is expected to issue many of the clarified standards in *one* SAS that will be codified in "AU Section" format. The ASB has decided that the effective date of the clarified SASs that have not yet been issued is for audits of financial statements for periods ending on or after December 15, 2012. Auditors should be alert to and monitor further developments in this area.

WHAT EVERY PRACTITIONER SHOULD KNOW

Basic Objectives and Requirements

Audit sampling is the "application of an audit procedure to less than 100 percent of the items within an account balance or class of transactions for the purpose of evaluating some characteristic of the balance or class." The auditor should adhere to the requirements of this Section whenever he or she tests less than 100% of a population for the purpose of reaching a conclusion about the entire population.

Once a decision is made that audit sampling is necessary, the auditor must choose between a statistical and nonstatistical sampling approach. Both statistical and nonstatistical sampling are satisfactory sampling methods and they can be used for substantive tests, for tests of controls, or for both. Both approaches require that the auditor use professional judgment in planning, performing, and evaluating a sample, and in relating the audit evidence produced by the sample to other audit evidence when forming a conclusion about the related account balance or class of transactions.

Statistical sampling is the use of mathematical measurement techniques to calculate formal statistical results and is based on probability concepts. Statistical sampling is highly technical (i.e., the sample must be statistically selected in such a way that each item in the sample must have a known probability of selection), and the sample results must be quantitatively or mathematically evaluated.

Nonstatistical sampling includes all other sampling selection and evaluation techniques. In nonstatistical sampling, the auditor does not quantify sampling risk; instead, conclusions are reached about populations on a more judgmental basis.

The discussion in this Section applies equally to statistical and nonstatistical sampling approaches.

Steps Involved in Applying Audit Sampling

There are five broad steps involved in applying audit sampling to both substantive tests and to tests of controls:

1. *Planning the sample*—The purposes of planning the sample are to make sure that the audit tests are performed in a manner to provide the desired sampling risk (e.g., 95% confidence level provides a 5% sampling risk) and to minimize the likelihood of nonsampling error.

2. *Determining the sample size*—This step involves predefining the various factors that affect the sample size (e.g., tolerable rate, expected population deviation rate).

3. *Selecting the sample*—This step involves deciding how to select sample items from the population. The auditor should select a sample size that is adequate, giving consideration to materiality, audit risk, and population characteristics.

4. *Performing the tests*—This step primarily involves the examination of documents and performing other audit procedures.

5. *Evaluating the sample results*—This step involves drawing conclusions about the likely effect on the total population based on the audit tests of the sample.

Sampling in substantive tests of details and in tests of controls is discussed below.

Sampling in Substantive Tests of Details

Substantive tests are audit procedures designed to obtain evidence about the validity and propriety of the accounting treatment of transactions and balances or to detect misstatements. Substantive tests differ from tests of controls in that the auditor is interested primarily in a conclusion about dollars.

Planning the sample for substantive tests The following steps are involved in planning the sample for substantive tests:

1. *Determine the audit objective of the test*—The auditor should decide whether the dollar value assigned by management to an account balance or group of transactions is reasonable (i.e., whether the population is fairly stated).

2. *Define the population:*
   a. Define the sampling unit (e.g., individual accounts receivable).
   b. Consider the completeness of the population (e.g., determine that the accounts receivable aged trial balance agrees with the general ledger, or if items are numerically sequenced, account for the numerical sequence of items in the population before selecting the sample from that sequence).
   c. Consider variations within the population. This is primarily to determine if the sample size selected is representative of the population. For example, an accounts receivable trial balance may be composed of a few large balances, several medium balances, and numerous

smaller balances. The auditor may review the accounts receivable trial balance or prior years' workpapers to determine the extent of variations within the population.

d. Identify individually significant items (e.g., large dollar items or delinquent accounts receivable). The cutoff amount for individually significant dollar items can be any amount up to tolerable misstatement and may include items that the auditor considers significant due to their nature.

e. Determine the sampling population. The auditor determines the sampling population by deducting any items that have been determined to be significant and that will be examined 100% from the total amount of the account balance or transaction class.

Determining the sample size for substantive tests The following steps are involved in determining the sample size for substantive tests:

1. *Consider sampling risk*—The auditor is concerned with two aspects of sampling risk: (a) the risk of incorrect acceptance which relates to the effectiveness of an audit in detecting an existing material misstatement, and (b) the risk of incorrect rejection, which relates solely to the efficiency of the audit. The auditor is primarily concerned with the risk of incorrect acceptance because it is the risk that the results of a sample will lead the auditor to conclude that the recorded account balance is not materially misstated when in fact it is. If the auditor assesses the combination of inherent risk and control risk at a lower level, he or she can accept a greater risk of incorrect acceptance for the planned substantive test. As the acceptable level of risk of incorrect acceptance increases, the appropriate sample size for the substantive test decreases. Conversely, if the auditor assesses the combination of inherent risk and control risk at a higher level, the acceptable level of risk of incorrect acceptance decreases, and the appropriate sample size increases.

2. *Determine tolerable misstatement*—This is the maximum monetary misstatement in an account balance or class of transactions that is acceptable without causing the financial statements to be materially misstated. Tolerable misstatement relates to and is based on the auditor's determination of planning materiality. There is an inverse relationship between tolerable misstatement and the required sample size. Therefore, as the tolerable misstatement decreases, the required sample size increases.

3. *Assess the expected misstatement likely to exist in the sampling population*—The *expected misstatement* is the auditor's best estimate of misstatements in the remaining population from which the sample is selected (sometimes referred to as "expected projected misstatement"). The expected misstatement does not include adjustments that the client expects the auditor to make (e.g., adjustments to accruals or prepaids). There is a direct relationship between expected misstatement and the required sample size. The required sample size increases as the auditor's estimate of the expected amount of misstatement in the population increases. The assessment of the expected misstatement likely to exist in the population

is a matter of professional judgment; however, it is based on several factors: (a) understanding of the client's business, (b) previous experience and prior years' tests of the population, (c) results of any tests of controls, and (d) knowledge of the population.

Illustration 1, which is adapted from AU Section 350, summarizes the effects of various factors on sample sizes for substantive tests of details.

Selecting the sample for substantive tests The auditor should select the sample in such a way that it can be expected to be representative of the population; each item in the population should have an equal opportunity (probability) of being selected. Common representative random-sampling methods used by auditors include systematic selection, random-number selection, and haphazard selection. See Issue 6 below for additional discussion of these methods of sample selection.

Performing the substantive tests Once the sample has been selected, the auditor should apply appropriate audit procedures. If the auditor is unable to perform an audit procedure on a sampling unit selected for testing, alternative auditing procedures should be considered. If the sampling unit does not have an effect on the conclusion reached by the auditor concerning the acceptability of the population, alternative audit procedures do not have to be applied, and the sampling unit may be treated as an error for evaluation purposes. In addition, the auditor should determine whether the inability to apply an audit procedure has an effect on (1) the planned assessed level of control risk, (2) the assessment of the risk of fraud, or (3) the degree of reliance on management representations.

Evaluating the sample results of substantive tests The auditor should project the misstatements found in the sample to the population from which the sample was selected, and should add that amount to the misstatements discovered in any items examined 100%. The auditor should give adequate consideration to the qualitative aspects of the misstatements, including the possible relationship of the misstatements to other phases of the audit. The nature and cause of the misstatements should be considered, including (a) whether they are errors or caused by fraud or (b) whether they are due to misunderstanding of instructions, carelessness, intentional failure to perform procedures, or due to other factors. The discovery of fraud generally would require more attention from the auditor than the discovery of an error.

Sampling in Tests of Controls

Tests of controls are intended to provide evidence about the effectiveness of the design or operation of a control in preventing or detecting material misstatements in a financial statement assertion. Tests of controls are necessary if the auditor plans to assess control risk below the maximum for a particular assertion.

Planning the sample for tests of controls The following steps are involved in planning the sample for tests of controls:

1. *Determine the audit objective of the test*—The objective of tests of controls is to provide the auditor with evidence about whether controls are operating effectively. For example, to determine whether disbursements have been authorized, the auditor could examine payment vouchers to deter-

mine if the authorized client personnel signed the payment voucher before processing.

2. *Define the population:*

   a. Define the sampling unit. A sampling unit may be, for example, a document, an entry, or a line item. If the objective of the test is to determine whether disbursements have been authorized and the prescribed control activity requires an authorized signature on the voucher before processing, the sampling unit might be defined as the voucher. On the other hand, if one voucher pays several invoices and the prescribed control activity requires each invoice to be authorized individually, the line item on the voucher representing the invoice might be defined as the sampling unit.

   b. Consider the completeness of the population. The population represents the body of data about which the auditor wishes to generalize. For example, in performing tests of recorded sales transactions, the auditor generally defines the population as all recorded sales for the year. If the auditor randomly samples from only one month's transactions, it is invalid to draw conclusions or generalizations about the sales for the entire year. To consider the completeness of the population, the auditor scans the sales journal for the year to account for the numerical sequence of invoice numbers issued.

   c. Define the period covered by the test. Tests of controls may be applied to transactions executed throughout the period under audit (e.g., the entire year) or during the period from the beginning of the year to an interim date. If the auditor decides to define the period covered by the test as less than the period under audit, the auditor might use audit sampling to reach a conclusion about compliance with the prescribed activity for the period up to the interim date. In this situation, the auditor should obtain reasonable assurance regarding the remaining period by performing additional procedures. The extent of these procedures depends on factors such as (1) the results of the tests during the interim period, (2) the length of the remaining period, (3) responses to inquiries concerning the remaining period, and (4) evidence of compliance within the remaining period obtained from substantive tests performed.

3. *Define the deviation conditions*—A *deviation* in tests of controls is a departure from adequate performance of the prescribed control activity. The auditor must make a precise statement of what constitutes a deviation so that the staff performing the audit procedure will have specific guidelines for identifying deviations.

Determining the sample size for tests of controls The following steps are involved in determining the sample size for tests of controls:

1. *Consider sampling risk*—The auditor is concerned with two aspects of sampling risk: (a) the risk of assessing control risk too low, which relates to the effectiveness of an audit in detecting an existing material misstatement and (b) the risk of assessing control risk too high, which relates

solely to the efficiency of the audit. The auditor is primarily concerned with the risk of assessing control risk too low because it is the risk that the assessed level of control risk based on the sample is less than the true operating of the control. If the auditor assesses control risk too low, he or she inappropriately reduces the evidence obtained from substantive tests. Samples taken for tests of controls are intended to provide evidence about the operating effectiveness of the controls. Because a test of controls is the primary source of evidence about whether the controls are operating effectively, the auditor generally wishes to obtain a high degree of assurance that the conclusions from the sample would not differ from the conclusions that would be reached if the test were applied in the same way to all transactions. Therefore, the auditor should allow for a low level of risk of assessing control risk too low. The auditor who prefers to think of risk levels in quantitative terms might consider, for example, a 5% to 10% risk of assessing control risk too low. There is an inverse relationship between the risk of assessing control risk too low and sample size. If the auditor is willing to accept only a low risk of assessing control risk too low, the sample size ordinarily would be larger than if a higher risk were acceptable.

2. *Consider the tolerable rate*—The tolerable rate is the maximum rate of deviation from a prescribed control activity that the auditor is willing to accept without altering the planned assessed level of control risk. There is an inverse relationship between the tolerable rate and the sample size (i.e., the lower the tolerable rate, the larger the sample size). If, after performing the sampling application, the auditor finds that the rate of deviation from the prescribed control activity is close to, or exceeds, the tolerable rate, the auditor might decide that there is an unacceptably high sampling risk that the deviation rate for the population exceeds the tolerable rate. In such situations, the auditor should increase the assessed level of control risk.

3. *Consider the expected population deviation rate*—The auditor should consider the expected rate of deviation from a particular control. It is common for the auditor to use the results of the preceding year's audit to make an estimate of the expected population deviation rate. If the prior year's results are not available, the auditor considers other factors, such as his or her assessment of the overall control environment. There is a direct relationship between the expected population deviation rate and the sample size (i.e., the higher the expected population deviation rate, the larger the sample size).

Selecting the sample for tests of controls The auditor should select sample items in such a way that the sample can be expected to be representative of the population. Therefore, all items in the population should have an opportunity to be selected. Common representative random-sampling methods used by auditors include systematic selection, random number selection, and haphazard selection. See Issue 6 below for additional discussion of these methods of sample selection.

Performing the tests of controls Once the sample has been selected, the auditor should apply appropriate audit procedures. If the auditor is unable to perform an audit procedure on a sampling unit selected for testing, alternative auditing procedures should be considered. If the sampling unit does not have an effect on the conclusion reached by the auditor concerning the acceptability of the population, alternative audit procedures do not have to be applied, and the sampling unit may be treated as a deviation for evaluation purposes. In addition, the auditor should determine whether the inability to apply an audit procedure has an effect on the planned assessed level of control risk.

Audit procedures should be applied to each sampling unit to determine whether there has been a deviation from the established internal control activity. Usually a deviation occurs if the auditor is unable to perform an audit procedure or apply alternative audit procedures to a sampling unit. As a general rule, sampling units that are selected but not examined, such as voided transactions or unused documents, should be replaced with new sampling units. Voided or unused documents are not considered deviations if the established procedure of accounting for these items has been properly followed.

Evaluating the sample results of tests of controls In addition to evaluating the frequency of the deviations from pertinent procedures, the auditor should consider the qualitative aspects of the deviations, including the possible relationship of the deviations to other phases of the audit. The nature and cause of the deviations should be considered, including (a) whether they are errors or caused by fraud or (b) whether they are due to misunderstanding of instructions, carelessness, intentional failure to perform procedures, or due to other factors. The discovery of fraud generally would require more attention from the auditor than the discovery of an error.

The auditor uses professional judgment to reach an overall conclusion about the effect that the evaluation of the results will have on his or her assessed level of control risk and thus on the nature, timing, and extent of planned substantive tests. If the sample results, along with other relevant audit evidence, support the planned assessed level of control risk, the auditor generally does not need to modify planned substantive tests. If the planned assessed level of control risk is not supported, the auditor would ordinarily either perform tests of other controls that could support the planned assessed level of control risk or increase the assessed level of control risk.

PRACTICE ISSUES AND FREQUENTLY ASKED QUESTIONS

Issue 1: What are some examples of audit procedures that do not constitute audit sampling?

Numerous situations exist in an audit when the auditor does not use audit sampling. The following are examples of audit procedures that do not constitute audit sampling:

- Performing a 100% examination of an account balance or transaction class because the auditor is not willing to accept sampling risk for the balance

- Performing a walk-through of the client's accounting system to gain an understanding of how transactions are processed
- Testing individually significant dollar amounts in an account balance and not testing the remaining balance because of immateriality
- Performing analytical review procedures
- Inquiry and observation (e.g., completing an internal control questionnaire)

Issue 2: Is there a practical approach that the auditor might follow when determining whether audit sampling in substantive tests of details is necessary or appropriate?

Yes. The auditor can follow the following basic steps to determine whether audit sampling in substantive tests of details is necessary or appropriate:

1. Identify individually significant items to be examined. (See Issue 3 below for further guidance.)

2. Determine whether the extent of audit evidence obtained from examining the individually significant items is sufficient. Generally, a coverage of two-thirds or higher of the total population would be considered sufficient. If the auditor can accept the evidence obtained as sufficient, ordinarily there is no need to apply audit sampling. (See Issue 4 below for further guidance.)

3. If the extent of audit evidence gathered in Step 2 is not sufficient, consider the contribution of other audit procedures and determine whether the resulting evidence is sufficient. Generally, if the auditor can accept such additional evidence as sufficient, there is no need to apply audit sampling.

4. If the extent of audit evidence obtained from examining individually significant items (Step 2) and the contribution of other audit procedures (Step 3) is not considered sufficient, it would be appropriate, and possibly necessary, for the auditor to apply audit sampling.

Issue 3: What factors should the auditor consider when selecting specific individually significant items to audit in substantive tests of details?

Ordinarily, the first step in selecting specific individually significant items to audit is to identify any transactions or accounts that are individually important because of their size or that the auditor believes have a high likelihood of misstatement. Generally, the auditor uses a cutoff amount for individually significant items to be tested 100%. In addition to the size of the item, the auditor should consider factors such as the following:

- Transactions involving estimates and requiring highly subjective judgments (e.g., allowance for doubtful accounts, inventory valuation adjustments, or percentage-of-completion estimates for a construction contractor)
- Large or unusual transactions recorded as of or near the end of the client's year end (e.g., large sales just before or after year end)
- Old items (e.g., past due accounts receivable or slow-moving inventory)

- Transactions having a high degree of management involvement (e.g., related-party transactions)
- Other large or unusual items

Issue 4: What factors should the auditor consider when evaluating the sufficiency of audit evidence obtained in substantive tests of details for a particular account balance or class of transactions?

When evaluating the sufficiency of audit evidence obtained in substantive tests of details for a particular account balance or class of transactions, the auditor should consider the following factors:

- The importance and significance of the individual items examined. If the items examined account for a high percentage of the total population, the auditor may be reasonably assured that there is an acceptably low risk of an undetected misstatement in the remaining population. The auditor should consider whether the dollar amount of the remaining population is equal to or greater than an amount that would be material to the financial statements.

- The nature and cause of the misstatements. If the auditor detects misstatements during the course of the audit, he or she should evaluate them to determine if they are (1) caused by differences in accounting principles or application thereof, (2) due to errors or fraud, (3) caused by misunderstanding of instructions, or (4) resulting from carelessness.

- Possible effect and relationship of the misstatements to other phases of the audit. For example, if the auditor determines that the misstatement is caused by fraud, this would require a broader consideration of the possible implications than would the discovery of an error.

- The characteristics of the sample compared to the population. The auditor may obtain some knowledge of the types of items in the population if the characteristics in the sample are similar in nature and the same controls are followed for processing the transactions. The auditor should consider the degree of risk involved (i.e., how susceptible the account is to misstatement and whether there have been problems with this area in prior audits).

Issue 5: What are some types of statistical sampling models?

There are two broad categories of statistical sampling models:

1. *Classical statistical sampling models:*

   a. *Attributes sampling*—Attributes sampling is a statistical sampling method used to estimate the rate (percentage) of occurrence of a specific quality (attribute) in a population. Attributes sampling is used primarily for tests of controls.

   b. *Discovery sampling*—Discovery sampling is a special kind of attributes sampling typically used when the auditor expects very few or no deviations. Discovery sampling is typically used for substantive testing in situations where few misstatements are expected.

c. *Variables sampling*—Variables sampling is a statistical technique applied when the auditor desires to reach a dollar or a quantitative conclusion about a population. Variables sampling is used primarily for substantive testing.

2. *Probability-proportionate-to-size (PPS) sampling*—PPS sampling enables the auditor to make dollar conclusions about the total dollar amount of misstatement in a population. Whereas the classical sampling techniques focus on physical units of the population, PPS sampling focuses on the dollar units of a population. That is to say, instead of the auditor viewing a $100,000 accounts receivable population as containing 500 individual customer balances, the auditor considers the population as 100,000 individual dollar units from which to draw a sample. In PPS sampling, each dollar is a sampling unit. Therefore, individual accounts with larger balances have a proportionally higher chance of being selected in a sample because they contain more sampling units, hence the name probability-proportionate-to-size sampling. PPS sampling is used by auditors for both tests of controls and substantive tests.

Issue 6: What are some common methods used by auditors for selecting a statistical or a nonstatistical sample in substantive tests of details and in tests of controls?

The following is a basic overview of common sample selection methods used by auditors that are appropriate for statistical and/or nonstatistical sampling applications:

1. *Random-number selection*—The auditor may select a random sample by matching random numbers generated by a computer or selected from a random-number table with, for example, document numbers. With this method, every sampling unit has the same probability of being selected as every other sampling unit in the population. This approach is appropriate for both statistical and nonstatistical sampling applications.

2. *Systematic selection*—Systematic sampling consists of determining a uniform interval and selecting throughout the population one item at each of the uniform intervals from the starting point (i.e., every nth item). The following steps should be observed when systematic sampling selection is used:

   a. Determine the population (N).

   b. Determine the sample size (n).

   c. Compute the interval size by dividing N by n.

   d. Select a random start (a random-number table can be used to determine the starting point). The starting point should be less than the interval size.

   e. Determine the sample items selected by successively adding the interval to the random starting point.

Systematic selection is useful for nonstatistical sampling, and if the starting point is a random number, it might be useful for statistical sampling.

3. *Haphazard selection*—A "haphazard sample" consists of a selection that is made without any special reason for including or excluding a given item from the sample. For example, the auditor may select disbursement vouchers from a client's file cabinet, without consideration to the size or location of such vouchers. Haphazard samples cannot be used in statistical sampling because they are not selected based on defined probability concepts. However, the auditor may find it useful, and is permitted, to use haphazard selection in nonstatistical sampling, as long as the auditor expects the selected sample to be representative of the population.

Issue 7: What effect does the selection of a voided item have on sampling in connection with tests of controls?

An auditor using random-number selection techniques might select a voided item to be included in a sample. If the auditor obtains reasonable assurance that the item selected has been properly voided and does not represent a deviation from the prescribed control, he or she should replace the voided item with another one.

Issue 8: Does this Section require specific documentation of audit sampling applications?

No. This Section does not require specific documentation of audit sampling applications. However, the documentation requirements set forth in other Sections (e.g., AU Section 339, Audit Documentation) apply to audit sampling applications just as they apply to other auditing procedures. Therefore, the following are examples of items that the auditor might consider documenting for audit sampling applications:

Tests of Controls	Substantive Tests of Details
• A description of the prescribed control being tested • The objectives of the sampling application, including its relationship to the assessment of control risk • The definition of the population and the sampling unit, including how the auditor considered the completeness of the population • The definition of the deviation condition • The risk of assessing control risk too low, the tolerable deviation rate, and the expected population deviation rate used in the application • The method of sample-size determination • The method of sample selection • A description of how the sampling procedure was performed and a list of the deviations identified in the sample • The evaluation of the sample and a summary of the overall conclusion	• The objectives of the test and a description of other audit procedures related to those objectives • The definition of the population and the sampling unit, including how the auditor determined the completeness of the population • The definition of a misstatement • The risk of incorrect acceptance, the risk of incorrect rejection, and the tolerable misstatement • The audit sampling technique used • The method of sample selection • A description of the performance of the sampling procedures and a list of misstatements identified in the sample • The evaluation of the sample and a summary of the overall conclusion

ILLUSTRATIONS AND PRACTICE AIDS

ILLUSTRATION 1—FACTORS INFLUENCING SAMPLE SIZES FOR A TEST OF DETAILS IN SAMPLE PLANNING

Conditions Leading to:

Factor	Smaller Sample Size	Larger Sample Size	Related Factor for Substantive Sample Planning
Assessment of inherent risk	Low assessed level of inherent risk	High assessed level of inherent risk	Allowable risk of incorrect acceptance
Assessment of control risk	Low assessed level of control risk	High assessed level of control risk	Allowable risk of incorrect acceptance
Assessment of risk for other substantive procedures related to the same assertion (including substantive analytical procedures and other relevant substantive procedures)	Low assessment of risk associated with other relevant substantive procedures	High assessment of risk associated with other relevant substantive procedures	Allowable risk of incorrect acceptance
Measure of tolerable misstatement for a specific account	Larger measure of tolerable misstatement	Smaller measure of tolerable misstatement	Tolerable misstatement
Expected size and frequency of misstatements	Smaller misstatements or lower frequency	Larger misstatements or higher frequency	Assessment of population characteristics

| | Conditions Leading to: | | |
Factor	Smaller Sample Size	Larger Sample Size	Related Factor for Substantive Sample Planning
Number of items in the population	Virtually no effect on sample size unless population is very small	Virtually no effect on sample size unless population is very small	
Choice between statistical and nonstatistical samplings	Ordinarily, sample sizes are comparable	Ordinarily, sample sizes are comparable	

AU SECTION 380
THE AUDITOR'S COMMUNICATION WITH THOSE CHARGED WITH GOVERNANCE

PRACTICE POINT: As part of its Clarity Project, the American Institute of Certified Public Accountants' (AICPA's) Auditing Standards Board (ASB) has finalized a clarified Statement on Auditing Standards (SAS) titled, "The Auditor's Communication with Those Charged with Governance (Redrafted)," which supersedes AU Section 380 The Auditor's Communication with Those Charged with Governance). The clarified SAS does not change or expand extant AU Section 380 in any significant respect. A requirement to communicate matters related to other information included in documents containing audited financial statements has been placed in clarified SAS-118 (Other Information in Documents Containing Audited Financial Statements).

The ASB is expected to issue many of the clarified standards in *one* SAS that will be codified in "AU Section" format. The ASB has decided that the effective date of the clarified SASs that have not yet been issued is for audits of financial statements for periods ending on or after December 15, 2012. Auditors should be alert to and monitor further developments in this area.

PRACTICE POINT: In March 2011, the American Institute of Certified Public Accountants' (AICPA's) Auditing Standards Board (ASB) issued an exposure draft (ED) of a proposed Statement on Auditing Standards (SAS) titled, "Omnibus Statement on Auditing Standards—2011." This proposed SAS, which is part of the AICPA's Clarity Project, would amend the following SASs that have been issued in the clarity format and are currently effective:

- SAS-117 (AU Section 801) (Compliance Audits). The amendment to SAS-117 conforms the auditor's report on compliance to the requirements of the clarified SAS, "Forming an Opinion and Reporting on Financial Statements." In addition, the amendment revises the appendix in SAS-117, "AU Sections That Are Not Applicable to Compliance Audits," to reflect conforming changes to affected references to AU Sections as a result of the ASB's Clarity Project.

- SAS-118 (AU Section 550) (Other Information in Documents Containing Audited Financial Statements). The amendment to SAS-118 clarifies the requirements with respect to identified material inconsistencies by categorizing the requirements based on when the inconsistencies are identified (prior to the date of the auditor's report on the audited financial statements; after the date of the auditor's report but prior to the report release date; and after the report release date). It also adds application material addressing electronic sites to include guidance from an interpretation of AU Section 550 (Other Information in Documents Containing Audited Financial Statements), which the ASB determined was appropriate to include in SAS-118.

In addition, in order to address other changes necessitated by the ASB's overall Clarity Project, the proposed SAS would amend the following clarified SASs that have been finalized and released, but not yet issued as authoritative:

- Clarified SAS, "Overall Objectives of the Independent Auditor and the Conduct of an Audit in Accordance with Generally Accepted Auditing Standards."
- Clarified SAS, "Modifications to the Opinion in the Independent Auditor's Report."
- Clarified SAS, "Reports on Application of Requirements of an Applicable Financial Reporting Framework.."
- Clarified SAS, "The Auditor's Communication with Those Charged with Governance (Redrafted)."
- Clarified SAS, "Audit Documentation (Redrafted)."

The proposed SAS would be effective for audits of financial statements for periods ending on or after December 15, 2012, except for the amendment to the clarified SAS, "Reports on Application of Requirements of an Applicable Financial Reporting Framework," which would be effective for engagements ending on or after December 15, 2012.

WHAT EVERY PRACTITIONER SHOULD KNOW

Basic Objectives and Requirements

This Section provides guidance to auditors on matters to be communicated to those charged with governance in connection with audits of financial statements of nonpublic entities. Specifically, this Section:

1. Describes the main objectives of the auditor's communication with "those charged with governance," including the importance of two-way communication. The term *those charged with governance* refers to the persons "with responsibility for overseeing the strategic direction of the entity and obligations related to the accountability of the entity," including the entity's financial reporting process (e.g., audit committee, board of directors, finance or budget committee, or an owner in an owner-managed entity).

2. Requires the auditor to decide on the appropriate person within the entity's governance structure with whom to communicate. When it is not clear to the auditor who at the client is charged with governance, the auditor and the client should agree on the persons with whom the auditor will communicate.

3. Indicates that, before communicating matters with those charged with governance, the auditor may discuss them with management, unless it is not appropriate to do so.

4. Includes specific communication requirements pertaining to the planned scope and timing of the audit, representations from management, and significant audit findings.

5. Requires the auditor to communicate in writing to those charged with governance all the significant audit findings when the auditor concludes that oral communication would not be adequate; all other communications may be oral or in writing.

6. Requires the auditor to evaluate the adequacy of the two-way communication between the auditor and those charged with governance, and to take appropriate action if the auditor believes the communication was inadequate.

7. Calls for the auditor to document any required matters that were communicated orally and to retain copies of the written communications.

8. Requires the auditor to communicate certain specific matters when events or conditions indicate there could be substantial doubt about the entity's ability to continue as a going concern for a reasonable period of time.

Communication with the Audit Committee or Similar Subgroup of Those Charged with Governance

If the auditor is considering communicating with a subgroup (e.g., audit committee or specific individual) of those charged with governance, this Section requires the auditor to evaluate whether such a communication with a subgroup sufficiently fulfills the auditor's responsibility to communicate with those charged with governance. In such circumstances, the auditor may consider matters, such as:

- The particular and relevant responsibilities of the subgroup and the governing body as a whole.
- The nature of the matter to be communicated.
- The pertinent legal or regulatory requirements.
- The authority of the subgroup to take action regarding the information communicated by the auditor.
- The ability of the subgroup to furnish additional information and explanations the auditor may need.
- Any potential conflicts of interest between the subgroup and members of the governing body.
- The need to communicate the information to the governing body as a whole.

Matters to Be Communicated to Those Charged with Governance

The following are specific matters that the auditor is required to communicate to those charged with governance:

1. *The auditor's responsibility under generally accepted auditing standards (GAAS)*—This should include, at a minimum, the auditor's responsibility for:

   a. Forming and expressing an opinion on whether the financial statements are presented fairly, in all material respects, in conformity with GAAP.

   b. Communicating that the audit of the financial statements does not relieve management or those charged with governance of their responsibilities.

   c. Other information included in documents containing audited financial statements, any procedures performed relating to the information, and the results obtained, if the entity includes such other information.

2. *An overview of the planned scope and timing of the audit*—For example:

   a. The auditor's approach to internal control relevant to the audit.

   b. The concept of materiality in planning and executing the audit.

   c. The extent to which the auditor will use the work of internal auditors, where applicable.

   d. The views of those charged with governance about the entity's business risks that may result in material misstatements and significant communications with regulators.

   e. The actions of those charged with governance in response to previous communications with the auditor.

3. *Significant findings from the audit*—This should include all of the following matters:

   a. The auditor's views about the qualitative aspects of the entity's significant accounting practices, including accounting policies, accounting estimates, and financial statement disclosures. If the auditor believes a significant accounting practice is not appropriate, the auditor should request proper changes when necessary. If the changes requested by the auditor are not made, the auditor should inform those charged with governance that he or she will consider the effect of this matter on the entity's financial statements for the current and future years, and on the auditor's report.

   b. Major difficulties encountered in performing the audit. This includes, for example, considerable delays by management in providing required information and unavailability of expected information.

   c. Uncorrected misstatements, including both known misstatements and likely misstatements (other than those the auditor believes are trivial). In connection with this requirement, the auditor should communicate the effect that such uncorrected misstatements may have on the opinion in the auditor's report and the potential implications of a failure to correct such misstatements to future financial statements.

   d. Disagreements with management, whether or not satisfactorily resolved, about matters that could be significant to the entity's financial statements or the auditor's report (e.g., matters relating to the scope of the audit, application of accounting principles, disclosures to be included in the financial statements, and wording of the auditor's report).

   e. Issues or findings that in the auditor's judgment are significant and relevant to those charged with governance relating to their oversight of the financial reporting process.

f. Material, corrected misstatements that were brought to management's attention (unless all of those charged with governance are involved in managing the entity).

g. Representations the auditor is requesting from management (unless all of those charged with governance are involved in managing the entity).

h. The auditor's view on significant matters that were the subject of management's consultation with other accountants (unless all of those charged with governance are involved in managing the entity).

i. Significant issues that were discussed, or the subject of correspondence, with management (unless all of those charged with governance are involved in managing the entity). For example, this includes major issues discussed with management in connection with the initial or recurring retention of the auditor, including the application of accounting principles and auditing standards.

4. *Events or conditions that indicate there could be substantial doubt about the entity's ability to continue as a going concern for a reasonable period of time—* This should include:

a. The possible effect on the financial statements and the adequacy of related disclosures in the financial statements.

b. The effects on the auditor's report.

Form and Timing of Communication

This Section requires the auditor to communicate to those charged with governance the form, timing, and expected general content of communications. The form of communication includes whether the communication is oral or in writing, the extent of detail or summarization in the communication, and whether the communication includes formal presentations or is conducted in an informal manner. Therefore, to achieve a mutual understanding with the client regarding the communication process, the auditor may find it useful to discuss with those charged with governance matters, such as: (1) the purpose of communications; (2) the persons on the audit team and among those charged with governance who will communicate regarding relevant matters; and (3) the process for taking action and reporting back on matters communicated by the auditor and those charged with governance.

This Section specifically requires the auditor to communicate in writing with those charged with governance all the significant audit findings when the auditor concludes that oral communication would not be adequate; all other communications may be oral or in writing. When the communication is in writing, the auditor should indicate that (1) it is intended only for the information and use of those charged with governance and, if appropriate, management; and (2) it is not intended to be and should not be used by anyone other than these specified parties. The communications required herein are incidental to the audit and should be made on a timely basis to enable those charged with governance to take appropriate action.

The form and timing of the auditor's communication will vary depending on several factors, including the specific client or engagement circumstances, the size of the entity, the effectiveness of the governance structure, and the significance of the matters to be communicated.

Adequacy of the Two-Way Communication Process

This Section requires the auditor to evaluate the adequacy of the two-way communication between the auditor and those charged with governance and to take appropriate action if the auditor believes the communication was inadequate. It does not dictate a specific set of audit procedures to perform and support this evaluation but, rather, indicates that such evaluation may be based on observations made by the auditor in connection with other audit procedures performed.

If the auditor believes that the two-way communication between the auditor and those charged with governance is not adequate, the auditor should consider the effect, if any, on the auditor's assessment of the risks of material misstatements and may find it necessary to discuss the situation with those charged with governance. If the auditor is unable to resolve the situation, the auditor may find it necessary to take actions, such as:

- Modify the auditor's opinion due to a scope limitation.
- Obtain legal advice about the consequences of different courses of action.
- Communicate with third parties (e.g., regulator, government agency).
- Withdraw from the engagement.

Documentation Requirements

AU Section 339 (Audit Documentation) requires the auditor to document significant findings or issues discussed with management and others (including those charged with governance), responses obtained, when the discussions took place, and with whom the discussions took place. This Section affirms the documentation requirements included in AU Section 339 and establishes certain additional documentation requirements. Specifically, under this Section, the auditor should:

- Document all matters that are required to be communicated with those charged with governance under this Section, when such matters have been communicated orally.
- Retain a copy of the communication, when matters that are required to be communicated with those charged with governance under this Section have been communicated in writing.

PRACTICE ISSUES AND FREQUENTLY ASKED QUESTIONS

Issue 1: Do the requirements to communicate with those charged with governance under this Section encompass communication with an entity's management?

This Section does not establish requirements regarding the auditor's communication with an entity's management or owners unless they are also charged with a governance role. This Section uses the term *those charged with governance* to refer to those persons "with responsibility for overseeing the strategic direction of the entity and obligations related to the accountability of the entity," including overseeing the entity's financial reporting process. While those charged with governance may include some or all of the entity's management, this Section uses the term *management* to refer to persons who are responsible (1) for the entity's financial statements, including designing, implementing, and maintaining effective internal control over financial reporting; and (2) for achieving the entity's objectives, and who have the authority to establish policies and make decisions by which those objectives are to be pursued.

In some cases, those charged with governance (e.g., board of directors or audit committee) are responsible for approving the entity's financial statements; in other cases, management has this responsibility. Accordingly, the auditor's communication with those charged with governance under this Section does not encompass an entity's management or owners unless they are also charged with a governance role.

Issue 2: Who is the appropriate party within the entity's governance structure with whom the auditor should communicate the matters required under this Section?

Because governance structures vary by entity, the auditor should use professional judgment to determine the appropriate party within the entity's governance structure with whom to communicate the matters required under this Section. In most entities, those charged with governance include the board of directors or trustees, partners, proprietors, audit committees, or equivalent persons. However, in most small businesses, the owner-manager is the person charged with governance. When it is not clear to the auditor who at the client is charged with governance, the auditor and the engaging party should agree on the relevant persons with whom the auditor will communicate.

Issue 3: What relation does the required communication with those charged with governance under this Section have to other required communications with the client?

The auditor should make sure that the information contained in the communication required under this Section is consistent with other communications and reports issued in the course of the audit, such as communication of internal control-related matters identified in an audit; see AU Section 325 (Communicating Internal Control Related Matters Identified in an Audit).

For example, a communication letter under this Section should not indicate that the auditor identified no significant deficiencies in performing the audit if the auditor has communicated to management certain significant deficiencies, as required by AU Section 325. Another obvious common inconsistency is when the auditor communicates to those charged with governance that no significant adjustments were proposed when the working papers, in fact, indicate significant adjustments.

Issue 4: What matters might the auditor address when communicating to those charged with governance his or her views about the qualitative aspects of the entity's significant accounting practices?

The auditor should communicate to those charged with governance his or her views about the qualitative aspects of the entity's significant accounting practices, including (1) accounting policies, (2) accounting estimates, (3) financial statement disclosures, and (4) other related matters. The auditor's communication may include matters such as the following, which are adapted from an appendix to AU Section 380:

- *Accounting policies*—The auditor's communication about the qualitative aspects of accounting policies may include matters, such as:
  - The appropriateness of the accounting policies to the particular circumstances of the entity, considering the need to balance the cost of providing information with the likely benefit to users of the entity's financial statements.
  - Where acceptable alternative accounting policies exist, an identification of the financial statement items that are affected by the choice of significant policies as well as information on accounting policies used by similar entities.
  - The initial selection of, and changes in, significant accounting policies, including the application of new accounting pronouncements. For example, the communication may include the effect of the timing and method of adoption of a change in accounting policy on the current and future earnings of the entity, and the timing of a change in accounting policies in relation to expected new accounting pronouncements.
  - The effect of significant accounting policies in controversial or emerging areas, or those unique to an industry.
  - The effect of the timing of transactions in relation to the period in which they are recorded.
- *Accounting estimates*—The auditor's communication about the qualitative aspects of accounting estimates that are significant may include matters, such as:
  - Management's identification of accounting estimates.
  - Management's process for making accounting estimates.
  - Risks of material misstatement.
  - Indicators of possible management bias.
  - Disclosure of estimation uncertainty in the financial statements.
- *Financial statement disclosures*—The auditor's communication about the qualitative aspects of financial statement disclosures may include matters, such as:
  - The issues involved, and related judgments made, in formulating particularly sensitive financial statement disclosures (e.g., disclosures related to revenue recognition, going concern, subsequent events, and contingency issues).
  - The overall neutrality, consistency, and clarity of the disclosures in the financial statements.

- *Other related* matters—The auditor's communication about the qualitative aspects of other matters related to the entity's accounting practices may include matters, such as:

  — The potential effect on the financial statements of significant risks and exposures, and uncertainties (e.g., pending litigation) that are disclosed in the financial statements.

  — The extent to which the financial statements are affected by unusual transactions, including nonrecurring amounts recognized during the period, and the extent to which such transactions are separately disclosed in the financial statements.

  — The factors affecting asset and liability carrying values, including the entity's bases for determining useful lives assigned to tangible and intangible assets. For example, the communication may explain how factors affecting carrying values were selected and how alternative selections would have affected the financial statements.

  — The selective correction of misstatements (e.g., correcting misstatements with the effect of increasing reported earnings, but not those that have the effect of decreasing reported earnings.

Issue 5: May the auditor discuss with management significant matters related to the audit before communicating them to those charged with governance?

Generally, yes. The auditor may discuss with management significant matters related to the audit before communicating them to those charged with governance, unless it is not appropriate to do so. For example, if the auditor's communication with those charged with governance involve matters relating to management's integrity or competence, it may not be appropriate for the auditor to discuss such matters directly with management. However, many matters may be discussed with management in the normal course of an audit, especially in light of management's responsibility for the financial statements. In addition, generally, the auditor may find it useful to hold initial discussions with management regarding matters that will be communicated to those charged with governance in order to clarify facts and issues and give management an opportunity to provide further information and explanations.

Issue 6: What factors might the auditor consider in determining whether to communicate matters to those charged with governance orally or in writing?

This Section requires the auditor to communicate in writing to those charged with governance all the significant audit findings when the auditor concludes that oral communication would not be adequate. The auditor may consider the following factors when determining whether to communicate orally or in writing with those charged with governance:

- The significance of a particular matter.
- Whether the matter has been satisfactorily resolved.
- Whether management has previously communicated the matter.
- The size, operating structure, control environment, and legal structure of the entity being audited.

- The legal or regulatory requirements that may require a written communication with those charged with governance.

- The expectations of those charged with governance, including arrangements made for periodic meetings or communications with the auditor.

- The amount of ongoing contact and dialogue the auditor has with those charged with governance.

- Whether there have been significant changes in the membership of a governing body.

- In the case of a special purpose financial statement audit, whether the auditor also audits the entity's general purpose financial statements.

Issue 7: Notwithstanding the requirements to communicate with those charged with governance under AU Section 380, are there any other requirements for the auditor to communicate with those charged with governance under generally accepted auditing standards (GAAS)?

Yes. In addition to the requirements under AU Section 380, there are other requirements under GAAS for the auditor to communicate with those charged with governance. Specifically, they require the auditor to:

- Communicate to the audit committee or others with equivalent authority and responsibility illegal acts that come to the auditor's attention (AU Section 317 [Illegal Acts by Clients]).

- Communicate to management and the audit committee (or others with equivalent authority and responsibility) when the auditor becomes aware during an audit, in accordance with GAAS, that the entity is subject to an audit requirement that may not be encompassed in the terms of the engagement, and that an audit in accordance with GAAS may not satisfy the relevant legal, regulatory, or contractual requirements (AU Section 801 [Compliance Auditing Considerations in Audits of Governmental Entities and Recipients of Governmental Financial Assistance]).

- Inquire directly of the audit committee (or at least its chair) regarding the audit committee's views about the risks of fraud and whether the audit committee has knowledge of any fraud or suspected fraud affecting the entity (AU Section 316 [Consideration of Fraud in a Financial Statement Audit]).

- Communicate with those charged with governance fraud involving senior management and fraud (whether caused by senior management or other employees) that causes a material misstatement of the financial statements. Also, the auditor should reach an understanding with those charged with governance regarding the nature and extent of communications with those charged with governance about misappropriations perpetrated by lower-level employees (AU Section 316 [Consideration of Fraud in a Financial Statement Audit]).

- Communicate in writing to management and those charged with governance control deficiencies identified during an audit that upon evaluation are considered significant deficiencies or material weaknesses (AU Section

325 [Communicating Internal Control Related Matters Identified in an Audit]).

ILLUSTRATIONS AND PRACTICE AIDS

ILLUSTRATION 1—THE AUDITOR'S COMMUNICATION WITH THOSE CHARGED WITH GOVERNANCE

To (*the body or individuals charged with governance*)

(*Name of client*)

We have audited the financial statements of (*insert name of client*) as of and for the year ended (*insert date*), and have issued our report thereon dated (*insert date*). Professional standards require that we advise you of the following matters relating to our audit.

Our Responsibility under Generally Accepted Auditing Standards

As communicated in our engagement letter dated (*insert date of engagement letter*), our responsibility, as described by professional standards, is to form and express an opinion about whether the financial statements that have been prepared by management with your oversight are presented fairly, in all material respects, in conformity with accounting principles generally accepted in the United States of America. Our audit of the financial statements does not relieve you or management of your respective responsibilities.

Our responsibility, as prescribed by professional standards, is to plan and perform our audit to obtain reasonable, rather than absolute, assurance about whether the financial statements are free of material misstatement. An audit of financial statements includes consideration of internal control over financial reporting as a basis for designing audit procedures that are appropriate in the circumstances, but not for the purpose of expressing an opinion on the effectiveness of the entity's internal control over financial reporting. Accordingly, as part of our audit, we considered the internal control of (*insert name of client*) solely for the purpose of determining our audit procedures and not to provide any assurance concerning such internal control.

We are also responsible for communicating significant matters related to the audit that are, in our professional judgment, relevant to your responsibilities in overseeing the financial reporting process. However, we are not required to design procedures for the purpose of identifying other matters to communicate to you.

We have provided our comments regarding significant control deficiencies (*and material weaknesses, if applicable*) and other matters noted during our audit in a separate letter to you dated (*insert date*).

Other Information in Documents Containing Audited Financial Statements

Pursuant to professional standards, our responsibility as auditors for other information in documents containing the Company's audited financial statements does not extend beyond the financial information identified in the audit report, and we are not required to perform any procedures to corroborate such other information. However, in accordance with such standards, we have:

> [*Describe the procedures performed on such other information, such as reading the information and considering whether such information, or the manner of its presentation, was materially inconsistent with its presentation in the financial statements.*]

Our responsibility also includes communicating to you any information which we believe is a material misstatement of fact. Nothing came to our attention that caused us to believe that such information, or its manner of presentation, is materially inconsistent with the information, or manner of its presentation, appearing in the financial statements.

Planned Scope and Timing of the Audit

We conducted our audit consistent with the planned scope and timing we previously communicated to you.

PRACTICE POINT 1: The auditor is required to communicate with those charged with governance an overview of the planned scope and timing of the audit. Such communication is ordinarily made during the planning phase of the audit either in a separate communication, in the engagement letter, or orally. Matters communicated may include, among other things, the following:

- The auditor's approach to internal control relevant to the audit.
- The concept of materiality in planning and executing the audit.
- The extent to which the auditor will use the work of internal auditors, where applicable.
- The views of those charged with governance about the entity's business risks that may result in material misstatements and significant communications with regulators.
- The actions of those charged with governance in response to previous communications with the auditor.

See AU Section 380 (The Auditor's Communication with Those Charged with Governance), paragraphs 29-33, for further guidance on communicating the planned scope and timing of the audit.

Qualitative Aspects of the Company's Significant Accounting Practices

Significant Accounting Policies

Management has the responsibility to select and use appropriate accounting policies. A summary of the significant accounting policies adopted by (insert name of client) is included in Note [X] to the financial statements. There have been no initial selection of accounting policies and no changes in significant accounting policies or their application during (insert year). No matters have come to our attention that would require us, under professional standards, to inform you about (1) the methods used to account for significant unusual transactions and (2) the effect of significant accounting policies in controversial or emerging areas for which there is a lack of authoritative guidance or consensus.

PRACTICE POINT 2: If there has been an accounting policy change during the year, the third sentence of the "Significant Accounting Policies" paragraph in this section would be modified as follows:

> As described in Note [X] to the financial statements, during the year the Company changed its method of accounting for revenue recognition by adopting ASC [XXX], [*title*]. Accordingly, the cumulative effect of the accounting change as of the beginning of the year has been reported in the Statement of Operations.

PRACTICE POINT 3: If there are significant unusual transactions, the last sentence of the "Significant Accounting Policies" paragraph in this section would be modified as follows:

> During the year, the Company disposed of the retail segment of the business, which resulted in a material loss on the disposition. This

transaction is reported as discontinued operations for financial statement purposes and is reflected net of tax on the Statement of Operations. The footnotes to the financial statements contain a more complete description of this transaction. No matters have come to our attention that would require us, under professional standards, to inform you about the effect of significant accounting policies in controversial or emerging areas for which there is a lack of authoritative guidance or consensus.

PRACTICE POINT 4: If there are significant accounting policies for which there is a lack of authoritative guidance, the last sentence of the "Significant Accounting Policies" paragraph in this section would be modified as follows:

As described in Note [X], management has accounted for [*description of transaction*] by [*describe accounting treatment*]. No authoritative accounting principles are available for this type of transaction. Management has applied accounting principles that it believes are applicable in similar situations. We have reviewed this approach for accounting for [*description of transaction*] and believe that it is appropriate in this circumstance.

Significant Accounting Estimates

Accounting estimates are an integral part of the financial statements prepared by management and are based on management's current judgments. Those judgments are normally based on knowledge and experience about past and current events and assumptions about future events. Certain accounting estimates are particularly sensitive because of their significance to the financial statements and because of the possibility that future events affecting them may differ markedly from management's current judgments.

The most sensitive accounting estimates affecting the financial statements are *(describe)*.

Management's estimate of the *(describe the accounting estimate)* is based on *(describe the process used by management and the basis for the estimate)*. We evaluated the key factors and assumptions used to develop the *(describe the accounting estimate)* and determined that it is reasonable in relation to the basic financial statements taken as a whole.

Financial Statement Disclosures

Certain financial statement disclosures involve significant judgment and are particularly sensitive because of their significance to financial statement users. The most sensitive disclosures affecting the Company's financial statements relate to: *(describe, for example, revenue recognition, contingencies, going-concern, and fair value estimates)*.

Significant Difficulties Encountered During the Audit

We encountered no significant difficulties in dealing with management relating to the performance of the audit.

PRACTICE POINT 5: If the auditor's difficulties in performing the audit pertained to audit schedule preparation, the "Significant Difficulties Encountered During the Audit" section should read as follows:

Although we ultimately received full cooperation of management and believe that we were given direct and unrestricted access to the Company's officers and senior management, we experienced significant difficulties in the performance of the audit owing to the failure of Company's accounting personnel to prepare the requested audit schedules as initially agreed. These difficulties in receiving incomplete or inaccurately prepared audit schedules, or not receiving the requested audit schedules at all, significantly added to the time and related cost of the audit.

PRACTICE POINT 6: If the auditor's difficulties in performing the audit pertained to unreasonable delays by management, the "Significant Difficulties Encountered during the Audit" section should read as follows:

> Although we ultimately received full cooperation of management and believe that we were given direct and unrestricted access to the Company's officers and senior management, we experienced significant difficulties in the performance of the audit owing to unreasonable delays by management in the overall audit process. These unreasonable delays, such as a lack of responsiveness to audit inquiries and a general unavailability of management, significantly added to the time and related cost of the audit.

PRACTICE POINT 7: If the auditor's difficulties in performing the audit pertained to unreasonable delays and other matters, the "Significant Difficulties Encountered during the Audit" section should read as follows:

> Although we ultimately received full cooperation of management and believe that we were given direct and unrestricted access to the Company's books and records, as we disclosed in the management letter, we encountered significant difficulties in performing and completing the audit process. Principally, these difficulties related to the poor condition of the books and records, lack of consistent and standard accounting procedures, lack of available documentation, and the lack of qualified internal staffing. All of these issues, as well as others, such as the constant turnover of senior-level executives, contributed to the problem and added to the time and related cost of the audit.

Uncorrected and Corrected Misstatements

For purposes of this communication, professional standards require us to accumulate all known and likely misstatements identified during the audit, other than those that we believe are trivial, and communicate them to the appropriate level of management. The attached schedule summarizes uncorrected financial statement misstatements whose effects, as determined by management, are immaterial, both individually and in the aggregate, to the financial statements taken as a whole.

PRACTICE POINT 8: The presentation of uncorrected misstatements to those charged with governance should be similar to the presentation of uncorrected misstatements included in, or attached to, the management representations letter obtained in connection with the audit. If there are no uncorrected misstatements, the second sentence in the preceding paragraph above should be replaced with the following: "Management has corrected all identified misstatements."

In addition, professional standards require us to communicate to you all material, corrected misstatements that were brought to the attention of management as a result of our audit procedures. The following material misstatements that we identified as a result of our audit procedures were brought to the attention of, and corrected by, management (*include all material misstatements that were corrected*).

PRACTICE POINT 9: Unless all of those charged with governance are involved in managing the entity, the auditor should also communicate all material, corrected misstatements that were brought to the attention of management as a result of the audit. If there are no material, corrected misstatements, the second sentence in the preceding paragraph above should be replaced with the following: "None of the misstatements identified by us as a result of our audit procedures and corrected by management were material, either individually or in the aggregate, to the financial statements taken as a whole."

Disagreements with Management

For purposes of this letter, professional standards define a disagreement with management as a matter, whether or not resolved to our satisfaction, concerning a financial accounting, reporting, or auditing matter, which could be significant to the Company's financial statements or the auditor's report. No such disagreements arose during the course of the audit.

Representations Requested from Management

We have requested certain written representations from management, which are included in the attached letter dated (*insert date of management representation letter*).

PRACTICE POINT 10: Unless all of those charged with governance are involved in managing the entity, the auditor should also communicate representations requested from management. The auditor may provide those charged with governance a copy of management's written representations.

Management's Consultations with Other Accountants

In some cases, management may decide to consult with other accountants about auditing and accounting matters. Management informed us that, and to our knowledge, there were no consultations with other accountants regarding auditing and accounting matters.

PRACTICE POINT 11: Unless all of those charged with governance are involved in managing the entity, the auditor should also communicate management's consultations with other accountants. When the auditor is aware that such consultation has occurred, the auditor should discuss with those charged with governance his or her views about significant matters that were the subject of such consultation.

Other Significant Findings or Issues

In the normal course of our professional association with (*insert name of client*), we generally discuss a variety of matters, including the application of accounting principles and auditing standards, business conditions affecting the Company, and business plans and strategies that may affect the risks of material misstatement. None of the matters discussed resulted in a condition to our retention as the Company's auditors.

PRACTICE POINT 12: The auditor should communicate to those charged with governance other findings or issues, if any, arising from the audit that are, in the auditor's professional judgment, significant and relevant to those charged with governance regarding their oversight of the financial reporting process. In addition, unless all of those charged with governance are involved in managing the entity, the auditor should communicate to those charged with governance any significant issues that were discussed or were the subject of correspondence with management, such as: (1) discussions or correspondence in connection with the initial or recurring retention of the auditor including, among other matters, any discussions or correspondence regarding the application of accounting principles and auditing standards and (2) business conditions affecting the entity, and business plans and strategies that may affect the risks of material misstatement.

This report is intended solely for the information and use of the (*identify the body or individuals charged with governance, for example, audit committee, board of directors*), and management of (*insert name of client*) and is not intended to be and should not be used by anyone other than these specified parties.

(*Signature of auditor*)

(*Date*)

AU SECTION 390
CONSIDERATION OF OMITTED PROCEDURES AFTER THE REPORT DATE

PRACTICE POINT: As part of its Clarity Project, the American Institute of Certified Public Accountants' (AICPA's) Auditing Standards Board (ASB) has finalized a clarified Statement on Auditing Standards (SAS) titled, "Consideration of Omitted Procedures After the Report Release Date," which supersedes AU Section 390 (Consideration of Omitted Procedures After the Report Date). The clarified SAS does not change or expand extant AU Section 390 in any significant respect.

The ASB is expected to issue many of the clarified standards in *one* SAS that will be codified in "AU Section" format. The ASB has decided that the effective date of the clarified SASs that have not yet been issued is for audits of financial statements for periods ending on or after December 15, 2012. Auditors should be alert to and monitor further developments in this area.

WHAT EVERY PRACTITIONER SHOULD KNOW

Basic Objectives

This Section provides guidance to the auditor on the considerations and procedures to be applied when omitted auditing procedures, considered necessary at the time of the audit, are discovered after the audit report has been issued. This circumstance should be distinguished from that described in AU Section 561 (Subsequent Discovery of Facts Existing at the Date of the Auditor's Report), which applies to circumstances that indicate possible misstatement of financial statements.

In determining an appropriate course of action, the auditor should consider consulting with his attorney when he or she encounters the circumstances to which this Section may apply because of legal implications that may be involved.

Consideration of Omitted Procedures

When the auditor concludes that an auditing procedure considered necessary at the time of the audit was omitted from the audit of financial statements, he or she should assess the importance of the omitted procedure to his or her present ability to support the previously expressed opinion regarding those financial statements taken as a whole. The following procedures may be helpful in making this assessment:

1. Review the working papers, paying particular attention to other procedures that were applied that compensate for the omitted procedures.

2. Discuss the circumstances with engagement personnel and others.

3. Reevaluate the overall scope of the audit.

If the auditor concludes that the existence of certain omitted audit procedures impairs his or her present ability to support the previously expressed opinion regarding the financial statements, and he or she believes there are persons currently relying, or likely to rely, on the audit report, the auditor should promptly undertake to apply the omitted procedures or alternative procedures that would provide a satisfactory basis for his or her opinion.

If the auditor is unable to apply the previously omitted procedures or alternative procedures, he or she should consult his or her attorney to determine an appropriate course of action concerning his or her responsibilities to the following parties:

1. The client;

2. Regulatory authorities, if any, having jurisdiction over the client; and

3. Persons relying, or likely to rely, on the audit report.

When, as a result of the subsequent application of the omitted procedures or alternative procedures, the auditor becomes aware that facts regarding the financial statements existed at the date of his or her report that would have affected that report had the auditor been aware of them, he or she should refer to the guidance in AU Section 561.

PRACTICE ISSUES AND FREQUENTLY ASKED QUESTIONS

Issue 1: Do the provisions of this Section apply in situations when a peer reviewer determines that the auditor did not comply with generally accepted auditing standards in performing the audit?

Yes. For example, if a peer review reveals that the auditor failed to obtain a client representation letter, as required by AU Section 333 (Management Representations), the provisions of this Section would apply and the auditor could remedy the situation by obtaining a representation letter retroactive to the date of the auditor's report.

Issue 2: Once the auditor has issued his or her report on the audited financial statements, does the auditor have a responsibility to carry out a review of his or her work to determine if omitted procedures exist?

No. Once the auditor has reported on audited financial statements, the auditor has no responsibility to carry out any retrospective review of his or her work. However, reports and working papers relating to particular engagements may be reviewed in connection with a firm's internal monitoring program, peer review, or otherwise. As a result, such reviews may disclose the omission of necessary auditing procedures.

Issue 3: What should the auditor do if he or she discovers, subsequent to the issuance of the auditor's report, that a confirmation of a material note receivable balance was not requested?

The first thing to do is assess the effect of this omitted audit procedure on the auditor's ability to support his or her opinion. It may be that other evidence obtained during the audit, such as a subsequent collection of the note, would provide support for the opinion, and make the confirmation unnecessary. If this is not the case, the confirmation should be sent out immediately. Assuming that the response supports the opinion as issued, no additional action need be taken.

Issue 4: How should a firm proceed if its inspection procedures reveal that it failed to perform tests of certain significant transactions in a previous year's audit, and the current year's audit is in progress and issuance of the report is imminent?

The firm should consider whether the current year's audit provides evidence about these transactions. If it does not provide sufficient evidence, those transactions should be tested during the current year's audit. The firm should also consider the results of that testing on its ability to support its previously issued opinion.

Issue 5: Does this Section require the auditor to notify the client of omitted audit procedures?

No. The auditor is not required to notify the client of the omitted auditing procedures.

ILLUSTRATIONS AND PRACTICE AIDS

There are no illustrations and practice aids for this Section.

AU Section 400
THE FIRST, SECOND, AND THIRD
STANDARDS OF REPORTING

AU SECTION 410
ADHERENCE TO GENERALLY ACCEPTED ACCOUNTING PRINCIPLES

PRACTICE POINT: As part of its Clarity Project, the American Institute of Certified Public Accountants' (AICPA's) Auditing Standards Board (ASB) has finalized a clarified Statement on Auditing Standards (SAS) titled, "Forming an Opinion and Reporting on Financial Statements," which supersedes:

- AU Section 410 (Adherence to Generally Accepted Accounting Principles), as amended;

- Paragraphs .01–.02 of AU Section 530 (Dating of the Independent Auditor's Report), as amended); and

- With the clarified SAS titled, "Modifications to the Opinion in the Independent Auditor's Report," and the clarified SAS, "Emphasis-of-Matter Paragraphs and Other-Matter Paragraphs in the Independent Auditor's Report," supersedes paragraphs .01–.11, .14–.15, .19–.32, .35–.52, .58–.70, and .74–.76 of AU Section 508 (Reports on Audited Financial Statements).

The clarified SAS includes extant guidance from AU Sections 410, 508, and 530 (along with some of the related interpretations). The clarified SAS also includes requirements and application material addressing comparative financial statements.

Extant AU Section 508 requires a statement in the auditor's report that the financial statements are the responsibility of the company's management. The clarified SAS prescribes a requirement to describe management's responsibility for the preparation and fair presentation of the financial statements in more detail than what is required in extant AU Section 508. The description includes an explanation that management is responsible for the preparation and fair presentation of the financial statements in accordance with the applicable financial reporting framework, and that this responsibility includes the design, implementation, and maintenance of internal control relevant to the preparation and fair presentation of financial statements that are free from material misstatement, whether due to fraud or error.

The clarified SAS also prescribes the use of headings throughout the auditor's report to clearly distinguish each section of the report.

The ASB is expected to issue many of the clarified standards in *one* SAS that will be codified in "AU Section" format. The ASB has decided that the effective date of the clarified SASs that have not yet been issued is for audits of financial statements for periods ending on or after December 15, 2012. Auditors should be alert to and monitor further developments in this area.

WHAT EVERY PRACTITIONER SHOULD KNOW

Basic Objectives

The first standard of reporting indicates that the auditor "must state in the auditor's report whether the financial statements are presented in accordance with generally accepted accounting principles." The term "generally accepted accounting principles" (GAAP) includes not only accounting principles and practices, but the methods of applying them. In addition, there may exist practices having general acceptance but that are not covered in an official pronouncement; in such circumstances, the auditor must use his or her judgment and expertise to determine whether such practices have found general acceptance for reporting purposes.

If limitations on the scope of the audit make it impossible for the auditor to form an opinion as to conformity in accordance with GAAP, the auditor should appropriately qualify his or her report. AU Section 508 (Reports on Audited Financial Statements) provides further guidance on modifications of the auditor's report.

Other Comprehensive Basis of Accounting

When an auditor reports on financial statements prepared in accordance with a comprehensive basis of accounting other than GAAP, the first standard of reporting is satisfied by disclosing in the auditor's report that the statements have been prepared in conformity with an other comprehensive basis of accounting other than GAAP, and by expressing an opinion (or disclaiming an opinion) on whether the financial statements are presented in conformity with the comprehensive basis of accounting used. AU Section 623 (Special Reports) provides further guidance on auditors' reports issued in connection with an other comprehensive basis of accounting (OCBOA).

The Impact on an Auditor's Report of Accounting Guidance Prior to Its Effective Date

There may be situations when (1) the auditor is reporting on financial statements issued before the effective date of accounting guidance currently reflected in the FASB Accounting Standards Codification (ASC) as "pending content" due to transition and open effective date information, and (2) these financial statements will have to be restated in the future because the pending content will require retroactive application of its provisions by prior period adjustment.

In such situations, the auditor should not qualify his or her opinion if a company does not adopt the accounting guidance that is currently reflected as pending content in the ASC due to transition and open effective date information, as long as the accounting guidance being followed is currently acceptable. However, the auditor should consider whether disclosure of the impending change in principle and the resulting restatement are essential data. If the auditor decides that the matter should be disclosed and it is not, the auditor should express a qualified or an adverse opinion as to conformity with GAAP, as required by AU Section 508. Additionally, the auditor should consider whether disclosure is needed for other effects that may result upon the required future adoption of an accounting principle. For example, the future adoption of an accounting principle may result in a reduction to stockholders' equity that may cause the company to be in violation of its debt covenants, which, in turn, may accelerate the due date for repayment of debt.

Even if the auditor decides that the disclosure of the forthcoming change and its effects are adequate and, consequently, decides not to qualify his or her opinion, the auditor nevertheless may decide to include an explanatory paragraph in his or her report if the effects of the change are expected to be unusually material. The explanatory paragraph should not be construed as a qualification of the auditor's opinion; it is only intended to highlight circumstances of particular importance and to help third-party users in interpreting the financial statements.

PRACTICE ISSUES AND FREQUENTLY ASKED QUESTIONS

Issue 1: What does the term "financial statements" encompass as referred to in the first standard of reporting?

The term "financial statements" as referred to in the first standard of reporting is intended to include the following:

1. Basic financial statements:
   a. Statement of financial position (balance sheet)
   b. Statement of income
   c. Statement of comprehensive income (alternatively, comprehensive income may be reported in a combined statement of income and comprehensive income, or in a statement of changes in stockholders' equity)
   d. Statement of changes in retained earnings or changes in stockholders' equity
   e. Statement of cash flows
2. Descriptions of accounting policies
3. Notes to financial statements
4. Schedules and explanatory material that are identified as being part of the basic financial statements

Issue 2: Do professional standards prescribe a specific method for disclosing or presenting the pro forma financial effect of a future change in accounting principle on an entity's financial statements?

No. Disclosure of the effect of a prospective change in accounting principle, if considered necessary, can best be made by supplementing the historical financial statements with pro forma financial data that give effect to the future adjustment as if it had occurred on the date of the balance sheet. The pro forma data may be presented in:

1. Columnar form alongside the historical financial statements.
2. The notes to the historical financial statements.
3. Separate pro forma statements presented with the historical financial statements.

Issue 3: Once the auditor is satisfied that the pro forma effect of a future change in accounting principle is adequately disclosed in the financial statements, should the auditor consider anything else before issuing the audit report?

The auditor should also consider any ancillary effects of a future change in accounting principle and whether disclosure is needed for such other effects, beyond the pro forma disclosure already made. For example, the future adoption of a new principle may have an impact on key financial ratios, which may cause the entity to be in violation of its debt covenants. Therefore, the auditor should consider the broader reporting implications of such matters, in addition to considerations that focus strictly upon the numbers within the financial statements.

Issue 4: How does the auditor reconcile "substance" versus "form" type issues when considering whether the financial statements are presented in accordance with GAAP?

Many transactions (e.g., related-party transactions) have substance over form implications, primarily because substance depends so much on the intentions of the parties involved. Certain transactions can be described by their legal form, such as a loan, a lease, a purchase or sale of products or services, and so on. They also can be described by their economic substance, which may be different from their legal form. For example, what is legally a lease may in economic reality be a purchase.

In such circumstances, the auditor should be aware that the substance of a particular transaction could be significantly different from its form and that financial statements should recognize the substance, rather than the legal form, of particular transactions. Therefore, because the substance of a transaction may differ materially from its form, the auditor should determine that the accounting principle selected account for the substance of a transaction.

ILLUSTRATIONS AND PRACTICE AIDS

There are no illustrations and practice aids for this Section.

AU SECTION 411
THE MEANING OF *PRESENT FAIRLY IN CONFORMITY WITH GENERALLY ACCEPTED ACCOUNTING PRINCIPLES*

PRACTICE POINT: The hierarchies of generally accepted accounting principles (GAAP) of nongovernmental, state and local, and federal reporting entities have resided in SAS-69 (AU Section 411) (The Meaning of *Present Fairly in Conformity with Generally Accepted Accounting Principles*) in the auditing literature. However, the Financial Accounting Standards Board (FASB), the Governmental Accounting Standards Board (GASB), and the Federal Accounting Standards Advisory Board (FASAB) have issued the following pronouncements that incorporate their respective GAAP hierarchy into their respective authoritative literature:

- FASB Statement No. 162, *The Hierarchy of Generally Accepted Accounting Principles*, as superseded by FASB Statement No. 168, *The FASB Accounting Standards Codification™ and the Hierarchy of Generally Accepted Accounting Principles—a Replacement of FASB Statement No. 162.*
- GASB Statement No. 55, *The Hierarchy of Generally Accepted Accounting Principles for State and Local Governments.*
- Statement of Federal Financial Accounting Standards No. 34, *The Hierarchy of Generally Accepted Accounting Principles, Including the Application of Standards Issued by the Financial Accounting Standards Board.*

Therefore, the Auditing Standards Board has withdrawn SAS-69 AU Section 411) and Interpretation No. 3, "The Auditor's Consideration of Management's Adoption of Accounting Principles for New Transactions or Events."

AU SECTION 420
CONSISTENCY OF APPLICATION OF GENERALLY ACCEPTED ACCOUNTING PRINCIPLES

PRACTICE POINT: As part of its Clarity Project, the American Institute of Certified Public Accountants' (AICPA's) Auditing Standards Board (ASB) has finalized a clarified Statement on Auditing Standards (SAS) titled, "Consistency of Financial Statements," which supersedes AU Section 420 (Consistency of Application of Generally Accepted Accounting Principles), as amended. The clarified SAS does not change or expand existing standards in any significant respect except as follows:

- Extant AU Section 420 states that changes and material reclassifications made in previously issued financial statements to enhance comparability with current financial statements ordinarily would not need to be referred to in the independent auditor's report. The clarified SAS requires the auditor to evaluate a material change in financial statement classification and the related disclosures to determine whether such a change is also a change in accounting principle or an adjustment to correct a material misstatement in previously issued financial statements. If so, the requirements in the clarified SAS apply.

- The clarified SAS recognizes that the applicable financial reporting framework usually sets forth the method of accounting for accounting changes and, therefore, the references to accounting guidance included in extant AU Section 420 have not been included in the clarified SAS. To reflect a more principles-based approach to standard setting, certain requirements that are duplicative of broader requirements in AU Section 420 have been moved to application and other explanatory material. In the ASB's view, this has not changed the overall effectiveness of the clarified SAS.

The ASB is expected to issue many of the clarified standards in *one* SAS that will be codified in "AU Section" format. The ASB has decided that the effective date of the clarified SASs that have not yet been issued is for audits of financial statements for periods ending on or after December 15, 2012. Auditors should be alert to and monitor further developments in this area.

WHAT EVERY PRACTITIONER SHOULD KNOW

Basic Objectives and Requirements

The second standard of reporting, commonly referred to as "the consistency standard," states that the auditor "must identify in the auditor's report those circumstances in which such principles have not been consistently observed in the current period in relation to the preceding period."

The auditor should distinguish between (1) changes that affect consistency and (2) changes that do not affect consistency, but may affect comparability. This is important because only changes that affect consistency, if material, require the addition of an explanatory paragraph in the auditor's report following the opinion paragraph.

Changes affecting consistency, if material, require recognition in the independent auditor's report by the addition of an explanatory paragraph after the opinion paragraph. On the other hand, changes not affecting consistency ordinarily would not require the addition of an explanatory paragraph about consistency in the independent auditor's report. However, such changes generally require disclosure in the notes to the financial statements. Therefore, if necessary disclosures are not made in the financial statements, the auditor should qualify his opinion for inadequate disclosure of the matter.

Illustration 1 is a sample auditor's report applicable when there is a change in accounting principles or in the method of their application that has a material effect on the comparability of the financial statements.

Effect on the Standard Auditor's Report as a Result of a Change Affecting Consistency

When a change in accounting principles materially affects the consistency standard in the financial statements, the auditor should include an explanatory paragraph in the standard auditor's report. The auditor should not modify his or her opinion, provided the change in accounting principles is properly accounted for and disclosed in the financial statements. The explanatory paragraph, following the opinion paragraph, should:

1. Identify the nature of the change in accounting principle.

2. Refer the reader to the note in the financial statements that discusses the change in detail.

The standard introductory, scope, and opinion paragraphs are not changed and should not refer to the explanatory paragraph.

Periods to Which the Consistency Standard Relates

The periods to which the consistency standard relates depend on what financial statement periods are covered by the auditor's report, as follows:

1. When the auditor reports only on the current period, he or she should obtain sufficient, appropriate audit evidence about consistency of the application of accounting principles, regardless of whether financial statements for the preceding period are presented. The term *current period* means the most recent year, or period of less than one year, upon which the auditor is reporting.

2. When the auditor reports on two or more years presented, he or she should address the consistency of the application of accounting principles between all such years presented.

3. When the auditor reports on two or more years presented, and a prior year is also presented but not reported on by the auditor, he or she should address the consistency of the application of accounting principles between years included in the report and also the consistency of such years with the prior year.

First Year Audits

When the auditor has not audited the financial statements of an entity for the preceding year, he or she should ascertain that the accounting principles adopted are consistent between the current and the preceding year. However, scope limitations (e.g., inadequate financial records, limitations imposed by the client) may prevent the auditor from forming an opinion about the consistent application of accounting principles between the current and the prior year, as well as to the amounts of assets or liabilities at the beginning of the current year. Where such amounts could materially affect current operating results, the auditor, in addition to modifying his or her report for a scope limitation as to consistency, would also be unable to express an opinion on the current year's results of operations and cash flows.

PRACTICE ISSUES AND FREQUENTLY ASKED QUESTIONS

Issue 1: If an accounting change has no material effect on the financial statements in the current year but is expected to have substantial effect in future years, is the auditor required to modify his or her report for this change?

No. The independent auditor is not required to modify his or her report for an accounting change that has no material effect in the current year, but is expected to have a material effect in future years. However, the change should be disclosed in the notes to the financial statements whenever the statements of the period of change are presented.

Issue 2: Is the auditor required to state in the audit report whether he or she concurs with the appropriateness of an accounting change affecting consistency?

No. When changes affecting consistency occur, the auditor should modify his or her report by adding an explanatory paragraph after the opinion paragraph that discusses the change. It is implicit in this explanatory paragraph that the auditor concurs with the appropriateness of the change. If the auditor does not concur, the change would be considered a violation of GAAP, and his or her opinion should be qualified. See AU Section 508 (Reports on Audited Financial Statements) for further guidance.

Issue 3: Does the auditor have a responsibility to address the consistency standard when engaged to audit a single year's financial statements and no comparative financial statements are presented?

Yes. The consistency standard applies regardless of whether financial statements for preceding periods are presented.

Issue 4: Does a change in an actuarial estimate that results in a significant increase in a client's pension liability and expense for the current year, when compared to the prior year, constitute an inconsistent application of an accounting principle that should be referred to in the auditor's report?

No. Changes in accounting estimates, such as the above, or depreciable lives of fixed assets or allowance for doubtful accounts ordinarily are not changes in the application of accounting principles, and therefore would not be reported on as such. However, the auditor should inquire about the circumstances giving rise to the change in the actuarial estimate in this case, and be satisfied that the change in reported amounts does not include the effects of a change in accounting principle, as well as a change in estimate.

ILLUSTRATIONS AND PRACTICE AIDS

ILLUSTRATION 1—AUDITOR'S REPORT WHEN THERE IS A CHANGE IN ACCOUNTING PRINCIPLES OR IN THE METHOD OF THEIR APPLICATION THAT HAS A MATERIAL EFFECT ON THE COMPARABILITY OF THE FINANCIAL STATEMENTS

Independent Auditor's Report

Board of Directors and Stockholders
ABC Company

We have audited the accompanying balance sheet of ABC Company as of December 31, 20X2, and the related statements of income, retained earnings, and cash flows for the year then ended. These financial statements are the responsibility of the Company's management. Our responsibility is to express an opinion on these financial statements based on our audit.

We conducted our audit in accordance with auditing standards generally accepted in the United States of America. Those standards require that we plan and perform the audit to obtain reasonable assurance about whether the financial statements are free of material misstatement. An audit includes examining, on a test basis, evidence supporting the amounts and disclosures in the financial statements. An audit also includes assessing the accounting principles used and significant estimates made by management, as well as evaluating the overall financial statement presentation. We believe that our audit provides a reasonable basis for our opinion.

In our opinion, the financial statements referred to above present fairly, in all material respects, the financial position of ABC Company as of December 31, 20X2, and the results of its operations and its cash flows for the year then ended in conformity with accounting principles generally accepted in the United States of America.

As discussed in Note [X] to the financial statements, the Company changed its method of computing depreciation in 20X2.

Seliga & Co., CPAs

March 14, 20X3

AU SECTION 431
ADEQUACY OF DISCLOSURE IN FINANCIAL STATEMENTS

PRACTICE POINT: As part of its Clarity Project, the American Institute of Certified Public Accountants' (AICPA's) Auditing Standards Board (ASB) has finalized a clarified Statement on Auditing Standards (SAS) titled, "Modifications to the Opinion in the Independent Auditor's Report," which supersedes:

- AU Section 431 (Adequacy of Disclosure in Financial Statements); and

- With the clarified SAS, "Forming an Opinion and Reporting on Financial Statements," and the clarified SAS, "Emphasis-of-Matter Paragraphs and Other-Matter Paragraphs in the Independent Auditor's Report," supersedes paragraphs .01–.11, .14–.15, .19–.32, .35–.52, .58–.70, and .74–.76 of AU Section 508 (Reports on Audited Financial Statements).

The clarified SAS includes extant guidance from AU Section 431 and AU Section 508. However, the clarified SAS does not change or expand extant standards in any significant respect.

The ASB is expected to issue many of the clarified standards in *one* SAS that will be codified in "AU Section" format. The ASB has decided that the effective date of the clarified SASs that have not yet been issued is for audits of financial statements for periods ending on or after December 15, 2012. Auditors should be alert to and monitor further developments in this area.

WHAT EVERY PRACTITIONER SHOULD KNOW

Basic Objectives and Requirements

The third standard of reporting states:

> When the auditor determines that informative disclosures are not reasonably adequate, the auditor must so state in the auditor's report.

The independent auditor should consider whether a particular matter should be disclosed in light of the facts and circumstances of the particular engagement. If management omits from the financial statements and the accompanying notes information that is required by GAAP, the auditor should:

1. Express a qualified or an adverse opinion, and

2. Provide the information in his or her report, if practicable, unless its omission from the auditor's report is recognized as appropriate by a specific Statement on Auditing Standards.

Ordinarily, the auditor should not, without the client's consent, make available information that is not required to be disclosed in financial statements to comply with GAAP.

PRACTICE ISSUES AND FREQUENTLY ASKED QUESTIONS

Issue 1: Small businesses with limited accounting expertise often rely entirely upon their auditors to draft the notes to the financial statements. How does this practice affect the auditor's ability to render an opinion on the financial statements?

The guidance in this Section is clear in stating that an independent auditor may participate in preparing financial statements, including the accompanying notes, and that such participation does not require the auditor to modify his or her report. The Section is equally clear in stating that the financial statements and accompanying notes, however, remain the representations of management.

Issue 2: How do auditors generally go about making sure that the financial statement disclosures are adequate and that all the necessary disclosures have been made?

To facilitate the review of financial statement disclosures, most auditors complete a financial statement disclosures checklist for each engagement. Such a checklist may be prepared by the auditor or obtained from an outside source, including publishers and the AICPA. The financial statement disclosures checklist is designed to remind the auditor of common disclosure requirements and to facilitate the final review of the disclosures by the engagement partner.

Issue 3: What are some useful considerations for the preparation of the notes to the financial statements?

The following factors are useful considerations in the preparation of notes to the financial statements:

- The notes should be individually numbered and clearly titled to facilitate review of the financial statements of which they are an integral part.

- The notes should be presented in a logical sequence. For example, they may be presented in the same order in which they are referred to in the financial statements; or, they may be presented in order of importance as perceived by the entity.

- The description of the entity's significant accounting policies generally appears as the first note to the financial statements.

- When financial statements for two or more years are presented, appropriate disclosures should be included for each year presented.

ILLUSTRATIONS AND PRACTICE AIDS

There are no illustrations and practice aids for this Section.

AU Section 500
THE FOURTH STANDARD OF REPORTING

AU SECTION 504
ASSOCIATION WITH FINANCIAL STATEMENTS

WHAT EVERY PRACTITIONER SHOULD KNOW

Basic Objectives and Requirements

The fourth standard of reporting states:

> The auditor must either express an opinion regarding the financial statements, taken as a whole, or state that an opinion cannot be expressed, in the auditor's report. When the auditor cannot express an overall opinion, the auditor should state the reasons therefor in the auditor's report. In all cases where an auditor's name is associated with financial statements, the auditor should clearly indicate the character of the auditor's work, if any, and the degree of responsibility the auditor is taking, in the auditor's report.

The objective of the fourth standard of reporting is to prevent misinterpretation of the degree of responsibility the accountant assumes when his or her name is *associated* with financial statements.

An accountant is *associated* with financial statements under the following conditions:

1. When the accountant has consented to the use of his or her name in a report, document, or written communication containing the statements.

2. When the accountant submits to the client or others financial statements that he or she has prepared or assisted in preparing.

This Section provides guidance to an accountant associated with:

1. The unaudited financial statements of a public entity prepared in accordance with GAAP or in accordance with a comprehensive basis of accounting other than GAAP (OCBOA).

2. The unaudited financial statements of a public entity when the accountant is not independent.

3. The unaudited financial statements of a public entity that are not in conformity with GAAP or OCBOA.

4. The audited and unaudited financial statements of a public or a nonpublic entity presented in comparative form.

Association with Unaudited Financial Statements of a Public Entity Prepared in Accordance with GAAP or OCBOA

When an accountant is associated with the unaudited financial statements of a public entity that are prepared in accordance with GAAP or OCBOA, but has not audited or reviewed such statements, the following requirements apply:

1. The accountant should disclaim an opinion. In addition, for OCBOA presentations, a note to the financial statements should describe how the basis of presentation differs from GAAP, but the monetary effect of such differences need not be stated. Illustrations 1 and 2 provide examples of

the forms of the accountant's reports to be issued in such circumstances for GAAP and OCBOA presentations, respectively.

2. Each page of the financial statements should be clearly marked as "unaudited."

3. The accountant should read the financial statements for obvious material misstatements.

4. The accountant should not describe any procedures that may have been applied, except as permissible in letters for underwriters in connection with a registration statement filed with the SEC. See AU Section 634 (Letters for Underwriters and Certain Other Requesting Parties).

5. For public entities that do not have annual audits, the accountant should refer to SSARS for guidance on the form of report applicable to such an engagement.

Association with Unaudited Financial Statements of a Public Entity When the Accountant Is Not Independent

When an accountant is not independent, any procedures he or she might perform would not be in accordance with GAAS, and the accountant would be precluded from expressing an opinion on such statements. If the financial statements are those of a nonpublic entity, the accountant should follow the guidance and reporting requirements in SSARS, which indicate that the auditor may only issue a compilation report.

If the financial statements are those of a public entity, the accountant should disclaim an opinion and follow the guidance above (under "Association with Unaudited Financial Statements of a Public Entity Prepared in Accordance with GAAP or OCBOA"); however, the disclaimer of opinion should be modified to state specifically that the accountant is not independent. Illustration 3 provides an example of such a report.

The accountant should consider the AICPA's Code of Professional Conduct and ethical requirements of his or her state CPA society or state board of accountancy in determining whether he or she is independent. The accountant's consideration of whether he or she is independent should be the same whether the financial statements are audited or unaudited.

Association with Unaudited Financial Statements of a Public Entity That Are Not in Conformity with GAAP or OCBOA

If the accountant concludes that the unaudited financial statements of a public entity on which he or she is disclaiming an opinion are not in conformity with GAAP or OCBOA, the accountant should suggest to the client that they be revised. If the client fails to revise them, the accountant should describe the departure in his disclaimer of opinion, and such description should:

1. Refer specifically to the nature of the departure, and

2. State, if practicable, the effects on the financial statements, or include the necessary information for adequate disclosure.

Illustration 4 provides an example of such a report.

When the effects of the departure on the financial statements are not reasonably determinable, the disclaimer of opinion should so state. If the client will not agree to a revision of the financial statements or will not accept the accountant's disclaimer of opinion with the description of the departure, the accountant should refuse to be associated with the statements and, if necessary, withdraw from the engagement.

Association with Audited and Unaudited Financial Statements in Comparative Form of a Public or Nonpublic Entity

When unaudited financial statements are presented in comparative form with audited financial statements in documents filed with the SEC, the unaudited financial statements should be clearly marked as "unaudited" but should not be referred to in the auditor's report.

When unaudited financial statements are presented in comparative form with audited financial statements in any other document, the unaudited financial statements should be clearly marked as "unaudited" *and* either (a) the report on the prior period should be reissued or (b) the report on the current period should include a separate paragraph describing the responsibility assumed for the financial statements of the prior period.

For reissuance of auditors' reports, see AU Section 530 (Dating of the Independent Auditor's Report). For reissuance of compilation or review reports, see AR Section 200 (Reporting on Comparative Financial Statements).

Prior-period financial statements audited When the financial statements of the prior period have been audited and the report on the current period is to contain a separate paragraph about those financial statements, the separate paragraph should indicate:

1. That the financial statements of the prior period were audited previously.
2. The date of the previous report.
3. The type of opinion expressed previously.
4. If the opinion was other than unqualified, the substantive reasons therefor.
5. That no auditing procedures were performed after the date of the previous report.

The following is an example of such a separate paragraph:

> The financial statements for the year ended December 31, 20X2, were audited by us (other accountants) and we (they) expressed an unqualified opinion on them in our (their) report dated March 1, 20X3, but we (they) have not performed any auditing procedures since that date.

Prior-period financial statements unaudited When the financial statements of the prior period have been unaudited and the report on the current period is to contain a separate paragraph about those financial statements, the separate paragraph should include:

1. A statement of the service performed in the prior period.

2. The date of the report on that service.

3. A description of any material modifications noted in that report.

4. A statement that the service was less in scope than an audit and does not provide the basis for the expression of an opinion on the financial statements taken as a whole.

When the financial statements are those of a public entity, the separate paragraph should include a disclaimer of opinion or a description of a review. When the financial statements are those of a nonpublic entity and the financial statements were compiled or reviewed, the separate paragraph should contain an appropriate description of the compilation or review. The following is an example of a separate paragraph describing a review:

> The 20X2 financial statements were reviewed by us (other accountants) and our (their) report thereon, dated March 1, 20X3, stated we (they) were not aware of any material modifications that should be made to those statements for them to be in conformity with generally accepted accounting principles. However, a review is substantially less in scope than an audit and does not provide a basis for the expression of an opinion on the financial statements taken as a whole.

The following is an example of a separate paragraph describing a compilation:

> The 20X2 financial statements were compiled by us (other accountants) and our (their) report thereon, dated March 1, 20X3, stated we (they) did not audit or review those financial statements and, accordingly, express no opinion or other form of assurance on them.

PRACTICE ISSUES AND FREQUENTLY ASKED QUESTIONS

Issue 1: What course of action should an accountant take if he or she is aware that his or her name is to be included in a client-prepared written communication of a public entity containing financial statements that have not been audited or reviewed?

If the accountant is aware that his or her name is to be included in a client-prepared written communication of a public entity containing financial statements that have not been audited or reviewed, the accountant should:

1. Request that his or her name not be included in the communication, or

2. Request that the financial statements be marked as "unaudited" and that there be a notation that the accountant does not express an opinion on them.

If the client does not comply, the accountant should (a) advise the client that he or she has not consented to the use of his or her name and (b) consider consulting with legal counsel.

Issue 2: Should the accountant describe the reasons for lack of independence in his or her report when the accountant is associated with unaudited financial statements of a public or nonpublic entity?

No. When the accountant is not independent, he or she should disclaim an opinion with respect to the financial statements and should state specifically that he or she is not independent. However, the reasons for lack of independence and any procedures the accountant has performed should not be described. The inclusion of such matters in the accountant's report might confuse the reader concerning the importance of the impairment of independence.

Issue 3: Does the auditor have an obligation to audit interim data presented in a note to annual audited financial statements?

No. Unless specifically engaged to do so, the auditor does not have an obligation to audit interim data as a result of his or her audit of the annual financial statements.

For example, disclosure of fourth quarter adjustments and other disclosures required by FASB Accounting Standards Codification (ASC) 270, *Interim Reporting*, would appear in a note to the annual financial statements of a publicly traded company only if fourth quarter data were not separately distributed or did not appear elsewhere in the annual report. Consequently, such disclosures are not essential for a fair presentation of the annual financial statements in conformity with GAAP, but are required under ASC 270. Such information would ordinarily be labeled "unaudited" or "not covered by auditor's report."

If a publicly traded company does not comply with the disclosure requirements of ASC 270, the auditor should call attention in his or her report to the omission of the information. However, the auditor need not qualify his or her opinion on the annual financial statements since the disclosure is not essential for a fair presentation of the annual statements in conformity with GAAP.

Issue 4: Is the auditor "associated" with condensed financial data when he is identified by a financial reporting service (e.g., Dunn & Bradstreet, Moody's Investors Service) as being a company's independent auditor or when his report is reproduced and presented with such data?

No. Financial reporting services, such as Dunn & Bradstreet and Moody's Investors Service, furnish subscribers with information concerning commercial businesses as a basis for credit, insurance, marketing, and other business purposes. Generally, neither the auditor nor the client has the ability to prohibit a financial reporting service from publishing such information. In such cases, the accountant has not *consented* to the use of his or her name when it is published by a financial reporting service. Therefore, there is no *association* with the financial data as defined in this Section and the auditor has no reporting obligation.

Furthermore, in this context, it is doubtful that a reasonable user of the financial reporting service would conclude that the firm had audited the financial information presented.

Issue 5: Is an accountant who maintains a general ledger for the client for the primary purpose of management's information and tax compliance "associated" with financial statements for purposes of this Section?

No. The provisions of this Section do not apply to data, such as tax returns and general ledgers, and the accountant does not have a reporting obligation in such circumstances.

Issue 6: Can an accountant, who disclaims an opinion on a client's financial statements due to a scope limitation, provide assurance in his or her report that there were no material departures from GAAP?

No. The expression of such a negative assurance is prohibited in connection with a disclaimer of an opinion on an audit of financial statements under generally accepted auditing standards. Such an assertion would contradict the auditor's disclaimer.

Issue 7: Are negative assurances permitted under the provisions of this Section?

Yes. The guidance in this Section indicates that negative assurances are permissible, for example, in letters for underwriters in which the auditor reports on his or her limited procedures applied to financial data pertaining to a registration statement filed with the SEC; see AU Section 634 (Letters for Underwriters and Certain Other Requesting Parties).

ILLUSTRATIONS AND PRACTICE AIDS

ILLUSTRATION 1—DISCLAIMER OF OPINION REPORT WHEN ACCOUNTANT IS ASSOCIATED WITH UNAUDITED FINANCIAL STATEMENTS OF A PUBLIC ENTITY PREPARED IN ACCORDANCE WITH GAAP

(Addressee)

The accompanying balance sheet of ABC Company as of December 31, 20X2, and the related statements of income, retained earnings, and cash flows for the year then ended were not audited by us and, accordingly, we do not express an opinion on them.

(Signature)

(Date)

ILLUSTRATION 2—DISCLAIMER OF OPINION REPORT WHEN ACCOUNTANT IS ASSOCIATED WITH UNAUDITED FINANCIAL STATEMENTS OF A PUBLIC ENTITY PREPARED IN ACCORDANCE WITH OCBOA

(Addressee)

The accompanying statement of assets and liabilities resulting from cash transactions of ABC Company as of December 31, 20X2, and the related statement of revenues collected and expenses paid during the year then ended were not audited by us and, accordingly, we do not express an opinion on them.

(Signature)

(Date)

ILLUSTRATION 3—ACCOUNTANT'S DISCLAIMER OF OPINION ON A PUBLIC ENTITY'S FINANCIAL STATEMENTS DUE TO LACK OF INDEPENDENCE

(Addressee)

We are not independent with respect to ABC Company, and the accompanying balance sheet as of December 31, 20X2, and the related statements of income, retained earnings, and cash flows for the year then ended were not audited by us and, accordingly, we do not express an opinion on them.

(Signature)

(Date)

ILLUSTRATION 4—ACCOUNTANT'S MODIFIED DISCLAIMER OF OPINION ON A PUBLIC ENTITY'S UNAUDITED FINANCIAL STATEMENTS THAT ARE NOT IN CONFORMITY WITH GAAP

(Addressee)

The accompanying balance sheet of ABC Company as of December 31, 20X2, and the related statements of income, retained earnings, and cash flows for the year then ended were not audited by us and, accordingly, we do not express an opinion on them.

Accounting principles generally accepted in the United States of America require that inventory cost consist of material, labor, and overhead. Management has informed us that the inventory of finished goods and work in process is stated in the accompanying financial statements at material and labor cost only, and that the effects of this departure from generally accepted accounting principles on financial position, results of operations, and cash flows have not been determined.

(Signature)

(Date)

AU SECTION 508
REPORTS ON AUDITED FINANCIAL STATEMENTS

PRACTICE POINT: As part of its Clarity Project, the American Institute of Certified Public Accountants' (AICPA's) Auditing Standards Board (ASB) has finalized a clarified Statement on Auditing Standards (SAS) titled, "Forming an Opinion and Reporting on Financial Statements," which supersedes:

- AU Section 410 (Adherence to Generally Accepted Accounting Principles), as amended;

- Paragraphs .01–.02 of AU Section 530 (Dating of the Independent Auditor's Report), as amended); and

- With the clarified SAS, "Modifications to the Opinion in the Independent Auditor's Report," and the clarified SAS, "Emphasis-of-Matter Paragraphs and Other-Matter Paragraphs in the Independent Auditor's Report," supersedes paragraphs .01–.11, .14–.15, .19–.32, .35–.52, .58–.70, and .74–.76 of AU Section 508 (Reports on Audited Financial Statements).

The clarified SAS includes extant guidance from AU Sections 410, 508, and 530 (along with some of the related interpretations). The clarified SAS also includes requirements and application material addressing comparative financial statements.

Extant AU Section 508 requires a statement in the auditor's report that the financial statements are the responsibility of the company's management. The clarified SAS prescribes a requirement to describe management's responsibility for the preparation and fair presentation of the financial statements in more detail than what is required in extant AU Section 508. The description includes an explanation that management is responsible for the preparation and fair presentation of the financial statements in accordance with the applicable financial reporting framework, and that this responsibility includes the design, implementation, and maintenance of internal control relevant to the preparation and fair presentation of financial statements that are free from material misstatement, whether due to fraud or error.

The clarified SAS also prescribes the use of headings throughout the auditor's report to clearly distinguish each section of the report.

The ASB is expected to issue many of the clarified standards in *one* SAS that will be codified in "AU Section" format. The ASB has decided that the effective date of the clarified SASs that have not yet been issued is for audits of financial statements for periods ending on or after December 15, 2012. Auditors should be alert to and monitor further developments in this area.

PRACTICE POINT: As part of its Clarity Project, the American Institute of Certified Public Accountants' (AICPA's) Auditing Standards Board (ASB) has finalized a clarified Statement on Auditing Standards (SAS) titled, "Modifications to the Opinion in the Independent Auditor's Report," which supersedes:

- AU Section 431 (Adequacy of Disclosure in Financial Statements); and

- With the clarified SAS, "Forming an Opinion and Reporting on Financial Statements," and the clarified SAS, "Emphasis-of-Matter Paragraphs and Other-Matter Paragraphs in the Independent Auditor's Report,." supersedes paragraphs .01–.11, .14–.15, .19–.32, .35–.52, .58–.70, and .74–.76 of AU Section 508 (Reports on Audited Financial Statements).

The clarified SAS includes extant guidance from AU Section 431 and AU Section 508. However, the clarified SAS does not change or expand extant standards in any significant respect.

The ASB is expected to issue many of the clarified standards in *one* SAS that will be codified in "AU Section" format. The ASB has decided that the effective date of the clarified SASs that have not yet been issued is for audits of financial statements for periods ending on or after December 15, 2012. Auditors should be alert to and monitor further developments in this area.

PRACTICE POINT: As part of its Clarity Project, the American Institute of Certified Public Accountants' (AICPA's) Auditing Standards Board (ASB) has finalized a clarified Statement on Auditing Standards (SAS) titled, "Emphasis-of-Matter Paragraphs and Other-Matter Paragraphs in the Independent Auditor's Report." This clarified SAS together with the clarified SAS, "Forming an Opinion and Reporting on Financial Statements," and the clarified SAS, "Modifications to the Opinion in the Independent Auditor's Report," supersedes paragraphs .01–.11, .14–.15, .19–.32, .35–.52, .58–.70, and .74–.76 of AU Section 508 (Reports on Audited Financial Statements).

Extant AU Section 508 indicates that certain circumstances (although not those affecting the auditor's unqualified opinion) may require that the auditor add an explanatory paragraph, or other explanatory language, to the standard report (e.g., auditors are required to include an explanatory paragraph when the auditor has concluded that there is substantial doubt about the entity's ability to continue as a going concern). Also, the auditor may add an explanatory paragraph to emphasize a matter regarding the financial statements. Under extant AU Section 508, emphasis paragraphs are never required; however, they may be added solely at the auditor's discretion.

The clarified SAS introduces the terms *emphasis-of-matter* and *other-matter paragraphs*. The clarified SAS describes an emphasis-of-matter as a paragraph included in the auditor's report that refers to a matter appropriately presented or disclosed in the financial statements. The clarified SAS describes an other-matter paragraph as a paragraph included in the auditor's report that refers to a matter other than those presented or disclosed in the financial statements that, in the auditor's judgment, is relevant to users' understanding of the audit, the auditor's responsibilities, or the auditor's report.

Under the clarified SAS, an emphasis-of-matter paragraph would refer to any paragraph added to the auditor's report that relates to a matter that is appropriately presented or disclosed in the financial statements. Some of these paragraphs would be required by certain SASs, whereas others would be added at the discretion of the auditor, consistent with current practice. However, all such paragraphs would be considered emphasis-of-matter paragraphs because they are intended to draw users' attention to a particular matter. Accordingly, the concept of an "explanatory paragraph" is no longer to be included in U.S. GAAS.

Instead, additional communications in the auditor's report are labeled as either "emphasis-of-matter" or "other-matter" paragraphs.

Further, extant AU Section 508 states that unless otherwise required by the provisions of that section, an explanatory paragraph may precede or follow the opinion paragraph in the auditor's report. The clarified SAS requires an emphasis-of-matter or other-matter paragraph to always follow the opinion paragraph and be included in a separate section of the auditor's report under the section heading "Emphasis of Matter" or "Other Matter."

The ASB is expected to issue many of the clarified standards in *one* SAS that will be codified in "AU Section" format. The ASB has decided that the effective date of the clarified SASs that have not yet been issued is for audits of financial statements for periods ending on or after December 15, 2012. Auditors should be alert to and monitor further developments in this area.

PRACTICE POINT: In March 2011, the American Institute of Certified Public Accountants' (AICPA's) Auditing Standards Board (ASB) issued an exposure draft (ED) of a proposed Statement on Auditing Standards (SAS) titled, "Omnibus Statement on Auditing Standards—2011." This proposed SAS, which is part of the AICPA's Clarity Project, would amend the following SASs that have been issued in the clarity format and are currently effective:

- SAS-117 (AU Section 801) (Compliance Audits). The amendment to SAS-117 conforms the auditor's report on compliance to the requirements of the clarified SAS, "Forming an Opinion and Reporting on Financial Statements." In addition, the amendment revises the appendix in SAS-117, "AU Sections That Are Not Applicable to Compliance Audits," to reflect conforming changes to affected references to AU Sections as a result of the ASB's Clarity Project.

- SAS-118 (AU Section 550) (Other Information in Documents Containing Audited Financial Statements). The amendment to SAS-118 clarifies the requirements with respect to identified material inconsistencies by categorizing the requirements based on when the inconsistencies are identified (prior to the date of the auditor's report on the audited financial statements; after the date of the auditor's report but prior to the report release date; and after the report release date). It also adds application material addressing electronic sites to include guidance from an interpretation of AU Section 550 (Other Information in Documents Containing Audited Financial Statements), which the ASB determined was appropriate to include in SAS-118.

In addition, in order to address other changes necessitated by the ASB's overall Clarity Project, the proposed SAS would amend the following clarified SASs that have been finalized and released, but not yet issued as authoritative:

- Clarified SAS, "Overall Objectives of the Independent Auditor and the Conduct of an Audit in Accordance with Generally Accepted Auditing Standards."

- Clarified SAS, "Modifications to the Opinion in the Independent Auditor's Report."

- Clarified SAS, "Reports on Application of Requirements of an Applicable Financial Reporting Framework.."

- Clarified SAS, "The Auditor's Communication with Those Charged with Governance (Redrafted)."
- Clarified SAS, "Audit Documentation (Redrafted)."

The proposed SAS would be effective for audits of financial statements for periods ending on or after December 15, 2012, except for the amendment to the clarified SAS, "Reports on Application of Requirements of an Applicable Financial Reporting Framework," which would be effective for engagements ending on or after December 15, 2012.

WHAT EVERY PRACTITIONER SHOULD KNOW

Basic Objectives and Requirements

The fourth standard of reporting states:

> The auditor must either express an opinion regarding the financial statements, taken as a whole, or state that an opinion cannot be expressed, in the auditor's report. When the auditor cannot express an overall opinion, the auditor should state the reasons therefor in the auditor's report. In all cases where an auditor's name is associated with financial statements, the auditor should clearly indicate the character of the auditor's work, if any, and the degree of responsibility the auditor is taking, in the auditor's report.

The objective of the fourth standard of reporting is to prevent misinterpretation of the degree of responsibility the auditor is assuming when his or her name is associated with audited financial statements.

Unqualified opinions An auditor may issue an unqualified opinion on an entity's financial statements only when both of the following conditions are met:

1. The audit has been conducted in accordance with GAAS.
2. The financial statements are presented in conformity with GAAP, in all material respects.

If either of these conditions is not met, one of the following opinions will have to be issued: (1) a qualified opinion, (2) an adverse opinion, or (3) a disclaimer of opinion.

See Illustrations 1 and 2 for examples of auditor's reports with unqualified opinions.

Qualified opinions A qualified opinion is issued when any of the following circumstances has a material impact on the financial statements:

a. *Scope limitations*—Sufficient audit evidence cannot be collected because of engagement circumstances or restrictions imposed by the client, and the auditor has concluded not to disclaim an opinion.

b. *Departures from GAAP*—Generally accepted accounting principles, which include adequate disclosures, have not been observed by the client in the presentation of the financial statements, and the auditor has concluded not to express an adverse opinion.

A qualified opinion excludes a specific item from the auditor's opinion. Therefore, the auditor expresses an opinion that the financial statements as a whole are presented fairly in conformity with generally accepted accounting principles, excluding the item or items specified in the auditor's report. A qualified opinion should include the word *except* or *exception* in a phrase such as "except for" or "with the exception of."

Examples of auditor's reports with qualified opinions are found in Illustrations 7, 9, 10, 12, 13, and 14.

Adverse opinions Departures from GAAP may be so material and pervasive that the financial statements taken as a whole are misstated or misleading and, therefore, cannot be relied on. Under these circumstances, the auditor should express an adverse opinion.

See Illustration 11 for an auditor's report that includes an adverse opinion due to departures from GAAP.

Disclaimer of opinion The necessity for disclaiming an opinion may arise because of either of the following conditions:

1. *A severe limitation on the scope of the audit*—Client-imposed circumstances or engagement circumstances may arise during the audit that prevent the auditor from applying one or more audit procedures the auditor considers necessary. Such conditions could be so highly material and severe that it would be inappropriate to issue a qualified opinion; therefore, the auditor should disclaim an opinion on the financial statements.

2. *Lack of independence*—If the auditor is not independent with respect to a public company, he or she must disclaim an opinion on the financial statements. For nonpublic entities, the auditor may only issue a compilation report. See AU Section 504 (Association with Financial Statements) for additional guidance and report illustration on this issue.

See Illustration 8 for an auditor's report that includes a disclaimer of opinion due to a scope limitation.

The Auditor's Standard Report

The auditor's standard report includes an introductory paragraph, a scope paragraph, and an opinion paragraph. The introductory paragraph describes the basic responsibilities of management and the auditor with respect to the financial statements. The scope paragraph provides a summarized description of the audit process. The auditor's opinion on the entity's financial statements is expressed in the opinion paragraph.

The auditor's report usually is addressed to the groups or individuals who appointed the auditor. For corporate clients, this may be the board of directors, the stockholders, or the audit committee. For an unincorporated client, this may be the partners or the proprietor. When an audit is performed at the request of a party other than the management or the owners of the audited entity, the auditor's report should be addressed to the party who requested the audit.

The auditor's standard report should include the following:

1. A title that includes the word *independent*.

2. A statement that the financial statements identified in the report were audited.

3. A statement that the financial statements are the responsibility of the entity's management and that the auditor's responsibility is to express an opinion on the financial statements based on the audit.

4. A statement that the audit was conducted in accordance with GAAS and an identification of the United States of America as the country of origin of those standards.

5. A statement that GAAS requires that the auditor plan and perform the audit to obtain reasonable assurance about whether the financial statements are free of material misstatement.

6. A statement that an audit includes:

   a. Examination of evidence supporting the amounts and disclosures in the financial statements on a test basis.

   b. Assessment of the accounting principles used and significant estimates made by management.

   c. Evaluation of the overall financial statement presentation.

7. A statement that the auditor believes that the audit provides a reasonable basis for his or her opinion.

8. An opinion on whether the financial statements present fairly, in all material respects, (a) the financial position of the entity as of the balance sheet date and (b) the results of its operations and its cash flows for the period then ended in conformity with GAAP. The opinion should also include an identification of the United States of America as the country of origin of those accounting principles.

9. Manual or printed signature of the auditor's firm.

10. Date of the audit report.

See Illustration 1 for an auditor's standard report covering single year financial statements. See Illustration 2 for an auditor's standard report covering comparative financial statements.

Explanatory Language Added to the Auditor's Standard Unqualified Report

Certain circumstances may require modification of the wording (e.g., explanatory paragraph) of the auditor's standard report, but not modification of the auditor's unqualified opinion on the financial statements. These circumstances include:

1. Lack of consistency in accounting principles or in the method of their application (see discussion below).

2. Emphasis of a matter (see discussion below).

3. Departure from a promulgated accounting principle (see discussion below).

4. The auditor's opinion is based in part on the report of another auditor (see discussion below).

5. Certain matters relating to reports on comparative financial statements (see discussion below).

6. Substantial doubt about the entity's ability to continue as a going concern (see AU Section 341, *The Auditor's Consideration of an Entity's Ability to Continue as a Going Concern,* for additional guidance).

7. Other information in a document containing audited financial statements is materially inconsistent with information appearing in the financial statements (see AU Section 550, *Other Information in Documents Containing Audited Financial Statements,* for additional guidance).

8. Certain matters relating to supplementary information required by the Financial Accounting Standards Board (FASB), the Governmental Accounting Standards Board (GASB), or the Federal Accounting Standards Advisory Board (FASAB) (see AU Section 558, *Required Supplementary Information,* for additional guidance).

9. Selected quarterly financial data required by SEC Regulation S-K has been omitted or has not been reviewed (see AU Section 722, *Interim Financial Information,* for additional guidance).

Lack of consistency in accounting principles or in the method of their application When a change in accounting principles or in the method of their application materially affects the comparability of the entity's financial statements, the auditor should include an explanatory paragraph in the standard report. The explanatory paragraph, following the opinion paragraph, should (1) identify the nature of the change and (2) refer the reader to the note in the financial statements that discusses the change in detail. The standard introductory, scope, and opinion paragraphs are not changed and should not refer to the explanatory paragraph.

The addition of the explanatory paragraph in the auditor's report is required in the auditor's reports on financial statements of subsequent years as long as the year of the change is presented and reported on. An exception to this requirement occurs when a change in accounting principle that does not require a cumulative effect adjustment is made at the beginning of the earliest year presented and reported on, such as a change from FIFO to LIFO. However, if the accounting change is accounted for by retroactive restatement of the financial statements affected, the explanatory paragraph is required only in the year of the change.

It should be noted that items that materially affect the comparability of the financial statements generally require disclosure in the notes to the financial statements. A qualified audit report for inadequate disclosure may be required if the client refuses to properly disclose the items.

See Illustration 3 for an unqualified auditor's report that includes an explanatory paragraph due to a change in accounting principles or in the method of their application.

Emphasis of a matter The auditor's report may emphasize a matter regarding the financial statements without qualifying the opinion. The following are examples of matters that the auditor may want to emphasize:

- The entity reported on is a component of a larger entity.
- The entity has had significant transactions with related parties.
- A significant subsequent event has taken place.
- Accounting matters, other than those involving changes in accounting principles, exist that affect the comparability of the financial statements with those of the preceding period.

When the auditor decides to emphasize a matter, an explanatory paragraph may be added, either following or preceding the opinion paragraph, and an unqualified opinion should be expressed. The standard introductory, scope, and opinion paragraphs should not refer to the explanatory paragraph.

See Illustrations 4 and 5 for auditor's reports that contain an emphasis of a matter paragraph.

Departure from a promulgated accounting principle Rule 203 of the AICPA's *Code of Professional Conduct* states that in unusual circumstances a departure from an accounting principle promulgated by a body designated by the AICPA to establish accounting principles may not require a qualified or adverse opinion. The unusual circumstances referred to are when a departure is necessary to keep the financial statements from being misleading. If the auditor agrees with the client's conclusion that the use of a promulgated rule would result in misleading financial statements, he or she may issue an unqualified opinion.

Under these rare circumstances, an explanatory paragraph, either following or preceding the opinion paragraph, should be included in the standard unqualified auditor's report and should describe:

1. The departure from GAAP;
2. The approximate effects of the departure, if practicable; and
3. The reasons why adherence to the principle would have resulted in misleading financial statements in that particular situation.

The standard introductory, scope, and opinion paragraphs are not modified, and no reference is made to the explanatory paragraph.

Although Rule 203 is needed to provide flexibility in the application of accounting principles, the rule must be used with a great deal of caution. When the rule is used, the auditor is, in effect, promulgating an accounting rule for a specific client, which is a heavy responsibility to take. Not surprisingly, there are very few examples where Rule 203 has been used regarding the departure from a promulgated principle.

Auditor's opinion is based in part on the report of another auditor More than one audit firm may participate in an audit of a client. An auditor may report on the financial statements of a consolidated or combined entity, even if he or she has not audited every single entity, branch, or component that is included in the consolidated or combined financial statements. For additional guidance in these circumstances, see AU Section 543 (Part of Audit Performed by Other Independent Auditors).

When the auditor decides to make reference to the report of another auditor as a basis, in part, for his or her opinion, the auditor should disclose this fact in his or her report to indicate division of responsibility for performance of the audit, as follows:

1. *Introductory paragraph*—This paragraph should be modified to identify, preferably by name, the subsidiaries that the principal auditor has not audited. Also, the magnitude of the portion of the financial statements audited by the other auditor should be disclosed; this may be done by indicating dollar amounts or percentages of total assets, total revenues, or other appropriate criteria. In addition, the principal auditor should specify that part of the audit was conducted by another auditor; however, the other auditor need not be, and usually is not, identified by name. The other auditor may be named by the principal auditor only with his or her express permission.

2. *Scope paragraph*—This paragraph should be modified to indicate that the principal auditor's audit and the report of other auditors provide a reasonable basis for the opinion on the financial statements.

3. *Opinion paragraph*—This paragraph is modified to indicate shared responsibility for the audit opinion (i.e., the opinion is based, in part, on the report of the other auditor).

See Illustration 6 for an auditor's opinion that is based in part on the report of another auditor.

Scope Limitations

The two major categories of scope limitations are:

1. Restrictions caused by a client (e.g., refusal to permit inquiry of outside legal counsel, refusal to permit confirmation of accounts receivable, refusal to furnish the auditor with a letter of representations); and

2. Limitations beyond the control of either the client or the auditor (e.g., timing of the auditor's work, such as when the auditor is engaged too late to observe physical inventory).

Scope limitations require the auditor either to express a qualified opinion or to disclaim an opinion. Note that an adverse opinion is not appropriate when limitations on the scope of the audit exist, because such an opinion relates to a deficiency in the financial statements rather than a deficiency in the scope of the audit.

While the effect on the auditor's report is the same for either restriction, the interpretation of materiality is likely to be different. For scope restrictions that are imposed by the client, the auditor should be concerned that management may be attempting to prevent discovery of misstated information; in these cases, the auditor usually would disclaim an opinion, if the condition is material. On the other hand, when restrictions are caused by conditions beyond the client's control, a qualified opinion is more likely. The description of the scope limitation should not be incorporated in the auditor's report by reference to a note to the financial statements, because the auditor, and not the client, is responsible for the description of the scope limitation.

Qualified opinion due to a scope limitation When the auditor concludes that a qualified opinion should be issued for a limitation on the scope of the engagement, the auditor's report should contain:

1. *An introductory paragraph*—The wording is the same as in the auditor's standard report.

2. *A scope paragraph*—The wording of the scope paragraph should be modified by adding the phrase "except as discussed in the following paragraph" to the beginning of the first sentence in the paragraph.

3. *An explanatory paragraph*—A separate paragraph should be added, following the scope paragraph, to explain the nature of the scope limitation.

4. *An opinion paragraph*—The opinion paragraph must be qualified by using the phrase "except for" or a similar phrase. In addition, the opinion paragraph must refer to the explanatory paragraph.

See Illustration 7 for an auditor's report that includes a qualified opinion due to a scope limitation.

Disclaimer of opinion due to a scope limitation When the auditor concludes that a disclaimer of opinion should be issued for a limitation on the scope of the engagement, the auditor's report should:

1. *Contain an introductory paragraph*—The wording of the introductory paragraph should be modified to state "We were engaged to audit" instead of "We have audited" and to delete the statement of the auditor's responsibility to express an opinion on the financial statements.

2. *Omit the scope paragraph*—The scope paragraph of the auditor's standard report is omitted to avoid overshadowing the disclaimer of opinion (i.e., to avoid stating anything that might lead readers to believe that other parts of the financial statements were audited and therefore might be fairly stated).

3. *Contain an explanatory paragraph*—A separate paragraph should be added, following the introductory paragraph, to explain the nature of the scope limitation.

4. *Contain a disclaimer of opinion paragraph*—In this paragraph the auditor specifically states that an opinion cannot be expressed on the financial statements because the significance of the scope limitation precluded the auditor from forming an opinion.

See Illustration 8 for an auditor's report that includes a disclaimer of opinion due to a scope limitation.

Departures from GAAP

Departures from GAAP include (1) using inappropriate accounting principles, such as valuing property and equipment at current values instead of historical cost; (2) improperly applying accounting methods (e.g., incorrect application of the LIFO costing method to inventory); and (3) inadequate disclosures in the financial statements or the related footnotes.

When a client does not observe accounting principles, the auditor must decide whether an unqualified, a qualified, or an adverse opinion should be issued on the financial statements. The selection of the appropriate opinion depends on the materiality amount of the departure, the number of financial statement items affected by the departure, and the effects of the departure on the financial statements taken as a whole. An unqualified opinion can be issued if the departure is not significant to the fair presentation of the financial statements. If the departure affects the fairness of the financial statements but overall the statements can be relied on, a qualified opinion can be issued. On the other hand, when the departure is so significant that the financial statements should not be relied on, an adverse opinion must be issued.

Qualified opinion due to a departure from GAAP When the auditor concludes that a qualified opinion should be issued due to a GAAP departure, the auditor's report should contain:

1. *An introductory paragraph*—The wording is the same as in the auditor's standard report.

2. *A scope paragraph*—The wording is the same as in the auditor's standard report because no limitations have been placed on the scope of the audit.

3. *An explanatory paragraph*—A separate paragraph should be added, following the scope paragraph, to explain all of the significant reasons for the qualified opinion and to describe the departure from GAAP and its effects, or potential effects, on the financial statements. If the effects are not reasonably determinable, the report should so state.

4. *An opinion paragraph*—The opinion paragraph must be qualified by using the phrase "except for" or a similar phrase. In addition, the opinion paragraph must refer to the explanatory paragraph.

See Illustrations 9 and 10 for auditor's reports that include a qualified opinion due to departures from GAAP.

Adverse opinion due to a departure from GAAP When the auditor concludes that an adverse opinion should be issued due to a GAAP departure, the auditor's report should contain:

1. *An introductory paragraph*—The wording is the same as in the auditor's standard report.

2. *A scope paragraph*—The wording is the same as in the auditor's standard report because no limitations have been placed on the scope of the audit.

3. *An explanatory paragraph*—A separate paragraph should be added, following the scope paragraph, to explain all of the significant reasons for the adverse opinion and to describe the departure from GAAP and its effects, or potential effects, on the financial statements.

4. *An opinion paragraph*—The opinion paragraph should state that because of the effects of the departures from GAAP, the financial statements are

not presented fairly in conformity with GAAP. In addition, the opinion paragraph must refer to the explanatory paragraph.

See Illustration 11 for an auditor's report that includes an adverse opinion due to departures from GAAP.

Omission of statement of cash flows If an entity issues financial statements that purport to present financial position and results of operations but omits the related statement of cash flows, the auditor will normally conclude that the omission requires qualification of his or her opinion. See Illustration 12 for an auditor's report that includes a qualified opinion in such circumstances.

Accounting changes The auditor should express a qualified opinion with respect to accounting changes if any of the following conditions exist:

1. A newly adopted accounting principle is not a generally accepted accounting principle.

2. The method of accounting for the effect of the change is not in conformity with GAAP.

3. Management has not provided reasonable justification for the change in accounting principle.

If the effect of the change is highly material, the auditor should express an adverse opinion on the financial statements.

In addition, in subsequent years, the auditor should continue to express his exception with respect to the financial statements for the year of change as long as they are presented and reported on. However, the auditor's exception relates to the accounting change and does not affect the status of a newly adopted principle as a generally accepted accounting principle. Therefore, the auditor's opinion regarding the subsequent years' statements need not express an exception to use of the newly adopted principle.

Whenever an accounting change causes an auditor to express a qualified or an adverse opinion on the conformity of financial statements with GAAP for the year of change, the auditor should consider the possible effects of that change when reporting on subsequent year's financial statements as follows:

1. The auditor's report should disclose his or her reservations with respect to the financial statements for the year of change, if such statements are presented and reported on with a subsequent year's financial statements.

2. If an entity has adopted an accounting principle that is not in accordance with GAAP, its continued use might have a material effect on the statements of a subsequent year on which the auditor is reporting. In this situation, the auditor should express either a qualified opinion or an adverse opinion, depending on the materiality of the departure in relation to the statements of the subsequent year.

3. If an entity accounts for the effect of a change prospectively when GAAP requires restatement or the inclusion of the cumulative effect of the change in the year of change, the auditor should express a qualified opinion or an adverse opinion on the subsequent year's financial statements.

See Illustrations 13 and 14 for auditor's qualified reports for departures from GAAP resulting from (a) change in accounting principle without reasonable justification and (b) change to an accounting principle not in conformity with GAAP, respectively.

Limited Reporting Engagements

An auditor may be asked to report on one basic financial statement (e.g., balance sheet) and not on the others (e.g., statements of income, retained earnings, or cash flows). Such engagements do not involve scope limitations if (a) the auditor applies all the procedures deemed necessary in the circumstances and (b) the auditor's access to information underlying the basic financial statements is not limited.

See Illustration 15 for an auditor's unqualified report on a balance sheet only audit.

Reporting on Comparative Financial Statements

When all financial statements presented have been audited by the same auditor, the introductory, scope, and opinion paragraphs refer to and report on all the financial statements presented. The auditor's report on comparative financial statements ordinarily should be dated as of the date of completion of fieldwork for the most recent audit. See Illustration 2 for an auditor's unqualified report covering comparative financial statements.

Because the auditor's report on comparative financial statements applies to the individual financial statements presented, an auditor may express one type of opinion (e.g., a qualified or an adverse opinion) with respect to one or more financial statements for one or more periods, while issuing a different report on the other financial statements presented. See Illustration 16 for an auditor's report on comparative financial statements that contains an unqualified opinion on the current year's financial statements and a qualified opinion on the prior year's statements.

Opinion on prior-period financial statements is different from the opinion previously expressed A *continuing auditor*—an auditor who has audited the financial statements of the current period and at least the immediately preceding period—has a responsibility to update the report on prior-period financial statements that have been audited and that are presented for comparative purposes. *Updating* requires the auditor to consider whether, based on information obtained in the audit of the current period financial statements, he or she should re-express the same opinion on prior-period financial statements or express a different opinion on them.

If the auditor believes that the prior opinion is not appropriate, the current report (which covers both years) must include an explanatory paragraph, immediately preceding the opinion paragraph, stating why a different opinion on the prior-period financial statements is being expressed. The explanatory paragraph must disclose the following:

1. That the updated opinion on the financial statements of the prior period is different from the prior original opinion on those statements.

2. The reason the opinion is being revised.

3. The type of opinion previously issued.

4. The date of the prior audit report.

When an explanatory paragraph is added because of a change in the opinion expressed on a previous year's financial statements, the introductory, scope, and opinion paragraphs in the updated report would not refer to the explanatory paragraph, and an unqualified opinion is expressed on both years' financial statements, assuming that unqualified opinions are appropriate under the circumstances. See Illustration 17 for an example of an auditor's updated opinion on prior-period financial statements that is different from the opinion previously expressed.

Predecessor auditor's report is not presented When comparative financial statements are presented and one or more prior periods included have been audited by a predecessor auditor, one of the following reporting approaches should be followed: (1) if the predecessor auditor's report is not presented, the successor (current) auditor may refer to the predecessor auditor's report in the report on the current-period financial statements; or (2) the predecessor auditor may reissue his or her report on the prior-period financial statements (see discussion below).

Most frequently, the successor auditor refers to the predecessor auditor's report. In that case, the successor auditor should modify the introductory paragraph of the current report to (1) state that the prior year's financial statements were audited by other auditors; (2) include the date of the predecessor auditor's report; and (3) state the type of opinion expressed by the predecessor auditor, including the reasons for any explanatory paragraph included in the predecessor auditor's report. See Illustration 18 for a successor auditor's report when a predecessor auditor's report is unqualified and is not presented.

If the predecessor auditor's report was other than a standard unqualified report, the successor auditor should describe the nature of and reasons for the explanatory paragraph added to the predecessor's report or his opinion qualification. See Illustration 19 for a successor auditor's report when a predecessor auditor's report included an explanatory paragraph and is not presented.

If the prior-period financial statements have been restated, the introductory paragraph in the successor auditor's report should indicate that a predecessor auditor reported on those financial statements before restatement; see Illustration 20 for a successor auditor's report when the prior year financial statements have been restated following issuance of the predecessor's original report. Also, if the successor auditor is engaged to audit and applies sufficient procedures to satisfy himself or herself about the appropriateness of the restatement adjustments, an additional paragraph may be added to the successor auditor's report; see Illustration 21 for a successor auditor's report when the prior year financial statements have been restated following issuance of the predecessor's original report, and the successor has audited the restatement adjustments.

Predecessor auditor's report reissued Ordinarily, a predecessor auditor will be in a position to reissue his or her report. Reissuing is different from updating a report, in that the predecessor auditor is not in a position to evaluate his or her opinion in the context of the current year's audit. However, before reissuing the report, the predecessor auditor is required to:

1. Read the current-period financial statements, primarily to determine whether they contain any significant information that might materially affect the report on the prior-period financial statements.

2. Compare the prior-period financial statements originally reported on with those that are presented in the current comparative financial statements, primarily to determine if the prior-period financial statements do not differ materially from their original presentation.

3. Obtain representation letters from management of the former client and from the successor auditor. The representation letter from management of the former client should state (a) whether any information has come to management's attention that would cause them to believe that any of the previous representations should be modified and (b) whether any events have occurred subsequent to the balance sheet date of the latest financial statements reported on by the predecessor auditor that would require adjustment to or disclosure in those financial statements. See Illustration 26 for such a management representation letter from the former client. The representation letter from the successor auditor should state whether the successor's audit revealed any matters that, in the successor's opinion, might have a material effect on, or require disclosure in, the financial statements reported on by the predecessor auditor; see Illustration 27 for such a representation letter from a successor auditor to a predecessor auditor.

If the predecessor auditor concludes, on the basis of these limited procedures, that the prior year's opinion still is appropriate, the predecessor auditor should reissue his or her report as it was originally. The reissued report should include the same original report date to avoid any implications that the predecessor auditor has performed any procedures with respect to any records, transactions, or events that have occurred subsequent to that date.

If the predecessor auditor concludes that the prior year's opinion is no longer appropriate, he or she should issue a revised report. In that case, the same reporting guidelines that apply to a continuing auditor's updated report, as discussed above, apply to the predecessor auditor (i.e., in an explanatory paragraph the predecessor auditor must fully describe the type of original opinion issued and the reason for changing that opinion). However, the predecessor auditor's updated report normally is dual-dated rather than redated to the report date on the current financial statements. Language such as the following should be used: "March 3, 20X2, except for Note X as to which the date is February 26, 20X3."

If the prior year's financial statements have been restated, the introductory paragraph of the successor auditor's report should state that the predecessor auditor reported on the previous year's financial statements before they were restated. See Illustration 20 for a successor auditor's report when the prior year financial statements have been restated following issuance of the predecessor's original report.

When the successor auditor has been engaged to audit the restatement adjustments, and has applied sufficient procedures to determine that the adjustments are appropriate, an additional paragraph may be added to the successor auditor's report. See Illustration 21 for a successor auditor's report when the prior year financial statements have been restated following issuance of the predecessor's original report, and the successor has audited the restatement adjustments.

Reporting on Financial Statements Prepared on a Liquidation Basis of Accounting

An entity is not viewed as a going concern if liquidation appears imminent. Therefore, a liquidation basis of accounting may be considered GAAP for entities in liquidation or for which liquidation appears imminent. In such circumstances, the auditor should issue an unqualified opinion on the financial statements, as long as the liquidation basis of accounting has been properly applied and adequate disclosures are made.

If the financial statements of an entity that adopts a liquidation basis of accounting are presented along with financial statements of a prior period that were prepared on the basis of GAAP for going concerns, the auditor's report ordinarily should include an explanatory paragraph that describes the change in the basis of accounting. For auditor's reports in year of adoption of liquidation basis, see Illustrations 22 and 23 for single year and comparative years' financial statements, respectively.

Reporting Considerations When Prior-Period Financial Statements Were Audited by a Predecessor Auditor Who Has Ceased Operations

An auditing interpretation of this Section discusses certain reporting considerations by a successor auditor when prior-period financial statements were audited by a predecessor auditor who has ceased operations. For purposes of determining whether an auditing firm has "ceased operations," the auditing interpretation indicates that such definition includes any firm that no longer issues audit opinions in its own name or in the name of a successor firm. Also, the auditing interpretation indicates that a "firm may cease operations with respect to public entities and still issue audit opinions with respect to non-public entities."

Reporting when prior-period financial statements are unchanged If the prior-period audited financial statements are unchanged and the predecessor auditor has ceased operations, then the successor auditor should indicate in his or her report the following:

- State that the prior-period financial statements were audited by another auditor (without naming the predecessor auditor);
- Include the date of the predecessor auditor's report;
- State the type of report issued by the predecessor auditor;

- If the report was other than a standard unqualified report, describe the nature of and reasons for the explanatory paragraph added to the predecessor's report or the opinion qualification; and

- Ordinarily indicate that the other auditor has ceased operations.

In such circumstances, the successor auditor should include the aforementioned items in the introductory paragraph of his or her report, such as follows:

> The financial statements of XYZ Company as of December 31, 20X1, and for the year then ended were audited by other auditors who have ceased operations. Those auditors expressed an unqualified opinion on those financial statements in their report dated March 29, 20X2.

Such reference to the predecessor auditor's report should be included even when the predecessor's report is *reprinted* and accompanies the successor auditor's report, because reprinting does not constitute *reissuance* of the predecessor auditor's report.

Reporting when prior-period financial statements have been restated If the prior-period financial statements have been restated and the entity does not file annual financial statements with the Securities and Exchange Commission (SEC), the introductory paragraph in the successor auditor's report should indicate that a predecessor auditor reported on those financial statements before restatement, such as follows:

> The financial statements of XYZ Company as of December 31, 20X1, and for the year then ended, before the restatement described in Note X, were audited by other auditors who have ceased operations. Those auditors expressed an unqualified opinion on those financial statements in their report dated March 29, 20X2.

When the prior-period financial statements have been restated, the successor auditor may be engaged either to reaudit the prior-period financial statements or to audit only the restatement adjustments. If the successor auditor is engaged to reaudit the prior-period financial statements, he or she should report on the financial statements following the guidance in this Section. If the successor auditor is engaged to audit the restatement adjustments and applies sufficient procedures to satisfy himself or herself about their appropriateness, an additional paragraph, following the opinion paragraph, may be added to the successor auditor's report. The following is an example:

> We also audited the adjustments described in Note X that were applied to restate the 20X1 financial statements. In our opinion, such adjustments are appropriate and have been properly applied.

The successor auditor may wish to indicate that he or she did not audit, review, or apply other procedures to the prior-period financial statements beyond the procedures applied to the restatement adjustments. In such circumstances, he or she may include a paragraph such as the following in his or her report:

> As discussed above, the financial statements of XYZ Company as of December 31, 20X1, and for the year then ended were audited by other auditors who have ceased operations. As described in Note X, these financial statements have been restated [revised]. We audited the adjustments described in Note X that were applied to restate [revise] the 20X1 financial statements. In our

opinion, such adjustments are appropriate and have been properly applied. However, we were not engaged to audit, review, or apply any procedures to the 20X1 financial statements of the Company other than with respect to such adjustments and, accordingly, we do not express an opinion or any other form of assurance on the 20X1 financial statements taken as a whole.

In some instances, when the successor auditor is auditing the restatement adjustments, he or she may determine that conducting a reaudit of the prior-period financial statements is necessary. The auditing interpretation indicates that a reaudit is ordinarily necessary when the restatement adjustments involve items such as the following:

- Corrections of errors
- Reflection of a change in reporting entity
- Retroactive accounting changes with material impact on previously reported amounts
- Retroactive accounting changes that affect previously reported net income or net assets
- Reporting discontinued operations
- Changes affecting previously reported net income or net assets

There may be circumstances where the successor auditor neither performs a reaudit of the prior-period financial statements nor audits only the restatement adjustments. In such situations, the note to the financial statements that describes the restatement adjustments should be marked "Unaudited." Also, it may be appropriate for the prior-period financial statements to be marked "Unaudited," depending on the nature and extent of the restatement adjustments.

If the entity files annual financial statements with the SEC, the auditing interpretation indicates that the predecessor auditor's latest signed and dated report on the prior-period financial statements should be reprinted with a legend indicating the following: (a) that the report is a copy of the previously issued report and (b) that the predecessor auditor has not reissued the report.

Procedures performed with respect to the restatement adjustments are identified in the successor auditor's report There may be instances where the successor auditor may wish to indicate in his or her report the procedures performed with respect to the restatement adjustments. The following is an example of a paragraph in the successor auditor's report identifying the procedures performed in connection with restatement adjustments for changes in segment composition:

> As discussed above, the financial statements of XYZ Company as of December 31, 20X1, and for the year then ended were audited by other auditors who have ceased operations. As described in Note X, the Company changed the composition of its reportable segments in 20X2, and the amounts in the 20X1 financial statements relating to reportable segments have been restated to conform to the 20X2 composition of reportable segments. We audited the adjustments that were applied to restate the disclosures for reportable segments reflected in the 20X1 financial statements. Our procedures included (a) agreeing the adjusted amounts of segment revenues, operating income, and assets to the Company's underlying records obtained from management and (b) testing the mathematical accuracy of the reconciliations of segment amounts to the consolidated financial statements. In our opinion, such adjust-

ments are appropriate and have been properly applied. However, we were not engaged to audit, review, or apply any procedures to the 20X1 financial statements of the Company other than with respect to such adjustments and, accordingly, we do not express an opinion or any other form of assurance on the 20X1 financial statements taken as a whole.

Reporting on restatement adjustments when the successor auditor has not yet completed an audit of current-period financial statements There may be situations where the prior-period financial statements audited by a predecessor auditor who has ceased operations have been subsequently restated; however, the successor auditor has not yet completed an audit of current-period financial statements. In such circumstances, the successor auditor is prohibited from reporting on the restatement adjustments. In other words, the successor auditor cannot report on prior-period financial statements that have been restated without also reporting on current-period audited financial statements. Alternatively, the successor auditor would need to reaudit the prior-period financial statements in order to report separately on them.

Clarification in the Audit Report of a Nonissuer That Testing of Internal Control under AICPA Standards Is Different Than Testing of Internal Control under PCAOB Standards

In connection with a nonpublic company's audit, the auditor is required to obtain a sufficient understanding of internal control to plan the audit and to determine the nature, timing, and extent of tests to be performed. The scope of the auditor's consideration of internal control, in accordance with GAAS as established by the AICPA, is significantly different and substantially less than that required for an attestation of internal control pursuant to PCAOB standards. Therefore, an audit performed in accordance with AICPA standards does not require the same level of testing and reporting on internal control over financial reporting as an audit of an issuer that is performed in accordance with PCAOB standards.

To clarify the extent of testing of internal control over financial reporting in accordance with GAAS, the AICPA has issued an auditing interpretation of AU Section 508, titled "Clarification in the Audit Report of the Extent of Testing of Internal Control over Financial Reporting in Accordance with Generally Accepted Auditing Standards." Specifically, this auditing interpretation addresses whether an auditor of a nonissuer may modify his or her audit report to state that the purpose and extent of the auditor's internal control testing was to determine the auditor's procedures under GAAS and was not sufficient to express an opinion on the effectiveness of internal control over financial reporting. According to the auditing interpretation, an auditor may modify his or her standard audit report on a nonissuer's financial statements to clarify the extent of the internal control testing. In such circumstances, the auditor's modification would be included in the scope paragraph (i.e., second paragraph) of the standard auditor's report; the first paragraph and the opinion paragraph remain the same as those in the standard auditor's report.

The auditing interpretation provides the following example of the additional language that may be included in the scope paragraph of the auditor's report (modified language is underlined):

Independent Auditor's Report

[*Same introductory paragraph as the standard auditor's report*]

We conducted our audit in accordance with auditing standards generally accepted in the United States of America. Those standards require that we plan and perform the audit to obtain reasonable assurance about whether the financial statements are free of material misstatement. An audit includes consideration of internal control over financial reporting as a basis for designing audit procedures that are appropriate in the circumstances, but not for the purpose of expressing an opinion on the effectiveness of the Company's internal control over financial reporting. Accordingly, we express no such opinion. An audit also includes examining, on a test basis, evidence supporting the amounts and disclosures in the financial statements, assessing the accounting principles used and significant estimates made by management, as well as evaluating the overall financial statement presentation. We believe that our audit provides a reasonable basis for our opinion.

[*Same opinion paragraph as the standard auditor's report*]

Reference to PCAOB Standards in an Audit Report on a Nonissuer

PCAOB Auditing Standard No. 1 (AS-1), "References in Auditors' Reports to the Standards of the Public Company Accounting Oversight Board," requires auditors of issuers to include in their audit reports a reference that the engagement was conducted in accordance with "the standards of the Public Company Accounting Oversight Board (United States)." In connection with issuing AS-1, the PCAOB has indicated that an accounting firm is not precluded from performing an audit of a nonissuer in accordance with the PCAOB standards and making reference to such standards in its audit report. That is to say, auditors of privately held entities are permitted to conduct their audits in accordance with the PCAOB standards and to make reference in their audit reports to such standards regardless of whether the accounting firm has registered with the PCAOB.

The AICPA has issued an auditing interpretation of AU Section 508 titled "Reference to PCAOB Standards in an Audit Report on a Nonissuer." This auditing interpretation clarifies the applicability of GAAS, as established by the AICPA, and how the auditor should report when he or she is engaged to perform an audit of a nonissuer in accordance with the PCAOB standards. Specifically, this auditing interpretation indicates that, if the auditor of a nonissuer conducted the audit in accordance with AICPA's generally accepted auditing standards *and* the auditing standards of the PCAOB, the auditor may indicate in the auditor's report that:

- The audit was conducted in accordance with both (1) generally accepted auditing standards as established by the AICPA's Auditing Standards Board and (2) the standards of the PCAOB; and

- The Company is not required to have an audit of its internal control over financial reporting and the purpose and extent of the auditor's internal control testing was to determine the auditor's procedures, but was not sufficient to express an opinion on the effectiveness of internal control.

In such circumstances, the auditor's modification would be included in the scope paragraph (i.e., second paragraph) of the standard auditor's report; the first paragraph and the opinion paragraph remain the same as those in the standard auditor's report. The auditing interpretation provides the following example of the additional language that may be included in the scope paragraph of the auditor's report (modified language is underlined):

Independent Auditor's Report

[*Same introductory paragraph as the standard auditor's report*]

We conducted our audit in accordance with generally accepted auditing standards as established by the Auditing Standards Board (United States) and in accordance with the auditing standards of the Public Company Accounting Oversight Board (United States). Those standards require that we plan and perform the audit to obtain reasonable assurance about whether the financial statements are free of material misstatement. The Company is not required to have, nor were we engaged to perform, an audit of its internal control over financial reporting. Our audit included consideration of internal control over financial reporting as a basis for designing audit procedures that are appropriate in the circumstances, but not for the purpose of expressing an opinion on the effectiveness of the Company's internal control over financial reporting. Accordingly we express no such opinion. An audit also includes examining, on a test basis, evidence supporting the amounts and disclosures in the financial statements, assessing the accounting principles used and significant estimates made by management, as well as evaluating the overall financial statement presentation. We believe that our audit provides a reasonable basis for our opinion.

[*Same opinion paragraph as the standard auditor's report*]

Reporting on Audits Conducted in Accordance with U.S. GAAS and International Standards on Auditing

There may be circumstances where an auditor conducts an audit in accordance with U.S. GAAS and, also, in accordance with the International Standards on Auditing (ISA) promulgated by the International Auditing and Assurance Standards Board (IAASB). Auditing Interpretation No. 14, *Reporting on Audits Conducted in Accordance with Auditing Standards Generally Accepted in the United States of America and in Accordance with International Standards on Auditing*, provides guidance to auditors when reporting on audits conducted in accordance with U.S. GAAS and the ISA.

The auditing interpretation states that the auditor is not precluded from indicating in his or her report that the audit also was conducted in accordance with another set of auditing standards, in addition to U.S. GAAS. Therefore, if the audit also was conducted in accordance with the ISA, the auditor may so indicate in his or her report. To determine whether an audit was conducted in accordance with the ISA, it is necessary for the auditor to consider the entire ISA text, including the basic principles, essential procedures, and the related guidance contained therein.

When reporting on an audit performed in accordance with U.S. GAAS and the ISA, the auditor should comply with reporting standards generally accepted in the U.S. See Illustration 25 for a sample auditor's report that would be appropriate when reporting on an audit conducted in accordance with U.S. GAAS and with the ISA.

Financial Statements Prepared in Conformity with International Financial Reporting Standards as Issued by the International Accounting Standards Board

Auditing Interpretation No. 19, *Financial Statements Prepared in Conformity with International Financial Reporting Standards as Issued by the International Accounting Standards Board*, of AU Section 508 provides guidance regarding whether an independent U.S. auditor may apply the guidance in AU Section 508 when engaged to report on financial statements presented in conformity with International Financial Reporting Standards (IFRS) as issued by the International Accounting Standards Board (IASB). The auditing interpretation indicates that the IASB has been designated by the AICPA Council as the body to establish international financial reporting standards for both private and public entities pursuant to Rule 202, *Compliance with Standards*, and Rule 203, *Accounting Principles*, of the AICPA *Code of Professional Conduct*. Therefore, an auditor may apply the guidance in AU Section 508 when reporting on general purpose financial statements presented in accordance with IFRS as issued by the IASB. In such circumstances, the opinion paragraph of the auditor's report would make reference to IFRS, rather than U.S. GAAP, for example, as follows:

> In our opinion, the financial statements referred to above present fairly, in all material respects, the financial position of ABC Company as of December 31, 20X2 and 20X1, and the results of its operations, comprehensive income, changes in equity and its cash flows for the years then ended in conformity with International Financial Reporting Standards as issued by the International Accounting Standards Board.

Reporting considerations when the financial statements are presented in conformity with a jurisdictional variation of IFRS. An entity may prepare financial statements in conformity with a jurisdictional variation of IFRS, for example, International Financial Reporting Standards as endorsed by the European Union. Because the AICPA Council has *not* designated bodies other than the IASB to establish international financial reporting standards, in such circumstances the auditor should follow the guidance in AU Section 534 (Reporting on Financial Statements Prepared for Use in Other Countries) when the financial statements are prepared for use outside the U.S.

When an entity prepares its financial statements in conformity with a jurisdictional variation of IFRS *and* such financial statements are prepared for more than limited distribution in the U.S., the auditing interpretation indicates that the auditor should follow the guidance in paragraphs 14 and 15 of AU Section 534 and paragraphs 35-60 of AU Section 508.

In addition, if financial statements are presented in conformity with *both* IFRS, as issued by the IASB, and a jurisdictional variation of IFRS, the auditor may follow the guidance previously discussed.

PRACTICE ISSUES AND FREQUENTLY ASKED QUESTIONS

Issue 1: May an auditor express an unqualified opinion on one of the financial statements presented and a different opinion (e.g., qualified, adverse, or disclaimer) on another?

Yes. The auditor may express an unqualified opinion on one of the financial statements (e.g., balance sheet) and express a qualified or adverse opinion or disclaim an opinion on another (e.g., income statement) if the circumstances warrant. For example, if an auditor did not observe the inventory taking at the beginning of the period for a new audit client, and did not become satisfied by other means with respect to the beginning inventory, the auditor may issue an opinion only on the balance sheet and disclaim an opinion on the income statement and statement of cash flows. See Illustration 24 for an example of such an auditor's report.

Issue 2: Is the auditor required to indicate in his or her report concurrence with a change in accounting principles that affects the comparability of the financial statements being reported on?

No. The auditor's concurrence with a change in accounting principles is implicit. Therefore, if the auditor does not concur with the change, the auditor should issue a qualified opinion due to a departure from GAAP. However, an adverse opinion would be appropriate if the GAAP departure is so highly material and pervasive that the financial statements are misleading and cannot be relied on.

Issue 3: When a principal auditor decides to make reference to the report of another auditor as a basis, in part, for his or her opinion, is the principal auditor required to identify the other auditor by name?

No. The principal auditor should only specify that part of the audit was conducted by another auditor; however, the other auditor need not be, and usually is not, identified by name (see Illustration 6). The other auditor may be named by the principal auditor only with his or her express permission.

Issue 4: Is a disclaimer of opinion appropriate when the auditor observes departures from GAAP?

No. A disclaimer of opinion is not appropriate when the auditor observes a departure from GAAP. This is because the auditor has gathered sufficient evidence to place him or her in a position to express an opinion and, therefore, cannot avoid disclosing a known departure from GAAP by denying an opinion on the financial statements.

Issue 5: May an auditor describe a scope limitation in notes to the financial statements as opposed to describing it in an explanatory paragraph in the audit report?

No. It is not appropriate for the scope of the audit to be described in a note to the financial statements, since the description of the audit scope is the responsibility of the auditor and not that of the client.

Issue 6: When reporting on comparative financial statements, should a successor auditor name a predecessor auditor in his or her report when the predecessor's report is not presented?

No. The successor auditor should not name the predecessor auditor in his or her report. However, the successor auditor may name the predecessor auditor if the predecessor's practice was acquired by, or merged with, that of the successor auditor.

Issue 7: When an auditor is appointed to a new engagement after the physical inventory count, is the report of an outside inventory-taking firm by itself a satisfactory substitute for the auditor's own observation sufficient to eliminate the scope limitation?

No. It is ordinarily necessary for the auditor to be present at the time of the count and to be satisfied about the effectiveness of the counting procedures used. Therefore, the report from an outside company that takes independent inventory counts is not, by itself, a satisfactory substitute for the auditor's own observation or taking of some physical counts. In such circumstances, the auditor should:

- Review the outside firm's inventory counting program.
- Observe the outside firm's inventory counting procedures and controls.
- Make or observe a test of physical counts.
- Recompute calculations of the submitted inventory on a test basis.
- Apply appropriate tests to the intervening transactions, if applicable.

The auditor ordinarily may reduce, but not eliminate, the extent of his or her work on the physical count of inventory if the procedures of the outside firm are deemed satisfactory. However, any restriction on the auditor's judgment concerning the extent of his contact with the inventory would be a scope limitation.

Issue 8: May the auditor's standard report refer to a separate report presented by management that describes management's financial reporting responsibilities?

No. For example, a client-prepared document that includes audited financial statements (e.g., an annual shareholders' report) may contain a management report that states the financial statements are the responsibility of management. The statement about management's responsibilities for the financial statements that is included in the auditor's standard report should not be further elaborated upon or referenced to management's report. Such modifications to the standard auditor's report may lead users to erroneously believe that the auditor is providing assurances about representations made by management about their responsibility for financial reporting, internal controls and other matters that might be discussed in the management report.

Issue 9: When an auditor disclaims an opinion on financial statements because of pervasive scope limitations, may the auditor express an opinion on certain identified items (e.g., cash) if he or she is satisfied about the fairness of such items?

No. This is not permissible, because expression of an opinion on certain specific identified items in such circumstances would overshadow or contradict the disclaimer of opinion. The same is true if the auditor had issued an adverse opinion on the financial statements taken as a whole.

Issue 10: When a principal auditor engages another auditor to observe the inventory at a client's subsidiary in another state, should the auditor refer in his or her report to the work of the other auditor?

No. In such circumstances, the auditor's inventory observation work in the other state would not be mentioned in the principal auditor's report. The inventory observation alone is not sufficient to enable the other auditor to express an opinion on the inventory.

Issue 11: What is the difference between updating a report on prior-period financial statements and reissuing a previous audit report?

Updating usually refers to the process that a continuing auditor goes through in considering the effect, on the prior period's financial statements, of information gathered during the audit of current period financial statements in a comparative presentation. Normally, the auditor's report on comparative statements is dated as of the last day of field work on the current period's audit.

On the other hand, *reissuance* of a report implies that no auditing procedures have been applied after the issuance of the original report. Reissuance of reports is covered in AU Section 530 (Dating of the Independent Auditor's Report).

Issue 12: Is it appropriate to include on each page of the basic audited financial statements a reference to the auditor's report such as "The accompanying notes and auditor's report are an integral part of these financial statements"?

No. The financial statements are the responsibility of the client and management and should be clearly distinguished from the auditor's responsibility. Therefore, the auditor's report cannot be an *integral part of the financial statements.* Accordingly, it is inappropriate to include such reference to the auditor's report as part of the reference to the notes to the financial statements. However, a reference such as the following is appropriate: "The accompanying notes are an integral part of these financial statements."

Issue 13: May an auditor express an opinion on financial statements covering a period longer than 12 months?

Yes, as long as the title of the financial statements is descriptive of the period covered and the auditor's report clearly indicates the period covered by the financial statements.

ILLUSTRATIONS AND PRACTICE AIDS

ILLUSTRATION 1—AUDITOR'S STANDARD UNQUALIFIED REPORT: SINGLE-YEAR FINANCIAL STATEMENTS

Independent Auditor's Report

Board of Directors and Stockholders
ABC Company

We have audited the accompanying balance sheet of ABC Company as of December 31, 20X2, and the related statements of income, retained earnings, and cash flows for the year then ended. These financial statements are the responsibility of the Company's management. Our responsibility is to express an opinion on these financial statements based on our audit.

We conducted our audit in accordance with auditing standards generally accepted in the United States of America. Those standards require that we plan and perform the audit to obtain reasonable assurance about whether the financial statements are free of material misstatement. An audit includes examining, on a test basis, evidence supporting the amounts and disclosures in the financial statements. An audit also includes assessing the accounting principles used and significant estimates made by management, as well as evaluating the overall financial statement presentation. We believe that our audit provides a reasonable basis for our opinion.

In our opinion, the financial statements referred to above present fairly, in all material respects, the financial position of ABC Company as of December 31, 20X2, and the results of its operations and its cash flows for the year then ended in conformity with accounting principles generally accepted in the United States of America.

[*Signature*]

[*Date*]

ILLUSTRATION 2—AUDITOR'S STANDARD UNQUALIFIED REPORT: COMPARATIVE FINANCIAL STATEMENTS

Independent Auditor's Report

Board of Directors and Stockholders
ABC Company

We have audited the accompanying balance sheets of ABC Company as of December 31, 20X2, and 20X1, and the related statements of income, retained earnings, and cash flows for the years then ended. These financial statements are the responsibility of the Company's management. Our responsibility is to express an opinion on these financial statements based on our audits.

We conducted our audits in accordance with auditing standards generally accepted in the United States of America. Those standards require that we plan and perform the audit to obtain reasonable assurance about whether the financial statements are free of material misstatement. An audit includes examining, on a test basis, evidence supporting the amounts and disclosures in the financial statements. An audit also includes assessing the accounting principles used and significant estimates made by management, as well as evaluating the overall financial statement presentation. We believe that our audits provide a reasonable basis for our opinion.

In our opinion, the financial statements referred to above present fairly, in all material respects, the financial position of ABC Company as of December 31, 20X2, and 20X1, and the results of its operations and its cash flows for the years then ended in conformity with accounting principles generally accepted in the United States of America.

[*Signature*]

[*Date*]

ILLUSTRATION 3—AUDITOR'S UNQUALIFIED OPINION WITH EXPLANATORY PARAGRAPH DUE TO CHANGE IN ACCOUNTING PRINCIPLES OR IN THE METHOD OF THEIR APPLICATION

Independent Auditor's Report

Board of Directors and Stockholders
ABC Company

We have audited the accompanying balance sheet of ABC Company as of December 31, 20X2, and the related statements of income, retained earnings, and cash flow for the year then ended. These financial statements are the responsibility of the Company's management. Our responsibility is to express an opinion on these financial statements based on our audit.

We conducted our audit in accordance with auditing standards generally accepted in the United States of America. Those standards require that we plan and perform the audit to obtain reasonable assurance about whether the financial statements are free of material misstatement. An audit includes examining, on a test basis, evidence supporting the amounts and disclosures in the financial statements. An audit also includes assessing the accounting principles used and significant estimates made by management, as well as evaluating the overall financial statement presentation. We believe that our audit provides a reasonable basis for our opinion.

In our opinion, the financial statements referred to above present fairly, in all material respects, the financial position of ABC Company as of December 31, 20X2, and the results of its operations and its cash flows for the year then ended in conformity with accounting principles generally accepted in the United States of America.

As discussed in Note [X] to the financial statements, the Company changed its method of computing depreciation in 20X2.

[*Signature*]

[*Date*]

ILLUSTRATION 4—AUDITOR'S UNQUALIFIED OPINION: EMPHASIS OF A MATTER PARAGRAPH DESCRIBING A SUBSEQUENT EVENT

Independent Auditor's Report

Board of Directors and Stockholders
ABC Company

We have audited the accompanying balance sheets of ABC Company as of December 31, 20X2, and 20X1, and the related statements of income, retained earnings, and cash flows for the years then ended. These financial statements are the responsibility of the Company's management. Our responsibility is to express an opinion on these financial statements based on our audits.

We conducted our audits in accordance with auditing standards generally accepted in the United States of America. Those standards require that we plan and perform the audit to obtain reasonable assurance about whether the financial statements are free of material misstatement. An audit includes examining, on a test basis, evidence supporting the amounts and disclosures in the financial statements. An audit also includes assessing the accounting principles used and significant estimates made by management, as well as evaluating the overall financial statement presentation. We believe that our audits provide a reasonable basis for our opinion.

In our opinion, the financial statements referred to above present fairly, in all material respects, the financial position of ABC Company as of December 31, 20X2, and 20X1, and the results of its operations and its cash flows for the years then ended in conformity with accounting principles generally accepted in the United States of America.

As discussed in Note [X] to the financial statements, on April 12, 20X3, the Company completed the sale of its DEF Subsidiary. This subsidiary accounted for 22% and 20% of the Company's total revenues for the years ended December 31, 20X2, and 20X1, respectively.

[*Signature*]

[*Date*]

ILLUSTRATION 5—AUDITOR'S UNQUALIFIED OPINION: EMPHASIS OF A MATTER PARAGRAPH DESCRIBING RELATED-PARTY TRANSACTIONS

Independent Auditor's Report

Board of Directors and Stockholders
ABC Company

We have audited the accompanying balance sheets of ABC Company as of December 31, 20X2, and 20X1, and the related statements of income, retained earnings, and cash flows for the years then ended. These financial statements are the responsibility of the Company's management. Our responsibility is to express an opinion on these financial statements based on our audits.

We conducted our audits in accordance with auditing standards generally accepted in the United States of America. Those standards require that we plan and perform the audit to obtain reasonable assurance about whether the financial statements are free of material misstatement. An audit includes examining, on a test basis, evidence supporting the amounts and disclosures in the financial statements. An audit also includes assessing the accounting principles used and significant estimates made by management, as well as evaluating the overall financial statement presentation. We believe that our audits provide a reasonable basis for our opinion.

In our opinion, the financial statements referred to above present fairly, in all material respects, the financial position of ABC Company as of December 31, 20X2, and 20X1, and the results of its operations and its cash flows for the years then ended in conformity with accounting principles generally accepted in the United States of America.

As discussed in Note [X] to the financial statements, the Company has had numerous significant transactions with businesses controlled by, and with people who are related to, the officers and directors of the Company.

[*Signature*]

[*Date*]

ILLUSTRATION 6—AUDITOR'S UNQUALIFIED OPINION: OPINION IS BASED IN PART ON REPORT OF ANOTHER AUDITOR

Independent Auditor's Report

Board of Directors and Stockholders
ABC Company and Subsidiaries

We have audited the consolidated balance sheets of ABC Company and subsidiaries as of December 31, 20X2, and 20X1, and the related consolidated statements of income, retained earnings, and cash flows for the years then ended. These financial statements are the responsibility of the Company's management. Our responsibility is to express an opinion on these financial statements based on our audits. We did not audit the financial statements of DEF Company, a wholly-owned subsidiary, whose statements reflect total assets of $_____ and $_____ as of December 31, 20X2, and 20X1, respectively, and total revenues of $_____ and $_____ for the years then ended. Those statements were audited by other auditors whose report has been furnished to us, and our opinion, insofar as it relates to the amounts included for DEF Company, is based solely on the report of the other auditors.

We conducted our audits in accordance with auditing standards generally accepted in the United States of America. Those standards require that we plan and perform the audit to obtain reasonable assurance about whether the financial statements are free of material misstatement. An audit includes examining, on a test basis, evidence supporting the amounts and disclosures in the financial statements. An audit also includes assessing the accounting principles used and significant estimates made by management, as well as evaluating the overall financial statement presentation. We believe that our audits and the report of other auditors provide a reasonable basis for our opinion.

In our opinion, based on our audits and the report of other auditors, the consolidated financial statements referred to above present fairly, in all material respects, the financial position of ABC Company and subsidiaries as of December 31, 20X2, and 20X1, and the results of their operations and their cash flows for the years then ended in conformity with accounting principles generally accepted in the United States of America.

[*Signature*]

[*Date*]

ILLUSTRATION 7—AUDITOR'S QUALIFIED OPINION DUE TO A SCOPE LIMITATION: INVESTMENT IN A FOREIGN AFFILIATE (THE AUDITOR HAS CONCLUDED THAT A DISCLAIMER OF OPINION IS NOT APPROPRIATE)

Independent Auditor's Report

Board of Directors and Stockholders
ABC Company

We have audited the accompanying balance sheets of ABC Company as of December 31, 20X2, and 20X1, and the related statements of income, retained earnings, and cash flows for the years then ended. These financial statements are the responsibility of the Company's management. Our responsibility is to express an opinion on these financial statements based on our audits.

Except as discussed in the following paragraph, we conducted our audits in accordance with auditing standards generally accepted in the United States of America. Those standards require that we plan and perform the audit to obtain reasonable assurance about whether the financial statements are free of material misstatement. An audit includes examining, on a test basis, evidence supporting the amounts and disclosures in the financial statements. An audit also includes assessing the accounting principles used and significant estimates made by management, as well as evaluating the overall financial statement presentation. We believe that our audits provide a reasonable basis for our opinion.

We were unable to obtain audited financial statements supporting the Company's investment in a foreign affiliate stated at $_____ and $_____ at December 31, 20X2, and 20X1, respectively, or its equity in earnings of that affiliate of $_____ and $_____, which is included in net income for the years then ended as described in Note [X] to the financial statements; nor were we able to satisfy ourselves as to the carrying value of the investment in the foreign affiliate or the equity in its earnings by other auditing procedures.

In our opinion, except for the effects of such adjustments, if any, as might have been determined to be necessary had we been able to examine evidence regarding the foreign affiliate investment and earnings, the financial statements referred to in the first paragraph above present fairly, in all material respects, the financial position of ABC Company as of December 31, 20X2, and 20X1, and the results of its operations and its cash flows for the years then ended in conformity with accounting principles generally accepted in the United States of America.

[*Signature*]

[*Date*]

ILLUSTRATION 8—AUDITOR'S DISCLAIMER OF OPINION DUE TO A SCOPE LIMITATION: INABILITY TO OBTAIN SUFFICIENT APPROPRIATE AUDIT EVIDENCE

Independent Auditor's Report

Board of Directors and Stockholders
ABC Company

We were engaged to audit the accompanying balance sheets of ABC Company as of December 31, 20X2, and 20X1, and the related statements of income, retained earnings, and cash flows for the years then ended. These financial statements are the responsibility of the Company's management.

The Company did not make a count of its physical inventory in 20X2 or 20X1, stated in the accompanying financial statements at $_____ as of December 31, 20X2, and at $_____ as of December 31, 20X1. Further, evidence supporting the cost of property and equipment acquired prior to December 31, 20X1, is no longer available. The Company's records do not permit the application of other auditing procedures to inventories or property and equipment.

Since the Company did not take physical inventories and we were not able to apply other auditing procedures to satisfy ourselves as to inventory quantities and the cost of property and equipment, the scope of our work was not sufficient to enable us to express, and we do not express, an opinion on these financial statements.

[*Signature*]

[*Date*]

ILLUSTRATION 9—AUDITOR'S QUALIFIED OPINION DUE TO A DEPARTURE FROM GAAP: LEASES NOT CAPITALIZED IN ACCORDANCE WITH ASC 840 (LEASES) AND PERTINENT FACTS ARE DISCLOSED IN A NOTE (THE AUDITOR HAS CONCLUDED THAT AN ADVERSE OPINION IS NOT APPROPRIATE)

Independent Auditor's Report

Board of Directors and Stockholders
ABC Company

We have audited the accompanying balance sheets of ABC Company as of December 31, 20X2, and 20X1, and the related statements of income, retained earnings, and cash flows for the years then ended. These financial statements are the responsibility of the Company's management. Our responsibility is to express an opinion on these financial statements based on our audits.

We conducted our audits in accordance with auditing standards generally accepted in the United States of America. Those standards require that we plan and perform the audit to obtain reasonable assurance about whether the financial statements are free of material misstatement. An audit includes examining, on a test basis, evidence supporting the amounts and disclosures in the financial statements. An audit also includes assessing the accounting principles used and significant estimates made by management, as well as evaluating the overall financial statement presentation. We believe that our audits provide a reasonable basis for our opinion.

As more fully described in Note [X] to the financial statements, the Company has excluded certain lease obligations from property and debt in the accompanying balance sheets. In our opinion, accounting principles generally accepted in the United States of America require that such obligations be included in the balance sheets.

In our opinion, except for the effects of not capitalizing certain lease obligations as discussed in the preceding paragraph, the financial statements referred to above present fairly, in all material respects, the financial position of ABC Company as of December 31, 20X2, and 20X1, and the results of its operations and its cash flows for the years then ended in conformity with accounting principles generally accepted in the United States of America.

[*Signature*]

[*Date*]

ILLUSTRATION 10—AUDITOR'S QUALIFIED OPINION DUE TO A DE-PARTURE FROM GAAP: OMISSION OF DISCLOSURES (THE AUDITOR HAS CONCLUDED THAT AN ADVERSE OPINION IS NOT APPROPRIATE)

Independent Auditor's Report

Board of Directors and Stockholders
ABC Company

We have audited the accompanying balance sheet of ABC Company as of December 31, 20X2, and the related statements of income, retained earnings, and cash flows for the year then ended. These financial statements are the responsibility of the Company's management. Our responsibility is to express an opinion on these financial statements based on our audit.

We conducted our audit in accordance with auditing standards generally accepted in the United States of America. Those standards require that we plan and perform the audit to obtain reasonable assurance about whether the financial statements are free of material misstatement. An audit includes examining, on a test basis, evidence supporting the amounts and disclosures in the financial statements. An audit also includes assessing the accounting principles used and significant estimates made by management, as well as evaluating the overall financial statement presentation. We believe that our audit provides a reasonable basis for our opinion.

The Company's financial statements do not disclose [*describe the nature of the omitted disclosures*]. In our opinion, disclosure of this information is required by accounting principles generally accepted in the United States of America.

In our opinion, except for the omission of the information discussed in the preceding paragraph, the financial statements referred to above present fairly, in all material respects, the financial position of ABC Company as of December 31, 20X2, and the results of its operations and its cash flows for the year then ended in conformity with accounting principles generally accepted in the United States of America.

[*Signature*]

[*Date*]

ILLUSTRATION 11—AUDITOR'S ADVERSE OPINION DUE TO DEPAR-TURES FROM GAAP

Independent Auditor's Report

Board of Directors and Stockholders
ABC Company

We have audited the accompanying balance sheets of ABC Company as of December 31, 20X2, and 20X1, and the related statements of income, retained earnings, and cash flows for the years then ended. These financial statements are the responsibility of the Company's management. Our responsibility is to express an opinion on these financial statements based on our audits.

We conducted our audits in accordance with auditing standards generally accepted in the United States of America. Those standards require that we plan and perform the audit to obtain reasonable assurance about whether the financial statements are free of material misstatement. An audit includes examining, on a test basis, evidence supporting the amounts and disclosures in the financial statements. An audit also includes assessing the accounting principles used and significant estimates made by management, as well as evaluating the overall financial statement presentation. We believe that our audits provide a reasonable basis for our opinion.

As discussed in Note [X] to the financial statements, the Company carries its property, plant, and equipment accounts at appraisal values and provides depreciation on the basis of such values. Further, the Company does not provide for income taxes with respect to differences between financial income and taxable income arising because of the use, for income tax purposes, of the installment method of reporting gross profit from certain types of sales. Accounting principles generally accepted in the United States of America require that property, plant, and equipment be stated at an amount not in excess of cost, reduced by depreciation based on such amount, and that deferred income taxes be provided.

Because of the departures from accounting principles generally accepted in the United States of America identified above, as of December 31, 20X2, and 20X1, inventories have been increased $_____ and $_____ by inclusion in manufacturing overhead of depreciation in excess of that based on cost; property, plant, and equipment, less accumulated depreciation, is carried at $_____ and $_____ in excess of an amount based on the cost to the Company; and deferred income taxes of $_____ and $_____ have not been recorded, resulting in an increase of $_____ and $_____ in retained earnings and in appraisal surplus of $_____ and $_____, respectively. For the years ended December 31, 20X2 and 20X1, cost of goods sold has been increased $_____ and $_____, respectively, because of the effects of the depreciation accounting referred to above and deferred income taxes of $_____ and $_____ have not been provided, resulting in an increase in net income of $_____ and $_____, respectively.

In our opinion, because of the effects of the matters discussed in the preceding paragraphs, the financial statements referred to above do not present fairly, in conformity with accounting principles generally accepted in the United States of America, the financial position of ABC Company as of December 31, 20X2, and 20X1, or the results of its operations or its cash flows for the years then ended.

[*Signature*]

[*Date*]

ILLUSTRATION 12—AUDITOR'S QUALIFIED OPINION DUE TO A DEPARTURE FROM GAAP: OMISSION OF STATEMENT OF CASHFLOWS

Independent Auditor's Report

Board of Directors and Stockholders
ABC Company

We have audited the accompanying balance sheets of ABC Company as of December 31, 20X2, and 20X1, and the related statements of income and retained earnings for the years then ended. These financial statements are the responsibility of the Company's management. Our responsibility is to express an opinion on these financial statements based on our audits.

We conducted our audits in accordance with auditing standards generally accepted in the United States of America. Those standards require that we plan and perform the audit to obtain reasonable assurance about whether the financial statements are free of material misstatement. An audit includes examining, on a test basis, evidence supporting the amounts and disclosures in the financial statements. An audit also includes assessing the accounting principles used and significant estimates made by management, as well as evaluating the overall financial statement presentation. We believe that our audits provide a reasonable basis for our opinion.

The Company declined to present a statement of cash flows for the years ended December 31, 20X2, and 20X1. Presentation of such statement summarizing the Company's operating, investing, and financing activities is required by accounting principles generally accepted in the United States of America.

In our opinion, except that the omission of a statement of cash flows results in an incomplete presentation as explained in the preceding paragraph, the financial statements referred to above present fairly, in all material respects, the financial position of ABC Company as of December 31, 20X2, and 20X1, and the results of its operations for the years then ended in conformity with accounting principles generally accepted in the United States of America.

[*Signature*]

[*Date*]

ILLUSTRATION 13—AUDITOR'S QUALIFIED OPINION DUE TO A DEPARTURE FROM GAAP: CHANGE IN ACCOUNTING PRINCIPLE WITHOUT REASONABLE JUSTIFICATION

Independent Auditor's Report

Board of Directors and Stockholders
ABC Company

We have audited the accompanying balance sheets of ABC Company as of December 31, 20X2, and 20X1, and the related statements of income, retained earnings, and cash flows for the years then ended. These financial statements are the responsibility of the Company's management. Our responsibility is to express an opinion on these financial statements based on our audits.

We conducted our audits in accordance with auditing standards generally accepted in the United States of America. Those standards require that we plan and perform the audit to obtain reasonable assurance about whether the financial statements are free of material misstatement. An audit includes examining, on a test basis, evidence supporting the amounts and disclosures in the financial statements. An audit also includes assessing the accounting principles used and significant estimates made by management, as well as evaluating the overall financial statement presentation. We believe that our audits provide a reasonable basis for our opinion.

As disclosed in Note [X] to the financial statements, the Company adopted in 20X2 the first-in, first-out (FIFO) method of accounting for its inventories, whereas it previously used the last-in, first-out (LIFO) method. Although use of the FIFO method is in conformity with accounting principles generally accepted in the United States of America, in our opinion the Company has not provided reasonable justification for making this change as required by accounting principles generally accepted in the United States of America.

In our opinion, except for the change in accounting principle discussed in the preceding paragraph, the financial statements referred to above present fairly, in all material respects, the financial position of ABC Company as of December 31, 20X2, and 20X1, and the results of its operations and its cash flows for the years then ended in conformity with accounting principles generally accepted in the United States of America.

[*Signature*]

[*Date*]

ILLUSTRATION 14—AUDITOR'S QUALIFIED OPINION DUE TO A DEPARTURE FROM GAAP: CHANGE TO AN ACCOUNTING PRINCIPLE NOT IN CONFORMITY WITH GAAP

Independent Auditor's Report

Board of Directors and Stockholders
ABC Company

We have audited the accompanying balance sheets of ABC Company as of December 31, 20X2, and 20X1, and the related statements of income, retained earnings, and cash flows for the years then ended. These financial statements are the responsibility of the Company's management. Our responsibility is to express an opinion on these financial statements based on our audits.

We conducted our audits in accordance with auditing standards generally accepted in the United States of America. Those standards require that we plan and perform the audit to obtain reasonable assurance about whether the financial statements are free of material misstatement. An audit includes examining, on a test basis, evidence supporting the amounts and disclosures in the financial statements. An audit also includes assessing the accounting principles used and significant estimates made by management, as well as evaluating the overall financial statement presentation. We believe that our audits provide a reasonable basis for our opinion.

In 20X2, the Company changed its method of valuing land from the cost method to appraised values. The increase resulting from the revaluation amounted to $500,000 and is presented as an increase in stockholder's equity. In our opinion, the new basis on which land is recorded is not in conformity with accounting principles generally accepted in the United States of America.

In our opinion, except for the change to recording appraised values for land as described above, the financial statements referred to above present fairly, in all material respects, the financial position of ABC Company as of December 31, 20X2, and 20X1, and the results of its operations and its cash flows for the years then ended in conformity with accounting principles generally accepted in the United States of America.

[*Signature*]

[*Date*]

ILLUSTRATION 15—AUDITOR'S UNQUALIFIED REPORT ON A BALANCE SHEET ONLY AUDIT

Independent Auditor's Report

Board of Directors and Stockholders
ABC Company

We have audited the accompanying balance sheet of ABC Company as of December 31, 20X2. This financial statement is the responsibility of the Company's management. Our responsibility is to express an opinion on this financial statement based on our audit.

We conducted our audit in accordance with auditing standards generally accepted in the United States of America. Those standards require that we plan and perform the audit to obtain reasonable assurance about whether the balance sheet is free of material misstatement. An audit includes examining, on a test basis, evidence supporting the amounts and disclosures in the balance sheet. An audit also includes assessing the accounting principles used and significant estimates made by management, as well as evaluating the overall balance sheet presentation. We believe that our audit provides a reasonable basis for our opinion.

In our opinion, the balance sheet referred to above presents fairly, in all material respects, the financial position of ABC Company as of December 31, 20X2, in conformity with accounting principles generally accepted in the United States of America.

[*Signature*]

[*Date*]

ILLUSTRATION 16—AUDITOR'S REPORT ON CURRENT YEAR IS UNQUALIFIED; OPINION ON PRIOR YEAR IS QUALIFIED

Independent Auditor's Report

Board of Directors and Stockholders
ABC Company

We have audited the accompanying balance sheets of ABC Company as of December 31, 20X2, and 20X1, and the related statements of income, retained earnings, and cash flows for the years then ended. These financial statements are the responsibility of the Company's management. Our responsibility is to express an opinion on these financial statements based on our audits.

We conducted our audits in accordance with auditing standards generally accepted in the United States of America. Those standards require that we plan and perform the audit to obtain reasonable assurance about whether the financial statements are free of material misstatement. An audit includes examining, on a test basis, evidence supporting the amounts and disclosures in the financial statements. An audit also includes assessing the accounting principles used and significant estimates made by management, as well as evaluating the overall financial statement presentation. We believe that our audits provide a reasonable basis for our opinion.

As more fully described in Note [X] to the financial statements, a net provision for loss on abandonment of equipment of $200,000 after related income taxes has been presented as an extraordinary charge against earnings for 20X1. In our opinion, accounting principles generally accepted in the United States of America require that the gross amount of such provision be part of the determination of income from operations before taxes and that the amount of the provision not be separately presented as an extraordinary item in the statement of income.

In our opinion, except for the effects of the matter described in the previous paragraph on the 20X1 statement of income, the financial statements referred to above present fairly, in all material respects, the financial position of ABC Company as of December 31, 20X2, and 20X1, and the results of its operations and its cash flows for the years then ended in conformity with accounting principles generally accepted in the United States of America.

[*Signature*]

[*Date*]

ILLUSTRATION 17—AUDITOR'S UPDATED OPINION ON PRIOR-PE-
RIOD FINANCIAL STATEMENTS IS DIFFERENT FROM PREVIOUS
OPINION

Independent Auditor's Report

Board of Directors and Stockholders
ABC Company

We have audited the accompanying balance sheets of ABC Company as of
December 31, 20X2, and 20X1, and the related statements of income, retained
earnings, and cash flows for the years then ended. These financial statements
are the responsibility of the Company's management. Our responsibility is to
express an opinion on these financial statements based on our audits.

We conducted our audits in accordance with auditing standards generally
accepted in the United States of America. Those standards require that we
plan and perform the audit to obtain reasonable assurance about whether the
financial statements are free of material misstatement. An audit includes
examining, on a test basis, evidence supporting the amounts and disclosures
in the financial statements. An audit also includes assessing the accounting
principles used and significant estimates made by management, as well as
evaluating the overall financial statement presentation. We believe that our
audits provide a reasonable basis for our opinion.

In our report dated March 31, 20X2, we expressed an opinion that the
20X1 financial statements did not fairly present financial position, results of
operations, and cash flows in conformity with accounting principles generally
accepted in the United States of America because of two departures from such
principles: (1) the Company carried its property, plant, and equipment at
appraisal values, and provided for depreciation on the basis of such values
and (2) the Company did not provide for deferred income taxes with respect
to differences between income for financial reporting purposes and taxable
income. As described in Note [X], the Company has changed its method of
accounting for these items and restated its 20X1 financial statements to
conform with accounting principles generally accepted in the United States of
America. Accordingly, our present opinion on the 20X1 financial statements,
as presented herein, is different from that expressed in our previous report.

In our opinion, the financial statements referred to above present fairly, in
all material respects, the financial position of ABC Company as of December
31, 20X2, and 20X1, and the results of its operations and its cash flows for the
years then ended in conformity with accounting principles generally accepted
in the United States of America.

[*Signature*]

[*Date*]

ILLUSTRATION 18—SUCCESSOR AUDITOR'S REPORT WHEN A PREDE-
CESSOR AUDITOR'S REPORT IS UNQUALIFIED AND IS NOT
PRESENTED

Independent Auditor's Report

Board of Directors and Stockholders
ABC Company

We have audited the balance sheet of ABC Company as of December 31, 20X2,
and the related statements of income, retained earnings, and cash flows for
the year then ended. These financial statements are the responsibility of the
Company's management. Our responsibility is to express an opinion on these
financial statements based on our audit. The financial statements of ABC
Company as of December 31, 20X1, were audited by other auditors whose

report dated March 31, 20X2, expressed an unqualified opinion on those statements.

We conducted our audit in accordance with auditing standards generally accepted in the United States of America. Those standards require that we plan and perform the audit to obtain reasonable assurance about whether the financial statements are free of material misstatement. An audit includes examining, on a test basis, evidence supporting the amounts and disclosures in the financial statements. An audit also includes assessing the accounting principles used and significant estimates made by management, as well as evaluating the overall financial statement presentation. We believe that our audit provides a reasonable basis for our opinion.

In our opinion, the 20X2 financial statements referred to above present fairly, in all material respects, the financial position of ABC Company as of December 31, 20X2, and the results of its operations and its cash flows for the year then ended in conformity with accounting principles generally accepted in the United States of America.

[*Signature*]

[*Date*]

ILLUSTRATION 19—SUCCESSOR AUDITOR'S REPORT WHEN A PREDE-CESSOR AUDITOR'S REPORT INCLUDED AN EXPLANATORY PARA-GRAPH AND IS NOT PRESENTED

Independent Auditor's Report

Board of Directors and Stockholders
ABC Company

We have audited the balance sheet of ABC Company as of December 31, 20X2, and the related statements of income, retained earnings, and cash flows for the year then ended. These financial statements are the responsibility of the Company's management. Our responsibility is to express an opinion on these financial statements based on our audit. The financial statements of ABC Company as of December 31, 20X1, were audited by other auditors whose report, dated March 31, 20X2, on those statements included an explanatory paragraph that described the change in the Company's method of computing depreciation discussed in Note [X] to the financial statements.

We conducted our audit in accordance with auditing standards generally accepted in the United States of America. Those standards require that we plan and perform the audit to obtain reasonable assurance about whether the financial statements are free of material misstatement. An audit includes examining, on a test basis, evidence supporting the amounts and disclosures in the financial statements. An audit also includes assessing the accounting principles used and significant estimates made by management, as well as evaluating the overall financial statement presentation. We believe that our audit provides a reasonable basis for our opinion.

In our opinion, the 20X2 financial statements referred to above present fairly, in all material respects, the financial position of ABC Company as of December 31, 20X2, and the results of its operations and its cash flows for the year then ended in conformity with accounting principles generally accepted in the United States of America.

[*Signature*]

[*Date*]

ILLUSTRATION 20—SUCCESSOR AUDITOR'S REPORT WHEN THE PRIOR YEAR FINANCIAL STATEMENTS HAVE BEEN RESTATED FOL-

LOWING ISSUANCE OF THE PREDECESSOR'S ORIGINAL REPORT (SUCCESSOR DID NOT AUDIT THE RESTATEMENT ADJUSTMENTS)

Independent Auditor's Report

Board of Directors and Stockholders
ABC Company

We have audited the balance sheet of ABC Company as of December 31, 20X2, and the related statements of income, retained earnings, and cash flows for the year then ended. These financial statements are the responsibility of the Company's management. Our responsibility is to express an opinion on these financial statements based on our audit. The financial statements of ABC Company as of December 31, 20X1, before the restatement described in Note [X], were audited by other auditors whose report, dated March 31, 20X2, expressed an unqualified opinion on those statements.

We conducted our audit in accordance with auditing standards generally accepted in the United States of America. Those standards require that we plan and perform the audit to obtain reasonable assurance about whether the financial statements are free of material misstatement. An audit includes examining, on a test basis, evidence supporting the amounts and disclosures in the financial statements. An audit also includes assessing the accounting principles used and significant estimates made by management, as well as evaluating the overall financial statement presentation. We believe that our audit provides a reasonable basis for our opinion.

In our opinion, the 20X2 financial statements referred to above present fairly, in all material respects, the financial position of ABC Company as of December 31, 20X2, and the results of its operations and its cash flows for the year then ended in conformity with accounting principles generally accepted in the United States of America.

[*Signature*]

[*Date*]

ILLUSTRATION 21—SUCCESSOR AUDITOR'S REPORT WHEN THE PRIOR YEAR FINANCIAL STATEMENTS HAVE BEEN RESTATED FOLLOWING ISSUANCE OF THE PREDECESSOR'S ORIGINAL REPORT AND THE SUCCESSOR HAS AUDITED THE RESTATEMENT ADJUSTMENTS

Independent Auditor's Report

Board of Directors and Stockholders
ABC Company

We have audited the balance sheet of ABC Company as of December 31, 20X2, and the related statements of income, retained earnings, and cash flows for the year then ended. These financial statements are the responsibility of the Company's management. Our responsibility is to express an opinion on these financial statements based on our audit. The financial statements of ABC Company as of December 31, 20X1, before the restatement described in Note [X], were audited by other auditors whose report, dated March 31, 20X2, expressed an unqualified opinion on those statements.

We conducted our audit in accordance with auditing standards generally accepted in the United States of America. Those standards require that we plan and perform the audit to obtain reasonable assurance about whether the financial statements are free of material misstatement. An audit includes examining, on a test basis, evidence supporting the amounts and disclosures in the financial statements. An audit also includes assessing the accounting principles used and significant estimates made by management, as well as evaluating the overall financial statement presentation. We believe that our audit provides a reasonable basis for our opinion.

In our opinion, the 20X2 financial statements referred to above present fairly, in all material respects, the financial position of ABC Company as of December 31, 20X2, and the results of its operations and its cash flows for the year then ended in conformity with accounting principles generally accepted in the United States of America.

We also audited the adjustments described in Note [X] that were applied to restate the 20X1 financial statements. In our opinion, such adjustments are appropriate and have been properly applied.

[*Signature*]

[*Date*]

ILLUSTRATION 22—AUDITOR'S REPORT ON SINGLE YEAR FINANCIAL STATEMENTS IN YEAR OF ADOPTION OF LIQUIDATION BASIS

Independent Auditor's Report

Board of Directors and Stockholders
ABC Company

We have audited the statement of net assets in liquidation of ABC Company as of December 31, 20X2, and the related statement of changes in net assets in liquidation for the period from April 26, 20X2, to December 31, 20X2. In addition, we have audited the statements of income, retained earnings, and cash flows for the period from January 1, 20X2, to April 25, 20X2. These financial statements are the responsibility of the Company's management. Our responsibility is to express an opinion on these financial statements based on our audit.

We conducted our audit in accordance with auditing standards generally accepted in the United States of America. Those standards require that we plan and perform the audit to obtain reasonable assurance about whether the financial statements are free of material misstatement. An audit includes examining, on a test basis, evidence supporting the amounts and disclosures in the financial statements. An audit also includes assessing the accounting principles used and significant estimates made by management, as well as evaluating the overall financial statement presentation. We believe that our audit provides a reasonable basis for our opinion.

As described in Note [X] to the financial statements, the stockholders of ABC Company approved a plan of liquidation on April 25, 20X2, and the company commenced liquidation shortly thereafter. As a result, the company has changed its basis of accounting for periods subsequent to April 25, 20X2, from the going-concern basis to a liquidation basis.

In our opinion, the financial statements referred to above present fairly, in all material respects, the net assets in liquidation of ABC Company as of December 31, 20X2, the changes in its net assets in liquidation for the period from April 26, 20X2, to December 31, 20X2, and the results of its operations and its cash flows for the period from January 1, 20X2, to April 25, 20X2, in conformity with accounting principles generally accepted in the United States of America applied on the bases described in the preceding paragraph.

[*Signature*]

[*Date*]

ILLUSTRATION 23—AUDITOR'S REPORT ON COMPARATIVE FINANCIAL STATEMENTS IN YEAR OF ADOPTION OF LIQUIDATION BASIS

Independent Auditor's Report

Board of Directors and Stockholders
ABC Company

We have audited the balance sheet of ABC Company as of December 31, 20X1, the related statements of income, retained earnings, and cash flows for the year then ended, and the statements of income, retained earnings, and cash flows for the period from January 1, 20X2, to April 25, 20X2. In addition, we have audited the statement of net assets in liquidation as of December 31, 20X2, and the related statement of changes in net assets in liquidation for the period from April 26, 20X2, to December 31, 20X2. These financial statements are the responsibility of the Company's management. Our responsibility is to express an opinion on these financial statements based on our audits.

We conducted our audits in accordance with auditing standards generally accepted in the United States of America. Those standards require that we plan and perform the audit to obtain reasonable assurance about whether the financial statements are free of material misstatements. An audit includes examining, on a test basis, evidence supporting the amounts and disclosures in the financial statements. An audit also includes assessing the accounting principles used and significant estimates made by management, as well as evaluating the overall financial statement presentation. We believe that our audits provide a reasonable basis for our opinion.

As described in Note [X] to the financial statements, the stockholders of ABC Company approved a plan of liquidation on April 25, 20X2, and the company commenced liquidation shortly thereafter. As a result, the company has changed its basis of accounting for periods subsequent to April 25, 20X2, from the going-concern basis to a liquidation basis.

In our opinion, the financial statements referred to above present fairly, in all material respects, the financial position of ABC Company as of December 31, 20X1, the results of its operations and its cash flows for the year then ended and for the period from January 1, 20X2, to April 25, 20X2, its net assets in liquidation as of December 31, 20X2, and the changes in its net assets in liquidation for the period from April 26, 20X2, to December 31, 20X2, in conformity with accounting principles generally accepted in the United States of America applied on the bases described in the preceding paragraph.

[*Signature*]

[*Date*]

ILLUSTRATION 24—AUDITOR'S UNQUALIFIED OPINION ON THE BALANCE SHEET AND DISCLAIMER OF OPINION ON THE INCOME STATEMENT AND STATEMENT OF CASH FLOWS

Independent Auditor's Report

Board of Directors and Stockholders
ABC Company

We have audited the accompanying balance sheet of ABC Company as of December 31, 20X2, and we were engaged to audit the related statements of income, retained earnings, and cash flows for the year then ended. These financial statements are the responsibility of the Company's management. Our responsibility is to express an opinion on these financial statements based on our audit.

Except as discussed in the following paragraph, we conducted our audit in accordance with auditing standards generally accepted in the United States of America. Those standards require that we plan and perform the audit to obtain reasonable assurance about whether the financial statements are free of material misstatement. An audit includes examining, on a test basis, evidence supporting the amounts and disclosures in the financial statements. An audit also includes assessing the accounting principles used and significant estimates made by management, as well as evaluating the overall financial statement presentation. We believe that our audit provides a reasonable basis for our opinion.

Because we were not engaged by the Company as auditors until after December 31, 20X1, we were not present to observe the physical inventory taken at that date, and we have not satisfied ourselves by means of other procedures concerning inventory quantities. The amount of the inventory at December 31, 20X1, enters materially into the determination of the results of operations and cash flows for the year ended December 31, 20X2. Therefore, we do not express an opinion on the accompanying statements of income, retained earnings, and cash flows for the year ended December 31, 20X2.

In our opinion, the balance sheet referred to above presents fairly, in all material respects, the financial position of ABC Company as of December 31, 20X2, in conformity with accounting principles generally accepted in the United States of America.

[*Signature*]

[*Date*]

ILLUSTRATION 25—AUDITOR'S REPORT IN CONNECTION WITH AN AUDIT CONDUCTED IN ACCORDANCE WITH U.S. GAAS AND IN ACCORDANCE WITH THE INTERNATIONAL STANDARDS ON AUDITING

Independent Auditor's Report

Board of Directors and Stockholders
ABC Company

We have audited the accompanying balance sheets of ABC Company as of December 31, 20X2, and 20X1, and the related statements of income, retained earnings, and cash flows for the years then ended. These financial statements are the responsibility of the Company's management. Our responsibility is to express an opinion on these financial statements based on our audits.

We conducted our audits in accordance with auditing standards generally accepted in the United States of America and in accordance with International Standards on Auditing. Those standards require that we plan and perform the audit to obtain reasonable assurance about whether the financial statements are free of material misstatement. An audit includes examining, on a test basis, evidence supporting the amounts and disclosures in the financial statements. An audit also includes assessing the accounting principles used and significant estimates made by management, as well as evaluating the overall financial statement presentation. We believe that our audits provide a reasonable basis for our opinion.

In our opinion, the financial statements referred to above present fairly, in all material respects, the financial position of ABC Company as of December 31, 20X2, and 20X1, and the results of its operations and its cash flows for the years then ended in conformity with accounting principles generally accepted in the United States of America.

[*Signature*]

[*Date*]

ILLUSTRATION 26—UPDATING MANAGEMENT REPRESENTATION LETTER

(Prepared on client's letterhead)

(Date)

To (*Independent auditor*)

In connection with your audit(s) of the [*identify the financial statements, e.g., balance sheet, statement of operations, and statement of cash flows*] of [*name of entity*] as of [*dates*] and for the [*periods*] then ended, for the purpose of expressing an opinion as to whether the [*consolidated*] financial statements present fairly, in all material respects, the financial position, results of operations, and cash flows of [*name of entity*] in conformity with accounting principles generally accepted in the United States of America, you were previously provided with a representation letter under date of [*date of previous representation letter*]. No information has come to our attention that would cause us to believe that any of those previous representations should be modified.

To the best of our knowledge and belief, no events have occurred subsequent to [*date of latest balance sheet reported on by the auditor*] and through the date of this letter that would require adjustment to or disclosure in the aforementioned financial statements.

[*Name of Chief Executive Officer and Title*]

[*Name of Chief Financial Officer and Title*]

PRACTICE POINT: If matters exist that should be disclosed to the auditor, they should be indicated by listing them following the representation. For example, if an event subsequent to the date of the balance sheet has been disclosed in the financial statements, the final paragraph could be modified as follows:

"To the best of our knowledge and belief, except as discussed in Note [X] to the financial statements, no events have occurred. . . . "

ILLUSTRATION 27—REPRESENTATION LETTER FROM SUCCESSOR AUDITOR TO PREDECESSOR AUDITOR

(*Prepared on successor auditor's letterhead*)

(Date)

To (*Predecessor auditor*)

In connection with the reissuance of your report on the financial statements of [*client's name*] for the year ended [*date*],which statements are to be included comparatively with similar statements for the year ended [*date*], we make the following representations.

We have audited, in accordance with auditing standards generally accepted in the United States of America, the balance sheet of [*client's name*] as of [*balance sheet date*] and the related statements of income, retained earnings, and cash flows for the year then ended. Our procedures in connection with the engagement did not disclose any events or transactions subsequent to [*predecessor's balance sheet date*] which, in our opinion, would have a material effect upon the financial statements, or which would require disclosure in the notes to the financial statements of [*client's name*] for the year then ended.

Should anything come to our attention prior to the date our report is issued which, in our judgment, would have a material effect upon the financial statements covered by your report, we shall notify you promptly.

Very truly yours,

[*Successor auditor's signature*]

AU SECTION 530
DATING OF THE INDEPENDENT AUDITOR'S REPORT

PRACTICE POINT: As part of its Clarity Project, the American Institute of Certified Public Accountants' (AICPA's) Auditing Standards Board (ASB) has finalized a clarified Statement on Auditing Standards (SAS) titled, "Forming an Opinion and Reporting on Financial Statements," which supersedes:

- AU Section 410 (Adherence to Generally Accepted Accounting Principles), as amended;

- Paragraphs .01–.02 of AU Section 530 (Dating of the Independent Auditor's Report), as amended); and

- With the clarified SAS, "Modifications to the Opinion in the Independent Auditor's Report," and the clarified SAS, "Emphasis-of-Matter Paragraphs and Other-Matter Paragraphs in the Independent Auditor's Report," supersedes paragraphs .01–.11, .14–.15, .19–.32, .35–.52, .58–.70, and .74–.76 of AU Section 508 (Reports on Audited Financial Statements).

The clarified SAS includes extant guidance from AU Sections 410, 508, and 530 (along with some of the related interpretations). The clarified SAS also includes requirements and application material addressing comparative financial statements.

Extant AU Section 508 requires a statement in the auditor's report that the financial statements are the responsibility of the company's management. The clarified SAS prescribes a requirement to describe management's responsibility for the preparation and fair presentation of the financial statements in more detail than what is required in extant AU Section 508. The description includes an explanation that management is responsible for the preparation and fair presentation of the financial statements in accordance with the applicable financial reporting framework, and that this responsibility includes the design, implementation, and maintenance of internal control relevant to the preparation and fair presentation of financial statements that are free from material misstatement, whether due to fraud or error.

The clarified SAS also prescribes the use of headings throughout the auditor's report to clearly distinguish each section of the report.

The ASB is expected to issue many of the clarified standards in *one* SAS that will be codified in "AU Section" format. The ASB has decided that the effective date of the clarified SASs that have not yet been issued is for audits of financial statements for periods ending on or after December 15, 2012. Auditors should be alert to and monitor further developments in this area.

WHAT EVERY PRACTITIONER SHOULD KNOW

Basic Objectives and Requirements

The auditor's report should not be dated earlier than the date on which the auditor has obtained sufficient audit evidence to support his or her opinion on the financial statements. Among other things, sufficient appropriate audit evidence includes evidence that

- The audit documentation has been reviewed;
- The entity's financial statements and related disclosures have been prepared; and
- Management has asserted that it has taken responsibility for the financial statements and related disclosures.

The auditor's responsibility for reviewing for subsequent events normally is limited to the period beginning with the balance sheet date and ending with the date of the auditor's report (commonly referred to as the *subsequent period*).

Events Occurring after the Original Date of the Auditor's Report but before Issuance of the Related Financial Statements

There are two types of subsequent events that require consideration and evaluation by the auditor:

1. Events that require adjustment (Type 1). Such events provide additional evidence with respect to conditions that existed at the balance sheet date and affect the estimates inherent in the process of preparing financial statements. These events have a direct effect on the financial statements and, if material, require *adjustment.*

2. Events that require disclosure (Type 2). Such events provide evidence with respect to conditions that did not exist at the date of the balance sheet but arose subsequent to that date. These events have no direct effect on the financial statements and should not result in an adjustment; however, if they are material, disclosure is required to keep the financial statements from being misleading.

See AU Section 560 (Subsequent Events) for additional guidance.

Effect of subsequent events requiring adjustment of the financial statements If the auditor becomes aware of a subsequent event requiring adjustment of the financial statements, the auditor should observe the following requirements:

1. *The adjustment is made in the financial statements, and disclosure of the event is made*—In such circumstances, the auditor should either "dual-date" the report or date it as of the later date (i.e., the date of the event). See "Methods available for dating the auditor's report for a subsequent event" below.

2. *The adjustment is made in the financial statements, but disclosure of the event is not made because it is not considered necessary*—In such circumstances, the auditor's report should be dated as of the date on which the auditor has obtained sufficient audit evidence to support his or her opinion on the financial statements.

3. *No adjustment is made to the financial statements*—In such circumstances, the auditor should qualify his or her opinion; in some cases, a disclaimer of opinion or an adverse opinion may be appropriate.

Effect of subsequent events requiring disclosure If the auditor becomes aware of a subsequent event requiring disclosure, the auditor should observe the following requirements:

1. *Disclosure of the event is made*—If disclosure of the event is made (either in a note or in the auditor's report), the auditor should either "dual-date" the report or date it as of the later date (i.e., the date of the event). See "Methods available for dating the auditor's report for a subsequent event" below.

2. *Disclosure of the event is* not *made*—In such circumstances, the auditor should qualify his or her opinion; in some cases, a disclaimer of opinion or an adverse opinion may be appropriate.

Methods available for dating the auditor's report for a subsequent event The auditor has the following two equally acceptable options available for dating his or her report for a subsequent event occurring after the original date of the auditor's report but before issuance of the related financial statements:

1. *Dual-date the audit report*—An example of dual-dating would be "March 19, 20X3, except for Note X, as to which the date is March 30, 20X3." In such instances, the auditor's responsibility for events occurring subsequent to the date on which the auditor has obtained sufficient audit evidence to support his or her opinion on the financial statements is limited to the specific event referred to in the note, or otherwise disclosed.

2. *Date the audit report as of the date of the subsequent event*—In such instances, the auditor's responsibility for subsequent events extends to a date subsequent to the original report date; accordingly, the auditor should extend to that date the subsequent events procedures prescribed under AU Section 560 (Subsequent Events).

Reissuance of the Auditor's Report

An auditor may reissue his or her report on a client's financial statements subsequent to the date of his or her original report on the basic financial statements. For example, an auditor may be requested by a client to furnish additional copies of a previously issued report. Use of the original report date in a reissued report removes any implication that records, transactions, or events after that date have been examined or reviewed. Therefore, when the auditor reissues his or her report and uses the original report date, the auditor has no responsibility to make any additional investigation or inquiry about events which may have occurred during the period between the original report date and the date of the release of additional reports.

If the auditor's report is included in a registration statement filed under the Securities Act of 1933, the auditor should perform certain additional procedures as discussed in AU Section 711 (Filings Under Federal Securities Statutes).

Effect of subsequent events on reissuance of the auditor's report In some cases, the auditor may become aware of an event that occurred subsequent to the date of his original report that requires adjustment or disclosure in the financial statements. When the auditor reissues the report in these circumstances (i.e., when the adjustment is made in the financial statements or the event is disclosed), the auditor should either "dual-date" the report or date it as of the date of the event. Events occurring between the time of original issuance and reissuance of financial statements should not result in adjustment of the financial statements unless the adjustment meets the criteria for the correction of an error or for prior period adjustments (see AU Section 560).

However, an event that requires disclosure only may be disclosed in a separate note to the financial statements using, for example, the following caption: "Event (Unaudited) Subsequent to the Date of the Independent Auditor's Report." Under these circumstances, the auditor's report would have the same date as the date in the original report.

PRACTICE ISSUES AND FREQUENTLY ASKED QUESTIONS

Issue 1: Are there any specific rules for determining what constitutes the date on which the auditor has obtained "sufficient appropriate audit evidence" to support the opinion on the financial statements for purposes of dating the auditor's report?

This Section does not define a particular event or stage of completion that constitutes the date on which the auditor has obtained "sufficient appropriate audit evidence" to support the opinion on the financial statements for purposes of dating the auditor's report. However, it does indicate that sufficient appropriate audit evidence includes, among other things, evidence (1) that the audit documentation has been reviewed, (2) that the entity's financial statements, including disclosures, have been prepared, and (3) that management has asserted that they have taken responsibility for the financial statements. In practice, the date on which the auditor has obtained sufficient appropriate audit evidence typically is the same date as the date of the management representation letter and the date of the lawyer's response concerning litigation, claims, and assessments.

Issue 2: After the original date of the auditor's report, but before issuance of the related financial statements, a fire destroyed a client's entire plant and all inventories. How does this event affect the auditor's report?

This event does not provide evidence about conditions that existed at the balance sheet date and, therefore, no adjustment to the financial statements is required. However, because the event is so significant, disclosure is required in order to prevent the financial statements from being misleading.

The auditor has two options for handling this event. The first option is to expand the subsequent events procedures through the date at which the auditor is satisfied that all events occurring in the intervening period are given proper financial statement consideration. In this case, the auditor's report will be dated as of this latter date.

The second option, which is equally acceptable, is to limit the extended subsequent events procedures to the fire and its effect on the financial statements. Under this option, the auditor's report should be "dual-dated."

Issue 3: When a client requests additional copies of a previously issued audit report, is the auditor required to change the date of the original report in order to reissue it?

No. In most cases it is not prudent to change the date of the original report because users may infer that records, transactions, or events have been audited through that new date. However, if the auditor becomes aware of any significant events subsequent to the date of the original report, he or she should consider their effects on the amounts and disclosures in the statements. These events may require the extension of subsequent events procedures, as discussed above, and the re-dating or dual-dating of the audit report.

ILLUSTRATIONS AND PRACTICE AIDS

There are no illustrations and practice aids for this Section.

AU SECTION 532
RESTRICTING THE USE OF AN AUDITOR'S REPORT

PRACTICE POINT: As part of its Clarity Project, the American Institute of Certified Public Accountants' (AICPA's) Auditing Standards Board (ASB) has issued an exposure draft (ED) of a proposed Statement on Auditing Standards (SAS) titled, "Alert as to the Intended Use of the Auditor's Written Communication," which would supersede AU Section 532 (Restricting the Use of an Auditor's Report). The proposed SAS has been clarified to indicate that it applies to auditor's reports and other written communications issued in connection with an engagement conducted in accordance with GAAS. Among other matters, the proposed SAS:

- Eliminates the use of the term *restricted use* and instead addresses the *intended use* of such communications.

- Establishes an umbrella requirement to include an alert as to the intended use of the auditor's written communication when the subject matter of that communication is based on:

  — Measurement or disclosure criteria that are determined by the auditor to be suitable only for a limited number of users who can be presumed to have an adequate understanding of the criteria;

  — Measurement or disclosure criteria that are available only to the specified parties; *or*

  — Matters identified or communicated by the auditor during the course of the engagement that are not the primary objective of the engagement (commonly referred to as a byproduct of the audit).

- Modifies the guidance pertaining to single combined reports covering both (*a*) communications that are required to include an alert as to intended use and (*b*) communications that are for general use, which do not ordinarily include such an alert. Extant AU Section 532 states that if an auditor issues a single combined report, the use of a single combined report should be "restricted" to the specified parties. The proposed SAS, however, indicates that the alert as to intended use pertains only to the communications required to include such an alert. Accordingly, the intended use of the communications that are for general use are not affected by this alert.

- Does not require the auditor to consider informing his or her client that restricted use reports are not intended for distribution to nonspecified parties (as is currently required in extant AU Section 532). Rather, the proposed SAS makes clear that an auditor is not responsible for controlling distribution of the written communication. The alert is designed to avoid misunderstandings related to the use of the written communication, particularly when taken out of the context in which it is intended to be used. An auditor may consider informing the entity that the written communication is not intended for distribution to parties other than those specified in the written communication.

The ASB is expected to issue many of the clarified standards in *one* SAS that will be codified in "AU Section" format. The ASB has decided that the effective date of the clarified SASs that have not yet been issued is for audits of financial statements for periods ending on or after December 15, 2012. Auditors should be alert to and monitor further developments in this area.

WHAT EVERY PRACTITIONER SHOULD KNOW

Basic Objectives and Requirements

A *general-use* report is one that is not restricted to specified parties; for example, auditors' reports on financial statements prepared in conformity with GAAP or certain other comprehensive basis of accounting (OCBOA).

A *restricted-use* report is one that is intended only for specified parties. The need for restriction on the use of a report may result from:

- The purpose of the report.
- The nature of the procedures applied.
- The basis of or assumptions used.
- The extent to which the procedures performed generally are known or understood.
- The potential for the report to be misunderstood.

An auditor is not precluded from restricting the use of any report. Also, if an auditor issues a single combined report covering both (a) subject matter that requires restriction to specified parties and (b) subject matter that ordinarily does not require such a restriction, then the auditor should restrict to the specified parties the use of such a single combined report.

An auditor should consider informing his or her client that restricted-use reports are not intended for distribution to nonspecified parties.

Circumstances Requiring Reports to Be Restricted

The auditor should restrict the use of a report in the following circumstances:

1. The subject matter of the accountant's report or the presentation being reported on is based on measurement or disclosure criteria contained in contractual agreements or regulatory provisions that are not in conformity with GAAP or OCBOA.

2. The accountant's report is issued as a *by-product* (herein referred to as "by-product report") of a financial statement audit. Such a report is based on the results of procedures designed to enable the auditor to express an opinion on the financial statements taken as a whole, not to provide assurance on the specific subject matter of the report. Examples of such by-product reports include those issued pursuant to: AU Section 325 (Communicating Internal Control Related Matters Identified in an Audit); AU Section 380 (The Auditor's Communication with Those Charged with Governance); and AU Section 623 (Special Reports).

Specified Parties in Restricted-Use Reports

The auditor should restrict the use of by-product reports to those charged with governance, management, others within the organization, specified regulatory agencies; and, in the case of reports on compliance with aspects of contractual agreements, to the parties to the contract or agreement.

An auditor may be asked to consider adding other parties as specified parties in a restricted-use report. The auditor should not agree to add other parties as specified parties of a by-product report. However, if an auditor is reporting on subject matter or a presentation based on criteria contained in contractual agreements or regulatory provisions, the auditor may agree to add other parties as specified parties; in such circumstances, the auditor should consider factors such as the identity of the other parties and the intended use of the report.

If the auditor agrees to add other parties as specified parties, the auditor should obtain affirmative acknowledgment, ordinarily in writing, from the other parties of their understanding of: (a) the nature of the engagement, (b) the measurement or disclosure criteria used in the engagement, and (c) the related report.

If the auditor agrees to add such other parties after he or she has issued the report, the auditor may either reissue the report or may provide other written acknowledgment that the other parties have been added as specified parties. If the report is reissued, the report date should not be changed. If the auditor provides written acknowledgment, it ordinarily should state that no procedures have been performed subsequent to the date of the report.

Restricted-Use Report Language

In a report that is restricted as to use, the auditor should add a separate paragraph at the end of the report that includes the following:

1. A statement that the report is intended solely for the information and use of the specified parties.

2. An identification of the specified parties.

3. A statement that the report is not intended to be and should not be used by anyone other than the specified parties.

The following is an example of such a paragraph:

> This report is intended solely for the information and use of [*the specified parties*] and is not intended to be and should not be used by anyone other than these specified parties.

The report may list the specified parties or refer the reader to the specified parties listed elsewhere in the report. For reports on engagements performed in accordance with U.S. Office of Management and Budget Circular A-133 (Audits of States, Local Governments, and Non-Profit Organizations), the specified parties may be identified as "federal awarding agencies and pass-through entities."

PRACTICE ISSUES AND FREQUENTLY ASKED QUESTIONS

Issue 1: Is an auditor responsible for controlling a client's distribution of restricted-use reports?

No. An auditor is not responsible for controlling a client's distribution of restricted-use reports. That is why restricted-use reports should alert readers to the restriction on the use of the report by indicating that the report is not intended to be, and should not be, used by anyone other than the specified parties.

Issue 2: Is an auditor prohibited from reaching an understanding with the client that the intended use of his or her report will be restricted?

No. The auditor is not prohibited from reaching an understanding with the client (e.g., in connection with establishing the terms of the engagement) that the intended use of the report will be restricted. The auditor is also not precluded from obtaining the client's agreement that the client and the specified parties will not distribute the report to parties other than those identified in the report.

Issue 3: May an auditor comply with a small business client's request to restrict the use of the audit report to the client's bank and management because they are the only intended users of the statements?

Yes. Although auditors' reports on financial statements prepared in conformity with GAAP or OCBOA normally are not restricted as to their use, nothing precludes an auditor from restricting the use of any report. In this case, it is good practice for the auditor to reach an understanding with the client, preferably in the engagement letter, that the intended use of the report will be restricted. The client should agree that it and the specified parties will not distribute the report to other than the named parties.

Issue 4: When a client asks an auditor to report on the entity's compliance with loan covenants, as part of the audit of the client's financial statements, should the auditor restrict the use of his or her report on such an engagement?

Yes. The report on compliance with loan covenants is a by-product of the financial statement audit and, therefore, its use should be restricted.

Issue 5: Is the auditor required to restrict the use of his or her report on audited financial statements made in accordance with a basis of accounting prescribed by a regulatory agency that, by law, will become a matter of public record?

Yes. The criteria for such regulatory-basis financial statements is developed by the regulatory agency for its own use and they may not provide useful or relevant data for any other purpose. The fact that the financial statements are public information does not change this fact. Therefore, the auditor should restrict the use of his or her report in these circumstances.

Issue 6: May an auditor remove, pursuant to a client request, the restrictive wording from a significant deficiencies letter issued in connection with an audit of the financial statements?

No. Because of the limited procedures applied to the internal control for purposes of a report on significant deficiencies (see AU Section 325), such a report is not appropriate for use by personnel outside the entity.

Issue 7: When an auditor issues restricted-use reports pursuant to an audit under the provisions of "Government Auditing Standards" and OMB Circular A-133, may the auditor include these reports in the same document that contains the entity's financial statements and independent auditor's report thereon?

Yes. The inclusion of restricted-use reports in a document that also contains general-use reports does not affect the intended use of either report. It is permissible, and even useful to some of the intended users, that these reports be submitted together.

ILLUSTRATIONS AND PRACTICE AIDS

There are no illustrations and practice aids for this Section.

AU SECTION 534
REPORTING ON FINANCIAL STATEMENTS PREPARED FOR USE IN OTHER COUNTRIES

PRACTICE POINT: As part of its Clarity Project, the American Institute of Certified Public Accountants' (AICPA's) Auditing Standards Board (ASB) has issued an exposure draft (ED) of a proposed Statement on Auditing Standards (SAS) titled, "Financial Statements Prepared in Accordance with a Financial Reporting Framework Generally Accepted in Another Country," which would supersede AU Section 534 (Reporting on Financial Statements Prepared for Use in Other Countries). The following are the primary proposed changes from extant AU Section 534:

- Extant AU Section 534 indicates that the auditor "should consider consulting" with persons having expertise in auditing and accounting standards of the other country. The proposed SAS would require the auditor to obtain an understanding of a relevant financial reporting framework generally accepted in another country and of relevant auditing standards other than U.S. GAAS; however, the ASB believes that the consideration of consulting with persons having expertise in auditing and accounting standards should not be a requirement. Therefore, these previous requirements have been converted to application and other explanatory material.

- Extant AU Section 534 requires that if financial statements prepared in accordance with a financial reporting framework generally accepted in another country would have more than limited use in the United States, the auditor should report using the U.S. form of report, modified as appropriate (qualified or adverse), because of departures from U.S. GAAP. Extant AU Section 534 further requires that when the financial statements would not have more than limited use in the United States, the auditor's report may have included, as appropriate, an opinion only with respect to the financial reporting framework generally accepted in the other country (and no opinion relative to U.S. GAAP). In the proposed SAS, the concept of limited use has been eliminated. In instances when a report that is to be used in the United States was prepared in accordance with a financial reporting framework generally accepted in another country, the proposed SAS requires the auditor to include an emphasis-of-matter paragraph to highlight the foreign financial reporting framework but permits the auditor to express an unqualified opinion.

The ASB is expected to issue many of the clarified standards in *one* SAS that will be codified in "AU Section" format. The ASB has decided that the effective date of the clarified SASs that have not yet been issued is for audits of financial statements for periods ending on or after December 15, 2012. Auditors should be alert to and monitor further developments in this area.

WHAT EVERY PRACTITIONER SHOULD KNOW

Basic Objectives and Requirements

This Section provides guidance for an auditor on engagements to report on the financial statements of a U.S. entity (i.e., an entity that is either organized or domiciled in the United States) that have been prepared in conformity with accounting principles generally accepted in another country for use outside the U.S.

Before reporting on financial statements prepared in conformity with the accounting principles of another country (herein referred to as "foreign accounting principles"), the auditor should:

1. Have a clear understanding of the purpose and uses of such financial statements, and

2. Obtain written representations from management regarding the purpose and uses of such statements.

Applicable Auditing Standards and Procedures

When auditing the financial statements of a U.S. entity prepared in conformity with foreign accounting principles, the auditor should:

1. Perform the necessary procedures to comply with the general and field-work standards of GAAS in the U.S. ("U.S. GAAS").

2. Modify the auditing procedures generally performed under U.S. GAAS, as necessary, for differences between U.S. GAAP and foreign accounting principles.

3. Obtain an understanding of the foreign accounting principles applicable in the other country by appropriate means such as:

    a. Reading the statutes or professional literature that establish the foreign accounting principles.

    b. Consulting with persons having adequate expertise in the accounting principles of the other country.

    c. Considering the International Accounting Standards established by the International Accounting Standards Committee.

If the auditor is requested to apply the auditing standards of another country, the auditor should:

1. Comply with the general and fieldwork standards of both the foreign country and U.S. GAAS.

2. Read the statutes or professional literature that establish the auditing standards generally accepted in the other country.

3. Consider consulting with persons having adequate expertise in the auditing standards of the other country.

Reporting Standards—Use Only Outside the U.S. or Limited Distribution Within the U.S.

The auditor has the following two options for reporting on financial statements prepared in conformity with foreign accounting principles for use only outside the U.S. or for only limited distribution within the U.S.:

1. A U.S. style report modified to report on the accounting principles of another country; or

2. The report form of the foreign country.

   Limited distribution within the U.S. means distribution of the financial statements to parties (such as banks, institutional investors, and other knowledgeable parties that may choose to rely on the report) within the U.S. that deal directly with the entity to discuss differences from U.S. GAAP.

Modified U.S. style report If this option is used, the auditor's report should include the following:

1. A title that includes the word *independent.*

2. A statement that the financial statements identified in the report were audited.

3. A statement referring to a note to the financial statements that describes the basis of presentation, including the nationality of the accounting principles.

4. A statement that the financial statements are the responsibility of the entity's management and that the auditor's responsibility is to express an opinion on the financial statements based on the audit.

5. A statement that the audit was conducted in accordance with auditing standards generally accepted in the United States of America and, if appropriate, with the auditing standards of the foreign country.

6. A statement that GAAS require that the auditor plan and perform the audit to obtain reasonable assurance about whether the financial statements are free of material misstatement.

7. A statement that an audit includes:

   a. Examination of evidence supporting the amounts and disclosures in the financial statements on a test basis;

   b. Assessment of the accounting principles used and significant estimates made by management; and

   c. Evaluation of the overall financial statement presentation.

8. A statement that the auditor believes that the audit provides a reasonable basis for his or her opinion.

9. An opinion on whether the financial statements are presented fairly, in all material respects, in conformity with the basis of accounting described. If they are not presented fairly, the reasons therefor should be disclosed in a separate paragraph.

10. If the described basis of accounting has not been consistently applied, an explanatory paragraph to that effect.

11. Manual or printed signature of the auditor's firm.

12. Date of the audit report.

See Illustration 1 for an example of such a report.

Foreign country report form The standard audit report of another country may be used if:

1. Such a report would be used by auditors in the foreign country in similar circumstances.

2. The auditor understands, and is in a position to make, the attestations contained in such a report.

3. The auditor identifies the foreign country in his or her report when there is a risk of misunderstanding because the standard report of another country or the financial statements resemble those prepared in conformity with U.S. standards.

When the auditor uses the standard report form of the foreign country, the auditor should:

1. Comply with the reporting standards of the foreign country.

2. Recognize that such standard report may convey a different meaning and entail a different responsibility on the part of the auditor due to custom or culture.

3. Recognize that he or she may be required to provide assurance of statutory compliance or understanding of local law.

4. Understand applicable legal responsibilities.

5. Consider consulting with persons having adequate expertise in the audit reporting practices of the foreign country.

Reporting Standards—Dual Statements

If financial statements are needed for use both in another country and within the United States, the auditor may report on two sets of financial statements for the entity, as follows:

1. One set prepared in conformity with foreign accounting principles for use outside the United States, and

2. Another set prepared in accordance with U.S. GAAP.

In such circumstances, the auditor may wish to include, in one or both reports, a statement that another report has been issued on the financial statements for the entity that have been prepared in accordance with foreign accounting principles. The auditor may also wish to refer to any note that describes significant differences between the foreign accounting principles and U.S. GAAP. The following is an example of such a statement:

> We also have reported separately on the financial statements of International Company for the same period presented in accordance with accounting principles generally accepted in [*name of country*]. (The significant differences between the accounting principles accepted in [*name of country*] and those generally accepted in the United States are summarized in Note [X].)

Reporting Standards—General Distribution in the U.S.

If the auditor is reporting on financial statements prepared in conformity with foreign accounting that will have more than limited distribution in the United States, he or she should use the U.S. standard form of report modified because of departures from U.S. GAAP. The auditor may also express, in a separate paragraph, an opinion on whether the financial statements are presented in conformity with the foreign accounting principles.

The auditor may also report on these financial statements using both (a) the standard report of the foreign country or a modified U.S. style report as discussed above for distribution outside the U.S. and (b) the U.S. standard form of report for distribution inside the U.S.

Financial Statements Prepared in Conformity with IFRS

AU Section 534 provides guidance for U.S. auditors who are engaged to report on the financial statements of a U.S. entity for use outside of the U.S. in conformity with accounting principles generally accepted in another country. Auditing Interpretation No. 2, *Financial Statements Prepared in Conformity with International Financial Reporting Standards as Issued by the International Accounting Standards Board*, of AU Section 534 indicates that the guidance in AU Section 534 does *not* apply to the financial statements of a U.S. entity presented in conformity with International Financial Reporting Standards (IFRS) as issued by the International Accounting Standards Board (IASB). This is because the IASB has been designated by the AICPA Council as the body to establish international financial reporting standards for both private and public entities. Therefore, when engaged to report on the financial statements of a U.S. entity presented in conformity with IFRS as issued by the IASB, the auditor should follow the guidance in AU Section 508 (Reports on Audited Financial Statements).

Reporting considerations when the financial statements are presented in conformity with a jurisdictional variation of IFRS An entity may prepare financial statements in conformity with a jurisdictional variation of IFRS, for example, International Financial Reporting Standards as endorsed by the European Union. Because the AICPA Council has *not* designated bodies other than the IASB to establish international financial reporting standards, in such circumstances the auditor should follow the guidance in AU Section 534 when the financial statements are prepared for use outside the U.S.

When an entity prepares its financial statements in conformity with a jurisdictional variation of IFRS *and* such financial statements are prepared for more than limited distribution in the U.S., the auditing interpretation indicates that the auditor should follow the guidance in paragraphs 14 and 15 of AU Section 534 and paragraphs 35-60 of AU Section 508.

In addition, if financial statements are presented in conformity with *both* IFRS as issued by the IASB and a jurisdictional variation of IFRS, the auditor may follow the guidance in AU Section 508 and its related auditing interpretations.

Financial Statements Audited in Accordance with International Standards on Auditing

There may be circumstances where a U.S. auditor is engaged to perform an audit of a U.S. entity in accordance with the International Standards on Auditing (ISA) whose financial statements are prepared in conformity with IFRS, U.S. GAAP, or accounting principles generally accepted in another country. Auditing Interpretation No. 3, *Financial Statements Audited in Accordance with International Standards on Auditing*, provides the following guidance to U.S. auditors under such circumstances.

Financial statements are for use outside the U.S. A U.S. auditor may be engaged to perform an audit of financial statements of a U.S. entity in accordance with the ISA for use outside the U.S. The financial statements subject to audit may be prepared in conformity with IFRS, U.S. GAAP, or accounting principles generally accepted in another country. In planning and performing such engagements, the auditor should follow the guidance in AU Section 534 and, therefore, comply with the general and fieldwork standards of U.S. GAAS *and* any additional requirements of the ISA. In addition, in such circumstances, the U.S. auditor may use either (1) a U.S. style report, consistent with the provisions of AU Section 534, or (2) the report form set forth in the ISA.

Financial statements are for use in the U.S. A U.S. auditor may be engaged to perform an audit of financial statements of a U.S. entity in accordance with the ISA for use in the U.S. The financial statements subject to audit may be prepared in conformity with IFRS, U.S. GAAP, or accounting principles generally accepted in another country. In such engagements, the auditor should follow the guidance in AU Section 508 (Reports on Audited Financial Statements) and its related interpretations.

PRACTICE ISSUES AND FREQUENTLY ASKED QUESTIONS

Issue 1: What are some situations in which a U.S. entity would prepare its financial statements in accordance with foreign accounting principles?

The following are examples of situations in which a U.S. entity would prepare its financial statements in accordance with foreign accounting principles:

- The financial statements of a U.S. entity are to be consolidated with those of a foreign parent.
- A U.S. entity may have a significant number of foreign investors or creditors.
- A U.S. entity may decide to raise capital in a foreign country.

Issue 2: What are some examples of situations where the auditor may find it necessary to modify the auditing procedures generally performed under U.S. GAAS as a result of differences between U.S. GAAP and foreign accounting principles?

The following are examples of situations where the auditor may find it necessary to modify the auditing procedures generally performed under U.S. GAAS as a result of differences between U.S. GAAP and foreign accounting principles:

- Foreign accounting principles may require that certain assets be revalued to adjust for the effects of inflation; in these circumstances, the auditor should perform procedures to test the revaluation adjustments.

- Foreign accounting principles may not require or allow recognition of deferred income taxes; in these circumstances, procedures for deferred income taxes would not be applicable.

- Foreign accounting principles may not require or allow disclosure of related-party transactions; in such circumstances, procedures for determining that related-party transactions are properly disclosed in the financial statements would not be applicable.

Issue 3: What effect do statements prepared in conformity with International Accounting Standards and audits performed under International Standards on Auditing have on the auditor's responsibilities under this Section?

For purposes of this Section, International Accounting Standards and International Standards on Auditing can be treated the same as GAAP and GAAS from another country.

ILLUSTRATIONS AND PRACTICE AIDS

ILLUSTRATION 1—MODIFIED U.S. STYLE REPORT FOR USE ONLY OUTSIDE THE U.S.

Independent Auditor's Report

Board of Directors and Stockholders
International Company

We have audited the accompanying balance sheet of International Company as of December 31, 20X2, and the related statements of income, retained earnings, and cash flows for the year then ended which, as described in Note [*X*], have been prepared on the basis of accounting principles generally accepted in [*name of country*]. These financial statements are the responsibility of the Company's management. Our responsibility is to express an opinion on these financial statements based on our audit.

We conducted our audit in accordance with auditing standards generally accepted in the United States of America [and in *(name of country)*]. U.S. standards require that we plan and perform the audit to obtain reasonable assurance about whether the financial statements are free of material misstatement. An audit includes examining, on a test basis, evidence supporting the amounts and disclosures in the financial statements. An audit also includes assessing the accounting principles used and significant estimates made by management, as well as evaluating the overall financial statement presentation. We believe that our audit provides a reasonable basis for our opinion.

In our opinion, the financial statements referred to above present fairly, in all material respects, the financial position of International Company as of December 31, 20X2, and the results of its operations and its cash flows for the year then ended in conformity with accounting principles generally accepted in [*name of country*].

[*Signature*]

[*Date*]

AU SECTION 543
PART OF AUDIT PERFORMED BY OTHER INDEPENDENT AUDITORS

PRACTICE POINT: As part of its Clarity Project, the American Institute of Certified Public Accountants' (AICPA's) Auditing Standards Board (ASB) has finalized a clarified Statement on Auditing Standards (SAS) titled, "Special Considerations—Audits of Group Financial Statements (Including the Work of Component Auditors)," which supersedes AU Section 543 (Part of Audit Performed by Other Independent Auditors).

The clarified SAS is significantly broader in scope than AU Section 543. The focus of AU Section 543 is on how to conduct an audit that involves other auditors, while the focus of the clarified SAS is on how to conduct an effective audit of group financial statements. The clarified SAS includes requirements of GAAS established in other SASs that are applied in audits of group financial statements. Extant AU Section 543 does not take into consideration the risk assessment standards. The clarified SAS strengthens existing standards by making it easier for auditors to understand and apply the requirements of GAAS, such as those contained in the risk assessment standards, in the context of an audit of group financial statements.

The ASB is expected to issue many of the clarified standards in *one* SAS that will be codified in "AU Section" format. The ASB has decided that the effective date of the clarified SASs that have not yet been issued is for audits of financial statements for periods ending on or after December 15, 2012. Auditors should be alert to and monitor further developments in this area.

WHAT EVERY PRACTITIONER SHOULD KNOW

Basic Objectives and Requirements

More than one audit firm may participate in an audit of a client. This Section provides guidance to the auditor in deciding:

1. Whether he or she may serve as principal auditor and use the work and reports of other independent auditors who have audited the financial statements of a subsidiary, division, branch, component, or investment included in the financial statements presented; and

2. The form and content of the principal auditor's report in these circumstances.

Deciding Whether to Serve as Principal Auditor

When involved in an audit in which part of the audit has been performed by other auditors, the auditor must first decide whether he or she can serve as principal auditor. In making this decision, the auditor should consider the following factors:

- The materiality of the portions of the financial statements that were audited by the other auditors.

- The extent of his or her knowledge of the overall financial statements.
- The importance of the subsidiaries, divisions, branches, or components that he or she has audited in relation to the reporting entity as a whole.

If the auditor decides that it is appropriate to serve as the principal auditor, he or she must further decide whether to refer to the other auditor in the report or to assume responsibility for the other auditor's work. These considerations are discussed below.

See Illustration 3 for an example of a letter from the principal auditor to the other auditor indicating that reliance will be placed on the other auditor's work and requesting certain information from the other auditor.

Guidance When No Reference to the Other Auditor Is Made

Generally, the principal auditor would decide not to refer to the other auditor under any of the following circumstances:

1. The financial statements audited by the other auditor are immaterial in relation to the consolidated or combined financial statements of the reporting entity covered by the principal auditor's opinion.

2. The other auditor is an associate or correspondent and whose work is acceptable to the principal auditor.

3. The principal auditor engaged the other auditor *and* the other auditor's work was performed under the principal auditor's guidance, control, and supervision.

4. The principal auditor takes necessary steps to be satisfied with respect to the work performed by the other auditor and with respect to the overall reasonableness of the accounts or financial statements of the other component.

If the principal auditor decides to accept responsibility for the other auditor's work, the principal auditor's standard report is issued without modification. In such a case, the principal auditor's report expresses an opinion on the financial statements as if he or she had conducted the entire audit; no reference is made to the other auditor, or the other auditor's work, in the principal auditor's report.

Guidance When Reference to the Other Auditor Is Made

Reference to the other auditor is generally appropriate when the portion of the financial statements audited by the other auditor is material in relation to the whole. (See Illustration 3 for an example of a letter from the principal auditor to the other auditor indicating that reliance will be placed on the other auditor's work and requesting certain information from the other auditor.) Reference to the other auditor by the principal auditor does not constitute a qualification of opinion, but rather a division of responsibility between the two auditors. Therefore, only the report wording, not the opinion, is modified.

The principal auditor's report should clearly indicate the degree of shared responsibility and the portions of the financial statements audited by each.

Therefore, the following modifications should be made to the introductory, scope, and opinion paragraphs:

- *Introductory paragraph*—This paragraph should be modified to identify, preferably by name, the subsidiaries that the principal auditor has not audited. Also, the magnitude of the portion of the financial statements audited by the other auditor should be disclosed; this may be done by indicating dollar amounts or percentages of total assets, total revenues, or other appropriate criteria. In addition, the principal auditor should specify that part of the audit was conducted by another auditor; however, the other auditor need not be, and usually is not, identified by name. The other auditor may be named by the principal auditor only with his or her express permission and provided the other auditor's report is presented together with that of the principal auditor.

- *Scope paragraph*—This paragraph should be modified to indicate that the principal auditor's audit and the report of other auditors provide a reasonable basis for the opinion on the financial statements.

- *Opinion paragraph*—This paragraph is modified to indicate shared responsibility for the audit opinion (i.e., the opinion is based, in part, on the report of the other auditor).

See Illustration 1 for an example of a principal auditor's unqualified report when making reference to the other auditor.

If the other auditor's opinion is qualified, the principal auditor must decide whether the subject of the qualification is material in relation to the financial statements taken as a whole. If it is not, the principal auditor does not need to refer to the qualification in the report. If the principal auditor concludes that the subject of the qualification in the other auditor's report is material, he or she also should qualify his or her opinion. See Illustration 2 for an example of a principal auditor's report that is qualified due to a qualification in the audit report of the other auditor.

If the principal auditor concludes that the report of the other auditor cannot be relied on, a scope limitation exists and a qualified opinion or a disclaimer of opinion, depending on materiality, should be expressed.

Applicable Procedures When Part of the Audit Is Performed by Other Auditors

Regardless of whether the principal auditor decides to refer to the other auditor, the principal auditor should perform the following procedures:

1. Determine the professional reputation and standing of the other auditor (e.g., inquiries of the AICPA, colleagues, and members of the business community).

2. Obtain a representation from the other auditor that he or she is independent of the client.

3. Notify the other auditor that the financial statements of the component that he or she is to audit will be included in the financial statements on which the principal auditor will report.

4. Notify the other auditor that his or her report will be relied on and, if applicable, referred to in the principal auditor's report.

5. Determine whether the other auditor is familiar with U.S. GAAP and GAAS, and that he or she will be using these standards to conduct his or her engagements and to prepare the resulting reports.

6. If applicable, determine whether the other auditor is familiar with SEC reporting requirements and practices.

7. Notify the other auditor that a review will be made of matters affecting elimination of intercompany transactions and accounts and the uniformity of accounting practices among the components included in the consolidated group.

Additional procedures under decision not to make reference to the other auditor When the principal auditor decides not to make reference to the audit of the other auditor, he or she should consider performing, and may find it necessary to perform, in addition to the procedures discussed above, one or more of the following procedures:

- Visit the other auditor and discuss the audit procedures used and the results obtained during the engagement.

- Review the other auditor's audit program and workpapers, including the understanding of the internal control and the assessment of control risk.

- Consider whether instructions should be given to the other auditor regarding the scope of his or her audit work.

- Consider whether to discuss relevant matters directly with the management of the component whose financial statements are being audited by the other auditor.

- Consider whether to apply additional tests or procedures.

Inquiries of the principal auditor by the other auditor Because the other auditor is always responsible for his or her own work and report, the other auditor should also make inquiries of the principal auditor about such significant matters as:

- Related parties.

- Transactions or relationships which are unusual or complex between the component the other auditor is auditing and the component the principal auditor is auditing.

- Transactions, adjustments, or other matters that have come to the principal auditor's attention that he or she believes require adjustment to or disclosure in the financial statements of the component being audited by the other auditor.

- Any relevant limitation on the scope of the audit performed by the principal auditor.

- Any matters or contentious issues that may be significant to the other auditor's audit.

See Illustration 4 for an illustrative inquiry letter from the other auditor to the principal auditor and Illustration 6 for an illustrative response by the principal auditor.

PRACTICE ISSUES AND FREQUENTLY ASKED QUESTIONS

Issue 1: Are there any strict quantitative measures or thresholds for determining whether an auditor should serve as a principal auditor?

No. There are no strict quantitative measures or thresholds for determining whether an auditor should serve as a principal auditor. When making such a decision, the auditor primarily relies on his or her professional judgment as discussed above.

Issue 2: May an auditor report on the financial statements of a consolidated or combined entity even if he or she has not audited every single entity or component that is included in the consolidated or combined financial statements?

Yes. An auditor may report on the financial statements of a consolidated or combined entity, even if he or she has not audited every single entity, branch, or component that is included in the consolidated or combined financial statements. However, if significant parts of the audit have been performed by other auditors, he or she must decide whether he or she can serve as the principal auditor.

Issue 3: Is a principal auditor's report that makes reference to another auditor inferior to a report without such a reference?

No. A principal auditor's report that makes reference to another auditor is not inferior to a report without such a reference. This sharing of responsibility in no way raises questions about the quality of the other auditor's work, nor does it imply less assurance about the reliability of the financial statements. Reference to the other auditor by the principal auditor does not constitute a qualification of opinion, but rather a division of responsibility between the two auditors.

Issue 4: When making reference to the other auditor, is the principal auditor required to identify the other auditor by name?

No. The other auditor need not be, and usually is not, identified by name in the principal auditor's report. The other auditor may be named by the principal auditor only with his or her express permission and provided the other auditor's report is presented together with that of the principal auditor.

Issue 5: When two or more auditors in addition to the principal auditor participate in the audit, is the principal auditor required to state separately the percentages covered by the other auditors?

No. When two or more auditors in addition to the principal auditor participate in the audit, the principal auditor is not required to state separately the percentages covered by the other auditors. The percentages covered by the other auditors may be, and generally are, stated in the aggregate in the principal auditor's report.

Issue 6: If a principal auditor decides to assume responsibility for the work of other auditors, should the principal auditor make reference in the audit report to the work of the other auditors?

No. If a principal auditor decides to assume responsibility for the work of other auditors, the principal auditor should not make reference in the audit report to the work of the other auditors. To do so may cause a reader to misinterpret the degree of responsibility being assumed.

Issue 7: What is the effect on the principal auditor's report if he or she concludes to neither assume responsibility for the work of the other auditors nor accept shared responsibility with the other auditors?

If the principal auditor concludes that he or she can neither assume responsibility for the work of the other auditors nor accept shared responsibility with the other auditors, the principal auditor should issue either a qualified opinion or a disclaimer of opinion on the financial statements taken as a whole. In addition, the principal auditor should state the reasons therefor and disclose the magnitude of the portion of the financial statements to which the qualification or disclaimer applies.

Issue 8: What is the effect on the principal auditor's report if the report of the other auditor is other than an unqualified report?

If the report of the other auditor is other than an unqualified report, the principal auditor should decide whether the reason for the departure from the standard report would require recognition in his or her own report. If the reason for the departure is not material and the other auditor's report is not presented, the principal auditor is not required to make reference in his or her report to such departure. If the other auditor's report is presented, the principal auditor may decide to make reference to such departure and its disposition.

Issue 9: When a principal auditor requests the other auditor to perform certain specific procedures, who is responsible for determining the extent of the procedures to be performed under these circumstances?

When the principal auditor requests the other auditor to perform certain procedures, the principal auditor is responsible for determining the extent of the procedures to be performed. Therefore, the principal auditor should provide specific instructions on (1) the procedures to be performed, (2) materiality considerations, and (3) other information that may be necessary in the circumstances. The other auditor should perform the requested procedures in accordance with the principal's instructions and report the findings solely for the use of the principal auditor.

Issue 10: When a principal auditor's response to the other auditor's inquiry is limited because his or her audit has not progressed to a point that enables a meaningful response, what course of action should the other auditor take?

A principal auditor's response to the other auditor's inquiry may indicate that it is limited because his or her audit has not progressed to a point that enables him or her to provide a response that satisfies the other auditor's need for information. In such circumstances, the other auditor should consider the following courses of action:

1. Apply acceptable alternative procedures.
2. Delay the issuance of the report until the principal auditor can respond.

3. Qualify or disclaim an opinion for a limitation on the scope of the audit.

Issue 11: Should a principal auditor's response to the other auditor's inquiry be written or oral?

A principal auditor's response to inquiries made by the other auditor may be written or oral, as requested by the other auditor. However, the principal auditor's response ordinarily should be in writing if it contains information that may have a significant effect on the other auditor's audit.

Issue 12: How should a principal auditor respond to the other auditor's inquiry?

The principal auditor should identify the stage of completion of his or her audit at the response date, and should indicate that no audit procedures were performed for purposes of identifying matters that would not affect his or her report and, therefore, that all the information requested might not be revealed.

Issue 13: What factors should the principal auditor consider when making a decision about the nature and extent of the additional procedures to be applied concerning the audit performed by the other auditor?

When the principal auditor decides not to make reference to the audit of the other auditor, he or she should consider performing certain additional procedures concerning the audit performed by the other auditor, as discussed in this Section. In making such a decision, the principal auditor should consider the following factors:

- Knowledge obtained of the other auditor's quality control policies and procedures.
- Previous experience with the other auditor.
- The materiality of the portion of the financial statements audited by the other auditor.
- The control exercised by the principal auditor over the other auditor's work.
- The results of the principal auditor's other procedures.

Issue 14: Can an auditor's report indicate a division of responsibility between the auditor and a specialist who was hired by the auditor to evaluate material financial statement assertions?

No. A specialist (e.g., actuary, appraiser, or geologist) is not a certified public accountant and is not in a position to share responsibility for any portion of an opinion on audited financial statements. See AU Section 336 (Using the Work of a Specialist) for evaluating the effect of the work of a specialist on the audit report.

ILLUSTRATIONS AND PRACTICE AIDS

ILLUSTRATION 1—PRINCIPAL AUDITOR'S UNQUALIFIED REPORT WHEN MAKING REFERENCE TO THE OTHER AUDITOR

Independent Auditor's Report

Board of Directors and Stockholders
ABC Company and Subsidiaries

We have audited the consolidated balance sheets of ABC Company and subsidiaries as of December 31, 20X2, and 20X1, and the related consolidated statements of income, retained earnings, and cash flows for the years then ended. These financial statements are the responsibility of the Company's management. Our responsibility is to express an opinion on these financial statements based on our audits. We did not audit the financial statements of DEF Company, a wholly-owned subsidiary, whose statements reflect total assets of $_____ and $_____ as of December 31, 20X2, and 20X1, respectively, and total revenues of $_____ and $_____ for the years then ended. Those statements were audited by other auditors whose report has been furnished to us, and our opinion, insofar as it relates to the amounts included for DEF Company, is based solely on the report of the other auditors.

We conducted our audits in accordance with auditing standards generally accepted in the United States of America. Those standards require that we plan and perform the audit to obtain reasonable assurance about whether the financial statements are free of material misstatement. An audit includes examining, on a test basis, evidence supporting the amounts and disclosures in the financial statements. An audit also includes assessing the accounting principles used and significant estimates made by management, as well as evaluating the overall financial statement presentation. We believe that our audits and the report of the other auditors provide a reasonable basis for our opinion.

In our opinion, based on our audits and the report of the other auditors, the consolidated financial statements referred to above present fairly, in all material respects, the financial position of ABC Company and subsidiaries as of December 31, 20X2, and 20X1, and the results of their operations and their cash flows for the years then ended in conformity with accounting principles generally accepted in the United States of America.

[*Signature*]

[*Date*]

ILLUSTRATION 2—PRINCIPAL AUDITOR'S REPORT QUALIFIED DUE TO A QUALIFICATION IN THE REPORT OF THE OTHER AUDITOR

Independent Auditor's Report

Board of Directors and Stockholders
ABC Company and Subsidiaries

We have audited the consolidated balance sheets of ABC Company and subsidiaries as of December 31, 20X2, and 20X1, and the related consolidated statements of income, retained earnings, and cash flows for the years then ended. These financial statements are the responsibility of the Company's management. Our responsibility is to express an opinion on these financial statements based on our audits. We did not audit the financial statements of DEF Company, a wholly-owned subsidiary, whose statements reflect total assets of $_____ and $_____ as of December 31, 20X2, and 20X1, respectively, and total revenues of $_____ and $_____ for the years then ended. Those statements were audited by other auditors whose report has been furnished to us, and our opinion, insofar as it relates to the amounts included for DEF Company, is based solely on the report of the other auditors.

We conducted our audits in accordance with auditing standards generally accepted in the United States of America. Those standards require that we plan and perform the audit to obtain reasonable assurance about whether the financial statements are free of material misstatement. An audit includes examining, on a test basis, evidence supporting the amounts and disclosures in the financial statements. An audit also includes assessing the accounting principles used and significant estimates made by management, as well as evaluating the overall financial statement presentation. We believe that our audits and the report of the other auditors provide a reasonable basis for our opinion.

The opinion of the other auditors referred to in the first paragraph above was qualified due to [*describe the nature of the qualification and the effects on the consolidated financial statements*].

In our opinion, based on our audits and the report of the other auditors, and except for the effects of [*describe the nature of the qualification*] as described in the preceding paragraph, the consolidated financial statements referred to above present fairly, in all material respects, the financial position of ABC Company and subsidiaries as of December 31, 20X2, and 20X1, and the results of their operations and their cash flows for the years then ended in conformity with accounting principles generally accepted in the United States of America.

[*Signature*]

[*Date*]

ILLUSTRATION 3—LETTER FROM THE PRINCIPAL AUDITOR TO THE OTHER AUDITOR INDICATING RELIANCE WILL BE PLACED ON THE OTHER AUDITOR'S WORK

(*Principal auditor's letterhead*)

To (*Other auditor*):

We are auditing the financial statements of (*client's name*). The financial statements of (*other auditor's client's name*) that you are auditing are to be included in the financial statements of (*client's name*). We will rely on your report on the financial statements in expressing an opinion on the consolidated financial statements of (*client's name*) and subsidiaries. In that connection, we will refer to your report.

Please confirm to us that your firm is independent with respect to (*client's name*) and (*other auditor's client's name*) within the meaning of Rule 101 of the Code of Professional Conduct of the American Institute of Certified Public Accountants.

Please provide us promptly, in writing, with the following information in connection with your current audit of the financial statements of (*other auditor's client's name*) with respect to:

1. Related-party transactions or other matters that have come to your attention. We are aware of the following related parties: (*names of known related parties*).

2. Any limitation on the scope of your audit that is related to the financial statements of (*client's name*), or that limits your ability to respond to this inquiry.

Please update your letter to indicate any additional matters of the type designated above that have come to your attention through the date of your report on the financial statements of (*other auditor's client's name*).

[*Signature of principal auditor*]

ILLUSTRATION 4—INQUIRY LETTER FROM THE OTHER AUDITOR TO THE PRINCIPAL AUDITOR

(*Other auditor's letterhead*)

To (*Principal auditor*):

We are auditing the financial statements of (*name of client*) as of (*date*) and for the (*period of audit*) for the purpose of expressing an opinion as to whether the financial statements present fairly, in all material respects, the financial position, results of operations, and cash flows of *(name of client)* in conformity with accounting principles generally accepted in the United States of America.

A draft of the financial statements referred to above and a draft of our report are enclosed solely to aid you in responding to this inquiry. Please provide us *(in writing/orally)* with the following information in connection with your current audit of the consolidated financial statements of *(name of parent company)*:

1. Transactions or other matters, including adjustments made during consolidation or contemplated at the date of your reply, that have come to your attention that you believe require adjustment to or disclosure in the financial statements of *(name of client)* being audited by us.

2. Any limitation on the scope of your audit that is related to the financial statements of *(name of client)* being audited by us, or that limits your ability to provide us with the information requested in this inquiry.

Please make your response as of a date near *(expected date of the other auditor's report)*.

[*Signature of other auditor*]

ILLUSTRATION 5—PRINCIPAL AUDITOR'S RESPONSE LETTER TO INQUIRIES FROM THE OTHER AUDITOR

(Principal auditor's letterhead)

To *(Other auditor)*:

This letter is furnished to you in response to your request that we provide you with certain information in connection with your audit of the financial statements of *(name of component)*, a *(subsidiary, division, branch or investment)* of Parent Company for the year ended *(date)*.

We are in the process of performing an audit of the consolidated financial statements of Parent Company for the year ended *(date)* [*insert the following, if applicable: "but have not completed our work as of this date"*]. The objective of our audit is to enable us to express an opinion on the consolidated financial statements of Parent Company and, accordingly, we have performed no procedures directed toward identifying matters that would not affect our audit or our report. However, solely for the purpose of responding to your inquiry, we have read the draft of the financial statements of *(name of component)* as of *(date)* and for the *(period of audit)* and the draft of your report on them, included with your inquiry dated *(date of inquiry)*.

Based solely on the work we have performed *(to date)* in connection with our audit of the consolidated financial statements, which would not necessarily reveal all or any of the matters covered in your inquiry, we advise you that:

1. No transactions or other matters, including adjustments made during consolidation or contemplated at this date, have come to our attention that we believe require adjustment to or disclosure in the financial statements of *(name of component)* being audited by you.

2. No limitation has been placed by Parent Company on the scope of our audit that, to our knowledge, is related to the financial statements of *(name of component)* being audited by you, that has limited our ability to provide you with the information requested in your inquiry.

[*Signature of principal auditor*]

AU SECTION 544
LACK OF CONFORMITY WITH GENERALLY ACCEPTED ACCOUNTING PRINCIPLES

PRACTICE POINT: As part of its Clarity Project, the American Institute of Certified Public Accountants' (AICPA's) Auditing Standards Board (ASB) has finalized a clarified Statement on Auditing Standards (SAS) titled, "Special Considerations—Audits of Financial Statements Prepared in Accordance with Special Purpose Frameworks," which supersedes AU Section 544 (Lack of Conformity with Generally Accepted Accounting Principles) and AU Section 623 (Special Reports), except paragraphs 19–21.

The clarified SAS addresses special considerations in the application of the AU sections to an audit of financial statements prepared in accordance with a special purpose framework. Special purpose frameworks are limited to cash, tax, regulatory, or contractual bases of accounting. The cash, tax, and regulatory bases of accounting are commonly referred to as other comprehensive bases of accounting (OCBOA). The term *OCBOA* was replaced with the term *special purpose framework*, which no longer includes a definite set of criteria having substantial support that is applied to all material items appearing in financial statements. Among other matters, the clarified SAS requires:

- The auditor to obtain an understanding of (*a*) the purpose for which the financial statements are prepared, (*b*) the intended users, and (*c*) the steps taken by management to determine that the special purpose framework is acceptable in the circumstances.

- The auditor to obtain the agreement of management that it acknowledges and understands its responsibility to include all informative disclosures that are appropriate for the special purpose framework used to prepare the financial statements, including, but not limited to, additional disclosures beyond those required by the applicable financial reporting framework that may be necessary to achieve fair presentation. The auditor is required to evaluate whether such disclosures are necessary.

- In the case of special purpose financial statements prepared in accordance with a contractual basis of accounting, the auditor to obtain an understanding of any significant interpretations of the contract that management made in the preparation of those financial statements and to evaluate whether the financial statements adequately describe such interpretations.

- When management has a choice of financial reporting frameworks in the preparation of the financial statements, the explanation of management's responsibility for the financial statements in the auditor's report to make reference to management's responsibility for determining that the applicable financial reporting framework is acceptable in the circumstances.

- In the case of financial statements prepared in accordance with a regulatory or contractual basis of accounting, the auditor's report to describe the purpose for which the financial statements are prepared or refer to a note in the special purpose financial statements that contains that information.

- The auditor's report to include an emphasis-of-matter paragraph under an appropriate heading that, among other things, states that the special purpose framework is a basis of accounting other than GAAP.

- The auditor's report to include specific elements if the auditor is required by law or regulation to use a specific layout, form, or wording of the auditor's report.

The ASB is expected to issue many of the clarified standards in *one* SAS that will be codified in "AU Section" format. The ASB has decided that the effective date of the clarified SASs that have not yet been issued is for audits of financial statements for periods ending on or after December 15, 2012. Auditors should be alert to and monitor further developments in this area.

WHAT EVERY PRACTITIONER SHOULD KNOW

Basic Objectives and Requirements

This Section is applicable to audits of regulated companies (e.g., public utilities, insurance companies) when their financial statements are presented for purposes *other than regulatory filings.*

GAAP, which pertain to business enterprises in general, apply also to companies whose accounting practices are prescribed by regulated companies. Therefore, when financial statements of regulated companies are presented for purposes other than regulatory filings, material variances from GAAP and their effects, if they exist, should be addressed in the auditor's report in the same manner followed for entities which are not regulated.

However, appropriate differences do exist between accounting practices for regulated and nonregulated businesses because of the effect in regulated businesses of the rate-making process. Generally, such differences concern primarily the time at which various items enter into the determination of net income in accordance with the principle of matching costs and revenues.

Modifications of the Auditor's Report Due to Departures from GAAP

A regulated entity may prepare its financial statements in accordance with a basis of accounting prescribed by a regulatory agency; and the auditor may be requested to report on their fair presentation in conformity with such prescribed basis of accounting for distribution to parties other than the regulatory agency. In those circumstances, the auditor ordinarily should issue a qualified or an adverse opinion on such statements, due to departures from GAAP. In addition, the auditor should, in an additional paragraph to that report, express an opinion on whether the financial statements are presented in conformity with the prescribed basis of accounting.

PRACTICE ISSUES AND FREQUENTLY ASKED QUESTIONS

Issue 1: May an auditor report on a regulated company's financial statements as being prepared in accordance with a comprehensive basis of accounting other than GAAP?

An auditor may report on a regulated company's financial statements as being prepared in accordance with a comprehensive basis of accounting other than GAAP (OCBOA) *only* if the financial statements are intended solely for filing with the regulatory agency. See AU Section 623 (Special Reports) for additional guidance.

ILLUSTRATIONS AND PRACTICE AIDS

There are no illustrations and practice aids for this Section.

AU SECTION 550
OTHER INFORMATION IN DOCUMENTS CONTAINING
AUDITED FINANCIAL STATEMENTS

PRACTICE POINT: In February 2010, the American Institute of Certified Public Accountants' (AICPA's) Auditing Standards Board (ASB) issued a set of three new Statements on Auditing Standards (SAS) related to: (1) other information in documents containing audited financial statements, (2) supplementary information presented outside the basic financial statements (excluding required supplementary information), and (3) required supplementary information that a designated accounting standard setter requires to accompany an entity's basic financial statements. The three standards are:

1. SAS-118 (AU Section 550) (Other Information in Documents Containing Audited Financial Statements).

2. SAS-119 (AU Section 551) (Supplementary Information in Relation to the Financial Statements as a Whole).

3. SAS-120 (AU Section 558) (Required Supplementary Information).

All three SASs were issued in the clarity format and are effective for audits of financial statements for periods beginning on or after December 15, 2010, with earlier application permitted.

SAS-118 (AU Section 550) supersedes SAS-8 (AU Section 550A), as amended, of the same name and, together with SAS-119 (AU Section 551), also supersedes SAS-29 (AU Section 551A) (Reporting on Information Accompanying the Basic Financial Statements in Auditor-Submitted Documents), as amended.

SAS-118 (AU Section 550) eliminates the distinction between (a) other information that is included in an auditor-submitted document containing the client's basic financial statements and the auditor's report thereon, and (b) other information that is in a client-prepared document. In addition, among other matters, SAS-118 (AU Section 550) establishes presumptively mandatory requirements that the auditor:

- Read the other information in order to identify material inconsistencies with the audited financial statements.

- Make appropriate arrangements with management or those charged with governance to obtain the other information prior to the report release date or, if it is not possible to obtain all of the other information prior to the report release date, that the auditor read such other information as soon as practicable.

- Communicate with those charged with governance the auditor's responsibility about the other information, any procedures performed relating to the other information, and the results.

- Carry out certain specific procedures (e.g., communicate with those charged with governance, modify the auditor's opinion, withhold the auditor's report, and/or withdraw from the engagement) if, prior to the report release date, the auditor identifies a material inconsistency that requires revision of the audited financial statements or the other information and management refuses to make the necessary revision.

- Apply the relevant requirements in AU Section 561 (Subsequent Discovery of Facts Existing at the Date of the Auditor's Report) when the auditor determines that revision of the audited financial statements is necessary as a result of a material inconsistency with other information and the auditor's report on the financial statements has already been released.

- Take appropriate action and carry out the procedures necessary in the circumstances when revision of the other information is necessary after the report release date.

- Communicate with management and, if applicable, request management to consult with a qualified third party (e.g., the entity's legal counsel) if the auditor becomes aware of an apparent material misstatement of fact.

- Notify those charged with governance of the auditor's concerns and take any further appropriate action if the auditor concludes that there is a material misstatement of fact in the other information and management refuses to correct it.

The provisions and requirements of SAS-118 (AU Section 550) are discussed in more detail below.

PRACTICE POINT: In March 2011, the American Institute of Certified Public Accountants' (AICPA's) Auditing Standards Board (ASB) issued an exposure draft (ED) of a proposed Statement on Auditing Standards (SAS) titled, "Omnibus Statement on Auditing Standards—2011." This proposed SAS, which is part of the AICPA's Clarity Project, would amend the following SASs that have been issued in the clarity format and are currently effective:

- SAS-117 (AU Section 801) (Compliance Audits). The amendment to SAS-117 conforms the auditor's report on compliance to the requirements of the clarified SAS, "Forming an Opinion and Reporting on Financial Statements." In addition, the amendment revises the appendix in SAS-117, "AU Sections That Are Not Applicable to Compliance Audits," to reflect conforming changes to affected references to AU Sections as a result of the ASB's Clarity Project.

- SAS-118 (AU Section 550) (Other Information in Documents Containing Audited Financial Statements). The amendment to SAS-118 clarifies the requirements with respect to identified material inconsistencies by categorizing the requirements based on when the inconsistencies are identified (prior to the date of the auditor's report on the audited financial statements; after the date of the auditor's report but prior to the report release date; and after the report release date). It also adds application material addressing electronic sites to include guidance from an interpretation of AU Section 550 (Other Information in Documents Containing Audited Financial Statements), which the ASB determined was appropriate to include in SAS-118.

In addition, in order to address other changes necessitated by the ASB's overall Clarity Project, the proposed SAS would amend the following clarified SASs that have been finalized and released, but not yet issued as authoritative:

- Clarified SAS, "Overall Objectives of the Independent Auditor and the Conduct of an Audit in Accordance with Generally Accepted Auditing Standards."

- Clarified SAS, "Modifications to the Opinion in the Independent Auditor's Report."
- Clarified SAS, "Reports on Application of Requirements of an Applicable Financial Reporting Framework."
- Clarified SAS, "The Auditor's Communication with Those Charged with Governance (Redrafted)".
- Clarified SAS, "Audit Documentation (Redrafted)"

The proposed SAS would be effective for audits of financial statements for periods ending on or after December 15, 2012, except for the amendment to the clarified SAS, "Reports on Application of Requirements of an Applicable Financial Reporting Framework," which would be effective for engagements ending on or after December 15, 2012.

WHAT EVERY PRACTITIONER SHOULD KNOW

Objectives and Scope of AU Section 550

AU Section 550 requires auditors to read the other information in documents containing audited financial statements and the auditor's report thereon ("other information"), and to respond appropriately to inconsistencies in it that may undermine the credibility of the financial statements or the auditor's report. The auditor's opinion on the financial statements does not ordinarily cover such other information, unless there is a separate requirement to do so in the particular engagement. Therefore, the auditor has no responsibility to determine whether such information is properly stated, unless there are other requirements to do so in the circumstances of the particular engagement.

AU Section 550 may also be applied, with such adaptations as are necessary in the circumstances, to other documents to which the auditor, at the request of management, devotes attention. AU Section 550 does not address supplementary information presented outside the basic financial statements or required supplementary information that a designated accounting standard setter requires to accompany an entity's basic financial statements, which are covered in AU Section 551 and AU Section 558, respectively.

Definitions

For purposes of generally accepted auditing standards (GAAS), AU Section 550 establishes the following definitions:

Other information Financial and nonfinancial information (other than the financial statements and auditor's report thereon) that is included in a document that contains audited financial statements and the auditor's report on those financial statements. AU Section 550 specifically excludes from this definition *required supplementary information,* which is information other than the basic financial statements that the Financial Accounting Standards Board (FASB), the Government Accounting Standards Board (GASB), the Federal Accounting Standards Advisory Board (FASAB), or the International Accounting Standards Board (IASB) requires to accompany the basic financial statements.

The application and other explanatory material to AU Section 550 provides the following examples of materials that are included in, or that are excluded from, the definition of *other information*:

Other information includes items, such as:

- Reports on operations by management or those charged with governance.
- Financial summaries or highlights.
- Employment data.
- Planned capital expenditures.
- Financial ratios.
- Names of officers and directors.
- Selected quarterly data.

Other information does not include items such as:

- Press releases, similar memoranda, or cover letters accompanying the document containing the audited financial statements and auditor's report.
- Information included in analyst briefings.
- Information included on the entity's Web site.

OBSERVATION: It is significant that the ASB has eliminated the distinction between (a) other information that is included in an auditor-submitted document that contains the client's basic financial statements and the auditor's report thereon, and (b) other information that is in a client-prepared document. This emphasizes the auditor's responsibility to read other information, whether it is in a document that the auditor submits to the client or bound up with the audited financial statements and auditor's report thereon in a document that the client prepares.

Inconsistency Other information that conflicts with information that is contained in the audited financial statements.

Misstatement of fact Other information (unrelated to matters appearing in the audited financial statements) that is incorrectly stated or presented.

OBSERVATION: For purposes of AU Section 550, the term *documents containing audited financial statements* refers to annual reports or similar documents that are issued to stakeholders and annual reports of governments and not-for-profit organizations that are available to the public that contain audited financial statements and the auditor's report thereon. This designation is intended to apply only for purposes of AU Section 550 and not for GAAS as a whole. For this reason, it is presented in the scope section of the pronouncement, rather than in the definitions section.

The Auditor's Responsibility for Reading Other Information

AU Section 550 requires the auditor to read the other information of which he or she is aware in order to identify material inconsistencies, if any, with the audited financial statements. The auditor should arrange with management or those charged with governance to obtain the other information before the report release date (i.e., the date the auditor grants the entity permission to use the auditor's report in connection with the financial statements). If such other information is not available by that date, the auditor should read it as soon as practicable. The auditor may delay release of the audit report until management furnishes the other information.

AU Section 550 also requires the auditor to communicate with those charged with governance the auditor's responsibility regarding the other information, any procedures performed relating to that information, and the results.

OBSERVATION: These requirements contain practical implications for two important auditor communications: the engagement letter and the communication with those charged with governance under AU Section 380 (The Auditor's Communication with Those Charged with Governance). Essentially, the communication to those charged with governance of the auditor's responsibility under GAAS should also address the auditor's responsibility for other information in documents containing the audited financial statements, any procedures performed relating to that information, and the results obtained.

Effect of Material Inconsistencies

When the auditor identifies a material inconsistency, the auditor should determine whether the audited financial statements or the other information needs to be revised. AU Section 550 discusses this determination at two relevant points in time: when material inconsistencies are identified in other information obtained (1) prior to the release date of the auditor's report, and (2) subsequent to the release date of the auditor's report.

Material inconsistencies identified in other information obtained prior to the release date of the auditor's report Obtaining the other information in advance of the report release date enables the auditor to timely resolve possible material inconsistencies (or misstatements of fact) with management. For example, a material inconsistency exists if the client refers to cash flow from operations as net income.

When material inconsistencies that require revisions to the audited financial statements are identified before the report release date, the auditor should express a modified opinion on the audited financial statements if management declines to make the necessary revisions. When those inconsistencies require revision of the other information, and management declines to make the revision, the auditor should communicate the matter to those charged with governance, and should:

- Include an explanatory paragraph in the auditor's report describing the material inconsistency;

- Withhold the auditor's report; or

- Withdraw from the engagement, when possible under law or regulation.

The auditor may base any decision on further actions to take under these circumstances on advice from the auditor's legal counsel. In some audits of governmental entities, withdrawal from the engagement or withholding the report may not be allowable under law or regulation. In these cases, the auditor may issue a report to those charged with governance and to the appropriate statutory body, if applicable, detailing the inconsistency.

Material inconsistencies identified in other information obtained after the release date of the auditor's report When a revision to the financial statements becomes necessary as a consequence of a material inconsistency with other information, and the auditor's report has already been released, the auditor should refer to and comply with the relevant requirements of AU Section 561 (Subsequent Discovery of Facts Existing at the Date of the Auditor's Report). If management agrees to make the needed revision, the auditor should carry out the procedures necessary in the circumstances. Such procedures may include reviewing the steps that management has taken to make sure that persons who have received the previously issued financial statements, auditor's report, and other information are informed of the need for revision.

When management refuses to make the necessary revision of other information, the auditor should:

- Notify those charged with governance of the auditor's concerns regarding the other information; and

- Take any further appropriate action, which may include obtaining the advice of legal counsel.

Effect of Material Misstatements of Fact

If the auditor becomes aware of an obvious material misstatement of fact while reading the other information, the auditor should discuss the matter with management. This discussion may reveal some disclosures within the other information, or may result in certain management's response to the auditor's inquiries, that the auditor may not be able to evaluate or validate. The auditor may, in these circumstances, reasonably conclude that valid differences of judgment or opinion exist. However, when the auditor considers, following such a discussion, that an obvious misstatement of fact still exists, the auditor should ask management to consult with a qualified third party, such as legal counsel. In such circumstances, the auditor should then consider the advice management received from that third party in determining whether a material misstatement of fact exists.

For example, a material misstatement of fact exists if the client indicates that the entity reached a favorable settlement with the IRS over a pending tax litigation, while in fact it has not.

If management declines to correct a material misstatement of fact in the other information, AU Section 550 indicates that the auditor should:

- Notify those charged with governance of the auditor's concerns regarding the other information; and
- Take any further appropriate action, which may include:
  — Obtaining the advice of legal counsel;
  — Withholding the auditor's report; or
  — Withdrawing from the engagement.

OBSERVATION: The distinction between an inconsistency and a misstatement of fact is important. An *inconsistency* relates to other information that conflicts with information in the audited financial statements. A *misstatement* of fact is not related to matters in the audited financial statements; rather, it is other information that is incorrectly stated or presented. Even though a material misstatement of fact is not directly related to the audited financial statements, it may cast doubt upon the credibility of the document containing the audited financial statements.

Example Explanatory Paragraph That the Auditor May Use to Disclaim an Opinion on Other Information

The application and other explanatory material of AU Section 550 presents the following example of an explanatory paragraph that an auditor may use to disclaim an opinion on other information:

> Our audit was conducted for the purpose of forming an opinion on the basic financial statements as a whole. The [*identify the other information*]is presented for purposes of additional analysis and is not a required part of the basic financial statements. Such information has not been subjected to the auditing procedures applied in the audit of the basic financial statements and, accordingly, we do not express an opinion or provide any assurance on it.

PRACTICE ISSUES AND FREQUENTLY ASKED QUESTIONS

Issue 1: May an auditor express an opinion on other information included in documents containing audited financial statements, based on his reading of such information?

No. The auditor's mere reading of such other information does not provide him or her with an adequate basis for expressing an opinion on that information.

Issue 2: Is the auditor obligated to review press releases or such other forms of financial event releases?

No. The auditor is not obligated to review such dissemination of financial information, unless requested by the client to do so.

Issue 3: What are some examples of other information in documents containing audited financial statements?

- The president's letter in the annual report might read, "Net income increased from $1,275,000 in 20X1 to $2,350,000 in 20X2."
- The vice president of operations might write, "This year's sales increased 36% over the prior year."
- Management's discussion and analysis (MD&A).

- Financial graphs and charts accompanied by explanations.

Issue 4: What are some common procedures that auditors perform when reading other information in documents containing audited financial statements?

Auditors commonly perform the following procedures when reading the other information in documents containing audited financial statements:

- Compare the other information with the audited financial statements.
- Compare the other information with information contained in the working papers.
- Compare the other information with a schedule or report prepared by the client.
- Prove the arithmetic accuracy of the financial information.
- Recompute ratios, such as current ratio or gross profit margin.

Issue 5: What degree of responsibility does the auditor take with respect to other information in documents containing audited financial statements?

An auditor's responsibility for information in a document does not go beyond the financial information identified in his or her report. Professional standards require only that the auditor read the other information in the document and consider whether it is inconsistent with the information in the financial statements. The auditor does not express any opinion or any form of assurance on such other information.

Issue 6: What is the auditor's responsibility with respect to other information included, along with the audited financial statements and the auditor's report thereon, on the client's website?

Electronic sites or venues are considered to be a means of distributing information for purposes of this Section; they are not "other information" as that term is used in this Section. Therefore, the auditor has no responsibility to read or perform any other procedures with respect to other information included in electronic sites. This is true whether such information is included on a client's own website or any other electronic venue, such as an electronic data-gathering, analysis, and retrieval (EDGAR) system or an electronic bulletin board.

ILLUSTRATIONS AND PRACTICE AIDS

There are no illustrations and practice aids for this Section.

AU SECTION 551
SUPPLEMENTARY INFORMATION IN RELATION TO THE
FINANCIAL STATEMENTS AS A WHOLE

> **PRACTICE POINT:** In February 2010, the American Institute of Certified Public Accountants' (AICPA's) Auditing Standards Board (ASB) issued a set of three new Statements on Auditing Standards (SAS) related to: (1) other information in documents containing audited financial statements, (2) supplementary information presented outside the basic financial statements (excluding required supplementary information), and (3) required supplementary information that a designated accounting standard setter requires to accompany an entity's basic financial statements. The three standards are:
>
> 1. SAS-118 (AU Section 550) (Other Information in Documents Containing Audited Financial Statements).
>
> 2. SAS-119 (AU Section 551) (Supplementary Information in Relation to the Financial Statements as a Whole).
>
> 3. SAS-120 (AU Section 558) (Required Supplementary Information).

All three SASs were issued in the clarity format and are effective for audits of financial statements for periods beginning on or after December 15, 2010, with earlier application permitted.

SAS-118 (AU Section 550) supersedes SAS-8 (AU Section 550A), as amended, of the same name and, together with SAS-119 (AU Section 551), supersedes SAS-29 (AU Section 551A) (Reporting on Information Accompanying the Basic Financial Statements in Auditor-Submitted Documents), as amended.

SAS-119 (AU Section 551) defines the term *supplementary information*, and significantly changes existing standards by requiring certain specified procedures, beyond those performed during the audit of financial statements, when auditors report on whether supplementary information is fairly stated in all material respects. It also introduces significant changes to the standard report wording for auditor's reports on supplementary information. In addition, among other matters, SAS-119 (AU Section 551) establishes presumptively mandatory requirements that the auditor:

- Determine that certain specified conditions are met in order to opine on whether supplementary information is fairly stated in relation to the financial statements as a whole.

- Obtain the agreement of management that it acknowledges and understands its responsibility for various matters (e.g., the fair presentation of the supplementary information in accordance with the applicable criteria).

- Perform certain specific procedures (in addition to the procedures performed during the audit of the financial statements) using the same materiality level used in the audit of the financial statements.

- Obtain written representations from management.

- When the audited financial statements are presented with the supplementary information, report on the supplementary information in either (1) an explanatory paragraph following the opinion paragraph in the auditor's report on the financial statements or (2) in a separate report on the financial statements. Either option also requires that the explanatory paragraph or separate report include certain specific elements.

- When the audited financial statements are not presented with the supplementary information, report on the supplementary information in a separate report that includes certain specific elements.

- Refrain from expressing an opinion on supplementary information when the auditor's report on the audited financial statements contains an adverse opinion or a disclaimer of opinion.

- Date the auditor's report on the supplementary information not earlier than the date on which the auditor completed the procedures required under SAS-119 (AU Section 551).

- When the supplementary information is materially misstated in relation to the financial statements as a whole, discuss the matter with management and propose appropriate revision of the supplementary information and, if management does not revise the supplementary information, take prescribed next steps.

The provisions and requirements of SAS-118 (AU Section 550) are discussed in more detail in "AU Section 550: Other Information in Documents Containing Audited Financial Statements" and the provisions and requirements of SAS-119 (AU Section 551) are discussed in more detail below.

WHAT EVERY PRACTITIONER SHOULD KNOW

Objectives and Scope of AU Section 551

When engaged to report on supplementary information in relation to the financial statements as a whole, the auditor's objectives are to:

- Evaluate the presentation of that supplementary information in relation to the financial statements as a whole; and

- Report on whether that supplementary information is fairly stated, in all material respects, in relation to the financial statements as a whole.

The supplementary information subject to this SAS is presented outside the basic financial statements and is not considered necessary for the fair presentation of the basic financial statements in accordance with the applicable financial reporting framework (e.g., GAAP, OCBOA).

PRACTICE POINT: AU Section 551 may also be applied, with appropriate adaptation of the report wording as necessary, when an auditor has been engaged to report on *required supplementary information*, as defined in AU Section 558. AU Section 558 defines *required supplementary information* as information other than the basic financial statements that the Financial Accounting Standards Board (FASB), the Government Accounting Standards Board (GASB), the Federal Accounting Standards Advisory Board (FASAB), or the International Accounting Standards Board (IASB) requires to accompany the basic financial statements.

AU Section 550 addresses *other information* (in documents containing audited financial statements), which it defines as financial and nonfinancial information (other than the financial statements and auditor's report thereon) that is included in a document that contains audited financial statements and the auditor's report on those statements.

AU Sections 550, 551, and 558 do not address engagements to express an opinion on specified elements, accounts or items of financial statements, for the purpose of a separate presentation. Requirements and guidance for such engagements are set forth in AU Section 623 (Special Reports).

Definition of Supplementary Information

AU Section 551 defines supplementary information as information presented outside the basic financial statements, excluding required supplementary information that is not considered necessary in order for the financial statements to be fairly presented in accordance with the applicable financial reporting framework. For purposes of AU Section 551, supplementary information may be presented (1) in a document containing the audited financial statements, or (2) separately from the financial statements.

The application and other explanatory material of AU Section 551 states that supplementary information may be prepared in accordance with an applicable financial reporting framework, regulatory or contractual requirements, other requirements, or management's criteria. Examples of supplementary information include:

- Additional details or explanations of items in or related to the basic financial statements.
- Consolidating information.
- Historical summaries of items extracted from the basic financial statements.
- Statistical data.
- Other material (e.g., material from sources outside the accounting system or entity).

Procedures to Determine Whether Supplementary Information Is Fairly Stated

Preconditions for rendering an opinion on the supplementary information AU Section 551 indicates that, in order to render an opinion on whether supplementary information is fairly stated, in all material respects, in relation to the financial statements as a whole, auditors should determine that all of the following conditions are satisfied:

- The supplementary information was derived from and directly relates to the accounting and other records the entity used to prepare the financial statements;
- The supplementary information relates to the same period as the financial statements;
- The financial statements were audited and the auditor served as the principal auditor;

- Neither an adverse opinion nor a disclaimer of opinion was issued on the financial statements; and

- The supplementary information will accompany the audited financial statements, or the entity will make the audited statements readily available. The application and other explanatory material states that posting the financial statements on the entity's website, or otherwise making them available without further action by the entity, qualifies as making them "readily available." However, if the financial statements are available only upon request, then they would not be considered "readily available."

Obtaining the agreement of management regarding its responsibility AU Section 551 explicitly states that auditors should obtain management's agreement and acknowledgement that it understands its responsibility for:

- Preparing the supplementary information in accordance with the applicable criteria.

- Providing the auditor with certain written representations, as detailed in the section captioned "obtaining written representations from management" below.

- Including the auditor's report on the supplementary information in any document containing such information that indicates that the auditor has reported on it.

- Presenting the supplementary information with the audited financial statements, or making those statements readily available to intended users of the supplementary information no later than the date that the entity issues that supplementary information and the related auditor's report.

PRACTICE POINT: AU Section 551 does not specify the form of this agreement; however, a widely accepted practice is to include it in the engagement letter for the audit.

Performing additional prescribed procedures on the supplementary information In order to render an opinion on whether the supplementary information is fairly stated, the auditor should perform the following procedures, in addition to those performed in the audit of the financial statements:

- Inquire of management about:
  - The purpose of the supplementary information.
  - The criteria management used to prepare the supplementary information (e.g., an applicable financial reporting framework, criteria established by a regulator).
  - Significant assumptions or interpretations underlying the measurement or presentation of the supplementary information.

- Determine whether the supplementary information complies with the applicable criteria in both form and content.

- Obtain an understanding about the methods management used to prepare the supplementary information.

- Determine whether the methods management used to prepare the supplementary information have changed since the prior period and, if so, the reasons for the changes.

- Compare and reconcile the supplementary information to either (1) the financial statements, or (2) the accounting and other records used in preparing those statements. (Note: The auditor may consider materiality in determining which supplementary information to compare and reconcile.)

- Evaluate the appropriateness and completeness of the supplementary information in light of (1) the procedures performed and results obtained, and (2) other knowledge obtained in the audit of the basic financial statements. When performing this evaluation, the auditor may consider testing accounting or other records through observation or examination of source documents or other procedures ordinarily performed in a financial statement audit.

AU Section 551 states that, in performing these additional procedures, the auditor should use the same level of materiality that is used in the audit of the basic financial statements. However, in audits of governmental entities where materiality is considered at the opinion unit level, the auditor's opinion on supplementary information is in relation to the financial statements as a whole. Accordingly, for purposes of AU Section 551, materiality is considered at a level that represents the entire governmental entity in this situation.

The application and other explanatory material to AU Section 551 also points out that auditors are not required to:

- Apply procedures as extensive as would be necessary to express an opinion on stand-alone supplementary information.

- Assess fraud risk for the supplementary information separately from the fraud risk assessment for the basic financial statements.

- Obtain an understanding of internal control with respect to the supplementary information separately from the internal control understanding for the basic financial statements.

Obtaining written representations from management Auditors are required to obtain the following written representations from management:

- Acknowledgement of management's responsibility for the presentation of the supplementary information in accordance with the applicable criteria.

- Management's belief that the supplementary information is fairly presented, both in form and content, in accordance with the applicable criteria.

- That the methods of measurement and presentation of the supplementary information are unchanged from those used in the prior period, or the reasons for any changes.

- Significant assumptions or interpretations underlying the measurement or presentation of the supplementary information.

- In cases when the supplementary information is not presented with the audited financial statements, acknowledgement that management will make the audited financial statements readily available to intended users of the supplementary information no later than the date that such information and the related auditor's report are issued.

Subsequent events AU Section 551 specifically exempts auditors from the responsibility to consider subsequent events with respect to supplementary information. It does, however, require auditors to apply the relevant requirements of AU Section 560 (Subsequent Events), or AU Section 561 (Subsequent Discovery of Facts Existing at the Date of the Auditor's Report), as applicable, when subsequent events come to the auditor's attention that might affect the financial statements.

Reporting on Supplementary Information

Standard report when supplementary information is presented with the audited financial statements When supplementary information is presented with the audited financial statements, the auditor should report on it in either an explanatory paragraph following the opinion paragraph of the independent auditor's report on the financial statements or in a separate report on the supplementary information. That explanatory paragraph or separate report should include statements to the effect that:

- The audit was conducted for the purpose of forming an opinion on the financial statements as a whole.

- The supplementary information is presented for purposes of additional analysis, and is not a required part of the financial statements.

- The supplementary information is management's responsibility.

- The supplementary information was derived from, and relates directly to, the underlying accounting and other records used to prepare the financial statements.

- The supplementary information has been subjected to:

  — The auditing procedures applied in the audit of the financial statements;

  — Certain additional procedures, including comparing and reconciling the supplementary information to (1) the financial statements, or (2) the underlying accounting and other records used to prepare those financial statements; and

  — Other additional procedures.

- In the auditor's opinion, the supplementary information is fairly stated, in all material respects, in relation to the financial statements as a whole, in cases where the auditor has both:

  — Issued an unqualified opinion on the financial statements; and

— Concluded that the supplementary information is fairly stated, in all material respects, in relation to the financial statements as a whole.

Standard report when supplementary information is NOT presented with the audited financial statements A separate report on the supplementary information is required when such information is not presented together with the audited financial statements. That separate report should include, in addition to the items listed in the preceding section, the following elements:

- A reference to the auditor's report on the financial statements.
- The date of the auditor's report on the financial statements.
- The nature of the opinion expressed on the financial statements.
- Any report modifications.

Variations of the standard report When a qualified opinion has been issued on the basic financial statements, and the qualification affects the supplementary information, the explanatory paragraph or separate report pertaining to the supplementary information should also indicate that, except for the effects of the qualification, the supplementary information is fairly stated, in all material respects, in relation to the financial statements as a whole.

When an adverse opinion or a disclaimer of opinion on the audited financial statements has been issued, the auditor is prohibited from expressing an opinion on the supplementary information. In such cases, the auditor may, when permitted by law or regulation, withdraw from the engagement to report on the supplementary information. When the auditor does not withdraw, the report on the supplementary information should state that because of the significance of the matter disclosed in the auditor's report, it is inappropriate to, and the auditor does not, express an opinion on the supplementary information.

Dating of the auditor's separate report on supplementary information When the auditor issues a separate report on the supplementary information, the date of that report should not be earlier than the date on which the auditor (1) obtained the required written representations from management with respect to the supplementary information as discussed above, and (2) completed the procedures described in the preceding section "Performing additional prescribed procedures on the supplementary information."

Restricting the use of the auditor's separate report on supplementary information AU Section 551 does not require auditors to restrict the use of a separate report on supplementary information to specified parties. However, auditors may consider restricting the use of their separate reports on supplementary information to appropriate specified parties under the provisions of AU Section 532 (Restricting the Use of an Auditor's Report) in order to avoid misunderstanding or misinterpretation of supplementary information that is presented separately from the financial statements.

Considerations when the supplementary information is materially misstated When the auditor concludes that the supplementary information is materially misstated in relation to the financial statements as a whole, the auditor should discuss the finding with management and propose appropriate revisions. If management declines to revise the supplementary information, SAS-119 requires the auditor to either:

- Modify the opinion on the supplementary information and describe the misstatement in the auditor's report; or
- Withhold the report on the supplementary information, if a separate report is to be issued.

PRACTICE ISSUES AND FREQUENTLY ASKED QUESTIONS

Issue 1: What are some examples of information that constitutes "supplementary information" as opposed to "basic financial statements" for purposes of AU Section 551?

The following table provides a comparison between information that constitutes "supplementary information" as opposed to information that is considered part of the basic financial statements:

Basic Financial Statements and Information Considered Part of Such Statements	Other Accompanying Information
• Balance sheet • Income statement • Statement of retained earnings • Statement of comprehensive income • Statement of changes in stockholders' equity • Statement of cash flows • Descriptions of accounting policies • Notes to financial statements • Schedules and explanatory material that are identified as being part of the basic financial statements	• Additional details or explanations of items in or related to the basic financial statements (e.g., schedules of costs of goods sold and operating expenses) • Consolidating information • Historical summaries of items extracted from the basic financial statements (e.g., a five-year summary presentation of sales, gross profit, net income, current assets, current liabilities, and stockholders' equity) • Statistical data (e.g., ratios and trends) • Other material, some of which may be from sources outside the accounting system or outside the entity (e.g., industry statistics)

Issue 2: In order to opine on whether supplementary information is fairly stated, in all material respects, in relation to the financial statements as a whole, is the auditor required to apply a different level of materiality than that used in forming an opinion on the basic financial statements?

No. For purposes of opining on whether supplementary information is fairly stated, in all material respects, in relation to the financial statements as a whole, the auditor should perform the necessary procedures using the same materiality level used in the audit of the financial statements. The auditor by no means is required, and need not, apply procedures as extensive as would be necessary to express an opinion on the information taken by itself.

Issue 3: May non-accounting information be included in the supplementary information accompanying the basic financial statements and, if so, what is the auditor's reporting responsibility for such information?

Non-accounting information (e.g., number of units produced related to royalties under a license agreement or number of employees related to a given payroll period) may be included in a document containing the basic financial statements.

Generally, such information would not have been subjected to the auditing procedures applied in the audit of the basic financial statements and, therefore, the auditor would not be able to opine on such information. However, if such information was obtained or derived from accounting records that have been tested by the auditor, the auditor may be in a position to express an opinion on such information in relation to the financial statements as a whole.

Issue 4: When engaged to report on supplementary information in relation to the financial statements as a whole, is the auditor required to obtain a separate understanding of the entity's internal control or to assess fraud risk?

No. When engaged to report on supplementary information in relation to the financial statements as a whole, the auditor is not required to obtain a separate understanding of the entity's internal control or to assess fraud risk.

Issue 5: When supplementary information is presented with the basic financial statements, should the auditor's report on the supplementary information be combined with the report on the basic financial statements or presented separately?

Either presentation is acceptable. The auditor should report on the supplementary information in either (1) an explanatory paragraph following the opinion paragraph in the auditor's report on the financial statements, or (2) in a separate report on the supplementary information.

ILLUSTRATIONS AND PRACTICE AIDS
Examples of Explanatory Paragraph Following the Opinion Paragraph in the Auditor's Report

ILLUSTRATION 1—EXPLANATORY PARAGRAPH FOLLOWING THE OPINION PARAGRAPH IN THE AUDITOR'S REPORT ON THE FINANCIAL STATEMENTS: UNQUALIFIED OPINION ON THE FINANCIAL STATEMENTS AND UNQUALIFIED OPINION ON THE SUPPLEMENTARY INFORMATION

Our audit was conducted for the purpose of forming an opinion on the financial statements as a whole. The [*identify accompanying supplementary information*] is presented for purposes of additional analysis and is not a required part of the financial statements. Such information is the responsibility of management and was derived from and relates directly to the underlying accounting and other records used to prepare the financial statements. The information has been subjected to the auditing procedures applied in the audit of the financial statements and certain additional procedures, including comparing and reconciling such information directly to the underlying accounting and other records used to prepare the financial statements or to the financial statements themselves, and other additional procedures in accordance with auditing standards generally accepted in the United States of America. In our opinion, the information is fairly stated in all material respects in relation to the financial statements as a whole.

ILLUSTRATION 2—EXPLANATORY PARAGRAPH FOLLOWING THE OPINION PARAGRAPH IN THE AUDITOR'S REPORT ON THE FINANCIAL STATEMENTS: QUALIFIED OPINION ON THE FINANCIAL STATEMENTS AND QUALIFIED OPINION ON THE SUPPLEMENTARY INFORMATION

Our audit was conducted for the purpose of forming an opinion on the financial statements as a whole. The [*identify accompanying supplementary information*]is presented for purposes of additional analysis and is not a required part of the financial statements. Such information is the responsibility of management and was derived from and relates directly to the underlying accounting and other records used to prepare the financial statements. The information has been subjected to the auditing procedures applied in the audit of the financial statements and certain additional procedures, including comparing and reconciling such information directly to the underlying accounting and other records used to prepare the financial statements or to the financial statements themselves, and other additional procedures in accordance with auditing standards generally accepted in the United States of America. In our opinion, except for the effect on the supplementary information of [*describe reason for qualification of the auditor's opinion on the financial statements and reference the explanatory paragraph*], the information is fairly stated in all material respects in relation to the financial statements as a whole.

ILLUSTRATION 3—EXPLANATORY PARAGRAPH FOLLOWING THE OPINION PARAGRAPH IN THE AUDITOR'S REPORT ON THE FINANCIAL STATEMENTS: DISCLAIMER OF OPINION ON THE FINANCIAL STATEMENTS

We were engaged for the purpose of forming an opinion on the basic financial statements as a whole. The [*identify accompanying supplementary information*] is presented for purposes of additional analysis and is not a required part of the financial statements. Because of the significance of the matter described above [*the auditor may describe the basis for the disclaimer of opinion*], it is inappropriate to and we do not express an opinion on the supplementary information referred to above.

ILLUSTRATION 4—EXPLANATORY PARAGRAPH FOLLOWING THE OPINION PARAGRAPH IN THE AUDITOR'S REPORT ON THE FINANCIAL STATEMENTS: ADVERSE OPINION ON THE FINANCIAL STATEMENTS

Our audit was conducted for the purpose of forming an opinion on the financial statements as a whole. The [*identify accompanying supplementary information*]is presented for purposes of additional analysis and is not a required part of the financial statements. Because of the significance of the matter described above [*the auditor may describe the basis for the adverse opinion*], it is inappropriate to and we do not express an opinion on the supplementary information referred to above.

Examples of Separate Report on Supplementary Information

ILLUSTRATION 5—SEPARATE REPORT ON SUPPLEMENTARY INFORMATION: UNQUALIFIED OPINION ON THE FINANCIAL STATEMENTS AND UNQUALIFIED OPINION ON THE SUPPLEMENTARY INFORMATION

We have audited the financial statements of ABC Company as of and for the year ended December 31, 20X2, and have issued our report thereon dated [*date of the auditor's report on the financial statements*], which contained an unqualified opinion on those financial statements. Our audit was performed for the purpose of forming an opinion on the financial statements as a whole. The [*identify supplementary information*] is presented for purposes of additional analysis and is not a required part of the financial statements. Such information is the responsibility of management and was derived from and relates directly to the underlying accounting and other records used to prepare the financial statements. The information has been subjected to the auditing procedures applied in the audit of the financial statements and certain additional procedures, including comparing and reconciling such information directly to the underlying accounting and other records used to prepare the financial statements or to the financial statements themselves, and other additional procedures in accordance with auditing standards generally accepted in the United States of America. In our opinion, the information is fairly stated in all material respects in relation to the financial statements as a whole.

ILLUSTRATION 6—SEPARATE REPORT ON SUPPLEMENTARY INFORMATION: QUALIFIED OPINION ON THE FINANCIAL STATEMENTS AND QUALIFIED OPINION ON THE SUPPLEMENTARY INFORMATION

We have audited the financial statements of ABC Company as of and for the year ended December 31, 20X2, and have issued our report thereon dated [*date of the auditor's report on the financial statements, the nature of the opinion expressed on the financial statements, and a description of the report modifications*]. Our audit was performed for the purpose of forming an opinion on the financial statements as a whole. The [*identify supplementary information*]is presented for purposes of additional analysis and is not a required part of the financial statements. Such information is the responsibility of management and was derived from and relates directly to the underlying accounting and other records used to prepare the financial statements. The information has been subjected to the auditing procedures applied in the audit of the financial statements and certain additional procedures, including comparing and reconciling such information directly to the underlying accounting and other records used to prepare the financial statements or to the financial statements themselves, and other additional procedures in accordance with auditing standards generally accepted in the United States of America. In our opinion, except for the effect on the accompanying information of the qualified opinion on the financial statements as described above, the information is fairly stated in all material respects in relation to the financial statements as a whole.

ILLUSTRATION 7—SEPARATE REPORT ON SUPPLEMENTARY INFORMATION: DISCLAIMER OF OPINION ON THE FINANCIAL STATEMENTS

We were engaged to audit the financial statements of ABC Company as of and for the year ended December 31, 20X2, and have issued our report thereon dated [*date of the auditor's report on the financial statements*]. However, the scope of our audit of the financial statements was not sufficient to enable us to express an opinion because [*describe reasons*]and accordingly we did not express an opinion on such financial statements. The [*identify the supplementary information*] is presented for purposes of additional analysis and is not a required part of the basic financial statements. Because of the significance of the matter discussed above, it is inappropriate to and we do not express an opinion on the supplementary information referred to above.

ILLUSTRATION 8—SEPARATE REPORT ON SUPPLEMENTARY INFORMATION: ADVERSE OPINION ON THE FINANCIAL STATEMENTS

We have audited the financial statements of ABC Company as of and for the year ended December 31, 20X2, and have issued our report thereon dated [*date of the auditor's report on the financial statements*], which stated that the financial statements are not presented fairly in accordance with [*identify the applicable financial reporting framework (for example, accounting principles generally accepted in the United States of America [GAAP])*] because [*describe reasons*]. The [*identify the supplementary information*]is presented for purposes of additional analysis and is not a required part of the basic financial statements. Because of the significance of the matter discussed above, it is inappropriate to and we do not express an opinion on the supplementary information referred to above.

AU SECTION 552
REPORTING ON CONDENSED FINANCIAL STATEMENTS AND SELECTED FINANCIAL DATA

PRACTICE POINT: As part of its Clarity Project, the American Institute of Certified Public Accountants' (AICPA's) Auditing Standards Board (ASB) has finalized a clarified Statement on Auditing Standards (SAS) titled, "Engagements to Report on Summary Financial Statements," which supersedes AU Section 552 (Reporting on Condensed Financial Statements and Selected Financial Data). The clarified SAS addresses the auditor's responsibilities when reporting on summary financial statements derived from financial statements audited by that same auditor. Accordingly, an auditor cannot report on summary financial statements unless the auditor has audited the financial statements from which the summary financial statements are derived. Among other matters, the clarified SAS:

- Eliminates reporting on selected financial data.

- Introduces the notion of criteria for preparing summary financial statements and requires the auditor to determine whether the criteria applied by management in the preparation of the summary financial statements are acceptable.

- Requires the auditor to obtain management's agreement that it acknowledges and understands its responsibilities for the summary financial statements, including its responsibility to make the audited financial statements readily available to the intended users of the summary financial statements. Being available upon request is not considered readily available.

- Stipulates specific procedures to be performed as the basis for the auditor's opinion on the summary financial statements.

- Stipulates specific elements of the auditor's report, including management's responsibility and a description of the auditor's procedures.

- Requires the auditor to request management to provide, in the form of a representation letter addressed to the auditor, written representations relating to the summary financial statements.

- Requires, when the auditor has concluded that an unmodified opinion on the summary financial statements is appropriate, the auditor's opinion to state that the summary financial statements are consistent, in all material respects, with the audited financial statements from which they have been derived, in accordance with the applied criteria. (Note: Extant AU Section 552 requires that the auditor's opinion state whether the information set forth in the summary financial statements is fairly presented, in all material respects, in relation to the complete set of financial statements from which it has been derived.)

- Requires, when the auditor's report on the audited financial statements contains an adverse opinion or a disclaimer of opinion, the auditor to withdraw from the engagement, when withdrawal is possible under applicable law or regulation. Otherwise, the auditor is required to state in the report that it is inappropriate to express, and the auditor does not express, an opinion on the summary financial statements.

- Clarifies the auditor's responsibilities related to subsequent events and subsequently discovered facts when the date of the auditor's report on the summary financial statements is later than the date of the auditor's report on the audited financial statements.

- Includes specific requirements relating to comparatives, unaudited information presented with summary financial statements, and other information included in a document containing the summary financial statements and related auditor's report.

- Addresses the auditor's responsibilities as they relate to the auditor's association with summary financial statements.

The ASB is expected to issue many of the clarified standards in *one* SAS that will be codified in "AU Section" format. The ASB has decided that the effective date of the clarified SASs that have not yet been issued is for audits of financial statements for periods ending on or after December 15, 2012. Auditors should be alert to and monitor further developments in this area.

WHAT EVERY PRACTITIONER SHOULD KNOW

Basic Objectives and Requirements

This Section applies when an auditor is engaged to report, in a client-prepared document, on:

1. Condensed financial statements that are derived from audited financial statements of a *public entity* that is required to file, at least annually, complete audited financial statements with a regulatory agency.

2. Selected financial data that are derived from audited financial statements of either *a public or a nonpublic entity* and (a) that are presented in a document that includes audited financial statements or (b) with respect to a public entity that incorporates such statements by reference to information filed with a regulatory agency.

The auditor should follow the guidance in AU Section 551 (Reporting on Information Accompanying the Basic Financial Statements in Auditor-Submitted Documents) when reporting on condensed financial statements or selected financial data that accompany audited financial statements in *auditor-submitted documents*.

Condensed financial statements are presented in considerably less detail than complete financial statements and, therefore, should be read in conjunction with an entity's complete financial statements that include all the disclosures required by GAAP.

Selected financial data include (a) selected components of financial statements (e.g., net sales, total assets) and (b) data calculated from amounts presented in the financial statements (e.g., working capital).

Reporting on Condensed Financial Statements

When the auditor reports on condensed financial statements that are derived from audited financial statements of a *public entity* that he or she has audited, the auditor's report should indicate:

1. That the auditor has audited and expressed an opinion on the complete financial statements.

2. The date of the auditor's report on the complete financial statements.

3. The type of opinion expressed.

4. Whether the information in the condensed financial statements is fairly stated in all material respects in relation to the complete financial statements from which it has been derived.

See Illustration 1 for an example of an auditor's unqualified opinion on condensed financial statements.

If condensed financial statements derived from audited financial statements of a public entity are presented on a comparative basis with interim financial information as of a subsequent date that is accompanied by the auditor's review report, the auditor should report on the condensed financial statements of each period. See Illustration 2 for an example of such report in these circumstances.

Statements made by client in a client-prepared document—condensed financial statements If a client makes a statement in a client-prepared document that identifies the auditor and states that condensed financial statements have been derived from audited financial statements, the auditor is not required to report on the condensed financial statements, provided that they are included in a document that contains audited financial statements (or incorporates such statements by reference). However, if such a statement is made in a client-prepared document of a *public* entity that does not include audited financial statements (or incorporates such statements by reference), the auditor should request that the client either:

1. Delete any reference to the auditor's name from the document, or

2. Include the auditor's report on the condensed financial statements, as discussed above (see Illustration 1).

If the client refuses to comply with either of these options, the auditor should advise the client that he or she does not consent to the use of, or reference to, his or her name. Also, the auditor should consider other appropriate courses of action, including consulting with legal counsel.

If a statement naming the auditor and stating that condensed financial statements have been derived from audited financial statements is made in a client-prepared document that does not include audited financial statements and the client is a *nonpublic* entity, the auditor would ordinarily express an adverse opinion on the condensed financial statements because of inadequate disclosure. See Illustration 3 for an example of an auditor's report on condensed financial statements in such circumstances when the auditor had previously audited and reported on the complete financial statements.

Reporting on Selected Financial Data

When an auditor is engaged to report on selected financial data that are included in a client-prepared document containing audited financial statements (or, with respect to a public entity, that incorporates such statements by reference), his or her report should be limited to data that are derived from audited financial statements. If the selected financial data include both data derived from audited financial statements and other information (e.g., number of employees, square footage of facilities), the auditor's report should specifically identify the data on which he or she is reporting. The auditor's report should indicate:

1. That the auditor has audited and expressed an opinion on the complete financial statements.

2. The type of opinion expressed.

3. Whether the information in the selected financial data is fairly stated in all material respects in relation to the complete financial statements from which it has been derived.

If the selected financial data for any of the years presented are derived from financial statements that were audited by another auditor, the auditor should state that fact and should not express an opinion on that data.

Illustration 4 is an example of an auditor's standard report that includes an additional paragraph reporting on selected financial data.

Statements made by client in a client-prepared document—selected financial data A client may make a statement in a client-prepared document that identifies the auditor and states that the selected financial data are derived from audited financial statements. In such circumstances, the auditor is not required to report on the selected financial data, provided that they are presented in a document that contains audited financial statements (or, with respect to a public entity, that incorporates such statements by reference). However, if such a statement is made in a client-prepared document that does not include audited financial statements (or incorporates such statements by reference), the auditor should either:

1. Ask the client that neither the auditor's name nor reference to him or her be associated with the information, or

2. Disclaim an opinion on the selected financial data and ask the client to include the disclaimer in the document.

If the client refuses to comply with either of these options, the auditor should advise the client that he or she does not consent to the use of, or reference to, his or her name. Also, the auditor should consider other appropriate courses of action, including consulting with legal counsel.

PRACTICE ISSUES AND FREQUENTLY ASKED QUESTIONS

Issue 1: Do condensed financial statements constitute fair and complete presentation of financial position, results of operations, and cash flows in conformity with GAAP?

No. Condensed financial statements do not constitute fair and complete presentation of financial position, results of operations, and cash flows in conformity with GAAP. That is why this Section prescribes more limited auditor reporting for condensed financial statements.

Issue 2: Is the auditor obligated to investigate events that may have occurred during the period between the date of the report on the complete financial statements and the date of the report on the condensed financial statements?

No. The auditor does not have a responsibility to investigate or inquire further into events that may have occurred during the period between the date of the report on the complete financial statements and the date of the report on the condensed financial statements. This is one reason why it is important to refer to the date of the auditor's report on the complete financial statements in the report on the condensed financial statements. However, if the condensed financial statements are part of a filing under federal securities statutes, see AU Section 711 (Filings under Federal Securities Statutes).

Issue 3: What is the effect on the auditor's report on condensed financial statements or selected financial data when the auditor's report on the complete financial statements was other than unqualified?

If the auditor's report on the complete financial statements was other than unqualified, the auditor's report on the condensed financial statements or selected financial data should describe the nature of, and the reasons for, the qualification. Also, if the auditor's report on the complete financial statements referred to another auditor, the report on the condensed financial statements or selected financial data should state that fact. However, no reference to lack of consistency is necessary if a change in accounting referred to in the auditor's report on the complete financial statements does not materially affect the comparability of the information being presented.

Issue 4: Is selected financial data a required part of the basic financial statements that should be audited?

No. Selected financial data is not a required part of the basic financial statements and is not required to be audited.

Issue 5: Is it required to have the condensed financial statements marked "condensed?"

No. However, in practice condensed financial statements are clearly marked "condensed."

Issue 6: How does an auditor report in situations where a client is required by the SEC to include, as a supplementary schedule to the consolidated financial statements in its filings, condensed financial information of the parent company?

Because the condensed financial information of the parent company is presented as supplementary information, the auditor should report on such condensed financial information in the same manner as other supplementary schedules, as discussed in AU Section 551 (Reporting on Information Accompanying the Basic Financial Statements in Auditor-Submitted Documents).

Issue 7: What should the report date be when the auditor is reporting on condensed financial statements or selected financial data?

This Section is silent on this issue. With respect to condensed financial statements, there is a presumption that the report date should be the same as the original report date on the complete financial statements. This is important because condensed financial statements are derived from audited financial statements and the auditor should remove any implication that he or she audited records, transactions, or events after that date. With respect to selected financial data, dating the report is generally not an issue because reporting on selected financial data is ordinarily included as a separate paragraph in the auditor's standard report.

ILLUSTRATIONS AND PRACTICE AIDS

ILLUSTRATION 1—AUDITOR'S UNQUALIFIED OPINION ON CONDENSED FINANCIAL STATEMENTS

Independent Auditor's Report

Board of Directors and Stockholders
ABC Company

We have audited, in accordance with auditing standards generally accepted in the United States of America, the consolidated balance sheet of ABC Company and subsidiaries as of December 31, 20X2, and the related consolidated statements of income, retained earnings, and cash flows for the year then ended (not presented herein); and in our report dated February 11, 20X3, we expressed an unqualified opinion on those consolidated financial statements.

In our opinion, the information set forth in the accompanying condensed consolidated financial statements is fairly stated, in all material respects, in relation to the consolidated financial statements from which it has been derived.

[*Signature*]

[*Date*]

ILLUSTRATION 2—REVIEW REPORT ON CONDENSED FINANCIAL STATEMENTS

Note: *This illustration assumes a presentation of a condensed balance sheet as of March 31, 20X2, and the related condensed statements of income and cash flows for the three-month periods ended March 31, 20X2, and 20X1, together with a report on a condensed balance sheet derived from audited financial statements as of December 31, 20X1.*

Independent Auditor's Report

Board of Directors and Stockholders
ABC Company

We have reviewed the condensed consolidated balance sheet of ABC Company and subsidiaries as of March 31, 20X2, and the related condensed consolidated statements of income and cash flows for the three-month periods ended March 31, 20X2, and 20X1. These financial statements are the responsibility of the Company's management.

We conducted our review in accordance with standards established by the American Institute of Certified Public Accountants. A review of interim financial information consists principally of applying analytical procedures to financial data and making inquiries of persons responsible for financial and accounting matters. It is substantially less in scope than an audit conducted in accordance with generally accepted auditing standards, the objective of which is the expression of an opinion regarding the financial statements taken as a whole. Accordingly, we do not express such an opinion.

Based on our review, we are not aware of any material modifications that should be made to the condensed consolidated financial statements referred to above for them to be in conformity with generally accepted accounting principles.

We have previously audited, in accordance with auditing standards generally accepted in the United States of America, the consolidated balance sheet as of December 31, 20X1, and the related consolidated statements of income, retained earnings, and cash flows for the year then ended (not presented herein); and in our report dated February 11, 20X2, we expressed an unqualified opinion on those consolidated financial statements. In our opinion, the information set forth in the accompanying condensed consolidated balance sheet as of December 31, 20X1, is fairly stated, in all material respects, in relation to the consolidated balance sheet from which it has been derived.

[*Signature*]

[*Date*]

ILLUSTRATION 3—AUDITOR'S ADVERSE OPINION ON CONDENSED FINANCIAL STATEMENTS DUE TO INADEQUATE DISCLOSURE

Independent Auditor's Report

Board of Directors and Stockholders
ABC Company

We have audited the consolidated balance sheet of ABC Company and subsidiaries as of December 31, 20X2, and the related consolidated statements of income, retained earnings, and cash flows for the year then ended (not presented herein). These financial statements are the responsibility of the Company's management. Our responsibility is to express an opinion on these financial statements based on our audit.

We conducted our audit in accordance with auditing standards generally accepted in the United States of America. Those standards require that we plan and perform the audit to obtain reasonable assurance about whether the financial statements are free of material misstatement. An audit includes examining, on a test basis, evidence supporting the amounts and disclosures in the financial statements. An audit also includes assessing the accounting principles used and significant estimates made by management, as well as evaluating the overall financial statement presentation. We believe that our audit provides a reasonable basis for our opinion.

The condensed consolidated balance sheet as of December 31, 20X2, and the related condensed statements of income, retained earnings, and cash flows for the year then ended, presented on pages X–Y, are presented as a summary and therefore do not include all of the disclosures required by accounting principles generally accepted in the United States of America.

In our opinion, because of the significance of the omission of the information referred to in the preceding paragraph, the condensed consolidated financial statements referred to above do not present fairly, in conformity with accounting principles generally accepted in the United States of America, the financial position of ABC Company and subsidiaries as of December 31, 20X2, or the results of its operations or its cash flows for the year then ended.

[*Signature*]

[*Date*]

ILLUSTRATION 4—AUDITOR'S STANDARD REPORT INCLUDES REPORTING ON SELECTED FINANCIAL DATA

Independent Auditor's Report

Board of Directors and Stockholders
ABC Company

We have audited the consolidated balance sheets of ABC Company and subsidiaries as of December 31, 20X5, and 20X4, and the related consolidated statements of income, retained earnings, and cash flows for each of the three years in the period ended December 31, 20X5. These financial statements are the responsibility of the Company's management. Our responsibility is to express an opinion on these financial statements based on our audits.

We conducted our audits in accordance with auditing standards generally accepted in the United States of America. Those standards require that we plan and perform the audit to obtain reasonable assurance about whether the financial statements are free of material misstatement. An audit includes examining, on a test basis, evidence supporting the amounts and disclosures in the financial statements. An audit also includes assessing the accounting principles used and significant estimates made by management, as well as evaluating the overall financial statement presentation. We believe that our audits provided a reasonable basis for our opinion.

In our opinion, the consolidated financial statements referred to above present fairly, in all material respects, the financial position of ABC Company and subsidiaries as of December 31, 20X5, and 20X4, and the results of their operations and their cash flows for each of the three years in the period ended December 31, 20X5, in conformity with accounting principles generally accepted in the United States of America.

We have also previously audited, in accordance with auditing standards generally accepted in the United States of America, the consolidated balance sheets as of December 31, 20X3, 20X2, and 20X1, and the related statements of income, retained earnings, and cash flows for the years ended December 31, 20X2, and 20X1 (none of which are presented herein); and we expressed unqualified opinions on those consolidated financial statements. In our opinion, the information set forth in the selected financial data for each of the five years in the period ended December 31, 20X5, appearing on page X, is fairly stated, in all material respects, in relation to the consolidated financial statements from which it has been derived.

[*Signature*]

[*Date*]

AU SECTION 558
REQUIRED SUPPLEMENTARY INFORMATION

PRACTICE POINT: In February 2010, the American Institute of Certified Public Accountants' (AICPA's) Auditing Standards Board (ASB) issued a set of three new Statements on Auditing Standards (SAS) related to: (1) other information in documents containing audited financial statements, (2) supplementary information presented outside the basic financial statements (excluding required supplementary information), and (3) required supplementary information that a designated accounting standard setter requires to accompany an entity's basic financial statements. The three standards are:

1. SAS-118 (AU Section 550) (Other Information in Documents Containing Audited Financial Statements).

2. SAS-119 (AU Section 551) (Supplementary Information in Relation to the Financial Statements as a Whole).

3. SAS-120 (AU Section 558) (Required Supplementary Information).

All three SASs were issued in the clarity format and are effective for audits of financial statements for periods beginning on or after December 15, 2010, with earlier application permitted.

SAS-120 (AU Section 558) supersedes AU Section 558A (Required Supplementary Information). The most significant change that SAS-120 (AU Section 558) introduces to previous standards is the requirement that auditors place an explanatory paragraph in their independent auditors' reports on the entity's basic financial statements in all cases in which required supplementary information is presented. Under previous standards, an explanatory paragraph was required only when departures from standards were present, such as: (1) the omission of some or all of the required supplementary information, (2) the inability of the auditor to apply certain limited procedures, (3) material departures from prescribed guidelines for measuring or presenting the required supplementary information, or (4) unresolved doubts about that information.

Among other matters, SAS-120 (AU Section 558) establishes presumptively mandatory requirements that the auditor:

- Inquire of management about the methods of preparing the required supplementary information.

- Compare the required supplementary information for consistency with (1) management's responses to the auditor's inquires, (2) the basic financial statements, and (3) other knowledge obtained during the audit of the basic financial statements.

- Obtain written representations from management.

- Consider whether management contributed to the auditor's inability to complete certain specified procedures, if the auditor is unable to apply those procedures.

- Inform those charged with governance if the auditor concludes that the inability to complete the specified procedures was due to significant difficulties encountered in dealing with management.

- Include an explanatory paragraph (after the opinion paragraph) in the auditor's report on the financial statements to refer to the required supplementary information and to explain certain specific circumstances.

The provisions and requirements of SAS-120 (AU Section 558) are discussed in more detail below.

WHAT EVERY PRACTITIONER SHOULD KNOW

Objectives and Scope of AU Section 558

AU Section 558 addresses the auditor's responsibility with respect to information that a designated accounting standard setter requires to accompany an entity's basic financial statements ("required supplementary information"). It establishes the auditor's objectives when a designated accounting standard setter requires information to accompany an entity's basic financial statements. Those objectives essentially pertain to performing procedures in order to enable the auditor to accomplish the following:

- Describe in the auditor's report whether that required supplementary information is presented.

- Communicate in the auditor's report when some or all of the required supplementary information has not been presented in accordance with guidelines established by the designated accounting standard setter.

- Communicate in the auditor's report when the auditor has identified material modifications that should be made to the required supplementary information in order for such information to be in accordance with guidelines established by the designated accounting standard setter.

PRACTICE POINT: AU Section 558 does not cover the auditor's responsibility for financial and nonfinancial information that is not required by a designated accounting standard setter, but which is included in a document containing audited financial statements and the auditor's report thereon. This subject is covered in AU Section 550. In addition, AU Section 558 does not cover traditional supplementary information that is related to, or derived from, the basic financial statements (e.g., detailed schedules supporting line items in the basic financial statements); rather, AU Section 551 addresses such reporting circumstances.

Definitions

AU Section 558 establishes the following definitions:

Required supplementary information Information that a designated accounting standard setter requires to accompany an entity's basic financial statements. Required supplementary information is not part of the basic financial statements; however, it is information that a designated accounting standard setter considers to be an essential part of financial reporting and for which authoritative guidelines for measuring and presenting the information have been established.

Designated accounting standard setter A body designated by the AICPA council to establish professional standards for financial accounting and reporting principles pursuant to Rule 202 (ET Section 202), Compliance with Standards, and Rule 203 (ET Section 203), Accounting Principles. The bodies so designated are:

- The Financial Accounting Standards Board (FASB);

- The Governmental Accounting Standards Board (GASB);

- The Federal Accounting Standards Advisory Board (FASAB); and

- The International Accounting Standards Board (IASB).

Basic financial statements Financial statements presented in accordance with an applicable financial reporting framework as established by a designated accounting standard setter, excluding required supplementary information.

Applicable financial reporting framework The financial reporting framework (e.g., GAAP, OCBOA, IFRS) that is (1) adopted by management or those charged with governance, or (2) required by law or regulation. For practical purposes, this term equates to the more familiar term, "basis of accounting."

Prescribed guidelines Authoritative guidelines that a designated accounting standard setter has established for measuring and presenting the required supplementary information.

Procedures for Required Supplementary Information

AU Section 558 establishes a presumptively mandatory requirement that the auditor (1) inquire of management about the methods of preparing the required supplementary information, (2) compare the required supplementary information for consistency, and (3) obtain written representations from management. These requirements are addressed in more detail in the following sections.

Inquiries of management Auditors should inquire of management about the methods of preparing the required supplementary information, including whether:

- The required supplementary information has been measured and presented in accordance with the prescribed guidelines;

- The methods of measurement or presentation have changed since the prior period and the reasons for such changes, if any; and

- There were any significant assumptions or interpretations underlying the measurement or presentation of the required supplementary information.

Comparison of information for consistency Auditors should compare the required supplementary information for consistency with:

- Management's responses to the auditor's inquiries described in the preceding section;

- The basic financial statements; and

- Other knowledge the auditor has obtained during the audit of the basic financial statements.

Management representations AU Section 558 explicitly states that auditors should obtain written representations from management covering the following matters:

- Management's acknowledgement of its responsibility for the required supplementary information;

- Whether the required supplementary information is measured and presented in accordance with prescribed guidelines;

- Whether the methods of measurement or presentation have changed since the prior period and the reasons for such changes, if any; and

- Any significant assumptions or interpretations underlying the measurement or presentation of the information.

PRACTICE POINT: These representations would ordinarily be obtained as a part of the written representations from management covering the audit of the basic financial statements.

Communication with those charged with governance When the auditor encounters significant difficulties in dealing with management that result in an inability to complete any of the required procedures, the auditor should inform those charged with governance as required by AU Section 380 (The Auditor's Communication with Those Charged with Governance).

Reporting on Required Supplementary Information

AU Section 558 establishes a presumptively mandatory requirement that the auditor (1) include an explanatory paragraph in the auditor's report on the basic financial statements to refer to the required supplementary information, and (2) position the explanatory paragraph after the opinion paragraph. This requirement is applicable for all circumstances when the auditor is reporting on required supplementary information; however, the elements or language that should be included in the explanatory paragraph vary depending on the various circumstances as discussed in the following sections.

Standard explanatory paragraph on required supplementary information (see Illustration 1) The standard explanatory paragraph is appropriate when all of the required supplementary information is included, the auditor has applied the procedures specified in AU Section 558, and no material departures from the prescribed guidelines have been identified. In such circumstances, the standard explanatory paragraph should include a statement that:

- Identifies the applicable financial reporting framework (e.g., GAAP) calling for the required supplementary information to be presented to supplement the basic financial statements.

- Identifies the required supplementary information.

- Indicates that the required supplementary information is not a part of the basic financial statements.

- Identifies the designated accounting standard setter (e.g., FASB, GASB) requiring the information and who considers it to be an essential part of financial reporting for placing the basic financial statements in an appropriate operational, economic, or historical context.

- Indicates that the auditor has applied certain limited procedures to the required supplementary information, in accordance with auditing standards generally accepted in the United States of America, which consisted of inquiries of management and comparing the information for consistency.

- Indicates that the auditor does not express an opinion or provide any assurance on the information.

PRACTICE POINT: This reporting requirement represents a significant change to previous standards. Under those standards, auditors were not required to add such an explanatory paragraph unless there were circumstances, such as discussed in the following sections that would have led to a modified report on the required supplementary information. There was no requirement for an explanatory paragraph otherwise.

According to the application and other explanatory material of AU Section 558, a discussion of the responsibility taken by the auditor for required supplementary information is included in the auditor's report because that information accompanies the basic financial statements. However, the required supplementary information is not a part of the basic financial statements. Therefore, the required supplementary information does not affect the auditor's opinion on the basic financial statements, even if it is omitted in whole or in part. Furthermore, the auditor has no obligation to present such information if the entity chooses to omit it.

PRACTICE POINT: There is no provision for a separate auditor's report on required supplementary information because such information would never be presented apart from the basic financial statements.

Explanatory paragraph language when all the required supplementary information is omitted (see Illustration 2) When all of the required supplementary information is omitted, the explanatory paragraph should include a statement that:

- Indicates that management has omitted the required supplementary information.

- Provides a description of the missing required supplementary information.

- Identifies the applicable financial reporting framework (e.g., GAAP) calling for the required supplementary information to be presented to supplement the basic financial statements.

- Indicates that the missing information is not a part of the basic financial statements.

- Identifies the designated accounting standard setter (e.g., FASB, GASB) requiring the missing information and who considers it to be an essential part of financial reporting for placing the basic financial statements in an appropriate operational, economic, or historical context.

- Indicates that the auditor's opinion on the basic financial statements is not affected by the missing information.

Explanatory paragraph language when some required supplementary information is omitted and some is presented in accordance with prescribed guidelines (see Illustration 3) When some of the required supplementary information is omitted and some is presented in accordance with prescribed guidelines, the explanatory paragraph should include a combination of the elements discussed in the preceding two sections.

Explanatory paragraph language when the auditor has identified material departures from the prescribed guidelines (see Illustration 4) If the measurement or presentation of the required supplementary information departs materially from the prescribed guidelines, the explanatory paragraph should include a statement that:

- Identifies the applicable financial reporting framework (e.g., GAAP) calling for the required supplementary information to be presented to supplement the basic financial statements.

- Identifies the required supplementary information.

- Indicates that the required supplementary information is not a part of the basic financial statements.

- Identifies the designated accounting standard setter (e.g., FASB, GASB) requiring the information and who considers it to be an essential part of financial reporting for placing the basic financial statements in an appropriate operational, economic, or historical context.

- Indicates that the auditor has applied certain limited procedures to the required supplementary information, in accordance with auditing standards generally accepted in the United States of America, which consisted of inquiries of management and comparing the information for consistency.

- Indicates that, although the auditor's opinion on the basic financial statements is not affected, material departures from the prescribed guidelines exist.

- Includes a description of those material departures from the prescribed guidelines.

- Indicates that the auditor does not express an opinion or provide any assurance on the information.

Explanatory paragraph language when the auditor is unable to complete the specific procedures prescribed in AU Section 558 (see Illustration 5) If the auditor is not able to complete the specific procedures required in AU Section 558, the explanatory paragraph should include a statement that:

- Identifies the applicable financial reporting framework (e.g., GAAP) calling for the required supplementary information to be presented to supplement the basic financial statements.
- Identifies the required supplementary information.
- Indicates that the required supplementary information is not a part of the basic financial statements.
- Identifies the designated accounting standard setter (e.g., FASB, GASB) requiring the information and who considers it to be an essential part of financial reporting for placing the basic financial statements in an appropriate operational, economic, or historical context.
- Indicates that the auditor was unable to apply certain limited procedures to the required supplementary information in accordance with auditing standards generally accepted in the United States of America.
- States the reasons for the auditor's inability to apply those procedures.
- Indicates that the auditor does not express an opinion or provide any assurance on the information.

Explanatory paragraph language when the auditor has unresolved doubts about whether the required supplementary information is measured or presented in accordance with the prescribed guidelines (see Illustration 6) If the auditor has unresolved doubts about whether the required supplementary information is measured or presented in accordance with the prescribed guidelines, the explanatory paragraph should include a statement that:

- Identifies the applicable financial reporting framework (e.g., GAAP) calling for the required supplementary information to be presented to supplement the basic financial statements.
- Identifies the required supplementary information.
- Indicates that the required supplementary information is not a part of the basic financial statements.
- Identifies the designated accounting standard setter (e.g., FASB, GASB) requiring the information and who considers it to be an essential part of financial reporting for placing the basic financial statements in an appropriate operational, economic, or historical context.
- Indicates that the auditor has applied certain limited procedures to the required supplementary information, in accordance with auditing standards generally accepted in the United States of America, which consisted of inquiries of management and comparing the information for consistency.
- Indicates that the auditor does not express an opinion or provide any assurance on the information.
- Indicates that, although the auditor's opinion on the basic financial statements is not affected, the results of the limited procedures have raised doubts about whether material modifications should be made to the

required supplementary information in order for it to be presented in accordance with the prescribed guidelines established by the applicable accounting standard setter.

PRACTICE POINT: The auditor may (but is not required to) include in the report the reasons he or she was unable to resolve his or her doubts.

PRACTICE ISSUES AND FREQUENTLY ASKED QUESTIONS

Issue 1: Do the provisions of AU Section 558 apply if an entity presents a supplementary schedule of cost of sales with its basic financial statements?

No. AU Section 558 deals strictly with supplementary information that a designated accounting standard setter (e.g., FASB, GASB, FASAB, or IASB) requires to accompany an entity's basic financial statements. Neither GAAP nor any of these accounting standard setters require the supplementary schedule of cost of sales that is commonly included with information accompanying the basic financial statements. Reporting on information such as the supplementary schedule of cost of sales is covered in AU Section 551 (Supplementary Information in Relation to the Financial Statements as a Whole).

Issue 2: How does "required supplementary information," as the term is used in AU Section 558, differ from other types of supplementary information?

In order to fall within the scope of AU Section 558, a designated accounting standard setter (e.g., FASB, GASB, FASAB, or IASB) must consider the information to be an essential part of financial reporting for placing the basic financial statements in an appropriate operational, economic, or historical context. In addition, authoritative guidelines for the methods of measurement and presentation of the information must have been established. Information that does not meet both of these criteria does not come within the purview of AU Section 558.

Issue 3: Is the auditor obligated to audit supplementary information required by the FASB, GASB, FASAB, or IASB?

No. Generally, an auditor is under no obligation to audit information that is not a part of the basic financial statements, unless he or she is engaged to do so. However, in the case of supplementary information required by the FASB, GASB, FASAB, or IASB, the auditor should apply certain limited procedures to the information. As discussed above, such procedures generally consist of (1) inquiries of management, (2) comparisons directed toward assessing the information's consistency, and (3) obtaining written representations from management.

Issue 4: If a client declines to present certain supplementary information required by the FASB, GASB, FASAB, or IASB, is the auditor obligated to prepare such information for the client?

No. Just as with basic financial statements, an auditor is not required to prepare on the client's behalf any data that the client chooses not to prepare. However, as a practical matter, auditors often assist clients in preparing such data, and may, by agreement, prepare that data for the client. It is important in such a case that management take responsibility for the data.

ILLUSTRATIONS AND PRACTICE AIDS

ILLUSTRATION 1—EXPLANATORY PARAGRAPH WHEN THE RE-QUIRED SUPPLEMENTARY INFORMATION IS INCLUDED, THE AUDI-TOR HAS APPLIED THE SPECIFIED PROCEDURES, AND NO MATERIAL DEPARTURES FROM PRESCRIBED GUIDELINES HAVE BEEN IDENTIFIED

[*Identify the applicable financial reporting framework (e.g., accounting principles generally accepted in the United States of America)*] require that the [*identify the required supplementary information*] on page XX be presented to supplement the basic financial statements. Such information, although not a part of the basic financial statements, is required by [*identify designated accounting standard setter*] who considers it to be an essential part of financial reporting for placing the basic financial statements in an appropriate operational, economic, or historical context. We have applied certain limited procedures to the required supplementary information in accordance with auditing standards generally accepted in the United States of America, which consisted of inquiries of management about the methods of preparing the information and comparing the information for consistency with management's responses to our inquiries, the basic financial statements, and other knowledge we obtained during our audit of the basic financial statements. We do not express an opinion or provide any assurance on the information because the limited procedures do not provide us with sufficient evidence to express an opinion or provide any assurance.

ILLUSTRATION 2—EXPLANATORY PARAGRAPH WHEN ALL THE RE-QUIRED SUPPLEMENTARY INFORMATION IS OMITTED

Management has omitted [*describe the missing required supplementary information*] that [*identify the applicable financial reporting framework (e.g., accounting principles generally accepted in the United States of America)*] require to be presented to supplement the basic financial statements. Such missing information, although not a part of the basic financial statements, is required by [*identify designated accounting standard setter*] who considers it to be an essential part of financial reporting for placing the basic financial statements in an appropriate operational, economic, or historical context. Our opinion on the basic financial statements is not affected by this missing information.

ILLUSTRATION 3—EXPLANATORY PARAGRAPH WHEN SOME RE-QUIRED SUPPLEMENTARY INFORMATION IS OMITTED AND SOME IS PRESENTED IN ACCORDANCE WITH PRESCRIBED GUIDELINES

[*Identify the applicable financial reporting framework (e.g., accounting principles generally accepted in the United States of America)*] require that [*identify the included required supplementary information*] be presented to supplement the basic financial statements. Such information, although not a part of the basic financial statements, is required by [*identify designated accounting standard setter*] who considers it to be an essential part of financial reporting for placing the basic financial statements in an appropriate operational, economic, or historical context. We have applied certain limited procedures to the required supplementary information in accordance with auditing standards generally accepted in the United States of America, which consisted of inquiries of management about the methods of preparing the information and comparing the information for consistency with management's responses to our inquiries, the basic financial statements, and other knowledge we obtained during our audit of the basic financial statements. We do not express an opinion or provide any assurance on the information because the limited procedures do not provide us with evidence sufficient to express an opinion or provide any assurance.

Management has omitted [*describe the missing required supplementary information*] that [*identify the applicable financial reporting framework*] require to be presented to supplement the basic financial statements. Such missing information, although not a part of the basic financial statements, is required by [*identify designated accounting standard setter*] who considers it to be an essential part of financial reporting for placing the basic financial statements in an appropriate operational, economic, or historical context. Our opinion on the basic financial statements is not affected by this missing information.

ILLUSTRATION 4—EXPLANATORY PARAGRAPH WHEN THE AUDITOR HAS IDENTIFIED MATERIAL DEPARTURES FROM THE PRESCRIBED GUIDELINES

[*Identify the applicable financial reporting framework (e.g., accounting principles generally accepted in the United States of America)*] require that the [*identify the required supplementary information*] on page XX be presented to supplement the basic financial statements. Such information, although not a part of the basic financial statements, is required by [*identify designated accounting standard setter*] who considers it to be an essential part of financial reporting for placing the basic financial statements in an appropriate operational, economic, or historical context. We have applied certain limited procedures to the required supplementary information in accordance with auditing standards generally accepted in the United States of America, which consisted of inquiries of management about the methods of preparing the information and comparing the information for consistency with management's responses to our inquiries, the basic financial statements, and other knowledge we obtained during our audit of the basic financial statements. Although our opinion on the basic financial statements is not affected, the following material departures from the prescribed guidelines exist [*identify the required supplementary information and describe the material departures from the prescribed guidelines*]. We do not express an opinion or provide any assurance on the information.

ILLUSTRATION 5—EXPLANATORY PARAGRAPH WHEN THE AUDITOR IS UNABLE TO COMPLETE THE SPECIFIC PROCEDURES PRESCRIBED IN SAS-120

[*Identify the applicable financial reporting framework (e.g., accounting principles generally accepted in the United States of America)*] require that the [*identify the required supplementary information*] on page XX be presented to supplement the basic financial statements. Such information, although not a part of the basic financial statements, is required by [*identify designated accounting standard setter*] who considers it to be an essential part of financial reporting for placing the basic financial statements in an appropriate operational, economic, or historical context. We were unable to apply certain limited procedures to the required supplementary information in accordance with auditing standards generally accepted in the United States of America because [*state the reasons*]. We do not express an opinion or provide any assurance on the information.

ILLUSTRATION 6—EXPLANATORY PARAGRAPH WHEN THE AUDITOR HAS UNRESOLVED DOUBTS ABOUT WHETHER THE REQUIRED SUPPLEMENTARY INFORMATION IS MEASURED OR PRESENTED IN ACCORDANCE WITH THE PRESCRIBED GUIDELINES

[*Identify the applicable financial reporting framework (e.g., accounting principles generally accepted in the United States of America)*] require that the [*identify the required supplementary information*] on page XX be presented to supplement the basic financial statements. Such information, although not a part of the basic financial statements, is required by [*identify designated accounting standard setter*] who considers it to be an essential part of financial reporting for placing the basic financial statements in an appropriate operational, economic, or historical context. We have applied certain limited procedures to the required supplementary information in accordance with auditing standards generally accepted in the United States of America, which consisted of inquiries of management about the methods of preparing the information and comparing the information for consistency with management's responses to our inquiries, the basic financial statements, and other knowledge we obtained during our audit of the basic financial statements. We do not express an opinion or provide any assurance on the information because the limited procedures do not provide us with sufficient evidence to express an opinion or provide any assurance. Although our opinion on the basic financial statements is not affected, the results of the limited procedures have raised doubts about whether material modifications should be made to the required supplementary information for it to be presented in accordance with guidelines established by [*identify designated accounting standard setter*].

[*The auditor may consider including in the report the reasons he or she was unable to resolve his or her doubts.*]

AU SECTION 560
SUBSEQUENT EVENTS

PRACTICE POINT: As part of its Clarity Project, the American Institute of Certified Public Accountants' (AICPA's) Auditing Standards Board (ASB) has finalized a clarified Statement on Auditing Standards (SAS) titled, "Subsequent Events and Subsequently Discovered Facts," which supersedes:

- AU Section 508 (Reports on Audited Financial Statements), paragraphs 71–73;

- AU Section 530 (Dating of the Independent Auditor's Report);

- AU Section 560 (Subsequent Events); and

- AU Section 561 (Subsequent Discovery of Facts Existing at the Date of the Auditor's Report).

The clarified SAS combines elements of existing standards and considers the impact of accounting guidance related to subsequent events, as follows:

- The clarified SAS combines the guidance pertaining to subsequent events (currently residing in AU Section 560) and subsequent discovery of facts (currently residing in AU Section 561) into one AU Section.

- The clarified SAS eliminates the accounting guidance related to subsequent events from the auditing literature. The Financial Accounting Standards Board (FASB) concluded that accounting guidance related to subsequent events should reside in the accounting literature established by the FASB and, accordingly, has included that guidance in its Accounting Standards Codification.

- The clarified SAS incorporates the guidance related to report reissuances (currently residing in AU Sections 530 and 508).

The ASB is expected to issue many of the clarified standards in *one* SAS that will be codified in "AU Section" format. The ASB has decided that the effective date of the clarified SASs that have not yet been issued is for audits of financial statements for periods ending on or after December 15, 2012. Auditors should be alert to and monitor further developments in this area.

WHAT EVERY PRACTITIONER SHOULD KNOW

Basic Objectives and Requirements

The auditor has a responsibility to perform procedures for transactions and events occurring after the balance sheet date to determine whether anything occurred that might affect the valuation or disclosure of the financial statements being audited. The auditor's responsibility for reviewing for subsequent events normally is limited to the period beginning with the balance sheet date and ending with the date of the auditor's report (commonly referred to as the "subsequent period").

Types of Subsequent Events

There are two types of subsequent events that require consideration by management and evaluation by the auditor:

1. Events that require *adjustment* (Type 1). Such events provide additional evidence with respect to conditions that existed at the balance sheet date and affect the estimates inherent in the process of preparing financial statements. These events have a direct effect on the financial statements and, if material, require *adjustment*.

2. Events that require *disclosure* (Type 2). Such events provide evidence with respect to conditions that did not exist at the date of the balance sheet but arose subsequent to that date. These events have no direct effect on the financial statements and should not result in an *adjustment*; however, if they are material, disclosure is required to keep the financial statements from being misleading. See Illustration 1 for examples of financial statement disclosures on subsequent events.

Auditing Procedures for Subsequent Events

Many audit procedures normally integrated as part of the verification of year-end account balances provide evidence of subsequent events. For example, subsequent period sales and purchases transactions are tested to determine whether the cutoff is accurate. Likewise, the auditor often tests the collectibility of accounts receivable by reviewing subsequent period cash receipts. However, in addition to these normal audit procedures, the auditor is required to perform other audit tests to determine specifically whether subsequent events exist that require either adjustment to or disclosure in the financial statements. Such audit procedures generally include:

1. *Reading the latest available interim financial statements*—The auditor should pay particular attention to major changes in the business or environment in which the client operates. The auditor should discuss with management whether the interim financial statements are prepared on the same basis as the current-period audited financial statements and inquire of management about any significant changes in operating results or financial condition in the subsequent period.

2. *Inquiring of management*—The auditor should inquire of management whether:

   a. Any substantial contingent liabilities or commitments exist;

   b. Any significant changes in capital stock, long-term debt, or working capital have occurred since the balance sheet date;

   c. There has been a change in the status of items that were not completely resolved at the balance sheet date; and

   d. Any material adjustments have been made during the subsequent period.

3. *Reading minutes of meetings of stockholders, directors, and appropriate committees*—The auditor also should inquire about any recent meetings for which minutes have not yet been prepared. When minutes have not

been prepared, the auditor should ask management about matters dealt with at such meetings, review summaries of actions pertinent to the financial statements, and obtain written representations from management regarding such matters.

4. *Inquiring of the client's legal counsel about litigation, claims, and assessments*—This correspondence generally takes place in connection with the audit inquiry letter to the client's legal counsel.

5. *Obtaining specific representations in the letter of representations from management, dated as of the date of the auditor's report*—In addition to obtaining representations about different matters throughout the audit, the auditor should obtain representations about whether any events occurred during the subsequent period that require adjustment to, or disclosure in, the financial statements.

6. *Performing additional procedures, if necessary*—The auditor should make additional inquiries or perform additional procedures that are deemed necessary, depending on the results of the procedures described above. For example, auditors frequently scan journals (e.g., cash receipts, cash disbursements) and ledgers prepared subsequent to the balance sheet date to determine the existence and nature of any unusual transactions. If the journals and ledgers are not kept up-to-date, the auditor should review the documents relating to these records.

See Illustration 2 for an audit procedures checklist for subsequent events.

Effect of Subsequent Events on the Auditor's Report

If the auditor becomes aware of a subsequent event requiring adjustment of the financial statements and the client refuses to reflect the adjustment, the auditor should qualify his or her opinion. In some cases, a disclaimer of opinion or an adverse opinion may be appropriate.

If the auditor becomes aware of a subsequent event requiring disclosure and the client refuses to make appropriate disclosures in the financial statements, the auditor should qualify his or her opinion. Also, in some cases, a disclaimer of opinion or an adverse opinion may be appropriate.

See AU Section 530 (Dating of the Independent Auditor's Report) for a more detailed discussion of the impact of subsequent events on the auditor's report, dating of the auditor's report, and reissuance of the auditor's report.

PRACTICE ISSUES AND FREQUENTLY ASKED QUESTIONS

Issue 1: What are some examples of subsequent events that have a direct effect on the financial statements and require adjustment?

Examples of subsequent events that have a direct effect on the financial statements and require an adjustment of account balances in the current year's financial statements, if material, include:

- A customer with an outstanding accounts receivable balance as of the balance sheet date that declares bankruptcy in the subsequent period.

- The subsequent settlement of a litigation at an amount that is different from the amount recorded in the financial statements.

- The subsequent sale of property not being used in operations at a price less than the carrying value in the financial statements.

- The subsequent sale of investments at a price less than the carrying value in the financial statements.

- Payment of contingent liabilities.

These types of events provide additional information to management and the auditor in evaluating the valuation of account balances as of the balance sheet date. For example, the auditor may be having difficulty determining the correct valuation of inventory because of obsolescence. The sale of raw material inventory as scrap in the subsequent period should be used as further evidence for determining the correct valuation of the inventory as of the balance sheet date.

Issue 2: What are some examples of subsequent events that do not result in an adjustment, but require disclosure in the financial statements, if significant?

Some subsequent events provide evidence of conditions that did not exist at the balance sheet date, but arose subsequently. These events do not result in an adjustment of financial statement accounts but may be so significant that they require disclosure for fair presentation of the financial statements. The following are examples of this second type of subsequent event:

- Issuance of bonds or equity securities

- Acquisition of a business

- Litigation that arises subsequent to the balance sheet date

- Loss of inventories or plant as a result of fire or a catastrophe

- Decline in market value of inventory as a consequence of government action barring further sale of the client's products

- Loss of receivables resulting from conditions that arose subsequent to the balance sheet date

Issue 3: If the auditor is responsible for considering the effects of subsequent events on the financial statements, doesn't that require him or her to do a complete audit of transactions occurring in the period between the balance sheet date and the date of the audit report?

No. Even if this were possible, it would be impractical and prohibitively expensive. Many subsequent events are routinely considered during the normal course of most audits. Although they are seldom thought of as subsequent event tests, they provide the auditor with pertinent evidence about items in the statements. For example, tracing outstanding checks to subsequent bank statements provides the auditor with evidence to support their existence and amounts; testing subsequent collections of accounts receivable can provide useful information about their valuation at the balance sheet date; and reviewing subsequent cash disbursements often reveal unrecorded accounts payable.

Issue 4: Is it sufficient to obtain in the representations letter a specific representation by management that no events have occurred subsequent to the balance sheet, without having to perform any additional procedures?

No. Like any other representation made by management, this one alone is not sufficient evidence. Therefore, additional subsequent events procedures must be performed to obtain corroborative evidence.

Issue 5: When disclosure of subsequent events is required in the financial statements, may such disclosure be made in the form of pro forma financial data?

Yes. Sometimes a certain subsequent event may be so significant that disclosure can best be made by supplementing the historical financial statements with pro forma financial data, as if the event had taken place as of the date of the balance sheet. Also, it may be desirable to present pro forma statements (usually a balance sheet only) in columnar form on the face of the historical financial statements. The auditor may label the pro forma presentation as "unaudited."

Issue 6: After the original date of the auditor's report, but before issuance of the related financial statements, a fire destroyed a client's entire plant and all inventories. How does this event affect the auditor's report?

This event does not provide evidence about conditions that existed at the balance sheet date and, therefore, no adjustment to the financial statements is required. However, because the event is so significant, disclosure is required in order to prevent the financial statements from being misleading.

The auditor has two options for handling this event. The first option is to expand the subsequent events procedures through the date at which the auditor is satisfied that all events occurring in the intervening period are given proper financial statement consideration. In this case, the auditor's report will be dated as of this latter date.

The second option, which is equally acceptable, is to limit the extended subsequent events procedures to the fire and its effect on the financial statements. Under this option, the auditor's report should be "dual-dated."

Issue 7: Is the auditor required to include in the audit report an explanatory paragraph directing the reader's attention to a subsequent event disclosed in notes to the financial statements?

No. The auditor may wish, but is not required, to include such an explanatory paragraph in his or her audit report. See Illustration 3 for an example of an auditor's report that includes an *optional* "emphasis-of-matter" paragraph describing a subsequent event.

Issue 8: Does the auditor have a responsibility to search for events subsequent to the date of his or her report on an entity's audited financial statements?

No. However, if subsequent to the date of his or her report on audited financial statements the auditor discovers facts that existed at the date of the report, the auditor should follow the guidance in AU Section 561 (Subsequent Discovery of Facts Existing at the Date of the Auditor's Report).

ILLUSTRATIONS AND PRACTICE AIDS

ILLUSTRATION 1—EXAMPLES OF FINANCIAL STATEMENT DISCLO-SURES DESCRIBING SUBSEQUENT EVENTS

Note: For purposes of the examples below, assume that the financial statements being reported on are as of and for the year ended December 31, 20X2.

Example 1: *Inventory destroyed in fire*

In February 20X3, the Company suffered a fire in its main warehouse located in Hillsborough, Virginia. The Company estimates that inventory with a recorded value of approximately $1,200,000 was destroyed. While the exact amount of the loss is not currently determinable, the Company expects to recover 50% to 75% of the value through insurance proceeds.

Example 2: *Contingent liability relating to lease termination*

In March 20X3, the Company notified the developer and landlord of its planned future headquarters in Paramount, California that the Company intends to terminate the project. The Company had previously entered into a 15-year lease agreement for the new site. Although groundbreaking for the new site has not occurred, the Company anticipates that it will incur lease termination costs. However, the Company is not able to make a meaningful estimate of the amount or range of loss that could result from an unfavorable resolution of this matter.

Example 3: *Patent infringement lawsuit*

On February 13, 20X3, the Company was named as a defendant in a patent infringement suit brought by Pasterine, Ltd. alleging that certain of the Company's products infringe seven patents that Pasterine Ltd. allegedly owns and is seeking a judgment of infringement for each of these asserted patents and other costs. The Company is reviewing the suit and, based on advice from legal counsel, believes that the complaints are without merit. However, no assurance can be given that this matter will be resolved in the Company's favor.

Example 4: *Purchase of assets*

On March 4, 20X3, the Company entered into an agreement to purchase a new warehouse and distribution center at a total cost of $4,700,000. The Company opened escrow and made a deposit of $500,000. The purchase price is expected to be financed by the Company's primary bank over five years at an interest rate of 1% above the bank's prime rate.

Example 5: *Sale of common stock*

On February 11, 20X3, the Company sold 300,000 shares of its common stock at $10 per share. The proceeds will be used for working capital purposes and to pay off long-term debt of approximately $1,300,000.

Example 6: *Stock split*

On March 1, 20X3, the Company's Board of Directors declared a two-for-one stock split of the common stock effected in the form of a 25% stock dividend, to be distributed on or about April 10, 20X3, to holders of record on March 23, 20X3. Accordingly all references to number of shares, except shares authorized, and to per share information in the consolidated financial statements have been adjusted to reflect the stock split on a retroactive basis.

ILLUSTRATION 2—AUDIT PROCEDURES CHECKLIST FOR SUBSEQUENT EVENTS

	Performed By	Workpaper Reference

1. Read the latest available interim financial statements, and:

   a. Compare them with the financial statements being reported on.

   b. Investigate any unexpected significant changes.

   c. Make any other comparisons considered appropriate in the circumstances.

   d. Inquire about whether the interim financial statements have been prepared on the same basis as that used for the audited statements.

2. Scan the following for the period subsequent to the financial statement date for unusual transactions:

   a. General ledger

   b. Cash receipts journals or records

   c. Cash disbursement journals

   d. Sales journal and accounts receivable ledger

   e. General journal entries

3. Inquire of management whether:

   a. Any substantial contingent liabilities or commitments exist.

   b. Any significant changes in capital stock, long-term debt, or working capital have occurred since the balance sheet date.

   c. There has been a change in the status of items that were not completely resolved at the balance sheet date.

   d. Any material adjustments have been made during the period subsequent to the date of the financial statements being reported on.

   e. Commitments or plans for major purchases of capital assets or inventory exist, and consideration of possible losses due to price changes.

   f. There has been any changes in accounting or financial policies.

   g. Any events have occurred that have caused a decline in the value of any assets or have made any significant portion of fixed assets idle or obsolete.

   h. There is any expiration or cancellation of significant insurance coverage.

   i. There are any new regulatory requirements or laws that could adversely affect the entity.

   j. There are any liabilities in dispute or being contested.

   k. There have been any losses of significant customers, major suppliers, or key executive employees.

   l. There are any related-party transactions.

	Performed By	Workpaper Reference

4. Read minutes of meetings of stockholders, directors, and appropriate committees held subsequent to the period being audited through the date of the auditor's report. If meetings were held for which minutes have not been prepared, inquire about significant matters discussed and resolutions made at such meetings. _____ _____

5. Inquire of client's legal counsel concerning litigation, claims, and assessments. _____ _____

6. Obtain written representations from management, dated as of the date of the auditor's report, about whether any events have occurred subsequent to the balance sheet date that would require adjustment to, or disclosure in, the financial statements. _____ _____

7. Consider adjustment of year-end financial statements or disclosure of any items as a result of the above procedures. _____ _____

ILLUSTRATION 3—AUDITOR'S REPORT INCLUDES "EMPHASIS OF A MATTER" PARAGRAPH DESCRIBING A SUBSEQUENT EVENT

Independent Auditor's Report

Board of Directors and Stockholders
ABC Company

We have audited the accompanying balance sheets of ABC Company as of December 31, 20X2, and 20X1, and the related statements of income, retained earnings, and cash flows for the years then ended. These financial statements are the responsibility of the Company's management. Our responsibility is to express an opinion on these financial statements based on our audits.

We conducted our audits in accordance with auditing standards generally accepted in the United States of America. Those standards require that we plan and perform the audit to obtain reasonable assurance about whether the financial statements are free of material misstatement. An audit includes examining, on a test basis, evidence supporting the amounts and disclosures in the financial statements. An audit also includes assessing the accounting principles used and significant estimates made by management, as well as evaluating the overall financial statement presentation. We believe that our audits provide a reasonable basis for our opinion.

In our opinion, the financial statements referred to above present fairly, in all material respects, the financial position of ABC Company as of December 31, 20X2, and 20X1, and the results of its operations and its cash flows for the years then ended in conformity with accounting principles generally accepted in the United States of America.

As discussed in Note [X] to the financial statements, on April 12, 20X3, the Company completed the sale of its DEF Subsidiary. This subsidiary accounted for 22% and 20% of the Company's total revenues for the years ended December 31, 20X2, and 20X1, respectively.

[*Signature*]

[*Date*]

AU SECTION 561
SUBSEQUENT DISCOVERY OF FACTS EXISTING AT THE DATE OF THE AUDITOR'S REPORT

PRACTICE POINT: As part of its Clarity Project, the American Institute of Certified Public Accountants' (AICPA's) Auditing Standards Board (ASB) has finalized a clarified Statement on Auditing Standards (SAS) titled, "Subsequent Events and Subsequently Discovered Facts," which supersedes:

- AU Section 508 (Reports on Audited Financial Statements), paragraphs 71–73;
- AU Section 530 (Dating of the Independent Auditor's Report);
- AU Section 560 (Subsequent Events); and
- AU Section 561 (Subsequent Discovery of Facts Existing at the Date of the Auditor's Report).

The clarified SAS combines elements of existing standards and considers the impact of accounting guidance related to subsequent events, as follows:

- The clarified SAS combines the guidance pertaining to subsequent events (currently residing in AU Section 560) and subsequent discovery of facts (currently residing in AU Section 561) into one AU Section.
- The clarified SAS eliminates the accounting guidance related to subsequent events from the auditing literature. The Financial Accounting Standards Board (FASB) concluded that accounting guidance related to subsequent events should reside in the accounting literature established by the FASB and, accordingly, has included that guidance in its Accounting Standards Codification.
- The clarified SAS incorporates the guidance related to report reissuances (currently residing in AU Sections 530 and 508).

The ASB is expected to issue many of the clarified standards in *one* SAS that will be codified in "AU Section" format. The ASB has decided that the effective date of the clarified SASs that have not yet been issued is for audits of financial statements for periods ending on or after December 15, 2012. Auditors should be alert to and monitor further developments in this area.

WHAT EVERY PRACTITIONER SHOULD KNOW

Basic Objectives and Requirements

AU Section 560The provisions of this Section are applicable if, subsequent to the date of the report on audited financial statements, the auditor becomes aware the facts:

1. Existed at the date of the audit report but were not known to him or her at that date, and

2. Would have affected the audit report had he or she then been aware of such facts.

In such circumstances, the auditor should promptly:

1. Determine whether the information he or she became aware of is reliable.
2. Determine whether the facts existed at the date of the audit report.
3. Discuss the matter with the client at the appropriate level, including the board of directors.
4. Request cooperation in whatever investigation may be necessary.
5. Consider whether there are persons currently relying, or likely to rely, on the financial statements and the related auditor's report who would attach importance to the information (herein referred to "interested third parties").
6. Consider consulting with legal counsel.

Action to Prevent Future Reliance on the Audit Report and Financial Statements

If the auditor concludes that action should be taken to prevent future reliance on the audit report, he or she should advise the client to make appropriate disclosure to interested third parties of (a) the newly discovered facts and (b) their impact on the financial statements. The method the client uses to make the appropriate disclosure will depend on the circumstances:

1. **Effect of discovered information can be determined promptly** If the effect on the financial statements or auditor's report can be determined promptly, disclosure should consist of issuing revised financial statements and auditor's report, as soon as practicable. The reasons for the revision usually should be described in a note to the financial statements and referred to in the auditor's report. In such circumstances, the auditor's report on the revised financial statements should be dual-dated. See Illustration 2 for an example of an auditor's revised report for subsequent discovery of facts.

2. **Issuance of financial statements and the auditor's report thereon for a subsequent period is imminent** When issuance of financial statements and the auditor's report thereon for a subsequent period is imminent, appropriate disclosure of the revision can be made in such subsequent statements instead of reissuing the earlier statements discussed in 1 above.

3. **Effect of discovered information cannot be determined promptly** If the effect on the financial statements or auditor's report cannot be promptly determined, the client should notify interested third parties that (a) they should not be relying on the statements and the auditor's report and (b) revised statements and auditor's report will be issued upon completion of an investigation. Also, if applicable, the auditor should advise the client to discuss with the Securities and Exchange Commission, stock exchanges, and appropriate regulatory agencies the disclosure to be made or other measures to be taken in the circumstances.

The auditor should be satisfied that the client has made the appropriate disclosures described above.

Auditor's Action If Client Refuses to Make the Appropriate Disclosures

If the client refuses to make the disclosures discussed above, the auditor should notify each member of the board of directors of such refusal and of the fact that the auditor, in order to prevent future reliance upon his or her audit report, will notify:

1. The client that the audit report must no longer be associated with the financial statements.

2. Regulatory agencies having jurisdiction over the client that the auditor's report should no longer be relied upon.

3. Each person known to the auditor to be relying on the financial statements that his report should no longer be relied upon.

The auditor should observe the following guidelines when making disclosures to persons other than the client:

1. **Auditor able to make a satisfactory investigation** If the auditor has been able to make a satisfactory investigation of the information, the auditor should disclose:

   a. The effect the subsequently acquired information would have had on the auditor's report if it had been known to him or her at the date of the report and had not been reflected in the financial statements.

   b. The nature of the subsequently acquired information and of its effect on the financial statements.

   c. The discovered information as precisely and factually as possible, without any comments about the conduct or motives of any persons involved.

2. **Auditor unable to make a satisfactory investigation** If the auditor has been unable to make a satisfactory investigation because the client refused to cooperate, the auditor should disclose:

   a. That information has come to his or her attention which the client has not cooperated in attempting to substantiate.

   b. That, if the information is true, the auditor believes that his or her report must no longer be relied upon or be associated with the financial statements.

PRACTICE ISSUES AND FREQUENTLY ASKED QUESTIONS

Issue 1: Does this Section apply to subsequent event matters identified by the auditor in connection with events occurring prior to the issuance of the financial statements?

No. This Section applies to the auditor's discovery of facts only *after* the issuance of an entity's financial statements. See AU Section 560 (Subsequent Events) for the auditor's responsibility to perform procedures for transactions and events occurring after the balance sheet date but prior to the issuance of the financial statements.

Issue 2: Does the auditor have a responsibility to search for events subsequent to the date of his or her report on an entity's audited financial statements?

No. However, if subsequent to the date of his or her report on audited financial statements, new information comes to the auditor's attention which may affect his or her report, the auditor should comply with the provisions of this Section.

Issue 3: Does the auditor's responsibility under this Section change if failure to discover material misstatement at the date of the auditor's report was the fault of the client or the auditor?

No. The auditor's responsibility remains the same regardless of whether the failure to discover material misstatement at the date of the auditor's report was the fault of the client or the auditor.

Issue 4: If the client refuses to make the appropriate disclosures pursuant to this Section, how should the auditor notify stockholders or investors at large that the audit report should no longer be relied on?

Generally, it will not be practicable for the auditor to give appropriate individual notification to stockholders or investors at large, whose identities ordinarily are unknown to the auditor. Therefore, notification to a regulatory agency having jurisdiction over the client will usually be the only practicable way for the auditor to provide appropriate disclosure. Such notification should be accompanied by a request that the agency take whatever steps it may deem appropriate to accomplish the necessary disclosure. Also, under these circumstances, it is highly advisable that the auditor consult with his or her legal counsel.

Issue 5: Is the auditor's responsibility with respect to subsequently discovered information different if the auditor has resigned or been discharged prior to undertaking or completing his or her investigation?

No. The auditor is responsible for determining whether the subsequently discovered information is reliable and whether the facts existed at the date of the audit report, even when the auditor has resigned or been discharged.

ILLUSTRATIONS AND PRACTICE AIDS

ILLUSTRATION 1—AUDIT PROCEDURES CHECKLIST FOR SUBSEQUENT DISCOVERY OF FACTS EXISTING AT THE DATE OF THE AUDITOR'S REPORT

		Performed By	Workpaper Reference
1.	Determine if the discovered facts are relevant to the financial statements by considering whether:		
	a. The auditor's report would have been affected if the auditor had known about the information at the date of his or her report.	————	————
	b. The matter would have been reflected in the financial statements.	————	————
	c. The auditor believes that there are third-party users relying on, or likely to rely on, the financial statements and who would place importance on the subsequently discovered information.	————	————

	Performed By	Workpaper Reference

2. If the conditions described in item 1 above exist, advise the client to inform third-party users currently relying on, or likely to rely on, the financial statements of the newly discovered facts and their impact on the financial statements, by one of the following methods:

    a. If the effects of the subsequently discovered information can be determined promptly and the issuance of more current financial statements is not imminent, revised financial statements and a revised auditor's report should be issued as soon as practicable. Both the financial statements and the auditor's report should describe the reasons for the revision. Also, the auditor's report on the revised financial statements should be dual-dated. _____ _____

    b. If issuance of financial statements accompanied by the auditor's report thereon for a subsequent period is imminent, appropriate disclosure of the revision should be made in such financial statements; the earlier financial statements need not be reissued. _____ _____

    c. If the effects of the subsequently discovered information cannot be determined without a prolonged investigation, ask the client to notify third-party users that they should not be relying on the financial statements and the auditor's report, and that revised financial statements and auditor's report will be issued when an investigation is complete. _____ _____

3. If the client refuses to make appropriate disclosures to third-party users, inform each member of the board of directors of the refusal. _____ _____

4. If the board of directors is notified but appropriate disclosures to third-party users still are not made, discuss the matter with legal counsel. _____ _____

5. If it appears that there are or will be third-party users relying on the financial statements and the client refuses to make the appropriate disclosures, take the following actions:

    a. Notify the client that the audit report should no longer be associated with the financial statements. _____ _____

    b. Notify regulatory agencies having jurisdiction over the client that the auditor's report should no longer be relied upon. _____ _____

    c. To the extent practical, notify each third-party user known to be relying on the financial statements that the auditor's report should no longer be relied upon. _____ _____

	Performed By	Workpaper Reference

6. If matters have been satisfactorily investigated and the subsequent information considered reliable, make the following disclosures to regulatory authorities and third-party users:

   a. The nature of the subsequently acquired information and its effect on the financial statements.   _____   _____

   b. The effect of the subsequently acquired information on the auditor's report, if the information had been known to him or her at the date of the report and had not been reflected in the financial statements.   _____   _____

   c. The discovered information as precisely and factually as possible, without any comments about the conduct or motives of any persons involved.   _____   _____

7. If a satisfactory investigation is not conducted, make the following disclosures to regulatory authorities and third-party users:

   a. Describe the general nature of the matter.   _____   _____

   b. State that the effect of the matter cannot be determined because the client did not cooperate in the investigation of the matter.   _____   _____

   c. State that if the information is correct, the auditor believes that his or her report should no longer be relied upon or be associated with the financial statements.   _____   _____

ILLUSTRATION 2—AUDITOR'S REVISED REPORT DUE TO SUBSEQUENT DISCOVERY OF FACTS

Independent Auditor's Report

Board of Directors and Stockholders
ABC Company

We have audited the accompanying balance sheets of ABC Company as of December 31, 20X2, and 20X1, and the related statements of income, retained earnings, and cash flows for the years then ended. These financial statements are the responsibility of the Company's management. Our responsibility is to express an opinion on these financial statements based on our audits.

We conducted our audits in accordance with auditing standards generally accepted in the United States of America. Those standards require that we plan and perform the audit to obtain reasonable assurance about whether the financial statements are free of material misstatement. An audit includes examining, on a test basis, evidence supporting the amounts and disclosures in the financial statements. An audit also includes assessing the accounting principles used and significant estimates made by management, as well as evaluating the overall financial statement presentation. We believe that our audits provide a reasonable basis for our opinion.

In our opinion, the financial statements referred to above, revised as described in Note [X], present fairly, in all material respects, the financial position of ABC Company as of December 31, 20X2, and 20X1, and the results of its operations and its cash flows for the years then ended in conformity with accounting principles generally accepted in the United States of America.

As discussed in Note [X] to the financial statements, the Company's 20X2 [*specify accounts corrected, for example accounts payable, inventory, etc.*] previously reported as $_____ should have been $_____. This discovery was made subsequent to the issuance of the financial statements. The financial statements have been restated to reflect this correction.

[*Signature*]

[*February 11, 20X3, except for Note X, as to which the date is March 18, 20X3.*]

AU Section 600
OTHER TYPES OF REPORTS

AU SECTION 623
SPECIAL REPORTS

PRACTICE POINT: As part of its Clarity Project, the American Institute of Certified Public Accountants' (AICPA's) Auditing Standards Board (ASB) has finalized a clarified Statement on Auditing Standards (SAS) titled, "Special Considerations—Audits of Financial Statements Prepared in Accordance with Special Purpose Frameworks," which supersedes AU Section 544 (Lack of Conformity with Generally Accepted Accounting Principles) and AU Section 623 (Special Reports), except paragraphs 19–21.

The clarified SAS addresses special considerations in the application of the AU sections to an audit of financial statements prepared in accordance with a special purpose framework. Special purpose frameworks are limited to cash, tax, regulatory, or contractual bases of accounting. The cash, tax, and regulatory bases of accounting are commonly referred to as other comprehensive bases of accounting (OCBOA). The term *OCBOA* was replaced with the term *special purpose framework,* which no longer includes a definite set of criteria having substantial support that is applied to all material items appearing in financial statements. Among other matters, the clarified SAS requires:

- The auditor to obtain an understanding of (*a*) the purpose for which the financial statements are prepared, (*b*) the intended users, and (*c*) the steps taken by management to determine that the special purpose framework is acceptable in the circumstances.

- The auditor to obtain the agreement of management that it acknowledges and understands its responsibility to include all informative disclosures that are appropriate for the special purpose framework used to prepare the financial statements, including, but not limited to, additional disclosures beyond those required by the applicable financial reporting framework that may be necessary to achieve fair presentation. The auditor is required to evaluate whether such disclosures are necessary.

- In the case of special purpose financial statements prepared in accordance with a contractual basis of accounting, the auditor to obtain an understanding of any significant interpretations of the contract that management made in the preparation of those financial statements and to evaluate whether the financial statements adequately describe such interpretations.

- When management has a choice of financial reporting frameworks in the preparation of the financial statements, the explanation of management's responsibility for the financial statements in the auditor's report to make reference to management's responsibility for determining that the applicable financial reporting framework is acceptable in the circumstances.

- In the case of financial statements prepared in accordance with a regulatory or contractual basis of accounting, the auditor's report to describe the purpose for which the financial statements are prepared or refer to a note in the special purpose financial statements that contains that information.

- The auditor's report to include an emphasis-of-matter paragraph under an appropriate heading that, among other things, states that the special purpose framework is a basis of accounting other than GAAP.

- The auditor's report to include specific elements if the auditor is required by law or regulation to use a specific layout, form, or wording of the auditor's report.

The ASB is expected to issue many of the clarified standards in *one* SAS that will be codified in "AU Section" format. The ASB has decided that the effective date of the clarified SASs that have not yet been issued is for audits of financial statements for periods ending on or after December 15, 2012. Auditors should be alert to and monitor further developments in this area.

PRACTICE POINT: As part of its Clarity Project, the American Institute of Certified Public Accountants' (AICPA's) Auditing Standards Board (ASB) has finalized a clarified Statement on Auditing Standards (SAS) titled, "Special Considerations—Audits of Single Financial Statements and Specific Elements, Accounts, or Items of a Financial Statement," which supersedes paragraphs .33-.34 of AU Section 508 (Reports on Audited Financial Statements) and paragraphs .11-.18 of AU Section 623 (Special Reports).

The clarified SAS addresses special considerations in the application of GAAS to an audit of a single financial statement or of a specific element, account, or item of a financial statement. It does not apply to the report of a component auditor issued as a result of work performed on the financial information of a component at the request of a group engagement team for purposes of an audit of group financial statements. Among other matters, the clarified SAS:

- Explains that a single financial statement and a specific element include the related notes, which ordinarily comprise a summary of significant accounting policies and other relevant explanatory information.

- Requires the auditor (if the auditor is not also engaged to audit the entity's complete set of financial statements) to determine whether the audit of a single financial statement or a specific element is practicable and to determine whether the auditor will be able to perform procedures on interrelated items. In the case of an audit of a specific element that is, or is based on, the entity's stockholders' equity or net income (or the equivalents thereto), the clarified SAS requires the auditor to perform procedures necessary to obtain sufficient appropriate audit evidence about financial position, or financial position and results of operations, respectively.

- Requires the auditor to obtain an understanding of (*a*) the purpose for which the single financial statement or specific element is prepared, (*b*) the intended users, and (*c*) the steps taken by management to determine that the application of the applicable financial reporting framework is acceptable in the circumstances.

- Requires the auditor to determine the acceptability of the financial reporting framework, including whether its application will result in a presentation that provides adequate disclosures to enable the intended users to understand the information conveyed and the effect of material transactions and events on such information.

- Requires the auditor (if the auditor undertakes an engagement to audit a single financial statement or a specific element in conjunction with an engagement to audit the complete set of financial statements) to issue a separate auditor's report and express a separate opinion for each engagement. In addition, the auditor is required to indicate, in the report on a specific element, the date of the auditor's report on the complete set of financial statements and the nature of opinion expressed under an appropriate heading.

- Permits, except as otherwise indicated, an audited single financial statement or a specific element to be published together with the audited complete set of financial statements, provided that the presentation of the single financial statement or specific element is sufficiently differentiated from the complete set of financial statements.

- Requires the auditor, if the opinion in the auditor's report on the complete set of financial statements is modified, to determine the effect that this may have on the auditor's opinion on a single financial statement or a specific element. In the case of an audit of a specific element, if the modified opinion is relevant to the audit of the specific element, the clarified SAS requires the auditor to:

    — Express an adverse opinion on the specific element when the modification on the complete set of financial statements arises from a material misstatement.

    — Disclaim an opinion on the specific element when the modification on the complete set of financial statements arises from an inability to obtain sufficient appropriate audit evidence.

- Permits the auditor, when it is necessary to express an adverse opinion or disclaim an opinion on the complete set of financial statements as a whole but, in the context of a separate audit of a specific element, the auditor nevertheless considers it appropriate to express an unmodified opinion on that element, to do so only if:

    — That opinion is expressed in an auditor's report that is neither published together with, nor otherwise accompanies, the auditor's report containing the adverse opinion or disclaimer of opinion; and

    — The specific element does not constitute a major portion of the complete set of financial statements or the specific element is not, or is not based on, the entity's stockholders' equity or net income or the equivalent.

- Prohibits the auditor from expressing an unmodified opinion on a single financial statement if the auditor expressed an adverse opinion or disclaimed an opinion on the complete set of financial statements as a whole.

- Requires the auditor, if the auditor's report on the complete set of financial statements includes an emphasis-of-matter or an other-matter paragraph that is relevant to the audit of the single financial statement or specific element, to include a similar emphasis-of-matter paragraph or an other-matter paragraph in the auditor's report on the single financial statement or specific element.

- Permits the auditor to report on an incomplete presentation but one that is otherwise in accordance with GAAP by including an emphasis-of-matter paragraph in the auditor's report that (a) states the purpose for which the presentation is prepared, (b) refers to the note that describes the basis of presentation, and (*c*) indicates that the presentation is not intended to be a complete presentation of the entity's assets, liabilities, revenues, or expenses.

The ASB is expected to issue many of the clarified standards in *one* SAS that will be codified in "AU Section" format. The ASB has decided that the effective date of the clarified SASs that have not yet been issued is for audits of financial statements for periods ending on or after December 15, 2012. Auditors should be alert to and monitor further developments in this area.

PRACTICE POINT: As part of its Clarity Project, the American Institute of Certified Public Accountants' (AICPA's) Auditing Standards Board (ASB) has issued an exposure draft (ED) of a proposed Statement on Auditing Standards (SAS) titled, "Reporting on Compliance with Aspects of Contractual Agreements or Regulatory Requirements in Connection with Audited Financial Statements (Redrafted)," which would supersede paragraphs .19–.21 of AU Section 623 (Special Reports).

The proposed SAS does not change or expand paragraphs .19–.21 of AU Section 623 in any significant respect. However, to reflect a more principles-based approach to standard setting, certain requirements that are duplicative of broader requirements in paragraphs .19–.21 of AU Section 623 have been moved to application and other explanatory material.

The ASB is expected to issue many of the clarified standards in *one* SAS that will be codified in "AU Section" format. The ASB has decided that the effective date of the clarified SASs that have not yet been issued is for audits of financial statements for periods ending on or after December 15, 2012. Auditors should be alert to and monitor further developments in this area.

WHAT EVERY PRACTITIONER SHOULD KNOW

Basic Objectives and Requirements

This Section is applicable to auditor's reports issued in connection with the following:

1. Audited financial statements prepared in conformity with a comprehensive basis of accounting other than generally accepted accounting principles (OCBOA).

2. Audited specified elements, accounts, or items of a financial statement.

3. Compliance with aspects of contractual agreements or regulatory requirements related to audited financial statements.

4. Special-purpose financial presentations to comply with contractual agreements or regulatory provisions.

5. Financial information presented in prescribed forms or schedules that require a prescribed form of auditor's reports.

The auditor's reporting requirements under each of these circumstances is discussed in the following sections.

Audited Financial Statements Prepared in Conformity with an OCBOA

For purposes of reporting under the provisions of this Section, a comprehensive basis of accounting other than generally accepted accounting principles (OCBOA) is a basis that is used by the entity under any of the following circumstances:

1. To comply with the requirements or financial reporting provisions of a governmental regulatory agency, such as the Department of Housing and Urban Development (HUD) or state insurance commissions.

2. To file its income tax return for the period covered by the financial statements (i.e., income tax basis accounting).

3. To prepare the financial statements on the cash receipts and disbursements basis of accounting (i.e., cash basis). This includes modifications of the cash basis having substantial support, such as recording depreciation on fixed assets or accruing income taxes (i.e., modified cash basis).

4. To apply a definite set of criteria having substantial support to all material items appearing in financial statements, such as the price-level basis of accounting.

OCBOA financial statements should include, in the accompanying notes, a summary of significant accounting policies that discusses the basis of presentation and describes how that basis differs from GAAP. However, the effects of the differences between GAAP and OCBOA need not be quantified. (See Issue 6 for examples). Also, when the OCBOA financial statements contain items that are the same as, or similar to, those in GAAP financial statements, similar informative disclosures are appropriate (e.g., property and equipment, and long-term debt).

When reporting on OCBOA financial statements, the auditor should consider whether the financial statements and the accompanying notes include all informative disclosures that are appropriate for the basis of accounting used. The auditor should also consider whether disclosures are adequate regarding matters that are not specifically identified on the face of the financial statements, such as: related party transactions, restrictions on assets and owners' equity, subsequent events, and uncertainties.

See Illustration 1 for a list of the items that should be included in the auditor's report on OCBOA financial statements. See Illustrations 2, 3, and 4 for examples of auditor's reports on OCBOA financial statements.

Auditor reports on financial statements prepared using accounting practices prescribed or permitted by a regulatory agency There may be instances when a regulated entity (including a state and local governmental entity) prepares its financial statements using accounting practices prescribed or permitted by a regulatory agency. An example is a basis of accounting that insurance companies use pursuant to the rules of a state insurance commission. If the financial statements are prepared in accordance with the requirements or financial reporting provisions of a governmental regulatory agency, the auditor should restrict the use of the report to the specified parties. Specifically, the auditor is required to add a separate paragraph at the end of the report stating that the report (1) is intended solely for the information and use of those *within* the entity and those regulatory agencies with jurisdiction over the entity, and (2) it is not intended to be and should not be used by anyone other than these specified parties. Such an additional paragraph, called a "restricted-use paragraph," is appropriate even though the auditor's report may be made a matter of public record by law or regulation.

An Auditing Interpretation of AU Section 623 addresses the appropriateness of using such additional paragraph and the form of the auditor's report when (1) the financial statements and report are intended for use by parties *outside* the entity and one or more regulatory agencies that have jurisdiction over the entity, or (2) the entity distributes, voluntarily or upon request, the financial statements and report to parties other than the regulatory agencies with jurisdiction over the entity. In such circumstances, the Auditing Interpretation provides the following guidance:

- The auditor is prohibited from adding a restricted-use paragraph to his or her report if the entity distributes, either voluntarily or upon specific request, its financial statements to outside parties other than the regulatory agency.

- If the financial statements and report are intended for use by parties other than those within the entity and one or more regulatory agencies with jurisdiction over the entity, the auditor should follow the guidance in AU Section 544 (Lack of Conformity with Generally Accepted Accounting Principles). Specifically, AU Section 544 indicates that the auditor should use the standard form of report, which should be modified, as appropriate, for the departures from GAAP and should express, in an additional paragraph, an opinion on whether the financial statements are presented in conformity with the regulatory basis of accounting.

Reports on financial statements included in Internal Revenue Form 990 Charitable organizations in some states may use Internal Revenue Form 990, "Return of Organizations Exempt from Income Tax," as a uniform annual report for reporting to both state and federal governments. Many states require an auditor's opinion on whether the financial statements included in the report are presented fairly in conformity with GAAP. However, financial statements included in a Form 990 by such charitable organizations may contain certain material departures from the accounting principles in certain AICPA Audit and Accounting Guides.

While the report is used primarily to satisfy statutory requirements, regulatory authorities sometimes make the financial statements and the accompanying auditor's report a matter of public record. In some situations, however, there may be public distribution of the report.

If the financial statements are in conformity with GAAP, the auditor can express an unqualified opinion. If the financial statements are *not* in conformity with GAAP, the auditor should consider, as follows, the distribution of the report to determine the type of report to be issued:

1. If the financial statements and report are intended solely for use by those within the entity and one or more regulatory agencies to whose jurisdiction the entity is subject, the auditor may issue the type of special report discussed in this Section. See Illustration 5 for an example of such a report. This type of report is appropriate, although the accountant's report may be made a matter of public record pursuant to law or regulation.

2. If there is public distribution of the report, the type of special report discussed in Item 1 above is not appropriate. Therefore, in such cases, the auditor should express a qualified or an adverse opinion and disclose the effects on the financial statements of the departures from GAAP. If the effects are not reasonably determinable, the report should so state. (Note: Public distribution exists when the charitable organization distributes to contributors or others the annual report without receiving a specific request for such distribution.)

Audited Specified Elements, Accounts, or Items of a Financial Statement

An auditor may be requested to express an opinion on one or more specified elements, accounts, or items of a financial statement, such as rentals, royalties, a profit participation, or a provision for income taxes. The auditor may undertake such engagement either in conjunction with an audit of financial statements or as a separate engagement. Because, in such engagements, the auditor expresses an opinion on the specified elements, accounts, or items encompassed by the auditor's report, the measurement of materiality must be related to each such item reported on rather than to the financial statements taken as a whole.

The auditor should not express an opinion on specified elements, accounts, or items included in financial statements on which he or she has expressed an adverse opinion or disclaimed an opinion based on an audit, if such reporting would be the same as expressing a piecemeal opinion on the financial statements. However, an auditor would be able to express an opinion on one or more specified elements, accounts, or items of a financial statement if the matters to be reported on and the related scope of the audit were not intended to, and did not, encompass so many elements, accounts, or items as to constitute a major portion of the financial statements.

If a specified element, account, or item is, or is based on, an entity's net income or stockholders' equity (or the equivalent thereof), the auditor should have audited the complete financial statements to express an opinion on the specified element, account, or item.

In addition, the auditor should consider the effect that any departure, including any additional explanatory language, from the standard report on the audited financial statements might have on the report on a specified element, account, or item thereof.

See Illustration 6 for a list of the items that should be included in the auditor's report on specified elements, accounts, or items of a financial statement. See Illustrations 7 to 11 for examples of auditor's reports on specified elements, accounts, or items of a financial statement.

Auditor's special reports on property and liability insurance companies' loss reserves Certain property and liability insurance companies are required to file with state regulatory agencies a statement of a qualified loss reserve specialist setting forth his or her opinion regarding loss and loss adjustment expense reserves. A *qualified loss reserve specialist* includes an independent auditor who has competency in loss reserve evaluation. Therefore, an auditor may be engaged to report on an insurance company's loss and loss adjustment expense reserves. In such circumstances, the guidance discussed herein is applicable. See Illustration 12 for an example of the auditor's report in such circumstances and the schedule of liabilities for losses and loss adjustment expenses that would accompany the report.

Compliance with Aspects of Contractual Agreements or Regulatory Requirements Related to Audited Financial Statements

Entities may be required by contractual agreements (e.g., bond indentures, loan agreements) or by regulatory agencies to furnish compliance reports by independent auditors. Also, in some situations, lenders or their trustees may request assurance from the auditor that the borrower has complied with certain covenants of the agreement relating to accounting matters. The auditor may satisfy such requests by giving negative assurance relative to the applicable covenants based on the audit of the financial statements, but should *not* extend to covenants that relate to matters that have not been subjected to audit procedures. However, the auditor should not give such assurance if:

1. He or she has not audited the financial statements to which the contractual agreements or regulatory requirements relate; or

2. He or she has expressed an adverse opinion or disclaimed an opinion on the financial statements to which these covenants relate.

The auditor may give assurance in a separate report or in one or more paragraphs of the auditor's report accompanying the financial statements. When the auditor's report is included in the report on the financial statements, the auditor should:

1. Include a paragraph, after the opinion paragraph, that:

    a. Provides negative assurance relative to compliance with the applicable covenants of the agreement, insofar as they relate to accounting matters.

    b. States that the negative assurance is being given in connection with the audit of the financial statements.

    c. States that the audit was not directed primarily toward obtaining knowledge regarding compliance.

2. Include another paragraph that indicates a description and source of significant interpretations made by the entity's management, if any.

3. Include a paragraph at the end of the report that restricts its use to those within the entity and the parties to the contract or agreement, or the regulatory agency with which the report is being filed.

See Illustration 13 for a list of the items that should be included in the auditor's report when a separate report is issued on compliance with contractual agreements or regulatory provisions. See Illustrations 14 to 16 for examples of auditor's reports that might be issued on compliance with contractual agreements or regulatory provisions.

Special-Purpose Financial Presentations to Comply with Contractual Agreements or Regulatory Provisions

An auditor may be engaged to report on special-purpose financial statements, typically intended solely for the use of the parties to an agreement or a regulatory body, that are prepared on a basis of accounting that is:

1. Prescribed in a contractual agreement or regulatory provision that does not constitute a complete presentation of the entity's assets, liabilities, revenues and expenses, but is otherwise prepared in conformity with GAAP or OCBOA *(incomplete presentations)*. Examples of incomplete presentations include:

   a. A schedule of gross income and certain expenses, as required by a governmental agency, measured in conformity with GAAP, but where expenses are defined to exclude certain items such as interest, depreciation, and income taxes.

   b. A schedule of an entity's gross assets and liabilities, as specified in a buy-sell agreement, measured in conformity with GAAP, but limited to the assets to be sold and liabilities to be transferred pursuant to the agreement.

2. Prescribed in an agreement that does not result in a presentation in conformity with GAAP or OCBOA *(non-GAAP or non-OCBOA basis presentations)*. Examples of such non-GAAP or non-OCBOA basis presentations include:

   a. Consolidated financial statements that are prepared pursuant to a loan agreement in which assets (e.g., inventory) are presented on a basis that is not in conformity with GAAP or OCBOA.

   b. Financial statements of an entity (or a segment of it) being acquired that are prepared pursuant to an acquisition agreement in conformity with GAAP, except for certain assets (e.g., receivables, inventories, and properties) for which a valuation basis is specified in the agreement.

Incomplete presentations These types of financial presentations should generally be regarded as financial statements, even though certain items may be excluded. Therefore, the measurement of materiality for purposes of expressing an opinion should be related to the presentations taken as a whole. Also, these presentations should differ from complete financial statements only to the extent necessary to meet the special purposes for which they were prepared. In addition, when these financial presentations contain items that are the same as, or similar to, those contained in a full set of financial statements prepared in conformity with GAAP, similar informative disclosures should be made. The auditor should also be satisfied that the financial statements presented are suitably titled to avoid any implication that these incomplete presentations are intended to present financial position, results of operations, or cash flows.

See Illustration 17 for a list of the items that should be included in the auditor's report on special-purpose financial statements that result in an incomplete presentation. See Illustrations 18 and 19 for examples of auditor's reports in such circumstances.

Non-GAAP or non-OCBOA basis presentations Special-purpose financial statements presented in conformity with a basis of accounting that departs from GAAP or an other comprehensive basis of accounting are *not* considered to be prepared in conformity with a "comprehensive basis of accounting" as discussed above. This is because the criteria used to prepare such special-purpose financial statements do not meet the requirement of being "criteria having substantial support" even though the criteria are definite.

See Illustration 20 for a list of the items that should be included in the auditor's report on special-purpose financial statements that result in non-GAAP or non-OCBOA basis presentations. See Illustration 21 for an example of an auditor's report in such circumstances.

Reporting on current-value financial statements that supplement historical-cost financial statements in presentations of real estate entities An auditor may accept an engagement to report on current-value financial statements that supplement historical-cost financial statements of a real estate entity only if the following two conditions exist:

1. The measurement and disclosure criteria used to prepare the current-value financial statements are reasonable, and

2. Competent persons using the measurement and disclosure criteria would ordinarily obtain materially similar measurements or disclosures.

An auditor may report on such current-value financial statements in a manner similar to that discussed under "Non-GAAP or non-OCBOA basis presentations" above. However, because the current-value financial statements only supplement the historical-cost financial statements and are not presented as a stand-alone presentation, it is not necessary to restrict the use of the auditor's report on the presentation. See Illustration 22 for an example of an auditor's report in such circumstances.

The auditor should also consider the adequacy of disclosures relating to the current-value financial statements. Such disclosures should describe:

1. The accounting policies applied.

2. The basis of presentation.

3. Nature of the entity's properties.

4. Status of construction-in-process.

5. Valuation bases used for each classification of assets and liabilities.

6. Sources of valuation.

Financial Information Presented in Prescribed Forms or Schedules

Printed forms or schedules designed or adopted by the bodies with which they are to be filed often prescribe the wording of an auditor's report. Generally, such wording does not conform to the applicable professional standards and, therefore, the prescribed reports are not acceptable to independent auditors. When a printed report form calls upon an auditor to make a statement that he or she is not justified in making, the auditor should either reword the form or attach a separate report.

Circumstances Requiring Explanatory Language in an Auditor's Special Report

The auditor may encounter certain circumstances that, although not affecting the auditor's unqualified opinion, may nevertheless require that the auditor add additional explanatory language to the special report. Such circumstances include the following:

1. *Lack of consistency in accounting principles*—In such circumstances, the auditor should add an explanatory paragraph, following the opinion paragraph, that (a) describes the change in accounting principles or in the method of their application and (b) refers to the note to the financial presentation (or specified elements, accounts, or items thereof) that discusses the change and its effect. However, the auditor need not follow this reporting requirement when the entity changes its method of presentation in the current year to an OCBOA basis, from a GAAP basis in prior years. Nonetheless, the auditor may wish to add an explanatory paragraph to the report to highlight (1) a difference in the basis of presentation from that used in prior years or (2) that another report has been issued on the entity's financial statements prepared in conformity with an other basis of presentation (e. g., when cash basis financial statements are issued in addition to GAAP financial statements). For further guidance, see AU Section 508 (Reports on Audited Financial Statements).

2. *Going-concern uncertainties*—If the auditor believes there is substantial doubt about the entity's ability to continue as a going concern for a reasonable period of time not to exceed one year beyond the date of the financial statements, the auditor should add an explanatory paragraph, following the opinion paragraph, if substantial doubt is relevant to the presentation.

3. *Other auditors*—When the auditor decides to make reference to the report of another auditor as a basis, in part, for his or her opinion, the auditor should (a) disclose that fact in the introductory paragraph of his or her report and (b) refer to the other auditors' report in the opinion paragraph. For further guidance, see AU Section 508 (Reports on Audited Financial Statements).

4. *Comparative financial statements (or specified elements, accounts, or items thereof)*—If the auditor expresses an opinion on prior-period financial presentations that is different from the opinion he or she previously

expressed on that same information, the auditor should disclose all of the substantive reasons for the different opinion in a separate explanatory paragraph preceding the opinion paragraph. For further guidance, see AU Section 508 (Reports on Audited Financial Statements).

PRACTICE ISSUES AND FREQUENTLY ASKED QUESTIONS

Reporting on OCBOA Financial Statements

Issue 1: Can titles of OCBOA financial statements be the same as titles for similar statements prepared in accordance with GAAP?

No. Terms such as *balance sheet, statement of financial position, statement of income, statement of operations, and statement of cash flows,* or similar unmodified titles are generally understood to be applicable only to financial statements in conformity with GAAP. Therefore, the auditor should make sure that titles of OCBOA financial statements are suitably modified. The following is a summary of appropriate titles for financial statements prepared on the cash and income tax bases of accounting versus GAAP:

GAAP	Cash Basis	Income Tax Basis
• Balance Sheet, *or* Statement of Financial Position	• Statement of Assets and Liabilities Arising From Cash Transactions, *or* Statement of Assets, Liabilities, and Equity— Cash Basis	• Statement of Assets, Liabilities, and Equity— Income Tax Basis
• Statement of Income, *or* Statement of Operations	• Statement of Revenues Collected and Expenses Paid, *or* Statement of Revenues and Expenses—Cash Basis	• Statement of Revenues and Expenses—Income Tax Basis
• Statement of Retained Earnings	• Statement of Retained Earnings—Cash Basis	• Statement of Retained Earnings—Income Tax Basis
• Statement of Changes in Stockholders' Equity	• Statement of Changes in Stockholders' Equity— Cash Basis	• Statement of Changes in Stockholders' Equity— Income Tax Basis
• Statement of Cash Flows	• Statement of Cash Flows—Cash Basis	• Statement of Cash Flows—Income Tax Basis

Issue 2: What is the effect on the auditor's report if titles of OCBOA financial statements are the same as those for similar statements prepared in accordance with GAAP?

If the auditor believes that the titles of OCBOA financial statements have not been properly modified, so that there is no implication that the statements are presented in conformity with GAAP, the auditor should disclose his or her reservations in an explanatory paragraph of the report and qualify the opinion.

Issue 3: Is a statement of cash flows required to be presented if the financial statements are prepared on an OCBOA basis?

No. ASC 230, *Statement of Cash Flows*, requires a statement of cash flows to be presented only whenever financial statements purport to present financial position and results of operations *in conformity with GAAP*. Therefore, a statement of cash flows is not required to be presented if the financial statements are prepared on a comprehensive basis of accounting other than GAAP, such as cash, modified cash, or income tax basis. Furthermore, the auditor's report should not refer to the omission of the statement of cash flows, because it is not required.

Issue 4: What is the effect on the auditor's report if, in connection with reporting on OCBOA financial statements, the auditor concludes that the statements are not presented fairly on the basis of accounting described?

If the auditor concludes that the financial statements are not presented fairly on the basis of accounting described, he or she should:

1. Disclose, in an explanatory paragraph preceding the opinion paragraph of the report, all the substantive reasons for the modified opinion; and

2. Include in the opinion paragraph the appropriate modifying language and a reference to such explanatory paragraph.

The foregoing modifications are also applicable in circumstances where there is a limitation on the scope of the audit.

Issue 5: In connection with describing the basis of presentation in OCBOA financial statements, is the auditor required to quantify the effects of differences between that basis and GAAP?

No. The summary of significant accounting policies should describe the basis of presentation used and indicate how that basis differs from GAAP. However, the effects of the differences do not have to be quantified. See Issue 6 below.

Issue 6: What are some examples of appropriate disclosures of an other comprehensive basis of accounting in notes to the financial statements?

The following are examples of appropriate note disclosures of an other comprehensive basis of accounting:

Example 1—Modified Cash Basis of Accounting

> The Company's policy is to prepare its financial statements on the modified cash basis of accounting, which is a comprehensive basis of accounting other than generally accepted accounting principles. Under this basis, certain revenues are recognized when received rather than when earned and certain expenditures are recognized when paid rather than when incurred. Also, depreciation of fixed assets and accruals for taxes are reported on the financial statements.

Example 2—Income Tax Basis of Accounting

> The financial statements are prepared on the accounting basis used for the Partnership's federal income tax return. Consequently, property and equipment are depreciated in accordance with the requirements of the Internal Revenue Code. Under generally accepted accounting principles (GAAP), property and equipment are depreciated over their estimated useful lives. Accordingly, the financial statements are not intended to present financial position, results of operations, and cash flows in accordance with GAAP.

Other Reporting Issues

Issue 7: Do the provisions of this Section apply if an auditor has been engaged to perform agreed-upon procedures to specified elements, accounts, or items of a financial statement?

No. See AT Section 201 (Agreed-Upon Procedures Engagements) for guidance when reporting on the results of applying agreed-upon procedures to one or more specified elements, accounts, or items of a financial statement.

Issue 8: Do the provisions of this Section apply if an auditor has been engaged to test compliance with laws and regulations in accordance with the "Yellow Book"?

No. If the auditor is engaged to test compliance with laws and regulations in accordance with *Government Auditing Standards* issued by the Comptroller General of the United States ("Yellow Book"), he or she should follow guidance contained in AU Section 801 (Compliance Audits).

In addition, AU Section 801 is the authoritative guidance that the auditor should follow when testing compliance with laws and regulations in connection with a single audit in accordance with an Office of Management Budget (OMB) Circular.

Issue 9: When issuing special reports under this Section, may the auditor add an explanatory paragraph to emphasize a matter regarding the financial presentation?

Yes. The auditor may add an explanatory paragraph to emphasize a matter regarding the financial presentation being reported on, as in reports on financial statements prepared in conformity with GAAP.

ILLUSTRATIONS AND PRACTICE AIDS

Illustrations Relating to Auditors' Reports on Financial Statements Prepared in Conformity with an Other Comprehensive Basis of Accounting (OCBOA) (Illustrations 1 through 5)

ILLUSTRATION 1—COMPONENTS OF THE AUDITOR'S REPORT ON FINANCIAL STATEMENTS PREPARED IN CONFORMITY WITH AN OCBOA

An auditor's report on financial statements prepared in conformity with an OCBOA should include the following:

1. A title that includes the word *independent.*
2. A paragraph stating that:
   a. The financial statements identified were audited;
   b. The financial statements are the responsibility of the Company's management; and
   c. The auditor is responsible for expressing an opinion on the financial statements based on the audit.
3. A paragraph stating that:
   a. The audit was conducted in accordance with GAAS, and an identification of the United States of America as the country of origin of those standards;

b. GAAS require that the auditor plan and perform the audit to obtain reasonable assurance about whether the financial statements are free of material misstatement;

c. An audit includes:

(1) Examining, on a test basis, evidence supporting the amounts and disclosures in the financial statements

(2) Assessing the accounting principles used and significant estimates made by management

(3) Evaluating the overall financial statement presentation

d. The auditor believes that the audit provides a reasonable basis for his or her opinion.

4. A paragraph stating:

a. The basis of presentation and referring to the note to the financial statements that describes the basis; and

b. That the basis of presentation is a comprehensive basis of accounting other than GAAP.

5. A paragraph that expresses the auditor's opinion, or disclaims an opinion, on whether the financial statements are presented fairly, in all material respects, in conformity with the basis of accounting described. If the auditor concludes that the financial statements are not presented fairly on the basis of accounting described, or if there has been a limitation on the scope of the audit, the auditor should:

a. Disclose, in an explanatory paragraph preceding the opinion paragraph of the report, all the substantive reasons for his or her conclusion; and

b. Include in the opinion paragraph the appropriate modifying language and a reference to such explanatory paragraph.

6. If the financial statements are prepared in conformity with the requirements or financial reporting provisions of a governmental regulatory agency, a separate paragraph at the end of the report stating that its use is restricted to those within the entity and the regulatory agency, and that it should not be used by anyone other than these specified parties.

7. Manual or printed signature of the auditor's firm.

8. Date of the audit report.

ILLUSTRATION 2—AUDITOR'S REPORT ON FINANCIAL STATEMENTS PREPARED ON A BASIS PRESCRIBED BY A REGULATORY AGENCY

Independent Auditor's Report

Board of Directors and Stockholders
ABC Insurance Company

We have audited the accompanying statements of admitted assets, liabilities, and surplus—statutory basis of ABC Insurance Company as of December 31, 20X2, and 20X1, and the related statements of income and cash flows—statutory basis and changes in surplus—statutory basis for the years then ended. These financial statements are the responsibility of the Company's management. Our responsibility is to express an opinion on these financial statements based on our audits.

We conducted our audits in accordance with auditing standards generally accepted in the United States of America. Those standards require that we plan and perform the audit to obtain reasonable assurance about whether the financial statements are free of material misstatement. An audit includes examining, on a test basis, evidence supporting the amounts and disclosures in the financial statements. An audit also includes assessing the accounting principles used and significant estimates made by management, as well as evaluating the overall financial statement presentation. We believe that our audits provide a reasonable basis for our opinion.

As described in Note [X], these financial statements were prepared in conformity with the accounting practices prescribed or permitted by the Insurance Department of *[State]*, which is a comprehensive basis of accounting other than generally accepted accounting principles.

In our opinion, the financial statements referred to above present fairly, in all material respects, the admitted assets, liabilities, and surplus of ABC Insurance Company as of December 31, 20X2, and 20X1, and the results of its operations and its cash flows for the years then ended, on the basis of accounting described in Note [X].

This report is intended solely for the information and use of the board of directors and management of ABC Insurance Company and *[name of regulatory agency]* and is not intended to be and should not be used by anyone other than these specified parties.

[*Signature*]

[*Date*]

ILLUSTRATION 3—AUDITOR'S REPORT ON FINANCIAL STATEMENTS PREPARED ON THE ENTITY'S INCOME TAX BASIS

Independent Auditor's Report

Board of Directors and Stockholders
ABC Partnership

We have audited the accompanying statements of assets, liabilities, and capital—income tax basis of ABC Partnership as of December 31, 20X2, and 20X1, and the related statements of revenue and expenses—income tax basis and of changes in partners' capital accounts—income tax basis for the years then ended. These financial statements are the responsibility of the Partnership's management. Our responsibility is to express an opinion on these financial statements based on our audits.

We conducted our audits in accordance with auditing standards generally accepted in the United States of America. Those standards require that we plan and perform the audit to obtain reasonable assurance about whether the financial statements are free of material misstatement. An audit includes examining, on a test basis, evidence supporting the amounts and disclosures in the financial statements.

An audit also includes assessing the accounting principles used and significant estimates made by management, as well as evaluating the overall financial statement presentation. We believe that our audits provide a reasonable basis for our opinion.

As described in Note [X], these financial statements were prepared on the basis of accounting the Partnership uses for income tax purposes, which is a comprehensive basis of accounting other than accounting principles generally accepted in the United States of America.

In our opinion, the financial statements referred to above present fairly, in all material respects, the assets, liabilities, and capital of ABC Partnership as of

December 31, 20X2, and 20X1, and its revenue and expenses and changes in partners' capital accounts for the years then ended, on the basis of accounting described in Note [X].

[*Signature*]

[*Date*]

ILLUSTRATION 4—AUDITOR'S REPORT ON FINANCIAL STATEMENTS PREPARED ON THE CASH BASIS

Independent Auditor's Report

Board of Directors and Stockholders
ABC Company

We have audited the accompanying statements of assets and liabilities arising from cash transactions of ABC Company as of December 31, 20X2, and 20X1, and the related statements of revenue collected and expenses paid for the years then ended. These financial statements are the responsibility of the Company's management. Our responsibility is to express an opinion on these financial statements based on our audits.

We conducted our audits in accordance with auditing standards generally accepted in the United States of America. Those standards require that we plan and perform the audit to obtain reasonable assurance about whether the financial statements are free of material misstatement. An audit includes examining, on a test basis, evidence supporting the amounts and disclosures in the financial statements. An audit also includes assessing the accounting principles used and significant estimates made by management, as well as evaluating the overall financial statement presentation. We believe that our audits provide a reasonable basis for our opinion.

As described in Note [X], these financial statements were prepared on the basis of cash receipts and disbursements, which is a comprehensive basis of accounting other than accounting principles generally accepted in the United States of America.

In our opinion, the financial statements referred to above present fairly, in all material respects, the assets and liabilities arising from cash transactions of ABC Company as of December 31, 20X2, and 20X1, and its revenue collected and expenses paid during the years then ended, on the basis of accounting described in Note [X].

[*Signature*]

[*Date*]

ILLUSTRATION 5—AUDITOR'S REPORT ON FINANCIAL STATEMENTS INCLUDED IN INTERNAL REVENUE FORM 990, "RETURN OF ORGANIZATIONS EXEMPT FROM INCOME TAX"

Independent Auditor's Report

Board of Directors
ABC Charity

We have audited the balance sheet (Part IV) of ABC Charity as of December 31, 20X2, and the related statement of revenue, expenses and changes in net assets (Part 1) and statement of functional expenses (Part II) for the year then ended included in the accompanying Internal Revenue Service Form 990. These financial statements are the responsibility of ABC Charity's management. Our responsibility is to express an opinion on these financial statements based on our audit.

We conducted our audit in accordance with auditing standards generally accepted in the United States of America. Those standards require that we plan and perform the audit to obtain reasonable assurance about whether the financial statements are free of material misstatement. An audit includes examining, on a test basis, evidence supporting the amounts and disclosures in the financial statements. An audit also includes assessing the accounting principles used and significant estimates made by management, as well as evaluating the overall financial statement presentation. We believe that our audit provides a reasonable basis for our opinion.

As described in Note [X], these financial statements were prepared in conformity with the accounting practices prescribed by the Internal Revenue Service and the Office of the State of _____, which is a comprehensive basis of accounting other than accounting principles generally accepted in the United States of America.

In our opinion, the financial statements referred to above present fairly, in all material respects, the assets, liabilities and fund balances of ABC Charity as of December 31, 20X2, and its revenue and expenses and changes in fund balances for the year then ended on the basis of accounting described in Note [X].

Our audit was made for the purpose of forming an opinion on the above financial statements taken as a whole. The accompanying information on pages X to Y is presented for purposes of additional analysis and is not a required part of the above financial statements. Such information, except for that portion marked "unaudited," on which we express no opinion, has been subjected to the auditing procedures applied in the audit of the above financial statements; and, in our opinion, the information is fairly stated in all material respects in relation to the financial statements taken as a whole.

This report is intended solely for the information and use of the board of directors and management of ABC Charity, the Internal Revenue Service, and the Office of the State of _____ and is not intended to be and should not be used by anyone other than these specified parties.

[*Signature*]

[*Date*]

Illustrations Relating to Auditors' Reports on Specified Elements, Accounts, or Items of a Financial Statement (Illustrations 6 through 12)

ILLUSTRATION 6—COMPONENTS OF THE AUDITOR'S REPORT ON SPECIFIED ELEMENTS, ACCOUNTS, OR ITEMS OF A FINANCIAL STATEMENT

An auditor's report on one or more specified elements, accounts, or items of a financial statement should include the following:

1. A title that includes the word *independent.*

2. A paragraph stating that:

   a. The specified elements, accounts, or items were audited. If the audit was in conjunction with an audit of the entity's financial statements, the paragraph should so state and indicate the date of the auditor's report on those financial statements. Also, any departure from the standard report on those statements should be disclosed if considered relevant;

   b. The specified elements, accounts, or items are the responsibility of the Company's management; and

    c. The auditor is responsible for expressing an opinion on the specified elements, accounts, or items based on the audit.

3. A paragraph stating that:

    a. The audit was conducted in accordance with GAAS, and an identification of the United States of America as the country of origin of those standards;

    b. GAAS require that the auditor plan and perform the audit to obtain reasonable assurance about whether the specified elements, accounts, or items are free of material misstatement;

    c. An audit includes:

        (1) Examining, on a test basis, evidence supporting the amounts and disclosures in the specified elements, accounts, or items

        (2) Assessing the accounting principles used and significant estimates made by management

        (3) Evaluating the overall presentation of the specified elements, accounts, or items

    d. The auditor believes that the audit provides a reasonable basis for his or her opinion.

4. A paragraph describing:

    a. The basis on which the specified elements, accounts, or items are presented and, if applicable, any agreements specifying such basis if the presentation is not prepared in conformity with GAAP; and

    b. If necessary, significant interpretations and the sources thereof, if any, made by management that relate to the provisions of a relevant agreement.

5. A paragraph that expresses the auditor's opinion, or disclaims an opinion, on whether the specified elements, accounts, or items are presented fairly, in all material respects, in conformity with the basis of accounting described. If the auditor concludes that such items are not presented fairly on the basis of accounting described, or if there has been a limitation on the scope of the audit, the auditor should:

    a. Disclose, in an explanatory paragraph preceding the opinion paragraph of the report, all the substantive reasons for his or her conclusion; and

    b. Include in the opinion paragraph the appropriate modifying language and a reference to such explanatory paragraph.

6. If the specified element, account, or item is prepared to comply with the requirements or financial reporting provisions of a contract or agreement that results in a presentation that is not in conformity with either GAAP or OCBOA, a separate paragraph at the end of the report stating that its use is restricted to those within the entity and the parties to the contract or agreement, and that it should not be used by anyone other than these specified parties.

7. Manual or printed signature of the auditor's firm.

8. Date of the audit report.

ILLUSTRATION 7—AUDITOR'S REPORT ON ACCOUNTS RECEIVABLE

Independent Auditor's Report

Board of Directors and Stockholders
ABC Company

We have audited the accompanying schedule of accounts receivable of ABC Company as of December 31, 20X2. This schedule is the responsibility of the Company's management. Our responsibility is to express an opinion on this schedule based on our audit.

We conducted our audit in accordance with auditing standards generally accepted in the United States of America. Those standards require that we plan and perform the audit to obtain reasonable assurance about whether the schedule of accounts receivable is free of material misstatement. An audit includes examining, on a test basis, evidence supporting the amounts and disclosures in the schedule of accounts receivable. An audit also includes assessing the accounting principles used and significant estimates made by management, as well as evaluating the overall schedule presentation. We believe that our audit provides a reasonable basis for our opinion.

In our opinion, the schedule of accounts receivable referred to above presents fairly, in all material respects, the accounts receivable of ABC Company as of December 31, 20X2, in conformity with accounting principles generally accepted in the United States of America.

[*Signature*]

[*Date*]

ILLUSTRATION 8—AUDITOR'S REPORT ON AMOUNT OF SALES FOR THE PURPOSE OF COMPUTING RENTAL

Independent Auditor's Report

Board of Directors and Stockholders
XYZ Stores Corporation

We have audited the accompanying schedule of gross sales (as defined in the lease agreement dated March 4, 20X1, between ABC Company, as lessor, and XYZ Stores Corporation, as lessee) of XYZ Stores Corporation at its Main Street store, [*City*], [*State*], for the year ended December 31, 20X2. This schedule is the responsibility of XYZ Stores Corporation's management. Our responsibility is to express an opinion on this schedule based on our audit.

We conducted our audit in accordance with auditing standards generally accepted in the United States of America. Those standards require that we plan and perform the audit to obtain reasonable assurance about whether the schedule of gross sales is free of material misstatement. An audit includes examining, on a test basis, evidence supporting the amounts and disclosures in the schedule of gross sales. An audit also includes assessing the accounting principles used and significant estimates made by management, as well as evaluating the overall schedule presentation. We believe that our audit provides a reasonable basis for our opinion.

In our opinion, the schedule of gross sales referred to above presents fairly, in all material respects, the gross sales of XYZ Stores Corporation at its Main Street store, [*City*], [*State*], for the year ended December 31, 20X2, as defined in the lease agreement referred to in the first paragraph.

This report is intended solely for the information and use of the boards of directors and managements of XYZ Stores Corporation and ABC Company and is not intended to be and should not be used by anyone other than these specified parties.

[*Signature*]

[*Date*]

ILLUSTRATION 9—AUDITOR'S REPORT ON ROYALTIES

Independent Auditor's Report

Board of Directors and Stockholders
ABC Company

We have audited the accompanying schedule of royalties applicable to engine production of the Q Division of ABC Company for the year ended December 31, 20X2, under the terms of a license agreement dated May 14, 20X1, between XYZ Corporation and ABC Company. This schedule is the responsibility of ABC Company's management. Our responsibility is to express an opinion on this schedule based on our audit.

We conducted our audit in accordance with auditing standards generally accepted in the United States of America. Those standards require that we plan and perform the audit to obtain reasonable assurance about whether the schedule of royalties is free of material misstatement. An audit includes examining, on a test basis, evidence supporting the amounts and disclosures in the schedule of royalties. An audit also includes assessing the accounting principles used and significant estimates made by management, as well as evaluating the overall schedule presentation. We believe that our audit provides a reasonable basis for our opinion.

We have been informed that, under ABC Company's interpretation of the agreement referred to in the first paragraph, royalties were based on the number of engines produced after giving effect to a reduction for production retirements that were scrapped, but without a reduction for field returns that were scrapped, even though the field returns were replaced with new engines without charge to customers.

In our opinion, the schedule of royalties referred to above presents fairly, in all material respects, the number of engines produced by the Q Division of ABC Company during the year ended December 31, 20X2, and the amount of royalties applicable thereto, under the license agreement referred to above.

This report is intended solely for the information and use of the boards of directors and managements of ABC Company and XYZ Corporation and is not intended to be and should not be used by anyone other than these specified parties.

[*Signature*]

[*Date*]

ILLUSTRATION 10—AUDITOR'S REPORT ON A PROFIT PARTICIPATION

Independent Auditor's Report

Board of Directors and Stockholders
ABC Company

We have audited, in accordance with auditing standards generally accepted in the United States of America, the financial statements of ABC Company for the year ended December 31, 20X2, and have issued our report thereon dated March 5, 20X3. We have also audited ABC Company's schedule of John Smith's profit participation for the year ended December 31, 20X2. This schedule is the responsibility of the Company's management. Our responsibility is to express an opinion on this schedule based on our audit.

We conducted our audit of the schedule in accordance with auditing standards generally accepted in the United States of America. Those standards require that we plan and perform the audit to obtain reasonable assurance about whether the schedule of profit participation is free of material misstatement. An audit includes examining, on a test basis, evidence supporting the amounts and disclosures in the schedule. An audit also includes assessing the accounting principles used and significant estimates made by management, as well as evaluating the overall schedule presentation. We believe that our audit provides a reasonable basis for our opinion.

We have been informed that the documents that govern the determination of John Smith's profit participation are (a) the employment agreement between John Smith and ABC Company dated February 1, 20X1, (b) the production and distribution agreement between ABC Company and Television Network Incorporated dated March 1, 20X1, and (c) the studio facilities agreement between ABC Company and QRX Studios dated April 1, 20X1, as amended November 1, 20X1.

In our opinion, the schedule of profit participation referred to above presents fairly, in all material respects, John Smith's participation in the profits of ABC Company for the year ended December 31, 20X2, in accordance with the provisions of the agreements referred to above.

This report is intended solely for the information and use of the boards of directors and managements of ABC Company and John Smith and is not intended to be and should not be used by anyone other than these specified parties.

[*Signature*]

[*Date*]

ILLUSTRATION 11—AUDITOR'S REPORT ON FEDERAL AND STATE INCOME TAXES INCLUDED IN FINANCIAL STATEMENTS

Independent Auditor's Report

Board of Directors and Stockholders
ABC Company

We have audited, in accordance with auditing standards generally accepted in the United States of America, the financial statements of ABC Company for the year ended June 30, 20X2, and have issued our report thereon dated August 13, 20X2. We have also audited the current and deferred provision for the Company's federal and state income taxes for the year ended June 30, 20X2, included in those financial statements, and the related asset and liability tax accounts as of June 30, 20X2. This income tax information is the responsibility of the Company's management. Our responsibility is to express an opinion on it based on our audit.

We conducted our audit of the income tax information in accordance with auditing standards generally accepted in the United States of America. Those standards require that we plan and perform the audit to obtain reasonable assurance about whether the federal and state income tax accounts are free of material misstatement. An audit includes examining, on a test basis, evidence supporting the amounts and disclosures related to the federal and state income tax accounts. An audit also includes assessing the accounting principles used and significant estimates made by management, as well as evaluating the overall presentation of the federal and state income tax accounts. We believe that our audit provides a reasonable basis for our opinion.

In our opinion, the Company has paid or, in all material respects, made adequate provision in the financial statements referred to above for the payment of all federal and state income taxes and for related deferred income taxes that could be reasonably estimated at the time of our audit of the financial statements of ABC Company for the year ended June 30, 20X2.

[*Signature*]

[*Date*]

ILLUSTRATION 12—AUDITOR'S REPORT ON AN INSURANCE COMPANY'S LOSS AND LOSS ADJUSTMENT EXPENSE RESERVES AND THE ACCOMPANYING SCHEDULE OF RELATED LIABILITIES

Independent Auditor's Report

Board of Directors and Stockholders
ABC Insurance Company

We are members of the American Institute of Certified Public Accountants (AICPA) and are the independent public accountants of ABC Insurance Company. We acknowledge our responsibility under the AICPA's *Code of Professional Conduct* to undertake only those engagements which we can complete with professional competence.

We have audited the financial statements prepared in conformity with accounting principles generally accepted in the United States of America [*or prepared in conformity with accounting practices prescribed or permitted by the Insurance Department of the State of* _____] of ABC Insurance Company as of December 31, 20X2, and have issued our report thereon dated March 5, 20X3. In the course of our audit, we have audited the estimated liabilities for unpaid losses and unpaid loss adjustment expenses of ABC Insurance Company as of December 31, 20X2, as set forth in the accompanying schedule including consideration of the assumptions and methods relating to the estimation of such liabilities.

In our opinion, the accompanying schedule presents fairly, in all material respects, the estimated unpaid losses and unpaid loss adjustment expenses of ABC Insurance Company that could be reasonably estimated at December 31, 20X2, in conformity with accounting practices prescribed or permitted by the Insurance Department of the State of _____ on a basis consistent with that of the preceding year.

This report is intended solely for the information and use of the board of directors and management of ABC Insurance Company and [*the state regulatory agencies to whose jurisdiction the entity is subject*] and is not intended to be and should not be used by anyone other than these specified parties.

[*Signature*]

[*Date*]

ABC Insurance Company
Schedule of Liabilities for Losses and Loss Adjustment Expenses
December 31, 20X2

Liability for losses	$XX,XXX,XXX
Liability for loss adjustment expenses	X,XXX,XXX
Total	$XX,XXX,XXX

Note 1—Basis of Presentation

The above schedule has been prepared in conformity with accounting practices prescribed or permitted by the Insurance Department of the State of_____ [*Significant differences between statutory practices and generally accepted accounting principles for the calculation of the above amounts should be described but the monetary effect of any such differences need not be stated.*]

Losses and loss adjustment expenses are provided for when incurred in accordance with the applicable requirements of the insurance laws [*and/or regulations*] of the State of _____. Such provisions include (1) individual case estimates for reported losses, (2) estimates received from other insurers with respect to reinsurance assumed, (3) estimates for unreported losses based on past experience modified for current trends, and (4) estimates of expenses for investigating and settling claims.

Note 2—Reinsurance

The Company reinsures certain portions of its liability insurance coverage to limit the amount of loss on individual claims and purchases catastrophe insurance to protect against aggregate single occurrence losses. Certain portions of property insurance are reinsured on a quota share basis.

The liability for losses and the liability for loss adjustment expenses were reduced by $_____ and $_____, respectively, for reinsurance ceded to other companies.

Contingent liability exists with respect to reinsurance which would become an actual liability in the event the reinsuring companies, or any of them, might be unable to meet their obligations to the Company under existing reinsurance agreements.

Illustrations Relating to Auditors' Compliance Reports with Contractual Agreements or Regulatory Requirements Related to Audited Financial Statements (Illustrations 13 through 16)

ILLUSTRATION 13—COMPONENTS OF A SEPARATE AUDITOR'S REPORT ON COMPLIANCE WITH CONTRACTUAL AGREEMENTS OR REGULATORY PROVISIONS

When an auditor's report on compliance with contractual agreements or regulatory provisions is issued in a separate report, the report should include the following:

1. A title that includes the word *independent.*

2. A paragraph:

   a. Stating that the financial statements were audited in accordance with GAAS and that includes an identification of the United States of America as the country of origin of those standards and the date of the auditor's report on those financial statements; and

   b. Disclosing any departure from the standard report on those financial statements.

3. A paragraph:

   a. Referring to the specific covenants or paragraphs of the agreement;

   b. Providing negative assurance relative to compliance with the applicable covenants of the agreement insofar as they relate to accounting matters;

   c. Specifying that the negative assurance is being given in connection with the audit of the financial statements; and

   d. Stating that the audit was not directed primarily toward obtaining knowledge regarding compliance.

4. A paragraph that includes a description and the source of any significant interpretations made by the Company's management relating to the provisions of a relevant agreement.

5. A separate paragraph at the end of the report stating that its use is restricted to those within the entity and the parties to the contract or

agreement or the regulatory agency with which the report is being filed, and that it should not be used by anyone other than these specified parties.

6. Manual or printed signature of the auditor's firm.

7. Date of the report.

ILLUSTRATION 14—AUDITOR'S REPORT ON COMPLIANCE WITH CONTRACTUAL PROVISIONS IS INCLUDED IN THE REPORT ON THE ENTITY'S AUDITED FINANCIAL STATEMENTS

Independent Auditor's Report

Board of Directors and Stockholders
ABC Company

We have audited the accompanying balance sheet of ABC Company as of December 31, 20X2, and the related statements of income, retained earnings, and cash flows for the year then ended. These financial statements are the responsibility of the Company's management. Our responsibility is to express an opinion on these financial statements based on our audit.

We conducted our audit in accordance with auditing standards generally accepted in the United States of America. Those standards require that we plan and perform the audit to obtain reasonable assurance about whether the financial statements are free of material misstatement. An audit includes examining, on a test basis, evidence supporting the amounts and disclosures in the financial statements. An audit also includes assessing the accounting principles used and significant estimates made by management, as well as evaluating the overall financial statement presentation. We believe that our audit provides a reasonable basis for our opinion.

In our opinion, the financial statements referred to above present fairly, in all material respects, the financial position of ABC Company as of December 31, 20X2, and the results of its operations and its cash flows for the year then ended in conformity with accounting principles generally accepted in the United States of America.

In connection with our audit, nothing came to our attention that caused us to believe that the Company failed to comply with the terms, covenants, provisions, or conditions of sections [XX] to [XX], inclusive, of the Indenture dated May 11, 20X0, with XYZ Bank insofar as they relate to accounting matters. However, our audit was not directed primarily toward obtaining knowledge of such noncompliance.

This report is intended solely for the information and use of the boards of directors and management of ABC Company and XYZ Bank and is not intended to be and should not be used by anyone other than these specified parties.

[*Signature*]

[*Date*]

ILLUSTRATION 15—AUDITOR'S SEPARATE REPORT ON COMPLIANCE WITH CONTRACTUAL PROVISIONS

Independent Auditor's Report

Board of Directors and Stockholders
ABC Company

We have audited, in accordance with auditing standards generally accepted in the United States of America, the balance sheet of ABC Company as of December 31, 20X2, and the related statements of income, retained earnings, and cash flows for the year then ended, and have issued our report thereon dated February 19, 20X3.

In connection with our audit, nothing came to our attention that caused us to believe that the Company failed to comply with the terms, covenants, provisions, or conditions of sections [XX] to [XX], inclusive, of the Indenture dated May 11, 20X0, with XYZ Bank insofar as they relate to accounting matters. However, our audit was not directed primarily toward obtaining knowledge of such noncompliance.

This report is intended solely for the information and use of the boards of directors and managements of ABC Company and XYZ Bank and is not intended to be and should not be used by anyone other than these specified parties.

[*Signature*]

[*Date*]

ILLUSTRATION 16—AUDITOR'S SEPARATE REPORT ON COMPLIANCE WITH REGULATORY REQUIREMENTS WHEN THE AUDITOR'S REPORT ON THE FINANCIAL STATEMENTS INCLUDED AN EXPLANATORY PARAGRAPH BECAUSE OF AN UNCERTAINTY

Independent Auditor's Report

Board of Directors and Stockholders
ABC Company

We have audited, in accordance with auditing standards generally accepted in the United States of America, the balance sheet of ABC Company as of December 31, 20X2, and the related statements of income, retained earnings, and cash flows for the year then ended, and have issued our report thereon dated February 19, 20X3, which included an explanatory paragraph that described the litigation discussed in Note [X] of those statements.

In connection with our audit, nothing came to our attention that caused us to believe that the Company failed to comply with the accounting provisions in sections (1), (2) and (3) of the [*name of state regulatory agency*]. However, our audit was not directed primarily toward obtaining knowledge of such noncompliance.

This report is intended solely for the information and use of the board of directors and managements of ABC Company and the [*name of state regulatory agency*] and is not intended to be and should not be used by anyone other than these specified parties.

[*Signature*]

[*Date*]

Illustrations Relating to Auditors' Reports on Special-Purpose Financial Presentations to Comply with Contractual Agreements or Regulatory Provisions (Illustrations 17 through 22)

ILLUSTRATION 17—COMPONENTS OF AN AUDITOR'S REPORT ON SPECIAL-PURPOSE FINANCIAL STATEMENTS THAT RESULT IN AN INCOMPLETE PRESENTATION

An auditor's report on special purpose-financial statements that result in an incomplete presentation should include the following:

    1. A title that includes the word *independent*.

    2. A paragraph stating that:

        a. The financial statements identified were audited;

b. The financial statements are the responsibility of the Company's management; and

c. The auditor is responsible for expressing an opinion on the financial statements based on the audit.

3. A paragraph stating that:

    a. The audit was conducted in accordance with GAAS, and an identification of the United States of America as the country of origin of those standards;

    b. GAAS require that the auditor plan and perform the audit to obtain reasonable assurance about whether the financial statements are free of material misstatement;

    c. An audit includes:

        (1) Examining, on a test basis, evidence supporting the amounts and disclosures in the financial statements

        (2) Assessing the accounting principles used and significant estimates made by management

        (3) Evaluating the overall financial statement presentation

    d. The auditor believes that the audit provides a reasonable basis for his or her opinion.

4. A paragraph that:

    a. Explains what the presentation is intended to present and refers to the note to the special-purpose financial statements that describes the basis of presentation; and

    b. States that the presentation is not intended to be a complete presentation of the entity's assets, liabilities, revenues and expenses, if the basis of presentation is in conformity with GAAP or OCBOA.

5. A paragraph that expresses the auditor's opinion, or disclaims an opinion, on whether the information the presentation is intended to present is fairly presented, in all material respects, in conformity with GAAP or OCBOA. If the auditor concludes that the information the presentation is intended to present is not presented fairly on the basis of accounting described, or if there has been a limitation on the scope of the audit, the auditor should:

    a. Disclose, in an explanatory paragraph preceding the opinion paragraph of the report, all the substantive reasons for his or her conclusion; and

    b. Include in the opinion paragraph the appropriate modifying language and a reference to such explanatory paragraph.

6. A separate paragraph at the end of the report stating that its use is restricted to (a) those within the entity, (b) the parties to the contract or agreement, (c) the regulatory agency with which the report is being filed, or (d) those with whom the entity is negotiating directly, and that it should not be used by anyone other than these specified parties. However, such a paragraph should not be included if the report and related financial presentation are to be filed with a regulatory agency (e.g., SEC), and are to be included in a document (e.g., prospectus) that is distributed to the general public.

7. Manual or printed signature of the auditor's firm.

8. Date of the audit report.

ILLUSTRATION 18—AUDITOR'S REPORT ON A SCHEDULE OF GROSS INCOME AND CERTAIN EXPENSES TO MEET A REGULATORY REQUIREMENT AND TO BE INCLUDED IN A DOCUMENT DISTRIBUTED TO THE GENERAL PUBLIC (INCOMPLETE PRESENTATION)

Independent Auditor's Report

Board of Directors and Stockholders
ABC Company

We have audited the accompanying Historical Summaries of Gross Income and Direct Operating Expenses of XYZ Apartments, City, State (Historical Summaries), for each of the three years in the period ended December 31, 20X2. These Historical Summaries are the responsibility of the Apartments' management. Our responsibility is to express an opinion on the Historical Summaries based on our audits.

We conducted our audits in accordance with auditing standards generally accepted in the United States of America. Those standards require that we plan and perform the audit to obtain reasonable assurance about whether the Historical Summaries are free of material misstatement. An audit includes examining, on a test basis, evidence supporting the amounts and disclosures in the Historical Summaries. An audit also includes assessing the accounting principles used and significant estimates made by management, as well as evaluating the overall presentation of the Historical Summaries. We believe that our audits provide a reasonable basis for our opinion.

The accompanying Historical Summaries were prepared for the purpose of complying with the rules and regulations of the Securities and Exchange Commission (for inclusion in the registration statement on Form S-11 of ABC Company) as described in Note [X] and are not intended to be a complete presentation of the Apartments' revenues and expenses.

In our opinion, the Historical Summaries referred to above present fairly, in all material respects, the gross income and direct operating expenses described in Note [X] of XYZ Apartments for each of the three years in the period ended December 31, 20X2, in conformity with accounting principles generally accepted in the United States of America.

[*Signature*]

[*Date*]

ILLUSTRATION 19—AUDITOR'S REPORT ON A STATEMENT OF ASSETS SOLD AND LIABILITIES TRANSFERRED TO COMPLY WITH A CONTRACTUAL AGREEMENT (INCOMPLETE PRESENTATION)

Independent Auditor's Report

Board of Directors and Stockholders
ABC Company

We have audited the accompanying statement of net assets sold of ABC Company as of May 9, 20X2. This statement of net assets sold is the responsibility of ABC Company's management. Our responsibility is to express an opinion on the statement of net assets sold based on our audit.

We conducted our audit in accordance with auditing standards generally accepted in the United States of America. Those standards require that we plan and perform the audit to obtain reasonable assurance about whether the statement of net assets sold is free of material misstatement. An audit includes examining, on a test basis, evidence supporting the amounts and disclosures in the statement. An audit also includes assessing the accounting principles used and significant estimates made by management, as well as evaluating the overall presentation of the statement of net assets sold. We believe that our audit provides a reasonable basis for our opinion.

The accompanying statement was prepared to present the net assets of ABC Company sold to XYZ Corporation pursuant to the purchase agreement described in Note [X], and is not intended to be a complete presentation of ABC Company's assets and liabilities.

In our opinion, the accompanying statement of net assets sold presents fairly, in all material respects, the net assets of ABC Company as of May 9, 20X2 sold pursuant to the purchase agreement referred to in Note [X], in conformity with accounting principles generally accepted in the United States of America.

This report is intended solely for the information and use of the boards of directors and managements of ABC Company and XYZ Corporation and is not intended to be and should not be used by anyone other than these specified parties.

[*Signature*]

[*Date*]

ILLUSTRATION 20—COMPONENTS OF AN AUDITOR'S REPORT ON SPECIAL-PURPOSE FINANCIAL STATEMENTS THAT RESULT IN NON-GAAP OR NON-OCBOA PRESENTATIONS

An auditor's report on special-purpose financial statements that result in non-GAAP or non-OCBOA presentations should include the following:

1. A title that includes the word *independent*.

2. A paragraph stating that:

   a. The financial statements identified were audited;

   b. The financial statements are the responsibility of the Company's management; and

   c. The auditor is responsible for expressing an opinion on the financial statements based on the audit.

3. A paragraph stating that:

   a. The audit was conducted in accordance with GAAS, and an identification of the United States of America as the country of origin of those standards;

   b. GAAS require that the auditor plan and perform the audit to obtain reasonable assurance about whether the financial statements are free of material misstatement;

   c. An audit includes:

      (1) Examining, on a test basis, evidence supporting the amounts and disclosures in the financial statements

      (2) Assessing the accounting principles used and significant estimates made by management

      (3) Evaluating the overall financial statement presentation

   d. The auditor believes that the audit provides a reasonable basis for his or her opinion.

4. A paragraph that:

        a. Explains what the presentation is intended to present and refers to the note to the special-purpose financial statements that describes the basis of presentation; and

        b. States that the presentation is not intended to be a presentation in conformity with GAAP.

5. A paragraph that includes a description and the source of any significant interpretations made by the Company's management relating to the provisions of a relevant agreement.

6. A paragraph that expresses the auditor's opinion, or disclaims an opinion, on whether the information the presentation is intended to present is fairly presented, in all material respects, on the basis of accounting specified. If the auditor concludes that the information the presentation is intended to present is not presented fairly on the basis of accounting described, or if there has been a limitation on the scope of the audit, the auditor should:

        a. Disclose, in an explanatory paragraph preceding the opinion paragraph of the report, all the substantive reasons for his or her conclusion; and

        b. Include in the opinion paragraph the appropriate modifying language and a reference to such explanatory paragraph.

7. A separate paragraph at the end of the report stating that its use is restricted to (a) those within the entity, (b) the parties to the contract or agreement, (c) the regulatory agency with which the report is being filed, or (d) those with whom the entity is negotiating directly, and that it should not be used by anyone other than these specified parties.

8. Manual or printed signature of the auditor's firm.

9. Date of the audit report.

ILLUSTRATION 21—AUDITOR'S REPORT ON SPECIAL-PURPOSE FINANCIAL STATEMENTS PREPARED PURSUANT TO A LOAN AGREEMENT THAT RESULTS IN NON-GAAP OR NON-OCBOA PRESENTATIONS

Independent Auditor's Report

Board of Directors and Stockholders
ABC Company

We have audited the special-purpose statement of assets and liabilities of ABC Company as of December 31, 20X2, and 20X1, and the related special-purpose statements of revenues and expenses and of cash flows for the years then ended. These financial statements are the responsibility of the Company's management. Our responsibility is to express an opinion on these financial statements based on our audits.

    We conducted our audits in accordance with auditing standards generally accepted in the United States of America. Those standards require that we plan and perform the audit to obtain reasonable assurance about whether the financial statements are free of material misstatement. An audit includes examining, on a test basis, evidence supporting the amounts and disclosures in the financial statements. An audit also includes assessing the accounting principles used and significant estimates made by management, as well as evaluating the overall financial statement presentation. We believe that our audits provide a reasonable basis for our opinion.

The accompanying special-purpose financial statements were prepared for the purpose of complying with Section 4 of a loan agreement between DEF Bank and the Company as discussed in Note [X], and are not intended to be a presentation in conformity with accounting principles generally accepted in the United States of America.

In our opinion, the special-purpose financial statements referred to above present fairly, in all material respects, the assets and liabilities of ABC Company at December 31, 20X2, and 20X1, and the revenues, expenses and cash flows for the years then ended, on the basis of accounting described in Note [X].

This report is intended solely for the information and use of the boards of directors and managements of ABC Company and DEF Bank and is not intended to be and should not be used by anyone other than these specified parties.

[*Signature*]

[*Date*]

ILLUSTRATION 22—AUDITOR'S REPORT ON CURRENT-VALUE FINAN-CIAL STATEMENTS THAT SUPPLEMENT HISTORICAL-COST FINANCIAL STATEMENTS OF A REAL ESTATE ENTITY

Independent Auditor's Report

Board of Directors and Stockholders
ABC Company

We have audited the accompanying historical-cost balance sheets of ABC Company as of December 31, 20X2, and 20X1, and the related historical-cost statements of income, shareholders' equity and cash flows for each of the three years in the period ended December 31, 20X2. We also have audited the supplemental current-value balance sheets of ABC Company as of December 31, 20X2, and 20X1, and the related supplemental current-value statements of income and shareholders' equity for each of the three years in the period ended December 31, 20X2. These financial statements are the responsibility of the Company's management. Our responsibility is to express an opinion on these financial statements based on our audits.

We conducted our audits in accordance with auditing standards generally accepted in the United States of America. Those standards require that we plan and perform the audit to obtain reasonable assurance about whether the financial statements are free of material misstatement. An audit includes examining, on a test basis, evidence supporting the amounts and disclosures in the financial statements. An audit also includes assessing the accounting principles used and significant estimates made by management, as well as evaluating the overall financial statement presentation. We believe that our audits provide a reasonable basis for our opinion.

In our opinion, the historical-cost financial statements referred to above present fairly, in all material respects, the financial position of ABC Company as of December 31, 20X2, and 20X1, and the results of its operations and its cash flows for each of the three years in the period ended December 31, 20X2, in conformity with accounting principles generally accepted in the United States of America.

As described in Note [X], the supplemental current-value financial statements have been prepared by management to present relevant financial information that is not provided by the historical-cost financial statements and are not intended to be a presentation in conformity with generally accepted accounting principles. In addition, the supplemental current-value financial statements do not purport to present the net realizable, liquidation, or market value of the Company as a whole. Furthermore, amounts ultimately realized by the Company from the disposal of properties may vary significantly from the current values presented.

In our opinion, the supplemental current-value financial statements referred to above present fairly, in all material respects, the information set forth in them on the basis of accounting described in Note [X].

[*Signature*]

[*Date*]

AU SECTION 625
REPORTS ON THE APPLICATION OF ACCOUNTING PRINCIPLES

PRACTICE POINT: As part of its Clarity Project, the American Institute of Certified Public Accountants' (AICPA's) Auditing Standards Board (ASB) has finalized a clarified Statement on Auditing Standards (SAS) titled, "Reports on Application of Requirements of an Applicable Financial Reporting Framework," which supersedes AU Section 625 (Reports on the Application of Accounting Principles). The clarified SAS does not change or expand extant AU Section 625 in any significant respect.

The term *financial reporting framework,* as defined in the clarified SAS, "Overall Objectives of the Independent Auditor and the Conduct of an Audit in Accordance with Generally Accepted Auditing Standards," replaces the term *generally accepted accounting principles.* Accordingly, the term *requirements of an applicable financial reporting framework* replaces the term *application of accounting principles.* These changes in terminology are not intended to create a difference in the application of AU Section 625 and this clarified SAS.

Auditing Interpretation No. 1, *Requirement to Consult with the Continuing Accountant*, of AU Section 625 (Reports on the Application of Accounting Principles: Auditing Interpretations of Section 625) uses the term *advisory accountant* rather than the term *reporting accountant* to distinguish that an accountant in this capacity is not engaged to provide a second opinion and is typically engaged to provide accounting and reporting advice on a recurring basis. The auditing interpretation addresses situations in which the advisory accountant may overcome the presumptive requirement to consult with the continuing accountant.

Although the extant AU Section 625 does not use the term *advisory accountant,* the clarified SAS acknowledges that a reporting accountant who is also engaged to provide accounting and reporting advice to a specific entity on a recurring basis is commonly referred to as an *advisory accountant.* The clarified SAS incorporates the auditing interpretation and distinguishes between the reporting accountant and the advisory accountant without broadening the extant AU Section 625.

The ASB is expected to issue many of the clarified standards in *one* SAS that will be codified in "AU Section" format. The ASB has decided that the effective date of the clarified SASs that have not yet been issued is for audits of financial statements for periods ending on or after December 15, 2012. Auditors should be alert to and monitor further developments in this area.

PRACTICE POINT: In March 2011, the American Institute of Certified Public Accountants' (AICPA's) Auditing Standards Board (ASB) issued an exposure draft (ED) of a proposed Statement on Auditing Standards (SAS) titled, "Omnibus Statement on Auditing Standards—2011." This proposed SAS, which is part of the AICPA's Clarity Project, would amend the following SASs that have been issued in the clarity format and are currently effective:

- SAS-117 (AU Section 801) (Compliance Audits). The amendment to SAS-117 conforms the auditor's report on compliance to the requirements of the clarified SAS, "Forming an Opinion and Reporting on Financial Statements." In addition, the amendment revises the appendix in SAS-117, "AU Sections That Are Not Applicable to Compliance Audits," to reflect conforming changes to affected references to AU Sections as a result of the ASB's Clarity Project.

- SAS-118 (AU Section 550) (Other Information in Documents Containing Audited Financial Statements). The amendment to SAS-118 clarifies the requirements with respect to identified material inconsistencies by categorizing the requirements based on when the inconsistencies are identified (prior to the date of the auditor's report on the audited financial statements; after the date of the auditor's report but prior to the report release date; and after the report release date). It also adds application material addressing electronic sites to include guidance from an interpretation of AU Section 550 (Other Information in Documents Containing Audited Financial Statements), which the ASB determined was appropriate to include in SAS-118.

In addition, in order to address other changes necessitated by the ASB's overall Clarity Project, the proposed SAS would amend the following clarified SASs that have been finalized and released, but not yet issued as authoritative:

- Clarified SAS, "Overall Objectives of the Independent Auditor and the Conduct of an Audit in Accordance with Generally Accepted Auditing Standards."

- Clarified SAS, "Modifications to the Opinion in the Independent Auditor's Report."

- Clarified SAS, "Reports on Application of Requirements of an Applicable Financial Reporting Framework."

- Clarified SAS, "The Auditor's Communication with Those Charged with Governance (Redrafted)".

- Clarified SAS, "Audit Documentation (Redrafted)."

The proposed SAS would be effective for audits of financial statements for periods ending on or after December 15, 2012, except for the amendment to the clarified SAS, "Reports on Application of Requirements of an Applicable Financial Reporting Framework," which would be effective for engagements ending on or after December 15, 2012.

WHAT EVERY PRACTITIONER SHOULD KNOW

Basic Objectives and Requirements

This Section applies to a reporting accountant (i.e., an accountant in public practice other than the accountant who has been engaged to report on an entity's financial statements) when providing:

1. A *written* report:

    a. On the application of accounting principles to specified transactions, either completed or proposed, involving facts and circumstances of a specific entity; or

   b. On the type of opinion that may be rendered on a specific entity's financial statements.

2. *Oral* advice, which is intended to be used by a principal to the transaction as an important factor considered in reaching a decision, in the following circumstances:

   a. On the application of accounting principles to a specific transaction; or

   b. On the type of opinion that may be rendered on a specific entity's financial statements.

Performance Standards

The reporting accountant should:

1. Exercise due professional care in performing the engagement.
2. Possess adequate technical training and proficiency.
3. Plan the engagement adequately.
4. Supervise the work of assistants.
5. Accumulate sufficient information to provide a reasonable basis for his or her judgment described in the report.
6. Consider who requested the report, the purpose of the request, the circumstances under which the request is made, and the intended use of the report or oral advice.

When making an informed judgment regarding the sufficiency of information, the reporting accountant should:

1. Obtain an understanding of the form and substance of the transactions.
2. Review applicable GAAP.
3. Consult with other professionals or experts.
4. Perform research or other procedures to determine the existence of creditable precedents or analogies.

When evaluating accounting principles or determining the type of opinion that may be rendered on an entity's financial statements, the reporting accountant should:

1. Consult with the entity's continuing accountant (i.e., accountant who has been engaged to report on an entity's financial statements) to identify all pertinent facts, including:

   a. The form and substance of the transaction;

   b. How management has applied accounting principles to similar transactions;

   c. Whether there is any dispute between the continuing accountant and management about the method of accounting; and

   d. Whether the continuing accountant has reached a different conclusion than the reporting accountant on the application of accounting principles or the type of opinion that may be rendered.

2. Inform the entity of the need to consult with the continuing accountant, request permission to do so, and request the entity's management to authorize the continuing accountant to respond fully to the reporting accountant's inquiries.

Reporting Standards

The reporting accountant should address his or her written report to the requesting entity (e.g., the entity's board of directors). The reporting accountant's report should ordinarily include the following:

1. A brief description of the engagement.

2. A statement that the engagement was performed in accordance with applicable AICPA standards.

3. Identification of the specific entity.

4. A description of the transaction.

5. A statement of the relevant facts, circumstances, and assumptions.

6. A statement about sources of the information.

7. A description of the appropriate accounting principles, including the country of origin, to be applied or type of opinion that maybe rendered and, if appropriate, a description of the reasons for the reporting accountant's conclusion.

8. A statement that the responsibility for the proper accounting treatment rests with the preparers of the financial statements, who should consult with their continuing accountants.

9. A statement that any difference in the facts, circumstances, or assumptions presented may change the continuing accountant's report.

10. A "restricted use" paragraph that includes (a) a statement that the report is intended only for the information and use of the specified parties, and that it should not be used by anyone other than these parties, and (b) an identification of the specified parties.

See Illustration 1 for an example of an accountant's report on the application of accounting principles.

Advisory Accountants Assisting Management and the Requirement to Consult with the Continuing Accountant

When the guidance in AU Section 625 was originally issued, it was intended to encompass such situations as "second opinion," or what is often referred to as opinion shopping. However, since the issuance of this guidance, a familiar trend in today's business environment has emerged whereby an entity may engage a secondary CPA in public practice (i.e., other than the reporting or continuing accountant) to assist management in certain accounting and reporting functions, such as bookkeeping; assistance in drafting the entity's financial statements or related notes before providing them to the entity's continuing accountant; assistance in preparing required filings with regulatory agencies, such as the Securities and Exchange Commission; and performing asset impairment tests. Often, the advisory, or secondary, accountant is engaged to perform such functions in order to compensate for lack of adequate staffing or experience within the entity, to mitigate or alleviate independence concerns, to effectively outsource the entity's controllership or financial reporting function, or for similar other reasons.

An Auditing Interpretation of AU Section 625 addresses the question of whether an accountant in public practice, who has been engaged to act in the capacity of an advisory accountant to management and to provide advice on the application of accounting principles to specified transactions, is required to consult with the continuing accountant pursuant to AU Section 625. In order to address this question, it is important to understand the roles and definitions of the continuing accountant, the reporting accountant, and the advisory accountant:

- *Continuing accountant*—An accountant in public practice who has been engaged to report on an entity's financial statements (i.e., the entity's auditor).

- *Reporting accountant*—An accountant in public practice who has been engaged to provide a second opinion on the application of accounting principles to specified transactions.

- *Advisory accountant*—An accountant in public practice who has been engaged to assist management in certain recurring accounting or reporting functions, including providing advice (not a second opinion) on the application of accounting principles to specified transactions.

When AU Section 625 was issued, it recognized that a reporting accountant who is engaged to provide a second opinion on the application of accounting principles to specific transactions may not have been provided complete details and all the relevant facts, circumstances, and information by management that are needed to form a second opinion. To address this matter, AU Section 625 requires the reporting accountant to consult with the continuing accountant so that the relevant facts and circumstances are conveyed by the continuing accountant to the reporting accountant. However, according to the Auditing Interpretation, an advisory accountant is *not* required to consult with the continuing accountant on the application of accounting principles to the client's specified transactions when he or she believes both of the following conditions have been met:

- The advisory accountant is not being asked to provide a second opinion, and

- The advisory accountant has obtained all relevant information from management to provide written or oral guidance regarding the application of accounting principles to the client's specified transactions.

The Auditing Interpretation makes it clear that an advisory accountant may be able to overcome the presumptive requirement to consult with the continuing accountant only on matters relating to the application of accounting principles. Accordingly, if the client requests the advisory accountant to provide oral advice or a written report on the type of opinion that may be rendered by the continuing accountant, the advisory accountant would be required to consult with the continuing accountant pursuant to the provisions of AU Section 625.

The Auditing Interpretation emphasizes that an advisory accountant should always be alert to instances in which the client uses his or her services to "opinion shop." Generally, engagements that involve the advisory accountant in certain recurring (as opposed to periodic) accounting and reporting functions would not be indicative of opinion shopping. If the advisory accountant concludes that the services involved do not encompass "opinion shopping" and, therefore, consultation with the continuing accountant is not required under AU Section 625, the Auditing Interpretation indicates that the advisory accountant should:

- Establish an understanding with the client that includes a statement that the responsibility for the proper accounting treatment rests with management, who should consult with its continuing accountant, and that the continuing accountant and members of any governance body (e.g., the audit committee or board of directors) will be notified of the arrangement;

- Document his or her conclusion that consultation with the continuing accountant was not considered necessary under the circumstances;

- Obtain an understanding of the form and substance of the transaction(s);

- Review applicable GAAP;

- Consult with other professionals or experts, if appropriate; and

- Perform research or other procedures to determine the existence of creditable precedents or analogies, if appropriate.

PRACTICE ISSUES AND FREQUENTLY ASKED QUESTIONS

Issue 1: Does this Section apply to situations that are commonly referred to as "opinion shopping"?

Yes. When the Auditing Standards Board developed the guidance in this Section, it intended to encompass such situations as "second opinion" or what is often referred to as "opinion shopping."

Issue 2: What are the responsibilities of the continuing accountant to respond to inquiries made by the reporting accountant under this Section?

The responsibilities of the continuing accountant to respond to inquiries by the reporting accountant are the same as the responsibilities of a predecessor auditor to respond to inquiries by a successor auditor. Therefore, the requirements of AU Section 315 (Communications between Predecessor and Successor Auditors) should be followed in such circumstances.

Issue 3: Can an accountant report on the application of accounting principles involving hypothetical transactions of a particular entity?

No. An accountant is prohibited from reporting on the application of accounting principles involving hypothetical transactions of a particular entity.

Issue 4: Is the reporting accountant required to obtain any written representations from the entity when reporting on the application of accounting principles under this Section?

No. There is no requirement to obtain written representations from the entity under such circumstances.

Issue 5: If an accountant in public practice, who has certain specialized industry knowledge, receives a call from another accountant regarding the application of an accounting principle in the specialized industry, do the provisions of this Section apply?

No. Consultations or professional advice given to other accountants in public practice are specifically exempted from reporting under this Section.

Issue 6: What should a reporting accountant do if a principal entity refuses to authorize the reporting accountant to communicate with the continuing accountant?

This Section requires the reporting accountant to consult with the continuing accountant. A refusal by management to authorize this consultation would ordinarily raise concern sufficient to cause most accountants to decline the engagement. This refusal is a limitation on the scope of the reporting accountant's procedures; however, the reporting standards for this type of engagement do not contain provisions for qualifying the report due to a scope limitation and do not provide any guidance in such circumstances. Therefore, sound business practice would suggest that the accountant should decline the engagement in such circumstances.

Issue 7: If, subsequent to reporting on the application of an accounting principle to a specified transaction, the reporting accountant is engaged to audit the principal entity, is the accountant required to inform those charged with governance of his or her previous engagement?

Yes. This is one of the specific items required to be communicated under AU Section 380 (The Auditor's Communication with Those Charged with Governance).

Issue 8: Does this Section require any specific documentation of the procedures performed in connection with reporting on the application of accounting principles?

No. There are no specified documentation requirements in connection with the accountant's reporting on the application of accounting principles. However, sound business practice would suggest that documentation of the following matters is advisable:

- A description of the transaction.
- A description of the procedures performed, including research conducted, to determine applicable GAAP under the circumstances (e.g., references or citations to authoritative literature).
- Any consultation with other experts or professionals.
- Any discussions with the continuing accountant.

ILLUSTRATIONS AND PRACTICE AIDS

ILLUSTRATION 1—ACCOUNTANT'S REPORT ON THE APPLICATION OF ACCOUNTING PRINCIPLES

Introduction

We have been engaged to report on the appropriate application of accounting principles generally accepted in [*country of origin of such accounting principles*] to the specific transaction described below. This report is being issued to the ABC Company for assistance in evaluating accounting principles for the described specific transaction. Our engagement has been conducted in accordance with standards established by the American Institute of Certified Public Accountants.

Description of Transaction

The facts, circumstances, and assumptions relevant to the specific transaction as provided to us by the management of ABC Company are as follows:

[*Text describing the specific transaction*]

Appropriate Accounting Principles

[*Text discussing generally accepted accounting principles*]

Concluding Comments

The ultimate responsibility for the decision on the appropriate application of accounting principles generally accepted in [*country of origin of such accounting principles*] for an actual transaction rests with the preparers of financial statements, who should consult with their continuing accountants. Our judgment on the appropriate application of accounting principles generally accepted in [*country of origin of such accounting principles*] for the described specific transaction is based solely on the facts provided to us as described above; should these facts and circumstances differ, our conclusion may change.

Restricted Use

This report is intended solely for the information and use of the Board of Directors and management of ABC Company and is not intended to be and should not be used by anyone other than these specified parties.

[*Signature*]

[*Date*]

AU SECTION 634
LETTERS FOR UNDERWRITERS AND CERTAIN OTHER REQUESTING PARTIES

PRACTICE POINT: As part of its Clarity Project, the American Institute of Certified Public Accountants' (AICPA's) Auditing Standards Board (ASB) has issued an exposure draft (ED) of a proposed Statement on Auditing Standards (SAS) titled, "Letters for Underwriters and Certain Other Requesting Parties (Redrafted)," which would supersede AU Section 634 (Letters for Underwriters and Certain Other Requesting Parties).

The proposed SAS does not change or expand existing requirements in extant AU Section 634 in any significant respect. However, to reflect a more principles-based approach to standard setting, certain requirements that are duplicative of broader requirements in AU Section 634 have been moved to application and other explanatory material.

The ASB is expected to issue many of the clarified standards in *one* SAS that will be codified in "AU Section" format. The ASB has decided that the effective date of the clarified SASs that have not yet been issued is for audits of financial statements for periods ending on or after December 15, 2012. Auditors should be alert to and monitor further developments in this area.

WHAT EVERY PRACTITIONER SHOULD KNOW

Applicability

Accountants may issue comfort letters to underwriters or to "other parties" in connection with financial statements and financial statement schedules included, or incorporated by reference, in registration statements filed with the Securities and Exchange Commission (SEC) under the Securities Act of 1933 ("1933 Act"). *Other parties* specifically refers to parties with a statutory due diligence defense under section 11 of the 1933 Act, other than a named underwriter. A comfort letter may be addressed to such "other parties" only when a law firm or an attorney for the requesting party issues a written opinion to the accountants stating that such a party has a due diligence defense under section 11 of the 1933 Act. If the requesting party cannot provide such an opinion letter, he or she must provide a written representation letter to the accountants in the form found in Illustration 19, in order for the accountant to issue a comfort letter.

Also, accountants may issue a comfort letter in the following circumstances:

1. To a broker-dealer or other financial intermediary (acting as principal or agent in an offering or a placement of securities) in connection with the following types of securities offerings:

    a. Foreign offerings, including Regulation S, Eurodollar, and other offshore offerings.

    b. Transactions that are exempt from the registration requirements of section 5 of the Act, including those pursuant to Regulation A, Regulation D, and Rule 144A.

    c. Offerings of securities issued or backed by governmental, municipal, banking, tax-exempt, or other entities that are exempt from registration under the Act.

2. In connection with acquisition transactions (e.g., cross-comfort letters in a typical Form S-4 or merger proxy situation) in which there is an exchange of stock and such comfort letters are requested by the buyer or seller, or both.

In the situations described in 1 and 2, accountants may provide a comfort letter *only* if the party provides a written representation letter to the accountants stating that the review process applied to the issuer is substantially consistent with the due diligence review process under the 1933 Act. See Illustration 19 for an example of such a representation letter.

When one of the parties identified above, other than an underwriter or other party with a due diligence defense under section 11 of the Act, requests a comfort letter but does not provide a representation letter, accountants should not provide a comfort letter but may provide another type of letter as found in Illustration 17.

General Requirements

In connection with a comfort letter, accountants should:

1. Suggest to the underwriter that they meet together with the client to discuss the procedures to be followed. In connection with such discussion, accountants should clearly state that they cannot furnish any assurance regarding the sufficiency of the procedures for the underwriter's purposes.

2. Obtain from the underwriter a draft of the underwriting agreement in order to indicate whether they will be able to furnish a comfort letter in acceptable form.

3. Preferably prepare a draft of the form of the comfort letter they expect to furnish. Such a draft should:

    a. To the extent possible, deal with all matters to be covered in the final letter and use exactly the same terms as those to be used in the final letter, subject to the understanding that the comments in the final letter cannot be determined until the underlying procedures have been performed.

    b. Be identified as a draft to avoid any misunderstanding.

    c. Avoid any statements or implications that the accountants are carrying out procedures as they consider necessary.

The following is suggested wording that accountants may place on the draft comfort letter for identification and explanation of its purposes and limitations:

This draft is furnished solely for the purpose of indicating the form of letter that we would expect to be able to furnish [*name of underwriter*] in response to their request, the matters expected to be covered in the letter, and the nature of the procedures that we would expect to carry out with respect to such matters. Based on our discussions with [*name of underwriter*], it is our understanding that the procedures outlined in this draft letter are those they wish us to follow. [*Note:* In the absence of any discussions with the underwriter, the preceding sentence should be revised as follows: "In the absence of any discussions with (*name of underwriter*), we have set out in this draft letter those procedures referred to in the draft underwriting agreement, of which we have been furnished a copy, that we are willing to follow."]. Unless [*name of underwriter*] informs us otherwise, we shall assume that there are no additional procedures they wish us to follow. The text of the letter itself will depend, of course, on the results of the procedures, which we would not expect to complete until shortly before the letter is given and in no event before the cutoff date indicated therein.

Shelf registration statement A company may register a designated amount of securities for continuous or delayed offerings during an extended period by filing one "shelf" registration statement. At the effective date of a shelf registration statement, the company may not have selected an underwriter. Under these circumstances, accountants should not furnish a comfort letter addressed to the client, legal counsel, or a nonspecific addressee such as "any or all underwriters to be selected." However, accountants may furnish the client or legal counsel for the underwriting group with a draft comfort letter describing the procedures performed and the comments the accountants are willing to express as a result. The draft comfort letter should include wording such as the following:

> This draft describes the procedures that we have performed and represents a letter we would be prepared to sign as of the effective date of the registration statement if the managing underwriter had been chosen at that date and requested such a letter. Based on our discussions with [*name of client or legal counsel*], the procedures set forth are similar to those that experience indicates underwriters often request in such circumstances. The text of the final letter will depend, of course, on whether the managing underwriter who is selected requests that other procedures be performed to meet his or her needs and whether the managing underwriter requests that any of the procedures be updated to the date of issuance of the signed letter.

Dating The comfort letter generally is dated on or shortly before the effective date of the registration statement. The underwriting agreement ordinarily specifies the "cutoff date" to which certain procedures described in the letter are to relate (e.g., a date five days before the date of the letter). The accountant should state in the comfort letter that the inquiries and other procedures described therein did not cover the period from the cutoff date to the date of the letter. Any subsequent comfort letters should relate only to information in the registration statement as most recently amended. See Illustration 3.

Addressee The following guidance applies:

1. The appropriate addressee is the intermediary who has negotiated the agreement with the client, and with whom the accountants deal in discussions regarding the scope and sufficiency of the comfort letter, e.g., "The ABC Company and XYZ & Co., as Representative of Several Underwriters."

2. When a comfort letter is furnished to other accountants, it should be addressed in accordance with item 1 above and copies should be furnished to the principal accountants and their client.

3. The comfort letter should not be addressed or given to any parties other than the client and the named underwriters, broker-dealer, financial intermediary or buyer or seller.

Contents of comfort letters Comfort letters usually cover one or more of the following:

1. The accountant's independence

2. An introductory paragraph

3. Compliance with SEC requirements

4. Commenting on information other than audited financial statements, for example: condensed interim financial information, capsule financial information, pro forma financial information, financial forecasts, and changes subsequent to the date and period of the latest financial statements included

5. Tables, statistics, and other financial information

6. Concluding paragraph

Each of these matters is discussed below. See Illustration 1 for a typical comfort letter and Illustration 2 when a short-form registration statement is filed incorporating previously filed forms 10-K and 10-Q by reference. Also, see Illustration 16 for an example of a comfort letter that is issued in a non-1933 Act offering.

The Accountant's Independence

If, in connection with SEC filings, the underwriting agreement requests the accountants to make a statement in the comfort letter concerning their independence, the accountants may use wording such as the following:

> We are independent certified public accountants with respect to ABC Company within the meaning of the Act and the applicable rules and regulations thereunder adopted by the SEC.

In a non-SEC filing, the accountants may refer to the AICPA's *Code of Professional Conduct* by using wording such as the following:

> We are independent certified public accountants with respect to ABC Company under rule 101 of the AICPA's *Code of Professional Conduct* and its interpretations and rulings.

Accountants for previously nonaffiliated companies recently acquired by the registrant would not be required to have been independent with respect to the company whose shares are being registered. In such circumstances, the accountants should make a statement similar to the following:

> As of [*insert date of the accountants' most recent report on the financial statements of their client*] and during the period covered by the financial statements on which we reported, we were independent certified public accountants with respect to [*insert the name of their client*] within the meaning of the Act and the applicable rules and regulations thereunder adopted by the SEC.

Introductory Paragraph in Comfort Letters

The accountant should observe the following matters applicable to the introductory paragraph of the accountant's comfort letter:

1. It is desirable to include a paragraph similar to the following:

   We have audited the [*identify the financial statements and financial statement schedules*] included [*incorporated by reference*] in the registration statement (No. 33-XXXXX) on Form _____ filed by the company under the Securities Act of 1933 (the Act); our reports with respect thereto are also included [*incorporated by reference*] in that registration statement. The registration statement, as amended as of _____, is herein referred to as the registration statement.

2. If the report on the audited financial statements and financial statement schedules included in the registration statement departs from the standard report, the accountant should:

   a. Refer to, and discuss the subject matter of, the departure from the standard report. However, the accountant need not refer to or discuss matters covering consistency of application of accounting principles. See Illustration 9.

   b. In those rare instances in which the SEC accepts a qualified opinion on historical financial statements, refer to and discuss the subject matter of the qualification.

3. The accountants should *not* repeat their opinion on the audited financial statements.

4. The accountants should *not* give negative assurance regarding:

   a. Their report on the audited financial statements.

   b. Financial statements and schedules that have been audited and are reported on in the registration statement by other accountants.

5. The accountants may refer to the fact that they have issued reports on:

   a. Condensed financial statements that are derived from audited financial statements.

   b. Selected financial data.

   c. Interim financial information.

   d. Pro forma financial information.

   e. A financial forecast.

   f. Management's discussion and analysis.

   If the foregoing reports are not included (incorporated by reference) in the registration statement, they may be attached to the comfort letter. However, the accountants should not repeat the reports in the comfort letter, imply that they are reporting as of the date of the comfort letter, or that they assume responsibility for the sufficiency of the procedures for the underwriter's purposes.

6. The accountants should *not*:

   a. Refer to reports issued on internal control pursuant to AU Section 325 (Communicating Internal Control Related Matters Identified in an Audit)

   b. Refer to any restricted-use reports concerning the client's internal control issued pursuant to AT Section 501 (Reporting on an Entity's Internal Control over Financial Reporting)

7. The accountants should *not*:

   a. Comment on unaudited interim financial information required by item 302(a) of Regulation S-K to which AU Section 722 (Interim Financial Information) pertains, unless the underwriter requests the accountant to perform procedures in addition to those required by AU Section 722.

   b. Comment on required supplementary information to which AU Section 558 (Required Supplementary Information) pertains, unless the underwriter requests the accountant to perform procedures in addition to those required by AU Section 558.

Compliance with SEC Requirements

The accountant should observe the following matters applicable to compliance with SEC requirements:

1. If, in connection with SEC filings, the accountants are requested to express an opinion on whether the financial statements covered by their report comply with the pertinent accounting requirements adopted by the SEC, the accountants may use wording such as the following:

   In our opinion [*include phrase "except as disclosed in the registration statement," if applicable*], the [*identify the financial statements and financial statement schedules*] audited by us and included [*incorporated by reference*] in the registration statement comply as to form in all material respects with the applicable accounting requirements of the Act and the related rules and regulations adopted by the SEC.

2. If there is a material departure from the pertinent SEC rules and regulations, the departure should be disclosed in the comfort letter. See Illustration 11.

3. Accountants may provide positive assurance on compliance as to form with requirements under the rules and regulations adopted by the SEC only as they apply to the form and content of financial statements and related schedules that they have audited; however, when the financial statements or related schedules have not been audited, accountants are limited to providing negative assurance.

Commenting in Comfort Letters on Information Other Than Audited Financial Statements

Comments made in comfort letters generally pertain to the following:

1. Unaudited condensed interim financial information

2. Capsule financial information

3. Pro forma financial information

4. Financial forecasts

5. Subsequent changes in capital stock, increases in long-term debt, and decreases in other specified financial statement items

The accountants should not comment in a comfort letter on items 1, 2, 4, and 5 above unless they have acquired knowledge of a client's internal control as it relates to the preparation of both annual and interim financial information. Therefore, when the accountants have not audited the most recent annual financial statements, and thus have not obtained sufficient knowledge of the entity's internal control, the accountants should perform procedures to acquire such knowledge.

Also, when commenting in comfort letters on the foregoing matters, accountants should observe the following guidance:

1. The procedures that the accountants performed should be stated in the letter; however, if the accountants have been requested to provide negative assurance on interim financial information or capsule financial information, the accountants need not specify the procedures involved in a review under AU Section 722.

2. The accountants should not make any statements or imply that they applied procedures that they determined to be necessary or sufficient for the underwriter's purposes. Any procedures performed at the underwriter's request, in addition to those specified in a review under AU Section 722, should be described in the letter along with the criteria specified by the underwriter.

3. The accountants should not use ambiguous terms such as *general review, limited review, reconcile, check,* or *test* in describing the work performed, unless the procedures contemplated by these terms are also described in the letter.

4. The accountants should not state in the letter that, as a result of the specified procedures performed, nothing else has come to their attention that would be of interest to the underwriter.

Unaudited condensed interim financial information The accountant should observe the following matters applicable to comments in comfort letters on unaudited condensed interim financial information:

1. Accountants may provide negative assurance only when they have conducted a review under AU Section 722 of the interim financial information.

2. If the accountants have issued a report on the review under AU Section 722 and they mention that fact in the comfort letter, they should attach the review report to the letter (unless the review report is included or incorporated by reference in the registration statement).

3. If the accountants have not conducted a review under AU Section 722, the accountants may only describe the procedures performed and findings obtained (i.e., they may not provide negative assurance). See Illustration 15.

4. The letter should identify any unaudited condensed interim financial information and should state that the accountants have not audited the information in accordance with GAAS and do not express an opinion on such information.

See Illustrations 1, 14, and 15.

Capsule financial information   In some registration statements, information shown in the audited financial statements or unaudited condensed interim financial information may be supplemented by unaudited summarized interim information for subsequent periods ("capsule financial information"). In such situations, the accountants may:

1. Give negative assurance regarding conformity with GAAP and may refer to whether the dollar amounts were determined on a basis substantially consistent with that of the corresponding amounts in the audited financial statements, if *both* of the following conditions are met:

   a. The capsule financial information is presented in accordance with the minimum disclosure requirements of FASB Accounting Standards Codification (ASC) 270-10-50-1; and

   b. The accountants have performed a review under AU Section 722 of the financial statements underlying the capsule financial information.

   If those conditions have not been met, the accountants are limited to reporting procedures performed and findings obtained.

2. Give negative assurance as to whether the dollar amounts were determined on a basis substantially consistent with that of the corresponding amounts in the audited financial statements if the capsule financial information is more limited than the minimum disclosures described in ASC 270-10-50-1, as long as the accountants have performed a review under AU Section 722 of the financial statements underlying the capsule financial information (see Illustration 12). If a review under AU Section 722 has not been performed, the accountants are limited to reporting procedures performed and findings obtained.

See Illustrations 1 and 12.

Pro forma financial information   Accountants should observe the following matters applicable to comments in comfort letters on pro forma financial information:

1. Unless they have sufficient knowledge of the accounting and financial reporting practices of the entity, accountants should not comment in the comfort letter on pro forma financial information.

2. Unless they have sufficient knowledge of the accounting and financial reporting practices of the entity and they performed an audit of the

annual financial statements, or a review under AU Section 722 of the interim financial statements, to which the pro forma adjustments were applied, accountants should not give negative assurance in the comfort letter on:

    a. The application of pro forma adjustments to historical amounts.

    b. The compilation of pro forma financial information.

    c. Whether the pro forma financial information complies as to form in all material respects with the applicable accounting requirements of rule 11-02 of Regulation S-X.

    d. Pro forma financial information.

3. For business combinations, the historical financial statements of each part of the combined entity on which the pro forma financial information is based should be audited or reviewed.

4. If the accountants have obtained sufficient knowledge of the entity's internal control, but have not met the requirements for providing negative assurance, the accountants may only report the procedures performed and findings obtained (see Illustration 15). In such circumstances, the accountants should comply with the guidance in AT Section 201 (Agreed-Upon Procedures Engagements).

See Illustrations 1, 4, and 15.

Financial forecasts Accountants should observe the following guidance applicable to financial forecasts:

1. To perform agreed-upon procedures on a financial forecast and provide comments on it in comfort letters, accountants should:

    a. Obtain sufficient knowledge of the entity's internal control.

    b. Perform procedures prescribed in AT Section 301 (Financial Forecasts and Projections) for reporting on compilation of a forecast.

    c. Attach their report on the forecast to the comfort letter. If the forecast is included in the registration statement, the forecast must indicate that the accountants have not examined the forecast and, therefore, do not express an opinion on it.

2. Accountants may perform additional procedures on financial forecasts and report their findings if the conditions in item 1 above have been met.

3. Accountants may not provide negative assurance on:

    a. The results of procedures performed; and

    b. Compliance of the forecast with rule 11-03 of Regulation S-X, unless they have performed an examination of the forecast in accordance with AT Section 301.

See Illustrations 1, 5, and 15.

Subsequent changes An entity may experience changes in capital stock, increases in long-term debt, or decreases in other specified financial statement items during a period subsequent to the date and period of the latest financial statements included in the registration statement ("change period"). Comments in comfort letters typically relate to such subsequent changes and changes in the amounts of (a) net current assets, (b) stockholders' equity, (c) net sales, and (d) the total and per-share amounts of income before extraordinary items and of net income.

The accountant's procedures with respect to the foregoing subsequent changes are generally limited to reading minutes and inquiring of company officials relating to the change period. Therefore, the accountants must base their comments in the comfort letter solely on the limited procedures actually performed with respect to that period. Furthermore, accountants should observe the following:

1. Accountants may provide negative assurance about subsequent changes in specified financial statement items as of a date less than 135 days from the end of the most recent period for which the accountants have performed an audit or a review. For periods of 135 days or more, the accountants may not provide negative assurance, but are limited to reporting procedures performed and findings obtained.

2. Accountants should not include comments in the comfort letter referring to "adverse changes" since that term is ambiguous and may be misunderstood.

3. If there has been a change in accounting principles during the change period, the accountants should indicate that fact in the comfort letter.

4. The accountants' comments on the subsequent changes should be limited to changes, increases, or decreases not disclosed in the registration statement. Therefore, when subsequent changes are disclosed in the registration statement, accountants should include the phrase "except for changes, increases, or decreases that the registration statement discloses have occurred or may occur" in the comfort letter.

5. Accountants should specify in the comfort letter, in both draft and final form, the dates as of which, and periods for which, data at the cutoff date and data for the change period are compared. See Illustrations 1, 10, 13, and 15.

Tables, Statistics, and Other Financial Information

The accountant should observe the following matters when requested to comment in the comfort letter on tables, statistics, and other financial information appearing in the registration statement:

1. Accountants may comment on:

   a. Information that is expressed in dollars (or percentages derived from such dollar amounts) and that has been obtained from accounting records that are subject to the entity's controls over financial reporting.

   b. Information that has been derived directly from accounting records by analysis or computation.

    c. Quantitative information that has been obtained from an accounting record, if the information is subject to the same controls over financial reporting as the dollar amounts.

2. The accountants should not comment on:

    a. Matters unless subjected to the entity's controls over financial reporting, including the square footage of facilities; number of employees, except as related to a given payroll period; and backlog information.

    b. Tables, statistics, and other financial information relating to an unaudited period unless the accountants:

      (1) Have audited the financial statements for a period including or immediately prior to the unaudited period or have completed an audit for a later period, or

      (2) Have otherwise obtained sufficient knowledge of the entity's internal control over financial reporting.

    c. Information or matters subject to legal interpretation.

    d. Segment information, or the appropriateness of allocations made to derive segment information, included in financial statements.

3. When financial information is included in registration statements because of specific requirements of Regulation S-K, accountants may comment as to whether such information is in conformity with the disclosure requirements of Regulation S-K, if the following conditions are met:

    a. The information is derived from the accounting records subject to the entity's controls over financial reporting, or has been derived directly from such accounting records by analysis or computation.

    b. The information is capable of evaluation against reasonable criteria that have been established by the SEC.

    The following are the disclosure requirements of Regulation S-K that generally meet these conditions:

    • Item 301, "Selected Financial Data"

    • Item 302, "Supplementary Financial Information"

    • Item 402, "Executive Compensation"

    • Item 503(d), "Ratio of Earnings to Fixed Charges"

4. With respect to specific information commented on in the comfort letter, the accountants:

    a. Should identify such information by reference to specific captions, tables, page numbers, paragraphs, or sentences.

    b. May state the procedures followed and the findings obtained individually for each item of specific information commented on. Alternatively, some or all of the descriptions may be grouped, summarized, or presented in a matrix listing the financial information and the procedures applied.

5. Comments in the comfort letter concerning tables, statistics, and other financial information should:

   a. Describe the procedures followed.

   b. Indicate the findings, ordinarily expressed in terms of agreement between items compared.

   c. Include, if appropriate, statements regarding the acceptability of methods of allocation used in deriving the figures commented on.

   d. Avoid using the expression "presents fairly" or a variation of it.

6. The procedures followed by the accountants with respect to the foregoing information should be clearly described in the comfort letter, in both draft and final form. Also, the accountants should state that:

   a. They are not furnishing any assurance with respect to the sufficiency of the procedures for the underwriter's purpose.

   b. They do not provide any representations about the completeness or adequacy of disclosure.

   c. The procedures performed would not necessarily disclose material misstatements or omissions in the information to which the comments relate.

See Illustrations 1, 6, 7, 8, and 18.

Concluding Paragraph

It is desirable that the comfort letter conclude with a paragraph using wording such as the following:

> This letter is solely for the information of the addressees and to assist the underwriters in conducting and documenting their investigation of the affairs of the company in connection with the offering of the securities covered by the registration statement. It is not to be used, circulated, quoted, or otherwise referred to within or without the underwriting group for any other purpose, including, but not limited to, the registration, purchase, or sale of securities, nor is it to be filed with or referred to in whole or in part in the registration statement or any other document, except that reference may be made to it in the underwriting agreement or in any list of closing documents pertaining to the offering of the securities covered by the registration statement.

Disclosure of Subsequently Discovered Matters

Accountants may discover matters that may require mention in the final comfort letter but that are not mentioned in the draft letter that has been furnished to the underwriter. Accountants should discuss such matters with the client to determine whether disclosure should be made in the registration statement. If disclosure is not to be made, the accountants should:

1. Inform the client that the matters will be mentioned in the comfort letter.

2. Suggest that the underwriter be informed promptly.

3. Preferably be present when the client and the underwriter discuss such matters.

PRACTICE ISSUES AND FREQUENTLY ASKED QUESTIONS

Issue 1: Does this Section apply when an accountant issues a report on a preliminary investigation in connection with a proposed merger or acquisition transaction?

No. An accountant's report on a preliminary investigation in connection with a proposed transaction (e.g., merger, acquisition, financing) is not covered by this Section. In such circumstances, the accountant should follow the guidance in AT Section 201 (Agreed-Upon Procedures Engagements).

Issue 2: What is a principal accountant's responsibility when more than one accountant is involved in the audit of the financial statements and the reports of those accountants appear in the registration statement?

There may be situations where more than one accountant is involved in the audit of an entity's financial statements and the reports of more than one accountant appear in the registration statement. Such situations include significant divisions, branches, or subsidiaries that have been audited by other accountants. In such circumstances, the principal accountant (i.e., the one reporting on the consolidated financial statements) should:

1. Read the comfort letters of the other accountants reporting on significant units.
2. State in his or her comfort letter that:
   a. Reading comfort letters of the other accountants was one of the procedures followed.
   b. The procedures performed by the principal accountant relate solely to companies audited by the principal accountant and to the consolidated financial statements.

See Illustration 10 for example of wording to be used in such circumstances.

Issue 3: May accountants comment in a comfort letter on compliance as to form of Management's Discussion & Analysis (MD&A) with rules and regulations adopted by the SEC?

No. Accountants should not comment in a comfort letter on compliance as to form of MD&A with rules and regulations adopted by the SEC. However, accountants may examine or review MD&A in accordance with AT Section 701 (Management's Discussion and Analysis).

Issue 4: May the auditor perform services at the request of an entity's board of directors in connection with the entity's annual report to the SEC on Form 10-K?

Yes. However, the auditor should observe the following guidance in connection with services performed relating to Form 10-K:

1. The auditor can express an opinion on whether the audited financial statements and schedules comply as to form with the applicable accounting requirements of the Securities Exchange Act of 1934 and the related rules and regulations thereunder adopted by the SEC.
2. The auditor should not provide any assurance on compliance with the provisions of the Securities Exchange Act of 1934 regarding controls.

3. The auditor may confirm that under GAAS he or she is required to read the information, in addition to audited financial statements, contained in the Form 10-K, for the purpose of considering whether such information may be materially inconsistent with information appearing in the financial statements (see AU Section 550, Other Information in Documents Containing Audited Financial Statements). However, the auditor should state that he or she has no obligation to corroborate such information.

4. The auditor may perform, at the request of the board of directors, specified procedures and report the results concerning various information contained in the Form 10-K such as tables, statistics, and other financial information.

5. The auditor may comment, and is limited to providing negative assurance, on whether certain financial information in Form 10-K is in conformity with the disclosure requirements of Regulation S-K, if the following conditions are met:

   a. The information is derived from the accounting records subject to the entity's controls over financial reporting, or has been derived directly from such accounting records by analysis or computation.

   b. The information is capable of evaluation against reasonable criteria that have been established by the SEC.

6. The auditor should not comment on matters that are primarily subjective or judgmental in nature such as those included in Item 7 of Form 10-K, "Management's Discussion and Analysis of Financial Condition and Results of Operations."

7. The auditor should clearly indicate to the board of directors that he or she cannot make any representations as to whether the agreed-upon procedures are sufficient for the directors' purposes.

8. If requested, the auditor may reaffirm his or her independence to the board of directors by making a statement similar to that described in the section above under "The Accountant's Independence."

Issue 5: What type of assurance may an accountant provide in a comfort letter regarding an entity's conformity with Item 305 of Regulation S-K?

Regulation S-K, Item 305—"Quantitative and Qualitative Disclosures about Market Risk"—requires certain disclosures about derivative financial instruments, other financial instruments, and derivative commodity instruments, such as commodity futures, forwards, and swaps.

Accountants may not provide either positive or negative assurance on conformity with Item 305 of Regulation S-K. The accountants are prohibited from providing positive assurance since the information is not in the form of financial statements and generally has not been audited. The accountants are also prohibited from giving negative assurance because a significant amount of information provided by the entity is not derived from accounting records subject to the entity's controls over financial reporting.

Issue 6: May an accountant provide comments in a comfort letter on an entity's qualitative disclosures made in accordance with Item 305 of Regulation S-K?

No, because such information is not:

1. Expressed in dollars (or percentages derived from such dollar amounts) and is not obtained from accounting records that are subject to the entity's controls over financial reporting; or

2. Derived directly from such accounting records by analysis or computation.

Issue 7: May an accountant provide comments in a comfort letter on an entity's quantitative disclosures made in accordance with Item 305 of Regulation S-K?

There are three alternative forms of quantitative disclosures under Item 305: tabular presentation, sensitivity analysis, and value at risk. The three alternative forms of quantitative disclosures under Item 305 reflect hypothetical effects on market-risk-sensitive instruments and result in differing presentations. The forward-looking information used to prepare these presentations may be substantially removed from the accounting records that are subject to the entity's controls over financial reporting. Therefore, an accountant's ability to comment on these disclosures is largely dependent upon the degree to which the forward-looking information used to prepare these disclosures is linked to such accounting records.

1. *Tabular presentation*—The tabular presentation contains the most limited number of assumptions and least complex mathematical calculations. Also, certain information, such as contractual terms, included in a tabular presentation is derived from the accounting records. As a result, accountants may perform limited procedures related to tabular presentations to the extent that such information is derived from the accounting records. However, the accountant should disclaim as to the reasonableness of the assumptions underlying the disclosures.

2. *Sensitivity analysis*—The disclosures under this alternative are dependent upon assumptions about theoretical future market conditions and, therefore, are not derived from the accounting records. As a result, accountants should not agree to make any comments or perform any procedures related to sensitivity analysis disclosures, due to the hypothetical and forward-looking nature of the disclosures.

3. *Value at risk*—The disclosures under this alternative are extremely aggregated and, in addition to the assumptions made for sensitivity analyses, may include additional assumptions regarding correlation between asset classes and future market volatilities. Therefore, they are not derived from the accounting records. As a result, accountants should not agree to make any comments or perform any procedures related to value-at-risk disclosures, due to the hypothetical and forward-looking nature of the disclosures.

Issue 8: Given that parties other than the registrant and the underwriters (e.g., attorneys) have input into the underwriting process, who really decides what procedures are to be applied in providing comfort letters for underwriters?

A comfort letter is a specialized form of an agreed-upon procedures engagement. Underwriters generally seek assistance on matters of concern or importance to them in requesting a comfort letter. Foremost among these is evidence that they have applied due diligence under the securities laws.

Accountants and others, such as attorneys, frequently recommend to underwriters procedures that can be, or in their opinion should be, applied in a given set of circumstances. However, what constitutes a reasonable set of procedures has never been authoritatively established. Therefore, the decision as to what constitute sufficient procedures is entirely the responsibility of the underwriters.

Issue 9: May an accountant, in response to an underwriter's request, comment in a comfort letter on a significant deficiencies letter that was issued in connection with an entity's financial statement audit?

No. This Section specifically prohibits the accountant from making such comments in the comfort letter. This is because the accountant will not have audited the subsequent period since the last year end, and the effectiveness of an internal control system cannot be projected into future periods; therefore, any comments about the significant deficiencies letter in a comfort letter might lead the underwriter to place more reliance than warranted by the limited procedures that were applied.

ILLUSTRATIONS AND PRACTICE AIDS

Most of the Illustrations below are reproduced or adapted from the appendix to AU Section 634.

ILLUSTRATION 1—TYPICAL COMFORT LETTER

Note to Illustration 1: This example assumes the following circumstances. The prospectus (part I of the registration statement) includes audited consolidated balance sheets as of December 31, 20X5, and 20X4, and audited consolidated statements of income, retained earnings (stockholders' equity), and cash flows for each of the three years in the period ended December 31, 20X5. Part I also includes an unaudited condensed consolidated balance sheet as of March 31, 20X6, and unaudited condensed consolidated statements of income, retained earnings (stockholders' equity), and cash flows for the three-month periods ended March 31, 20X6, and 20X5, reviewed in accordance with AU Section 722 but not previously reported on by the accountants. Part II of the registration statement includes audited consolidated financial statement schedules for the three years ended December 31, 20X5. The cutoff date is June 23, 20X6, and the letter is dated June 28, 20X6. The effective date is June 28, 20X6.

Each of the comments in the letter is in response to a requirement of the underwriting agreement. For purposes of Illustration 1, the income statement items of the current interim period are to be compared with those of the corresponding period of the preceding year.

June 28, 20X6

[*Addressee*]

Dear _____:

We have audited the consolidated balance sheets of ABC Company (the company) and subsidiaries as of December 31, 20X5, and 20X4, and the consolidated statements of income, retained earnings (stockholders' equity), and cash flows for each of the three years in the period ended December 31, 20X5, and the related financial statement schedules all included in the registration statement (No. 33-XXXXX) on Form S-1 filed by the company under the Securities Act of 1933 (the Act); our reports with respect thereto are also included in that registration statement. The registration statement, as amended on June 28, 20X6, is herein referred to as the registration statement.[1]

In connection with the registration statement:

1. We are independent certified public accountants with respect to the company within the meaning of the Act and the applicable rules and regulations thereunder adopted by the SEC.

2. In our opinion [*include the phrase "except as disclosed in the registration statement," if applicable*], the consolidated financial statements and financial statement schedules audited by us and included in the registration statement comply as to form in all material respects with the applicable accounting requirements of the Act and the related rules and regulations adopted by the SEC.

3. We have not audited any financial statements of the company as of any date or for any period subsequent to December 31, 20X5; although we have conducted an audit for the year ended December 31, 20X5, the purpose, and therefore the scope, of the audit was to enable us to express our opinion on the consolidated financial statements as of December 31, 20X5, and for the year then ended, but not on the financial statements for any interim period within that year. Therefore, we are unable to and do not express any opinion on the unaudited condensed consolidated balance sheet as of March 31, 20X6, and the unaudited condensed consolidated statements of income, retained earnings (stockholders' equity), and cash flows for the three-month periods ended March 31, 20X6, and 20X5, included in the registration statement, or on the financial position, results of operations, or cash flows as of any date or for any period subsequent to December 31, 20X5.

4. For purposes of this letter we have read the 20X6 minutes of meetings of the stockholders, the board of directors, and [*include other appropriate committees, if any*] of the company and its subsidiaries as set forth in the minute books at June 23, 20X6, officials of the company having advised us that the minutes of all such meetings[2] through that date were set forth therein; we have carried out other procedures to June 23, 20X6, as follows (our work did not extend to the period from June 24, 20X6, to June 28, 20X6, inclusive):

    a. With respect to the three-month periods ended March 31, 20X6, and 20X5, we have:

        (i) Performed the procedures specified by the American Institute of Certified Public Accountants for a review of interim financial information as described in AU Section 722, *Interim Financial Information*, on the unaudited condensed consolidated balance sheet as of March

---

[1] The example assumes that the accountants have not previously reported on the interim financial information. If the accountants have previously reported on the interim financial information, they may refer to that fact in the introductory paragraph of the comfort letter as follows:

Also, we have reviewed the unaudited condensed consolidated financial statements as of March 31, 20X6, and 20X5, and for the three-month periods then ended, as indi-

cated in our report dated May 15, 20X6, which is included (incorporated by reference) in the registration statement.

[2] The accountants should discuss with the secretary those meetings for which minutes have not been approved. The letter should be modified to identify specifically the unapproved minutes of meetings that the accountants have discussed with the secretary.

31, 20X6, and unaudited condensed consolidated statements of income, retained earnings (stockholders' equity), and cash flows for the three month periods ended March 31, 20X6, and 20X5, included in the registration statement.

(ii) Inquired of certain officials of the company who have responsibility for financial and accounting matters whether the unaudited condensed consolidated financial statements referred to in item a(i) above comply as to form in all material respects with the applicable accounting requirements of the Act and the related rules and regulations adopted by the SEC.

b. With respect to the period from April 1, 20X6, to May 31, 20X6, we have:

(i) Read the unaudited consolidated financial statements[3] of the company and subsidiaries for April and May of both 20X5 and 20X6 furnished us by the company, officials of the company having advised us that no such financial statements as of any date or for any period subsequent to May 31, 20X6, were available.

(ii) Inquired of certain officials of the company who have responsibility for financial and accounting matters whether the unaudited consolidated financial statements referred to in item b(i) above are stated on a basis substantially consistent with that of the audited consolidated financial statements included in the registration statement.

The foregoing procedures do not constitute an audit conducted in accordance with auditing standards generally accepted in the United States of America. Also, they would not necessarily reveal matters of significance with respect to the comments in the following paragraph. Accordingly, we make no representations regarding the sufficiency of the foregoing procedures for your purposes.

5. Nothing came to our attention as a result of the foregoing procedures, however, that caused us[4] to believe that:

a. Any material modifications should be made to the unaudited condensed consolidated financial statements described in item 4a(i) above, included in the registration statement, for them to be in conformity with accounting principles generally accepted in the United States of America.[5]

---

[3] If the interim financial information is incomplete, a sentence similar to the following should be added: "The financial information for April and May is incomplete in that it omits the statements of cash flows and other disclosures."

[4] If there has been a change in accounting principle during the interim period, a reference to that change should be included herein.

[5] AU Section 722 does not require the accountants to modify the report on a review of interim financial

b. The unaudited condensed consolidated financial statements described in item 4a(i) above do not comply as to form in all material respects with the applicable accounting requirements of the Act and the related rules and regulations adopted by the SEC.

c. At May 31, 20X6, there was any change in the capital stock, increase in long-term debt, or decrease in consolidated net current assets or stockholders' equity of the consolidated companies as compared with amounts shown in the March 31, 20X6, unaudited condensed consolidated balance sheet included in the registration statement, or for the period from April 1, 20X6, to May 31, 20X6, there were any decreases, as compared to the corresponding period in the preceding year, in consolidated net sales or in the total or per-share amounts of income before extraordinary items or of net income, except in all instances for changes, increases, or decreases that the registration statement discloses have occurred or may occur.

6. As mentioned in item 4b above, company officials have advised us that no consolidated financial statements as of any date or for any period subsequent to May 31, 20X6, are available; accordingly, the procedures carried out by us with respect to changes in financial statement items after May 31, 20X6, have, of necessity, been even more limited than those with respect to the periods referred to in item 4 above. We have inquired of certain officials of the company who have responsibility for financial and accounting matters whether (a) at June 23, 20X6, there was any change in the capital stock, increase in long-term debt or any decreases in consolidated net current assets or stockholders' equity of the consolidated companies as compared with amounts shown on the March 31, 20X6, unaudited condensed consolidated balance sheet included in the registration statement or (b) for the period from April 1, 20X6, to June 23, 20X6, there were any decreases, as compared with the corresponding period in the preceding year, in consolidated net sales or in the total or per-share amounts of income before extraordinary items or of net income. On the basis of these inquiries and our reading of the minutes as described in item 4 above, nothing came to our attention that caused us to believe that there was any such change, increase, or decrease, except in all instances for changes, increases, or decreases that the registration statement discloses have occurred or may occur.

7. This letter is solely for the information of the addressees and to assist the underwriters in conducting and documenting their investigation of the affairs of the company in connection with the offering of the securities covered by the registration statement, and it is not to be used, circulated, quoted, or otherwise referred to within or without the underwriting group for any purpose, including but not limited to the registration, purchase, or sale of securities, nor is it to be filed with or referred to in whole or in part in the registration statement or any other document, except that reference may be made to it in the underwriting agreement or in any list of closing documents pertaining to the offering of the securities covered by the registration statement.

(Footnote Continued)

information for a lack of consistency in the application of accounting principles provided that the interim financial information appropriately discloses such matters.

ILLUSTRATION 2—COMFORT LETTER WHEN A SHORT-FORM REGISTRATION STATEMENT IS FILED INCORPORATING PREVIOUSLY FILED FORMS 10-K AND 10-Q BY REFERENCE

Note to Illustration 2: *This example is applicable when a registrant uses a short-form registration statement (Form S-2 or S-3) which, by reference, incorporates previously filed Forms 10-K and 10-Q. It assumes that the short-form registration statement and prospectus include the Form 10-K for the year ended December 31, 20X5, and Form 10-Q for the quarter ended March 31, 20X6, which have been incorporated by reference. In addition to the information presented below, the letter would also contain paragraphs 6 and 7 of the typical letter in Illustration 1. A Form S-2 registration statement will often both incorporate and include the registrant's financial statements. In such situations, the language in the following example should be appropriately modified to refer to such information as being both incorporated and included.*

June 28, 20X6

[*Addressee*]

Dear _____:

We have audited the consolidated balance sheets of ABC Company (the company) and subsidiaries as of December 31, 20X5, and 20X4, and the consolidated statements of income, retained earnings (stockholders' equity), and cash flows for each of the three years in the period ended December 31, 20X5, and the related financial statement schedules, all included (incorporated by reference) in the company's annual report on Form 10-K for the year ended December 31, 20X5, and incorporated by reference in the registration statement (No. 33-XXXXX) on Form S-3 filed by the company under the Securities Act of 1933 (the Act); our report with respect thereto is also incorporated by reference in that registration statement. The registration statement, as amended on June 28, 20X6, is herein referred to as the registration statement.

In connection with the registration statement:

1. We are independent certified public accountants with respect to the company within the meaning of the Act and the applicable rules and regulations thereunder adopted by the SEC.

2. In our opinion, the consolidated financial statements and financial statement schedules audited by us and incorporated by reference in the registration statement comply as to form in all material respects with the applicable accounting requirements of the Act and the Securities Exchange Act of 1934 and the related rules and regulations adopted by the SEC.

3. We have not audited any financial statements of the company as of any date or for any period subsequent to December 31, 20X5; although we have conducted an audit for the year ended December 31, 20X5, the purpose, and therefore the scope, of the audit was to enable us to express our opinion on the consolidated financial statements as of December 31, 20X5, and for the year then ended, but not on the consolidated financial statements for any interim period within that year. Therefore, we are unable to and do not express any opinion on the unaudited condensed consolidated balance sheet as of March 31, 20X6, and the unaudited condensed consolidated statements of income, retained earnings (stockholders' equity), and cash flows for the three-month periods ended March 31, 20X6, and 20X5, included in the company's quarterly report on Form 10-Q for the quarter ended March 31, 20X6, incorporated by reference in the registration state-

ment, or on the financial position, results of operations, or cash flows as of any date or for any period subsequent to December 31, 20X5.

4. For purposes of this letter, we have read the 20X6 minutes of the meetings of the stockholders, the board of directors, and [*include other appropriate committees, if any*] of the company and its subsidiaries as set forth in the minute books at June 23, 20X6, officials of the company having advised us that the minutes of all such meetings[6] through that date were set forth therein; we have carried out other procedures to June 23, 20X6, as follows (our work did not extend to the period from June 24, 20X6, to June 28, 20X6, inclusive):

    a. With respect to the three-month periods ended March 31, 20X6, and 20X5, we have:

        (i) Performed the procedures specified by the American Institute of Certified Public Accountants for a review of interim financial information as described in AU Section 722, *Interim Financial Information,* on the unaudited condensed consolidated financial statements for these periods, described in item 3 above, included in the company's quarterly report on Form 10-Q for the quarter ended March 31, 20X6, incorporated by reference in the registration statement.

        (ii) Inquired of certain officials of the company who have responsibility for financial and accounting matters whether the unaudited condensed consolidated financial statements referred to in item a(i) above comply as to form in all material respects with the applicable accounting requirements of the Securities Exchange Act of 1934 as it applies to Form 10-Q and the related rules and regulations adopted by the SEC.

    b. With respect to the period from April 1, 20X6, to May 31, 20X6, we have:

        (i) Read the unaudited consolidated financial statements[7] of the company and subsidiaries for April and May of both 20X5 and 20X6 furnished us by the company, officials of the company having advised us that no such financial statements as of any date or for any period subsequent to May 31, 20X6, were available.

        (ii) Inquired of certain officials of the company who have responsibility for financial and accounting matters whether the unaudited consolidated financial statements referred to in item b(i) above are stated on a basis substantially consistent with that of the audited consolidated financial statements incorporated by reference in the registration statement.

The foregoing procedures do not constitute an audit conducted in accordance with auditing standards gener-

---

ally accepted in the United States of America. Also, they would not necessarily reveal matters of significance with respect to the comments in the following paragraph. Accordingly, we make no representations about the sufficiency of the foregoing procedures for your purposes.

5. Nothing came to our attention as a result of the foregoing procedures, however, that caused us to believe that:

   a. Any material modifications should be made to the unaudited condensed consolidated financial statements described in item 3 above, incorporated by reference in the registration statement, for them to be in conformity with accounting principles generally accepted in the United States of America.

   b. The unaudited condensed consolidated financial statements described in item 3 above do not comply as to form in all material respects with the applicable accounting requirements of the Securities Exchange Act of 1934 as it applies to Form 10-Q and the related rules and regulations adopted by the SEC.

   c. At May 31, 20X6, there was any change in the capital stock, increase in long-term debt, or any decreases in consolidated net current assets or stockholders' equity of the consolidated companies as compared with amounts shown in the March 31, 20X6, unaudited condensed consolidated balance sheet incorporated by reference in the registration statement, or for the period from April 1, 20X6, to May 31, 20X6, there were any decreases, as compared with the corresponding period in the preceding year, in consolidated net sales or in the total or per-share amounts of income before extraordinary items or of net income, except in all instances for changes, increases, or decreases that the registration statement discloses have occurred or may occur.

ILLUSTRATION 3—COMFORT LETTER REAFFIRMING INFORMATION IN AN INITIAL COMFORT LETTER AS OF A LATER DATE

Note to Illustration 3: *If more than one comfort letter is requested, the later letter may, in appropriate situations, refer to information appearing in the earlier letter without repeating such information. This example reaffirms and updates the information in Illustration 1.*

July 25, 20X6

[*Addressee*]

Dear _____:

We refer to our letter of June 28, 20X6, relating to the registration statement (No. 33-XXXXX) of ABC Company (the company). We reaffirm as of the date hereof (and as though made on the date hereof) all statements made in that letter except that, for the purposes of this letter:

1. The registration statement to which this letter relates is as amended on July 13, 20X6 [*effective date*].

2. The reading of minutes described in paragraph 4 of that letter has been carried out through July 20, 20X6 [*the new cutoff date*].

3. The procedures and inquiries covered in paragraph 4 of that letter were carried out to July 20, 20X6 [*the new cutoff date*] (our work did

not extend to the period from July 21, 20X6, to July 25, 20X6 [*date of letter*], inclusive).

4. The period covered in paragraph 4b of that letter is changed to the period from April 1, 20X6, to June 30, 20X6, officials of the company having advised us that no such financial statements as of any date or for any period subsequent to June 30, 20X6, were available.

5. The references to May 31, 20X6, in paragraph 5c of that letter are changed to June 30, 20X6.

6. The references to May 31, 20X6, and June 23, 20X6, in paragraph 6 of that letter are changed to June 30, 20X6, and July 20, 20X6, respectively.

This letter is solely for the information of the addressees and to assist the underwriters in conducting and documenting their investigation of the affairs of the company in connection with the offering of the securities covered by the registration statement, and it is not to be used, circulated, quoted, or otherwise referred to within the underwriting group for any other purpose, including but not limited to the registration, purchase, or sale of securities, nor is it to be filed with or referred to in whole or in part in the registration statement or any other document, except that reference may be made to it in the underwriting agreement or any list of closing documents pertaining to the offering of the securities covered by the registration statement.

ILLUSTRATION 4—COMMENTS ON PRO FORMA FINANCIAL INFORMATION

Note to Illustration 4: *This example is applicable when the accountants are asked to comment on (a) whether the pro forma financial information included in a registration statement complies as to form in all material respects with the applicable accounting requirements of rule 11-02 of Regulation S-X and (b) the application of pro forma adjustments to historical amounts in the compilation of the pro forma financial information. The material in this example is intended to be inserted between paragraphs 6 and 7 in Illustration 1. The accountants have audited the December 31, 20X5, financial statements and have conducted a review under AU Section 722 of the March 31, 20X6, interim financial information of the acquiring company. Other accountants conducted a review of the March 31, 20X6, interim financial information of XYZ Company, the company being acquired. The example assumes that the accountants have not previously reported on the pro forma financial information. If the accountants did previously report on the pro forma financial information, they may refer in the introductory paragraph of the comfort letter to the fact that they have issued a report, and the report may be attached to the comfort letter. In that circumstance, therefore, the procedures in paragraphs 7b(i) and 7c of this Illustration ordinarily would not be performed, and the accountants should not separately comment on the application of pro forma adjustments to historical financial information, since that assurance is encompassed in the accountants' report on pro forma financial information. The accountants may, however, agree to comment on compliance as to form with the applicable accounting requirements of rule 11-02 of Regulation S-X.*

7. At your request, we have:

a. Read the unaudited pro forma condensed consolidated balance sheet as of March 31, 20X6, and the unaudited pro forma condensed consolidated statements of income for the year ended December 31, 20X5, and the three-month period ended March 31, 20X6, included in the registration statement.

    b. Inquired of certain officials of the company and of XYZ Company (the company being acquired) who have responsibility for financial and accounting matters about:

        (i) The basis for their determination of the pro forma adjustments, and

        (ii) Whether the unaudited pro forma condensed consolidated financial statements referred to in item 7a above comply as to form in all material respects with the applicable accounting requirements of rule 11-02 of Regulation S-X.

    c. Proved the arithmetic accuracy of the application of the pro forma adjustments to the historical amounts in the unaudited pro forma condensed consolidated financial statements.

The foregoing procedures are substantially less in scope than an examination, the objective of which is the expression of an opinion on management's assumptions, the pro forma adjustments, and the application of those adjustments to historical financial information. Accordingly, we do not express such an opinion. The foregoing procedures would not necessarily reveal matters of significance with respect to the comments in the following paragraph. Accordingly, we make no representation about the sufficiency of such procedures for your purposes.

8. Nothing came to our attention as a result of the procedures specified in paragraph 7, however, that caused us to believe that the unaudited pro forma condensed consolidated financial statements referred to in item 7a above included in the registration statement do not comply as to form in all material respects with the applicable accounting requirements of rule 11-02 of Regulation S-X and that the pro forma adjustments have not been properly applied to the historical amounts in the compilation of those statements. Had we performed additional procedures or had we made an examination of the pro forma condensed consolidated financial statements, other matters might have come to our attention that would have been reported to you.

ILLUSTRATION 5—COMMENTS ON A FINANCIAL FORECAST

Note to Illustration 5: *This example is applicable when accountants are asked to comment on a financial forecast. The material in this example is intended to be inserted between paragraphs 6 and 7 in Illustration 1. The example assumes that the accountants have previously reported on the compilation of the financial forecast and that the report is attached to the letter (see Illustration 15).*

7. At your request, we performed the following procedure with respect to the forecasted consolidated balance sheet and consolidated statements of income and cash flows as of December 31, 20X6, and for the year then ending. With respect to forecasted rental income, we compared the occupancy statistics about expected demand for rental of the housing units to statistics for existing comparable properties and found them to be the same.

8. Because the procedure described above does not constitute an examination of prospective financial statements in accordance with stan-

dards established by the American Institute of Certified Public Accountants, we do not express an opinion on whether the prospective financial statements are presented in conformity with AICPA presentation guidelines or on whether the underlying assumptions provide a reasonable basis for the presentation.

Had we performed additional procedures or had we made an examination of the forecast in accordance with standards established by the American Institute of Certified Public Accountants, matters might have come to our attention that would have been reported to you. Furthermore, there will usually be differences between the forecasted and actual results, because events and circumstances frequently do not occur as expected, and those differences may be material.

ILLUSTRATION 6—COMMENTS ON TABLES, STATISTICS, AND OTHER FINANCIAL INFORMATION—COMPLETE DESCRIPTION OF PROCEDURES AND FINDINGS

Note to Illustration 6: This example is applicable when the accountants are asked to comment on tables, statistics, or other compilations of information appearing in a registration statement. Each of the comments is in response to a specific request. The paragraphs in this example are intended to follow paragraph 6 in Illustration 1.

7. For purposes of this letter, we have also read the following, set forth in the registration statement on the indicated pages:[8]

Item	Page	Description
a.	4	"Capitalization." The amounts under the captions "Amount Outstanding as of June 15, 20X6" and "As Adjusted." The related notes, except the following in Note 2: "See 'Transactions with Interested Persons.' From the proceeds of this offering the company intends to repay $900,000 on these notes, pro rata. See 'Use of Proceeds.'"
b.	13	"History and Business—Sales and Marketing." The table following the first paragraph.
c.	22	"Executive Compensation—20X5 Compensation."
d.	33	"Selected Financial Data."[9]

---

[9] In some cases the company or the underwriter may request that the independent accountants report on "selected financial data" as described in AU Section 552 (Reporting on Condensed Financial Statements and Selected Financial Data). When the accountants report on this data and the report is included in the registration statement, separate comments should not be included in the comfort letter.

8. Our audit of the consolidated financial statements for the periods referred to in the introductory paragraph of this letter comprised audit tests and procedures deemed necessary for the purpose of expressing an opinion on such financial statements taken as a whole. For none of the periods referred to therein, or any other period, did we perform audit tests for the purpose of expressing an opinion on

---

[8] In some cases it may be considered desirable to combine in one paragraph the substance of paragraphs 7 and 9. This may be done by expanding the identification of items in paragraph 9 to provide the identification information contained in paragraph 7. In such cases, the introductory sentences in paragraphs 7 and 9 and the text of paragraph 8 might be combined as follows: "*For purposes of this letter, we have also read the following information and have performed the additional procedures stated below with respect to such information. Our audit of the consolidated financial statements . . .*"

individual balances of accounts or summaries of selected transactions such as those enumerated above, and, accordingly, we express no opinion thereon.

9. However, for purposes of this letter we have performed the following additional procedures, which were applied as indicated with respect to the items enumerated above:

Item in 7	*Procedures and Findings*
a.	We compared the amounts and numbers of shares listed under the caption "Amount Outstanding as of June 15, 20X6" with the balances in the appropriate accounts in the company's general ledger at May 31, 20X6 (the latest date for which posting had been made), and found them to be in agreement. We were informed by company officials who have responsibility for financial and accounting matters that there have been no changes in such amounts and numbers of shares between May 31, 20X6, and June 15, 20X6. We compared the amounts and numbers of shares listed under the caption "Amount Outstanding as of June 15, 20X6," adjusted for the issuance of the debentures to be offered by means of the registration statement and for the proposed use of a portion of the proceeds thereof to prepay portions of certain notes, as described under "Use of Proceeds," with the amounts and numbers of shares shown under the caption "As adjusted" and found such amounts and numbers of shares to be in agreement. (However, we make no comments regarding the reasonableness of the "Use of Proceeds" or whether such use will actually take place.) We compared the description of the securities and the information (except certain information in Note 2, referred to in 7) included in the notes to the table with the corresponding descriptions and information in the company's consolidated financial statements, including the notes thereto included in the registration statement, and found such description and information to be in agreement.
b.	We compared the amounts of military sales, commercial sales, and total sales shown in the registration statement with the balances in the appropriate accounts in the company's accounting records for the respective fiscal years and for the unaudited interim periods and found them to be in agreement. We proved the arithmetic accuracy of the percentages of such amounts of military sales and commercial sales to total sales for the respective fiscal years and for the unaudited interim periods. We compared such computed percentages with the corresponding percentages appearing in the registration statement and found them to be in agreement.

Item in 7	*Procedures and Findings*
c.	We compared the dollar amounts of compensation (salary, bonus, and other compensation) for each individual listed in the table "Annual Compensation" with the corresponding amounts shown by the individual employee earnings records for the year 20X5 and found them to be in agreement. We compared the dollar amount of aggregate executive officers' cash compensation on page 22 with the corresponding amount shown in an analysis prepared by the company and found the amounts to be in agreement. We traced every item over $10,000 on the analysis to the individual employee records for 20X5. We compared the dollar amounts shown under the heading of "Long-Term Compensation" on page 24 for each listed individual and the aggregate amounts for executive officers with corresponding amounts shown in an analysis prepared by the company and found such amounts to be in agreement.
	We compared the executive compensation information with the requirements of item 402 of Regulation S-K. We also inquired of certain officials of the company who have responsibility for financial and accounting matters whether the executive compensation information conforms in all material respects with the disclosure requirements of item 402 of Regulation S-K.
	Nothing came to our attention as a result of the foregoing procedures that caused us to believe that this information does not conform in all material respects with the disclosure requirements of item 402 of Regulation S-K.
d.	We compared the amounts of net sales, income from continuing operations, income from continuing operations per common share, and cash dividends declared per common share for the years ended December 31, 20X5, 20X4, and 20X3, with the respective amounts in the consolidated financial statements on pages 27 and 28 and the amounts for the years ended December 31, 20X2, and 20X1, with the respective amounts in the consolidated financial statements included in the company's annual reports to stockholders for 20X2 and 20X1 and found them to be in agreement.

Item in 7	*Procedures and Findings*
	We compared the amounts of total assets, long-term obligations, and redeemable preferred stock at December 31, 20X5, and 20X4, with the respective amounts in the consolidated financial statements on pages 27 and 28 and the amounts at December 31, 20X3, 20X2, and 20X1 with the corresponding amounts in the consolidated financial statements included in the company's annual reports to stockholders for 20X3, 20X2, and 20X1 and found them to be in agreement.
	We compared the information included under the heading "Selected Financial Data" with the requirements of item 301 of Regulation S-K. We also inquired of certain officials of the company who have responsibility for financial and accounting matters whether this information conforms in all material respects with the disclosure requirements of item 301 of Regulation S-K. Nothing came to our attention as a result of the foregoing procedures that caused us to believe that this information does not conform in all material respects with the disclosure requirements of item 301 of Regulation S-K.

10. It should be understood that we make no representations regarding questions of legal interpretation or regarding the sufficiency for your purposes of the procedures enumerated in the preceding paragraph; also, such procedures would not necessarily reveal any material misstatement of the amounts or percentages listed above. Further, we have addressed ourselves solely to the foregoing data as set forth in the registration statement and make no representations regarding the adequacy of disclosure or regarding whether any material facts have been omitted.

11. This letter is solely for the information of the addressees and to assist the underwriters in conducting and documenting their investigation of the affairs of the company in connection with the offering of the securities covered by the registration statement, and it is not to be used, circulated, quoted, or otherwise referred to within or without the underwriting group for any other purpose, including but not limited to the registration, purchase, or sale of securities, nor is it to be filed with or referred to in whole or in part in the registration statement or any other document, except that reference may be made to it in the underwriting agreement or in any list of closing documents pertaining to the offering of the securities covered by the registration statement.

ILLUSTRATION 7—COMMENTS ON TABLES, STATISTICS, AND OTHER FINANCIAL INFORMATION—SUMMARIZED DESCRIPTION OF PROCEDURES AND FINDINGS REGARDING TABLES, STATISTICS, AND OTHER FINANCIAL INFORMATION

Note to Illustration 7: *This example illustrates, in paragraph 9a, a method of summarizing the descriptions of procedures and findings regarding tables, statistics, and other financial information in order to avoid repetition in the comfort letter. The summarization of the descriptions is permitted. Each of the comments is in response to* *a specific request. The paragraphs in this example are intended to follow paragraph 6 in Illustration 1.*[10]

7. For purposes of this letter, we have also read the following, set forth in the registration statement on the indicated pages:

Item	Page	Description
a.	4	"Capitalization." The amounts under the captions "Amount Outstanding as of June 15, 20X6" and "As Adjusted." The related notes, except the following in Note 2: "See 'Transactions With Interested Persons.' From the proceeds of this offering the company intends to prepay $900,000 on these notes, pro rata. See 'Use of Proceeds.'"
b.	13	"History and Business—Sales and Marketing." The table following the first paragraph.
c.	22	"Executive Compensation—20X5 Compensation."
d.	33	"Selected Financial Data."[11]

[11] See footnote 9 of Illustration 6.

8. Our audit of the consolidated financial statements for the periods referred to in the introductory paragraph of this letter comprised audit tests and procedures deemed necessary for the purpose of expressing an opinion on such financial statements taken as a whole. For none of the periods referred to therein, or any other period, did we perform audit tests for the purpose of expressing an opinion on individual balances of accounts or summaries of selected transactions such as those enumerated above, and, accordingly, we express no opinion thereon.

9. However, for purposes of this letter and with respect to the items enumerated in paragraph 7 above:

   a. Except for item 7a above, we have (i) compared the dollar amounts either with the amounts in the audited consolidated financial statements described in the introductory paragraph of this letter or, for prior years, included in the company's annual report to stockholders for the years 20X1, 20X2, and 20X3, or with amounts in the unaudited consolidated financial statements described in paragraph 3 to the extent such amounts are included in or can be derived from such statements and found them to be in agreement; (ii) compared the amounts of military sales, commercial sales, and total sales and the dollar amounts of compensation for each listed individual with amounts in the company's accounting records and found them to be in agreement; (iii) compared other dollar amounts with amounts shown in analyses prepared by the company and found them to be in agreement; and (iv) proved the arithmetic accuracy of the percentages based on the data in the above-mentioned financial statements, accounting records, and analyses.

   We compared the information in items 7c and 7d above with the disclosure requirements of Regulation

---

[10] Other methods of summarizing the descriptions may also be appropriately used. For example, the letter may present a matrix listing the financial information and common procedures employed and indicating the procedures applied to specific items.

S-K. We also inquired of certain officials of the company who have responsibility for financial and accounting matters whether this information conforms in all material respects with the disclosure requirements of Regulation S-K. Nothing came to our attention as a result of the foregoing procedures that caused us to believe that this information does not conform in all material respects with the disclosure requirements of items 402 and 301, respectively, of Regulation S-K.

b. With respect to item 7a above, we compared the amounts and numbers of shares listed under the caption "Amount Outstanding as of June 15, 20X6" with the balances in the appropriate accounts in the company's general ledger at May 31, 20X6 (the latest date for which postings had been made), and found them to be in agreement. We were informed by officials of the company who have responsibility for financial and accounting matters that there had been no changes in such amounts and numbers of shares between May 31, 20X6, and June 15, 20X6. We compared the amounts and numbers of shares listed under the caption "Amount Outstanding as of June 15, 20X6" adjusted for the issuance of the debentures to be offered by means of the registration statement and for the proposed use of a portion of the proceeds thereof to prepay portions of certain notes, as described under "Use of Proceeds," with the amounts and numbers of shares shown under the caption "As Adjusted" and found such amounts and numbers of shares to be in agreement. (However, we make no comments regarding the reasonableness of "Use of Proceeds" or whether such use will actually take place.) We compared the description of the securities and the information (except certain information in Note 2, referred to in item 7 above) included in the notes to the table with the corresponding descriptions and information in the company's consolidated financial statements, including the notes thereto, included in the registration statement and found such descriptions and information to be in agreement.

10. It should be understood that we make no representations regarding questions of legal interpretation or regarding the sufficiency for your purposes of the procedures enumerated in the preceding paragraph; also, such procedures would not necessarily reveal any material misstatement of the amounts or percentages listed above. Further, we have addressed ourselves solely to the foregoing data as set forth in the registration statement and make no representations regarding the adequacy of disclosure or regarding whether any material facts have been omitted.

11. This letter is solely for the information of the addressees and to assist the underwriters in conducting and documenting their investigation of the affairs of the company in connection with the offering of the securities covered by the registration statement, and it is not to be used, circulated, quoted, or otherwise referred to within or without the underwriting group for any other purpose, including but not limited to the registration, purchase, or sale of securities, nor is it to

be filed with or referred to in whole or in part in the registration statement or any other document, except that reference may be made to it in the underwriting agreement or in any list of closing documents pertaining to the offering of the securities covered by the registration statement.

ILLUSTRATION 8—COMMENTS ON TABLES, STATISTICS, AND OTHER FINANCIAL INFORMATION: DESCRIPTIONS OF PROCEDURES AND FINDINGS REGARDING TABLES, STATISTICS, AND OTHER FINANCIAL INFORMATION—ATTACHED REGISTRATION STATEMENT (OR SELECTED PAGES) IDENTIFIES WITH DESIGNATED SYMBOLS ITEMS TO WHICH PROCEDURES WERE APPLIED

Note to Illustration 8: This example illustrates an alternate format which could facilitate reporting when the accountant is requested to perform procedures on numerous statistics included in a registration statement. Each of the comments is in response to a specific request. Paragraph 7 in this example is intended to follow paragraph 6 in Illustration 1. The letter would also contain paragraphs 8, 10, and 11 of the letter in Illustration 6.

7. For purposes of this letter, we have also read the items identified by you on the attached copy of the registration statement (prospectus), and have performed the following procedures, which were applied as indicated with respect to the symbols explained below:

R   Compared the amount with the XYZ (Predecessor Company) financial statements for the period indicated and found them to be in agreement.

Ø   Compared the amount with the XYZ (Predecessor Company) financial statements for the period indicated contained in the registration statement and found them to be in agreement.

V   Compared the amount with ABC Company's financial statements for the period indicated contained in the registration statement and found them to be in agreement.

X   Compared with a schedule or report prepared by the Company and found them to be in agreement.

[*The following is an extract from a registration statement that illustrates how an accountant can document procedures performed on numerous statistics included in the registration statement.*]

The following summary is qualified in its entirety by the financial statements and detailed information appearing elsewhere in this Prospectus.

The Company

ABC Company (the "Company") designs, constructs, sells, and finances single family homes for the entry-level and move-up homebuyer. The Company and its predecessor have built and delivered more single-family homes in the metropolitan area than any other homebuilder for each of the last five years. The Company delivered $1,000^X$ homes in the year ending December 31, 20X5, and at December 31, 20X5, had 500 homes under contract with an aggregate sales price of approximately $45,000,000. The Company's wholly owned mortgage banking subsidiary, which commenced operations in March 20X5, currently originates a substantial portion of the mortgages for homes sold by the Company.

The Company typically does not engage in land development without related home-building operations and limits speculative building. The Company purchases only that land which it is prepared to begin developing immediately for home production. A substantial portion of the Company's homes are under contract for sale before construction commences.

The DEF area has been among the top five markets in the country in housing starts for each of the last five years, with more than 90,000 single-family starts during that period. During the same period, the DEF metropolitan area has experienced increases in population, personal income, and employment at rates above the national average. The Company is a major competitive factor in three of the seven market areas, and is expanding significantly in a fourth area.

The Offering

Common Stock Offered by the Company	750,000^X shares of Common Stock—$.0l par value (the "Common Stock")*
Common Stock to Be Outstanding	3,250,000^X shares*
Use of Proceeds	To repay indebtedness incurred for the acquisition of the Company.
Proposed NASDAQ Symbol	ABC

* Assumes no exercise of the Underwriters' over allotment option. See "Underwriting."

Summary Financial Information
(In thousands, except per-share data)

Income Statement Data	XYZ (Predecessor Company) Year Ended December 31,				ABC Company Year Ended December 31,
	20X1	20X2	20X3	20X4	20X5
Revenue from home sales	$106,603^R	$88,977^R	$140,110$^∅$	$115,837$^∅$	$131,032^V
Gross profit from sales	$15,980^R	21,138^R	23,774$^∅$	17,099$^∅$	22,407^V
Income from home building net of tax	490^R	3,473^R	7,029$^∅$	1,000$^∅$	3,425^V
Earnings per share	—	—	—	—	$1.37^V

ILLUSTRATION 9—ALTERNATE WORDING WHEN ACCOUNTANTS' REPORT ON AUDITED FINANCIAL STATEMENTS CONTAINS AN EXPLANATORY PARAGRAPH

Note to Illustration 9: This example is applicable when the accountants' report on the audited financial statements included in the registration statement contains an explanatory paragraph regarding a matter that would also affect the unaudited condensed consolidated interim financial statements included in the registration statement.

The introductory paragraph of Illustration 1 would be revised as follows:

Our reports with respect thereto (which contain an explanatory paragraph that describes a lawsuit to which the Company is a defendant, discussed in note 8 to the consolidated financial statements) are also included in the registration statement.

The matter described in the explanatory paragraph should also be evaluated to determine whether it also requires mention in the comments on the unaudited condensed consolidated interim financial information (item 5c of Illustration 1). If it is concluded that mention of such a matter in the comments on unaudited condensed consolidated financial statements is appropriate, a sentence should be added at the end of paragraph 5c in Illustration 1, as follows:

> Reference should be made to the introductory paragraph of this letter which states that our audit report covering the consolidated financial statements as of and for the year ended December 31, 20X5, includes an explanatory paragraph that describes a lawsuit to which the company is a defendant, discussed in note 8 to the consolidated financial statements.

ILLUSTRATION 10—ALTERNATE WORDING WHEN MORE THAN ONE ACCOUNTANT IS INVOLVED

Note to Illustration 10: This example applies when more than one accountant is involved in the audit of the financial statements of a business and the principal accountants have obtained a copy of the comfort letter of the other accountants. This example consists of an addition to paragraph 4c, a substitution for the applicable part of paragraph 5, and an addition to paragraph 6 of Illustration 1.

[4]c. We have read the letter dated_____of [*the other accountants*] with regard to [*the related company.*]

5. Nothing came to our attention as a result of the foregoing procedures (which, so far as [*the related company*] is concerned, consisted solely of reading the letter referred to in item 4c above), however, that caused us to believe that. . . .

6. On the basis of these inquiries and our reading of the minutes and the letter dated _____ of the [*the other accountants*] with regard to [*the related company*], as described in item 4 above, nothing came to our attention that caused us to believe that there was any such change, increase, or decrease, except in all instances for changes, increases, or decreases that the registration statement discloses have occurred or may occur.

ILLUSTRATION 11—ALTERNATE WORDING WHEN THE SEC HAS AGREED TO A DEPARTURE FROM ITS ACCOUNTING REQUIREMENTS

Note to Illustration 11: This example is applicable when (a) there is a departure from the applicable accounting requirements of the Act and the related rules and regulations adopted by the SEC and (b) representatives of the SEC have agreed to the departure. Paragraph 2 of Illustration 1 would be revised to read as follows:

2. In our opinion [*include the phrase "except as disclosed in the registration statement," if applicable*], the consolidated financial statements and financial statement schedules audited by us and included (incorporated by reference) in the registration statement comply as to form in all material respects with the applicable accounting requirements of the Act and the related rules and regulations adopted by the SEC; however, as agreed to by representatives of the SEC, separate financial statements and financial statement schedules of ABC Company (an equity investee) as required by rule 3-09 of Regulation S-X have been omitted.

ILLUSTRATION 12—ALTERNATE WORDING WHEN RECENT EARNINGS DATA ARE PRESENTED IN CAPSULE FORM

Note to Illustration 12: This example is applicable when (a) the statement of income in the registration statement is supplemented by later information regarding sales and earnings (capsule financial information), (b) the accountants are asked to comment on that information, and (c) the accountants have conducted a review under AU Section

722 *of the financial statements from which the capsule financial information is derived. The same facts exist as in Illustration 1, except for the following:*

- *Sales, net income (no extraordinary items), and earnings per share for the six-month periods ended June 30, 20X6, and 20X5 (both unaudited), are included in capsule form more limited than that specified by FASB Accounting Standards Codification (ASC) 270, Interim Reporting.*

- *No financial statements later than those for June 20X6 are available.*

- *The letter is dated July 25, 20X6, and the cutoff date is July 20, 20X6.*

Paragraphs 4, 5, and 6 of Illustration 1 should be revised to read as follows:

4. For purposes of this letter we have read the 20X6 minutes of the meetings of the stockholders, the board of directors, and [*include other appropriate committees, if any*] of the company and its subsidiaries as set forth in the minute books at July 20, 20X6, officials of the company having advised us that the minutes of all such meetings[12] through that date were set forth therein; we have carried out other procedures to July 20, 20X6, as follows (our work did not extend to the period from July 21, 20X6, to July 25, 20X6, inclusive):

   a. With respect to the three-month periods ended March 31, 20X6 and 20X5, we have:

      (i) Performed the procedures specified by the American Institute of Certified Public Accountants for a review of interim financial information as described in AU Section 722, *Interim Financial Information,* on the unaudited condensed consolidated balance sheet as of March 31, 20X6, and the unaudited condensed consolidated statements of income, retained earnings (stockholders' equity), and cash flows for the three-month periods ended March 31, 20X6, and 20X5, included in the registration statement.

      (ii) Inquired of certain officials of the company who have responsibility for financial and accounting matters whether the unaudited condensed consolidated financial statements referred to in item a(i) above comply as to form in all material respects with the applicable accounting requirements of the Act and the related rules and regulations adopted by the SEC.

   b. With respect to the six-month periods ended June 30, 20X6, and 20X5, we have:

      (i) Read the unaudited amounts for sales, net income, and earnings per share for the six-month periods ended June 30, 20X6, and 20X5, as set forth in paragraph [*identify location*].

      (ii) Performed the procedures specified by the American Institute of Certified Public Accountants for a review of financial information as described in AU Section 722, *Interim Financial Information,* on the unaudited condensed con-

---

[12] See footnote 2 of Illustration 1.

solidated balance sheet as of June 30, 20X6, and the unaudited condensed consolidated statements of income, retained earnings (stockholders' equity), and cash flows for the six-month periods ended June 30, 20X6, and 20X5, from which the unaudited amounts referred to in item b(i) above are derived.

(iii) Inquired of certain officials of the company who have responsibility for financial and accounting matters whether the unaudited amounts referred to in item b(i) above are stated on a basis substantially consistent with that of the corresponding amounts in the audited consolidated statements of income.

The foregoing procedures do not constitute an audit conducted in accordance with auditing standards generally accepted in the United States of America. Also, they would not necessarily reveal matters of significance with respect to the comments in the following paragraph. Accordingly, we make no representations regarding the sufficiency of the foregoing procedures for your purposes.

5. Nothing came to our attention as a result of the foregoing procedures, however, that caused us to believe that:

a. Any material modifications should be made to the unaudited condensed consolidated financial statements described in item 4a(i) above, included in the registration statement, for them to be in conformity with accounting principles generally accepted in the United States of America.

b. The unaudited condensed consolidated financial statements described in item 4a(i) above do not comply as to form in all material respects with the applicable accounting requirements of the Act and the related rules and regulations adopted by the SEC.

c. The unaudited amounts for sales, net income and earnings per share for the six-month periods ended June 30, 20X6, and 20X5, referred to in item 4b(i) above do not agree with the amounts set forth in the unaudited consolidated financial statements for those same periods.

d. The unaudited amounts referred to in item 5c above were not determined on a basis substantially consistent with that of the corresponding amounts in the audited consolidated statements of income.

e. At June 30, 20X6, there was any change in the capital stock, increase in long-term debt or any decreases in consolidated net current assets or stockholders' equity of the consolidated companies as compared with amounts shown in the March 31, 20X6, unaudited condensed consolidated balance sheet included in the registration statement, except in all instances for changes, increases, or decreases that the registration statement discloses have occurred or may occur.

6. Company officials have advised us that no consolidated financial statements as of any date or for any period subsequent to June 30, 20X6, are available; accordingly, the procedures carried out by us with respect to changes in financial statement items after June 30, 20X6, have been, of necessity, even more limited than those with respect to the periods referred to in item 4 above. We have inquired of certain officials of the company who have responsibility for financial and accounting matters regarding whether (a) at July 20, 20X6, there was any change in the capital stock, increase in long-term debt or any decreases in consolidated net current assets or stockholders' equity of the consolidated companies as compared with amounts shown on the March 31, 20X6, unaudited condensed consolidated balance sheet included in the registration statement; or (b) for the period from July 1, 20X6, to July 20, 20X6, there were any decreases, as compared with the corresponding period in the preceding year, in consolidated net sales or in the total or per-share amounts of income before extraordinary items or of net income. On the basis of these inquiries and our reading of the minutes as described in item 4 above, nothing came to our attention that caused us to believe that there was any such change, increase, or decrease, except in all instances for changes, increases, or decreases that the registration statement discloses have occurred or may occur.

ILLUSTRATION 13—ALTERNATE WORDING WHEN ACCOUNTANTS ARE AWARE OF A DECREASE IN A SPECIFIED FINANCIAL STATEMENT ITEM

Note to Illustration 13: This example covers a situation in which accountants are aware of a decrease in a financial statement item on which they are requested to comment. The same facts exist as in Illustration 1, except for the decrease covered in the following change in paragraph 5c.

c. At May 31, 20X6, there was any change in the capital stock, increase in long-term debt or any decrease in consolidated stockholders' equity of the consolidated companies as compared with amounts shown in the March 31, 20X6, unaudited condensed consolidated balance sheet included in the registration statement, or for the period from April 1, 20X6, to May 31, 20X6, there were any decreases, as compared with the corresponding period in the preceding year, in consolidated net sales or the total or per-share amounts of income before extraordinary items or of net income, except in all instances for changes, increases, or decreases that the registration statement discloses have occurred or may occur and except that the unaudited consolidated balance sheet as of May 31, 20X6, which we were furnished by the company, showed a decrease from March 31, 20X6, in consolidated net current assets as follows (in thousands of dollars):

	Current Assets	Current Liabilities	Net Current Assets
March 31, 20X6	$4,251	$1,356	$2,895
May 31, 20X6	3,986	1,732	2,254

6. As mentioned in item 4b above, company officials have advised us that no consolidated financial statements as of any date or for any period subsequent to May 31, 20X6, are available; accordingly, the procedures carried out by us with respect to changes in financial statement items after May 31, 20X6, have been, of necessity, even more limited than those with respect to the periods referred to in item 4 above. We have inquired of certain officials of the company

who have responsibility for financial and accounting matters regarding whether (a) there was any change at June 23, 20X6, in the capital stock, increase in long-term debt or any decreases in consolidated net current assets or stockholders' equity of the consolidated companies as compared with amounts shown on the March 31, 20X6, unaudited condensed consolidated balance sheet included in the registration statement; or (b) for the period from April 1, 20X6, to June 23, 20X6, there were any decreases, as compared with the corresponding period in the preceding year, in consolidated net sales or in the total or per-share amounts of income before extraordinary items or of net income. On the basis of these inquiries and our reading of the minutes as described in item 4 above, nothing came to our attention that caused us to believe that there was any such change, increase, or decrease, except in all instances for changes, increases, or decreases that the registration statement discloses have occurred or may occur and except as described in the following sentence. We have been informed by officials of the company that there continues to be a decrease in net current assets that is estimated to be approximately the same amount as set forth in item 5c above [*or whatever other disclosure fits the circumstances*].

ILLUSTRATION 14—ALTERNATE WORDING OF THE COMFORT LETTER FOR COMPANIES THAT ARE PERMITTED TO PRESENT INTERIM EARNINGS DATA FOR A 12-MONTH PERIOD

Note to Illustration 14: *Certain types of companies are permitted to include earnings data for a twelve-month period to the date of the latest balance sheet furnished in lieu of earnings data for both the interim period between the end of the latest fiscal year and the date of the latest balance sheet and the corresponding period of the preceding fiscal year. The following would be substituted for the applicable part of paragraph 3 of Illustration 1.*

3. . . . was to enable us to express our opinion on the financial statements as of December 31, 20X5, and for the year then ended, but not on the financial statements for any period included in part within that year. Therefore, we are unable to and do not express any opinion on the unaudited condensed consolidated balance sheet as of March 31, 20X6, and the related unaudited condensed consolidated statements of income, retained earnings (stockholders' equity), and cash flows for the twelve months then ended included in the registration statement. . . .

ILLUSTRATION 15—ALTERNATE WORDING WHEN THE PROCEDURES THAT THE UNDERWRITER HAS REQUESTED THE ACCOUNTANT TO PERFORM ON INTERIM FINANCIAL INFORMATION ARE LESS THAN A REVIEW UNDER AU SECTION 722

Note to Illustration 15: *This example assumes that the underwriter has asked the accountants to perform specified procedures on the interim financial information and report thereon in the comfort letter. The letter is dated June 28, 20X6; procedures were performed through June 23, 20X6, the cutoff date. Since a review under AU Section 722 was not performed on the interim financial information as of March 31, 20X6, and for the quarter then ended, the accountants are limited to reporting procedures performed and findings obtained on the interim financial information.*

June 28, 20X6

[*Addressee*]

Dear _____:

We have audited the consolidated balance sheets of ABC Company (the company) and the subsidiaries as of December 31, 20X5, and 20X4, and the consolidated statements of income, retained earnings (stockholders' equity), and cash flows for each of the three years in the period ended December 31, 20X5, and the related financial statement schedules all included in the registration statement (No. 33-XXXXX) on Form S-1 filed by the company under the Securities Act of 1933 (the Act); our reports with respect thereto are included in that registration statement. The registration statement, as amended on June 28, 20X6, is herein referred to as the registration statement.

Also, we have compiled the forecasted balance sheet and consolidated statements of income, retained earnings (stockholders' equity), and cash flows as of December 31, 20X6, and for the year then ending, attached to the registration statement, as indicated in our report dated May 15, 20X6, which is attached.

In connection with the registration statement:

1. We are independent certified public accountants with respect to the company within the meaning of the Act and the applicable rules and regulations thereunder adopted by the SEC.

2. In our opinion [*include the phrase "except as disclosed in the registration statement," if applicable*], the consolidated financial statements and financial statement schedules audited by us and included in the registration statement comply as to form in all material respects with the applicable accounting requirements of the Act and the related rules and regulations adopted by the SEC.

3. We have not audited any financial statements of the company as of any date or for any period subsequent to December 31, 20X5; although we have conducted an audit for the year ended December 31, 20X5, the purpose, and therefore the scope, of the audit was to enable us to express our opinion on the consolidated financial statements as of December 31, 20X5, and for the year then ended, but not on the financial statements for any interim period within that year. Therefore, we are unable to and do not express any opinion on the unaudited condensed consolidated balance sheet as of March 31, 20X6, and the unaudited condensed consolidated statements of income, retained earnings (stockholders' equity), and cash flows for the three-month periods ended March 31, 20X6, and 20X5, included in the registration statement, or on the financial position, results of operations, or cash flows as of any date or for any period subsequent to December 31, 20X5.

4. For purposes of this letter, we have read the 20X6 minutes of meetings of the stockholders, the board of directors, and [*include other appropriate committees, if any*] of the company as set forth in the minute books at June 23, 20X6, officials of the company having advised us that the minutes of all such meetings[13] through that date were set forth therein; we have carried out other procedures to June 23, 20X6, as follows (our work did not extend to the period from June 24, 20X6, to June 28, 20X6, inclusive):

    a. With respect to the three-month periods ended March 31, 20X6, and 20X5, we have:

        (i) Read the unaudited condensed consolidated balance sheet as of March 31, 20X6, and unaudited condensed consolidated statements

---

[13] See footnote 2 of Illustration 1.

of income, retained earnings (stockholders' equity), and cash flows for the three-month periods ended March 31, 20X6 and 20X5, included in the registration statement, and agreed the amounts contained therein with the company's accounting records as of March 31, 20X6 and 20X5, and for the three-month periods then ended.

(ii) Inquired of certain officials of the company who have responsibility for financial and accounting matters whether the unaudited condensed consolidated financial statements referred to in item a(i) above: (1) are in conformity with generally accepted accounting principles[14] applied on a basis substantially consistent with that of the audited consolidated financial statements included in the registration statement and (2) comply as to form in all material respects with the applicable accounting requirements of the Act and the related rules and regulations adopted by the SEC. Those officials stated that the unaudited condensed consolidated financial statements (1) are in conformity with accounting principles generally accepted in the United States of America applied on a basis substantially consistent with that of the audited financial statements, and (2) comply as to form in all material respects with the applicable accounting requirements of the Act and the related rules and regulations adopted by the SEC.

b. With respect to the period from April 1, 20X6, to May 31, 20X6, we have:

(i) Read the unaudited condensed consolidated financial statements of the company[15] for April and May of both 20X5 and 20X6 furnished us by the company, and agreed the amounts contained therein to the company's accounting records. Officials of the company have advised us that no such financial statements as of any date or for any period subsequent to May 31, 20X6, were available.

(ii) Inquired of certain officials of the company who have responsibility for financial and accounting matters whether (1) the unaudited financial statements referred to in item b(i) above are stated on a basis substantially consistent with that of the audited consolidated financial statements included in the registration statement, (2) at May 31, 20X6, there was any change in the capital stock, increase in long-term debt or any decrease in consolidated net current assets or stockholders' equity of the

---

[14] See footnote 4 of Illustration 1.   [15] See footnote 3 of Illustration 1.

consolidated companies as compared with amounts shown in the March 31, 20X6, unaudited condensed consolidated balance sheet included in the registration statement, and (3) for the period from April 1, 20X6, to May 31, 20X6, there were any decreases, as compared with the corresponding period in the preceding year, in consolidated net sales or in the total or per-share amounts of income before extraordinary items or of net income.

Those officials stated that (1) the unaudited consolidated financial statements referred to in item 4b(i) above are stated on a basis substantially consistent with that of the audited consolidated financial statements included in the registration statement, (2) at May 31, 20X6, there was no change in the capital stock, no increase in long-term debt, and no decrease in net current assets or stockholders' equity of the consolidated companies as compared with amounts shown in the March 31, 20X6, unaudited condensed consolidated balance sheet included in the registration statement, and (3) there were no decreases for the period from April 1, 20X6, to May 31, 20X6, as compared with the corresponding period in the preceding year, in consolidated net sales or in the total or per-share amounts of income before extraordinary items or of net income.

c. As mentioned in item 4b(i) above, company officials have advised us that no financial statements as of any date or for any period subsequent to May 31, 20X6, are available; accordingly, the procedures carried out by us with respect to changes in financial statement items after May 31, 20X6, have, of necessity, been even more limited than those with respect to the periods referred to in items 4a and 4b above. We have inquired of certain officials of the company who have responsibility for financial and accounting matters whether (a) at June 23, 20X6, there was any change in the capital stock, increase in long-term debt or any decreases in consolidated net current assets or stockholders' equity of the consolidated companies as compared with amounts shown on the March 31, 20X6, unaudited condensed consolidated balance sheet included in the registration statement, or (b) for the period from April 1, 20X6, to June 23, 20X6, there were any decreases, as compared with the corresponding period in the preceding year, in consolidated net sales or in the total or per-share amounts of income before extraordinary items or of net income. Those officials stated that (1) at June 23, 20X6, there was no change in the capital stock, no increase in long-term debt and no decreases in consolidated net current assets or stockholders' equity of the consolidated companies as compared with amounts shown on the March 31, 20X6, unaudited condensed consolidated balance sheet and (2) for the period from April 1, 20X6, to June 23, 20X6, there were no decreases, as compared with the corresponding period in the preceding year, in consolidated net sales or in the total or per-share amounts of income before extraordinary items or of net income.

The foregoing procedures do not constitute an audit conducted in accordance with auditing standards generally accepted in the United States of America. We make no representations regarding the sufficiency of the foregoing procedures for your purposes. Had we performed additional procedures or had we conducted an audit or a review, other matters might have come to our attention that would have been reported to you.

5. At your request, we also performed the following procedures:

   a. Read the unaudited pro forma condensed consolidated balance sheet as of March 31, 20X6, and the unaudited pro forma condensed consolidated statements of income for the year ended December 31, 20X5, and the three-month period ended March 31, 20X6, included in the registration statement.

   b. Inquired of certain officials of the company and of XYZ Company (the company being acquired) who have responsibility for financial and accounting matters as to whether all significant assumptions regarding the business combination had been reflected in the pro forma adjustments and whether the unaudited pro forma condensed consolidated financial statements referred to in item 5a above comply as to form in all material respects with the applicable accounting requirements of rule 11-02 of Regulation S-X.

   Those officials referred to above stated, in response to our inquiries, that all significant assumptions regarding the business combination had been reflected in the pro forma adjustments and that the unaudited pro forma condensed consolidated financial statements referred to in item 5a above comply as to form in all material respects with the applicable accounting requirements of rule 11-02 of Regulation S-X.

   c. Compared the historical financial information for the company included on page 20 in the registration statement with historical financial information for the company on page 12 and found them to be in agreement.

   We also compared the financial information included on page 20 of the registration statement with the historical information for XYZ Company on page 13 and found them to be in agreement.

d. Proved the arithmetic accuracy of the application of the pro forma adjustments to the historical amounts in the unaudited pro forma condensed consolidated financial statements.

The foregoing procedures are less in scope than an examination, the objective of which is the expression of an opinion on management's assumptions, the pro forma adjustments, and the application of those adjustments to historical financial information. Accordingly, we do not express such an opinion. We make no representation about the sufficiency of the foregoing procedures for your purposes. Had we performed additional procedures or had we made an examination of the pro forma financial information, other matters might have come to our attention that would have been reported to you.

6. At your request, we performed the following procedures with respect to the forecasted consolidated balance sheet and consolidated statements of income and cash flows as of December 31, 20X6, and for the year then ending. With respect to forecasted rental income, we compared the occupancy statistics about expected demand for rental of the housing units to statistics for existing comparable properties and found them to be the same.

Because the procedures described above do not constitute an examination of prospective financial statements in accordance with standards established by the American Institute of Certified Public Accountants, we do not express an opinion on whether the prospective financial statements are presented in conformity with AICPA presentation guidelines or on whether the underlying assumptions provide a reasonable basis for the presentation. Furthermore, there will usually be differences between the forecasted and actual results, because events and circumstances frequently do not occur as expected, and those differences may be material. We make no representations about the sufficiency of such procedures for your purposes. Had we performed additional procedures or had we made an examination of the forecast in accordance with standards established by the AICPA, matters might have come to our attention that would have been reported to you.

7. This letter is solely for the information of the addressees and to assist the underwriters in conducting and documenting their investigation of the affairs of the company in connection with the offering of the securities covered by the registration statement, and it is not to be used, circulated, quoted, or otherwise referred to within or without the underwriting group for any purpose, including but not limited to the registration, purchase, or sale of securities, nor is it to be filed with or referred to in whole or in part in the registration statement or

any other document, except that reference may be made to it in the underwriting agreement or in any list of closing documents pertaining to the offering of the securities covered by the registration statement.

ILLUSTRATION 16—A TYPICAL COMFORT LETTER IN A NON-1933 ACT OFFERING, INCLUDING THE REQUIRED UNDERWRITER REPRESENTATIONS

Note to Illustration 16: *This example is applicable when a comfort letter is issued in a non-1933 Act offering. The underwriter has given the accountants a letter including the representations regarding their due diligence review process, and the comfort letter refers to those representations. In addition, the example assumes that the accountants were unable or were not requested to perform a review under AU Section 722 of a subsequent interim period and therefore no negative assurance has been given.*

November 30, 20X5

[*Addressee*]

Dear _____:

We have audited the balance sheets of ABC City, Any State Utility System as of June 30, 20X5, and 20X4, and the statements of revenues, expenses, and changes in retained earnings and cash flows for the years then ended, included in the Official Statement for $30,000,000 of ABC City, Any State Utility System Revenue Bonds due November 30, 20X5. Our report with respect thereto is included in the Official Statement. This Official Statement, dated November 30, 20X5, is herein referred to as the Official Statement.

This letter is being furnished in reliance upon your representation to us that:

- You are knowledgeable with respect to the due diligence review process that would be performed if this placement of securities were being registered pursuant to the Securities Act of 1933 (the Act).

- In connection with the offering of revenue bonds, the review process you have performed is substantially consistent with the due diligence review process that you would have performed if this placement of securities were being registered pursuant to the Act.

In connection with the Official Statement:

1. We are independent certified public accountants with respect to ABC City, Any State and its Utility System under rule 101 of the AICPA's *Code of Professional Conduct*, and its interpretations and rulings.

2. We have not audited any financial statements of ABC City, Any State Utility System as of any date or for any period subsequent to June 30, 20X5; although we have conducted an audit for the year ended June 30, 20X5, the purpose, and therefore the scope, of the audit was to enable us to express our opinion on the financial statements as of June 30, 20X5, and for the year then ended, but not on the financial statements for any interim period within that year. Therefore, we are unable to and do not express any opinion on the financial position, results of operations, or cash flows as of any date or for any period subsequent to June 30, 20X5, for the ABC City, Any State Utility System.

3. For purposes of this letter we have read the 20X5 minutes of the meetings of the City Council of ABC City, Any State as set forth in the minutes books as of November 25, 20X5, the City Clerk of ABC City having advised us that the minutes of all such meetings through that date were set forth therein.

4. With respect to the period subsequent to June 30, 20X5, we have carried out other procedures to November 25, 20X5, as follows (our work did not extend to the period from November 26, 20X5, to November 30, 20X5, inclusive):

   a. We have inquired of, and received assurance from, city officials who have responsibility for financial and accounting matters, that no financial statements as of any date or for any period subsequent to June 30, 20X5, are available.

   b. We have inquired of those officials regarding whether (a) at November 25, 20X5, there was any increase in long-term debt or any decrease in net current assets of ABC City, Any State Utility System as compared with amounts shown on the June 30, 20X5, balance sheet, included in the Official Statement or (b) for the period from July 1, 20X5, to November 25, 20X5, there were any decreases, as compared with the corresponding period in the preceding year, in total operating revenues, income from operations or net income. Those officials stated that (1) at November 25, 20X5, there was no increase in long-term debt and no decrease in net current assets of the ABC City, Any State Utility System as compared with amounts shown in the June 30, 20X5, balance sheet and (2) there were no decreases for the period from July 1, 20X5, to November 25, 20X5, as compared with the corresponding period in the preceding year, in total operating revenues, income from operations, or net income, except in all instances for changes, increases, or decreases that the Official Statement discloses have occurred or may occur.

5. For accounting data pertaining to the years 20X3 through 20X5, inclusive, shown on page 11 of the Official Statement, we have (i) for data shown in the audited financial statements, compared such data with the audited financial statements of the ABC City, Any State Utility System for 20X3 through 20X5 and found them to be in agreement; and (ii) for data not directly shown in the audited financial statements, compared such data with the general ledger and accounting records of the Utility System from which such information was derived, and found them to be in agreement.

6. The procedures enumerated in the preceding paragraphs do not constitute an audit conducted in accordance with generally accepted auditing standards. Accordingly, we make no representations regarding the sufficiency of the foregoing procedures for your purposes.

7. This letter is solely for the information of the addressees and to assist the underwriters in conducting and documenting their investigation of the affairs of the ABC City, Any State Utility System in connection with the offering of securities covered by the Official Statement, and it is not to be used, circulated, quoted, or otherwise referred to for any other purpose, including but not limited to the purchase or sale of securities, nor is it to be filed with or referred to in whole or in part in the Official Statement or any other document, except that reference may be made to it in the Purchase Contract or in any list of closing documents pertaining to the offering of securities covered by the Official Statement.

ILLUSTRATION 17—LETTER TO A REQUESTING PARTY THAT HAS NOT PROVIDED THE REQUIRED REPRESENTATION LETTER

Note to Illustration 17: This example assumes that these procedures are being performed at the request of the placement agent on information included in an offering circular in connection with a private placement of unsecured notes with two insurance companies. The letter is dated June 30, 20X6; procedures were performed through the cutoff date of June 25, 20X6.

June 30, 20X6

[*Addressee*]

Dear _____:

We have audited the consolidated balance sheets of ABC Company, Inc. (the company) and subsidiaries as of December 31, 20X5, and 20X4, and the consolidated statements of income, retained earnings (stockholders' equity), and cash flows for each of the three years in the period ended December 31, 20X5, included in the offering circular for $50,000,000 of notes due June 30, 20X6. Our report with respect thereto is included in the offering circular. The offering circular dated June 30, 20X6, is herein referred to as the offering circular.

We are independent certified public accountants with respect to the company under rule 101 of the AICPA's *Code of Professional Conduct,* and its interpretations and rulings.

We have not audited any financial statements of the company as of any date or for any period subsequent to December 31, 20X5; although we have conducted an audit for the year ended December 31, 20X5, the purpose (and, therefore, the scope) of the audit was to enable us to express our opinion on the consolidated financial statements as of December 31, 20X5, and for the year then ended, but not on the financial statements for any interim period within that year. Therefore, we are unable to and do not express any opinion on the unaudited condensed consolidated balance sheet as of March 31, 20X6, and the unaudited condensed consolidated statements of income, retained earnings (stockholders' equity), and cash flows for the three-month periods ended March 31, 20X6, and 20X5, included in the offering circular, or on the financial position, results of operations, or cash flows as of any date or for any period subsequent to December 31, 20X5.

1. At your request, we have read the 20X6 minutes of meetings of the stockholders, the board of directors, and [*include other appropriate committees, if any*] of the company as set forth in the minute books at June 25, 20X6, officials of the company having advised us that the minutes[16] of all such meetings through that date were set forth therein; we have carried out other procedures to June 25, 20X6 (our work did not extend to the period from June 26, 20X6, to June 30, 20X6, inclusive), as follows:

   a. With respect to the three-month periods ended March 31, 20X6 and 20X5, we have:

      (i) Read the unaudited condensed consolidated balance sheet as of March 31, 20X6, and the unaudited condensed consolidated statements of income, retained earnings (stockholders' equity), and cash flows[17] of the company for the three-month periods ended March 31, 20X6, and 20X5, included in the offering circular, and agreed the amounts contained therein with the company's accounting records as of March 31,

---

[16] See footnote 2 of Illustration 1.　　　　　　[17] See footnotes 3 and 4 of Illustration 1.

20X6, and 20X5, and for the three-month periods then ended.

    (ii) Inquired of certain officials of the company who have responsibility for financial and accounting matters whether the unaudited condensed consolidated financial statements referred to in item a(i) above are in conformity with generally accepted accounting principles applied on a basis substantially consistent with that of the audited consolidated financial statements included in the offering circular. Those officials stated that the unaudited condensed consolidated financial statements are in conformity with accounting principles generally accepted in the United States of America applied on a basis substantially consistent with that of the audited consolidated financial statements.

b. With respect to the period from April 1, 20X6, to May 31, 20X6, we have:

    (i) Read the unaudited condensed consolidated financial statements of the company for April and May of both 20X5 and 20X6, furnished us by the company, and agreed the amounts contained therein with the company's accounting records. Officials of the company have advised us that no financial statements as of any date or for any period subsequent to May 31, 20X6, were available.

    (ii) Inquired of certain officials of the company who have responsibility for financial and accounting matters whether (1) the unaudited condensed consolidated financial statements referred to in item b(i) above are stated on a basis substantially consistent with that of the audited consolidated financial statements included in the offering circular, (2) at May 31, 20X6, there was any change in the capital stock, increase in long-term debt or any decrease in consolidated net current assets or stockholders' equity of the consolidated companies as compared with amounts shown in the March 31, 20X6, unaudited condensed consolidated balance sheet included in the offering circular, and (3) for the period from April 1, 20X6, to May 31, 20X6, there were any decreases, as compared with the corresponding period in the preceding year, in consolidated net sales or in the total or per-share amounts of income before extraordinary items or of net income.

Those officials stated that (1) the unaudited condensed consolidated financial statements referred to in item b(ii) above are stated on a basis substantially consistent with that of the audited consolidated financial statements included in the offering circular, (2) at May 31, 20X6, there was no change in the capital stock, no increase in long-term debt, and no decrease in consolidated net current assets or stockholders' equity of the consolidated companies as compared with amounts shown in the March 31, 20X6, unaudited condensed consolidated balance sheet included in the offering circular, and (3) there were no decreases for the period from April 1, 20X6, to May 31, 20X6, as compared with the corresponding period in the preceding year, in consolidated net sales or in the total or per-share amounts of income before extraordinary items or of net income.

c. As mentioned in item 1b above, company officials have advised us that no financial statements as of any date or for any period subsequent to May 31, 20X6, are available; accordingly, the procedures carried out by us with respect to changes in financial statement items after May 31, 20X6, have, of necessity, been even more limited than those with respect to the periods referred to in items 1a and 1b above. We have inquired of certain officials of the company who have responsibility for financial and accounting matters whether (i) at June 25, 20X6, there was any change in the capital stock, increase in long-term debt, or any decreases in consolidated net current assets or stockholders' equity of the consolidated companies as compared with amounts shown on the March 31, 20X6, unaudited condensed consolidated balance sheet included in the offering circular or (ii) for the period from April 1, 20X6, to June 25, 20X6, there were any decreases, as compared with the corresponding period in the preceding year, in consolidated net sales or in the total or per-share amounts of income before extraordinary items or of net income.

Those officials referred to above stated that (i) at June 25, 20X6, there was no change in the capital stock, no increase in long-term debt, and no decreases in consolidated net current assets or stockholders' equity of the consolidated companies as compared with amounts shown on the March 31, 20X6, unaudited condensed consolidated balance sheet, and there were no decreases for the period from April 1, 20X6, to June 25, 20X6, as compared with the corresponding period in the preceding year, in consolidated net sales or in the total or per-share amounts of income before extraordinary items or of net income.

2. At your request, we have read the following items in the offering circular on the indicated pages:

Item	Page	Description
a.	13	"History and Business—Sales and Marketing." The table following the first paragraph.
b.	22	"Executive Compensation—20X5 Compensation."
c.	33	"Selected Financial Data."[18]

[18] See footnote 9 of Illustration 6.

3. Our audits of the consolidated financial statements for the periods referred to in the introductory paragraph of this letter comprised audit tests and procedures deemed necessary for the purpose of expressing an opinion on such financial statements taken as a whole. For none of the periods referred to therein, nor for any other period, did we perform audit tests for the purpose of expressing an opinion on individual balances of accounts or summaries of selected transactions such as those enumerated above, and, accordingly, we express no opinion thereon.

4. However, at your request, we have performed the following additional procedures, which were applied as indicated with respect to the items enumerated above.

Item in 2	Procedures and Findings
a.	We compared the amounts of military sales, commercial sales, and total sales shown in the registration statement with the balances in the appropriate accounts in the company's accounting records for the respective fiscal years and for the unaudited interim periods and found them to be in agreement. We proved the arithmetic accuracy of the percentages of such amounts of military sales and commercial sales to total sales for the respective fiscal years and for the unaudited interim periods. We compared such computed percentages with the corresponding percentages appearing in the registration statement and found them to be in agreement.
b.	We compared the dollar amounts of compensation (salary, bonus, and other compensation) for each individual listed in the table "Annual Compensation" with the corresponding amounts shown by the individual employee earnings records for the year 20X5 and found them to be in agreement. We compared the dollar amounts shown under the heading of "Long-Term Compensation" on page 24 for each listed individual and the aggregate amounts for executive officers with corresponding amounts shown in an analysis prepared by the company and found such amounts to be in agreement.

Item in 2	Procedures and Findings
c.	We compared the amounts of net sales, income from continuing operations, income from continuing operations per common share, and cash dividends declared per common share for the years ended December 31, 20X5, 20X4, and 20X3, with the respective amounts in the consolidated financial statements on pages 27 and 28 and the amounts for the years ended December 31, 20X2, and 20X1, with the respective amounts in the consolidated financial statements included in the company's annual reports to stockholders for 20X2 and 20X1 and found them to be in agreement.
	We compared the amounts of total assets, long-term obligations, and redeemable preferred stock at December 31, 20X5, and 20X4, with the respective amounts in the consolidated financial statements on pages 27 and 28 and the amounts at December 31, 20X3, 20X2, and 20X1 with the corresponding amounts in the consolidated financial statements included in the company's annual reports to stockholders for 20X3, 20X2, and 20X1 and found them to be in agreement.

5. It should be understood that we have no responsibility for establishing (and did not establish) the scope and nature of the procedures enumerated in paragraphs 1 through 4 above; rather, the procedures enumerated therein are those the requesting party asked us to perform. Accordingly, we make no representations regarding questions of legal interpretations or regarding the sufficiency for your purposes of the procedures enumerated in the preceding paragraphs; also, such procedures would not necessarily reveal any material misstatement of the amounts or percentages listed above as set forth in the offering circular. Further, we have addressed ourselves solely to the foregoing data and make no representations regarding the adequacy of disclosures or whether any material facts have been omitted. This letter relates only to the financial statement items specified above and does not extend to any financial statement of the company taken as a whole.

6. The foregoing procedures do not constitute an audit conducted in accordance with auditing standards generally accepted in the United States of America. Had we performed additional procedures or had we conducted an audit or a review of the company's March 31, April 30, or May 31, 20X6, and 20X5, condensed consolidated financial statements in accordance with standards established by the American Institute of Certified Public Accountants, other matters might have come to our attention that would have been reported to you.

7. These procedures should not be taken to supplant any additional inquiries or procedures that you would undertake in your consideration of the proposed offering.

8. This letter is solely for your information and to assist you in your inquiries in connection with the offering of the securities covered by the offering circular, and it is not to be used, circulated, quoted, or otherwise referred to for any other purpose, including but not limited to the registration, purchase, or sale of securities, nor is it to

be filed with or referred to in whole or in part in the offering document or any other document, except that reference may be made to it in any list of closing documents pertaining to the offering of the securities covered by the offering document.

9. We have no responsibility to update this letter for events and circumstances occurring after June 25, 20X6.

ILLUSTRATION 18—COMFORT LETTER THAT INCLUDES REFERENCE TO EXAMINATION OF ANNUAL MD&A AND REVIEW OF INTERIM MD&A

Note to Illustration 18: This example assumes the following circumstances. The prospectus (part I of the registration statement) includes audited consolidated balance sheets as of December 31, 20X5, and 20X4, and audited consolidated statements of income, retained earnings (stockholders' equity), and cash flows for each of the three years in the period ended December 31, 20X5. Part I also includes an unaudited condensed consolidated balance sheet as of March 31, 20X6, and unaudited condensed consolidated statements of income, retained earnings (stockholders' equity), and cash flows for the three-month periods ended March 31, 20X6, and 20X5. Part II of the registration statement includes audited consolidated financial statement schedules for the three years ended December 31, 20X5. The accountants have examined the company's management's discussion and analysis (MD&A) for the year ended December 31, 20X5, in accordance with AT Section 701, "Management's Discussion and Analysis." The accountants have also performed reviews under AU Section 722 of the company's unaudited condensed consolidated financial statements, referred to above, in accordance with AU Section 722, and the company's MD&A for the three-month period ended March 31, 20X6, in accordance with AT Section 701. The accountant's reports on the examination and review of MD&A have been previously issued, but not distributed publicly; none of these reports is included in the registration statement. The cutoff date is June 23, 20X6, and the letter is dated June 28, 20X6. The effective date is June 28, 20X6.

Each of the comments in the letter is in response to a requirement of the underwriting agreement. For purposes of this example, the income statement items of the current interim period are to be compared with those of the corresponding period of the preceding year.

June 28, 20X6

[*Addressee*]

Dear _____:

We have audited the consolidated balance sheets of ABC Company (the company) and subsidiaries as of December 31, 20X5, and 20X4, and the consolidated statements of income, retained earnings (stockholders' equity), and cash flows for each of the three years in the period ended December 31, 20X5, and the related financial statement schedules, all included in the registration statement (No. 33-XXXXX) on Form S-1 filed by the company under the Securities Act of 1933 (the Act); our reports with respect thereto are also included in that registration statement. The registration statement, as amended on June 28, 20X6, is herein referred to as the registration statement. Also, we have examined[19] the company's Management's Discussion and Analysis for the year ended December 31, 20X5, included in the registration statement, as indicated in our report dated March 28, 20X6; our report with respect thereto is attached. We have also reviewed the unaudited condensed consolidated financial statements as of March 31, 20X6, and 20X5, and for the

---

[19] If the accountant has performed a review of the company's annual MD&A, the opening paragraph of the comfort letter should be revised accordingly.

three-month periods then ended, included in the registration statement, as indicated in our report dated May 15, 20X6, and have also reviewed the company's Management's Discussion and Analysis for the three-month period ended March 31, 20X6, included in the registration statement, as indicated in our report dated May 15, 20X6; our reports with respect thereto are attached.

In connection with the registration statement:

1. We are independent certified public accountants with respect to the company within the meaning of the Act and the applicable rules and regulations thereunder adopted by the SEC.

2. In our opinion [*include the phrase "except as disclosed in the registration statement," if applicable*], the consolidated financial statements and financial statement schedules audited by us and included in the registration statement comply as to form in all material respects with the applicable accounting requirements of the Act and the related rules and regulations adopted by the SEC.

3. We have not audited any financial statements of the company as of any date or for any period subsequent to December 31, 20X5; although we have conducted an audit for the year ended December 31, 20X5, the purpose, and therefore the scope, of the audit was to enable us to express our opinion on the consolidated financial statements as of December 31, 20X5, and for the year then ended, but not on the financial statements for any interim period within that year. Therefore, we are unable to and do not express any opinion on the unaudited condensed consolidated balance sheet as of March 31, 20X6, and the unaudited condensed consolidated statements of income, retained earnings (stockholders' equity), and cash flows for the three-month periods ended March 1, 20X6, and 20X5, included in the registration statement, or on the financial position, results of operations, or cash flows as of any date or for any period subsequent to December 31, 20X5.

4. We have not examined any management's discussion and analysis of the company as of or for any period subsequent to December 31, 20X5; although we have made an examination of the company's Management's Discussion and Analysis for the year ended December 31, 20X5, included in the company's registration statement, the purpose, and therefore the scope, of the examination was to enable us to express our opinion on such Management's Discussion and Analysis, but not on the management's discussion and analysis for any interim period within that year. Therefore, we are unable to and do not express any opinion on the Management's Discussion and Analysis for the three-month period ended March 31, 20X6, included in the registration statement, or for any period subsequent to March 31, 20X6.

5. For purposes of this letter we have read the 20X6 minutes of meetings of the stockholders, the board of directors, and [*include other appropriate committees, if any*] of the company and its subsidiaries as set forth in the minute books at June 23, 20X6, officials of the company having advised us that the minutes of all such meetings[20] through that date were set forth therein; we have carried out other procedures to June 23, 20X6, as follows (our work did not extend to the period from June 24, 20X6, to June 28, 20X6, inclusive):

---

[20] See footnote 2 of Illustration 1.

a. With respect to the three-month periods ended March 31, 20X6, and 20X5, we have inquired of certain officials of the company who have responsibility for financial and accounting matters whether the unaudited condensed consolidated balance sheet as of March 31, 20X6, and the unaudited condensed consolidated statements of income, retained earnings (stockholders' equity), and cash flows for the three-month periods ended March 31, 20X6, and 20X5, included in the registration statement, comply as to form in all material respects with the applicable accounting requirements of the Act and the related rules and regulations adopted by the SEC.

b. With respect to the period from April 1, 20X6, to May 31, 20X6, we have:

(i) Read the unaudited consolidated financial statements[21] of the company and subsidiaries for April and May of both 20X5 and 20X6 furnished to us by the company, officials of the company having advised us that no such financial statements as of any date or for any period subsequent to May 31, 20X6, were available.

(ii) Inquired of certain officials of the company who have responsibility for financial and accounting matters whether the unaudited consolidated financial statements referred to in item b(i) above are stated on a basis substantially consistent with that of the audited consolidated financial statements included in the registration statement.

The foregoing procedures do not constitute an audit of financial statements conducted in accordance with auditing standards generally accepted in the United States of America. Also, they would not necessarily reveal matters of significance with respect to the comments in the following paragraph. Accordingly, we make no representations regarding the sufficiency of the foregoing procedures for your purposes.

6. Nothing came to our attention as a result of the foregoing procedures, however, that caused us[22] to believe that:

a. The unaudited condensed consolidated financial statements described in item 5a above do not comply as to form in all material respects with the applicable accounting requirements of the Act and the related rules and regulations adopted by the SEC.

b. At May 31, 20X6, there was any change in the capital stock, increase in long-term debt, or decrease in consolidated net current assets or stockholders' equity of the consolidated companies as compared with amounts shown in the March 31, 20X6, unaudited condensed consolidated balance sheet included in the registration statement, or for the period

---

[21] See footnote 3 of Illustration 1.   [22] See footnote 4 of Illustration 1.

from April 1, 20X6, to May 31, 20X6, there were any decreases, as compared to the corresponding period in the preceding year, in consolidated net sales or in the total or per-share amounts of income before extraordinary items or of net income, except in all instances for changes, increases, or decreases that the registration statement discloses have occurred or may occur.

7. As mentioned in item 5b above, company officials have advised us that no consolidated financial statements as of any date or for any period subsequent to May 31, 20X6, are available; accordingly, the procedures carried out by us with respect to changes in financial statement items after May 31, 20X6, have, of necessity, been even more limited than those with respect to the periods referred to in item 5 above. We have inquired of certain officials of the company who have responsibility for financial and accounting matters whether (a) at June 23, 20X6, there was any change in the capital stock, increase in long-term debt or any decreases in consolidated net current assets or stockholders' equity of the consolidated companies as compared with amounts shown on the March 31, 20X6, unaudited condensed consolidated balance sheet included in the registration statement or (b) for the period from April 1, 20X6, to June 23, 20X6, there were any decreases, as compared with the corresponding period in the preceding year, in consolidated net sales or in the total or per-share amounts of income before extraordinary items or of net income. On the basis of these inquiries and our reading of the minutes as described in item 5 above, nothing came to our attention that caused us to believe that there was any such change, increase, or decrease, except in all instances for changes, increases, or decreases that the registration statement discloses have occurred or may occur.

8. This letter is solely for the information of the addressees and to assist the underwriters in conducting and documenting their investigation of the affairs of the company in connection with the offering of the securities covered by the registration statement, and it is not to be used, circulated, quoted, or otherwise referred to within or without the underwriting group for any purpose, including but not limited to the registration, purchase, or sale of securities, nor is it to be filed with or referred to in whole or in part in the registration statement or any other document, except that reference may be made to it in the underwriting agreement or in any list of closing documents pertaining to the offering of the securities covered by the registration statement.

ILLUSTRATION 19—REPRESENTATION LETTER FROM A PARTY REQUESTING A COMFORT LETTER FROM THE ACCOUNTANT

Dear ABC Accountants:

[*Name of financial intermediary*], as principal or agent, in the placement of [*identify securities*] to be issued by [*name of issuer*], will be reviewing certain information relating to [*issuer*] that will be included [*incorporated by reference*] in the document [*if appropriate, the document should be identified*], which may be delivered to investors and utilized by them as a basis for their investment decision. This review process, applied to the information relating to the issuer, is [*will be*] substantially consistent with the due diligence review process that we would perform if this placement of securities were being registered pursuant to the Securities Act of 1933 ("the Act"). We are knowledgeable with respect to the due diligence review process that would be performed if this placement of securities were being registered pursuant to the Act. We hereby request that you deliver to us a "comfort" letter concerning the financial statements of the issuer and certain statistical and other data included in the offering document. We will contact you to identify the procedures we wish you to follow and the form we wish the comfort letter to take.

Very truly yours,

[*Name of financial intermediary*]

AU Section 700
SPECIAL TOPICS

AU SECTION 711
FILINGS UNDER FEDERAL SECURITIES STATUTES

PRACTICE POINT: As part of its Clarity Project, the American Institute of Certified Public Accountants' (AICPA's) Auditing Standards Board (ASB) has finalized a clarified Statement on Auditing Standards (SAS) titled, "Filings with the U.S. Securities and Exchange Commission Under the Securities Act of 1933," which supersedes AU Section 711 (Filings Under Federal Securities Statutes).

The clarified SAS does not change or expand existing requirements in extant AU Section 711 in any significant respect.

The ASB is expected to issue many of the clarified standards in *one* SAS that will be codified in "AU Section" format. The ASB has decided that the effective date of the clarified SASs that have not yet been issued is for audits of financial statements for periods ending on or after December 15, 2012. Auditors should be alert to and monitor further developments in this area.

WHAT EVERY PRACTITIONER SHOULD KNOW

Basic Objectives and Requirements

A statement is frequently made in a prospectus, in connection with filings under the Securities Act of 1933, that certain information is included in reliance upon the report of certain named experts. The accountant should read the relevant section of the prospectus to make sure that it does not indicate or imply more responsibility than the accountant intends. There should be no implication that the financial statements have been prepared by the accountant or that they are not the direct representations of management.

An accountant's report on a review of interim financial information may be presented or incorporated by reference in a registration statement. In such circumstances, the Securities and Exchange Commission (SEC) requires that a prospectus that includes a statement about the accountant's involvement should clarify that his or her review report is not a "report" or "part" of the registration statement within the meaning of sections 7 and 11 of the Securities Act of 1933. Illustration 1 includes wording that would be considered a satisfactory description for the accountant's purposes of the status of his or her review report that was included in a Form 10-Q filing that was later presented or incorporated by reference in a registration statement.

Also, the accountant should read other sections of the prospectus to make sure that his or her name is not being used in a way that indicates or implies more responsibility than the accountant intends.

Subsequent Events Procedures in 1933 Act Filings

The auditor should extend his or her procedures with respect to subsequent events from the date of the audit report up to the effective date of the registration statement, or as close thereto as is reasonably possible. In addition to performing the procedures discussed in AU Section 560 (Subsequent Events), the auditor generally should perform the following procedures at or near the effective date:

1. Arrange with the client to stay informed of the progress of the registration proceedings.

2. Read the entire prospectus and other pertinent portions of the registration statement.

3. Inquire of and obtain written representations from officers and other executives responsible for financial and accounting matters about whether any events have occurred, other than those reflected or disclosed in the registration statement, that have a material effect on the audited financial statements included therein or that should be disclosed in order to keep those statements from being misleading.

See Illustration 2 for a subsequent events procedures checklist in 1933 Act filings, which also includes the procedures required by AU Section 560.

A registration statement may also contain the report of an auditor who has audited the financial statements for prior periods but has not audited the financial statements for the most recent audited period included in the registration statement ("predecessor auditor"). The predecessor auditor has a responsibility relating to events subsequent to the date of the prior-period financial statements, and extending to the effective date, that bear materially on the financial statements on which he or she reported. Generally, the predecessor auditor should:

1. Read pertinent portions of the prospectus and the registration statement.

2. Obtain a letter of representation from the successor auditor regarding whether the successor's audit, including procedures performed with respect to subsequent events, revealed any matters (a) that might have a material effect on the financial statements reported on by the predecessor auditor or (b) that would require disclosure in the notes thereto.

3. Make inquiries and perform other procedures deemed necessary to become satisfied regarding the appropriateness of any adjustment or disclosure affecting the financial statements covered by the audit report.

Response to Subsequent Events and Subsequently Discovered Facts

In response to events and discovered facts subsequent to the date of his or her report on *audited* financial statements, the auditor (including a successor auditor) should:

1. Follow the guidance and procedures in AU Section 560 (Subsequent Events), if he or she discovers subsequent events that require adjustment or disclosure in the audited financial statements.

2. Follow the guidance and procedures in AU Section 561 (Subsequent Discovery of Facts Existing at the Date of the Auditor's Report), if the auditor becomes aware that facts may have existed at the date of the audit report that might have affected that report had he or she then been aware of those facts.

3. Follow the guidance and procedures in AU Section 530 (Dating of the Independent Auditor's Report) with respect to dating the report, if the financial statements are appropriately adjusted or the required additional disclosure is made.

4. Follow the guidance and procedures in AU Section 561, if the client refuses to make appropriate adjustment or disclosure in the financial statements for a subsequent event or subsequently discovered facts. Also, in such circumstances, the auditor should consider (a) consulting with his or her legal counsel and (b) withholding his or her consent to the use of the report on the audited financial statements in the registration statement.

If an accountant believes that *unaudited* financial statements or *unaudited* interim financial information presented or incorporated by reference in a registration statement are not in conformity with GAAP, the accountant should insist that the client makes the appropriate revisions. If the client refuses to, the accountant should:

1. Follow the guidance and procedures in AU Section 561, if the accountant has reported on a review of interim financial information and the subsequently discovered facts are such that they would have affected the report had they been known to the accountant at the date of the report.

2. Modify his or her report on the audited financial statements to describe the departure from GAAP in the unaudited financial statements or interim financial information, if the accountant has *not* reported on a review of the unaudited financial statements or interim financial information.

3. Consider (a) consulting with his or her legal counsel and (b) withholding his or her consent to the use of the report on the audited financial statements in the registration statement.

PRACTICE ISSUES AND FREQUENTLY ASKED QUESTIONS

Issue 1: Is an accountant required to update his or her subsequent events procedures when a shelf registration statement is updated by a supplemental or "sticker" prospectus?

No. Under these circumstances, the supplemental prospectus is not considered to be an amendment to the registration statement. Therefore, an accountant has no duty to update his or her performance of subsequent events procedures through the date of the supplemental prospectus.

Issue 2: In connection with the offering of securities other than those under the 1933 Act, should the auditor consent to be named, or referred to, as an "expert" in an offering document?

No. The term "expert" has a specific statutory meaning under the 1933 Act. However, outside the 1933 Act, the term "expert" is generally not defined and the auditor's responsibility, as a result, is also undefined. However, if the term "expert" is defined, for instance under applicable state law, the auditor may agree to be named as an expert in an offering document, as long as the auditor's responsibility as a result of the use of that term is explicitly defined.

Issue 3: May an auditor permit a client to make reference in an offering document to the auditor's role in connection with a securities offering that is not registered under the 1933 Act?

Yes, as long as the caption "Experts" is *not* used and the auditor is *not* referred to as "expert" anywhere in the offering document. In those circumstances when a client wishes to make reference in the document to the auditor's role, a caption titled "Independent Auditors" should be used in the offering document. Also, the following paragraph should be used to describe the auditor's role:

Independent Auditors

> The financial statements as of December 31, 20X2 and for the year then ended, included in this offering circular, have been audited by Jones & Smith, independent auditors, as stated in their report(s) appearing herein.

If the client refuses to delete all references to the auditor as "expert," the auditor should not permit the client to include his or her audit report in the offering document.

Issue 4: May the auditor consent to the use of the audit report in an offering document in connection with securities offerings other than ones registered under the 1933 Act?

Yes. Although it is not generally necessary for the auditor to provide a consent in connection with securities offerings other than ones registered under the 1933 Act, an auditor may be requested to do so. In such circumstances, the auditor may use the following language in such a consent:

> We agree to the inclusion in this offering circular of our report, dated February 12, 20X3, on our audit of the financial statements of ABC Company for the year ended December 31, 20X2.

ILLUSTRATIONS AND PRACTICE AIDS

ILLUSTRATION 1—WORDING IN A PROSPECTUS REGARDING AN AC-COUNTANT'S REVIEW REPORT INCLUDED IN A FORM 10-Q

Report of Independent Registered Public Accounting Firm

> The consolidated balance sheets as of December 31, 20X2 and 20X1, and the consolidated statements of income, retained earnings, and cash flows for each of the three years in the period ended December 31, 20X2, incorporated by reference in this prospectus, have been included herein in reliance on the report of _____, independent public accountants, given on the authority of that firm as experts in auditing and accounting.
>
> With respect to the unaudited interim financial information for the periods ended March 31, 20X3 and 20X2, incorporated by reference in this prospectus, the independent public accountants have reported that they have applied limited procedures in accordance with professional standards for a review of such information. However, their separate report included in the company's quarterly report on Form 10-Q for the quarter ended March 31, 20X3, and incorporated by reference herein, states that they did not audit and they do not express an opinion on that interim financial information. Accordingly, the degree of reliance on their report on such information should be restricted in light of the limited nature of the review procedures applied. The

accountants are not subject to the liability provisions of section 11 of the Securities Act of 1933 for their report on the unaudited interim financial information because that report is not a "report" or a "part" of the registration statement prepared or certified by the accountants within the meaning of sections 7 and 11 of the Act.

ILLUSTRATION 2—SUBSEQUENT EVENTS PROCEDURES CHECKLIST IN 1933 ACT FILINGS

	Performed By	Workpaper Reference
1. Read the latest available interim financial statements, and:	————	————
a. Compare them with the financial statements being reported on.	————	————
b. Investigate any unexpected significant changes.	————	————
c. Make any other comparisons considered appropriate in the circumstances.	————	————
d. Inquire about whether the interim financial statements have been prepared on the same basis as that used for the audited statements.	————	————
2. Scan the following for the period subsequent to the financial statement date for unusual transactions:	————	————
a. General ledger	————	————
b. Cash receipts journals or records	————	————
c. Cash disbursement journals or records	————	————
d. General journal entries	————	————
3. Inquire of management whether:	————	————
a. Any substantial contingent liabilities or commitments exist.	————	————
b. Any significant changes in capital stock, long-term debt, or working capital have occurred since the balance sheet date.	————	————
c. There has been a change in the status of items that were not completely resolved at the balance sheet date.	————	————
d. Any material adjustments have been made during the period subsequent to the date of the financial statements being reported on.	————	————
e. Commitments or plans for major purchases of capital assets or inventory exist, and consideration of possible losses due to price changes.	————	————
f. There have been any changes in accounting or financial policies.	————	————
g. Any events have occurred that have caused a decline in the value of any assets or have made any significant portion of fixed assets idle or obsolete.	————	————
h. There is any expiration or cancellation of significant insurance coverage.	————	————

	Performed By	Workpaper Reference

    i.   There are any new regulatory requirements or laws that could adversely affect the entity.

    j.   There are any liabilities in dispute or being contested.

    k.   There have been any losses of significant customers, major suppliers, or key executive employees.

    l.   There are any related-party transactions.

    m.   Any events have occurred, other than those reflected or disclosed in the registration statement, that have a material effect on the audited financial statements included therein or that should be disclosed in order to keep those statements from being misleading.

4.   Inquire of client's legal counsel concerning litigation, claims, and assessments.

5.   Obtain written representations from management about whether any events have occurred subsequent to the balance sheet date that would require adjustment to, or disclosure in, the financial statements.

6.   Consider adjustment of year-end financial statements or disclosure of any items as a result of the above procedures.

7.   Arrange with the client to stay informed of the progress of the registration proceedings.

8.   Read the entire prospectus and other pertinent portions of the registration statement.

AU SECTION 722
INTERIM FINANCIAL INFORMATION

> **PRACTICE POINT:** As part of its Clarity Project, the American Institute of Certified Public Accountants' (AICPA's) Auditing Standards Board (ASB) has issued an exposure draft (ED) of a proposed Statement on Auditing Standards (SAS) titled, "Interim Financial Information" (Redrafted), which would supersede AU Section 722 (Interim Financial Information). The proposed SAS does not change or expand existing requirements in extant AU Section 722 in any significant respect.
>
> The ASB is expected to issue many of the clarified standards in *one* SAS that will be codified in "AU Section" format. The ASB has decided that the effective date of the clarified SASs that have not yet been issued is for audits of financial statements for periods ending on or after December 15, 2012. Auditors should be alert to and monitor further developments in this area.

WHAT EVERY PRACTITIONER SHOULD KNOW

Basic Objectives and Applicability

The objective of a review of interim financial information is to determine whether any material modifications should be made to the interim financial information in order for it to be in conformity with *the applicable financial reporting framework*, for example: U.S. GAAP; International Financial Reporting Standards (IFRS) issued by the International Accounting Standards Board (IASB); or a comprehensive basis of accounting other than GAAP (OCBOA).

An accountant may conduct a review of interim financial information of a nonissuer in accordance with this Section only if all of the following conditions are met:

1. The accountant or a predecessor has audited the entity's latest annual financial statements;

2. The accountant either (*a*) has been engaged to audit the entity's current-year financial statements, or (*b*) audited the entity's latest annual financial statements and expects to be engaged to audit the entity's current-year financial statements;

3. The entity prepares its interim financial information in accordance with the same financial reporting framework that is used to prepare the annual financial statements; and

4. The accountant has assessed management's ability to acknowledge its responsibility for establishing and maintaining controls that are sufficient to provide a reasonable basis for the preparation of reliable interim financial information in accordance with the applicable financial reporting framework.

> **PRACTICE POINT:** In February 2011, the American Institute of Certified Public Accountants' (AICPA's) Auditing Standards Board (ASB) issued Statement on

Auditing Standards (SAS) No. 121, "Revised Applicability of Statement on Auditing Standards No. 100, 'Interim Financial Information,'" which amends the applicability of SAS-100 as codified in paragraph .05 of AU Section 722 (Interim Financial Information). Specifically, SAS-121 revises the applicability paragraph of AU Section 722 such that AU Section 722 would be applicable when the accountant audited the entity's latest annual financial statements, and the appointment of another accountant to audit the current-year financial statements is not effective prior to the beginning of the period covered by the review (i.e., revising item 2 above).

Essentially, SAS-121 revises the condition specified in item 2 above, as follows:

> The accountant either (*a*) has been engaged to audit the entity's current-year financial statements, or (*b*) audited the entity's latest annual financial statements and, when it is expected that the current-year financial statements will be audited, the appointment of another accountant to audit the current-year financial statements is not effective prior to the beginning of the period covered by the review.

This amendment is effective for interim reviews of interim financial information for periods beginning after December 15, 2011 (i.e., beginning in 2012 for calendar-year entities). Early application is permitted.

Except for the revised applicability of AU Section 722, the discussion in this chapter remains unaffected by SAS-121.

Also, in a related action, the AICPA's Accounting and Review Services Committee issued Statement on Standards for Accounting and Review Services (SSARS) No. 20, "Revised Applicability of Statements on Standards for Accounting and Review Services." SSARS-20 revises paragraph .01 of AR Section 90 (Review of Financial Statements) so that SSARS do not apply when the provisions of SAS-100, as amended by SAS-121 (AU Section 722), apply. Consistent with the effective date of SAS-121, the amendment in SSARS-20 is effective for reviews of financial statements for periods beginning after December 15, 2011 (i.e., beginning in 2012 for calendar-year entities). Early application is permitted.

In addition, if the interim financial information is condensed information, the following conditions are required to be met:

1. The condensed interim financial information purports to conform with an appropriate financial reporting framework (e.g., FASB Accounting Standards Codification (ASC) 270, *Interim Reporting*), and Article 10 of SEC Regulation S-X);

2. The condensed interim financial information includes a note that the financial information does not represent complete financial statements and should be read in conjunction with the entity's latest annual audited financial statements; and

3. The condensed interim financial information accompanies the entity's latest audited annual financial statements, or such audited annual financial statements are made readily available by the entity (e.g., financial statements on an entity's Web site may be considered readily available, but being available upon request is not considered readily available).

If the previous requisite conditions are not met, reviews of interim financial information of nonissuers should be performed in accordance with Statements on Standards for Accounting and Review Services (SSARS).

This Section defines *interim financial information* as "financial information or statements covering a period less than a full year or for a 12-month period ending on a date other than the entity's fiscal year end." In addition, interim financial information may be condensed or in the form of a complete set of financial statements.

Reaching an Understanding with the Client Regarding the Services to Be Performed

This Section requires the accountant to reach a clear understanding with the client regarding the services to be performed and to document such understanding through a written communication with the client. Such an understanding should include the following matters:

- The objectives of a review of interim financial information (e.g., to provide the accountant with a basis for communicating whether he or she is aware of any material modifications that should be made to the interim financial information for it to conform with the applicable financial reporting framework);
- The limitations of the engagement (i.e., the engagement is not designed to provide assurance on internal control or to identify significant deficiencies and material weaknesses in internal control);
- Management's responsibilities (e.g., to establish and maintain effective internal control over financial reporting, and to make all financial records and related information available to the accountant);
- The accountant's responsibilities (e.g., to conduct the review in accordance with AICPA standards); and
- The expected form of the communication upon completion of the engagement (i.e., written or oral report).

In addition, the accountant should not accept the engagement if he or she believes that management does not have the ability to acknowledge its responsibility to establish and maintain controls that are sufficient to provide a reasonable basis for the preparation of reliable interim financial information in accordance with the applicable financial reporting framework.

See Illustration 1 for an engagement letter applicable to reviews of interim financial information.

Obtaining Knowledge of the Entity's Business and Its Internal Control

In connection with a review of interim financial information, the accountant should obtain adequate knowledge of an entity's business and its internal control pertaining to the preparation of both annual and interim financial information. In planning a review of interim financial information, this Section requires the accountant to perform the following specified procedures to identify matters that may affect the engagement:

1. Read documentation of the prior year's audit and reviews of prior interim periods of the current year and corresponding interim periods of the prior year and consider any:

   a. Corrected material misstatements.

   b. Uncorrected misstatements.

   c. Risks of material misstatement due to fraud, including the risk of management override of controls.

   d. Financial accounting and reporting matters of continuing significance (e.g., significant deficiencies and material weaknesses).

2. Read the most recent annual and comparable prior interim period financial information.

3. Consider the results of any audit procedures performed with respect to the current year's financial statements.

4. Inquire of management about changes in the entity's business activities.

5. Inquire of management about whether there have been any significant changes in the entity's internal control and, if so, their potential effect on the preparation of the interim financial information.

In addition, this Section indicates that an accountant performing an initial review of interim financial information (i.e., where the accountant has not audited the previous year end's financial statements) should perform the following procedures:

1. Inquire of the predecessor accountant and review the predecessor accountant's documentation for the preceding annual audit and for any prior interim periods in the current year that have been reviewed by the predecessor accountant. When performing this procedure, the successor accountant should specifically consider the nature of the items specified in 1a–1d above.

2. If the predecessor accountant does not allow access to his or her documentation or does not respond to the successor accountant's inquiries, the successor accountant should use alternative procedures to obtain the applicable knowledge.

Performing Interim Review Procedures

This Section requires the accountant to perform the following procedures in connection with a review of interim financial information:

1. Apply analytical procedures to the interim financial information to identify unusual changes or fluctuations that may indicate a material misstatement. Such procedures should include:

   a. Comparing the current period financial information with that of the immediately preceding interim period.

   b. Comparing the current period financial information with that of the corresponding period of the previous fiscal year.

   c. Considering plausible relationships between financial and nonfinancial information.

   d. Comparing recorded amounts (or ratios developed from such amounts) to expectations the accountant developed.

   e. Comparing disaggregated revenue data (e.g., comparing current period revenue reported by month and operating segment to prior periods).

2. Read the minutes of the board of directors, shareholders, and appropriate committees and inquire about relevant matters discussed at meetings for which minutes are not available.

3. Obtain reports from other accountants, if any, when relying on their review work or reports in connection with significant components of the reporting entity.

4. Inquire of management personnel who are responsible for financial and accounting matters about:

   a. Whether the interim financial information has been prepared in conformity with the applicable financial reporting framework, consistently applied.

   b. Unusual or complex situations that may affect the interim financial information.

   c. Significant transactions that occurred or were recognized in the last several days of the interim period.

   d. The status of uncorrected misstatements identified during the previous audit and interim review.

   e. Matters that caused the accountant to raise questions in connection with the review procedures (e.g., discontinued operations, extraordinary items).

   f. Any material subsequent events.

   g. Knowledge of any fraud that has been perpetrated on the entity or any suspected fraud involving (a) management, (b) employees who have significant roles in internal control, or (c) others, if the fraud could have a material effect on the interim financial information.

   h. Allegations of fraud or suspected fraud affecting the entity.

   i. Significant journal entries and other adjustments.

   j. Communications from regulatory agencies.

   k. Significant deficiencies and material weaknesses in the design or operation of internal controls.

5. Obtain evidence that the interim financial information agrees or reconciles with the accounting records, including inquiries of management about the reliability of the records to which the interim financial information was traced or reconciled.

6. Read the interim financial information for conformity with the applicable financial reporting framework.

7. Read other information in documents containing the interim financial information to consider whether such information or the manner of its presentation is materially inconsistent with the interim financial information.

8. Consider whether inquiry of the entity's lawyer concerning litigation, claims, and assessments is necessary.

9. Consider conditions or events that might be indicative of the entity's possible inability to continue as a going concern, and:

   a. Inquire of management about its plans for dealing with the adverse effects of the conditions and events.

   b. Consider whether such matters are adequately disclosed in the interim financial information.

See Illustration 2 for an interim review procedures checklist.

Obtaining a Management Representation Letter

This Section requires the accountant to obtain an appropriate letter of representations from management for all interim financial information presented and for all periods covered by the review. The accountant has the option of obtaining either one of the following letters:

- A representation letter that is used in conjunction with the one provided by management in connection with the prior year's audit (see Illustration 3); or

- A representation letter that may be used independently of any other representation letter (see Illustration 4).

Evaluating the Results of Interim Review Procedures

The accountant may become aware of *likely misstatements*, which is defined as "the accountant's best estimate of the total misstatement in the account balances or classes of transactions on which he or she has performed review procedures." For purposes of evaluating the results of interim review procedures, the accountant should:

- Accumulate for further evaluation likely misstatements identified in performing the review procedures.

- Recognize that aggregated misstatements of relatively small amounts could have a material effect on the interim financial information.

- Evaluate, individually and in the aggregate, misstatements identified by the accountant or brought to his or her attention (including inadequate disclosure) and determine whether the interim financial information should be modified. In connection with such evaluation, the accountant should evaluate the materiality of any likely misstatements that the entity has not corrected and consider matters such as:

  — The nature, cause, and amount of the misstatements.

  — Whether the misstatements occurred in the preceding year or interim periods of the current year.

— Materiality judgments made in connection with the current or prior year's annual audit.

— The potential effect of the misstatements on future interim or annual periods.

— The appropriateness of offsetting a misstatement of an estimated amount with a misstatement of an item that is subject to more precise measurement.

— Whether the accumulation of immaterial misstatements in the current period could contribute to material misstatements in future periods.

Communicating with Management, Those Charged with Governance, and Others

This Section requires the accountant to communicate with the appropriate level of management when *either* of the following conditions exist:

1. The accountant has determined that the interim financial information should be modified because of material departures from the applicable financial reporting framework; or

2. The entity issued the interim financial information before the accountant completed his or her review, in those circumstances in which a review is required.

If, after being notified, management does not respond in a timely, appropriate, and responsible manner, the matter should be brought to the attention of those charged with governance (e.g., the client's audit committee or equivalent body). The communication with those charged with governance may be written or oral; however, in the case of an oral communication, documentation should be made in the workpapers.

If those charged with governance do not respond in a timely, appropriate, and responsible manner, the accountant should consider resigning from the engagement related to interim financial information. In addition, the accountant should evaluate whether to remain the auditor of the entity's financial statements.

In addition, during the course of performing the interim review procedures, the accountant may become aware of illegal acts or fraud by the client, significant deficiencies and material weaknesses in internal control, or other matters that should be communicated to those charged with governance. In such circumstances, the accountant should communicate these matters to management and/or those charged with governance and refer to the applicable guidance found in the following sections:

- AU Section 316 (Consideration of Fraud in a Financial Statement Audit)
- AU Section 317 (Illegal Acts by Clients)
- AU Section 325 (Communicating Internal Control Related Matters Identified in an Audit)
- AU Section 380 (The Auditor's Communication with Those Charged with Governance)

Documentation

This Section indicates that the accountant should prepare documentation in connection with a review of interim financial information, the form and content of which should be designed to meet the circumstances of the particular engagement. While any documentation that the accountant prepares in connection with an interim review engagement is a matter of professional judgment, the documentation should:

- Include significant findings or issues, actions taken to address such findings or issues, and the basis for the final conclusions reached.
- Enable supervisory and review engagement personnel to understand the nature, timing, extent, and results of the procedures performed.
- Identify the engagement team members who performed and reviewed the work.
- Identify the evidence obtained that enabled the accountant to conclude that the interim financial information agreed or reconciled with the accounting records.

The Accountant's Report on a Review of Interim Financial Information

An accountant is not required to issue a report on a review of interim financial information. However, if the accountant is engaged to issue a written report or determines to issue a written report, the report should be in appropriate form and include all the required elements.

The accountant's standard review report on interim financial information should include the following:

1. A title that includes the word *independent*.

2. A statement that the interim financial information identified in the report was reviewed by the accountant and is the responsibility of the entity's management.

3. A statement that the review of interim financial information was conducted in accordance with standards established by the AICPA.

4. A description of the procedures for a review of interim financial information.

5. A statement that a review of interim financial information is substantially less in scope than an audit conducted in accordance with auditing standards generally accepted in the United States, the objective of which is an expression of an opinion regarding the financial information taken as a whole, and accordingly, no such opinion is expressed.

6. A statement about whether the accountant is aware of any material modifications that should be made to the accompanying interim financial information for it to conform with the applicable financial reporting framework, including an identification of the country of origin of those accounting principles (e.g., accounting principles generally accepted in the United States).

7. The manual or printed signature of the accountant's firm.

8. The date of the review report, which is generally the date of completion of the review procedures.

See Illustration 5 for an example of an accountant's standard review report on interim financial information.

In addition, in some circumstances, the accountant's standard report on a review of interim financial information may need to be modified. The following sections discuss circumstances under which the accountant's standard report requires modification.

Reference to other accountants The accountant may use and make reference to the report of other accountants who have performed a review of the interim financial information of a significant component of the reporting entity (e.g., subsidiary). In such circumstances, the accountant's standard review report should be modified. See Illustration 6.

Departure from the applicable financial reporting framework The accountant's report should be modified if he or she has proposed, but effect has not been given to, a material adjustment that is necessary to conform the interim financial information with the applicable financial reporting framework. The modification should describe the nature of the departure and, if practicable, should state the effects on the interim financial information. See Illustration 7.

Inadequate disclosure If the interim financial information does not include necessary disclosures to comply with the applicable financial reporting framework (e.g., disclosures about the entity's ability to continue as a going concern), the accountant's report should be modified. In addition, if practicable, the accountant should include the necessary information in his or her report. See Illustration 8.

Conditions that gave rise to a going-concern paragraph that was included in the prior year's audit report continue to exist In such circumstances, the accountant is *not* required to modify his or her interim review report if all of the following conditions exist:

- The prior year end audit report included an explanatory paragraph indicating substantial doubt about the entity's ability to continue as a going concern;

- The conditions that raised such doubt still exist as of the interim review reporting date; and

- The interim financial information includes adequate disclosures about these conditions.

However, the accountant may add an explanatory paragraph to the interim review report, after the concluding paragraph, which emphasizes the going-concern matter. See Illustration 9.

Conditions or events pertaining to the entity's possible inability to continue as a going concern exist as of the interim review reporting date; a going-concern paragraph was not included in the prior year's audit report In such circumstances, the accountant is *not* required to modify his or her interim review report if the following conditions exist:

- Conditions or events pertaining to the entity's possible inability to continue as a going concern exist as of the interim review reporting date; and

- The interim financial information includes adequate disclosures about these conditions and events.

However, the accountant may add an explanatory paragraph to the interim review report, after the concluding paragraph, which emphasizes the going-concern matter. See Illustration 10.

The accountant's responsibility after the report date The accountant has no responsibility to continue investigating or apply additional procedures to interim financial information after the date of his or her review report. However, the accountant should not ignore the subsequent discovery of facts that existed at the date of the report and that may have had an effect on his or her report. Under such circumstances, the accountant should consider the guidance in AU Section 561 (Subsequent Discovery of Facts Existing at the Date of the Auditor's Report).

Client's Representations Concerning a Review of Interim Financial Information

The accountant's review report must be included in any client document, report, or written communication containing the reviewed interim financial information in which the client represents that the accountant has reviewed the interim financial information. If the client refuses to include the accountant's review report, the accountant should:

1. Inform the client that the accountant's name is not to be associated with the interim financial information or referred to in the document. If the client does not comply with the accountant's request, the accountant should inform the client that he or she will not permit either the use of, or reference to, the accountant's name.

2. Communicate the client's noncompliance with the accountant's request to those charged with governance.

3. Recommend that the client consult with legal counsel about the application of relevant laws and regulations to the circumstances.

4. Consider other appropriate actions, including consultation with his or her legal counsel.

Similarly, if a client represents in a document filed with a regulatory agency, or issued to stockholders or third parties, that the accountant has reviewed the interim financial information included in the document, and the accountant has been unable to complete his or her review, the accountant should follow the preceding steps.

Interim Financial Information Accompanying Audited Financial Statements

The interim financial information ordinarily would be presented as supplementary information outside the audited financial statements. Each page of the interim financial information should be clearly marked as "unaudited." If the information is presented in a note to the audited financial statements, the information should also be clearly marked as "unaudited."

Generally, the auditor's report on audited annual financial statements need not refer to the review of the accompanying interim financial information because this information (1) has not been audited and (2) is not required for fair presentation of the audited financial statements in conformity with the applicable financial reporting framework. However, exceptions to this general rule apply in the situations described below.

1. **The interim financial information is included as a note to the audited financial statements and has been reviewed, but is not appropriately marked as "unaudited."** The auditor's report should include a separate explanatory paragraph indicating that the information was not audited and, therefore, the auditor expresses no opinion on it. The following is a sample of a separate explanatory paragraph in the auditor's report:

   Note X, "Summary of Quarterly Results of Operations," contains information that we did not audit and, accordingly, we do not express an opinion on that information.

2. **The interim financial information accompanying audited financial statements does not appear to be presented in accordance with the applicable financial reporting framework.** The auditor's report should include an additional paragraph describing the circumstances (e.g., inadequate disclosures, departure from the applicable financial reporting framework) and, if practical, the effects on the interim financial information, unless such matters are addressed in the accountant's separate review report and his or her report is presented with the information. The following is a sample of a separate explanatory paragraph in the auditor's report:

   The selected quarterly financial data on page XX [*or in Note X, "Unaudited Summary of Quarterly Results of Operations"*] contain data that we did not audit and, accordingly, we do not express an opinion on that data. However, we did perform a review of that data in accordance with standards established by the American Institute of Certified Public Accountants. Based on our review, we believe that an adjustment should have been made to the quarterly data to reflect the effect of the extraordinary charge described in Note Y to the financial statements during the quarter ended June 30, 20X2, rather than as an equal charge to each of the quarters ended June 30, September 30, and December 31, 20X2.

   The effect of this adjustment would be to decrease net income for the quarter ended June 30, 20X2 by $_____ and increase net income for each of the quarters ended September 30 and December 31, 20X2 by $_____.

PRACTICE ISSUES AND FREQUENTLY ASKED QUESTIONS

Issue 1: Is the accountant required to confirm with the client in writing the terms and scope of a review engagement of interim financial information?

Yes. The accountant should establish a clear understanding with the client regarding the services to be performed and should document such understanding through a written communication with the client.

Issue 2: May an accountant accept an engagement to review interim financial information under this Section if management is unable to acknowledge its responsibility to establish and maintain sufficient controls as a basis for the preparation of reliable interim financial information?

No. The accountant is required to assess management's ability to acknowledge its responsibility to establish and maintain controls that are sufficient to provide a reasonable basis for the preparation of reliable interim financial information. However, if management is not able to make such an acknowledgement, the accountant is precluded from accepting the engagement.

Issue 3: Does a review of interim financial information in accordance with this Section provide the accountant with a basis for expressing an opinion on such information?

No. A review of interim financial information does not provide the accountant with a basis for expressing an opinion on such information. This is primarily because the review does not contemplate (1) tests of accounting records (e.g., inspection, observation, or confirmation); (2) tests of controls; (3) obtaining corroborating evidence in response to inquiries; or (4) the application of certain other procedures ordinarily performed during an audit.

Issue 4: Should each page of the interim financial information be marked as "unaudited"?

Yes. When the accountant's report accompanies interim financial information that he or she has reviewed, each page of the interim financial information should be marked as "unaudited."

Issue 5: What are examples of scope limitations that would prevent the accountant from completing a review of interim financial information?

The following are examples of scope limitations that would prevent the accountant from completing a review of interim financial information:

1. Restrictions imposed by a client on the timing, nature, or extent of procedures to be performed.
2. Timing of the accountant's work.
3. Inadequacy of the entity's accounting records.
4. Inadequacy of the entity's internal control.
5. Management's refusal to provide the accountant with the written representations the accountant believes are necessary.

The accountant should not consent to be associated with interim financial information if he or she cannot issue a review report due to the inability to complete the review procedures prescribed in this Section.

Issue 6: Is the accountant required to issue a review report in connection with his or her review of interim financial information under this Section?

No. Typically, a review report is not issued on interim financial information, although this Section provides that a report may be issued. However, if the accountant is engaged to issue a written report or determines to issue a written report, the report should be in appropriate form and include all the required elements.

Issue 7: Is there a requirement for a concurring partner review when performing a review of interim financial information?

No. Currently, there is no AICPA requirement for a concurring partner review when performing a review of interim financial information. However, significant judgmental matters would likely warrant consultation with the concurring review partner.

Issue 8: Is the accountant required to corroborate management's responses with other evidence in a review of interim financial information?

No. Generally, the accountant is not required to corroborate management's responses with other evidence. However, if the accountant determines that management's responses are not reasonable or consistent, based on the results of other review procedures and his or her knowledge of the client, the accountant should make further inquiries or perform additional procedures.

Issue 9: Is the accountant required to send an inquiry letter to an entity's lawyer concerning litigation, claims, and assessments, in connection with a review of interim financial information?

No. The accountant is not required, and generally it is not necessary, to send an inquiry letter to an entity's lawyer concerning litigation, claims, and assessments, in connection with a review of interim financial information. However, the accountant is required to consider whether inquiry of the entity's lawyer concerning litigation, claims, and assessments is necessary. For example, an inquiry letter to the entity's lawyer might be considered necessary if the accountant believes the interim financial information departs from GAAP with respect to contingencies that the entity's lawyer may have pertinent information about.

Issue 10: In an initial review of an entity's interim financial information, is the successor accountant required to communicate with the predecessor accountant?

Yes. Before accepting an engagement to perform an initial review of an entity's interim financial information, the successor accountant should contact the predecessor accountant and make those inquiries prescribed in AU Section 315 (Communications between Predecessor and Successor Auditors).

Issue 11: Can the accountant issue a review report if a client refuses to provide a written representation letter?

No. If a client refuses to provide a written representation letter to the accountant, the review is considered incomplete and the accountant does not have an adequate basis to issue a review report. In addition, in such circumstances, the accountant should inform those charged with governance of this matter. If those charged with governance do not respond in a timely manner, the accountant should consider resigning from the engagement.

ILLUSTRATIONS AND PRACTICE AIDS

ILLUSTRATION 1—ENGAGEMENT LETTER FOR REVIEW OF INTERIM FINANCIAL INFORMATION

(Prepared on accountant's letterhead)

December 18, 20X1

Mr. John Smith
Seliga Enterprises
2960 Champion Way
Tustin, California 92782

Dear Mr. Smith:

This letter confirms our understanding of the arrangements for the review of interim financial information of Seliga Enterprises ("Company") for each of the quarters in the year ending December 31, 20X2.

Objectives of the Engagement

The objectives of our review of the Company's interim financial information is to provide us with a basis for communicating whether we are aware of any material modifications that should be made to the interim financial information for it to conform with [*identify the applicable financial reporting framework, for example, "accounting principles generally accepted in the United States of America"*].

A review includes obtaining sufficient knowledge of the Company's business and its internal control relating to the preparation of both annual and interim financial information to (1) identify the types of potential material misstatements in the interim financial information and consider the likelihood of their occurrence, and (2) select the inquiries and analytical procedures to be performed.

Management's Responsibilities

Management of Seliga Enterprises is responsible for (1) the Company's interim financial information; (2) establishing and maintaining effective internal control over financial reporting; (3) safeguarding of assets; (4) identifying and ensuring that the Company complies with the laws and regulations applicable to its activities; (5) making all financial records and related information available to us; and (6) adjusting the interim financial information to correct material misstatements.

At the conclusion of the engagement, we will request that management provide us with a letter confirming certain representations made during the review. Although a review of interim financial information is not designed to obtain reasonable assurance that the interim financial information is free from material misstatement, management also is responsible for affirming in its representation letter to us that the effects of any uncorrected misstatements aggregated by us during the current engagement and pertaining to the current-year period(s) under review are immaterial, both individually and in the aggregate, to the interim financial information taken as a whole.

Our Responsibilities

Our review will be conducted in accordance with standards established by the American Institute of Certified Public Accountants. A review of interim financial information consists principally of performing analytical procedures and making inquiries of persons responsible for financial and accounting matters. It is substantially less in scope than an audit conducted in accordance with auditing standards generally accepted in the United States of America, the objective of which is the expression of an opinion regarding the financial information taken as a whole. Accordingly, we will not express an opinion on the Company's interim financial information.

Expected Form of Our Communication

Upon completion of the engagement, we will communicate to you in a [*written or oral*] report our conclusion and findings consistent with the objectives of the engagement described above. In addition, if the Company states in any report, document, or written communication containing the interim financial information that the information has been reviewed by us or makes other reference to our association with the interim financial information, then our review report will be required to be included in the document.

Limitations of the Engagement

A review of interim financial information does not provide a basis for expressing an opinion about whether the financial information is presented fairly in all material respects in conformity with [*identify the applicable financial reporting framework, for example, "accounting principles generally accepted in the United States of America"*]. In addition, such a review does not provide assurance that we will become aware of all significant matters that would be identified in an audit. Due to the limited nature of the procedures to be performed, such a review engagement is not designed to provide assurance on internal control or to identify significant deficiencies and material weaknesses in internal control; however, we will inform the appropriate level of management and [*those charged with governance*] of any significant deficiencies or material weaknesses in internal control that we identify.

Our fees are based on the amount of time required at various levels of responsibility, plus actual out-of-pocket expenses. Invoices will be rendered every two weeks and are payable upon presentation.

If the foregoing is in accordance with your understanding, please indicate your agreement by signing the duplicate copy of this letter and returning it to us. If you have any questions, please let us know.

Very truly yours,

Christensen & Company

****

RESPONSE:

This letter correctly sets forth the understanding of Seliga Enterprises.

Approved by: _____

Title: _____

Date: _____

ILLUSTRATION 2—INTERIM REVIEW PROCEDURES CHECKLIST

	Yes	No	N/A	Workpaper Reference
General				
1. Has an engagement letter been obtained or a written understanding been reached with the client regarding the scope of the engagement?				

	Yes	No	N/A	Workpaper Reference

2. In connection with planning the engagement, have the following prescribed procedures been performed to obtain sufficient knowledge about the entity's business and its internal control:

    a. Obtain an understanding of the entity's business and its internal control relating to the preparation of both interim and annual financial information?   ___ ___ ___ _____

    b. Read the documentation of the prior year's audit and of reviews of prior interim periods of the current year and corresponding interim periods of the prior year and consider any:

       (1) Corrected material misstatements?   ___ ___ ___ _____

       (2) Uncorrected material misstatements?   ___ ___ ___ _____

       (3) Risks of material misstatements due to fraud, including the risk of management override of controls?   ___ ___ ___ _____

       (4) Financial accounting and reporting matters of continuing significance (e.g., significant deficiencies and material weaknesses)?   ___ ___ ___ _____

    c. Read the most recent annual and comparable prior interim period financial information?   ___ ___ ___ _____

    d. Consider the results of any audit procedures performed with respect to the current year's financial statements?   ___ ___ ___ _____

    e. Inquire of management about changes in the entity's business activities?   ___ ___ ___ _____

    f. Inquire of management about whether there have been any significant changes in the entity's internal control and, if so, their potential effect on the preparation of the interim financial reporting information, including:

       (1) Changes in the entity's policies and procedures?   ___ ___ ___ _____

       (2) Changes in the entity's personnel?   ___ ___ ___ _____

	Yes	No	N/A	Workpaper Reference

   (3) The nature and extent of such changes? _____ _____ _____ _____

3. Is this an initial review of interim financial information (i.e., the accountant has not audited the previous year-end's financial statements)? If yes, have the following prescribed procedures been performed:

  a. Inquire of the predecessor accountant and review the predecessor accountant's documentation for the preceding annual audit and for any prior interim periods in the current year that have been reviewed by the predecessor accountant? _____ _____ _____ _____

  b. Consider the nature of the following items:

    (1) Corrected material misstatements? _____ _____ _____ _____

    (2) Uncorrected misstatements? _____ _____ _____ _____

    (3) Risks of material misstatements due to fraud, including the risk of management override of controls? _____ _____ _____ _____

    (4) Financial accounting and reporting matters of continuing significance (e.g., significant deficiencies and material weaknesses)? _____ _____ _____ _____

4. Did you read the minutes of the board of directors, shareholders, and appropriate committees and inquire about relevant matters discussed at meetings for which minutes are not available? _____ _____ _____ _____

5. Did you obtain reports from other accountants, if any, when relying on their review work or reports in connection with significant components of the reporting entity? _____ _____ _____ _____

6. Did you obtain evidence that the interim financial information agrees or reconciles with the accounting records, including inquiries of management about the reliability of the records to which the interim financial information was traced or reconciled? _____ _____ _____ _____

	Yes	No	N/A	Workpaper Reference

7. Did you read the interim financial information and other information included in company-prepared reports (e.g., prospectus, quarterly report to shareholders) for compliance with the applicable financial reporting framework (e.g., U.S. GAAP; IFRS)? _____ _____ _____ _____

8. Is the interim financial information consistent with other information (e.g., Management's Discussion &Analysis) included in the entity's document? _____ _____ _____ _____

9. Are there events that occurred after the end of the interim period that have a significant effect on the financial statements? _____ _____ _____ _____

10. Has consideration been given to conditions or events that might be indicative of the entity's possible inability to continue as a going concern, and:

    a. Have inquiries been made of management about its plans for dealing with the adverse effects of the conditions and events? _____ _____ _____ _____

    b. Has consideration been given to the adequacy of the disclosure about such matters in the interim financial information? _____ _____ _____ _____

11. Has a management representation letter been obtained for all interim financial information presented and for all periods covered by the review? _____ _____ _____ _____

Analytical Procedures

1. Have the following prescribed analytical procedures been performed:

    a. Comparison of current period interim financial information with that of the immediately preceding interim period? _____ _____ _____ _____

    b. Comparison of current period interim financial information with that of the corresponding period of the previous fiscal year? _____ _____ _____ _____

    c. Consideration of plausible relationships between financial and nonfinancial information? _____ _____ _____ _____

    d. Comparison of recorded amounts, or ratios developed from recorded amounts, to expectations developed by the accountant? _____ _____ _____ _____

		Yes	No	N/A	Workpaper Reference
e.	Comparison of disaggregated revenue data (e.g., comparing current period revenue reporting by month and operating segment to prior periods)?	___	___	___	_____

2. Has consideration been given to performing other analytical procedures such as the following:

		Yes	No	N/A	Workpaper Reference
a.	Comparison of current interim financial information to budgets and forecasts?	___	___	___	_____
b.	Comparison of current interim financial information to that of others in the same industry?	___	___	___	_____
c.	Vertical analysis of financial information in comparison to prior periods (e.g., expenses by type as a percentage of sales; assets by type as a percentage of total assets)?	___	___	___	_____
d.	Gross profit analysis by product line and business segment?	___	___	___	_____
e.	Comparison of disaggregated data by period (e.g., financial statement items disaggregated into quarterly or monthly amounts)?	___	___	___	_____
f.	Comparison of disaggregated data by operating line or product segment?	___	___	___	_____
g.	Comparison of disaggregated data by location (e.g., subsidiary, division, or branch)?	___	___	___	_____
h.	Comparison of selected ratios and indicators to expectations based on prior periods and industry averages (e.g., current ratio, receivable turnover, inventory turnover, gross profit percentage)? (See Illustration 1 in AU Section 329, "Analytical Procedures.")	___	___	___	_____

Management Inquiries

1. Have specific inquiries been made of management and appropriate officials about the following:

		Yes	No	N/A	Workpaper Reference
a.	Whether the interim financial information has been prepared in conformity with the applicable financial reporting framework (e.g., GAAP; IFRS) consistently applied?	___	___	___	_____
b.	Unusual or complex situations that affect the interim financial information?				

		Yes	No	N/A	Workpaper Reference
c.	Significant transactions that occurred or were recognized in the last several days of the interim period?	____	____	____	_____
d.	The status of uncorrected misstatements identified during the previous audit and interim review?	____	____	____	_____
e.	Matters which caused the accountant to raise questions in connection with the review procedures, for example, discontinued operations, extraordinary items?	____	____	____	_____
f.	Any material subsequent events?	____	____	____	_____
g.	Knowledge of any fraud that has been perpetrated on the entity or any suspected fraud involving (1) management, (2) employees who have significant roles in internal control, or (3) others, if the fraud could have a material effect on the interim financial information?	____	____	____	_____
h.	Allegations of fraud or suspected fraud affecting the entity?	____	____	____	_____
i.	Significant journal entries and other adjustments?	____	____	____	_____
j.	Communications from regulatory agencies?	____	____	____	_____
k.	Significant deficiencies and material weaknesses in the design or operation of internal controls as it relates to the preparation of both annual and interim financial information?	____	____	____	_____

2. Have inquiries been made of management about the existence of any of the following unusual or complex situations:

		Yes	No	N/A	Workpaper Reference
a.	Business combinations?	____	____	____	_____
b.	New or complex revenue recognition methods?	____	____	____	_____
c.	Impairment of assets?	____	____	____	_____
d.	Disposal of a segment of a business?	____	____	____	_____
e.	Use of derivative instruments and hedging activities?	____	____	____	_____

		Yes	No	N/A	Workpaper Reference
f.	Sales and transfers that may affect the classification of investments in securities, including management's intent and ability with respect to the remaining securities classified as held to maturity?	___	___	___	___
g.	If presented, computation of earnings per share in a complex capital structure?	___	___	___	___
h.	Adoption of new stock compensation plans or changes to existing plans?	___	___	___	___
i.	Restructuring charges taken in the current and prior quarters?	___	___	___	___
j.	Significant, unusual, or infrequently occurring transactions?	___	___	___	___
k.	Changes in litigation or contingencies?	___	___	___	___
l.	Changes in major contracts with customers or suppliers?	___	___	___	___
m.	Application of new accounting principles?	___	___	___	___
n.	Changes in accounting principles or the methods of applying them?	___	___	___	___
o.	Trends and developments affecting accounting estimates?	___	___	___	___
p.	Compliance with debt covenants?	___	___	___	___
q.	Changes in related parties or significant new related-party transactions?	___	___	___	___
r.	Material off-balance-sheet transactions, special-purpose entities, and other equity investments?	___	___	___	___
s.	Unique terms for debt or capital stock that could affect classification?	___	___	___	___

Evaluation and Documentation of Procedures

		Yes	No	N/A	Workpaper Reference
1.	Have likely misstatements that were identified during the engagement been accumulated and evaluated?	___	___	___	___
2.	Have the following matters been considered in connection with the evaluation of the materiality of any likely misstatements that the entity has not corrected:				
a.	The nature, cause, and amount of the misstatements?	___	___	___	___

	Yes	No	N/A	Workpaper Reference
b. Whether the misstatements occurred in the preceding year or interim periods of the current year?	___	___	___	_____
c. Materiality judgments made in connection with the current or prior year's annual audit?	___	___	___	_____
d. The potential effect of the misstatements on future interim or annual periods?	___	___	___	_____
e. The appropriateness of offsetting a misstatement of an estimated amount with a misstatement of an item that is subject to more precise measurement?	___	___	___	_____
f. The contribution of immaterial misstatements in the current period to material misstatements in future periods?	___	___	___	_____
3. Has consideration been given to the fact that aggregated misstatements of relatively small amounts could have a material effect on the interim financial information?	___	___	___	_____
4. Have appropriate and timely communications been made with management and those charged with governance with respect to the following, where applicable:				
a. Fraud?	___	___	___	_____
b. Illegal acts?	___	___	___	_____
c. Internal control-related matters?	___	___	___	_____
d. Matters described in AU Section 380 (The Auditor's Communication with Those Charged with Governance)?	___	___	___	_____
5. Does documentation in connection with the review of interim financial information encompass the following:				
a. Include significant findings or issues, actions taken to address such findings or issues, and the basis for the final conclusions reached?	___	___	___	_____
b. Enable supervisory and review engagement personnel to understand the nature, timing, extent, and results of the procedures performed?	___	___	___	_____

	Yes	No	N/A	Workpaper Reference
c. Identify the engagement team members who performed and reviewed the work?	____	____	____	_____
d. Identify the evidence obtained that enabled the accountant to conclude that the interim financial information agreed or reconciled with the accounting records?	____	____	____	_____

Cash

	Yes	No	N/A	Workpaper Reference
1. Have bank balances been reconciled with book balances?	____	____	____	_____
2. Have old or unusual reconciling items between bank balances and book balances been reviewed and adjustments made where necessary?	____	____	____	_____
3. Has a proper cutoff of cash transactions been made?	____	____	____	_____
4. Are there any restrictions on the availability of cash balances?	____	____	____	_____
5. Have cash funds been counted and reconciled with control accounts?	____	____	____	_____

Accounts Receivable

	Yes	No	N/A	Workpaper Reference
1. Has an adequate allowance been made for doubtful accounts, discounts, and sales returns?	____	____	____	_____
2. Have receivables considered uncollectible been written off?	____	____	____	_____
3. If appropriate, has interest been reflected?	____	____	____	_____
4. Has a proper cutoff of sales transactions been made?	____	____	____	_____
5. Are there any receivables from employees and related parties?	____	____	____	_____
6. Are any receivables pledged, discounted, or factored?	____	____	____	_____
7. Have receivables been properly classified between current and noncurrent?	____	____	____	_____

Inventories

	Yes	No	N/A	Workpaper Reference
1. Have inventories been physically counted? If not, how have inventories been determined?	____	____	____	_____
2. Have general ledger control accounts been adjusted to agree with physical inventories?	____	____	____	_____

		Yes	No	N/A	Workpaper Reference
3.	If physical inventories are taken at a date other than the balance-sheet date, what procedures were used to record changes in inventory between the date of the physical inventory and the balance sheet date?	___	___	___	___
4.	Were consignments in or out considered in taking physical inventories?	___	___	___	___
5.	What is the method of determining inventory cost, for example, FIFO,LIFO?	___	___	___	___
6.	Has inventory been valued at the lower of cost or market?	___	___	___	___
7.	Does inventory cost include material, labor, and overhead where applicable?	___	___	___	___
8.	Have write-downs for obsolescence, scrap, or cost in excess of net realizable value been made?	___	___	___	___
9.	Have proper cutoffs of purchases, goods in transit, and returned goods been made?	___	___	___	___
10.	Are there any inventory encumbrances?	___	___	___	___

Prepaid Expenses

		Yes	No	N/A	Workpaper Reference
1.	Have the nature and propriety of the amounts included in prepaid expenses been considered?	___	___	___	___
2.	Are these amounts properly amortized?	___	___	___	___

Investments

		Yes	No	N/A	Workpaper Reference
1.	Have gains and losses on disposal been reflected?	___	___	___	___
2.	Has investment income been reflected?	___	___	___	___
3.	Has appropriate consideration been given to the classification of investments between current and noncurrent, and the difference between the cost and market value of investments?	___	___	___	___
4.	Have consolidation or equity accounting requirements been considered?	___	___	___	___
5.	Has the basis of valuation of marketable equity securities been properly applied?	___	___	___	___
6.	Are investments unencumbered?	___	___	___	___

Property and Equipment

		Yes	No	N/A	Workpaper Reference
1.	Have gains or losses on disposal of property or equipment been reflected?	___	___	___	___
2.	Are the criteria for capitalization of property and equipment consistently applied?	___	___	___	___
3.	Does the repairs and maintenance account only include items of an expense nature?	___	___	___	___

	Yes	No	N/A	Workpaper Reference
4. Are property and equipment stated at cost?				
5. Are the depreciation methods and rates appropriate and consistent?				
6. Are there any unrecorded additions, retirements, abandonments, sales, or trade-ins?				
7. Does the entity have material lease agreements? Have they been properly reflected?				
8. Is any property or equipment mortgaged or otherwise encumbered?				

Other Assets

1. Do these assets represent costs that will benefit future periods?				
2. Is the amortization policy for deferred costs and intangible assets appropriate?				
3. Have other assets been properly classified between current and noncurrent?				
4. Are any of these assets mortgaged or otherwise encumbered?				

Accounts and Notes Payable and Accrued Liabilities

1. Have all significant payables been reflected?				
2. Are all bank and other short-term liabilities properly classified?				
3. Have all significant accruals, such as payroll, interest, and provisions for pension and profit-sharing plans been reflected?				
4. Are there any collateralized liabilities?				
5. Are there any payables to employees and related parties?				

Long-Term Liabilities

1. Are the terms and other provisions of long-term liability agreements properly accounted for?				
2. Have liabilities been properly classified between current and noncurrent?				
3. Has interest expense been reflected?				
4. Has there been compliance with restrictive covenants of loan agreements?				
5. Are any long-term liabilities collateralized or subordinated?				

Income and Other Taxes

	Yes	No	N/A	Workpaper Reference
1. Has provision been made for current and prior-year federal income taxes payable?	___	___	___	_____
2. Have any assessments or reassessments been received?	___	___	___	_____
3. Are there tax examinations in process?	___	___	___	_____
4. Are there temporary differences? If so, have deferred taxes been reflected?	___	___	___	_____
5. Has provision been made for state and local income, franchise, sales, and other taxes payable?	___	___	___	_____

Other Liabilities, Commitments, and Contingencies

	Yes	No	N/A	Workpaper Reference
1. Have other liabilities been properly classified between current and noncurrent?	___	___	___	_____
2. Are there any contingent liabilities, such as discounted notes, drafts, endorsements, warranties, litigation, and unsettled asserted claims?	___	___	___	_____
3. Are there any unasserted potential claims?	___	___	___	_____
4. Are there any material contractual obligations for construction or purchase of real property and equipment?	___	___	___	_____
5. Are there any commitments or options to purchase or sell company securities?	___	___	___	_____
6. Has adequate consideration been given as to whether inquiry of the entity's lawyer concerning litigation, claims, and assessments is necessary?	___	___	___	_____

Equity

	Yes	No	N/A	Workpaper Reference
1. Is the nature of any changes in equity accounts considered and properly accounted for?	___	___	___	_____
2. Have classes of capital stock been authorized?	___	___	___	_____
3. Is the par or stated value of the various classes of stock properly stated?	___	___	___	_____
4. Do amounts of outstanding shares of capital stock agree with subsidiary records?	___	___	___	_____
5. Have capital stock preferences, if any, been disclosed?	___	___	___	_____
6. Have stock options been granted?	___	___	___	_____
7. Has the entity made any acquisitions of its own capital stock?	___	___	___	_____
8. Are there any restrictions on retained earnings or other capital?	___	___	___	_____

Revenue and Expenses

	Yes	No	N/A	Workpaper Reference
1. Are revenues from the sale of major products and services recognized in the appropriate period?	_____	_____	_____	_____
2. Are purchases and expenses recognized in the appropriate period and properly classified?	_____	_____	_____	_____
3. Do the financial statements include discontinued operations or items that might be considered extraordinary?	_____	_____	_____	_____
4. Are the company's revenue recognition methods in compliance with the applicable financial reporting framework (e.g., GAAP; IFRS)?	_____	_____	_____	_____

Prepared By: _____ Date: _____

Approved By: _____ Date: _____

ILLUSTRATION 3—MANAGEMENT REPRESENTATION LETTER FOR A REVIEW OF INTERIM FINANCIAL INFORMATION (SHORT FORM TO BE USED IN CONJUNCTION WITH THE LETTER PROVIDED BY MANAGEMENT IN CONNECTION WITH THE PRIOR YEAR'S AUDIT)

(Prepared on client's letterhead)

(Date of accountant's report)

To *(Accountant)*

We are providing this letter in connection with your review of the [*identification of interim financial information*] of [*name of entity*] as of [*dates*] and for the [*periods*] for the purpose of determining whether any material modifications should be made to the [*consolidated*] interim financial information for it to conform with [*identify the applicable financial reporting framework, for example, "accounting principles generally accepted in the United States of America"; including, if appropriate, an indication as to the appropriate form and content of interim financial information, for example, "Article 10 of SEC Regulation S-X"*]. We confirm that we are responsible for the fair presentation of the [*consolidated*] interim financial information in conformity with [*identify the applicable financial reporting framework, for example, "accounting principles generally accepted in the United States of America"*] and that we are responsible for establishing and maintaining controls that are sufficient to provide a reasonable basis for the preparation of reliable interim financial information in accordance with [*identify the applicable financial reporting framework, for example, "accounting principles generally accepted in the United States of America"*].

Certain representations in this letter are described as being limited to matters that are material. Items are considered material, regardless of size, if they involve an omission or misstatement of accounting information that, in the light of surrounding circumstances, makes it probable that the judgment of a reasonable person relying on the information would be changed or influenced by the omission or misstatement.

We confirm, to the best of our knowledge and belief, [*as of (date of accountant's report or the completion of the review)*], the following representations made to you during your review.

1. The interim financial information referred to above has been prepared and presented in conformity with [*identify the applicable financial reporting framework, for example, "accounting principles generally accepted in the United States of America"*] applicable to interim financial information.

2. We have made available to you:

   a. All financial records and related data.

   b. All minutes of the meetings of stockholders, directors, and committees of directors, or summaries of actions of recent meetings for which minutes have not yet been prepared. All significant board and committee actions are included in the summaries.

3. We believe that the effects of any uncorrected financial statement misstatements aggregated by you during the current review engagement and pertaining to the interim period(s) in the current year, as summarized in the accompanying schedule, are immaterial, both individually and in the aggregate, to the interim financial information taken as a whole.

PRACTICE POINT: If no uncorrected misstatements were identified, this item should be eliminated.

---

4. There are no significant deficiencies or material weaknesses in the design or operation of internal controls as it relates to the preparation of both annual and interim financial information.

5. We acknowledge our responsibility for the design and implementation of programs and controls to prevent and detect fraud.

6. We have no knowledge of any fraud or suspected fraud affecting the Company involving:

   a. Management.

   b. Employees who have significant roles in internal control.

   c. Others where the fraud could have a material effect on the interim financial information.

7. We have no knowledge of any allegations of fraud or suspected fraud affecting the Company received in communications from employees, former employees, analysts, regulators, short sellers, or others.

8. We have reviewed our representation letter to you dated [*date of representation letter relating to most recent audit*] with respect to the audited financial statements for the year ended [*prior year-end date*]. We believe that representations [*A*], [*B*], and [*C*] within that representation letter do not apply to the interim financial information referred to above. We now confirm those representations 1 through [*X*], as they apply to the interim financial information referred to above, and incorporate them herein, with the following changes: [*Indicate any changes.*]

9. [*Add any representations related to new accounting or auditing standards that are being implemented for the first time.*]

To the best of our knowledge and belief, no events have occurred subsequent to the balance sheet date and through the date of this letter that would require adjustment to or disclosure in the aforementioned interim financial information.

[*Name of Chief Executive Officer and Title*]

[*Name of Chief Financial Officer and Title*]

[*Name of Chief Accounting Officer and Title*]

ILLUSTRATION 4—MANAGEMENT REPRESENTATION LETTER FOR A REVIEW OF INTERIM FINANCIAL INFORMATION (LONG FORM TO BE USED INDEPENDENTLY OF ANY OTHER LETTER)

(*Prepared on client's letterhead*)

(*Date of accountant's report*)

To (*Accountant*)

We are providing this letter in connection with your review of the [*identification of interim financial information*] of [*name of entity*] as of [*dates*] and for the [*periods*] for the purpose of determining whether any material modifications should be made to the [*consolidated*] interim financial information for it to conform with [*identify the applicable financial reporting framework, for example, "accounting principles generally accepted in the United States of America"; including, if appropriate, an indication as to the appropriate form and content of interim financial information, for example, "Article 10 of SEC Regulation S-X"*]. We confirm that we are responsible for the fair presentation of the [*consolidated*] interim financial information in conformity with [*identify the applicable financial reporting framework, for example, "accounting principles generally accepted in the United States of America"*] and that we are responsible for establishing and maintaining controls that are sufficient to provide a reasonable basis for the preparation of reliable interim financial information in accordance with [*identify the applicable financial reporting framework, for example, "accounting principles generally accepted in the United States of America"*].

Certain representations in this letter are described as being limited to matters that are material. Items are considered material, regardless of size, if they involve an omission or misstatement of accounting information that, in the light of surrounding circumstances, makes it probable that the judgment of a reasonable person relying on the information would be changed or influenced by the omission or misstatement.

We confirm, to the best of our knowledge and belief, [*as of (date of accountant's report or the completion of the review)*], the following representations made to you during your review.

1. The interim financial information referred to above has been prepared and presented in conformity with [*identify the applicable financial reporting framework, for example, "accounting principles generally accepted in the United States of America"*] applicable to interim financial information.

2. We have made available to you:

   a. All financial records and related data.

   b. All minutes of the meetings of stockholders, directors, and committees of directors, or summaries of actions of recent meetings for which minutes have not yet been prepared.

All significant board and committee actions are included in the summaries.

3. There have been no communications from regulatory agencies concerning noncompliance with or deficiencies in financial reporting practices.

4. There are no material transactions that have not been properly recorded in the accounting records underlying the interim financial information.

5. We believe that the effects of any uncorrected financial statement misstatements aggregated by you during the current review engagement and pertaining to the interim period(s) in the current year, as summarized in the accompanying schedule, are immaterial, both individually and in the aggregate, to the interim financial information taken as a whole.

PRACTICE POINT: If no uncorrected misstatements were identified, this item should be eliminated.

---

6. There are no significant deficiencies or material weaknesses in the design or operation of internal controls as it relates to the preparation of both annual and interim financial information.

7. We acknowledge our responsibility for the design and implementation of programs and controls to prevent and detect fraud.

8. We have no knowledge of any fraud or suspected fraud affecting the Company involving:

   a. Management.

   b. Employees who have significant roles in internal control.

   c. Others where the fraud could have a material effect on the interim financial information.

9. We have no knowledge of any allegations of fraud or suspected fraud affecting the Company received in communications from employees, former employees, analysts, regulators, short sellers, or others.

10. The Company has no plans or intentions that may materially affect the carrying value or classification of assets and liabilities.

11. The following have been properly recorded or disclosed in the interim financial information:

    a. Related-party transactions, including sales, purchases, loans, transfers, leasing arrangements, and guarantees, and amounts receivable from or payable to related parties.

    b. Guarantees, whether written or oral, under which the company is contingently liable.

    c. Significant estimates and material concentrations known to management that are required to be disclosed in accordance with ASC 275, *Risks and Uncertainties*. Significant estimates are estimates at the balance sheet date that could change materially within the next year. Concentrations refer to volumes of business, revenues, available sources of supply, or markets or geographic areas for which events could occur that would significantly disrupt normal finances within the next year.

12. There are no violations or possible violations of laws or regulations whose effects should be considered for disclosure in the interim financial information or as a basis for recording a loss contingency.

13. There are no unasserted claims or assessments that are probable of assertion and must be disclosed in accordance with ASC 450, *Contingencies.*

14. There are no other liabilities or gain or loss contingencies that are required to be accrued or disclosed by ASC 450.

15. The Company has satisfactory title to all owned assets, and there are no liens or encumbrances on such assets; nor has any asset been pledged as collateral.

16. The Company has complied with all aspects of contractual agreements that would have a material effect on the interim financial information in the event of noncompliance.

17. [*Add additional representations that are unique to the entity's business or industry. See AU Section 333, "Management Representations."*]

18. [*Add any representations related to new accounting or auditing standards that are being implemented for the first time.*]

To the best of our knowledge and belief, no events have occurred subsequent to the balance sheet date and through the date of this letter that would require adjustment to or disclosure in the aforementioned interim financial information.

[*Name of Chief Executive Officer and Title*]

[*Name of Chief Financial Officer and Title*]

[*Name of Chief Accounting Officer and Title*]

ILLUSTRATION 5—ACCOUNTANT'S STANDARD REVIEW REPORT ON INTERIM FINANCIAL INFORMATION

Independent Accountant's Report

Board of Directors and Stockholders
ABC Company

We have reviewed the accompanying [*describe the interim financial information or statements reviewed*] of ABC Company and consolidated subsidiaries as of September 30, 20X2, and for the three-month and nine-month periods then ended.[1] This interim financial information is the responsibility of the Company's management.

We conducted our review in accordance with standards established by the American Institute of Certified Public Accountants. A review of interim financial information consists principally of applying analytical procedures and making inquiries of persons responsible for financial and accounting matters. It is substantially less in scope than an audit conducted in accordance with auditing standards generally accepted in the United States of America,

---

[1] If interim financial information of a prior period is presented with that of the current period, and the accountant has reviewed that information, the accountant should report on his or her review of the prior period. The first sentence should be modified as follows:

We have reviewed the accompanying [*describe the statements or information reviewed*] of ABC Company and consolidated subsidiaries as of September 30, 20X2, and 20X1, and for the three-month and nine-month periods then ended.

the objective of which is the expression of an opinion regarding the financial information taken as a whole. Accordingly, we do not express such an opinion.

Based on our review, we are not aware of any material modifications that should be made to the accompanying interim financial information for it to be in conformity with [*identify the applicable financial reporting framework, for example, "accounting principles generally accepted in the United States of America"*].

[*Signature*]

[*Date*]

ILLUSTRATION 6—ACCOUNTANT'S REVIEW REPORT ON INTERIM FINANCIAL INFORMATION MAKES REFERENCE TO OTHER ACCOUNTANTS

Independent Accountant's Report

Board of Directors and Stockholders
ABC Company

We have reviewed the accompanying [*describe the interim financial information or statements reviewed*] of ABC Company and consolidated subsidiaries as of September 30, 20X2, and for the three-month and nine-month periods then ended. This interim financial information is the responsibility of the Company's management.

We were furnished with the report of other accountants on their review of the interim financial information of DEF subsidiary, whose total assets as of September 30, 20X2, and whose revenues for the three-month and nine-month periods then ended, constituted 15%, 20%, and 22%, respectively, of the related consolidated totals.

We conducted our review in accordance with standards established by the American Institute of Certified Public Accountants. A review of interim financial information consists principally of applying analytical procedures and making inquiries of persons responsible for financial and accounting matters. It is substantially less in scope than an audit conducted in accordance with auditing standards generally accepted in the United States of America, the objective of which is the expression of an opinion regarding the financial information taken as a whole. Accordingly, we do not express such an opinion.

Based on our review and the report of other accountants, we are not aware of any material modifications that should be made to the accompanying interim financial information for it to be in conformity with [*identify the applicable financial reporting framework, for example, "accounting principles generally accepted in the United States of America"*].

[*Signature*]

[*Date*]

ILLUSTRATION 7—ACCOUNTANT'S REVIEW REPORT ON INTERIM FINANCIAL INFORMATION MODIFIED DUE TO A DEPARTURE FROM THE APPLICABLE FINANCIAL REPORTING FRAMEWORK

Independent Accountant's Report

Board of Directors and Stockholders
ABC Company

We have reviewed the accompanying [*describe the interim financial information or statements reviewed*] of ABC Company and consolidated subsidiaries as of September 30, 20X2, and for the three-month and nine-month periods then ended. This interim financial information is the responsibility of the Company's management.

We conducted our review in accordance with standards established by the American Institute of Certified Public Accountants. A review of interim financial information consists principally of applying analytical procedures to financial data and making inquiries of persons responsible for financial and accounting matters. It is substantially less in scope than an audit conducted in accordance with auditing standards generally accepted in the United States of America, the objective of which is the expression of an opinion regarding the financial information taken as a whole. Accordingly, we do not express such an opinion.

Based on information furnished to us by management, we believe that the Company has excluded from property and debt in the accompanying balance sheet certain lease obligations that should be capitalized to conform with [*identify the applicable financial reporting framework, for example, "accounting principles generally accepted in the United States of America"*]. This information indicates that if these lease obligations were capitalized at September 30, 20X2, property would be increased by $_____, long-term debt by $_____, and net income would be increased [*decreased*] by $_____, and $_____, respectively, for the three-month and nine-month periods then ended.

Based on our review, with the exception of the matter(s) described in the preceding paragraph(s), we are not aware of any material modifications that should be made to the accompanying interim financial information for it to be in conformity with [*identify the applicable financial reporting framework, for example, "accounting principles generally accepted in the United States of America"*].

[*Signature*]

[*Date*]

ILLUSTRATION 8—ACCOUNTANT'S REVIEW REPORT ON INTERIM FINANCIAL INFORMATION MODIFIED DUE TO INADEQUATE DISCLOSURE

Independent Accountant's Report

Board of Directors and Stockholders
ABC Company

We have reviewed the accompanying [*describe the interim financial information or statements reviewed*] of ABC Company and consolidated subsidiaries as of September 30, 20X2, and for the three-month and nine-month periods then ended. This interim financial information is the responsibility of the Company's management.

We conducted our review in accordance with standards established by the American Institute of Certified Public Accountants. A review of interim financial information consists principally of applying analytical procedures and making inquiries of persons responsible for financial and accounting matters. It is substantially less in scope than an audit conducted in accordance with auditing standards generally accepted in the United States of America, the objective of which is the expression of an opinion regarding the financial statements taken as a whole. Accordingly, we do not express such an opinion.

Management has informed us that the Company is presently defending a claim regarding [*describe the nature of the loss contingency*] and that the extent of the Company's liability, if any, and the effect on the accompanying information is not determinable at this time. The information fails to disclose these matters, which we believe are required to be disclosed in conformity with [*identify the applicable financial reporting framework, for example, "accounting principles generally accepted in the United States of America"*].

Based on our review, with the exception of the matter(s) described in the preceding paragraph(s), we are not aware of any material modifications that should be made to the accompanying interim financial information for it to be in conformity with [*identify the applicable financial reporting framework, for example, "accounting principles generally accepted in the United States of America"*].

[*Signature*]

[*Date*]

ILLUSTRATION 9—ACCOUNTANT'S REVIEW REPORT ON INTERIM FINANCIAL INFORMATION INCLUDES A PARAGRAPH EMPHASIZING A GOING-CONCERN MATTER DISCLOSED IN THE AUDITED FINANCIAL STATEMENTS AND THE INTERIM FINANCIAL INFORMATION

Independent Accountant's Report

Board of Directors and Stockholders
ABC Company

We have reviewed the accompanying [*describe the interim financial information or statements reviewed*] of ABC Company and consolidated subsidiaries as of September 30, 20X2, and for the three-month and nine-month periods then ended. This interim financial information is the responsibility of the Company's management.

We conducted our review in accordance with standards established by the American Institute of Certified Public Accountants. A review of interim financial information consists principally of applying analytical procedures and making inquiries of persons responsible for financial and accounting matters. It is substantially less in scope than an audit conducted in accordance with auditing standards generally accepted in the United States of America, the objective of which is the expression of an opinion regarding the financial statements taken as a whole. Accordingly, we do not express such an opinion.

Based on our review, we are not aware of any material modifications that should be made to the accompanying interim financial information for it to be in conformity with [*identify the applicable financial reporting framework, for example, "accounting principles generally accepted in the United States of America"*].

Note [X] of the Company's audited financial statements as of December 31, 20X1, and for the year then ended discloses that the Company was unable to renew its line of credit or obtain alternative financing at December 31, 20X1. Our auditor's report on those financial statements includes an explanatory paragraph referring to the matters in Note [X] of those financial statements and indicating that these matters raised substantial doubt about the Company's ability to continue as a going concern. As indicated in Note [Y] of the Company's unaudited interim financial information as of September 30, 20X2, and for the nine months then ended, the Company was still unable to renew its line of credit or obtain alternative financing as of September 30, 20X2. The accompanying interim financial information does not include any adjustments that might result from the outcome of this uncertainty.

[*Signature*]

[*Date*]

ILLUSTRATION 10—ACCOUNTANT'S REVIEW REPORT ON INTERIM FINANCIAL INFORMATION INCLUDES A PARAGRAPH EMPHASIZING A GOING-CONCERN MATTER THAT WAS NOT INCLUDED IN THE PRIOR YEAR'S AUDIT REPORT

Independent Accountant's Report

Board of Directors and Stockholders
ABC Company

We have reviewed the accompanying [*describe the interim financial information or statements reviewed*] of ABC Company and consolidated subsidiaries as of September 30, 20X2, and for the three-month and nine-month periods then ended. This interim financial information is the responsibility of the Company's management.

We conducted our review in accordance with standards established by the American Institute of Certified Public Accountants. A review of interim financial information consists principally of applying analytical procedures and making inquiries of persons responsible for financial and accounting matters. It is substantially less in scope than an audit conducted in accordance with auditing standards generally accepted in the United States of America, the objective of which is the expression of an opinion regarding the financial statements taken as a whole. Accordingly, we do not express such an opinion.

Based on our review, we are not aware of any material modifications that should be made to the accompanying interim financial information for it to be in conformity with [*identify the applicable financial reporting framework, for example, "accounting principles generally accepted in the United States of America"*].

As discussed in Note [X], certain conditions indicate that the Company may be unable to continue as a going concern. The accompanying interim financial information does not include any adjustments that might result from the outcome of this uncertainty.

[*Signature*]

[*Date*]

AU Section 800
COMPLIANCE AUDITING

AU SECTION 801
COMPLIANCE AUDITS

PRACTICE POINT: This codified AU Section 801 is for Statement on Auditing Standards (SAS) No. 117 titled, "Compliance Audits," which has superseded SAS-74 (Compliance Auditing Considerations in Audits of Governmental Entities and Recipients of Governmental Financial Assistance). SAS-117, which was issued in the clarity format, is effective for compliance audits for fiscal periods ending on or after June 15, 2010, with earlier application permitted.

SAS-117 was developed in response to a study by the President's Council on Integrity and Efficiency (the PCIE study) of the quality of audits conducted under Office of Management and Budget (OMB) Circular A-133, *Audits of States, Local Governments, and Non-Profit Organizations*, which was released in 2007. This PCIE study showed that improvements to the compliance auditing process were needed in many areas.

SAS-117 establishes standards and provides guidance on performing and reporting on an audit of an entity's compliance with applicable governmental audit compliance requirements. This includes audits under:

- OMB Circular A-133 (also referred to as *single audits*); and
- U.S. Department of Housing and Urban Development (HUD), *Consolidated Audit Guide for Audits of HUD Programs.*

SAS-117 changes SAS-74 in several significant respects. The most important of those are that it:

- Incorporates the risk assessment standards (SAS Nos. 104-111);
- Requires auditors to adapt and apply generally accepted auditing standards (GAAS), including the fraud and risk assessment standards, to a compliance audit;
- Identifies AU Sections that are applicable to compliance audits and those that are not;
- Defines terms related to compliance audits;
- Identifies requirements that are unique to a compliance audit;
- Identifies elements to be included in an auditor's report on a compliance audit;
- Reflects changes in the compliance auditing environment;
- Provides guidance for evaluating whether an entity has materially complied with applicable compliance requirements; and
- Clarifies the applicability of the standard.

SAS-117 is effective for compliance audits for fiscal periods ending on or after June 15, 2010. Earlier application is permitted.

The provisions and requirements of SAS-117 (AU Section 801) are discussed in more detail below.

PRACTICE POINT: In March 2011, the American Institute of Certified Public Accountants' (AICPA's) Auditing Standards Board (ASB) issued an exposure draft (ED) of a proposed Statement on Auditing Standards (SAS) titled, "Omnibus Statement on Auditing Standards—2011." This proposed SAS, which is part of the AICPA's Clarity Project, would amend the following SASs that have been issued in the clarity format and are currently effective:

- SAS-117 (AU Section 801) (Compliance Audits). The amendment to SAS-117 conforms the auditor's report on compliance to the requirements of the clarified SAS, "Forming an Opinion and Reporting on Financial Statements." In addition, the amendment revises the appendix in SAS-117, "AU Sections That Are Not Applicable to Compliance Audits," to reflect conforming changes to affected references to AU Sections as a result of the ASB's Clarity Project.

- SAS-118 (AU Section 550) (Other Information in Documents Containing Audited Financial Statements). The amendment to SAS-118 clarifies the requirements with respect to identified material inconsistencies by categorizing the requirements based on when the inconsistencies are identified (prior to the date of the auditor's report on the audited financial statements; after the date of the auditor's report but prior to the report release date; and after the report release date). It also adds application material addressing electronic sites to include guidance from an interpretation of AU Section 550 (Other Information in Documents Containing Audited Financial Statements), which the ASB determined was appropriate to include in SAS-118.

In addition, in order to address other changes necessitated by the ASB's overall Clarity Project, the proposed SAS would amend the following clarified SASs that have been finalized and released, but not yet issued as authoritative:

- Clarified SAS, "Overall Objectives of the Independent Auditor and the Conduct of an Audit in Accordance with Generally Accepted Auditing Standards."

- Clarified SAS, "Modifications to the Opinion in the Independent Auditor's Report."

- Clarified SAS, "Reports on Application of Requirements of an Applicable Financial Reporting Framework."

- Clarified SAS, "The Auditor's Communication with Those Charged with Governance (Redrafted)."

- Clarified SAS, "Audit Documentation (Redrafted)."

The proposed SAS would be effective for audits of financial statements for periods ending on or after December 15, 2012, except for the amendment to the clarified SAS, "Reports on Application of Requirements of an Applicable Financial Reporting Framework," which would be effective for engagements that end on or after December 15, 2012.

WHAT EVERY PRACTITIONER SHOULD KNOW

Summary of Significant Changes to Existing Standards and Practice

The impact of SAS-117 on a firm's compliance auditing practice likely will depend on how closely the firm has been following the AICPA Audit Guide, *Government Auditing Standards and Circular A-133 Audits* (the AICPA Audit

Guide) and adapting the existing standards (e.g., risk assessment and fraud standards) to its compliance audits. The PCIE study identified half of the audits in its statistical sample as being unacceptable or of limited reliability. It is expected that SAS-117 will result in significant improvements to, and changes in, such engagements.

SAS-117 brings the following significant changes to compliance auditing:

- Expanded applicability of SAS-117, to include not only audits under OMB Circular A-133 but those under certain federal agency audit guides, such as the HUD consolidated audit guide;

- Expanded discussion of management's responsibilities for compliance;

- A more detailed description of auditor requirements than those in SAS-74;

- Increased guidance related to applying auditor requirements;

- Inclusion as professional requirements in SAS-117 of certain compliance auditing considerations that had previously been non-authoritative guidance under the AICPA Audit Guide; and

- Clarification of the applicability of other AU Sections to compliance audits. (*Note:* SAS-117 states that all AU Sections are applicable to compliance audits, except those specifically exempted in Appendix A of SAS-117.)

Applicability

This Section is applicable when an auditor is engaged, or is required by law or regulation, to perform a compliance audit in accordance with *all three* of the following:

1. GAAS;
2. The standards for financial audits under *Government Auditing Standards* (GAGAS), also referred to as the "Yellow Book"; and
3. A governmental audit that requires the expression of an auditor opinion on compliance.

This Section does not apply to:

- The financial statement component of a compliance audit that is performed in conjunction with a financial statement audit.

- Engagements in which governmental audit requirements call for an examination under the Statements on Standards for Attestation Engagements (SSAE) of an entity's compliance with specified requirements or internal control over compliance.

PRACTICE POINT: Common examples of engagements to which this Section applies are audits performed under OMB Circular A-133, or HUD's *Audit Requirements Related to Entities Such as Public Housing Agencies, Nonprofit and For-Profit Housing Projects, and Certain Lenders.* Both of these engagements are conducted under GAAS and the Yellow Book, and require the auditor to express an opinion on compliance.

Examples of engagements to which this Section does not apply include an examination of an entity's compliance with specified requirements of the U.S. Department of Education's Audit Guide, *Audits of Federal Student Financial Assistance Programs at Participating Institutions and Institution Servicers*, under AT Section 601 (Compliance Attestation). Another case in which this Section does not apply is an engagement performed to satisfy a law or regulation requiring an entity to have an auditor determine whether transportation excise taxes have been spent in accordance with specific purposes described in law or regulation, but not requiring an audit under both GAAS and the Yellow Book. Such an engagement could be performed under AT Section 101 (Attest Engagements), AT Section 201 (Agreed-Upon Procedures Engagements), or AT Section 601, depending on the government's requirements.

Primary Objectives of this Section

This Section sets forth two main objectives for the auditor:

1. To obtain sufficient appropriate audit evidence to enable the auditor to express an opinion on whether the entity has complied with the applicable compliance requirements. This objective includes reporting at the level specified in the governmental audit requirements. In most cases, this is at the program level; however, some governmental audit requirements may specify a different level, such as the applicable compliance requirement level.

2. To identify additional audit and reporting requirements imposed by the governmental audit requirements that go beyond GAAS and GAGAS, and to perform procedures that address those requirements.

Terms and Definitions

This Section defines 21 terms that are applicable to compliance audits and clusters them into several conceptual areas. The most significant of these groupings and definitions are discussed below.

Audit risk in a compliance audit This Section presents three terms that adapt the definitions of risk assessment in the risk assessment standards for financial statement audits to the compliance auditing environment. These terms are comparable to those used for financial statement audits, and mainly replace the word *misstatement* with the word *noncompliance*. The three terms are:

1. Audit risk of noncompliance;

2. Detection risk of noncompliance; and

3. Risk of material noncompliance.

Audit risk in a financial statement audit is focused on material misstatement of the financial statements. In a compliance audit, this focus shifts to noncompliance. Audit risk of noncompliance (AR) is a function of the risk of material noncompliance (RMN) and detection risk of noncompliance (DR).

This Section defines *audit risk of noncompliance* as the risk that an auditor will express an inappropriate opinion on compliance, when material noncompliance exists.

Detection risk of noncompliance is the risk that auditing procedures will not detect an instance of noncompliance that could be material, either by itself or in combination with other instances of noncompliance.

Risk of material noncompliance contains two components, similar to its counterpart, risk of material misstatement in a financial statement audit. These are inherent risk of noncompliance and control risk of noncompliance. This Section defines *inherent risk of noncompliance* (IR) as the susceptibility of a compliance requirement to noncompliance that could be material, either by itself or in combination with other instances of noncompliance, before consideration of any controls over compliance. *Control risk of noncompliance* (CR) is the risk that material noncompliance could occur and not be prevented, or detected and corrected, on a timely basis by the entity's internal control over compliance.

Audit risk of noncompliance can thus be expressed as the following formula:

$$AR = DR \times IR \times CR$$

Deficiencies in internal control over compliance This Section conforms the definitions and classifications of deficiencies in internal control over compliance to those of AU Section 325 (Communicating Internal Control Related Matters Identified in an Audit) for financial statement audits. *Deficiencies in internal control over compliance* may be of two types:

1. *Design deficiencies*, in which a control necessary to meet the compliance objective is either missing or is not properly designed to meet the control objective, or

2. *Operating deficiencies*, in which a properly designed control either does not operate as designed or the person performing the control does not have the authority or the competence to perform it effectively.

A *deficiency in internal control over compliance* exists when the design or operation of that control does not allow management or employees, in the ordinary course of performing their assigned functions to prevent or to timely detect and correct noncompliance.

A *material weakness in internal control over compliance* is a deficiency or a combination of deficiencies such that there is a reasonable possibility that material noncompliance will not be prevented or timely detected and corrected. This Section indicates that a *reasonable possibility* exists when the likelihood of the event is either reasonably possible or probable, as defined using the following constructs:

- *Remote*—The chance of a future occurrence is slight.

- *Probable*—A future occurrence is likely.

- *Reasonably possible*—The chance of a future occurrence is more than remote but less than likely.

A *significant deficiency in internal control over compliance* is a deficiency or combination of deficiencies that is less severe than a material weakness, but still important enough to warrant attention by those charged with governance.

Material noncompliance In the absence of a more specific definition in the particular governmental audit requirement, *material noncompliance* is a failure to follow compliance requirements or a violation of prohibitions in an applicable compliance requirement that results in noncompliance that is quantitatively or qualitatively material to the affected government program, either individually or when aggregated with other noncompliance.

Questioned costs Questioned costs are those questioned by the auditor because of:

- A violation or possible violation of applicable compliance requirements;
- Lack of adequate documentary support; or
- Costs that appear unreasonable and do not reflect actions that a prudent person would take in the circumstances.

Known questioned costs are those specifically identified by the auditor, and are a subset of likely questioned costs. *Likely questioned costs* are defined as the auditor's best estimate of total questioned costs, including known questioned costs. This estimate is developed by extrapolation from audit evidence obtained, such as by projecting sample results to an entire population.

Compliance audit Compliance audits may be either organization-wide or program-specific.

An *organization-wide audit* encompasses both an audit of the entity's financial statements and an audit of its compliance with the applicable compliance requirements of one or more government programs that the entity administers.

A *program-specific audit* is an audit of the entity's compliance with applicable compliance requirements as they relate to one government program that the entity administers. The compliance portion of a program-specific audit is performed in conjunction with an audit of either the entity's or the program's financial statements.

Governmental audit requirement A governmental audit requirement is a requirement established by law, regulation, rule, or by the provisions of contracts or grant agreements. These requirements may also set forth specific supplementary requirements of the compliance audit, such as procedures to be performed by the auditor, documentation requirements, the form of reporting, or continuing education requirements for the auditor.

Management's Responsibilities

This Section states that compliance audits are based on the concept that compliance with an entity's compliance requirements is a management responsibility. Those responsibilities include:

- Identifying the entity's government programs;
- Understanding those programs;
- Complying with the compliance requirements of the government programs;

- Establishing and maintaining effective controls to provide reasonable assurance that government programs are administered in compliance with the compliance requirements;

- Evaluating and monitoring compliance with the compliance requirements; and

- Taking corrective action on identified instances of noncompliance, including the audit findings of a compliance audit.

PRACTICE POINT: This discussion adds emphasis on management's responsibilities in several areas that were not mentioned in SAS-74 (AU Section 801A): Management's Understanding of Its Government Programs, Evaluation and Monitoring Compliance, and Corrective Actions. This emphasis is consistent with one of the Auditing Standards Board's (ASB) general philosophical directions in standards that have been released in recent years, which is to draw a more sharply defined distinction between management's responsibilities and those of the auditor. In the case of this Section, this emphasis counteracts possible misperceptions by either management or the public that the auditor is responsible, for example, for identifying government programs or for monitoring compliance.

Adapting and Applying the AU Sections to a Compliance Audit

This Section requires auditors to adapt and apply the other AU Sections to the objectives of a compliance audit, using their professional judgment. The AU Sections that are not applicable to a compliance audit are listed in appendix A of AU Section 801. AU Sections 100-300 and 500, which deal with auditor responsibilities, competence and independence, field work, and reporting, can generally be adapted to the objectives of a compliance audit. However, with certain exceptions, AU Sections 400, 600, 700, and 900 generally cannot be adapted because they address reporting standards for an audit of financial statements and other topics (e.g., special reports, interim financial information, and public warehouses) that do not apply to compliance audits.

The application guidance and explanatory material to this Section observes that some AU Sections can be easily adapted to a compliance audit. For example, the word *misstatement* can generally be replaced with the word *noncompliance*. Others will entail additional modification. Auditors are not required to make a literal translation of each procedure that might be performed in a financial statement audit, but rather to obtain sufficient appropriate evidence to support an opinion on compliance. Auditors are also not expected to prepare specific documentation of how they applied each applicable AU Section to the compliance audit. Rather, the documentation in the audit strategy, audit plan, and the work performed cumulatively demonstrate auditor compliance with the requirement of this Section.

Establishing Materiality Levels

This Section requires auditors to establish and apply materiality levels for compliance audits based on the governmental audit requirement. This Section's application guidance states that the purpose for establishing materiality levels in a compliance audit is to:

- Determine the nature and extent of risk assessment procedures;
- Identify and assess the risks of material noncompliance;
- Determine the nature, timing, and extent of further audit procedures;
- Evaluate compliance with the applicable compliance requirements; and
- Report findings of noncompliance and other matters required to be reported by the governmental audit requirement.

Consideration of materiality is generally in relation to the government program taken as a whole, unless a different level of materiality is specified. OMB Circular A-133, for example, requires reporting of noncompliance that is material in relation to any of the applicable compliance requirements in the OMB *Compliance Supplement.*

The auditor's materiality determination is usually influenced by the needs of the grantors, because the report on compliance is primarily for their use. However, the auditor's judgment about matters that are material to users of the report is also based on consideration of the needs of the users as a group, including grantors.

Identifying Government Programs and Applicable Compliance Requirements

It is management's responsibility, not the auditor's, to identify the entity's government programs and to understand and comply with the applicable compliance requirements. The auditor's responsibility is to determine which of those government programs and compliance requirements to test in accordance with the governmental audit requirement.

Some governmental audit requirements specifically identify the applicable compliance requirements, whereas others (e.g., the OMB *Compliance Supplement*) provide a framework for the auditor to use in identifying the applicable compliance requirements.

The application guidance of this Section suggests the following procedures that an auditor may perform to identify and obtain an understanding of applicable compliance requirements in the absence of a program-specific audit guide or if the OMB *Compliance Supplement* is not applicable:

- Reading pertinent laws, regulations, rules, contractual or grant provisions;
- Inquiring of management and other knowledgeable persons within the entity (e.g., legal counsel, compliance or chief financial officer);
- Inquiring of knowledgeable persons outside of the entity (e.g., governmental officials or auditors, appropriate oversight organizations or regulators, or third-party specialists such as attorneys);
- Reading the minutes of the entity's governing board;
- Reading prior years' audit or other engagement documentation; and

- Discussing compliance requirements with prior years' auditors or those performing other engagements.

Performing Risk Assessment Procedures

Risk assessment procedures primarily consist of (a) inquiries of management and others within the entity, (b) analytical procedures, and (c) observation and inspection. Under this Section, the auditor is required to:

- Perform risk assessment procedures to obtain a sufficient understanding of the applicable compliance requirements and the entity's internal control over compliance for each of the government programs and compliance requirements selected for testing. The application guidance and explanatory material notes that risk assessment procedures include evaluation of the design and implementation of internal controls over compliance. The nature and extent of risk assessment procedures will vary between entities, and may be influenced by various factors, for example:
  - The newness, nature, and complexity of the applicable compliance requirements;
  - The auditor's knowledge of the entity's internal control over compliance;
  - The services that the entity provides and the extent to which they are affected by external factors;
  - The level of oversight exercised by the grantor or pass-through entity; and
  - How findings are addressed by management.
- Inquire of management whether there are findings and recommendations directly related to the compliance objectives of the audit in written communications from previous audits, attestation engagements, and internal or external monitoring, such as program reviews by government agencies or pass-through entities. The purpose of these inquiries is to assist the auditor in understanding whether management has responded appropriately to the findings.
- Gain an understanding of management's responses, such as taking corrective actions, to such findings and recommendations.
- Based on the information obtained, assess risk and determine the nature, timing, and extent of audit procedures for the compliance audit. This includes determining the extent to which testing of the implementation of corrective actions is applicable to the audit.

Assessing the Risks of Material Noncompliance and Performing Further Audit Procedures in Response to Those Risks

This Section requires the auditor to assess the risks of material noncompliance, whether due to error or fraud, for each applicable compliance requirement and to consider the pervasiveness of those risks to the entity's compliance. The application guidance and explanatory material lists the following factors that auditors may consider in assessing the risks of material noncompliance with the applicable requirements:

- The complexity of the requirement;
- The susceptibility of the requirement to noncompliance;
- The length of time that the entity has been subject to the requirement;
- The auditor's observations about compliance/noncompliance in previous years;
- The potential effect of noncompliance on the entity;
- The degree of judgment involved; and
- The auditor's assessment of the risks of material misstatement in the financial statement audit.

When performing a compliance audit, the auditor may identify a risk of material noncompliance that is pervasive to the entity's compliance. For example, the risk that grant funds will be diverted for unauthorized purposes might be higher in an entity that is experiencing financial difficulty. If the auditor identifies risks of material noncompliance that are pervasive to the entity's compliance, the auditor should develop an overall response to those risks. The auditor's overall response may include emphasizing to the audit team the need to maintain professional skepticism, assigning more experienced staff or those with specialized skills, providing more supervision, or incorporating additional elements of unpredictability in the selection of further audit procedures to be performed.

In addition, the auditor should design and perform further audit procedures in response to the assessed risks of material noncompliance. This Section indicates that these procedures should include the following:

- Tests of details, which may include tests of transactions, to obtain sufficient appropriate audit evidence about compliance with each applicable compliance requirement. The application guidance and explanatory material suggests that tests of details and/or tests of transactions may be performed in the following areas:
  - Grant disbursements or expenditures;
  - Eligibility files;
  - Cost allocation plans; and
  - Periodic reports filed with grantor agencies.
- Tests of controls over compliance (including tests of the operating effectiveness of controls over each applicable compliance requirement) if *any* of the following conditions are met:
  - The auditor's risk assessment includes an expectation of the operating effectiveness of controls over compliance.
  - Substantive procedures do not by themselves provide sufficient appropriate audit evidence.
  - A governmental audit requirement mandates tests of controls over compliance.

PRACTICE POINT: Risk assessment procedures, tests of controls, and analytical procedures alone are not sufficient to address the risk of material noncompliance. In addition, the use of analytical procedures to obtain substantive evidence is generally less effective in a compliance audit than it is in a financial statement audit. Nonetheless, when used in conjunction with tests of transactions or other auditing procedures, they may contribute some evidence.

Supplementary Audit Requirements

This Section requires auditors to determine whether audit requirements that are supplementary to GAAS and GAGAS are specified, and to perform procedures to address those requirements, if any. Examples of such additional requirements are the requirements in OMB Circular A-133 for the auditor to perform specified procedures to identify major programs, and to follow up on prior audit findings and assess the reasonableness of the summary schedule of prior audit findings.

In addition, this Section makes it clear that auditors should comply with the most current applicable GAAS and GAGAS in cases where audit guidance provided by a governmental agency for performing compliance audits is either in conflict with or has not been updated to conform to changes in those standards.

Written Representations from Management

Written representations from management are not a substitute for other audit procedures but, nevertheless, represent an essential component of audit evidence. This Section requires the auditor to obtain written representations from management related to the entity's compliance with the applicable compliance requirements in which management:

1. Acknowledges its responsibility for:

   a. Understanding and complying with the compliance requirements;

   b. Establishing and maintaining controls that provide reasonable assurance that the entity administers government programs in accordance with the compliance requirements; and

   c. Taking corrective action on audit findings of the compliance audit.

2. States that it has disclosed to the auditor:

   a. All of its government programs and related activities (that management has identified) subject to the governmental audit requirement;

   b. All known noncompliance with the applicable compliance requirements or stating that there was no such noncompliance;

   c. Any communications from grantors and pass-through entities concerning possible noncompliance with the applicable compliance requirements, including communications received from the end of the period covered by the compliance audit to the date of the auditor's report;

d. The findings received and related corrective actions taken for previous audits, attestation engagements, and internal or external monitoring that directly relate to the objectives of the compliance audit, including findings received and corrective actions taken from the end of the period covered by the compliance audit to the date of the auditor's report; and

e. All known noncompliance with the applicable compliance requirements subsequent to the period covered by the auditor's report or stating that there were no such known instances.

3. States that it has made available to the auditor:

a. All contracts and grant agreements, including amendments, if any, and any other correspondence relevant to the programs and related activities subject to the governmental audit requirement; and

b. All documentation related to compliance with the applicable compliance requirements.

4. States whether it believes that the entity has complied with the applicable compliance requirements, except for noncompliance it has disclosed to the auditor.

5. Identifies its interpretation of any applicable compliance requirements that are subject to varying interpretations.

Management's written representations should be tailored to the entity and the governmental audit requirement. Representations other than those specifically required should be requested if the auditor determines that they are necessary.

Management may sometimes add qualifying language to its representations to the effect that they are made "to the best of management's knowledge and belief." According to the application guidance and explanatory material in this Section, such language is not appropriate for the representations related to management's responsibility for:

- Understanding and complying with the compliance requirements;
- Establishing and maintaining controls that provide reasonable assurance that the entity administers government programs in accordance with the compliance requirements; and
- Taking corrective action on audit findings of the compliance audit.

Subsequent Events Procedures

This Section requires the auditor to perform audit procedures up to the date of the auditor's report to obtain sufficient appropriate audit evidence that subsequent events related to compliance during the period covered by the auditor's report on compliance have been identified. The types of subsequent events that the auditor is concerned with fall into the following categories:

- *Events that provide additional evidence about conditions that existed at the end of the reporting period that affect the entity's compliance during the reporting period.*

- *Events of noncompliance that did not exist at the end of the reporting period, but arose subsequent to the reporting period*—Before the report release date, the auditor may become aware of noncompliance in the period subsequent to the period covered by the auditor's report. Depending on the nature and significance of the noncompliance, the auditor may determine that its disclosure is necessary to prevent report users from being misled. An example of such an event would be the discovery of noncompliance in the subsequent period serious enough to cause the grantor to cease funding a program. In such circumstances that warrant disclosure, the auditor is required to discuss the matter with management, and if appropriate, with those charged with governance, and include an explanatory paragraph in the auditor's report describing the nature of the noncompliance.

In determining the nature and extent of subsequent event procedures to be performed, the auditor is required to take into account the auditor's risk assessment. Nonetheless, such subsequent event procedures should include, at a minimum, inquiries of management about and considerations of:

- The following reports, if any, pertaining to noncompliance that were issued during the subsequent period: (a) relevant internal auditors' reports; (b) other auditors' reports; and (c) reports from grantors and pass-through entities.

- Information about the entity's noncompliance obtained through other professional engagements performed for the entity.

Evaluating the Audit Evidence and Forming an Opinion

In determining and opining on whether an entity has materially complied with the applicable compliance requirements, this Section requires the auditor to:

- Evaluate the sufficiency and appropriateness of the audit evidence obtained;

- Form an opinion, at the level specified by the governmental audit requirement, on whether the entity complied in all material respects with the applicable compliance requirements, and report appropriately; and

- Evaluate known questioned costs, likely questioned costs, and other material instances of noncompliance that may not result in questioned costs in forming the opinion. This includes consideration of all material noncompliance, regardless of whether the entity subsequently corrected it.

The application guidance and explanatory material offers the following factors for the auditor's consideration in determining whether an entity has materially complied with the applicable compliance requirements:

- The frequency of noncompliance identified;

- The nature of the noncompliance;

- The adequacy of the entity's system for monitoring compliance;

- The potential effect of any noncompliance on the entity; and

- Whether identified noncompliance resulted in likely questioned costs that are material to the government program.

Reporting Requirements

This Section lists in detail the components that are required in the several types of auditor's reports. These report types are:

- A report on compliance only;
- A combined report on compliance and internal control over compliance; and
- A separate report on internal control over compliance.

The required elements for each type of report are described below.

Required elements in a report on compliance only In a report on compliance only, the auditor's report should include the following:

1. A title that includes the word *independent*.

2. Identification of the following:

    a. The one or more government programs covered by the compliance audit or reference to a separate schedule containing that information;

    b. The applicable compliance requirements or a reference to where they can be found; and

    c. The period covered by the auditor's report.

3. A statement that compliance with the applicable compliance requirements is management's responsibility.

4. A statement that the auditor's responsibility is to express an opinion on the entity's compliance with the applicable compliance requirements based on the compliance audit.

5. A statement that the compliance audit:

    a. Was conducted in accordance with auditing standards generally accepted in the United States of America, the standards applicable to financial audits contained in *Government Auditing Standards,* and the governmental audit requirement;

    b. Included examining, on a test basis, evidence about the entity's compliance with those requirements and performing such other procedures as considered necessary in the circumstances; and

    c. Does not provide a legal determination of the entity's compliance.

6. A statement that the auditor believes the compliance audit provides a reasonable basis for his or her opinion.

7. The auditor's opinion, at the level specified by the governmental audit requirement, on whether the entity complied, in all material respects, with the applicable compliance requirements.

8. If the auditor's opinion is modified as a result of identified noncompliance, a description of such noncompliance or a reference to a description of such noncompliance in an accompanying schedule.

9. If noncompliance that does not result in an opinion modification is identified but that is required to be reported by the governmental audit requirement, a description of such noncompliance or a reference to a description of such noncompliance in an accompanying schedule.

10. A separate paragraph at the end of the report that includes restricted-use language if the criteria used to evaluate compliance are:

    a. Established or determined by contractual agreement or regulatory provisions that are developed solely for the parties to the agreement or regulatory agency responsible for the provisions; *or*

    b. Available only to the specified parties.

11. Manual or printed signature of the auditor's firm.

12. Date of the auditor's report.

Required elements in a combined report on compliance and internal control over compliance There may be circumstances in which the governmental audit requirement requires the auditor to report on internal control over compliance. In such situations, the auditor may combine the auditor's report on compliance with a report on internal control over compliance. If the auditor issues a combined report on compliance and internal control over compliance, this Section requires the auditor to add the following elements to the ones listed above for a report on compliance only:

1. A statement that:

    a. Management is responsible for establishing and maintaining effective internal control over compliance with the requirements of laws, regulations, rules, and provisions of contracts or grant agreements applicable to government programs.

    b. The auditor considered the entity's internal control over compliance with the applicable compliance requirements to determine the auditing procedures for the purpose of expressing an opinion on compliance, but not for the purpose of expressing an opinion on the effectiveness of internal control over compliance.

    c. The auditor is not expressing an opinion on internal control over compliance.

    d. The auditor's consideration of the entity's internal control over compliance was not designed to identify all deficiencies in internal control that might be significant deficiencies or material weaknesses in internal control over compliance.

2. The definition of "deficiency in internal control over compliance" and "material weakness in internal control over compliance."

3. A description of any material weaknesses in internal control over compliance that have been identified or a reference to an accompanying schedule that contains such a description.

4. If significant deficiencies in internal control over compliance were identified, the definition of "significant deficiency in internal control over

compliance" and a description of the deficiencies or a reference to an accompanying schedule that contains such a description.

5. If no material weaknesses in internal control over compliance were identified, a statement to that effect.

6. A restricted-use paragraph.

See Illustration 1 for an auditor's combined report on compliance and internal control over compliance. This reporting example presents an unqualified opinion on compliance with no material weaknesses or significant deficiencies in internal control over compliance. The AICPA Audit Guide, *Government Auditing Standards and Circular A-133 Audits*, contains illustrative language for other types of reports in which other than an unqualified opinion is issued, or significant deficiencies or material weaknesses are identified.

Required elements in a separate report on internal control over compliance There may be circumstances in which the governmental audit requirement requires the auditor to report on internal control over compliance and the auditor may choose to issue a separate report on internal control over compliance. In such situations, this Section requires the auditor to include in that separate report the six elements described above for a combined report and the following additional elements:

1. A title that includes the word *independent*.

2. A statement that the auditor audited the entity's compliance with applicable compliance requirements pertaining to [*identify the government program(s) and the period audited*] and a reference to the auditor's report on compliance.

3. A statement that the compliance audit was conducted in accordance with auditing standards generally accepted in the United States of America, the standards applicable to financial audits contained in *Government Auditing Standards*, and the governmental audit requirement.

4. Manual or printed signature of the auditor's firm.

5. Date of the auditor's report.

Other reporting requirements and considerations In addition to the required reporting elements in the various types of the auditor's reports discussed above, this Section requires the auditor to:

- Report noncompliance and other matters that are required to be reported, and in the manner specified, by the governmental audit requirement.

- Modify his or her opinion on compliance if the audit identifies material noncompliance, or there is a restriction on the scope of the compliance audit.

- Modify the auditor's report when making reference to the report of another auditor as the basis, in part, for the auditor's report.

- Issue a written communication to management and those charged with governance when significant deficiencies or material weaknesses in internal control over compliance are identified and the governmental audit requirement does not otherwise require them to be reported. This communication is comparable to the communication made in a financial statement audit under AU Section 325. Under GAGAS, the auditor is also required to obtain a response from responsible officials, preferably in writing, to the auditor's findings, conclusions and recommendations, and to include a copy of a written response in the auditor's report. In such cases, the auditor may include a paragraph in his or her written communication disclaiming an opinion on that response.

- Communicate to those charged with governance (a) the auditor's responsibilities under GAAS, GAGAS, and the governmental audit requirement, (b) an overview of the planned scope and timing of the compliance audit, and (c) significant findings. This communication is comparable to the communication made in a financial statement audit under AU Section 380 (The Auditor's Communication with Those Charged with Governance).

In addition, if a printed form, schedule, or report designed by a government agency requires an auditor to make a statement that he or she has no basis to make, or if a governmental audit requirement requires other matters to be reported on that are not appropriate, the auditor is required to attach an appropriately worded separate report, or reword the governmental agency's form, schedule, or report. The auditor may, in such cases, include a separate communication to the agency explaining why the auditor's report was modified.

Reissuance of the compliance report An auditor might reissue his or her compliance report, for example, if a quality control review performed by a government agency indicates that the auditor did not test an applicable compliance requirement, or if subsequent to the date of the compliance report another government program was discovered that was required to be tested. If an auditor reissues his or her compliance report, this Section requires the auditor to include an explanatory paragraph in the reissued report that:

- States that the report is replacing a previously issued report;
- Describes the reasons why the report is being reissued; and
- Describes any changes from the previous report.

The report date should be updated to reflect the date that the auditor obtained sufficient appropriate evidence, if additional procedures are performed for all of the government programs being reported. If additional procedures are performed for only some of the government programs being reported, the reissued report should be dual dated, retaining the original date for those programs not affected.

This Section states that the reissuance of an auditor-prepared document required by a governmental audit requirement that is incorporated by reference into the auditor's report, such as the schedule of findings and questioned costs required by OMB Circular A-133, is considered to be a reissuance of the report.

Specific Audit Documentation Requirements

This Section contains requirements to document the following four specific items:

1. The risk assessment procedures performed, including those related to obtaining an understanding of internal control over compliance;

2. Responses to the assessed risks of material noncompliance, including procedures performed to test compliance, tests of controls over compliance, and the results of those tests;

3. Materiality levels and the basis on which they were determined; and

4. How the auditor complied with the supplementary governmental audit requirements, if any.

PRACTICE ISSUES AND FREQUENTLY ASKED QUESTIONS

Issue 1: When adapting and applying the various AU Sections to a compliance audit, is the auditor required or expected to adapt and apply all the audit procedures prescribed in those AU Sections?

No. Because the various AU Sections often identify audit procedures and contain examples that are specific to a financial statement audit, the auditor is neither required nor expected to adapt or apply all such procedures to the compliance audit. However, the auditor should adapt and apply those procedures that, in the auditor's professional judgment, are relevant and necessary to meet the objectives of the compliance audit.

Issue 2: Is the auditor's consideration of materiality in a compliance audit the same as that in an audit of the financial statements?

No. In a financial statement audit, the auditor is concerned with materiality at the financial statement and account balance or transaction level. In a compliance audit, the auditor's consideration of materiality is in relation to the government program taken as a whole and is usually influenced by the needs of users as a group, including the needs of grantors.

Issue 3: What are general examples of "questioned costs" for purposes of reporting in a compliance audit?

What constitutes questioned costs depends on the specific government program or compliance requirement, and varies from one agency to another. However, questioned costs generally include unallowable costs, undocumented costs, unapproved costs, and unreasonable costs. The following are examples of expenses that usually would be considered questioned costs if charged to funded programs:

- Penalties and interest
- Fund-raising expenses
- Entertainment expenses
- Expenditures that exceed the funding source's budget guidelines
- Expenditures that cannot be substantiated (e.g., supporting invoices or canceled checks cannot be located)

Issue 4: How can the auditor make a determination and issue an opinion on compliance, which might be construed as a legal opinion?

The standard wording in the auditor's report contains a statement that the compliance audit does not provide a legal determination of the entity's compliance. Within the context of the assurance that the auditor is asked to provide under this Section, it is understood that he or she, although not trained as an attorney, has specific expertise that confers the ability to render an opinion on compliance that stops short of a legal determination.

Issue 5: Do provisions of the OMB's Compliance Supplement that are pertinent to a client's federal awards provide a sufficient basis for the auditor's determination of the compliance requirements for those awards?

No. Auditors are widely cautioned that the OMB's Compliance Supplements are not updated with each change in program compliance requirements. Accordingly, the auditor is well advised to read the award documents and to check with the awarding agencies (or determine that the client has done so) to ascertain that the most current compliance requirements have been identified. In addition, a program that does not appear in the OMB's Compliance Supplement may still have compliance requirements. Furthermore, when an award is passed through a state or local government agency, these agencies sometimes impose compliance requirements in addition to those originating at the federal level. Therefore, a careful reading of each award document is necessary.

Issue 6: Is the auditor required or expected to prepare specific documentation of how he or she adapted and applied each of the applicable AU Sections to the objectives of a compliance audit?

No. The documentation of the audit strategy, audit plan, and work performed cumulatively and adequately demonstrate whether the auditor has complied with the documentation requirements prescribed in this Section.

ILLUSTRATIONS AND PRACTICE AIDS

ILLUSTRATION 1—AUDITOR'S COMBINED REPORT ON COMPLIANCE AND INTERNAL CONTROL OVER COMPLIANCE

Independent Auditor's Report

[*Governing Body or Board*]
[*Entity*]

Compliance

We have audited [*Entity Name*]'s compliance with the [*identify the applicable compliance requirements, or refer to the document that describes the applicable compliance requirements*] applicable to [*Entity Name*]'s [*identify the government program(s) audited, or refer to a separate schedule that identifies the program(s)*] for the year ended June 30, 20X1. Compliance with the requirements referred to above is the responsibility of [*Entity Name*]'s management. Our responsibility is to express an opinion on [*Entity Name*]'s compliance based on our audit.

We conducted our audit of compliance in accordance with auditing standards generally accepted in the United States of America; the standards applicable to financial audits contained in *Government Auditing Standards* issued by the Comptroller General of the United States; and [*insert the name of the governmental audit requirement or program-specific audit guide*]. Those standards and [*insert the name of the governmental audit requirement or program-specific audit guide*] require that we plan and perform the audit to obtain reasonable assurance about whether noncompliance with the compliance requirements referred to above that could have a material effect on [*identify the government program(s) audited, or refer to a separate schedule that identifies the program(s)*]. An audit includes examining, on a test basis, evidence about

[*Entity Name*]'s compliance with those requirements and performing such other procedures as we considered necessary in the circumstances. We believe that our audit provides a reasonable basis for our opinion. Our audit does not provide a legal determination of [*Entity Name*]'s compliance with those requirements.

In our opinion, [*Entity Name*]complied, in all material respects, with the compliance requirements referred to above that are applicable to [*identify the government program(s) audited*] for the year ended June 30, 20X1.

Internal Control over Compliance

Management of [*Entity Name*]is responsible for establishing and maintaining effective internal control over compliance with the compliance requirements referred to above. In planning and performing our audit, we considered [*Entity Name*]'s internal control over compliance to determine the auditing procedures for the purpose of expressing our opinion on compliance, but not for the purpose of expressing an opinion on the effectiveness of internal control over compliance. Accordingly, we do not express an opinion on the effectiveness of [*Entity Name*]'s internal control over compliance.

A *deficiency in internal control over compliance* exists when the design or operation of a control does not allow management or employees, in the normal course of performing their assigned functions, to prevent, or detect and correct, noncompliance on a timely basis. A *material weakness* in internal control over compliance is a deficiency, or combination of deficiencies in internal control over compliance, such that there is a reasonable possibility that material noncompliance with a compliance requirement will not be prevented, or detected and corrected, on a timely basis.

Our consideration of internal control over compliance was for the limited purpose described in the first paragraph of this section and was not designed to identify all deficiencies in internal control that might be deficiencies, significant deficiencies, or material weaknesses in internal control over compliance. We did not identify any deficiencies in internal control over compliance that we consider to be material weaknesses, as defined above.

This report is intended solely for the information and use of management, [*identify the body or individuals charged with governance*], others within the entity, [*identify the legislative or regulatory body*], and [*identify the grantor agency(ies)*]and is not intended to be and should not be used by anyone other than these specified parties.

[*Signature*]

[*Date*]

AU Section 900
SPECIAL REPORTS OF THE COMMITTEE ON AUDITING PROCEDURE

AU SECTION 901
PUBLIC WAREHOUSES—CONTROLS AND AUDITING PROCEDURES FOR GOODS HELD

PRACTICE POINT: The American Institute of Certified Public Accountants' (AICPA's) Auditing Standards Board (ASB) has finalized a clarified Statement on Auditing Standards (SAS) titled, "Audit Evidence—Specific Considerations for Selected Items," which supersedes:

- AU Section 331 (Inventories);
- AU Section 332 (Auditing Derivative Instruments, Hedging Activities and Investments in Securities);
- AU Section 337 (Inquiry of a Client's Lawyer Concerning Litigation, Claims, and Assessments);
- AU Section 337A (Appendix—Illustrative Audit Inquiry Letter to Legal Counsel); and
- AU Section 337C (Exhibit II—American Bar Association Statement of Policy Regarding Lawyers' Responses to Auditors' Requests for Information).

The clarified SAS also rescinds AU Section 337B (Exhibit I—Excerpts from Financial Accounting Standards Board Accounting Standards Codification 450, Contingencies) and AU Section 901 (Public Warehouses—Controls and Auditing Procedures for Goods Held).

The following are noteworthy changes from extant GAAS:

- The clarified SAS combines the requirements and guidance from extant AU Sections 331, 332, and 337.
- Many of the requirements of extant AU Section 332 are essentially the same as requirements in other clarified standards, primarily the risk assessment standards and the clarified SAS, "Auditing Accounting Estimates, Including Fair Value Accounting Estimates and Related Disclosures." Therefore, the ASB concluded that the application of those requirements in the other clarified standards to the subject matter addressed by extant AU Section 332 is most appropriately addressed as interpretative guidance in the AICPA Audit Guide, *Auditing Derivative Instruments, Hedging Activities, and Investments in Securities*. Consideration of these requirements and related application guidance will be a specific focus in updating the audit guide.
- Requirements and guidance addressing auditing investments accounted for using the equity method have been excluded from this clarified SAS because the auditing of equity investees is addressed more broadly by the clarified SAS, "Special Considerations—Audits of Group Financial Statements (Including the Work of Component Auditors)."
- Extant AU Section 337 states, in part, that "the auditor should request the client's management to send a letter of inquiry to those lawyers with whom management consulted concerning litigation, claims, and assessments." In contrast, the clarified SAS takes a more principles-based approach and requires the auditor to seek direct communication with the entity's external legal counsel (through a letter of inquiry) if the auditor

assesses a risk of material misstatement regarding litigation or claims, or when audit procedures performed indicate that material litigation or claims may exist.

The ASB is expected to issue many of the clarified standards in *one* SAS that will be codified in "AU Section" format. The ASB has decided that the effective date of the clarified SASs that have not yet been issued is for audits of financial statements for periods ending on or after December 15, 2012. Auditors should be alert to and monitor further developments in this area.

WHAT EVERY PRACTITIONER SHOULD KNOW

Basic Objectives and Requirements

This Section discusses controls of a public warehouse and provides guidance about the procedures to be performed by an auditor of:

1. The public warehouse with respect to goods in the warehouse's custody.
2. The owner of goods in the public warehouse.

A primary document in warehousing is the warehouse receipt. Article 7 of the Uniform Commercial Code regulates the issuance of warehouse receipts, prescribes certain terms that must be contained in such receipts, provides for their negotiation and transfer, and establishes the rights of receipt holders. Warehouse receipts may be in negotiable form or non-negotiable form and may be used as evidence of collateral for loans or other forms of credit.

Illustration 1 is an internal control checklist for public warehouses, based on elements discussed in this Section. Illustration 2 is an internal control checklist for an owner of goods stored in public warehouses, based on elements discussed in this Section.

Procedures of the Auditor of the Warehouseman

The auditor of a public warehouse should perform the following procedures:

1. Obtain an understanding of controls relating to the accountability for and the custody of all goods placed in the warehouse and perform tests of controls to evaluate their effectiveness.
2. Test the warehouseman's records relating to accountability for all goods placed in his or her custody.
3. Test the warehouseman's accountability under recorded outstanding warehouse receipts. Such procedures might include, on a test basis:
   a. Comparing documentary evidence of goods received and delivered with warehouse receipts records;
   b. Accounting for issued and unissued warehouse receipts by number; and
   c. Comparing records of goods stored with billings for storage.
4. Observe physical counts of the goods in custody and reconcile tests of such counts with records of goods stored. In the case of field warehouses

where goods are stored at many scattered locations, the auditor may observe the procedures at certain selected locations.

5. Confirm accountability by direct communication with the holders of warehouse receipts.

6. Review the nature and extent of insurance coverage.

7. Review the adequacy of any reserves for losses under damage claims.

8. Apply such other procedures as may be considered necessary in the circumstances.

Procedures of the Auditor of the Owner of Goods Stored in Public Warehouses

Generally, direct confirmation with the custodian of inventory held in public warehouses provides sufficient evidence to validate the existence and ownership of the inventory. However, if such inventory is significant in relation to current assets and total assets, the auditor should supplement confirmation of the inventory with the performance of additional procedures such as the following:

1. Test the client's control activities used in investigating and evaluating the performance of the warehouseman.

2. Observe the warehouseman's or client's count of goods whenever practical and reasonable.

3. If warehouse receipts have been pledged as collateral, confirm details with the lenders.

4. Obtain an independent auditor's report on the warehouseman's system of internal control relevant to custody of goods and, if applicable, pledge of receipts, or apply alternative procedures at the warehouse to gain reasonable assurance that information received from the warehouseman is reliable.

PRACTICE ISSUES AND FREQUENTLY ASKED QUESTIONS

Issue 1: What procedures should an auditor perform with respect to a client that has pledged the warehouse receipts for certain inventory as collateral for a bank loan?

The auditor should confirm the details of the warehouse receipts with the warehouse and the bank and reconcile any differences with the client's records. Also, the auditor should read the financing arrangement with the bank and confirm the terms and the outstanding balance at the balance sheet date. With this information available, the client's portion of the payment for the inventory, plus the amount of the advance from the bank should equal the stated cost of the goods. Because these arrangements are usually short term financing devices, tests of subsequent sale of the inventory, release from the warehouse, and liquidation of the related advances should also be feasible.

Issue 2: Is the report of an outside inventory-taking firm that takes independent inventory counts a satisfactory substitute for the auditor's own observation of the physical count of inventory?

No. The auditor's responsibility with regard to the count and other tasks performed by an inventory-taking company is similar to the tasks that normally would be performed directly by the client. Therefore, the report from an outside company that takes independent inventory counts is not, by itself, a satisfactory substitute for the auditor's own observation of the physical count of inventory. In such circumstances, the auditor should:

- Review the outside firm's inventory-counting program.
- Observe the outside firm's inventory counting procedures and controls.
- Make or observe a test of physical counts.
- Recompute calculations of the submitted inventory on a test basis.
- Apply appropriate tests to the intervening transactions, if applicable.

The auditor ordinarily may reduce, but not eliminate, the extent of his or her work on the physical count of inventory if the procedures of the outside firm are deemed satisfactory.

Issue 3: May the auditor use the work of a specialist to determine whether certain special inventory actually is as represented by the client?

Yes. If the auditor is unfamiliar with the identification or measurement of quantity or quality of certain inventory (e.g., precious metals, diamonds, coal piles), the auditor may find it necessary to obtain the services of specialists to determine whether the inventory actually is as represented by the client. In these circumstances, the auditor should refer to AU Section 336 (Using the Work of a Specialist) for the appropriate procedures to be followed.

ILLUSTRATIONS AND PRACTICE AIDS

ILLUSTRATION 1—INTERNAL CONTROL CHECKLIST FOR PUBLIC WAREHOUSES

	Yes	No	N/A
Receiving, Storing, and Delivering Goods			
1. Are receipts issued for all goods admitted into storage?	___	___	___
2. Do receiving clerks prepare reports for all goods received?	___	___	___
3. Are receiving reports compared with quantities shown on bills of lading or other documents received from the owner or other outside sources by an employee independent of receiving, storing, and shipping?	___	___	___
4. Are goods received inspected, counted, weighed, measured, or graded in accordance with applicable requirements?	___	___	___
5. Is a periodic check performed of the accuracy of any mechanical facilities used for inspecting, counting, weighing, measuring or grading goods?	___	___	___
6. Are goods stored so that each lot is segregated and identified with the pertinent warehouse receipt, unless commingling is unavoidable?	___	___	___

	Yes	No	N/A

7. Do the warehouse office records show the location of the goods represented by each outstanding receipt?

8. Are instructions issued that goods may be released only on proper authorization including, where applicable, surrender of the receipt?

9. Is access to the storage area limited to those employees whose duties require it, and is the custody of keys controlled?

10. Do periodic statements to customers identify the goods held and request that discrepancies be reported to a specified employee who is not connected with receiving, storing, and delivery of goods?

11. Are stored goods physically counted or tested periodically, and quantities agreed to the records by an employee independent of the storage function?

12. Where the goods held are perishable, is a regular schedule for inspection of condition established?

13. Are protective devices such as burglar alarms, fire alarms, sprinkler systems, and temperature and humidity controls inspected regularly?

14. Are goods released from the warehouse only on the basis of written instructions received from an authorized employee who does not have access to the goods?

15. Are counts of goods released, as made by stock clerks, independently checked by shipping clerks or others, and the two counts compared before the goods are released?

Warehouse Receipts

16. Are prenumbered receipt forms used, and procedures established for accounting for all forms used and for cancellation of negotiable receipts when goods have been delivered?

17. Are unused forms safeguarded against theft or misuse and their custody assigned to a responsible employee who is not authorized to prepare or sign receipts?

18. Are receipt forms furnished only to authorized persons, and in a quantity limited to the number required for current use?

19. Does the signer of receipts ascertain that the receipts are supported by receiving records or other underlying documents?

20. Are receipts prepared and completed in a manner designed to prevent alteration?

21. Is the number of authorized signers limited to a few responsible employees?

Insurance

	Yes	No	N/A
22. Is the adequacy, as to both type and amount, of insurance coverage carried reviewed at appropriate intervals?			

Additional Controls for Field Warehouses

	Yes	No	N/A
23. Has adequate consideration been given to the business reputation and financial standing of the depositor?			
24. Has a field warehouse contract been prepared in accordance with the particular requirements of the depositor and the lender?			
25. Do the leased warehouse premises meet the physical requirements for segregation and effective custody of goods?			
26. Have legal matters been satisfied relative to the lease of the warehouse premises?			
27. Are background checks performed on employees at the field locations?			
28. Are employees at the field locations bonded?			
29. Are employees at field locations provided with written instructions covering their duties and responsibilities?			
30. Are inventory records maintained at the central office and do they show the quantity (and stated value, where applicable) of goods represented by each outstanding warehouse receipt?			
31. Is the field warehouse examined by representatives of the central office?			
32. Does the field warehouse examination by representatives of the central office include the following:			
a. Inspection of the facilities?			
b. Observation as to adherence to prescribed procedures?			
c. Physical counts or tests of goods in custody?			
d. Reconcilement of quantities to records at the central office and at field locations?			
e. Accounting for all receipt forms furnished to the field locations?			
f. Confirmation (on a test basis, where appropriate) of outstanding warehouse receipts with the registered holders?			

ILLUSTRATION 2—INTERNAL CONTROL CHECKLIST FOR AN OWNER OF GOODS STORED IN PUBLIC WAREHOUSES

	Yes	No	N/A

Controls before Placing the Goods in a Warehouseman's Custody

1. Has adequate consideration been given to the business reputation and financial standing of the warehouseman? ____ ____ ____

2. Has an inspection been conducted of the physical facilities? ____ ____ ____

3. Have inquiries been made as to the warehouseman's controls and whether the warehouseman holds goods for his own account? ____ ____ ____

4. Have inquiries been made as to type and adequacy of the warehouseman's insurance? ____ ____ ____

5. Have inquiries been made as to government or other licensing and bonding requirements? ____ ____ ____

6. Have inquiries been made about the nature, extent, and results of any inspection by government or other agencies? ____ ____ ____

7. Has a review been made of the warehouseman's financial statements and related reports of independent auditors? ____ ____ ____

Controls after Placing the Goods in a Warehouseman's Custody

8. Is the information developed from the procedures in items 1–7 above reviewed and updated as necessary? ____ ____ ____

9. Are physical counts, or test counts, of the goods taken periodically? ____ ____ ____

10. Are quantities shown on statements received from the warehouseman reconciled with the owner's records? ____ ____ ____

11. Is the adequacy of insurance on goods in the custody of the warehouseman reviewed periodically? ____ ____ ____

ILLUSTRATION 3—REQUEST FOR CONFIRMATION OF INVENTORIES HELD BY WAREHOUSES OR OTHER THIRD PARTIES WHEN LISTING OF INVENTORIES IS PROVIDED BY THE CLIENT AND ENCLOSED WITH THE CONFIRMATION REQUEST

(*Prepared on client's letterhead*)

(*Date*)

(*Name and address of warehouse or other third party*)

Dear _____:

Our auditors (*insert name and address of auditors*) are conducting an audit of our financial statements as of (*insert date*) and for the (*insert period [e.g., year, quarter]*) then ended. We have furnished our auditors with a copy of the attached listing, which reflects the inventory held by you for our account as of (*insert date*). Accordingly, please review the listing carefully and confirm directly to our auditors the information requested below as of (*insert date*).

After completing the information in the space provided below, please sign and date your reply and mail it directly to our auditors in the enclosed return envelope.

Thank you for your anticipated timely cooperation with this request.

Respectfully,

(Name of client)

(Client's authorized signature and title)

****

RESPONSE:

To: *(Insert auditor's name)*

1. The enclosed inventory listing is in agreement with our records as of *(insert date)* with the following exceptions, if any. (If no exceptions are noted, please state "None.")

   _____

   _____

   _____

2. The correctness of the quantities we are confirming to you was determined as follows (please check the appropriate items):

   _____ Physical count

   _____ Weight

   _____ Measure

   _____ Book record only

   _____ Other (specify) _____

3. The following is a list of negotiable and nonnegotiable warehouse receipts issued. (If none were issued, please state "None.") Also, please state whether such receipts have, to your knowledge, been assigned or pledged.

   _____

   _____

   _____

4. The following are known liens against the merchandise. (If none are known to your knowledge, please state "None.")

   _____

   _____

   _____

5. The amount of unpaid charges, if any, as of *(insert date)* is $_____.

Signature: _____

Title: _____

Date: _____

ILLUSTRATION 4—REQUEST FOR CONFIRMATION OF INVENTORIES HELD BY WAREHOUSES OR OTHER THIRD PARTIES WHEN LISTING OF INVENTORIES IS NOT PROVIDED BY THE CLIENT AND NOT EN-CLOSED WITH THE CONFIRMATION REQUEST

(Prepared on client's letterhead)

(Date)

(Name and address of warehouse or other third party)

Dear _____:

Our auditors (*insert name and address of auditors*) are conducting an audit of our financial statements as of (*insert date*) and for the (*insert period [e.g., year, quarter]*) then ended. Please furnish directly to our auditors the information requested below about merchandise held in your custody for our account as of (*insert date*):

1. Quantities on hand, including:

   a. Lot number

   b. Date received

   c. Type of merchandise

   d. Unit of measure or package including number of units and kind of units (e.g., box, can, dozen)

In addition to the above-requested quantities, please complete the information requested below with respect to the merchandise. After completing the information requested, please sign and date your reply and mail it directly to our auditors in the enclosed return envelope.

Thank you for your anticipated timely cooperation with this request.

Respectfully,

(Name of client)

(Client's authorized signature and title)

****

RESPONSE:

To: *(Insert auditor's name)*

1. The correctness of the quantities we are confirming to you was determined as follows (please check the appropriate items):

   _____ Physical count

   _____ Weight

   _____ Measure

   _____ Book record only

   _____ Other (specify) _____

2. The following is a list of negotiable and nonnegotiable warehouse receipts issued (if none were issued, please state "None"). Also, please state whether such receipts have, to your knowledge, been assigned or pledged.

   _____

   _____

   _____

3. The following are known liens against the merchandise. (If none are known to your knowledge, please state "None.")

   _____

   _____

4. The amount of unpaid charges, if any, as of *(insert date)* is $_____.

Signature: _____

Title: _____

Date: _____

AT Section
STATEMENTS ON STANDARDS FOR ATTESTATION ENGAGEMENTS

AT SECTION 20
DEFINING PROFESSIONAL REQUIREMENTS IN STATEMENTS ON STANDARDS FOR ATTESTATION ENGAGEMENTS

WHAT EVERY PRACTITIONER SHOULD KNOW

Basic Objectives and Requirements

This Section defines the terminology the AICPA uses to describe the degree of responsibility that the attestation standards impose on practitioners. It specifically defines two types of responsibility that the standards impose on practitioners: (1) unconditional responsibility to comply with a requirement in all cases, for which responsibility is communicated by the terms "must" or "is required" and (2) presumptive responsibility to comply with a requirement in all cases, for which responsibility is communicated by the term "should" and places the burden of proof on the practitioner if he or she departs from the presumptive requirement.

Categories of Professional Requirements

This Section uses, describes, and imposes the following two categories of professional requirements on the practitioner:

- *Unconditional requirements*—The practitioner is required to comply with a requirement in all cases in which the circumstances exist to which the requirement applies. An unconditional requirement is indicated by the words "must" or "is required."

- *Presumptively mandatory requirements*—The practitioner is also required to comply with a presumptively mandatory requirement in all cases in which the circumstances exist to which the presumptively mandatory requirement applies. In rare circumstances, the practitioner may depart from a presumptively mandatory requirement provided he or she documents the justification for departure and how alternative procedures performed in the circumstances were sufficient to achieve the objectives of the presumptively mandatory requirement. A presumptively mandatory requirement is indicated by the word "should."

The following is a summary of the imperatives/terms used in this Section and the degrees of responsibility they impose on practitioners:

Imperatives/Terms	What They Mean
"must" and "is required"	These words impose an unconditional responsibility or requirement on the practitioner to comply with requirements of this type specified in professional standards.
"should"	This indicates a presumptively mandatory requirement. Compliance with requirements of this type specified in professional standards is required, unless the practitioner can demonstrate that the alternative procedures or actions that he or she applied were appropriate and sufficient to accomplish the objectives of the particular standard.
"should consider"	This indicates that the consideration of the procedure or action provided in professional standards is presumptively required; however, carrying out the action or procedure is not required.
"may," "might," and "could"	These words do not impose a professional requirement for the practitioner to perform the suggested procedures or actions. Rather, these words impose on the practitioner a responsibility to consider certain actions, procedures, or matters specified in professional standards. Whether and how the practitioner implements these matters in the conduct of an audit is subject to the practitioner's professional judgment.

Required Documentation When a Presumptively Mandatory Requirement Is Not Complied With

The imperative "should" indicates a presumptively mandatory activity. There are only rare circumstances in which the practitioner would be able to meet the objectives of the standards by alternative means. Therefore, if the practitioner departs from a presumptively mandatory requirement, the practitioner must document in the working papers the following: (1) the reasons why the presumptively mandatory requirement was not complied with and (2) how the alternative procedures performed adequately achieved the objectives of the presumptively mandatory requirement. Since the practitioner must already document the work performed as part of an audit, adding a concise (but complete) explanation as to why the practitioner chose to perform the alternative procedures should not increase the volume of documentation to an unreasonable level.

PRACTICE ISSUES AND FREQUENTLY ASKED QUESTIONS

Issue 1: Do the words "may," "might," and "could" impose a professional requirement for the practitioner to perform the suggested procedures or actions described in professional standards?

No. Professional standards generally include explanatory material that provides further clarification or guidance on the professional requirements, or identifies and describes other procedures or actions relating to the practitioner's activities. Such explanatory material generally explains why the practitioner might consider certain particular procedures and provides additional information for the practitioner to consider in exercising professional judgment in performing the audit engagement. The words *may, might,* and *could* are typically used to describe these actions and procedures. Therefore, explanatory material that uses such terms is not intended to impose a professional requirement for the practitioner to perform the suggested procedures or actions. Rather, these procedures or actions require the practitioner's attention and understanding; accordingly, how and whether the practitioner carries out the suggested procedures or actions depends on the exercise of professional judgment in the specific engagement.

ILLUSTRATIONS AND PRACTICE AIDS

There are no illustrations and practice aids for this Section.

AT SECTION 50
SSAE HIERARCHY

WHAT EVERY PRACTITIONER SHOULD KNOW

Basic Objectives and Requirements

This Section establishes three levels of literature within the SSAE hierarchy: (1) attestation standards, (2) attestation interpretations, and (3) other attestation publications.

There are eleven attestation standards approved by the AICPA, which are divided into the following three groups:

1. *General Standards*—There are five standards in this group, which relate to (1) the professional qualifications, independence, and personal integrity of the practitioner; and (2) the practitioner's knowledge of the subject matter and considerations regarding its suitability.

2. *Standards of Field Work*—There are two standards in this group, which set forth quality criteria for the actual conduct of the attest engagement, including the proper design and execution of attest procedures.

3. *Standards of Reporting*—There are four standards in this group, which guide the practitioner when issuing a report in connection with attestation engagements.

See Illustration 1 for these eleven attestation standards.

The SSAEs are codified within the framework of the eleven standards. Therefore, the practitioner should have sufficient knowledge of the SSAEs to identify those that are applicable to his or her attestation engagement and should be prepared to justify departures from them.

PRACTICE POINT: The SSAEs use the word *should* to indicate a "presumptively mandatory requirement." When the practitioner departs from a "presumptively mandatory requirement," the practitioner must document in the working papers his or her justification for the departure and how the alternative procedures performed in the circumstances were sufficient to achieve the objectives of the presumptively mandatory requirement. See AT Section 20 (Defining Professional Requirements in Statements on Standards for Attestation Engagements) for further guidance.

The practitioner also should be aware of and consider *attestation interpretations* applicable to his or her engagement. Attestation interpretations are recommendations on the application of SSAEs in specific circumstances, including engagements for entities in specialized industries. If the practitioner does not apply the guidance included in an applicable attestation interpretation, the practitioner should be prepared to explain how he or she complied with the provisions of the SSAE addressed by such guidance.

While *other attestation publications* may help practitioners understand and apply the SSAEs, they have no authoritative status. However, if a practitioner applies the guidance included in an other attestation publication, he or she should be satisfied that, in his or her judgment, it is both appropriate and relevant to the circumstances of his or her engagement. Other attestation publications published by the AICPA that have been reviewed by the AICPA Audit and Attest Standards staff are presumed to be appropriate.

PRACTICE ISSUES AND FREQUENTLY ASKED QUESTIONS

Issue 1: What is the difference between "attestation standards" and "attestation procedures" as they appear in professional literature?

"Attestation procedures" are acts that a practitioner performs in an attestation engagement in order to meet the standards. Procedures are specific in nature and have the primary purpose of gathering evidence to provide a reasonable basis for the conclusion that is expressed in the practitioner's report. "Attestation standards" are broader, more authoritative, and are criteria for the quality of engagement performance. They deal with the objectives to be accomplished by those procedures, the quality of their performance, and the practitioner's judgment in performing and reporting on an attestation engagement. Attestation procedures vary depending on the size, nature, complexity, and other unique characteristics of each engagement, whereas attestation standards do not change from engagement to engagement and provide guidance and requirements for all attestation engagements.

Issue 2: The fifth general standard states that the practitioner must exercise due professional care in the planning and performance of the attestation engagement and the preparation of the report. What is generally meant by "due professional care"?

The exercise of due professional care in an attestation engagement requires that the practitioner develop a healthy skepticism when conducting the attestation engagement. This is generally exhibited by a disposition to question and test all material representations made by management, whether they are oral, written, or incorporated into the client's records. At the same time, such an attitude of skepticism should be balanced by an open mind about the integrity of management; in other words, the practitioner should not blindly assume that management is dishonest or perfectly and unquestionably honest.

Issue 3: What are "attestation interpretations" and what do they consist of?

Attestation interpretations are recommendations on the application of SSAEs in specific circumstances, including engagements for entities in specialized industries. Attestation interpretations consist of:

1. Interpretations of the SSAEs;
2. Appendices to the SSAEs;
3. Attestation guidance included in AICPA Audit and Accounting Guides; and
4. AICPA attestation Statements of Position.

While attestation interpretations are "level 2" in the SSAE hierarchy, the practitioner is expected to apply the guidance included in an applicable attestation interpretation. If the practitioner does not apply such applicable guidance in an attestation engagement, he or she should be prepared to explain how he or she complied with the provisions of the SSAE addressed by such guidance.

Issue 4: Is the practitioner required or expected to follow the guidance included in an other attestation publication, for example an article in the Journal of Accountancy or other such professional journals?

No. *Other attestation publications* have no authoritative status, although they may help the practitioner understand and apply the SSAEs. *Other attestation publications* under this Section include the following:

- AICPA attestation publications other than SSAEs and attestation interpretations referred to above.
- Attestation articles in the *Journal of Accountancy* and other professional journals.
- Attestation articles in the AICPA's The *CPA Letter*.
- Continuing professional education programs.
- Other instruction materials.
- Textbooks.
- Guide books.
- Attest programs and checklists.
- Other attestation publications from state CPA societies, other organizations, and individuals.

If a practitioner applies the guidance included in another attestation publication, such as the ones listed above, he or she should be satisfied that, in his or her judgment, such guidance is both appropriate and relevant to the circumstances of his or her engagement.

ILLUSTRATIONS AND PRACTICE AIDS

ILLUSTRATION 1—THE ELEVEN ATTESTATION STANDARDS

General Standards

1. The practitioner must have adequate technical training and proficiency to perform the attestation engagement.
2. The practitioner must have adequate knowledge of the subject matter.
3. The practitioner must have reason to believe that the subject matter is capable of evaluation against criteria that are suitable and available to users.
4. The practitioner must maintain independence in mental attitude in all matters relating to the engagement.
5. The practitioner must exercise due professional care in the planning and performance of the engagement and the preparation of the report.

Standards of Field Work

1. The practitioner must adequately plan the work and must properly supervise any assistants.

2. The practitioner must obtain sufficient evidence to provide a reasonable basis for the conclusion that is expressed in the report.

Standards of Reporting

1. The practitioner must identify the subject matter or the assertion being reported on and state the character of the engagement in the report.

2. The practitioner must state the practitioner's conclusion about the subject matter or the assertion in relation to the criteria against which the subject matter was evaluated in the report.

3. The practitioner must state all of the practitioner's significant reservations about the engagement, the subject matter, and, if applicable, the assertion related thereto in the report.

4. The practitioner must state in the report that the report is intended solely for the information and use of the specified parties under the following circumstances:

    a. When the criteria used to evaluate the subject matter are determined by the practitioner to be appropriate only for a limited number of parties who either participated in their establishment or can be presumed to have an adequate understanding of the criteria.

    b. When the criteria used to evaluate the subject matter are available only to specified parties.

    c. When reporting on subject matter and a written assertion have not been provided by the responsible party.

    d. When the report is on an attestation engagement to apply agreed-upon procedures to the subject matter.

AT SECTION 101
ATTEST ENGAGEMENTS

PRACTICE POINT: In July 2010, the AICPA's Auditing Standards Board issued Interpretation No. 8 of AT Section 101, *Including a Description of Tests of Controls or Other Procedures, and the Results Thereof, in an Examination Report.* The Interpretation includes considerations that are relevant when practitioners are determining whether to include, in a separate section of the examination report, a description of tests of controls or other procedures performed in support of the practitioner's opinion. Also, the Interpretation discusses the potential need to restrict use of the practitioner's report to specified parties.

The discussion in this Section has been updated to reflect the guidance in Interpretation No. 8 of AT Section 101.

WHAT EVERY PRACTITIONER SHOULD KNOW

Basic Objectives and Requirements

This Section applies to engagements in which a practitioner is engaged to issue or does issue an examination, a review, or an agreed-upon procedures report on subject matter, or an assertion about the subject matter, that is the responsibility of another party. The subject matter may be as of a point in time or for a period of time.

A practitioner may report either on a written assertion or directly on the subject matter. In either case, the practitioner ordinarily should obtain a *written* assertion in an examination or a review engagement. A practitioner may nevertheless report on the subject matter when a written assertion has not been obtained; however, the form of the report will vary depending on the circumstances and its use should be restricted.

The practitioner should not take on the role of the responsible party in an attest engagement. A practitioner may accept an attest engagement on subject matter, or an assertion related thereto, provided that one of the following conditions is met:

1. The party engaging the practitioner is responsible for the subject matter, or has a reasonable basis for providing a written assertion about the subject matter if a responsible party does not otherwise exist, *or*

2. The party engaging the practitioner is not responsible for the subject matter but is able to provide, directly or through a third party who is responsible for the subject matter, evidence of the third party's responsibility for the subject matter.

The practitioner should obtain written acknowledgment or other evidence of the responsible party's responsibility for the subject matter, or the written assertion. Such acknowledgment can be obtained in a number of ways, such as in: an engagement letter, a representation letter, or the presentation of the subject matter or the written assertion. If the practitioner is unable to directly obtain such written acknowledgment, he or she should obtain other evidence of the responsible party's responsibility for the subject matter, for example by reference to legislation, a regulation, or a contract.

When a practitioner performs an attest engagement for the benefit of a government body or agency and agrees to follow specified government standards or requirements, the practitioner should follow the applicable attestation standards as well as those governmental requirements.

Attestation Standards

There are eleven attestation standards which are divided into the following three groups: general standards (5 in total), fieldwork standards (2 in total), and reporting standards (4 in total).

While the attestation standards are a natural extension of the ten generally accepted auditing standards, they do not supersede any of the existing standards in Statements on Auditing Standards (SASs) and Statements on Standards for Accounting and Review Services (SSARSs). Therefore, a practitioner who is engaged to perform an engagement subject to existing SASs or SSARSs should follow such standards, not the attestation standards.

Illustration 1 provides a comparison between the eleven attestation standards and the ten generally accepted auditing standards.

General standards When observing the five general standards (see Illustration 1), the practitioner should:

1. Determine and evaluate whether the criteria used to measure and present the subject matter are suitable. *Suitable criteria* must be:

    a. Objective (i.e., free from bias).

    b. Measurable (i.e., reasonably consistent measurements, qualitative or quantitative, of subject matter).

    c. Complete (i.e., relevant factors that would alter a conclusion about subject matter are not omitted).

    d. Relevant (i.e., criteria should be relevant to the subject matter).

2. Determine that the criteria used to measure and present the subject matter are *available to users* in one or more of the following ways:

    a. Available publicly.

    b. Available to all users through inclusion in a clear manner in the presentation of the subject matter or in the assertion.

    c. Available to all users through inclusion in a clear manner in the practitioner's report.

    d. Well understood by most users, although not formally available.

    e. Available only to specified parties (e.g., terms of a contract or criteria issued by an industry association that are available only to those in the industry).

3. Restrict the use of the attest report to the specified parties, if the practitioner determines that the criteria used are appropriate or available only for a limited number of parties who either participated in their

establishment or can be presumed to have an adequate understanding of the criteria.

4. Not perform a review engagement if the practitioner concludes that an examination cannot be performed because competent persons using the same criteria would not be able to obtain materially similar evaluations.

Fieldwork standards When observing the two fieldwork standards (see Illustration 1), the practitioner should:

1. Develop an overall strategy for the expected conduct and scope of the engagement and plan the attest engagement by considering relevant factors, including the following:

   a. The criteria to be used.

   b. Preliminary judgments about attestation risk and materiality for attest purposes.

   c. The nature of the subject matter or the items within the assertion that are likely to require revision or adjustment.

   d. Conditions that may require extension or modification of attest procedures.

   e. The nature of the report expected to be issued.

2. Establish an understanding with the client, preferably in writing, regarding the attest services including: (a) the objectives of the engagement, (b) management's responsibilities, (c) the practitioner's responsibilities, and (d) limitations of the engagement. If such an understanding with the client has not been established, the practitioner should decline to accept or perform the engagement.

3. Consider the nature, extent, and timing of the work to be performed to accomplish the objectives of the attest engagement, including supervising and directing the efforts of assistants to accomplish the engagement objectives.

4. Direct assistants to bring to his or her attention significant questions raised during the attest engagement so that their significance may be assessed.

5. Review the work performed by each assistant on the engagement.

6. Consider the following presumptions when establishing procedures to gather sufficient evidence:

   a. Evidence obtained from independent sources outside an entity provides greater assurance than evidence gathered solely from within the entity.

   b. Information obtained from the independent attester's direct personal knowledge (e.g., through physical examination, observation, computation, operating tests, or inspection) is more persuasive than information obtained indirectly.

   c. The more effective the controls over the subject matter, the more assurance they provide about the subject matter or the assertion.

7. Consider the written assertion ordinarily provided by the responsible party. If a written assertion cannot be obtained from the responsible party, the practitioner should take one of the following actions depending on whether the practitioner's client is the responsible party:

   a. When the practitioner's client is the responsible party, the practitioner should conclude that a scope limitation exists. Therefore, in an examination engagement, the practitioner should modify his or her report for the scope limitation. In a review engagement, such a scope limitation results in an incomplete review and the practitioner should withdraw from the engagement.

   b. When the practitioner's client is *not* the responsible party, the practitioner may be able to conclude that he or she has sufficient evidence to form a conclusion about the subject matter.

8. Consider obtaining a representation letter from the responsible party in an examination or a review engagement. See Illustration 2 for examples of matters that might appear in such a representation letter. If the client or the responsible party refuses to furnish the requested written representations, the practitioner should consider the effects of such a refusal on whether he or she can issue a conclusion about the subject matter. The responsible party's or the client's refusal to furnish the written representations deemed necessary by the practitioner constitutes a limitation on the scope of an attest engagement. Ordinarily, this is sufficient for the practitioner to disclaim an opinion or withdraw from an examination engagement. When such a scope limitation exists in a review engagement, the practitioner should withdraw from the review engagement.

Reporting standards When observing the four reporting standards (see Illustration 1), the practitioner should:

1. Issue a report on the subject matter or the assertion or withdraw from the attest engagement. If the practitioner is reporting on the assertion, the assertion should (a) be bound with the practitioner's report, or (b) accompany the practitioner's report, or (c) be clearly stated in the practitioner's report.

2. State the character of the engagement in his or her report and include the following two elements in such statement:

   a. A description of the nature and scope of the work performed. The terms *examination* and *review* should be used to describe the level of assurance provided.

   b. A reference to the professional standards governing the engagement (i.e., "attestation standards established by the American Institute of Certified Public Accountants" or, for engagements performed in accordance with PCAOB standards, a reference to the "standards of the Public Company Accounting Oversight Board (United States))."

3. Modify the report and should ordinarily express his or her conclusion directly on the subject matter, not on the assertion, if conditions exist that result in material misstatements or deviations from the criteria.

4. Consider the materiality of an omission or a misstatement and how that might influence a reasonable person relying on the subject matter or the assertion. The practitioner should consider both quantitative and qualitative aspects of omissions and misstatements.

5. Limit general-use attest reports to the following two levels of assurance:

   a. *Examination.* Such an engagement provides a high level of assurance and the practitioner's conclusion should be expressed in the form of an opinion. See discussion in the section below.

   b. *Review.* Such an engagement provides only a moderate level of assurance and the practitioner's conclusion should be expressed in the form of negative assurance. See discussion in the section below.

6. Determine whether the criteria are clearly stated or described for each of the dates or periods and whether the changes have been adequately disclosed, when reporting on subject matter or an assertion at multiple dates or covering multiple periods during which criteria have changed.

7. Consider the effects on the report or the engagement of any significant reservations about the engagement, the subject matter, or the assertion, as follows:

   a. *Reservations about the engagement (i.e., unresolved problems in complying with the attestation standards or the specific procedures agreed to by the specified parties)*—Any such reservations about, or restrictions on the scope of, the engagement ordinarily should cause the practitioner, in an examination engagement, to provide a qualified opinion, to disclaim an opinion, or to withdraw from the engagement. In a review engagement, the practitioner should withdraw from the engagement when (i) the client is the responsible party and does not provide a written assertion to the practitioner *or* (ii) the practitioner is unable to perform the procedures deemed necessary in a review.

   b. *Reservations about the subject matter or the assertion (i.e., unresolved reservations about the assertion or about the conformity of the subject matter with the criteria, including the adequacy of the disclosure of material matters)*—Any such reservations ordinarily should cause the practitioner to provide a qualified or an adverse opinion in an examination engagement, or a modified conclusion in a review engagement.

8. Restrict the use of his or her report to specified parties in the circumstances described in the fourth standard of reporting (see Illustration 1) and should:

   a. Consider informing the client that restricted-use reports are not intended for distribution to nonspecified parties. However, a practitioner is not responsible for controlling a client's distribution of restricted-use reports.

    b. Include a separate paragraph at the end of the report alerting readers to the restriction, such as the following: "This report is intended solely for the information and use of [*the specified parties*] and is not intended to be and should not be used by anyone other than these specified parties."

Reporting on attestation engagements performed in accordance with Government Auditing Standards Practitioners who perform attestation engagements pursuant to generally accepted government auditing standards (GAGAS) are also required to follow the general, fieldwork, and reporting standards for attestation engagements set forth in *Government Auditing Standards* (the "Yellow Book"). GAGAS prescribe additional reporting standards that go beyond the reporting standards included in AT Section 101. The additional GAGAS standards relate to:

- Reporting auditors' compliance with GAGAS;
- Reporting deficiencies in internal control, fraud, illegal acts, violations of provisions of contracts or grant agreements, and abuse;
- Reporting views of responsible officials;
- Reporting privileged and confidential information; and
- Issuance and distribution of the attestation report.

An AICPA Attestation Interpretation indicates that, when a practitioner performs an attestation engagement in accordance with GAGAS, the practitioner should modify his or her report to comply with the additional Yellow Book requirements as well. Specifically, the practitioner should:

- Modify the scope paragraph of the attestation report to indicate that the examination or review was "conducted in accordance with attestation standards established by the American Institute of Certified Public Accountants and the standards applicable to attestation engagements contained in *Government Auditing Standards* issued by the Comptroller General of the United States."

- Disclose (a) deficiencies in internal control, including internal control over compliance with laws, regulations, and provisions of contracts or grant agreements that are material to the subject matter or assertion, (b) all instances of fraud and illegal acts unless clearly inconsequential, and (c) violations of provisions of contracts or grant agreements and abuse that are material to the subject matter or assertion of the engagement.

- Make reference in the attestation report to the management letter, if any, that the practitioner issued to communicate findings related to internal control deficiencies, fraud, illegal acts, violations of provisions of contracts or grant agreements, or abuse that were not deemed material to the subject matter or assertion.

- Place the findings in proper perspective by providing a description of the work performed that resulted in the finding and, to the extent possible, use the following elements in reporting a finding: criteria, condition, cause, and effect.

- Include in the attestation report a copy of the client officials' written comments or a summary of the comments received in response to the practitioner's findings, conclusions, or recommendations.

- If certain pertinent information is prohibited from general disclosure, state the nature of any information omitted from the attestation report and the requirement that makes the omission necessary.

Examination Reports

In addition to complying with the reporting standards above, when expressing an opinion the practitioner should state:

    a. Whether the subject matter is based on [*or in conformity with*] the criteria in all material respects, *or*

    b. Whether the assertion is presented [*or fairly stated*], in all material respects, based on the criteria.

Reports expressing an opinion may be qualified or modified for some aspect of, or may emphasize certain matters relating to, the subject matter, the assertion, or the attest engagement.

The form of the examination report depends on whether the practitioner's opinion is on the subject matter or on the assertion. See Illustration 3 for a list of the items that should be included in the practitioner's examination report on a subject matter or on an assertion. See Illustration 4 for a standard examination report on a subject matter and Illustration 5 for a standard examination report on an assertion.

Also, the practitioner may examine management's assertion, but issue an opinion directly on the subject matter. See Illustration 6 for an example of such a report in these circumstances.

The following additional illustrations of examination reports are provided:

- Illustration 7—Examination report on subject matter that is restricted because the criteria are available only to specified parties.

- Illustration 8—Examination report with a qualified opinion due to material misstatements or deviations from the criteria.

- Illustration 9—Examination report with a disclaimer of opinion due to a scope restriction.

- Illustration 10—Examination report on subject matter that is the responsibility of a party other than the client and that is restricted since a written assertion has not been provided by the responsible party.

Review Reports

In providing negative assurance, the practitioner should state whether any information came to his or her attention that indicates that (a) the subject matter is not based on (or in conformity with) the criteria or (b) the assertion is not presented (or fairly stated) in all material respects based on the criteria.

The review will be incomplete:

1. When the practitioner is unable to perform the inquiry and the analytical, or other, procedures considered necessary to achieve the limited assurance contemplated by a review, *or*

2. When the client is the responsible party and does not provide the practitioner with a written assertion.

A review that is incomplete does not provide the practitioner with an adequate basis for issuing a review report and, accordingly, the practitioner should withdraw from the engagement under such circumstances.

The form of the review report depends on whether the practitioner is providing limited assurance on a subject matter or on an assertion. See Illustration 11 for a list of the items that should be included in the practitioner's review report on a subject matter or on an assertion.

The following illustrations of review reports are provided:

- Illustration 12—Standard review report on subject matter for general use.
- Illustration 13—Review report on subject matter that is the responsibility of a party other than the client and that is restricted since a written assertion has not been provided by the responsible party.
- Illustration 14—Review report on an assertion that is restricted since the criteria are available only to the specified parties.

Other Information in a Client-Prepared Document Containing the Practitioner's Attest Report

A client may publish various documents that contain information (herein referred to as "other information") in addition to the practitioner's attest report on subject matter or on an assertion related thereto. The guidance herein applies when the other information is contained in the following documents:

1. Annual reports to holders of securities or beneficial interests.

2. Annual reports of organizations for charitable or philanthropic purposes distributed to the public.

3. Annual reports filed with regulatory authorities under the Securities Exchange Act of 1934 (e.g., 10-K reports).

4. Documents to which the practitioner, at the client's request, devotes attention.

In these circumstances, the practitioner should read the other information not covered by the practitioner's report and determine whether such other information, or the manner of its presentation, is materially inconsistent with the information appearing in the practitioner's report.

Effect of material inconsistencies If the practitioner concludes there is a material inconsistency, he or she should determine whether the practitioner's report requires revision. If the practitioner concludes that the report does not require revision, he or she should request the client to revise the other information to eliminate the material inconsistency. If the client refuses to revise the other information, the practitioner should consider other actions such as the following:

1. Revise the report to include an explanatory paragraph describing the material inconsistency.

2. Withhold the use of his or her report in the document.

3. Withdraw from the engagement.

Effect of material misstatement of fact If the practitioner believes that the other information is a material misstatement of fact that is not a material inconsistency, he or she should discuss the matter with the client and consider whether:

1. He or she has the expertise to assess the validity of the statement.

2. There may be no standards by which to assess the presentation of the statement.

3. There may be valid differences of judgment or opinion.

If the practitioner concludes he or she has a valid basis for concern, the practitioner should propose that the client consult other advisers (e.g., the client's legal counsel, specialists). If, after such discussions, the practitioner concludes that a material misstatement of fact remains, the practitioner should consider notifying the client's management and those charged with governance in writing of his or her views concerning the information and consulting with legal counsel on an appropriate course of action.

Subsequent Events Considerations

In performing an attest engagement, the practitioner should consider information about the following types of subsequent events, through the date of the attest report, that come to his or her attention:

1. Events that provide additional information with respect to conditions that existed at the point in time or during the period of time of the subject matter being tested. For these types of events, the practitioner should consider whether the subject matter is presented in conformity with the criteria and may affect the presentation of the subject matter, the assertion, or the practitioner's report.

2. Events that provide information with respect to conditions that arose subsequent to the point in time or period of time of the subject matter being tested, and whose disclosure is necessary to keep the subject matter from being misleading. The practitioner's report generally will not be affected if the discovered information is appropriately disclosed.

The practitioner should inquire of the client and/or the responsible party about whether they are aware of any subsequent events that would have a material effect on the subject matter or assertion.

If subsequent to the date of his or her attest report the practitioner becomes aware of conditions that existed at that date that might have affected the attest report, the practitioner should consider the guidance in AU Section 561 (Subsequent Discovery of Facts Existing at the Date of the Auditor's Report).

Attest Documentation

The practitioner is required to prepare and maintain attest documentation (i.e., working papers) for every attest engagement. The type, form, quantity, and content of attest documentation are matters of the practitioner's judgment; however, they should be tailored to meet the circumstances of the individual attest engagement. Attest documentation includes: work programs, confirmations, representation letters, memoranda, analyses, abstracts or copies of client documents, and client-prepared schedules.

Specifically, attest documentation should be sufficient to:

1. Enable engagement personnel with supervision and review responsibilities to understand the nature, timing, extent, and results of the procedures performed, and the information obtained.

2. Indicate the engagement staff who performed and reviewed the work.

3. For examinations of prospective financial statements, indicate that the practitioner considered the process the entity uses to develop its prospective financial statements in determining the scope of his or her examination.

Retention and confidentiality of attest documentation The practitioner should adopt reasonable procedures to:

1. Retain attest documentation for a period of time sufficient to meet the needs of the firm's practice and to satisfy legal or regulatory requirements, if any, for records retention;

2. Enable the practitioner to access electronic attest documentation throughout the retention period;

3. Maintain the confidentiality of client information that is confidential and is contained in the attest documentation; and

4. Prevent unauthorized access to the attest documentation.

Providing access to or copies of attest documentation to regulators A regulator may request access to or copies of attest documentation in an attest engagement. In such circumstances, the practitioner should follow the same guidance pertaining to audit documentation as discussed in AU Section 339 (Audit Documentation). However, the letter to a regulator should be tailored to meet the individual engagement characteristics or the purpose of the regulatory request, for example, a quality control review. See Illustration 15 for a sample letter to a regulator for an examination engagement performed in accordance with AT Section 601 (Compliance Attestation) and Illustration 16 for an agreed-upon procedures engagement performed in accordance with AT Section 201 (Agreed-Upon Procedures Engagements).

Attest Services Related to Consulting Service Engagements

When a practitioner provides an attest service as part of a consulting service engagement, the attestation standards apply only to the attest service. Statements on Standards for Consulting Services apply to the balance of the consulting service engagement. When the practitioner determines that an attest service is to be provided as part of a consulting service engagement, the practitioner should:

1. Inform the client of the relevant differences between the two types of services.

2. Obtain the client's acknowledgment that the attest service is to be performed in accordance with the appropriate professional requirements.

3. Issue separate reports on the attest engagement and the consulting service engagement. If the report on the attestation engagement is submitted in the same document with the report on the consulting service engagement, it should be clearly identified and segregated from the consulting service engagement.

Assurances on Matters Relating to Solvency

A practitioner should not provide any form of assurance, through examination, review or agreed-upon procedures engagements, that an entity:

1. Is not insolvent at the time the debt is incurred or would not be rendered insolvent thereby.

2. Does not have unreasonably small capital.

3. Has the ability to pay its debts as they mature.

However, a practitioner is not prohibited from providing expert testimony on matters relating to solvency.

Reporting on the Design of Internal Control

Attestation Interpretation No. 7 of AT Section 101, *Reporting on the Design of Internal Control*, addresses the following four issues:

1. Whether a practitioner may report on the suitability of the design of an entity's internal control over financial reporting ("internal control") based on the risk assessment procedures the auditor performs in a financial statement audit to obtain a sufficient understanding of the entity and its environment, including its internal control;

2. How a practitioner may report on the suitability of the design of an entity's internal control (or a portion thereof);

3. The practitioner's responsibilities when requested to sign a prescribed form regarding the design of an entity's internal control if it includes language that is not consistent with the practitioner's function or responsibility or with professional standards; and

4. Whether a practitioner may issue a report about an entity's *ability* to establish suitably designed internal control, or its assertion thereon, based on (a) the risk assessment procedures related to existing internal control that the auditor performs in an audit of an entity's financial statements or (b) the performance of an attest engagement.

May a practitioner report on the suitability of the design of an entity's internal control based on the risk assessment procedures the auditor performs in a

financial statement audit to obtain a sufficient understanding of the entity and its environment, including its internal control? No. Obtaining an understanding of the entity and its environment, including its internal control, is an essential aspect of performing a financial statement audit in accordance with GAAS. Such understanding enables the auditor to assess the risk of material misstatement of the financial statements whether due to error or fraud, and to design the nature, timing, and extent of further audit procedures. However, such understanding does not provide the practitioner with a sufficient basis to report on the suitability of the design of an entity's internal control.

How may a practitioner report on the suitability of the design of an entity's internal control (or a portion thereof)? The Attestation Interpretation indicates that a practitioner may report on the suitability of the design of an entity's internal control, or a portion thereof, in one of the following ways:

1. By performing an examination under AT Section 101; or
2. By applying agreed-upon procedures under AT Section 201 (Agreed-Upon Procedures Engagements) to management's written assertion about the suitability of the design of the entity's internal control. In addition, when such engagement involves the application of agreed-upon procedures to a written assertion about the suitability of the design of an entity's internal control over compliance with specified requirements, the practitioner should follow the provisions of paragraphs 9 and 11-29 of AT Section 601 (Compliance Attestation).

PRACTICE POINT: AT Section 501 (An Examination of an Entity's Internal Control over Financial Reporting That Is Integrated with an Audit of Its Financial Statements) applies when a practitioner is engaged to perform an examination of the design and operating effectiveness of an entity's internal control over financial reporting that is integrated with an audit of financial statements ("integrated audit"). AT Section 501 does not directly apply when an auditor is engaged to examine the suitability of design of an entity's internal control. However, footnote 4 of AT Section 501 states that although AT Section 501 does not directly apply when an auditor is engaged to examine the suitability of design of an entity's internal control, it may be useful in planning and performing such engagements.

See Illustration 17 for an accountant's report when reporting on the suitability of the design of an entity's internal control that has been implemented.

If the practitioner is asked to report on the suitability of the design of an entity's internal control that has *not* yet been implemented, the practitioner should modify his or her report to (1) inform readers, in the scope paragraph of the report, that the controls identified in the report have not yet been implemented and (2) change the inherent limitations paragraph of the report to reflect the related risk. See Illustration 18 for an accountant's report when controls have not yet been implemented.

What are the practitioner's responsibilities when requested to sign a prescribed form regarding the design of an entity's internal control if it includes language that is not consistent with the practitioner's function or responsibil-

ity or with professional standards? There may be situations where a practitioner is requested to sign a prescribed form developed by the party to whom the form is to be submitted regarding the design of an entity's internal control. Generally, the language in such forms is not consistent with the practitioner's function or responsibility or with the reporting requirements of professional standards. In such circumstances, the practitioner should either revise the prescribed form or attach a separate report in place of the prescribed form that conforms with the practitioner's function or responsibility and professional standards.

May a practitioner issue a report about an entity's *ability* to establish suitably designed internal control, or its assertion thereon, based on (1) the risk assessment procedures related to existing internal control that the auditor performs in an audit of an entity's financial statements or (2) the performance of an attest engagement? No. The Attestation Interpretation states that there are no suitable criteria for evaluating an entity's *ability* to establish suitably designed internal control. Accordingly, neither the risk assessment procedures the auditor performs in an audit of an entity's financial statements nor the performance of an attest engagement provide the practitioner with a basis for issuing such a report. However, if acceptable to the requesting party, the practitioner may issue a consulting service report that includes the following elements:

- A statement that the practitioner is unable to perform an attest engagement that addresses the entity's ability to establish suitably designed internal control because there are no suitable criteria for evaluating the entity's ability to do so;

- A description of the nature and scope of the practitioner's consulting services; and

- The practitioner's findings.

Guidance on consulting services is provided in CS Section 100 (Consulting Services: Definitions and Standards).

Including a Description of Tests of Controls or Other Procedures, and the Results Thereof, in an Examination Report

AT Section 801 (Reporting on Controls at a Service Organization) addresses examination engagements undertaken by a service auditor to report on controls at organizations that provide services to user entities when those controls are likely to be relevant to user entities' internal control over financial reporting (ICFR). When, as a result of such an examination engagement, a service auditor issues a type 2 report, AT Section 801 provides for a separate section of the service auditor's report that includes a description of the tests of controls likely to be relevant to user entities' ICFR and the results of those tests.

However, there may be circumstances when a practitioner is engaged to examine and report on controls at a service organization other than those likely to be relevant to user entities' ICFR, for example, controls at a service provider that are relevant to user entities' compliance with laws or regulations or that are relevant to the privacy of user entities' information. In such circumstances, AT Section 801 directs the practitioner to AT Section 101 (because AT Section 801 is not intended to permit a report that combines reporting on a service organization's controls likely to be relevant to user entities' ICFR with reporting on controls that are not likely to be relevant to user entities' ICFR).

Accordingly, if a practitioner performs an examination engagement under AT Section 101 under those circumstances, the question is whether the practitioner's examination report may include, in a separate section, a description of tests of controls or other procedures performed in support of the practitioner's opinion resulting from such an engagement. Attestation Interpretation No. 8 of AT Section 101, *Including a Description of Tests of Controls or Other Procedures, and the Results Thereof, in an Examination Report*, provides further guidance in such circumstances. It specifically indicates that, although nothing in AT Section 101 precludes a practitioner from including in a separate section of his or her examination report a description of tests of controls or other procedures performed and the results thereof, such a description may overshadow the practitioner's overall opinion or may cause report users to misunderstand the opinion. The Interpretation indicates that, in determining whether to include such a description in the practitioner's examination report, the circumstances of the particular engagement are relevant to the practitioner's consideration, including the following:

- Whether there has been a request for such information and whether the specified parties making the request have an appropriate business need or reasonable basis for requesting the information;

- Whether the specified parties have an understanding of the nature and subject matter of the engagement and experience in using the information in such reports;

- Whether including such a description in the examination report is likely to cause report users to misunderstand the opinion; and

- Whether the practitioner's tests of controls or other procedures performed directly relate to the subject matter of the engagement.

Also, the Interpretation states that the addition of a description of tests of controls or other procedures performed, and the results thereof, in a separate section of an examination report may increase the need for use of the report to be restricted to specified parties.

PRACTICE ISSUES AND FREQUENTLY ASKED QUESTIONS

Issue 1: May a practitioner report on an assertion when a written assertion has not been provided by the responsible party?

No. A practitioner may only report on the subject matter when a written assertion has not been obtained. Furthermore, when reporting on subject matter and a written assertion has not been provided by the responsible party, the use of the practitioner's report should be restricted.

Issue 2: What are some services that are typically provided by practitioners under the attestation standards?

Services that typically are provided by practitioners under the attestation standards include:

- Examining, compiling, or performing agreed-upon procedures related to a management financial forecast or projection.
- Examining or performing agreed-upon procedures related to management's assertion about the effectiveness of internal controls over financial reporting.
- Examining or performing agreed-upon procedures related to management's assertion about compliance with specified legal, contractual, and regulatory requirements.

Issue 3: What are some services that are provided by practitioners that would not be considered attest engagements?

Examples of professional services typically provided by practitioners that would *not* be considered attest engagements include:

- Management consulting engagements whereby the practitioner provides advice or recommendations to a client.
- Engagements to advocate a client's position, for example, tax matters being reviewed by the Internal Revenue Service.
- Tax engagements involving the preparation of tax returns or providing tax advice.
- Compilations or reviews of financial statements.
- Engagements in which the practitioner's role is solely to assist the client, for example, acting as the company's accountant in preparing information other than financial statements.
- Engagements to testify as an expert witness in accounting, auditing, taxation, or other matters.
- Engagements to provide an expert opinion on certain points of principle, such as the application of tax laws or accounting standards, given certain stipulated facts provided by another party as long as the expert opinion does not express a conclusion about the reliability of the facts provided by another party.

Issue 4: What is the difference between an examination and a review attest engagement?

The fundamental difference is that an examination is designed to provide positive assurance, that is to say an opinion, on the subject matter or the assertion. It requires the practitioner to accumulate sufficient evidence to reduce to an appropriately low level the risk that his or her procedures will result in an improper assurance. The standards and procedures for performing an examination are in many ways analogous to those for performing an audit.

A review, on the other hand, offers only a limited level of assurance. The practitioner's objective in such an engagement is to accumulate evidence to limit his or her attestation risk to a moderate level. Generally, inquiries and analytical procedures will be sufficient to accomplish this objective.

Issue 5: May a practitioner use a specialist in connection with acquiring knowledge in the subject matter of the assertion to be reported on?

Yes. A practitioner may use a specialist on a particular attest engagement as long as he or she has sufficient knowledge of the subject matter to achieve both of the following:

1. Communicate to the specialist the objectives of the work.
2. Evaluate the specialist's work to determine if the objectives were achieved.

Issue 6: What are considered "suitable criteria" against which a practitioner can evaluate the subject matter in an attest engagement?

Criteria issued by regulatory agencies and other bodies composed of experts that follow due-process procedures, including procedures for broad distribution of proposed criteria for public comment, normally should be considered suitable criteria. Criteria promulgated by a body designated by the AICPA's Governing Council are, by definition, considered to be suitable. Examples include the Financial Accounting Standards Board (FASB), the Governmental Accounting Standards Board (GASB), and the Federal Accounting Standards Advisory Board (FASAB).

Issue 7: What effect do restrictions on the scope of an attest engagement have on the practitioner's report?

When there are restrictions on the scope of an attest engagement, whether imposed by the client or other circumstances, the practitioner should (a) qualify the assurance provided, (b) disclaim any assurance, or (c) withdraw from the examination or review engagement. Generally a disclaimer of opinion or withdrawal from an examination engagement is appropriate under the following circumstances:

1. If the scope limitation is imposed by the client or the responsible party.
2. If the potential effects of the scope limitation are pervasive to the subject matter or the assertion.

In a review engagement, the practitioner should withdraw from the attest engagement under the following circumstances:

1. When the practitioner is unable to perform the inquiry and the analytical, or other, procedures deemed necessary to achieve the limited assurance contemplated by a review.
2. When the client is the responsible party and does not provide the practitioner with a written assertion.

Issue 8: Is a practitioner responsible for controlling a client's distribution of restricted-use reports?

No. The statement provided in a restricted-use report indicating that the report is not intended to be and should not be used by anyone other than the specified parties is sufficient.

Issue 9: Can attest documentation be a substitute for the client's accounting records?

No. Although attest documentation often may be useful to the client, it is not a part of, nor is it a substitute for, the client's accounting records.

Issue 10: Who owns the attest documentation, the practitioner or the client?

The practitioner, not the client, owns the attest documentation. Some states have already recognized this right of ownership in their statutes. Attest documentation is the practitioner's evidence of the procedures performed, evidence obtained, and conclusions reached. Therefore, they belong to the practitioner and are necessary for the practitioner to support any legal questions regarding the work performed. Attest documentation should be retained for a period that meets the legal requirements and the needs of the practitioner.

Issue 11: What is the practitioner's responsibility for confidential client information contained in attest documentation?

At a minimum, the practitioner has an ethical responsibility and obligation to maintain the confidentiality of client information. In addition, in some cases, a legal obligation exists as well.

Rule 301 of the AICPA's Code of Professional Conduct, which requires the practitioner to maintain the confidentiality of working papers, states:

> A member in public practice shall not disclose any confidential client information without the specific consent of the client.

During the course of an attest engagement, practitioners obtain a considerable amount of information of a confidential nature. Therefore, the practitioner should not reveal information gathered in the course of an attest engagement without the client's express consent. Rule 301, however, does *not* preclude the practitioner from responding to a subpoena, a peer review, or an ethics inquiry. Communications between the client and the practitioner are not considered privileged, unless declared privileged by statute.

Issue 12: Is the practitioner required to let the working papers out of his or her custody in response to a regulator's request, pursuant to law or regulation, to access the working papers?

No. While the practitioner is required in such circumstances to provide the regulator access to the working papers, authoritative literature specifically recognizes that the practitioner should maintain custody of the working papers. This is necessary to insure their continued integrity. Therefore, the working papers may be made available to a regulator at the offices of the client, the practitioner, or a mutually agreed-upon location, as long as the practitioner maintains control. In addition, the practitioner should take appropriate steps to maintain custody of the original working papers.

Issue 13: Are practitioners required to comply with quality control standards when performing attest engagements?

Yes. Practitioners, in the conduct of a firm's attest practice, should comply with quality control standards. Therefore, a firm should establish quality control policies and procedures to provide it with reasonable assurance of conforming with attestation standards in its attest engagements. While attestation standards relate to the conduct of individual attest engagements, quality control standards relate to the conduct of a firm's attest practice as a whole. Therefore, attestation standards and quality control standards are related and the quality control policies and procedures that a firm adopts may affect both the conduct of individual attest engagements and the conduct of a firm's attest practice as a whole.

Issue 14: Do deficiencies in a firm's quality control system indicate that an attest engagement was not performed in accordance with attestation standards?

No. This Section specifically states that deficiencies in a firm's quality control system, or noncompliance therewith, do not necessarily indicate that an attest engagement was not performed in accordance with attestation standards.

ILLUSTRATIONS AND PRACTICE AIDS

ILLUSTRATION 1—COMPARISON BETWEEN ATTESTATION STANDARDS AND GENERALLY ACCEPTED AUDITING STANDARDS

Generally Accepted Auditing Standards	Attestation Standards
General Standards	
1. The auditor must have adequate technical training and proficiency to perform the audit.	1. The practitioner must have adequate technical training and proficiency to perform the attestation engagement.
	2. The practitioner must have adequate knowledge of the subject matter.
	3. The practitioner must have reason to believe that the subject matter is capable of evaluation against criteria that are suitable and available to users.
2. The auditor must maintain independence in mental attitude in all matters relating to the audit.	4. The practitioner must maintain independence in mental attitude in all matters relating to the engagement.
3. The auditor must exercise due professional care in the performance of the audit and in the preparation of the report.	5. The practitioner must exercise due professional care in the planning and performance of the engagement and in the preparation of the report.
Standards of Field Work	
1. The auditor must adequately plan the work and properly supervise any assistants.	1. The practitioner must adequately plan the work and properly supervise any assistants.
2. The auditor must obtain a sufficient understanding of the entity and its environment, including its internal control, to assess the risk of material misstatement of the financial statements whether due to error or fraud, and to design the nature, timing, and extent of further audit procedures.	

Generally Accepted Auditing Standards	Attestation Standards
3. The auditor must obtain sufficient appropriate audit evidence by performing audit procedures to afford a reasonable basis for an opinion regarding the financial statements under audit.	2. The practitioner must obtain sufficient evidence to provide a reasonable basis for the conclusion that is expressed in the report.

Standards of Reporting

1. The auditor must state in the auditor's report whether the financial statements are presented in accordance with generally accepted accounting principles.	1. The practitioner must identify the subject matter or the assertion being reported on and state the character of the engagement in the report.
2. The auditor must identify in the auditor's report those circumstances in which such principles have not been consistently observed in the current period in relation to the preceding period.	2. The practitioner must state his or her conclusion about the subject matter or the assertion in relation to the criteria against which the subject matter was evaluated in the report.
3. When the auditor determines that informative disclosures are not reasonably adequate, the auditor must state so in the auditor's report.	3. The practitioner must state all of his or her significant reservations about the engagement, the subject matter, and, if applicable, the assertion related thereto in the report.
4. The auditor must either express an opinion regarding the financial statements, taken as a whole, or state that an opinion cannot be expressed, in the auditor's report. When the auditor cannot express an overall opinion, he or she should state the reasons therefor in the auditor's report. In all cases where an auditor's name is associated with financial statements, the auditor should clearly indicate the character of the auditor's work, if any, and the degree of responsibility the auditor is taking in the auditor's report.	4. The practitioner must state in the report that the report is intended solely for the information and use of the specified parties under the following circumstances: • When the criteria used to evaluate the subject matter are determined by the practitioner to be appropriate only for a limited number of parties who either participated in the establishment or can be presumed to have an adequate understanding of the criteria. • When the criteria used to evaluate the subject matter are available only to specified parties. • When reporting on subject matter and a written assertion has not been provided by the responsible party. • When the report is on an attestation engagement to apply agreed-upon procedures to the subject matter.

ILLUSTRATION 2—EXAMPLES OF MATTERS THAT MIGHT APPEAR IN A REPRESENTATION LETTER FOR AN ATTEST ENGAGEMENT

Examples of Representation Letter Items When the Client Is the Responsible Party

- A statement acknowledging responsibility for the subject matter and, when applicable, the assertion.

- A statement acknowledging responsibility for selecting the criteria, where applicable.

- A statement acknowledging responsibility for determining that such criteria are appropriate for the responsible party's purposes.

- The assertion about the subject matter based on the criteria selected.

- A statement that all known matters contradicting the assertion and any communication from regulatory agencies affecting the subject matter or the assertion have been disclosed to the practitioner.

- Availability of all records relevant to the subject matter.

- A statement that any known events subsequent to the period (or point in time) of the subject matter being reported on that would have a material effect on the subject matter, or the assertion, have been disclosed to the practitioner.

- Other matters that the practitioner deems appropriate.

- A statement acknowledging the client's responsibility for selecting the criteria, where applicable.

- A statement acknowledging the client's responsibility for determining that such criteria are appropriate for its purposes.

- A statement that any known events subsequent to the period (or point in time) of the subject matter being reported on that would have a material effect on the subject matter, or the assertion, have been disclosed to the practitioner.

- Other matters that the practitioner deems appropriate.

ILLUSTRATION 3—COMPONENTS OF THE PRACTITIONER'S EXAMINATION REPORT ON A SUBJECT MATTER OR ON AN ASSERTION

Item in the Practitioner's Examination Report	Applicability of Item to an Examination Report on:	
	A Subject Matter	An Assertion
1. A title that includes the word *independent*.	✓	✓
2. An introductory paragraph that:		
a. Identifies the [*subject matter or assertion, whichever is applicable*] and the responsible party. (For an examination report on an assertion, when the assertion does not accompany the practitioner's report, the introductory paragraph should also contain a statement of the assertion.)	✓	✓
b. States that the [*subject matter or assertion, whichever is applicable*] is the responsibility of the responsible party.	✓	✓
c. States that the practitioner's responsibility is to express an opinion on the [*subject matter or assertion, whichever is applicable*] based on his or her examination.	✓	✓

	Applicability of Item to an Examination Report on:	
Item in the Practitioner's Examination Report	A Subject Matter	An Assertion
3. A scope paragraph stating that:		
a. The examination was conducted in accordance with attestation standards established by the American Institute of Certified Public Accountants and, accordingly, included procedures that the practitioner considered necessary in the circumstances.	✓	✓
b. The practitioner believes the examination provides a reasonable basis for his or her opinion.	✓	✓
4. An opinion paragraph stating:		
a. Whether the subject matter is based on (or in conformity with) the criteria in all material respects.	✓	N/A
b. Whether the assertion is presented (or fairly stated), in all material respects, based on the criteria. (However, the practitioner should modify the report and should ordinarily express his or her conclusion directly on the subject matter, not on the assertion, if conditions exist that result in material misstatements or deviations from the criteria.)	N/A	✓
5. A statement restricting the use of the report to specified parties under the following circumstances:		
a. When the criteria used to evaluate the subject matter are determined by the practitioner to be appropriate only for a limited number of parties who either participated in their establishment or can be presumed to have an adequate understanding of the criteria.	✓	✓
b. When the criteria used to evaluate the subject matter are available only to the specified parties.	✓	✓
c. When a written assertion has not been provided by the responsible party. (The practitioner should also include a statement to that effect in the introductory paragraph of the report.)	✓	N/A
6. Manual or printed signature of the practitioner's firm.	✓	✓
7. Date of the examination report.	✓	✓

ILLUSTRATION 4—STANDARD EXAMINATION REPORT ON SUBJECT MATTER FOR GENERAL USE

Independent Accountant's Report

We have examined the [*identify the subject matter—for example, the accompanying schedule of investment returns of XYZ Company for the year ended December 31, 20X2*]. XYZ Company's management is responsible for the schedule of investment returns. Our responsibility is to express an opinion based on our examination.

Our examination was conducted in accordance with attestation standards established by the American Institute of Certified Public Accountants and, accordingly, included examining on a test basis, evidence supporting the [*identify the subject matter—for example, XYZ Company's schedule of investment returns*] and performing such other procedures as we considered necessary in the circumstances. We believe that our examination provides a reasonable basis for our opinion.

[*Additional paragraph(s) may be added to emphasize certain matters relating to the attest engagement or the subject matter.*]

In our opinion, the schedule referred to above presents, in all material respects, [*identify the subject matter—for example, the investment returns of XYZ Company for the year ended December 31, 20X2*] based on [*identify criteria—for example, the ABC criteria set forth in Note 1*].

[*Signature*]

[*Date*]

ILLUSTRATION 5—STANDARD EXAMINATION REPORT ON AN ASSERTION FOR GENERAL USE

Independent Accountant's Report

We have examined management's assertion that [*identify the assertion—for example, the accompanying schedule of investment returns of XYZ Company for the year ended December 31, 20X2, is presented in accordance with the ABC criteria set forth in Note 1*]. XYZ Company's management is responsible for the assertion. Our responsibility is to express an opinion on the assertion based on our examination.

Our examination was conducted in accordance with attestation standards established by the American Institute of Certified Public Accountants and, accordingly, included examining on a test basis, evidence supporting management's assertion and performing such other procedures as we considered necessary in the circumstances. We believe that our examination provides a reasonable basis for our opinion.

[*Additional paragraph(s) may be added to emphasize certain matters relating to the attest engagement or the assertion.*]

In our opinion, management's assertion referred to above is fairly stated, in all material respects, based on [*identify criteria—for example, the ABC criteria set forth in Note 1*].

[*Signature*]

[*Date*]

ILLUSTRATION 6—EXAMINATION REPORT ON AN ASSERTION BUT OPINION ISSUED IS ON THE SUBJECT MATTER

Independent Accountant's Report

We have examined management's assertion that [*identify the assertion—for example, the accompanying schedule of investment returns of XYZ Company for the year ended December 31, 20X2, is presented in accordance with the ABC criteria set forth in Note 1*]. XYZ Company's management is responsible for the assertion. Our responsibility is to express an opinion based on our examination.

Our examination was conducted in accordance with attestation standards established by the American Institute of Certified Public Accountants and, accordingly, included examining on a test basis evidence supporting the [*identify the subject matter—for example, XYZ Company's schedule of investment returns*] and performing such other procedures as we considered necessary in the circumstances. We believe that our examination provides a reasonable basis for our opinion.

[*Additional paragraph(s) may be added to emphasize certain matters relating to the attest engagement or the assertion.*]

In our opinion, the schedule referred to above presents, in all material respects, [*identify the subject matter—for example, the investment returns of XYZ Company for the year ended December 31, 20X2*] based on [*identify criteria—for example, the ABC criteria set forth in Note 1*].

[*Signature*]

[*Date*]

ILLUSTRATION 7—EXAMINATION REPORT ON SUBJECT MATTER THAT IS RESTRICTED BECAUSE THE CRITERIA ARE AVAILABLE ONLY TO SPECIFIED PARTIES

Independent Accountant's Report

We have examined the accompanying schedule of investment returns of XYZ Company for the year ended December 31, 20X2. XYZ Company's management is responsible for the schedule of investment returns. Our responsibility is to express an opinion based on our examination.

Our examination was conducted in accordance with attestation standards established by the American Institute of Certified Public Accountants and, accordingly, included examining on a test basis evidence supporting the [*identify the subject matter—for example, XYZ Company's schedule of investment returns*] and performing such other procedures as we considered necessary in the circumstances. We believe that our examination provides a reasonable basis for our opinion.

[*Additional paragraph(s) may be added to emphasize certain matters relating to the attest engagement or the assertion.*]

In our opinion, the schedule referred to above presents, in all material respects, [*identify the subject matter—for example, the investment returns of XYZ Company for the year ended December 31, 20X2*] based on the ABC criteria referred to in the investment management agreement between XYZ Company and DEF Investment Managers, Ltd., dated August 13, 20X1.

This report is intended solely for the information and use of XYZ Company and [*identify other specified parties—for example, DEF Investment Managers, Ltd.*] and is not intended to be and should not be used by anyone other than these specified parties.

[*Signature*]

[*Date*]

ILLUSTRATION 8—EXAMINATION REPORT WITH A QUALIFIED OPINION DUE TO MATERIAL MISSTATEMENTS OR DEVIATIONS FROM THE CRITERIA

Independent Accountant's Report

We have examined the accompanying schedule of investment returns of XYZ Company for the year ended December 31, 20X2. XYZ Company's management is responsible for the schedule of investment returns. Our responsibility is to express an opinion based on our examination.

Our examination was conducted in accordance with attestation standards established by the American Institute of Certified Public Accountants and, accordingly, included examining on a test basis evidence supporting the [*identify the subject matter—for example, XYZ Company's schedule of investment returns*] and performing such other procedures as we considered necessary in the circumstances. We believe that our examination provides a reasonable basis for our opinion.

Our examination disclosed the following [*describe condition(s) that, individually or in the aggregate, resulted in a material misstatement or deviation from the criteria*].

In our opinion, except for the material misstatement [*or deviation from the criteria*] described in the preceding paragraph, the schedule referred to above presents, in all material respects, [*identify the subject matter—for example, the investment returns of XYZ Company for the year ended December 31, 20X2*] based on [*identify criteria—for example, the ABC criteria set forth in Note 1*].

[*Signature*]

[*Date*]

ILLUSTRATION 9—EXAMINATION REPORT WITH A DISCLAIMER OF OPINION DUE TO A SCOPE RESTRICTION

Independent Accountant's Report

We were engaged to examine the accompanying schedule of investment returns of XYZ Company for the year ended December 31, 20X2. XYZ Company's management is responsible for the schedule of investment returns.

[*Include paragraph to describe scope restrictions.*]

Because of the restriction on the scope of our examination discussed in the preceding paragraph, the scope of our work was not sufficient to enable us to express, and we do not express, an opinion on whether the schedule referred to above presents, in all material respects, [*identify the subject matter—for example, the*] *investment returns of XYZ Company for the year ended December 31, 20X2]* based on *[identify criteria—for example, the ABC criteria set forth in Note 1]*.

[Signature]

[Date]

ILLUSTRATION 10—EXAMINATION REPORT ON SUBJECT MATTER THAT IS THE RESPONSIBILITY OF A PARTY OTHER THAN THE CLIENT AND THAT IS RESTRICTED SINCE A WRITTEN ASSERTION HAS NOT BEEN PROVIDED BY THE RESPONSIBLE PARTY

Independent Accountant's Report

We have examined the *[identify the subject matter—for example, the accompanying schedule of investment returns of XYZ Company for the year ended December 31, 20X2]*. XYZ Company's management is responsible for the schedule of investment returns. XYZ management did not provide us a written assertion about their schedule of investment returns for the year ended December 31, 20X2. Our responsibility is to express an opinion based on our examination.

Our examination was conducted in accordance with attestation standards established by the American Institute of Certified Public Accountants and, accordingly, included examining on a test basis, evidence supporting the *[identify the subject matter—for example, XYZ Company's schedule of investment returns]* and performing such other procedures as we considered necessary in the circumstances. We believe that our examination provides a reasonable basis for our opinion.

[Additional paragraph(s) may be added to emphasize certain matters relating to the attest engagement or the subject matter.]

In our opinion, the schedule referred to above presents, in all material respects, *[identify the subject matter—for example, the investment returns of XYZ Company for the year ended December 31, 20X2]* based on *[identify criteria—for example, the ABC criteria set forth in Note 1]*.

This report is intended solely for the information and use of the management and board of Directors of DEF Company and is not intended to be and should not be used by anyone other than these specified parties.

[Signature]

[Date]

ILLUSTRATION 11—COMPONENTS OF THE PRACTITIONER'S REVIEW REPORT ON A SUBJECT MATTER OR ON AN ASSERTION

Item in the Practitioner's Review Report	Applicability of Item to a Review Report on:	
	A Subject Matter	An Assertion
1. A title that includes the word *independent*.	✓	✓
2. An introductory paragraph that:		

Item in the Practitioner's Review Report	Applicability of Item to a Review Report on:	
	A Subject Matter	An Assertion
a. Identifies the [*subject matter or assertion, whichever is applicable*] and the responsible party. (For a review report on an assertion, when the assertion does not accompany the practitioner's report, the introductory paragraph should also contain a statement of the assertion.)	✓	✓
b. States that the [*subject matter or assertion, whichever is applicable*] is the responsibility of the responsible party.	✓	✓
3. A scope paragraph stating that:		
a. The review was conducted in accordance with attestation standards established by the American Institute of Certified Public Accountants.	✓	✓
b. A review is substantially less in scope than an examination, the objective of which is an expression of opinion on the [*subject matter or assertion, whichever is applicable,*] and accordingly no such opinion is expressed.	✓	✓
4. A conclusion paragraph stating:		
a. Whether the practitioner is aware of any material modifications that should be made to the subject matter in order for it to be based on (or in conformity with), in all material respects, the criteria, other than those modifications, if any, indicated in his or her report.	✓	N/A
b. Whether the practitioner is aware of any material modifications that should be made to the assertion in order for it to be presented (or fairly stated), in all material respects, based on (or in conformity with) the criteria, other than those modifications, if any, indicated in his or her report.	N/A	✓
5. A statement restricting the use of the report to specified parties under the following circumstances:		
a. When the criteria used to evaluate the subject matter are determined by the practitioner to be appropriate only for a limited number of parties who either participated in their establishment or can be presumed to have an adequate understanding of the criteria.	✓	✓
b. When the criteria used to evaluate the subject matter are available only to the specified parties.	✓	✓

	Applicability of Item to a Review Report on:	
Item in the Practitioner's Review Report	A Subject Matter	An Assertion
c. When a written assertion has not been provided by the responsible party. (The practitioner should also include a statement to that effect in the introductory paragraph of the report.)	✓	N/A
6. Manual or printed signature of the practitioner's firm.	✓	✓
7. Date of the review report.	✓	✓

ILLUSTRATION 12—STANDARD REVIEW REPORT ON SUBJECT MATTER FOR GENERAL USE

Independent Accountant's Report

We have reviewed the [*identify the subject matter—for example, the accompanying schedule of investment returns of XYZ Company for the year ended December 31, 20X2*]. XYZ Company's management is responsible for the schedule of investment returns.

Our review was conducted in accordance with attestation standards established by the American Institute of Certified Public Accountants. A review is substantially less in scope than an examination, the objective of which is the expression of an opinion on the [*identify the subject matter—for example, XYZ Company's schedule of investment returns*]. Accordingly, we do not express such an opinion.

[*Additional paragraph(s) may be added to emphasize certain matters relating to the attest engagement or the subject matter.*]

Based on our review, nothing came to our attention that caused us to believe that the [*identify the subject matter—for example, the schedule of investment returns of XYZ Company for the year ended December 31, 20X2*] is not presented, in all material respects, in conformity with [*identify the criteria—for example, the ABC criteria set forth in Note 1*].

[*Signature*]

[*Date*]

ILLUSTRATION 13—REVIEW REPORT ON SUBJECT MATTER THAT IS THE RESPONSIBILITY OF A PARTY OTHER THAN THE CLIENT AND THAT IS RESTRICTED SINCE A WRITTEN ASSERTION HAS NOT BEEN PROVIDED BY THE RESPONSIBLE PARTY

Independent Accountant's Report

We have reviewed the [*identify the subject matter—for example, the accompanying schedule of investment returns of XYZ Company for the year ended December 31, 20X2*]. XYZ Company's management is responsible for the schedule of investment returns. XYZ Company's management did not provide us a written assertion about their schedule of investment returns for the year ended December 31, 20X2.

Our review was conducted in accordance with attestation standards established by the American Institute of Certified Public Accountants. A review is substantially less in scope than an examination, the objective of which is the expression of an opinion on the [*identify the subject matter—for example, XYZ Company's schedule of investment returns*]. Accordingly, we do not express such an opinion.

[*Additional paragraph(s) may be added to emphasize certain matters relating to the attest engagement or the subject matter.*]

Based on our review, nothing came to our attention that caused us to believe that the [*identify the subject matter—for example, the schedule of investment returns of XYZ Company for the year ended December 31, 20X2*] is not presented, in all material respects, in conformity with [*identify the criteria—for example, the ABC criteria set forth in Note 1*].

This report is intended solely for the information and use of the management and board of Directors of DEF Company and is not intended to be and should not be used by anyone other than these specified parties.

[*Signature*]

[*Date*]

ILLUSTRATION 14—REVIEW REPORT ON AN ASSERTION THAT IS RESTRICTED SINCE THE CRITERIA ARE AVAILABLE ONLY TO THE SPECIFIED PARTIES

Independent Accountant's Report

We have reviewed management's assertion that [*identify the assertion—for example, the accompanying schedule of investment returns of XYZ Company for the year ended December 31, 20X2, is presented in accordance with the ABC criteria referred to in Note 1*]. XYZ Company's management is responsible for the assertion.

Our review was conducted in accordance with attestation standards established by the American Institute of Certified Public Accountants. A review is substantially less in scope than an examination, the objective of which is the expression of an opinion on management's assertion. Accordingly, we do not express such an opinion.

[*Additional paragraph(s) may be added to emphasize certain matters relating to the attest engagement or the assertion.*]

Based on our review, nothing came to our attention that caused us to believe that management's assertion referred to above is not fairly stated, in all material respects, based on [*identify the criteria—for example, the ABC criteria referred to in the investment management agreement between XYZ Company and DEF Investment Managers, Ltd., dated August 13, 20X1*].

This report is intended solely for the information and use of XYZ Company and [*identify other specified parties—for example, DEF Investment Managers, Ltd.*] and is not intended to be and should not be used by anyone other than these specified parties.

[*Signature*]

[*Date*]

ILLUSTRATION 15—SAMPLE LETTER TO A REGULATOR'S REQUEST FOR ACCESS TO ATTEST DOCUMENTATION IN AN EXAMINATION ENGAGEMENT

[*Date*]

[*Name and Address of Regulatory Agency*]

Your representatives have requested access to our attest documentation in connection with our engagement to examine [*identify the subject matter examined or restate management's assertion*]. It is our understanding that the purpose of your request is [*state purpose, for example, "to facilitate your regulatory examination"*].[1]

Our examination was conducted in accordance with attestation standards established by the American Institute of Certified Public Accountants, the objective of which is to form an opinion as to whether management's assertion is fairly stated, in all material respects, based on [*identify criteria*]. Under these standards, we have the responsibility to plan and perform our examination to provide a reasonable basis for our opinion and to exercise due professional care in the performance of our examination. Our examination is subject to the inherent risk that material noncompliance, if it exists, would not be detected. In addition, our examination does not address the possibility that material noncompliance may occur in the future. Also, our use of professional judgment and the assessments of attestation risk and materiality for the purpose of our examination means that matters may have existed that would have been assessed differently by you. Our examination does not provide a legal determination on [*name of entity*]'s compliance with specified requirements.

The attest documentation was prepared for the purpose of providing the principal support for our opinion on [*name of entity's*] compliance and to aid in the performance and supervision of our examination. The attest documentation is the principal record of attest procedures performed, information obtained, and conclusions reached in the examination. The procedures that we performed were limited to those we considered necessary under attestation standards established by the American Institute of Certified Public Accountants to provide us with reasonable basis for our opinion. Accordingly, we make no representation as to the sufficiency or appropriateness, for your purposes, of either the procedures or information documented in our audit documentation. In addition, any notations, comments, and individual conclusions appearing on any of the attest documentation do not stand alone and should not be read as an opinion on any part of management's assertion or the related subject matter.

---

[1] If the practitioner is not required by law, regulation, or engagement contract to provide a regulator access to the attest documentation but otherwise intends to provide such access, the letter should include a statement that: "Management of (*name of client*) has authorized us to provide you access to our attest documentation for (*state purpose*)."

Our examination was performed for the purpose stated above and was not planned or performed in contemplation of your [*state purpose, for example, "regulatory examination"*]. Therefore, items of possible interest to you may not have been specifically addressed. Accordingly, our examination, and the attest documentation prepared in connection therewith, should not supplant other inquiries and procedures that should be undertaken by the [*name of regulatory agency*] for the purpose of monitoring and regulating [*name of entity*]. In addition, we have not performed any procedures since the date of our report with respect to management's assertion, and significant events or circumstances may have occurred since that date.

The attest documentation constitutes and reflects work performed or information obtained by us in the course of our examination. The documents contain trade secrets and confidential commercial and financial information of our firm and [*name of entity*] that is privileged and confidential, and we expressly reserve all rights with respect to disclosures to third parties. Accordingly, we request confidential treatment under the Freedom of Information Act or similar laws and regulations when requests are made for the attest documentation or information contained therein or any documents created by the [*name of regulatory agency*] containing information derived there-from. We further request that written notice be given to our firm before distribution of the information in the attest documentation (or copies thereof) to others, including other governmental agencies, except when such distribution is required by law or regulation.

(If it is expected that copies will be requested, add:

Any copies of our attest documentation we agree to provide you will contain a legend "Confidential Treatment Requested by [*name of practitioner, address, telephone number*]."*)*

[*Firm signature*]

ILLUSTRATION 16—SAMPLE LETTER TO A REGULATOR'S REQUEST FOR ACCESS TO ATTEST DOCUMENTATION IN AN AGREED-UPON PROCEDURES ENGAGEMENT

[*Date*]

[*Name and Address of Regulatory Agency*]

Your representatives have requested access to our attest documentation in connection with our engagement to perform agreed-upon procedures on [*identify the subject matter or management's assertion*]. It is our understanding that the purpose of your request is [*state purpose, for example, "to facilitate your regulatory examinations"*].[2]

Our agreed-upon procedures engagement was performed in accordance with attestation standards established by the American Institute of Certified Public Accountants. Under these standards, we have the responsibility to per-

---

[2] If the practitioner is not required by law, regulation, or engagement contract to provide a regulator access to the attest documentation but otherwise intends to provide such access, the letter should include a statement that: "Management of (*name of client*) has authorized us to provide you access to our attest documentation for (*state purpose*)."

form the agreed-upon procedures to provide a reasonable basis for the findings expressed in our report. We were not engaged to, and did not, perform an examination, the objective of which would be to form an opinion on [*identify the subject matter or management's assertion*]. Our engagement is subject to the inherent risk that material misstatement of [*identify the subject matter or management's assertion*], if it exists, would not be detected. [*The practitioner may add the following:* "*In addition, our engagement does not address the possibility that material misstatement of the subject matter or management's assertion may occur in the future.*"] The procedures that we performed were limited to those agreed to by the specified users, and the sufficiency of these procedures is solely the responsibility of the specified users of the report. Further, our engagement does not provide a legal determination on [*name of entity*]'s compliance with specified requirements.

The attest documentation was prepared to document agreed-upon procedures applied, information obtained, and findings reached in the engagement. Accordingly, we make no representation, for your purposes, as to the sufficiency or appropriateness of the information documented in our attest documentation. In addition, any notations, comments, and individual findings appearing on any of the attest documentation should not be read as an opinion on management's assertion or the related subject matter, or any part thereof.

Our engagement was performed for the purpose stated above and was not performed in contemplation of your [*state purpose, for example, "regulatory examination"*]. Therefore, items of possible interest to you may not have been specifically addressed. Accordingly, our engagement, and the attest documentation prepared in connection therewith, should not supplant other inquiries and procedures that should be undertaken by the [*name of regulatory agency*] for the purpose of monitoring and regulating [*name of client*]. In addition, we have not performed any procedures since the date of our report with respect to the subject matter or management's assertion related thereto, and significant events or circumstances may have occurred since that date.

The attest documentation constitutes and reflects procedures performed or information obtained by us in the course of our engagement. The documents contain trade secrets and confidential commercial and financial information of our firm and [*name of client*] that is privileged and confidential, and we expressly reserve all rights with respect to disclosures parties. Accordingly, we request confidential treatment under the Freedom of Information Act or similar laws and regulations when requests are made for the attest documentation or information contained therein or any documents created by the [*name of regulatory agency*] containing information derived therefrom. We further request that written notice be given to our firm before distribution of the information in the attest documentation (or copies thereof) to others, including other governmental agencies, except when such distribution is required by law or regulation.

(*If it is expected that copies will be requested, add:*

Any copies of our attest documentation we agree to provide you will contain a legend "Confidential Treatment Requested by [*name of practitioner, address, telephone number*].")

[*Firm signature*]

ILLUSTRATION 17—ACCOUNTANT'S REPORT ON THE SUITABILITY OF THE DESIGN OF AN ENTITY'S INTERNAL CONTROL THAT HAS BEEN IMPLEMENTED

Independent Accountant's Report

We have examined the suitability of the design of XYZ Company's internal control over financial reporting to prevent or detect and correct material misstatements in its financial statements on a timely basis as of December 31, 20X2, based on [*identify criteria*]. XYZ Company's management is responsible for the suitable design of internal control over financial reporting. Our responsibility is to express an opinion on the design of internal control based on our examination.

Our examination was conducted in accordance with attestation standards established by the American Institute of Certified Public Accountants and, accordingly, included obtaining an understanding of internal control over financial reporting, evaluating the design of internal control, and performing such other procedures as we considered necessary in the circumstances. We believe that our examination provides a reasonable basis for our opinion. We were not engaged to examine and report on the operating effectiveness of XYZ Company's internal control over financial reporting as of December 31, 20X2, and, accordingly, we express no opinion on operating effectiveness.

Because of its inherent limitations, internal control over financial reporting may not prevent or detect and correct misstatements. Also, projections of any evaluation of effectiveness to future periods are subject to the risk that controls may become inadequate because of changes in conditions, or that the degree of compliance with the policies or procedures may deteriorate.

In our opinion, XYZ Company's internal control over financial reporting was suitably designed, in all material respects, to prevent or detect and correct material misstatements in the financial statements on a timely basis as of December 31, 20X2, based on [*identify criteria*].

[*Signature*]

[*Date*]

ILLUSTRATION 18—ACCOUNTANT'S REPORT ON THE SUITABILITY OF THE DESIGN OF AN ENTITY'S INTERNAL CONTROL THAT HAS NOT YET BEEN IMPLEMENTED

Independent Accountant's Report

We have examined the suitability of the design of XYZ Company's internal control over financial reporting to prevent or detect and correct material misstatements in its financial statements on a timely basis as of December 31, 20X2, based on [*identify criteria*]. XYZ Company's management is responsible for the suitable design of internal control over financial reporting. Our responsibility is to express an opinion on the design of internal control based on our examination.

Our examination was conducted in accordance with attestation standards established by the American Institute of Certified Public Accountants and, accordingly, included obtaining an understanding of internal control over financial reporting, evaluating the design of internal control, and performing such other procedures as we considered necessary in the circumstances. We believe that our examination provides a reasonable basis for our opinion. Because operations had not begun as of December 31, 20X2, we could not confirm that the specified controls were implemented. Accordingly, our report solely addresses the suitability of the design of the Company's internal control and does not address whether the controls were implemented. Furthermore, because the specified controls have not yet been implemented, we were unable to test, and did not test, the operating effectiveness of XYZ Company's internal control over financial reporting as of December 31, 20X2, and, accordingly, we express no opinion on operating effectiveness.

Because of its inherent limitations, internal control over financial reporting may not prevent or detect and correct misstatements. Also, projections of any evaluation of effectiveness to future periods are subject to the risk that controls may not be implemented as intended when operations begin or may become inadequate because of changes in conditions.

In our opinion, XYZ Company's internal control over financial reporting was suitably designed, in all material respects, to prevent or detect and correct material misstatements in the financial statements on a timely basis as of December 31, 20X2, based on [*identify criteria*].

[*Signature*]

[*Date*]

AT SECTION 201
AGREED-UPON PROCEDURES ENGAGEMENTS

WHAT EVERY PRACTITIONER SHOULD KNOW

Basic Objectives and Requirements

This Section is applicable to all agreed-upon procedures engagements, except those engagements noted in Illustration 1. In addition, when performing agreed-upon procedures on prospective financial information or on compliance matters, the practitioner should refer to AT Section 301 (Financial Forecasts and Projections) and AT Section 601 (Compliance Attestation), respectively.

In an agreed-upon procedures engagement, the practitioner does not provide an opinion or negative assurance. Rather, the practitioner's report should be in the form of procedures and findings and should indicate that its use is restricted to those parties, including the client, who agreed to the procedures performed or to be performed (herein referred to as "specified parties").

In addition, the practitioner should comply with attest documentation requirements prescribed in AT Section 101 (Attest Engagements).

Conditions for Engagement Performance

The following conditions must be met before a practitioner may perform an agreed-upon procedures attest engagement:

1. The practitioner is independent.
2. One of the following conditions is met:
   a. The party wishing to engage the practitioner is responsible for the subject matter, or has a reasonable basis for providing a written assertion about the subject matter, *or*
   b. The party wishing to engage the practitioner is *not* responsible for the subject matter but is able to provide the practitioner, or have a third party who is responsible for the subject matter provide the practitioner, with evidence of the third party's responsibility for the subject matter.
3. The practitioner and the specified parties agree on the procedures that the practitioner has performed or will perform.
4. The specified parties take responsibility for the sufficiency of the agreed-upon procedures for their purposes.
5. The specific subject matter to which the procedures are applied is subject to reasonably consistent measurement.
6. Criteria to be used in the determination of findings are agreed upon between the practitioner and the specified parties.
7. The application of the agreed-upon procedures is expected to generate reasonably consistent findings.

8. Audit evidence related to the specific subject matter is expected to exist and to provide a reasonable basis for the practitioner's findings.

9. Where applicable, the practitioner and the specified parties agree on any materiality limits for reporting purposes.

10. Use of the practitioner's report is restricted to the specified parties.

11. For agreed-upon procedures engagements on prospective financial information, the prospective financial statements include a summary of significant assumptions. See AT Section 301 (Financial Forecasts and Projections).

The practitioner should establish an understanding with the client regarding the services to be performed, for example through the use of an engagement letter. See Illustration 2 for matters that might be included in such an understanding with the client.

Procedures to Be Performed

The procedures that the practitioner agrees to perform should not be so general as to be subject to various interpretations. Terms that are ambiguous and subject to varying degrees of interpretation (such as *limited review, general review, reconcile, check,* or *test*) should not be used to describe procedures unless they are defined. Also, certain procedures are limited in nature (such as the mere reading of information furnished) and, therefore, cannot be the basis for the engagement. Illustration 3 provides examples of appropriate and inappropriate procedures in engagements to apply agreed-upon procedures.

Involvement of a specialist The practitioner may use the work of a specialist to assist in the execution of an agreed-upon procedures engagement when the engagement requires expertise beyond that of the practitioner. The role of the specialist should be agreed to by the practitioner and the specified parties, and should be described in the practitioner's report. However, the practitioner should not agree to merely read the report of a specialist solely for the purpose of describing or repeating the specialist's findings. Also, the practitioner should not take any responsibility for all or a portion of any procedures performed by a specialist or the specialist's work product.

Use of internal auditors and client personnel The practitioner may use internal auditors and other client personnel for preparing schedules and analyses for the practitioner's use in the engagement. However, the agreed-upon procedures enumerated, or referred to, in the practitioner's report should be performed solely and entirely by the practitioner, except where a specialist is involved as described above.

Reporting Requirements

The practitioner should report all findings in his or her report regardless of materiality, unless the definition of materiality is agreed to by the specified parties. If the specified parties have specifically agreed that the practitioner should report only those amounts greater than an agreed-upon materiality threshold, then the practitioner's report should include a description of the agreed-upon materiality limits.

The practitioner is prohibited from providing negative assurance about whether the subject matter or the assertion is fairly stated based on the criteria. For example, it would be inappropriate to state in the report that "nothing came to our attention that caused us to believe that the [*identify subject matter*] is not presented based on (or the assertion is not fairly stated based on) [*identify criteria*]."

Required elements in the practitioner's report The practitioner's report on agreed-upon procedures engagements should be in the form of procedures and findings and should contain the following elements:

1. A title that includes the word *independent.*

2. Identification of the specified parties.

3. Identification of the subject matter, or the written assertion related thereto, and the character of the engagement.

4. Identification of the responsible party.

5. A statement that the subject matter is the responsibility of the responsible party.

6. A statement that the procedures performed were those agreed to by the specified parties.

7. A reference to AICPA attestation standards.

8. A statement that the specified parties are solely responsible for the sufficiency of the procedures and a disclaimer of responsibility for the sufficiency of those procedures.

9. A list of the procedures performed (or reference thereto) and related findings.

10. A description of any agreed-upon materiality limits, if applicable.

11. A statement that the practitioner was not engaged to and did not conduct an examination of the subject matter.

12. A disclaimer of opinion on the subject matter.

13. A statement that, if additional procedures had been performed, other matters might have come to the practitioner's attention that would have been reported.

14. A statement of restrictions on the use of the report because it is intended to be used solely by the specified parties.

15. Any reservations or restrictions regarding procedures or description findings.

16. For an agreed-upon procedures engagement on prospective financial information, all items required by AT Section 301 (Financial Forecasts and Projections).

17. Where applicable, a description of the role of any specialists in the engagement.

18. Manual or printed signature of the practitioner's firm.

19. Date of the report, which is the date of completion of the agreed-upon procedures.

See Illustration 4 for an example of a practitioner's report on an agreed-upon procedures engagement under this Section.

Explanatory language The practitioner's report in an agreed-upon procedures engagement may include explanatory language for conditions such as the following:

- Description of stipulated facts, assumptions, or interpretations (including the source thereof) used in the application of the agreed-upon procedures.

- Description of the condition of records, data, or controls that were subjected to the agreed-upon procedures.

- Statement that the practitioner has no responsibility to update his or her report.

- Explanation of sampling risk.

Scope restrictions When circumstances preclude the practitioner from performing the agreed-upon procedures, the practitioner should obtain agreement from the specified parties for modification of the procedures. If the specified parties do not or cannot agree (for instance, a regulatory agency) to the modification, the practitioner should describe the restrictions in his or her report or withdraw from the engagement.

Adding other parties as specified parties After the completion of the agreed-upon procedures engagement, the practitioner may be requested to add another party as a specified party (a nonparticipant party). When considering whether to add a nonparticipant party, the practitioner should consider such factors as the identity of the nonparticipant party and the intended use of the report. If the practitioner agrees to the addition of other specified parties, the practitioner should obtain acknowledgment, preferably in writing, from the added parties indicating that they agree to the procedures performed and they are responsible for the sufficiency of the procedures for their purposes.

Also, the practitioner may be requested to add another party as a specified party after the agreed-upon procedures report has been issued. Under this circumstance, the practitioner may reissue the original report or provide some other form of written communication that acknowledges the addition of the specified party. When the practitioner agrees to reissue the report, the original date of the report should be used.

Written Representations

While the practitioner is *not* required to obtain a representation letter in an agreed-upon procedures engagement, he or she may find the use of one helpful in obtaining representations from the responsible party. If the practitioner determines that a representation letter should be obtained but the responsible party refuses to provide one, the practitioner should take one of the following actions:

1. Disclose in the practitioner's report the inability to obtain representations from the responsible party.

2. Change the nature of the agreed-upon procedures engagement to another type of engagement, such as a consulting engagement.

3. Withdraw from the engagement.

Change to an Agreed-Upon Procedures Engagement from Another Form of Engagement

During the course of another form of engagement (e.g., an audit), the practitioner may be requested by the client to change the other engagement to an agreed-upon procedures engagement. In determining whether to agree to the change in engagements, the practitioner should consider the following factors:

1. Whether procedures performed as part of another type of engagement are appropriate for an agreed-upon procedures engagement.

2. The reason for the requested change in engagement, particularly the implications of scope restrictions imposed on the original engagement or matters to be reported.

3. The amount of effort that would be needed to complete the original engagement.

4. If applicable, the reasons for changing from a general-use report to a restricted-use report.

When the practitioner concludes that it is appropriate to change from the original engagement to an agreed-upon procedures engagement, the practitioner's report should not refer to the original engagement or any performance limitations that resulted in the changed engagement.

PRACTICE ISSUES AND FREQUENTLY ASKED QUESTIONS

Issue 1: Is a written assertion required in an agreed-upon procedures engagement?

No. Generally, a written assertion is not required in an agreed-upon procedures engagement unless specifically required by another attest standard (for example, an attest engagement about compliance with specified requirements or internal control over compliance). However, if the practitioner requests the responsible party to provide an assertion, the assertion may be presented in a representation letter or another written communication from the responsible party, such as in a statement or a narrative description.

Issue 2: When performing an agreed-upon procedures engagement under this Section, is the practitioner required to comply with the general, fieldwork, and reporting standards for attest engagements described in AT Section 101?

Yes. In addition to complying with the specific requirements discussed in this Section, the practitioner should comply with the five general standards, the two fieldwork standards, and the four reporting standards described in AT Section 101 (Attest Engagements).

Issue 3: Is the practitioner or the specified parties responsible for the sufficiency of the nature, timing, and extent of the agreed-upon procedures?

Specified parties, not the practitioner, are responsible for the nature, timing, and extent of agreed-upon procedures because they best understand their own needs. However, the practitioner must have adequate knowledge in the specific subject matter to which the agreed-upon procedures will be applied. In addition, the practitioner assumes the risk (1) for misapplication of the procedures that may lead to inappropriate findings and (2) that appropriate findings may not be reported or may be incorrectly reported.

Issue 4: Should the practitioner generally communicate with the specified parties regarding the nature of the procedures to be performed and their sufficiency for the parties' purposes?

Yes. To determine if the specified parties agree with and assume responsibility for the procedures, the practitioner should communicate directly with the specified parties and obtain an "affirmative acknowledgment" from each of them. This may be accomplished by:

1. Using engagement letters.

2. Meeting with the specified parties.

3. Distributing a draft of the anticipated report to the specified parties.

If the practitioner is unable to communicate directly with all of the specified parties, he or she may satisfy these requirements by applying procedures such as the following:

1. Compare the written requirements established by the specified parties with the proposed agreed-upon procedures.

2. Discuss the procedures to be applied with appropriate representatives of the specified parties.

3. Review relevant contracts with, or correspondence from, the specified parties.

Issue 5: Is there a minimum number of specified procedures that the practitioner is required to apply in an agreed-upon procedures engagement?

No. This Section does not specify a list of minimum procedures that the practitioner must perform in an agreed-upon procedures engagement. Therefore, the scope of such an engagement is flexible and procedures may be modified as long as the specified parties agree to the changes and accept responsibility for the sufficiency of the procedures.

Issue 6: May a practitioner report on an engagement when specified parties do not agree upon the procedures performed, or to be performed, or do not take responsibility for the sufficiency of the procedures?

No. The practitioner should not report on an engagement when the specified parties do not agree upon the procedures performed, or to be performed, or do not take responsibility for the sufficiency of the procedures for their purposes.

Issue 7: Can reports on applying agreed-upon procedures be combined with reports on other services, such as reviews, compilations, or attest and nonattest services?

Yes, the practitioner may combine reports on applying agreed-upon procedures with reports on such other services provided that (1) the types of services performed can be clearly distinguished and (2) the applicable standards for each service are followed.

Issue 8: Is a written engagement letter required for agreed-upon procedures engagements?

No. This Section requires only that the practitioner establish a clear understanding regarding the services to be performed. It states that this understanding may be in the form of an engagement letter, but does not require one. The engagement procedures can be as broad or as narrow as the parties agree to. There are no standards, other than the parties' agreement, that define what constitutes sufficient procedures for agreed-upon procedures engagements. Therefore, it is good business practice to obtain an engagement letter for all such engagements. See Illustration 2 for examples of matters that might be included in engagement letters for agreed-upon procedures engagements.

Issue 9: Is the practitioner obligated to report all findings from the application of agreed-upon procedures, regardless of materiality?

Yes. The practitioner should report all findings in his or her report regardless of materiality, unless the definition of materiality is agreed to by the specified parties. Unlike the standards for audits under GAAS, the agreed-upon procedures standards do not embrace the concept of materiality as a fundamental precept. They recognize, however, that the parties may agree to a definition of materiality for purposes of an engagement. When they do so, the practitioner must describe the agreed-upon materiality limits in his or her report and, if applicable, in the engagement letter.

Issue 10: Is the practitioner required to enumerate all of the agreed-upon procedures and findings in the body of his or her report, or can they be presented in a schedule accompanying the report?

Either method is acceptable. Generally, when the procedures or the findings are lengthy, a presentation in a separate schedule or schedules is more practical for ease of use by the specified parties.

Issue 11: If the practitioner decides to obtain a representation letter from the responsible party, what matters might the practitioner consider including in such a letter?

If the practitioner decides to obtain a representation letter from the responsible party, the following are examples of matters that might be included in such a letter:

- A statement acknowledging responsibility for the subject matter and, when applicable, the assertion.
- A statement acknowledging responsibility for selecting the criteria and for determining that such criteria are appropriate for their purposes.

- The assertion about the subject matter based on the criteria selected.
- A statement that all known matters contradicting the subject matter or the assertion have been disclosed to the practitioner.
- A statement that any communications from regulatory agencies affecting the subject matter or the assertion have been disclosed to the practitioner.
- Availability of all records relevant to the subject matter and the agreed-upon procedures.
- Other matters that the practitioner deems appropriate.

ILLUSTRATIONS AND PRACTICE AIDS

ILLUSTRATION 1—ENGAGEMENTS FOR WHICH AT SECTION 201 DOES NOT APPLY

Type of Engagement	Applicable Guidance
1. Engagements to report on specified compliance requirements based solely on an audit of financial statements.	1. AU Section 623 (Special Reports.)
2. Engagements to report in accordance with *Government Auditing Standards,* the Single Audit Act, or the Office of Management and Budget (OMB) Circulars.	2. AU Section 801 (Compliance Audits). However, AT Section 201 would apply when the terms of the engagement specify that the engagement be performed pursuant to SSAEs.
3. Situations covered by AU Section 324 (Service Organizations) when the service auditor is requested to apply substantive procedures to user transactions or assets at the service organization and he or she makes specific reference in the service auditor's report to having carried out designated procedures.	3. AU Section 324 (Service Organizations). However, AT Section 201 would apply when the service auditor provides a separate report on the performance of agreed-upon procedures in an attestation engagement.
4. Engagements to issue comfort letters for under writers and certain other requesting parties, pursuant to AU Section 634.	4. AU Section 634 (Letters for Underwriters and Certain Other Requesting Parties).
5. Engagements to express an opinion on specified elements, accounts, or items of a financial statement based on an audit.	5. AU Section 623 (Special Reports).

ILLUSTRATION 2—MATTERS THAT MIGHT BE INCLUDED IN ENGAGEMENT LETTERS FOR AGREED-UPON PROCEDURES ENGAGEMENTS

- The nature of the engagement.
- Identification of the subject matter, or the assertion related thereto, the responsible party, and the criteria to be used.
- Identification of the specified parties.
- Specified parties' acknowledgment of their responsibility for the sufficiency of the procedures.
- The practitioner's responsibilities.

- Reference to AICPA attestation standards.
- Agreement on procedures by enumerating or referring to them.
- Disclaimers that are expected to be part of the practitioner's report.
- Restrictions on the use of the agreed-upon procedures report.
- If applicable, description of assistance to be provided to the practitioner.
- Involvement of specialists.
- Agreed-upon materiality limits.

ILLUSTRATION 3—EXAMPLES OF APPROPRIATE AND INAPPROPRIATE PROCEDURES IN ENGAGEMENTS TO APPLY AGREED-UPON PROCEDURES

Examples of Appropriate Agreed-Upon Procedures	Examples of Inappropriate Agreed-Upon Procedures
• Performing a sampling application after agreeing on pertinent parameters.	• Mere reading of the work performed by others (e.g., specialists, internal auditors) solely to describe or repeat their findings.
• Examining specified documents evidencing certain types of transactions or detailed attributes thereof.	• Evaluating the competency or objectivity of another party.
• Confirming specific information with outside third parties.	• Obtaining an understanding about a particular subject.
• Comparing documents, schedules, or analyses with certain specified attributes.	• Interpreting documents that are not within the scope of the practitioner's professional expertise.
• Performing specific procedures on work performed by others, including the work of internal auditors.	• Taking responsibility for any portion of the client's internal auditors' procedures by reporting those findings as the practitioner's own.
• Performing mathematical computations.	• Reporting in any manner that implies shared responsibility for the procedures with the client's internal auditors.
• Performing all or some of the procedures previously performed by the client's internal auditors.	

ILLUSTRATION 4—STANDARD REPORT ON AN AGREED-UPON PROCEDURES ENGAGEMENT

Independent Accountant's Report on Applying Agreed-Upon Procedures

To the Audit Committees and Managements of
ABC Company and XYZ Fund

We have performed the procedures enumerated below, which were agreed to by the audit committees and managements of ABC Company and XYZ Fund, solely to assist you in evaluating the accompanying Statement of Investment Performance Statistics of XYZ Fund (prepared in accordance with the criteria specified therein) for the year ended December 31, 20X2. XYZ Fund's management is responsible for the statement of investment performance statistics. This agreed-upon procedures engagement was conducted in accordance with attestation standards established by the American Institute of Certified Public Accountants. The sufficiency of these procedures is solely the responsibility of those parties specified in this report. Consequently, we make no representation regarding the sufficiency of the procedures described below either for the purpose for which this report has been requested or for any other purpose.

[*Include paragraphs to enumerate procedures and findings.*]

We were not engaged to and did not conduct an examination, the objective of which would be the expression of an opinion on the accompanying Statement of Investment Performance Statistics of XYZ Fund. Accordingly, we do not express such an opinion. Had we performed additional procedures, other matters might have come to our attention that would have been reported to you.

This report is intended solely for the information and use of the audit committees and managements of ABC Company and XYZ Fund, and is not intended to be and should not be used by anyone other than these specified parties.

[*Signature*]

[*Date*]

ILLUSTRATION 5—REPORT ON APPLYING AGREED-UPON PROCEDURES IN CONNECTION WITH A PROPOSED ACQUISITION

Independent Accountant's Report on Applying Agreed-Upon Procedures

Board of Directors and Management
ABC Company

We have performed the procedures enumerated below, which were agreed to by the Board of Directors and Management of ABC Company, solely to assist you in connection with the proposed acquisition of XYZ Company as of December 31, 20X2. XYZ Company is responsible for its cash and accounts receivable records. This agreed-upon procedures engagement was conducted in accordance with attestation standards established by the American Institute of Certified Public Accountants. The sufficiency of these procedures is solely the responsibility of the parties specified in this report. Consequently, we make no representation regarding the sufficiency of the procedures described below either for the purpose for which this report has been requested or for any other purpose.

The procedures and the associated findings are as follows:

Cash

1. We obtained confirmation of the cash on deposit from the following banks, and we agreed the confirmed balance to the amount shown on the bank reconciliations maintained by XYZ Company. We mathematically checked the bank reconciliations and compared the resultant cash balances per book to the respective general ledger account balances.

Bank	General Ledger Account Balances as of December 31, 20X2
First National Bank	$ 107,000
Second State Bank	213,000
Global Trust Company-regular account	411,000
Global Trust Company-payroll account	72,000
	$803,000

We found no exceptions as a result of the procedures.

Accounts Receivable

2. We added the individual customer account balances shown in an aged trial balance of accounts receivable (identified as Exhibit A) and compared the resultant total with the balance in the general ledger account.

   We found no difference.

3. We compared the individual customer account balances shown in the aged trial balance of accounts receivable (Exhibit A) as of December 31, 20X2, to the balances shown in the accounts receivable subsidiary ledger.

   We found no exceptions as a result of the comparisons.

4. We traced the aging (according to invoice dates) for 50 customer account balances shown in Exhibit A to the details of outstanding invoices in the accounts receivable subsidiary ledger. The balances selected for tracing were determined by starting at the eighth item and selecting every fifteenth item thereafter.

   We found no exceptions in the aging of the amounts of the 50 customer account balances selected. The sample size traced was 10 percent of the aggregate amount of the customer account balances.

5. We mailed confirmations directly to the customers representing the 150 largest customer account balances selected from the accounts receivable trial balance, and we received responses as indicated below. We also traced the items constituting the outstanding customer account balance to invoices and supporting shipping documents for customers from which there was no reply. As agreed, any individual differences in a customer account balance of less than $300 were to be considered minor, and no further procedures were performed.

   Of the 150 customer balances confirmed, we received responses from 140 customers; 10 customers did not reply. No exceptions were identified in 120 of the confirmations received. The differences disclosed in the remaining 20 confirmation replies were either minor in amount (as defined above) or were reconciled to the customer account balance without proposed adjustment thereto. A summary of the confirmation results according to the respective aging categories is as follows:

Accounts Receivable December 31, 20X2

Aging Categories	Customer Account Balances	Confirmations Requested	Confirmation Replies Received
Current	$156,000	$76,000	$65,000
Past due:			
Less than one month	60,000	30,000	19,000
One to three months	36,000	18,000	10,000
Over three months	48,000	48,000	8,000
	$300,000	$172,000	$102,000

We were not engaged to and did not conduct an audit, the objective of which would be the expression of an opinion on cash and accounts receivable. Accordingly, we do not express such an opinion. Had we performed additional procedures, other matters might have come to our attention that would have been reported to you.

This report is intended solely for the information and use of the board of directors and management of ABC Company and is not intended to be and should not be used by anyone other than these specified parties.

[*Signature*]

[*Date*]

ILLUSTRATION 6—REPORT ON APPLYING AGREED-UPON PROCEDURES IN CONNECTION WITH CLAIMS OF CREDITORS

Independent Accountant's Report on Applying Agreed-Upon Procedures

To the Trustee of ABC Company:

We have performed the procedures described below, which were agreed to by the Trustee of ABC Company, with respect to the claims of creditors solely to assist you in determining the validity of claims of ABC Company as of May 31, 20X2, as set forth in the accompanying Schedule A. ABC Company is responsible for maintaining records of claims submitted by creditors of ABC Company. This agreed-upon procedures engagement was conducted in accordance with attestation standards established by the American Institute of Certified Public Accountants. The sufficiency of these procedures is solely the responsibility of the party specified in this report. Consequently, we make no representation regarding the sufficiency of the procedures described below either for the purpose for which this report has been requested or for any other purpose.

The procedures and associated findings are as follows:

1. Compare the total of the trial balance of accounts payable at May 31, 20X2, prepared by ABC Company, to the balance in the related general ledger account.

   The total of the accounts payable trial balance agreed with the balance in the related general ledger account.

2. Compare the amounts for claims received from creditors (as shown in claim documents provided by ABC Company) to the respective amounts shown in the trial balance of accounts payable. Using the data included in the claims documents and in ABC Company's accounts payable detail records, reconcile any differences found to the accounts payable trial balance.

   All differences noted are presented in column 3 of Schedule A. Except for those amounts shown in column 4 of Schedule A, all such differences were reconciled.

3. Obtain the documentation submitted by creditors in support of the amounts claimed and compare it to the following documentation in ABC Company's files: invoices, receiving reports, and other evidence of receipt of goods or services.

   No exceptions were found as a result of these comparisons.

We were not engaged to and did not conduct an audit, the objective of which would be the expression of an opinion on the claims of creditors set forth in the accompanying Schedule A. Accordingly, we do not express such an opinion. Had we performed additional procedures, other matters might have come to our attention that would have been reported to you.

This report is intended solely for the information and use of the Trustee of ABC Company and is not intended to be and should not be used by anyone other than this specified party.

[*Signature*]

[*Date*]

AT SECTION 301
FINANCIAL FORECASTS AND PROJECTIONS

PRACTICE POINT: In December 2010, the American Institute of Certified Public Accountants issued Statement on Standards for Attestation Engagements (SSAE) No. 17, "Reporting on Compiled Prospective Financial Statements When the Practitioner's Independence Is Impaired," which amends paragraph 23 of AT Section 301 (Financial Forecasts and Projections). The amendment removes the extant prohibition against disclosing the reasons for an independence impairment. Accordingly, the amendment permits, but does not require, the practitioner to disclose the reasons for an independence impairment in a report on compiled prospective financial information. This brings AT Section 301 into alignment with the guidance in SSARS-19, "Compilation and Review Engagements."

The amendment in SSAE-17 is effective for compilations of prospective financial statements for periods ending on or after December 15, 2010. Early application is permitted.

The provisions and requirements of SSAE-17, which is codified in AT Section 301, have been incorporated into this chapter.

WHAT EVERY PRACTITIONER SHOULD KNOW

Basic Objectives and Requirements

AT Section 20A practitioner should compile, examine, or apply agreed-upon procedures to prospective financial statements whenever the practitioner either:

1. Submits to a client or others prospective financial statements that he or she has assembled, or assisted in assembling, that are or reasonably might be expected to be used by another third party, *or*

2. Is engaged to report on prospective financial statements that are or reasonably might be expected to be used by another third party.

Prospective financial statements refers to either financial forecasts or financial projections, including the summaries of significant assumptions and accounting policies. Although they may cover a period that has partially expired, statements for periods that have completely expired are not considered to be prospective financial statements. They are for either "general use" or "limited use" as follows:

1. *General use*—This refers to use of the statements by persons with whom the responsible party is not negotiating directly, for example, in an offering statement of an entity's debt or equity interests. Because recipients of prospective financial statements distributed for general use are unable to ask the responsible party directly about the presentation, the presentation most useful to them is one that presents the expected results. Therefore, *only a financial forecast is appropriate for general use.*

2. *Limited use*—This refers to use of the statements by the responsible party alone or by the responsible party and third parties with whom the responsible party is negotiating directly. Examples include use in negoti-

ations for a bank loan, submission to a regulatory agency, and use solely within the entity. Recipients of prospective financial statements intended for limited use can ask questions of, and negotiate terms directly with, the responsible party. Therefore, *either a financial forecast or a financial projection is appropriate for limited use.*

In addition, a practitioner may accept and perform an engagement to compile, examine, or apply agreed-upon procedures to *partial presentations*, that is, presentations of prospective financial information that excludes one or more of the items required for prospective financial statements as described in Illustration 1. Because partial presentations are generally appropriate only for limited use, a practitioner's report on partial presentations of both forecasted and projected information should include a description of any limitations on the usefulness of the presentation.

The practitioner should comply with the attest documentation requirements prescribed in AT Section 101 (Attest Engagements) which, among other things, require the practitioner to document his or her consideration of the process the entity uses to develop its prospective financial statements.

This Section is not applicable:

1. When prospective financial statements are used solely in connection with litigation support services *and* the practitioner's work is subject to detailed analysis and challenge by each party to a dispute in a legal proceeding.

2. When the practitioner is engaged to prepare a financial analysis of a potential project where the practitioner obtains the information, makes appropriate assumptions, and assembles the presentation. Such an analysis is not a forecast or projection and would not be appropriate for general use. However, if the responsible party reviewed and adopted the assumptions and presentation, or based its assumptions and presentation on the analysis, the practitioner could perform one of the engagements described in this Section.

3. For budgets that do not extend beyond the end of the current fiscal year and that are presented with interim historical financial statements for the current year.

Compilation of Prospective Financial Statements

A compilation of prospective financial statements does not provide assurance that the practitioner will become aware of significant matters that might be disclosed by more extensive procedures, such as in an examination engagement. In a compilation engagement, the practitioner should observe the following:

1. The practitioner should not compile prospective financial statements that omit disclosure of the summary of significant assumptions, because such disclosure is essential to the reader's understanding of the statements.

2. The practitioner should not compile a financial projection that excludes (a) an identification of the hypothetical assumptions or (b) a description of the limitations on the usefulness of the presentation.

3. If the practitioner believes that information he or she has received is incomplete, inappropriate, or otherwise misleading, the practitioner should obtain additional or revised information. If he or she does not receive such information, the practitioner should ordinarily withdraw from the compilation engagement.

Illustration 15 is a procedures checklist that the practitioner can use in connection with compilations of prospective financial statements.

Reports on compiled prospective financial statements The practitioner's report on a compilation of prospective financial statements should include:

1. A paragraph that identifies the prospective financial statements presented by the responsible party.

2. A paragraph stating that:

   a. The practitioner has compiled the prospective financial statements in accordance with attestation standards established by the AICPA.

   b. A compilation is limited in scope and does not enable the practitioner to express an opinion or any other form of assurance on the prospective financial statements or the assumptions.

   c. The prospective results may not be achieved.

   d. The practitioner assumes no responsibility to update the report for events and circumstances occurring after the date of the report.

3. The date of the report, which is the date of completion of the compilation procedures.

4. Manual or printed signature of the practitioner's firm.

5. If the practitioner is not independent, the practitioner's report should be modified to indicate his or her lack of independence in a separate paragraph of the practitioner's report, for example:

   "We are not independent with respect to ABC Company."

   Also, if the practitioner *elects* to disclose a description about the reasons his or her independence is impaired, the practitioner should ensure that all reasons are included in the description. The following is an example of a description the practitioner may use:

   "We are not independent with respect to ABC Company as of and for the year ended [*or ending, as applicable*] December 31, 20X2, because a member of the engagement team had a direct financial interest in ABC Company."

See Illustration 2 for an example of the practitioner's standard report on the compilation of a forecast that does not contain a range.

When the presentation is a projection, the practitioner's compilation report should also include (1) a statement describing the special purpose for which the projection was prepared and (2) a separate paragraph that restricts the use of the report because it is intended to be used solely by the specified parties. See

Illustration 3 for an example of the practitioner's standard report on the compilation of a projection that does not contain a range.

When the prospective financial statements contain a range, the practitioner's standard report should also include a separate paragraph stating that the responsible party has elected to portray the expected results of one or more assumptions as a range. See Illustration 4 for an example of such a separate paragraph.

Modifications of the standard compilation report If prospective financial statements contain presentation deficiencies or omit disclosures, other than those relating to significant assumptions, the practitioner should describe the deficiency or omission in the report. See Illustration 5.

If the compiled prospective financial statements are presented on a comprehensive basis of accounting other than GAAP and do not include disclosure of the basis of accounting used, the practitioner should disclose the basis in his or her report.

Examination of Prospective Financial Statements

An examination engagement provides the practitioner with a basis for reporting on (a) whether the prospective financial statements are presented in conformity with AICPA guidelines and (b) whether the assumptions provide a reasonable basis for the responsible party's forecast or projection given the hypothetical assumptions. In an examination engagement, the practitioner should follow the general, fieldwork, and reporting standards for attestation engagements set forth and discussed in AT Section 101 (Attest Engagements).

Illustration 16 is a procedures checklist that the practitioner can use in connection with examinations of prospective financial statements.

Reports on examined prospective financial statements The practitioner's report on an examination of prospective financial statements should include:

1. A title that includes the word *independent.*

2. An introductory paragraph that:

   a. Identifies the prospective financial statements presented.

   b. Identifies the responsible party and contains a statement that the prospective financial statements are the responsibility of the responsible party.

   c. States that the practitioner's responsibility is to express an opinion on the prospective financial statements based on his or her examination.

3. A scope paragraph stating that:

   a. The examination was conducted in accordance with attestation standards established by the AICPA.

   b. The practitioner believes that the examination provides a reasonable basis for his or her opinion.

4. An opinion paragraph stating:

a. The practitioner's opinion that the prospective financial statements are presented in conformity with AICPA presentation guidelines and that the underlying assumptions provide a reasonable basis for the forecast, or the projection given the hypothetical assumptions.

b. That the prospective results may not be achieved.

c. That the practitioner assumes no responsibility to update the report for events and circumstances occurring after the date of the report.

5. Manual or printed signature of the practitioner's firm.

6. The date of the report, which is the date of completion of the examination procedures.

See Illustration 6 for an example of the practitioner's standard report on the examination of a forecast that does not contain a range.

When the presentation is a projection, the practitioner's opinion regarding the assumptions should be conditioned on the hypothetical assumptions and the examination report should also include (1) a statement describing the special purpose for which the projection was prepared and (2) a separate paragraph that restricts the use of the report because it is intended to be used solely by the specified parties. See Illustration 7 for an example of the practitioner's standard report on an examination of a projection that does not contain a range.

When the prospective financial statements contain a range, the practitioner's standard report should also include a separate paragraph stating that the responsible party has elected to portray the expected results of one or more assumptions as a range. See Illustration 8 for an example of such a separate paragraph.

Modifications to the practitioner's opinion in an examination engagement The practitioner should modify his or her opinion in the following circumstances:

1. If the prospective financial statements depart from AICPA presentation guidelines, the practitioner should express a qualified opinion or an adverse opinion.

2. If the prospective financial statements contain a measurement departure (e.g., failure to capitalize a capital lease), the practitioner should express an adverse opinion.

3. If the prospective financial statements omit disclosure of significant assumptions, the practitioner should express an adverse opinion.

4. If the practitioner believes that one or more significant assumptions do not provide a reasonable basis for the forecast, he or she should express an adverse opinion.

5. If the practitioner believes that one or more significant assumptions do not provide a reasonable basis for the projection given the hypothetical assumptions, he or she should express an adverse opinion.

6. If the practitioner is unable to apply the necessary procedures due to a scope limitation, he or she should disclaim an opinion and describe the scope limitation in the report.

Qualified opinion When the practitioner expresses a qualified opinion, he or she should:

1. State, in a separate paragraph, all of the substantive reasons for qualifying the opinion.

2. Describe the departure from AICPA presentation guidelines.

3. Include, in the opinion paragraph, the words "except" or "exception" and refer to the separate explanatory paragraph.

See Illustration 9 for an example of a qualified opinion.

Adverse opinion When the practitioner expresses an adverse opinion, he or she should:

1. State, in a separate paragraph, all of the substantive reasons for the adverse opinion.

2. Indicate in the opinion paragraph that the presentation is not in conformity with AICPA presentation guidelines and refer to the explanatory paragraph.

3. State in the opinion paragraph, when applicable, that the assumptions do not provide a reasonable basis for the prospective financial statements.

4. Describe in the report any significant assumptions that are not disclosed in the prospective presentation.

See Illustration 10 for an example of an adverse opinion.

Disclaimer of opinion When the practitioner expresses a disclaimer of opinion, he or she should:

1. Indicate, in a separate paragraph, how the examination did not comply with the standards.

2. State that the scope of the examination was not sufficient to enable him or her to express an opinion on the presentation or the underlying assumptions.

3. Include, in the opinion paragraph, a direct reference to the separate explanatory paragraph.

See Illustration 11 for an example of a disclaimer of opinion.

Other modifications to the standard examination report The practitioner should modify his or her examination report in the following circumstances, which do not result in modifications to the practitioner's opinion:

1. *Emphasis of a matter*—The practitioner may present other explanatory information and comments on the prospective financial statements in a separate paragraph of his or her report.

2. *Evaluation based in part on a report of another practitioner*—When more than one practitioner is involved in the examination, the guidance provided for that situation in connection with examinations of historical financial statements is generally applicable. See AU Section 543 (Part of Audit Performed by Other Independent Auditors) for more guidance.

3. *Comparative historical financial information*—Prospective financial statements may be included in a document that also contains historical financial statements and a practitioner's report thereon. Also, the historical financial statements that appear in the document may be summarized and presented with the prospective financial statements for comparative purposes. In such circumstances, the practitioner should add a concluding sentence to the last paragraph of the practitioner's report on the examination of the prospective financial statements as follows:

> The historical financial statements for the year ended December 31, 20X2 (from which the historical data are derived), and our report thereon are set forth on pages XX of this document.

4. *Reporting when the examination is part of a larger engagement*—The practitioner's examination of prospective financial statements may be a part of a larger engagement, such as a financial feasibility study or business acquisition study. In such circumstances, the practitioner may expand the report on the examination of the prospective financial statements to describe the entire engagement. See Illustration 12 for an example.

Applying Agreed-Upon Procedures to Prospective Financial Statements

A practitioner may perform an agreed-upon procedures attest engagement on prospective financial statements, provided all of the following conditions are met:

1. The practitioner is independent.

2. The practitioner and the specified parties agree upon the scope and nature of the agreed-upon procedures.

3. The specified parties take responsibility for the sufficiency of the agreed-upon procedures.

4. The prospective financial statements include a summary of significant assumptions.

5. The prospective financial statements are subject to reasonably consistent evaluation against criteria that are suitable and available to the specified parties.

6. The practitioner and the specified parties agree upon the criteria to be used in the determination of findings.

7. The procedures to be applied are expected to result in reasonably consistent findings using the criteria.

8. Audit evidence is expected to exist to provide a reasonable basis for expressing the findings in the practitioner's report.

9. The practitioner and the specified parties agree on materiality limits for reporting purposes.

10. Use of the report is restricted to the specified parties.

Practitioner's report on the results of applying agreed-upon procedures The practitioner's report on the results of applying agreed-upon procedures should be in the form of procedures and findings and should include the following:

1. A title that includes the word *independent*.

2. Identification of the specified parties.

3. An introductory paragraph that:

   a. Identifies the prospective financial statements covered by the practitioner's report and the character of the engagement.

   b. Indicates that the procedures performed were agreed to by the specified parties.

   c. Identifies the responsible party and contains a statement that the prospective financial statements are the responsibility of the responsible party.

4. A scope paragraph stating that:

   a. The agreed-upon procedures engagement was conducted in accordance with attestation standards established by the AICPA.

   b. The sufficiency of the procedures is solely the responsibility of the specified parties and a disclaimer of responsibility for the sufficiency of those procedures.

5. A list of the procedures performed and related findings.

6. A description of any agreed-upon materiality limits.

7. A conclusion paragraph stating:

   a. That the practitioner was not engaged to and did not conduct an examination of prospective financial statements, and related caveats.

   b. Any reservations or restrictions concerning procedures or findings.

   c. That the prospective results may not be achieved.

   d. That the practitioner assumes no responsibility to update the report for events and circumstances occurring after the date of the report.

8. A statement of restrictions on the use of the report.

9. Where applicable, a description of the nature of any assistance provided by specialists.

10. The date of the report, which is the date of completion of the agreed-upon procedures.

11. Manual or printed signature of the practitioner's firm.

See Illustration 13 for an example of the practitioner's report on applying agreed-upon procedures to prospective financial statements.

Practitioner-Submitted Documents

A practitioner's compilation, review, or audit report on historical financial statements may be included in a practitioner-submitted document containing prospective financial statements. In such circumstances, the practitioner should examine, compile, or apply agreed-upon procedures to the prospective financial statements and report accordingly, unless all of the following conditions exist:

1. The prospective financial statements are labeled as a "budget";

2. The budget does not extend beyond the end of the current fiscal year; and

3. The budget is presented with interim historical financial statements for the current year.

When these conditions exist, the practitioner need not examine, compile, or apply agreed-upon procedures to the budget; however, the practitioner should report on the budget and (a) indicate that he or she did not examine or compile it and (b) disclaim an opinion or any other form of assurance on it.

The budgeted information may omit the summaries of significant assumptions and accounting policies required by the AICPA guidelines for presentation of prospective financial statements, provided such omission (a) is not undertaken with the intention to mislead users and (b) is disclosed in the practitioner's report. See Illustration 14 for an example of the paragraphs to be added to the practitioner's report in such circumstances.

Client-Prepared Documents

A practitioner's compilation, review, or audit report on historical financial statements may be included in a client-prepared document containing prospective financial statements. In such circumstances, the practitioner should not consent to the use of his or her name in the document unless one of the following conditions exists:

1. The practitioner has examined, compiled, or applied agreed-upon procedures to the prospective financial statements and the practitioner's report accompanies such statements.

2. The prospective financial statements are accompanied by an indication that the practitioner has not performed such a service on the prospective financial statements and that the practitioner assumes no responsibility for them.

3. Another practitioner has examined, compiled, or applied agreed-upon procedures to the prospective financial statements and his or her report is included in the document.

If the practitioner's report on prospective financial statements is included in a client-prepared document containing historical financial statements, the practitioner should not consent to the use of his or her name in the document unless one of the following conditions exists:

1. The practitioner has compiled, reviewed, or audited the historical financial statements and the practitioner's report accompanies such statements.

2. The historical financial statements are accompanied by an indication that the practitioner has not performed such a service on the historical

financial statements and that the practitioner assumes no responsibility for them.

3. Another practitioner has compiled, reviewed, or audited the historical financial statements and his or her report is included in the document.

PRACTICE ISSUES AND FREQUENTLY ASKED QUESTIONS

Issue 1: Does this Section apply to pro forma financial statements?

No. The objective of pro forma financial information is to show what the significant effects on the historical financial information might have been if a consummated or proposed transaction, or event, had occurred at an earlier date. Pro forma presentations are basically historical financial statements and are not intended to be prospective financial statements. AT Section 401 (Reporting on Pro Forma Financial Information) applies to pro forma financial information.

Issue 2: Does this Section apply to prospective financial statements that are restricted to internal use?

No. This Section applies only when the prospective financial statements are, or reasonably might be, expected to be used by another third party.

Issue 3: What is the difference between financial forecasts and financial projections?

Financial forecasts present, to the best of the responsible party's knowledge and belief, an entity's expected financial position, results of operations, and cash flows. It is based on that party's assumptions regarding the conditions it expects to exist and the course of action it expects to take.

Financial projections present, to the best of the responsible party's knowledge and belief, given one or more hypothetical assumptions, an entity's expected financial position, results of operations, and cash flows. Financial projections are generally prepared as in response to a question such as "What would happen if . . . ?"

Both financial forecasts and financial projections are prospective financial statements.

Issue 4: May a practitioner compile, examine, or apply agreed-upon procedures to prospective financial statements that omit the summary of significant assumptions?

No. A practitioner may not perform such engagements when the prospective financial statements omit the summary of significant assumptions. By definition, financial forecasts and projections include the summaries of significant assumptions and accounting policies.

Issue 5: Are the practitioner's reports discussed in this Section and the examples shown in the Illustrations appropriate when the presentation of prospective financial statements is based on an other comprehensive basis of accounting?

Yes. The forms of reports provided in this Section are appropriate whether the presentation is based on GAAP or on an other comprehensive basis of accounting.

Issue 6: May a practitioner examine a financial projection that omits an identification of the hypothetical assumptions?

No. The practitioner should not examine a financial projection that omits an identification of the hypothetical assumptions or a description of the limitations on the usefulness of the presentation.

Issue 7: May a practitioner report on an agreed-upon procedures engagement when specified parties do not agree upon the procedures to be performed and do not take responsibility for the sufficiency of the procedures?

No. The practitioner should not report on an engagement when specified parties do not agree upon the procedures performed or to be performed and do not take responsibility for the sufficiency of the procedures for their purposes.

Issue 8: For purposes of this Section, what is the effect of a practitioner's lack of independence on his or her ability to render the various levels of service?

Lack of independence precludes a practitioner from reporting on examinations or agreed-upon procedures engagements involving forecasts and projections. However, a practitioner who is not independent may compile financial forecasts and projections, but should modify the practitioner's report to indicate his or her lack of independence in a separate paragraph of the compilation report.

Issue 9: How is materiality calculated in an examination of prospective financial statements?

Generally, a practitioner starts with the same financial measure that he or she would use in an audit of historical financial statements. Typically, this would be based on total assets or total revenues, or some modification of either of the bases. Professional standards do not specify a particular method for calculating materiality. However, in prospective financial statements, materiality should be judged in light of the expected range of reasonableness of the information. Information about events that have yet to occur will necessarily be less precise than historical information. For this reason, the materiality levels in an examination of prospective financial statements would normally be larger than those for an audit of historical financial statements.

Issue 10: What is the difference between prospective financial information and pro forma financial information?

Prospective financial information portrays the expected results of future transactions or events, in a future period. Pro forma financial information, on the other hand, shows the effects of an actual or a proposed transaction or event on historical financial information. In other words, it shows what the historical information would have been had the event or transaction taken place within, rather than after the close of, the historical period.

Issue 11: What course of action should the practitioner take if he or she examines or compiles prospective financial statements included in a document published by a client containing inconsistent information?

If the practitioner examines prospective financial statements included in a document containing inconsistent information, he or she should consider whether the prospective financial statements, the report, or both require revision. Depending on the conclusion reached, the practitioner should consider other actions that may be appropriate, such as:

1. Issuing an adverse opinion.
2. Disclaiming an opinion because of a scope limitation.
3. Withholding the use of his or her report in the document.
4. Withdrawing from the engagement.

If the practitioner compiles prospective financial statements included in a document containing inconsistent information, he or she should attempt to obtain additional or revised information. If the practitioner does not receive such information, he or she should withhold the use of the report or withdraw from the compilation engagement.

If the practitioner becomes aware of information that he or she believes is a material misstatement of fact, he or she should discuss the matter with the responsible party. If the practitioner concludes that there is a valid basis for concern, he or she should propose that the responsible party consult with some other party whose advice might be useful, such as the entity's legal counsel. If the practitioner nevertheless concludes that a material misstatement of fact remains, he or she should consider notifying the responsible party in writing and consulting his or her legal counsel.

Issue 12: Are partial presentations of prospective financial information appropriate for general use?

No. Ordinarily, partial presentations of prospective financial information are not appropriate for general use. Therefore, partial presentations should be restricted for use by specified parties who will be negotiating directly with the responsible party.

ILLUSTRATIONS AND PRACTICE AIDS

ILLUSTRATION 1—MINIMUM PRESENTATION GUIDELINES FOR PROSPECTIVE FINANCIAL STATEMENTS

Prospective financial statements may take the form of complete basic financial statements or may be limited to the following items at a minimum:

1. Sales or gross revenues.
2. Gross profit or cost of sales.
3. Unusual or infrequently occurring items.
4. Provision for income taxes.
5. Discontinued operations or extraordinary items.
6. Income from continuing operations.
7. Net income.
8. Basic and diluted earnings per share.
9. Significant changes in financial position. (This item does *not* require a balance sheet, a statement of changes in financial position, or a statement of cash flows.)

10. A description of what the responsible party intends the prospective financial statements to present.

11. A statement that the assumptions are based on the responsible party's judgment at the time the prospective information was prepared.

12. A caveat that the prospective results may not be achieved.

13. Summary of significant assumptions.

14. Summary of significant accounting policies.

Note: *A presentation that omits any of the items in 1 through 9 is a partial presentation, which would not ordinarily be appropriate for general use. A presentation that contains items 1 through 9 but omits items 10 through 14 is subject to all of the provisions of this Section applicable to complete presentations.*

ILLUSTRATION 2—STANDARD COMPILATION REPORT ON A FORECAST THAT DOES NOT CONTAIN A RANGE

We have compiled the accompanying forecasted balance sheet, statements of income, retained earnings, and cash flows of ABC Company as of December 31, 20X2, and for the year then ending, in accordance with attestation standards established by the American Institute of Certified Public Accountants.

A compilation is limited to presenting in the form of a forecast information that is the representation of management and does not include evaluation of the support for the assumptions underlying the forecast. We have not examined the forecast and, accordingly, do not express an opinion or any other form of assurance on the accompanying statements or assumptions. Furthermore, there will usually be differences between the forecasted and actual results, because events and circumstances frequently do not occur as expected, and those differences may be material. We have no responsibility to update this report for events and circumstances occurring after the date of this report.

[*Signature*]

[*Date*]

ILLUSTRATION 3—STANDARD COMPILATION REPORT ON A PROJECTION THAT DOES NOT CONTAIN A RANGE

We have compiled the accompanying projected balance sheet, statements of income, retained earnings, and cash flows of ABC Company as of December 31, 20X2, and for the year then ending, in accordance with attestation standards established by the American Institute of Certified Public Accountants. The accompanying projection was prepared for [*State special purpose, for example, "the purpose of negotiating a loan to expand ABC Company's plant"*].

A compilation is limited to presenting, in the form of a projection, information that is the representation of management and does not include evaluation of the support for the assumptions underlying the projection. We have not examined the projection and, accordingly, do not express an opinion or any other form of assurance on the accompanying statements or assumptions. Furthermore, even if [*describe hypothetical assumption, for example, "the loan is granted and the plant is expanded,"*] there will usually be differences between the projected and actual results, because events and circumstances frequently do not occur as expected, and those differences may be material. We have no responsibility to update this report for events and circumstances occurring after the date of this report.

The accompanying projection and this report are intended solely for the information and use of [*identify specified parties, for example, "ABC Company and DEF Bank"*] and is not intended to be and should not be used by anyone other than these specified parties.

[*Signature*]

[*Date*]

ILLUSTRATION 4—SEPARATE PARAGRAPH IN A COMPILATION REPORT ON PROSPECTIVE FINANCIAL STATEMENTS THAT CONTAIN A RANGE

As described in the summary of significant assumptions, management of ABC Company has elected to portray forecasted [*describe financial statement element or elements for which the expected results of one or more assumptions fall within a range, and identify the assumptions expected to fall within a range, for example, "revenue at the amounts of $_____ and $_____, which is predicated upon occupancy rates of _____ percent and _____ percent of available apartments"*], rather than as a single point estimate. Accordingly, the accompanying forecast presents forecasted financial position, results of operations, and cash flows [*describe one or more assumptions expected to fall within a range, for example, "at such occupancy rate"*]. However, there is no assurance that the actual results will fall within the range of [*describe one or more assumptions expected to fall within a range, for example, "occupancy rates"*] presented.

ILLUSTRATION 5—SEPARATE PARAGRAPH IN A COMPILATION REPORT ON PROSPECTIVE FINANCIAL STATEMENTS THAT OMIT THE SUMMARY OF SIGNIFICANT ACCOUNTING POLICIES

Management has elected to omit the summary of significant accounting policies required by the guidelines for presentation of a forecast established by the American Institute of Certified Public Accountants. If the omitted disclosures were included in the forecast, they might influence the user's conclusions about the Company's financial position, results of operations, and cash flows for the forecast period. Accordingly, this forecast is not designed for those who are not informed about such matters.

ILLUSTRATION 6—STANDARD EXAMINATION REPORT ON A FORECAST THAT DOES NOT CONTAIN A RANGE

Independent Accountant's Report

We have examined the accompanying forecasted balance sheet, statements of income, retained earnings, and cash flows of ABC Company as of December 31, 20X2, and for the year then ending. ABC Company's management is responsible for the forecast. Our responsibility is to express an opinion on the forecast based on our examination.

Our examination was conducted in accordance with attestation standards established by the American Institute of Certified Public Accountants and, accordingly, included such procedures as we considered necessary to evaluate both the assumptions used by management and the preparation and presentation of the forecast. We believe that our examination provides a reasonable basis for our opinion.

In our opinion, the accompanying forecast is presented in conformity with guidelines for presentation of a forecast established by the American Institute of Certified Public Accountants, and the underlying assumptions provide a reasonable basis for management's forecast. However, there will usually be differences between the forecasted and actual results, because events and circumstances frequently do not occur as expected, and those differences may be material. We have no responsibility to update this report for events and circumstances occurring after the date of this report.

[*Signature*]

[*Date*]

ILLUSTRATION 7—STANDARD EXAMINATION REPORT ON A PROJECTION THAT DOES NOT CONTAIN A RANGE

Independent Accountant's Report

We have examined the accompanying projected balance sheet, statements of income, retained earnings, and cash flows of ABC Company as of December 31, 20X2, and for the year then ending. ABC Company's management is responsible for the projection, which was prepared for [*state special purpose, for example, "the purpose of negotiating a loan to expand ABC Company's plant"*]. Our responsibility is to express an opinion on the projection based on our examination.

Our examination was conducted in accordance with attestation standards established by the American Institute of Certified Public Accountants and, accordingly, included such procedures as we considered necessary to evaluate both the assumptions used by management and the preparation and presentation of the projection. We believe that our examination provides a reasonable basis for our opinion.

In our opinion, the accompanying projection is presented in conformity with guidelines for presentation of a projection established by the American Institute of Certified Public Accountants, and the underlying assumptions provide a reasonable basis for management's projection [*describe the hypothetical assumption, for example, "assuming the granting of the requested loan for the purpose of expanding ABC Company's plant as described in the summary of significant assumptions"*]. However, even if [*describe hypothetical assumption, for example, "the loan is granted and the plant is expanded"*], there will usually be differences between the projected and actual results, because events and circumstances frequently do not occur as expected, and those differences may be material. We have no responsibility to update this report for events and circumstances occurring after the date of this report.

The accompanying projection and this report are intended solely for the information and use of [*identify specified parties, for example, "ABC Company and DEF Bank"*] and is not intended to be and should not be used by anyone other than these specified parties.

[*Signature*]

[*Date*]

ILLUSTRATION 8—SEPARATE PARAGRAPH IN AN EXAMINATION REPORT ON PROSPECTIVE FINANCIAL STATEMENTS THAT CONTAIN A RANGE

As described in the summary of significant assumptions, management of ABC Company has elected to portray forecasted [*describe financial statement element or elements for which the expected results of one or more assumptions fall within a range, and identify the assumptions expected to fall within a range, for example, "revenue at the amounts of $_____ and $_____, which is predicated upon occupancy rates of _____ percent and _____ percent of available apartments"*], rather than as a single point estimate. Accordingly, the accompanying forecast presents forecasted financial position, results of operations, and cash flows [*describe one or more assumptions expected to fall within a range, for example, "at such occupancy rates"*]. However, there is no assurance that the actual results will fall within the range of [*describe one or more assumptions expected to fall within a range, for example, "occupancy rates"*] presented.

ILLUSTRATION 9—QUALIFIED OPINION IN AN EXAMINATION REPORT ON A FORECAST

Independent Accountant's Report

We have examined the accompanying forecasted balance sheet, statements of income, retained earnings, and cash flows of ABC Company as of December 31, 20X2, and for the year then ending. ABC Company's management is responsible for the forecast. Our responsibility is to express an opinion on the forecast based on our examination.

Our examination was conducted in accordance with attestation standards established by the American Institute of Certified Public Accountants and, accordingly, included such procedures as we considered necessary to evaluate both the assumptions used by management and the preparation and presentation of the forecast. We believe that our examination provides a reasonable basis for our opinion.

The forecast does not disclose significant accounting policies. Disclosure of such policies is required by guidelines for presentation of a forecast established by the American Institute of Certified Public Accountants.

In our opinion, except for the omission of the disclosure of the significant accounting policies as discussed in the preceding paragraph, the accompanying forecast is presented in conformity with guidelines for presentation of a forecast established by the American Institute of Certified Public Accountants, and the underlying assumptions provide a reasonable basis for management's forecast. However, there will usually be differences between the forecasted and actual results, because events and circumstances frequently do not occur as expected, and those differences may be material. We have no responsibility to update this report for events and circumstances occurring after the date of this report.

[*Signature*]

[*Date*]

ILLUSTRATION 10—ADVERSE OPINION IN AN EXAMINATION REPORT ON A FORECAST

Independent Accountant's Report

We have examined the accompanying forecasted balance sheet, statements of income, retained earnings, and cash flows of ABC Company as of December 31, 20X2, and for the year then ending. ABC Company's management is responsible for the forecast. Our responsibility is to express an opinion on the forecast based on our examination.

Our examination was conducted in accordance with attestation standards established by the American Institute of Certified Public Accountants and, accordingly, included such procedures as we considered necessary to evaluate both the assumptions used by management and the preparation and presentation of the forecast. We believe that our examination provides a reasonable basis for our opinion.

As discussed under the caption "Sales" in the summary of significant forecast assumptions, the forecasted sales include, among other things, revenue from the Company's federal defense contracts continuing at the current level. The Company's present federal defense contracts will expire in March 20X6. No new contracts have been signed and no negotiations are under way for new federal defense contracts. Furthermore, the federal government has entered into contracts with another company to supply the items being manufactured under the Company's present contracts.

In our opinion, the accompanying forecast is not presented in conformity with guidelines for presentation of a financial forecast established by the American Institute of Certified Public Accountants because management's assumptions, as discussed in the preceding paragraph, do not provide a reasonable basis for management's forecast. We have no responsibility to update this report for events or circumstances occurring after the date of this report.

[*Signature*]

[*Date*]

ILLUSTRATION 11—DISCLAIMER OF OPINION IN AN EXAMINATION REPORT ON A FORECAST

Independent Accountant's Report

We were engaged to examine the accompanying forecasted balance sheet, statements of income, retained earnings, and cash flows of ABC Company as of December 31, 20X2, and for the year then ending. ABC Company's management is responsible for the forecast.

As discussed under the caption "Income From Investee" in the summary of significant forecast assumptions, the forecast includes income from an equity investee constituting 22 percent of forecasted net income, which is management's estimate of the Company's share of the investee's income to be accrued for 20X2. The investee has not prepared a forecast for the year ending December 31, 20X2, and we were therefore unable to obtain suitable support for this assumption.

Because, as described in the preceding paragraph, we are unable to evaluate management's assumption regarding income from an equity investee and other assumptions that depend thereon, the scope of our work was not sufficient to express, and we do not express, an opinion with respect to the presentation of or the assumptions underlying the accompanying forecast. We have no responsibility to update this report for events and circumstances occurring after the date of this report.

[*Signature*]

[*Date*]

ILLUSTRATION 12—EXAMINATION REPORT EXPANDED FOR A FINANCIAL FEASIBILITY STUDY

Independent Accountant's Report

The Board of Directors
ABC Hospital
Anywhere, State

We have prepared a financial feasibility study of ABC Hospital's (the Hospital's) plans to expand and renovate its facilities. The study was undertaken to evaluate the ability of the Hospital to meet its operating expenses, working capital needs, and other financial requirements, including the debt service requirements associated with the proposed $50,000,000 [*legal title of bonds*] issue, at an assumed average annual interest rate of 10 percent during the five years ending December 31, 20X6.

The proposed capital improvements program (the Program) consists of a new two-level addition, which is to provide fifty additional medical-surgical beds, increasing the complement to 300 beds. In addition, various administrative and support service areas in the present facilities are to be remodeled. The Hospital administration anticipates that construction is to begin June 30, 20X2, and to be completed by December 31, 20X3.

The estimated total cost of the Program is approximately $55,000,000. It is assumed that the $50,000,000 of revenue bonds that the ABC Hospital Finance Authority proposes to issue would be the primary source of funds for the Program. The responsibility for payment of debt service on the bonds is solely that of the Hospital. Other necessary funds to finance the Program are assumed to be provided from the Hospital's funds, from a local fund drive, and from interest earned on funds held by the bond trustee during the construction period.

Our procedures included analysis of:

1. Program history, objectives, timing and financing.

2. The future demand for the Hospital's services, including consideration of:

   a. Economic and demographic characteristics of the Hospital's defined service area.

   b. Locations, capacities, and competitive information pertaining to other existing and planned area hospitals.

   c. Physician support for the Hospital and its programs.

   d. Historical utilization levels.

3. Planning agency applications and approvals.

4. Construction and equipment costs, debt service requirements, and estimated financing costs.

5. Staffing patterns and other operating considerations.

6. Third-party reimbursement policy and history.

7. Revenue/expense/volume relationships.

We also participated in gathering other information, assisted management in identifying and formulating its assumptions, and assembled the accompanying financial forecast based on those assumptions.

The accompanying financial forecast for the annual periods ending December 31, 20X2, through 20X6, is based on assumptions that were provided by or reviewed with and approved by management. The financial forecast includes:

1. Balance sheets.

2. Statements of operations.

3. Statements of cash flows.

4. Statements of changes in net assets.

We have examined the financial forecast. ABC Hospital's management is responsible for the forecast. Our responsibility is to express an opinion on the forecast based on our examination. Our examination was conducted in accordance with attestation standards established by the American Institute of Certified Public Accountants and, accordingly, included such procedures as we considered necessary to evaluate both the assumptions used by management and the preparation and presentation of the forecast. We believe that our examination provides a reasonable basis for our opinion.

Legislation and regulations at all levels of government have affected and may continue to affect revenues and expenses of hospitals. The financial forecast is based on legislation and regulations currently in effect. If future legislation or regulations related to hospital operations are enacted, such legislation or regulations could have a material effect on future operations.

The interest rate, principal payments, Program costs, and other financing assumptions are described in the section entitled "Summary of Significant Forecast Assumptions and Rationale." If actual interest rates, principal payments, and funding requirements are different from those assumed, the amount of the bond issue and debt service requirements would need to be adjusted accordingly from those indicated in the forecast. If such interest rates, principal payments, and funding requirements are lower than those assumed, such adjustments would not adversely affect the forecast.

Our conclusions are presented below:

1. In our opinion, the accompanying financial forecast is presented in conformity with guidelines for presentation of a financial forecast established by the American Institute of Certified Public Accountants.

2. In our opinion, the underlying assumptions provide a reasonable basis for management's forecast. However, there will usually be differences between the forecasted and actual results, because events and circumstances frequently do not occur as expected, and those differences may be material.

3. The accompanying financial forecast indicates that sufficient funds could be generated to meet the Hospital's operating expenses, working capital needs, and other financial requirements, including the debt service requirements associated with the proposed $50,000,000 bond issue, during the forecast periods. However, the achievement of any financial forecast is dependent on future events, the occurrence of which cannot be assured.

We have no responsibility to update this report for events and circumstances occurring after the date of this report.

[*Signature*]

[*Date*]

ILLUSTRATION 13—REPORT ON APPLYING AGREED-UPON PROCEDURES TO PROSPECTIVE FINANCIAL STATEMENTS

Independent Accountant's Report on Applying Agreed-Upon Procedures

The Board of Directors—XYZ Corporation
The Board of Directors—ABC Company

At your request, we have performed certain agreed-upon procedures, as enumerated below, with respect to the forecasted balance sheet and the related forecasted statements of income, retained earnings, and cash flows of DEF Company, a subsidiary of ABC Company, as of December 31, 20X2, and for the year then ending. These procedures, which were agreed to by the Boards of Directors of XYZ Corporation and ABC Company, were performed solely to assist you in evaluating the forecast in connection with the proposed sale of DEF Company to XYZ Corporation. DEF Company's management is responsible for the forecast.

This agreed-upon procedures engagement was conducted in accordance with attestation standards established by the American Institute of Certified Public Accountants. The sufficiency of these procedures is solely the responsibility of the specified parties. Consequently, we make no representation regarding the sufficiency of the procedures described below either for the purpose for which this report has been requested or for any other purpose.

[*Include paragraphs to enumerate procedures and findings.*]

We were not engaged to and did not conduct an examination, the objective of which would be the expression of an opinion on the accompanying prospective financial statements. Accordingly, we do not express an opinion on whether the prospective financial statements are presented in conformity with AICPA presentation guidelines or on whether the underlying assumptions provide a reasonable basis for the presentation. Had we performed additional procedures, other matters might have come to our attention that would have been reported to you. Furthermore, there will usually be differences between the forecasted and actual results, because events and circumstances frequently do not occur as expected, and those differences may be material. We have no responsibility to update this report for events and circumstances occurring after the date of this report.

This report is intended solely for the information and use of the Boards of Directors of ABC Company and XYZ Corporation and is not intended to be and should not be used by anyone other than these specified parties.

[*Signature*]

[*Date*]

ILLUSTRATION 14—PARAGRAPHS TO BE ADDED TO THE PRACTITIONER'S REPORT IN A PRACTITIONER-SUBMITTED DOCUMENT WHEN THE SUMMARIES OF SIGNIFICANT ASSUMPTIONS AND ACCOUNTING POLICIES HAVE BEEN OMITTED FROM THE BUDGETED INFORMATION

The accompanying budgeted balance sheet, statements of income, retained earnings, and cash flows of ABC Company as of December 31, 20X2, and for the six months then ending, have not been compiled or examined by us, and, accordingly, we do not express an opinion or any other form of assurance on them.

Management has elected to omit the summaries of significant assumptions and accounting policies required under established guidelines for presentation of prospective financial statements. If the omitted summaries were included in the budgeted information, they might influence the user's conclusions about the company's budgeted information. Accordingly, this budgeted information is not designed for those who are not informed about such matters.

ILLUSTRATION 15—COMPILATION ENGAGEMENT CHECKLIST: PROSPECTIVE FINANCIAL STATEMENTS

	Yes	No	N/A	Workpaper Reference
1. Obtain familiarity with the guidelines for the preparation and presentation of prospective financial statements contained in the AICPA's Audit and Accounting *Guide for Prospective Financial Information.*	___	___	___	_____
2. Obtain adequate knowledge of the industry and the accounting principles and practices of the industry in which the entity operates, or will operate.	___	___	___	_____

	Yes	No	N/A	Workpaper Reference

3. For an existing entity, obtain a general knowledge of the nature of the entity's business transactions and the key factors upon which its future financial results appear to depend, including an understanding of the accounting principles and practices of the entity to determine if they are comparable to those used within the industry in which the entity operates. _____ _____ _____ _____

4. For a proposed entity, obtain knowledge of the proposed operations and the key factors upon which its future results appear to depend and that have affected the performance of entities in the same industry. _____ _____ _____ _____

5. Establish an understanding with the client, preferably in writing, regarding the services to be performed, including the following:

   a. The objectives of the engagement. _____ _____ _____ _____

   b. The client's responsibilities. _____ _____ _____ _____

   c. The practitioner's responsibilities. _____ _____ _____ _____

   d. Limitations of the engagement. _____ _____ _____ _____

6. Inquire about the accounting principles used in the preparation of the prospective financial statements and perform the following:

   a. For existing entities, (i) compare the accounting principles used to those used in the preparation of previous historical financial statements and (ii) inquire whether such principles are the same as those expected to be used in the historical financial statements covering the prospective period. _____ _____ _____ _____

   b. For entities to be formed or entities formed that have not commenced operations, (i) compare specialized industry accounting principles used, if any, to those typically used in the industry and (ii) inquire about whether the accounting principles used for the prospective financial statements are those that are expected to be used when, or if, the entity commences operations. _____ _____ _____ _____

7. Inquire how the responsible party identifies the key factors and develops its assumptions. _____ _____ _____ _____

	Yes	No	N/A	Workpaper Reference

8. List, or obtain a list of, the responsible party's significant assumptions providing the basis for the prospective financial statements and consider whether there are any obvious omissions in light of the key factors upon which the prospective results of the entity appear to depend. ____ ____ ____ _____

9. Consider whether there appear to be any obvious internal inconsistencies in the assumptions. ____ ____ ____ _____

10. Perform, or test the mathematical accuracy of, the computations that translate the assumptions into prospective financial statements. ____ ____ ____ _____

11. Read the prospective financial statements, including the summary of significant assumptions, and consider whether:

   a. The statements, including the disclosures of assumptions and accounting policies, are not presented in conformity with the AICPA presentation guidelines for prospective financial statements. ____ ____ ____ _____

   b. The statements, including the summary of significant assumptions, are not obviously inappropriate in relation to the knowledge obtained of the entity and its industry and:

     (i) For a financial forecast, the expected conditions and course of action in the prospective period. ____ ____ ____ _____

     (ii) For a financial projection, the purpose of the presentation. ____ ____ ____ _____

12. If a significant part of the prospective period has expired, inquire about the results of operations or significant portions of the operations (such as sales volume), and significant changes in financial position, and consider their effect in relation to the prospective financial statements. If historical financial statements have been prepared for the expired portion of the period, read such statements and consider those results in relation to the prospective financial statements. ____ ____ ____ _____

13. Obtain written representations from the responsible party, and ascertain that:

	Yes	No	N/A	Workpaper Reference

a. For a financial forecast, the representations include the responsible party's assertion that the financial forecast presents, to the best of its knowledge and belief, the expected financial position, results of operations, and cash flows for the forecast period and that the forecast reflects the responsible party's judgment, based on present circumstances, of the expected conditions and its expected course of action. If the forecast contains a range, the representation should also include a statement that, to the best of the responsible party's knowledge and belief, the item or items subject to the assumption are expected to actually fall within the range and that the range was not selected in a biased or misleading manner.

b. For a financial projection, the representations include the responsible party's assertion that the financial projection presents, to the best of its knowledge and belief, the expected financial position, results of operations, and cash flows for the projection period given the hypothetical assumptions, and that the projection reflects its judgment, based on present circumstances, of expected conditions and its expected course of action given the occurrence of the hypothetical events. The representations should also:

(i) Identify the hypothetical assumptions and describe the limitations on the usefulness of the presentation.

(ii) State that the assumptions are appropriate.

(iii) Indicate if the hypothetical assumptions are improbable.

	Yes	No	N/A	Workpaper Reference

(iv) If the projection contains a range, include a statement that, to the best of the responsible party's knowledge and belief, given the hypothetical assumptions, the item or items subject to the assumption are expected to actually fall within the range and that the range was not selected in a biased or misleading manner.   _____ _____ _____ _____

(v) Include a statement that the projection is presented in conformity with guidelines for presentation of a projection established by the American Institute of Certified Public Accountants.   _____ _____ _____ _____

14. Consider whether any representations or other information received appears to be obviously inappropriate, incomplete, or otherwise misleading and, if so, attempt to obtain additional or revised information. Otherwise, consider withdrawing from the engagement.   _____ _____ _____ _____

ILLUSTRATION 16—EXAMINATION ENGAGEMENT CHECKLIST: PROSPECTIVE FINANCIAL STATEMENTS

	Yes	No	N/A	Workpaper Reference

1. Obtain familiarity with the guidelines for the preparation and presentation of prospective financial statements contained in the AICPA's Audit and Accounting *Guide for Prospective Financial Information.*   _____ _____ _____ _____

2. Obtain adequate knowledge of the industry and the accounting principles and practices of the industry in which the entity operates, or will operate.   _____ _____ _____ _____

3. Develop an overall strategy for the expected scope and conduct of the engagement and obtain sufficient knowledge and understanding of the events, transactions, and practices that may have a significant effect on the prospective financial statements.   _____ _____ _____ _____

4. In planning the examination engagement, consider the following factors:

   a. The accounting principles to be used and the type of presentation.   _____ _____ _____ _____

	Yes	No	N/A	Workpaper Reference
b. The anticipated level of attestation risk related to the prospective financial statements.	___	___	___	___
c. Preliminary judgments about materiality levels.	___	___	___	___
d. Items within the prospective financial statements that are likely to require revision or adjustment.	___	___	___	___
e. Conditions that may require extension or modification of the examination procedures.	___	___	___	___
f. Knowledge of the entity's business and its industry.	___	___	___	___
g. The responsible party's experience in preparing prospective financial statements.	___	___	___	___
h. The length of the period covered by the prospective financial statements.	___	___	___	___
i. The process by which the responsible party develops its prospective financial statements.	___	___	___	___

5. Obtain knowledge of the entity's business, accounting principles, and the key factors upon which its future financial results appear to depend, including the following:

	Yes	No	N/A	Workpaper Reference
a. The availability and cost of resources needed to operate, such as raw materials, labor, short-term and long-term financing, and plant and equipment.	___	___	___	___
b. The nature and condition of markets in which the entity sells its goods or services, including final consumer markets if the entity sells to intermediate markets.	___	___	___	___
c. Factors specific to the industry, including competitive conditions, sensitivity to economic conditions, accounting policies, specific regulatory requirements, and technology.	___	___	___	___
d. Patterns of past performance for the entity or comparable entities, including trends in revenue and costs, turnover of assets, uses and capacities of physical facilities, and management policies.	___	___	___	___

6. Establish an understanding with the responsible party and/or client, preferably in writing, regarding the services to be performed, including the following:

	Yes	No	N/A	*Workpaper Reference*
a. The objectives of the engagement.	___	___	___	_____
b. The responsible party's and / or client's responsibilities.	___	___	___	_____
c. The practitioner's responsibilities.	___	___	___	_____
d. Limitations of the engagement.	___	___	___	_____

7. In determining the nature of procedures to be performed, consider the following factors:

a. The nature and materiality of the information to the prospective financial statements taken as a whole.	___	___	___	_____
b. The likelihood of misstatements.	___	___	___	_____
c. Knowledge obtained during current and previous engagements.	___	___	___	_____
d. The responsible party's competence with respect to prospective financial statements.	___	___	___	_____
e. The extent to which the prospective financial statements are affected by the responsible party's judgment, for example, its judgment in selecting the assumptions used to prepare the prospective financial statements.	___	___	___	_____
f. The adequacy of the responsible party's underlying data.	___	___	___	_____

8. For a financial forecast, determine whether:

a. The responsible party represents that the presentation reflects, to the best of its knowledge and belief, its estimate of expected financial position, results of operations, and cash flows for the prospective period. (Note: If the forecast contains a range, the representation should also include a statement that, to the best of the responsible party's knowledge and belief, the item or items subject to the assumption are expected to actually fall within the range and that the range was not selected in a biased or misleading manner.)	___	___	___	_____
b. The responsible party has explicitly identified all factors expected to materially affect the operations of the entity during the prospective period and has developed appropriate assumptions with respect to such factors.	___	___	___	_____
c. The assumptions are suitably supported.	___	___	___	_____

	Yes	No	N/A	Workpaper Reference

9. For a financial projection, determine whether:

    a. The responsible party represents that the presentation reflects, to the best of its knowledge and belief, expected financial position, results of operations, and cash flows for the prospective period given the hypothetical assumptions. (Note: If the projection contains a range, the representation should also include a statement that, to the best of the responsible party's knowledge and belief, given the hypothetical assumptions, the item or items subject to the assumption are expected to actually fall within the range and that the range was not selected in a biased or misleading manner.)

    b. The responsible party has explicitly identified all factors that would materially affect the operations of the entity during the prospective period if the hypothetical assumptions were to materialize and has developed appropriate assumptions with respect to such factors.

    c. The other assumptions are suitably supported given the hypothetical assumptions.

10. Evaluate the support for the assumptions and determine:

    a. For a financial forecast, whether the preponderance of information supports each significant assumption.

    b. For a financial projection, whether the preponderance of information supports each significant assumption given the hypothetical assumptions.

11. In evaluating the support for assumptions, consider:

	Yes	No	N/A	Workpaper Reference
a. Whether sufficient pertinent sources of information about the assumptions have been considered. Examples of external sources are government publications, industry publications, economic forecasts, existing or proposed legislation, and reports of changing technology. Examples of internal sources are budgets, labor agreements, patents, royalty agreements and records, sales backlog records, debt agreements, and actions of the board of directors involving entity plans.	_____	_____	_____	_____
b. Whether the assumptions are consistent with the sources from which they are derived.	_____	_____	_____	_____
c. Whether the assumptions are consistent with each other.	_____	_____	_____	_____
d. Whether the historical financial information and other data used in developing the assumptions are sufficiently reliable for that purpose:				
(i) If historical financial statements have been prepared for an expired part of the prospective period, consider the historical data in relation to the prospective results for the same period, where applicable.	_____	_____	_____	_____
(ii) If the prospective financial statements incorporate such historical financial results and that period is significant to the presentation, perform a review of the historical information in conformity with the applicable standards for a review.	_____	_____	_____	_____
e. Whether the historical financial information and other data used in developing the assumptions are comparable over the periods specified or whether the effects of any lack of comparability were considered in developing the assumptions.	_____	_____	_____	_____
f. Whether the logical arguments or theory, considered with the data supporting the assumptions, are reasonable.	_____	_____	_____	_____

		Yes	No	N/A	Workpaper Reference

12. In evaluating the preparation and presentation of the prospective financial statements, perform procedures that will provide reasonable assurance that the:

    a. Presentation reflects the identified assumptions.

    b. Computations made to translate the assumptions into prospective amounts are mathematically accurate.

    c. Assumptions are internally consistent.

    d. Accounting principles used in a financial forecast are consistent with the accounting principles expected to be used in the historical financial statements covering the prospective period and those used in the most recent historical financial statements, if any.

    e. Accounting principles used in a financial projection are consistent with the accounting principles expected to be used in the prospective period and those used in the most recent historical financial statements, if any, or that they are consistent with the purpose of the presentation.

    f. Presentation of the prospective financial statements follows the AICPA guidelines applicable for such statements.

    g. Assumptions have been adequately disclosed based on AICPA presentation guidelines for prospective financial statements.

13. Consider whether the prospective financial statements, including related disclosures, should be revised because of:

    a. Mathematical errors.

    b. Unreasonable or internally inconsistent assumptions.

    c. Inappropriate or incomplete presentation.

    d. Inadequate disclosure.

14. Obtain written representations from the responsible party, and ascertain that:

		Yes	No	N/A	Workpaper Reference

a. For a financial forecast, the representations include a statement that the financial forecast presents, to the best of the responsible party's knowledge and belief, the expected financial position, results of operations, and cash flows for the forecast period and that the forecast reflects the responsible party's judgment, based on present circumstances, of the expected conditions and its expected course of action. If the forecast contains a range, the representation should also include a statement that, to the best of the responsible party's knowledge and belief, the item or items subject to the assumption are expected to actually fall within the range and that the range was not selected in a biased or misleading manner.   ____ ____ ____ ____

b. For a financial projection, the representations should include a statement that the financial projection presents, to the best of the responsible party's knowledge and belief, the expected financial position, results of operations, and cash flows for the projection period given the hypothetical assumptions, and that the projection reflects its judgment, based on present circumstances, of expected conditions and its expected course of action given the occurrence of the hypothetical events. The representations should also:

(i) Identify the hypothetical assumptions and describe the limitations on the usefulness of the presentation.   ____ ____ ____ ____

(ii) State that the assumptions are appropriate.   ____ ____ ____ ____

(iii) Indicate if the hypothetical assumptions are improbable.   ____ ____ ____ ____

	Yes	No	N/A	Workpaper Reference
(iv) If the projection contains a range, include a statement that, to the best of the responsible party's knowledge and belief, given the hypothetical assumptions, the item or items subject to the assumption are expected to actually fall within the range and that the range was not selected in a biased or misleading manner.	———	———	———	———
15. Consider whether any representations or other information received appears to be obviously inappropriate, incomplete, or otherwise misleading and, if so, attempt to obtain additional or revised information. Otherwise, consider withdrawing from the engagement.	———	———	———	———

AT SECTION 401
REPORTING ON PRO FORMA FINANCIAL INFORMATION

WHAT EVERY PRACTITIONER SHOULD KNOW

Basic Objectives and Requirements

A practitioner may report on an *examination* or a *review* of pro forma financial information if all of the following conditions are met:

1. The document that contains the pro forma information includes (or incorporates by reference) the entity's complete historical financial statements for the most recent year, or for the preceding year if financial statements for the most recent year are not yet available. If pro forma information is presented for an interim period, the document also includes (or incorporates by reference) historical interim financial information for that period. For business combinations, the document should include (or incorporate by reference) the appropriate historical financial information for the significant components comprising the combined entity.

2. The practitioner has audited or reviewed the entity's historical financial statements on which the pro forma information is based.

3. The practitioner reporting on the pro forma information should have an appropriate level of knowledge of the accounting and financial reporting practices of each significant component comprising the combined entity.

In addition to the requirements of this Section, the practitioner should comply with the attest documentation requirements prescribed in AT Section 101 (Attest Engagements).

Procedures for an Examination or Review Procedures

The practitioner should perform the following procedures on the assumptions and pro forma adjustments for either an examination or a review engagement:

1. Obtain an understanding of the underlying transaction or event.

2. Obtain appropriate knowledge of each component of the combined entity in a business combination that is sufficient to enable the practitioner to perform the required procedures.

3. Discuss with management its assumptions regarding the effects of the transaction or event.

4. Evaluate whether pro forma adjustments are included for all significant effects directly attributable to the transaction or event.

5. Obtain sufficient evidence in support of such adjustments.

6. Evaluate whether management's assumptions underlying the pro forma adjustments:

   a. Are presented in a sufficiently clear and comprehensive manner.

b. Are consistent with each other and with the data used to develop them.

7. Determine that computations of pro forma adjustments are mathematically correct and that the pro forma column reflects the proper application of those adjustments to the historical financial statements.

8. Obtain management's written representations that management:

a. Is responsible for the assumptions used in determining the pro forma adjustments.

b. Asserts that the assumptions provide a reasonable basis for presenting all of the significant effects directly attributable to the transaction or event.

c. Asserts that the related pro forma adjustments give appropriate effect to the assumptions.

d. Asserts that the pro forma column reflects the proper application of those adjustments to the historical financial statements.

e. Asserts that the significant effects directly attributable to the transaction or event are appropriately disclosed.

9. Read the pro forma financial information and evaluate whether:

a. There is an appropriate description of the (i) underlying transaction or event, (ii) pro forma adjustments, (iii) significant assumptions, and (iv) significant uncertainties, if any, about those assumptions.

b. The source of the historical financial information on which the pro forma financial information is based is appropriately identified.

Reporting on Pro Forma Financial Information

The practitioner's report on pro forma financial information for an examination or a review engagement should include the items listed in Illustration 1.

See Illustrations 2 and 3 for examples of reports on an examination and a review, respectively, of pro forma financial information.

The practitioner should modify his or her report for:

1. Restrictions on the scope of the engagement.

2. Reservations about the propriety of the assumptions and conformity of the presentation with those assumptions, including inadequate disclosure of significant matters.

3. Other reservations.

In these circumstances, the practitioner should issue a qualified opinion, disclaim an opinion, or withdraw from the engagement. In addition, the practitioner should disclose all substantive reasons for any report modifications. See Illustrations 5 through 7 for examples of modified reports.

PRACTICE ISSUES AND FREQUENTLY ASKED QUESTIONS

Issue 1: What is the difference between pro forma financial information and prospective financial information?

Pro forma financial information shows the effects of an actual or a proposed transaction or event on historical financial information. In other words, it shows what the historical information would have been had the event or transaction taken place within, rather than after the close of, the historical period. Prospective financial information, on the other hand, portrays the expected results of future transactions or events, in a future period.

Issue 2: When reporting on pro forma financial information under this Section, is the practitioner required to comply with any of the other attestation standards?

Yes. An engagement to report on pro forma financial information should comply with the five general standards and two fieldwork standards described in AT Section 101 (Attest Engagements), in addition to complying with the specific requirements discussed in this Section.

Issue 3: Can a practitioner accept an engagement to report on pro forma financial information if the historical financial statements for the most recent year are not yet available?

Yes. In these circumstances, the historical financial statements for the preceding year should be included.

Issue 4: If the report on the historical financial statements is qualified, should a practitioner's report on pro forma financial information make reference to the qualification?

Yes. The practitioner's report on pro forma financial information should refer to any modification in the practitioner's report on the historical financial statements.

Issue 5: May a practitioner combine his or her report on an examination of pro forma financial information with his or her report on the audit of an entity's historical financial statements?

Yes. The practitioner's report on pro forma financial information may be added to the practitioner's audit report on historical financial information or may appear separately.

Issue 6: May a practitioner examine pro forma financial information that is related to historical financial statements that the practitioner has previously reviewed?

No. The rule is that the level of assurance expressed on the pro forma financial information cannot be higher than that expressed on the underlying historical financial statements. On the other hand, the practitioner may review pro forma financial information that is related to historical financial statements that the practitioner has previously audited.

Issue 7: May a practitioner examine pro forma information pertaining to a business combination whereby all the constituent entities comprising the combined entity have audited historical financial statements, except for one significant entity which has reviewed statements?

No. As discussed in Issue 6 above, a practitioner cannot report on pro forma information at a higher level of assurance than is available on the underlying historical information. Since the entity with the reviewed historical financial statements is a significant component of the combined entity, the practitioner does not have a basis for expressing the level of positive assurance that an examination report conveys. Accordingly, in such circumstances, a practitioner is limited to performing a review of the pro forma information.

Issue 8: *May a practitioner restrict the use of his or her report on pro forma financial information?*

Yes. A practitioner may restrict the use of his or her report on pro forma financial information.

ILLUSTRATIONS AND PRACTICE AIDS

ILLUSTRATION 1—COMPONENTS OF THE PRACTITIONER'S REPORT ON PRO FORMA FINANCIAL INFORMATION FOR AN EXAMINATION OR A REVIEW ENGAGEMENT

		Applicability of Item to:	
	The Practitioner's Report on Pro Forma Information Should:	*An Examination Engagement*	*A Review Engagement*
1.	Have a title that includes the word *independent*.	✓	✓
2.	Identify the pro forma financial information.	✓	✓
3.	Refer to the financial statements from which the historical financial information is derived and state whether such financial statements were audited or reviewed.	✓	✓
4.	Refer to any modification in the practitioner's report on the historical financial information.	✓	✓
5.	Identify the responsible party and state that the responsible party is responsible for the proforma financial information.	✓	✓
6.	In an examination engagement, state that:		
	a. The practitioner's responsibility is to express an opinion on the pro forma financial information based on his or her examination.	✓	N/A
	b. The examination of the pro forma financial information was conducted in accordance with attestation standards established by the AICPA and, accordingly, included such procedures deemed necessary in the circumstances.	✓	N/A
	c. The practitioner believes that the examination provides a reasonable basis for his or her opinion.	✓	N/A
7.	In a review engagement, state that		
	a. The review of the pro forma financial information was conducted in accordance with attestation standards established by the AICPA.	✓	N/A

The Practitioner's Report on Pro Forma Information Should:	Applicability of Item to:	
	An Examination Engagement	A Review Engagement
b. A review is substantially less in scope than an examination, the objective of which is the expression of an opinion on the pro forma financial information and, accordingly, the practitioner does not express such an opinion.	N/A	✓
8. Explain the objective of pro forma financial information and its limitations	✓	✓
9. Include the practitioner's opinion in an examination engagement, or the practitioner's conclusion in a review engagement, regarding whether:		
a. Management's assumptions provide a reasonable basis for presenting the significant effects directly attributable to the transaction or event.	✓	✓
b. The related pro forma adjustments give appropriate effect to those assumptions.	✓	✓
c. The pro forma column reflects the proper application of those adjustments to the historical financial statements.	✓	✓
10. Include the manual or printed signature of the practitioner's firm.	✓	✓
11. Include the date of the report.	✓	✓

ILLUSTRATION 2—REPORT ON EXAMINATION OF PRO FORMA FINANCIAL INFORMATION

Independent Accountant's Report

We have examined the pro forma adjustments reflecting the transaction [*or event*] described in Note [*X*] and the application of those adjustments to the historical amounts in [*the assembly of*][1] the accompanying pro forma financial condensed balance sheet of ABC Company as of December 31, 20X2, and the pro forma condensed statement of income for the year then ended. The historical condensed financial statements are derived from the historical financial statements of ABC Company, which were audited by us, and of DEF Company, which were audited by other accountants,[2] appearing elsewhere herein [*or incorporated by reference*]. Such pro forma adjustments are based upon management's assumptions described in Note [*Y*]. ABC Company's management is responsible for the pro forma financial information. Our responsibility is to express an opinion on the pro forma financial information based on our examination.

Our examination was conducted in accordance with attestation standards established by the American Institute of Certified Public Accountants and, ac-

---

[1] This wording is appropriate when one column of pro forma financial information is presented without separate columns of historical financial information and pro forma adjustments.

[2] If either accountant's report includes an explanatory paragraph or is other than unqualified, that fact should be referred to within this report.

cordingly, included such procedures as we considered necessary in the circumstances. We believe that our examination provides a reasonable basis for our opinion.

The objective of this pro forma financial information is to show what the significant effects on the historical financial information might have been had the transaction [*or event*] occurred at an earlier date. However, the pro forma condensed financial statements are not necessarily indicative of the results of operations or related effects on financial position that would have been attained had the above-mentioned transaction [*or event*] actually occurred earlier.

[*Additional paragraph(s) may be added to emphasize certain matters relating to the attest engagement or the subject matter.*]

In our opinion, management's assumptions provide a reasonable basis for presenting the significant effects directly attributable to the above-mentioned transaction [*or event*] described in Note [*X*], the related pro forma adjustments give appropriate effect to those assumptions, and the pro forma column reflects the proper application of those adjustments to the historical financial statement amounts in the pro forma condensed balance sheet as of December 31, 20X2, and the pro forma condensed statement of income for the year then ended.

[*Signature*]

[*Date*]

ILLUSTRATION 3—REPORT ON REVIEW OF PRO FORMA FINANCIAL INFORMATION

Independent Accountant's Report

We have reviewed the pro forma adjustments reflecting the transaction [*or event*] described in Note [*X*] and the application of those adjustments to the historical amounts in [*the assembly of*][3] the accompanying pro forma condensed balance sheet of ABC Company as of March 31, 20X3, and the pro forma condensed statement of income for the three months then ended. These historical condensed financial statements are derived from the historical unaudited financial statements of ABC Company, which were reviewed by us, and of DEF Company, which were reviewed by other accountants,[4][,5] appearing elsewhere herein [*or incorporated by reference*]. Such pro forma adjustments are based on management's assumptions as described in Note [*Y*]. ABC Company's management is responsible for the pro forma financial information.

Our review was conducted in accordance with attestation standards established by the American Institute of Certified Public Accountants. A review is

---

[3] This wording is appropriate when one column of pro forma financial information is presented without separate columns of historical financial information and pro forma adjustments.

[4] If either accountant's report includes an explanatory paragraph or is modified, that fact should be referred to within this report.

[5] Where one set of historical financial statements is audited and the other set is reviewed, wording similar to the following would be appropriate:

The historical condensed financial statements are derived from the historical financial statements of ABC Company, which were audited by us, and of DEF Company, which were reviewed by other accountants, appearing elsewhere herein [*or incorporated by reference*].

substantially less in scope than an examination, the objective of which is the expression of an opinion on management's assumptions, the pro forma adjustments and the application of those adjustments to historical financial information. Accordingly, we do not express such an opinion.

The objective of this pro forma financial information is to show what the significant effects on the historical financial information might have been had the transaction [*or event*] occurred at an earlier date. However, the pro forma condensed financial statements are not necessarily indicative of the results of operations or related effects on financial position that would have been attained had the above-mentioned transaction [*or event*] actually occurred earlier.

[*Additional paragraph(s) may be added to emphasize certain matters relating to the attest engagement or the subject matter.*]

Based on our review, nothing came to our attention that caused us to believe that management's assumptions do not provide a reasonable basis for presenting the significant effects directly attributable to the above-mentioned transaction [*or event*] described in Note [X], that the related pro forma adjustments do not give appropriate effect to those assumptions, or that the pro forma column does not reflect the proper application of those adjustments to the historical financial statement amounts in the pro forma condensed balance sheet as of March 31, 20X3, and the pro forma condensed statement of income for the three months then ended.

[*Signature*]

[*Date*]

ILLUSTRATION 4—REPORT ON EXAMINATION OF PRO FORMA FINANCIAL INFORMATION AT YEAR-END WITH A REVIEW OF PRO FORMA FINANCIAL INFORMATION FOR A SUBSEQUENT INTERIM DATE

Independent Accountant's Report

We have examined the pro forma adjustments reflecting the transaction [*or event*] described in Note [X] and the application of those adjustments to the historical amounts in [*the assembly of*][6] the accompanying pro forma condensed balance sheet of ABC Company as of December 31, 20X2, and the pro forma condensed statement of income for the year then ended. The historical condensed financial statements are derived from the historical financial statements of ABC Company, which were audited by us, and of DEF Company, which were audited by other accountants,[7] appearing elsewhere herein [*or incorporated by reference*]. Such pro forma adjustments are based upon management's assumptions described in Note [Y]. ABC Company's management is responsible for the pro forma financial information. Our responsibility is to express an opinion on the pro forma financial information based on our examination.

---

[6] This wording is appropriate when one column of pro forma financial information is presented without separate columns of historical financial information and pro forma adjustments.

[7] If either accountant's report includes an explanatory paragraph or is other than unqualified, that fact should be referred to within this report.

Our examination was conducted in accordance with attestation standards established by the American Institute of Certified Public Accountants and, accordingly, included such procedures as we considered necessary in the circumstances. We believe that our examination provides a reasonable basis for our opinion.

In addition, we have reviewed the pro forma adjustments and the application of those adjustments to the historical amounts in [*the assembly of*][1] the accompanying pro forma condensed balance sheet of ABC Company as of March 31, 20X3, and the pro forma condensed statement of income for the three months then ended. The historical condensed financial statements are derived from the historical financial statements of ABC Company, which were reviewed by us, and of DEF Company, which were reviewed by other accountants,[8] appearing elsewhere herein [*or incorporated by reference*]. Such pro forma adjustments are based upon management's assumptions described in Note [Y]. Our review was conducted in accordance with attestation standards established by the American Institute of Certified Public Accountants. A review is substantially less in scope than an examination, the objective of which is the expression of an opinion on management's assumptions, the pro forma adjustments and the application of those adjustments to historical financial information. Accordingly, we do not express such an opinion on the pro forma adjustments or the application of such adjustments to the pro forma condensed balance sheet as of March 31, 20X3, and the pro forma condensed statement of income for the three months then ended.

The objective of this pro forma financial information is to show what the significant effects on the historical financial information might have been had the transaction [*or event*] occurred at an earlier date. However, the pro forma condensed financial statements are not necessarily indicative of the results of operations or related effects on financial position that would have been attained had the above-mentioned transaction [*or event*] actually occurred earlier.

[*Additional paragraph(s) may be added to emphasize certain matters relating to the attest engagements or the subject matter.*]

In our opinion, management's assumptions provide a reasonable basis for presenting the significant effects directly attributable to the above-mentioned transaction [*or event*] described in Note [X], the related pro forma adjustments give appropriate effect to those assumptions, and the pro forma column reflects the proper application of those adjustments to the historical financial statement amounts in the pro forma condensed balance sheet as of December 31, 20X2, and the pro forma condensed statement of income for the year then ended.

Based on our review, nothing came to our attention that caused us to believe that management's assumptions do not provide a reasonable basis for presenting the significant effects directly attributable to the above-mentioned transaction [*or event*] described in Note [X], that the related pro forma adjustments do not give

---

[8] Where one set of historical financial statements is audited and the other set is reviewed, wording similar to the following would be appropriate:

The historical condensed financial statements are derived from the historical financial statements of ABC Company, which were audited by us, and of DEF Company, which were reviewed by other accountants, appearing elsewhere herein [*or incorporated by reference*].

appropriate effect to those assumptions, or that the pro forma column does not reflect the proper application of those adjustments to the historical financial statement amounts in the pro forma condensed balance sheet as of March 31, 20X3, and the pro forma condensed statement of income for the three months then ended.

[*Signature*]

[*Date*]

ILLUSTRATION 5—EXAMINATION REPORT QUALIFIED FOR A SCOPE LIMITATION

Independent Accountant's Report

We have examined the pro forma adjustments reflecting the transaction [*or event*] described in Note [*X*] and the application of those adjustments to the historical amounts in [*the assembly of*][9] the accompanying pro forma condensed balance sheet of ABC Company as of December 31, 20X2, and the pro forma condensed statement of income for the year then ended. The historical condensed financial statements are derived from the historical financial statements of ABC Company, which were audited by us, and of DEF Company, which were audited by other accountants,[10] appearing elsewhere herein [*or incorporated by reference*]. Such pro forma adjustments are based upon management's assumptions described in Note [*Y*]. ABC Company's management is responsible for the pro forma financial information. Our responsibility is to express an opinion on the pro forma financial information based on our examination.

Except as described below, our examination was conducted in accordance with attestation standards established by the American Institute of Certified Public Accountants and, accordingly, included such procedures as we considered necessary in the circumstances. We believe that our examination provides a reasonable basis for our opinion.

We are unable to perform the examination procedures we considered necessary with respect to assumptions relating to the proposed loan described as Adjustment 1 in Note [*Y*].

The objective of this pro forma financial information is to show what the significant effects on the historical financial information might have been had the transaction [*or event*] occurred at an earlier date. However, the pro forma condensed financial statements are not necessarily indicative of the results of operations or related effects on financial position that would have been attained had the above-mentioned transaction [*or event*] actually occurred earlier.

In our opinion, except for the effects of such changes, if any, as might have been determined to be necessary had we been able to satisfy ourselves as to the assumptions relating to the proposed loan, management's assumptions provide a reasonable basis for presenting the significant effects directly attributable to the

---

[9] This wording is appropriate when one column of pro forma financial information is presented without separate columns of historical financial information and pro forma adjustments.

[10] If either accountant's report includes an explanatory paragraph or is other than unqualified, that fact should be referred to within this report.

above-mentioned transaction [*or event*] described in Note [*X*], the related pro forma adjustments give appropriate effect to those assumptions, and the pro forma column reflects the proper application of those adjustments to the historical financial statement amounts in the pro forma condensed balance sheet as of December 31, 20X2, and the pro forma condensed statement of income for the year then ended.

[*Signature*]

[*Date*]

ILLUSTRATION 6—EXAMINATION REPORT QUALIFIED FOR RESERVATIONS ABOUT THE PROPRIETY OF ASSUMPTIONS ON AN ACQUISITION TRANSACTION

Independent Accountant's Report

We have examined the pro forma adjustments reflecting the transaction [*or event*] described in Note [*X*] and the application of those adjustments to the historical amounts in [*the assembly of*][11] the accompanying pro forma financial condensed balance sheet of ABC Company as of December 31, 20X2, and the pro forma condensed statement of income for the year then ended. The historical condensed financial statements are derived from the historical financial statements of ABC Company, which were audited by us, and of DEF Company, which were audited by other accountants,[12] appearing elsewhere herein [*or incorporated by reference*]. Such pro forma adjustments are based upon management's assumptions described in Note [*Y*]. ABC Company's management is responsible for the pro forma financial information. Our responsibility is to express an opinion on the pro forma financial information based on our examination.

Our examination was conducted in accordance with attestation standards established by the American Institute of Certified Public Accountants and, accordingly, included such procedures as we considered necessary in the circumstances. We believe that our examination provides a reasonable basis for our opinion.

The objective of this pro forma financial information is to show what the significant effects on the historical financial information might have been had the transaction [*or event*] occurred at an earlier date. However, the pro forma condensed financial statements are not necessarily indicative of the results of operations or related effects on financial position that would have been attained had the above-mentioned transaction [*or event*] actually occurred earlier.

As discussed in Note [*Y*] to the pro forma financial statements, the pro forma adjustments reflect management's assumption that XYZ Division of the acquired company will be sold. The net assets of this division are reflected at their historical carrying amount; generally accepted accounting principles require these net assets to be recorded at estimated net realizable value.

---

[11] This wording is appropriate when one column of pro forma financial information is presented without separate columns of historical financial information and pro forma adjustments.

[12] If either accountant's report includes an explanatory paragraph or is other than unqualified, that fact should be referred to within this report.

In our opinion, except for inappropriate valuation of the net assets of XYZ Division, management's assumptions described in Note [Y] provide a reasonable basis for presenting the significant effects directly attributable to the above-mentioned transaction [*or event*] described in Note [X], the related pro forma adjustments give appropriate effect to those assumptions, and the pro forma column reflects the proper application of those adjustments to the historical financial statement amounts in the pro forma condensed balance sheet as of December 31, 20X2, and the pro forma condensed statement of income for the year then ended.

[*Signature*]

[*Date*]

ILLUSTRATION 7—DISCLAIMER OF OPINION BECAUSE OF A SCOPE LIMITATION

Independent Accountant's Report

We were engaged to examine the pro forma adjustments reflecting the transaction [*or event*] described in Note [X] and the application of those adjustments to the historical amounts in [*the assembly of*][13] the accompanying pro forma financial condensed balance sheet of ABC Company as of December 31, 20X2, and the pro forma condensed statement of income for the year then ended. The historical condensed financial statements are derived from the historical financial statements of ABC Company, which were audited by us, and of DEF Company which were audited by other accountants,[14] appearing elsewhere herein [*or incorporated by reference.*] Such pro forma adjustments are based upon management's assumptions described in Note [Y]. ABC Company's management is responsible for the pro forma financial information.

As discussed in Note [Y] to the pro forma financial statements, the pro forma adjustments reflect management's assumptions that the elimination of duplicate facilities would have resulted in a 40 percent reduction in operating costs. Management could not supply us with sufficient evidence to support this assertion.

The objective of this pro forma financial information is to show what the significant effects on the historical financial information might have been had the transaction [*or event*] occurred at an earlier date. However, the pro forma condensed financial statements are not necessarily indicative of the results of operations or related effects on financial position that would have been attained had the above-mentioned transaction [*or event*] actually occurred earlier.

Since we were unable to evaluate management's assumptions regarding the reduction in operating costs and other assumptions related thereto, the scope of our work was not sufficient to express and, therefore, we do not express an opinion on the pro forma adjustments, management's underlying assumptions regarding those adjustments, and the application of those adjustments to the

---

[13] This wording is appropriate when one column of pro forma financial information is presented without separate columns of historical financial information and pro forma adjustments.

[14] If either accountant's report includes an explanatory paragraph or is other than unqualified, that fact should be referred to within this report.

historical financial statement amounts in the pro forma condensed financial statement amounts in the pro forma condensed balance sheet as of December 31, 20X2, and the pro forma condensed statement of income for the year then ended.

[*Signature*]

[*Date*]

AT SECTION 501
AN EXAMINATION OF AN ENTITY'S INTERNAL CONTROL OVER FINANCIAL REPORTING THAT IS INTEGRATED WITH AN AUDIT OF ITS FINANCIAL STATEMENTS

WHAT EVERY PRACTITIONER SHOULD KNOW

Basic Objectives and Requirements

This Section establishes requirements and provides guidance when a practitioner is engaged to perform an examination of the design and operating effectiveness of an entity's internal control over financial reporting that is integrated with an audit of its financial statements. The auditor's objective in an examination of internal control is to form an opinion on the effectiveness of the entity's internal control. An effective internal control means that no *material weaknesses* exist. Therefore, the auditor should plan and perform the examination to obtain appropriate evidence that is sufficient to provide reasonable assurance about whether material weaknesses exist as of the date specified in management's assertion. To achieve this objective, the auditor should use the same suitable and available control criteria to perform his or her examination of internal control as management uses for its evaluation of the effectiveness of the entity's internal control.

The examination of ICFR should be integrated with an audit of financial statements. This Section specifically states that the auditor should plan and perform the integrated audit to achieve the objectives of both engagements simultaneously. Accordingly, the auditor should design tests of controls to obtain sufficient appropriate evidence to support the auditor's (a) opinion on internal control as of the period-end, and (b) control risk assessments for the financial statement audit.

In an integrated audit, the date specified in management's assertion should correspond to the balance sheet date, or period ending date, of the period covered by the financial statements.

In this Section, the phrase "examination of internal control" means an engagement to report directly on internal control or on management's assertion thereon and, therefore, the guidance in this Section applies equally to either reporting alternative.

Management's responsibility This Section indicates that, in order for the auditor to perform an examination of ICFR, management has to fulfill its responsibilities to accomplish the following:

- Accept responsibility for the effectiveness of the entity's internal control;

- Evaluate the effectiveness of the entity's internal control using suitable and available control criteria, for example, The Committee of Sponsoring Organizations of the Treadway Commission's (COSO) report *Internal Control-Integrated Framework*;

- Support its assertion about the effectiveness of the entity's internal control with sufficient appropriate evidence; and

- Provide its assertion about the effectiveness of the entity's internal control in a report that accompanies the auditor's report.

Broad steps in performing an examination of internal control Performing an examination of ICFR under this Section involves:

1. Planning the examination engagement;
2. Using a top-down approach to select the controls to test;
3. Testing controls;
4. Evaluating identified deficiencies; and
5. Forming an opinion on the effectiveness of ICFR and wrapping-up the engagement.

The following paragraphs provide additional guidance on the application of these steps.

Planning the Examination Engagement

When planning and performing the examination of ICFR, the auditor should (1) use the same materiality used in planning and performing the audit of the entity's financial statements; (2) incorporate the results of the fraud risk assessment performed in the financial statement audit; and (3) focus more of his or her attention on the areas of highest risk. In addition, the auditor should evaluate whether the entity's controls sufficiently address identified risks of material misstatement due to fraud and the risk of management override of other controls.

Matters that may be important to the entity's financial statements and internal control, which may assist the auditor in planning the examination of ICFR, include the following:

- Knowledge of the entity's internal control obtained during the course of other professional engagements performed by the auditor for the client.

- Matters affecting the industry in which the entity operates (e.g., financial reporting practices, economic conditions, laws and regulations, technological changes).

- Matters pertaining to the entity's business (e.g., operating characteristics, capital structure).

- The nature and extent of any recent changes in the entity, its operations, or its internal control.

- Preliminary judgments about materiality, risk, and other factors relating to the determination of material weaknesses.

- Internal control deficiencies previously communicated to management or those charged with governance.

- Legal or regulatory matters that the entity is aware of.

- The nature and extent of available evidence pertaining to the effectiveness of the entity's ICFR.

- Preliminary judgments about the effectiveness of internal control.
- Public information about the entity pertinent to the evaluation of the likelihood of material financial statement misstatements and the effectiveness of its ICFR.
- Knowledge about specific risks related to the entity that were evaluated as part of the auditor's acceptance and retention evaluation.
- Complexity of the entity's operations.

The auditor should focus more attention on the areas of highest risk. Therefore, it is not necessary for the auditor to test controls that would not present a reasonable possibility of material misstatement to the financial statements, even if such controls are deficient. In addition, the auditor should incorporate the results of the fraud risk assessment performed in the financial statement audit and should evaluate whether the entity's controls sufficiently address identified risks of material misstatement due to fraud and the risk of management override of other controls. If the auditor identifies deficiencies in controls designed to prevent, or detect and correct, misstatements caused by fraud during the examination of internal control, the auditor should take into account those deficiencies when developing his or her response to risks of material misstatement during the financial statement audit. AU Section 316 (Consideration of Fraud in a Financial Statement Audit) provides additional guidance when addressing the risk of fraud.

Considering and using the work of others Work of others includes work performed by internal auditors, other entity personnel, and third parties working under the direction of management or those charged with governance. Before using this work, the auditor should obtain a sufficient understanding of the work performed by others in order to identify those activities related to the effectiveness of ICFR that are relevant to planning the examination of internal control. To determine the extent to which the auditor may use the work of others, the auditor is required to:

- Evaluate the competence of the individuals who performed the work, including assessment of the person's qualifications and ability to perform the work that the auditor plans to use;
- Evaluate the objectivity of the individuals who performed the work, including whether factors exist that might restrict or enhance the individual's ability to perform with the necessary degree of objectivity the work that the auditor plans to use; and
- Apply the provisions of AU Section 322 (The Auditor's Consideration of the Internal Audit Function in an Audit of Financial Statements) to assess the competence and objectivity of internal auditors and apply the principles therein to assess the competence and objectivity of persons other than internal auditors whose work the auditor plans to use.

Using a Top-Down Approach to Select the Controls to Test

This Section requires the auditor to use a top-down approach to the examination of internal control to select the controls to test. A top-down approach begins at the financial statement level and with the auditor's understanding of the overall risks to ICFR. The auditor then focuses on entity-level controls and works down to significant accounts and disclosures and their relevant assertions. This approach directs the auditor's attention to accounts, disclosures, and assertions that present a reasonable possibility of material misstatement to the financial statements and related disclosures. The auditor then verifies his or her understanding of the risks in the entity's processes and selects for testing those controls that sufficiently address the assessed risk of material misstatement to each relevant assertion. Note that the top-down approach describes the auditor's sequential thought process in identifying risks and the controls to test, not necessarily the order in which the auditor will perform the examination procedures.

Identifying entity-level controls This Section states that the auditor should test those entity-level controls that are important to his or her conclusion about whether the entity has effective internal control. Entity-level controls include, but are not limited to, the following: controls related to the control environment, controls over management override, and controls over the period-end financial reporting process.

The auditor is required to evaluate the control environment at the entity and, as part of this evaluation, to assess:

- Whether management's philosophy and operating style promote effective ICFR;
- Whether sound integrity and ethical values, particularly of top management, are developed and understood; and
- Whether those charged with governance understand and exercise oversight responsibility over financial reporting and internal control.

In addition, the auditor is required to evaluate the period-end financial reporting process, which includes procedures the entity uses to (1) enter transaction totals into the general ledger; (2) select and apply accounting policies; (3) initiate, authorize, record, and process journal entries in the general ledger; (4) record recurring and nonrecurring adjustments to the financial statements; and (5) prepare financial statements and related disclosures. As part of this evaluation, the auditor should assess:

- Inputs, procedures performed, and outputs of the processes the entity uses to produce its financial statements;
- The extent of information technology (IT) involvement in the period-end financial reporting process;
- Who participates from management;
- The locations involved in the period-end financial reporting process;
- The types of adjusting and consolidating entries; and
- The nature and extent of the oversight of the process by management and those charged with governance.

Identifying significant accounts and disclosures and their relevant assertions The auditor should identify significant accounts and disclosures and their relevant assertions. During this process, the auditor should:

- Evaluate the qualitative and quantitative risk factors related to the financial statement line items and disclosures. Such risk factors include, for example: (1) size and composition of the account; (2) susceptibility to misstatement due to errors or fraud; (3) nature of the account, class of transactions, or disclosure; (4) exposure to losses in the account; and (5) existence of related-party transactions in the account.

- Determine the likely sources of potential misstatements that would cause the financial statements to be materially misstated (e.g., what could go wrong within a given significant account or disclosure).

- Identify significant accounts and disclosures and their relevant assertions based on the consolidated financial statements, when an entity has multiple locations or business units.

Understanding likely sources of misstatement As part of selecting the controls to test, and in order to further understand the likely sources of potential misstatement, this Section requires the auditor to:

- Understand the flow of transactions related to the relevant assertions, including how such transactions are initiated, authorized, processed, and recorded;

- Identify the points within the entity's processes at which a material misstatement could arise;

- Identify the controls that management has implemented to address these potential misstatements; and

- Identify the controls that management has implemented over the prevention or timely detection and correction of unauthorized acquisition, use, or disposition of the entity's assets that could result in a material misstatement of the financial statements.

The auditor should either perform these procedures personally, or supervise the work of others (as described in AU Section 322) who provide direct assistance to the auditor in achieving the objectives contemplated herein.

Selecting controls to test The auditor is required to test those controls that are important to the auditor's conclusion about whether the entity's controls sufficiently address the assessed risk of material misstatement to each relevant assertion. However, the auditor is not required to test *all* controls related to a relevant assertion or to test redundant controls, unless redundancy is itself a control objective.

Testing Controls

This Section requires the auditor to evaluate the design effectiveness of controls by determining whether the entity's controls (1) satisfy its control objectives, and (2) can effectively prevent, or detect and correct, material misstatements caused by errors or fraud. Generally, walkthroughs that include a mix of inquiry of appropriate personnel, observation of the entity's operations, and inspection of relevant documentation are sufficient to evaluate design effectiveness.

The auditor is also required to test the operating effectiveness of a control by determining whether it is operating as designed and whether the person performing the control possesses the necessary authority and competence to perform the control effectively.

This Section provides the following additional directives when testing controls:

- When the auditor identifies deviations from the entity's controls, he or she should determine the effect of the deviations on his or her assessment of the risk associated with the control being tested and the evidence to be obtained, as well as on the operating effectiveness of the control.

- The auditor should balance performing the tests of controls closer to the "as-of" date with the need to test controls over a sufficient period of time to obtain sufficient appropriate evidence of operating effectiveness.

- Prior to the date specified in management's assertion, management might implement changes to the entity's controls to make them more effective or efficient, or to address control deficiencies. If the new controls achieve the related control objectives and have been in effect for a sufficient period to enable the auditor to perform tests of controls to assess their design and operating effectiveness, the auditor is not required to test the superseded controls for purposes of expressing an opinion on ICFR. However, if the operating effectiveness of the superseded controls is important to the auditor's control risk assessment in the financial statement audit, the auditor should test the design and operating effectiveness of those superseded controls, as appropriate.

- When the auditor reports on the effectiveness of controls as of a specific date and obtains evidence about the operating effectiveness of controls at an interim date, the auditor should determine what additional evidence is necessary concerning the operation of the controls for the remaining period.

- In subsequent years' examinations, the auditor should incorporate into the decision-making process for tests of controls knowledge obtained during past examinations he or she performed of the entity's ICFR.

- The auditor should vary the nature, timing, and extent of testing of controls from period to period to introduce unpredictability into the testing, and respond to changes in circumstances (e.g., testing controls at a different interim period each year).

Evaluating Identified Deficiencies

This Section provides the following definitions related to deficiencies in internal control over financial reporting:

- *Deficiency*—A deficiency in internal control exists when the design or operation of a control does not allow management or employees, in the normal course of performing their assigned functions, to prevent, or detect and correct misstatements on a timely basis. There are two types of deficiencies:

— *Deficiency in design*—A deficiency in design exists when (a) a control necessary to meet the control objective is missing, or (b) an existing control is not properly designed so that, even if the control operates as designed, the control objective would not be met.

— *Deficiency in operation*—A deficiency in operation exists when (a) a properly designed control does not operate as designed, or (b) the person performing the control does not possess the necessary authority or competence to perform the control effectively.

- *Significant deficiency*—A deficiency, or a combination of deficiencies, in internal control that is less severe than a material weakness, yet important enough to merit attention by those charged with governance.

- *Material weakness*—A deficiency, or a combination of deficiencies, in internal control, such that there is a reasonable possibility that a material misstatement of the entity's financial statements will not be prevented, or detected and corrected, on a timely basis.

This Section requires the auditor to evaluate the severity of each control deficiency that comes to his or her attention to determine whether the deficiency, individually or in combination, is a material weakness as of the date of management's assertion. Although compensating controls can limit the severity of a deficiency and prevent it from being a material weakness, they do not eliminate the deficiency. Therefore, the auditor should evaluate the effect of compensating controls when determining whether a control deficiency or combination of deficiencies is a material weakness. In addition, for purposes of determining whether compensating controls have a mitigating effect, the auditor should test the operating effectiveness of compensating controls.

If the auditor determines that a deficiency, or a combination of deficiencies, is not a material weakness, the auditor is required to consider whether prudent officials, having knowledge of the same facts and circumstances, would likely reach the same conclusion.

Forming an Opinion on the Effectiveness of ICFR and Wrapping Up the Engagement

The auditor should evaluate evidence obtained from all sources and form an opinion on the effectiveness of ICFR. Sources of evidence for the auditor's evaluation include the auditor's testing of controls, misstatements detected during the financial statement audit, and any identified control deficiencies. In connection with this evaluation, the auditor should review reports issued during the year by internal audit, or similar functions, that address controls related to ICFR and evaluate control deficiencies identified in those reports.

Evaluating management's report and determining that it contains the required elements This Section states that, after forming an opinion on the effectiveness of the entity's ICFR, the auditor should evaluate management's report to determine that it appropriately includes the following elements:

- A statement regarding management's responsibility for internal control;

- A description of the subject matter of the examination (e.g., controls over the preparation of the entity's financial statements in accordance with GAAP);
- An identification of the criteria against which internal control is measured (e.g., COSO);
- Management's assertion about the effectiveness of internal control;
- A description of the material weaknesses, if any; and
- The date as of which management's assertion is made.

See Illustration 10 for an illustrative management report containing these required elements.

If any of these required elements is incomplete or improperly presented in management's report, the auditor should request management to revise its report. If management does not revise its report, the auditor should modify his or her report to include an explanatory paragraph describing the reasons for this determination.

This Section indicates that, if management refuses to furnish a report to the auditor, management's refusal should cause the auditor to withdraw from the engagement. However, if law or regulation does not allow the auditor to withdraw from the engagement and management refuses to furnish a written assertion, the auditor should disclaim an opinion on internal control.

Obtaining written representations The auditor should obtain written representations from management in which it:

1. Acknowledges its responsibility for establishing and maintaining effective internal control.

2. States that it has performed an evaluation of the effectiveness of the entity's internal control and specifies the control criteria.

3. States that it did not use the auditor's procedures performed during the integrated audit as part of the basis for its assertion.

4. States its assertion about the effectiveness of the entity's internal control based on the control criteria as of a specified date.

5. States that it has disclosed to the auditor all deficiencies in the design or operation of internal control, including separately disclosing all such deficiencies that it believes to be significant deficiencies or material weaknesses in internal control.

6. Describes any material fraud and any other fraud that, although not material, involves senior management or management or other employees who have a significant role in the entity's internal control.

7. States whether the significant deficiencies and material weaknesses identified and communicated to management and those charged with governance during previous engagements have been resolved and specifically identified any that have not.

8. States whether there were any subsequent changes in internal control or other factors that might significantly affect internal control, including

any corrective actions taken by management with respect to significant deficiencies and material weaknesses.

Management's refusal to furnish all appropriate written representations constitutes a limitation on the scope of the examination, sufficient to cause the auditor to withdraw from the engagement or disclaim an opinion. Further, in such circumstances, the auditor should evaluate the effects of management's refusal on his or her ability to rely on other representations, including those obtained in the audit of the entity's financial statements.

Communicating certain matters The auditor should communicate, in writing, to management and those charged with governance all significant deficiencies or material weaknesses identified during the integrated audit, including those that were previously communicated but have not yet been remediated. In addition, if the auditor concludes that the oversight of the entity's financial reporting and internal control by the audit committee or its equivalent is ineffective, the auditor should communicate that conclusion, in writing, to the board of directors or other similar governing body. These required communications should be made by the report release date, which is the date the auditor grants the entity permission to use the auditor's report. However, under certain circumstances, for governmental entities, the required written communications can be made up to 60 days following the report release date.

In addition, for all deficiencies that are not considered significant deficiencies or material weaknesses, the auditor is required to communicate to management, in writing, all such deficiencies identified during the integrated audit on a timely basis, but no later than 60 days following the report release date. The auditor should also inform those charged with governance when such communication was made to management.

The auditor should not issue a report stating that no such deficiencies were identified during the integrated audit. In addition, the auditor is precluded from issuing a report indicating that no material weaknesses were identified during the integrated audit.

See Illustration 9 for a sample written communication of significant deficiencies and material weaknesses.

Reporting on the Examination of Internal Control

The auditor's report on the examination of internal control should include certain specified elements. See Illustration 2 for a list of the items that should be included in the auditor's report when reporting directly on internal control or on management's assertion thereon.

The auditor may issue either separate reports or a combined report on the entity's financial statements and on internal control over financial reporting. If a separate report on internal control is issued, the auditor is required to:

- Add the following additional paragraph to the auditor's report on the financial statements making reference to the auditor's report on internal control: "We also have examined [*or audited*] in accordance with attestation standards established by the American Institute of Certified Public

Accountants, [*entity name*]'s internal control over financial reporting as of December 31, 20X8, based on [*identify control criteria*] and our report dated [*date of report, which should be the same as the date of the report on the financial statements*]expressed [*include nature of opinion*]."

- Add the following additional paragraph to the auditor's report on internal control making reference to the auditor's report on the financial statements: "We also have audited, in accordance with auditing standards generally accepted in the United States of America, the [*identify financial statements*]of [*entity name*] and our report dated [*date of report, which should be the same as the date of the report on internal control*] expressed [*include nature of opinion*]." See Illustrations 3 through 7.

The auditor should date the report no earlier than the date on which the auditor has obtained sufficient appropriate evidence to support the auditor's opinion. Because the examination of internal control is integrated with the audit of the financial statements, the dates of the reports should be the same.

See Illustration 3 for a sample separate report expressing an unqualified opinion directly on internal control, Illustration 4 for a sample separate report expressing an unqualified opinion on management's assertion, and Illustration 8 for a sample combined report expressing an unqualified opinion directly on internal control and on the financial statements.

Adverse opinions This Section requires the auditor to express an adverse opinion on the entity's internal control if there are deficiencies that, individually or in combination, result in one or more material weaknesses as of the date specified in management's assertion. However, if there are restrictions on the scope of the engagement, the auditor should withdraw from the engagement or disclaim an opinion (see discussion below for report modifications when scope limitations exist). See Illustration 5 for a sample report expressing an adverse opinion on internal control.

In addition, the auditor should observe the following directives when one or more material weaknesses exist:

- *No opinion on management's assertion*—The auditor is prohibited from expressing an opinion on management's assertion and should report directly on the effectiveness of internal control. The auditor's report should include (1) the definition of a material weakness, and (2) a statement that one or more material weaknesses have been identified and an identification of the material weaknesses described in management's assertion.

- *Material weaknesses not included in management's report*—If one or more material weaknesses have not been included in management's report accompanying the auditor's report, the auditor's report should be modified to state that one or more material weaknesses have been identified but not included in management's report. In addition, the auditor's report should (1) include a description of each material weakness not included in management's report, and (2) communicate, in writing, to those charged with governance that one or more material weaknesses were not disclosed or identified as a material weakness in management's report.

- *Disclosure of material weaknesses in management's report is not fairly presented*—If one or more material weaknesses have been included in management's report but the auditor concludes that the disclosure of such material weaknesses is not fairly presented in all material respects, the auditor's report should describe this conclusion as well as the information necessary to fairly describe each material weakness.

- *Effect of an adverse opinion on internal control on the auditor's opinion on the financial statements*—The auditor should determine the effect that an adverse opinion on internal control has on his or her opinion on the financial statements. In this case, the auditor should disclose whether his or her opinion on the financial statements was affected by the material weaknesses.

Report modifications This Section requires the auditor to modify his or her standard report on internal control over financial reporting in the following circumstances:

1. *Elements of management's report are incomplete or improperly presented*—If any required element of management's report (e.g., management's assertion about the effectiveness of internal control; a description of the material weaknesses, if any) is incomplete or improperly presented, the auditor should ask management to revise it. If management does not revise its report, the auditor should modify his or her report on internal control to include an explanatory paragraph describing the reasons for this determination. If the auditor concludes that the required disclosure about one or more material weaknesses is not fairly presented in all material respects, the auditor should follow the guidance previously discussed.

2. *Scope limitations exist*—If the auditor cannot apply all the necessary procedures due to restrictions imposed by the engagement circumstances, the auditor should either withdraw from the engagement or disclaim an opinion. See Illustration 6 for a sample report expressing a disclaimer of opinion on internal control. If the auditor decides to disclaim an opinion due to scope limitations, the auditor should observe the following directives:

   a. The auditor should state that he or she does not express an opinion on the effectiveness of internal control and include the substantive reasons for the disclaimer.

   b. The auditor should not identify the procedures that were performed nor include the statements describing the characteristics of an examination of internal control.

   c. When the limited procedures performed by the auditor caused him or her to conclude that one or more material weaknesses exist, the auditor's report should include (1) the definition of a material weakness, and (2) a description of any material weaknesses identified in the entity's internal control, including specific information about the nature of any material weakness and its actual and potential effect on the presentation of the entity's financial statements issued during the existence of the weakness.

    d. The auditor should communicate, in writing, to management and those charged with governance that the examination of internal control cannot be satisfactorily completed.

3. *The auditor's opinion is based in part on the report of another auditor*—An auditor may report on the effectiveness of a combined or consolidated entity's internal control over financial reporting even if he or she has not audited all the individual components within such entity (e.g., subsidiary, division, branch). Under these circumstances, the auditor should decide whether it is appropriate for him or her to serve as the principal auditor of internal control and whether to make reference to the other auditor. In such circumstances, the auditor's considerations are similar to those of the independent auditor when reporting on an entity's financial statements, as discussed in AU Section 543 (Part of Audit Performed by Other Independent Auditors). When the principal auditor of internal control decides to make reference to the report of the other auditor as a basis, in part, for his or her opinion on the entity's internal control, the principal auditor should refer to the report of the other auditor when describing the scope of the examination and when expressing the opinion. See Illustration 7 for a sample report expressing an unqualified opinion on internal control when the auditor decides to refer to the report of another auditor as the basis, in part, for the auditor's own report.

4. *Other information is contained in management's report on internal control over financial reporting*—Management's report on internal control over financial reporting may contain certain additional information, for example, about the entity's plans to implement new controls or about corrective actions taken by the entity after the date of management's assessment. If such additional information is included in management's assessment, the auditor should disclaim an opinion on the information, by including language such as the following as the last paragraph of the auditor's report:

> We do not express an opinion or any other form of assurance on [*describe additional information, such as management's cost-benefit statement*].

If the auditor believes that the additional information is a material misstatement of fact, the auditor should discuss the matter with the client. If the auditor concludes he or she has a valid basis for concern, the auditor should suggest that the client consult other advisers (e.g., the client's legal counsel). If, after such discussions, the auditor concludes that a material misstatement of fact remains, the auditor should notify management and those charged with governance, in writing, of his or her views concerning the information.

Subsequent Events

The auditor should inquire and obtain information about changes in internal control, or other factors that might significantly affect internal control, that have occurred subsequent to the date at which internal control is being examined but before the date of the auditor's report. In addition to obtaining written representations from management relating to such matters, the auditor should inquire about and examine the following items for the subsequent period:

1. Reports issued by internal auditors, if any.
2. Reports issued by other independent auditors relating to deficiencies in internal control.
3. Regulatory agency reports on the entity's internal control.
4. Information about the effectiveness of the entity's internal control obtained through other professional engagements.

If the auditor obtains knowledge about a material weakness that existed as of the date specified in management's assertion, the auditor should report directly on internal control and issue an adverse opinion. If the auditor is unable to determine the effect of the subsequent event on the effectiveness of the entity's internal control, he or she should disclaim an opinion.

The auditor may become aware of conditions that did not exist at the date specified in management's assertion but arose subsequent to that date and before the release of the auditor's report. In such circumstances, if the subsequent event has a material effect on the entity's internal control, the auditor should include an explanatory paragraph that (1) describes the event and its effects or (2) directs the reader's attention to the event and its effects as disclosed in management's report.

Special Considerations Relating to Examinations of an Entity's Internal Control

Multi-location considerations Entities with multiple locations or business units present the auditor with additional decision points when planning and performing the audit. The auditor is required to employ a risk-based approach in determining the proper strategy for auditing multiple locations. In determining the locations or business units at which to perform tests of controls, the auditor should assess the risk of misstatement to the financial statements associated with the location or business unit and correlate the amount of audit attention devoted to the location or business unit with the degree of risk.

This Section provides the following additional guidance and directives for entities with multiple locations:

- The auditor may eliminate from further consideration those locations or business units that, individually or when aggregated with others, do not present a reasonable possibility of misstatement to the consolidated financial statements.

- The auditor should test controls over specific risks that present a reasonable possibility of material misstatement to the consolidated financial statements. In lower-risk locations or business units, the auditor first might evaluate whether testing entity-level controls provides the auditor with sufficient evidence.

- The auditor may consider the work performed by others on behalf of management and may coordinate work with the internal auditors and reduce the number of locations or business units that would otherwise be subjected to the auditor's examination procedures.

- The auditor should vary the nature, timing, and extent of testing controls at locations or business units from year to year.

Acquisitions, dispositions, equity-method investments, and allowed exclusions This Section states that the scope of the auditor's examination of an entity's internal control should include the following:

- Entities that are acquired on or before the date of management's assertion;

- Operations that are accounted for as discontinued operations on the date of management's assertion; and

- For equity method investments, controls over the reporting of the entity's portion of the investees' income or loss, the investment balance, adjustments to the income or loss and investment balance, and related disclosures. (*Note:* The scope of the auditor's examination generally would not extend to controls at the equity method investee.)

There may be situations in which a regulator allows management to limit its assertion by excluding certain entities, which would not be considered a scope limitation. While the auditor may limit the examination in the same manner, this Section states that the auditor should apply the following procedures in such circumstances:

- Include, either in an additional explanatory paragraph or as part of the scope paragraph of the auditor's report on internal control, a disclosure similar to management's regarding the exclusion of an entity from the scope of both management's assertion and the auditor's examination of internal control.

- Evaluate the reasonableness of management's conclusion that the situation meets the criteria of the regulator's allowed exclusion and the appropriateness of any required disclosure related to such a limitation.

- If management's disclosure about the limitation requires modification, communicate the matter to the appropriate level of management and, if management does not respond appropriately and timely, inform those charged with governance of the matter. If management and those charged with governance do not respond appropriately, the auditor should modify his or her report on the examination of internal control; such modification should include an explanatory paragraph describing the reasons why the auditor believes management's disclosure requires modification.

Use of service organizations If a service organization's services are part of an entity's information system, then they are part of the information and communication component of the entity's internal controls and the auditor should include the activities of the service organization when determining the evidence required to support his or her opinion on the entity's internal control. In such circumstances, the auditor may apply the relevant concepts described in AU Section 324 (Service Organizations) to the examination of internal control.

Specifically, the auditor should perform the procedures in paragraphs .07 to .16 of AU Section 324, which include:

- Obtaining an understanding of the controls at the service organization that are relevant to the entity's internal control and the controls at the user organization over the activities of the service organization; and

- Obtaining evidence that the controls that are relevant to the auditor's opinion are operating effectively (e.g., obtaining a service auditor's report).

It is important to note that the auditor should not refer to the service auditor's report when expressing an opinion on internal control. If a service auditor's report on controls placed in operation and tests of operating effectiveness is available, the auditor may evaluate whether this report provides sufficient evidence to support his or her opinion. In evaluating whether such a service auditor's report provides sufficient appropriate evidence, the auditor should assess the following factors:

- The time period covered by the tests of controls and its relation to the "as of" date of management's assessment;

- The scope of the examination and applications covered, the controls tested, and the way in which tested controls relate to the entity's controls; and

- The results of those tests of controls and the service auditor's opinion on the operating effectiveness of the controls.

These factors are similar to factors the auditor would consider in determining whether the report provides sufficient evidence to support the auditor's assessed level of control risk in an audit of the financial statements. In determining whether the service auditor's report provides sufficient appropriate evidence to support the auditor's opinion, the auditor should make inquiries concerning the service auditor's reputation, competence, and independence.

When a significant period of time has elapsed between the time period covered by the tests of controls in the service auditor's report and the date specified in management's assertion, the auditor should perform the following additional procedures:

- Inquire of management to determine whether it has identified any changes in the service organization's controls subsequent to the period covered by the service auditor's report (e.g., changes communicated to management from the service organization; changes in reports or other data received from the service organization; or errors identified in the service organization's processing), and evaluate the effect of any such changes on the effectiveness of the entity's internal control; and

- Evaluate whether the results of other procedures he or she performed indicate that there have been changes in the controls at the service organization.

Benchmarking of automated controls This Section allows auditors to incorporate the knowledge they obtained during past examinations of the entity's internal control over financial reporting into the nature, timing, and extent of testing necessary for a current examination. This principle may allow auditors to reduce testing in later years. Auditors are cautioned, however, to be aware of any changes in the control or the process in which it operates since the previous examination.

Auditors are also permitted to use a benchmarking strategy for automated application controls in subsequent years' examinations. Benchmarking involves establishing a baseline and verifying that the automated control has not changed since the baseline's establishment. This would allow the auditor to conclude that the automated control is still effective without repeating the prior year's tests.

This Section requires the auditor to assess the following factors when determining whether to use a benchmarking strategy:

- The extent to which the application control can be matched to a defined program within an application;
- The extent to which the application is stable (i.e., few changes from period to period); and
- The availability and reliability of a report of the compilation dates of the programs placed in production.

The baseline of the operation of an automated application control should be reestablished after a period of time. This Section requires the auditor to evaluate the following factors for purposes of determining when to reestablish a baseline:

- The effectiveness of the IT control environment (e.g., controls over application and system software acquisition and maintenance; access controls; and computer operations);
- The auditor's understanding of the nature of changes, if any, on the specific programs containing the controls;
- The nature and timing of other related tests;
- The consequences of errors pertaining to the application control that was benchmarked; and
- Whether the control is sensitive to other business factors that may have changed.

Integration with the financial statement audit The objective of the tests of controls in an examination of internal control is to obtain evidence about the effectiveness of controls to support the auditor's opinion on the entity's internal control. The auditor's opinion relates to the effectiveness of the entity's internal control (i) as of a point in time, and (ii) taken as a whole, as follows:

- *Point in time*—The auditor should obtain evidence that internal control has operated effectively for a sufficient period of time, which may be less than the entire period covered by the entity's financial statements.

- *Taken as a whole*—The auditor should obtain evidence about the effectiveness of *selected* controls over *all* relevant assertions. This requires that auditors test the design and operating effectiveness of controls they ordinarily would not test if expressing an opinion only on the financial statements.

When concluding on the effectiveness of internal control for purposes of expressing an opinion on internal control, this Section requires the auditor to incorporate the results of any additional tests of controls performed to achieve the objective related to expressing an opinion on the financial statements, as follows:

- *Tests of controls in an audit of financial statements*—When concluding on the effectiveness of controls for the purpose of the financial statement audit, the auditor should also evaluate the results of any additional tests of controls performed to achieve the objective related to expressing an opinion on the entity's internal control. Consideration of these results may require the auditor to modify the nature, timing, and extent of substantive procedures and to plan and perform further tests of controls, particularly in response to identified control deficiencies.

- *Effect of tests of controls on substantive procedures*—Auditors identifying a deficiency during the examination of internal control should determine the effect of the deficiency on the nature, timing, and extent of substantive procedures to be performed to reduce audit risk in the audit of the financial statements to an appropriately low level. Further, regardless of the assessed risk of material misstatement in connection with the financial statement audit, the auditor should perform substantive procedures for all relevant assertions related to each material class of transactions, account balance, and disclosure. Note that performing procedures to express an opinion on internal control does not diminish this requirement.

- *Effect of substantive procedures on conclusions about the operating effectiveness of controls*—In an examination of internal control, the auditor should evaluate the effect of the findings of the substantive auditing procedures performed in the audit of financial statements on the effectiveness of internal controls, including at a minimum the following:

  — The auditor's risk assessments in connection with the selection and application of substantive auditing procedures, particularly those related to fraud;

  — Findings involving illegal acts and related-party transactions;

  — Indications of management bias in making accounting estimates and selecting accounting principles; and

  — Misstatements detected by substantive auditing procedures that might alter the auditor's judgment about the effectiveness of controls.

This Section cautions that the effectiveness of a control cannot be inferred from the absence of misstatements detected by substantive auditing procedures. Rather, to obtain evidence about whether a selected control is effective, the control must be tested directly.

Pre-Award Surveys

In connection with its application for a government grant or contract, an entity may be required to submit a written pre-award assertion (survey) about the effectiveness of the design of the entity's internal control, together with a practitioner's report thereon. A practitioner may not issue such a report based solely on the consideration of internal control in an audit of the entity's financial statements.

In order to issue a report on a written pre-award assertion by management about the effectiveness of the design of the entity's internal control, or a portion thereof, the practitioner should perform an examination of or apply agreed-upon procedures to management's written assertion. For an examination engagement, the practitioner should follow the requirements of this Section (AT 501). For an agreed-upon procedures engagement, the practitioner should, in addition, follow the provisions of AT Section 201 (Agreed-Upon Procedures Engagements) and AT Section 601 (Compliance Attestation).

The practitioner should refuse to sign any form prescribed by a government agency in connection with a pre-award survey unless he or she has performed an examination or an agreed-upon procedures attestation engagement. If the practitioner has performed such an attestation engagement, he or she should determine whether the wording of the prescribed form conforms to professional standards; if not, the practitioner should either make the necessary revisions or attach a separate report.

In addition, the practitioner should not issue a report on the *ability* of an entity to establish suitably designed internal control because the assertion about ability is not capable of reasonably consistent estimation or measurement. This is true in either an audit or an attestation engagement.

PRACTICE ISSUES AND FREQUENTLY ASKED QUESTIONS

Issue 1: When performing an examination of internal control under this Section, is the auditor required to comply with any of the other attestation standards?

Yes. An auditor engaged to perform an examination of internal control should comply with the five general standards, the two fieldwork standards, and the four reporting standards described in AT Section 101 (Attest Engagements), in addition to complying with the specific requirements discussed in this Section.

Issue 2: Does this Section apply if management engages the practitioner to provide recommendations on improvements to the entity's internal control?

No. An engagement to provide recommendations on improvements to the entity's internal control is not an attest service. While the practitioner may accept such an engagement, he or she should follow the guidance in Statement on

Standards for Consulting Services No. 1, "Consulting Services: Definitions and Standards."

Issue 3: May an auditor accept an engagement to "review" an entity's internal control or a written assertion thereon?

No. An auditor is prohibited from accepting an engagement to *review* an entity's internal control or a written assertion thereon.

Issue 4: What is the effect on an engagement to examine an entity's internal control if management refuses to furnish a written assertion to the auditor?

Management's refusal to furnish a written assertion as part of an examination engagement should cause the auditor to withdraw from the engagement, unless law or regulation does not allow the auditor to withdraw from the engagement. In that instance, the auditor should disclaim an opinion on internal control and follow the directives in this Section for disclaiming an opinion.

Issue 5: In planning and performing the examination of internal control, may the auditor use a different materiality than the one used in planning and performing the audit of the entity's financial statements?

No. This Section explicitly states that, in planning and performing the examination of internal control, the auditor should use the same materiality used in planning and performing the audit of the entity's financial statements.

Issue 6: What types of walkthrough procedures may the auditor perform in connection with obtaining an understanding of the likely sources of potential misstatements?

Performing walkthroughs is often the most effective way of obtaining an understanding of the likely sources of potential misstatements. A walkthrough involves following a transaction from origination through the entity's processes, including information systems, until it is reflected in the entity's financial records, using the same documents and IT that entity personnel use. A walkthrough includes questioning the entity's personnel about their understanding of what is required by the entity's prescribed procedures and controls at the points at which important processing procedures occur.

Walkthrough procedures may include a combination of the following:

- Inquiry;
- Observation;
- Inspection of relevant documentation;
- Recalculation; and
- Control reperformance.

Issue 7: Is it necessary to test all controls related to a relevant assertion or to test redundant controls?

There might be more than one control that addresses the assessed risk of material misstatement to a particular relevant assertion; conversely, one control might address the assessed risk of material misstatement to more than one relevant assertion. It may not be necessary to test all controls related to a relevant assertion nor necessary to test redundant controls, unless redundancy is, itself, a control objective.

Issue 8: Is the auditor responsible for obtaining sufficient appropriate evidence to support an opinion about the effectiveness of each individual control for each relevant assertion?

No. Although the auditor should obtain evidence about the effectiveness of controls for each relevant assertion, he or she is not responsible for obtaining sufficient appropriate evidence to support an opinion about the effectiveness of each individual control. Instead, the auditor's objective is to express an opinion on the entity's internal control overall. This inherently allows the auditor to vary the evidence obtained regarding the effectiveness of individual controls selected for testing based on the risk associated with the individual control.

Issue 9: Does an individual control have to operate without any deviation to be considered effective?

No. Because effective internal control cannot, and does not, provide absolute assurance of achieving the entity's control objectives, an individual control does not necessarily have to operate without any deviation to be considered effective.

Issue 10: What are some examples of tests that produce greater evidence of the effectiveness of controls than other tests?

Some types of tests, by their nature, produce greater evidence of the effectiveness of controls than other tests. This Section indicates that the following tests that the auditor might perform are presented in order of the evidence that they ordinarily would produce, from least to most: (1) inquiry, (2) observation, (3) inspection of relevant documentation, (4) recalculation, and (5) reperformance of a control. However, inquiry alone does not provide sufficient appropriate evidence to support a conclusion about the effectiveness of a control.

Issue 11: Are there any circumstances under which the auditor might be required to test superseded controls for purposes of expressing an opinion on internal control over financial reporting?

Yes. Prior to the date specified in management's assertion, management might implement changes to the entity's controls to make them more effective or efficient, or to address control deficiencies. If the new controls achieve the related control objectives and have been in effect for a sufficient period to enable the auditor to perform tests of controls to assess their design and operating effectiveness, the auditor is not required to test the superseded controls for purposes of expressing an opinion on internal control over financial reporting. However, if the operating effectiveness of the superseded controls is important to the auditor's control risk assessment in the financial statement audit, the auditor should test the design and operating effectiveness of those superseded controls, as appropriate.

Issue 12: What factors might the auditor consider when determining the extent of the additional evidence needed to update the results of testing from an interim date to the entity's period-end?

When the auditor reports on the effectiveness of controls as of a specific date and obtains evidence about the operating effectiveness of controls at an interim date, he or she should determine what additional evidence is necessary concerning the operation of the controls for the remaining period. This Section indicates that the additional evidence that is necessary to update the results of testing from an interim date to the entity's period-end depends on the following factors:

- The specific control tested prior to the as-of date, including the risks associated with the control, the nature of the control, and the results of those tests;
- The sufficiency of the evidence of operating effectiveness obtained at an interim date;
- The length of the remaining period; and
- The possibility that there have been any significant changes in internal control subsequent to the interim date.

Issue 13: What are some indicators of material weaknesses in internal control?

Indicators of material weaknesses in internal control include the following:

- Identification of fraud on the part of senior management, regardless of materiality.
- Restatement of previously issued financial statements for material misstatement(s).
- Identification by the auditor of a material misstatement in circumstances that indicate that the misstatement would not have been detected and corrected by the entity's internal control.
- Ineffective oversight of the entity's financial reporting and internal control by those charged with governance.

Issue 14: When determining whether a deficiency, or combination of deficiencies, is not a material weakness, how does the auditor address the requirement to consider whether prudent officials would likely reach the same conclusion as the auditor's?

If the auditor determines that a deficiency, or a combination of deficiencies, is not a material weakness, the auditor is required to consider whether prudent officials, having knowledge of the same facts and circumstances, would likely reach the same conclusion. However, this Section does not define the term "prudent official" and does not provide any specific examples of how the auditor might achieve such conclusion. Practically, the auditor would have to take into account various factors, such as the following:

- The severity of the deficiency.
- Ineffective oversight of the entity's ICFR.
- Whether other controls accomplish the same control objective.
- Compensating controls.

The concept of the prudent official test is that an auditor should "stand back" and objectively assess the severity of the deficiency through the skeptical eyes of a prudent official, such as a regulator or an official from an oversight agency. If the auditor does not have a robust basis for his or her conclusion and would not be comfortable defending such conclusion, the auditor should reconsider his or her evaluation of the significance of the deficiency.

Issue 15: If no significant deficiencies were noted during the integrated audit, can the auditor issue a written report stating that no significant deficiencies were noted?

No. The auditor is not required to perform procedures that are sufficient to identify all deficiencies; rather, the auditor communicates deficiencies of which he or she is aware. Because the integrated audit does not provide the auditor with assurance that he or she has identified all deficiencies less severe than a material weakness, the auditor should not issue a report stating that no such deficiencies were identified during the integrated audit.

Issue 16: May the auditor issue a report indicating that no material weaknesses were identified during the integrated audit?

No. Because the auditor's objective in an examination of internal control is to form an opinion on the effectiveness of the entity's internal control, the auditor should not issue a report indicating that no material weaknesses were identified during the integrated audit.

Issue 17: What is the effect on an examination engagement to report on an entity's internal control if management refuses to furnish the appropriate written representations required under this Section?

Management's refusal to furnish all appropriate written representations required under this Section constitutes a limitation on the scope of the examination, which is sufficient to cause the auditor to withdraw from the engagement or disclaim an opinion. In addition, in such circumstances, the auditor should evaluate the effects of management's refusal on his or her ability to rely on other management representations, including those obtained in the audit of the entity's financial statements.

Issue 18: For an entity with operations in multiple locations, is it necessary for the auditor to understand and test controls at each location in order to report on the entity's internal control?

No. For an entity with operations in several locations, the auditor may *not* find it necessary to understand and test controls at each location. The auditor is required to employ a risk-based approach in determining the proper strategy for auditing multiple locations. In determining the locations or business units at which to perform tests of controls, the auditor should assess the risk of misstatement to the financial statements associated with the location or business unit and correlate the amount of audit attention devoted to the location or business unit with the degree of risk.

The auditor's selection of locations may be affected by factors such as the following:

- The variations in operations and internal control at the various locations.
- The degree of centralization of records.
- The effectiveness of the control environment.

- The nature and amount of transactions executed and related assets at the various locations.

ILLUSTRATIONS AND PRACTICE AIDS

ILLUSTRATION 1—APPLICABILITY OF ATTESTATION AND AUDITING STANDARDS TO DIFFERENT TYPES OF INTERNAL CONTROL ENGAGEMENTS

Type of Engagement	*Applicable Standards*
1. Engagements to examine the design and operating effectiveness of an entity's internal control over financial reporting that is integrated with an audit of financial statements.	1. AT Section 501 (An Examination of an Entity's Internal Control over Financial Reporting That Is Integrated with an Audit of Its Financial Statements)
2. Engagements to examine only the suitability of design of an entity's internal control over financial reporting.	2. AT Section 101 (Attest Engagements)
3. Engagements to examine controls over the effectiveness and efficiency of operations.	3. AT Section 101 (Attest Engagements)
4. Engagements to perform agreed-upon procedures on controls.	4. AT Section 201 (Agreed-Upon Procedures Engagements)
5. Engagements to examine controls over compliance with laws and regulations.	5. AT Section 601 (Compliance Attestation)

ILLUSTRATION 2—CONDITIONS FOR ENGAGEMENT PERFORMANCE FOR EXAMINATION AND AGREED-UPON PROCEDURES ENGAGEMENTS

Item in the Auditor's Examination Report	*Auditor's Opinion Directly on Internal Control*	*Auditor's Opinion on Management's Assertion*
1. A title that includes the word *independent*.	✓	✓
2. An introductory paragraph that:		
a. States that management is responsible for maintaining effective internal control and for evaluating the effectiveness of internal control.	✓	✓
b. Identifies management's assertion on internal control that accompanies the auditor's report, including a reference to management's report.	✓	✓
c. States that the auditor's responsibility is to express an opinion on the entity's internal control based on his or her examination.	✓	N/A
d. States that the auditor's responsibility is to express an opinion on management's assertion based on his or her examination.	N/A	✓
3. A scope paragraph stating that:		
a. The examination was conducted in accordance with attestation standards established by the AICPA.	✓	✓

Item in the Auditor's Examination Report	Auditor's Opinion Directly on Internal Control	Auditor's Opinion on Management's Assertion
b. Such standards require the auditor to plan and perform the examination to obtain reasonable assurance about whether effective internal control was maintained in all material respects.	✓	✓
c. An examination includes (1) obtaining an understanding of internal control, (2) assessing the risk that a material weakness exists, (3) testing and evaluating the design and operating effectiveness of internal control based on the assessed risk, and (4) performing such other procedures as the auditor considers necessary in the circumstances.	✓	✓
d. The auditor believes the examination provides a reasonable basis for his or her opinion.	✓	✓
4. A definition of internal control paragraph (Note: The auditor should use the same description of the entity's internal control as management uses in its report).	✓	✓
5. An inherent limitations paragraph stating that internal control may not prevent, or detect and correct, misstatements, and that projections of any evaluation of effectiveness to future periods are subject to the risk that controls may become inadequate because of changes in conditions, or that the degree of compliance with the policies or procedures may deteriorate.	✓	✓
6. An opinion paragraph stating the auditor's opinion on whether:		
a. The entity maintained, in all material respects, effective internal control as of the specified date, based on the control criteria.	✓	N/A
b. Management's assertion about the effectiveness of the entity's internal control as of the specified date is fairly stated, in all material respects, based on the control criteria.	N/A	✓
7. Manual or printed signature of the auditor's firm.	✓	✓
8. Date of the examination report.	✓	✓

ILLUSTRATION 3—SEPARATE REPORT EXPRESSING AN UNQUALIFIED OPINION DIRECTLY ON INTERNAL CONTROL

Independent Auditor's Report

We have examined ABC Company's internal control over financial reporting as of December 31, 20X2, based on [*identify criteria, for example* "criteria established in *Internal Control—Integrated Framework* issued by the Committee of Sponsoring Organizations of the Treadway Commission (COSO)"]. ABC Company's management is responsible for maintaining effective internal control over financial reporting, and for its assertion of the effectiveness of internal control over financial reporting, included in the accompanying [*title of management's report*]. Our responsibility is to express an opinion on ABC Company's internal control over financial reporting based on our examination.

We conducted our examination in accordance with attestation standards established by the American Institute of Certified Public Accountants. Those standards require that we plan and perform the examination to obtain reasonable assurance about whether effective internal control over financial reporting was maintained in all material respects. Our examination included obtaining an understanding of internal control over financial reporting, assessing the risk that a material weakness exists, and testing and evaluating the design and operating effectiveness of internal control based on the assessed risk. Our examination also included performing such other procedures as we considered necessary in the circumstances. We believe that our examination provides a reasonable basis for our opinion.

An entity's internal control over financial reporting is a process effected by those charged with governance, management, and other personnel, designed to provide reasonable assurance regarding the preparation of reliable financial statements in accordance with [*applicable financial reporting framework, such as* "accounting principles generally accepted in the United States of America"]. An entity's internal control over financial reporting includes those policies and procedures that (1) pertain to the maintenance of records that, in reasonable detail, accurately and fairly reflect the transactions and dispositions of the assets of the entity; (2) provide reasonable assurance that transactions are recorded as necessary to permit preparation of financial statements in accordance with [*applicable financial reporting framework, such as* "accounting principles generally accepted in the United States of America"], and that receipts and expenditures of the entity are being made only in accordance with authorizations of management and those charged with governance; and (3) provide reasonable assurance regarding prevention, or timely detection and correction of unauthorized acquisition, use, or disposition of the entity's assets that could have a material effect on the financial statements.

Because of its inherent limitations, internal control over financial reporting may not prevent, or detect and correct misstatements. Also, projections of any evaluation of effectiveness to future periods are subject to the risk that controls may become inadequate because of changes in conditions, or that the degree of compliance with the policies or procedures may deteriorate.

In our opinion, ABC Company maintained, in all material respects, effective internal control over financial reporting as of December 31, 20X2, based on [*identify criteria, for example,* "criteria established in *Internal Control—Integrated Framework* issued by the Committee of Sponsoring Organizations of the Treadway Commission (COSO)"].

We also have audited, in accordance with auditing standards generally accepted in the United States of America, the [*identify financial statements*] of ABC Company and our report dated [*date of report, which should be the same as the date of the report on the examination of internal control*] expressed [*include nature of opinion*].

[*Signature*]

[*Date*]

ILLUSTRATION 4—SEPARATE REPORT EXPRESSING AN UNQUALIFIED OPINION ON MANAGEMENT'S ASSERTION

Independent Auditor's Report

We have examined management's assertion, included in the accompanying [*title of management report*], that ABC Company maintained effective internal control over financial reporting as of December 31, 20X2, based on [*identify criteria, for example* "criteria established in *Internal Control—Integrated Framework* issued by the Committee of Sponsoring Organizations of the Treadway Commission (COSO)"]. ABC Company's management is responsible for maintaining effective internal control over financial reporting, and for its assertion of the effectiveness of internal control over financial reporting, included in the accompanying [*title of management's report*]. Our responsibility is to express an opinion on management's assertion based on our examination.

We conducted our examination in accordance with attestation standards established by the American Institute of Certified Public Accountants. Those standards require that we plan and perform the examination to obtain reasonable assurance about whether effective internal control over financial reporting was maintained in all material respects. Our examination included obtaining an understanding of internal control over financial reporting, assessing the risk that a material weakness exists, and testing and evaluating the design and operating effectiveness of internal control based on the assessed risk. Our examination also included performing such other procedures as we considered necessary in the circumstances. We believe that our examination provides a reasonable basis for our opinion.

An entity's internal control over financial reporting is a process effected by those charged with governance, management, and other personnel, designed to provide reasonable assurance regarding the preparation of reliable financial statements in accordance with [*applicable financial reporting framework, such as* "accounting principles generally accepted in the United States of America"]. An entity's internal control over financial reporting includes those policies and procedures that (1) pertain to the maintenance of records that, in reasonable detail, accurately and fairly reflect the transactions and dispositions of the assets of the entity; (2) provide reasonable assurance that transactions are recorded as necessary to permit preparation of financial statements in accordance with [*applicable financial reporting framework, such as* "accounting principles generally accepted in the United States of America"], and that receipts and expenditures of the entity are being made only in accordance with authorizations of management and those charged with governance; and (3) provide reasonable assurance regarding prevention, or timely detection and correction of unauthorized acquisition, use, or disposition of the entity's assets that could have a material effect on the financial statements.

Because of its inherent limitations, internal control over financial reporting may not prevent, or detect and correct misstatements. Also, projections of any evaluation of effectiveness to future periods are subject to the risk that controls may become inadequate because of changes in conditions, or that the degree of compliance with the policies or procedures may deteriorate.

In our opinion, management's assertion that ABC Company maintained effective internal control over financial reporting as of December 31, 20X2, is fairly stated, in all material respects, based on [*identify criteria, for example* "criteria established in *Internal Control—Integrated Framework* issued by the Committee of Sponsoring Organizations of the Treadway Commission (COSO)"].

We also have audited, in accordance with auditing standards generally accepted in the United States of America, the [*identify financial statements*] of ABC Company and our report dated [*date of report, which should be the same as the date of the report on the examination of internal control*] expressed [*include nature of opinion*].

[*Signature*]

[*Date*]

ILLUSTRATION 5—SEPARATE REPORT EXPRESSING AN ADVERSE OPINION ON INTERNAL CONTROL

Independent Auditor's Report

We have examined ABC Company's internal control over financial reporting as of December 31, 20X2, based on [*identify criteria, for example,* "criteria established in *Internal Control—Integrated Framework* issued by the Committee of Sponsoring Organizations of the Treadway Commission (COSO)"]. ABC Company's management is responsible for maintaining effective internal control over financial reporting, and for its assertion of the effectiveness of internal control over financial reporting, included in the accompanying [*title of management's report*]. Our responsibility is to express an opinion on ABC Company's internal control over financial reporting based on our examination.

We conducted our examination in accordance with attestation standards established by the American Institute of Certified Public Accountants. Those standards require that we plan and perform the examination to obtain reasonable assurance about whether effective internal control over financial reporting was maintained in all material respects. Our examination included obtaining an understanding of internal control over financial reporting, assessing the risk that a material weakness exists, and testing and evaluating the design and operating effectiveness of internal control based on the assessed risk. Our examination also included performing such other procedures as we considered necessary in the circumstances. We believe that our examination provides a reasonable basis for our opinion.

An entity's internal control over financial reporting is a process effected by those charged with governance, management, and other personnel, designed to provide reasonable assurance regarding the preparation of reliable financial statements in accordance with [*applicable financial reporting framework, such as* "accounting principles generally accepted in the United States of America"]. An entity's internal control over financial reporting includes those policies and procedures that (1) pertain to the maintenance of records that, in reasonable detail, accurately and fairly reflect the transactions and dispositions of the assets of the entity; (2) provide reasonable assurance that transactions are recorded as necessary to permit preparation of financial statements in accordance with [*applicable financial reporting framework, such as* "accounting principles generally accepted in the United States of America"], and that receipts and expenditures of the entity are being made only in accordance with authorizations of management and those charged with governance; and (3) provide reasonable assurance regarding prevention, or timely detection and correction of unauthorized acquisition, use, or disposition of the entity's assets that could have a material effect on the financial statements.

Because of its inherent limitations, internal control over financial reporting may not prevent, or detect and correct misstatements. Also, projections of any evaluation of effectiveness to future periods are subject to the risk that controls may become inadequate because of changes in conditions, or that the degree of compliance with the policies or procedures may deteriorate.

A material weakness is a deficiency, or a combination of deficiencies, in internal control over financial reporting, such that there is a reasonable possibility that a material misstatement of the entity's financial statements will not be prevented, or detected and corrected on a timely basis. The following material weakness has been identified and included in the accompanying [*title of management's report*].

[*Identify the material weakness described in management's report.*]

In our opinion, because of the effect of the material weakness described above on the achievement of the objectives of the control criteria, ABC Company has not maintained effective internal control over financial reporting as of December 31, 20X2, based on [*identify criteria, for example* "criteria established in *Internal Control—Integrated Framework* issued by the Committee of Sponsoring Organizations of the Treadway Commission (COSO)"].

We also have audited, in accordance with auditing standards generally accepted in the United States of America, the [*identify financial statements*] of ABC Company. We considered the material weakness identified above in determining the nature, timing, and extent of audit tests applied in our audit of the 20X2 financial statements, and this report does not affect our report dated [*date of report, which should be the same as the date of the report on the examination of internal control*], which expressed [*include nature of opinion*].

[*Signature*]

[*Date*]

ILLUSTRATION 6—SEPARATE REPORT EXPRESSING A DISCLAIMER OF OPINION ON INTERNAL CONTROL DUE TO A SCOPE LIMITATION

Independent Auditor's Report

We were engaged to examine ABC Company's internal control over financial reporting as of December 31, 20X2, based on [*identify criteria, for example,* "criteria established in *Internal Control—Integrated Framework* issued by the Committee of Sponsoring Organizations of the Treadway Commission (COSO)"]. ABC Company's management is responsible for maintaining effective internal control over financial reporting, and for its assertion of the effectiveness of internal control over financial reporting, included in the accompanying [*title of management's report*].

[*Paragraph that describes the substantive reasons for the scope limitation.*] Accordingly, we were unable to perform auditing procedures necessary to form an opinion on ABC Company's internal control over financial reporting as of December 31, 20X2.

An entity's internal control over financial reporting is a process effected by those charged with governance, management, and other personnel, designed to provide reasonable assurance regarding the preparation of reliable financial statements in accordance with [*applicable financial reporting framework, such as* "accounting principles generally accepted in the United States of America"]. An entity's internal control over financial reporting includes those policies and procedures that (1) pertain to the maintenance of records that, in reasonable detail, accurately and fairly reflect the transactions and dispositions of the assets of the entity; (2) provide reasonable assurance that transactions are recorded as necessary to permit preparation of financial statements in accordance with [*applicable financial reporting framework, such as* "accounting principles generally accepted in the United States of America"], and that receipts and expenditures of the entity are being made only in accordance with authorizations of management and those charged with governance; and (3) provide reasonable assurance regarding prevention, or timely detection and correction of unauthorized acquisition, use, or disposition of the entity's assets that could have a material effect on the financial statements.

Because of its inherent limitations, internal control over financial reporting may not prevent, or detect and correct misstatements. Also, projections of any evaluation of effectiveness to future periods are subject to the risk that controls may become inadequate because of changes in conditions, or that the degree of compliance with the policies or procedures may deteriorate.

A material weakness is a deficiency, or a combination of deficiencies, in internal control over financial reporting, such that there is a reasonable possibility that a material misstatement of the entity's financial statements will not be prevented, or detected and corrected on a timely basis. If one or more material weaknesses exist, an entity's internal control over financial reporting cannot be considered effective. The following material weakness has been identified and included in the accompanying [*title of management's report*].

[*Identify the material weakness described in management's report and include a description of the material weakness, including its nature and its actual and potential effect on the presentation of the entity's financial statements issued during the existence of the material weakness.*]

Because of the limitation on the scope of our audit described in the second paragraph, the scope of our work was not sufficient to enable us to express, and we do not express, an opinion on the effectiveness of ABC Company's internal control over financial reporting.

We have audited, in accordance with auditing standards generally accepted in the United States of America, the [*identify financial statements*] of ABC Company and our report dated [*date of report*] expressed [*include nature of opinion*]. We considered the material weakness identified above in determining the nature, timing, and extent of audit tests applied in our audit of the 20X2 financial statements, and this report does not affect such report on the financial statements.

[*Signature*]

[*Date*]

ILLUSTRATION 7—SEPARATE REPORT EXPRESSING AN UNQUALIFIED OPINION ON INTERNAL CONTROL BASED, IN PART, ON THE REPORT OF ANOTHER AUDITOR

Independent Auditor's Report

We have examined ABC Company's internal control over financial reporting as of December 31, 20X2, based on [*identify criteria, for example,* "criteria established in *Internal Control—Integrated Framework* issued by the Committee of Sponsoring Organizations of the Treadway Commission (COSO)"]. ABC Company's management is responsible for maintaining effective internal control over financial reporting, and for its assertion of the effectiveness of internal control over financial reporting, included in the accompanying [*title of management's report*]. Our responsibility is to express an opinion on ABC Company's internal control over financial reporting based on our examination. We did not examine the effectiveness of internal control over financial reporting of XYZ Company, a wholly owned subsidiary, whose financial statements reflect total assets and revenues constituting 20 percent and 30 percent, respectively, of the related consolidated financial statement amounts as of and for the year ended December 31, 20X2. The effectiveness of XYZ Company's internal control over financial reporting was examined by other auditors whose report has been furnished to us, and our opinion, insofar as it relates to the effectiveness of XYZ Company's internal control over financial reporting, is based solely on the report of the other auditors.

We conducted our examination in accordance with attestation standards established by the American Institute of Certified Public Accountants. Those standards require that we plan and perform the examination to obtain reasonable assurance about whether effective internal control over financial reporting was maintained in all material respects. Our examination included obtaining an understanding of internal control over financial reporting, assessing the risk that a material weakness exists, and testing and evaluating the design and operating effectiveness of internal control based on the assessed risk. Our examination also included performing such other procedures as we considered necessary in the circumstances. We believe that our examination and the report of the other auditors provide a reasonable basis for our opinion.

An entity's internal control over financial reporting is a process effected by those charged with governance, management, and other personnel, designed to provide reasonable assurance regarding the preparation of reliable financial statements in accordance with [*applicable financial reporting framework, such as* "accounting principles generally accepted in the United States of America"]. An entity's internal control over financial reporting includes those policies and procedures that (1) pertain to the maintenance of records that, in reasonable detail, accurately and fairly reflect the transactions and dispositions of the assets of the entity; (2) provide reasonable assurance that transactions are recorded as necessary to permit preparation of financial statements in accordance with [*applicable financial reporting framework, such as* "accounting principles generally accepted in the United States of America"], and that receipts and expenditures of the entity are being made only in accordance with authorizations of management and those charged with governance; and (3) provide reasonable assurance regarding prevention, or timely detection and correction of unauthorized acquisition, use, or disposition of the entity's assets that could have a material effect on the financial statements.

Because of its inherent limitations, internal control over financial reporting may not prevent, or detect and correct misstatements. Also, projections of any evaluation of effectiveness to future periods are subject to the risk that controls may become inadequate because of changes in conditions, or that the degree of compliance with the policies or procedures may deteriorate.

In our opinion, based on our examination and the report of the other auditors, ABC Company maintained, in all material respects, effective internal control over financial reporting as of December 31, 20X2, based on [*identify criteria, for example* "criteria established in *Internal Control—Integrated Framework* issued by the Committee of Sponsoring Organizations of the Treadway Commission (COSO)"].

We also have audited, in accordance with auditing standards generally accepted in the United States of America, the [*identify financial statements*] of ABC Company and our report dated [*date of report, which should be the same as the date of the report on the examination of internal control*] expressed [*include nature of opinion*].

[*Signature*]

[*Date*]

ILLUSTRATION 8—COMBINED REPORT EXPRESSING AN UNQUALIFIED OPINION ON INTERNAL CONTROL AND ON THE FINANCIAL STATEMENTS

Independent Auditor's Report

We have audited the accompanying balance sheet of ABC Company as of December 31, 20X2, and the related statements of income, retained earnings, and cash flows for the year then ended. We also have audited ABC Company's internal control over financial reporting as of December 31, 20X2, based on [*identify criteria, for example,* "criteria established in *Internal Control—Integrated Framework* issued by the Committee of Sponsoring Organizations of the Treadway Commission (COSO)"]. ABC Company's management is responsible for these financial statements, for maintaining effective internal control over financial reporting, and for its assertion of the effectiveness of internal control over financial reporting, included in the accompanying [*title of management's report*].

Our responsibility is to express an opinion on these financial statements and an opinion on ABC Company's internal control over financial reporting based on our audits.

We conducted our audit of the financial statements in accordance with auditing standards generally accepted in the United States of America and our audit of internal control over financial reporting in accordance with attestation standards established by the American Institute of Certified Public Accountants. Those standards require that we plan and perform the audits to obtain reasonable assurance about whether the financial statements are free of material misstatement and whether effective internal control over financial reporting was maintained in all material respects. Our audit of the financial statements included examining, on a test basis, evidence supporting the amounts and disclosures in the financial statements, assessing the accounting principles used and significant estimates made by management, as well as evaluating the overall financial statement presentation. Our audit of internal control over financial reporting included obtaining an understanding of internal control over financial reporting, assessing the risk that a material weakness exists, and testing and evaluating the design and operating effectiveness of internal control based on the assessed risk. Our audits also included performing such other procedures as we considered necessary in the circumstances. We believe that our audits provide a reasonable basis for our opinions.

An entity's internal control over financial reporting is a process effected by those charged with governance, management, and other personnel, designed to provide reasonable assurance regarding the preparation of reliable financial statements in accordance with [*applicable financial reporting framework, such as* "accounting principles generally accepted in the United States of America"]. An entity's internal control over financial reporting includes those policies and procedures that (1) pertain to the maintenance of records that, in reasonable detail, accurately and fairly reflect the transactions and dispositions of the assets of the entity; (2) provide reasonable assurance that transactions are recorded as necessary to permit preparation of financial statements in accordance with [*applicable financial reporting framework, such as* "accounting principles generally accepted in the United States of America"], and that receipts and expenditures of the entity are being made only in accordance with authorizations of management and those charged with governance; and (3) provide reasonable assurance regarding prevention, or timely detection and correction of unauthorized acquisition, use, or disposition of the entity's assets that could have a material effect on the financial statements.

Because of its inherent limitations, internal control over financial reporting may not prevent, or detect and correct misstatements. Also, projections of any evaluation of effectiveness to future periods are subject to the risk that controls may become inadequate because of changes in conditions, or that the degree of compliance with the policies or procedures may deteriorate.

In our opinion, the financial statements referred to above present fairly, in all material respects, the financial position of ABC Company as of December 31, 20X2, and the results of its operations and its cash flows for the year then ended in conformity with accounting principles generally accepted in the United States of America. Also in our opinion, ABC Company maintained, in all material respects, effective internal control over financial reporting as of December 31, 20X2, based on [*identify criteria, for example,* "criteria established in *Internal Control—Integrated Framework* issued by the Committee of Sponsoring Organizations of the Treadway Commission (COSO)"].

[*Signature*]

[*Date*]

ILLUSTRATION 9—COMMUNICATION OF SIGNIFICANT DEFICIENCIES AND MATERIAL WEAKNESSES

In connection with our audit of ABC Company's (the "Company") financial statements as of December 31, 20X2, and for the year then ended, and our audit of the Company's internal control over financial reporting as of December 31, 20X2 ("integrated audit"), the standards established by the American Institute of Certified Public Accountants require that we advise you of the following internal control matters identified during our integrated audit.

Our responsibility is to plan and perform our integrated audit to obtain reasonable assurance about whether the financial statements are free of material misstatement, whether caused by error or fraud, and whether effective internal control over financial reporting was maintained in all material respects (that is, whether material weaknesses exist as of the date specified in management's assertion). The integrated audit is not designed to detect deficiencies that, individually or in combination, are less severe than a material weakness. However, we are responsible for communicating to management and those charged with governance significant deficiencies and material weaknesses identified during the integrated audit. We are also responsible for communicating to management deficiencies that are of a lesser magnitude than a significant deficiency, unless previously communicated, and inform those charged with governance when such a communication was made.

A deficiency in internal control over financial reporting exists when the design or operation of a control does not allow management or employees, in the normal course of performing their assigned functions, to prevent, or detect and correct misstatements on a timely basis. [*A material weakness is a deficiency, or a combination of deficiencies, in internal control over financial reporting, such that there is a reasonable possibility that a material misstatement of the Company's financial statements will not be prevented, or detected and corrected on a timely basis. We believe the following deficiencies constitute material weaknesses:*]

[*Describe the material weaknesses that were identified during the integrated audit. The auditor may separately identify those material weaknesses that exist as of the date of management's assertion by referring to the auditor's report.*]

[*A significant deficiency is a deficiency, or a combination of deficiencies, in internal control over financial reporting that is less severe than a material weakness, yet important enough to merit attention by those charged with governance. We consider the following deficiencies to be significant deficiencies:*]

[*Describe the significant deficiencies that were identified during the integrated audit.*]

This communication is intended solely for the information and use of management, [*identify the body or individuals charged with governance*], others within the organization, and [*identify any specified governmental authorities*] and is not intended to be and should not be used by anyone other than these specified parties.

[*Signature*]

[*Date*]

ILLUSTRATION 10—SAMPLE MANAGEMENT REPORT ON INTERNAL CONTROL OVER FINANCIAL REPORTING CONTAINING THE REQUIRED REPORTING ELEMENTS

Management's Report on Internal Control Over Financial Reporting

ABC Company's internal control over financial reporting is a process effected by those charged with governance, management, and other personnel, designed to provide reasonable assurance regarding the preparation of reliable financial statements in accordance with [*applicable financial reporting framework, such as* "accounting principles generally accepted in the United States of America"]. An entity's internal control over financial reporting includes those policies and procedures that (1) pertain to the maintenance of records that, in reasonable detail, accurately and fairly reflect the transactions and dispositions of the assets of the entity; (2) provide reasonable assurance that transactions are recorded as necessary to permit preparation of financial statements in accordance with [*applicable financial reporting framework, such as* "accounting principles generally accepted in the United States of America"], and that receipts and expenditures of the entity are being made only in accordance with authorizations of management and those charged with governance; and (3) provide reasonable assurance regarding prevention, or timely detection and correction of unauthorized acquisition, use, or disposition of the entity's assets that could have a material effect on the financial statements.

Management is responsible for establishing and maintaining effective internal control over financial reporting. Management assessed the effectiveness of ABC Company's internal control over financial reporting as of December 31, 20X2, based on the framework set forth by the Committee of Sponsoring Organizations of the Treadway Commission in *Internal Control—Integrated Framework*. Based on that assessment, management concluded that, as of December 31, 20X2, ABC Company's internal control over financial reporting is effective based on the criteria established in *Internal Control—Integrated Framework*.

[*ABC Company*]

[*Report signers, if applicable*]

[*Date*]

AT SECTION 601
COMPLIANCE ATTESTATION

WHAT EVERY PRACTITIONER SHOULD KNOW

Basic Objectives and Requirements

This Section is applicable to *agreed-upon procedures* engagements related to:

1. An entity's compliance with requirements of specified laws, regulations, rules, contracts, or grants (herein referred to as "compliance with specified requirements").

2. The effectiveness of an entity's internal control over compliance with specified requirements (herein referred to as "internal control over compliance").

3. Both 1. and 2.

This Section is also applicable to *examination* engagements related to an entity's compliance with specified requirements or a written assertion thereon. However, if a practitioner is engaged to examine the effectiveness of an entity's internal control over compliance or an assertion thereon, he or she should follow the guidance in AT Section 101 (Attest Engagements) and in AT Section 501 (Reporting on an Entity's Internal Control over Financial Reporting).

As part of engagement performance, the practitioner should obtain from the responsible party a written assertion about compliance with specified requirements or internal control over compliance.

This Section does not affect the auditor's responsibility in an audit of financial statements performed in accordance with GAAS and does not apply to the situations described in Illustration 1.

Certain conditions must be met in order for the practitioner to perform (a) an agreed-upon procedures engagement related to an entity's compliance with specified requirements or the effectiveness of internal control over compliance or (b) an examination engagement related to an entity's compliance with specified requirements. These conditions are summarized in Illustration 2.

In addition to the requirements of this Section, the practitioner should comply with the attest documentation requirements prescribed in AT Section 101 (Attest Engagements).

Agreed-Upon Procedures Engagement

The practitioner should communicate directly with, and obtain affirmative acknowledgment from each of, the specified users to (a) agree upon the procedures performed or to be performed and (b) ascertain that the specified users take responsibility for the sufficiency of the agreed-upon procedures for their purposes. When it is not practical for the practitioner to communicate directly with all of the specified users, the practitioner should apply any one or more of the following, or similar, procedures:

1. Compare the procedures to be applied to written requirements of the specified users.

2. Discuss the procedures to be applied with appropriate representatives of the specified users involved.

3. Review relevant contracts with or correspondence from the specified users.

4. Distribute a draft of the anticipated report or a copy of the proposed engagement letter to the specified users involved and obtain their agreement.

Obtaining an understanding of the specified compliance requirements in agreed-upon procedures engagements In an agreed-upon procedures engagement, the practitioner should obtain an understanding of the specified compliance requirements by considering the following:

1. Laws, regulations, rules, contracts, and grants that pertain to the specified compliance requirements, including published requirements.

2. Knowledge about the specified compliance requirements obtained through:

   a. Prior engagements and regulatory reports.

   b. Discussions with appropriate individuals within the entity (e.g., chief financial officer or legal counsel).

   c. Discussions with appropriate individuals outside the entity (e.g., a regulator or a third-party specialist).

Reporting requirements for agreed-upon procedures engagements The practitioner's report on agreed-upon procedures related to an entity's compliance with specified requirements or the effectiveness of an entity's internal control over compliance should be in the form of procedures and findings and should include all the elements contained in Illustration 3.

See Illustration 4 for an example of an agreed-upon procedures report on an entity's compliance with specified requirements. See Illustration 5 for an example of an agreed-upon procedures report on the effectiveness of an entity's internal control over compliance.

In agreed-upon procedures engagements that relate to both compliance with specified requirements and the effectiveness of the internal control over compliance, the practitioner may issue one report that addresses both. In such circumstances, the first sentence of the introductory paragraph would be modified to read as follows:

> We have performed the procedures enumerated below, which were agreed to by [*list specified parties*], solely to assist the specified parties in evaluating ABC Company's compliance with [*list specified requirements*] during the [*period*] ended [*date*] and the effectiveness of ABC Company's internal control over compliance with the aforementioned compliance requirements as of [*date*].

Report modifications in agreed-upon procedures engagements Restrictions on the scope of an agreed-upon procedures engagement, whether imposed by the client or by such other circumstances as the timing of the work or the inability to obtain sufficient evidence, require the practitioner to obtain agreement from the users to modify the agreed-upon procedures. When the practitioner cannot obtain such an agreement (e.g., when the agreed-upon procedures are published by a regulatory agency that will not modify the procedures), the practitioner should describe such restrictions in his or her report or withdraw from the engagement.

If noncompliance comes to the practitioner's attention, the practitioner should include such information in his or her report. If the practitioner becomes aware of noncompliance that occurs subsequent to the period addressed by the practitioner's report, but before the date of the report, the practitioner should consider including information about such noncompliance in his or her report. However, the practitioner has no responsibility to perform procedures to detect such noncompliance other than obtaining the responsible party's representations about noncompliance in the subsequent period.

Examination Engagement

In order to express an opinion on an entity's compliance with specified requirements, or assertion related thereto, based on specified criteria, the practitioner accumulates sufficient evidence about the entity's compliance to limit *attestation risk* to an appropriately low level. *Attestation risk* is the risk that the practitioner may unknowingly fail to appropriately modify his or her opinion. For purposes of a compliance examination, attestation risk is comprised of the following three components:

1. *Inherent risk*—This is the risk that material noncompliance with specified requirements could occur, assuming there are no related controls. In assessing inherent risk, the practitioner should consider risk factors similar to those an auditor would consider when planning audits of financial statements, as discussed in AU Section 316 (Consideration of Fraud in a Financial Statement Audit). In addition, the practitioner should consider inherent risk factors unique to compliance engagements, such as the following:

   a. The complexity of the specified compliance requirements.

   b. The length of time the entity has been subject to the specified compliance requirements.

   c. Prior experience with the entity's compliance.

   d. The potential impact of noncompliance.

2. *Control risk*—This is the risk that material noncompliance that could occur will not be prevented or detected on a timely basis by the entity's controls. The practitioner should assess control risk by obtaining an understanding of relevant portions of the entity's internal control over compliance and performing procedures such as the following: (a) inquiries of appropriate management, supervisory, and staff personnel, (b) inspection of the entity's documents, and (c) observation of the entity's activities and operations. When the practitioner seeks to assess control

risk below the maximum, he or she should perform tests of controls to obtain evidence to support the assessed level of control risk.

3. *Detection risk*—This is the risk that the practitioner's procedures will lead him or her to conclude that material noncompliance does not exist when, in fact, such noncompliance does exist. The acceptable level of detection risk increases as assessed inherent risk or control risk decreases. Therefore, in determining an appropriate level of detection risk, the practitioner may modify the nature, timing, and extent of compliance tests performed based on the assessments of inherent risk and control risk.

Obtaining an understanding of the specified compliance requirements in an examination engagement In an examination engagement, the practitioner should obtain an understanding of the specified compliance requirements by considering the following:

1. Laws, regulations, rules, contracts, and grants that pertain to the specified compliance requirements, including published requirements.

2. Knowledge about the specified compliance requirements obtained through:

   a. Prior engagements and regulatory reports.

   b. Discussions with appropriate individuals within the entity, e.g., chief financial officer or legal counsel.

   c. Discussions with appropriate individuals outside the entity, e.g., a regulator or a third-party specialist.

Materiality considerations in an examination engagement The practitioner's consideration of materiality in a compliance examination engagement is different from materiality considerations applied in an audit of financial statements. In compliance examination engagements, the practitioner should consider the following factors:

1. The nature of the compliance requirements, which may or may not be quantifiable in monetary terms.

2. The nature and frequency of noncompliance identified, including consideration of sampling risk.

3. Qualitative considerations, including the needs and expectations of users of the report.

Other considerations in an examination engagement In addition to the factors discussed above, when planning the examination engagement, the practitioner should consider the following:

1. If the entity has multiple components (e.g., subsidiaries, locations), the practitioner should determine the extent of testing compliance with requirements at every component, if any, by considering factors such as the following:

   a. The degree to which the specified compliance requirements apply at the component level.

   b. Judgments about materiality.

   c. The degree of centralization of records.

   d. The effectiveness of the control environment.

   e. The nature and extent of operations conducted at the various components.

   f. The similarity of operations and controls over compliance for different components.

2. The need for a specialist. See AU Section 336 (Using the Work of a Specialist).

3. The extent to which internal auditors, if any, are involved in monitoring compliance with the specified requirements. See AU Section 322 (The Auditor's Consideration of the Internal Audit Function in an Audit of Financial Statements).

Nature and extent of examination procedures to obtain sufficient evidence Determining procedures to provide reasonable assurance of detecting material noncompliance and evaluating the sufficiency of the evidence obtained are matters of professional judgment. However, the practitioner's procedures should include the following:

1. For engagements involving compliance with regulatory requirements, the practitioner should:

   a. Review reports of significant examinations by regulatory agencies.

   b. Review communications between the regulatory agencies and the entity related to significant examinations.

   c. Make inquiries of the regulatory agencies, including inquiries about any examinations in progress.

2. The practitioner should perform procedures to identify subsequent events that provide additional information about compliance during the reporting period, including inquiries about and consideration of the following:

   a. Relevant reports issued during the subsequent period, including:

     (1) Internal auditors' reports.

     (2) Other practitioners' reports identifying noncompliance.

     (3) Regulatory agencies' reports on the entity's noncompliance.

   b. Information about the entity's noncompliance, obtained through other professional engagements for the entity.

Reporting requirements for examination engagements In order to be able to form an opinion on an entity's compliance, the practitioner should consider (a) the nature and frequency of the noncompliance identified and (b) whether such noncompliance is material relative to the nature of the compliance requirements. The form of the examination report depends on whether the practitioner is reporting directly on an entity's compliance with specified requirements or on the responsible party's written assertion. See Illustration 6 for a list of the items that should be included in the practitioner's examination report on an entity's compliance or on the responsible party's written assertion.

See Illustration 7 for an example of a practitioner's examination report directly on an entity's compliance with specified requirements. See Illustration 8 for an example of a practitioner's examination report on a written assertion about compliance with specified requirements.

The practitioner should modify the standard examination reports in Illustrations 7 and 8, if any of the following conditions exist:

1. *There is material noncompliance with specified requirements.* If the practitioner's examination of an entity's compliance with specified requirements discloses material noncompliance with the applicable requirements, the practitioner should appropriately modify his or her report and state his or her opinion on the entity's specified compliance requirements, not on the responsible party's assertion. In such circumstances, the practitioner should issue a qualified opinion or an adverse opinion, depending on the pervasiveness of the material noncompliance. See Illustration 9 for a sample report when a qualified opinion is appropriate and Illustration 10 when an adverse opinion is appropriate.

   If the practitioner's examination report on the entity's compliance with specified requirements is issued within the same document that includes his or her audit report on the entity's financial statements, the practitioner should include the following sentence in the paragraph of the examination report that describes the material noncompliance: "These conditions were considered in determining the nature, timing, and extent of audit tests applied in our audit of the 20X2 financial statements, and this report does not affect our report dated [*date of report*] on these financial statements." This sentence may also be included in situations where the two reports are not included within the same document.

2. *Scope restrictions exist.* The practitioner should refer to AT Section 101 (Attest Engagements) for guidance on scope restrictions.

3. *The practitioner's opinion is based in part on the report of another practitioner.* The practitioner must decide whether it is appropriate for him or her to serve as the principal practitioner and whether to make reference to the other practitioner. In such circumstances, the practitioner's considerations are similar to those of the independent auditor as discussed in AU Section 543 (Part of Audit Performed by Other Independent Auditors). See AT Section 501 (Reporting on an Entity's Internal Control over Financial Reporting), Illustration 8, for a sample report in such circumstances which may be adapted to the standard reports in this Section.

Written Representations

In an agreed-upon procedures engagement or an examination engagement, the practitioner should obtain written representations from the responsible party in which it:

1. Recognizes its responsibility for complying with the specified requirements.

2. Recognizes its responsibility for establishing and maintaining effective internal control over compliance.

3. States that it has performed an evaluation of (1) the entity's compliance with specified requirements or (2) the entity's controls for ensuring compliance and detecting noncompliance with requirements, as applicable.

4. States its assertion about the entity's compliance with the specified requirements or about the effectiveness of internal control over compliance, as applicable, based upon the stated or established criteria.

5. States that it has disclosed to the practitioner all known noncompliance.

6. States that it has made available all documentation related to compliance with the specified requirements.

7. States its interpretation of any compliance requirements that have varying interpretations.

8. States that it has disclosed any communications from regulatory agencies, internal auditors, and other practitioners concerning possible noncompliance with the specified requirements.

9. States that it has disclosed any known noncompliance occurring subsequent to the period for which, or date as of which, the responsible party selects to make its assertion.

The responsible party's refusal to furnish all appropriate written representations constitutes a limitation on the scope of the engagement. In such circumstances, the practitioner should:

a. *In an examination engagement,* disclaim an opinion or withdraw from the engagement. However, based on the nature of the representations not obtained or the circumstances of the refusal, the practitioner may conclude that a qualified opinion is appropriate.

b. *In an agreed-upon procedures engagement,* withdraw from the engagement if the client is the responsible party. However, the practitioner is not required to withdraw when the client is not the responsible party; in these circumstances, the practitioner should consider the effects of the responsible party's refusal on his or her report and ability to rely on other representations.

PRACTICE ISSUES AND FREQUENTLY ASKED QUESTIONS

Issue 1: When performing a compliance attestation engagement under this Section, is the practitioner required to comply with any of the other attestation standards?

Yes. In addition to complying with the specific requirements discussed in this Section, the practitioner should comply with the five general standards, the two fieldwork standards, and the four reporting standards described in AT Section 101 (Attest Engagements).

Issue 2: *May a practitioner accept an engagement to "review" an entity's compliance with specified requirements or the effectiveness of an entity's internal control over compliance?*

No. A practitioner may only *examine* or *perform agreed-upon procedures* relating to an entity's compliance with specified requirements or the effectiveness of an entity's internal control over compliance. The practitioner is prohibited from performing a *review* engagement related to such matters.

Issue 3: *What is the effect on an examination engagement, related to an entity's compliance with specified requirements, if the responsible party refuses to furnish a written assertion to the practitioner?*

A responsible party's refusal to furnish a written assertion as part of an examination engagement should cause the practitioner to withdraw from the engagement, unless the examination of an entity's compliance with specified requirements is required by law or regulation. In that instance, the practitioner should either disclaim an opinion or express an adverse opinion on compliance. If the practitioner expresses an adverse opinion and the responsible party does not provide an assertion, the practitioner's report should be restricted as to use.

Issue 4: *What is the effect on an agreed-upon procedures engagement, related to an entity's compliance with specified requirements or the effectiveness of internal control over compliance, if the responsible party refuses to furnish a written assertion to the practitioner?*

The answer depends on whether the practitioner's client is the responsible party:

1. The practitioner's client is the responsible party—A refusal to provide an assertion in this instance requires the practitioner to withdraw from the engagement. However, the practitioner is not required to withdraw if the engagement is required by law or regulation.

2. The practitioner's client is *not* the responsible party—A refusal to provide an assertion in this instance does not require the practitioner to withdraw from the engagement. However, the practitioner should consider the effects of the responsible party's refusal on the engagement and his or her report.

Issue 5: *Does this Section apply if management engages the practitioner to provide recommendations on improvements to the entity's compliance with specified requirements or the entity's internal control over compliance?*

No. Engagements to provide recommendations on how to improve the entity's compliance with specified requirements or related internal control are not attest services. While the practitioner may accept such engagements, he or she should follow the guidance in Statement on Standards for Consulting Services No. 1 (Consulting Services: Definitions and Standards).

Issue 6: *Is this Section applicable if a regulatory agency requires a client to submit a report on the entity's compliance with certain regulatory requirements based on an audit of its financial statements?*

No. Such a service is governed by AU Section 623 (Special Reports).

Issue 7: Can the responsible party present its written assertion about an entity's compliance with specified requirements or about the effectiveness of an entity's internal control over compliance in a representation letter to the practitioner?

Yes. The responsible party's written assertion about the entity's compliance with specified requirements or about the effectiveness of an entity's internal control over compliance may be presented either in a representation letter to the practitioner or in a separate report that accompanies the practitioner's report.

Issue 8: What is the practitioner's responsibility in an examination engagement for detecting noncompliance that occurs subsequent to the period being reported on but before the date of the practitioner's report?

The practitioner has no responsibility to detect noncompliance that occurs subsequent to the period being reported on but before the date of the practitioner's report. However, if the practitioner becomes aware of such noncompliance that is considered significant, he or she should include in his or her report an explanatory paragraph describing the nature of the noncompliance.

Issue 9: If, in a multiple-party arrangement, the practitioner's client is not the responsible party, does the practitioner have a responsibility to communicate significant deficiencies to the responsible party?

No. The practitioner has no responsibility to communicate significant deficiencies to the responsible party if, in a multiple-party arrangement, the practitioner's client is not the responsible party. For example, if the practitioner is engaged by his or her client to examine the compliance of another entity, the practitioner has no obligation to communicate any significant deficiencies that he or she becomes aware of to the other entity. However, the practitioner is not precluded from making such a communication.

Issue 10: Can the practitioner provide assurance on an assertion that states the entity maintains "very effective" or "excellent" internal control over compliance with specified requirements?

No. The practitioner should not provide assurance on an assertion about compliance that is subjective, for example using terms such as "very effective," "superior," "excellent," or "outstanding." This is important in order to avoid potential misunderstanding or misinterpretation of the practitioner's assurance provided regarding an assertion.

Issue 11: Is the practitioner permitted to examine an assertion about compliance with specified requirements but to issue an opinion directly on an entity's compliance with specified requirements?

Yes. The practitioner may examine an assertion about compliance with specified requirements and issue an opinion directly on an entity's compliance with specified requirements.

ILLUSTRATIONS AND PRACTICE AIDS

ILLUSTRATION 1—ENGAGEMENTS FOR WHICH AT SECTION 601 DOES NOT APPLY

Type of Engagement	Applicable Guidance
1. Engagements to report on specified compliance requirements based solely on an audit of financial statements.	1. AU Section 623 (Special Reports).
2. Engagements to report in accordance with *Government Auditing Standards,* the Single Audit Act, or the Office of Management and Budget (OMB) Circulars.	2. AU Section 801 (Compliance Audits). However, AT Section 601 would apply when the terms of the engagement specify an attest report under that Section.
3. Program-specific audits as addressed in AU Section 801 performed in accordance with federal audit guides issued prior to June 15, 1994.	3. AU Section 801.
4. Engagements to issue comfort letters for underwriters and certain other requesting parties, pursuant to AU Section 634.	4. AU Section 634 (Letters for Underwriters and Certain Other Requesting Parties).
5. Engagements to report on the internal control over compliance for a broker or dealer in securities as required by rule 17a-5 of the Securities Exchange Act of 1934.	5. AICPA Audit and Accounting Guide *Brokers and Dealers in Securities.*
6. Engagements to provide recommendations on how to improve the entity's compliance with specified requirements or related internal control.	6. Statement on Standards for Consulting Services No. 1 (Consulting Services: Definitions and Standards).

ILLUSTRATION 2—CONDITIONS FOR ENGAGEMENT PERFORMANCE FOR EXAMINATION AND AGREED-UPON PROCEDURES ENGAGEMENTS

	Condition Must Be Met for:	
Condition for Engagement Performance	Examination Engagements	Agreed-Upon Procedures Engagements
1. The responsible party accepts responsibility for the entity's compliance with specified requirements and the effectiveness of the entity's internal control over compliance.	Yes	Yes
2. The responsible party evaluates the entity's compliance with specified requirements.	Yes	Yes
3. The responsible party evaluates the effectiveness of the entity's internal control over compliance.	No	Yes
4. Sufficient evidential matter exists or could be developed to support management's evaluation.	Yes	No
5. The practitioner obtains from the responsible party a written assertion about compliance with specified requirements or internal control over compliance.	Yes	Yes

Condition for Engagement Performance	Condition Must Be Met for:	
	Examination Engagements	Agreed-Upon Procedures Engagements
6. Conditions that apply to acceptance of all agreed-upon procedures engagements, as discussed in AT Section 201 (Agreed-Upon Procedures Engagements).	No	Yes

ILLUSTRATION 3—COMPONENTS OF A PRACTITIONER'S REPORT ON AGREED-UPON PROCEDURES RELATED TO AN ENTITY'S COMPLIANCE WITH SPECIFIED REQUIREMENTS OR THE EFFECTIVENESS OF INTERNAL CONTROL OVER COMPLIANCE

The practitioner's report should include the following:

1. A title that includes the word *independent*.

2. Identification of the specified parties.

3. Identification of the subject matter of the engagement (or management's assertion thereon), including the period or point in time addressed and the character of the engagement. Generally, management's assertion about compliance with specified requirements will address a *period* of time, whereas an assertion about internal control over compliance will address a *point* in time.

4. Identification of the responsible party.

5. A statement that the subject matter is the responsibility of the responsible party.

6. A statement that the procedures performed were agreed to by the specified parties and are intended to assist them in evaluating the entity's compliance with specified requirements or the effectiveness of its internal control over compliance.

7. Reference that the engagement was conducted pursuant to attestation standards established by the AICPA.

8. A statement that the sufficiency of the procedures is solely the responsibility of the specified parties and a disclaimer of responsibility for the sufficiency of those procedures.

9. A list of the procedures performed, or reference thereto, and related findings.

10. A description of any agreed-upon materiality limits, where applicable.

11. A statement that the practitioner was not engaged to, and did not, perform an examination, a disclaimer of opinion, and a statement that if additional procedures had been performed, other matters might have come to the practitioner's attention that would have been reported.

12. A statement restricting the use of the report to the specified parties.

13. Any reservations or restrictions concerning procedures or findings.

14. A description of the nature of any assistance provided by specialists.

15. Manual or printed signature of the practitioner's firm.

16. Date of the report.

ILLUSTRATION 4—AGREED-UPON PROCEDURES REPORT ON AN ENTITY'S COMPLIANCE WITH SPECIFIED REQUIREMENTS

Independent Accountant's Report on Applying Agreed-Upon Procedures

We have performed the procedures enumerated below, which were agreed to by [*list specified parties*], solely to assist the specified parties in evaluating ABC Company's compliance with [*list specified requirements*] during the [*period*] ended [date].[1] Management is responsible for ABC Company's compliance with those requirements. This agreed-upon procedures engagement was conducted in accordance with attestation standards established by the American Institute of Certified Public Accountants. The sufficiency of these procedures is solely the responsibility of those parties specified in this report. Consequently, we make no representation regarding the sufficiency of the procedures described below either for the purpose for which this report has been requested or for any other purpose.

[*Include paragraphs to enumerate procedures and findings.*][2]

We were not engaged to and did not conduct an examination, the objective of which would be the expression of an opinion on compliance. Accordingly, we do not express such an opinion. Had we performed additional procedures, other matters might have come to our attention that would have been reported to you.

This report is intended solely for the information and use of [*list or refer to specified parties*] and is not intended to be and should not be used by anyone other than these specified parties.

[*Signature*]

[*Date*]

ILLUSTRATION 5—AGREED-UPON PROCEDURES REPORT ON THE EFFECTIVENESS OF AN ENTITY'S INTERNAL CONTROL OVER COMPLIANCE

Independent Accountant's Report on Applying Agreed-Upon Procedures

We have performed the procedures enumerated below, which were agreed to by [*list specified parties*], solely to assist the specified parties in evaluating the effectiveness of ABC Company's internal control over compliance with [*list*

---

[1] If the agreed-upon procedures have been published by a third-party user (for example, a regulator in regulatory policies or a lender in a debt agreement), this sentence might begin as follows: "We have performed the procedures included in [*title of publication or other document*] and enumerated below, which were agreed to by [*list specified parties*], solely to assist the specified parties in evaluating . . . ."

[2] Evaluating compliance with certain requirements may require interpretation of the laws, regulations, rules, contracts, or grants that establish those requirements. If these interpretations are significant, the practitioner may include a paragraph stating the description and the source of interpretations made by management. The following is an example of such a paragraph, which should precede the procedures and findings paragraph(s):

> We have been informed that, under ABC Company's interpretation of [*identify the compliance requirement*], [*explain the nature and source of the relevant interpretation*].

specified requirements] as of [*date*].[3] Management is responsible for ABC Company's internal control over compliance with those requirements. This agreed-upon procedures engagement was conducted in accordance with attestation standards established by the American Institute of Certified Public Accountants. The sufficiency of these procedures is solely the responsibility of those parties specified in this report. Consequently, we make no representation regarding the sufficiency of the procedures described below either for the purpose for which this report has been requested or for any other purpose.

[*Include paragraphs to enumerate procedures and findings.*]

We were not engaged to and did not conduct an examination, the objective of which would be the expression of an opinion on the effectiveness of internal control over compliance. Accordingly, we do not express such an opinion. Had we performed additional procedures, other matters might have come to our attention that would have been reported to you.

This report is intended solely for the information and use of [*list or refer to specified parties*] and is not intended to be and should not be used by anyone other than these specified parties.

[*Signature*]

[*Date*]

ILLUSTRATION 6—COMPONENTS OF THE PRACTITIONER'S EXAMINATION REPORT ON AN ENTITY'S COMPLIANCE WITH SPECIFIED REQUIREMENTS OR ON THE RESPONSIBLE PARTY'S WRITTEN ASSERTION

	Applicability of Item to an Examination Report	
Item in the Practitioner's Examination Report	*Directly on the Effectiveness of an Entity's Internal Control*	*On a Written Assertion*
1. A title that includes the word *independent*.	✓	✓
2. An introductory paragraph that:		
a. Identifies the specified compliance requirements, including the period covered.	✓	✓
b. Identifies the responsible party's assertion about the entity's compliance with specified requirements, including the period covered. (When the assertion does not accompany the practitioner's report, the introductory paragraph should also contain a statement of the responsible party's assertion.)	N/A	✓
c. Identifies the responsible party.	✓	✓

---

[3] If the agreed-upon procedures have been published by a third-party user (for example, a regulator in regulatory policies or a lender in a debt agreement), this sentence might begin: "We have performed the procedures included in [*title of publication or other document*] and enumerated below, which were agreed to by [*list specified parties*], solely to assist the specified parties in evaluating the effectiveness of ABC Company's internal control over compliance . . . ."

Item in the Practitioner's Examination Report	Applicability of Item to an Examination Report	
	Directly on the Effectiveness of an Entity's Internal Control	On a Written Assertion
d. States that compliance with the specified requirements is the responsibility of the entity's management.	✓	✓
e. States that the practitioner's responsibility is to express an opinion on the entity's compliance with those requirements based on his or her examination.	✓	✓
3. A scope paragraph stating that:		
a. The examination was conducted in accordance with attestation standards established by the American Institute of Certified Public Accountants, and a brief description of the scope of such examination.	✓	✓
b. The practitioner believes the examination provides a reasonable basis for his or her opinion.	✓	✓
c. The examination does not provide a legal determination on the entity's compliance.	✓	✓
4. An opinion paragraph stating:		
a. Whether the entity complied, in all material respects, with specified requirements based on the specified criteria.	✓	N/A
b. Whether the responsible party's assertion about compliance with specified requirements is fairly stated in all material respects based on the specified criteria.	N/A	✓
5. A statement restricting the use of the report to specified parties under the following circumstances:		
a. When the criteria used to evaluate compliance are determined by the practitioner to be appropriate only for a limited number of parties who either participated in their establishment or can be presumed to have an adequate understanding of the criteria.	✓	✓
b. When the criteria used to evaluate compliance are available only to specified parties.	✓	✓
6. Manual or printed signature of the practitioner's firm.	✓	✓
7. Date of the examination report.	✓	✓

ILLUSTRATION 7—EXAMINATION REPORT ON AN ENTITY'S COMPLIANCE WITH SPECIFIED REQUIREMENTS

Independent Accountant's Report

We have examined ABC Company's compliance with [*list specified compliance requirements*] during the [*period*] ended [*date*]. Management is responsible for ABC Company's compliance with those requirements. Our responsibility is to express an opinion on ABC Company's compliance based on our examination.

Our examination was conducted in accordance with attestation standards established by the American Institute of Certified Public Accountants and, accordingly, included examining, on a test basis, evidence about ABC Company's compliance with those requirements and performing such other procedures as we considered necessary in the circumstances. We believe that our examination provides a reasonable basis for our opinion. Our examination does not provide a legal determination on ABC Company's compliance with specified requirements.[4]

In our opinion, ABC Company complied, in all material respects, with the aforementioned requirements for the year ended December 31, 20X2.

[*Signature*]

[*Date*]

ILLUSTRATION 8—EXAMINATION REPORT ON MANAGEMENT'S ASSERTION ABOUT COMPLIANCE WITH SPECIFIED REQUIREMENTS

Independent Accountant's Report

We have examined management's assertion, included in the accompanying [*title of management report*], that ABC Company complied with [*list specified compliance requirements*] during the [*period*] ended [*date*].[5] Management is responsible for ABC Company's compliance with those requirements. Our responsibility is to express an opinion on management's assertion about ABC Company's compliance based on our examination.

Our examination was conducted in accordance with attestation standards established by the American Institute of Certified Public Accountants and, accordingly, included examining, on a test basis, evidence about ABC Company's compliance with those requirements and performing such other procedures as we considered necessary in the circumstances. We believe that our examination provides a reasonable basis for our opinion. Our examination does not provide a legal determination on ABC Company's compliance with specified requirements.[6]

---

[4] Evaluating compliance with certain requirements may require interpretation of the laws, regulations, rules, contracts, or grants that establish those requirements. If these interpretations are significant, the practitioner may include a paragraph stating the description and the source of interpretations made by management. The following is an example of such a paragraph, which should directly follow the scope paragraph:

We have been informed that, under ABC Company's interpretation of [*identify the compliance requirement*], [*explain the nature and source of the relevant interpretation*].

[5] If management's assertion is stated in the practitioner's report and does not accompany the practitioner's report, the phrase "included in the accompanying [*title of management report*]" would be omitted.

[6] Evaluating compliance with certain requirements may require interpretation of the laws, regulations, rules, contracts, or grants that establish those requirements. If these interpretations are significant, the practitioner may include a paragraph stating the description and the source of interpretations made by management. The following is an example of such a paragraph, which should directly follow the scope paragraph:

We have been informed that, under ABC Company's interpretation of [*identify the com-*

In our opinion, management's assertion that ABC Company complied with the aforementioned requirements during the [*period*] ended [*date*] is fairly stated, in all material respects.

[*Signature*]

[*Date*]

ILLUSTRATION 9—EXAMINATION REPORT WITH A QUALIFIED OPINION WHEN THERE IS MATERIAL NONCOMPLIANCE WITH SPECIFIED REQUIREMENTS

Independent Accountant's Report

We have examined ABC Company's compliance with [*list specified compliance requirements*] for the [*period*] ended [*date*]. Management is responsible for compliance with those requirements. Our responsibility is to express an opinion on ABC Company's compliance based on our examination.

Our examination was conducted in accordance with attestation standards established by the American Institute of Certified Public Accountants and, accordingly, included examining, on a test basis, evidence about ABC Company's compliance with those requirements and performing such other procedures as we considered necessary in the circumstances. We believe that our examination provides a reasonable basis for our opinion. Our examination does not provide a legal determination on ABC Company's compliance with specified requirements.

Our examination disclosed the following material noncompliance with [*type of compliance requirement*] applicable to ABC Company during the [*period*] ended [*date*]. [*Describe noncompliance.*]

In our opinion, except for the material noncompliance described in the third paragraph, ABC Company complied, in all material respects, with the aforementioned requirements for the [*period*] ended [*date*].

[*Signature*]

[*Date*]

ILLUSTRATION 10—EXAMINATION REPORT WITH AN ADVERSE OPINION WHEN THERE IS MATERIAL NONCOMPLIANCE WITH SPECIFIED REQUIREMENTS

Independent Accountant's Report

We have examined ABC Company's compliance with [*list specified compliance requirements*] for the [*period*] ended [*date*]. Management is responsible for compliance with those requirements. Our responsibility is to express an opinion on ABC Company's compliance based on our examination.

Our examination was conducted in accordance with attestation standards established by the American Institute of Certified Public Accountants and, accordingly, included examining, on a test basis, evidence about ABC Company's

---

(Footnote Continued)

pliance requirement], [*explain the nature and source of the relevant interpretation*].

compliance with those requirements and performing such other procedures as we considered necessary in the circumstances. We believe that our examination provides a reasonable basis for our opinion. Our examination does not provide a legal determination on ABC Company's compliance with specified requirements.

Our examination disclosed the following material noncompliance with [*type of compliance requirement*] applicable to ABC Company during the [*period*] ended [*date*]. [*Describe noncompliance.*]

In our opinion, because of the effect of the noncompliance described in the third paragraph, ABC Company has not complied with the aforementioned requirements for the [*period*] ended [*date*].

[*Signature*]

[*Date*]

AT SECTION 701
MANAGEMENT'S DISCUSSION AND ANALYSIS

WHAT EVERY PRACTITIONER SHOULD KNOW

Basic Objectives and Requirements

This Section is applicable when a practitioner is engaged to *examine* or *review* management's discussion and analysis (MD&A) by:

1. A public entity that prepares MD&A in accordance with SEC rules and regulations.
2. A nonpublic entity that prepares an MD&A presentation and whose management provides a written assertion that the presentation has been prepared using SEC rules and regulations.

This Section does not affect the auditor's responsibility in an audit of financial statements performed in accordance with GAAS and does not apply to the situations described in Illustration 1.

In addition to the requirements of this Section, the practitioner should comply with the attest documentation requirements prescribed in AT Section 101 (Attest Engagements).

Overall Engagement Considerations in an Examination or a Review of an MD&A Presentation

The practitioner should consider the concept of materiality in planning and performing the engagement. The practitioner should consider the omission or misstatement of an individual assertion to be material if its magnitude is such that a reasonable person using the MD&A presentation would be influenced by the inclusion or correction of the individual assertion. Also, the practitioner's examination or review procedures of MD&A should cover:

1. Pro forma financial information with respect to any business combination or other transactions included in MD&A.
2. Information external to the entity that is included in MD&A, such as the rating of an entity's debt by certain rating agencies or comparisons with statistics from a trade association.
3. Forward-looking disclosures in the MD&A presentation.
4. Voluntary information in the MD&A presentation that is not required by SEC rules and regulations.

Examination Engagement

Before accepting an engagement to examine MD&A, the practitioner should consider whether management, and others involved in the preparation of MD&A (e.g., legal counsel), have appropriate knowledge of the SEC rules and regulations relating to MD&A. In addition, in order to perform such an engagement, all the conditions summarized in Illustration 2 should be met.

In planning an examination of MD&A, the practitioner should consider factors such as the following:

1. The anticipated level of attestation risk related to assertions embodied in the MD&A.

2. Preliminary judgments about materiality.

3. The items within the MD&A presentation that are likely to require revision or adjustment.

4. Conditions that may require extension or modification of attest procedures.

Procedures in an examination engagement The practitioner should perform the following procedures when engaged to examine an entity's MD&A:

1. Obtain an understanding of the SEC rules and regulations for MD&A and management's method for the preparation of MD&A.

2. Plan the examination engagement.

3. Consider relevant portions of the entity's internal control applicable to the preparation of MD&A.

4. Obtain sufficient evidence, including testing completeness.

5. Consider the effect of events subsequent to the balance sheet date.

6. Obtain written representations from management.

7. Form an opinion on the examination of MD&A.

See Illustration 4 for a procedures checklist for engagements to examine MD&A.

Reporting on an examination of MD&A In order for the practitioner to issue a report on an examination of MD&A, the financial statements for the periods covered by the MD&A presentation and the related auditor's report(s) should accompany the MD&A presentation. For a public entity, alternatively, the financial statements for the periods covered by the MD&A presentation and the related auditor's report(s) may be incorporated in the document containing the MD&A by reference to information filed with a regulatory agency. In addition, if the entity is a nonpublic entity, either (1) a statement should be included in the body of the MD&A presentation that it has been prepared using the rules and regulations adopted by the SEC or (2) a separate written assertion should accompany the MD&A presentation or be included in a representation letter from the entity.

The practitioner's report on an examination of MD&A should include all the elements contained in Illustration 5. See Illustration 6 for an example of a standard examination report on MD&A.

The practitioner should modify the standard examination report in Illustration 6 if any of the following conditions exist:

1. The MD&A presentation excludes a material required element under the SEC rules and regulations (see Illustration 7).

2. The historical financial amounts have not been accurately derived, in all material respects, from the entity's financial statements.

3. The underlying information, determinations, estimates, and assumptions used by management do not provide the entity with a reasonable basis for the disclosure in the MD&A presentation (see Illustration 8).

4. There is a restriction on the scope of the engagement.

5. The practitioner decides to refer to the report of another practitioner as the basis, in part, for his or her report (see Illustration 9).

6. The practitioner is engaged to examine the MD&A presentation after it has been filed with the SEC or other regulatory agency.

Review Engagement

Before accepting an engagement to review MD&A, the practitioner should consider whether management, and others involved in the preparation of MD&A (e.g., legal counsel), have appropriate knowledge of the SEC rules and regulations relating to MD&A. In addition, in order to perform such an engagement, all the applicable conditions summarized in Illustration 3 should be met.

Procedures in a review engagement The practitioner should perform the following procedures when engaged to review an entity's MD&A:

1. Obtain an understanding of the published SEC rules and regulations for MD&A and management's method for the preparation of MD&A.

2. Plan the review engagement.

3. Consider relevant portions of the entity's internal control applicable to the preparation of MD&A.

4. Apply analytical procedures to the financial statements and related MD&A and make inquiries of management and others.

5. Consider the effect of events subsequent to the balance sheet date.

6. Obtain written representations from management.

7. Form a conclusion on the MD&A presentation.

See Illustration 10 for a procedures checklist for engagements to review MD&A.

Reporting on a review of MD&A In order for the practitioner to issue a report on a review of MD&A for an annual period, the financial statements for the periods covered by the MD&A presentation and the related auditor's report(s) should accompany the MD&A presentation. For a public entity, alternatively, the financial statements for the periods covered by the MD&A presentation and the related auditor's report(s) may be incorporated in the document containing the MD&A by reference to information filed with a regulatory agency.

If the MD&A presentation relates to an interim period and the entity is a public entity, the financial statements for the interim periods covered by the MD&A presentation and the related accountant's review report(s) should accompany the MD&A presentation, or be incorporated in the document containing the MD&A by reference to information filed with a regulatory agency.

If the MD&A presentation relates to an interim period and the entity is a nonpublic entity, the following conditions should be met in order for the practitioner to issue a review report:

1. The MD&A presentation for the most recent fiscal year and related accountant's examination or review reports should accompany the interim MD&A presentation.

2. The financial statements for the periods covered by the respective MD&A presentations (i.e., most recent fiscal year and interim periods and the related auditor's reports and accountant's review reports) should accompany the interim MD&A presentation.

3. One of the following conditions should be met:

   a. A statement should be included in the body of the MD&A presentation that it has been prepared using the SEC rules and regulations.

   b. A separate written assertion should accompany the MD&A presentation or be included in a representation letter from the entity.

The practitioner's report on a review of MD&A should include all the elements contained in Illustration 11. See Illustration 12 for an example of a standard review report on an annual MD&A presentation and Illustration 13 for a standard review report on an interim MD&A presentation.

The practitioner should modify the standard review reports in Illustrations 12 and 13 if any of the following conditions exist:

1. The MD&A presentation excludes a material required element of the SEC rules and regulations (see Illustration 14).

2. The historical financial amounts have not been accurately derived, in all material respects, from the entity's financial statements.

3. The underlying information, determinations, estimates, and assumptions used by management do not provide the entity with a reasonable basis for the disclosures in the MD&A presentation.

4. The practitioner decides to refer to the report of another practitioner as the basis, in part, for his or her report.

5. The practitioner is engaged to review the MD&A presentation after it has been filed with the SEC or other regulatory agency.

If the practitioner is unable to perform the inquiry and analytical procedures considered necessary for the MD&A review, the review is incomplete and the practitioner does not have a basis for issuing a review report. When the practitioner is unable to complete a review because of a scope limitation, the practitioner should consider the implications of that limitation with respect to possible misstatements of the MD&A presentation. In such circumstances, the practitioner should also refer to the guidance discussed below under "Communications with Audit Committee."

Combined Examination and Review Report on MD&A

A practitioner may be engaged both (1) to examine MD&A as of the most recent fiscal year end and (2) to review a separate MD&A presentation for a subsequent interim period. If the examination and review engagements are completed at the same time, the practitioner may issue a combined report. Illustration 15 provides an example of a combined report on an examination of an annual MD&A presentation and the review of a separate MD&A presentation for an interim period.

An entity may prepare a combined MD&A presentation for annual and interim periods in which there is a discussion of liquidity and capital resources only as of the most recent interim period but not as of the most recent annual period. In such circumstances, the practitioner is limited to performing the highest level of service that is provided with respect to the historical financial statements for any of the periods covered by the MD&A presentation. Illustration 16 provides an example of a review report on a combined MD&A presentation for annual and interim periods.

Engagement of Practitioner Subsequent to the Filing of MD&A

If the practitioner is engaged to examine or review an MD&A presentation of a public entity that has already been filed with the SEC, or other regulatory agency, the practitioner should consider whether material subsequent events are appropriately disclosed in a Form 8-K or Form 10-Q, or a registration statement that includes or incorporates by reference such MD&A presentation, as follows:

1. **Subsequent event disclosed, or there are no subsequent events.** If subsequent events of a public entity are appropriately disclosed in a Form 8-K or Form 10-Q, or in a registration statement, or if there have been no material subsequent events, the practitioner should add the following paragraph to his or her examination or review report following the opinion or concluding paragraph:

   > The accompanying Management's Discussion and Analysis does not consider events that have occurred subsequent to July 15, 20X3, the date as of which it was filed with the Securities and Exchange Commission.

2. **Subsequent event *not* disclosed.** If there has been a material subsequent event that has not been appropriately disclosed, and if the practitioner determines that it is appropriate to issue a report even though the MD&A presentation has not been updated for such material subsequent event, the practitioner should express a qualified or an adverse opinion (or appropriately modify the review report) on the MD&A presentation. If such material subsequent event is not appropriately disclosed, the practitioner should evaluate (a) whether to resign from the engagement related to the MD&A presentation and (b) whether to remain as the entity's auditor or stand for reelection to audit the entity's financial statements.

Because a nonpublic entity is not subject to the filing requirements of the SEC, an MD&A presentation of a nonpublic entity should be updated for material subsequent events through the date of the practitioner's report.

Situations Involving a Predecessor Auditor Who Has Audited Prior Period Financial Statements

If a predecessor auditor has audited the financial statements for a prior period covered by the MD&A, the successor practitioner reporting on the MD&A should consider reviewing the predecessor auditor's working papers with respect to audits of financial statements and examinations or reviews of MD&A presentations for such prior periods.

In addition, if at the time of the appointment as auditor, the practitioner is also being engaged to examine or review MD&A, the practitioner should also make specific inquiries of the predecessor auditor regarding matters that may affect the examination or review engagement of MD&A.

Situations Involving Another Auditor of a Significant Part of the Financial Statements

When another auditor audits a significant part of the financial statements, the practitioner may request that such other auditor perform procedures with respect to the MD&A or the practitioner may perform the procedures directly with respect to such components. The practitioner should consider whether he or she has sufficient industry expertise and experience with respect to a subsidiary audited by another auditor to take sole responsibility for the consolidated MD&A presentation.

Unless the other auditor issues an examination or a review report on a separate MD&A presentation of such components, the principal practitioner should not make reference to the work of the other practitioner on MD&A in his or her report on MD&A. Therefore, if the practitioner has requested such other auditor to perform procedures, the principal practitioner should perform those procedures that he or she considers necessary to take responsibility for the work of the other auditor. Such procedures may include one or more of the following:

1. Visit the other auditor and discuss the procedures performed and the results obtained.

2. Review the working papers of the other auditor with respect to the component.

3. Participate in discussions with the component's management regarding matters that may affect the preparation of MD&A.

4. Perform additional tests with respect to such component.

Communications with Audit Committee

The practitioner may become aware of certain matters that require communication with the audit committee, such as the following:

1. Material inconsistencies between the MD&A presentation and other information included in the document containing the MD&A presentation.

2. Material inconsistencies between the MD&A presentation and the historical financial statements.

3. Material omissions.

4. Material misstatements of fact.

If management refuses to take corrective action in the circumstances, the practitioner should inform the audit committee or others with equivalent authority and responsibility. If the MD&A is not revised, the practitioner should consider consulting with his or her legal counsel and evaluate:

1. Whether to resign from the engagement related to the MD&A.

2. Whether to remain as the entity's auditor or stand for reelection to audit the entity's financial statements.

A practitioner who is engaged after the MD&A presentation has been filed with the SEC (or other regulatory agency) may become aware that such MD&A presentation on file has not been revised for a matter for which the practitioner has qualified or would qualify his or her opinion. In such circumstances, the practitioner should discuss such matter with the audit committee and request that the MD&A presentation be revised. If the audit committee fails to take appropriate action, the practitioner should consider whether to resign as the independent auditor of the company. See AU Section 317 (Illegal Acts by Clients) for additional guidance.

Written Representations

The practitioner should obtain written representations from management in an examination or a review engagement. The types of representations to be obtained will depend on the circumstances of the engagement and the nature of the MD&A presentation. See Illustration 4 (item 26), and Illustration 10 (item 19), for specific representations to be obtained in an examination or review engagement of MD&A, respectively.

PRACTICE ISSUES AND FREQUENTLY ASKED QUESTIONS

Issue 1: When performing an examination or a review of MD&A under this Section, is the practitioner required to comply with the general, fieldwork, and reporting standards for attestation engagements described in AT Section 101?

Yes. In addition to complying with the specific requirements discussed in this Section, the practitioner should comply with the five general standards, the two fieldwork standards, and the four reporting standards described in AT Section 101 (Attest Engagements).

Issue 2: Under what circumstances may the practitioner permit a client to make reference in a client-prepared document to the practitioner's examination or review of MD&A?

An entity should not name the practitioner in a client-prepared document as having examined or reviewed MD&A unless the following information is included in the document (or, for a public entity, incorporated by reference):

1. The MD&A presentation and related practitioner's report, and

2. The related financial statements and auditor's (or accountant's review) report.

If an entity names the practitioner in a document that does not include (or incorporate by reference) such information, the practitioner should request that neither his or her name nor reference to the practitioner be made with respect to the MD&A information. Or, such document should be revised to include the required presentations and reports. If the client does not comply, the practitioner should advise the client that he or she does not consent to either the use of his or her name or the reference to the practitioner, and should consider consulting with his or her legal counsel.

Issue 3: In an examination of an MD&A presentation, is the practitioner required to document his or her understanding of an entity's internal control applicable to the preparation of MD&A?

Yes. The practitioner is required to document his or her understanding of the entity's internal control applicable to the preparation of MD&A used to plan the examination and the assessment of the level of control risk. The form and extent of this documentation is influenced by the size and complexity of the entity, as well as the nature of the entity's controls applicable to the preparation of MD&A.

Issue 4: What is the practitioner's responsibility in an examination engagement regarding significant deficiencies in the design or operation of internal control applicable to the preparation of MD&A?

If during the course of the examination engagement, the practitioner becomes aware of significant deficiencies in the design or operation of internal control applicable to the preparation of MD&A, the practitioner should consider the implications of such deficiencies on his or her ability to rely on management's representations and on comparisons to summary accounting records. The practitioner's responsibility to communicate these control deficiencies in an examination of MD&A is similar to the auditor's responsibility described in AU Section 325 (Communicating Internal Control Related Matters Identified in an Audit) and AU Section 380 (The Auditor's Communication with Those Charged with Governance).

Issue 5: What course of action should the practitioner take if management refuses to provide a written letter of representations in an examination or a review engagement of MD&A?

In an examination engagement, management's refusal to furnish the practitioner with a written letter of representations constitutes a limitation on the scope of the MD&A engagement sufficient to preclude an unqualified opinion. Ordinarily, this is sufficient cause for the practitioner to disclaim an opinion or withdraw from the engagement. However, based on the nature of the representations not obtained or the circumstances of the refusal, the practitioner may conclude that a qualified opinion is appropriate in an examination engagement.

In a review engagement, management's refusal to furnish written representations constitutes a limitation on the scope of the engagement sufficient to require withdrawal from the review engagement.

In addition, if management refuses to provide a written letter of representations, the practitioner should consider and evaluate the effects of management's refusal on his or her ability to rely on other management representations.

Issue 6: Does a review of MD&A require the practitioner to test accounting records or obtain corroborating evidence in response to inquiries made of management?

No. A review of MD&A does not contemplate tests of accounting records (e.g., through confirmation, observation, or inspection), obtaining corroborating audit evidence in response to inquiries, or the application of certain other procedures ordinarily performed during an examination of MD&A. Instead, a review of MD&A consists primarily of applying analytical procedures and making inquiries of persons responsible for financial, accounting, and operational matters.

Issue 7: What is the practitioner's responsibility, in an examination or a review engagement, for other information in documents containing MD&A?

The guidance in AU Section 550 (Other Information in Documents Containing Audited Financial Statements) is also pertinent to other information in annual reports containing MD&A and other documents to which the practitioner devotes attention. Therefore, the practitioner should read the other information and consider whether such information, or the manner of its presentation, is materially inconsistent with information appearing in the MD&A presentation that has been reported on by the practitioner. If there is a material inconsistency or material misstatement of fact, the practitioner should take such actions as described in AU Section 550 for audited financial statements.

When the practitioner's report on MD&A is included in a registration statement, proxy statement, or periodic report filed under the federal securities statutes, the practitioner should follow the guidance in AU Section 711 (Filings under Federal Securities Statutes).

Issue 8: How does a practitioner gauge materiality in relation to an MD&A presentation which typically includes both specific quantifiable data and a wide range of qualitative assertions?

The objective of an examination or a review of MD&A is to report on the presentation as a whole, not on its individual components. The most important consideration is whether an omission or misstatement within the MD&A presentation would influence a reasonable person's judgment.

With respect to quantitative data, materiality is gauged relative to size. However, consideration should be given to the expected precision or range of reasonableness of that data. Historical data generally will be more precise than prospective information.

Qualitative considerations also enter into the consideration of materiality in determining, for example, whether the company's estimates and assumptions provide a reasonable basis for the disclosures in the MD&A.

Issue 9: Currently, where can a practitioner find the rules and regulations for MD&A adopted by the SEC?

The rules and regulations for MD&A adopted by the SEC are presently found in:

1. Item 303 of Regulation S-K, as interpreted by Financial Reporting Release (FRR) No. 36, which is titled "Management's Discussion and Analysis of Financial Condition and Results of Operations; Certain

Investment Company Disclosures" (Section 501 of the "Codification of Financial Reporting Policies").

2. Item 303 of Regulation S-B for small business issuers.

3. Item 9 of Form 20-F for Foreign Private Issuers.

The SEC requirements for MD&A may, and do, change periodically. Therefore, in an engagement to examine or review an MD&A presentation, the practitioner should consider whether the SEC has adopted additional rules and regulations with respect to MD&A.

ILLUSTRATIONS AND PRACTICE AIDS

ILLUSTRATION 1—ENGAGEMENTS FOR WHICH AT SECTION 701 DOES NOT APPLY

Type of Engagement	Applicable Guidance
1. Engagements to perform agreed-upon procedures on MD& A.	1. AT Section 201 (Agreed-Upon Procedures Engagements).
2. Engagements to provide attest services with respect to an MD&A presentation that is prepared based on criteria other than the SEC rules and regulations.	2. AT Section 101 (Attest Engagements) or AT Section 201 (Agreed-Upon Procedures Engagements).
3. Engagements to provide recommendations on how to improve the MD&A rather than to provide assurance.	3. Statement on Standards for Consulting Services No. 1 (Consulting Services: Definitions and Standards).
4. Engagements to perform agreed-upon procedures on MD&A and to report thereon in a letter for underwriters.	4. AU Section 634 (letters for Underwriters and Certain Other Requesting Parties).

ILLUSTRATION 2—CONDITIONS FOR PERFORMING AN EXAMINATION ENGAGEMENT OF MD&A

Before accepting an engagement to examine the MD&A of a public or nonpublic entity, the practitioner should observe the following conditions:

1. The practitioner must audit, in accordance with GAAS, the financial statements for at least the latest period to which the MD&A presentation relates.

2. The financial statements for the other periods covered by the MD&A presentation must have been audited by the practitioner or a predecessor auditor.

3. If a predecessor auditor has audited the financial statements for a prior period covered by the MD&A, the practitioner (successor auditor) should consider whether he or she can acquire sufficient knowledge of the entity's business, and accounting and financial reporting practices for such period to enable him or her to:

   a. Identify types of potential material misstatements in the MD&A and consider the likelihood of their occurrence.

   b. Perform the necessary procedures in order to express an opinion on whether the MD&A presentation includes the required elements of the rules and regulations adopted by the SEC.

c. Perform the necessary procedures in order to express an opinion on the MD&A presentation with respect to whether the historical financial amounts have been accurately derived from the entity's financial statements for such period.

d. Perform the necessary procedures in order to express an opinion on whether the underlying information, determinations, estimates, and assumptions of the entity provide a reasonable basis for the disclosures contained therein.

ILLUSTRATION 3—CONDITIONS FOR PERFORMING A REVIEW ENGAGEMENT OF MD&A

Before accepting an engagement to review the MD&A of a public or nonpublic entity, the practitioner should observe the following conditions:

Public Entities

For annual periods:

1. The practitioner has audited, in accordance with PCAOB standards, the financial statements for at least the latest annual period to which the MD&A presentation relates.

2. The financial statements for the other periods covered by the MD&A presentation have been audited by the practitioner or a predecessor auditor.

3. If a predecessor auditor has audited the financial statements for a prior period covered by the MD&A, the practitioner (successor auditor) should consider whether he or she can acquire sufficient knowledge of the entity's business, and accounting and financial reporting practices for such period to enable him or her to:

    a. Identify types of potential material misstatements in the MD&A and consider the likelihood of their occurrence.

    b. Perform the procedures that will provide the practitioner with a basis for reporting whether any information has come to the practitioner's attention to cause him or her to believe any of the following:

        (1) The MD&A presentation does not include the required elements of the SEC rules and regulations.

        (2) The historical financial amounts included therein have not been accurately derived from the entity's financial statements for such period.

        (3) The underlying information, determinations, estimates, and assumptions of the entity do not provide a reasonable basis for the disclosures contained therein.

For interim periods:

1. The practitioner performs either of the following:

    a. A review of the historical financial statements for the related comparative interim periods and issues a review report thereon in accordance with AU Section 722 (Interim Financial Information).

   b. An audit of the interim financial statements.

2. The MD&A presentation for the most recent fiscal year has been or will be examined or reviewed by either the practitioner or a predecessor auditor.

Nonpublic Entities

For annual periods:

1. The annual financial statements for the periods covered by the MD&A presentation have been or will be audited and the practitioner has audited or will audit the most recent year.

2. If a predecessor auditor has audited the financial statements for a prior period covered by the MD&A, the practitioner should consider whether he or she can acquire sufficient knowledge of the entity's business, and accounting and financial reporting practices for such period to enable him or her to:

   a. Identify types of potential material misstatements in the MD&A and consider the likelihood of their occurrence.

   b. Perform the procedures that will provide the practitioner with a basis for reporting whether any information has come to the practitioner's attention to cause him or her to believe any of the following:

     (1) The MD&A presentation does not include the required elements of the SEC rules and regulations.

     (2) The historical financial amounts included therein have not been accurately derived from the entity's financial statements for such period.

     (3) The underlying information, determinations, estimates, and assumptions of the entity do not provide a reasonable basis for the disclosures contained therein.

3. Management will provide a written assertion that the presentation has been prepared using the SEC rules and regulations as the criteria.

For interim periods:

1. The practitioner performs one of the following:

   a. A review of the historical financial statements for the related interim periods under the Statements on Standards for Accounting and Review Services and issues a review report thereon.

   b. A review of the condensed interim financial information for the related interim periods under AU Section 722 (Interim Financial Information) and issues a review report thereon, and such interim financial information is accompanied by complete annual financial statements for the most recent fiscal year that have been audited.

   c. An audit of the interim financial statements.

2. The MD&A presentation for the most recent fiscal year has been or will be examined or reviewed.

3. Management will provide a written assertion stating that the presentation has been prepared using the SEC rules and regulations as the criteria.

ILLUSTRATION 4—PROCEDURES CHECKLIST FOR ENGAGEMENTS TO EXAMINE MD&A

	Performed By	*Workpaper Reference*
1. Consider whether management, and others involved in the preparation of MD&A (e.g., legal counsel), have appropriate knowledge of the SEC rules and regulations relating to MD&A.	_____	_____
2. Obtain an understanding of the SEC rules and regulations for MD&A and management's method for the preparation of MD&A, and make inquiries about:		
a. The sources of the information.	_____	_____
b. How the information is gathered.	_____	_____
c. How management evaluates the types of factors having a material effect on financial condition, results of operations, and cash flows.	_____	_____
d. Whether there have been any changes in the procedures from the prior year.	_____	_____
3. Obtain an understanding of the entity's internal control applicable to the preparation of MD&A sufficient to plan the engagement and to assess control risk, by performing procedures such as the following:		
a. Making inquiries of appropriate management, supervisory, and staff personnel.	_____	_____
b. Inspecting relevant documents and records.	_____	_____
c. Observing the entity's relevant activities and operations, including controls over matters discussed in MD&A, nonfinancial data included, and management evaluation of the reasonableness of information included.	_____	_____
4. Develop an overall strategy for the expected scope and performance of the engagement, by considering factors such as the following:		
a. The industry in which the entity operates and matters affecting the industry, such as financial reporting practices, economic conditions, laws and regulations, and technological changes.	_____	_____
b. Knowledge of the entity's internal control applicable to the preparation of MD&A obtained during the audit of the financial statements and any subsequent changes.	_____	_____
c. The entity's business, including its organization structure, operating characteristics, capital structure, and distribution methods.	_____	_____
d. The types of relevant information that management reports to external analysts, e.g., press releases and presentations to lenders and rating agencies concerning past and future performance.	_____	_____

		Performed By	Workpaper Reference
e.	How the entity analyzes actual performance versus budgets and the types of information provided to the board of directors for day-to-day operations and long-range planning.	_____	_____
f.	The extent of management's knowledge of and experience with the SEC rules and regulations for MD&A.	_____	_____
g.	For nonpublic entities, the intended use of the MD&A presentation.	_____	_____
h.	Preliminary judgments about (1) materiality, (2) inherent risk at the individual assertion level, and (3) factors relating to significant deficiencies in internal control applicable to the preparation of MD&A.	_____	_____
i.	The fraud risk factors or other conditions identified during the audit of the most recent annual financial statements and the practitioner's response to such risk factors.	_____	_____
j.	The type and extent of evidential matter supporting management's assertions and disclosures in the MD&A.	_____	_____
k.	The nature of complex or subjective matters potentially material to the MD&A that may require specialized skill or knowledge or using the work of a specialist to obtain sufficient evidential matter.	_____	_____
l.	The presence of an internal audit function and the extent to which internal auditors are involved in directly testing the MD&A presentation, in monitoring the entity's internal control applicable to the preparation of MD&A, or in testing the underlying records supporting disclosures in the MD&A.	_____	_____

5. Consider the results of the audits of the financial statements for the periods covered by the MD&A on the examination engagement, including such matters as:

a.	The availability and condition of the entity's records.	_____	_____
b.	The nature and magnitude of audit adjustments.	_____	_____
c.	Likely misstatements that were not corrected in the financial statements that may affect MD&A disclosures, such as misclassifications between financial statement line items.	_____	_____
d.	Modification of the auditor's report, including matters addressed in the auditor's report explanatory paragraph.	_____	_____

6. When MD&A has not previously been examined:

a.	Consider the degree to which the entity has information available for such prior periods and the continuity of the entity's personnel and their ability to respond to inquiries with respect to such periods.	_____	_____
b.	Obtain an understanding of the entity's internal control in prior years applicable to the preparation of MD&A.	_____	_____

	Performed By	Workpaper Reference

7. When the entity has operations in several components (for example, locations, subsidiaries), determine the components to which procedures should be applied. In such cases, consider such factors as:

   a. The relative significance of each component to the applicable MD&A disclosure. _____ _____

   b. The extent to which pertinent records are centralized. _____ _____

   c. The effectiveness of controls, particularly oversight controls at the various locations. _____ _____

   d. The nature and extent of operations conducted at the various components. _____ _____

   e. The similarity of operations and internal control for the different components. _____ _____

8. Read the MD&A presentation and determine whether the information presented is consistent with the audited financial statements, or related accounting records and analyses. _____ _____

9. Recompute increases, decreases, and percentages disclosed. _____ _____

10. Compare nonfinancial data to the audited financial statements or, if inapplicable, to other records. _____ _____

11. Consider whether explanations presented in the MD&A are consistent with information obtained during the audit; for items or explanations that cannot be substantiated by information in the audit working papers, investigate through inquiry of client executives and inspection of relevant records. _____ _____

12. Examine internally generated documents (e.g., sales analyses, business plans) and externally generated documents (e.g., contracts, loan agreements) to support the explanations, events, and items disclosed in the MD&A. _____ _____

13. Obtain available prospective financial information (e.g., budgets, financial forecasts and projections) and compare such information to forward-looking MD&A disclosures; consider whether the underlying information and assumptions provide a reasonable basis for the MD&A disclosures. _____ _____

14. Consider obtaining prospective financial information relating to prior periods and comparing actual results with forecasted and projected amounts. _____ _____

15. Make inquiries of company officials responsible for operational, financial, and accounting matters about their future plans and expectations that could affect the entity's liquidity and capital resources. _____ _____

16. Consider obtaining independent information about industry trends, inflation, and changing prices and comparing the related MD&A disclosures to such information. _____ _____

	Performed By	Workpaper Reference
17. Compare the information in the MD&A with the rules and regulations adopted by the SEC.	_____	_____
18. Read the minutes of meetings of the board of directors and other significant committees to identify matters that may affect MD&A and consider whether such matters are appropriately addressed in the MD&A.	_____	_____
19. Inquire of management about the entity's prior experience with the SEC and the extent of comments received in connection with documents filed by the entity with the SEC; read related correspondence between the entity and the SEC.	_____	_____
20. Obtain public communications made by the entity (e.g., press releases, quarterly reports) dealing with historical and future results; consider whether the MD&A is consistent with such communications.	_____	_____
21. Consider obtaining other types of publicly available information (e.g., analyst reports and news articles) and compare the MD&A presentation with such information.	_____	_____
22. If the MD&A presentation includes certain nonfinancial data (e.g., units produced, units sold, major customers, plant utilization, or square footage), consider whether:		
a. The definitions used by management for such nonfinancial data are reasonable.	_____	_____
b. Industry standards exist for the nonfinancial data.	_____	_____
c. There are different methods of measurement that may be used, and if such methods could result in materially different results.	_____	_____
d. The method of measurement selected by management is reasonable and consistent between periods covered by the MD&A presentation.	_____	_____
23. Consider whether the MD&A discloses matters that could significantly impact future financial condition and results of operations of the entity, as follows:		
a. Inquire of the entity's management about current events, conditions, economic changes, commitments and uncertainties.	_____	_____
b. Consider information obtained through the audit of the financial statements.	_____	_____
c. Obtain other information through procedures performed during the engagement.	_____	_____
24. Consider information about subsequent events after the end of the period addressed by MD&A and prior to the issuance of the report that may have a material effect on the entity's financial condition (including liquidity and capital resources), changes in financial condition, results of operations, and material commitments for capital resources. Events and matters that should be disclosed in the MD&A include those that:		

	Performed By	Workpaper Reference

a. Are reasonably expected to have a material favorable or unfavorable impact on net sales or revenues or income from continuing operations. _____ _____

b. Are reasonably likely to result in a material increase or decrease in the entity's liquidity. _____ _____

c. Will have a material effect on the entity's capital resources. _____ _____

d. Would cause reported financial information not to be necessarily indicative of future operating results or of future financial condition. _____ _____

25. Perform the following subsequent events procedures:

a. Read available minutes of meetings of stockholders, directors, and appropriate committees. _____ _____

b. Inquire about any recent meetings for which minutes have not yet been prepared. When minutes have not been prepared, inquire of management about matters dealt with at such meetings, and obtain written representation from management regarding such matters. _____ _____

c. Read the latest available interim financial statements and compare them with the financial statements for the periods covered by the MD&A. Pay special attention to major changes in the business or environment in which the client operates, and inquire of and discuss with management:

(1) Whether the interim financial statements have been prepared on the same basis as the current period audited financial statements. _____ _____

(2) Whether there were any significant changes in the entity's operations, liquidity, or capital resources in the subsequent period. _____ _____

(3) The current status of items in the financial statements for which the MD&A has been prepared, that were accounted for on the basis of tentative, preliminary, or inconclusive data. _____ _____

(4) Whether any unusual adjustments were made during the period from the balance sheet date to the date of inquiry. _____ _____

d. Inquire of management about the current status of litigation, claims, and assessments identified during the audit of the financial statements and consider obtaining updated legal letters from legal counsel. _____ _____

e. Consider whether there have been any changes in economic conditions or in the industry that could have a significant effect on the entity. _____ _____

f. Obtain written representations from appropriate officials as to whether any events occurred during the subsequent period that would require disclosure in the MD&A. _____ _____

	Performed By	Workpaper Reference

g.   Make additional inquiries or perform additional procedures that are deemed necessary depending on the results of the procedures described above.   _____   _____

26.   Obtain a letter of representations from management that addresses:

a.   Management's acknowledgment of its responsibility for the preparation of MD&A and management's assertion that the MD&A presentation has been prepared in accordance with the rules and regulations adopted by the SEC for MD&A. (For nonpublic entities, also obtain a written assertion that the presentation has been prepared using the rules and regulations adopted by the SEC.)   _____   _____

b.   That the historical financial amounts included in the MD&A have been accurately derived from the entity's financial statements.   _____   _____

c.   That the entity's underlying information, determinations, estimates, and assumptions of the entity provide a reasonable basis for the disclosures contained in the MD&A.   _____   _____

d.   That the entity has made available to the practitioner all significant documentation related to compliance with the SEC rules and regulations for MD&A.   _____   _____

e.   Completeness and availability of all minutes of meetings of stockholders, directors, and committees of directors.   _____   _____

f.   For public entities, that management has provided to the practitioner communications from the SEC concerning noncompliance with or deficiencies in MD&A reporting practices.   _____   _____

g.   Whether any events occurred subsequent to the latest balance sheet date that would require disclosure in the MD&A.   _____   _____

h.   If forward-looking information is included, a statement that:

   (1)   The forward-looking information is based on management's best estimate of expected events and operations, and is consistent with budgets, forecasts, or operating plans prepared for such periods.   _____   _____

   (2)   The accounting principles expected to be used for the forward-looking information are consistent with the principles used in preparing the historical financial statements.   _____   _____

   (3)   Management has provided the latest version of such budgets, forecasts, or operating plans, and has informed the practitioner of any anticipated changes or modifications to such information that could affect the disclosures contained in the MD&A presentation.   _____   _____

	Performed By	Workpaper Reference

i.   If voluntary information is included that is subject to the rules and regulations adopted by the SEC (e.g., information required by Item 305, *Quantitative and Qualitative Disclosures About Market Risk*), a statement that such voluntary information has been prepared in accordance with the related rules and regulations adopted by the SEC for such information.   _____   _____

j.   If pro forma information is included, a statement that:

   (1) Management is responsible for the assumptions used in determining the pro forma adjustments.   _____   _____

   (2) Management believes that the assumptions provide a reasonable basis for presenting all the significant effects directly attributable to the transaction or event, that the related pro forma adjustments give appropriate effect to those assumptions, and that the pro-forma column reflects the proper application of those adjustments to the historical financial statements.   _____   _____

   (3) Management believes that the significant effects directly attributable to the transaction or event are appropriately disclosed in the pro forma financial information.   _____   _____

ILLUSTRATION 5—COMPONENTS OF A PRACTITIONER'S REPORT ON AN EXAMINATION OF MD&A

The practitioner's report on an examination of MD&A should include the following:

1. A title that includes the word *independent.*

2. An identification of the MD&A presentation, including the period covered.

3. A statement that management is responsible for the preparation of the MD&A pursuant to the SEC rules and regulations, and a statement that the practitioner's responsibility is to express an opinion on the presentation based on his or her examination.

4. A reference to the auditor's report on the related financial statements, and if the report was other than a standard report, the substantive reasons therefor.

5. A statement that the examination was made in accordance with attestation standards established by the AICPA and a description of the scope of an examination of MD&A.

6. A statement that the practitioner believes that his or her examination provides a reasonable basis for his or her opinion.

7. A paragraph stating that:

    a. The preparation of MD&A requires management to interpret the criteria, make determinations as to the relevancy of information to be included, and make estimates and assumptions that affect reported information.

    b. Actual results in the future may differ materially from management's present assessment of information regarding the estimated future impact of transactions and events that have occurred or are expected to occur, expected sources of liquidity and capital resources, operating trends, commitments, and uncertainties.

8. If the entity is a nonpublic entity, a statement that, although the entity is not subject to the rules and regulations of the SEC, the MD&A presentation is intended to be a presentation in accordance with the SEC rules and regulations.

9. The practitioner's opinion on whether:

    a. The presentation includes, in all material respects, the required elements of the SEC rules and regulations.

    b. The historical financial amounts have been accurately derived, in all material respects, from the entity's financial statements.

    c. The underlying information, determinations, estimates, and assumptions of the entity provide a reasonable basis for the disclosures contained therein.

10. Manual or printed signature of the practitioner's firm.

11. Date of the examination report, which is the date as of the completion of the examination procedures (such date should not precede the date of the auditor's report on the latest historical financial statements covered by the MD&A).

ILLUSTRATION 6—STANDARD UNQUALIFIED EXAMINATION REPORT ON MD&A

Independent Accountant's Report

We have examined ABC Company's Management's Discussion and Analysis taken as a whole, included [*incorporated by reference*] in the Company's [insert *description of registration statement or document*]. Management is responsible for the preparation of the Company's Management's Discussion and Analysis pursuant to the rules and regulations adopted by the Securities and Exchange Commission. Our responsibility is to express an opinion on the presentation based on our examination. We have audited, in accordance with auditing standards generally accepted in the United States of America, the financial statements of ABC Company as of December 31, 20X2, and 20X1, and for each of the years in the three-year period ended December 31, 20X2, and in our report dated February 12, 20X3, we expressed an unqualified opinion on those financial statements.[1]

---

[1] If prior financial statements were audited by other auditors, this sentence would be replaced by the following:

    We have audited, in accordance with auditing standards generally accepted in the United States of America, the financial statements of ABC Company as of and for the year ended December 31, 20X2, and in our report dated February 12, 20X3, we expressed an unqualified opinion on those fi-

Our examination of Management's Discussion and Analysis was made in accordance with attestation standards established by the American Institute of Certified Public Accountants and, accordingly, included examining, on a test basis, evidence supporting the historical amounts and disclosures in the presentation. An examination also includes assessing the significant determinations made by management as to the relevancy of information to be included and the estimates and assumptions that affect reported information. We believe that our examination provides a reasonable basis for our opinion.

The preparation of Management's Discussion and Analysis requires management to interpret the criteria, make determinations as to the relevancy of information to be included, and make estimates and assumptions that affect reported information. Management's Discussion and Analysis includes information regarding the estimated future impact of transactions and events that have occurred or are expected to occur, expected sources of liquidity and capital resources, operating trends, commitments, and uncertainties. Actual results in the future may differ materially from management's present assessment of this information because events and circumstances frequently do not occur as expected.[2]

In our opinion, the Company's presentation of Management's Discussion and Analysis includes, in all material respects, the required elements of the rules and regulations adopted by the Securities and Exchange Commission; the historical financial amounts included therein have been accurately derived, in all material respects, from the Company's financial statements; and the underlying information, determinations, estimates, and assumptions of the Company provide a reasonable basis for the disclosures contained therein.

[*Signature*]

[*Date*]

ILLUSTRATION 7—EXAMINATION REPORT ON MD&A WITH A QUALIFIED OPINION DUE TO A MATERIAL OMISSION

Independent Accountant's Report

We have examined ABC Company's Management's Discussion and Analysis taken as a whole, included [*incorporated by reference*] in the Company's [*insert*

(Footnote Continued)

nancial statements. The financial statements of ABC Company as of December 31, 20X1, and for each of the years in the two-year period then ended were audited by other auditors, whose report dated January 30, 20X2, expressed an unqualified opinion on those financial statements.

If the practitioner's opinion on the financial statements is based on the report of other auditors, this sentence would be replaced by the following:

We have audited, in accordance with auditing standards generally accepted in the United States of America, the financial statements of ABC Company as of December 31, 20X2, and 20X1, and for each of the years in

the three-year period ended December 31, 20X2, and in our report dated February 12, 20X3, we expressed an unqualified opinion on those financial statements based on our audits and the report of other auditors.

[2] If the entity is a nonpublic entity, the following sentence should be added to the beginning of this explanatory paragraph:

Although ABC Company is not subject to the rules and regulations of the Securities and Exchange Commission, the accompanying Management's Discussion and Analysis is intended to be a presentation in accordance with the rules and regulations adopted by the Securities and Exchange Commission.

description of registration statement or document]. Management is responsible for the preparation of the Company's Management's Discussion and Analysis pursuant to the rules and regulations adopted by the Securities and Exchange Commission. Our responsibility is to express an opinion on the presentation based on our examination. We have audited, in accordance with auditing standards generally accepted in the United States of America, the financial statements of ABC Company as of December 31, 20X2, and 20X1, and for each of the years in the three-year period ended December 31, 20X2, and in our report dated February 12, 20X3, we expressed an unqualified opinion on those financial statements.

Our examination of Management's Discussion and Analysis was made in accordance with attestation standards established by the American Institute of Certified Public Accountants and, accordingly, included examining, on a test basis, evidence supporting the historical amounts and disclosures in the presentation. An examination also includes assessing the significant determinations made by management as to the relevancy of information to be included and the estimates and assumptions that affect reported information. We believe that our examination provides a reasonable basis for our opinion.

The preparation of Management's Discussion and Analysis requires management to interpret the criteria, make determinations as to the relevancy of information to be included, and make estimates and assumptions that affect reported information. Management's Discussion and Analysis includes information regarding the estimated future impact of transactions and events that have occurred or are expected to occur, expected sources of liquidity and capital resources, operating trends, commitments, and uncertainties. Actual results in the future may differ materially from management's present assessment of this information because events and circumstances frequently do not occur as expected.

Based on information furnished to us by management, we believe that the Company has excluded a discussion of the significant capital outlay required for its plans to expand into the telecommunications industry and the possible effects on the Company's financial condition, liquidity, and capital resources.

In our opinion, except for the omission of the matter described in the preceding paragraph, the Company's presentation of Management's Discussion and Analysis includes, in all material respects, the required elements of the rules and regulations adopted by the Securities and Exchange Commission; the historical financial amounts included therein have been accurately derived, in all material respects, from the Company's financial statements; and the underlying information, determinations, estimates, and assumptions of the Company provide a reasonable basis for the disclosures contained therein.

[*Signature*]

[*Date*]

ILLUSTRATION 8—EXAMINATION REPORT ON MD&A WITH A QUALIFIED OPINION WHEN OVERLY SUBJECTIVE ASSERTIONS ARE INCLUDED IN MD&A

Independent Accountant's Report

We have examined ABC Company's Management's Discussion and Analysis taken as a whole, included [*incorporated by reference*] in the Company's [*insert description of registration statement or document*]. Management is responsible for the preparation of the Company's Management's Discussion and Analysis pursuant to the rules and regulations adopted by the Securities and Exchange Commission. Our responsibility is to express an opinion on the presentation based on our examination. We have audited, in accordance with auditing standards generally accepted in the United States of America, the financial statements of ABC Company as of December 31, 20X2, and 20X1, and for each of the years in the three-year period ended December 31, 20X2, and in our report dated February 12, 20X3, we expressed an unqualified opinion on those financial statements.

Our examination of Management's Discussion and Analysis was made in accordance with attestation standards established by the American Institute of Certified Public Accountants and, accordingly, included examining, on a test basis, evidence supporting the historical amounts and disclosures in the presentation. An examination also includes assessing the significant determinations made by management as to the relevancy of information to be included and the estimates and assumptions that affect reported information. We believe that our examination provides a reasonable basis for our opinion.

The preparation of Management's Discussion and Analysis requires management to interpret the criteria, make determinations as to the relevancy of information to be included, and make estimates and assumptions that affect reported information. Management's Discussion and Analysis includes information regarding the estimated future impact of transactions and events that have occurred or are expected to occur, expected sources of liquidity and capital resources, operating trends, commitments, and uncertainties. Actual results in the future may differ materially from management's present assessment of this information because events and circumstances frequently do not occur as expected.

Based on information furnished to us by management, we believe that the underlying information, determinations, estimates, and assumptions used by management do not provide the company with a reasonable basis for the disclosure concerning [*describe*] in the Company's Management's Discussion and Analysis.

In our opinion, except for the disclosure regarding [*describe*] discussed in the preceding paragraph, the Company's presentation of Management's Discussion and Analysis includes, in all material respects, the required elements of the rules and regulations adopted by the Securities and Exchange Commission; the historical financial amounts included therein have been accurately derived, in all material respects, from the Company's financial statements; and the underlying information, determinations, estimates, and assumptions of the Company provide a reasonable basis for the disclosures contained therein.

[*Signature*]

[*Date*]

ILLUSTRATION 9—EXAMINATION REPORT ON MD&A WITH REFERENCE MADE TO THE REPORT OF ANOTHER PRACTITIONER

Independent Accountant's Report

We have examined ABC Company's Management's Discussion and Analysis taken as a whole, included [*incorporated by reference*] in the Company's [*insert description of registration statement or document*]. Management is responsible for the preparation of the Company's Management's Discussion and Analysis pursuant to the rules and regulations adopted by the Securities and Exchange Commission. Our responsibility is to express an opinion on the presentation based on our examination. We did not examine Management's Discussion and Analysis of DEF Corporation, a wholly-owned subsidiary, included in DEF Corporation's [*insert description of registration statement or document*]. Such Management's Discussion and Analysis was examined by other accountants, whose report has been furnished to us, and our opinion, insofar as it relates to information included for DEF Corporation, is based solely on the report of the other accountants.

We have audited, in accordance with auditing standards generally accepted in the United States of America, the consolidated financial statements of ABC Company as of December 31, 20X2, and 20X1, and for each of the years in the three-year period ended December 31, 20X2, and in our report dated February 12, 20X3, we expressed an unqualified opinion on those financial statements based on our audits and the report of other auditors.

Our examination of Management's Discussion and Analysis was made in accordance with attestation standards established by the American Institute of Certified Public Accountants and, accordingly, included examining, on a test basis, evidence supporting the historical amounts and disclosures in the presentation. An examination also includes assessing the significant determinations made by management as to the relevancy of information to be included and the estimates and assumptions that affect reported information. We believe that our examination and the report of the other accountants provide a reasonable basis for our opinion.

The preparation of Management's Discussion and Analysis requires management to interpret the criteria, make determinations as to the relevancy of information to be included, and make estimates and assumptions that affect reported information. Management's Discussion and Analysis includes information regarding the estimated future impact of transactions and events that have occurred or are expected to occur, expected sources of liquidity and capital resources, operating trends, commitments, and uncertainties. Actual results in the future may differ materially from management's present assessment of this information because events and circumstances frequently do not occur as expected.[3]

---

[3] If the entity is a nonpublic entity, the following sentence should be added to the beginning of the explanatory paragraph:

Although ABC Company is not subject to the rules and regulations of the Securities and Exchange Commission, the accompanying Management's Discussion and Analysis is intended to be a presentation in accordance with the rules and regulations adopted by the Securities and Exchange Commission.

In our opinion, based on our examination and the report of other accountants, the Company's presentation of Management's Discussion and Analysis included [*incorporated by reference*] in the Company's [*insert description of registration statement or document*] includes, in all material respects, the required elements of the rules and regulations adopted by the Securities and Exchange Commission; the historical financial amounts included therein have been accurately derived, in all material respects, from the Company's financial statements; and the underlying information, determinations, estimates, and assumptions of the Company provide a reasonable basis for the disclosures contained therein.

[*Signature*]

[*Date*]

ILLUSTRATION 10—PROCEDURES CHECKLIST FOR ENGAGEMENTS TO REVIEW MD&A

		Performed By	Workpaper Reference
1.	Consider whether management, and others involved in the preparation of MD&A (e.g., legal counsel), have appropriate knowledge of the SEC rules and regulations relating to MD&A.	_____	_____
2.	Obtain an understanding of the SEC rules and regulations for MD&A and management's method for the preparation of MD&A, and make inquiries about:		
a.	The sources of the information.	_____	_____
b.	How the information is gathered.	_____	_____
c.	How management evaluates the types of factors having a material effect on financial condition, results of operations, and cash flows.	_____	_____
d.	Whether there have been any changes in the procedures from the prior year.	_____	_____
3.	Develop an overall strategy for the expected scope and performance of the engagement, by considering factors such as the following:		
a.	The industry in which the entity operates and matters affecting the industry, such as financial reporting practices, economic conditions, laws and regulations, and technological changes.	_____	_____
b.	The entity's business, including its organization structure, operating characteristics, capital structure, and distribution methods.	_____	_____
c.	The types of relevant information that management reports to external analysts, e.g., press releases and presentations to lenders and rating agencies concerning past and future performance.	_____	_____
d.	The extent of management's knowledge of and experience with the SEC rules and regulations for MD&A.	_____	_____
e.	For nonpublic entities, the intended use of the MD&A presentation.	_____	_____

	Performed By	Workpaper Reference

f. Matters identified during the audit or review of the historical financial statements relating to MD&A reporting, including knowledge of the entity's internal control applicable to the preparation of MD&A and the extent of recent changes, if any. _____ _____

g. Matters identified during prior engagements to examine or review MD&A. _____ _____

h. Preliminary judgments about materiality. _____ _____

i. Any complex or subjective matters potentially material to the MD&A that may require specialized skill or knowledge. _____ _____

j. The presence of an internal audit function and the extent to which internal auditors are involved in directly testing the MD&A presentation or underlying records. _____ _____

4. Obtain a sufficient understanding of the entity's internal control applicable to the preparation of MD&A to:

a. Identify types of potential misstatements in MD&A, including types of material omissions, and consider the likelihood of their occurrence. _____ _____

b. Select the inquiries and analytical procedures that will provide a basis for reporting whether:

(1) The MD&A presentation does not include, in all material respects, the required elements of the rules and regulations adopted by the SEC, or the historical financial amounts included therein have not been accurately derived, in all material respects, from the entity's financial statements. _____ _____

(2) The underlying information, determinations, estimates, and assumptions of the entity do not provide a reasonable basis for the disclosures contained therein. _____ _____

5. Read the MD&A presentation and determine whether the information presented is consistent with the audited financial statements (or reviewed interim financial information if the MD&A includes interim information). _____ _____

6. Compare financial amounts to the audited or reviewed financial statements or related accounts and analyses. _____ _____

7. Recompute the increases, decreases, and percentages disclosed. _____ _____

8. Compare nonfinancial data to the audited or reviewed financial statements or, if inapplicable, to other records. _____ _____

9. Consider whether explanations presented in the MD&A are consistent with information obtained during the audit or the review of interim financial information; make further inquiries of management as necessary. _____ _____

	Performed By	Workpaper Reference

10. Obtain available prospective financial information (e.g., budgets, financial forecasts and projections) and compare such information to forward-looking MD&A disclosures; consider whether the underlying information, determinations, estimates, and assumptions do not provide a reasonable basis for the MD&A disclosures of trends, demands, commitments, events, or uncertainties.   _____   _____

11. Make inquiries of company officials responsible for operational, financial, and accounting matters about their future plans and expectations that could affect the entity's liquidity and capital resources.   _____   _____

12. Compare the information in the MD&A with the SEC rules and regulations.   _____   _____

13. Read the minutes of meetings of the board of directors and other significant committees to identify matters that may affect MD&A and consider whether such matters are appropriately addressed in the MD&A.   _____   _____

14. Inquire of management about the entity's prior experience with the SEC and the extent of comments received in connection with documents filed by the entity with the SEC; read related correspondence between the entity and the SEC.   _____   _____

15. Inquire of management regarding the nature of public communications (e.g., press releases, quarterly reports) dealing with historical and future results and consider whether the MD&A presentation is consistent with such communications.   _____   _____

16. If the MD&A presentation includes certain nonfinancial data (e.g., units produced, units sold, major customers, plant utilization, or square footage), inquire about whether the definitions used by management for such nonfinancial data are consistent between periods covered by the MD&A presentation.   _____   _____

17. Consider information about subsequent events after the end of the period addressed by MD&A and prior to the issuance of the report that may have a material effect on the entity's financial condition (including liquidity and capital resources), changes in financial condition, results of operations, and material commitments for capital resources. Events and matters that should be disclosed in the MD&A include those that:

   a. Are reasonably expected to have a material favorable or unfavorable impact on net sales or revenues or income from continuing operations.   _____   _____

   b. Are reasonably likely to result in a material increase or decrease in the entity's liquidity.   _____   _____

   c. Will have a material effect on the entity's capital resources.   _____   _____

   d. Would cause reported financial information not to be necessarily indicative of future operating results or of future financial condition.   _____   _____

	Performed By	Workpaper Reference

18. Perform the following subsequent events procedures:

   a. Read available minutes of meetings of stockholders, directors, and appropriate committees. _____ _____

   b. Inquire about any recent meetings for which minutes have not yet been prepared. When minutes have not been prepared, inquire of management about matters dealt with at such meetings, and obtain written representation from management regarding such matters. _____ _____

   c. Read the latest available interim financial statements and compare them with the financial statements for the periods covered by the MD&A. Pay special attention to major changes in the business or environment in which the client operates, and inquire of and discuss with management: _____ _____

     (1) Whether the interim financial statements have been prepared on the same basis as the current period audited financial statements. _____ _____

     (2) Whether there were any significant changes in the entity's operations, liquidity, or capital resources in the subsequent period. _____ _____

     (3) The current status of items in the financial statements for which the MD&A has been prepared, that were accounted for on the basis of tentative, preliminary, or inconclusive data. _____ _____

     (4) Whether any unusual adjustments were made during the period from the balance sheet date to the date of inquiry. _____ _____

   d. Inquire of management about the current status of litigation, claims, and assessments identified during the audit of the financial statements and consider obtaining updated legal letters from legal counsel. _____ _____

   e. Consider whether there have been any changes in economic conditions or in the industry that could have a significant effect on the entity. _____ _____

   f. Obtain written representations from appropriate officials as to whether any events occurred during the subsequent period that would require disclosure in the MD&A. _____ _____

   g. Make additional inquiries or perform additional procedures that are deemed necessary depending on the results of the procedures described above. _____ _____

19. Obtain a letter of representations from management that addresses:

	Performed By	Workpaper Reference

a. Management's acknowledgment of its responsibility for the preparation of MD&A and management's assertion that the MD&A presentation has been prepared in accordance with the rules and regulations adopted by the SEC for MD&A. (For nonpublic entities, also obtain a written assertion that the presentation has been prepared using the rules and regulations adopted by the SEC.)   ————   ————

b. That the historical financial amounts included in the MD&A have been accurately derived from the entity's financial statements.   ————   ————

c. That the entity's underlying information, determinations, estimates, and assumptions of the entity provide a reasonable basis for the disclosures contained in the MD&A.   ————   ————

d. That the entity has made available to the practitioner all significant documentation related to compliance with the SEC rules and regulations for MD&A.   ————   ————

e. Completeness and availability of all minutes of meetings of stockholders, directors, and committees of directors.   ————   ————

f. For public entities, that management has provided to the practitioner communications from the SEC concerning noncompliance with or deficiencies in MD&A reporting practices.   ————   ————

g. Whether any events occurred subsequent to the latest balance sheet date that would require disclosure in the MD&A.   ————   ————

h. If forward-looking information is included, a statement that:

(1) The forward-looking information is based on management's best estimate of expected events and operations, and is consistent with budgets, forecasts, or operating plans prepared for such periods.   ————   ————

(2) The accounting principles expected to be used for the forward-looking information are consistent with the principles used in preparing the historical financial statements.   ————   ————

(3) Management has provided the latest version of such budgets, forecasts, or operating plans, and has informed the practitioner of any anticipated changes or modifications to such information that could affect the disclosures contained in the MD&A presentation.   ————   ————

	Performed By	Workpaper Reference
i. If voluntary information is included that is subject to the rules and regulations adopted by the SEC (e.g., information required by Item 305, *Quantitative and Qualitative Disclosures About Market Risk*), a statement that such voluntary information has been prepared in accordance with the related rules and regulations adopted by the SEC for such information.	_____	_____
j. If pro forma information is included, a statement that:		
(1) Management is responsible for the assumptions used in determining the pro forma adjustments.	_____	_____
(2) Management believes that the assumptions provide a reasonable basis for presenting all the significant effects directly attributable to the transaction or event, that the related pro forma adjustments give appropriate effect to those assumptions, and that the pro forma column reflects the proper application of those adjustments to the historical financial statements.	_____	_____
(3) Management believes that the significant effects directly attributable to the transaction or event are appropriately disclosed in the pro forma financial information.	_____	_____

ILLUSTRATION 11—COMPONENTS OF A PRACTITIONER'S REPORT ON A REVIEW OF MD&A

The practitioner's report on a review of MD&A should include the following:

1. A title that includes the word *independent*.

2. An identification of the MD&A presentation, including the period covered.

3. A statement that management is responsible for the preparation of the MD&A pursuant to the rules and regulations adopted by the SEC.

4. A reference to the auditor's report on the related financial statements, and if the report was other than a standard report, the substantive reasons therefor.

5. A statement that the review was conducted in accordance with attestation standards established by the AICPA.

6. A description of the procedures for a review of MD&A.

7. A statement that a review of MD&A is substantially less in scope than an examination, the objective of which is an expression of opinion regarding the MD&A presentation, and accordingly, no such opinion is expressed.

8. A paragraph stating that:

a. The preparation of MD&A requires management to interpret the criteria, make determinations as to the relevancy of information to be included, and make estimates and assumptions that affect reported information.

b. Actual results in the future may differ materially from management's present assessment of information regarding the estimated future impact of transactions and events that have occurred or are expected to occur, expected sources of liquidity and capital resources, operating trends, commitments, and uncertainties.

9. If the entity is a nonpublic entity, a statement that, although the entity is not subject to the rules and regulations of the SEC, the MD&A presentation is intended to be a presentation in accordance with the rules and regulations adopted by the SEC.

10. A statement about whether any information came to the practitioner's attention that caused him or her to believe that:

a. The MD&A presentation does not include, in all material respects, the required elements of the rules and regulations adopted by the SEC.

b. The historical financial amounts included therein have not been accurately derived, in all material respects, from the entity's financial statements.

c. The underlying information, determinations, estimates, and assumptions of the entity do not provide a reasonable basis for the disclosures contained therein.

11. If the entity is a public entity, or a nonpublic entity that is making or has made an offering of securities and it appears that the securities may subsequently be registered or subject to a filing with the SEC or other regulatory agency, a statement of restrictions on the use of the report to specified parties because it is not intended to be filed with the SEC as a report under the 1933 Act or the 1934 Act.

12. Manual or printed signature of the practitioner's firm.

13. Date of the review report, which is the date as of the completion of the review procedures (such date should not precede the date of the practitioner's report on the latest historical financial statements covered by the MD&A).

ILLUSTRATION 12—STANDARD REVIEW REPORT ON AN ANNUAL MD&A PRESENTATION

Independent Accountant's Report

We have reviewed ABC Company's Management's Discussion and Analysis taken as a whole, included [*incorporated by reference*] in the Company's [*insert description of registration statement or document*]. Management is responsible for the preparation of the Company's Management's Discussion and Analysis pursuant to the rules and regulations adopted by the Securities and Exchange Commission. We have audited, in accordance with auditing standards generally accepted in the United States of America, the financial statements of ABC Company as of December 31, 20X2, and 20X1, and for each of the years in the three-year period ended December 31, 20X2, and in our report dated February 12, 20X3, we expressed an unqualified opinion on those financial statements.

We conducted our review of Management's Discussion and Analysis in accordance with attestation standards established by the American Institute of Certified Public Accountants. A review of Management's Discussion and Analysis consists principally of applying analytical procedures and making inquiries of persons responsible for financial, accounting, and operational matters. It is substantially less in scope than an examination, the objective of which is the expression of an opinion on the presentation. Accordingly, we do not express such an opinion.

The preparation of Management's Discussion and Analysis requires management to interpret the criteria, make determinations as to the relevancy of information to be included, and make estimates and assumptions that affect reported information. Management's Discussion and Analysis includes information regarding the estimated future impact of transactions and events that have occurred or are expected to occur, expected sources of liquidity and capital resources, operating trends, commitments, and uncertainties. Actual results in the future may differ materially from management's present assessment of this information because events and circumstances frequently do not occur as expected.[4]

Based on our review, nothing came to our attention that caused us to believe that the Company's presentation of Management's Discussion and Analysis does not include, in all material respects, the required elements of the rules and regulations adopted by the Securities and Exchange Commission, that the historical financial amounts included therein have not been accurately derived, in all material respects, from the Company's financial statements, or that the underlying information, determinations, estimates, and assumptions of the Company do not provide a reasonable basis for the disclosures contained therein.

This report is intended solely for the information and use of [*list or refer to specified parties*], and is not intended to be and should not be used by anyone other than the specified parties.

[*Signature*]

[*Date*]

ILLUSTRATION 13—STANDARD REVIEW REPORT ON AN INTERIM MD&A PRESENTATION

Independent Accountant's Report

We have reviewed ABC Company's Management's Discussion and Analysis taken as a whole, included in the Company's [*insert description of registration*

---

[4] If the entity is a nonpublic entity, the following sentence should be added to the beginning of this explanatory paragraph:

Although ABC Company is not subject to the rules and regulations of the Securities and Exchange Commission, the accompanying Management's Discussion and Analysis is intended to be a presentation in accordance with the rules and regulations adopted by the Securities and Exchange Commission.

statement or document]. Management is responsible for the preparation of the Company's Management's Discussion and Analysis pursuant to the rules and regulations adopted by the Securities and Exchange Commission. We have reviewed, in accordance with standards established by the American Institute of Certified Public Accountants, the interim financial information of ABC Company as of June 30, 20X3, and 20X2, and for the three-month and six-month periods then ended, and have issued our report thereon dated July 27, 20X3.

We conducted our review of Management's Discussion and Analysis in accordance with attestation standards established by the American Institute of Certified Public Accountants. A review of Management's Discussion and Analysis consists principally of applying analytical procedures and making inquiries of persons responsible for financial, accounting, and operational matters. It is substantially less in scope than an examination, the objective of which is the expression of an opinion on the presentation. Accordingly, we do not express such an opinion.

The preparation of Management's Discussion and Analysis requires management to interpret the criteria, make determinations as to the relevancy of information to be included, and make estimates and assumptions that affect reported information. Management's Discussion and Analysis includes information regarding the estimated future impact of transactions and events that have occurred or are expected to occur, expected sources of liquidity and capital resources, operating trends, commitments, and uncertainties. Actual results in the future may differ materially from management's present assessment of this information because events and circumstances frequently do not occur as expected.[5]

Based on our review, nothing came to our attention that caused us to believe that the Company's presentation of Management's Discussion and Analysis does not include, in all material respects, the required elements of the rules and regulations adopted by the Securities and Exchange Commission, that the historical financial amounts included therein have not been accurately derived, in all material respects, from the Company's financial statements, or that the underlying information, determinations, estimates, and assumptions of the Company do not provide a reasonable basis for the disclosures contained therein.

This report is intended solely for the information and use of [*list or refer to specified parties*], and is not intended to be and should not be used by anyone other than the specified parties.

[*Signature*]

[*Date*]

ILLUSTRATION 14—MODIFIED REVIEW REPORT ON AN MD&A PRESENTATION FOR A MATERIAL MISSTATEMENT

---

[5] If the entity is a nonpublic entity, the following sentence should be added to the beginning of this explanatory paragraph:

Although ABC Company is not subject to the rules and regulations of the Securities and Exchange Commission, the accompanying Management's Discussion and Analysis is intended to be a presentation in accordance with the rules and regulations adopted by the Securities and Exchange Commission.

Independent Accountant's Report

We have reviewed ABC Company's Management's Discussion and Analysis taken as a whole, included [*incorporated by reference*] in the Company's [*insert description of registration statement or document*]. Management is responsible for the preparation of the Company's Management's Discussion and Analysis pursuant to the rules and regulations adopted by the Securities and Exchange Commission. We have audited, in accordance with auditing standards generally accepted in the United States of America, the financial statements of ABC Company as of December 31, 20X2, and 20X1, and for each of the years in the three-year period ended December 31, 20X2, and in our report dated February 12, 20X3, we expressed an unqualified opinion on those financial statements.

We conducted our review of Management's Discussion and Analysis in accordance with attestation standards established by the American Institute of Certified Public Accountants. A review of Management's Discussion and Analysis consists principally of applying analytical procedures and making inquiries of persons responsible for financial, accounting, and operational matters. It is substantially less in scope than an examination, the objective of which is the expression of an opinion on the presentation. Accordingly, we do not express such an opinion.

The preparation of Management's Discussion and Analysis requires management to interpret the criteria, make determinations as to the relevancy of information to be included, and make estimates and assumptions that affect reported information. Management's Discussion and Analysis includes information regarding the estimated future impact of transactions and events that have occurred or are expected to occur, expected sources of liquidity and capital resources, operating trends, commitments, and uncertainties. Actual results in the future may differ materially from management's present assessment of this information because events and circumstances frequently do not occur as expected.[6]

Based on information furnished to us by management, we believe that the Company has excluded a discussion of the significant capital outlay required for its plans to expand into the telecommunications industry and the possible effects on the Company's financial condition, liquidity, and capital resources.

Based on our review, with the exception of the matter described in the preceding paragraph, nothing came to our attention that caused us to believe that the Company's presentation of Management's Discussion and Analysis does not include, in all material respects, the required elements of the rules and regulations adopted by the Securities and Exchange Commission, that the historical financial amounts included therein have not been accurately derived, in all material respects, from the Company's financial statements, or that the underly-

---

[6] If the entity is a nonpublic entity, the following sentence should be added to the beginning of this explanatory paragraph:

Although ABC Company is not subject to the rules and regulations of the Securities and Exchange Commission, the accompanying Management's Discussion and Analysis is intended to be a presentation in accordance with the rules and regulations adopted by the Securities and Exchange Commission.

ing information, determinations, estimates, and assumptions of the Company do not provide a reasonable basis for the disclosures contained therein.

This report is intended solely for the information and use of [*list or refer to specified parties*], and is not intended to be and should not be used by anyone other than the specified parties.

[*Signature*]

[*Date*]

ILLUSTRATION 15—COMBINED REPORT ON AN EXAMINATION OF AN ANNUAL MD&A PRESENTATION AND REVIEW OF MD&A FOR AN INTERIM PERIOD

Independent Accountant's Report

We have examined ABC Company's Management's Discussion and Analysis taken as a whole for the three-year period ended December 31, 20X2, included [*incorporated by reference*] in the Company's [*insert description of registration statement or document*]. Management is responsible for the preparation of the Company's Management's Discussion and Analysis pursuant to the rules and regulations adopted by the Securities and Exchange Commission. Our responsibility is to express an opinion on the annual presentation based on our examination. We have audited, in accordance with auditing standards generally accepted in the United States of America, the financial statements of ABC Company as of December 31, 20X2, and 20X1, and for each of the years in the three-year period ended December 31, 20X2, and in our report dated February 12, 20X3, we expressed an unqualified opinion on those financial statements.

Our examination of Management's Discussion and Analysis was conducted in accordance with attestation standards established by the American Institute of Certified Public Accountants and, accordingly, included examining, on a test basis, evidence supporting the historical amounts and disclosures in the presentation. An examination also includes assessing the significant determinations made by management as to the relevancy of information to be included and the estimates and assumptions that affect reported information. We believe that our examination provides a reasonable basis for our opinion.

The preparation of Management's Discussion and Analysis requires management to interpret the criteria, make determinations as to the relevancy of information to be included, and make estimates and assumptions that affect reported information. Management's Discussion and Analysis includes information regarding the estimated future impact of transactions and events that have occurred or are expected to occur, expected sources of liquidity and capital resources, operating trends, commitments, and uncertainties. Actual results in the future may differ materially from management's present assessment of this information because events and circumstances frequently do not occur as expected.[7]

---

[7] If the entity is a nonpublic entity, the following sentence should be added to the beginning of this explanatory paragraph:

Although ABC Company is not subject to the rules and regulations of the Securities and Exchange Commission, the accompanying Management's Discussion and Analysis is

In our opinion, the Company's presentation of Management's Discussion and Analysis for the three-year period ended December 31, 20X2, includes, in all material respects, the required elements of the rules and regulations adopted by the Securities and Exchange Commission; the historical financial amounts included therein have been accurately derived, in all material respects, from the Company's financial statements; and the underlying information, determinations, estimates, and assumptions of the Company provide a reasonable basis for the disclosures contained therein.

We have also reviewed ABC Company's Management's Discussion and Analysis taken as a whole for the six-month period ended June 30, 20X3, included [*incorporated by reference*] in the Company's [*insert description of registration statement or document*]. We have reviewed, in accordance with standards established by the American Institute of Certified Public Accountants, the interim financial information of ABC Company as of June 30, 20X3, and 20X2, and for the six-month periods then ended, and have issued our report thereon dated July 27, 20X3.

We conducted our review of Management's Discussion and Analysis in accordance with attestation standards established by the American Institute of Certified Public Accountants. A review of Management's Discussion and Analysis consists principally of applying analytical procedures and making inquiries of persons responsible for financial, accounting, and operational matters. It is substantially less in scope than an examination, the objective of which is the expression of an opinion on the presentation. Accordingly, we do not express such an opinion.

Based on our review, nothing came to our attention that caused us to believe that the Company's presentation of Management's Discussion and Analysis for the six-month period ended June 30, 20X3, does not include, in all material respects, the required elements of the rules and regulations adopted by the Securities and Exchange Commission, that the historical financial amounts included therein have not been accurately derived, in all material respects, from the Company's unaudited interim financial statements, or that the underlying information, determinations, estimates, and assumptions of the Company do not provide a reasonable basis for the disclosures contained therein.

This report is intended solely for the information and use of [*list or refer to specified parties*], and is not intended to be and should not be used by anyone other than the specified parties.

[*Signature*]

[*Date*]

ILLUSTRATION 16—REVIEW REPORT ON A COMBINED ANNUAL AND INTERIM MD&A PRESENTATION

Independent Accountant's Report

(Footnote Continued)

intended to be a presentation in accordance with the rules and regulations adopted by the Securities and Exchange Commission.

We have reviewed ABC Company's Management's Discussion and Analysis taken as a whole, included [*incorporated by reference*] in the Company's [*insert description of registration statement or document*]. Management is responsible for the preparation of the Company's Management's Discussion and Analysis pursuant to the rules and regulations adopted by the Securities and Exchange Commission. We have audited, in accordance with auditing standards generally accepted in the United States of America, the financial statements of ABC Company as of December 31, 20X2, and 20X1, and for each of the years in the three-year period ended December 31, 20X2, and in our report dated February 12, 20X3, we expressed an unqualified opinion on those financial statements. We have reviewed, in accordance with standards established by the American Institute of Certified Public Accountants, the interim financial information of ABC Company as of June 30, 20X3, and 20X2, and for the six-month periods then ended, and have issued our report thereon dated July 27, 20X3.

We conducted our review of Management's Discussion and Analysis in accordance with attestation standards established by the American Institute of Certified Public Accountants. A review of Management's Discussion and Analysis consists principally of applying analytical procedures and making inquiries of persons responsible for financial, accounting, and operational matters. It is substantially less in scope than an examination, the objective of which is the expression of an opinion on the presentation. Accordingly, we do not express such an opinion.

The preparation of Management's Discussion and Analysis requires management to interpret the criteria, make determinations as to the relevancy of information to be included, and make estimates and assumptions that affect reported information. Management's Discussion and Analysis includes information regarding the estimated future impact of transactions and events that have occurred or are expected to occur, expected sources of liquidity and capital resources, operating trends, commitments, and uncertainties. Actual results in the future may differ materially from management's present assessment of this information because events and circumstances frequently do not occur as expected.[8]

Based on our review, nothing came to our attention that caused us to believe that the Company's presentation of Management's Discussion and Analysis does not include, in all material respects, the required elements of the rules and regulations adopted by the Securities and Exchange Commission, that the historical financial amounts included therein have not been accurately derived, in all material respects, from the Company's financial statements, or that the underlying information, determinations, estimates, and assumptions of the Company do not provide a reasonable basis for the disclosures contained therein.

---

[8] If the entity is a nonpublic entity, the following sentence should be added to the beginning of the explanatory paragraph:

Although ABC Company is not subject to the rules and regulations of the Securities and Exchange Commission, the accompanying Management's Discussion and Analysis is intended to be a presentation in accordance with the rules and regulations adopted by the Securities and Exchange Commission.

This report is intended solely for the information and use of [*list or refer to specified parties*], and is not intended to be and should not be used by anyone other than the specified parties.

[*Signature*]

[*Date*]

AT SECTION 801
REPORTING ON CONTROLS AT A SERVICE ORGANIZATION

PRACTICE POINT: In April 2010, the American Institute of Certified Public Accountants' (AICPA's) Auditing Standards Board (ASB) issued Statement on Standards for Attestation Engagements (SSAE) No. 16, "Reporting on Controls at a Service Organization," which contains the requirements and guidance for a service auditor reporting on a service organization's controls. Prior to the issuance of SSAE-16, Statement on Auditing Standards (SAS) No. 70 (AU Section 324), "Service Organizations," contained guidance for auditors auditing the financial statements of entities that use a service organization ("user auditors") and for auditors reporting on controls at a service organization ("service auditors"). The ASB, as part of its project to converge audit, attest, and quality control standards with those of the International Auditing and Assurance Standards Board (IAASB), decided that the guidance for service auditors in SAS-70 (AU Section 324) should be moved to the SSAEs (attestation standards), and the guidance for user auditors should be retained in the SASs (auditing standards). Accordingly, SSAE-16 only contains guidance for service auditors reporting on controls at a service organization and supersedes the guidance for service auditors in SAS-70 (AU Section 324). Guidance for user auditors is contained in a new clarified SAS, "Audit Considerations Relating to an Entity Using a Service Organization," as part of the Clarity Project, which will supersede the guidance for user auditors in SAS-70 (AU Section 324).

SSAE-16 is based on the IAASB's International Standard on Assurance Engagements (ISAE) No. 3402, "Assurance Reports on Controls at a Service Organization." The following are some of the more significant changes in the requirements for a service auditor's engagement introduced by SSAE-16:

- In a type 2 engagement (i.e., a service auditor's report on the fairness of the presentation of management's description of the service organization's system and the suitability of the design and operating effectiveness of controls), the description of the service organization's system and the service auditor's opinion on the description will cover a specified *period*. In SAS-70, the description of the service organization's system in a type 2 report was as of a specified *date*, rather than for a period.

- Management of the service organization is now required to provide the service auditor with a written assertion about the following matters:

  — The fairness of the presentation of the description of the service organization's system;

  — The suitability of the design of the controls to achieve the related control objectives stated in the service organization's description; and

  — In a type 2 engagement, the operating effectiveness of those controls to achieve the related control objectives stated in the service organization's description.

- The service auditor may not use evidence obtained in prior engagements about the satisfactory operation of controls in prior periods to provide a basis for a reduction in testing, even if it is supplemented with evidence obtained during the current period.

- The service auditor is required to identify in the description of tests of controls any tests of controls performed by internal auditors and the service auditor's procedures with respect to that work.

SSAE-16 is effective for service auditors' reports for periods ending on or after June 15, 2011, with earlier application permitted.

The provisions and requirements of SSAE-16, which is codified in AT Section 801 (Reporting on Controls at a Service Organization), are discussed in more detail below.

WHAT EVERY PRACTITIONER SHOULD KNOW

Scope and Objectives

Many entities outsource business tasks or functions to other entities. AT Section 801 is applicable when an entity outsources a business task or function to another entity and the data resulting from that task or function is incorporated in the outsourcer's financial statements. For purposes of AT Section 801, an entity that performs a specialized task or function for other entities is known as a *service organization* and an entity that outsources the task or function to a service organization is known as a *user entity*. The following are examples of service organizations:

- An investment adviser that invests assets for user entities, maintains the accountability for those assets, and provides statements to user entities that contain information that is incorporated in the user entities' financial statements (e.g., the fair value of exchange-traded securities, or dividend and interest income).

- An entity that provides payroll processing and related payroll tax administration.

- An entity that processes medical claims for health insurance companies.

- A data center that provides applications and technology that enable user entities to process financial transactions.

One way a user auditor may obtain evidence about the quality and accuracy of the data provided to a user entity by a service organization is to obtain a service auditor's report on controls at the service organization that affect data provided to the user entities and incorporated in the user entities' financial statements.

Types of service auditors' reports   AT Section 801 enables service auditors to provide the following two types of reports:

1. *Type 1 report—A report on management's description of a service organization's system and the suitability of the design of controls.* In a type 1 report, the service auditor expresses an opinion on whether:

   a. Management's description of the service organization's system fairly presents the system that was designed and implemented as of a specified date; and

    b. The controls related to the control objectives stated in management's description of the service organization's system were suitably designed to achieve those control objectives as of the specified date.

2. *Type 2 report—A report on management's description of a service organization's system and the suitability of the design and operating effectiveness of controls.* In a type 2 report, the service auditor expresses an opinion on whether:

    a. Management's description of the service organization's system fairly presents the system that was designed and implemented throughout the specified period;

    b. The controls related to the control objectives stated in management's description of the service organization's system were suitably designed throughout the specified period to achieve those control objectives; and

    c. The controls related to the control objectives stated in management's description of the service organization's system operated effectively throughout the specified period to achieve those control objectives.

Also, in a type 2 report, the service auditor's report includes a description of the tests of controls and the results thereof.

Acceptance and Continuance of Engagements to Report on Controls at a Service Organization

The service auditor should accept or continue an engagement to report on controls at a service organization only if all of the following conditions are met:

- The service auditor has the capability and competence to perform the engagement;
- The criteria to be used will be suitable and available to the intended user entities and their auditors;
- The service auditor will have access to sufficient, appropriate evidence;
- The scope of the engagement and the description of the service organization's system will not be so limited that they are unlikely to be useful to user entities and their auditors;
- Management of the service organization acknowledges and accepts its responsibility to:
  - Prepare the description of the service organization's system and the assertion, including their completeness, accuracy, and method of presentation;
  - Have a reasonable basis for its assertion;
  - Select the criteria to be used and state them in the assertion;
  - Specify the control objectives and state them in the description of the service organization's system;

— Identify in the description of the service organization's system the party specifying the control objectives when the control objectives are specified by law, regulation, or another party;

— Identify the risks that threaten the achievement of the control objectives stated in management's description;

— Design, implement, and document controls that are suitably designed and operating effectively to provide reasonable assurance that the control objectives stated in management's description will be achieved;

— Provide the service auditor with (1) access to all relevant information of which management is aware; (2) additional information that the service auditor may request from management; (3) unrestricted access to personnel within the service organization; and (4) written representations at the conclusion of the engagement; and

— Provide a written assertion that will be included in or attached to management's description of the service organization's system, and provided to user entities.

PRACTICE POINT: Illustrations 1 and 2 below provide examples of assertions by management of a service organization for a type 1 and type 2 report, respectively.

PRACTICE POINT: If management refuses to provide the service auditor with a written assertion, then a scope limitation exists and the service auditor should withdraw from the engagement. However, if law or regulation precludes the service auditor from withdrawing from the engagement, then the service auditor should disclaim an opinion.

In addition, if management refuses to provide the service auditor with a written assertion, the service auditor is prohibited from performing an engagement to report on controls at a service organization under AT Section 101 (Attest Engagements).

Considerations when management requests a change in the scope of the engagement Before the completion of the engagement, management may request a change in the scope of the engagement. Before agreeing to the change, the service auditor should be satisfied that management has a reasonable justification for the change. For example, management's request to change the scope of the engagement may not have a reasonable justification if the request is made to exclude certain control objectives at the service organization because of the likelihood that the service auditor's opinion would be modified with respect to those control objectives.

Assessing Whether Management Has Used Suitable Criteria

AT Section 801 requires the service auditor to assess whether management has used suitable criteria in:

1. *Preparing the description of the service organization's system.* In making this assessment, the service auditor should determine if the criteria include, at a minimum, whether management's description of the service organization's system:

   a. Presents how the service organization's system was designed and implemented, including (if applicable):

      (1) The types of services provided;

      (2) The classes of transactions processed;

      (3) The procedures within both automated and manual systems by which services are provided and by which transactions are initiated, authorized, recorded, processed, corrected (as necessary), and transferred to the reports and other information prepared for user entities;

      (4) The related accounting records and supporting information involved in initiating, authorizing, recording, processing, and reporting transactions;

      (5) How the service organization's system captures and addresses significant events and conditions (other than transactions);

      (6) The process used to prepare reports and other information for user entities;

      (7) The specified control objectives and controls designed to achieve those objectives, including complementary user entity controls contemplated in the design of the service organization's controls; and

      (8) Other aspects of the service organization's control environment, risk assessment process, information and communication systems, control activities, and monitoring controls that are relevant to the services provided.

   b. Includes relevant details of changes to the service organization's system during the period covered by the description (in the case of a type 2 report).

   c. Does not omit or distort information relevant to the service organization's system, while acknowledging that the description of the service organization's system is prepared to meet the common needs of a broad range of user entities and their auditors.

2. *Evaluating whether controls were suitably designed to achieve the control objectives stated in management's description.* In making this assessment, the service auditor should determine if the criteria include, at a minimum, whether:

   a. Management has identified the risks that threaten the achievement of the control objectives stated in its description of the service organization's system.

b. The identified controls would, if operating as described, provide reasonable assurance that those risks would not prevent the control objectives stated in the description from being achieved.

3. *In a type 2 report, evaluating whether controls operated effectively throughout the specified period to achieve the control objectives stated in management's description.* In making this assessment, the service auditor should determine if the criteria include, at a minimum, whether the controls were consistently applied as designed, including whether manual controls were applied by individuals who have the appropriate competence and authority.

Materiality Considerations

In an engagement to report on controls at a service organization, the concept of materiality relates to the information being reported on, not to the financial statements of user entities. Materiality regarding the fair presentation of management's description of the service organization's system and regarding the design of controls primarily includes the consideration of qualitative factors, for example, whether management's description omits or misrepresents relevant information. Materiality regarding the operating effectiveness of controls includes the consideration of both quantitative and qualitative factors, for example, (1) the tolerable rate and observed rate of deviation (a quantitative matter) and (2) the nature and cause of any observed deviations (a qualitative matter).

AT Section 801 requires the service auditor to evaluate materiality with respect to the following:

- The fair presentation of management's description of the service organization's system;

- The suitability of the design of controls to achieve the related control objectives stated in management's description; and

- In a type 2 report, the operating effectiveness of the controls.

Requisite Understanding and Evidence to Report on Controls at a Service Organization

In a type 1 or type 2 engagement, the service auditor should perform the following procedures in order to obtain an understanding of the service organization's system, evidence regarding management's description of that system, and evidence regarding the design of controls:

- Obtain an understanding of the service organization's system, including controls that are included in the scope of the engagement. The service auditor's procedures to obtain this understanding may include inquiries of management and others within the service organization; observing operations; inspecting documents, reports, and agreements; and reperforming the application of a control.

- Obtain and read management's description of the service organization's system, and evaluate whether those aspects of the description that are included in the scope of the engagement are presented fairly. Specifically, the service auditor should evaluate whether:

— The control objectives stated in management's description are reasonable;

— The controls identified in management's description were implemented;

— Any complementary user entity controls are adequately described; and

— Services performed by a subservice organization, if any, are adequately described, including whether the inclusive method or the carve-out method has been used in relation to them.

PRACTICE POINT: AT Section 801 defines the carve-out method and the inclusive method as follows:

Carve-out method—Method of addressing the services provided by a subservice organization, whereby management's description of the service organization's system identifies the nature of the services performed by the subservice organization and excludes from the description and from the scope of the service auditor's engagement, the subservice organization's relevant control objectives and related controls. Management's description of the service organization's system and the scope of the service auditor's engagement include controls at the service organization that monitor the effectiveness of controls at the subservice organization, which may include management of the service organization's review of a service auditor's report on controls at the subservice organization.

Inclusive method—Method of addressing the services provided by a subservice organization, whereby management's description of the service organization's system includes a description of the nature of the services provided by the subservice organization as well as the subservice organization's relevant control objectives and related controls.

• Determine whether the service organization's system described in management's description has been implemented, which should be made through inquiries, observation, and inspection.

• Determine which of the controls at the service organization are necessary to achieve the control objectives stated in the description of the service organization's system and assess whether such controls were suitably designed to achieve the control objectives by:

— Identifying the risks that threaten the achievement of the control objectives stated in the description; and

— Evaluating the linkage of the controls identified in the description with those risks.

Additional procedures required regarding the operating effectiveness of controls in a type 2 engagement In addition to the preceding required procedures, when performing a type 2 engagement, the service auditor should obtain evidence regarding the operating effectiveness of controls by performing the following procedures:

- Test those controls that the service auditor has determined are necessary to achieve the control objectives stated in the description of the service organization's system and assess their operating effectiveness throughout the period. (*Note:* Evidence obtained by service auditors in prior engagements about the satisfactory operation of controls in prior periods does not provide a basis for a reduction in testing in the current period, even if supplemented with evidence obtained during the current period.) When designing and performing tests of controls, the service auditor should:

  - Perform other procedures in combination with inquiry to obtain evidence about: (a) how the control was applied; (b) the consistency with which the control was applied; and (c) by whom or by what means the control was applied;

  - Determine whether the controls to be tested depend on other controls and, if applicable, whether it is necessary to obtain evidence supporting the operating effectiveness of those other controls; and

  - Determine an effective method for selecting the items to be tested to meet the objectives of the test.

- Consider, in connection with determining the extent of tests of controls and whether sampling is appropriate, the following: (a) the characteristics of the population of the controls to be tested; (b) the nature of the controls; (c) the frequency of their application (e.g., monthly, daily); and (d) the expected rate of deviation.

- Investigate the nature and cause of any deviations identified and consider whether the deviations may be the result of intentional acts by service organization personnel. If any identified deviations have resulted from intentional acts by service organization personnel, the service auditor should assess the risk that management's description of the service organization's system is not fairly presented, the controls are not suitably designed, and the controls are not operating effectively. When addressing the nature and cause of deviations, the service auditor should determine whether:

  - Identified deviations are within the expected rate of deviation and are acceptable;

  - Additional testing of the control or of other controls is necessary; and

  - The testing that has been performed provides an appropriate basis for concluding that the control did not operate effectively throughout the specified period.

- Inquire about changes in the service organization's controls that were implemented during the period covered by the service auditor's report, and:

  - If the changes were deemed significant, they should be included in the description of the service organization's system.

— If the changes that were deemed significant are not included in the description of the service organization's system, the service auditor should describe the changes in, and determine their effect on, his or her report.

— If the superseded controls are relevant to the achievement of the control objectives stated in the description of the service organization's system, the service auditor should test the superseded controls before the change. If it is not possible to test the superseded controls, the service auditor should determine the effect on his or her report.

Using the Work of the Internal Audit Function

The service auditor should obtain an understanding of the aspects of the internal audit function, if any, that are relevant to the engagement. Such understanding should encompass the nature of the internal audit function's responsibilities and of the activities it performs in order to determine its relevance to the engagement. Also, when the service auditor intends to use the work of the internal audit function, he or she should evaluate:

- The competence and objectivity of the members of the internal audit function;
- Whether the internal audit function's work is likely to be undertaken with due professional care;
- Whether it is likely that effective communication will occur between the internal audit function and the service auditor;
- The effect of any constraints or restrictions that the service organization places on the internal audit function;
- The nature and scope of specific work performed, or to be performed, by the internal audit function and the significance of that work to the service auditor's conclusions; and
- The degree of subjectivity involved in the evaluation of the evidence gathered

In addition, when the service auditor uses specific work of the internal audit function, the service auditor should perform procedures on that work and evaluate its adequacy. When making this assessment, the service auditor should evaluate the following:

- Whether the work was performed by persons having adequate technical training and proficiency;
- Whether the work was properly supervised, reviewed, and documented;
- Whether the evidence obtained was sufficient and appropriate to enable the internal audit function to draw reasonable conclusions;
- Whether conclusions reached are appropriate in the circumstances, and any reports prepared are consistent with the results of the work performed; and
- Whether any exceptions or unusual matters disclosed by the internal audit function are properly resolved.

Effect of the use of the work of the internal audit function on the service auditor's report AT Section 801 indicates that if the service auditor uses specific work of the internal audit function, the service auditor should not make any reference to that work in his or her auditor's report. However, in a type 2 report, if the service auditor has used the work of the internal audit function in performing tests of controls, the service auditor's description of tests of controls and results thereof should include a description of (a) the internal auditor's work, and (b) the service auditor's procedures with respect to that work.

Obtaining Written Representations from Management

AT Section 801 requires the service auditor to obtain a written representation letter from the service organization's management, as of the same date as the date of the service auditor's report, that includes the following items:

- A statement indicating that management reaffirms its assertion included in or attached to the description of the service organization's system;
- An affirmation that management has provided the service auditor with all the relevant information and agreed access; and
- A statement that management has disclosed to the service auditor any of the following items of which it is aware:
  — Instances of noncompliance with laws and regulations;
  — Uncorrected errors;
  — Knowledge of any actual, suspected, or alleged intentional acts by the service organization's management or employees (e.g., overrides of controls or misappropriation of user entity assets) that could adversely affect the fairness of the presentation of the description of the service organization's system or the completeness or achievement of the control objectives stated in the description;
  — Design deficiencies in controls;
  — Instances when controls have not operated as described; and
  — Any subsequent events that could have a significant effect on management's assertion.

Also, the service auditor should obtain these written representations from management of the subservice organization, if a service organization uses a subservice organization and the description of the service organization's system uses the inclusive method.

Management's refusal to provide the required representations If management does not provide one or more of the required written representations, AT Section 801 states that the service auditor should:

- Discuss the matter with management;
- Evaluate the effect of management's refusal on the service auditor's assessment of the integrity of management and on the reliability of management's representations and evidence in general; and
- Take appropriate actions, which may include disclaiming an opinion or withdrawing from the engagement.

In addition, AT Section 801 indicates that the service auditor should disclaim an opinion or withdraw from the engagement if management refuses to (1) reaffirm its assertion included in or attached to the description of the service organization's system, and (2) represent that it has provided the service auditor with all the relevant information and agreed access.

Service Auditor's Responsibility for Other Information Included in a Document Containing Management's Description of the Service Organization's System and the Service Auditor's Report

Other information may be included in a document containing management's description of the service organization's system and the service auditor's report. For example:

- Information is provided by the service organization and is included in a section of the service auditor's report.
- Information outside the service auditor's report is included in a document that contains the service auditor's report.

In such circumstances, the service auditor should read the other information to identify material inconsistencies, if any, with management's description of the service organization's system. Also, while reading the other information, the service auditor may become aware of an apparent misstatement of fact in the other information. If the service auditor becomes aware of a material inconsistency or an apparent misstatement of fact in the other information, the service auditor should discuss the matter with management and request that the information be corrected. If management refuses to correct it, the service auditor should take further appropriate action (*Note*: AT Section 101, paragraphs .91–.94, addresses the practitioner's additional responsibility in such circumstances).

Subsequent Events

The service auditor should inquire of management whether it is aware of any events subsequent to the period covered by its description of the service organization's system up to the date of the service auditor's report that could have a significant effect on management's assertion. If the service auditor becomes aware of such an event or any other event that is of such a nature and significance that its disclosure is necessary to prevent the service auditor's report from being misleading, the service auditor should determine that information about that event is disclosed by management in its description. If information about that event is not disclosed by management in its description, the service auditor should disclose such event in his or her report.

After the release of the service auditor's report, the service auditor may become aware of conditions that existed at the report date that might have affected management's assertion and the service auditor's report had the service auditor been aware of them. In such circumstances, the service auditor should evaluate the subsequently discovered information by adapting and applying the guidance in AU Section 561 (Subsequent Discovery of Facts Existing at the Date of the Auditor's Report).

Documentation Requirements

AT Section 801 indicates that the service auditor should prepare documentation that would enable an experienced service auditor, having no previous connection with the engagement, to understand the following:

- The nature, timing, and extent of the procedures performed, including the following:
  - The identifying characteristics of the specific items or matters tested;
  - Who performed the procedures and the date such procedures were completed; and
  - Who reviewed the work performed and the date and extent of such review.
- The results of the procedures performed and the evidence obtained.
- Significant matters arising during the engagement, the conclusions reached, and significant professional judgments made in reaching those conclusions.
- If work of the internal audit function was used, the service auditor's conclusions regarding the evaluation of the adequacy of the work of the internal audit function and the procedures the service auditor performed on that work.
- Discussions of significant findings or issues with the service organization's management and others, including when and with whom the discussions took place and the nature of the significant findings or issues discussed.
- If information regarding a significant finding or issue was identified that is inconsistent with the service auditor's final conclusion, how the service auditor addressed the inconsistency in forming the final conclusion.

The engagement documentation should be assembled in an engagement file on a timely basis, no later than 60 days following the service auditor's report release date. Once the assembly of the final engagement file has been completed, the service auditor should not delete or discard documentation before the end of its retention period.

If the service auditor finds it necessary to modify the engagement documentation or add new documentation after the assembly of the final engagement file, the service auditor should document the following:

- The specific reasons for making the changes;
- When and by whom the changes were made; and
- When and by whom the changes were reviewed.

The Service Auditor's Report

The following is a summary of the elements that should be included in a service auditor's type 1 and type 2 reports under AT Section 801.

		Type 1 Report	Type 2 Report
1.	A title that includes the word "independent."	Yes	Yes
2.	An addressee.	Yes	Yes
3.	Identification of management's description of the service organization's system and the function performed by the system.	Yes	Yes
4.	Identification of any parts of management's description of the service organization's system that are not covered by the service auditor's report.	Yes	Yes
5.	Identification of any information included in a document containing the service auditor's report that is not covered by the service auditor's report.	Yes	Yes
6.	Identification of the criteria.	Yes	Yes
7.	Identification of any services performed by a subservice organization and whether the carve-out method or the inclusive method was used in relation to them, and:	Yes	Yes
a.	If the carve-out method was used, a statement that management's description of the service organization's system excludes the control objectives and related controls at relevant subservice organizations, and that the service auditor's procedures do not extend to the subservice organization.	Yes	Yes
b.	If the inclusive method was used, a statement that management's description of the service organization's system includes the subservice organization's specified control objectives and related controls, and that the service auditor's procedures included procedures related to the subservice organization.	Yes	Yes
8.	If management's description of the service organization's system refers to the need for complementary user entity controls, a statement that (1) the service auditor has not evaluated the suitability of the design or operating effectiveness of complementary user entity controls, and (2) the control objectives stated in the description can be achieved only if complementary user entity controls are suitably designed and operating effectively, along with the controls at the service organization.	Yes	Yes
9.	A reference to management's assertion and a description of management's responsibilities.	Yes	Yes
10.	A description of the service auditor's responsibilities.	Yes	Yes
11.	A statement that the examination engagement was conducted in accordance with the AICPA's attestation standards and a description of the related objectives, requirements, and procedures to obtain reasonable assurance in order to provide a basis for the service auditor's opinion.	Yes	Yes
12.	A statement that the service auditor has not performed any procedures regarding the operating effectiveness of controls and, therefore, expresses no opinion thereon.	Yes	No

	Type 1 Report	Type 2 Report
13. A statement that the examination engagement included testing the operating effectiveness of those controls that the service auditor considers necessary to provide reasonable assurance that the stated control objectives were achieved.	No	Yes
14. A statement about the inherent limitations of controls at the service organization and of the risk of projecting to the future:	Yes	Yes
a. Any evaluation of the fairness of the presentation of management's description of the service organization's system.	Yes	Yes
b. Conclusions about the suitability of the design of controls.	Yes	Yes
c. Conclusions about the operating effectiveness of controls.	No	Yes
15. The service auditor's opinion on whether, in all material respects, based on the criteria described in management's assertion:		
a. Management's description of the service organization's system fairly presents the service organization's system that was designed and implemented ("*as of the specified date*" in a type 1 report; "*throughout the specified period*" in a type 2 report).	Yes	Yes
b. The controls related to the control objectives stated in management's description of the service organization's system were suitably designed to provide reasonable assurance that those control objectives would be achieved if the controls operated effectively ("*as of the specified date*" in a type 1 report; "*throughout the specified period*" in a type 2 report). (*Note*: Modifying language should be added if the application of complementary user entity controls is necessary to achieve the described control objectives.)	Yes	Yes
c. The controls the service auditor tested operated effectively throughout the specified period. (*Note*: Modifying language should be added if the application of complementary user entity controls is necessary to achieve the described control objectives.)	No	Yes
16. A reference to a description of the service auditor's tests of controls and the results thereof.	No	Yes
17. A statement restricting the use the service auditor's report to (1) management of the service organization; (2) user entities of the service organization's system ("*as of the end of the period covered by the service auditor's report*" in a type 1 report; "*during some or all of the period covered by the service auditor's report*" in a type 2 report); and (3) the auditors of such user entities.	Yes	Yes

	Type 1 Report	Type 2 Report
18. The date of the service auditor's report.	Yes	Yes
19. The name of the service auditor and the city and state where the service auditor maintains the office that has responsibility for the engagement.	Yes	Yes

Service auditor's report date The service auditor's report date should not be earlier than the date on which he or she has obtained sufficient appropriate evidence to support the service auditor's opinion.

Modified service auditor's opinions AT Section 801 states that the service auditor should modify his or her opinion and include a clear description of all the reasons for the modification under *any* of the following circumstances:

- The service auditor concludes that management's description of the service organization's system is not fairly presented, in all material respects;
- The service auditor believes the controls are not suitably designed to provide reasonable assurance that the control objectives stated in management's description of the service organization's system would be achieved if the controls operated as described;
- The service auditor is unable to obtain sufficient appropriate evidence; or
- In a type 2 report, the controls did not operate effectively throughout the specified period to achieve the related control objectives stated in management's description of the service organization's system.

Disclaimer of opinion There may be circumstances under which the auditor may not be able to obtain sufficient appropriate evidence and, based on the limited procedures performed, has concluded that:

- Certain aspects of management's description of the service organization's system are not fairly presented, in all material respects;
- Certain controls were not suitably designed to provide reasonable assurance that the stated control objectives would be achieved if the controls operated as described; *or*
- In a type 2 report, certain controls did not operate effectively throughout the specified period to achieve the stated control objectives.

If the service auditor plans to disclaim an opinion under these circumstances, the service auditor should identify these findings in his or her report. However, the service auditor's report should not identify the procedures that were performed, and should not include statements describing the characteristics of a service auditor's engagement.

Illustrative service auditor's reports Illustrations 3 through 10 below provide examples of service auditor's reports under various circumstances.

Other Communication Requirements

The service auditor may become aware of incidents of noncompliance with laws and regulations, fraud, or uncorrected errors attributable to management or other service organization personnel that are not clearly trivial and that may affect one or more user entities. Under these circumstances, the auditor should determine the effect of such matters on the following:

- Management's description of the service organization's system;
- The achievement of the control objectives; and
- The service auditor's report.

Also, the service auditor should determine whether management of the service organization has communicated appropriately this information to affected user entities. If the auditor determines that the information has not been properly communicated, and the service organization's management is unwilling to do so, the service auditor should take appropriate action, such as the following:

- Seek legal advice about the consequences of different courses of action;
- Communicate with those charged with governance of the service organization;
- Modify, or add an emphasis paragraph in, the service auditor's opinion;
- Disclaim an opinion;
- Communicate with third parties (e.g., a regulator, when required to do so); and
- Withdraw from the engagement.

Including a Description of Tests of Controls or Other Procedures, and the Results Thereof, in an Examination Report

AT Section 801 addresses examination engagements undertaken by a service auditor to report on controls at organizations that provide services to user entities when those controls are likely to be relevant to user entities' internal control over financial reporting (ICFR). When, as a result of such an examination engagement, a service auditor issues a type 2 report, AT Section 801 provides for a separate section of the service auditor's report that includes a description of the tests of controls likely to be relevant to user entities' ICFR and the results of those tests.

However, there may be circumstances when a practitioner is engaged to examine and report on controls at a service organization other than those likely to be relevant to user entities' ICFR, for example, controls at a service provider that are relevant to user entities' compliance with laws or regulations or that are relevant to the privacy of user entities' information. In such circumstances, AT Section 801 directs the practitioner to AT Section 101 (because AT Section 801 is not intended to permit a report that combines reporting on a service organization's controls likely to be relevant to user entities' ICFR with reporting on controls that are not likely to be relevant to user entities' ICFR).

Accordingly, if a practitioner performs an examination engagement under AT Section 101 under those circumstances, the question is whether the practitioner's examination report may include, in a separate section, a description of tests of controls or other procedures performed in support of the practitioner's opinion resulting from such an engagement. Attestation Interpretation No. 8 of AT Section 101, *Including a Description of Tests of Controls or Other Procedures, and* the Results Thereof, in an Examination Report, provides further guidance in such circumstances. It specifically indicates that, although nothing in AT Section 101 precludes a practitioner from including in a separate section of his or her examination report a description of tests of controls or other procedures performed and the results thereof, such a description may overshadow the practitioner's overall opinion or may cause report users to misunderstand the opinion. The Interpretation indicates that, in determining whether to include such a description in the practitioner's examination report, the circumstances of the particular engagement are relevant to the practitioner's consideration, including the following:

- Whether there has been a request for such information and whether the specified parties making the request have an appropriate business need or reasonable basis for requesting the information;
- Whether the specified parties have an understanding of the nature and subject matter of the engagement and experience in using the information in such reports;
- Whether including such a description in the examination report is likely to cause report users to misunderstand the opinion; and
- Whether the practitioner's tests of controls or other procedures performed directly relate to the subject matter of the engagement.

Also, the Interpretation states that the addition of a description of tests of controls or other procedures performed, and the results thereof, in a separate section of an examination report may increase the need for use of the report to be restricted to specified parties.

PRACTICE ISSUES AND FREQUENTLY ASKED QUESTIONS

Issue 1: In connection with a service auditor's engagement to report on the processing of transactions by a service organization, is it necessary for the service auditor to be independent from each user entity?

No. It is not necessary for the service auditor to be independent from each user entity. However, the service auditor should be independent from the service organization.

Issue 2: What does the concept of materiality relate to in an engagement to report on controls at a service organization?

In an engagement to report on controls at a service organization, the concept of materiality relates to the information on which the service auditor is reporting, not the financial statements of user entities. The concept of materiality takes into account that the service auditor's report provides information about the service organization's system to meet the common information needs of a broad range of user entities and their auditors who have an understanding of the manner in which the system is being used by a particular user entity for financial reporting.

The concept of materiality is not applied when disclosing, in the description of the tests of controls, the results of those tests when deviations have been identified. This is because, in the particular circumstances of a specific user entity or user auditor, a deviation may have significance beyond whether, in the opinion of the service auditor, it prevents a control from operating effectively. For example, the control to which the deviation relates may be particularly significant in preventing a certain type of error that may be material in the particular circumstances of a user entity's financial statements.

Issue 3: What types of procedures does the service auditor typically use to evaluate the fair presentation of management's description of the service organization's system?

When evaluating the fair presentation of management's description of the service organization's system, the service auditor typically employs procedures such as the following:

- Reading contracts with user entities to gain an understanding of the service organization's contractual obligations.
- Observing procedures performed by service organization personnel.
- Reviewing the service organization's policy and procedure manuals and other documentation of the system (e.g., flowcharts and narratives).
- Performing walkthroughs of transactions through the service organization's system.
- Considering the nature of the user entities and how the services provided by the service organization are likely to affect them (e.g., the predominant types of user entities and whether the user entities are regulated by government agencies).

Issue 4: If the service auditor is unable to obtain written representations regarding relevant control objectives and related controls at the subservice organization, can management of the service organization nevertheless use the inclusive method?

No. If the service auditor is unable to obtain written representations regarding relevant control objectives and related controls at the subservice organization, management of the service organization would not be able to use the inclusive method. Rather, management of the service organization could use the carve-out method.

Issue 5: What actions may a service auditor take when he or she becomes aware of noncompliance with laws and regulations, fraud, or uncorrected errors at the service organization?

The following are examples of the types of actions that a service auditor may take when he or she becomes aware of noncompliance with laws and regulations, fraud, or uncorrected errors at the service organization:

- Communicating with those charged with governance of the service organization.
- Disclaiming an opinion, modifying the service auditor's opinion, or adding an emphasis paragraph.
- Obtaining legal advice about the consequences of different courses of action.

- Communicating with third parties (e.g., a regulator) when required to do so.
- Withdrawing from the engagement.

The service auditor may take such actions after giving consideration to instances in which the service organization has not appropriately communicated the relevant information to affected user entities, and the service organization is unwilling to do so.

ILLUSTRATIONS AND PRACTICE AIDS

ILLUSTRATION 1—A SERVICE ORGANIZATION MANAGEMENT'S ASSERTION FOR A TYPE 1 REPORT

[*Service Organization Name*]'s Assertion

We have prepared the description of [*Service Organization Name*]'s [*type or name of*] system (description) for user entities of the system as of [*Month XX, 20X2*], and their user auditors who have a sufficient understanding to consider it, along with other information including information about controls implemented by user entities themselves, when obtaining an understanding of user entities' information and communication systems relevant to financial reporting. We confirm, to the best of our knowledge and belief, that:

1. The description fairly presents the [*type or name of*] system made available to user entities of the system as of [*Month XX, 20X2*], for processing their transactions [*or identification of the function performed by the system*]. The criteria we used in making this assertion were that the description:

    a. Presents how the system made available to user entities of the system was designed and implemented to process relevant transactions, including:

       (1) The classes of transactions processed.

       (2) The procedures, within both automated and manual systems, by which those transactions are initiated, authorized, recorded, processed, corrected, as necessary, and transferred to the reports presented to user entities of the system.

       (3) The related accounting records, supporting information, and specific accounts that are used to initiate, authorize, record, process, and report transactions; this includes the correction of incorrect information and how information is transferred to the reports provided to user entities of the system.

       (4) How the system captures and addresses significant events and conditions, other than transactions.

       (5) The process used to prepare reports or other information provided to user entities of the system.

       (6) Specified control objectives and controls designed to achieve those objectives.

       (7) Other aspects of our control environment, risk assessment process, information and communication systems (including the

related business processes), control activities, and monitoring controls that are relevant to processing and reporting transactions of user entities of the system.

   b. Does not omit or distort information relevant to the scope of the [*type or name of*] system, while acknowledging that the description is prepared to meet the common needs of a broad range of user entities of the system and the independent auditors of those user entities, and may not, therefore, include every aspect of the [*type or name of*] system that each individual user entity of the system and its auditor may consider important in its own particular environment.

2. The controls related to the control objectives stated in the description were suitably designed as of [*Month XX, 20X2*], to achieve those control objectives. The criteria we used in making this assertion were that:

   a. The risks that threaten the achievement of the control objectives stated in the description have been identified by the service organization.

   b. The controls identified in the description would, if operating as described, provide reasonable assurance that those risks would not prevent the control objectives stated in the description from being achieved.

ILLUSTRATION 2—A SERVICE ORGANIZATION MANAGEMENT'S ASSERTION FOR A TYPE 2 REPORT

[*Service Organization Name*]'s Assertion

We have prepared the description of [*Service Organization Name*]'s [*type or name of*] system (description) for user entities of the system during some or all of the period [*Month XX, 20X2*], to [*Month XX, 20X2*], and their user auditors who have a sufficient understanding to consider it, along with other information, including information about controls implemented by user entities of the system themselves, when assessing the risks of material misstatements of user entities' financial statements. We confirm, to the best of our knowledge and belief, that:

1. The description fairly presents the [*type or name of*] system made available to user entities of the system during some or all of the period [*Month XX, 20X2*]to [*Month XX, 20X2*], for processing their transactions [*or identification of the function performed by the system*]. The criteria we used in making this assertion were that the description:

   a. Presents how the system made available to user entities of the system was designed and implemented to process relevant transactions, including:

      (1) The classes of transactions processed.

      (2) The procedures, within both automated and manual systems, by which those transactions are initiated, authorized, recorded, processed, corrected, as necessary, and transferred to the reports presented to user entities of the system.

(3) The related accounting records, supporting information, and specific accounts that are used to initiate, authorize, record, process, and report transactions; this includes the correction of incorrect information and how information is transferred to the reports provided to user entities of the system.

(4) How the system captures and addresses significant events and conditions, other than transactions.

(5) The process used to prepare reports or other information provided to user entities of the system.

(6) Specified control objectives and controls designed to achieve those objectives.

(7) Other aspects of our control environment, risk assessment process, information and communication systems (including the related business processes), control activities, and monitoring controls that are relevant to processing and reporting transactions of user entities of the system.

b. Does not omit or distort information relevant to the scope of the [*type or name of*] system, while acknowledging that the description is prepared to meet the common needs of a broad range of user entities of the system and the independent auditors of those user entities, and may not, therefore, include every aspect of the [*type or name of*] system that each individual user entity of the system and its auditor may consider important in its own particular environment.

2. The description includes relevant details of changes to the service organization's system during the period covered by the description when the description covers a period of time.

3. The controls related to the control objectives stated in the description were suitably designed and operated effectively throughout the period [*Month XX, 20X2*] to [*Month XX, 20X2*], to achieve those control objectives. The criteria we used in making this assertion were that:

a. The risks that threaten the achievement of the control objectives stated in the description have been identified by the service organization.

b. The controls identified in the description would, if operating as described, provide reasonable assurance that those risks would not prevent the control objectives stated in the description from being achieved.

c. The controls were consistently applied as designed, including whether manual controls were applied by individuals who have the appropriate competence and authority.

ILLUSTRATION 3—SERVICE AUDITOR'S UNQUALIFIED OPINION ON A DESCRIPTION OF A SERVICE ORGANIZATION'S SYSTEM AND THE SUITABILITY OF THE DESIGN OF CONTROLS (TYPE 1 REPORT)

Independent Service Auditor's Report

To: [*Service Organization Name*]

We have examined [*Service Organization Name*]'s description of its [*type or name of*] system for processing user entities' transactions [*or identification of the function performed by the system*]as of [Month XX, 20X2], and the suitability of the design of controls to achieve the related control objectives stated in the description.

Note: When the description of the service organization's system refers to the need for complementary user entity controls, the above scope paragraph should be modified as follows:

"We have examined [*Service Organization Name*]'s description of its [*type or name of*] system for processing user entities' transactions [*or identification of the function performed by the system*] as of [*Month XX, 20X2*], and the suitability of the design of controls to achieve the related control objectives stated in the description. The description indicates that certain complementary user entity controls must be suitably designed and implemented at user entities for related controls at the service organization to be considered suitably designed to achieve the related control objectives. We have not evaluated the suitability of the design or operating effectiveness of such complementary user entity controls."

On page [*XX*]of the description, [*Service Organization Name*] has provided an assertion about the fairness of the presentation of the description and suitability of the design of the controls to achieve the related controls objectives stated in the description. [*Service Organization Name*] is responsible for preparing the description and for its assertion, including the completeness, accuracy, and method of presentation of the description and the assertion, providing the services covered by the description, specifying the control objectives and stating them in the description, identifying the risks that threaten the achievement of the control objectives, selecting the criteria, and designing, implementing, and documenting controls to achieve the related control objectives stated in the description.

Note: When the control objectives have been specified by an outside party, the above paragraph describing the service organization's responsibilities should be modified as follows:

"On page [*XX*] of the description, [*Service Organization Name*] has provided an assertion about the fairness of the presentation of the description and suitability of the design of the controls to achieve the related controls objectives stated in the description. [*Service Organization Name*] is responsible for preparing the description and for its assertion, including the completeness, accuracy, and method of presentation of the description and the assertion, providing the services covered by the description, specifying the control objectives and stating them in the description, identifying the risks that threaten the achievement of the control objectives, selecting the criteria, and designing, implementing, and documenting controls to achieve the related control objectives stated in the description. The control objectives have been specified by [*name of party specifying the control objectives*]and are stated on page [*XX*] of the description."

Our responsibility is to express an opinion on the fairness of the presentation of the description and on the suitability of the design of the controls to achieve the related control objectives stated in the description, based on our examination. We conducted our examination in accordance with attestation standards established by the American Institute of Certified Public Accountants. Those standards require that we plan and perform our examination to obtain reasonable assurance, in all material respects, about whether the description is fairly presented and the controls were suitably designed to achieve the related control objectives stated in the description as of [*Month XX, 20X2*].

An examination of a description of a service organization's system and the suitability of the design of the service organization's controls to achieve the related control objectives stated in the description involves performing procedures to obtain evidence about the fairness of the presentation of the description of the system and the suitability of the design of the controls to achieve the related control objectives stated in the description. Our procedures included assessing the risks that the description is not fairly presented and that the controls were not suitably designed to achieve the related control objectives stated in the description. An examination engagement of this type also includes evaluating the overall presentation of the description and the suitability of the control objectives stated therein, and the suitability of the criteria specified by the service organization and described at page [*XX*].

We did not perform any procedures regarding the operating effectiveness of the controls stated in the description and, accordingly, do not express an opinion thereon.

We believe that the evidence we obtained is sufficient and appropriate to provide a reasonable basis for our opinion.

Because of their nature, controls at a service organization may not prevent, or detect and correct, all errors or omissions in processing or reporting transactions [*or identification of the function performed by the system*]. The projection to the future of any evaluation of the fairness of the presentation of the description, or any conclusions about the suitability of the design of the controls to achieve the related control objectives, is subject to the risk that controls at a service organization may become ineffective or fail.

In our opinion, in all material respects, based on the criteria described in [*Service Organization Name*]'s assertion:

  a. The description fairly presents the [*type or name of*] system that was designed and implemented as of [*Month XX, 20X2*], and

  b. The controls related to the control objectives stated in the description were suitably designed to provide reasonable assurance that the control objectives would be achieved if the controls operated effectively as of [*Month XX, 20X2*].

Note: If the application of complementary user entity controls is necessary to achieve the control objectives stated in management's description of the service organization's system, item b. above should be modified as follows:

"b. The controls related to the control objectives stated in the description were suitably designed to provide reasonable assurance that the control objectives would be achieved if the controls operated effectively as of [*Month XX, 20X2*], and user entities applied the complementary user entity controls contemplated in the design of [*Service Organization Name*]'s controls as of [*Month XX, 20X2*]."

This report is intended solely for the information and use of [*Service Organization Name*], user entities of [*Service Organization Name*]'s [*type or name of*] system as of [*Month XX, 20X2*], and the independent auditors of such user entities, who have a sufficient understanding to consider it, along with other information including information about controls implemented by user entities themselves, when obtaining an understanding of user entities' information and communication systems relevant to financial reporting. This report is not intended to be and should not be used by anyone other than these specified parties.

[*Service auditor's signature*]

[*Date of the service auditor's report*]

[*Service auditor's city and state*]

ILLUSTRATION 4—SERVICE AUDITOR'S UNQUALIFIED OPINION ON A DESCRIPTION OF A SERVICE ORGANIZATION'S SYSTEM AND THE SUITABILITY OF THE DESIGN AND OPERATING EFFECTIVENESS OF CONTROLS (TYPE 2 REPORT)

Independent Service Auditor's Report

To: [*Service Organization Name*]

We have examined [*Service Organization Name*]'s description of its [*type or name of*] system for processing user entities' transactions [*or identification of the function performed by the system*]throughout the period [*Month XX, 20X2*] to [*Month XX, 20X2*] (description) and the suitability of the design and operating effectiveness of controls to achieve the related control objectives stated in the description.

Note: When the description of the service organization's system refers to the need for complementary user entity controls, the above scope paragraph should be modified as follows:

"We have examined [*Service Organization Name*]'s description of its [*type or name of*] system for processing user entities' transactions [*or identification of the function performed by the system*] throughout the period [*Month XX, 20X2*] to [*Month XX, 20X2*] (description) and the suitability of the design and operating effectiveness of controls to achieve the related control objectives stated in the description. The description indicates that certain control objectives specified in the description can be achieved only if complementary user entity controls contemplated in the design of [*Service Organization Name*]'s controls are suitably designed and operating effectively, along with related controls at the service organization. We have not evaluated the suitability of the design or operating effectiveness of such complementary user entity controls."

On page [*XX*]of the description, [*Service Organization Name*] has provided an assertion about the fairness of the presentation of the description and suitability of the design and operating effectiveness of the controls to achieve the related control objectives stated in the description. [*Service Organization Name*]is responsible for preparing the description and for the assertion, including the completeness, accuracy, and method of presentation of the description and the assertion, providing the services covered by the description, specifying the control objectives and stating them in the description, identifying the risks that threaten the achievement of the control objectives, selecting the criteria, and designing, implementing, and documenting controls to achieve the related control objectives stated in the description.

Note: When the control objectives have been specified by an outside party, the above paragraph describing the service organization's responsibilities should be modified as follows:

"On page [*XX*] of the description, [*Service Organization Name*] has provided an assertion about the fairness of the presentation of the description and suitability of the design and operating effectiveness of the controls to achieve the related control objectives stated in the description. [*Service Organization Name*] is responsible for preparing the description and for the assertion, including the completeness, accuracy, and method of presentation of the description and the assertion, providing the services covered by the description, specifying the control objectives and stating them in the description, identifying the risks that threaten the achievement of the control objectives, selecting the criteria, and designing, implementing, and documenting controls to achieve the related control objectives stated in the description. The control objectives have been specified by [*name of party specifying the control objectives*] and are stated on page [*XX*]of the description."

Our responsibility is to express an opinion on the fairness of the presentation of the description and on the suitability of the design and operating effectiveness of the controls to achieve the related control objectives stated in the description, based on our examination. We conducted our examination in accordance with attestation standards established by the American Institute of Certified Public Accountants. Those standards require that we plan and perform our examination to obtain reasonable assurance about whether, in all material respects, the description is fairly presented and the controls were suitably designed and operating effectively to achieve the related control objectives stated in the description throughout the period [*Month XX, 20X2*] to [*Month XX, 20X2*].

An examination of a description of a service organization's system and the suitability of the design and operating effectiveness of the service organization's controls to achieve the related control objectives stated in the description involves performing procedures to obtain evidence about the fairness of the presentation of the description and the suitability of the design and operating effectiveness of those controls to achieve the related control objectives stated in the description. Our procedures included assessing the risks that the description is not fairly presented and that the controls were not suitably designed or operating effectively to achieve the related control objectives stated in the description. Our procedures also included testing the operating effectiveness of those controls that we consider necessary to provide reasonable assurance that the related control objectives stated in the description were achieved. An examination engagement of this type also includes evaluating the overall presentation of the description and the suitability of the control objectives stated therein, and the suitability of the criteria specified by the service organization and described at page [XX]. We believe that the evidence we obtained is sufficient and appropriate to provide a reasonable basis for our opinion.

Because of their nature, controls at a service organization may not prevent, or detect and correct, all errors or omissions in processing or reporting transactions [or *identification of the function performed by the system*]. Also, the projection to the future of any evaluation of the fairness of the presentation of the description, or conclusions about the suitability of the design or operating effectiveness of the controls to achieve the related control objectives is subject to the risk that controls at a service organization may become inadequate or fail.

In our opinion, in all material respects, based on the criteria described in [*Service Organization Name*]'s assertion on page [XX]:

a. The description fairly presents the [type or name of]system that was designed and implemented throughout the period [*Month XX, 20X2*] to [*Month XX, 20X2*].

b. The controls related to the control objectives stated in the description were suitably designed to provide reasonable assurance that the control objectives would be achieved if the controls operated effectively throughout the period [*Month XX, 20X2*]to [*Month XX, 20X2*].

c. The controls we tested, which were those necessary to provide reasonable assurance that the control objectives stated in the description were achieved, operated effectively throughout the period [*Month XX, 20X2*] to [*Month XX, 20X2*].

Note: If the application of complementary user entity controls is necessary to achieve the control objectives stated in management's description of the service organization's system, items b. and c. above should be modified as follows:

"b. The controls related to the control objectives stated in the description were suitably designed to provide reasonable assurance that the control objectives would be achieved if the controls operated effectively throughout the period [*Month XX, 20X2*] to [*Month XX, 20X2*], and user entities applied the complementary user entity controls contemplated in the design of [*Service Organization Name*]'s controls throughout the period [*Month XX, 20X2*] to [*Month XX, 20X2*].

c. The controls we tested, which together with the complementary user entity controls referred to in the scope paragraph of this report, if operating effectively, were those necessary to provide reasonable assurance that the control objectives stated in the description were achieved, operated effectively throughout the period [*Month XX, 20X2*] to [*Month XX, 20X2*]."

The specific controls tested and the nature, timing, and results of those tests are listed on pages [*YY–ZZ*].

This report, including the description of tests of controls and results thereof on pages [*YY–ZZ*], is intended solely for the information and use of [*Service Organization Name*], user entities of [*Service Organization Name*]'s [*type or name of*] system during some or all of the period [*Month XX, 20X2*] to [*Month XX, 20X2*], and the independent auditors of such user entities, who have a sufficient understanding to consider it, along with other information including information about controls implemented by user entities themselves, when assessing the risks of material misstatements of user entities' financial statements. This report is not intended to be and should not be used by anyone other than these specified parties.

[*Service auditor's signature*]

[*Date of the service auditor's report*]

[*Service auditor's city and state*]

PRACTICE POINT: Attest Interpretation 9101.8, *Including a Description of Tests of Controls or Other Procedures, and the Results Thereof, in an Examination Report*, issued in July 2010, addresses whether a practitioner who performs an examination engagement under AT Section 101 may include in a separate section of his examination report a description of tests of controls or other procedures performed in support of the practitioner's opinion resulting from such an engagement.

The Interpretation indicates that nothing in AT Section 101 precludes a practitioner from including in a separate section of his or her examination report a description of tests of controls or other procedures performed and the results thereof. However, in some cases, such a description may overshadow the practitioner's overall opinion or may cause report users to misunderstand the opinion. Therefore, the circumstances of the particular engagement are relevant to the practitioner's consideration regarding whether to include a description of tests of controls or other procedures performed, and the results thereof, in a separate section of the practitioner's examination report. In determining whether to include such a description in the practitioner's examination report, the following considerations are relevant:

- Whether there has been a request for such information and whether the specified parties making the request have an appropriate business need or reasonable basis for requesting the information (e.g., the specified parties are required to maintain and monitor controls that either encompass or are dependent on controls that are the subject of the examination and, therefore, need information about the tests of controls to enable them to have a basis for concluding that they have met the requirements applicable to them);

- Whether the specified parties have an understanding of the nature and subject matter of the engagement and experience in using the information in such reports;

- Whether including such a description in the examination report is likely to cause report users to misunderstand the opinion; and

- Whether the practitioner's tests of controls or other procedures performed directly relate to the subject matter of the engagement.

The Interpretation further alerts practitioners that the addition of a description of tests of controls or other procedures performed, and the results thereof, in a separate section of an examination report may increase the need for use of the report to be restricted to specified parties.

ILLUSTRATION 5—SERVICE AUDITOR'S QUALIFIED OPINION BECAUSE THE DESCRIPTION OF THE SERVICE ORGANIZATION'S SYSTEM IS NOT FAIRLY PRESENTED (TYPE 2 REPORT)

Independent Service Auditor's Report

To: [*Service Organization Name*]

We have examined [*Service Organization Name*]'s description of its [*type or name of*] system for processing user entities' transactions [*or identification of the function performed by the system*]throughout the period [*Month XX, 20X2*] to [*Month XX, 20X2*] (description) and the suitability of the design and operating effectiveness of controls to achieve the related control objectives stated in the description.

Note: When the description of the service organization's system refers to the need for complementary user entity controls, the above scope paragraph should be modified as follows:

"We have examined [*Service Organization Name*]'s description of its [*type or name of*] system for processing user entities' transactions [*or identification of the function performed by the system*] throughout the period [*Month XX, 20X2*] to [*Month XX, 20X2*] (description) and the suitability of the design and operating effectiveness of controls to achieve the related control objectives stated in the description. The description indicates that certain control objectives specified in the description can be achieved only if complementary user entity controls contemplated in the design of [*Service Organization Name*]'s controls are suitably designed and operating effectively, along with related controls at the service organization. We have not evaluated the suitability of the design or operating effectiveness of such complementary user entity controls."

On page [*XX*]of the description, [*Service Organization Name*] has provided an assertion about the fairness of the presentation of the description and suitability of the design and operating effectiveness of the controls to achieve the related control objectives stated in the description. [*Service Organization Name*] is responsible for preparing the description and for the assertion, including the completeness, accuracy, and method of presentation of the description and the assertion, providing the services covered by the description, specifying the control objectives and stating them in the description, identifying the risks that threaten the achievement of the control objectives, selecting the criteria, and designing, implementing, and documenting controls to achieve the related control objectives stated in the description.

Note: When the control objectives have been specified by an outside party, the above paragraph describing the service organization's responsibilities should be modified as follows:

> "On page [XX] of the description, [*Service Organization Name*] has provided an assertion about the fairness of the presentation of the description and suitability of the design and operating effectiveness of the controls to achieve the related control objectives stated in the description. [*Service Organization Name*] is responsible for preparing the description and for the assertion, including the completeness, accuracy, and method of presentation of the description and the assertion, providing the services covered by the description, specifying the control objectives and stating them in the description, identifying the risks that threaten the achievement of the control objectives, selecting the criteria, and designing, implementing, and documenting controls to achieve the related control objectives stated in the description. The control objectives have been specified by [*name of party specifying the control objectives*] and are stated on page [XX]of the description."

Our responsibility is to express an opinion on the fairness of the presentation of the description and on the suitability of the design and operating effectiveness of the controls to achieve the related control objectives stated in the description, based on our examination. We conducted our examination in accordance with attestation standards established by the American Institute of Certified Public Accountants. Those standards require that we plan and perform our examination to obtain reasonable assurance about whether, in all material respects, the description is fairly presented and the controls were suitably designed and operating effectively to achieve the related control objectives stated in the description throughout the period [*Month XX, 20X2*] to [*Month XX, 20X2*].

An examination of a description of a service organization's system and the suitability of the design and operating effectiveness of the service organization's controls to achieve the related control objectives stated in the description involves performing procedures to obtain evidence about the fairness of the presentation of the description and the suitability of the design and operating effectiveness of those controls to achieve the related control objectives stated in the description. Our procedures included assessing the risks that the description is not fairly presented and that the controls were not suitably designed or operating effectively to achieve the related control objectives stated in the description. Our procedures also included testing the operating effectiveness of those controls that we consider necessary to provide reasonable assurance that the related control objectives stated in the description were achieved. An examination engagement of this type also includes evaluating the overall presentation of the description and the suitability of the control objectives stated therein, and the suitability of the criteria specified by the service organization and described at page [XX]. We believe that the evidence we obtained is sufficient and appropriate to provide a reasonable basis for our opinion.

Because of their nature, controls at a service organization may not prevent, or detect and correct, all errors or omissions in processing or reporting transactions [*or identification of the function performed by the system*]. Also, the projection to the future of any evaluation of the fairness of the presentation of the description, or conclusions about the suitability of the design or operating effectiveness of the controls to achieve the related control objectives is subject to the risk that controls at a service organization may become inadequate or fail.

The accompanying description states on page [XX]that [*Service Organization Name*] uses operator identification numbers and passwords to prevent unauthorized access to the system. Based on inquiries of staff personnel and observation of activities, we have determined that operator identification numbers and passwords are employed in applications [A] and [B]but are not required to access the system in applications [C]and [D].

In our opinion, except for the matter described in the preceding paragraph, and based on the criteria described in [*Service Organization Name*]'s assertion on page [XX], in all material respects:

a. The description fairly presents the [*type or name of*] system that was designed and implemented throughout the period [*Month XX, 20X2*] to [*Month XX, 20X2*].

b. The controls related to the control objectives stated in the description were suitably designed to provide reasonable assurance that the control objectives would be achieved if the controls operated effectively throughout the period [*Month XX, 20X2*]to [*Month XX, 20X2*].

c. The controls we tested, which were those necessary to provide reasonable assurance that the control objectives stated in the description were achieved, operated effectively throughout the period [*Month XX, 20X2*] to [*Month XX, 20X2*].

Note: If the application of complementary user entity controls is necessary to achieve the control objectives stated in management's description of the service organization's system, items b. and c. above should be modified as follows:

"b. The controls related to the control objectives stated in the description were suitably designed to provide reasonable assurance that the control objectives would be achieved if the controls operated effectively throughout the period [*Month XX, 20X2*] to [*Month XX, 20X2*], and user entities applied the complementary user entity controls contemplated in the design of [*Service Organization Name*]'s controls throughout the period [*Month XX, 20X2*] to [*Month XX, 20X2*].

c. The controls we tested, which together with the complementary user entity controls referred to in the scope paragraph of this report, if operating effectively, were those necessary to provide reasonable assurance that the control objectives stated in the description were achieved, operated effectively throughout the period [*Month XX, 20X2*] to [*Month XX, 20X2*]."

The specific controls tested and the nature, timing, and results of those tests are listed on pages [*YY–ZZ*].

This report, including the description of tests of controls and results thereof on pages [*YY–ZZ*], is intended solely for the information and use of [*Service Organization Name*], user entities of [*Service Organization Name*]'s [*type or name of*] system during some or all of the period [*Month XX, 20X2*] to [*Month XX, 20X2*], and the independent auditors of such user entities, who have a sufficient understanding to consider it, along with other information including information about controls implemented by user entities themselves, when assessing the risks of material misstatements of user entities' financial statements. This report is not intended to be and should not be used by anyone other than these specified parties.

[*Service auditor's signature*]

[*Date of the service auditor's report*]

[*Service auditor's city and state*]

PRACTICE POINT: Attest Interpretation 9101.8, *Including a Description of Tests of Controls or Other Procedures, and the Results Thereof, in an Examination Report,* issued in July 2010, addresses whether a practitioner who performs an examination engagement under AT Section 101 may include in a separate section of his examination report a description of tests of controls or other procedures performed in support of the practitioner's opinion resulting from such an engagement.

The Interpretation indicates that nothing in AT Section 101 precludes a practitioner from including in a separate section of his or her examination report a description of tests of controls or other procedures performed and the results thereof. However, in some cases, such a description may overshadow the practitioner's overall opinion or may cause report users to misunderstand the opinion. Therefore, the circumstances of the particular engagement are relevant to the practitioner's consideration regarding whether to include a description of tests of controls or other procedures performed, and the results thereof, in a separate section of the practitioner's examination report. In determining whether to include such a description in the practitioner's examination report, the following considerations are relevant:

- Whether there has been a request for such information and whether the specified parties making the request have an appropriate business need or reasonable basis for requesting the information (e.g., the specified parties are required to maintain and monitor controls that either encompass or are dependent on controls that are the subject of the examination and, therefore, need information about the tests of controls to enable them to have a basis for concluding that they have met the requirements applicable to them);

- Whether the specified parties have an understanding of the nature and subject matter of the engagement and experience in using the information in such reports;

- Whether including such a description in the examination report is likely to cause report users to misunderstand the opinion; and

- Whether the practitioner's tests of controls or other procedures performed directly relate to the subject matter of the engagement.

The Interpretation further alerts practitioners that the addition of a description of tests of controls or other procedures performed, and the results thereof, in a separate section of an examination report may increase the need for use of the report to be restricted to specified parties.

ILLUSTRATION 6—SERVICE AUDITOR'S QUALIFIED OPINION BECAUSE THE CONTROLS ARE NOT SUITABLY DESIGNED (TYPE 2 REPORT)

Independent Service Auditor's Report

To: [*Service Organization Name*]

We have examined [*Service Organization Name*]'s description of its [*type or name of*] system for processing user entities' transactions [*or identification of the function performed by the system*]throughout the period [*Month XX, 20X2*] to [*Month XX, 20X2*] (description) and the suitability of the design and operating effectiveness of controls to achieve the related control objectives stated in the description.

Note: When the description of the service organization's system refers to the need for complementary user entity controls, the above scope paragraph should be modified as follows:

"We have examined [*Service Organization Name*]'s description of its [*type or name of*] system for processing user entities' transactions [*or identification of the function performed by the system*] throughout the period [*Month XX, 20X2*] to [*Month XX, 20X2*] (description) and the suitability of the design and operating effectiveness of controls to achieve the related control objectives stated in the description. The description indicates that certain control objectives specified in the description can be achieved only if complementary user entity controls contemplated in the design of [*Service Organization Name*]'s controls are suitably designed and operating effectively, along with related controls at the service organization. We have not evaluated the suitability of the design or operating effectiveness of such complementary user entity controls."

On page [*XX*]of the description, [*Service Organization Name*] has provided an assertion about the fairness of the presentation of the description and suitability of the design and operating effectiveness of the controls to achieve the related control objectives stated in the description. [*Service Organization Name*] is responsible for preparing the description and for the assertion, including the completeness, accuracy, and method of presentation of the description and the assertion, providing the services covered by the description, specifying the control objectives and stating them in the description, identifying the risks that threaten the achievement of the control objectives, selecting the criteria, and designing, implementing, and documenting controls to achieve the related control objectives stated in the description.

Note: When the control objectives have been specified by an outside party, the above paragraph describing the service organization's responsibilities should be modified as follows:

> "On page [*XX*] of the description, [*Service Organization Name*] has provided an assertion about the fairness of the presentation of the description and suitability of the design and operating effectiveness of the controls to achieve the related control objectives stated in the description. [*Service Organization Name*] is responsible for preparing the description and for the assertion, including the completeness, accuracy, and method of presentation of the description and the assertion, providing the services covered by the description, specifying the control objectives and stating them in the description, identifying the risks that threaten the achievement of the control objectives, selecting the criteria, and designing, implementing, and documenting controls to achieve the related control objectives stated in the description. The control objectives have been specified by [*name of party specifying the control objectives*] and are stated on page [*XX*]of the description."

Our responsibility is to express an opinion on the fairness of the presentation of the description and on the suitability of the design and operating effectiveness of the controls to achieve the related control objectives stated in the description, based on our examination. We conducted our examination in accordance with attestation standards established by the American Institute of Certified Public Accountants. Those standards require that we plan and perform our examination to obtain reasonable assurance about whether, in all material respects, the description is fairly presented and the controls were suitably designed and operating effectively to achieve the related control objectives stated in the description throughout the period [*Month XX, 20X2*] to [*Month XX, 20X2*].

An examination of a description of a service organization's system and the suitability of the design and operating effectiveness of the service organization's controls to achieve the related control objectives stated in the description involves performing procedures to obtain evidence about the fairness of the presentation of the description and the suitability of the design and operating effectiveness of those controls to achieve the related control objectives stated in the description. Our procedures included assessing the risks that the description is not fairly presented and that the controls were not suitably designed or operating effectively to achieve the related control objectives stated in the description. Our procedures also included testing the operating effectiveness of those controls that we consider necessary to provide reasonable assurance that the related control objectives stated in the description were achieved. An examination engagement of this type also includes evaluating the overall presentation of the description and the suitability of the control objectives stated therein, and the suitability of the criteria specified by the service organization and described at page [*XX*]. We believe that the evidence we obtained is sufficient and appropriate to provide a reasonable basis for our opinion.

Because of their nature, controls at a service organization may not prevent, or detect and correct, all errors or omissions in processing or reporting transactions [*or identification of the function performed by the system*]. Also, the projection to the future of any evaluation of the fairness of the presentation of the description, or conclusions about the suitability of the design or operating effectiveness of the controls to achieve the related control objectives, is subject to the risk that controls at a service organization may become inadequate or fail.

As discussed on page [*XX*] of the accompanying description, from time to time, [*Service Organization Name*]makes changes in application programs to correct deficiencies or to enhance capabilities. The procedures followed in determining whether to make changes, in designing the changes, and in implementing them do not include review and approval by authorized individuals who are independent from those involved in making the changes. There are also no specified requirements to test such changes or provide test results to an authorized reviewer prior to implementing the changes. As a result, the controls are not suitably designed to achieve the control objective, "Controls provide reasonable assurance that changes to existing applications are authorized, tested, approved, properly implemented, and documented."

In our opinion, except for the matter described in the preceding paragraph, and based on the criteria described in [*Service Organization Name*]'s assertion on page [*XX*], in all material respects:

a. The description fairly presents the [*type or name of*] system that was designed and implemented throughout the period [*Month XX, 20X2*] to [*Month XX, 20X2*].

b. The controls related to the control objectives stated in the description were suitably designed to provide reasonable assurance that the control objectives would be achieved if the controls operated effectively throughout the period [*Month XX, 20X2*]to [*Month XX, 20X2*].

c. The controls we tested, which were those necessary to provide reasonable assurance that the control objectives stated in the description were achieved, operated effectively throughout the period [*Month XX, 20X2*] to [*Month XX, 20X2*].

Note: If the application of complementary user entity controls is necessary to achieve the control objectives stated in management's description of the service organization's system, items b. and c. above should be modified as follows:

"b. The controls related to the control objectives stated in the description were suitably designed to provide reasonable assurance that the control objectives would be achieved if the controls operated effectively throughout the period [*Month XX, 20X2*] to [*Month XX, 20X2*], and user entities applied the complementary user entity controls contemplated in the design of [*Service Organization Name*]'s controls throughout the period [*Month XX, 20X2*] to [*Month XX, 20X2*].

c. The controls we tested, which together with the complementary user entity controls referred to in the scope paragraph of this report, if operating effectively, were those necessary to provide reasonable assurance that the control objectives stated in the description were achieved, operated effectively throughout the period [*Month XX, 20X2*] to [*Month XX, 20X2*]."

The specific controls tested and the nature, timing, and results of those tests are listed on pages [*YY–ZZ*].

This report, including the description of tests of controls and results thereof on pages [*YY–ZZ*], is intended solely for the information and use of [*Service Organization Name*], user entities of [*Service Organization Name*]'s [*type or name of*] system during some or all of the period [*Month XX, 20X2*] to [*Month XX, 20X2*], and the independent auditors of such user entities, who have a sufficient understanding to consider it, along with other information including information about controls implemented by user entities themselves, when assessing the risks of material misstatements of user entities' financial statements. This report is not intended to be and should not be used by anyone other than these specified parties.

[*Service auditor's signature*]

[*Date of the service auditor's report*]

[*Service auditor's city and state*]

> **PRACTICE POINT:** Attest Interpretation 9101.8, *Including a Description of Tests of Controls or Other Procedures, and the Results Thereof, in an Examination Report,* issued in July 2010, addresses whether a practitioner who performs an examination engagement under AT Section 101 may include in a separate section of his examination report a description of tests of controls or other procedures performed in support of the practitioner's opinion resulting from such an engagement.
>
> The Interpretation indicates that nothing in AT Section 101 precludes a practitioner from including in a separate section of his or her examination report a description of tests of controls or other procedures performed and the results thereof. However, in some cases, such a description may overshadow the practitioner's overall opinion or may cause report users to misunderstand the opinion. Therefore, the circumstances of the particular engagement are relevant to the practitioner's consideration regarding whether to include a description of tests of controls or other procedures performed, and the results thereof, in a separate section of the practitioner's examination report. In determining whether to include such a description in the practitioner's examination report, the following considerations are relevant:
>
> - Whether there has been a request for such information and whether the specified parties making the request have an appropriate business need or reasonable basis for requesting the information (e.g., the specified parties are required to maintain and monitor controls that either encompass or are dependent on controls that are the subject of the examination and, therefore, need information about the tests of controls to enable

them to have a basis for concluding that they have met the requirements applicable to them);

- Whether the specified parties have an understanding of the nature and subject matter of the engagement and experience in using the information in such reports;

- Whether including such a description in the examination report is likely to cause report users to misunderstand the opinion; and

- Whether the practitioner's tests of controls or other procedures performed directly relate to the subject matter of the engagement.

The Interpretation further alerts practitioners that the addition of a description of tests of controls or other procedures performed, and the results thereof, in a separate section of an examination report may increase the need for use of the report to be restricted to specified parties.

ILLUSTRATION 7—SERVICE AUDITOR'S QUALIFIED OPINION BECAUSE THE CONTROLS DID NOT OPERATE EFFECTIVELY THROUGHOUT THE SPECIFIED PERIOD (TYPE 2 REPORT)

Independent Service Auditor's Report

To: [*Service Organization Name*]

We have examined [*Service Organization Name*]'s description of its [type or name of] system for processing user entities' transactions [*or identification of the function performed by the system*] throughout the period [*Month XX, 20X2*] to [*Month XX, 20X2*] (description) and the suitability of the design and operating effectiveness of controls to achieve the related control objectives stated in the description.

Note: When the description of the service organization's system refers to the need for complementary user entity controls, the above scope paragraph should be modified as follows:

"We have examined [*Service Organization Name*]'s description of its [*type or name of*] system for processing user entities' transactions [*or identification of the function performed by the system*] throughout the period [*Month XX, 20X2*] to [*Month XX, 20X2*] (description) and the suitability of the design and operating effectiveness of controls to achieve the related control objectives stated in the description. The description indicates that certain control objectives specified in the description can be achieved only if complementary user entity controls contemplated in the design of [*Service Organization Name*]'s controls are suitably designed and operating effectively, along with related controls at the service organization. We have not evaluated the suitability of the design or operating effectiveness of such complementary user entity controls."

On page [*XX*]of the description, [*Service Organization Name*] has provided an assertion about the fairness of the presentation of the description and suitability of the design and operating effectiveness of the controls to achieve the related control objectives stated in the description. [*Service Organization Name*] is responsible for preparing the description and for the assertion, including the completeness, accuracy, and method of presentation of the description and the assertion, providing the services covered by the description, specifying the control objectives and stating them in the description, identifying the risks that threaten the achievement of the control objectives, selecting the criteria, and designing, implementing, and documenting controls to achieve the related control objectives stated in the description.

Note: When the control objectives have been specified by an outside party, the above paragraph describing the service organization's responsibilities should be modified as follows:

"On page [XX] of the description, [*Service Organization Name*] has provided an assertion about the fairness of the presentation of the description and suitability of the design and operating effectiveness of the controls to achieve the related control objectives stated in the description. [*Service Organization Name*] is responsible for preparing the description and for the assertion, including the completeness, accuracy, and method of presentation of the description and the assertion, providing the services covered by the description, specifying the control objectives and stating them in the description, identifying the risks that threaten the achievement of the control objectives, selecting the criteria, and designing, implementing, and documenting controls to achieve the related control objectives stated in the description. The control objectives have been specified by [*name of party specifying the control objectives*] and are stated on page [XX] of the description."

Our responsibility is to express an opinion on the fairness of the presentation of the description and on the suitability of the design and operating effectiveness of the controls to achieve the related control objectives stated in the description, based on our examination. We conducted our examination in accordance with attestation standards established by the American Institute of Certified Public Accountants. Those standards require that we plan and perform our examination to obtain reasonable assurance about whether, in all material respects, the description is fairly presented and the controls were suitably designed and operating effectively to achieve the related control objectives stated in the description throughout the period [*Month XX, 20X2*] to [*Month XX, 20X2*].

An examination of a description of a service organization's system and the suitability of the design and operating effectiveness of the service organization's controls to achieve the related control objectives stated in the description involves performing procedures to obtain evidence about the fairness of the presentation of the description and the suitability of the design and operating effectiveness of those controls to achieve the related control objectives stated in the description. Our procedures included assessing the risks that the description is not fairly presented and that the controls were not suitably designed or operating effectively to achieve the related control objectives stated in the description. Our procedures also included testing the operating effectiveness of those controls that we consider necessary to provide reasonable assurance that the related control objectives stated in the description were achieved. An examination engagement of this type also includes evaluating the overall presentation of the description and the suitability of the control objectives stated therein, and the suitability of the criteria specified by the service organization and described at page [XX]. We believe that the evidence we obtained is sufficient and appropriate to provide a reasonable basis for our opinion.

Because of their nature, controls at a service organization may not prevent, or detect and correct, all errors or omissions in processing or reporting transactions [*or identification of the function performed by the system*]. Also, the projection to the future of any evaluation of the fairness of the presentation of the description, or conclusions about the suitability of the design or operating effectiveness of the controls to achieve the related control objectives, is subject to the risk that controls at a service organization may become inadequate or fail.

[*Service Organization Name*] states in its description that it has automated controls in place to reconcile loan payments received with the various output reports. However, as noted on page [XX] of the description of tests of controls and results thereof, this control was not operating effectively throughout the period [*insert date*] to [*insert date*]due to a programming error. This resulted in the nonachievement of the control objective, "Controls provide reasonable assurance that loan payments received are properly recorded" throughout the period [*January 1, 20X2*] to [*April 30, 20X2*]. [*Service Organization Name*] implemented a change to the program performing the calculation as of [*May 1, 20X2*], and our tests indicate that it was operating effectively throughout the period [*May 1, 20X2*] to [*December 31, 20X2*].

In our opinion, except for the matter described in the preceding paragraph, and based on the criteria described in [*Service Organization Name*]'s assertion on page [XX], in all material respects:

a. The description fairly presents the [*type or name of*] system that was designed and implemented throughout the period [*Month XX, 20X2*] to [*Month XX, 20X2*].

b. The controls related to the control objectives stated in the description were suitably designed to provide reasonable assurance that the control objectives would be achieved if the controls operated effectively throughout the period [*Month XX, 20X2*]to [*Month XX, 20X2*].

c. The controls we tested, which were those necessary to provide reasonable assurance that the control objectives stated in the description were achieved, operated effectively throughout the period [*Month XX, 20X2*] to [*Month XX, 20X2*].

Note: If the application of complementary user entity controls is necessary to achieve the control objectives stated in management's description of the service organization's system, items b. and c. above should be modified as follows:

"b. The controls related to the control objectives stated in the description were suitably designed to provide reasonable assurance that the control objectives would be achieved if the controls operated effectively throughout the period [*Month XX, 20X2*] to [*Month XX, 20X2*], and user entities applied the complementary user entity controls contemplated in the design of [*Service Organization Name*]'s controls throughout the period [*Month XX, 20X2*] to [*Month XX, 20X2*].

c. The controls we tested, which together with the complementary user entity controls referred to in the scope paragraph of this report, if operating effectively, were those necessary to provide reasonable assurance that the control objectives stated in the description were achieved, operated effectively throughout the period [*Month XX, 20X2*] to [*Month XX, 20X2*]."

The specific controls tested and the nature, timing, and results of those tests are listed on pages [*YY–ZZ*].

This report, including the description of tests of controls and results thereof on pages [*YY–ZZ*], is intended solely for the information and use of [*Service Organization Name*], user entities of [*Service Organization Name*]'s [*type or name of*] system during some or all of the period [*Month XX, 20X2*] to [*Month XX, 20X2*], and the independent auditors of such user entities, who have a sufficient understanding to consider it, along with other information including information about controls implemented by user entities themselves, when assessing the risks of material misstatements of user entities' financial statements. This report is not intended to be and should not be used by anyone other than these specified parties.

[*Service auditor's signature*]

[*Date of the service auditor's report*]

[*Service auditor's city and state*]

PRACTICE POINT: Attest Interpretation 9101.8, *Including a Description of Tests of Controls or Other Procedures, and the Results Thereof, in an Examination Report,* issued in July 2010, addresses whether a practitioner who performs an examination engagement under AT Section 101 may include in a separate section of his examination report a description of tests of controls or other procedures performed in support of the practitioner's opinion resulting from such an engagement.

The Interpretation indicates that nothing in AT Section 101 precludes a practitioner from including in a separate section of his or her examination report a description of tests of controls or other procedures performed and the results thereof. However, in some cases, such a description may overshadow the practitioner's overall opinion or may cause report users to misunderstand the opinion. Therefore, the circumstances of the particular engagement are relevant to the practitioner's consideration regarding whether to include a description of tests of controls or other procedures performed, and the results thereof, in a separate section of the practitioner's examination report. In determining whether to include such a description in the practitioner's examination report, the following considerations are relevant:

- Whether there has been a request for such information and whether the specified parties making the request have an appropriate business need or reasonable basis for requesting the information (e.g., the specified parties are required to maintain and monitor controls that either encompass or are dependent on controls that are the subject of the examination and, therefore, need information about the tests of controls to enable them to have a basis for concluding that they have met the requirements applicable to them);

- Whether the specified parties have an understanding of the nature and subject matter of the engagement and experience in using the information in such reports;

- Whether including such a description in the examination report is likely to cause report users to misunderstand the opinion; and

- Whether the practitioner's tests of controls or other procedures performed directly relate to the subject matter of the engagement.

The Interpretation further alerts practitioners that the addition of a description of tests of controls or other procedures performed, and the results thereof, in a separate section of an examination report may increase the need for use of the report to be restricted to specified parties.

ILLUSTRATION 8—SERVICE AUDITOR'S QUALIFIED OPINION BECAUSE OF THE AUDITOR'S INABILITY TO OBTAIN SUFFICIENT APPROPRIATE EVIDENCE (TYPE 2 REPORT)

Independent Service Auditor's Report

To: [*Service Organization Name*]

We have examined [*Service Organization Name*]'s description of its [*type or name of*] system for processing user entities' transactions [*or identification of the function performed by the system*]throughout the period [*Month XX, 20X2*] to [*Month XX, 20X2*] (description) and the suitability of the design and operating effectiveness of controls to achieve the related control objectives stated in the description.

Note: When the description of the service organization's system refers to the need for complementary user entity controls, the above scope paragraph should be modified as follows:

"We have examined [*Service Organization Name*]'s description of its [*type or name of*] system for processing user entities' transactions [*or identification of the function performed by the system*] throughout the period [*Month XX, 20X2*] to [*Month XX, 20X2*] (description) and the suitability of the design and operating effectiveness of controls to achieve the related control objectives stated in the description. The description indicates that certain control objectives specified in the description can be achieved only if complementary user entity controls contemplated in the design of [*Service Organization Name*]'s controls are suitably designed and operating effectively, along with related controls at the service organization. We have not evaluated the suitability of the design or operating effectiveness of such complementary user entity controls."

On page [*XX*]of the description, [*Service Organization Name*] has provided an assertion about the fairness of the presentation of the description and suitability of the design and operating effectiveness of the controls to achieve the related control objectives stated in the description. [*Service Organization Name*] is responsible for preparing the description and for the assertion, including the completeness, accuracy, and method of presentation of the description and the assertion, providing the services covered by the description, specifying the control objectives and stating them in the description, identifying the risks that threaten the achievement of the control objectives, selecting the criteria, and designing, implementing, and documenting controls to achieve the related control objectives stated in the description.

Note: When the control objectives have been specified by an outside party, the above paragraph describing the service organization's responsibilities should be modified as follows:

"On page [XX] of the description, [*Service Organization Name*] has provided an assertion about the fairness of the presentation of the description and suitability of the design and operating effectiveness of the controls to achieve the related control objectives stated in the description. [*Service Organization Name*] is responsible for preparing the description and for the assertion, including the completeness, accuracy, and method of presentation of the description and the assertion, providing the services covered by the description, specifying the control objectives and stating them in the description, identifying the risks that threaten the achievement of the control objectives, selecting the criteria, and designing, implementing, and documenting controls to achieve the related control objectives stated in the description. The control objectives have been specified by [*name of party specifying the control objectives*] and are stated on page [XX]of the description."

Our responsibility is to express an opinion on the fairness of the presentation of the description and on the suitability of the design and operating effectiveness of the controls to achieve the related control objectives stated in the description, based on our examination. We conducted our examination in accordance with attestation standards established by the American Institute of Certified Public Accountants. Those standards require that we plan and perform our examination to obtain reasonable assurance about whether, in all material respects, the description is fairly presented and the controls were suitably designed and operating effectively to achieve the related control objectives stated in the description throughout the period [*Month XX, 20X2*] to [*Month XX, 20X2*].

An examination of a description of a service organization's system and the suitability of the design and operating effectiveness of the service organization's controls to achieve the related control objectives stated in the description involves performing procedures to obtain evidence about the fairness of the presentation of the description and the suitability of the design and operating effectiveness of those controls to achieve the related control objectives stated in the description. Our procedures included assessing the risks that the description is not fairly presented and that the controls were not suitably designed or operating effectively to achieve the related control objectives stated in the description. Our procedures also included testing the operating effectiveness of those controls that we consider necessary to provide reasonable assurance that the related control objectives stated in the description were achieved. An examination engagement of this type also includes evaluating the overall presentation of the description and the suitability of the control objectives stated therein, and the suitability of the criteria specified by the service organization and described at page [XX]. We believe that the evidence we obtained is sufficient and appropriate to provide a reasonable basis for our opinion.

Because of their nature, controls at a service organization may not prevent, or detect and correct, all errors or omissions in processing or reporting transactions [*or identification of the function performed by the system*]. Also, the projection to the future of any evaluation of the fairness of the presentation of the description, or conclusions about the suitability of the design or operating effectiveness of the controls to achieve the related control objectives, is subject to the risk that controls at a service organization may become inadequate or fail.

[*Service Organization Name*] states in its description that it has automated controls in place to reconcile loan payments received with the output generated. However, electronic records of the performance of this reconciliation for the period from [*Month XX, 20X2*] to [*Month XX, 20X2*], were deleted as a result of a computer processing error and, therefore, we were unable to test the operation of this control for that period. Consequently, we were unable to determine whether the control objective, "Controls provide reasonable assurance that loan payments received are properly recorded" was achieved throughout the period [*Month XX, 20X2*]to [*Month XX, 20X2*].

In our opinion, except for the matter described in the preceding paragraph, and based on the criteria described in [*Service Organization Name*]'s assertion on page [XX], in all material respects:

a. The description fairly presents the [*type or name of*] system that was designed and implemented throughout the period [*Month XX, 20X2*] to [*Month XX, 20X2*].

b. The controls related to the control objectives stated in the description were suitably designed to provide reasonable assurance that the control objectives would be achieved if the controls operated effectively throughout the period [*Month XX, 20X2*]to [*Month XX, 20X2*].

c. The controls we tested, which were those necessary to provide reasonable assurance that the control objectives stated in the description were achieved, operated effectively throughout the period [*Month XX, 20X2*] to [*Month XX, 20X2*].

Note: If the application of complementary user entity controls is necessary to achieve the control objectives stated in management's description of the service organization's system, items b. and c. above should be modified as follows:

"b. The controls related to the control objectives stated in the description were suitably designed to provide reasonable assurance that the control objectives would be achieved if the controls operated effectively throughout the period [*Month XX, 20X2*] to [*Month XX, 20X2*], and user entities applied the complementary user entity controls contemplated in the design of [*Service Organization Name*]'s controls throughout the period [*Month XX, 20X2*] to [*Month XX, 20X2*].

c. The controls we tested, which together with the complementary user entity controls referred to in the scope paragraph of this report, if operating effectively, were those necessary to provide reasonable assurance that the control objectives stated in the description were achieved, operated effectively throughout the period [*Month XX, 20X2*] to [*Month XX, 20X2*]."

The specific controls tested and the nature, timing, and results of those tests are listed on pages [*YY–ZZ*].

This report, including the description of tests of controls and results thereof on pages [*YY–ZZ*], is intended solely for the information and use of [*Service Organization Name*], user entities of [*Service Organization Name*]'s [*type or name of*] system during some or all of the period [*Month XX, 20X2*] to [*Month XX, 20X2*], and the independent auditors of such user entities, who have a sufficient understanding to consider it, along with other information including information about controls implemented by user entities themselves, when assessing the risks of material misstatements of user entities' financial statements. This report is not intended to be and should not be used by anyone other than these specified parties.

[*Service auditor's signature*]

[*Date of the service auditor's report*]

[*Service auditor's city and state*]

PRACTICE POINT: Attest Interpretation 9101.8, *Including a Description of Tests of Controls or Other Procedures, and the Results Thereof, in an Examination Report*, issued in July 2010, addresses whether a practitioner who performs an examination engagement under AT Section 101 may include in a separate section of his examination report a description of tests of controls or other procedures performed in support of the practitioner's opinion resulting from such an engagement.

The Interpretation indicates that nothing in AT Section 101 precludes a practitioner from including in a separate section of his or her examination report a description of tests of controls or other procedures performed and the results thereof. However, in some cases, such a description may overshadow the practitioner's overall opinion or may cause report users to misunderstand the opinion. Therefore, the circumstances of the particular engagement are relevant to the practitioner's consideration regarding whether to include a description of tests of controls or other procedures performed, and the results thereof, in a separate section of the practitioner's examination report. In determining whether to include such a description in the practitioner's examination report, the following considerations are relevant:

- Whether there has been a request for such information and whether the specified parties making the request have an appropriate business need or reasonable basis for requesting the information (e.g., the specified parties are required to maintain and monitor controls that either encompass or are dependent on controls that are the subject of the examination and, therefore, need information about the tests of controls to enable them to have a basis for concluding that they have met the requirements applicable to them);

- Whether the specified parties have an understanding of the nature and subject matter of the engagement and experience in using the information in such reports;

- Whether including such a description in the examination report is likely to cause report users to misunderstand the opinion; and

- Whether the practitioner's tests of controls or other procedures performed directly relate to the subject matter of the engagement.

The Interpretation further alerts practitioners that the addition of a description of tests of controls or other procedures performed, and the results thereof, in a separate section of an examination report may increase the need for use of the report to be restricted to specified parties.

ILLUSTRATION 9—SERVICE AUDITOR'S REPORT FOR ENGAGEMENTS IN WHICH THE SERVICE ORGANIZATION USES A SUBSERVICE ORGANIZATION: CARVE-OUT METHOD (TYPE 2 REPORT)

Independent Service Auditor's Report

To: [*Service Organization Name*]

We have examined [*Service Organization Name*]'s description of its [type or name of] system for processing user entities' transactions [or identification of the function performed by the system] throughout the period [*Month XX, 20X2*] to [*Month XX, 20X2*] (description) and the suitability of the design and operating effectiveness of controls to achieve the related control objectives stated in the description.

Note: When the description of the service organization's system refers to the need for complementary user entity controls, the above scope paragraph should be modified as follows:

"We have examined [*Service Organization Name*]'s description of its [*type or name of*] system for processing user entities' transactions [*or identification of the function performed by the system*] throughout the period [*Month XX, 20X2*] to [*Month XX, 20X2*] (description) and the suitability of the design and operating effectiveness of controls to achieve the related control objectives stated in the description. The description indicates that certain control objectives specified in the description can be achieved only if complementary user entity controls contemplated in the design of [*Service Organization Name*]'s controls are suitably designed and operating effectively, along with related controls at the service organization. We have not evaluated the suitability of the design or operating effectiveness of such complementary user entity controls."

[*Service Organization Name*] uses a computer processing service organization for all of its computerized application processing. The description on pages [*BB–CC*] includes only the controls and related control objectives of [*Service Organization*

Name]and excludes the control objectives and related controls of the computer processing service organization. Our examination did not extend to controls of the computer processing service organization.

On page [XX] of the description, [*Service Organization Name*] has provided an assertion about the fairness of the presentation of the description and suitability of the design and operating effectiveness of the controls to achieve the related control objectives stated in the description. [*Service Organization Name*] is responsible for preparing the description and for the assertion, including the completeness, accuracy, and method of presentation of the description and the assertion, providing the services covered by the description, specifying the control objectives and stating them in the description, identifying the risks that threaten the achievement of the control objectives, selecting the criteria, and designing, implementing, and documenting controls to achieve the related control objectives stated in the description.

Note: When the control objectives have been specified by an outside party, the above paragraph describing the service organization's responsibilities should be modified as follows:

> "On page [XX] of the description, [*Service Organization Name*] has provided an assertion about the fairness of the presentation of the description and suitability of the design and operating effectiveness of the controls to achieve the related control objectives stated in the description. [*Service Organization Name*] is responsible for preparing the description and for the assertion, including the completeness, accuracy, and method of presentation of the description and the assertion, providing the services covered by the description, specifying the control objectives and stating them in the description, identifying the risks that threaten the achievement of the control objectives, selecting the criteria, and designing, implementing, and documenting controls to achieve the related control objectives stated in the description. The control objectives have been specified by [*name of party specifying the control objectives*] and are stated on page [XX] of the description."

Our responsibility is to express an opinion on the fairness of the presentation of the description and on the suitability of the design and operating effectiveness of the controls to achieve the related control objectives stated in the description, based on our examination. We conducted our examination in accordance with attestation standards established by the American Institute of Certified Public Accountants. Those standards require that we plan and perform our examination to obtain reasonable assurance about whether, in all material respects, the description is fairly presented and the controls were suitably designed and operating effectively to achieve the related control objectives stated in the description throughout the period [*Month XX, 20X2*] to [*Month XX, 20X2*].

An examination of a description of a service organization's system and the suitability of the design and operating effectiveness of the service organization's controls to achieve the related control objectives stated in the description involves performing procedures to obtain evidence about the fairness of the presentation of the description and the suitability of the design and operating effectiveness of those controls to achieve the related control objectives stated in the description. Our procedures included assessing the risks that the description is not fairly presented and that the controls were not suitably designed or operating effectively to achieve the related control objectives stated in the description. Our procedures also included testing the operating effectiveness of those controls that we consider necessary to provide reasonable assurance that the related control objectives stated in the description were achieved. An examination engagement of this type also includes evaluating the overall presentation of the description and the suitability of the control objectives stated therein, and the suitability of the criteria specified by the service organization and described at page [XX]. We believe that the evidence we obtained is sufficient and appropriate to provide a reasonable basis for our opinion.

Because of their nature, controls at a service organization may not prevent, or detect and correct, all errors or omissions in processing or reporting transactions [*or identification of the function performed by the system*]. Also, the projection to the future of any evaluation of the fairness of the presentation of the description, or conclusions about the suitability of the design or operating effectiveness of the controls to achieve the related control objectives, is subject to the risk that controls at a service organization may become inadequate or fail.

In our opinion, in all material respects, based on the criteria described in [*Service Organization Name*]'s assertion on page [XX]:

a. The description fairly presents the [type or name of]system that was designed and implemented throughout the period [*Month XX, 20X2*] to [*Month XX, 20X2*].

b. The controls related to the control objectives stated in the description were suitably designed to provide reasonable assurance that the control objectives would be achieved if the controls operated effectively throughout the period [*Month XX, 20X2*]to [*Month XX, 20X2*].

c. The controls we tested, which were those necessary to provide reasonable assurance that the control objectives stated in the description were achieved, operated effectively throughout the period [*Month XX, 20X2*] to [*Month XX, 20X2*].

Note: If the application of complementary user entity controls is necessary to achieve the control objectives stated in management's description of the service organization's system, items b. and c. above should be modified as follows:

"b. The controls related to the control objectives stated in the description were suitably designed to provide reasonable assurance that the control objectives would be achieved if the controls operated effectively throughout the period [*Month XX, 20X2*] to [*Month XX, 20X2*], and user entities applied the complementary user entity controls contemplated in the design of [*Service Organization Name*]'s controls throughout the period [*Month XX, 20X2*] to [*Month XX, 20X2*].

c. The controls we tested, which together with the complementary user entity controls referred to in the scope paragraph of this report, if operating effectively, were those necessary to provide reasonable assurance that the control objectives stated in the description were achieved, operated effectively throughout the period [*Month XX, 20X2*] to [*Month XX, 20X2*]."

The specific controls tested and the nature, timing, and results of those tests are listed on pages [*YY–ZZ*].

This report, including the description of tests of controls and results thereof on pages [*YY–ZZ*], is intended solely for the information and use of [*Service Organization Name*], user entities of [*Service Organization Name*]'s [*type or name of*] system during some or all of the period [*Month XX, 20X2*] to [*Month XX, 20X2*], and the independent auditors of such user entities, who have a sufficient understanding to consider it, along with other information including information about controls implemented by user entities themselves, when assessing the risks of material misstatements of user entities' financial statements. This report is not intended to be and should not be used by anyone other than these specified parties.

[*Service auditor's signature*]

[*Date of the service auditor's report*]

[*Service auditor's city and state*]

PRACTICE POINT: Attest Interpretation 9101.8, *Including a Description of Tests of Controls or Other Procedures, and the Results Thereof, in an Examination Report,* issued in July 2010, addresses whether a practitioner who performs an examination engagement under AT Section 101 may include in a separate section of his examination report a description of tests of controls or other procedures performed in support of the practitioner's opinion resulting from such an engagement.

The Interpretation indicates that nothing in AT Section 101 precludes a practitioner from including in a separate section of his or her examination report a description of tests of controls or other procedures performed and the results thereof. However, in some cases, such a description may overshadow the practitioner's overall opinion or may cause report users to misunderstand the opinion. Therefore, the circumstances of the particular engagement are relevant to the practitioner's consideration regarding whether to include a description of tests of controls or other procedures performed, and the results thereof, in a separate section of the practitioner's examination report. In determining whether to include such a description in the practitioner's examination report, the following considerations are relevant:

- Whether there has been a request for such information and whether the specified parties making the request have an appropriate business need or reasonable basis for requesting the information (e.g., the specified parties are required to maintain and monitor controls that either encompass or are dependent on controls that are the subject of the examination and, therefore, need information about the tests of controls to enable them to have a basis for concluding that they have met the requirements applicable to them);

- Whether the specified parties have an understanding of the nature and subject matter of the engagement and experience in using the information in such reports;

- Whether including such a description in the examination report is likely to cause report users to misunderstand the opinion; and

- Whether the practitioner's tests of controls or other procedures performed directly relate to the subject matter of the engagement.

The Interpretation further alerts practitioners that the addition of a description of tests of controls or other procedures performed, and the results thereof, in a separate section of an examination report may increase the need for use of the report to be restricted to specified parties.

ILLUSTRATION 10—SERVICE AUDITOR'S REPORT FOR ENGAGEMENTS IN WHICH THE SERVICE ORGANIZATION USES A SUBSERVICE ORGANIZATION: INCLUSIVE METHOD (TYPE 2 REPORT)

Independent Service Auditor's Report

To: [*Service Organization Name*]

We have examined [*Service Organization Name*]'s and [*Subservice Organization*]'s description of their [*type or name of*] system for processing user entities' transactions [*or identification of the function performed by the system*] throughout the period [*Month XX, 20X2*] to [*Month XX, 20X2*](description) and the suitability of the design and operating effectiveness of [*Service Organization Name*]'s and [*Subservice Organization*]'s controls to achieve the related control objectives stated in the description. [*Subservice Organization*]is an independent service organization that provides computer processing services to [*Service Organization Name*]. [*Service Organization Name*]'s description includes a description of [*Subservice Organization*]'s [*type or name of*] system used by [*Service Organization Name*] to process transactions for its user entities, as well as relevant control objectives and controls of [*Subservice Organization*].

Note: When the description of the service organization's system refers to the need for complementary user entity controls, the above scope paragraph should be modified as follows:

"We have examined [*Service Organization Name*]'s and [*Subservice Organization*]'s description of their [*type or name of*] system for processing user entities' transactions [*or identification of the function performed by the system*] throughout the period [*Month XX, 20X2*] to [*Month XX, 20X2*] (description) and the suitability of the design and operating effectiveness of [*Service Organization Name*]'s and [*Subservice Organization*]'s controls to achieve the related control objectives stated in the description. [*Subservice Organization*] is an independent service organization that provides computer processing services to [*Service Organization Name*]. [*Service Organization Name*]'s description includes a description of [*Subservice Organization*]'s [*type or name of*] system used by [*Service Organization Name*] to process transactions for its user entities, as well as relevant control objectives and controls of [*Subservice Organization*].The description indicates that certain control objectives specified in the description can be achieved only if complementary user entity controls contemplated in the design of [*Service Organization Name*]'s controls are suitably designed and operating effectively, along with related controls at the service organization. We have not evaluated the suitability of the design or operating effectiveness of such complementary user entity controls."

On page [*XX*]of the description, [*Service Organization Name*] and [*Subservice Organization*] have provided their assertions about the fairness of the presentation of the description and suitability of the design and operating effectiveness of the controls to achieve the related control objectives stated in the description. [*Service Organization Name*] and [*Subservice Organization*]are responsible for preparing the description and for the assertions, including the completeness, accuracy, and method of presentation of the description and the assertions, providing the services covered by the description, specifying the control objectives and stating them in the description, identifying the risks that threaten the achievement of the control objectives, selecting the criteria, and designing, implementing, and documenting controls to achieve the related control objectives stated in the description.

Note: When the control objectives have been specified by an outside party, the above paragraph describing the service organization's responsibilities should be modified as follows:

"On page [*XX*] of the description, [*Service Organization Name*] and [Subservice Organization] have provided their assertions about the fairness of the presentation of the description and suitability of the design and operating effectiveness of the controls to achieve the related control objectives stated in the description. [*Service Organization Name*] and [*Subservice Organization*]are responsible for preparing the description and for the assertions, including the completeness, accuracy, and method of presentation of the description and the assertions, providing the services covered by the description, specifying the control objectives and stating them in the description, identifying the risks that threaten the achievement of the control objectives, selecting the criteria, and designing, implementing, and documenting controls to achieve the related control objectives stated in the description. The control objectives have been specified by [*name of party specifying the control objectives*]and are stated on page [*XX*] of the description."

Our responsibility is to express an opinion on the fairness of the presentation of the description and on the suitability of the design and operating effectiveness of the controls to achieve the related control objectives stated in the description, based on our examination. We conducted our examination in accordance with attestation standards established by the American Institute of Certified Public Accountants. Those standards require that we plan and perform our examination to obtain reasonable assurance about whether, in all material respects, the description is fairly presented and the controls were suitably designed and operating effectively to achieve the related control objectives stated in the description throughout the period [*Month XX, 20X2*] to [*Month XX, 20X2*].

An examination of a description of a service organization's system and the suitability of the design and operating effectiveness of the service organization's controls to achieve the related control objectives stated in the description involves performing procedures to obtain evidence about the fairness of the presentation of the description and the suitability of the design and operating effectiveness of those controls to achieve the related control objectives stated in the description. Our procedures included assessing the risks that the description is not fairly presented and that the controls were not suitably designed or operating effectively to achieve the related control objectives stated in the description. Our procedures also included testing the operating effectiveness of those controls that we consider necessary to provide reasonable assurance that the related control objectives stated in the description were achieved. An examination engagement of this type also includes evaluating the overall presentation of the description and the suitability of the control objectives stated therein, and the suitability of the criteria specified by the service organization and described at page [*XX*]. We believe that the evidence we obtained is sufficient and appropriate to provide a reasonable basis for our opinion.

Because of their nature, controls at a service organization or subservice organization may not prevent, or detect and correct, all errors or omissions in processing or reporting transactions [*or identification of the function performed by the system*]. Also, the projection to the future of any evaluation of the fairness of the presentation of the description, or conclusions about the suitability of the design or operating effectiveness of the controls to achieve the related control objectives is subject to the risk that controls at a service organization or subservice organization may become inadequate or fail.

In our opinion, in all material respects, based on the criteria described in [*Service Organization Name*]'s and [*Subservice Organization*]'s assertions on page [*XX*]:

a. The description fairly presents [*Service Organization Name*]'s [*type or name of*] system and [*Subservice Organization*]'s [*type or name of*] system used by [*Service Organization Name*]to process transactions for its user entities [*or identification of the function performed by the service organization's system*]that were designed and implemented throughout the period [*Month XX, 20X2*] to [*Month XX, 20X2*].

b. The controls related to the control objectives of [*Service Organization Name*] and [*Subservice Organization*]stated in the description were suitably designed to provide reasonable assurance that the control objectives would be achieved if the controls operated effectively throughout the period [*Month XX, 20X2*]to [*Month XX, 20X2*].

c. The controls of [*Service Organization Name*]and [*Subservice Organization*] that we tested, which were those necessary to provide reasonable assurance that the control objectives stated in the description were achieved, operated effectively throughout the period [*Month XX, 20X2*] to [*Month XX, 20X2*].

Note: If the application of complementary user entity controls is necessary to achieve the control objectives stated in management's description of the service organization's system, items b. and c. above should be modified as follows:

"b. The controls related to the control objectives of [*Service Organization Name*] and [*Subservice Organization*] stated in the description were suitably designed to provide reasonable assurance that the control objectives would be achieved if the controls operated effectively throughout the period [*Month XX, 20X2*]to [*Month XX, 20X2*], and user entities applied the complementary user entity controls contemplated in the design of [*Service Organization Name*]'s controls throughout the period [*Month XX, 20X2*] to [*Month XX, 20X2*].

c. The controls of [*Service Organization Name*] and [*Subservice Organization*] that we tested, which together with the complementary user entity controls referred to in the scope paragraph of this report, if operating effectively, were those necessary to provide reasonable assurance that the control objectives stated in the description were achieved, operated effectively throughout the period [*Month XX, 20X2*] to [*Month XX, 20X2*]."

The specific controls tested and the nature, timing, and results of those tests are listed on pages [*YY–ZZ*].

This report, including the description of tests of controls and results thereof on pages [*YY–ZZ*], is intended solely for the information and use of [*Service Organization Name*], user entities of [*Service Organization Name*]'s [*type or name of*] system during some or all of the period [*Month XX, 20X2*] to [*Month XX, 20X2*], and the independent auditors of such user entities, who have a sufficient understanding to consider it, along with other information including information about controls implemented by user entities themselves, when assessing the risks of material misstatements of user entities' financial statements. This report is not intended to be and should not be used by anyone other than these specified parties.

[*Service auditor's signature*]

[*Date of the service auditor's report*]

[*Service auditor's city and state*]

PRACTICE POINT: Attest Interpretation 9101.8, *Including a Description of Tests of Controls or Other Procedures, and the Results Thereof, in an Examination Report,* issued in July 2010, addresses whether a practitioner who performs an examination engagement under AT Section 101 may include in a separate section of his examination report a description of tests of controls or other procedures performed in support of the practitioner's opinion resulting from such an engagement.

The Interpretation indicates that nothing in AT Section 101 precludes a practitioner from including in a separate section of his or her examination report a description of tests of controls or other procedures performed and the results thereof. However, in some cases, such a description may overshadow the practitioner's overall opinion or may cause report users to misunderstand the opinion. Therefore, the circumstances of the particular engagement are relevant to the practitioner's consideration regarding whether to include a description of tests of controls or other procedures performed, and the results thereof, in a separate section of the practitioner's examination report. In determining whether to include such a description in the practitioner's examination report, the following considerations are relevant:

- Whether there has been a request for such information and whether the specified parties making the request have an appropriate business need or reasonable basis for requesting the information (e.g., the specified parties are required to maintain and monitor controls that either encompass or are dependent on controls that are the subject of the examination and, therefore, need information about the tests of controls to enable them to have a basis for concluding that they have met the requirements applicable to them);
- Whether the specified parties have an understanding of the nature and subject matter of the engagement and experience in using the information in such reports;
- Whether including such a description in the examination report is likely to cause report users to misunderstand the opinion; and
- Whether the practitioner's tests of controls or other procedures performed directly relate to the subject matter of the engagement.

The Interpretation further alerts practitioners that the addition of a description of tests of controls or other procedures performed, and the results thereof, in a separate section of an examination report may increase the need for use of the report to be restricted to specified parties.

AR Section
STATEMENTS ON STANDARDS FOR ACCOUNTING AND REVIEW SERVICES

AR SECTION 60
FRAMEWORK FOR PERFORMING AND REPORTING ON COMPILATION AND REVIEW ENGAGEMENTS

PRACTICE POINT: The American Institute of Certified Public Accountants' (AICPA's) Accounting and Review Services Committee has published an exposure draft of a proposed Statement on Standards for Accounting and Review Services (SSARS) titled, "The Use of the Accountant's Name in a Document or Communication Containing Unaudited Financial Statements That Have Not Been Compiled or Reviewed." This proposal would amend AR Section 60 (Framework for Performing and Reporting on Compilation and Review Engagements), SSARS-19, "Compilation and Review Engagements," to address the accountant's responsibilities when he or she permits the use of his or her name in a document or written communication containing unaudited financial statements that have not been compiled or reviewed. Specifically, this proposal would establish a:

- Requirement that, prior to permitting the use of his or her name in a document or written communication containing unaudited financial statements that have not been compiled or reviewed, the accountant should read the financial statements and other information in the document and consider whether such financial statements and other information appears free from obvious material misstatements and from material inconsistencies with other knowledge or information that the accountant may have obtained.

- Nonreporting option when the accountant permits the use of his or her name in a document or written communication containing unaudited financial statements that have not been compiled or reviewed provided that the accountant requests that the client clearly indicate that the unaudited financial statements were not compiled or reviewed by the accountant.

As proposed, this guidance would be effective for unaudited financial statements that have not been compiled or reviewed for periods ending on or after December 15, 2011.

WHAT EVERY PRACTITIONER SHOULD KNOW

Basic Objectives and Requirements

AR Section 60 provides a framework for, and defines and describes the objectives and elements of, compilation and review engagements. It also defines certain terms as used in the SSARSs. It is intended to help accountants better understand their professional responsibilities when engaged to compile or review financial statements or financial information. Additional standards of SSARSs have been established to set forth specific performance and reporting requirements. Such additional standards are based on the framework provided by AR Section 60.

Relevant Definitions

The following terms are defined in AR Section 60 for purposes of the SSARSs:

- *Applicable financial reporting framework*—This is the financial reporting framework the entity adopted in the preparation of the financial statements that is acceptable in view of the nature of the entity and objective of the financial statements, or that is required by law or regulation, for example, U.S. generally accepted accounting principles (GAAP).

- *Assurance engagement*—An engagement in which an accountant issues a report designed to enhance the degree of confidence of third parties and management about the outcome of an evaluation or measurement of financial statements (subject matter) against an applicable financial reporting framework (criteria).

- *Attest engagement*—An engagement that requires independence, as defined in *AICPA Professional Standards*.

- *Financial reporting framework*—A set of criteria used to determine measurement, recognition, presentation, and disclosure of all material items appearing in the financial statements. It is similar to the commonly used term *basis of accounting*.

- *Financial statements*—A structured representation of historical financial information, including the related notes, that is intended to communicate an entity's economic resources and obligations at a point in time, or the changes therein for a period of time in accordance with a financial reporting framework. This term ordinarily refers to a complete set of financial statements, but can also refer to a single financial statement, or financial statements without notes.

- *Management*—Persons with executive responsibility for the conduct of the entity's operations. For some entities, this may include some or all of *those charged with governance*, as defined below.

- *Nonissuer*—All entities except those registered or required to file reports with the Securities and Exchange Commission (SEC) under the provisions of certain specific laws.

- *Other comprehensive basis of accounting (OCBOA)*—A definite set of criteria other than GAAP or International Financial Reporting Standards (IFRS) having substantial support underlying the preparation of financial statements prepared pursuant to that basis; for example, regulatory basis, income tax basis, and cash basis.

- *Review evidence*—The information used by the accountant to provide a reasonable basis for obtaining limited assurance.

- *Submission of financial statements*—Financial statements prepared by the accountant and presented to management.

- *Third party*—All persons, except members of management. The definition of "third party" includes *those charged with governance*, as defined below.

- *Those charged with governance*—Persons with responsibility for overseeing the strategic direction of the entity and obligations related to its accountability, including the financial reporting process. Those charged with governance are specifically excluded from management unless they perform management functions.

Objectives and Limitations of Compilation and Review Services

AR Section 60 identifies and distinguishes between compilation and review services, their objectives, and their limitations, as discussed below.

Compilations The objective of a compilation is to assist management in presenting financial information in the form of financial statements. A compilation does not undertake to obtain or provide any assurance about whether material modifications should be made to the financial statements. It differs significantly from a review or an audit, in that it does not contemplate:

- Performing inquiry or analytical procedures;
- Performing other procedures normally performed in a review;
- Obtaining an understanding of the entity's internal controls;
- Assessing fraud risk;
- Testing accounting records through inspection, observation, confirmation, or examination of source documents;
- Performing other procedures normally performed in an audit; and
- Providing any assurance regarding the financial statements.

A compilation is classified as an attest engagement, but not an assurance engagement.

Reviews The objective of a review is to obtain limited assurance that no material modifications should be made to the financial statements in order for them to be in conformity with the applicable financial reporting framework. The accountant should gather review evidence to obtain that limited level of assurance. A review differs significantly from an audit in that it does not contemplate:

- Obtaining a high level of assurance (i.e., reasonable assurance) about the financial statements;
- Obtaining an understanding of the entity's internal control;
- Assessing fraud risk;
- Testing accounting records through inspection, observation, confirmation, or examination of source documents; and
- Performing other procedures normally performed in an audit.

A review is classified as both an attest and assurance engagement.

Categories of Professional Requirements

AR Section 60 emphasizes that accountants are responsible for considering the entire text of a SSARS in performing engagements, and for understanding and applying the relevant professional requirements. Not every paragraph of a SSARS contains a professional requirement. AR Section 60 establishes two categories of professional requirements (similar to the auditing standards). They are:

1. *Unconditional requirements*—The accountant is required to comply with an unconditional requirement in all cases in which the circumstances exist to which the requirement applies. An unconditional requirement is indicated by the words "must" or "is required."

2. *Presumptively mandatory requirements*—The accountant also is required to comply with a presumptively mandatory requirement in all cases in which the circumstances exist to which the requirement applies, except in rare cases in which the accountant documents a justification for the departure and how alternative procedures achieved the requirement's objectives. A presumptively mandatory requirement is indicated by the word "should." (*Note*: When the SSARSs use the words "should consider," the consideration of the procedure or action is presumptively mandatory, but its performance is not.)

The SSARSs also contain explanatory material, which is identified by the words" may," "might," and "could." This material is not intended to impose professional requirements. It is descriptive, not imperative, and provides further guidance and explanation on the professional requirements, or identifies and describes other procedures or actions relating to the accountant's activities. Whether or how those procedures or actions are performed is a matter of professional judgment.

The following is a summary of the imperatives/terms used in AR Section 60 and the degrees of responsibility they impose on accountants:

Imperatives/Terms	Meaning
"must" and "is required"	These words impose an unconditional responsibility or requirement on the accountant to comply with requirements of this type specified in SSARSs.
"should"	This indicates a presumptively mandatory requirement. Compliance with requirements of this type specified in SSARSs is required, unless the accountant can demonstrate that the alternative procedures or actions that he or she applied were appropriate and sufficient to accomplish the objectives of the particular standard.
"should consider"	This indicates that the consideration of the procedure or action provided in the is presumptively required; however, carrying out the action or procedure is not required.
"may," "might," and "could"	These words do not impose a professional requirement for the accountant to perform the suggested procedures or actions. Rather, they impose on the accountant a responsibility to consider certain actions, procedures, or matters specified in SSARSs. Whether and how the accountant implements these matters in the conduct a compilation or review engagement is subject to the accountant's professional judgment.

The imperative "should" indicates a presumptively mandatory activity. There are only rare circumstances in which the accountant would be able to meet the objectives of the standards by alternative means. Therefore, if the accountant departs from a presumptively mandatory requirement, the accountant must document (1) the reasons and justification for why the presumptively mandatory requirement was not complied with and (2) how the alternative procedures performed adequately achieved the objectives of the presumptively mandatory requirement.

Hierarchy of Compilation and Review Standards and Guidance

AR Section 60 states, as an unconditional requirement, that accountants perform compilation and review engagements of a nonissuer in accordance with the SSARSs, except for certain reviews of interim financial information, to which AU Section 722 (Interim Financial Information) applies.

The SSARSs hierarchy includes (1) *interpretive publications* (e.g., compilation and review interpretations of the SSARSs) and (2) *other compilation and review publications* (e.g., articles and textbooks). AR Section 60 is intended to make practitioners aware of the literature and the various publications' standing in the SSARSs hierarchy.

Interpretive publications provide recommendations to practitioners on the application of the SSARSs in specific circumstances, including engagements involving specialized industries. Although interpretive publications are not accounting and review services standards, the accountant should be aware of and consider interpretive publications applicable to his or her compilation or review engagements. Therefore, if the accountant does not apply the guidance included in an applicable interpretive publication, the accountant should be prepared to explain how he or she complied with the SSARSs provisions addressed by such guidance in the applicable interpretive publication.

Although *other compilation and review publications* may help accountants understand and apply the SSARSs, they have no authoritative status. However, if an accountant applies the guidance included in another compilation and review publication, he or she should be satisfied that, in his or her judgment, it is both appropriate and relevant to the circumstances of his or her engagement. Other compilation and review publications published by the AICPA that have been reviewed by the AICPA Audit and Attest Standards staff are considered appropriate.

In addition to the SSARSs, AICPA members who perform compilations and reviews are governed by the AICPA *Code of Professional Conduct* and Statements on Quality Control Standards. Accordingly, they are responsible for adopting a system of quality control to provide reasonable assurance that firm personnel comply with the SSARSs in compilation and review engagements.

Elements of a Compilation or Review Engagement

AR Section 60 discusses the following elements of compilation and review engagements:

- *Three-party relationship*—A compilation or review engagement is a three-party relationship, involving management (or the responsible party), the accountant, and the intended users, as follows:
  - Management (or the responsible party) is responsible for the preparation and fair presentation of the financial statements, and for designing, implementing, and maintaining internal control. This includes

identifying the applicable financial reporting framework and establishing accounting policies.

— Accountants may make recommendations about the form or content of financial statements or may prepare them based on information represented by management. Accountants are precluded from issuing an unmodified compilation report or a review report on financial statements when management is not willing to accept its responsibility as described in the preceding paragraph.

— Intended users are presumed to understand the limitations of both (1) the financial statements and (2) compilation and review engagements. Accountants are not responsible for identifying the intended users.

- *Applicable financial reporting framework*—Examples of financial reporting frameworks include GAAP, IFRS, and OCBOA.

- *Financial statements or financial information*—An accountant may be engaged to compile or review a complete set of financial statements or an individual financial statement for an annual period or for a shorter or longer period, depending on the needs of management. The applicable financial reporting framework determines what constitutes a complete set of financial statements.

- *Evidence*—An accountant has no responsibility to gather any evidence about the accuracy or completeness of financial statements in a compilation engagement. In a review engagement, the accountant is responsible for obtaining review evidence to provide a reasonable basis for obtaining limited assurance that no material modifications should be made to the financial statements in order for them to be in conformity with the applicable financial reporting framework. Analytical procedures and inquiries ordinarily are sufficient for this purpose.

- *Compilation and review reports*—Written accountants' reports are required on compilation or review engagements unless the accountant withdraws from the engagement or, in the case of compiled financial statements that are not expected to be submitted to a third party, the accountant issues a written communication to management.

Materiality

AR Section 60 contains a discussion of materiality that is designed to guide accountants whenever an applicable financial reporting framework does not contain more specific guidance. It includes the following concepts:

- Misstatements, including omissions, are material if they could reasonably be expected to influence the economic decisions of users.

- Judgments about materiality are made in the context of surrounding circumstances, and are affected by the size or nature of the misstatement.

- Judgments about materiality are based on a consideration of the common needs of the users as a group, and not on specific individual users.

Accountants use professional judgment in determining materiality, taking into consideration the needs of financial statement users. AR Section 60 indicates that it is reasonable for accountants to assume that users:

- Have reasonable business and economic knowledge.
- Are willing to study the financial statements with reasonable diligence.
- Understand that financial statements are prepared, presented, and reviewed according to levels of materiality.
- Understand that there are inherent uncertainties involving estimates, judgment, and consideration of future events.
- Make reasonable economic decisions based on the financial statement information.

PRACTICE ISSUES AND FREQUENTLY ASKED QUESTIONS

Issue 1: Do the words "may," "might," and "could" impose a professional requirement for the accountant to perform the suggested procedures or actions described in SSARS?

No. SSARS generally include explanatory material that provides further clarification or guidance on the professional requirements, or identifies and describes other procedures or actions relating to the accountant's activities. Such explanatory material generally explains why the accountant might consider certain particular procedures and provides additional information for the accountant to consider in exercising professional judgment in performing the compilation or review engagement. The words *may, might,* and *could* are typically used to describe these actions and procedures. Therefore, explanatory material that uses such terms is not intended to impose a professional requirement for the accountant to perform the suggested procedures or actions. Rather, these procedures or actions require the accountant's attention and understanding; accordingly, how and whether the accountant carries out the suggested procedures or actions depends on the exercise of professional judgment in the specific engagement.

Issue 2: What are examples of interpretive publications under SSARS?

Interpretive publications under SSARS consist of:

- Compilation and review Interpretations of the SSARS.
- Appendices to the SSARS.
- Compilation and review guidance included in AICPA Audit and Accounting Guides.
- AICPA Statements of Position, to the extent they are applicable to compilation and review engagements.

Issue 3: What are examples of other compilation and review publications under SSARS?

Other compilation and review publications under SSARS include:

- AICPA accounting and review publications, other than the SSARS and the interpretive publications referred to above.
- AICPA's annual *Compilation and Review Alert.*

- Articles in the *Journal of Accountancy* and other professional journals.
- Articles in the AICPA's *The CPA Letter*.
- Continuing professional education programs.
- Other instruction materials.
- Textbooks.
- Guide books.
- Compilation and review programs and checklists.
- Other publications from state CPA societies, other organizations, and individuals.

ILLUSTRATIONS AND PRACTICE AIDS

There are no illustrations and practice aids for this Section.

AR SECTION 80
COMPILATION OF FINANCIAL STATEMENTS

WHAT EVERY PRACTITIONER SHOULD KNOW

Basic Objectives and Requirements

The guidance and requirements in AR Section 80 are based on the framework provided by AR Section 60 (Framework for Performing and Reporting on Compilation and Review Engagements).

AR Section 80 establishes standards and provides guidance on compilations of financial statements. The accountant is required to comply with the provisions of AR Section 80 whenever he or she is engaged to report on compiled financial statements or submits financial statements to a client or to third parties.

Establishing an Understanding with the Client in a Compilation Engagement

AR Section 80 contains a presumptively mandatory requirement for the accountant to establish an understanding with management (and, if applicable, those charged with governance) regarding the services to be performed and to document the understanding through a written communication (i.e., engagement letter). This is a significant change from previous standards, which stated only that the client understanding should *preferably* be in writing. The engagement letter should address the following:

- *Objectives of the engagement*—Essentially, the primary objective of the compilation is to assist management in presenting financial information in the form of financial statements, without undertaking to obtain or provide any assurance that there are no material modifications that should be made to the financial statements.

- *Management's responsibilities*—Management is responsible for the following:

  — The preparation and fair presentation of the financial statements in accordance with the applicable financial reporting framework.

  — Designing, implementing, and maintaining internal control relevant to the preparation and fair presentation of the financial statements.

  — Preventing and detecting fraud.

  — Identifying and ensuring that the entity complies with the laws and regulations applicable to its activities.

  — Making all financial records and related information available to the accountant.

- *Accountant's responsibilities*—The accountant is responsible for the following:

  — Conducting the engagement in accordance with SSARSs issued by the AICPA.

— Informing the appropriate level of management of any material errors and any evidence or information that comes to the accountant's attention that fraud or an illegal act may have occurred. (*Note:* The accountant is not required to report any matters regarding illegal acts that may have occurred that are clearly inconsequential and may reach agreement in advance with the entity on the nature of any such matters to be communicated.)

— Addressing the effect of any independence impairments on the expected form of the accountant's compilation report, if applicable.

- *Limitations of the engagement*—A compilation conducted in accordance with SSARSs:

— Differs significantly from a review or an audit of financial statements and, therefore, does not contemplate: (1) performing inquiry, analytical procedures, or other procedures performed in a review; (2) obtaining an understanding of the entity's internal control; (3) assessing fraud risk; (4) testing accounting records by obtaining sufficient appropriate audit evidence through inspection, observation, confirmation, or the examination of source documents (e.g., cancelled checks or bank images); or (5) performing other procedures ordinarily performed in an audit. Accordingly, the accountant will not express an opinion or provide any assurance regarding the financial statements.

— Cannot be relied on to disclose errors, fraud, or illegal acts.

- *Other additional matters*—The engagement letter should address the following additional matters, if applicable:

— Material departures from the applicable financial reporting framework may exist, and the effects of those departures, if any, on the financial statements may not be disclosed.

— Substantially all disclosures (and statement of cash flows, if applicable) required by the applicable financial reporting framework may be omitted.

— Reference to supplementary information.

In addition to the required matters discussed above, AR Section 80 indicates that an understanding with the client also may include other matters, such as the following:

- Arrangements regarding fees and billings.

- Any limitation of or other arrangements regarding the liability of the accountant or the client, for example, indemnification to the accountant for liability arising from knowing misrepresentations to the accountant by management (certain regulators may restrict or prohibit such liability limitation arrangements).

- Conditions under which access to compilation documentation may be granted to others.

- Additional services to be provided relating to regulatory requirements.

Furthermore, if the compiled financial statements are not expected to be used by a third party and the accountant does not expect to issue a compilation report on the financial statements, the accountant should include in the engagement letter an acknowledgment of management's representation and agreement that the financial statements are not to be used by a third party.

See Illustration 1 for an example of a standard engagement letter that is appropriate for a compilation, and Illustration 2 for an example of an engagement letter for a compilation of financial statements not intended for third-party use.

Compilation Performance Requirements

AR Section 80 sets forth the following specific performance requirements for compilation engagements:

- *Understanding the industry*—The accountant should obtain an understanding of the client's industry sufficient to compile financial statements in appropriate form for an entity operating in that industry. This requirement does not preclude an accountant from accepting a compilation engagement in an industry in which the accountant has no previous experience. However, it does make the accountant responsible for obtaining that understanding by, for example, consulting professional literature, other knowledgeable individuals, or taking continuing education courses.

- *Knowledge of the client*—Knowledge of the client should include an understanding of the client's business and its accounting principles and practices. This understanding is ordinarily obtained through experience with the client or its industry and inquiries of client personnel. In gaining this understanding, AR Section 80 states that the accountant should be alert to unusual accounting policies or practices that come to the accountant's attention as a result of having knowledge of the industry.

- *Reading the financial statements*—The accountant should read the financial statements before submission to consider whether they appear to be in appropriate form and free from obvious material errors, including arithmetical or clerical mistakes, mistakes in the application of accounting principles, and inadequate disclosures.

- *Other compilation procedures*—Accountants are not required to make inquiries or perform other procedures to verify, corroborate, or review the client's information in a compilation engagement. However, they may become aware that information is incorrect, incomplete, otherwise unsatisfactory, or that fraud or an illegal act has occurred. In such cases, they should request management to consider the effects of these matters on the financial statements, and should ask for additional or revised information when they believe the financial statements are materially misstated. A refusal on management's part to provide this information should cause the accountant to withdraw from the engagement.

Documentation in a Compilation Engagement

AR Section 80 contains specific documentation requirements and requires the accountant to prepare documentation in connection with each compilation engagement in sufficient detail to provide a clear understanding of the work performed. At a minimum, accountants should prepare the following documentation in a compilation engagement:

- An engagement letter;
- Any findings or issues that are significant in the accountant's judgment; and
- Oral or written communications to the appropriate level of management regarding fraud or illegal acts that come to the accountant's attention.

Reporting on Compiled Financial Statements

Compiled financial statements should be accompanied by a written accountant's report under either of the following circumstances:

- When the accountant is engaged by the client to report on compiled financial statements; or
- When the accountant submits financial statements to the client that are reasonably expected to be used by a third party.

AR Section 80 states that the accountant's standard compilation report should include the following elements:

- *Title*—The title should clearly indicate that it is the accountant's compilation report. (*Note:* If applicable, the accountant may indicate that he or she is independent in the title. Appropriate titles would be "Accountant's Compilation Report" or "Independent Accountant's Compilation Report.")
- *Addressee*—The report should be addressed as appropriate in the circumstances of the engagement.
- *Introductory paragraph*—The accountant's report should include an introductory paragraph that:
  — Identifies the entity whose financial statements have been compiled;
  — States that the financial statements have been compiled;
  — Identifies the financial statements that have been compiled (e.g., balance sheet, statement of operations);
  — Specifies the date or period covered by the financial statements; and
  — States that the accountant has not audited or reviewed the financial statements and, accordingly, does not express an opinion or provide any assurance about whether the financial statements are in accordance with the applicable financial reporting framework (e.g., GAAP, OCBOA).
- *Management's responsibility paragraph*—The accountant's report should include a paragraph that describes management's responsibility for the

financial statements and for internal control over financial reporting, specifically stating that management is responsible for:

— The preparation and fair presentation of the financial statements in accordance with the applicable financial reporting framework (e.g., GAAP, OCBOA); and

— Designing, implementing, and maintaining internal control relevant to the preparation and fair presentation of the financial statements.

• *Accountant's responsibility paragraph*—The accountant's report should include a paragraph that states:

— The accountant's responsibility is to conduct the compilation in accordance with SSARSs issued by the AICPA; and

— The objective of a compilation is to assist management in presenting financial information in the form of financial statements without undertaking to obtain or provide any assurance that there are no material modifications that should be made to the financial statements.

• *Signature*—The accountant's report should include a manual or printed signature of the accounting firm or the accountant, as appropriate.

• *Date*—The accountant's compilation report should be dated the date of completion of the compilation.

In addition, each page of the compiled financial statements should include a reference to the accountant's compilation report, such as "See Accountant's Compilation Report" or "See Independent Accountant's Compilation Report."

See Illustration 3 for an example of a compilation report on full disclosure GAAP financial statements, Illustration 4 applicable to full disclosure cash basis financial statements, and Illustration 5 applicable to full disclosure income tax basis financial statements.

Reporting on Compiled Financial Statements That Omit Substantially All Disclosures

An accountant may compile financial statements that omit substantially all of the disclosures required by an applicable financial reporting framework (e.g., GAAP, OCBOA), provided the following conditions are met:

1. The omission of substantially all disclosures is not undertaken with the intention to mislead those who might reasonably be expected to use such financial statements.

2. The accountant includes (after the paragraph describing the accountant's responsibility) a paragraph in the compilation report that states:

   a. Management has elected to omit substantially all the disclosures (and the statement of cash flows, if applicable) required by the applicable financial reporting framework (or ordinarily included in the financial statements if the financial statements are prepared in accordance with an OCBOA);

   b. If the omitted disclosures (and statement of cash flows, if applicable) were included in the financial statements, they might influence the user's conclusions about the entity's financial position, results of operations, and cash flows (or equivalent for presentations other than GAAP); and

c. The financial statements are not designed for those who are not informed about such matters.

See Illustration 6 for an example of a compilation report on GAAP financial statements that omit substantially all disclosures, Illustration 7 for an example of a compilation report on cash basis financial statements that omit substantially all disclosures, and Illustration 8 for an example of such a report when the financial statements are prepared on the income tax basis of accounting.

If the entity decides to include disclosures about only a few matters in the form of notes to compiled financial statements that otherwise omit substantially all disclosures, the selected notes should be labeled "Selected Information— Substantially All Disclosures Required by [*identify the applicable financial reporting framework (e.g., 'Accounting Principles Generally Accepted in the United States of America')*] Are Not Included." However, this label cannot and should not be used when an entity has substantially included all disclosures but omitted a few (e.g., one or two notes); the omission of one or two notes, when substantially all other required disclosures are included, should be treated similar to any other departure from an applicable financial reporting framework and should be addressed in the accountant's compilation report.

Omission of the Display of Comprehensive Income in Compiled Financial Statements

GAAP requires comprehensive income and its components to be reported when a company presents a full set of financial statements that report financial position, results of operations, and cash flows. The term *comprehensive income* refers to net income plus other comprehensive income (i.e., certain revenues, expenses, gains, and losses that are reported as separate components of stockholders' equity instead of net income). Examples of other comprehensive income include unrealized holding gains or losses on available-for-sale securities and foreign currency translation adjustments.

GAAP requires that comprehensive income be displayed in one of three alternative presentation formats: (1) in a single statement of income and comprehensive income, (2) in a separate statement of comprehensive income, or (3) in the statement of changes in equity. When an element of comprehensive income is present, the presentation of comprehensive income can be omitted when issuing a compilation report on financial statements that omit substantially all the disclosures. However, the omission of the display of comprehensive income should be identified in the compilation report.

The following example provides wording that the accountant can use to identify the omission of the display of comprehensive income when compiled financial statements omit substantially all the disclosures and the display of comprehensive income but include the statement of cash flows:

> Management has elected to omit substantially all of the disclosures and the display of comprehensive income required by accounting principles generally

accepted in the United States of America. If the omitted disclosures and the display of comprehensive income were included in the financial statements, they might influence the user's conclusions about the company's financial position, results of operations, and cash flows. Accordingly, these financial statements are not designed for those who are not informed about such matters.

It should be noted that the preceding guidance applies only when issuing compilation reports on GAAP financial statements *that omit substantially all of the disclosures.* If the compiled financial statements include all of the required disclosures but omit the presentation of comprehensive income, the accountant should treat the omission as a departure from GAAP and modify his or her report accordingly. In addition, if an entity has not computed an element of comprehensive income (e.g., unrealized holding gains or losses on available-for-sale securities), the accountant should consider a departure from GAAP and follow the guidance in AR Section 80 for instances in which departures from GAAP exist.

Reporting When the Accountant Is Not Independent in a Compilation Engagement

Accountants are permitted, but are not required, to include a general description in the compilation report about the reasons that the accountant's independence is impaired. When accountants elect to describe the reasons for independence impairment, they should include all of the reasons for impairment.

See Illustrations 9 and 10 for examples of compilation reports under AR Section 80 when the accountant's independence has been impaired.

Accountant's Communications with the Client When the Compiled Financial Statements Are Not Expected to Be Used by a Third Party

When an accountant submits compiled financial statements to a client that are not expected to be used by a third party, the accountant is not required to issue a compilation report. However, under such circumstances, the accountant should include a reference on each page of the financial statements restricting their use. The following are examples of such restricted-use language:

- "Restricted for management's use only."

- "Solely for the information and use by the management of ABC Company and not intended to be and should not be used by any other party."

If the accountant becomes aware that the financial statements have been distributed to third parties, the accountant should (1) discuss the situation with the client, (2) determine the appropriate course of action, and (3) consider requesting that the client have the statements returned. If the client does not comply with an accountant's request to return the financial statements within a reasonable period of time, the accountant should notify known third parties that the financial statements are not intended for third-party use, preferably in consultation with his or her attorney.

Departures from the Applicable Financial Reporting Framework in Compilation Engagements

In connection with a compilation of an entity's financial statements, the accountant may become aware of a departure from the applicable financial reporting framework (e.g., GAAP, OCBOA) that is considered material to the financial statements and that require such statements to be revised. If the client does not revise the financial statements, the accountant should consider whether modification of his or her standard report is adequate to disclose the departure from the applicable financial reporting framework.

If modification of the standard report is appropriate, the accountant should disclose in a separate paragraph of the report:

- The departure from the applicable financial reporting framework; and

- The effects of the departure on the financial statements if (a) such effects have been determined by management or (b) are known as the result of the accountant's procedures.

If management has not determined the effects of a departure from the applicable financial reporting framework, the accountant is not required to do so; however, he or she should state in the report that such determination has not been made.

See Illustrations 11 and 12 for examples of compilation reports that are modified for departures from the applicable financial reporting framework.

It should be emphasized that the accountant should not make a statement in his or her report that the financial statements are not in conformity with the applicable financial reporting framework. Including such a statement would be tantamount to expressing an adverse opinion on the financial statements taken as a whole, which can be expressed only in the context of an audit engagement. However, depending on the significance of the departure and the pervasiveness and overall impact of the misstatements, the accountant may wish to emphasize the limitations of the financial statements in a separate paragraph. Such separate paragraph, which would follow the other modifications of the accountant's report, might read as follows:

> Because the significance and pervasiveness of the matters discussed above make it difficult to assess their impact on the financial statements taken as a whole, users of these financial statements should recognize that they might reach different conclusions about the company's financial position, results of operations, and cash flows if they had access to revised financial statements prepared in conformity with [identify the applicable financial reporting framework (*e.g.*, *"Accounting Principles Generally Accepted in the United States of America"*)].

If the accountant believes that modification of the standard compilation report is not adequate, he or she should withdraw from the engagement and provide no further services with respect to those financial statements. In such circumstances, the accountant should consider consulting with his or her legal counsel.

Supplementary Information Accompanying the Compiled Financial Statements

When the basic financial statements are accompanied by information presented for supplementary analysis purposes, the accountant should indicate the degree of responsibility, if any, that he or she is taking regarding such information.

When the accountant has compiled both the basic financial statements and the other supplementary data, the accountant should report on the other supplementary data, either in the compilation report or in a separate report on the other data. If the accountant issues a separate report on the other supplementary data, the separate report should state that:

- The other data accompanying the financial statements are presented only for the purposes of additional analysis;
- The information has been compiled from information that is the representation of management, without audit or review; and
- The accountant does not express an opinion or provide any assurance on such data.

See Illustration 13 for an example of an accountant's compilation report that covers supplementary information.

Emphasis of a Matter in Compilation Reports

Accountants are permitted (but not required) to include an emphasis-of-matter paragraph in their compilation reports, as long as the matter is appropriately disclosed in the financial statements. Therefore, an accountant may not include an emphasis-of-matter paragraph in a compilation report on financial statements that omit substantially all disclosures, unless the matter is disclosed in the financial statements. The following are examples of matters that the accountant may want to emphasize:

- Uncertainties;
- The entity reported on is a component of a larger entity;
- The entity has had significant transactions with related parties;
- A significant subsequent event has taken place; or
- Accounting matters, other than those involving changes in accounting principles, exist that affect the comparability of the financial statements with those of the preceding period.

Restricting the Use of an Accountant's Compilation Report

AR Section 80 provides guidance to accountants on restricting the use of their reports issued in connection with compilation engagements. A key distinction is made between reports issued for "general use" and "restricted use":

- *General use*—A general-use report is one that is not restricted to specified parties, for example, accountants' compilation reports on financial statements prepared in conformity with an applicable financial reporting framework (e.g., GAAP, OCBOA).

- *Restricted use*—A restricted-use report is one that is intended only for specified parties. The need for restriction on the use of a report may result from varying circumstances, such as the purpose of the report or the potential for the compilation report to be misunderstood.

An accountant is not precluded from restricting the use of any report. However, the accountant *should* restrict the use of his or her report when the subject matter of the report or the presentation being reported on is based on measurement or disclosure criteria contained in contractual agreements or regulatory provisions that are not in conformity with an applicable financial reporting framework (e.g., GAAP, OCBOA). This is because, in such circumstances, the basis, assumptions, or purpose of such presentations are developed for the parties to the agreement or regulatory agency for their own use, and may not provide useful or relevant data for any other purpose. The inclusion of restricted-use reports in a document that also contains general-use reports does not affect the intended use of either report. It is permissible, and even useful to some of the intended users, that these reports be submitted together.

If an accountant issues a single combined report covering matters that require restriction, as well as other matters that generally do not require restriction, then the accountant should restrict to the specified parties the use of such a single combined report.

Adding other specified parties in restricted-use reports An accountant may be asked to consider adding other parties as specified parties in a restricted-use report. If an accountant is reporting on subject matter or a presentation based on criteria contained in contractual agreements or regulatory provisions, the accountant is allowed to add other parties as specified parties. However, in such circumstances, the accountant should consider factors such as the identity of the other parties, their knowledge of the basis of the measurement or disclosure criteria, and the intended use of the report.

If the accountant agrees to add other parties as specified parties, the accountant should obtain acknowledgment from the other parties, preferably in writing, of their understanding of (a) the nature of the engagement; (b) the measurement or disclosure criteria used in the engagement; and (c) the related report.

If the accountant agrees to add such other parties after he or she has issued the report, the accountant may either reissue the report or provide other written acknowledgment that the other parties have been added as specified parties. However, if the report is reissued, the accountant should not change the report date. If the accountant provides written acknowledgment, he or she should ordinarily state that no procedures have been performed subsequent to the date of the accountant's report.

Limiting report distribution An accountant should consider informing the client that restricted-use reports are not intended for distribution to nonspecified parties. An auditor is not responsible for controlling a client's distribution of restricted-use reports. That is why restricted-use reports should alert readers to the restriction on the use of the report by indicating that the report is not intended to be, and should not be, used by anyone other than the specified parties.

Restricted-use report language In a compilation report that is restricted as to use, the accountant should add a separate paragraph at the end of the report that:

- States that the report is intended solely for the information and use of the specified parties.
- Identifies the specified parties.
- States that the report is not intended to be used and should not be used by anyone other than the specified parties.

The following is an example of such a paragraph: "This report is intended solely for the information and use of [*the specified parties*] and is not intended to be and should not be used by anyone other than these specified parties."

Uncertainties Related to Going Concern Matters in Compilation Engagements

During a compilation engagement, the accountant may become aware of conditions or events that indicate that there may be an uncertainty about the entity's ability to continue as a going concern for a reasonable period of time, not to exceed one year beyond the date of the financial statements. Such conditions or events include, but are not limited to (1) recurring operating losses, (2) working capital deficiencies, (3) negative cash flows from operating activities, (4) default on loan agreements or similar agreements, (5) restructuring of debt, (6) substantial dependence on the success of a particular project, and (7) legal proceedings.

The going-concern concept is based on the presumption that the entity will continue to exist as a business entity in the foreseeable future (usually one year) in the absence of information to the contrary. However, business failure is not uncommon, and conditions may require the accountant to exercise professional judgment in evaluating the adequacy of going-concern disclosures in the financial statements. Therefore, if evidence or information comes to the accountant's attention that indicates that an uncertainty may exist about the entity's ability to continue as a going concern for a reasonable period of time, not to exceed one year beyond the date of the financial statements, the accountant should request that management consider the possible effects of the going concern uncertainty on the financial statements, including the need for related disclosure. The accountant also should consider the reasonableness of management's conclusions, including the adequacy of the related disclosures, if applicable.

If the accountant determines that management's conclusions are unreasonable or the disclosure of the uncertainty regarding the entity's ability to continue as a going concern is not adequate, the accountant should follow the preceding guidance regarding departures from an applicable financial reporting framework.

An uncertainty about an entity's ability to continue as a going concern would not cause the accountant to modify the standard compilation report provided the financial statements appropriately disclose the going concern uncertainty. In addition, the accountant is not precluded from emphasizing in a separate paragraph of his or her report a matter regarding a going concern uncertainty. Therefore, when an uncertainty related to an entity's ability to continue as a going concern exists but is adequately disclosed in the financial statements, it is not necessary to add a paragraph to the standard compilation report describing the uncertainty. However, the accountant may wish to draw attention to such uncertainty in an emphasis-of-matter paragraph in the accountant's report, using language such as the following:

> As discussed in Note [X], certain conditions indicate that the Company may be unable to continue as a going concern. The accompanying financial statements do not include any adjustments to the financial statements that might be necessary should the Company be unable to continue as a going concern.

It should be noted that the accountant's report should not use the term substantial doubt in the additional paragraph to highlight a going concern matter in the client's financial statements. This is because substantial doubt is an audit-evidence-based concept that should only be used in audit reports.

Other Uncertainties in Compilation Engagements

The preparation of financial statements in conformity with an applicable financial reporting framework (e.g., GAAP, OCBOA) requires management to make estimates and assumptions that affect the reported amounts of assets and liabilities, disclosure of contingent assets and liabilities, and reported amounts of revenues and expenses. Generally, significant estimates relate to matters, such as allowance for uncollectible accounts receivable, inventory obsolescence, depreciation, asset valuations and useful lives, and contingencies.

Consistent with the guidance previously discussed regarding uncertainties related to going-concern matters, if the disclosures required by an applicable financial reporting framework regarding an uncertainty are not included in the compiled financial statements, the accountant's report on the financial statements should include a paragraph describing the departure from the applicable financial reporting framework. On the other hand, if the accountant concludes that management's disclosure of the uncertainty is adequate and in accordance with the applicable financial reporting framework, there is no need for the accountant to modify the compilation report; however, the accountant may add an emphasis of a matter paragraph with respect to the uncertainty in the compilation review report that contains wording similar to the following:

> As discussed in Note [X], the Company is currently named in a legal action. The Company has determined that it is not possible to predict the eventual outcome of the legal action but has determined that the resolution of the action will not result in an adverse judgment that would materially affect the financial statements. Accordingly, the accompanying financial statements do not include any adjustments related to this legal action.

Subsequent Events in Compilation Engagements

During the performance of compilation procedures, or subsequent to the date of the accountant's compilation report (but prior to the release of the report), the accountant may become aware of evidence or information that a subsequent event that has a material effect on the financial statements has occurred. In such circumstances, the accountant should request that management consider the possible effects of the subsequent event on the financial statements, including the adequacy of any related disclosure, if applicable.

If the accountant determines that the subsequent event is not adequately accounted for in the financial statements or disclosed in the notes, he or she should follow the preceding guidance regarding departures from an applicable financial reporting framework.

Therefore, when a subsequent event that has a material impact on the entity is adequately disclosed in the financial statements, it is not necessary for the accountant to add an explanatory paragraph to the standard compilation report describing the subsequent event. However, the accountant may wish to draw attention to such uncertainty in an emphasis-of-matter paragraph in the accountant's report.

Subsequent Discovery of Facts Existing at the Date of the Compilation Report

Subsequent to the date of the accountant's compilation report, the accountant may become aware that facts may have existed at that date that suggest that information supplied by the client was incorrect, incomplete, or otherwise unsatisfactory. In such circumstances, the accountant should determine the appropriate specific actions to be taken by considering:

- *The reliability of the information and whether the facts existed at the date of the accountant's report*—The accountant should discuss the matter with the client at the appropriate management level, including those charged with governance, and request cooperation in whatever investigation may be necessary. The accountant ordinarily would conclude that persons known to be using or likely to use the financial statements should be notified in an appropriate manner if the information (a) is deemed reliable and existed at the date of his or her report and (b) indicates that the financial statements, the report, or both need revision.

- *The existence of persons known to be using or likely to use the financial statements*—In evaluating the likelihood that persons are currently using or likely to use the financial statements, the accountant should consider the time elapsed since the financial statements were issued.

If the accountant determines that the subsequently discovered information is reliable and existed at the date of his or her report, he or she should, as soon as practicable, request that management consider the effect of the information on the previously issued financial statements. In addition, the accountant should consider the effect of the discovered matter on his or her report.

If the nature and effect of the matter are such that (a) the accountant's compilation report or the financial statements would have been affected if the information had been known to the accountant at the date of his or her report and had not been reflected in the financial statements and (b) the accountant believes that there are persons currently using or likely to use the financial statements who would attach importance to the information, the accountant should obtain additional or revised information.

Action to prevent future use of the accountant's compilation report If the accountant concludes that action should be taken to prevent future use of the compilation report or the financial statements, he or she should advise the client to make appropriate disclosure to interested third parties of (a) the newly discovered facts and (b) their impact on the financial statements. The method the client uses to make the appropriate disclosure will depend on the circumstances using the following guidance:

- *Effect of discovered information can be determined promptly*—If the effect on the financial statements or accountant's report can be determined promptly, disclosure should consist of issuing revised financial statements and accountant's report, as soon as practicable. The reasons for the revision usually should be described in a note to the financial statements and referred to in the accountant's report.

- *Issuance of financial statements and the accountant's report thereon for a subsequent period is imminent*—When issuance of financial statements and the accountant's report thereon for a subsequent period is imminent, appropriate disclosure of the revision can be made in such subsequent financial statements instead of reissuing the earlier financial statements.

- *Effect of discovered information cannot be determined promptly*—If the effect on the financial statements or accountant's report cannot be promptly determined, the client should notify persons who are known to be using or who are likely to use the financial statements that (a) they should not be using the financial statements, (b) revised financial statements will be issued, and (c) where applicable, the accountant's report will be issued as soon as practicable.

The accountant should be satisfied that the client has made the appropriate disclosures described above.

Accountant's action if the client refuses to make the appropriate disclosures If the client refuses to make the disclosures discussed above, the accountant should notify the appropriate personnel at the highest levels within the entity (e.g., owner or those charged with governance) of such refusal and of the fact that the accountant will notify:

- The client that the accountant's compilation or review report must no longer be associated with the financial statements.

- Regulatory agencies having jurisdiction over the client that the accountant's report should no longer be used.

- Each person known to the accountant to be using the financial statements that the financial statements and the accountant's report should no longer be used. (*Note*: Generally, notification to a regulatory agency having jurisdiction over the client will usually be the only practicable way for the accountant to provide appropriate disclosure. Any such notification to a regulatory agency should be accompanied by a request that the agency take whatever steps it deems appropriate to accomplish the necessary disclosure).

The accountant should observe the following guidelines when making disclosures to persons other than the client:

- The disclosure should include a description of the nature of the subsequently acquired information and its effect on the financial statements.

- The discovered information should be disclosed as precisely and factually as possible, without any comments about the conduct or motives of any persons involved.

- If the client refused to cooperate, the accountant should disclose (a) that information has come to his or her attention that the client has not cooperated in attempting to substantiate, and (b) that, if the information is true, the accountant believes that his or her report must no longer be used or be associated with the financial statements. (*Note*: No such disclosure should be made unless the accountant believes that the financial statements are likely to be misleading and that the accountant's compilation report should not be used.)

As a practical matter, the accountant should consult his or her legal counsel before making any disclosures to third parties.

Communicating Fraud and Illegal Acts to Management and Others in Compilation Engagements

For purposes of the SSARSs, fraud and illegal acts are defined as follows:

- *Fraud*—An intentional act that results in a misstatement in compiled or reviewed financial statements.

- *Illegal acts*—Violations of laws or government regulations, excluding fraud.

When evidence or information comes to the accountant's attention during the performance of compilation procedures that fraud or an illegal act may have occurred, it should be brought to the attention of the appropriate level of management. For purposes of communicating fraud and illegal acts to an appropriate level of management, an appropriate level of management generally should involve an individual or a group at a higher level within the entity than the level at which the fraud or illegal act may have occurred. For instances of fraud or illegal acts involving senior management, the related matters should be reported to an individual or group at a higher level within the entity (e.g., manager/owner, those charged with governance). When the instances of fraud or illegal acts involve an owner of the business, the accountant should consider resigning from the engagement. The accountant also should consider consulting his or her legal counsel and insurance provider under such circumstances.

In addition, while the communication to management and others regarding fraud and illegal acts may be oral or written, AR Section 80 requires the accountant to document such communication if it is made orally.

The accountant need not report matters regarding illegal acts that are clearly inconsequential and may reach agreement in advance with the entity on the nature of such items to be communicated.

Communications to third parties outside the entity AR Section 80 indicates that, generally, the accountant is not responsible to notify third parties—other than the client's senior management or those charged with governance, if applicable—of matters related to fraud or illegal acts. Owing to ethical and legal obligations of confidentiality, the accountant ordinarily would be precluded from communicating fraud or illegal acts to third parties outside the entity. However, AR Section 80 recognizes that the accountant may have a duty to disclose these matters to parties outside the entity in the following circumstances:

- To comply with certain legal and regulatory requirements;

- To respond to a successor accountant's inquiries that are made in accordance with AR Section 400 (Communications between Predecessor and Successor Accountants) for purposes of determining whether to accept a compilation engagement; and

- To respond to a subpoena.

Because of potential conflicts in the confidential relationship between the accountant and the client, the accountant may find it advisable to contact legal counsel before matters related to fraud or illegal acts are disclosed to parties outside the entity. This is particularly important because unjustified third-party notification could result in a lawsuit against the accountant for damages, slander, or similar reasons.

Impact of fraud and illegal acts on other aspects of the compilation engagement In a compilation engagement, no expression of assurance is contemplated or provided. Therefore, because of the limited nature of the procedures performed in a compilation engagement, the accountant is not required to perform any additional procedures to determine whether a suspected fraud or an illegal act has in fact occurred, or has probably occurred. However, the accountant should consider the effect of the suspected fraud or illegal act on the reliability and integrity of management's representations.

Change in Engagement from Audit or Review to Compilation

Before the completion of an audit or a review engagement, a client may request the accountant to change the engagement to a compilation engagement. In such circumstances, before an accountant agrees to change the engagement to a compilation, he or she should consider, at a minimum, the following:

1. The reasons given for the client's request, particularly the implications of a restriction on the scope of the audit or review, whether imposed by the client or by the engagement circumstances.

2. The additional effort required to complete the audit or review.

3. The estimated additional cost to complete the audit or review.

AR Section 80 states that changes in circumstances affecting the entity's requirement for an audit or review, or a misunderstanding about the nature of an audit, review, or compilation would ordinarily be a reasonable basis for such a request.

If the audit or review is substantially complete, or the cost to complete it is relatively insignificant, the accountant should consider the propriety of accepting a change to a compilation. If a limitation on the scope of the audit or review is involved, the accountant should evaluate the possibility that incorrect, incomplete, or otherwise unsatisfactory information may be affected. In any case, when the scope limitation restricts the accountant's ability to correspond with the entity's legal counsel or when the client would have refused to sign a representation letter in an audit or review engagement, the accountant would ordinarily be precluded from issuing a compilation report.

When an accountant concludes that a change in the engagement is appropriate, and complies with applicable standards for a compilation engagement, an appropriate compilation report should be issued. However, that report should not refer to the original audit or review engagement, any audit or review procedures that were performed, or any scope limitations that resulted in a changed engagement.

PRACTICE ISSUES AND FREQUENTLY ASKED QUESTIONS

Issue 1: Do accounting principles generally accepted in the United States (GAAP) apply to compilations of financial statements?

Yes. GAAP is one of the financial reporting frameworks that may be used in financial statements when performing compilations of financial statements. Other financial reporting frameworks would include IFRS and OCBOA.

Issue 2: What is the primary difference between a review engagement and a compilation engagement?

In a review engagement, the accountant performs inquiry and analytical procedures that provide the accountant with a reasonable basis for expressing limited assurance that there are no material modifications that should be made to the financial statements. However, no expression of assurance is contemplated or provided in a compilation engagement.

Issue 3: Is the accountant precluded from accepting a compilation engagement for an entity in an industry with which he or she has no prior experience?

No, as long as the accountant obtains the required level of knowledge before completing the compilation engagement.

Issue 4: May an accountant issue a compilation report on one financial statement, such as a balance sheet, and not on other related financial statements?

Yes. An accountant may issue a compilation report on one financial statement (e.g., balance sheet) and not on other related financial statements (e.g., income statement, cash flows statement).

Issue 5: Is a separate statement of retained earnings required to be presented as part of compiled financial statements that are prepared in accordance with GAAP?

No. A separate statement of retained earnings is not required to be presented as a financial statement. GAAP requires only disclosure of a change in capital. This can be accomplished by (1) preparation of a separate statement, (2) disclosure in the notes to the financial statements, or (3) presentation as part of another basic statement.

Issue 6: Should compilation reports be modified when a statement of comprehensive income is presented as part of compiled financial statements?

Yes. If a statement of comprehensive income is presented as part of compiled financial statements, the first paragraph of the compilation report should also refer to the statement of comprehensive income.

Issue 7: Are accountants permitted to include an emphasis-of-matter paragraph in their compilation reports to emphasize a matter regarding the financial statements?

Yes. Accountants are permitted (not required) to include an emphasis-of-matter paragraph in their compilation reports, as long as the matter is appropriately disclosed in the financial statements. However, emphasis paragraphs in the accountant's report should *not*:

- Introduce new information about the financial statements (i.e., they should only emphasize a matter that is already disclosed in the financial statements).

- Include information about or describe the procedures the accountant has or has not performed.

- Contain any conclusions or opinions.

   In addition, because an emphasis-of-matter paragraph should not be used in lieu of management disclosures, the accountant should not include an emphasis paragraph in a compilation report on financial statements that omit substantially all disclosures unless the matter is disclosed in the financial statements.

Issue 8: Does an uncertainty, such as uncertainty about an entity's ability to continue as a going concern, require the accountant to modify the standard report in a compilation engagement?

No. Generally, an uncertainty, including an uncertainty about an entity's ability to continue as a going concern, would not cause the accountant to modify the standard compilation report, provided the financial statements appropriately disclose the uncertainty. However, the accountant is not precluded from emphasizing in a separate paragraph of his or her report this type of matter regarding the financial statements. The following is an example of such a paragraph:

> As discussed in Note [X], certain conditions indicate that the Company may be unable to continue as a going concern. The accompanying financial statements do not include any adjustments to the financial statements that might be necessary should the Company be unable to continue as a going concern.

   Note that the accountant's report should not use the term "substantial doubt" in the additional paragraph to highlight a going concern disclosure in the client's financial statements. This is because "substantial doubt" is an audit-evidence-based concept that should only be used in audit reports.

Issue 9: What type of report should the accountant issue if he or she has provided more than one level of service on the same financial statements?

If the accountant has provided more than one level of service on the same financial statements, he or she should issue a report that is appropriate for the highest level of service rendered. For example, if the accountant both compiled and reviewed the financial statements that he or she was engaged to review, the accountant would need to issue only a review report.

Issue 10: May an accountant accept an engagement to perform a compilation of financial statements for an interim period (e.g., monthly) and an engagement to review the financial statements for another period (e.g., quarterly) that ends on the same date?

Yes, as long as the accountant complies with the applicable standards for each engagement.

Issue 11: Is an accountant precluded from accepting an engagement to perform a higher level of service with respect to financial statements that he or she previously compiled?

No. An accountant is not precluded from accepting an engagement to perform a higher level of service with respect to financial statements that he or she previously compiled. For example, an accountant who has issued a compilation report on a set of financial statements may later issue an audit or review report on the same set of financial statements.

Issue 12: Under what circumstances would it ordinarily be necessary for the accountant to withdraw from a compilation engagement?

Ordinarily, it would be necessary for the accountant to withdraw from a compilation engagement under the following circumstances:

- When the nature, extent, and probable effect of the departures from the applicable financial reporting framework (e.g., GAAP, OCBOA) cause the accountant to question whether such departures were undertaken with the intention to mislead potential users of the financial statements.

- When the client does not revise the financial statements, including disclosures, that the accountant requests to be made, and the client refuses to accept the modified standard report that the accountant believes is appropriate.

Issue 13: If, in connection with a compilation engagement, the accountant performs certain additional procedures (e.g., confirmation or inventory observation procedures), is he or she required to upgrade the engagement to an audit?

No. An accountant may perform additional procedures in connection with a compilation engagement, such as confirmations of accounts receivable, inventory observation procedures, or such other "auditing procedures." The accountant is not required to change the engagement level in such circumstances.

Issue 14: Are financial forecasts and projections considered financial statements for purposes of AR Section 80?

No. Financial forecasts, projections, and similar presentations are not financial statements for purposes of AR Section 80.

Issue 15: Why does AR Section 80 require that a reference to the accountant's compilation report appear on each page of the financial statements?

First, this is a reminder to the user of the financial statements of what level of service was performed. Second, it is believed to provide some protection for the accountant. Absent such a reference, it would be impossible to tell what level of service the accountant had performed if the report became separated from the financial statements.

Issue 16: Are practitioners required to comply with quality control standards when performing compilation engagements?

Yes. Practitioners in the conduct of a firm's accounting practice should comply with quality control standards. Therefore, a firm should establish quality control policies and procedures to provide it with reasonable assurance of conforming to SSARSs. While SSARSs relate to the conduct of individual compilation and review engagements, quality control standards relate to the conduct of a firm's accounting practice as a whole. Therefore, SSARSs and quality control standards are related and the quality control policies and procedures that a firm adopts may affect both the conduct of individual engagements and the conduct of a firm's accounting practice as a whole.

Issue 17: Do deficiencies in a firm's quality control system indicate that a compilation engagement was not performed in accordance with SSARSs?

No. AR Section 80 specifically states that deficiencies in a firm's quality control system or noncompliance therewith do not necessarily indicate that a compilation engagement was not performed in accordance with SSARSs.

Issue 18: Does AR Section 80 apply when an accountant derives financial information from an entity's tax return and such information is presented as part of the accountant's business valuation report?

No. Accountants are sometimes engaged to perform a business valuation of an entity. Oftentimes, in connection with such business valuations, it may be necessary for the accountant to derive financial information from the client's tax return to be used in the business valuation. This is common if the entity does not have audited, reviewed, or compiled financial statements. The financial information that is derived from the tax return and presented as part of a business valuation is not deemed to be submission of financial statements. Therefore, AR Section 80 does not apply when an accountant derives financial information from an entity's tax return and such information is presented as part of the accountant's business valuation report.

Issue 19: Do the provisions of AU Section 316 (Consideration of Fraud in a Financial Statement Audit) apply to compilation engagements?

No. AU Section 316 (Consideration of Fraud in a Financial Statement Audit) does not apply to compilation engagements. Accordingly, the accountant is not required to plan or perform a compilation engagement to obtain reasonable assurance about whether the financial statements are free of material misstatement, whether caused by error or fraud. In addition, compilation performance standards do not require the accountant to document his or her assessment of fraud risk in a compilation engagement.

However, this does not mean that the accountant has no responsibility to be alert to the possibility of the existence of errors or fraud. For example, if the accountant determines that information supplied by the client is incorrect, incomplete, or otherwise unsatisfactory as it relates to a compilation engagement, the accountant should obtain additional or revised information.

Issue 20: Is the accountant required, in a compilation engagement, to make inquiries or perform other procedures to corroborate, verify, or review information supplied by the client?

No. In a compilation engagement, the accountant is not required to make inquiries or perform other procedures to substantiate or review information furnished by the client.

Issue 21: Is the accountant required to obtain a representation letter from management in a compilation engagement?

No. The accountant is not required to obtain a representation letter from management in a compilation engagement.

Issue 22: If, in connection with a compilation engagement, the accountant performs some analytical procedures, is he or she required to upgrade the report to a review?

No. If, in connection with a compilation engagement, the accountant performs other accounting services or procedures beyond those required for a compilation (e.g., analytical procedures), he or she is not required to "upgrade" the report to a review in such circumstances.

Issue 23: May the accountant issue a standard compilation report on financial statements that have previously been compiled for management's use only?

Yes, as long as the accountant complies with the reporting requirements of AR Section 80 before issuing the compilation report.

ILLUSTRATIONS AND PRACTICE AIDS

ILLUSTRATION 1—STANDARD ENGAGEMENT LETTER FOR A COMPILATION

(Prepared on accountant's letterhead)

January 18, 20X2
ABC Company

Dear _____:

This letter is to confirm our understanding of the terms and objectives of our engagement and the nature and limitations of the services we will provide.

We will compile, from information you provide, the annual [*and interim, if applicable*] financial statements of ABC Company as of December 31, 20X2, and issue an accountant's report thereon in accordance with Statements on Standards for Accounting and Review Services (SSARSs) issued by the American Institute of Certified Public Accountants (AICPA).

The objective of a compilation is to assist you in presenting financial information in the form of financial statements. We will utilize information that is your representation without undertaking to obtain or provide any assurance that there are no material modifications that should be made to the financial statements in order for the statements to be in conformity with [*the applicable financial reporting framework (e.g., accounting principles generally accepted in the United States of America)*].

You are responsible for:

1. The preparation and fair presentation of the financial statements in accordance with [*the applicable financial reporting framework (e.g., accounting principles generally accepted in the United States of America)*].

2. Designing, implementing, and maintaining internal control relevant to the preparation and fair presentation of the financial statements.

3. Preventing and detecting fraud.

4. Identifying and ensuring that the entity complies with the laws and regulations applicable to its activities.

5. Making all financial records and related information available to us.

We are responsible for conducting the engagement in accordance with SSARSs issued by the AICPA.

A compilation differs significantly from a review or an audit of financial statements. A compilation does not contemplate performing inquiry, analytical procedures, or other procedures performed in a review. Additionally, a compilation does not contemplate obtaining an understanding of the entity's internal control; assessing fraud risk; testing accounting records by obtaining sufficient appropriate audit evidence through inspection, observation, confirmation, or the examination of source documents (e.g., cancelled checks or bank images); or other procedures ordinarily performed in an audit. Accordingly, we will not express an opinion or provide any assurance regarding the financial statements being compiled.

Our engagement cannot be relied upon to disclose errors, fraud, or illegal acts. However, we will inform the appropriate level of management of any material errors, and of any evidence or information that comes to our attention during the performance of our compilation procedures that fraud may have occurred. In addition, we will report to you any evidence or information that comes to our attention during the performance of our compilation procedures regarding illegal acts that may have occurred, unless they are clearly inconsequential.

[*If, during the period covered by the engagement letter, the accountant's independence is or will be impaired, insert the following:*

We are not independent with respect to ABC Company. We will disclose that we are not independent in our compilation report.]

If, for any reason, we are unable to complete the compilation of your financial statements, we will not issue a report on such statements as a result of this engagement.

Our fees for these services are based on the amount of time required at various levels of responsibility, plus actual out-of-pocket expenses.

We will be pleased to discuss this letter with you at any time. If the foregoing is in accordance with your understanding, please sign the copy of this letter in the space provided and return it to us.

Very truly yours,

Christensen & Company

****

Acknowledged by (ABC Company): _____

Title: _____

Date: _____

ILLUSTRATION 2—ENGAGEMENT LETTER—COMPILATION OF FINANCIAL STATEMENTS NOT INTENDED FOR THIRD-PARTY USE

(Prepared on accountant's letterhead)

January 18, 20X2
ABC Company

Dear _____:

This letter is to confirm our understanding of the terms and objectives of our engagement and the nature and limitations of the services we will provide.

We will compile, from information you provide, the [monthly, quarterly, or other frequency] financial statements of ABC Company for the year ended December 31, 20X2.

The objective of a compilation is to assist you in presenting financial information in the form of financial statements. We will utilize information that is your representation without undertaking to obtain or provide any assurance that there are no material modifications that should be made to the financial statements in order for the statements to be in conformity with [*the applicable financial reporting framework (e.g., accounting principles generally accepted in the United States of America)*].

You are responsible for:

1. The preparation and fair presentation of the financial statements in accordance with [*the applicable financial reporting framework (e.g., accounting principles generally accepted in the United States of America)*].
2. Designing, implementing, and maintaining internal control relevant to the preparation and fair presentation of the financial statements.
3. Preventing and detecting fraud.
4. Identifying and ensuring that the entity complies with the laws and regulations applicable to its activities.

5. Making all financial records and related information available to us.

We are responsible for conducting the engagement in accordance with Statements on Standards for Accounting and Review Services issued by the American Institute of Certified Public Accountants.

A compilation differs significantly from a review or an audit of financial statements. A compilation does not contemplate performing inquiry, analytical procedures, or other procedures performed in a review. Additionally, a compilation does not contemplate obtaining an understanding of the entity's internal control; assessing fraud risk; testing accounting records by obtaining sufficient appropriate audit evidence through inspection, observation, confirmation, or the examination of source documents (e.g., cancelled checks or bank images); or other procedures ordinarily performed in an audit. Accordingly, we will not express an opinion or provide any assurance regarding the financial statements being compiled.

Our engagement cannot be relied upon to disclose errors, fraud, or illegal acts. However, we will inform the appropriate level of management of any material errors, and of any evidence or information that comes to our attention during the performance of our compilation procedures that fraud may have occurred. In addition, we will report to you any evidence or information that comes to our attention during the performance of our compilation procedures regarding illegal acts that may have occurred, unless they are clearly inconsequential.

The financial statements will not be accompanied by a report and are for management's use only and are not to be used by a third party.

[*If, during the period covered by the engagement letter, the accountant's independence is or will be impaired, insert the following:*

  We are not independent with respect to ABC Company..]

Our fees for these services are based on the amount of time required at various levels of responsibility, plus actual out-of-pocket expenses.

We will be pleased to discuss this letter with you at any time. If the foregoing is in accordance with your understanding, please sign the copy of this letter in the space provided and return it to us.

Very truly yours,

Christensen & Company

****

Acknowledged by (ABC Company): _____

Title: _____

Date: _____

ILLUSTRATION 3—COMPILATION REPORT ON FULL DISCLOSURE GAAP FINANCIAL STATEMENTS

Accountant's Compilation Report

To the Board of Directors of ABC Company:

I (We) have compiled the accompanying balance sheet of ABC Company as of December 31, 20X2, and the related statements of income, retained earnings, and cash flows for the year then ended. I (We) have not audited or reviewed the accompanying financial statements and, accordingly, do not express an opinion or provide any assurance about whether the financial statements are in accordance with accounting principles generally accepted in the United States of America.

Management is (Owners are) responsible for the preparation and fair presentation of the financial statements in accordance with accounting principles generally accepted in the United States of America and for designing, implementing, and maintaining internal control relevant to the preparation and fair presentation of the financial statements.

My (Our) responsibility is to conduct the compilation in accordance with Statements on Standards for Accounting and Review Services issued by the American Institute of Certified Public Accountants. The objective of a compilation is to assist management in presenting financial information in the form of financial statements without undertaking to obtain or provide any assurance that there are no material modifications that should be made to the financial statements.

[*Signature of accounting firm or accountant*]

[*Date*]

ILLUSTRATION 4—COMPILATION REPORT ON FULL DISCLOSURE CASH BASIS FINANCIAL STATEMENTS

Accountant's Compilation Report

To the Board of Directors of ABC Company:

I (We) have compiled the accompanying statement of assets and liabilities arising from cash transactions of ABC Company as of December 31, 20X2, and the related statement of revenue collected and expenses paid for the year then ended. I (We) have not audited or reviewed the accompanying financial statements and, accordingly, do not express an opinion or provide any assurance about whether the financial statements are in accordance with the cash basis of accounting.

Management is (Owners are) responsible for the preparation and fair presentation of the financial statements in accordance with the cash basis of accounting and for designing, implementing, and maintaining internal control relevant to the preparation and fair presentation of the financial statements.

My (Our) responsibility is to conduct the compilation in accordance with Statements on Standards for Accounting and Review Services issued by the American Institute of Certified Public Accountants. The objective of a compilation is to assist management in presenting financial information in the form of financial statements without undertaking to obtain or provide any assurance that there are no material modifications that should be made to the financial statements.

[*Signature of accounting firm or accountant*]

[*Date*]

ILLUSTRATION 5—COMPILATION REPORT ON FULL DISCLOSURE IN-COME TAX BASIS FINANCIAL STATEMENTS

Accountant's Compilation Report

To the Board of Directors of ABC Company:

I (We) have compiled the accompanying statement of assets, liabilities, and equity-income tax basis of ABC Company as of December 31, 20X2, and the related statement of revenue and expenses-income tax basis for the year then ended. I (We) have not audited or reviewed the accompanying financial statements and, accordingly, do not express an opinion or provide any assurance about whether the financial statements are in accordance with the income tax basis of accounting.

Management is (Owners are) responsible for the preparation and fair presentation of the financial statements in accordance with the income tax basis of accounting and for designing, implementing, and maintaining internal control relevant to the preparation and fair presentation of the financial statements.

My (Our) responsibility is to conduct the compilation in accordance with Statements on Standards for Accounting and Review Services issued by the American Institute of Certified Public Accountants. The objective of a compilation is to assist management in presenting financial information in the form of financial statements without undertaking to obtain or provide any assurance that there are no material modifications that should be made to the financial statements.

[*Signature of accounting firm or accountant*]

[*Date*]

ILLUSTRATION 6—COMPILATION REPORT ON GAAP FINANCIAL STATE-MENTS THAT OMIT SUBSTANTIALLY ALL DISCLOSURES

Accountant's Compilation Report

To the Board of Directors of ABC Company:

I (We) have compiled the accompanying balance sheet of ABC Company as of December 31, 20X2, and the related statements of income, retained earnings, and cash flows for the year then ended. I (We) have not audited or reviewed the accompanying financial statements and, accordingly, do not express an opinion or provide any assurance about whether the financial statements are in accordance with accounting principles generally accepted in the United States of America.

Management is (Owners are) responsible for the preparation and fair presentation of the financial statements in accordance with accounting principles generally accepted in the United States of America and for designing, implementing, and maintaining internal control relevant to the preparation and fair presentation of the financial statements.

My (Our) responsibility is to conduct the compilation in accordance with Statements on Standards for Accounting and Review Services issued by the

American Institute of Certified Public Accountants. The objective of a compilation is to assist management in presenting financial information in the form of financial statements without undertaking to obtain or provide any assurance that there are no material modifications that should be made to the financial statements.

Management has elected to omit substantially all of the disclosures required by accounting principles generally accepted in the United States of America. If the omitted disclosures were included in the financial statements, they might influence the user's conclusions about the company's financial position, results of operations, and cash flows. Accordingly, the financial statements are not designed for those who are not informed about such matters.

[*Signature of accounting firm or accountant*]

[*Date*]

ILLUSTRATION 7—COMPILATION REPORT ON CASH BASIS FINANCIAL STATEMENTS THAT OMIT SUBSTANTIALLY ALL DISCLOSURES

Accountant's Compilation Report

To the Board of Directors of ABC Company:

I (We) have compiled the accompanying statement of assets and liabilities arising from cash transactions of ABC Company as of December 31, 20X2, and the related statement of revenue collected and expenses paid for the year then ended. I (We) have not audited or reviewed the accompanying financial statements and, accordingly, do not express an opinion or provide any assurance about whether the financial statements are in accordance with the cash basis of accounting.

Management is (Owners are) responsible for the preparation and fair presentation of the financial statements in accordance with the cash basis of accounting and for designing, implementing, and maintaining internal control relevant to the preparation and fair presentation of the financial statements.

My (Our) responsibility is to conduct the compilation in accordance with Statements on Standards for Accounting and Review Services issued by the American Institute of Certified Public Accountants. The objective of a compilation is to assist management in presenting financial information in the form of financial statements without undertaking to obtain or provide any assurance that there are no material modifications that should be made to the financial statements.

Management has elected to omit substantially all of the disclosures ordinarily included in financial statements prepared in accordance with the cash basis of accounting. If the omitted disclosures were included in the financial statements, they might influence the user's conclusions about the company's assets, liabilities, equity, revenue, and expenses. Accordingly, these financial statements are not designed for those who are not informed about such matters.

[*Signature of accounting firm or accountant*]

[*Date*]

ILLUSTRATION 8—COMPILATION REPORT ON INCOME TAX BASIS FI-NANCIAL STATEMENTS THAT OMIT SUBSTANTIALLY ALL DISCLOSURES

Accountant's Compilation Report

To the Board of Directors of ABC Company:

I (We) have compiled the accompanying statement of assets, liabilities, and equity-income tax basis of ABC Company as of December 31, 20X2, and the related statement of revenue and expenses-income tax basis for the year then ended. I (We) have not audited or reviewed the accompanying financial statements and, accordingly, do not express an opinion or provide any assurance about whether the financial statements are in accordance with the income tax basis of accounting.

Management is (Owners are) responsible for the preparation and fair presentation of the financial statements in accordance with the income tax basis of accounting and for designing, implementing, and maintaining internal control relevant to the preparation and fair presentation of the financial statements.

My (Our) responsibility is to conduct the compilation in accordance with Statements on Standards for Accounting and Review Services issued by the American Institute of Certified Public Accountants. The objective of a compilation is to assist management in presenting financial information in the form of financial statements without undertaking to obtain or provide any assurance that there are no material modifications that should be made to the financial statements.

Management has elected to omit substantially all of the disclosures ordinarily included in financial statements prepared in accordance with the income tax basis of accounting. If the omitted disclosures were included in the financial statements, they might influence the user's conclusions about the company's assets, liabilities, equity, revenue, and expenses. Accordingly, these financial statements are not designed for those who are not informed about such matters.

[*Signature of accounting firm or accountant*]

[*Date*]

ILLUSTRATION 9—COMPILATION REPORT WHEN THE ACCOUNTANT'S INDEPENDENCE HAS BEEN IMPAIRED, AND THE ACCOUNTANT DETER-MINES TO NOT DISCLOSE THE REASON FOR THE INDEPENDENCE IMPAIRMENT

Accountant's Compilation Report

To the Board of Directors of ABC Company:

I (We) have compiled the accompanying balance sheet of ABC Company as of December 31, 20X2, and the related statements of income, retained earnings, and cash flows for the year then ended. I (We) have not audited or reviewed the accompanying financial statements and, accordingly, do not express an opinion or provide any assurance about whether the financial statements are in accordance with accounting principles generally accepted in the United States of America.

Management is (Owners are) responsible for the preparation and fair presentation of the financial statements in accordance with accounting principles generally accepted in the United States of America and for designing, implementing, and maintaining internal control relevant to the preparation and fair presentation of the financial statements.

My (Our) responsibility is to conduct the compilation in accordance with Statements on Standards for Accounting and Review Services issued by the American Institute of Certified Public Accountants. The objective of a compilation is to assist management in presenting financial information in the form of financial statements without undertaking to obtain or provide any assurance that there are no material modifications that should be made to the financial statements.

I am (We are) not independent with respect to ABC Company.

[*Signature of accounting firm or accountant*]

[*Date*]

ILLUSTRATION 10—COMPILATION REPORT WHEN THE ACCOUNTANT'S INDEPENDENCE HAS BEEN IMPAIRED, AND THE ACCOUNTANT DECIDES TO DISCLOSE THE REASON FOR THE INDEPENDENCE IMPAIRMENT

Accountant's Compilation Report

To the Board of Directors of ABC Company:

I (We) have compiled the accompanying balance sheet of ABC Company as of December 31, 20X2, and the related statements of income, retained earnings, and cash flows for the year then ended. I (We) have not audited or reviewed the accompanying financial statements and, accordingly, do not express an opinion or provide any assurance about whether the financial statements are in accordance with accounting principles generally accepted in the United States of America.

Management is (Owners are) responsible for the preparation and fair presentation of the financial statements in accordance with accounting principles generally accepted in the United States of America and for designing, implementing, and maintaining internal control relevant to the preparation and fair presentation of the financial statements.

My (Our) responsibility is to conduct the compilation in accordance with Statements on Standards for Accounting and Review Services issued by the American Institute of Certified Public Accountants. The objective of a compilation is to assist management in presenting financial information in the form of financial statements without undertaking to obtain or provide any assurance that there are no material modifications that should be made to the financial statements.

I am (We are) not independent with respect to ABC Company because during the year ended December 31, 20X2, I (a member of the engagement team) had a direct financial interest in ABC Company.

Note: The following are other examples of descriptions that the accountant may use to disclose the reason for the independence impairment:

- I am (We are) not independent with respect to ABC Company as of and for the year ended December 31, 20X2, because an individual of my immediate family (an immediate family member of one of the members of the engagement team) was employed by ABC Company.

- I am (We are) not independent with respect to ABC Company as of and for the year ended December 31, 20X2, because I (we) performed certain accounting services (the accountant may include a specific description of those services) that impaired my (our) independence.

[*Signature of accounting firm or accountant*]

[*Date*]

ILLUSTRATION 11—COMPILATION REPORT MODIFIED FOR A DEPARTURE FROM GAAP: ACCOUNTING PRINCIPLE NOT GENERALLY ACCEPTED

Accountant's Compilation Report

To the Board of Directors of ABC Company:

I (We) have compiled the accompanying balance sheet of ABC Company as of December 31, 20X2, and the related statements of income, retained earnings, and cash flows for the year then ended. I (We) have not audited or reviewed the accompanying financial statements and, accordingly, do not express an opinion or provide any assurance about whether the financial statements are in accordance with accounting principles generally accepted in the United States of America.

Management is (Owners are) responsible for the preparation and fair presentation of the financial statements in accordance with accounting principles generally accepted in the United States of America and for designing, implementing, and maintaining internal control relevant to the preparation and fair presentation of the financial statements.

My (Our) responsibility is to conduct the compilation in accordance with Statements on Standards for Accounting and Review Services issued by the American Institute of Certified Public Accountants. The objective of a compilation is to assist management in presenting financial information in the form of financial statements without undertaking to obtain or provide any assurance that there are no material modifications that should be made to the financial statements. During our compilation, I (we) did become aware of a departure (certain departures) from accounting principles generally accepted in the United States of America that is (are) described in the following paragraph.

As disclosed in Note [X] to the financial statements, accounting principles generally accepted in the United States of America require that land be stated at cost. Management has informed me (us) that the company has stated its land at appraised value and that, if accounting principles generally accepted in the United States of America had been followed, the land account and stockholders' equity would have been decreased by $650,000.

[*Signature of accounting firm or accountant*]

[*Date*]

ILLUSTRATION 12—COMPILATION REPORT MODIFIED FOR A DEPARTURE FROM GAAP: STATEMENT OF CASH FLOWS IS OMITTED

Accountant's Compilation Report

To the Board of Directors of ABC Company:

I (We) have compiled the accompanying balance sheet of ABC Company as of December 31, 20X2, and the related statements of income and retained earnings for the year then ended. I (We) have not audited or reviewed the accompanying financial statements and, accordingly, do not express an opinion or provide any assurance about whether the financial statements are in accordance with accounting principles generally accepted in the United States of America.

Management is (Owners are) responsible for the preparation and fair presentation of the financial statements in accordance with accounting principles generally accepted in the United States of America and for designing, implementing, and maintaining internal control relevant to the preparation and fair presentation of the financial statements.

My (Our) responsibility is to conduct the compilation in accordance with Statements on Standards for Accounting and Review Services issued by the American Institute of Certified Public Accountants. The objective of a compilation is to assist management in presenting financial information in the form of financial statements without undertaking to obtain or provide any assurance that there are no material modifications that should be made to the financial statements. During our compilation, I (we) did become aware of a departure from accounting principles generally accepted in the United States of America that is described in the following paragraph.

A statement of cash flows for the year ended December 31, 20X2, has not been presented. Accounting principles generally accepted in the United States of America require that such a statement be presented when financial statements purport to present financial position and results of operations.

[*Signature of accounting firm or accountant*]

[*Date*]

ILLUSTRATION 13—COMPILATION REPORT COVERS SUPPLEMENTARY INFORMATION

Accountant's Compilation Report

To the Board of Directors of ABC Company:

I (We) have compiled the accompanying balance sheet of ABC Company as of December 31, 20X2, and the related statements of income, retained earnings, and cash flows for the year then ended, and the accompanying supplementary information [*identify the supplementary information, for example, schedule of cost of goods sold, schedule of general and administrative expenses*], which are presented only for supplementary analysis purposes. I (We) have not audited or reviewed the accompanying financial statements and supplementary information and, accordingly, do not express an opinion or provide any assurance about whether the financial statements and supplementary information are in accordance with accounting principles generally accepted in the United States of America.

Management is (Owners are) responsible for the preparation and fair presentation of the financial statements and supplementary information in accordance with accounting principles generally accepted in the United States of America and for designing, implementing, and maintaining internal control relevant to the preparation and fair presentation of the financial statements and supplementary information.

My (Our) responsibility is to conduct the compilation in accordance with Statements on Standards for Accounting and Review Services issued by the American Institute of Certified Public Accountants. The objective of a compilation is to assist management in presenting financial information in the form of financial statements and supplementary information without undertaking to obtain or provide any assurance that there are no material modifications that should be made to the financial statements and supplementary information.

[*Signature of accounting firm or accountant*]

[*Date*]

AR SECTION 90
REVIEW OF FINANCIAL STATEMENTS

WHAT EVERY PRACTITIONER SHOULD KNOW

Basic Objectives and Requirements

The guidance and requirements in AR Section 90 are based on the framework provided by AR Section 60 (Framework for Performing and Reporting on Compilation and Review Engagements).

AR Section 90 establishes standards and provides guidance on reviews of financial statements other than reviews of interim financial information to which AU Section 722 (Interim Financial Information) applies. It precludes accountants from performing a review engagement if independence is impaired for any reason.

The accountant is required to comply with the provisions of AR Section 90 whenever he or she has been engaged to review financial statements, except for reviews of interim financial information that meet all of the following conditions:

1. The accountant or a predecessor has audited the entity's latest annual financial statements;

2. The accountant either (*a*) has been engaged to audit the entity's current-year financial statements, or (*b*) audited the entity's latest annual financial statements and expects to be engaged to audit the entity's current-year financial statements; and

3. The entity prepares its interim financial information in accordance with the same financial reporting framework that is used to prepare the annual financial statements.

Accountants engaged to perform reviews of interim financial information when the conditions in (1)–(3) are met should perform such reviews in accordance with AU Section 722 (Interim Financial Information).

PRACTICE POINT: In February 2011, the American Institute of Certified Public Accountants' (AICPA's) Auditing Standards Board (ASB) issued Statement on Auditing Standards (SAS) No. 121, "Revised Applicability of Statement on Auditing Standards No. 100, Interim Financial Information," which amends the applicability of SAS-100 as codified in paragraph .05 of AU Section 722 (Interim Financial Information). Specifically, SAS-121 revises the applicability paragraph of AU Section 722 such that AU Section 722 would be applicable when the accountant audited the entity's latest annual financial statements, and the appointment of another accountant to audit the current-year financial statements is not effective prior to the beginning of the period covered by the review (i.e., revising item 2 above).

Essentially, SAS-121 revises the condition specified in item 2 above, as follows:

The accountant either (*a*) has been engaged to audit the entity's current-year financial statements, or (*b*) audited the entity's latest annual financial statements and, when it is expected that the current-year financial statements will be audited, the appointment of another accountant to audit the current-year financial statements is not effective prior to the beginning of the period covered by the review.

This amendment is effective for interim reviews of interim financial information for periods beginning after December 15, 2011 (i.e., beginning in 2012 for calendar-year entities). Early application is permitted.

Also, in a related action, the AICPA's Accounting and Review Services Committee issued Statement on Standards for Accounting and Review Services (SSARS) No. 20, "Revised Applicability of Statements on Standards for Accounting and Review Services." SSARS-20 revises paragraph .01 of AR Section 90 (Review of Financial Statements) so that SSARS do not apply when the provisions of SAS-100, as amended by SAS-121 (AU Section 722), apply (i.e., revising item 2 above). Consistent with the effective date of SAS-121, the amendment in SSARS-20 is effective for reviews of financial statements for periods beginning after December 15, 2011 (i.e., beginning in 2012 for calendar-year entities). Early application is permitted.

Except for the revised applicability of AR Section 90, the discussion in this chapter remains unaffected by SSARS-20.

Establishing an Understanding with the Client in a Review Engagement

AR Section 90 contains a presumptively mandatory requirement for the accountant to establish an understanding with management (and, if applicable, those charged with governance) regarding the services to be performed and to document the understanding through a written communication (i.e., engagement letter). This is a significant change from previous standards, which stated only that the client understanding should *preferably* be in writing. The engagement letter should address the following:

- *Objectives of the engagement*—Essentially, the primary objective of the review is to obtain limited assurance there are no material modifications that should be made to the financial statements in order for them to be in conformity with the applicable financial reporting framework (e.g., GAAP, OCBOA).

- *Management's responsibilities*—Management is responsible for the following:

  — The preparation and fair presentation of the financial statements in accordance with the applicable financial reporting framework.

  — Designing, implementing, and maintaining internal control relevant to the preparation and fair presentation of the financial statements.

  — Preventing and detecting fraud.

  — Identifying and ensuring that the entity complies with the laws and regulations applicable to its activities.

- Making all financial records and related information available to the accountant.

- Providing the accountant, at the conclusion of the engagement, with a letter that confirms certain representations made during the review.

- *Accountant's responsibilities*—The accountant is responsible for the following:

  - Conducting the engagement in accordance with SSARSs issued by the AICPA, which includes primarily applying analytical procedures to management's financial data and making inquiries of company management.

  - Informing the appropriate level of management of any material errors and any evidence or information that comes to the accountant's attention that fraud or an illegal act may have occurred. (*Note*: The accountant is not required to report any matters regarding illegal acts that may have occurred that are clearly inconsequential and may reach agreement in advance with the entity on the nature of any such matters to be communicated.)

- *Limitations of the engagement*—A review conducted in accordance with SSARSs:

  - Is substantially less in scope than an audit, the objective of which is the expression of an opinion regarding the financial statements as a whole, and, therefore, does not contemplate: (1) obtaining an understanding of the entity's internal control; (2) assessing fraud risk; (3) testing accounting records by obtaining sufficient appropriate audit evidence through inspection, observation, confirmation, or the examination of source documents (e.g., cancelled checks or bank images); or (4) performing other procedures ordinarily performed in an audit. Accordingly, the accountant will not express an opinion regarding the financial statements as a whole.

  - Cannot be relied on to disclose errors, fraud, or illegal acts.

- *Other additional matters*—The engagement letter should address the following additional matters, if applicable:

  - Material departures from the applicable financial reporting framework may exist, and the effects of those departures, if any, on the financial statements may not be disclosed.

  - Reference to supplementary information.

In addition to the required matters discussed above, AR Section 90 indicates that an understanding with the client also may include other matters, such as the following:

- Arrangements regarding fees and billings.

- Any limitation of or other arrangements regarding the liability of the accountant or the client, for example, indemnification to the accountant for liability arising from knowing misrepresentations to the accountant by management (certain regulators may restrict or prohibit such liability limitation arrangements).

- Conditions under which access to review documentation may be granted to others.

- Additional services to be provided relating to regulatory requirements.

See Illustration 1 for an example of a standard engagement letter that is appropriate for a review.

Review Performance Requirements

AR Section 90 requires the accountant to perform procedures designed to accumulate review evidence that will provide a reasonable basis for obtaining limited assurance that there are no material modifications that should be made to the financial statements in order for them to be in conformity with the applicable financial reporting framework. The specific nature, timing, and extent of these procedures are a matter of professional judgment; however, they should be tailored based on the accountant's knowledge of the client and its industry. Analytical procedures and inquiry will ordinarily provide a reasonable basis for obtaining limited assurance that the financial statements are not materially misstated; however, additional procedures should be performed if necessary to obtain such limited assurance.

AR Section 90 sets forth the following specific performance requirements for review engagements:

- *Understanding the industry*—The accountant should obtain an understanding of the client's industry sufficient to enable the accountant to determine the nature, timing, and extent of review procedures to be performed. This requirement does not preclude an accountant from accepting a review engagement in an industry in which the accountant has no previous experience. However, it does make the accountant responsible for obtaining that understanding by, for example, consulting professional literature, other knowledgeable individuals, or taking continuing education courses.

- *Knowledge of the client*—Knowledge of the client should include an understanding of the client's business and its accounting principles and practices. This understanding is ordinarily obtained through experience with the client or its industry and inquiries of client personnel. In gaining this understanding, AR Section 90 states that the accountant should be alert to unusual accounting policies or practices that come to the accountant's attention as a result of having knowledge of the industry.

Designing and Performing Review Procedures

AR Section 90 states that the accountant should (1) design and perform analytical procedures, (2) make inquiries, and (3) perform other procedures, as appropriate, to obtain review evidence sufficient to achieve limited assurance that no material modifications should be made to the financial statements. These procedures should focus on areas that, in the accountant's judgment, may have increased risks of misstatements. Results of analytical procedures and inquiries may modify the accountant's risk awareness. For example, discovery through inquiry that the accounts receivable detail listing was not reconciled to the general ledger control account would ordinarily cause the accountant to have increased awareness of the risk of misstatement of accounts receivable.

Analytical procedures Analytical procedures involve comparing expectations developed by the accountant to recorded amounts or ratios developed from recorded amounts. An understanding of financial and nonfinancial relationships is important in both developing analytical procedures and evaluating their results. Expectations are developed by identifying plausible relationships based on knowledge of the client and understanding of the industry. Sources of information for developing expectations include:

- Prior period information, considering known changes.
- Budgets, forecasts, or other anticipated results, including extrapolations from interim or annual data.
- Relationships between elements of financial information within the period.
- Information about the client's industry, such as gross margin information.
- Relationships of financial information with relevant nonfinancial information, such as payroll costs to number of employees.

Analytical procedures may be performed at either the financial statement level or at the detailed account level. AR Section 90 requires that accountants investigate, by inquiry and other procedures as necessary in the circumstances, fluctuations or relationships that are inconsistent with other relevant information or that differ significantly from expected values. There is no requirement to corroborate management's responses with other evidence. However, the accountant may need to perform other procedures when management is unable to provide an explanation or when management's response appears inadequate.

> *Note: For a detailed analytical procedures form that may be used, see Illustration 1 in AU Section 329 (Analytical Procedures), included in this Manual.*

Inquiries and other review procedures AR Section 90 indicates that the accountant should consider performing the following inquiries and other review procedures:

1. Inquiring of members of management having responsibility for financial and accounting matters (and others within the entity and those charged with governance, if appropriate) concerning:
   a. Whether the financial statements have been prepared in conformity with the applicable financial reporting framework.
   b. The entity's accounting principles and practices and the methods used in applying them.
   c. The entity's procedures for recording, classifying, and summarizing transactions, and accumulating information for disclosure in the financial statements.

    d. Unusual or complex situations that may have an effect on the entity's financial statements.

    e. Significant transactions occurring or recognized close to the end of the period being reported on.

    f. The status of uncorrected misstatements identified during the previous engagement.

    g. Matters as a result of questions raised when applying the review procedures.

    h. Material subsequent events.

    i. Any fraud or suspected fraud affecting the entity involving management or others where the effect could be material to the financial statements.

    j. Significant journal entries and other adjustments.

    k. Communications from regulatory agencies.

    l. Actions taken at meetings of stockholders, board of directors, committees, or comparable meetings that may affect the financial statements.

2. Inquiring about actions taken at meetings of stockholders, the board of directors, committees of the board of directors, or comparable meetings that may affect the financial statements.

3. Reading the financial statements to consider whether they appear to conform to the applicable financial reporting framework.

4. Obtaining reports from other accountants, if any, who have been engaged to audit or review the financial statements of significant components of the reporting entity, its subsidiaries, and other investees.

See Illustration 2 for a review procedures checklist.

    In a review engagement, unlike in an audit, the accountant is not ordinarily required to corroborate management's responses with other evidence. However, the accountant should consider whether those responses are reasonable and consistent within the context of other review procedures and the accountant's knowledge of the client's business and industry.

Incorrect, incomplete or otherwise unsatisfactory information During the course of a review engagement, it may come to the accountant's attention that information in the financial statements is incorrect, incomplete, or otherwise unsatisfactory. In such circumstances, AR Section 90 requires the accountant to perform the following procedures:

1. Request management to consider the effect of such matters on the financial statements and communicate its results to the accountant;

2. Consider management's response and the effect, if any, on the accountant's review report; and

3. If the accountant believes the financial statements may be materially misstated, perform additional necessary procedures to obtain the limited level of assurance contemplated in a review engagement.

If, based on the foregoing procedures, the accountant concludes that the financial statements are materially misstated, the accountant should follow the guidance regarding departures from the applicable financial reporting framework, as discussed later in this chapter.

Representation Letter From Management

AR Section 90 requires written representations from management for all financial statements and periods covered by the accountant's review report. The management representation letter should be addressed to the accountant and tailored to each individual review engagement; however, it should, at a minimum, contain specific representations about the following:

- Management's acknowledgement of its responsibility for the financial statements;
- Management's belief that the financial statements are fairly presented in conformity with the applicable financial reporting framework;
- Management's acknowledgement of its responsibility for designing, implementing, and maintaining internal control;
- Management's acknowledgement of its responsibility to prevent and detect fraud;
- Management's knowledge of any fraud or suspected fraud affecting the entity that could have a material effect on the financial statements;
- Management's full and truthful response to all inquiries;
- The completeness of information;
- Information about subsequent events; and
- Matters specific to the entity's business or industry.

PRACTICE POINT: When comparative financial statements are presented, it is important that the representation letter for the current engagement also cover all prior periods presented. This is true even when the accountant has a representation letter covering the prior periods in the files from those previous engagements, because management's representations for those periods might have changed since that time.

The representations from management should be made as of the date of the accountant's review report. In addition, the accountant is required to obtain written representations from current management for all periods covered by the accountant's report, even if current management was not present during all such periods. The letter should be signed by members of management who are responsible for and knowledgeable about the matters covered in the letter (i.e., normally the CEO and CFO, or others with equivalent positions).

If the client does not provide the accountant with a representation letter, the review will be incomplete and, therefore, the accountant would be precluded from issuing a review report under the circumstances.

See Illustration 3 for a management representation letter for a review engagement.

The accountant's consideration of obtaining an updating management representation letter AR Section 90 indicates that, in connection with a review engagement, the accountant should consider obtaining an updating representation letter from management in certain circumstances, for example, when a significant period of time has elapsed after the accountant has obtained the original management representation letter and before the issuance of the review report; or, when a material subsequent event occurs after obtaining the original management representation letter, but before the review report is issued.

In addition, AR Section 90 indicates that the accountant should obtain an updating management representation letter from a former client if the accountant is requested to reissue his or her report on the financial statements of a prior period that are being presented on a comparative basis with reviewed financial statements of a subsequent period reported on by a successor accountant.

When the accountant obtains an updating management representation letter, such letter should indicate (a) whether management believes if any of its previous representations should be modified and (b) whether any subsequent events have occurred that would require adjustment to, or disclosure in, the company's financial statements.

See Illustration 4 for an updating management representation letter for a review engagement.

Documentation in a Review Engagement

AR Section 90 contains requirements for accountants to prepare documentation in connection with review engagements to provide a clear understanding of the work performed, the review evidence obtained and its source, and the conclusions reached. This documentation provides the principal support for (a) the accountant's representation in the review report that the review was performed in accordance with the SSARSs, and (b) the conclusion that the accountant is not aware of any material modifications that should be made to the financial statements.

Although the form, content, and extent of the documentation is a matter of professional judgment and depends on the circumstances of the engagement, AR Section 90 indicates that the accountant's documentation should include:

- A signed engagement letter.
- The analytical procedures performed, including:
  - The expectations, when not otherwise obvious from the documentation;
  - The factors considered in developing the expectations;
  - The results of the comparisons of the expectations to recorded amounts or ratios derived from recorded amounts; and

— Management's responses to inquiries regarding fluctuations or relationships that are inconsistent with other relevant information or that differ from expected values by a significant amount.

- Additional review procedures performed to respond to significant unexpected differences discovered by analytical procedures, and the results of those procedures.

- Significant matters covered in the inquiry procedures, and management's responses. These may be documented in memorandum, checklist, or other form.

- Significant findings or issues, such as the results of review procedures indicating that the financial statements could be materially misstated, actions taken to address the findings, and the basis for final conclusions.

- Significant unusual matters the accountant considered during the review, and their disposition.

- Communications (written or oral) to the appropriate level of management of instances of fraud or illegal acts that come to the accountant's attention.

- The signed management representation letter.

Reporting on Reviewed Financial Statements

AR Section 90 requires the accountant's standard review report to include the following elements:

- *Title*—The title should clearly indicate that it is the accountant's review report and include the word "independent." (*Note*: An appropriate title would be "Independent Accountant's Review Report.")

- *Addressee*—The report should be addressed as appropriate in the circumstances of the engagement.

- *Introductory paragraph*—The accountant's report should include an introductory paragraph that:

  — Identifies the entity whose financial statements have been reviewed;

  — States that the financial statements have been reviewed;

  — Identifies the financial statements that have been reviewed (e.g., balance sheet, statement of operations);

  — Specifies the date or period covered by the financial statements;

  — States that a review includes primarily applying analytical procedures to management's financial data and making inquiries of company management; and

  — States that a review is substantially less in scope than an audit, the objective of which is the expression of an opinion regarding the financial statements as a whole, and that, accordingly, the accountant does not express such an opinion.

- *Management's responsibility paragraph*—The accountant's report should include a paragraph that describes management's responsibility for the financial statements and for internal control over financial reporting, specifically stating that management is responsible for:

— The preparation and fair presentation of the financial statements in accordance with the applicable financial reporting framework (e.g., GAAP, OCBOA); and

— Designing, implementing, and maintaining internal control relevant to the preparation and fair presentation of the financial statements that are free from material misstatement.

• *Accountant's responsibility paragraph*—The accountant's report should include a paragraph that states:

— The accountant's responsibility is to conduct the review in accordance with SSARSs issued by the AICPA;

— Those standards require the accountant to perform the procedures to obtain limited assurance that there are no material modifications that should be made to the financial statements; and

— The accountant believes that the results of his or her procedures provide a reasonable basis for his or her report.

• *Results of engagement (conclusion) paragraph*—The accountant's report should include a paragraph that states, based on the review, the accountant is not aware of any material modifications that should be made to the financial statements in order for them to be in conformity with the applicable financial reporting framework (other than those modifications, if any, indicated in the report).

• *Signature*—The accountant's report should include a manual or printed signature of the accounting firm or the accountant, as appropriate.

• *Date*—The accountant's review report should not be dated earlier than the date on which the accountant has accumulated review evidence sufficient to provide a reasonable basis for concluding that the accountant has obtained limited assurance that there are no material modifications that should be made to the financial statements in order for them to be in conformity with the applicable financial reporting framework.

In addition, each page of the reviewed financial statements should include a reference to the accountant's review report, such as "See Independent Accountant's Review Report."

AR Section 90 states that an accountant cannot issue a report on a review that is incomplete, such as when the accountant is not able to perform necessary inquiry and analytical procedures or when the client does not provide the accountant with a representation letter. Otherwise stated, review reports, unlike auditor's reports, cannot contain scope limitations. Under such circumstances, the accountant should consider whether it may be appropriate to issue a compilation report on the financial statements. For further guidance, see the discussion under "Change in Engagement From Audit or Review to Compilation" in AR Section 80 (Compilation of Financial Statements) of this Manual.

See Illustration 5 for an example of a standard review report on financial statements prepared in accordance with GAAP, Illustration 6 applicable to cash basis financial statements, and Illustration 7 applicable to income tax basis financial statements.

Lack of the Accountant's Independence in a Review Engagement

If the accountant is not independent in a review engagement, he or she is precluded from issuing a review report on the entity's financial statements.

Departures from the Applicable Financial Reporting Framework in Review Engagements

In connection with a review of an entity's financial statements, the accountant may become aware of a departure from the applicable financial reporting framework (e.g., GAAP, OCBOA) that is considered material to the financial statements and that require such statements to be revised. If the client does not revise the financial statements, the accountant should consider whether modification of his or her standard report is adequate to disclose the departure from the applicable financial reporting framework.

If modification of the standard report is appropriate, the accountant should disclose in a separate paragraph of the report:

- The departure from the applicable financial reporting framework; and
- The effects of the departure on the financial statements if (a) such effects have been determined by management or (b) are known as the result of the accountant's procedures.

If management has not determined the effects of a departure from the applicable financial reporting framework, the accountant is not required to do so; however, he or she should state in the report that such determination has not been made.

See Illustrations 8 and 9 for examples of review reports that are modified for departures from the applicable financial reporting framework.

It should be emphasized that the accountant should not make a statement in his or her report that the financial statements are not in conformity with the applicable financial reporting framework. Including such a statement would be tantamount to expressing an adverse opinion on the financial statements taken as a whole, which can be expressed only in the context of an audit engagement. In addition, such a statement in a review report would confuse users because it would contradict the expression of limited assurance contemplated in a review report. However, depending on the significance of the departure and the pervasiveness and overall impact of the misstatements, the accountant may wish to emphasize the limitations of the financial statements in a separate paragraph. Such separate paragraph, which would follow the other modifications of the accountant's report, might read as follows:

> Because the significance and pervasiveness of the matters discussed above make it difficult to assess their impact on the financial statements taken as a whole, users of these financial statements should recognize that they might reach different conclusions about the company's financial position, results of

operations, and cash flows if they had access to revised financial statements prepared in conformity with [*identify the applicable financial reporting framework (e.g., "Accounting Principles Generally Accepted in the United States of America")*].

If the accountant believes that modification of the standard review report is not adequate, he or she should withdraw from the engagement and provide no further services with respect to those financial statements. In such circumstances, the accountant should consider consulting with his or her legal counsel.

Supplementary Information Accompanying the Reviewed Financial Statements

When the basic financial statements are accompanied by information presented for supplementary analysis purposes, the accountant should indicate the degree of responsibility, if any, he or she is taking regarding such information. The accountant should include an explanation in the review report, or in a separate report on the other data, stating that the review was made for the purpose of expressing a conclusion that there are no material modifications that should be made to the financial statements in order for them to be in conformity with the applicable financial reporting framework, and *either* of the following depending on whether the other data was subjected to the inquiry and analytical procedures:

- *Other data was subjected to the inquiry and analytical procedures*—A statement should be made that the other data accompanying the financial statements are presented only for purposes of additional analysis and have been subjected to the inquiry and analytical procedures applied in the review of the basic financial statements, and the accountant did not become aware of any material modifications that should be made to such data. (See Illustration 10 for an example of a review report when the supplementary data has been subjected to the inquiry and analytical procedures applied in the review of the basic financial statements.)

- *Other data was not subjected to the inquiry and analytical procedures*—A statement should be made that the other data accompanying the financial statements are presented only for purposes of additional analysis and have not been subjected to the inquiry and analytical procedures applied in the review of the basic financial statements but were compiled from information that is the representation of management, without audit or review, and the accountant does not express an opinion or provide any assurance on such data. (See Illustration 11 for an example of a review report when the supplementary data has not been subjected to the inquiry and analytical procedures applied in the review of the basic financial statements.)

Emphasis of a Matter in Review Reports

Accountants are permitted (but not required) to include an emphasis-of-matter paragraph in their review reports, as long as the matter is appropriately disclosed in the financial statements. The following are examples of matters that the accountant may want to emphasize:

- Uncertainties;
- The entity reported on is a component of a larger entity;
- The entity has had significant transactions with related parties;
- A significant subsequent event has taken place; or
- Accounting matters, other than those involving changes in accounting principles, exist that affect the comparability of the financial statements with those of the preceding period.

Restricting the Use of an Accountant's Review Report

AR Section 90 provides guidance to accountants on restricting the use of their reports issued in connection with review engagements. A key distinction is made between reports issued for "general use" and "restricted use":

- *General use*—A *general-use* report is one that is not restricted to specified parties, for example, accountants' review reports on financial statements prepared in conformity with an applicable financial reporting framework (e.g., GAAP, OCBOA).
- *Restricted use*—A *restricted-use* report is one that is intended only for specified parties. The need for restriction on the use of a report may result from varying circumstances, such as the purpose of the report or the potential for the review report to be misunderstood.

An accountant is not precluded from restricting the use of any report. However, the accountant *should* restrict the use of his or her report when the subject matter of the report or the presentation being reported on is based on measurement or disclosure criteria contained in contractual agreements or regulatory provisions that are not in conformity with an applicable financial reporting framework (e.g., GAAP, OCBOA). This is because, in such circumstances, the basis, assumptions, or purpose of such presentations are developed for the parties to the agreement or regulatory agency for their own use, and may not provide useful or relevant data for any other purpose. The inclusion of restricted-use reports in a document that also contains general-use reports does not affect the intended use of either report. It is permissible, and even useful to some of the intended users, that these reports be submitted together.

If an accountant issues a single combined report covering matters that require restriction, as well as other matters that generally do not require restriction, then the accountant should restrict to the specified parties the use of such a single combined report.

Adding other specified parties in restricted-use reports An accountant may be asked to consider adding other parties as specified parties in a restricted-use report. If an accountant is reporting on subject matter or a presentation based on criteria contained in contractual agreements or regulatory provisions, the accountant is allowed to add other parties as specified parties. However, in such circumstances, the accountant should consider factors such as the identity of the other parties, their knowledge of the basis of the measurement or disclosure criteria, and the intended use of the report.

If the accountant agrees to add other parties as specified parties, the accountant should obtain acknowledgment from the other parties, preferably in writing, of their understanding of (a) the nature of the engagement; (b) the measurement or disclosure criteria used in the engagement; and (c) the related report.

If the accountant agrees to add such other parties after he or she has issued the report, the accountant may either reissue the report or may provide other written acknowledgment that the other parties have been added as specified parties. However, if the report is reissued, the accountant should not change the report date. If the accountant provides written acknowledgment, he or she should ordinarily state that no procedures have been performed subsequent to the date of the accountant's report.

Limiting report distribution An accountant should consider informing the client that restricted-use reports are not intended for distribution to nonspecified parties. An auditor is not responsible for controlling a client's distribution of restricted-use reports. That is why restricted-use reports should alert readers to the restriction on the use of the report by indicating that the report is not intended to be, and should not be, used by anyone other than the specified parties.

Restricted-use report language In a review report that is restricted as to use, the accountant should add a separate paragraph at the end of the report that:

- States that the report is intended solely for the information and use of the specified parties.
- Identifies the specified parties.
- States that the report is not intended to be used and should not be used by anyone other than the specified parties.

The following is an example of such a paragraph: "This report is intended solely for the information and use of [*the specified parties*] and is not intended to be and should not be used by anyone other than these specified parties."

Uncertainties Related to Going Concern Matters in Review Engagements

During a review engagement, the accountant may become aware of conditions or events that indicate that there may be an uncertainty about the entity's ability to continue as a going concern for a reasonable period of time, not to exceed one year beyond the date of the financial statements. Such conditions or events include, but are not limited to (1) recurring operating losses, (2) working capital deficiencies, (3) negative cash flows from operating activities, (4) default on loan agreements or similar agreements, (5) restructuring of debt, (6) substantial dependence on the success of a particular project, and (7) legal proceedings.

The going-concern concept is based on the presumption that the entity will continue to exist as a business entity in the foreseeable future (usually one year) in the absence of information to the contrary. However, business failure is not uncommon, and conditions may require the accountant to exercise professional judgment in evaluating the adequacy of going-concern disclosures in the financial statements. Therefore, if evidence or information comes to the accountant's attention that indicate that an uncertainty may exist about the entity's ability to continue as a going concern for a reasonable period of time, not to exceed one year beyond the date of the financial statements, the accountant should request that management consider the possible effects of the going concern uncertainty on the financial statements, including the need for related disclosure. The accountant also should consider the reasonableness of management's conclusions, including the adequacy of the related disclosures, if applicable.

If the accountant determines that management's conclusions are unreasonable or the disclosure of the uncertainty regarding the entity's ability to continue as a going concern is not adequate, the accountant should follow the preceding guidance regarding departures from an applicable financial reporting framework.

An uncertainty about an entity's ability to continue as a going concern would not cause the accountant to modify the standard review report provided the financial statements appropriately disclose the going concern uncertainty. In addition, the accountant is not precluded from emphasizing in a separate paragraph of his or her report a matter regarding a going concern uncertainty. Therefore, when an uncertainty related to an entity's ability to continue as a going concern exists but is adequately disclosed in the financial statements, it is not necessary to add a paragraph to the standard review report describing the uncertainty. However, the accountant may wish to draw attention to such uncertainty in an emphasis-of-matter paragraph in the accountant's report, using language such as the following:

> As discussed in Note [X], certain conditions indicate that the Company may be unable to continue as a going concern. The accompanying financial statements do not include any adjustments to the financial statements that might be necessary should the Company be unable to continue as a going concern.

It should be noted that the accountant's report should not use the term *substantial doubt* in the additional paragraph to highlight a going concern matter in the client's financial statements. This is because substantial doubt is an audit-evidence-based concept that should only be used in audit reports.

Other Uncertainties in Review Engagements

The preparation of financial statements in conformity with an applicable financial reporting framework (e.g., GAAP, OCBOA) requires management to make estimates and assumptions that affect the reported amounts of assets and liabilities, disclosure of contingent assets and liabilities, and reported amounts of revenues and expenses. Generally, significant estimates relate to matters, such as allowance for uncollectible accounts receivable, inventory obsolescence, depreciation, asset valuations and useful lives, and contingencies.

Consistent with the guidance previously discussed regarding uncertainties related to going-concern matters, if the disclosures required by an applicable financial reporting framework regarding an uncertainty are not included in the reviewed financial statements, the accountant's report on the financial statements should include a paragraph describing the departure from the applicable financial reporting framework. On the other hand, if the accountant concludes that management's disclosure of the uncertainty is adequate and in accordance with the applicable financial reporting framework, there is no need for the accountant to modify the review report; however, the accountant may add an emphasis of a matter paragraph with respect to the uncertainty in the review report that contains wording similar to the following:

> As discussed in Note [X], the Company is currently named in a legal action. The Company has determined that it is not possible to predict the eventual outcome of the legal action but has determined that the resolution of the action will not result in an adverse judgment that would materially affect the financial statements. Accordingly, the accompanying financial statements do not include any adjustments related to this legal action.

Subsequent Events in Review Engagements

During the performance of review procedures, or subsequent to the date of the accountant's review report (but prior to the release of the report), the accountant may become aware of evidence or information that a subsequent event that has a material effect on the financial statements has occurred. In such circumstances, the accountant should request that management consider the possible effects of the subsequent event on the financial statements, including the adequacy of any related disclosure, if applicable.

If the accountant determines that the subsequent event is not adequately accounted for in the financial statements or disclosed in the notes, he or she should follow the preceding guidance regarding departures from an applicable financial reporting framework.

Therefore, when a subsequent event that has a material impact on the entity is adequately disclosed in the financial statements, it is not necessary for the accountant to add an explanatory paragraph to the standard review report describing the subsequent event. However, the accountant may wish to draw attention to such uncertainty in an emphasis-of-matter paragraph in the accountant's report.

Subsequent Discovery of Facts Existing at the Date of the Review Report

Subsequent to the date of the accountant's review report, the accountant may become aware that facts may have existed at that date that suggest that information supplied by the client was incorrect, incomplete, or otherwise unsatisfactory. In such circumstances, the accountant should determine the appropriate specific actions to be taken by considering:

- *The reliability of the information and whether the facts existed at the date of the accountant's report*—The accountant should discuss the matter with the client at the appropriate management level, including those charged with governance, and request cooperation in whatever investigation may be necessary. The accountant ordinarily would conclude that persons known to be using or likely to use the financial statements should be notified in an appropriate manner if the information (a) is deemed reliable and existed at the date of his or her report and (b) indicates that the financial statements, the report, or both need revision.

- *The existence of persons known to be using or likely to use the financial statements*—In evaluating the likelihood that persons are currently using or likely to use the financial statements, the accountant should consider the time elapsed since the financial statements were issued.

If the accountant determines that the subsequently discovered information is reliable and existed at the date of his or her report, he or she should, as soon as practicable, request that management consider the effect of the information on the previously issued financial statements. In addition, the accountant should consider the effect of the discovered matter on his or her report.

If the nature and effect of the matter are such that (a) the accountant's review report or the financial statements would have been affected if the information had been known to the accountant at the date of his or her report and had not been reflected in the financial statements and (b) the accountant believes that there are persons currently using or likely to use the financial statements who would attach importance to the information, the accountant should perform additional procedures deemed necessary to achieve limited assurance that there are no material modifications that should be made to the financial statements in order for them to be in conformity with the applicable financial reporting framework (e.g., GAAP, OCBOA).

Action to prevent future use of the accountant's review report If the accountant concludes that action should be taken to prevent future use of the review report or the financial statements, he or she should advise the client to make appropriate disclosure to interested third parties of (a) the newly discovered facts and (b) their impact on the financial statements. The method the client uses to make the appropriate disclosure will depend on the circumstances using the following guidance:

- *Effect of discovered information can be determined promptly*—If the effect on the financial statements or accountant's report can be determined promptly, disclosure should consist of issuing revised financial statements and accountant's report, as soon as practicable. The reasons for the revision usually should be described in a note to the financial statements and referred to in the accountant's report.

- *Issuance of financial statements and the accountant's report thereon for a subsequent period is imminent*—When issuance of financial statements and the accountant's report thereon for a subsequent period is imminent, appropriate disclosure of the revision can be made in such subsequent financial statements instead of reissuing the earlier financial statements.

- *Effect of discovered information cannot be determined promptly*—If the effect on the financial statements or accountant's report cannot be promptly determined, the client should notify persons who are known to be using or who are likely to use the financial statements that (a) they should not be using the financial statements, (b) revised financial statements will be issued, and (c) where applicable, the accountant's report will be issued as soon as practicable.

The accountant should be satisfied that the client has made the appropriate disclosures described above.

Accountant's action if the client refuses to make the appropriate disclosures If the client refuses to make the disclosures discussed above, the accountant should notify the appropriate personnel at the highest levels within the entity (e.g., owner or those charged with governance) of such refusal and of the fact that the accountant will notify:

- The client that the accountant's review report must no longer be associated with the financial statements.
- Regulatory agencies having jurisdiction over the client that the accountant's report should no longer be used.
- Each person known to the accountant to be using the financial statements that the financial statements and the accountant's report should no longer be used. (*Note:* Generally, notification to a regulatory agency having jurisdiction over the client will usually be the only practicable way for the accountant to provide appropriate disclosure. Any such notification to a regulatory agency should be accompanied by a request that the agency take whatever steps it deems appropriate to accomplish the necessary disclosure).

The accountant should observe the following guidelines when making disclosures to persons other than the client:

- The disclosure should include a description of the nature of the subsequently acquired information and its effect on the financial statements.
- The discovered information should be disclosed as precisely and factually as possible, without any comments about the conduct or motives of any persons involved.
- If the client refused to cooperate, the accountant should disclose (a) that information has come to his or her attention which the client has not cooperated in attempting to substantiate, and (b) that, if the information is true, the accountant believes that his or her report must no longer be used or be associated with the financial statements. (*Note:* No such disclosure should be made unless the accountant believes that the financial statements are likely to be misleading and that the accountant's review report should not be used.)

As a practical matter, the accountant should consult his or her legal counsel before making any disclosures to third parties.

Communicating Fraud and Illegal Acts to Management and Others in Review Engagements

For purposes of the SSARSs, fraud and illegal acts are defined as follows:

- *Fraud*—An intentional act that results in a misstatement in reviewed financial statements.
- *Illegal acts*—Violations of laws or government regulations, excluding fraud.

When evidence or information comes to the accountant's attention during the performance of review procedures that fraud or an illegal act may have occurred, it should be brought to the attention of the appropriate level of management. For purposes of communicating fraud and illegal acts to an appropriate level of management, an appropriate level of management generally should involve an individual or a group at a higher level within the entity than the level at which the fraud or illegal act may have occurred. For instances of fraud or illegal acts involving senior management, the related matters should be reported to an individual or group at a higher level within the entity (e.g., manager/owner, those charged with governance). When the instances of fraud or illegal acts involve an owner of the business, the accountant should consider resigning from the engagement. The accountant also should consider consulting his or her legal counsel and insurance provider under such circumstances.

In addition, while the communication to management and others regarding fraud and illegal acts may be oral or written, AR Section 90 requires the accountant to document such communication if it is made orally.

The accountant need not report matters regarding illegal acts that are clearly inconsequential and may reach agreement in advance with the entity on the nature of such items to be communicated.

Communications to third parties outside the entity AR Section 90 indicates that, generally, the accountant is not responsible to notify third parties—other than the client's senior management or those charged with governance, if applicable—of matters related to fraud or illegal acts. Owing to ethical and legal obligations of confidentiality, the accountant ordinarily would be precluded from communicating fraud or illegal acts to third parties outside the entity. However, AR Section 90 recognizes that the accountant may have a duty to disclose these matters to parties outside the entity in the following circumstances:

- To comply with certain legal and regulatory requirements
- To respond to a successor accountant's inquiries that are made in accordance with AR Section 400 (Communications between Predecessor and Successor Accountants) for purposes of determining whether to accept a review engagement
- To respond to a subpoena

Because of potential conflicts in the confidential relationship between the accountant and the client, the accountant may find it advisable to contact legal counsel before matters related to fraud or illegal acts are disclosed to parties outside the entity. This is particularly important because unjustified third-party notification could result in a lawsuit against the accountant for damages, slander, or similar reasons.

Impact of fraud and illegal acts on other aspects of the review engagement In a review engagement, the accountant performs inquiry and analytical procedures that provide the accountant with a reasonable basis for expressing limited assurance that there are no material modifications that should be made to the financial statements in order for them to be in conformity with the applicable financial reporting framework. Therefore, because of the limited nature of the procedures performed in a review engagement, the accountant is not required to perform any additional procedures to determine whether a suspected fraud or an illegal act has in fact occurred, or has probably occurred. However, the account-ant should consider the effect of the suspected fraud or illegal act on his or her ability to perform the necessary inquiries and review procedures and on the reliability and integrity of management's representations.

Change in Engagement from Audit to Review

Before the completion of an audit engagement, a client may request the account-ant to change the engagement to a review engagement. In such circumstances, before an accountant agrees to change the audit to a review engagement, he or she should consider, at a minimum, the following:

1. The reasons given for the client's request, particularly the implications of a restriction on the scope of the audit, whether imposed by the client or by the engagement circumstances.

2. The additional effort required to complete the audit.

3. The estimated additional cost to complete the audit.

AR Section 90 states that changes in circumstances affecting the entity's requirement for an audit or a misunderstanding about the nature of an audit or a review would ordinarily be a reasonable basis for such a request.

If the audit is substantially complete, or the cost to complete it is relatively insignificant, the accountant should consider the propriety of accepting a change to a review. If a limitation on the scope of the audit is involved, the accountant should evaluate the possibility that incorrect, incomplete, or otherwise unsatis-factory information may be affected. In any case, when the scope limitation restricts the accountant's ability to correspond with the entity's legal counsel or when the client would have refused to sign a representation letter in an audit, the accountant would ordinarily be precluded from issuing a review report.

When an accountant concludes that a change in the engagement is appropri-ate, and complies with applicable standards for a review engagement, an appro-priate review report should be issued. However, that report should not refer to the original audit engagement, any audit procedures that were performed, or any scope limitations that resulted in a changed engagement.

PRACTICE ISSUES AND FREQUENTLY ASKED QUESTIONS

Issue 1: Do accounting principles generally accepted in the United States (GAAP) apply to reviews of financial statements?

Yes. GAAP is one of the financial reporting frameworks that may be used in financial statements when performing reviews of financial statements. Other financial reporting frameworks would include IFRS and OCBOA.

Issue 2: What is the primary difference between a review engagement and a compilation engagement?

In a review engagement, the accountant performs inquiry and analytical proce-dures that provide the accountant with a reasonable basis for expressing limited assurance that there are no material modifications that should be made to the financial statements. However, no expression of assurance is contemplated or provided in a compilation engagement.

Issue 3: Is the accountant precluded from accepting a review engagement for an entity in an industry with which he or she has no prior experience?

No, as long as the accountant obtains the required level of knowledge before completing the review engagement.

Issue 4: May an accountant issue a review report on one financial statement, such as a balance sheet, and not on other related financial statements?

Yes. An accountant may issue a review report on one financial statement (e.g., balance sheet) and not on other related financial statements (e.g., income statement, cash flows statement).

Issue 5: Is a separate statement of retained earnings required to be presented as part of reviewed financial statements that are prepared in accordance with GAAP?

No. A separate statement of retained earnings is not required to be presented as a financial statement. GAAP requires only disclosure of a change in capital. This can be accomplished by (1) preparation of a separate statement, (2) disclosure in the notes to the financial statements, or (3) presentation as part of another basic statement.

Issue 6: Should review reports be modified when a statement of comprehensive income is presented as part of reviewed financial statements?

Yes. If a statement of comprehensive income is presented as part of reviewed financial statements, the first paragraph of the review report should also refer to the statement of comprehensive income.

Issue 7: Are accountants permitted to include an emphasis-of-matter paragraph in their review reports to emphasize a matter regarding the financial statements?

Yes. Accountants are permitted (not required) to include an emphasis-of-matter paragraph in their review reports, as long as the matter is appropriately disclosed in the financial statements. However, emphasis paragraphs in the accountant's report should *not*:

- Introduce new information about the financial statements (i.e., they should only emphasize a matter that is already disclosed in the financial statements).
- Include information about or describe the procedures the accountant has or has not performed.
- Contain any conclusions or opinions.

Issue 8: Does an uncertainty, such as uncertainty about an entity's ability to continue as a going concern, require the accountant to modify the standard report in a review engagement?

No. Generally, an uncertainty, including an uncertainty about an entity's ability to continue as a going concern, would not cause the accountant to modify the standard review report, provided the financial statements appropriately disclose the uncertainty. However, the accountant is not precluded from emphasizing in a separate paragraph of his or her report such a matter regarding the financial statements. The following is an example of such a paragraph:

> As discussed in Note [X], certain conditions indicate that the Company may be unable to continue as a going concern. The accompanying financial statements do not include any adjustments to the financial statements that might be necessary should the Company be unable to continue as a going concern.

It should be noted that the accountant's report should not use the term "substantial doubt" in the additional paragraph to highlight a going concern disclosure in the client's financial statements. This is because "substantial doubt" is an audit-evidence-based concept that should only be used in audit reports.

Issue 9: What type of report should the accountant issue if he or she has provided more than one level of service on the same financial statements?

If the accountant has provided more than one level of service on the same financial statements, he or she should issue a report that is appropriate for the highest level of service rendered. For example, if the accountant both compiled and reviewed the financial statements that he or she was engaged to review, the accountant would need to issue only a review report.

Issue 10: May an accountant accept an engagement to perform a compilation of financial statements for an interim period (e.g., monthly) and an engagement to review the financial statements for another period (e.g., quarterly) that ends on the same date?

Yes, as long as the accountant complies with the applicable standards for each engagement.

Issue 11: Is an accountant precluded from accepting an engagement to perform a higher level of service with respect to financial statements that he or she previously compiled or reviewed?

No. An accountant is not precluded from accepting an engagement to perform a higher level of service with respect to financial statements that he or she previously compiled or reviewed. For example, an accountant who has issued a review report on a set of financial statements may later issue an audit report on the same set of financial statements.

Issue 12: Under what circumstances would it ordinarily be necessary for the accountant to withdraw from a review engagement?

Ordinarily, it would be necessary for the accountant to withdraw from a review engagement under the following circumstances:

- When the nature, extent, and probable effect of the departures from the applicable financial reporting framework (e.g., GAAP, OCBOA) cause the accountant to question whether such departures were undertaken with the intention to mislead potential users of the financial statements.

- When the client does not revise the financial statements, including disclosures, that the accountant requests to be made, and the client refuses to accept the modified standard report that the accountant believes is appropriate.

Issue 13: If, in connection with a review engagement, the accountant performs certain additional procedures (e.g., confirmation or inventory observation procedures), is he or she required to "upgrade" the engagement to an audit?

No. An accountant may perform additional procedures in connection with a review engagement, such as confirmations of accounts receivable, inventory observation procedures, or such other "auditing procedures." The accountant is not required to change the engagement level in such circumstances.

Issue 14: Are financial forecasts and projections considered financial statements for purposes of AR Section 90?

No. Financial forecasts, projections, and similar presentations are not financial statements for purposes of AR Section 90.

Issue 15: When supplementary information accompanies the basic financial statements, should the accountant's report on such information be combined with the report on the basic statements or presented separately?

Either presentation is acceptable. Many accountants prefer to present the reports separately when compiled supplementary information accompanies reviewed basic financial statements, because they feel that this more clearly distinguishes between the two levels of service.

In some cases, a client may wish to present the basic financial statements with supplementary information to some users, while omitting it for others. In such circumstances, it is usually more convenient to report separately on the supplementary information, thus making the related report a "detachable" document from the basic financial statements.

Issue 16: Why does AR Section 90 require that a reference to the accountant's review report appear on each page of the financial statements?

First, this is a reminder to the user of the financial statements of what level of service was performed. Second, it is believed to provide some protection for the accountant. Absent such a reference, it would be impossible to tell what level of service the accountant had performed if the report became separated from the financial statements.

Issue 17: Are practitioners required to comply with quality control standards when performing review engagements?

Yes. Practitioners in the conduct of a firm's accounting practice should comply with quality control standards. Therefore, a firm should establish quality control policies and procedures to provide it with reasonable assurance of conforming to SSARSs. While, SSARSs relate to the conduct of individual compilation and review engagements, quality control standards relate to the conduct of a firm's accounting practice as a whole. Therefore, SSARSs and quality control standards are related and the quality control policies and procedures that a firm adopts may affect both the conduct of individual engagements and the conduct of a firm's accounting practice as a whole.

Issue 18: Do deficiencies in a firm's quality control system indicate that a review engagement was not performed in accordance with SSARSs?

No. This AR Section 90 specifically states that deficiencies in a firm's quality control system or noncompliance therewith do not necessarily indicate that a review engagement was not performed in accordance with SSARSs.

Issue 19: Does AR Section 90 apply when an accountant derives financial information from an entity's tax return and such information is presented as part of the accountant's business valuation report?

No. Accountants are sometimes engaged to perform a business valuation of an entity. Oftentimes, in connection with such business valuations, it may be necessary for the accountant to derive financial information from the client's tax return to be used in the business valuation. This is common if the entity does not have audited, reviewed, or compiled financial statements. The financial information that is derived from the tax return and presented as part of a business valuation is not deemed to be submission of financial statements. Therefore, AR Section 90 does not apply when an accountant derives financial information from an entity's tax return and such information is presented as part of the accountant's business valuation report.

Issue 20: Do the provisions of AU Section 316 (Consideration of Fraud in a Financial Statement Audit) apply to review engagements?

No. AU Section 316 (Consideration of Fraud in a Financial Statement Audit) does not apply to review engagements. Accordingly, the accountant is not required to plan or perform a review engagement to obtain reasonable assurance about whether the financial statements are free of material misstatement, whether caused by error or fraud. In addition, review performance standards do not require the accountant to document his or her assessment of fraud risk in a review engagement.

However, this does not mean that the accountant has no responsibility to be alert to the possibility of the existence of errors or fraud. For example, if the accountant determines that information supplied by the client is incorrect, incomplete, or otherwise unsatisfactory as it relates to a review engagement, the accountant should obtain additional or revised information. Further, the accountant should perform the additional procedures he or she deems necessary to achieve limited assurance that there are no material modifications that should be made to the financial statements for them to be in conformity with the applicable financial reporting framework.

Issue 21: Is the accountant required to obtain an understanding of an entity's internal control and to assess control risk in a review engagement?

No. In a review engagement, the accountant is not required to perform procedures that are generally performed in an audit, such as the following:

- Obtaining an understanding of internal control

- Assessing control risk

- Obtaining corroborating evidence through inspection, observation, or confirmation procedures

Issue 22: What factors would the accountant typically consider in determining the nature and extent of analytical procedures to be performed and inquiries to be made in a review engagement?

In determining the nature and extent of analytical procedures to be performed and inquiries to be made in a review engagement, the accountant generally would consider the following factors:

- The nature and materiality of the financial statement items
- The likelihood that a misstatement exists in the financial statements
- Knowledge of the client's business and the quality of the accounting principles and practices
- The qualifications and competence of the client's accounting personnel
- Whether the particular financial statement item is subject to management's judgments and estimates
- Whether the entity's underlying financial data is adequate

Issue 23: Is the accountant required to obtain a representation letter from management in a review engagement?

Yes. The accountant is required to obtain a representation letter from management in a review engagement.

Issue 24: In connection with a review engagement, may the accountant issue a review report if the client refuses to provide the accountant with a representation letter?

No. If the client does not provide the accountant with a representation letter in a review engagement, the review will be considered incomplete. Therefore, in such circumstances, the accountant does not have an adequate basis for, and is precluded from, issuing a review report. Furthermore, the accountant is ordinarily precluded from issuing a compilation report on the financial statements in these circumstances.

Issue 25: In connection with a review engagement, may the accountant issue a review report if he or she is unable to perform the inquiry and analytical procedures considered necessary?

No. If the accountant is unable to perform the inquiry and analytical procedures he or she considers necessary in a review engagement, the review will be considered incomplete. Therefore, in such circumstances, the accountant does not have an adequate basis for, and is precluded from, issuing a review report.

Issue 26: May an accountant accept an engagement to review financial statements that omit substantially all the disclosures required by an applicable financial reporting framework (e.g., GAAP, OCBOA)?

No. An accountant is precluded from accepting an engagement to review financial statements that omit substantially all the disclosures required by an applicable financial reporting framework (e.g., GAAP, OCBOA). An accountant may only accept an engagement to *compile* financial statements that omit substantially all the disclosures required by an applicable financial reporting framework.

ILLUSTRATIONS AND PRACTICE AIDS

ILLUSTRATION 1—REVIEW ENGAGEMENT LETTER

(Prepared on accountant's letterhead)

January 18, 20X2
ABC Company

Dear _____:

This letter is to confirm our understanding of the terms and objectives of our engagement and the nature and limitations of the services we will provide.

We will review the financial statements of ABC Company as of December 31, 20X2, and issue an accountant's report thereon in accordance with Statements on Standards for Accounting and Review Services (SSARSs) issued by the American Institute of Certified Public Accountants (AICPA).

The objective of a review is to obtain limited assurance that there are no material modifications that should be made to the financial statements in order for the statements to be in conformity with [*the applicable financial reporting framework (e.g., accounting principles generally accepted in the United States of America)*].

You are responsible for:

1. The preparation and fair presentation of the financial statements in accordance with [*the applicable financial reporting framework (e.g., accounting principles generally accepted in the United States of America)*].

2. Designing, implementing, and maintaining internal control relevant to the preparation and fair presentation of the financial statements.

3. Preventing and detecting fraud.

4. Identifying and ensuring that the entity complies with the laws and regulations applicable to its activities.

5. Making all financial records and related information available to us.

6. Providing us, at the conclusion of the engagement, with a letter that confirms certain representations made during the review.

We are responsible for conducting the engagement in accordance with SSARSs issued by the AICPA.

A review includes primarily applying analytical procedures to your financial data and making inquiries of company management. A review is substantially less in scope that an audit, the objective of which is the expression of an opinion regarding the financial statements as a whole. A review does not contemplate obtaining an understanding of the entity's internal control; assessing fraud risk; testing accounting records by obtaining sufficient appropriate audit evidence through inspection, observation, confirmation, or the examination of source documents (e.g., cancelled checks or bank images); or other procedures ordinarily performed in an audit. Accordingly, we will not express an opinion regarding the financial statements as a whole.

Our engagement cannot be relied upon to disclose errors, fraud, or illegal acts. However, we will inform the appropriate level of management of any material errors and evidence or information that comes to our attention during the performance of our review procedures that fraud may have occurred. In addition, we will report to you any evidence or information that comes to our attention during the performance of our review procedures regarding illegal acts that may have occurred, unless they are clearly inconsequential.

If, for any reason, we are unable to complete the review of your financial statements, we will not issue a report on such statements as a result of this engagement.

Our fees for these services are based on the amount of time required at various levels of responsibility, plus actual out-of-pocket expenses.

We will be pleased to discuss this letter with you at any time. If the foregoing is in accordance with your understanding, please sign the copy of this letter in the space provided and return it to us.

Very truly yours,

Christensen & Company

****

Acknowledged by (ABC Company): _____

Title: _____

Date: _____

ILLUSTRATION 2—REVIEW PROCEDURES CHECKLIST

	Yes	No	N/A	Workpaper Reference
1. General				
a. Has an engagement letter been obtained?	____	____	____	_____
b. Has an understanding been obtained of the client's business and the accounting principles and practices of the industry in which the client operates, including an understanding of the following:				
(1) The entity's organization?	____	____	____	_____
(2) The entity's operating characteristics?	____	____	____	_____
(3) The nature of the entity's assets, liabilities, revenues, and expenses?	____	____	____	_____
(4) The entity's production, distribution, and compensation methods; types of products and services; operating locations; and material transactions with related parties?	____	____	____	_____

		Yes	No	N/A	Workpaper Reference
c.	Has an understanding been obtained of the procedures the entity uses for recording, classifying, and summarizing transactions and accumulating information relating to financial statement disclosures?	___	___	___	_____
d.	Have there been any changes in accounting principles and methods of applying them?	___	___	___	_____
e.	Have the financial statements been prepared in accordance with an applicable financial reporting framework (e.g., GAAP, OCBOA)?	___	___	___	_____
f.	Have there been any changes in the entity's business activities or accounting practices?	___	___	___	_____
g.	Are there any unusual or complex situations (e.g., business combinations, restructuring plans, or litigation) that may have an effect on the financial statements?	___	___	___	_____
h.	Have there been any instances of fraud or illegal acts within the entity?	___	___	___	_____
i.	Have there been any allegations or suspicions that fraud or illegal acts might have occurred or might be occurring within the entity? If yes, where and how?	___	___	___	_____
j.	Are any entities, other than the reporting entity, commonly controlled by the stockholders? If yes, has a determination been made about whether those entities should be consolidated into the financial statements of the reporting entity?	___	___	___	_____
k.	Are there any entities in which the stockholders or the reporting entity have significant investments (e.g., variable interest entities)? If yes, has a determination been made about whether the reporting entity is the primary beneficiary related to the activities of these other entities?	___	___	___	_____
l.	Have any significant transactions occurred or been recognized near the end of the reporting period?	___	___	___	_____
m.	Has adequate consideration been given to the status of uncorrected misstatements identified during the previous engagement?	___	___	___	_____

		Yes	No	N/A	Workpaper Reference
n.	If other accountants have been engaged to audit or review the financial statements of significant components of the reporting entity, have the reports from such other accountants been obtained?	___	___	___	_____
o.	Have all questions that have arisen during the course of applying the review procedures been adequately resolved?	___	___	___	_____

2. Analytical Procedures

		Yes	No	N/A	Workpaper Reference
a.	Have appropriate analytical procedures been applied, including the following:				
(1)	Comparison of the financial statements being reported on with statements for comparable prior periods?	___	___	___	_____
(2)	Comparison of the financial statements being reported on with anticipated results, if available (e.g., budgets and forecasts)?	___	___	___	_____
(3)	Study of the relationships of the elements of the financial statements that would be expected to conform to a predictable pattern based on the entity's experience (e.g., changes in sales compared to changes in accounts receivable or changes in fixed assets compared to changes in depreciation expense and repairs and maintenance)? *(Note: For a detailed analytical procedures form that may be used, see Illustration 1 in AU Section 329 Analytical Procedures).)*	___	___	___	_____
(4)	Comparison of current period financial information with relevant nonfinancial information?	___	___	___	_____
(5)	Comparison of financial information, ratios, and performance indicators for the current period with those of prior periods or with expectations based on prior periods?	___	___	___	_____
(6)	Comparison of financial information, ratios, and performance indicators for the current period with those of other entities in the same industry?	___	___	___	_____

	Yes	No	N/A	Workpaper Reference
(7) Vertical analysis of financial information in comparison to prior periods (e.g., expenses by type as a percentage of sales; assets by type as a percentage of total assets)?	____	____	____	_____
(8) Gross profit analysis by product line and business segment?	____	____	____	_____

3. Cash and Cash Equivalents

	Yes	No	N/A	Workpaper Reference
a. Are all cash accounts reconciled on a timely basis?	____	____	____	_____
b. Have old or unusual reconciling items between bank balances and book balances been reviewed and adjustments made where necessary?	____	____	____	_____
c. Has a proper cutoff of cash receipts and disbursements been made?	____	____	____	_____
d. Has a reconciliation of intercompany transfers been prepared?	____	____	____	_____
e. Have checks written but not yet mailed as of the balance sheet date been properly reclassified into liabilities?	____	____	____	_____
f. Have material bank overdrafts been properly reclassified into liabilities?	____	____	____	_____
g. Are there any compensating balances or other restrictions on the availability of cash balances? If yes, has consideration been given to reclassifying the amounts as noncurrent assets?	____	____	____	_____
h. Have cash funds been counted and reconciled with control accounts?	____	____	____	_____
i. Is the entity's policy regarding the composition of cash and cash equivalents in accordance with ASC 230, *Statement of Cash Flows,* and has that policy been applied on a consistent basis?	____	____	____	_____

4. Accounts Receivable

	Yes	No	N/A	Workpaper Reference
a. Has an adequate allowance for doubtful accounts, discounts, and sales returns been properly reflected in the financial statements?	____	____	____	_____
b. Have receivables considered uncollectible been written off?	____	____	____	_____
c. Has interest earned on receivables been properly reflected in the financial statements?	____	____	____	_____
d. Has a proper cutoff of sales transactions been made?	____	____	____	_____

		Yes	No	N/A	Workpaper Reference
e.	Are there any receivables from employees or other related parties?	___	___	___	___
f.	Have receivables from stockholders been evaluated to determine if they should be reflected in the equity section (vs. the asset section) of the balance sheet?	___	___	___	___
g.	Are any receivables that are pledged, discounted, or factored, along with any recourse provisions, properly reflected in the financial statements?	___	___	___	___
h.	Have receivables been properly classified between current and noncurrent assets?	___	___	___	___
i.	Has the entity issued significant numbers or amounts of sales returns or credit memos subsequent to the balance sheet date?	___	___	___	___
j.	Is the accounts receivable subsidiary ledger reconciled to the general ledger account balance on a regular basis?	___	___	___	___

5. Inventories

		Yes	No	N/A	Workpaper Reference
a.	Are physical inventory counts performed on a regular basis, including at the end of the period being reported on?	___	___	___	___
b.	Are physical count procedures adequate to ensure an appropriate count? If yes, what procedures were used to take the latest physical inventory and on what date was the inventory taken? If no, how have amounts related to inventories been determined for financial statement purposes?	___	___	___	___
c.	Have general ledger control accounts been adjusted to agree with physical inventory counts? If yes, were the adjustments significant?	___	___	___	___
d.	If physical inventory counts were taken at a date other than the balance sheet date, what procedures were used to determine changes in inventory between the date of the physical inventory counts and the balance sheet date?	___	___	___	___
e.	Were consignments in or out considered in taking physical inventories?	___	___	___	___
f.	What is the method of determining inventory cost (e.g., FIFO, LIFO)?	___	___	___	___

		Yes	No	N/A	Workpaper Reference

g. Has inventory been valued at the lower of cost or market?

h. Does inventory cost include material, labor, and overhead where applicable?

i. Has inventory been reviewed for obsolescence or cost in excess of net realizable value? If yes, how are these costs reflected in the financial statements?

j. Have proper cutoffs of purchases, goods in transit, and returned goods been made?

k. Are there any inventory encumbrances?

l. Is scrap inventoried and controlled?

6. Prepaid Expenses

a. What is the nature of the amounts included in prepaid expenses?

b. How are these amounts being amortized?

7. Investments

a. What is the basis of accounting for the various investments reported in the financial statements (e.g., marketable securities, joint ventures, or closely held businesses)?

b. Are derivative instruments properly measured and disclosed in the financial statements? If such derivatives are utilized in hedge transactions, have the documentation or assessment requirements related to hedge accounting been met?

c. Are investments in marketable debt and equity securities properly classified as trading, available-for-sale, or held-to-maturity?

d. How were fair values determined for the investments reported in the financial statements?

e. Have unrealized gains and losses been properly reported in the financial statements?

f. If the fair values of marketable debt and equity securities are below cost, have the declines in value been evaluated to determine whether they are other-than-temporary?

	Yes	No	N/A	Workpaper Reference

g. For debt securities classified as held-to-maturity, does management have the positive ability and intent to hold the securities until they mature? If yes, have the debt securities been properly measured?

h. Have gains and losses on disposal of investments been properly determined and reflected in the financial statements?

i. Has investment income been properly determined and reflected in the financial statements?

j. Has appropriate consideration been given to the classification of investments between current and noncurrent assets?

k. Have consolidation, equity, or cost method accounting requirements been considered for investments made by the entity?

l. Are any investments encumbered?

8. **Property and Equipment**

a. Are property and equipment items stated at cost or other appropriate value and properly depreciated?

b. Has the entity taken a recent physical inventory of property and equipment? If no, has the entity evaluated the need to take a physical inventory of property and equipment?

c. Are all items reflected in property and equipment held for use? If no, have items that are held for sale been properly segregated from property and equipment and appropriately disclosed in the financial statements?

d. Have gains or losses on disposal of property and equipment been properly reflected?

e. What are the criteria for capitalization of property and equipment? Have such criteria been consistently and appropriately applied?

f. Are repairs and maintenance expenditures properly reflected as an expense in the income statement?

g. What depreciation methods and rates are used for financial reporting? Are they appropriate and consistently applied?

		Yes	No	N/A	Workpaper Reference
h.	Are there any unrecorded additions, retirements, abandonments, sales, or trade-ins?	___	___	___	___
i.	Does the entity have any material lease agreements? If yes, have they been properly evaluated for financial statement presentation?	___	___	___	___
j.	Is any property or equipment mortgaged or otherwise encumbered? If yes, are they properly reflected and disclosed in the financial statements?	___	___	___	___
k.	Are there any asset retirement obligations associated with tangible long-lived assets? If yes, is the liability properly reflected in the balance sheet and has the recorded amount of the related asset been increased because of the obligation?	___	___	___	___
l.	Has the entity constructed any of its property and equipment items? If yes, have all components of cost been properly reflected in measuring these items, including capitalized interest?	___	___	___	___
m.	Has there been any significant impairment in the value of property and equipment items? If yes, has an impairment loss been properly reflected in the financial statements?	___	___	___	___

9. Intangibles and Other Assets

		Yes	No	N/A	Workpaper Reference
a.	What is the nature of the amounts included in other assets?	___	___	___	___
b.	Do these assets represent costs that will benefit future periods?	___	___	___	___
c.	What is the amortization policy for deferred costs? Is it appropriate?	___	___	___	___
d.	Have other assets been properly classified between current and noncurrent assets?	___	___	___	___
e.	Are intangible assets with finite lives being properly amortized?	___	___	___	___
f.	Are the costs associated with computer software properly reflected as intangible assets (rather than property and equipment) in the financial statements?	___	___	___	___
g.	Are the costs associated with goodwill and other intangible assets with indefinite lives properly reflected as intangible assets in the financial statements?	___	___	___	___

		Yes	No	N/A	Workpaper Reference

h. Has amortization ceased for goodwill and other intangible assets with indefinite lives? ___ ___ ___ ___

i. Has there been any significant impairment in value of intangibles and other assets? If yes, has an impairment loss been properly reflected in the financial statements? ___ ___ ___ ___

j. Are any of these assets mortgaged or otherwise encumbered? ___ ___ ___ ___

10. Accounts Payable, Short-Term Notes Payable, and Accrued Liabilities

a. Have all significant payables been properly reflected? ___ ___ ___ ___

b. Are loans from financial institutions and other short-term liabilities properly classified? ___ ___ ___ ___

c. Have all significant accruals (e.g., payroll, interest, and provisions for pension and profit-sharing plans) been properly reflected? ___ ___ ___ ___

d. Has a liability for employees' compensation for future absences been properly accrued and disclosed? ___ ___ ___ ___

e. Are there any collateralized or subordinated liabilities? If yes, have appropriate disclosures been made of such items? ___ ___ ___ ___

f. Are there any payables to employees and related parties? ___ ___ ___ ___

11. Long-Term Liabilities

a. Are the terms and other provisions of long-term liability agreements properly disclosed? ___ ___ ___ ___

b. Have liabilities been properly classified between current and non-current? ___ ___ ___ ___

c. Has interest expense been properly reflected? ___ ___ ___ ___

d. Is the entity in compliance with loan covenants and agreements? If no, is appropriate disclosure made of the noncompliance? ___ ___ ___ ___

e. Are any long-term liabilities collateralized or subordinated? If yes, have appropriate disclosures been made of such items? ___ ___ ___ ___

	Yes	No	N/A	Workpaper Reference

f. Are there any obligations that, by their terms, are due on demand within one year from the balance sheet date? If yes, have such obligations been reclassified into current liabilities?   _____ _____ _____ _____

12. Income and Other Taxes

a. Is an appropriate provision reflected in the financial statements for current and prior-year income taxes payable?   _____ _____ _____ _____

b. Have any assessments or reassessments been received?   _____ _____ _____ _____

c. Are there tax authority examinations in process?   _____ _____ _____ _____

d. Are there any temporary differences between book and tax amounts? If yes, have deferred taxes on these differences been properly reflected?   _____ _____ _____ _____

e. Do the financial statements reflect an appropriate provision for taxes other than income taxes (e.g., sales or franchise tax)?   _____ _____ _____ _____

f. Have all required tax payments been made timely?   _____ _____ _____ _____

13. Other Liabilities, Commitments, and Contingencies

a. What is the nature of the amounts included in other liabilities?   _____ _____ _____ _____

b. Have other liabilities been properly classified between current and noncurrent?   _____ _____ _____ _____

c. Are there any written or verbal guarantees that require the entity to stand ready to perform or be contingently liable under the terms of the guarantee? If yes, are the guarantees properly reflected and disclosed in the financial statements?   _____ _____ _____ _____

d. Are there any contingent liabilities (e.g., discounted notes, drafts, endorsements, warranties, litigation and unsettled asserted claims)? If yes, are they properly measured and disclosed in the financial statements?   _____ _____ _____ _____

e. Are there any potential unasserted claims? If yes, are they properly measured and disclosed in the financial statements?   _____ _____ _____ _____

		Yes	No	N/A	*Workpaper Reference*
f.	Are there any material contractual obligations for construction or purchase of property and equipment? If yes, are these facts adequately disclosed?	___	___	___	___
g.	Are there any commitments or options to purchase or sell company securities? If yes, are these facts adequately disclosed?	___	___	___	___
h.	Is the entity responsible for any environmental remediation liability? If yes, is the liability properly measured and disclosed?	___	___	___	___
i.	Does the entity have any agreements to repurchase items that previously were sold? If yes, have such agreements been properly reflected and disclosed?	___	___	___	___
j.	Does the entity have any sales commitments at prices expected to result in a loss at the consummation of the sale? If yes, are these commitments properly reflected?	___	___	___	___
k.	Are there any violations, or possible violations, of laws or regulations whose effects should be considered for accrual or disclosure in the financial statements?	___	___	___	___
l.	Has the entity received any communications from regulatory agencies?	___	___	___	___

14. Equity

		Yes	No	N/A	*Workpaper Reference*
a.	What is the nature of any changes in equity accounts?	___	___	___	___
b.	What classes of stock, or other ownership interests, have been authorized?	___	___	___	___
c.	What is the par or stated value of the various classes of stock or other ownership interests?	___	___	___	___
d.	Do amounts of outstanding shares of stock, or other ownership interests, agree with subsidiary records?	___	___	___	___
e.	Are the pertinent rights and privileges of the various classes of stock, or other ownership interests, properly disclosed?	___	___	___	___

		Yes	No	N/A	Workpaper Reference

f. Does the entity have mandatorily redeemable ownership interests? If yes, has an appropriate determination been made regarding whether these ownership interests should be measured and reported as liabilities?

g. Are redemption features associated with ownership interests properly disclosed?

h. Do disclosures related to ownership interests include the following items, if applicable: (1) dividend, distribution, and liquidation preferences; (2) call provisions, including prices and dates; (3) conversion provisions, including prices and dates; (4) unusual voting rights; (5) contractual arrangements to issue additional ownership interests; and (6) any other unusual features associated with the ownership interests?

i. Are syndication fees properly classified as a reduction of equity, rather than as an asset?

j. Have stock options or other compensation awards been granted to employees or others? If yes, are they properly measured and disclosed?

k. Has the entity made any acquisitions of its own stock? If yes, are the related amounts properly reflected as a reduction in equity and is the presentation consistent with applicable state laws?

l. Are there any restrictions or appropriations on retained earnings or other capital accounts? If yes, are such restrictions and appropriations properly reflected and disclosed in the financial statements?

15. Revenue and Expenses

a. What is the entity's revenue recognition policy?

b. Is the entity's revenue recognition policy appropriate and has it been consistently applied and adequately disclosed?

		Yes	No	N/A	Workpaper Reference
c.	Are revenues from the sale of products and services recognized in the appropriate period (i.e., when the products are delivered or when the services are performed)?	___	___	___	___
d.	Has the entity recorded any sales under a "bill and hold" arrangement? If yes, have the criteria been met to recognize the transaction as a sale?	___	___	___	___
e.	Are purchases and expenses recognized in the appropriate period, properly classified, and matched against revenue?	___	___	___	___
f.	Do the financial statements include discontinued operations and items that might be considered extraordinary? If yes, are the related amounts properly presented and the transactions properly disclosed in the financial statements?	___	___	___	___
g.	Are elements of comprehensive income (e.g., gains or losses on available-for-sale securities) properly displayed in the financial statements?	___	___	___	___

16. Other

		Yes	No	N/A	Workpaper Reference
a.	Are there any subsequent events that would require adjustment to, or disclosure in, the financial statements?	___	___	___	___
b.	Have actions taken at stockholders, directors, committees of directors, or comparable meetings that affect the financial statements been appropriately reflected in the financial statements?	___	___	___	___
c.	Are significant estimates and material concentrations (e.g., customers, vendors) properly disclosed?	___	___	___	___
d.	Does management have any plans or intentions that may materially affect the carrying amounts or classification of reported assets and liabilities?	___	___	___	___
e.	Have there been any material transactions between related parties? If yes, are such transactions adequately disclosed?	___	___	___	___
f.	Are there any uncertainties that could materially affect the financial statements?	___	___	___	___
g.	Is there any change in the status of material uncertainties that were previously disclosed?	___	___	___	___

			Yes	No	N/A	*Workpaper Reference*

h. Are all uncertainties, including those relating to going-concern matters, that could materially affect the financial statements properly disclosed? _____ _____ _____ _____

i. Are nonmonetary transactions, including barter transactions, properly measured, recorded, and disclosed? _____ _____ _____ _____

17. Documentation

a. Does documentation of the review engagement include the following:

   (1) The engagement letter documenting the understanding with the client? _____ _____ _____ _____

   (2) The analytical procedures performed? _____ _____ _____ _____

   (3) The expectations (when the expectations are not otherwise readily determinable from the documentation of the work performed) and the factors considered in the development of the expectations? _____ _____ _____ _____

   (4) The results of the comparison of the expectations developed to the amounts recorded by the client or to ratios developed from amounts recorded by the client? _____ _____ _____ _____

   (5) Management's responses to the accountant's inquiries regarding fluctuations or relationships that are inconsistent with other relevant information or that differ from expected values by a significant amount? _____ _____ _____ _____

   (6) Any additional review procedures that were performed in response to significant unexpected differences arising from the analytical procedures and the results obtained? _____ _____ _____ _____

   (7) The significant matters covered in the accountant's inquiry procedures and the responses thereto? _____ _____ _____ _____

   (8) Significant issues or findings (e.g., findings that indicate that the financial statements could be materially misstated, the procedures performed to address such findings, and the basis for the final conclusions reached)? _____ _____ _____ _____

	Yes	No	N/A	Workpaper Reference
(9) Significant unusual matters that were considered during the performance of the review procedures and their disposition?	___	___	___	___
(10) Any oral or written communications to the appropriate level of management regarding fraud or illegal acts?	___	___	___	___
(11) A signed management representation letter?	___	___	___	___

Prepared By: _____

Date: _____

Approved By: _____

Date: _____

ILLUSTRATION 3—MANAGEMENT REPRESENTATION LETTER: REVIEW ENGAGEMENT

(Prepared on client's letterhead)

(Date) [**Note:** *This date should be the date that the client presents and signs the letter, but not prior to the date of the accountant's review report.*]

To *(Accountant)*

We are providing this letter in connection with your review of the [*identification of financial statements*]of [*name of client*] as of [*dates*]and for the [*periods of review*] for the purpose of obtaining limited assurance that there are no material modifications that should be made to the financial statements in order for them to be in conformity with [*the applicable financial reporting framework (e.g., accounting principles generally accepted in the United States of America)*]. We confirm that we are responsible for the fair presentation of the financial statements in accordance with [*the applicable financial reporting framework*] and the selection and application of the accounting policies.

Certain representations in this letter are described as being limited to matters that are material. Items are considered material, regardless of size, if they involve an omission or misstatement of accounting information that, in the light of surrounding circumstances, makes it probable that the judgment of a reasonable person using the information would be changed or influenced by the omission or misstatement.

We confirm, to the best of our knowledge and belief, as of [*the date of the accountant's review report*], the following representations made to you during your review:

1. The financial statements referred to above are fairly presented in accordance with [*the applicable financial reporting framework (e.g., accounting principles generally accepted in the United States of America)*].

   2. We have made available to you:

      a. Financial records and related data.

      b. Minutes of the meetings of stockholders, directors, and committees of directors, or summaries of actions of recent meetings for which minutes have not yet been prepared.

   3. No material transactions exist that have not been properly recorded in the accounting records underlying the financial statements.

   4. We acknowledge our responsibility for the preparation and fair presentation of the financial statements in accordance with [*the applicable financial reporting framework (e.g., accounting principles generally accepted in the United States of America)*].

   5. We acknowledge our responsibility for designing, implementing, and maintaining internal control relevant to the preparation and fair presentation of the financial statements.

   6. We acknowledge our responsibility to prevent and detect fraud.

   7. We have no knowledge of any fraud or suspected fraud affecting the entity involving management or others where the fraud could have a material effect on the financial statements, including any communications received from employees, former employees, or others.

   8. We have no plans or intentions that may materially affect the carrying amounts or classification of assets and liabilities.

   9. No material losses exist (such as from obsolete inventory or purchase or sales commitments) that have not been properly accrued or disclosed in the financial statements.

  10. None of the following exist:

      a. Violations or possible violations of laws or regulations, whose effects should be considered for disclosure in the financial statements or as a basis for recording a loss contingency.

      b. Unasserted claims or assessments that our lawyer has advised us are probable of assertion that must be disclosed in accordance with Financial Accounting Standards Board (FASB) Accounting Standards Codification (ASC) 450, *Contingencies.*[1]

      c. Other material liabilities or gain or loss contingencies that are required to be accrued or disclosed by ASC 450.

  11. The Company has satisfactory title to all owned assets, and no liens or encumbrances on such assets exist, nor has any asset been pledged as collateral, except as disclosed to you and reported in the financial statements.

---

[1] If management has not consulted a lawyer regarding litigation, claims, and assessments, the representation might be worded as follows:

We are not aware of any pending or threatened litigation, claims, or assessments or unasserted claims or assessments that are required to be accrued or disclosed in the financial statements in accordance with Financial Accounting Standards Board Accounting Standards Codification (ASC) 450, *Contingencies,* and we have not consulted a lawyer concerning litigation, claims, or assessments.

12. We have complied with all aspects of contractual agreements that would have a material effect on the financial statements in the event of noncompliance.

13. The following have been properly recorded or disclosed in the financial statements:

    a. Related-party transactions, including sales, purchases, loans, transfers, leasing arrangements, and guarantees, and amounts receivable from or payable to related parties.

    b. Guarantees, whether written or oral, under which the Company is contingently liable.

    c. Significant estimates and material concentrations known to management, which are required to be disclosed in accordance with ASC 275, *Risks and Uncertainties*. Significant estimates are estimates at the balance sheet date that could change materially within the next year. Concentrations refer to volumes of business, revenues, available sources of supply, or markets or geographic areas for which events could occur that would significantly disrupt normal finances within the next year.

(Add additional representations that are unique to the entity's business or industry. See Note 2 below for illustrative examples of additional representations.)[2]

14. We are in agreement with the adjusting journal entries you have recommended, and they have been posted to the Company's accounts (*if applicable*).

15. To the best of our knowledge and belief, no events have occurred subsequent to the balance sheet date and through the date of this letter that would require adjustment to or disclosure in the aforementioned financial statements. (*Note: If the accountant dual dates his or her report, the accountant should consider whether obtaining additional representations relating to the subsequent event is appropriate.*)

16. We have responded fully and truthfully to all inquiries made to us by you during your review(s).

(Name of Owner or Chief Executive Officer and Title)

(Name of Chief Financial Officer and Title)

General

Accounting Changes

The effect of a new accounting principle is not known.

---

[2] The following additional representations may be appropriate in certain situations. This list of additional representations is not intended to be all-inclusive. In drafting a representation letter, the effects of other applicable pronouncements should be considered.

We have not completed the process of evaluating the effect that will result from adopting Financial Accounting Standards Board (FASB) Accounting Standards Codification (ASC) XXX, [*title*], as discussed in Note [*X*]. The Company is therefore unable to disclose the effect that adopting ASC XXX will have on its financial position and results of operations when such standard is adopted.

There is justification for a change in accounting principles.

We believe that [*describe the newly adopted accounting principle*] is preferable to [*describe the former accounting principle*] because [*describe management's justification for the change in accounting principles*].

Going Concern

Financial circumstances are strained with disclosure of management's intentions and the Company's ability to continue as a going concern.

Note [*X*] to the financial statements discloses all of the matters of which we are aware that are relevant to the Company's ability to continue as a going concern, including significant conditions and events, and management's plans.

Long-Lived Assets and Certain Identifiable Intangibles

The possibility exists that the value of specific significant long-lived assets or certain identifiable intangibles may be impaired.

We have reviewed long-lived assets and certain identifiable intangibles to be held and used for impairment whenever events or changes in circumstances have indicated that the carrying amount of the assets might not be recoverable, and have appropriately recorded the adjustment.

Variable Interest Entities

The Company has a variable interest in another entity:

- Variable interest entities (VIEs) and potential VIEs and transactions with VIEs and potential VIEs have been properly recorded and disclosed in the financial statements in accordance with GAAP.

- We have considered both implicit and explicit variable interests in (a) determining whether potential VIEs should be considered VIEs; (b) calculating expected losses and residual returns; and (c) determining which party, if any, is the primary beneficiary.

- We have provided you with lists of all identified variable interests in (a) VIEs, (b) potential VIEs that we considered but judged not to be VIEs, and (c) entities that were afforded the scope exceptions of ASC 810, *Consolidation*.

- We have advised you of all transactions with identified VIEs, potential VIEs, or entities afforded the scope exceptions of ASC 810.

- We have made available all relevant information about financial interests and contractual arrangements with related parties, de facto agents, and other entities, including but not limited to, their governing documents, equity and debt instruments, contracts, leases, guarantee arrangements, and other financial contracts and arrangements.

- The information we provided about financial interests and contractual arrangements with related parties, de facto agents, and other entities includes information about all transactions, unwritten understandings, agreement modifications, and written and oral side agreements.

- Our computations of expected losses and expected residual returns of entities that are VIEs and potential VIEs are based on the best information available and include all reasonably possible outcomes.

- Regarding entities in which the Company has variable interests (implicit and explicit), we have provided all information about events and changes in circumstances that could potentially cause reconsideration about whether the entities are VIEs or whether the Company is the primary beneficiary or has a significant variable interest in the entity.

- We have made and continue to make exhaustive efforts to obtain information about entities in which the Company has an implicit or explicit interest but that were excluded from complete analysis under ASC 810 due to lack of essential information to determine one or more of the following: whether the entity is a VIE, whether the Company is the primary beneficiary, or the accounting required to consolidate the entity.

Use of a Specialist

The Company has used the work of a specialist.

We agree with the findings of specialists in evaluating the [*describe assertion*] and have adequately considered the qualifications of the specialist in determining the amounts and disclosures used in the financial statements and underlying accounting records. We did not give or cause any instructions to be given to specialists with respect to the values or amounts derived in an attempt to bias their work, and we are not otherwise aware of any matters that have had impact on the independence or objectivity of the specialists.

Assets

Cash

Disclosure is required of compensating balances or other arrangements involving restrictions on cash balances, lines of credit, or similar arrangements.

Arrangements with financial institutions involving compensating balances or other arrangements involving restrictions on cash balances, lines of credit, or similar arrangements have been properly disclosed.

Financial Instruments

Management intends, and has the ability, to hold to maturity debt securities classified as held-to-maturity.

Debt securities classified as held-to-maturity have been so classified due to management's intent to hold such securities to maturity and the Company's ability to do so. All other debt securities have been classified as available-for-sale or trading.

Management considers the decline in value of debt or equity securities to be temporary.

We consider the decline in value of debt or equity securities classified as either available-for-sale or held-to-maturity to be temporary.

Management has determined the fair value of significant financial instruments that do not have readily determinable market values.

The methods and significant assumptions used to determine fair values of financial instruments are as follows: [*describe methods and significant assumptions used to determine fair values of financial instruments*]. The methods and significant assumptions used result in a measure of fair value appropriate for financial statement measurement and disclosure purposes.

There are financial instruments with off-balance-sheet risk and financial instruments with concentrations of credit risk.

The following information about financial instruments with off-balance-sheet risk and financial instruments with concentrations of credit risk has been properly disclosed in the financial statements: (a) the extent, nature, and terms of financial instruments with off-balance-sheet risk; (b) the amount of credit risk of financial instruments with off-balance-sheet risk and information about the collateral supporting such financial instruments; and (c) significant concentrations of credit risk arising from all financial instruments and information about the collateral supporting such financial instruments.

Receivables

Receivables have been recorded in the financial statements.

Receivables recorded in the financial statements represent valid claims against debtors for sales or other charges arising on or before the balance sheet date and have been appropriately reduced to their estimated net realizable value.

Inventories

Excess or obsolete inventories exist.

Provision has been made to reduce excess or obsolete inventories to their estimated net realizable value.

Investments

There are unusual considerations involved in determining the application of equity accounting:

- The equity method is used to account for the Company's investment in the common stock of [*investee*] because the Company has the ability to exercise significant influence over the investee's operating and financial policies.

- The cost method is used to account for the Company's investment in the common stock of [*investee*] because the Company does not have the ability to exercise significant influence over the investee's operating and financial policies.

Deferred Charges

Material expenditures have been deferred.

We believe that all material expenditures that have been deferred to future periods will be recoverable.

Deferred Tax Assets

A deferred tax asset exists at the balance sheet date:

- The valuation allowance has been determined pursuant to the provisions of ASC 740, *Income Taxes*, including the Company's estimation of future taxable income, if necessary, and is adequate to reduce the total deferred tax asset to an amount that will more likely than not be realized. [*Complete with appropriate wording detailing how the Company determined the valuation allowance against the deferred tax asset.*]

- A valuation allowance against deferred tax assets at the balance sheet date is not considered necessary because it is more likely than not the deferred tax asset will be fully realized.

Liabilities

Debt

Short-term debt could be refinanced on a long-term basis and management intends to do so.

The Company has excluded short-term obligations totaling $[*amount*]from current liabilities, because the Company intends to refinance the obligations on a long-term basis. [*Complete with appropriate wording detailing how amounts will be refinanced, as follows:*]

- The Company has issued a long-term obligation (debt security) after the date of the balance sheet but prior to the issuance of the financial statements for the purpose of refinancing the short-term obligations on a long-term basis.

- The Company has the ability to consummate the refinancing, by using the financing agreement referred to in Note [X] to the financial statements.

Tax-exempt bonds have been issued.

Tax-exempt bonds issued have retained their tax-exempt status.

Taxes

Management intends to reinvest undistributed earnings of a foreign subsidiary.

We intend to reinvest the undistributed earnings of [*name of foreign subsidiary*].

Contingencies

Estimates and disclosures have been made of environmental remediation liabilities and related loss contingencies.

Provision has been made for any material loss that is probable from environmental remediation liabilities associated with [*name of site*]. We believe that such estimate is reasonable based on available information and that the liabilities and related loss contingencies and the expected outcome of uncertainties have been adequately described in the Company's financial statements.

Agreements may exist to repurchase assets previously sold.

Agreements to repurchase assets previously sold have been properly disclosed.

Pension and Postretirement Benefits

An actuary has been used to measure pension liabilities and costs.

We believe that the actuarial assumptions and methods used to measure pension liabilities and costs for financial accounting purposes are appropriate in the circumstances.

There is involvement with a multiemployer plan:

- We are unable to determine the possibility of a withdrawal liability in a multiemployer benefit plan.
- We have determined that there is the possibility of a withdrawal liability in a multiemployer plan in the amount of $XX.

Postretirement benefits have been eliminated:

- We do not intend to compensate for the elimination of postretirement benefits by granting an increase in pension benefits.
- We plan to compensate for the elimination of postretirement benefits by granting an increase in pension benefits in the amount of $XX.

Employee layoffs that would otherwise lead to a curtailment of a benefit plan are intended to be temporary.

Current employee layoffs are intended to be temporary.

Management intends to either continue to make or not make frequent amendments to its pension or other postretirement benefit plans, which may affect the amortization period of prior service cost, or has expressed a substantive commitment to increase benefit obligations:

- We plan to continue to make frequent amendments to the Company's pension or other postretirement benefit plans, which may affect the amortization period of prior service cost.
- We do not plan to make frequent amendments to the Company's pension or other postretirement benefit plans.

Equity

There are capital stock repurchase options or agreements or capital stock reserved for options, warrants, conversions, or other requirements.

Capital stock repurchase options or agreements or capital stock reserved for options, warrants, conversions, or other requirements have been properly disclosed.

Income Statement

There may be a loss from sales commitments.

Provisions have been made for losses to be sustained in the fulfillment of, or from the inability to fulfill, any sales commitments.

There may be losses from purchase commitments.

Provisions have been made for losses to be sustained as a result of purchase commitments for inventory quantities in excess of normal requirements or at prices in excess of prevailing market prices.

Nature of the product or industry indicates the possibility of undisclosed sales returns.

We have fully disclosed to you all sales terms, including all rights of return or price adjustments and all warranty provisions.

ILLUSTRATION 4—UPDATING MANAGEMENT REPRESENTATION LETTER: REVIEW ENGAGEMENT

(Prepared on client's letterhead)

(Date) [**Note:** *The accountant may either (1) use dual dating, for example, "February 16, 20XX, except for Note Y, as to which the date is March 1, 20XX," or (2) date the report as of the later date.*]

To *(Accountant)*

In connection with your review(s) of the [*identification of financial statements*] of [*name of client*] as of [*dates*] and for the [*periods of review*] for the purpose of obtaining limited assurance that there are no material modifications that should be made to the financial statements in order for them to be in conformity with [*the applicable financial reporting framework (for example, accounting principles generally accepted in the United States of America)*], you were previously provided with a representation letter under date of [*date of previous representation letter*]. No information has come to our attention that would cause us to believe that any of those previous representations should be modified.

　　To the best of our knowledge and belief, no events have occurred subsequent to [*date of latest balance sheet reported on by the accountant or date of previous representation letter*]and through the date of this letter that would require adjustment to or disclosure in the aforementioned financial statements.

_____

(Name of Owner or Chief Executive Officer and Title)

_____

(Name of Chief Financial Officer and Title)

ILLUSTRATION 5—REVIEW REPORT ON GAAP FINANCIAL STATEMENTS

Independent Accountant's Review Report

To the Board of Directors of ABC Company:

I (We) have reviewed the accompanying balance sheet of ABC Company as of December 31, 20X2, and the related statements of income, retained earnings, and cash flows for the year then ended. A review includes primarily applying analytical procedures to management's (owners') financial data and making inquiries of company management (owners). A review is substantially less in scope than an audit, the objective of which is the expression of an opinion regarding the financial statements as a whole. Accordingly, I (we) do not express such an opinion.

Management is (Owners are) responsible for the preparation and fair presentation of the financial statements in accordance with accounting principles generally accepted in the United States of America and for designing, implementing, and maintaining internal control relevant to the preparation and fair presentation of the financial statements.

My (Our) responsibility is to conduct the review in accordance with Statements on Standards for Accounting and Review Services issued by the American Institute of Certified Public Accountants. Those standards require me (us) to perform procedures to obtain limited assurance that there are no material modifications that should be made to the financial statements. I (We) believe that the results of my (our) procedures provide a reasonable basis for my (our) report.

Based on my (our) review, I am (we are) not aware of any material modifications that should be made to the accompanying financial statements in order for them to be in conformity with accounting principles generally accepted in the United States of America.

[*Signature of accounting firm or accountant*]

[*Date*]

ILLUSTRATION 6—REVIEW REPORT ON CASH BASIS FINANCIAL STATEMENTS

Independent Accountant's Review Report

To the Board of Directors of ABC Company:

I (We) have reviewed the accompanying statement of assets and liabilities arising from cash transactions of ABC Company as of December 31, 20X2, and the related statement of revenue collected and expenses paid for the year then ended. A review includes primarily applying analytical procedures to management's (owners') financial data and making inquiries of company management (owners). A review is substantially less in scope than an audit, the objective of which is the expression of an opinion regarding the financial statements as a whole. Accordingly, I (we) do not express such an opinion.

Management is (Owners are) responsible for the preparation and fair presentation of the financial statements in accordance with the cash basis of accounting and for designing, implementing, and maintaining internal control relevant to the preparation and fair presentation of the financial statements.

My (Our) responsibility is to conduct the review in accordance with Statements on Standards for Accounting and Review Services issued by the American Institute of Certified Public Accountants. Those standards require me (us) to perform procedures to obtain limited assurance that there are no material modifications that should be made to the financial statements. I (We) believe that the results of my (our) procedures provide a reasonable basis for my (our) report.

Based on my (our) review, I am (we are) not aware of any material modifications that should be made to the accompanying financial statements in order for them to be in conformity with the cash basis of accounting, as described in Note [X].

[Signature of accounting firm or accountant]

[Date]

ILLUSTRATION 7—REVIEW REPORT ON INCOME TAX BASIS FINANCIAL STATEMENTS

Independent Accountant's Review Report

To the Board of Directors of ABC Company:

I (We) have reviewed the accompanying statement of assets, liabilities, and equity—income tax basis of ABC Company as of December 31, 20X2, and the related statement of revenue and expenses—income tax basis for the year then ended. A review includes primarily applying analytical procedures to management's (owners') financial data and making inquiries of company management (owners). A review is substantially less in scope than an audit, the objective of which is the expression of an opinion regarding the financial statements as a whole. Accordingly, I (we) do not express such an opinion.

Management is (Owners are) responsible for the preparation and fair presentation of the financial statements in accordance with the income tax basis of accounting and for designing, implementing, and maintaining internal control relevant to the preparation and fair presentation of the financial statements.

My (Our) responsibility is to conduct the review in accordance with Statements on Standards for Accounting and Review Services issued by the American Institute of Certified Public Accountants. Those standards require me (us) to perform procedures to obtain limited assurance that there are no material modifications that should be made to the financial statements. I (We) believe that the results of my (our) procedures provide a reasonable basis for my (our) report.

Based on my (our) review, I am (we are) not aware of any material modifications that should be made to the accompanying financial statements in order for them to be in conformity with the income tax basis of accounting, as described in Note [X].

[Signature of accounting firm or accountant]

[Date]

ILLUSTRATION 8—REVIEW REPORT MODIFIED FOR A DEPARTURE FROM GAAP: ACCOUNTING PRINCIPLE NOT GENERALLY ACCEPTED

Independent Accountant's Review Report

To the Board of Directors of ABC Company:

I (We) have reviewed the accompanying balance sheet of ABC Company as of December 31, 20X2, and the related statements of income, retained earnings, and cash flows for the year then ended. A review includes primarily applying analytical procedures to management's (owners') financial data and making inquiries of company management (owners). A review is substantially less in scope than an audit, the objective of which is the expression of an opinion regarding the financial statements as a whole. Accordingly, I (we) do not express such an opinion.

Management is (Owners are) responsible for the preparation and fair presentation of the financial statements in accordance with accounting principles generally accepted in the United States of America and for designing, implementing, and maintaining internal control relevant to the preparation and fair presentation of the financial statements.

My (Our) responsibility is to conduct the review in accordance with Statements on Standards for Accounting and Review Services issued by the American Institute of Certified Public Accountants. Those standards require me (us) to perform procedures to obtain limited assurance that there are no material modifications that should be made to the financial statements. I (We) believe that the results of my (our) procedures provide a reasonable basis for my (our) report.

Based on my (our) review, with the exception of the matter(s) described in the following paragraph(s), I am (we are) not aware of any material modifications that should be made to the accompanying financial statements in order for them to be in conformity with accounting principles generally accepted in the United States of America.

As disclosed in Note [X] to the financial statements, accounting principles generally accepted in the United States of America require that inventory cost consists of material, labor, and overhead. Management has informed me (us) that the inventory of finished goods and work in process is stated in the accompanying financial statements at material and labor cost only, and that the effects of this departure from accounting principles generally accepted in the United States of America on financial position, results of operations, and cash flows have not been determined.

[*Signature of accounting firm or accountant*]

[*Date*]

ILLUSTRATION 9—REVIEW REPORT MODIFIED FOR A DEPARTURE FROM GAAP: CHANGE IN ACCOUNTING PRINCIPLE WITHOUT REASONABLE JUSTIFICATION

Independent Accountant's Review Report

To the Board of Directors of ABC Company:

I (We) have reviewed the accompanying balance sheet of ABC Company as of December 31, 20X2, and the related statements of income, retained earnings, and cash flows for the year then ended. A review includes primarily applying analytical procedures to management's (owners') financial data and making inquiries of company management (owners). A review is substantially less in scope than an audit, the objective of which is the expression of an opinion regarding the financial statements as a whole. Accordingly, I (we) do not express such an opinion.

Management is (Owners are) responsible for the preparation and fair presentation of the financial statements in accordance with accounting principles generally accepted in the United States of America and for designing, implementing, and maintaining internal control relevant to the preparation and fair presentation of the financial statements.

My (Our) responsibility is to conduct the review in accordance with Statements on Standards for Accounting and Review Services issued by the American Institute of Certified Public Accountants. Those standards require me (us) to perform procedures to obtain limited assurance that there are no material modifications that should be made to the financial statements. I (We) believe that the results of my (our) procedures provide a reasonable basis for my (our) report.

Based on my (our) review, with the exception of the matter(s) described in the following paragraph(s), I am (we are) not aware of any material modifications that should be made to the accompanying financial statements in order for them to be in conformity with accounting principles generally accepted in the United States of America.

As disclosed in Note [X] to the financial statements, the Company has adopted [*describe the newly adopted method*], whereas it previously used [*describe the previous method*]. Although the [*description of the newly adopted method*]is in conformity with accounting principles generally accepted in the United States of America, the Company does not appear to have reasonable justification for making a change as required by Financial Accounting Standards Board Accounting Standards Codification 250, *Accounting Changes and Error Corrections.*

[*Signature of accounting firm or accountant*]

[*Date*]

ILLUSTRATION 10—REVIEW REPORT COVERS SUPPLEMENTARY INFORMATION THAT HAS BEEN SUBJECTED TO REVIEW PROCEDURES

Independent Accountant's Review Report

To the Board of Directors of ABC Company:

I (We) have reviewed the accompanying balance sheet of ABC Company as of December 31, 20X2, and the related statements of income, retained earnings, and cash flows for the year then ended. A review includes primarily applying analytical procedures to management's (owners') financial data and making inquiries of company management (owners). A review is substantially less in scope than an audit, the objective of which is the expression of an opinion regarding the financial statements as a whole. Accordingly, I (we) do not express such an opinion.

Management is (Owners are) responsible for the preparation and fair presentation of the financial statements in accordance with accounting principles generally accepted in the United States of America and for designing, implementing, and maintaining internal control relevant to the preparation and fair presentation of the financial statements.

My (Our) responsibility is to conduct the review in accordance with Statements on Standards for Accounting and Review Services issued by the American Institute of Certified Public Accountants. Those standards require me (us) to perform procedures to obtain limited assurance that there are no material modifications that should be made to the financial statements. I (We) believe that the results of my (our) procedures provide a reasonable basis for my (our) report.

Based on my (our) review, I am (we are) not aware of any material modifications that should be made to the accompanying financial statements in order for them to be in conformity with accounting principles generally accepted in the United States of America.

My (Our) review was made for the purpose of expressing a conclusion that there are no material modifications that should be made to the financial statements in order for them to be in conformity with accounting principles generally accepted in the United States of America. The information included in the accompanying [*identify the supplementary information, for example, schedule of cost of goods sold, schedule of general and administrative expenses*] is presented only for supplementary analysis purposes. Such information has been subjected to the inquiry and analytical procedures applied in the review of the basic financial statements and I am (we are) not aware of any material modifications that should be made thereto.

[*Signature of accounting firm or accountant*]

[*Date*]

ILLUSTRATION 11—REVIEW REPORT COVERS SUPPLEMENTARY INFORMATION THAT HAS NOT BEEN SUBJECTED TO REVIEW PROCEDURES

Independent Accountant's Review Report

To the Board of Directors of ABC Company:

I (We) have reviewed the accompanying balance sheet of ABC Company as of December 31, 20X2, and the related statements of income, retained earnings, and cash flows for the year then ended. A review includes primarily applying analytical procedures to management's (owners') financial data and making inquiries of company management (owners). A review is substantially less in scope than an audit, the objective of which is the expression of an opinion regarding the financial statements as a whole. Accordingly, I (we) do not express such an opinion.

Management is (Owners are) responsible for the preparation and fair presentation of the financial statements in accordance with accounting principles generally accepted in the United States of America and for designing, implementing, and maintaining internal control relevant to the preparation and fair presentation of the financial statements.

My (Our) responsibility is to conduct the review in accordance with Statements on Standards for Accounting and Review Services issued by the American Institute of Certified Public Accountants. Those standards require me (us) to perform procedures to obtain limited assurance that there are no material modifications that should be made to the financial statements. I (We) believe that the results of my (our) procedures provide a reasonable basis for my (our) report.

Based on my (our) review, I am (we are) not aware of any material modifications that should be made to the accompanying financial statements in order for them to be in conformity with accounting principles generally accepted in the United States of America.

My (Our) review was made for the purpose of expressing a conclusion that there are no material modifications that should be made to the financial statements in order for them to be in conformity with accounting principles generally accepted in the United States of America. The information included in the accompanying [*identify the supplementary information, for example, schedule of cost of goods sold, schedule of general and administrative expenses*] is presented only for supplementary analysis purposes. Such information has not been subjected to the inquiry and analytical procedures applied in the review of the basic financial statements, but was compiled from information that is the representation of management, without audit or review. Accordingly, I (we) do not express an opinion or provide any other form of assurance on the supplementary information.

[*Signature of accounting firm or accountant*]

[*Date*]

AR SECTION 110
COMPILATION OF SPECIFIED ELEMENTS, ACCOUNTS, OR ITEMS OF A FINANCIAL STATEMENT

PRACTICE POINT: SSARS-13, "Compilation of Specified Elements, Accounts, or Items of a Financial Statement," is codified in AR Section 110. As this Manual goes to press, the AICPA has not yet made any conforming changes to SSARS-13 (AR Section 110) as a result of the issuance of SSARS-19, "Compilation and Review Engagements." For example, extant AR Section 110 states that the accountant should establish an understanding with the client, *preferably* in writing, regarding the services to be performed in connection with a compilation of specified elements, accounts, or items of a financial statement. However, an engagement letter is now required under SSARS-19. Therefore, once the AICPA makes conforming changes to SSARS-13 (AR Section 110), an engagement letter will be required as well and the content of such engagement letters will be similar to the items discussed in detail in AR Section 80 (Compilation of Financial Statements) of this Manual. The discussion in this chapter has been updated to reflect the requirements of SSARS-13 (AR Section 110), with conforming changes made for the issuance of SSARS-19 (AR Section 80).

WHAT EVERY PRACTITIONER SHOULD KNOW

Basic Objectives and Requirements

An accountant may be requested to compile certain specified elements, accounts, or items of a financial statement, such as rentals, royalties, profit participation, or a provision for income taxes. An accountant may undertake such a compilation engagement either as a separate engagement or in conjunction with a compilation of an entity's financial statements. In addition, such a compilation engagement is limited to presenting financial information that is the representation of management, without any responsibility to convey any assurance on that information. However, the accountant might find it necessary to perform other accounting services to compile such financial information.

AR Section 110 specifies the basic elements of the accountant's compilation report on specified elements, accounts, or items of a financial statement. In addition, in connection with such engagements, the accountant must comply with the compilation performance requirements in AR Section 80 (Compilation of Financial Statements).

Establishing an Understanding with the Client

The accountant should establish an understanding with the client regarding the services to be performed in connection with a compilation of specified elements, accounts, or items of a financial statement. AR Section 110 indicates that such an understanding should include the following:

- A description of the nature and limitations of the services to be performed.
- A description of the report to be issued.

- A statement that the engagement cannot be relied upon to disclose errors, fraud, or illegal acts.
- A statement that the accountant will inform the appropriate level of management of any material errors, and of any evidence or information that fraud or an illegal act may have occurred.

> (*Note:* However, the accountant need not report any matters regarding illegal acts that may have occurred that are clearly inconsequential.)

PRACTICE POINT: SSARS-13, "Compilation of Specified Elements, Accounts, or Items of a Financial Statement," is codified in AR Section 110. As this Manual goes to press, the AICPA has not yet made any conforming changes to SSARS-13 (AR Section 110) as a result of the issuance of SSARS-19, "Compilation and Review Engagements." Therefore, once the AICPA makes conforming changes to SSARS-13 (AR Section 110), an engagement letter will be required and the content of such engagement letters will be similar to the items discussed in detail in AR Section 80 (Compilation of Financial Statements) of this Manual.

Performance and Reporting Requirements

In connection with a compilation to report on specified elements, accounts, or items of a financial statement, the accountant must comply with the compilation performance requirements in AR Section 80. Also, prior to issuing the compilation report, the accountant should read the compiled information and consider whether it is appropriate in form and is free of obvious material errors.

PRACTICE POINT: SSARS-13, "Compilation of Specified Elements, Accounts, or Items of a Financial Statement," is codified in AR Section 110. As this Manual goes to press, the AICPA has not yet made any conforming changes to SSARS-13 (AR Section 110) as a result of the issuance of SSARS-19, "Compilation and Review Engagements." Therefore, once the AICPA makes conforming changes to SSARS-13 (AR Section 110), the content of the accountant's compilation report on specified elements, accounts, or items of a financial statement will be similar to the items discussed in detail in AR Section 80 (Compilation of Financial Statements) of this Manual.

An accountant's compilation report on specified elements, accounts, or items of a financial statement should include the following elements (this list reflects conforming changes made for the issuance of SSARS-19):

- *Title*—The title should clearly indicate that it is the accountant's compilation report. (*Note*: If applicable, the accountant may indicate that he or she is independent in the title. Appropriate titles would be "Accountant's Compilation Report" or "Independent Accountant's Compilation Report.")
- *Addressee*—The report should be addressed as appropriate in the circumstances of the engagement.

- *Introductory paragraph*—The accountant's report should include an introductory paragraph that:
  - — Identifies the entity whose specified elements, accounts, or items have been compiled;
  - — States that the specified elements, accounts, or items have been compiled;
  - — Identifies the financial information that has been compiled;
  - — Specifies the date or period covered by the financial information; and
  - — States that the accountant has not audited or reviewed the specified elements, accounts, or items and, accordingly, does not express an opinion or provide any assurance about whether the financial information is in accordance with the applicable financial reporting framework (e.g., GAAP, OCBOA).
- *Management's responsibility paragraph*—The accountant's report should include a paragraph that states that management is responsible for:
  - — The preparation and fair presentation of the specified elements, accounts, or items in accordance with the applicable financial reporting framework (e.g., GAAP, OCBOA); and
  - — Designing, implementing, and maintaining internal control relevant to the preparation and fair presentation of the financial information.
- *Accountant's responsibility paragraph*—The accountant's report should include a paragraph that states:
  - — The accountant's responsibility is to conduct the compilation in accordance with SSARSs issued by the AICPA; and
  - — The objective of a compilation is to assist management in presenting financial information without undertaking to obtain or provide any assurance that there are no material modifications that should be made to the financial information.
- *Signature*—The accountant's report should include a manual or printed signature of the accounting firm or the accountant, as appropriate.
- *Date*—The accountant's compilation report should be dated the date of completion of the compilation.

Also, each page of the compiled specified elements, accounts, or items of a financial statement should include a reference to the accountant's compilation report, such as "See Accountant's Compilation Report" or "See Independent Accountant's Compilation Report."

In addition, if the compilation of the specified elements, accounts, or items of a financial statement was performed in conjunction with a compilation of the entity's financial statements, then the accountant should state that, specify the date of the accountant's compilation report on those financial statements, and disclose any departure from the standard report on those statements, if relevant to the presentation of the specified elements, accounts, or items.

See Illustrations 1 and 2 for examples of compilation reports on specified elements, accounts, or items of a financial statement (with conforming changes made for the issuance of SSARS-19).

PRACTICE ISSUES AND FREQUENTLY ASKED QUESTIONS

Issue 1: Do the provisions of AR Section 110 apply if the specified element, account, or item of a financial statement is included as accompanying information to the basic financial statements?

No. The provisions of AR Section 110 do not apply if the specified element, account, or item of a financial statement is included as accompanying information to the basic financial statements. In such circumstances, the accountant should refer to the guidance in AR Section 80 (Compilation of Financial Statements).

Issue 2: May an accountant prepare or assist the client in the preparation of one or more specified elements, accounts, or items of a financial statement without the issuance of a compilation report?

Yes. An accountant is not precluded from preparing or assisting the client in the preparation of one or more specified elements, accounts, or items of a financial statement and submitting them to the client without the issuance of a compilation report, unless the accountant has been specifically engaged to compile such specified elements, accounts, or items of a financial statement.

Issue 3: May an accountant accept and perform an engagement to compile one or more specified elements, accounts, or items of a financial statement in conjunction with a compilation of an entity's financial statements?

Yes. An engagement to compile one or more specified elements, accounts, or items of a financial statement may be accepted either as a separate engagement or in conjunction with an engagement to compile an entity's financial statements.

ILLUSTRATIONS AND PRACTICE AIDS

ILLUSTRATION 1—ACCOUNTANT'S COMPILATION REPORT RELATED TO ACCOUNTS RECEIVABLE

Accountant's Compilation Report

To the Board of Directors of ABC Company:

I (We) have compiled the accompanying schedule of accounts receivable of ABC Company as of December 31, 20X2. I (We) have not audited or reviewed the accompanying schedule of accounts receivable and, accordingly, do not express an opinion or provide any assurance about whether the schedule of accounts receivable is in accordance with accounting principles generally accepted in the United States of America.

Management is (Owners are) responsible for the preparation and fair presentation of the schedule of accounts receivable in accordance with accounting principles generally accepted in the United States of America and for designing, implementing, and maintaining internal control relevant to the preparation and fair presentation of the schedule of accounts receivable.

My (Our) responsibility is to conduct the compilation in accordance with Statements on Standards for Accounting and Review Services issued by the American Institute of Certified Public Accountants. The objective of a compilation is to assist management in presenting financial information in the form of a schedule of accounts receivable without undertaking to obtain or provide any assurance that there are no material modifications that should be made to the schedule of accounts receivable.

[*Signature of accounting firm or accountant*]

[*Date*]

ILLUSTRATION 2—ACCOUNTANT'S COMPILATION REPORT RELATED TO THE SCHEDULE OF DEPRECIATION—INCOME TAX BASIS

Accountant's Compilation Report

To the Board of Directors of ABC Company:

I (We) have compiled the accompanying schedule of depreciation—income tax basis of ABC Company as of December 31, 20X2. The schedule of depreciation—income tax basis has been prepared on the accounting basis used by ABC Company for federal income tax purposes, which is a comprehensive basis of accounting other than accounting principles generally accepted in the United States of America. I (We) have not audited or reviewed the accompanying schedule of depreciation and, accordingly, do not express an opinion or provide any assurance about whether the schedule of depreciation is in accordance with the income tax basis of accounting.

Management is (Owners are) responsible for the preparation and fair presentation of the schedule of preciation in accordance with the income tax basis of accounting and for designing, implementing, and maintaining internal control relevant to the preparation and fair presentation of the schedule of depreciation.

My (Our) responsibility is to conduct the compilation in accordance with Statements on Standards for Accounting and Review Services issued by the American Institute of Certified Public Accountants. The objective of a compilation is to assist management in presenting financial information in the form of a schedule of depreciation without undertaking to obtain or provide any assurance that there are no material modifications that should be made to the schedule of depreciation.

[*Signature of accounting firm or accountant*]

[*Date*]

AR SECTION 120
COMPILATION OF PRO FORMA FINANCIAL INFORMATION

PRACTICE POINT: SSARS-14, "Compilation of Pro Forma Financial Information", is codified in AR Section 120. As this Manual goes to press, the AICPA has not yet made any conforming changes to SSARS-14 (AR Section 120) as a result of the issuance of SSARS-19, "Compilation and Review Engagements." For example, extant AR Section 120 states that the accountant should establish an understanding with the client, *preferably* in writing, regarding the services to be performed in connection with a compilation of pro forma financial information. However, an engagement letter is now required under SSARS-19. Therefore, once the AICPA makes conforming changes to SSARS-14 (AR Section 120), an engagement letter will be required as well and the content of such engagement letters will be similar to the items discussed in detail in AR Section 80 (Compilation of Financial Statements) of this Manual. The discussion in this chapter has been updated to reflect the requirements of SSARS-14 (AR Section 120), with conforming changes made for the issuance of SSARS-19 (AR Section 80).

WHAT EVERY PRACTITIONER SHOULD KNOW

Basic Objectives and Requirements

Pro forma financial information shows the effects of an actual or a proposed transaction or event on historical financial information. In other words, it shows what the historical information would have been had the event or transaction taken place within, rather than after the close of, the historical period. Therefore, the pro forma financial information should be clearly labeled "pro forma" to distinguish it from historical financial information. In addition, a presentation of pro forma financial information should:

- Describe (a) the transaction, or event, that is reflected in the pro forma financial information, (b) the source of the historical financial information on which it is based, (c) the significant assumptions that management used in developing the pro forma adjustments, and (d) any important uncertainties about those assumptions.

- Indicate that the pro forma financial information should be read in conjunction with the related historical financial information.

- State that the pro forma financial information is not necessarily indicative of the results that would have been achieved had the transaction, or event, taken place earlier.

AR Section 120 specifies the basic elements of the accountant's compilation report on pro forma financial information. In addition, in connection with such engagements, the accountant must comply with the compilation performance requirements in AR Section 80 (Compilation of Financial Statements).

Conditions for Engagement Performance

An accountant may undertake an engagement to compile pro forma financial information either as a separate engagement or in conjunction with a compilation of an entity's financial statements, if all of the following conditions are met:

- The document that contains the pro forma information includes (or incorporates by reference) the entity's complete historical financial statements for the most recent year, or for the preceding year if the financial statements for the most recent year are not yet available. If pro forma information is presented for an interim period, the document also should include (or incorporate by reference) historical interim financial information for that period. For business combinations, the document should include (or incorporate by reference) the appropriate historical financial information for the significant components comprising the combined entity.

- The entity's historical financial statements on which the pro forma information is based have been compiled, reviewed, or audited.

- The accountant's compilation, review, or audit report on the historical financial statements is included (or incorporated by reference) in the document containing the pro forma financial information.

Establishing an Understanding with the Client

AR Section 120 indicates that the accountant should establish an understanding with the client regarding the services to be performed in connection with a compilation of pro forma financial information. AR Section 120 indicates that such an understanding should include the following:

- A description of the nature and limitations of the services to be performed.

- A description of the report to be issued.

- A statement that the engagement cannot be relied upon to disclose errors, fraud, or illegal acts.

- A statement that the accountant will inform the appropriate level of management of any material errors, and of any evidence or information that fraud or an illegal act may have occurred.

  (*Note:* However, the accountant need not report any matters regarding illegal acts that may have occurred that are clearly inconsequential.)

PRACTICE POINT: SSARS-14, "Compilation of Pro Forma Financial Information," is codified in AR Section 120. As this Manual goes to press, the AICPA has not yet made any conforming changes to SSARS-14 (AR Section 120) as a result of the issuance of SSARS-19, "Compilation and Review Engagements." Therefore, once the AICPA makes conforming changes to SSARS-14 (AR Section 120), an engagement letter will be required and the content of such engagement letters will be similar to the items discussed in detail in AR Section 80 (Compilation of Financial Statements) of this Manual.

Performance and Reporting Requirements

In connection with a compilation to report on pro forma financial information, the accountant must comply with the compilation performance requirements in AR Section 80. Also, prior to issuing the compilation report, the accountant should read the compiled information and the summary of significant assumptions and consider whether they are appropriate in form and are free of obvious material errors.

PRACTICE POINT: SSARS-14, "Compilation of Pro Forma Financial Information," is codified in AR Section 120. As this Manual goes to press, the AICPA has not yet made any conforming changes to SSARS-14 (AR Section 120) as a result of the issuance of SSARS-19, "Compilation and Review Engagements." Therefore, once the AICPA makes conforming changes to SSARS-14 (AR Section 120), the content of the accountant's compilation report on pro forma financial information will be similar to the items discussed in detail in AR Section 80 (Compilation of Financial Statements) of this Manual.

An accountant's compilation report on pro forma financial information should include the following elements (this list reflects conforming changes made for the issuance of SSARS-19):

- *Title*—The title should clearly indicate that it is the accountant's compilation report. (*Note*: If applicable, the accountant may indicate that he or she is independent in the title. Appropriate titles would be "Accountant's Compilation Report" or "Independent Accountant's Compilation Report.")
- *Addressee*—The report should be addressed as appropriate in the circumstances of the engagement.
- *Introductory paragraph*—The accountant's report should include an introductory paragraph that:
  - Identifies the entity whose pro forma financial information has been compiled;
  - States that the pro forma financial information has been compiled;
  - Identifies the pro forma financial information that has been compiled;
  - Specifies the date or period covered by the pro forma financial information; and
  - Refers to the financial statements from which the historical financial information is derived, states whether such financial statements were compiled, reviewed, or audited, and includes a reference to any modifications in the accountant's report on historical financial statements; and
  - States that the accountant has not audited or reviewed the pro forma financial information and, accordingly, does not express an opinion or provide any assurance about whether the financial information is in accordance with the applicable financial reporting framework (e.g., GAAP, OCBOA).

- *Management's responsibility paragraph*—The accountant's report should include a paragraph that states that management is responsible for:

  — The preparation and fair presentation of the pro forma financial information in accordance with the applicable financial reporting framework (e.g., GAAP, OCBOA); and

  — Designing, implementing, and maintaining internal control relevant to the preparation and fair presentation of the financial information.

- *Accountant's responsibility paragraph*—The accountant's report should include a paragraph that states:

  — The accountant's responsibility is to conduct the compilation in accordance with SSARSs issued by the AICPA; and

  — The objective of a compilation is to assist management in presenting financial information in the form of pro forma information without undertaking to obtain or provide any assurance that there are no material modifications that should be made to the financial information.

- *Pro forma explanatory paragraph*—The accountant's report should include a paragraph that describes the objective of pro forma financial information and its limitations.

- *Signature*—The accountant's report should include a manual or printed signature of the accounting firm or the accountant, as appropriate.

- *Date*—The accountant's compilation report should be dated the date of completion of the compilation.

Also, each page of the compiled pro forma financial information should include a reference to the accountant's compilation report, such as "See Accountant's Compilation Report" or "See Independent Accountant's Compilation Report."

In addition, if the compilation of the pro forma financial information was performed in conjunction with a compilation of the entity's financial statements, then the accountant should state that, specify the date of the accountant's compilation report on those financial statements, and disclose any departure from the standard report on those statements, if relevant to the presentation of the pro forma financial information.

See Illustrations 1 and 2 for examples of compilation reports on pro forma financial information (with conforming changes made for the issuance of SSARS-19).

PRACTICE ISSUES AND FREQUENTLY ASKED QUESTIONS

Issue 1: Do the provisions of AR Section 120 apply if the pro forma financial information is included as accompanying information to the basic financial statements?

No. The provisions of AR Section 120 do not apply if the pro forma financial information is included as accompanying information to the basic financial statements. In such circumstances, the accountant should refer to the guidance in AR Section 80 (Compilation of Financial Statements).

Issue 2: May an accountant prepare or assist the client in the preparation of pro forma financial information without the issuance of a compilation report?

Yes. An accountant is not precluded from preparing or assisting the client in the preparation of pro forma financial information and submitting them to the client without the issuance of a compilation report, unless the accountant has been specifically engaged to compile such pro forma financial information.

Issue 3: May an accountant report on compiled pro forma financial information if the summary of significant assumptions is not presented?

No. An accountant is precluded from reporting on compiled pro forma financial information if the summary of significant assumptions is not presented.

ILLUSTRATIONS AND PRACTICE AIDS

ILLUSTRATION 1—ACCOUNTANT'S COMPILATION REPORT ON PRO FORMA FINANCIAL INFORMATION

Accountant's Compilation Report

To the Board of Directors of ABC Company:

I (We) have compiled the accompanying pro forma financial information as of and for the year ended December 31, 20X2, reflecting the business combination of ABC Company and XYZ Company. The historical condensed financial statements are derived from the historical unaudited financial statements of ABC Company, which were compiled by me (us), and of XYZ Company, which were compiled by another (other) accountant(s). I (We) have not audited or reviewed the accompanying pro forma financial information and, accordingly, do not express an opinion or provide any assurance about whether the pro forma financial information is in accordance with accounting principles generally accepted in the United States of America.

Note: *Where one set of historical financial statements is audited or reviewed and the other is audited, reviewed, or compiled, the second sentence in the paragraph above should be modified to include wording similar to the following:*

> *"The historical condensed financial statements are derived from the historical financial statements of ABC Company, which were compiled by me (us), and of XYZ Company, which were reviewed by another (other) accountant(s), appearing elsewhere herein (or incorporated by reference)."*

If either accountant's review report or auditor's report includes an explanatory paragraph or is modified, that fact should be referred to within this report.

Management is (Owners are) responsible for the preparation and fair presentation of the pro forma financial information in accordance with accounting principles generally accepted in the United States of America and for designing, implementing, and maintaining internal control relevant to the preparation and fair presentation of the pro forma financial information.

My (Our) responsibility is to conduct the compilation in accordance with Statements on Standards for Accounting and Review Services issued by the

American Institute of Certified Public Accountants. The objective of a compilation is to assist management in presenting financial information in the form of pro forma information without undertaking to obtain or provide any assurance that there are no material modifications that should be made to the pro forma financial information.

The objective of this pro forma financial information is to show what the significant effects on the historical financial information might have been had the business combination occurred at an earlier date. However, the pro forma financial information is not necessarily indicative of the results of operations or related effects on financial position that would have been attained had the above-mentioned business combination actually occurred earlier.

[*Signature of accounting firm or accountant*]

[*Date*]

ILLUSTRATION 2—ACCOUNTANT'S COMPILATION REPORT ON PRO FORMA FINANCIAL INFORMATION IS MODIFIED BECAUSE THE PRESENTATION DOES NOT INCLUDE ALL APPLICABLE DISCLOSURES (HOWEVER, IT DOES INCLUDE THE SUMMARY OF SIGNIFICANT ASSUMPTIONS)

Accountant's Compilation Report

To the Board of Directors of ABC Company:

I (We) have compiled the accompanying pro forma financial information as of and for the year ended December 31, 20X2, reflecting the business combination of ABC Company and XYZ Company. The historical condensed financial statements are derived from the historical unaudited financial statements of ABC Company, which were compiled by me (us), and of XYZ Company, which were compiled by another (other) accountant(s). I (We) have not audited or reviewed the accompanying pro forma financial information and, accordingly, do not express an opinion or provide any assurance about whether the pro forma financial information is in accordance with accounting principles generally accepted in the United States of America.

Note: *Where one set of historical financial statements is audited or reviewed and the other is audited, reviewed, or compiled, the second sentence in the paragraph above should be modified to include wording similar to the following:*

> "*The historical condensed financial statements are derived from the historical financial statements of ABC Company, which were compiled by me (us), and of XYZ Company, which were reviewed by another (other) accountant(s), appearing elsewhere herein (or incorporated by reference).*"

If either accountant's review report or auditor's report includes an explanatory paragraph or is modified, that fact should be referred to within this report.

Management is (Owners are) responsible for the preparation and fair presentation of the pro forma financial information in accordance with accounting principles generally accepted in the United States of America and for designing, implementing, and maintaining internal control relevant to the preparation and fair presentation of the pro forma financial information.

My (Our) responsibility is to conduct the compilation in accordance with Statements on Standards for Accounting and Review Services issued by the American Institute of Certified Public Accountants. The objective of a compilation is to assist management in presenting financial information in the form of pro forma information without undertaking to obtain or provide any assurance that there are no material modifications that should be made to the pro forma financial information.

The objective of this pro forma financial information is to show what the significant effects on the historical financial information might have been had the business combination occurred at an earlier date. However, the pro forma financial information is not necessarily indicative of the results of operations or related effects on financial position that would have been attained had the above-mentioned business combination actually occurred earlier.

Management has elected to omit all of the disclosures ordinarily included in pro forma financial information. The omitted disclosures might have added significant information regarding the company's pro forma financial position and results of operations. Accordingly, this pro forma financial information is not designed for those who are not informed about such matters.

[*Signature of accounting firm or accountant*]

[*Date*]

AR SECTION 200
REPORTING ON COMPARATIVE FINANCIAL STATEMENTS

PRACTICE POINT: As this Manual goes to press, the AICPA has not yet made any conforming changes to AR Section 200 (Reporting on Comparative Financial Statements) as a result of the issuance of SSARS-19, "Compilation and Review Engagements." For example, the illustrative accountants' reports in extant AR Section 200 have not been revised to reflect the new wording of compilation and review reports under SSARS-19. To facilitate compliance with SSARS-19, the illustrative accountants' reports in this chapter have been updated to reflect the requirements of AR Section 200, with conforming changes made for the issuance of SSARS-19.

WHAT EVERY PRACTITIONER SHOULD KNOW

Basic Objectives and Requirements

This Section is applicable when an accountant is reporting on comparative financial statements of a nonissuer (generally, a nonpublic entity) and the financial statements of one or more periods presented have been compiled or reviewed.

The accountant should not issue a report on comparative financial statements when statements for one or more, but not all, of the periods presented omit substantially all of the disclosures required by GAAP (or OCBOA).

Also, when the current period financial statements of a nonissuer are audited and the prior period statements are compiled or reviewed, the accountant should follow the guidance in Statements on Auditing Standards (AU Sections).

Continuing Accountant's Standard Report

When comparative financial statements are presented, a continuing accountant who performs the same or a higher level of service with respect to the current period financial statements should update his or her report on the prior period financial statements. A *review* is a higher level of service, while a *compilation* is a lower level of service. For examples of a continuing accountant's standard report on comparative financial statements when the same level of service has been performed for both periods, see Illustrations 1 (compilation) and 2 (review). For an example of a continuing accountant's standard report on comparative financial statements for two periods when the current period financial statements have been reviewed and the prior period statements have been compiled, see Illustration 3.

In addition, a continuing accountant who performs a lower level of service with respect to the current period financial statements (i.e., current period compiled, prior period reviewed) should report in either one of the following forms:

1. Describe, in a separate paragraph of the report, the responsibility assumed for the prior period financial statements. The description should

(a) include the original date of the accountant's report and (b) state that the accountant has not performed any review procedures after that date. See Illustration 4.

2. Reissue the report on the prior period financial statements. Under this option, the reissued review report on the prior period financial statements may be:

   a. Combined with the compilation report on the current period financial statements. The combined report should state that the accountant has not performed any review procedures after the date of the review report. See Illustration 5.

   b. Presented separately.

Continuing Accountant's Changed Reference to a Departure from GAAP

In a current engagement, the continuing accountant should consider the effects on his or her prior period report of circumstances or events coming to his or her attention.

When the accountant's report on the prior period financial statements contains a changed reference to a departure from GAAP, his or her report should include a separate explanatory paragraph indicating:

1. The date of the previous report.

2. The circumstances or events that caused the change.

3. That the prior period financial statements have been changed, if applicable.

For examples of an accountant's report in such circumstances, see Illustrations 6 (compilation) and 7 (review).

Predecessor Accountant's Compilation or Review Report

A predecessor accountant may, but is not required to, reissue his or her compilation or review report on the prior period financial statements. If the predecessor does not reissue his or her report on the prior period financial statements, a successor accountant should either:

1. Make reference, in an additional paragraph of his or her report on the current-period financial statements, to the predecessor's report, including:

   a. A statement that the prior period financial statements were compiled or reviewed by another accountant. (*Note:* The successor accountant should not name the predecessor accountant in his or her report; however, the successor accountant may name the predecessor accountant if the predecessor accountant's practice was acquired by, or merged with, that of the successor accountant.)

   b. The date of the predecessor's report.

   c. A description of the standard form of disclaimer or limited assurance, as applicable, included in the predecessor's report.

   d. A description of any modifications of the predecessor's standard report and of any emphasis-of-matter paragraphs.

   See Illustrations 8–12 for examples of the accountant's report under this option.

2. Perform a compilation, review, or audit of the prior period financial statements and report on them accordingly.

Predecessor's compilation or review report reissued Before reissuing his or her compilation or review report on the financial statements of a prior period, a predecessor should:

1. Determine whether his or her report is still appropriate by considering:

   a. The current form and manner of presentation of the prior period financial statements.

   b. Subsequent events not previously known.

   c. Changes in the financial statements that require the addition or deletion of modifications to the report.

2. Perform the following procedures:

   a. Read the current period financial statements and the successor's report.

   b. Compare the prior period financial statements with those previously issued and with those of the current period.

   c. Obtain a letter from the successor that indicates whether he or she is aware of any matter that might have a material effect on the financial statements, including disclosures, reported on by the predecessor.

When reissuing the compilation or review report on the prior period financial statements, a predecessor should use the date of the previous report. If the predecessor revises his or her report, or if the financial statements are restated, the predecessor should:

1. Dual-date the reissued report.

2. Obtain a written statement from the former client that:

   a. Describes the information currently acquired and its effect on the prior period financial statements.

   b. Expresses an understanding of the effect of the new information on the predecessor's reissued report.

If a predecessor is unable to complete the reissuance procedures discussed herein, he or she should (a) not reissue the report and (b) consider consulting with legal counsel.

Restated Prior-Period Financial Statements

When the prior-period financial statements have been restated, either the predecessor or the successor accountant should report on them as restated. If the predecessor accountant does not reissue his or her report and the successor accountant is not engaged to report on the prior-period financial statements, the successor accountant should indicate in the introductory paragraph of his or her report that a predecessor accountant reported on the prior-period financial statements, before the restatement. If the successor accountant is engaged to compile or review the restatement adjustments, the successor accountant's report may indicate that he or she compiled or reviewed the adjustments that were applied to restate the prior-period financial statements.

Reporting When One Period Is Audited

When the current period financial statements of a nonissuer are audited and the prior-period statements are compiled or reviewed, the accountant should follow the guidance in Statements on Auditing Standards (AU Sections).

When the current period financial statements of a nonissuer are compiled or reviewed and the prior-period statements are audited, the accountant should issue a compilation or review report on the current period financial statements and either:

1. Reissue the audit report on the prior period, or
2. Include a separate paragraph in the report on the current period which indicates:
   a. That the prior-period financial statements were audited.
   b. The date of the previous audit report.
   c. The type of opinion expressed.
   d. The substantive reasons for an opinion that was other than unqualified.
   e. That no auditing procedures were performed after the date of the previous report.

See Illustrations 13 and 14 for examples of the accountant's report under option 2.

Reporting on Financial Statements That Previously Did Not Omit Substantially All Disclosures

When comparative financial statements are presented, an accountant who has previously compiled, reviewed, or audited financial statements that included all required disclosures may compile statements for the same period that omit such disclosures, provided he or she includes an additional paragraph in the report that indicates:

1. The nature of the previous service rendered.
2. The date of the previous report.
3. Whether he or she expressed a qualified, an adverse, or a disclaimer of, opinion and the substantive reasons therefor, if the statements were previously audited.
4. A description or a quotation of any report modifications or emphasis matter, if the statements were previously compiled or reviewed.

See Illustration 15 for an example of the accountant's report under these circumstances.

PRACTICE ISSUES AND FREQUENTLY ASKED QUESTIONS

Issue 1: Can client-prepared financial statements of some periods that have not been audited, reviewed, or compiled be presented on separate pages of a document that also contains financial statements of other periods on which the accountant has reported?

Yes, as long as the client-prepared financial statements are accompanied by an indication by the client that the accountant:

1. Has not audited, reviewed, or compiled those financial statements; *and*

2. Does not assume any responsibility for them.

Issue 2: Can client-prepared financial statements of some periods that have not been audited, reviewed, or compiled be presented in columnar form in a document that also contains financial statements of other periods on which the accountant has reported?

No. If the accountant becomes aware of such circumstances and his or her name, or report, is used in the document, the accountant should advise the client that this is not appropriate and should consider consulting with legal counsel about an appropriate course of action.

Issue 3: Are financial statements with disclosures considered comparative to financial statements without disclosures for purposes of reporting under this Section?

No. For purposes of reporting under this Section, financial statements in columnar form with disclosures are not comparative to financial statements without disclosures. Therefore, for purposes of reporting on comparative financial statements under this Section, the statements for all periods presented should either be with disclosures, or all without disclosures. As a result, an accountant is precluded from reporting on comparative financial statements when statements for some of the periods presented omit substantially all disclosures, while the statements for other periods include the required disclosures.

Issue 4: When a successor accountant makes reference to a predecessor's report, should the successor identify the predecessor accountant by name?

No. The successor accountant should not name the predecessor accountant in his or her report.

Issue 5: What course of action should a predecessor accountant take if, in connection with reissuing the compilation or review report on the prior-period financial statements, he or she becomes aware of information that may affect such statements or the report thereon?

In connection with reissuing the compilation or review report on the prior-period financial statements, a predecessor accountant may become aware of information that may affect such statements or his or her report on them. For example, such information might include events or transactions occurring subsequent to the date of the predecessor's report. In such circumstances, the predecessor should:

1. Make inquiries or perform analytical procedures similar to those he or she would have performed had he or she been aware of such information at the date of the report.

2. Perform any other procedures deemed necessary in the circumstances, such as:

   a. Discussing the information with the successor.

   b. Reviewing the successor's working papers that relate to the matters affecting the prior-period financial statements.

Issue 6: If the entity is an issuer in the current period and was a nonissuer in the prior period, should an accountant reissue or refer to a compilation or review report previously issued on the prior-period financial statements?

No. The current status of the entity should govern whether the accountant should follow Statements on Auditing Standards (AU Sections) or Statements on Standards for Accounting and Review Services (AR Sections). Therefore, a previously issued report that is not appropriate for the current status of the entity should not be reissued or referred to in the report on the current period financial statements.

ILLUSTRATIONS AND PRACTICE AIDS

ILLUSTRATION 1—CONTINUING ACCOUNTANT'S REPORT: BOTH PERIODS COMPILED

Accountant's Compilation Report

To the Board of Directors of ABC Company:

I (We) have compiled the accompanying balance sheets of ABC Company as of December 31, 20X2, and 20X1, and the related statements of income, retained earnings, and cash flows for the years then ended. I (We) have not audited or reviewed the accompanying financial statements and, accordingly, do not express an opinion or provide any assurance about whether the financial statements are in accordance with accounting principles generally accepted in the United States of America.

Management is (Owners are) responsible for the preparation and fair presentation of the financial statements in accordance with accounting principles generally accepted in the United States of America and for designing, implementing, and maintaining internal control relevant to the preparation and fair presentation of the financial statements.

My (Our) responsibility is to conduct the compilations in accordance with Statements on Standards for Accounting and Review Services issued by the American Institute of Certified Public Accountants. The objective of a compilation is to assist management (owners) in presenting financial information in the form of financial statements without undertaking to obtain or provide any assurance that there are no material modifications that should be made to the financial statements.

[*Signature of accounting firm or accountant*]

[*Date*]

ILLUSTRATION 2—CONTINUING ACCOUNTANT'S REPORT: BOTH PERIODS REVIEWED

Independent Accountant's Review Report

To the Board of Directors of ABC Company:

I (We) have reviewed the accompanying balance sheets of ABC Company as of December 31, 20X2, and 20X1, and the related statements of income, retained earnings, and cash flows for the years then ended. A review includes primarily applying analytical procedures to management's (owners') financial data and making inquiries of company management (owners). A review is substantially less in scope than an audit, the objective of which is the expression of an opinion regarding the financial statements as a whole. Accordingly, I (we) do not express such an opinion.

Management is (Owners are) responsible for the preparation and fair presentation of the financial statements in accordance with accounting principles generally accepted in the United States of America and for designing, implementing, and maintaining internal control relevant to the preparation and fair presentation of the financial statements.

My (Our) responsibility is to conduct the reviews in accordance with Statements on Standards for Accounting and Review Services issued by the American Institute of Certified Public Accountants. Those standards require me (us) to perform procedures to obtain limited assurance that there are no material modifications that should be made to the financial statements. I (We) believe that the results of my (our) procedures provide a reasonable basis for my (our) report.

Based on my (our) reviews, I am (we are) not aware of any material modifications that should be made to the accompanying financial statements in order for them to be in conformity with accounting principles generally accepted in the United States of America.

[*Signature of accounting firm or accountant*]

[*Date*]

ILLUSTRATION 3—CONTINUING ACCOUNTANT'S REPORT: CURRENT PERIOD REVIEWED, PRIOR PERIOD COMPILED

Independent Accountant's Review Report

To the Board of Directors of ABC Company:

I (We) have reviewed the accompanying balance sheet of ABC Company as of December 31, 20X2, and the related statements of income, retained earnings, and cash flows for the year then ended. A review includes primarily applying analytical procedures to management's (owners') financial data and making inquiries of company management (owners). A review is substantially less in scope than an audit, the objective of which is the expression of an opinion regarding the financial statements as a whole. Accordingly, I (we) do not express such an opinion.

Management is (Owners are) responsible for the preparation and fair presentation of the financial statements in accordance with accounting principles generally accepted in the United States of America and for designing, implementing, and maintaining internal control relevant to the preparation and fair presentation of the financial statements.

My (Our) responsibility is to conduct the review in accordance with Statements on Standards for Accounting and Review Services issued by the American Institute of Certified Public Accountants. Those standards require me (us) to perform procedures to obtain limited assurance that there are no material modifications that should be made to the financial statements. I (We) believe that the results of my (our) procedures provide a reasonable basis for my (our) report.

Based on my (our) review, I am (we are) not aware of any material modifications that should be made to the accompanying 20X2 financial statements in order for them to be in conformity with accounting principles generally accepted in the United States of America.

The accompanying 20X1 financial statements of ABC Company were compiled by me (us). The objective of a compilation is to assist management (owners) in presenting financial information in the form of financial statements without undertaking to obtain or provide any assurance that there are no material modifications that should be made to the financial statements. Accordingly, I (we) do not express an opinion or provide any assurance about whether the 20X1 financial statements are in accordance with accounting principles generally accepted in the United States of America.

[*Signature of accounting firm or accountant*]

[*Date*]

ILLUSTRATION 4—CONTINUING ACCOUNTANT'S REPORT: CURRENT PERIOD COMPILED, WITH REFERENCE MADE TO PRIOR-PERIOD REVIEW REPORT

Accountant's Compilation Report

To the Board of Directors of ABC Company:

I (We) have compiled the accompanying balance sheet of ABC Company as of December 31, 20X2, and the related statements of income, retained earnings, and cash flows for the year then ended. I (We) have not audited or reviewed the accompanying 20X2 financial statements and, accordingly, do not express an opinion or provide any assurance about whether the financial statements are in accordance with accounting principles generally accepted in the United States of America.

Management is (Owners are) responsible for the preparation and fair presentation of the financial statements in accordance with accounting principles generally accepted in the United States of America and for designing, implementing, and maintaining internal control relevant to the preparation and fair presentation of the financial statements.

My (Our) responsibility is to conduct the compilation in accordance with Statements on Standards for Accounting and Review Services issued by the

American Institute of Certified Public Accountants. The objective of a compilation is to assist management (owners) in presenting financial information in the form of financial statements without undertaking to obtain or provide any assurance that there are no material modifications that should be made to the financial statements.

The accompanying 20X1 financial statements of ABC Company were previously reviewed by me (us), and my (our) report dated March 12, 20X2, stated that I was (we were) not aware of any material modifications that should be made to those statements in order for them to be in conformity with accounting principles generally accepted in the United States of America. I (We) have not performed any procedures in connection with that review engagement after the date of my (our) report on the 20X1 financial statements.

[*Signature of accounting firm or accountant*]

[*Date*]

ILLUSTRATION 5—CONTINUING ACCOUNTANT'S COMBINED COMPILATION AND REVIEW REPORT: CURRENT PERIOD COMPILED, PRIOR PERIOD REVIEWED

Independent Accountant's Compilation (20X2) and Review (20X1) Reports

To the Board of Directors of ABC Company:

I (We) have compiled the accompanying balance sheet of ABC Company as of December 31, 20X2, and the related statements of income, retained earnings, and cash flows for the year then ended. I (We) have not audited or reviewed the accompanying 20X2 financial statements and, accordingly, do not express an opinion or provide any assurance about whether the financial statements are in accordance with accounting principles generally accepted in the United States of America.

Management is (Owners are) responsible for the preparation and fair presentation of the financial statements in accordance with accounting principles generally accepted in the United States of America and for designing, implementing, and maintaining internal control relevant to the preparation and fair presentation of the financial statements.

My (Our) responsibility is to conduct the compilation in accordance with Statements on Standards for Accounting and Review Services issued by the American Institute of Certified Public Accountants. The objective of a compilation is to assist management (owners) in presenting financial information in the form of financial statements without undertaking to obtain or provide any assurance that there are no material modifications that should be made to the financial statements.

The accompanying 20X1 financial statements of ABC Company were previously reviewed by me (us). A review includes primarily applying analytical procedures to management's (owners') financial data and making inquiries of company management (owners). A review is substantially less in scope than an audit, the objective of which is the expression of an opinion regarding the financial statements as a whole. Accordingly, I (we) do not express such an opinion.

Management is (Owners are) responsible for the preparation and fair presentation of the financial statements in accordance with accounting principles generally accepted in the United States of America and for designing, implementing, and maintaining internal control relevant to the preparation and fair presentation of the financial statements.

My (Our) responsibility is to conduct the review in accordance with Statements on Standards for Accounting and Review Services issued by the American Institute of Certified Public Accountants. Those standards require me (us) to perform procedures to obtain limited assurance that there are no material modifications that should be made to the financial statements. I (We) believe that the results of my (our) procedures provide a reasonable basis for my (our) report.

Based on my (our) review, I am (we are) not aware of any material modifications that should be made to the accompanying 20X1 financial statements in order for them to be in conformity with accounting principles generally accepted in the United States of America. I (We) have not performed any procedures in connection with that review engagement after March 12, 20X2, the date of my (our) report on the accompanying 20X1 financial statements.

[*Signature of accounting firm or accountant*]

[*Date*]

ILLUSTRATION 6—CONTINUING ACCOUNTANT'S REPORT: BOTH PERIODS COMPILED, WITH A CHANGED REFERENCE TO A GAAP DEPARTURE

Accountant's Compilation Report

To the Board of Directors of ABC Company:

I (We) have compiled the accompanying balance sheets of ABC Company as of December 31, 20X2, and 20X1, and the related statements of income, retained earnings, and cash flows for the years then ended. I (We) have not audited or reviewed the accompanying financial statements and, accordingly, do not express an opinion or provide any assurance about whether the financial statements are in accordance with accounting principles generally accepted in the United States of America.

Management is (Owners are) responsible for the preparation and fair presentation of the financial statements in accordance with accounting principles generally accepted in the United States of America and for designing, implementing, and maintaining internal control relevant to the preparation and fair presentation of the financial statements.

My (Our) responsibility is to conduct the compilations in accordance with Statements on Standards for Accounting and Review Services issued by the American Institute of Certified Public Accountants. The objective of a compilation is to assist management (owners) in presenting financial information in the form of financial statements without undertaking to obtain or provide any assurance that there are no material modifications that should be made to the financial statements.

In my (our) previous compilation report dated March 12, 20X2, on the 20X1 financial statements, I (we) referred to a departure from accounting principles generally accepted in the United States of America because the company carried its land at appraised values. However, as disclosed in note [X], the company has restated its 20X1 financial statements to reflect its land at cost in accordance with accounting principles generally accepted in the United States of America.

[*Signature of accounting firm or accountant*]

[*Date*]

ILLUSTRATION 7—CONTINUING ACCOUNTANT'S REPORT: BOTH PERIODS REVIEWED, WITH A CHANGED REFERENCE TO A GAAP DEPARTURE

Independent Accountant's Review Report

To the Board of Directors of ABC Company:

I (We) have reviewed the accompanying balance sheets of ABC Company as of December 31, 20X2, and 20X1, and the related statements of income, retained earnings, and cash flows for the years then ended. A review includes primarily applying analytical procedures to management's (owners') financial data and making inquiries of company management (owners). A review is substantially less in scope than an audit, the objective of which is the expression of an opinion regarding the financial statements as a whole. Accordingly, I (we) do not express such an opinion.

Management is (Owners are) responsible for the preparation and fair presentation of the financial statements in accordance with accounting principles generally accepted in the United States of America and for designing, implementing, and maintaining internal control relevant to the preparation and fair presentation of the financial statements.

My (Our) responsibility is to conduct the reviews in accordance with Statements on Standards for Accounting and Review Services issued by the American Institute of Certified Public Accountants. Those standards require me (us) to perform procedures to obtain limited assurance that there are no material modifications that should be made to the financial statements. I (We) believe that the results of my (our) procedures provide a reasonable basis for my (our) report.

Based on my (our) reviews, I am (we are) not aware of any material modifications that should be made to the accompanying financial statements in order for them to be in conformity with accounting principles generally accepted in the United States of America.

In my (our) previous review report dated March 12, 20X2, on the 20X1 financial statements, I (we) referred to a departure from accounting principles generally accepted in the United States of America because the company carried its land at appraised values. However, as disclosed in note [X], the company has restated its 20X1 financial statements to reflect its land at cost in accordance with accounting principles generally accepted in the United States of America.

[*Signature of accounting firm or accountant*]

[*Date*]

ILLUSTRATION 8—SUCCESSOR ACCOUNTANT'S COMPILATION REPORT MAKES REFERENCE TO THE PREDECESSOR'S COMPILATION REPORT

Accountant's Compilation Report

To the Board of Directors of ABC Company:

I (We) have compiled the accompanying balance sheet of ABC Company as of December 31, 20X2, and the related statements of income, retained earnings, and cash flows for the year then ended. I (We) have not audited or reviewed the accompanying 20X2 financial statements and, accordingly, do not express an opinion or provide any assurance about whether the financial statements are in accordance with accounting principles generally accepted in the United States of America.

Management is (Owners are) responsible for the preparation and fair presentation of the financial statements in accordance with accounting principles generally accepted in the United States of America and for designing, implementing, and maintaining internal control relevant to the preparation and fair presentation of the financial statements.

My (Our) responsibility is to conduct the compilation in accordance with Statements on Standards for Accounting and Review Services issued by the American Institute of Certified Public Accountants. The objective of a compilation is to assist management (owners) in presenting financial information in the form of financial statements without undertaking to obtain or provide any assurance that there are no material modifications that should be made to the financial statements.

The 20X1 financial statements of ABC Company were compiled by other accountants whose report dated March 12, 20X2, stated that they have not audited or reviewed the 20X1 financial statements and, accordingly, do not express an opinion or provide any assurance about whether the financial statements are in accordance with accounting principles generally accepted in the United States of America.

[*Signature of accounting firm or accountant*]

[*Date*]

ILLUSTRATION 9—SUCCESSOR ACCOUNTANT'S COMPILATION REPORT MAKES REFERENCE TO THE PREDECESSOR'S REVIEW REPORT

Accountant's Compilation Report

To the Board of Directors of ABC Company:

I (We) have compiled the accompanying balance sheet of ABC Company as of December 31, 20X2, and the related statements of income, retained earnings, and cash flows for the year then ended. I (We) have not audited or reviewed the accompanying 20X2 financial statements and, accordingly, do not express an opinion or provide any assurance about whether the financial statements are in accordance with accounting principles generally accepted in the United States of America.

Management is (Owners are) responsible for the preparation and fair presentation of the financial statements in accordance with accounting principles generally accepted in the United States of America and for designing, implementing, and maintaining internal control relevant to the preparation and fair presentation of the financial statements.

My (Our) responsibility is to conduct the compilation in accordance with Statements on Standards for Accounting and Review Services issued by the American Institute of Certified Public Accountants. The objective of a compilation is to assist management (owners) in presenting financial information in the form of financial statements without undertaking to obtain or provide any assurance that there are no material modifications that should be made to the financial statements.

The 20X1 financial statements of ABC Company were reviewed by other accountants whose report dated March 12, 20X2 stated that, based on their review, they are not aware of any material modifications that should be made to the 20X1 financial statements in order for them to be in conformity with accounting principles generally accepted in the United States of America.

[*Signature of accounting firm or accountant*]

[*Date*]

ILLUSTRATION 10—SUCCESSOR ACCOUNTANT'S COMPILATION REPORT MAKES REFERENCE TO A PREDECESSOR'S COMPILATION REPORT THAT INCLUDED AN EMPHASIS-OF-MATTER PARAGRAPH

Accountant's Compilation Report

To the Board of Directors of ABC Company:

I (We) have compiled the accompanying balance sheet of ABC Company as of December 31, 20X2, and the related statements of income, retained earnings, and cash flows for the year then ended. I (We) have not audited or reviewed the accompanying 20X2 financial statements and, accordingly, do not express an opinion or provide any assurance about whether the financial statements are in accordance with accounting principles generally accepted in the United States of America.

Management is (Owners are) responsible for the preparation and fair presentation of the financial statements in accordance with accounting principles generally accepted in the United States of America and for designing, implementing, and maintaining internal control relevant to the preparation and fair presentation of the financial statements.

My (Our) responsibility is to conduct the compilation in accordance with Statements on Standards for Accounting and Review Services issued by the American Institute of Certified Public Accountants. The objective of a compilation is to assist management (owners) in presenting financial information in the form of financial statements without undertaking to obtain or provide any assurance that there are no material modifications that should be made to the financial statements.

The 20X1 financial statements of ABC Company were compiled by other accountants whose report dated March 12, 20X2, stated that they have not audited or reviewed the 20X1 financial statements and, accordingly, do not express an opinion or provide any assurance about whether the financial statements are in accordance with accounting principles generally accepted in the United States of America; however, the report emphasized that during 20X1 the company changed its method of depreciation from the straight-line method to the double-declining method.

[*Signature of accounting firm or accountant*]

[*Date*]

ILLUSTRATION 11—SUCCESSOR ACCOUNTANT'S REVIEW REPORT MAKES REFERENCE TO THE PREDECESSOR'S REVIEW REPORT

Independent Accountant's Review Report

To the Board of Directors of ABC Company:

I (We) have reviewed the accompanying balance sheet of ABC Company as of December 31, 20X2, and the related statements of income, retained earnings, and cash flows for the year then ended. A review includes primarily applying analytical procedures to management's (owners') financial data and making inquiries of company management (owners). A review is substantially less in scope than an audit, the objective of which is the expression of an opinion regarding the financial statements as a whole. Accordingly, I (we) do not express such an opinion.

Management is (Owners are) responsible for the preparation and fair presentation of the financial statements in accordance with accounting principles generally accepted in the United States of America and for designing, implementing, and maintaining internal control relevant to the preparation and fair presentation of the financial statements.

My (Our) responsibility is to conduct the review in accordance with Statements on Standards for Accounting and Review Services issued by the American Institute of Certified Public Accountants. Those standards require me (us) to perform procedures to obtain limited assurance that there are no material modifications that should be made to the financial statements. I (We) believe that the results of my (our) procedures provide a reasonable basis for my (our) report.

Based on my (our) review, I am (we are) not aware of any material modifications that should be made to the accompanying 20X2 financial statements in order for them to be in conformity with accounting principles generally accepted in the United States of America.

The 20X1 financial statements of ABC Company were reviewed by other accountants whose report dated March 12, 20X2, stated that, based on their review, they are not aware of any material modifications that should be made to the 20X1 financial statements in order for them to be in conformity with accounting principles generally accepted in the United States of America.

[*Signature of accounting firm or accountant*]

[*Date*]

ILLUSTRATION 12—SUCCESSOR ACCOUNTANT'S REVIEW REPORT MAKES REFERENCE TO THE PREDECESSOR'S COMPILATION REPORT

Independent Accountant's Review Report

To the Board of Directors of ABC Company:

I (We) have reviewed the accompanying balance sheet of ABC Company as of December 31, 20X2, and the related statements of income, retained earnings, and cash flows for the year then ended. A review includes primarily applying analytical procedures to management's (owners') financial data and making inquiries of company management (owners). A review is substantially less in scope than an audit, the objective of which is the expression of an opinion regarding the financial statements as a whole. Accordingly, I (we) do not express such an opinion.

Management is (Owners are) responsible for the preparation and fair presentation of the financial statements in accordance with accounting principles generally accepted in the United States of America and for designing, implementing, and maintaining internal control relevant to the preparation and fair presentation of the financial statements.

My (Our) responsibility is to conduct the review in accordance with Statements on Standards for Accounting and Review Services issued by the American Institute of Certified Public Accountants. Those standards require me (us) to perform procedures to obtain limited assurance that there are no material modifications that should be made to the financial statements. I (We) believe that the results of my (our) procedures provide a reasonable basis for my (our) report.

Based on my (our) review, I am (we are) not aware of any material modifications that should be made to the accompanying 20X2 financial statements in order for them to be in conformity with accounting principles generally accepted in the United States of America.

The 20X1 financial statements of ABC Company were compiled by other accountants whose report dated March 12, 20X2, stated that they have not audited or reviewed the 20X1 financial statements and, accordingly, do not express an opinion or provide any assurance about whether the financial statements are in accordance with accounting principles generally accepted in the United States of America.

[*Signature of accounting firm or accountant*]

[*Date*]

ILLUSTRATION 13—CONTINUING ACCOUNTANT'S REPORT: CURRENT PERIOD COMPILED, WITH REFERENCE MADE TO PRIOR-PERIOD AUDIT REPORT

Accountant's Compilation Report

To the Board of Directors of ABC Company:

I (We) have compiled the accompanying balance sheet of ABC Company as of December 31, 20X2, and the related statements of income, retained earnings, and cash flows for the year then ended. I (We) have not audited or reviewed the accompanying 20X2 financial statements and, accordingly, do not express an opinion or provide any assurance about whether the financial statements are in accordance with accounting principles generally accepted in the United States of America.

Management is (Owners are) responsible for the preparation and fair presentation of the financial statements in accordance with accounting principles generally accepted in the United States of America and for designing, implementing, and maintaining internal control relevant to the preparation and fair presentation of the financial statements.

My (Our) responsibility is to conduct the compilation in accordance with Statements on Standards for Accounting and Review Services issued by the American Institute of Certified Public Accountants. The objective of a compilation is to assist management (owners) in presenting financial information in the form of financial statements without undertaking to obtain or provide any assurance that there are no material modifications that should be made to the financial statements.

The financial statements for the year ended December 31, 20X1, were audited by us (other accountants) and we (they) expressed an unqualified opinion on them in our (their) report dated March 12, 20X2, but we (they) have not performed any auditing procedures since that date.

[*Signature of accounting firm or accountant*]

[*Date*]

ILLUSTRATION 14—CONTINUING ACCOUNTANT'S REPORT: CURRENT PERIOD REVIEWED, WITH REFERENCE MADE TO PRIOR-PERIOD AUDIT REPORT

Independent Accountant's Review Report

To the Board of Directors of ABC Company:

I (We) have reviewed the accompanying balance sheet of ABC Company as of December 31, 20X2, and the related statements of income, retained earnings, and cash flows for the year then ended. A review includes primarily applying analytical procedures to management's (owners') financial data and making inquiries of company management (owners). A review is substantially less in scope than an audit, the objective of which is the expression of an opinion regarding the financial statements as a whole. Accordingly, I (we) do not express such an opinion.

Management is (Owners are) responsible for the preparation and fair presentation of the financial statements in accordance with accounting principles generally accepted in the United States of America and for designing, implementing, and maintaining internal control relevant to the preparation and fair presentation of the financial statements.

My (Our) responsibility is to conduct the review in accordance with Statements on Standards for Accounting and Review Services issued by the American Institute of Certified Public Accountants. Those standards require me (us) to perform procedures to obtain limited assurance that there are no material modifications that should be made to the financial statements. I (We) believe that the results of my (our) procedures provide a reasonable basis for my (our) report.

Based on my (our) review, I am (we are) not aware of any material modifications that should be made to the accompanying 20X2 financial statements in order for them to be in conformity with accounting principles generally accepted in the United States of America.

The financial statements for the year ended December 31, 20X1, were audited by us (other accountants) and we (they) expressed an unqualified opinion on them in our (their) report dated March 12, 20X2, but we (they) have not performed any auditing procedures since that date.

[*Signature of accounting firm or accountant*]

[*Date*]

ILLUSTRATION 15—CONTINUING ACCOUNTANT'S REPORT: PRIOR PERIOD FINANCIAL STATEMENTS HAVE BEEN COMPILED FROM PREVIOUSLY REVIEWED OR COMPILED STATEMENTS THAT DID NOT OMIT THE REQUIRED DISCLOSURES

Accountant's Compilation Report

To the Board of Directors of ABC Company:

I (We) have compiled the accompanying balance sheets of ABC Company as of December 31, 20X2, and 20X1, and the related statements of income, retained earnings, and cash flows for the years then ended. I (We) have not audited or reviewed the accompanying financial statements and, accordingly, do not express an opinion or provide any assurance about whether the financial statements are in accordance with accounting principles generally accepted in the United States of America.

Management is (Owners are) responsible for the preparation and fair presentation of the financial statements in accordance with accounting principles generally accepted in the United States of America and for designing, implementing, and maintaining internal control relevant to the preparation and fair presentation of the financial statements.

My (Our) responsibility is to conduct the compilations in accordance with Statements on Standards for Accounting and Review Services issued by the American Institute of Certified Public Accountants. The objective of a compilation is to assist management in presenting financial information in the form of financial statements without undertaking to obtain or provide any assurance that there are no material modifications that should be made to the financial statements.

Management has elected to omit substantially all of the disclosures required by accounting principles generally accepted in the United States of America. If the omitted disclosures were included in the financial statements, they might influence the user's conclusions about the company's financial position, results of operations, and cash flows. Accordingly, the financial statements are not designed for those who are not informed about such matters.

The accompanying 20X1 financial statements were compiled by me (us) from financial statements that did not omit substantially all of the disclosures required by accounting principles generally accepted in the United States of America and that I (we) previously reviewed (compiled) as indicated in my (our) report dated March 12, 20X2.

[*Signature of accounting firm or accountant*]

[*Date*]

ILLUSTRATION 16—SUCCESSOR ACCOUNTANT'S COMPILATION REPORT WHEN THE PREDECESSOR ACCOUNTANT'S REPORT IS NOT PRESENTED AND THE SUCCESSOR ACCOUNTANT IS ENGAGED TO COMPILE THE RESTATEMENT ADJUSTMENTS

Accountant's Compilation Report

To the Board of Directors of ABC Company:

I (We) have compiled the accompanying balance sheet of ABC Company as of December 31, 20X2, and the related statements of income, retained earnings, and cash flows for the year then ended. I (We) also compiled the adjustment(s) described in Note [X] that was (were) applied to restate the 20X1 financial statements. I (We) have not audited or reviewed the accompanying 20X2 financial statements or the adjustment(s) described in Note [X]and, accordingly, do not express an opinion or provide any assurance about whether the 20X2 financial statements or the adjustment(s) described in Note [X] are in accordance with accounting principles generally accepted in the United States of America. The 20X1 financial statements of ABC Company, before the adjustment(s) described in Note [X] that was (were) applied to restate the 20X1 financial statements, were compiled by other accountants whose report dated March 12, 20X2, stated that they have not audited or reviewed the 20X1 financial statements and, accordingly, do not express an opinion or provide any assurance about whether the 20X1 financial statements are in accordance with accounting principles generally accepted in the United States of America.

Management is (Owners are) responsible for the preparation and fair presentation of the financial statements in accordance with accounting principles generally accepted in the United States of America and for designing, implementing, and maintaining internal control relevant to the preparation and fair presentation of the financial statements.

My (Our) responsibility is to conduct the compilation in accordance with Statements on Standards for Accounting and Review Services issued by the American Institute of Certified Public Accountants. The objective of a compilation is to assist management (owners) in presenting financial information in the form of financial statements without undertaking to obtain or provide any assurance that there are no material modifications that should be made to the financial statements.

[*Signature of accounting firm or accountant*]

[*Date*]

ILLUSTRATION 17—SUCCESSOR ACCOUNTANT'S REVIEW REPORT WHEN THE PREDECESSOR ACCOUNTANT'S REPORT IS NOT PRESENTED AND THE SUCCESSOR ACCOUNTANT IS ENGAGED TO REVIEW THE RESTATEMENT ADJUSTMENTS

Independent Accountant's Review Report

To the Board of Directors of ABC Company:

I (We) have reviewed the accompanying balance sheet of ABC Company as of December 31, 20X2, and the related statements of income, retained earnings, and cash flows for the year then ended. A review includes primarily applying analytical procedures to management's (owners') financial data and making inquiries of company management (owners). A review is substantially less in scope than an audit, the objective of which is the expression of an opinion regarding the financial statements as a whole. Accordingly, I (we) do not express such an opinion. The 20X1 financial statements of ABC Company, before the adjustment(s) described in Note [X]that was (were) applied to restate the 20X1 financial statements, were reviewed by other accountants whose report dated March 12, 20X2, stated that, based on their review, they are not aware of any material modifications that should be made to the 20X1 financial statements in order for them to be in conformity with accounting principles generally accepted in the United States of America.

Management is (Owners are) responsible for the preparation and fair presentation of the financial statements in accordance with accounting principles generally accepted in the United States of America and for designing, implementing, and maintaining internal control relevant to the preparation and fair presentation of the financial statements.

My (Our) responsibility is to conduct the review in accordance with Statements on Standards for Accounting and Review Services issued by the American Institute of Certified Public Accountants. Those standards require me (us) to perform procedures to obtain limited assurance that there are no material modifications that should be made to the financial statements. I (We) believe that the results of my (our) procedures provide a reasonable basis for my (our) report.

Based on my (our) review, I am (we are) not aware of any material modifications that should be made to the accompanying 20X2 financial statements in order for them to be in conformity with accounting principles generally accepted in the United States of America.

I (We) also reviewed the adjustment(s) as described in Note [X] that was (were) applied to restate the 20X1 financial statements. Based on my (our) review, nothing came to my (our) attention to indicate that the adjustment(s) is (are) not appropriate and properly applied.

[*Signature of accounting firm or accountant*]

[*Date*]

AR SECTION 300
COMPILATION REPORTS ON FINANCIAL STATEMENTS INCLUDED IN CERTAIN PRESCRIBED FORMS

PRACTICE POINT: As this Manual goes to press, the AICPA has not yet made any conforming changes to AR Section 300 (Compilation Reports on Financial Statements Included in Certain Prescribed Forms) as a result of the issuance of SSARS-19, "Compilation and Review Engagements." For example, the illustrative accountants' compilation reports in extant AR Section 300 have not been revised to reflect the new wording of compilation reports under SSARS-19. To facilitate compliance with SSARS-19, the illustrative accountants' reports in this chapter have been updated to reflect the requirements of AR Section 300, with conforming changes made for the issuance of SSARS-19.

WHAT EVERY PRACTITIONER SHOULD KNOW

Basic Objectives and Requirements

This Section provides for an *alternative* form of standard compilation report on financial statements included in certain prescribed forms that call for departure from GAAP by either:

1. Specifying a measurement principle not in conformity with GAAP.

2. Failing to request the disclosures required by GAAP.

Therefore, an accountant may issue either a compilation report pursuant to AR Section 80 (Compilation of Financial Statements) or the alternative type of report discussed and illustrated in this Section.

Note: *Unless otherwise indicated, reference to generally accepted accounting principles (GAAP) in this Section includes, where applicable, another comprehensive basis of accounting (OCBOA).*

A prescribed form is any standard preprinted form designed or adopted by the body to which it is to be submitted, such as forms used by industry trade associations, credit agencies, banks, and governmental and regulatory bodies.

An accountant who has reviewed the financial statements of a nonissuer (generally, a nonpublic entity) may issue a compilation report on financial statements for the same period in a prescribed form that calls for a departure from GAAP. When the difference between the previously reviewed financial statements and the statements included in the prescribed form is limited to the omission of disclosures not requested by the form, the accountant may wish to refer to the review report in his or her report on the compiled financial statements included in the prescribed form.

PRACTICE ISSUES AND FREQUENTLY ASKED QUESTIONS

Issue 1: Does this Section apply to review engagements?

No. This Section applies only to compilation engagements.

Issue 2: Does this Section apply when the financial statements to be compiled are included in a form designed solely by the client's management?

No. A form designed or adopted by the entity is not considered to be a prescribed form.

Issue 3: Does this Section apply to a tax return that is to be submitted to a client's bank as a part of a credit application?

No. A tax return does not meet the definition of financial statements submitted on a prescribed form. Therefore, an accountant is not required to attach any form of report to a tax return even though it is to be submitted to others.

Issue 4: Is the accountant required to call attention to departures from GAAP in his or her compilation report when such departures are required by the prescribed form?

No, because there is a presumption that the information required by a prescribed form is sufficient to meet the needs of the body that designed or adopted the form.

Issue 5: If the accountant becomes aware of GAAP departures other than those called for by the prescribed form, should he or she describe such departures in the compilation report?

Yes. If the accountant becomes aware of GAAP departures other than those called for by the prescribed form, he or she should follow the guidance in AR Section 80 (Compilation of Financial Statements). In such circumstances, the wording in the accountant's compilation report disclosing the departure might read as follows:

> However, I (we) did become aware of a departure from generally accepted accounting principles that is not called for by the prescribed form or related instructions, as described in the following paragraph.

Issue 6: May an accountant sign a preprinted report form that does not conform with the guidance in this Section?

No. The accountant is precluded from signing a preprinted report form that does not conform to the guidance in this Section or in AR Section 80. In such circumstances, the accountant should attach an acceptable report to the prescribed form.

ILLUSTRATIONS AND PRACTICE AIDS

ILLUSTRATION 1—ACCOUNTANT'S COMPILATION REPORT ON FINANCIAL STATEMENTS INCLUDED IN CERTAIN PRESCRIBED FORMS

Accountant's Compilation Report

To the Board of Directors of ABC Company:

I (We) have compiled the balance sheet of ABC Company as of December 31, 20X2, and the related statements of income, retained earnings, and cash flows for the year then ended included in the accompanying prescribed form. I (We) have not audited or reviewed the accompanying financial statements and, accordingly, do not express an opinion or provide any assurance about whether the financial statements are in accordance with the form prescribed by [*name of body, for example, "First National Bank"*].

Management is (Owners are) responsible for the preparation and fair presentation of the financial statements in accordance with the requirements prescribed by [*name of body, for example, "First National Bank"*] and for designing, implementing, and maintaining internal control relevant to the preparation and fair presentation of the financial statements.

My (Our) responsibility is to conduct the compilation in accordance with Statements on Standards for Accounting and Review Services issued by the American Institute of Certified Public Accountants. The objective of a compilation is to assist management (owners) in presenting financial information in the form of financial statements without undertaking to obtain or provide any assurance that there are no material modifications that should be made to the financial statements.

These financial statements (including related disclosures) are presented in accordance with the requirements of [*name of body, for example, "First National Bank"*], which differ from accounting principles generally accepted in the United States of America. Accordingly, these financial statements are not designed for those who are not informed about such differences.

[*Signature of accounting firm or accountant*]

[*Date*]

AR SECTION 400
COMMUNICATIONS BETWEEN PREDECESSOR AND SUCCESSOR ACCOUNTANTS

WHAT EVERY PRACTITIONER SHOULD KNOW

Basic Objectives and Requirements

A successor accountant:

1. May, but is not required to, communicate with a predecessor accountant regarding acceptance of a compilation or review engagement.

2. Is required to request the client to communicate with the predecessor accountant when the successor believes that the financial statements reported on by the predecessor may require revision.

Inquiries Regarding Engagement Acceptance

A successor accountant may decide to communicate with a predecessor accountant in connection with acceptance of a compilation or review engagement when circumstances such as the following exist:

1. The information obtained about the prospective client is limited or appears to require special attention.

2. The change in accountants takes place substantially after the end of the accounting period for which financial statements are to be compiled or reviewed.

3. Frequent changes in accountants have occurred.

When a successor accountant decides to communicate with the predecessor, he or she should ask the prospective client (a) to grant permission to make inquiries of the predecessor and (b) to authorize the predecessor to respond fully to the successor accountant's inquiries. The successor's inquiries may be oral or written and, generally, would include the following:

1. Information that might bear on the integrity of management.

2. Disagreements with management over the application of accounting principles, performance of engagement procedures, or other similarly significant matters.

3. The cooperation of management in providing needed information.

4. Knowledge of any fraud or illegal acts.

5. The predecessor accountant's understanding as to the reasons for the change of accountants.

PRACTICE POINT: Illustration 1 provides a form that the successor accountant can use when making inquiries of the predecessor.

The predecessor accountant should respond promptly and fully to the successor's inquiries. If, due to unusual circumstances (e.g., litigation, disciplinary proceedings), the predecessor decides not to respond fully, he or she should indicate that such response is limited.

Financial Statements Reported on by Predecessor Accountant

During a compilation or review engagement, the successor accountant may become aware of information that leads him or her to believe that financial statements reported on by the predecessor accountant may require revision. In such circumstances:

1. The successor should request the client to communicate this information to the predecessor.

2. The predecessor should follow the guidance in AR Section 80 (Compilation of Financial Statements) for compilation engagements, or AR Section 90 (Review of Financial Statements) for review engagements, in determining an appropriate course of action.

If the client refuses to communicate with the predecessor, or if the successor is not satisfied with the predecessor's course of action, the successor should consider the implications for the engagement and determine whether to resign. Also, the successor should consider consulting with legal counsel.

PRACTICE ISSUES AND FREQUENTLY ASKED QUESTIONS

Issue 1: Is a successor accountant required to communicate with a predecessor accountant regarding acceptance of a compilation or review engagement?

No. A successor accountant may, but is not required to, communicate with a predecessor accountant regarding acceptance of a compilation or review engagement. This is unlike the *required* communications between accountants in connection with an audit engagement, as discussed in AU Section 315 (Communications between Predecessor and Successor Auditors). However, many accountants in practice communicate with a predecessor in connection with a compilation or review engagement, as a matter of "good practice."

Issue 2: Is a successor accountant required to review the predecessor's working papers in connection with a compilation or review engagement?

No. A successor accountant may wish, but is not required, to review the predecessor's working papers in connection with a compilation or review engagement. In such circumstances, the successor should request the client to authorize the predecessor to allow such review. The predecessor should determine which working papers are to be made available and which may be copied.

Issue 3: Should the predecessor accountant provide the successor access to his or her working papers?

Ordinarily, yes. However, this Section recognizes that the predecessor accountant may have valid business reasons (e.g., unpaid fees, litigation) to deny the successor accountant access to his or her working papers. Before permitting access to the working papers, the predecessor accountant may want, but is not required, to reach an understanding with the successor about the use of the working papers. Illustration 2, which is adapted from an appendix of AR Section 400, provides an example of a letter that the predecessor accountant may wish to obtain from the successor accountant about the use of the working papers.

Issue 4: What additional assurances might the successor accountant give the predecessor accountant to obtain broader access to the predecessor's working papers?

Experience has shown that the predecessor accountant may be willing to grant the successor accountant broader access to his or her working papers if the successor accountant provides additional assurance concerning the use of the predecessor's working papers. Accordingly, the successor accountant might consider agreeing to the following limitations on the review of the predecessor accountant's working papers in order to obtain broader access:

- The successor accountant will not comment, orally or in writing, to anyone as a result of the review as to whether the predecessor accountant's engagement was performed in accordance with SSARSs.

- The successor accountant will not provide expert testimony or litigation support services or otherwise accept an engagement to comment on issues relating to the quality of the predecessor accountant's engagement.

The successor accountant can incorporate the aforementioned points in the acknowledgment letter to the predecessor accountant, as shown in Illustration 2.

Issue 5: What steps can the successor accountant take if the predecessor accountant will not provide a comprehensive response to the successor's inquiries?

The successor accountant should seriously consider the desirability of accepting a prospective client, without considerable other investigation, if the predecessor accountant will not provide a comprehensive response to the successor's inquiries. In practice, many CPA firms investigate the prospective client to determine its acceptability. Sources of information include local attorneys, banks, other CPAs, and other businesses. In some cases, the accountant may hire a professional investigator to obtain information about the reputation, background, and integrity of key members of management.

Issue 6: Are the communications between successor and predecessor accountants required to be in writing?

No. The communications between successor and predecessor accountants may be either written or oral.

Issue 7: Is a successor accountant prohibited from accepting a compilation or review engagement if the predecessor does not respond, or provides only a limited response, to the successor accountant's inquiries?

No. This Section does *not* prohibit a CPA firm from accepting a compilation or review engagement when the predecessor accountant does not respond, or limits his or her response, to the successor accountant's inquiries. Such situations, however, should lead to a heightened awareness on the part of the successor accountant that matters relating to the prospective client's integrity or to disagreements over accounting issues may potentially exist.

Issue 8: How should the communications between the successor and predecessor accountants be documented?

SSARSs do not require any formal letters between any of the parties, or any specific documentation as a result of the communications. However, good business practice suggests that notations in the working papers indicating the names of the persons communicated with, the dates of communication, and the substance of the conversations, as a minimum level of documentation. Also, although the "Successor Accountant Acknowledgment Letter" in Illustration 2 below is not required by SSARSs, it is good practice to obtain such letter and include it in the workpapers.

Issue 9: Does this Section apply when an accountant is asked to provide written or oral advice on the application of accounting principles to specified transactions by an entity whose financial statements are compiled or reviewed by another accountant?

No. This Section does not apply when requests are made by an entity to obtain a second opinion from another accountant. In such circumstances, the accountant who is requested to provide the advice should follow the guidance in AU Section 625 (Reports on the Application of Accounting Principles).

ILLUSTRATIONS AND PRACTICE AIDS

ILLUSTRATION 1—COMMUNICATIONS WITH PREDECESSOR ACCOUNTANT FORM

Note: Any "Yes" answers to the following questions indicate a higher level of risk than normal, and the accountant should expand on those answers.

Client Name: _____

Date of Financial Statements: _____

		Yes	No	N/A
1.	Are you aware of any situations that might bear on the integrity of management?			
2.	Have you had any significant disagreements with management over the application of accounting principles, practices, or financial statement disclosures?			
3.	Has management ever attempted to restrict or direct the scope of the engagement?			
4.	Are you aware of any incidents of management intervention in, or circumvention of, the company's internal control?			
5.	Is management unwilling to accept primary responsibility for the content of the financial statements?			
6.	Does management discourage its key employees from cooperating fully with the independent accountant?			
7.	Are you aware of any fraud or illegal acts perpetrated within the client?			
8.	Inquire of the predecessor accountant about his or her understanding of reasons for change in accountants and summarize:			

_____

9.   Name of predecessor accountant:

10.   Name and position of person inquired of:

11.   Date of inquiry:

ILLUSTRATION 2—SUCCESSOR ACCOUNTANT ACKNOWLEDGMENT LETTER

[*Date*]

[*Successor Accountant*]

[*Address*]

We have previously [*reviewed or compiled*], in accordance with Statements on Standards for Accounting and Review Services, the December 31, 20X1, financial statements of ABC Enterprises ("ABC"). In connection with your [*review or compilation*] of ABC's 20X2 financial statements, you have requested access to our working papers prepared in connection with that engagement. ABC has authorized our firm to allow you to review those working papers.

Our [*review or compilation*], and the working papers prepared in connection therewith, of ABC's financial statements were not planned or conducted in contemplation of your [*review or compilation*]. Therefore, items of possible interest to you may not have been specifically addressed. Our use of professional judgment for the purpose of this engagement means that matters may have existed that would have been assessed differently by you. We make no representation as to the sufficiency or appropriateness of the information in our working papers for your purposes.

We understand that the purpose of your review is to obtain information about ABC and our 20X1 results to assist you in your 20X2 engagement of ABC. For that purpose only, we will provide you access to our working papers that relate to that objective.

Because your review of our working papers is undertaken solely for the purpose described above and may not entail a review of all our working papers, you agree that (1) the information obtained from the review will not be used by you for any other purpose; (2) you will not comment, orally or in writing, to anyone as a result of that review as to whether our engagement was performed in accordance with Statements on Standards for Accounting and Review Services; and (3) you will not provide expert testimony or litigation services or otherwise accept an engagement to comment on issues relating to the quality of our engagement.

Upon request, we will provide copies of those working papers that provide factual information about ABC. You agree to subject any such copies or information otherwise derived from our working papers to your normal policy for retention of working papers and protection of confidential client information. Furthermore, in the event of a third-party request for access to your working papers prepared in connection with your [*reviews or compilations*] of ABC, you agree to obtain our permission before voluntarily allowing any such access to our working papers or information otherwise derived from our working papers, and to obtain on our behalf any releases that you obtain from such third party. You agree to advise us promptly and provide us a copy of any subpoena, summons, or other court order for access to your working papers that include copies of our working papers or information otherwise derived therefrom.

Please confirm your agreement with the foregoing by signing and dating a copy of this letter and returning it to us.

Very truly yours,

[*Predecessor accountant*]

By: _____

Accepted: _____

[*Successor accountant*]

By: _____ Date: _____

AR SECTION 600
REPORTING ON PERSONAL FINANCIAL STATEMENTS INCLUDED IN WRITTEN PERSONAL FINANCIAL PLANS

WHAT EVERY PRACTITIONER SHOULD KNOW

Basic Objectives and Requirements

An accountant may submit a written personal financial plan containing unaudited personal financial statements to a client without complying with the requirements of AR Section 80 (Compilation of Financial Statements) for compilation engagements, or AR Section 90 (Review of Financial Statements) for review engagements, if all of the following conditions are met:

1. The accountant establishes an understanding with the client, preferably in writing, that the personal financial statements:

   a. Will be used solely to assist the client, and the client's advisers, to develop the client's personal financial goals and objectives, including implementation of the financial plan.

   b. Will not be used to obtain credit or for any purposes other than in a. above.

2. Nothing comes to the accountant's attention during the engagement that would lead him or her to believe that the financial statements will be used for any purposes other than permitted in 1. above.

However, this Section does not preclude an accountant from complying with AR Section 80 (Compilation of Financial Statements) for compilation engagements, or AR Section 90 (Review of Financial Statements) for review engagements when reporting on personal financial statements included in written personal financial plans.

Report Requirements

An accountant's written report issued pursuant to this Section should state that the unaudited personal financial statements:

1. Are designed solely to help develop the financial plan.

2. May be incomplete or contain other GAAP departures.

3. Should not be used to obtain credit or for any purposes other than developing the personal financial plan.

4. Have not been audited, reviewed, or compiled.

Each page of the personal financial statements should include a reference to the accountant's report.

See Illustration 1 for an example of an accountant's report.

PRACTICE ISSUES AND FREQUENTLY ASKED QUESTIONS

Issue 1: What is the accountant's reporting responsibility if the client, in connection with implementing the personal financial plan, expects to refinance certain debts and may be requested to submit the statements to obtain credit?

This Section creates an exemption for the accountant from complying with AR Section 80 (Compilation of Financial Statements) or AR Section 90 (Review of Financial Statements) for personal financial statements that are included in written personal financial plans if certain conditions exist. One of the conditions of this exemption is that the personal financial statements will not be used to obtain credit. Because, in this case, the client is expected to use the statements to obtain credit, the accountant has the following reporting options:

a. Compile a complete set of personal financial statements under AR Section 80 (Compilation of Financial Statements) for compilation engagements or AR Section 90 (Review of Financial Statements) for review engagements, including all relevant disclosures, and report on them accordingly. This set of statements could be submitted to others to obtain credit, and could also be incorporated in a personal financial plan. However, the financial plan need not, and preferably should not, be submitted to potential grantors of credit because it often contains personal information unnecessary for purposes of a credit decision.

b. Report on two sets of personal financial statements: (1) one pursuant to AR Section 80 (Compilation of Financial Statements) for compilation engagements or AR Section 90 (Review of Financial Statements) for review engagements, for use by outside parties, and (2) another one pursuant to AR Section 600 for use in the financial plan. Because it is often useful that statements prepared for planning purposes contain certain departures from GAAP or an other comprehensive basis of accounting, this alternative may be preferable. However, the client should clearly understand the different reporting levels and uses of these two sets of statements

Issue 2: May an accountant report, pursuant to this Section, on personal financial statements included in a written personal financial plan if the client plans to take the financial plan to an attorney for the purpose of drafting a will or trust documents?

Yes. In the process of implementing a financial plan, it is contemplated that the client will share the document with other advisers such as attorneys, investment advisers and insurance brokers.

ILLUSTRATIONS AND PRACTICE AIDS

ILLUSTRATION 1—ACCOUNTANT'S REPORT ON PERSONAL FINANCIAL STATEMENTS INCLUDED IN WRITTEN PERSONAL FINANCIAL PLANS

The accompanying Statement of Financial Condition of John Doe as of December 31, 20X2, was prepared solely to help you develop your personal financial plan. Accordingly, it may be incomplete or contain other departures from accounting principles generally accepted in the United States of America and should not be used to obtain credit or for any purposes other than developing your financial plan. We have not audited, reviewed, or compiled the statement.

[*Signature*]

[*Date*]

Accounting Resources on the Web

The following World Wide Web addresses are just a few of the resources on the Internet that are available to practitioners. Because of the evolving nature of the Internet, some addresses may change. In such a case, refer to one of the many Internet search engines, such as Yahoo! (http://www.yahoo.com).

Accounting Research Manager
http://www.accountingresearchmanager.com

AICPA   http://www.aicpa.org

American Accounting Association
http://aaahq.org

CCH   http://tax.CCHGroup.com

FASAB   http://www.fasab.gov

FASB   http://www.fasb.org

Federal Tax Law   http://www.taxsites.com/federal.html

Fedworld   http://www.fedworld.gov

GASB   http://www.gasb.org

Government Accountability Office   http://www.gao.gov

House of Representatives   http://www.house.gov

International Accounting Standards Board
http://www.iasb.org.uk

IRS Digital Daily   http://www.irs.gov

Learning Center   http://cch.learningcenter.com

Library of Congress   http://thomas.loc.gov

Office of Management and Budget
http://www.whitehouse.gov/omb

ProSystem*fx* Engagement   http://tax.cchgroup.com/Engagement/default

Public Company Accounting Oversight Board
http://www.pcaobus.org or http://www.pacobus.com

Securities and Exchange Commission   http://www.sec.gov

The CCH Accounting and Auditing Series Libraries   http://tax.cchgroup.com

Thomas Legislative Research   http://thomas.loc.gov

Cross-Reference

GAAS Practice Manual (AU Sections)

AU	Title	SAS No.
330	The Confirmation Process	SAS-67
331	Inventories	SAS-1*
332	Auditing Derivative Instruments, Hedging Activities, and Investments in Securities	SAS-92
333	Management Representations	SAS-85, SAS-113
334	Related Parties	SAS-45
336	Using the Work of a Specialist	SAS-73
337	Inquiry of a Client's Lawyer Concerning Litigation, Claims, and Assessments	SAS-12
339	Audit Documentation	SAS-96, SAS-103
341	The Auditor's Consideration of an Entity's Ability to Continue as a Going Concern	SAS-59, SAS-113
342	Auditing Accounting Estimates	SAS-57, SAS-113
350	Audit Sampling	SAS-39, SAS-111
380	The Auditor's Communication with Those Charged with Governance	SAS-114
390	Consideration of Omitted Procedures after the Report Date	SAS-46
410	Adherence to Generally Accepted Accounting Principles	SAS-1*
411	The Meaning of *Present Fairly in Conformity with Generally Accepted Accounting Principles*	SAS-69
420	Consistency of Application of Generally Accepted Accounting Principles	SAS-1*
431	Adequacy of Disclosure in Financial Statements	SAS-32
504	Association with Financial Statements	SAS-26
508	Reports on Audited Financial Statements	SAS-58
530	Dating of the Independent Auditor's Report	SAS-1*
532	Restricting the Use of an Auditor's Report	SAS-87
534	Reporting on Financial Statements Prepared for Use in Other Countries	SAS-51
543	Part of Audit Performed by Other Independent Auditors	SAS-1*
544	Lack of Conformity with Generally Accepted Accounting Principles	SAS-1*
550	Other Information in Documents Containing Audited Financial Statements	SAS-118

AU	Title	SAS No.
551	Supplementary Information in Relation to the Financial Statements as a Whole	SAS-119
552	Reporting on Condensed Financial Statements and Selected Financial Data	SAS-42
558	Required Supplementary Information	SAS-120
560	Subsequent Events	SAS-1*, SAS-113
561	Subsequent Discovery of Facts Existing at the Date of the Auditor's Report	SAS-1*
623	Special Reports	SAS-62
625	Reports on the Application of Accounting Principles	SAS-50
634	Letters for Underwriters and Certain Other Requesting Parties	SAS-72
711	Filings Under Federal Securities Statutes	SAS-37
722	Interim Financial Information	SAS-116, SAS-121
801	Compliance Audits	SAS-117
901	Public Warehouses—Controls and Auditing Procedures for Goods Held	SAS-1*

GAAS Practice Manual (AT Sections)

AT	Title	SSAE No.
20	Defining Professional Requirements in Statements on Standards for Attestation Engagements	SSAE-13
50	SSAE Hierarchy	SSAE-14
101	Attest Engagements	SSAE-10
201	Agreed-Upon Procedures Engagements	SSAE-10
301	Financial Forecasts and Projections	SSAE-10, SSAE-17
401	Reporting on Pro Forma Financial Information	SSAE-10
501	An Examination of an Entity's Internal Control over Financial Reporting That Is Integrated with an Audit of Its Financial Statements	SSAE-15
601	Compliance Attestation	SSAE-10
701	Management's Discussion and Analysis	SSAE-10
801	Reporting on Controls at a Service Organization	SSAE-16

GAAS Practice Manual (AR Sections)

AR	Title	SSARS No.
60	Framework for Performing and Reporting on Compilation and Review Engagements	SSARS-19
80	Compilation of Financial Statements	SSARS-19
90	Review of Financial Statements	SSARS-19, SSARS-20
110	Compilation of Specified Elements, Accounts, or Items of a Financial Statement	SSARS-13
120	Compilation of Pro Forma Financial Information	SSARS-14
200	Reporting on Comparative Financial Statements	SSARS-2
300	Compilation Reports on Financial Statements Included in Certain Prescribed Forms	SSARS-3
400	Communications between Predecessor and Successor Accountants	SSARS-4
600	Reporting on Personal Financial Statements Included in Written Personal Financial Plans	SSARS-6

Outstanding Statements on Auditing Standards, Statements on Standards for Attestation Engagements, and Statements on Standards for Accounting and Review Services Issued to Date

Outstanding Statements on Auditing Standards

SAS	Title	AU Section
1	Codification of Auditing Standards and Procedures	Various
12	Inquiry of a Client's Lawyer Concerning Litigation, Claims, and Assessments	337
25	The Relationship of Generally Accepted Auditing Standards to Quality Control Standards	161
26	Association with Financial Statements	504
32	Adequacy of Disclosure in Financial Statements	431
37	Filings Under Federal Securities Statutes	711
39	Audit Sampling	350
42	Reporting on Condensed Financial Statements and Selected Financial Data	552
43	Omnibus Statement on Auditing Standards	150, 331, 350, 420, 901

SAS	Title	AU Section
87	Restricting the Use of an Auditor's Report	325, 532
88	Service Organizations and Reporting on Consistency	324, 420
89	Audit Adjustments	333, 380
91	Federal GAAP Hierarchy	411
92	Auditing Derivative Instruments, Hedging Activities, and Investments in Securities	332
93	Omnibus Statement on Auditing Standards—2000	315, 411, 508
95	Generally Accepted Auditing Standards	150
97	Amendment to Statement on Auditing Standards No. 324, *Reports on the Application of Accounting Principles*	625
98	Omnibus Statement on Auditing Standards—2002	150, 161, 312, 324, 508, 530, 560, 561
99	Consideration of Fraud in a Financial Statement Audit	316
101	Auditing Fair Value Measurements and Disclosures	328
102	Defining Professional Requirements in Statements on Auditing Standards	120
103	Audit Documentation	339
104	Amendment to SAS-1, "Codification of Auditing Standards and Procedures" ("Due Professional Care in the Performance of Work")	230
105	Amendment to SAS-95, "Generally Accepted Auditing Standards"	150
106	Audit Evidence	326
107	Audit Risk and Materiality in Conducting an Audit	312
108	Planning and Supervision	311
109	Understanding the Entity and Its Environment and Assessing the Risks of Material Misstatement	314
110	Performing Audit Procedures in Response to Assessed Risks and Evaluating the Audit Evidence Obtained	318
111	Audit Sampling	350
113	Omnibus Statement on Auditing Standards—2006	150, 316, 328, 333, 341, 342, 560
114	The Auditor's Communication with Those Charged with Governance	380
115	Communicating Internal Control Related Matters Identified in an Audit	325

SAS	Title	AU Section
116	Interim Financial Information	722
117	Compliance Audits	801
118	Other Information in Documents Containing Audited Financial Statements	550
119	Supplementary Information in Relation to the Financial Statements as a Whole	551
120	Required Supplementary Information	558
121	Revised Applicability of Statement on Auditing Standards No. 100, "Interim Financial Information"	722

OUTSTANDING STATEMENTS ON STANDARDS FOR ATTESTATION ENGAGEMENTS

SSAE	Title	AT Section
10	Attestation Standards: Revision and Recodification	101–701
11	Attest Documentation	101, 201, 301
12	Amendment to Statement on Standards for Attestation Engagements No. 10, *Attestation Standards: Revision and Recodification*	101
13	Defining Professional Requirements in Statements on Standards for Attestation Engagements	20
14	SSAE Hierarchy	50
15	An Examination of an Entity's Internal Control over Financial Reporting That Is Integrated with an Audit of Its Financial Statements	501
16	Reporting on Controls at a Service Organization	801
17	Reporting on Compiled Prospective Financial Statements When the Practitioner's Independence Is Impaired	301

OUTSTANDING STATEMENTS ON STANDARDS FOR ACCOUNTING AND REVIEW SERVICES

SSARS	Title	AR Section
2	Reporting on Comparative Financial Statements	200
3	Compilation Reports on Financial Statements Included in Certain Prescribed Forms	300
4	Communications between Predecessor and Successor Accountants	400

SSARS	Title	AR Section
6	Reporting on Personal Financial Statements Included in Written Personal Financial Plans	600
7	Omnibus Statement on Standards for Accounting and Review Services—1992	200, 300, 400
9	Omnibus Statement on Standards for Accounting and Review Services—2002	400
13	Compilation of Specified Elements, Accounts, or Items of a Financial Statement	110
14	Compilation of Pro Forma Financial Information	120
15	Elimination of Certain References to Statements on Auditing Standards and Incorporation of Appropriate Guidance into Statements on Standards for Accounting and Review Services	200, 300, 400
17	Omnibus Statement on Standards for Accounting and Review Services—2008	200, 300, 400
19	Compilation and Review Engagements	60, 80, 90
20	Revised Applicability of Statements on Standards for Accounting and Review Services	90

* Portions of SAS No. 1 have been superseded by subsequent pronouncements.

Index

References are to page numbers. Alphabetization is letter-by-letter (e.g., "Profitability" precedes "Profit participation").

D

EXA

S

About the CD-ROM

Using the CD-ROM

SYSTEM REQUIREMENTS

- IBM PC or compatible computer with CD-ROM drive
- Windows 95 or higher
- Microsoft® Word 7.0 for Windows™ or compatible word processsor
- 10 MB available on hard drive

The CD-ROM provided with the 2012 *GAAS Practice Manual* contains electronic versions of the more than 350 separate sample checklists, questionnaires, working papers, correspondence letters, and accountant's reports contained in the book. See the CD-ROM Contents for a listing of these practice aids.

Subject to the conditions in the license agreement and the limited warranty, which are reproduced at the end of this book, you may duplicate the files on this disc, modify them as necessary, and create your own customized versions. Using the disc in any way indicates that you accept the terms of the license agreement.

USING THE CD-ROM

The disc data is intended for use with your word processing software. Each document is provided in Rich Text Format. These files can be read by all compatible word processors, including Microsoft Word for Windows and WordPerfect 7 or above. Check your owners manual for information on the conversion of the documents as required.

USING THE DOCUMENTS

The list of the Disc Contents is available on your disc in a file called _contents.rtf. The listing includes each individual example exhibit, checklist, correspondence, and workpaper and identifies its location in a particular file. You can open this file and view it on your screen and use it to link to the documents you're interested in, or print a hard copy to use for reference.

1. Open the file _contents.rtf in your word processor.
2. Locate the file you wish to access, and click on the hyperlinked file name. Your word processor will then open the file.
3. You may copy files from the CD-ROM to your hard disk. To edit files you have copied, remember to clear the read-only attribute from the file. To do this, select the name of the file in My Computer, right-click the filename, then choose Properties, and clear the Read-only checkbox.

SOFTWARE SUPPORT

If you experience any difficulties installing or running the electronic files and cannot resolve the problem using the information presented here, call our toll-free software support hotline at 800 835 0105 or visit our website at http://support.cch.com.

CD-ROM Contents

Disc contents by short file name are listed as shown. For more information about the CD-ROM, please turn to page 15,003 of the manual and see "Using the CD-ROM."

Title	File Name	File Type
AU SECTION		
Management's Responsibility for Financial Reporting	AU110-01	RTF
Client Acceptance and Retention Evaluation Form	AU161-01	RTF
Independence Representation Form	AU220-01	RTF
Sample Engagement Letter	AU311-01	RTF
Additional Audit Procedures for Initial Audit Engagements	AU311-02	RTF
Audit Review and Approval Checklist	AU311-03	RTF
Differences of Professional Opinion Form	AU311-04	RTF
Unconditional and Presumptively Mandatory Requirements of AU Section 311	AU311-05	RTF
Inherent Risk Assessment Form	AU312-01	RTF
Guidelines to Calculate Materiality Based on Operating Results or on Financial Position	AU312-02	RTF
Worksheet for Analysis of Uncorrected Misstatements	AU312-03	RTF
Unconditional and Presumptively Mandatory Requirements of AU Section 312	AU312-04	RTF
Questionnaire for Understanding the Control Environment Component of Internal Control	AU314-01	RTF
Questionnaire for Understanding the Risk Assessment Component of Internal Control	AU314-02	RTF
Questionnaire for Understanding the Control Activities Component of Internal Control	AU314-03	RTF
Questionnaire for Understanding the Information and Communication Component of Internal Control	AU314-04	RTF
Questionnaire for Understanding the Monitoring Component of Internal Control	AU314-05	RTF
Unconditional and Presumptively Mandatory Requirements of AU Section 314	AU314-06	RTF
Communication with Predecessor Auditor Form	AU315-01	RTF
Audit Program for Reviewing the Predecessor Auditor's Working Papers and Planning the New Audit Engagement	AU315-02	RTF
Client Consent and Acknowledgment Letter	AU315-03	RTF
Successor Auditor Acknowledgment Letter	AU315-04	RTF
Fraud Risk Assessment Form	AU316-03	RTF
Examples of Substantive Procedures for Inventories	AU318-01	RTF

Title	File Name	File Type
Accounts Receivable Confirmation Audit Program	AU330-01	RTF
Confirmation Request for Cutoff Bank Statement	AU330-02	RTF
Confirmation Request for Accounts Receivable: Positive Request of Dollar Amounts	AU330-03	RTF
Confirmation Request for Accounts Receivable: Positive Request of Open Invoices	AU330-04	RTF
Confirmation Request for Accounts Receivable: Negative Request	AU330-05	RTF
Confirmation Request for Notes Receivable	AU330-06	RTF
Confirmation Request for Accounts Payable	AU330-07	RTF
Confirmation Request for Notes Payable	AU330-08	RTF
Confirmation Request for Lease Agreement	AU330-09	RTF
Confirmation Control Summary	AU330-10	RTF
Accounts Receivable Confirmation Results Summary	AU330-11	RTF
Accounts Receivable Roll-Forward from Confirmation Date to Balance Sheet Date	AU330-12	RTF
Request for Confirmation of Inventories Held by Warehouses or Other Third Parties When Listing of Inventories Is Provided by the Client and Enclosed with the Confirmation Request	AU331-01	RTF
Request for Confirmation of Inventories Held by Warehouses or Other Third Parties When Listing of Inventories Is Not Provided by the Client and Not Enclosed with the Confirmation Request	AU331-02	RTF
Inventory Observation Checklist	AU331-03	RTF
Inventory Test Count Sheet	AU331-04	RTF
Inventory Audit Program	AU331-05	RTF
Auditor's Report: Disclaimer of Opinion-Auditor Did Not Observe Beginning Inventory	AU331-06	RTF
Auditor's Report: Disclaimer of Opinion-Company Did Not Make a Count of Its Physical Inventory	AU331-07	RTF
Request for Confirmation of Securities Held by Brokers or Other Third Parties When Listing of Securities Is Included in the Confirmation Request	AU332-01	RTF
Request for Confirmation of Securities Held by Brokers or Other Third Parties When Listing of Securities Is Not Included in the Confirmation Request	AU332-02	RTF
Count Sheet of Securities	AU332-03	RTF
Investments in Securities Workpaper	AU332-04	RTF
Illustrative Audit Procedures for Derivative Instruments, Hedging Activities, and Investments in Securities	AU332-06	RTF
Management Representations Letter	AU333-01	RTF
Additional Illustrative Management Representations	AU333-02	RTF
Updating Management Representations Letter	AU333-03	RTF
Audit Program for Identifying and Substantiating Related-Party Transactions	AU334-04	RTF
Related-Party Confirmation Letter	AU334-05	RTF

Title	File Name	File Type
Comments on Tables, Statistics, and Other Financial Information-Summarized Description of Procedures and Findings Regarding Tables, Statistics, and Other Financial Information	AU634-07	RTF
Comments on Tables, Statistics, and Other Financial Information: Descriptions of Procedures and Findings Regarding Tables, Statistics, and Other Financial Information-Attached Registration Statement (or Selected Pages) Identifies with Designated Symbols Items to Which Procedures Were Applied	AU634-08	RTF
Alternate Wording When Accountant's Report on Audited Financial Statements Contains an Explanatory Paragraph	AU634-09	RTF
Alternate Wording When More Than One Accountant Is Involved	AU634-10	RTF
Alternate Wording When the SEC Has Agreed to a Departure From Its Accounting Requirements	AU634-11	RTF
Alternate Wording When Recent Earnings Data Are Presented in Capsule Form	AU634-12	RTF
Alternate Wording When Accountants Are Aware of a Decrease in a Specified Financial Statement Item	AU634-13	RTF
Alternate Wording of the Comfort Letter for Companies That Are Permitted to Present Interim Earnings Data for a 12-Month Period	AU634-14	RTF
Alternate Wording When the Procedures That the Underwriter Has Requested the Accountant to Perform on Interim Financial Information Are Less than a Review under AU Section 722	AU634-15	RTF
A Typical Comfort Letter in a Non-1933 Act Offering, Including the Required Underwriter Representations	AU634-16	RTF
Letter to a Requesting Party That Has Not Provided the Required Representation Letter	AU634-17	RTF
Comfort Letter That Includes Reference to Examination of Annual MD&A and Review of Interim MD&A	AU634-18	RTF
Representation Letter from a Party Requesting a Comfort Letter from the Accountant	AU634-19	RTF
Wording in a Prospectus Regarding an Accountant's Review Report Included in a Form 10-Q	AU711-01	RTF
Subsequent Events Procedures Checklist in 1933 Act Filings	AU711-02	RTF
Engagement Letter for Review of Interim Financial Information	AU 722-01	RTF
Interim Review Procedures Checklist	AU 722-02	RTF
Management Representation Letter for a Review of Interim Financial Information (Short Form to Be Used in Conjunction with the Letter Provided by Management in Connection with the Prior Year's Audit)	AU 722-03	RTF
Management Representation Letter for a Review of Interim Financial Information (Long Form to Be Used Independently of Any Other Letter)	AU 722-04	RTF
Accountant's Standard Review Report on Interim Financial Information	AU 722-05	RTF

Title	File Name	File Type
Accountant's Review Report on Interim Financial Information Makes Reference to Other Accountants	AU 722-06	RTF
Accountant's Review Report on Interim Financial Information Modified Due to a Departure from the Applicable Financial Reporting Framework	AU 722-07	RTF
Accountant's Review Report on Interim Financial Information Modified Due to Inadequate Disclosure	AU 722-08	RTF
Accountant's Review Report on Interim Financial Information Includes a Paragraph Emphasizing a Going-Concern Matter Disclosed in the Audited Financial Statements and the Interim Financial Information	AU 722-09	RTF
Accountant's Review Report on Interim Financial Information Includes a Paragraph Emphasizing a Going-Concern Matter That Was Not Included in the Prior Year's Audit Report	AU 722-10	RTF
Auditor's Combined Report on Compliance and Internal Control over Compliance	AU801-01	RTF
Internal Control Checklist for Public Warehouses	AU901-01	RTF
Internal Control Checklist for an Owner of Goods Stored in Public Warehouses	AU901-02	RTF
Request for Confirmation of Inventories Held by Warehouses or Other Third Parties When Listing of Inventories Is Provided by the Client and Enclosed with the Confirmation Request	AU901-03	RTF
Request for Confirmation of Inventories Held by Warehouses or Other Third Parties When Listing of Inventories Is Not Provided by the Client and Not Enclosed with the Confirmation Request	AU901-04	RTF

AT SECTION

Title	File Name	File Type
Standard Examination Report on Subject Matter for General Use	AT101-04	RTF
Standard Examination Report on an Assertion for General Use	AT101-05	RTF
Examination Report on an Assertion but Opinion Issued Is on the Subject Matter	AT101-06	RTF
Examination Report on Subject Matter That Is Restricted Because the Criteria Are Available Only to Specified Parties	AT101-07	RTF
Examination Report with a Qualified Opinion Due to Material Misstatements or Deviations from the Criteria	AT101-08	RTF
Examination Report with a Disclaimer of Opinion Due to a Scope Restriction	AT101-09	RTF
Examination Report on Subject Matter That Is the Responsibility of a Party Other Than the Client and That Is Restricted Since a Written Assertion Has Not Been Provided by the Responsible Party	AT101-10	RTF
Standard Review Report on Subject Matter for General Use	AT101-12	RTF

Title	File Name	File Type
Review Report on Subject Matter That Is the Responsibility of a Party Other Than the Client and That Is Restricted Since a Written Assertion Has Not Been Provided by the Responsible Party	AT101-13	RTF
Review Report on an Assertion That Is Restricted Since the Criteria Are Available Only to the Specified Parties	AT101-14	RTF
Sample Letter to a Regulator's Request for Access to Attest Documentation in an Examination Engagement	AT101-15	RTF
Sample Letter to a Regulator's Request for Access to Attest Documentation in an Agreed-Upon Procedures Engagement	AT101-16	RTF
Accountant's Report on the Suitability of the Design of an Entity's Internal Control That Has Been Implemented	AT101-17	RTF
Accountant's Report on the Suitability of the Design of an Entity's Internal Control That Has Not Yet Been Implemented	AT101-18	RTF
Standard Report on an Agreed-Upon Procedures Engagement	AT201-04	RTF
Report on Applying Agreed-Upon Procedures in Connection with a Proposed Acquisition	AT201-05	RTF
Report on Applying Agreed-Upon Procedures in Connection with Claims of Creditors	AT201-06	RTF
Standard Compilation Report on a Forecast That Does Not Contain a Range	AT301-02	RTF
Standard Compilation Report on a Projection That Does Not Contain a Range	AT301-03	RTF
Separate Paragraph in a Compilation Report on Prospective Financial Statements That Contain a Range	AT301-04	RTF
Separate Paragraph in a Compilation Report on Prospective Financial Statements That Omit the Summary of Significant Accounting Policies	AT301-05	RTF
Standard Examination Report on a Forecast That Does Not Contain a Range	AT301-06	RTF
Standard Examination Report on a Projection That Does Not Contain a Range	AT301-07	RTF
Separate Paragraph in an Examination Report on Prospective Financial Statements That Contain a Range	AT301-08	RTF
Qualified Opinion in an Examination Report on a Forecast	AT301-09	RTF
Adverse Opinion in an Examination Report on a Forecast	AT301-10	RTF
Disclaimer of Opinion in an Examination Report on a Forecast	AT301-11	RTF
Examination Report Expanded for a Financial Feasibility Study	AT301-12	RTF
Report on Applying Agreed-Upon Procedures to Prospective Financial Statements	AT301-13	RTF
Paragraphs to Be Added to the Practitioner's Report in a Practitioner-Submitted Document When the Summaries of Significant Assumptions and Accounting Policies Have Been Omitted from the Budgeted Information	AT301-14	RTF
Compilation Engagement Checklist: Prospective Financial Statements	AT301-15	RTF

Title	File Name	File Type
Examination Engagement Checklist: Prospective Financial Statements	AT301-16	RTF
Report on Examination of Pro Forma Financial Information	AT401-02	RTF
Report on Review of Pro Forma Financial Information	AT401-03	RTF
Report on Examination of Pro Forma Financial Information at Year-End with a Review of Pro Forma Financial Information for a Subsequent Interim Date	AT401-04	RTF
Examination Report Qualified for a Scope Limitation	AT401-05	RTF
Examination Report Qualified for Reservations About the Propriety of Assumptions on an Acquisition Transaction	AT401-06	RTF
Disclaimer of Opinion Because of a Scope Limitation	AT401-07	RTF
Applicability of Attestation and Auditing Standards to Different Types of Internal Control Engagements	AT501-01	RTF
Components of the Auditor's Report on the Examination of an Entity's Internal Control	AT501-02	RTF
Separate Report Expressing an Unqualified Opinion Directly on Internal Control	AT501-03	RTF
Separate Report Expressing an Unqualified Opinion on Management's Assertion	AT501-04	RTF
Separate Report Expressing an Adverse Opinion on Internal Control	AT501-05	RTF
Separate Report Expressing a Disclaimer of Opinion on Internal Control Due to a Scope Limitation	AT501-06	RTF
Separate Report Expressing an Unqualified Opinion on Internal Control Based, in Part, on the Report of Another Auditor	AT501-07	RTF
Combined Report Expressing an Unqualified Opinion on Internal Control and on the Financial Statements	AT501-08	RTF
Communication of Significant Deficiencies and Material Weaknesses	AT501-09	RTF
Sample Management Report on Internal Control over Financial Reporting Containing the Required Reporting Elements	AT501-10	RTF
Agreed-Upon Procedures Report on an Entity's Compliance with Specified Requirements	AT601-04	RTF
Agreed-Upon Procedures Report on the Effectiveness of an Entity's Internal Control over Compliance	AT601-05	RTF
Examination Report on an Entity's Compliance with Specified Requirements	AT601-07	RTF
Examination Report on Management's Assertion About Compliance with Specified Requirements	AT601-08	RTF
Examination Report with a Qualified Opinion When There Is Material Noncompliance with Specified Requirements	AT601-09	RTF
Examination Report with an Adverse Opinion When There Is Material Noncompliance with Specified Requirements	AT601-10	RTF
Procedures Checklist for Engagements to Examine MD&A	AT701-04	RTF
Standard Unqualified Examination Report on MD&A	AT701-06	RTF

Title	File Name	File Type
Examination Report on MD&A with a Qualified Opinion Due to a Material Omission	AT701-07	RTF
Examination Report on MD&A with a Qualified Opinion When Overly Subjective Assertions Are Included in MD&A	AT701-08	RTF
Examination Report on MD&A with Reference Made to the Report of Another Practitioner	AT701-09	RTF
Procedures Checklist for Engagements to Review MD&A	AT701-10	RTF
Standard Review Report on an Annual MD&A Presentation	AT701-12	RTF
Standard Review Report on an Interim MD&A Presentation	AT701-13	RTF
Modified Review Report on an MD&A Presentation for a Material Misstatement	AT701-14	RTF
Combined Report on an Examination of an Annual MD&A Presentation and Review of MD&A for an Interim Period	AT701-15	RTF
Review Report on a Combined Annual and Interim MD&A Presentation	AT701-16	RTF
A Service Organization Management's Assertion for a Type 1 Report	AT801-01	RTF
A Service Organization Management's Assertion for a Type 2 Report	AT801-02	RTF
Service Auditor's Unqualified Opinion on a Description of a Service Organization's System and the Suitability of the Design of Controls (Type 1 Report)	AT801-03	RTF
Service Auditor's Unqualified Opinion on a Description of a Service Organization's System and the Suitability of the Design and Operating Effectiveness of Controls (Type 2 Report)	AT801-04	RTF
Service Auditor's Qualified Opinion Because the Description of the Service Organization's System Is Not Fairly Presented (Type 2 Report)	AT801-05	RTF
Service Auditor's Qualified Opinion Because the Controls Are Not Suitably Designed (Type 2 Report)	AT801-06	RTF
Service Auditor's Qualified Opinion Because the Controls Did Not Operate Effectively Throughout the Specified Period (Type 2 Report)	AT801-07	RTF
Service Auditor's Qualified Opinion Because of the Auditor's Inability to Obtain Sufficient Appropriate Evidence (Type 2 Report)	AT801-08	RTF
Service Auditor's Report for Engagements in Which the Service Organization Uses A Subservice Organization: Carve-Out Method (Type 2 Report)	AT801-09	RTF
Service Auditor's Report for Engagements in Which the Service Organization Uses a Subservice Organization: Inclusive Method (Type 2 Report)	AT801-10	RTF

AR SECTION

Title	File Name	File Type
Standard Engagement Letter for a Compilation	AR80-01	RTF
Engagement Letter-Compilation of Financial Statements Not Intended for Third-Party Use	AR80-02	RTF

Title	File Name	File Type
Compilation Report on Full Disclosure GAAP Financial Statements	AR80-03	RTF
Compilation Report on Full Disclosure Cash Basis Financial Statements	AR80-04	RTF
Compilation Report on Full Disclosure Income Tax Basis Financial Statements	AR80-05	RTF
Compilation Report on GAAP Financial Statements That Omit Substantially All Disclosures	AR80-06	RTF
Compilation Report on Cash Basis Financial Statements That Omit Substantially All Disclosures	AR80-07	RTF
Compilation Report on Income Tax Basis Financial Statements That Omit Substantially All Disclosures	AR80-08	RTF
Compilation Report When the Accountant's Independence Has Been Impaired, and the Accountant Determines to *Not* Disclose the Reason for the Independence Impairment	AR80-09	RTF
Compilation Report When the Accountant's Independence Has Been Impaired, and the Accountant Decides to Disclose the Reason for the Independence Impairment	AR80-10	RTF
Compilation Report Modified for a Departure from GAAP: Accounting Principle Not Generally Accepted	AR80-11	RTF
Compilation Report Modified for a Departure from GAAP: Statement of Cash Flows Is Omitted	AR80-12	RTF
Compilation Report Covers Supplementary Information	AR80-13	RTF
Review Engagement Letter	AR90-01	RTF
Review Procedures Checklist	AR90-02	RTF
Management Representation Letter: Review Engagement	AR90-03	RTF
Updating Management Representation Letter: Review Engagement	AR90-04	RTF
Review Report on GAAP Financial Statements	AR90-05	RTF
Review Report on Cash Basis Financial Statements	AR90-06	RTF
Review Report on Income Tax Basis Financial Statements	AR90-07	RTF
Review Report Modified for a Departure fromGAAP: Accounting Principle Not Generally Accepted	AR90-08	RTF
Review Report Modified for a Departure from GAAP: Change in Accounting Principle without Reasonable Justification	AR90-09	RTF
Review Report Covers Supplementary Information That Has Been Subjected to Review Procedures	AR90-10	RTF
Review Report Covers Supplementary Information That Has *Not* Been Subjected to Review Procedures	AR90-11	RTF
Accountant's Compilation Report Related to Accounts Receivable	AR110-01	RTF
Accountant's Compilation Report Related to the Schedule of Depreciation— Income Tax Basis	AR110-02	RTF
Accountant's Compilation Report on Pro Forma Financial Information	AR120-01	RTF

SOFTWARE LICENSE AGREEMENT FOR ELECTRONIC FILES TO ACCOMPANY 2012 GAAS PRACTICE MANUAL (THE "BOOK").

PLEASE READ THE TERMS AND CONDITIONS OF THIS LICENSE AGREEMENT CAREFULLY BEFORE INSTALLING THE FILES FROM THE CD-ROM.

THE ELECTRONIC FILES ARE COPYRIGHTED AND LICENSED (NOT SOLD). BY INSTALLING THE ELECTRONIC FILES ("THE SOFTWARE"), YOU ARE ACCEPTING AND AGREEING TO THE TERMS OF THIS LICENSE AGREEMENT. IF YOU ARE NOT WILLING TO BE BOUND BY THE TERMS OF THIS LICENSE AGREEMENT, YOU SHOULD REMOVE THE SOFTWARE FROM YOUR COMPUTER AT THIS TIME AND PROMPTLY RETURN THE PACKAGE IN RESELLABLE CONDITION AND YOU WILL RECEIVE A REFUND OF YOUR MONEY. THIS LICENSE AGREEMENT REPRESENTS THE ENTIRE AGREEMENT CONCERNING THE SOFTWARE BETWEEN YOU AND CCH (REFERRED TO AS "LICENSOR"), AND IT SUPERSEDES ANY PRIOR PROPOSAL, REPRESENTATION, OR UNDERSTANDING BETWEEN THE PARTIES.

1. License Grant. Licensor hereby grants to you, and you accept, a nonexclusive license to use the Software, and any computer programs contained therein in machine-readable, object code form only, and the accompanying User Documentation, only as authorized in this License Agreement. The Software may be used only on a single computer owned, leased, or otherwise controlled by you, or in the event of the inoperability of that computer, on a backup computer selected by you. Neither ___ computers nor use in a ___ ork is permitted without ___ possible payment of ___ you will not assign, ___ ent, or share your ___ t. You agree that ___ pile, disassemble, ___ e the Software.

___ computer, you ___

remain with Licensor. This License Agreement does not convey to you an interest in or to the Software, but only a limited right of use revocable in accordance with the terms of this License Agreement.

3. License Fees. The license fees paid by you are paid in consideration of the licenses granted under this License Agreement.

4. Term. This License Agreement is effective upon your installing this software and shall continue until terminated. You may terminate this License Agreement at any time by removing all copies of the Software and returning the CD-ROM to Licensor. Licensor may terminate this License Agreement upon the breach by you of any term hereof. Upon such termination by Licensor, you agree to return to Licensor the Software and all copies and portions thereof.

5. Limited Warranty. Licensor warrants, for our benefit alone, for a period of 90 days from the date of commencement of this License Agreement (referred to as the "Warranty Period") that the Program CD-ROM in which the software is contained is free from defects in material and workmanship. If during the Warranty Period, a defect appears in the Program CD-ROM, you may return the Program to Licensor for either replacement or, at Licensor's option, refund of amounts paid by you under this License Agreement. You agree that the foregoing constitutes your sole and exclusive remedy for breach by Licensor of any warranties made under this Agreement. EXCEPT FOR THE WARRANTIES SET FORTH ABOVE, THE PROGRAM CD-ROM, AND THE SOFTWARE CONTAINED THEREIN, ARE LICENSED "AS-IS," AND LICENSOR DISCLAIMS ANY AND ALL OTHER WARRANTIES, WHETHER EXPRESS OR IMPLIED, INCLUDING, WITHOUT LIMITATION, ANY IMPLIED WARRANTIES OF MERCHANTABILITY OR FITNESS FOR A PARTICULAR PURPOSE.

6. Li___ Liability. Licensor's ___ ative liability to you or any other party for any loss or damages ___ lting from any claims, demands, or actions arising ___ relating to this Agreement shall not exceed ___ d to Licensor for the use of the Soft-
___ SHALL LICENSOR BE LIABLE ___ , INCIDENTAL, CONSEQUEN-
___ R EXEMPLARY DAMAGES ___ MITED TO, LOSS OF ___ PROF-